T5-AEU-290

Western Civilization: Its Genesis and Destiny

CRITICAL READERS:

Herman Ausubel, Columbia University
Geoffrey Barraclough, Oxford University
David D. Bien, University of Michigan
Rudolph Binion, Brandeis University
Theodore S. Hamerow, University of Wisconsin
Francis L. Loewenheim, Rice University
Val R. Lorwin, University of Oregon
Jack J. Roth, Case Western Reserve University
A. William Salomone, University of Rochester
A. P. Thornton, University of Toronto
Warner Arms Wick, University of Chicago

SCOTT, FORESMAN AND COMPANY

VOLUME TWO

Western Civilization

Its Genesis and Destiny

FROM 1650 TO THE PRESENT DAY

NORMAN F. CANTOR

Leff Professor of History
Brandeis University

Southern Baptist College
FELIX·GOODSON
LIBRARY
Walnut Ridge, Ark.

Library of Congress catalog card number 69-15757. Copyright © by Scott, Foresman and Company, Glenview, Illinois 60025. Philippines copyright 1969 by Scott, Foresman and Company.
All rights Reserved. Printed in the United States of America.
Regional offices of Scott, Foresman and Company are located in Atlanta, Dallas, Glenview, Palo Alto, Oakland, N.J., and London, England.

PICTURE CREDITS

Part One—Introduction. p. 17 Giraudon.
Chapter One Environment Essay. p. 20 top: Gundermann; *bottom:* Bavaria Verlag. *p. 21* Mansell Collection, London. *p. 22 top:* Pierpont Morgan Library; *bottom:* Mansell Collection. *p. 23 left:* Zwicker, Art Reference Bureau; *right:* "Reproduced by courtesy of the Secretary of State for Foreign and Commonwealth Affairs." *p. 24* Bibliotheque Nationale, Paris. *p. 25 top:* The Metropolitan Museum of Art, New York, Harris Brisbane Dick Fund, 1932; *bottom:* Musée Carnavolet, Paris.

Chapter Two Heritage Essay. p. 114 top and middle: Bibliotheque Nationale, Paris; *bottom: Time-Life Books,* © Time Inc. *p. 114a top:* Photo by Yale University Audio-Visual Center; *bottom:* courtesy Trustees of the Tate Gallery, London. *p. 114b* courtesy of Victoria and Albert Museum, London. *p. 114c top:* Louvre, Paris, from Art Reference Bureau; *bottom:* Kunsthistorisches Museum, Vienna. *p. 114d top:* courtesy of Trustees, The National Gallery, London; *bottom:* Major Peter Samuel, London. *p. 114e* collection of the John and Mable Ringling Museum of Art, Sarasota. *p. 114f* The Metropolitan Museum of Art, New York, Harris Brisbane Dick Fund, 1941. *p. 114g* Guildhall Art Gallery, London. *p. 114h* Musée des Beaux-Arts, Rouen, from Giraudon. *p. 114i* Copyright Reserved. *p. 114j* Trustees of the Wallace Collection, London, Art Reference Bureau. *p. 114k left:* Louvre, Paris, Cliché Musées Nationaux; *right:* Louvre, Paris, from Giraudon. *p. 114l* The National Portrait Gallery, London.

Chapter Three Heritage Essay. p. 174 top: Bibliotheque Nationale, Paris, photo by Françoise Foliot; *bottom:* J. E. Bulloz from Art Reference Bureau. *p. 175 top:* J. E. Bulloz from Art Reference Bureau; *bottom:* Bibliotheque Nationale, Paris. *p. 176 top:* Philip Gendreau; *bottom:* New York Public Library Picture Collection. *p. 177 top:* J. E. Bulloz from Art Reference Bureau; *bottom:* Louvre, Paris, from Giraudon. *p. 178 top:* New York Public Library Print Collection; *bottom:* Bibliotheque Nationale, Paris. *p. 179* Musée du Mans, from Giraudon. *p. 180 top:* Musée National de Malmaison, Archives Photographiques, Paris; *bottom:* Musée Condé, Chantilly, from Giraudon. *p. 181* Louvre, Paris, from Giraudon. *p. 182* Musée National de Versailles, Cliché Musées Nationaux. *p. 183 top:* New York Public Library Picture Collection; *bottom:* Granger Collection. *p. 184 and p. 185* Bibliotheque Nationale, Paris.

Chapter Four Environment Essay. p. 189 top: The Metropolitan Museum of Art, New York, Harris Brisbane Dick Fund, 1933; *bottom:* Science Museum, London. *p. 190 top:* Science Museum, London; *bottom:* Radio Times Hulton Picture Library. *p. 191* Mansell Collection. *p. 192 top and bottom:* Philip Gendreau. *p. 193* Mansell Collection. *p. 194 top:* Mansell Collection; *bottom:* Earl Mountbatten of Burma.
Heritage Essay. p. 222 top: Culver Pictures, Inc.; *bottom:* Granger Collection. *p. 223 top:* J. E. Bulloz from Art Reference Bureau. *p. 224* Historical Pictures Service. *p. 225* Radio Times Hulton Picture Library. *p. 226* The National Buildings Record, "The Bank of England." *p. 227 top:* Mansell Collection; *bottom:* Mansell Collection. *p. 228* Bettmann Archive. *p. 229* Radio Times Hulton Picture Library. *p. 230* Historical Pictures Service. *p. 231* Mansell Collection. *p. 232 and p. 233* Historical Pictures Service.

Part Two—Introduction. p. 235 Historical Pictures Service.
Chapter Five Heritage Essay p. 274 Giraudon. *p. 274a* The Tate Gallery, London. *p. 274b top:* Nationalgalerie, Berlin; *bottom:* Southampton Art Gallery. *p. 274c* Trustees, the National Gallery, London. *p. 274d* Kunstmuseum der Stadt, Dusseldorf. *p. 274e top:* Neue Pinakothek, Munich; *bottom:* The Tate Gallery, London. *p. 274f top:* Art Reference Bureau; *bottom:* Shostal Assoc. Inc.

914.03
C168w
Cop. 2

p. 274g top: Musée National de Malmaison, Paris; *bottom:* Musée des Beaux-Arts de Bordeaux, from Giraudon. *p. 274h* Phillips Collection, Washington. *p. 274i top and bottom:* Louvre, Paris, Cliché Musées Nationaux. *p. 274j* Courtesy of the Fogg Art Museum, Harvard University. *p. 274k top:* The Royal Pavilion, Brighton, colour photo by Fine Art Photography Ltd.; *bottom:* Louvre, Paris, from Art Reference Bureau. *p. 274l top and bottom:* The Tate Gallery, London. *p. 275* The Tate Gallery, London.

Chapter Six Environment Essay. p. 278 Science Museum, London. *p. 279 top:* Mansell Collection; *bottom:* The Tate Gallery, London. *p. 280 top:* Mansell Collection; *bottom:* National Buildings Record. *p. 281* Mansell Collection. *p. 282* Granger Collection. *p. 283 top and bottom:* London Electrotype Agency.
Heritage Essay. p. 328 Mansell Collection. *p. 329 top:* Culver Pictures, Inc.; *bottom:* Peter A. Juley and Son. *p. 330* British Museum, London. *p. 331* Phillips Collection, Washington. *p. 332* London Electrotype Agency. *p. 333 top:* British Museum, London; *bottom:* from *The Rise of the Working Class*, published by Weidenfeld and Nicolson. *p. 334 top:* from *The Age of Revolution*, published by Weidenfeld and Nicolson; *bottom:* Bibliotheque Nationale, Paris. *p. 335* Musée Carnavolet, Paris.

Chapter Seven. p. 361 top left: Louvre, Paris, from Giraudon; *top right:* Musée Fabre, Montpellier; *bottom:* Courtesy, John G. Johnson Collection, Philadelphia.
Heritage Essay. p. 366 Victoria and Albert Museum, London. *p. 367* London Electrotype Agency. *p. 368 top:* Royal Institution, London; *bottom:* New York Public Library Picture Collection. *p. 369* London Electrotype Agency. *p. 370* Radio Times Hulton Picture Library. *p. 371* from *The Age of Optimism*, published by Weidenfeld and Nicolson. *p. 372 top:* Manchester City Art Galleries; *bottom:* Victoria and Albert Museum, London. *p. 373* Birmingham Museum and Art Gallery. *p. 374* Plate 13 from *Napoleon III and the Rebuilding of Paris*, David H. Pinkney (Princeton University Press, 1958). *p. 375* British Crown Copyright.

Chapter Eight. p. 395 Roger-Viollet. *p. 398 top:* Museum of Fine Arts, Boston, Allen Fund; *bottom:* Mansell Collection. *p. 403* British Museum, London. *p. 419 top:* Brown Brothers; *bottom:* Granger Collection. *p. 424* Bettmann Archive.

Part Three—Introduction. p. 427 Radio Times Hulton Picture Library.
Chapter Nine Environment Essay. p. 430 Chevejon Frères, permission SPADEM 1968 by French Reproduction Rights, Inc. *p. 431 top:* Radio Times Hulton Picture Library; *bottom:* Philip Gendreau. *p. 433 top:* Osterreichische Galerie, Vienna; *bottom:* Max Pohly from Black Star. *p. 432 and p. 434* Culver Pictures, Inc. *p. 435 top and bottom:* Brown Brothers. *p. 436* Leslie Bailey's BBC Scrapbooks, Vol. I, 1898–1914, Allen and Unwin Ltd.
p. 448 Culver Pictures Inc. *p. 455* Jones and Laughlin Steel Corp., Pittsburgh. *p. 465* Gott Strafe England. *p. 471* Illustrite Zeitung, 1881–I, Leipzig.

Chapter Ten. p. 492 Culver Pictures, Inc. *p. 511* Kaufman and Fabry Co. *p. 521* Graphic, Vol. 85, London.
Heritage Essay. p. 528 from *The Age of Optimism*, published by Weidenfeld and Nicolson, London. *p. 529 top:* The Macmillan Co.; *bottom:* Photo Deutsche Fotothek, Dresden. *p. 530* The Macmillan Co. *p. 531 top:* Radio Times Hulton Picture Library; *bottom:* Royal Holloway College, Surrey. *p. 532* I. Sheppard. *p. 533 top:* Radio Times Hulton Picture Library; *bottom:* The Granger Collection. *p. 534 top:* Leslie Bailey's BBC Scrapbooks, Vol. I, 1896–1914, Allen and Unwin, London; *bottom:* The Macmillan Co. *p. 535* Musée de Roermond.

Chapter Eleven Heritage Essay. p. 570a Private collection, Zurich. *p. 570a top:* Louvre, Paris, from Art Reference Bureau; *bottom:* Shostal Assoc., Inc. *p. 570c* Folkwang Museum, Essen. *p. 570d top:* Fogg Art Museum, Harvard University; *bottom:* Galleria Nazionale d'Arte Moderna, Rome, photo courtesy Skira, Geneva. *p. 570e* By kind permission of Baroness Horta, photo courtesy Skira, Geneva. *p. 570 f top:* Kunsthaus Zurich, Gottfried Keller-Foundation; *bottom:* Musée Royal des Beaux-Arts, Antwerp. *p. 570g* Collection: Richard S. Zeisler, photo by Paulus Leeser, New York. *p. 570h top:* Rasmus Meyers Samlinger, courtesy Munch Museet, Oslo; *bottom:* Rijksmuseum Kroller-Muller Foundation, Otterlo. *p. 570i* The Museum of Modern Art, New York. *p. 570j top:*

Collection of the Philadelphia Museum of Art, photo by A. J. Wyatt; *bottom:* Kunstmuseum, Basle, Colorphoto HINZ, Basle, Permission ADAGP 1969 by French Reproduction Rights, Inc. *p. 570k* Kunstmuseum, Basle, Color HINZ, Basle, Permission ADAGP 1969 by French Reproduction Rights, Inc. *p. 570l* by kind permission of Campbell Lawson, Esq., Studio 7 Photo, Glasgow. *p. 571 left:* Museum of Modern Art, N.Y.; *right:* Hedrich-Blessing, Chicago.

Chapter Twelve Environment Essay. p. 574 top: A Press Association Photograph, London; *bottom:* Leslie Bailey's BBC Scrapbooks, Vol. I, 1896–1914, Allen and Unwin Ltd., London. *p. 575 top and bottom:* Brown Brothers. *p. 576 top:* Radio Times Hulton Picture Library; *bottom:* Museum of the City of New York. *p. 577 top:* Mansell Collection; *bottom:* Harrods of Knightbridge, London. *p. 578* Granger Collection. *p. 579* British Motor Corp. Ltd., Morris Division. *p. 609* Historical Pictures Service. *p. 625* U.S. Signal Corps.
Heritage Essay. p. 630 Brown Brothers. *p. 631 top and bottom:* Brown Brothers. *p. 632 top:* The Press Association; *bottom:* Topix. *p. 633 top and bottom:* Manchester Evening News and Chronicle. *p. 634 top:* London Electrotype Agency, Ltd.; *bottom:* Musée de la Guerre, Paris. *p. 635* Radio Times Hulton Picture Library. *p. 636 and p. 637* Trustees of the Imperial War Museum, London. *p. 638 top:* Slavonic Division, N.Y. Public Library, Astor, Lenox and Tilden Foundations; *bottom:* U.P.I. *p. 639 top:* Sovfoto; *bottom:* Mansell Collection.

Part Four – Introduction. p. 641 White House Collection.
Chapter Thirteen Environment Essay. p. 646 top: Culver Pictures, Inc.; *bottom:* Paul Popper Ltd. London. *p. 647* Radio Times Hulton Picture Library. *p. 648 and p. 649* Brown Brothers. *p. 650 top and bottom:* Brown Brothers. *p. 651* Max Pohly from Black Star. *p. 652 top:* Wide World Photos; *bottom:* Philip Gendreau. *p. 667* Wide World Photos.

Chapter Fourteen Environment Essay. p. 692 top: Wide World Photos; *bottom: The Times*, London. *p. 694* Roger Schall, Paris. *p. 695* Fox Photos Ltd. *p. 696* U. S. Army Photograph. *p. 697 top:* Wide World Photos; *bottom:* U.S. Official Photo, Planet News Ltd., London.

Chapter Fifteen. p. 752 U.S. Air Force. *p. 753* N.A.S.A.
Heritage Essay. p. 778 Collection, Museum of Modern Art, N.Y., Purchase. *p. 778a* Kunstmuseum, Basle, Permission SPADEM 1969 by French Reproduction Rights, Inc. *p. 778b* Collection Roland Penrose, London. *p. 778c top:* Collection Haags Gemeentemuseum, The Hague, Colorphoto HINZ, Basle; *bottom:* Collection of the Museum of Modern Art, N.Y., Purchase. *p. 778d top:* Trustees of the Tate Gallery, London; *bottom:* Collection of the Museum of Modern Art, N.Y., Purchase. *p. 778e* Collection of the Museum of Modern Art, N.Y., Purchase. *p. 778f* Roger Tory Peterson from Photo Researchers, Inc. *p. 778g* George Holton from Photo Researchers, Inc. *p. 778h* D. G. MacLean from Shostal Assoc., Inc. *p. 778i* Robert Mottar from Photo Researchers, Inc. *p. 778j top:* Collection, Cedar Rapids Art Center, Cedar Rapids, Iowa; *bottom:* Collection Walter Netsch, Chicago. *p. 778k top:* U.S. Army; *bottom:* Institut fur Denkmalpflege, Berlin.

Chapter Sixteen Environment Essay. p. 780 Philip Gendreau. *p. 781 top:* Cornell Capa from Magnum; *bottom:* Philip Gendreau. *p. 782* Burt Glinn from Magnum. *p. 783 top:* John Laundis from Black Star; *bottom:* Alfred Eisenstaedt, LIFE Magazine © Time Inc. *p. 787* Howard Sochurek. *p. 786 top:* Black Star; *bottom:* Photo Wayne Andrews.
Heritage Essay. p. 840 Erick Leasing from Magnum. *p. 841 top:* Wide World Photos; *bottom:* Sovfoto and Eastfoto. *p. 842 top:* Wide World Photos; *bottom:* U.P.I. *p. 843* Henri Cartier-Bresson from Magnum. *p. 844* Wide World Photos. *p. 845* Lee Lockwood from Black Star. *p. 846* C. Capa, M. Bar-Am from Magnum. *p. 847 top:* Wide World Photos; *bottom:* Ghislain Bellorget from Black Star. *p. 848 top:* Ted Cowell from Black Star; *bottom:* Eugene Anthony from Black Star. *p. 849 top:* Wide World Photos; *bottom:* G. A. Laney, Benyas, Kaufman from Black Star.

PREFACE

In this second volume as in the first, a three-track approach to the study of Western civilization is used to communicate a synthesis of prevailing historical knowledge and interpretation in the clearest and most effective way.

The central track is a narrative of political, economic, and social change and an analysis of major institutional forms, cultural patterns, policies, and ideologies. An effort has been made to delineate key historiographical problems and the conflicting interpretations involved, to report consensus where consensus exists, and, where it does not, to offer a balanced and judicious view. Each chapter in this main, central track has been criticized by experts; it has undergone several drafts; and every effort has been made to arrive at an authoritative, clear, and readable summation of current scholarship.

The second track introduces each era with an illustrated *environment essay* that describes the way of life, stresses significant aspects of the physical and social environment, and generally attempts to establish the ambience for events that will be traced in the succeeding central track. The third track consists of *heritage essays*, which follow several of the chapters. Each of these consists of an expository essay, quotations from primary sources, and an elaborate picture assemblage. Through the heritage essays, the reader will gain a sense of the cultural layers that together make up the intellectual traditions of the contemporary world.

In this book, pictures and maps are used pedagogically as source documents and not merely as illustrative materials. Long captions—in many instances brief essays—accompany the pictures and maps, explicate their significance, and invite the student to examine these graphic materials carefully for their historical information.

Modern history—the period from 1715 to the present, with which this volume is concerned—presents a special challenge to the author of a general survey of this nature: it is necessary to strike a balance between broad patterns on the one hand and specific regional and national developments on the other. In accordance with recent trends in historiographical thought—which have replaced the nation-state with the era as the prime unit of historical inquiry for the modern period—I have followed certain basic principles of organization and exposition in those chapters dealing with political history. First, I have sought to view an era—comprising several decades with specific and definable issues and trends—as the distinguishing subject of each chapter. Second, *within* the era, I have then discussed regional and national developments. Third, I have compared the contemporary political and social developments in the leading states and attempted to account for national characteristics and the variations among them. This approach gives primary emphasis to the era and allows the contemporary patterns of change in Europe and America to be seen as a whole—as an interrelated entity. At the same time, since national identities and destinies are crucial to modern history, this approach also provides a sufficient view of distinctive national developments.

The Prologue to this volume, a survey of the period 1650–1715, is a recapitulation and summary of Chapter 16 and parts of Chapters 14 and 15 of Volume I. The Prologue is intended mainly for those who have not read Volume I.

The literature on modern history is vast, and the problems it presents are many and difficult. In preparing this volume, I have benefited from the assistance of the following: Mrs. Clarissa Atkinson, Miss Zane Berzins, Dr. Barbara Delman, Mr. Joel Doerfler, Mrs. Kathleen Greenfield, Mrs. Michela Mago, Mrs. Nancy Melia, and Mr. James Reed. In addition, Mrs. Melia, Mrs. Atkinson, and Mr. Michael Werthman researched points raised by the critical readers. Miss Berzins and Mr. Alan Walach helped me choose the illustrations; Mrs. Christine Masson assisted in the preparation of the maps, and Mrs. Melia with the map captions. Miss Marlene Aronin assisted in the preparation of the bibliographical essay.

Above all, I wish to acknowledge the assistance of my friend, Professor Francis L. Loewenheim of Rice University, who acted as general consultant on the volume, placing at my disposal his profound erudition in modern history. Professor Loewenheim saved me from many errors and made innumerable suggestions for improving the manuscript, many of which I have incorporated into the published version. Professor Loewenheim is not in agreement with all my interpretations, and he is no way responsible for any shortcomings or errors in the book.

In drawing to a close two and a half years of arduous labor on this project, I wish to acknowledge with respect to this volume, as I did in connection with Volume I, the editorial assistance of Miss Mary Wilkins and Mr. David R. Ebbitt of the Scott, Foresman staff. This is also the appropriate time to mention the help of my wife, whose constant support and encouragement made the completion of the work possible within a reasonable time.

At this point I think it also appropriate to dedicate the two volumes to the memory of my teacher and friend, Theodor E. Mommsen, scion of a most distinguished German academic family, a lover of freedom, a defender of civilization, an implacable enemy of tyranny. "Through thee I believe in the great and the good who are gone."

N. F. C.

CONTENTS

LIST OF MAPS

Prologue
to Modern History

Europe 1650-1715

I THE GEOGRAPHICAL AND ECONOMIC EXPANSION OF EUROPE

In the years between 1650 and 1715, the nation-states of the West continued the transition from the medieval to the modern era. The decisive break with the Middle Ages, which began at the end of the fifteenth century, was complete by the beginning of the eighteenth. The secular motives of personal profit and national interest had become central to the outlook of western Europeans. In the development of governmental institutions the latter half of the seventeenth century was extremely significant: between 1650 and 1715 England developed its unique judicial and political system, while on the Continent absolute monarchy reached its fullest expression. The major implementation of the new politics of nation-states was inextricably related to the revolution in trade and commerce that marked the Age of Expansion.

The economic expansion of the sixteenth century was revived in the late seventeenth century. In general, both population and prices rose between 1650 and 1715. There was no industrial revolution: piecemeal technical improvements (particularly in shipbuilding) had important effects, but no revolutionary change occurred in industrial or agricultural production nor were any new sources of power put to use in manufacture or transportation. European overseas expansion was accomplished in sailing ships, and the industrial output of the nation-states came from workers' cottages, not factories. It was a revolution in trade and commerce, rather, that sparked the economic advance, and this was both a cause and a result of geographical expansion.

The expansion that pushed Westerners out of the limits of the accessible world was motivated by greed, by the missionary impulse, and by nationalist and imperialist ambitions. By the middle of the seventeenth century the Atlantic Ocean had replaced the Mediterranean as the great highway of European commerce. Medieval shipbuilding techniques had been much improved—notably by the Dutch—and the Iberian conquests of the sixteenth century had been matched by the expansion of the Netherlands, England, and France. The Netherlands was the greatest commercial power in Europe in 1650; but it lacked the manpower and financial resources to maintain a far-flung empire, and eventually the Dutch were forced to concentrate on their East Indian possessions and the carrying trade.

By the end of the seventeenth century the English and French confronted each other in North America, in the West Indies, and in India. The English colonies, in particular, attracted permanent settlers. In North America the English colonists had French neighbors, and conflict between the two groups helped bring about the colonial wars that raged throughout the eighteenth century. By 1700, colonies in North America and elsewhere had begun to return new and valuable products to the home countries, and the commercial value of colonies became an accepted tenet of Western political economy.

The establishment of colonies and the development of overseas trade had several important effects on life in Europe. New products from the colonies (including cocoa, coffee, tobacco, tea, and sugar) became staples of the European diet, and corn and potatoes helped reduce the ever present threat of famine. Advanced ship design met the demands of long voyages and heavy cargoes. Fighting ships were developed to defend merchant fleets and to create the powerful navies the nation-states demanded. The influx of bullion from the New World was at least partly responsible for the great increase in available coinage and for the continuing inflation of the sixteenth and seventeenth centuries. Competition for colonies and trade routes became an important part of international relations, with incalculable effects on the course of modern European history.

The economic expansion of the Age of Discovery culminated in the seventeenth century in the development of institutions and theories to fit the new economic facts. Capitalism—the operation of a free market in a money economy based on acceptance of monetary gain as a valid human goal—was well entrenched in the cities of northern Europe by the middle of the seventeenth century. As money and credit came into general use, financial institutions became more efficient and more sophisticated. The joint-stock company, the national bank, and the stock exchange flourished by the end of the seventeenth century.

European social and political structure was affected but not transformed by capitalism. Modern financial institutions did not, after all, help farmers through bad years: seventeenth-century peasants were not much better off than their medieval predecessors, and most of the population of Europe still lived on the land. Except in England, where land retained its value, the old aristocracy felt the stress and strain of a money economy. Nobles began to depend on royal favor for a living, even for a profession, as private war became obsolete and judicial and political centralization took place. For their part, middle-class townsmen, particularly in France, envied the power and prestige of the nobility but neither attempted nor wanted to overturn the social system that gave top status to landed families. Instead, they hoped to buy or marry their way into the privileged class.

In the seventeenth century the state became the chief arbiter of economic affairs. In the newly complicated and competitive economy of the period, it was an indispensable element in business and finance. And as the state as a national political unit emerged, so did the conception of a national economic unit. The attempt to work toward national goals through state regulation of trade, commerce, and financial affairs has been given the name *mercantilism,* but mercantilism was never a coherent body of economic doctrine. It was rather a series of loosely defined assumptions. Throughout the period, localism and vested interests tended to vitiate national economic policies.

Colbert, the chief architect of French mercantilism, used the guilds as arms of the state in the supervision of production. In England, monopolies were granted by the Crown to favored producers and commercial companies. Home industries were encouraged by subsidies and by protective tariffs. The race for colonies was motivated in part by the desire to avoid buying colonial products from competitors. For underlying all the mercantilist activities was the belief that the total wealth of the world was strictly limited by the amount of bullion in existence—that one nation could enrich itself only at the expense of another. As a philosophy, it was perfectly suited to the era of rising nation-states.

In all, the late seventeenth century was a period of economic upswing and general prosperity. The growth of cities provided new opportunities for all classes and immeasurably enriched European life, but it produced urban problems hitherto unknown. Even piecemeal technological improvements put some workers out of jobs. The rise of the nation-states and the establishment of European colonies around the globe produced wars, suffering, and economic devastation. Like any period of rapid transition, the seventeenth century was a time of challenge and insecurity.

II SEVENTEENTH-CENTURY CULTURE AND SCIENCE

Baroque Culture

Toward the end of the sixteenth century, the style known as "Baroque" came more and more to predominate in the arts. *Baroque,* a rather vague term, refers to certain common characteristics of the highly diversified output in art, literature, and music during the seventeenth and early eighteenth centuries. In many ways it was merely an extension of Renaissance classicism and realism; but the dominant interests of Baroque artists were light, color, and motion, and the simplicity and unity of Renaissance art were lost in the new emphasis on decoration and dynamism. If Michelangelo's sculpture of David—that classic study of the young hero in repose—can be said to represent the style of the Renaissance, the "David" of Giovanni Lorenzo Bernini (1598–1680)—a crouching figure about to hurl the stone at an invisible Goliath—typifies the Baroque emphasis on motion and emotion.

Both the artist and the patron of Baroque differed from their Renaissance predecessors. The era of the "whole man" really ended with Leonardo da Vinci; in the Baroque period, the increasing intricacy of science and philosophy and the professionalization of art and literature demanded specialization. The Baroque patron could appreciate the arts without attempting to practice them. The opera, the theater, and the chateau provided a background for the dramatic, colorful lives of seventeenth-century aristocrats. Association with artists, playwrights, architects, musicians, and men of letters was a valuable asset in the pursuit of status.

The Scientific Revolution

Baroque artists spared no effort, neglected no technique, refrained from no excess to achieve the absolute in art. Similarly, the scientists of the period exhibited a wonderful restlessness, audacity, and selfless passion in creating a new intellectual system. Baroque artists never worried about their many failures, their lapses into awkwardness and bad taste; they simply tried again in their pursuit of aesthetic perfection. The scientists, too, made error after error and blundered into many wrong answers; but in the Baroque spirit, they never doubted that success was attainable, that the great breakthrough was not far off. They learned their mathematics and developed their instruments and even established their method of inquiry at the same time they were formulating their new view of the universe.

The scientific movement, which began with the New Learning of the late Middle Ages at Oxford, the Sorbonne, and the University of Padua, called into question the Aristotelian-Ptolemaic universe of classical and Christian natural philosophy. But the questions raised by the late medieval thinkers were much more significant than their answers; medieval mathematics was an inadequate basis for a new science, and the social and religious environment of the fifteenth century was not well suited to inquiry into natural phenomena. As a result, the scientific movement lapsed until the mid-sixteenth century, when Copernicus began a new investigation of the universe; and its first real turning point came with the achievements of Galileo in the early seventeenth century. Baconian empiricism and Cartesian mathematical rationalism contributed support and direction to the new science, which culminated in the publication of Newton's *Mathematical Principles of Natural Philosophy* in 1687.

Sir Isaac Newton (1642–1727) was a genius by any definition. His synthesis of physical science dominated the world view of Western man until the twentieth century. Newton's particular contributions included differential and integral calculus, the law of gravity, and a greatly improved theory of light, but even more important was his general conception of the universe as a huge mechanism in which all motion could be described in quantitative terms. Newton's system was simple and useful; it excluded unanswerable questions (such as, What is gravity?) and left a place for a Deity who created the universe, set it in motion, and stepped back to allow it to operate.

Newton's major achievement was the quantification of nature, the formulation of a theory of both terrestrial and celestial physics that could be expressed in mathematical terms. This quantification distinguishes modern science from ancient and medieval natural philosophy; it also distinguishes Western civilization as it has existed since the late seventeenth century from all other cultures. Only in the West has the conviction existed that nature can be absolutely comprehended and therefore manipulated for the betterment of man. Newton's laws of a mechanical universe made it possible for Europeans to establish hegemony in the world; essentially, it was the new physics that give rise to the industrial technology of the eighteenth and nineteenth centuries.

With the development of a methodology in physics, breakthroughs in other fields were inevitable. The microscope followed the telescope, and the rudiments of modern chemistry and biology were established in the seventeenth century. A scientific community emerged to answer the questions raised by the scientific revolution, and science became an independent discipline (separate from theology or metaphysics) whose practitioners were specialists, with professional societies and learned journals. By the end of the seventeenth century, the professionalization of science had gone so far that the average educated gentleman could no longer pretend to scientific competence.

The second half of the seventeenth century was a suitable period for an intellectual revolution, and England an appropriate environment for its greatest leader. First, the secularization of thought that had been accomplished during the Renaissance and the Reformation allowed seventeenth-century scientists to advance far beyond their late medieval predecessors. The invention of the telescope and the great advances in mathematics gave impetus to new inquiry and provided the tools for the quantification of nature. Perhaps equally significant, Sir Isaac Newton produced his most important work during a period when troublesome religious and political questions appeared to be settled—when the great passions of an earlier day had died down and the best minds of the era were freed to devote themselves to abstract speculation.

III CONSTITUTIONAL MONARCHY IN ENGLAND

The major outlines of the unique English political and judicial system were established during the latter part of the seventeenth century. It was in that period that the English gentry circumscribed the royal power within the common law and established the right of propertied men to share in national government as members of Parliament and to dominate local government as magistrates and justices of the peace.

Like their Continental cousins, the Tudor monarchs of the sixteenth century had vastly increased the power of the Crown. The Tudors, however—particularly Henry VIII and his daughter, Elizabeth I—rooted their new powers firmly in three important elements of English society: in Parliament, in the Church, and in the large and amorphous class of country gentlemen. These groups combined to check the royal power of the succeeding Stuart kings and managed to maintain themselves in authority into the great age of aristocratic government in England—the eighteenth century. Forced to share their power with the new industrial class in the nineteenth century and with the masses of an industrial democracy in the twentieth, this ancient "upper class" of England survives even today as an influential element in British society.

In the middle of the seventeenth century, the royal power had declined to its nadir in English history. In 1649 Charles I was tried and executed, a fantastic occurrence in seventeenth-century Europe. Both Charles and his father, James I, had confidently followed the course successfully pursued by contemporary Continental monarchs: absolute monarchy by divine right. But Puritan dissent was a powerful voice in England, and Parliament had become a strong and self-conscious body. After four years of civil war, Charles I was defeated by a coalition of Puritan dissenters and Parliamentarians. Most of the leaders of Parliament were lawyers, utterly devoted to the tradition of English common law that the attempted absolutism of the Stuarts appeared to defy.

The coalition was able to defeat the king's party and to establish a revolutionary government, but after the execution of Charles in 1649, differences among the victors made government by Parliament impossible. The real power fell into the hands of military leaders of the civil war—notably Oliver Cromwell, a Puritan of the gentry class. In the 1650's, Cromwell's Protectorate, a genuine attempt to found a "godly" society ruled by "saints," became in reality a military dictatorship. The gentry won none of the political privileges for which they had fought, and the democratic ideas that had been expressed in radical political pamphlets during the 1640's by Leveller agitators were firmly repressed. Cromwell strengthened England's hold on Ireland and the West Indies. His government was, by the standards of the day, highly efficient. But his rules concerning dress, manners, amusements, and the Sabbath were very unpopular.

Cromwell died in 1658, and in 1660 General Monk (himself a Puritan and Cromwell's replacement as head of the army) met the son of Charles I in London and presided over his restoration as Charles II (1660–1685). Charles had watched events in England from his sanctuary in France, and he was determined not to repeat his father's and grandfather's mistakes. He was an extremely popular king, and he profited from the country's relief at its liberation from the dreary days of Puritan rule. England's prosperity increased, and the arts and letters flourished. Sir Christopher Wren built a new St. Paul's Cathedral and other beautiful buildings after the Great Fire of 1666 burned much of London. Restoration comedy revived the English theater —closed down under the Protectorate—and a brilliant court reflected the general prosperity and the release from Puritan gloom.

The two-party system which still dominates English politics came into existence under Charles, who found his major source of support in the "Tories"—country gentlemen, for the most part, who had been frightened by the Civil War and the Protectorate and were prepared to devote themselves to monarchy, security, and religious moderation (which implied a sympathetic attitude toward Roman Catholics). But when Charles was succeeded by his Catholic brother James II in 1685, the new "Whig" party grew much more powerful. The Whigs were strongly anti-Catholic, favored toleration for Protestant dissenters, and suspected the king of plotting to restore the Roman Catholic religion in England. Many of the Whig leaders were members of great aristocratic families; this kind of great nobleman had, with few exceptions, been politically inert since the late fifteenth century. They allied themselves with financiers and businessmen of London and other growing cities, many of whom, as radical Protestants, were excluded from government. Whigs and businessmen alike favored political and commercial expansion, which implied fierce opposition to the expansionist designs of France under Louis XIV.

James II was remarkably untactful about his personal religious faith as well as his determination to dominate Parliament. Not only did he rush a Catholic priest to the deathbed of Charles II, but he had his son baptized a Roman Catholic, alarming Protestants of both parties. When the king went on to prosecute several leaders of the Anglican Church for seditious libel, he alienated almost every influential group in the country. Not only Whigs were involved in the negotiations that brought the Dutch prince William of Orange and his wife Mary (a Protestant daughter of James) to England in 1688. James was forced to flee to France when the commander of the English army declared for the invader.

William of Orange (William III of England) was more interested in leading a grand alliance against Louis XIV than in English constitutional questions. He was a willing partner in the Glorious Revolution, as the events of 1688 and 1689 have been called—a bloodless settlement of great constitutional issues. Before William succeeded to the throne, he agreed to the Bill of

Rights, which clarified the position of the king under the law, reaffirmed the sanctity of due process and the common law, and established the position of Parliament. The ultimate sovereignty of the king-in-Parliament was settled, Roman Catholics were permanently barred from the English throne, and governmental tyranny and absolutism were effectively forestalled.

The Glorious Revolution was as conservative as it was revolutionary. It enshrined property rights as well as common law (which favored the rich in any case, being slow and expensive). Rule by the rich, landowning classes was perpetuated, to the great satisfaction of most Englishmen, or at least of most articulate Englishmen. The settlement of 1689 was so successful in terms of political stability, and so satisfying to its beneficiaries, that it survived for almost a hundred and fifty years. Even then, it took the Industrial Revolution to bring about political reform.

William III was succeeded by Queen Anne (another Protestant daughter of James II, and the last Stuart monarch), whose reign was marked by party conflict and a search for political stability. The system of parliamentary government, in which the king ruled through patronage and pressure, relying on his ministers in Parliament to form and pass legislative policies, took shape under Anne. Parliament accepted the obligation of raising money to run the government, and the creation of the national Bank of England made this possible. The idea of a national debt became respectable, and loans to the government were regarded as attractive investments, placing England's government on a much sounder financial footing than the government of any other European nation. By 1715 the supreme age of the English aristocracy had begun; great noblemen led the army and the state, while the gentry maintained their virtual monopoly of local government.

The union of England and Scotland in 1707 brought a traditional enemy into permanent alliance and put an end to one chronically difficult situation. But Ireland remained as troublesome as ever. It had supported the Stuarts through the Civil War and had been viciously repressed under Cromwell; the Restoration failed to improve the situation. Ireland remained a thorn in England's side through the eighteenth century and beyond, but its problems seemed quite remote to England's ruling classes in the reign of Queen Anne.

The general prosperity and stability of the later Stuart period allowed English intellectuals to abandon religious passion and political unrest in favor of intellectual pursuits. In political thought as well as science, England led the Western world in the seventeenth century. Adopting the methodology of the natural sciences, Thomas Hobbes and John Locke deduced their views of the state from what they knew of human nature. Hobbes, believing the nature of man to be self-seeking and irrational, regarded the state as a necessary defense against the war that would inevitably break out if men were allowed to live in a state of nature. To achieve order and security, men gave up their freedom to a common sovereign with absolute authority. For Hobbes, as for many Continental thinkers, the sovereign and the state were identical, and the authority of the sovereign was limited only by his ability to impose his will on society.

John Locke (1632–1704) formed a more characteristically English political theory, but he, too, based his view of government on an examination of human nature. His major work, *The Second Treatise on Civil Government*, became the theoretical defense of the Glorious Revolution. Locke believed that men were motivated by self-interest but that in wise men self-interest was controlled by reasonable rules. Sensible men enter into civil society in order to provide a common judge for their inevitable differences, giving up only whatever part of their individual liberty is necessary to ensure the security of their life, liberty, and property.

Locke saw government as a contract between governors and governed, and he favored constitutional systems limited by the natural rights of the individual. His ideas were widely appreciated in England during his own lifetime and on the Continent during the eighteenth century. They were transported to North America by English colonists and permeate the Declaration of Independence and the United States Constitution. Locke's political theory became the most important expression of English liberalism and survived as such down to the nineteenth century.

IV ABSOLUTE MONARCHY IN FRANCE

The Rise of Absolutism

In the later Middle Ages and the sixteenth century, western Europe experienced great upheavals, and men had a variety of visions of the ways in which the consequences might be integrated into a viable social order. Humanists dreamed of a utopian commonwealth, Protestant reformers longed for the rule of the godly people, aristocrats advocated the leadership of representative estates, and the bourgeoisie were inclined to republican ideals. But between the late fifteenth century and the first half of the seventeenth century, these visions of a just society faded before the establishment of the system of government called absolute monarchy. By the early seventeenth century, Continental peoples generally accepted absolute monarchy as the most viable form of government.

This political solution to change and upheaval was, in part, a throwback to the thirteenth century. The early modern state perpetuated the medieval doctrine of the divine right of kings—that is, the divine right of the royal bloodline to decide on the holder of sovereign authority. But in the sixteenth century the concomitant medieval limitations on royal power, mainly through parliaments and estates, were greatly reduced, while the effectiveness of bureaucratic and ministerial institutions was greatly enhanced. Thus the "new monarchy" of the late fifteenth and the sixteenth century advanced far beyond medieval kings in developing both the theory and the institutions of royal power.

What is most striking about the "new monarchy" is its intense self-consciousness. Kingship was not simply an inheritance from the past; it was regarded as a way of solving the problems of contemporary European society. The servants and ideological justifiers of absolute monarchy thought of the king's sovereign authority as the most effective means of achieving peace, prosperity, and order. Kingship was supported on pragmatic grounds; energetic and intelligent monarchs and their officials were ever on the watch for ways of enhancing not only the wealth and privileges of the Crown but the effectiveness of its leadership in society.

The clearest exposition of the doctrine of absolute monarchy was made by the French lawyer Jean Bodin, member of a group called the *politiques*. The *politiques* believed that the only solution to the religious civil wars that were ruining France was to vest all authority in a king who would make decisions on the basis of the welfare of the nation rather than in accordance with sectarian ideology. In other words, Bodin and his colleagues sought a secular, political solution to the upheaval caused by the Reformation: "Monarchy is the sacred anchor on which, of necessity, all must in the last instance rely."[1] In the seventeenth century, Bodin's views gained wide acceptance on the Continent, largely due to the success of Henry IV, who reconstituted the power of the French Crown.

It remained to work out the institutional format of absolute monarchy. The most important achievement in this direction was the development of ministerial bureaucracy: the king chose a great minister, to whom he turned over the reins of day-to-day government, and this minister recruited a group of civil servants who were his own creatures. The king might devote himself to major issues of war and peace or simply to the pleasures of the court and the hunt; meanwhile, the ministerial bureaucracy imposed law and brought in revenue for the Crown. This system had been experimented with in England in the 1530's, and the Habsburg emperor Charles V also favored it; but it was employed to an unprecedented degree in France in the reign of Louis XIII (1610–1643) by the king's minister, Cardinal Richelieu.

Ministerial bureaucracy was a halfway house on the road to the modern state. It allowed the king to retain supreme power while it compensated for the inability or reluctance of most monarchs to do the hard work of the central government. But there were still many defects in the early seventeenth-century state. First, the reliance of the great minister on the king's favor encouraged court intrigues, and a minister's dismissal or death caused sudden disruptions in administrative continuity. Second, the king's admiration for great lords and his chronic need for money brought about the sale of offices to the aristocracy, as well as to the "middle sort" of people. Although

---

1. Jean Bodin, *Six Books of the Commonwealth*, trans. M. J. Tooley. Oxford: Blakewell, n.d., p. 198.

the latter usually did their jobs well, the aristocrats often treated Crown offices as hereditary private property and thereby impeded the effective operation of royal government. Third, in the sixteenth and the early seventeenth century the state was interminably involved in war, and while war brought accretions of territory and provided employment and markets for industrial goods, it also sapped the financial resources of the state.

Louis XIV

Even while the English were developing the special institutions of their constitutional monarchy, a French king was bringing absolute monarchy to its highest development. Louis XIV (1643–1715) was the absolute monarch *par excellence* — the embodiment of the glory of a great nation.

Louis inherited the throne at the age of five, but France was ruled by a regent — Louis' mother, Anne of Austria, and her adviser, the Italian minister Mazarin — until the latter's death in 1661. Mazarin's clever diplomacy allowed France to wring profit from the Thirty Years' War, which impoverished so much of Europe; but like his predecessor, Richelieu, Mazarin trampled on local interests and private feelings in order to achieve efficiency, centralization, and powerful monarchy — and he was cordially hated for it.

Louis grew up in the shadow of the Frondes of 1648 and 1652 — rebellions led by the French aristocracy in which all classes joined in revolt against the central government and the monarchy itself. Louis never allowed any similar occurrence to mar his personal reign; by diligence, determination, and war he mobilized all the resources of France — human as well as economic — to the service of the state. To do so, he used devices that were intended to rob the nobles of power and independence while leaving their pride and prestige unchallenged. Nobles were separated, when possible, from local power bases; they were supplanted in high administrative and military posts by bureaucrats who did the work while the nobles took the glory. Under Louis, the royal bureaucracy became an integral part of French government and French life, and the administrative achievements of the king and his bureaucrats were impressive. As described by the contemporary apologist for absolute monarchy, Bossuet, government by divine right was orderly, reasonable, and lawful — at the opposite extreme from the "arbitrary" government of an illegitimate tyrant.

Most of Louis' domestic reforms and bureaucratic accomplishments were achieved during the 1660's and early 1670's, before foreign wars distracted and impoverished the state. The once-spirited local courts, or *parlements*, submitted humbly to the king; rebellious aristocrats were tamed, and many became courtiers at the king's palace at Versailles. A class of loyal and devoted *commissaires* was established to supervise every detail of government in every part of France.

Louis' finance minister, Colbert, was the chief exponent and organizer of French mercantilism. It was he who insisted that French industries compete with European rivals in the manufacture of luxury goods and that overseas trading companies be launched to compete with such political rivals as England and Holland. Colbert's aim was to reconstruct French economic life in terms of efficiency, volume, and quality of production and distribution so that France might better compete in the world market. This was entirely compatible with the aims of his royal master, and indeed it is probable that both of them saw the strengthening of the French economy as a prerequisite for any increase in French military power. Colbert did not, however, accomplish any meaningful reform in the tax system or the financial structure, which remained totally inferior to those of Louis' major enemies, Holland and England.

Even the Church was forced to back down by the mighty king, who made the clergy produce an unequivocal declaration of the liberties of the Gallican Church—which really meant the temporal power of the French king. This brought him into conflict with the strong pope Innocent XI. To support his contention that "modernized" religion must serve the state, Louis in 1685 revoked the Edict of Nantes, which had provided toleration for Protestants. Although Louis has been soundly chastised for this act by historians, in its own context the revocation was not particularly radical; it was part of Louis' campaign to impose order and unity on France. But it had serious implications. The persecution of the French Huguenots (Protestants) was infuriating to Protestants everywhere, and France lost a sizable community of skilled and hard-working farmers and artisans to Holland and Germany.

No petty triumphs over the French nobility or even the pope could satisfy the Sun King, who believed that war was "the king's craft." Long after dynastic power politics had become obsolete, he persisted in the idea that the Habsburg king of Spain and the Habsburg emperor were his natural enemies and his only worthy foes. He never recognized the political implications of the revolution in trade and commerce, and he did not realize that England and Holland, with their fine navies and commercial predominance, had enormous natural advantages in any conflict. Louis kept Europe at war for fifty years, and the devastating (and unsuccessful) campaigns of the later years of his reign did much to vitiate his domestic reforms.

Louis began by fighting the Netherlands in Flanders in the late 1660's. His brilliant generals won town after town, but the Dutch allied themselves with England and Sweden and forced Louis to give back much of what his generals had gained. Louis kept on fighting and provoking other states to retaliate in coalition, but the showdown was delayed until the 1680's, primarily because of the renewed Turkish threat, which occupied the Austrian emperor until 1683. In that year the imperial armies won a decisive victory against the Turks at Kahlenberg, and in 1689 William of Orange succeeded to the throne of England: together, these events made Louis' defeat almost inevitable. William was determined to lead Protestant Europe against France, and he did so

SOUTHERN BAPTIST COLLEGE LIBRARY

in the War of the League of Augsburg in the 1690's. After 1689, France was continually on the defensive.

Louis' final war, which has been described as the last of the great European dynastic conflicts, was the War of the Spanish Succession, which dragged on from 1701 to 1714. When Louis' grandson, Philip of Anjou, inherited the Spanish throne, Louis predictably decided to support Philip's claim without regard to preexisting treaty obligations. France and Spain together opposed England, Holland, and the Austrian Empire, with a variety of lesser powers joining one side or the other (or both, in succession). In Europe the outcome was indecisive: Philip kept the Spanish throne, but Louis' conquests in the Spanish Netherlands, Germany, and Italy were lost. After the beginning of the eighteenth century, however, wars were fought in the colonies as well as in Europe, and colonial arrangements and rearrangements were part of every peace treaty, with incalculable results in later centuries. The most significant clauses in the Treaty of Utrecht, which ended the War of the Spanish Succession, gave England the lion's share of colonial concessions.

Warfare itself changed during the seventeenth century: it has been described as less violent and vicious than the religious wars of the Reformation and less devastating than the wars that occurred after the Industrial Revolution provided sophisticated modern weapons. The most spectacular military change was in the size of armies. At the beginning of the century an army of fifty thousand was considered very large, but by the 1660's, Louis could deploy a hundred thousand men, and from the 1690's on France kept as many as 400,000 soldiers in the field, sometimes for years at a time. In the enormous armies of the absolute monarchies, soldiers became instruments of the king rather than followers of any individual general or local magnate. War offices increased their power and tightened their control over generals; indeed, war justified and advanced the central bureaucratic power in every department of state. It absorbed the energies of the aristocratic class, discouraging domestic rebellion, and it provided a career for thousands of ambitious men.

Continuous war encouraged in France and elsewhere a new kind of professional diplomacy as well. Louis was his own foreign minister, and during his reign there was a new order and regularity in the conduct of foreign affairs. Ambassadors (with well-defined duties) were officially and permanently attached to the foreign offices, and diplomacy became a recognized form of service to the state.

V EASTERN EUROPE

The relationship between absolute monarchy and the warfare state is best exemplified in the history of eastern Europe and especially in the rise of Brandenburg-Prussia. In 1640, Frederick William Hohenzollern (known to history as the Great Elector) inherited the impoverished territories of his obscure German dynasty. He became elector of Brandenburg and had at least nominal power as head of state in a variety of other territories between the Baltic and the Rhineland. These included, after 1660, the frontier duchy of Prussia, formerly a remote, isolated Polish fief outside the Empire and the community of German states. Frederick William did not inherit much personal power; traditionally, the elector was not much more than *primus inter pares* among the east German nobility.

East German society was much more primitive than that of England or France. The important cities of the era of the Hanseatic League had diminished in size and prosperity when trade turned to the Atlantic, and the Thirty Years' War devastated towns and countryside alike. What remained of urban society had few resources to throw into the struggle against an ambitious, aggressive head of state. Frederick William regarded both urban independence and rural localism as obstacles to his ambition to unify and strengthen his scattered domains.

The Junker aristocrats of eastern Germany in the mid-seventeenth century were bucolic, backward landowners with no interests beyond their own estates. They certainly were not sympathetic to the elector's foreign wars, which were designed to enhance the status of the Hohenzollern dynasty and to unify his own domains. Frederick William allowed the landowners to deal as they wished with their own serfs but gradually deprived them of all political power. At the same time he used his small but efficient standing army to obliterate even the shadow of urban self-government from the impoverished towns. This he accomplished first in Brandenburg and later in Prussia, where the spirited resistance of Königsberg—the one prosperous city in the duchy—was crushed by the elector's army.

Frederick William entered foreign wars even though his country was far too small and weak to hope for more than judicious alliances, minor gains, and recognition from the great powers. He joined in the War of the North between Poland and Sweden in the late 1650's, and he managed to put more than forty thousand men into the field against Louis XIV in the 1670's. These wars did nothing for the people of eastern Germany but a great deal for absolutism and militarism in the Hohenzollern lands.

In Prussia, the absolute monarchy and its supportive bureaucracy were militaristic from the beginning. The war commissariat directed the economic life of the state, and civilian and military affairs were merged to an extent inconceivable in France or England. Despite their poverty, the elector's subjects paid twice as much in war taxes as those of Louis XIV. The Junkers soon discovered that military service offered an escape from rural poverty and obscurity. The prestige of the army was steadily enhanced in Prussia until soldiers were honored above all other men. The officer corps became fanatically loyal to the Prussian monarchy.

Determined to make the country prosperous in order to pay for its army, Frederick William applied to the Prussian economy a variety of the economic medicines of the age. He encouraged the immigration of refugees from France and Holland (notably French Huguenots), many of whom were skilled farmers and artisans. With their help, the countryside around Berlin became a productive market gardening area, while homesteads in distant frontier regions were settled by pioneers who were exempted from taxation in reward for their efforts. Infant industries were encouraged by strict protectionism and state monopolies.

Prussian autocracy developed with spectacular rapidity. The Great Elector accomplished in a single lifetime the task that had taken the French kings a century or more. The Hohenzollerns were upstarts in the royal community of Europe; their kingdom remained small and poor and insignificant until after the Industrial Revolution of the nineteenth century. But because Prussia was at the bottom of the international pecking order, a dynamic, restless ambition was built into its leaders. Free from the dead hand of national tradition and medieval ideas, the Prussians developed government efficiency, religious tolerance, and aggressive foreign policies along with despotic militarism.

While seventeenth-century Europe was expanding geographically, economically, and intellectually, Russia remained static. Absolute monarchy, a new force in Continental Europe, had been a fact in Russia for centuries; no institutional bulwarks existed to limit the authority of the czar. Russian "cities" were pathetic little villages without independence or urban privileges, and the parliament — the *zemskii sobor* — held no real power.

The czar was severely limited, however, by the size of his enormous land and the diversity of its peoples. Of all the troublesome groups within Russia, the Don Cossacks — a semiautonomous frontier people on the southern steppes — were the most difficult to control. In 1668 the Cossacks organized themselves under Stephen Razin and fought the central government until 1672. The rebellion had no politics and no program; it was a desperate, anarchistic protest against government as such and Russian government in particular.

The czar's administration was not only arbitrary and tyrannical but chaotic and corrupt. There was no tradition of devoted and efficient service to the state, and the nobles on whom the obligation of service rested were selfish, lazy, and unprincipled. Even the army was uncoordinated and poorly trained and equipped. Its most prestigious group — the palace guard, or *streltsy* — had power and status, but it was a continuing source of palace revolution and attempted coups.

When Peter the Great became czar in 1689, there was an enormous gulf between Russia and western Europe. In 1697 a "great embassy" of some 250 Russians led by the czar himself set forth to study the ships and arsenals of the West. Peter had decided that Russia must have a navy to protect itself from the expansionist designs of its neighbors. He brought home several hundred sailors, soldiers, engineers, and mathematicians. This was one of the most significant educational expeditions in history, if only for its effect upon the czar. Peter returned to Russia convinced of the value of Western skills and determined to acquire for his own country the technological and scientific wonders of the West.

Peter succeeded in a remarkable number of his ambitions. He made technological education compulsory for the children of landowners, and he promoted native industries, particularly shipbuilding and the heavy industry essential to war. His attempts at religious reform were less successful, and he earned the undying opposition of the clergy and of conservative landowners, who resisted coercion and change. Early in Peter's reign, Russia fought Turkey; later, Russia entered the Great Northern War against Sweden and emerged as a European power. As elsewhere, war had far-reaching social consequences. Peasants and nobles alike were conscripted for service. Peter introduced graded ranks in military and civilian organizations, undermining the position of the old nobility and creating a new elite whose first loyalty was to the state. But peasants were exploited more and more viciously by landowners with new taxes to pay, and once-free peasants and laborers sank into serfdom in Russia (as in Prussia) even while peasants and workers in western Europe were becoming more prosperous and more free.

Russia remained relatively backward despite Peter's immense accomplishments. The czar was widely detested, yet Russia had no tradition of organized resistance to the central government, and no political or legal ideas were imported from the West along with Western technology. The Russian police state discouraged treason on a high level, and without local self-government, resistance on the village level was impossible. While a small class of nobles was superficially Westernized, the great mass of Russians was almost untouched by Peter's reforms. The chasm in Russia between the sophisticated, traveled few and the illiterate, primitive many widened during the reign of Peter the Great. Russia became a European power in Peter's time, but it also developed its lasting tradition of progress by coercion.

VI THE TRIUMPH OF ABSOLUTISM AND AUTOCRACY

In the long-range perspective of history, Peter the Great did for Russia what the Great Elector did for Brandenburg-Prussia and what various kings and ministers had accomplished in France during the previous century. All these rulers had aimed at the modernization of government and the rational organization of the resources of society in the interest of state power and political order. In Russia the limitations upon the authority of the monarch that existed in France and Prussia were absent, but the tasks of modernization and social reorganization that confronted the czars were much more arduous. This is, essentially, the difference between French and Prussian absolutism and Russian autocracy.

Everywhere in the Europe of 1715, political authority was the exclusive province of very few people—the king, his ministers, a larger or smaller group of nobility. The peasant masses, the urban workers, even the lesser nobles and the wealthy merchants, had very little if anything to say about the decisions affecting the societies in which they lived. It is remarkable how much of the authoritarian and hierarchic political and social pattern that had emerged so long ago in the ancient Near East still prevailed. There was very little evidence of the perpetuation of the contrasting democratic institutions of the Greek polis. England was the only important exception to this general situation, and the degree to which England was an exception is a moot point.

Yet the *ancien régime* that prevailed everywhere from Paris to St. Petersburg in 1715 would, within half a century, undergo tremendous internal strain, experience fundamental economic and social change, and be openly challenged by liberal and democratic ideologies. To the men at the top of European society in 1715, the world had reached its point of perfection; absolutism and autocracy seemed the best forms of government that Western civilization could provide. But there was too much ingenuity in European intellectual life, too much enterprise in its economic life, and generally too much restlessness to allow the status quo to survive for very long.

Russia, lacking many of the social and cultural characteristics of the West, was destined never to escape the trammels of autocracy. In western Europe the political and social order of the early eighteenth century would soon reel under the onslaught of political and economic revolutions motivated by visions of a yet better life for human society.

PART ONE

The
Transformation
of Western
Civilization

**From the *Ancien Regime*
to the Napoleonic Wars**

Through several decades of the eighteenth century the traditional pattern of the *ancien régime* appeared to persist unchanged. Kings contended with each other for territory and hegemony, nobles cultivated an elegant life style, and the European states sought to expand their overseas empires. But behind this facade, the critical attitudes and rationalist doctrines of Enlightenment culture were challenging the morality and utility of the old order. The American Revolution brought ideals of liberty and equality into the arena of practical politics and demonstrated the weakness of royal and aristocratic institutions. Finally, when the *ancien régime* in France was unable to modernize and rationalize the political and social system, it disintegrated before the onslaught of the series of upheavals that comprised the French Revolution. This historic turning point in European political life marked the emergence of a democratic republic and the dissemination of egalitarian ideals. In the end, the revolutionaries could not establish a viable governmental system, and the welfare of France was subordinated to the expansionist ambitions of Napoleon Bonaparte, who replaced the Republic with a military dictatorship.

Napoleon's temporary conquest of much of Europe further served to export the egalitarian social ideals of the Revolution and also stirred popular yearnings for national liberation and rejuvenation. At the same time, Britain was beginning its advance toward an industrialized, urbanized economy. The Industrial Revolution joined with the democratic upheaval to inaugurate the transformation of Western civilization from the pattern of the *ancien régime* into the way of life of modern society.

A revolution can be neither made nor stopped.
The only thing that can be done is for one or several
of its children to give it a direction . . . ,
or else for its enemies to stifle it temporarily
by the strength of arms.
But in the latter case the revolutionary fire
smolders under the ashes, and sooner or later
the conflagration flares up again with new vigor
and devours all obstacles.

Napoleon Bonaparte

Page 17: a portrait of Napoleon I in 1808, by Jacques Louis David, court painter to the emperor.

Absolutism and Empire

ENVIRONMENT ESSAY

By modern standards the economy of Europe in the second and third quarters of the eighteenth century was preindustrial and its society was politically undeveloped. The great majority of the people lived on the land. The factory system had not yet emerged, and commerce remained the basis of urban wealth. Despite some improvements, transportation and communication were painfully slow. Wealth, power, and high culture were concentrated in the hands of the landed aristocracy and a narrow urban oligarchy, and government still served principally the interests of these elite groups.

Yet the persistence of these fundamental characteristics of the stage of economic, political, and social development that historians now identify with the *ancien régime* did not engender a mood of futility and pessimism. On the contrary, the pervasive attitude, at least among educated men and women, was a benign optimism with regard to what reason could do to further the welfare of mankind. These people who lived in the autumnal years of the preindustrial world constantly expressed what seems to us a naive faith in man's ability to control and utilize the physical environment for the general welfare and in society's continued progress from barbarism and violence toward civilization and universal peace.

Writing in 1793, the French social theorist Condorcet eloquently affirmed the common faith of educated men in his day:

Nature has set no term to the perfection of human faculties; . . . the perfectibility of man is truly indefinite; . . . the progress of this perfectibility . . . has no other limit than the duration of the globe upon which nature has cast us. This progress will doubtless vary in speed, but it will never be reversed as long as the earth occupies its present place in the system of the universe, and as long as the general laws of this

The Aristocratic World. In the eighteenth century and the early years of the nineteenth century, the aristocratic elite, when and where it was still untroubled by the onslaught of democracy and industrialization, applied its vast wealth to the creation of palaces and imposing urban dwellings. Many of these still stand as monuments to the classical tastes and extravagant opulence of the old order. Right: the palace of Würzburg, typical of the courtly centers of Germany and Austria in the eighteenth century. Below: Frederick the Great's palace of Sans Souci at Potsdam. The ornate classicism symbolizes the upstart arrogance of the Prussian monarchy. Facing page: the quadrant of Regent Street, London, designed between 1811 and 1817 by the architect John Nash at the behest of the Prince Regent, the last of the carefree grandees of the old order.

system produce neither a general cataclysm nor such changes as will deprive the human race of its present faculties and its present resources.[1]

We of the twentieth century, painfully aware of the agonies, terrors, and upheavals that continue to rack the modern world, are inclined to be critical of eighteenth-century optimism. Yet Condorcet was no smug, ignorant aristocrat; he was a man of learning and of deep feeling, a humanitarian and a liberal reformer. We must try to understand the conditions that underlay his idea of progress.

The key words are "present faculties" and "present resources." In eighteenth-century Europe, man's intellect and his social institutions seemed to have triumphed over nature, and there was every expectation that the environment would become steadily more hospitable to the peace and beauty

1. Marie Jean Antoine Nicolas Caritat, Marquis de Condorcet, *Sketch for a Historical Picture of the Progress of the Human Mind*, trans. J. Barraclough. New York: Noonday Press, 1955, pp. 4–5.

The Face of Power. The two most successful governments in the mid-eighteenth-century struggle for power were Great Britain and Prussia. Britain was ruled by an aristocratic oligarchy and Prussia by a ruthless autocrat. Left: the British House of Commons about 1740. Below: Frederick the Great of Prussia in a characteristic military pose.

The Impact of Empire. The vast overseas territories of the European powers greatly augmented the wealth and, therefore, the arrogant self-satisfaction of the old order. But experience with alien societies and problems of imperial government helped lead to a reexamination of Europe's own political and social systems. Facing page, left: exotic America as portrayed in a ceiling fresco at the Würzburg palace. Facing page, right: British fort at Calcutta, India.

mankind sought to achieve. When an eighteenth-century gentleman gazed upon the magnificent buildings erected by princes, lords, and rich merchants, he was delighted by the manner in which the artistic heritage of many centuries had been used to create their imposing elegance. Nor were such buildings isolated monuments; they dotted the landscape throughout western Europe, from England to Austria. In the cities, where handsome rows of colonnaded facades flanked the broad avenues, it seemed obvious that many could now share pleasures of urban living formerly enjoyed only by the most highborn in European society.

Gentlemen of good will like Condorcet were by no means content with the political situation that prevailed in the eighteenth century. Indeed, they were often vociferously critical of the absolutist regimes. But the fault they saw in government was that it was irrational: it catered to the interests of too narrow an aristocratic elite and failed to respond to the will of "the people"—by whom they meant the petty nobility and the high bourgeoisie. They believed that if government could be made more rational and more responsive to the people, it would be better able to apply human and natural resources to the further improvement of the physical and social environment.

Imperial ventures overseas taught educated Europeans of the eighteenth century two lessons. First, the existence of novel political and social institutions in other lands meant that there was nothing inevitable or sacrosanct about their own systems; these could and should be changed in accordance with human need. Second, the tremendous inflow of wealth from overseas encouraged the buoyant belief that there was no limit to the material possessions and aesthetic pleasures they might enjoy. The right of Europeans to live high on imperial pillage and the labor of the native peoples of Asia, Africa, and the Americas was seldom questioned or even seriously considered.

Naive as it may appear in retrospect, the faith of the eighteenth century in material and social progress was well grounded in the conditions and values of the age. But there was one aspect of their environment to which the prophets of progress gave insufficient notice—the horrible poverty and unrelieved misery of the great mass of society in both town and country. Man's reason

The Underside of the *Ancien Régime*. Alongside the elegance and order of eighteenth-century Europe there was widespread poverty and horrible squalor, for which the *ancien régime* had no solution—and little concern. Facing page: "Act of Humanity" by Jean Defraine. Humanitarian largess on the part of lords and ladies was the prescribed cure for the misery of the poor in the eighteenth century. Above: "Gin Lane" by William Hogarth, whose work frequently depicts life in the London slums. Gin was the first hard liquor accessible to the European working class. (Brandy was too expensive, and whisky was undrinkable until the late eighteenth century.) For the London poor, alcoholic delirium was the one escape from the horrors of reality. Right: the dungeons of the *Palais de Justice*, Paris, in the eighteenth century. The law was invariably brutal in its treatment of the poor and biased in favor of the rich and highborn. French courts, which followed the draconian traditions of Roman law, were particularly notorious.

EUROPE OF THE OLD REGIME
1721

	House of Bourbon in France and Spain
	House of Habsburg
	Brandenburg-Prussia
—	Boundary of the Holy Roman Empire

NORWAY SWEDEN •Nystad INGRIA

•Christiania •Stockholm ESTONIA RUSSIA

LIVONIA

BALTIC COURLAND

SEA •Smolensk

Western Dvina R.

DENMARK

NORTH •Copenhagen PRUSSIA

SEA •Danzig

•Dublin •York GREAT Hamburg

BRITAIN HANOVER BRANDENBURG Vistula R. •Warsaw

UNITED •Berlin POLAND •Kiev

NETHERLANDS Rhine SAXONY Oder R.

•London Utrecht AUSTRIAN HOLY •Prague GALICIA

ATLANTIC NETHERLANDS •Aachen ROMAN Dniester R.

ENGLISH CHANNEL EMPIRE MOLDAVIA

OCEAN •Brest •Paris Seine R. •Strasbourg Munich AUSTRIA •Vienna

Loire R. Danube R. Buda••Pest

FRANCE •Bern HUNGARY

BAY SWITZERLAND WALLACHIA BLACK

OF •Lyons SAVOY MILAN VENICE BOSNIA •Bucharest SEA

BISCAY •Bordeaux Rhône R. PIEDMONT •Milan •Venice •Belgrade OTTOMAN

Garonne R. •Genoa ADRIATIC MONTENEGRO •Constantinople

•Toulouse •Avignon TUSCANY PAPAL SEA EMPIRE

ANDORRA •Marseilles STATES •Ragusa

CORSICA •Rome AEGEAN

Genoa •Naples SEA

Tagus R. •Madrid SARDINIA NAPLES

PORTUGAL SPAIN MINORCA Austria, 1714; •Athens

•Lisbon Great Britain, 1713 Savoy, 1720 TYRRHENIAN SEA

BALEARIC IS.

•Gibraltar SICILY IONIAN SEA

•Tangier MEDITERRANEAN

•Algiers •Tunis SEA

The Great Powers. The War of the Spanish Succession (1701–1714) was precipitated by the expansionist policy of Louis XIV and particularly by the French king's declaration that the Bourbon Philip V of Spain and his descendants retained their rights of succession to the throne of France—a policy statement that created the prospect of the eventual union of France with the Spanish Empire. The war involved all the great powers of western Europe. The settlement of 1713–1714 and an adjustment made in 1720 established a peace that lasted until 1740. According to the treaty arrangements, the French and Spanish thrones would remain separate forever; Spain ceded the Spanish Netherlands, Sardinia, Naples, and Milan to Austria (with Sardinia going to the duke of Savoy in 1720); and Spain granted Gibraltar and Minorca to Great Britain. In addition, Britain gained Newfoundland, Nova Scotia, and the Hudson Bay region from France and trading rights in Spain's American empire from Spain.

and society's resources offered no solution to this blight. Indeed, in celebrating the beauty and order that distinguished their world, men of learning and sensibility seldom cared to comment on its dark side.

Jonathan Swift might rage at the sufferings of the Irish peasantry, and William Hogarth might portray the stinking rot of the London slums; but like all other preindustrial, underdeveloped, essentially aristocratic societies, eighteenth-century Europe accepted poverty and misery as part of the natural order. It was, in fact, a necessary part: the landed aristocracy could afford its way of life only with income obtained through the unending toil of hordes of poor peasants, and the elegant houses of nobles and rich merchants could function only with droves of servants on miserable wages. Admiration for the elegance of the eighteenth century should not blind us to the fact that the satisfaction of aristocratic taste depended upon the perpetual labor and unrelieved subjection of the majority of the people.

I **THE *ANCIEN RÉGIME***

Europe After the Death of Louis XIV

The death of Louis XIV in September 1715 marked the end of a turbulent period of European political history. French ambitions had united the rest of Europe in a war against France which neither side could afford. The death of the Sun King—who had personified the French state—made possible an era of peace. As regent, the duke of Orléans (1715–1723) exercised regal power while Louis' five-year-old great-grandson grew into his inheritance. Philip V (1700–1746), the Bourbon king of Spain and grandson of Louis XIV, sat upon his throne by virtue of the Treaty of Utrecht, fully aware that only that treaty kept him from the French throne as well.

George I (1714–1727) and his successors in the new Hanoverian dynasty in Great Britain strove to translate their parliamentary mandate to rule into political power, while the Stuart pretender—the son of James II—waited in the French court for an opportunity to cross the channel. George I lacked a clear and distinctive title to his throne, and as a king chosen by Parliament, he could not rule without parliamentary support. Fortunately for the Hanoverians, the English country gentlemen in Parliament hated the Catholicism of the Stuart pretender at least as much as they hated new taxes. In addition to his problematical relationship with France—Britain's recent enemy and present host to the Pretender—George I had to balance his interests as king of England with his interests as elector of Hanover. The king's Hanoverian connection brought up the inflammatory question of the need to maintain a standing army for use in Germany as well as the possibility of British involvement in Baltic wars, and neither issue met sympathetic understanding in the British Parliament.

The oldest and most venerable European state—if indeed it could be called a state at all—was, of course, the Holy Roman Empire. By the beginning of the eighteenth century, however, that empire was weak and decrepit. Rent by mighty power struggles since the High Middle Ages, it had become the hereditary preserve of the Habsburg family. But assurance of succession had not brought a greater sense of political community. On the contrary, by 1715 — during the reign of Charles VI of Austria—the Holy Roman Empire was divided by unbridgeable political, regional, and religious differences and incapable either of reforming itself or even—as the dramatic mid-century wars were once more to show—of preserving peace and order among its leading members.

Meanwhile, Prussia, Austria, and Russia jostled each other for shares in the disintegrating kingdoms in eastern Europe—Sweden, Poland, and Turkey. Prussia needed land to support its ever expanding army. Charles VI (1711–1740) of Austria strove to pass his lands on intact to his daughter, Maria Theresa. Russia, during the reign of Peter the Great, sought almost continuously to push its borders to the south and west while at the same time bringing Western forms of culture, administration, and technology to Russia. Control of northern and southern Italy was sought by many and secure to none, and the declining effectiveness of Spain as an imperial power was both an invitation and a danger to Britain and France. Spain's inability to fill the needs of its colonial markets tempted foreign powers.

The long series of wars terminated by the Treaty of Utrecht (1713) was not without its positive results. To begin with, it marked the beginning of the end of the long-standing conflict between the Bourbons of France and the Habsburgs of Spain and Austria, who since the late fifteenth century had been jockeying for power and position along the Rhine, the Pyrenees, and France's northern border—the French seeking to expand their natural frontiers, the Habsburgs attempting to contain or reduce them. Although France and Austria were frequently to be on opposite sides in the eighteenth century, it was not until the wars of the French Revolution and Napoleon that they again confronted each other in a military showdown.

Europe escaped general warfare between 1715 and 1740 despite the hectic atmosphere of European politics because the great powers, especially France and Britain, consistently sought peace. In November 1716 this common goal was formally stated in an alliance between the two former adversaries. The Netherlands soon joined the other two maritime powers, and Austria entered the alliance when Spain sent an expedition against Sardinia and southern Italy in 1718. The Quadruple Alliance set up a new balance-of-power system which established the outlines of European diplomacy for the next two decades, effectively preventing the outbreak of another general war.

The new alliance system was characterized by its flexibility. Thus when Spain invaded Italy in 1718 and when France and Prussia disputed the Polish succession in 1733, general war did not follow. Instead, after brief and limited campaigns, the problems were settled — or at least postponed — by international agreement. Diplomatic negotiations between 1715 and 1740 were admittedly protracted and indecisive, but they did succeed in avoiding a ruinous war at a time when no major power in Europe could afford such a conflict.

Problems of Central Government

The internal conditions of European states between 1715 and 1740 limited freedom of action in international affairs. In 1715 new dynasties in Spain and England were struggling to secure their thrones and to establish themselves in the domestic political structure, while in France and Sweden central government was weakened by the loss of powerful monarchs. Charles VI of Austria, with no male heir, schemed to secure the throne for his daughter. The 1720's brought the death of Peter the Great of Russia and also of the king of Poland. The new king of Prussia, Frederick William I (1713–1740), was an unusually able monarch who suffered from neither dynastic nor constitutional uncertainties but placed the major emphasis of his government upon internal affairs. The debts of the wars of Louis XIV had fallen due, and no major state was in a position to ignore internal problems or to launch a consistently aggressive and ambitious foreign policy. By no means satiated but much less bellicose than in the preceding century, the nations of Europe turned their attention to setting their respective houses in order.

The seventeenth century had witnessed a significant continuation of the rapid growth of central power begun in many European states in the late fifteenth and the sixteenth century. This growth continued throughout the eighteenth century, accompanied and reinforced by an ever increasing emphasis on, and acceptance of, theories of national sovereignty and *raison d'état*. This is not to say, however, that this political theory viewed the monarchical rulers as unlimited in their power and authority. Even the sixteenth-century theorist of absolutism, Jean Bodin, had recognized that within every state there must be subsidiary corporate bodies such as municipalities, trading companies, and other kinds of semiautonomous organizations. But Bodin — and his successors in the seventeenth and eighteenth centuries — believed that such corporate bodies should exist only with the consent of the sovereign and should derive their power from the sovereign.

The theoretical conception of the centralized state — even when further buttressed by the divine-right theory of Bishop Bossuet and his school — was much simpler than the political realities. It is true that the central government's scope of action increased enormously during the seventeenth century. At the same time, however, behind the legal and bureaucratic structure of the state there were many obstructions to the monolithic exercise of power.

The power of the French monarchy reached its height under Louis XIV, whose dominating personality and carefully calculated policies reduced the nobility to subservience. Court ritual and the economic and social dependence of the nobles at Versailles magnified the king's position. Louis XIV was powerful enough to defy even the *parlements*, the bastion of the nobility. But though Louis managed to keep most of the government in his own hands, the greatest days of the monarchy were fast slipping away, and during the last few years of his long reign, his weary subjects waited for him to die. His system of governing did not survive his death. During the childhood of his great-grandson, who succeeded him, France was ruled by the duke of Orléans, a nephew of the late king. The greatest problem facing the government was that of revenue. The wars of Louis XIV had left the state virtually bankrupt, and its financial condition could no longer be ignored, but the regency's clever—and ultimately unsuccessful—scheme to improve its impoverished position spoke volumes about the nature of the French government in the eighteenth century, as well as about the influence of clever international financiers.

Impressed by the early success of the Bank of England (likewise chartered in an age of financial stress in 1694), the regent gave eager approval to a proposal put forth by the Scotsman John Law (1671–1729) for a similar funding of the French national debt, and, indeed, it must be noted that Law's approach was not wholly without merit. His basic objectives were to bail out the government and simultaneously to increase the money supply in France. In order to achieve these twin goals, he suggested the establishment of a royal bank to manage the currency and trade of the country, collect its taxes, and, finally, wipe out the national debt.

In 1716 Law, by no means a novice in financial matters, obtained a royal charter for a general bank, a joint-stock company authorized to issue notes acceptable as currency. The bank rapidly proved an enormous success, and Law soon began to extend his area of operations. He purchased the monopoly of the Mississippi trade and formed the Louisiana Company. This enterprise, too, flourished. In 1718 the bank became a state institution. Next Law moved to consolidate the old companies of the East Indies and China with his own Louisiana Company, thus giving himself a virtual monopoly on France's overseas trade. Finally in 1719, having reached the pinnacle of social success and political influence, Law assumed the management of the national debt and acquired the right to collect indirect taxes and carry through a substantial simplification of the whole tax collection process.

But Law had overreached himself. Jealous financiers began to enter the field against him in France. His enterprises became the center of vast, unheard-of, and dangerous speculation. By early 1720 it became clear that shares in Law's company were vastly overpriced, and within a few months, he and his company tumbled into hopeless bankruptcy, taking with them thousands of small French investors. The collapse of Law's enterprise discredited not only its founder but his notable efforts to reorganize the French system of taxation as well. The best the duke of Orléans could do for Law was to help him escape across the French frontier with his life.

John Law's grandiose "Mississippi Bubble" had an English counterpart, possibly related to it, called the South Sea Bubble. The British government accepted a scheme for the liquidation of the national debt put forth by the South Sea Company and evidently promoted with substantial inducements to leading politicians and royal mistresses. As in France, the flotation of company stock produced a wild outburst of speculation, but when the South Sea Bubble burst in August 1720, the effects were much less severe than those caused by the collapse of Law's Mississippi Bubble in France. Perhaps the outstanding result of the South Sea Bubble was that it brought to power the one political leader who had actively opposed the scheme, Robert Walpole.

The most lasting result of the Mississippi Bubble was that it instilled in the French middle class a peculiar kind of thrift and caution in financial matters, a trait it has not yet fully overcome. But the failure of Law's grandiose schemes had other unfortunate consequences. Most important, the cause of tax reform was largely abandoned. When, a generation later, a controller general attempted to put France's financial house in order by imposing a general 5 per cent income tax, the privileged elements in the country quickly succeeded in putting an end to the dangerous proposal and to the official's career as well.

The striking success of the privileged elements in France in escaping or terminating the reform efforts of the monarchy, especially in fiscal affairs, was notable evidence of their resurgent power after the death of Louis XIV. But if it was the tragedy of the *ancien régime* that the privileged classes could not be reformed, neither could they govern the country on their own. The regent established a system of seven or eight councils to handle important affairs in place of the seven or eight top ministers formerly in charge; but this system — the so-called Polysynody — did not work properly either and collapsed after three years.

The French nobility, it was clear, had neither the training nor the inclination for the dull and difficult task of administration. As the memoirs of the Duc de Saint-Simon indicate in devastating detail, questions of precedence concerned the nobles more than the daily tasks of government. But if they could not govern, they could still exert enormous influence in matters which interested them. The regent was forced to recognize the rights of the *parlements* which Louis XIV had been able to strike down. When Louis XV came to power in 1723, this tendency continued; the nobles moved away from the court to Paris, escaping the social dependence which had helped keep them under control during the reign of the Sun King.

Louis XIV had been strong-willed, perhaps to a fault, but a weak will was only one of Louis XV's many failings. Far from wearing down his opposition through tireless pressure, he tended to give in when opposed. Thus, while the early eighteenth century did not bring any real attempt to curb the powers of the French monarchy, it was a conservative era in which the forces of particularism and localism successfully forestalled government attempts to wipe out the privileges of class or the autonomy of church, guild, or town; in so doing, they prevented any resurgence of the royal power. Indeed, conservative was the most appropriate description for the single most important action of Louis' reign — his decision to appoint his old tutor Abbé (soon Cardinal) Fleury (1653 – 1743) to head up his government. Fleury, whose maturity spanned the turbulent years of Louis xiv, knew what France needed most — peace abroad and consolidation at home — and though he was unable to prevent France's involvement in the War of the Austrian Succession, which broke out in December 1740, Fleury's policies seemed on the way toward giving France the era of tranquility it craved and required.

This trend in France was not an isolated phenomenon. In the early eighteenth century several European countries took steps to strengthen the old order and to improve its functioning. When Peter the Great died in 1725, he left Russia in a position similar to that of France after Louis xiv. During his long and eventful reign, Peter forced dramatic and far-reaching changes upon Russia. Like many Russian nobles, his son Alexis opposed the autocratic manner in which Peter attempted to enforce the westernization of the aristocracy; and he disliked the expansive foreign policy which made Peter's reign one of constant warfare. Alexis was done away with, probably with his father's approval, and Peter the Great left only an infant grandson as his heir.

The throne was given to Peter's wife, Catherine i, who ruled from 1725 to 1727, when she was succeeded by the twelve-year-old son of the unfortunate Alexis, Peter ii, who died of smallpox in 1730. During both reigns the supreme privy council of nobles actually governed, and the earlier attempts to modernize Russian society and government were curtailed. When Anne (1730 – 1740), a daughter of Peter the Great's half-brother Ivan v, came to the throne, the council forced her to accept serious limitations upon her power, but she abolished the council and ruled through her German advisers. Although Anne continued the policy of westernization, the entire period was characterized mainly by the disorganization and weakness of the central government. The nobles were given virtually a free hand with the peasantry, whose status had gradually been reduced to that of serfs who could be bought and sold. In Russia the *ancien régime* survived the eighteenth century largely intact. It underwent few important changes until the middle of the nineteenth century.

The decline of central power in France and Russia in the early eighteenth century was minor in comparison with its decline in Sweden and Poland. At the end of the seventeenth century Sweden had experienced a last burst of monarchical achievement at home and abroad. Charles xi (1660 – 1697) broke the power of the landed nobility and established an effective bureaucracy and standing army. Upon his death he was succeeded by his fifteen-year-old son Charles xii, who at once found himself confronted with a concerted effort on the part of his country's long-standing enemies—Russia, Denmark, and Poland—to drive Sweden from the Continent. At first Charles' brilliant generalship confounded his powerful enemies, but his disastrous invasion of Russia led to humiliating defeat at the Battle of Poltava in December 1709, which in turn led to his exile in Turkey in 1709–1714.

Returning to Sweden in the latter year, Charles resumed the struggle against his old enemies, now reinforced by Hanover and the rising state of Prussia. In 1718 Charles was mortally wounded. The disastrous peace treaty that ended the Great Northern War in 1720 put an end to Sweden's pretensions on the Continent. Hanover and Prussia took over many of Sweden's holdings on German soil, and most of the remainder—including Estonia, Livonia, and Karelia—went to Russia.

The humiliating Peace of Nystad did not mean the end of Sweden's misfortunes, however. The country now entered into a calamitous era of aristocratic misrule, which lasted until the early 1770's. With the new monarch little more than a figurehead, Sweden's policy was largely directed for the next twenty years by Count Arvid Bernhard Horn, a cautious chancellor who eschewed foreign involvements as a matter of principle. But by the late 1730's a new generation had arisen which had forgotten the disastrous experiences of the early 1700's and which derided the aging Horn for perpetuating "an inglorious peace." As a result, Sweden in 1741 became involved in a new series of unsuccessful wars with Russia.

This new era of aristocratic reaction was to last for another thirty years, ending only with the accession of Gustavus III in June 1771. Within a year, the new monarch had summarily forced the Swedish parliament to accept a constitution that provided for a more equitable balance between Crown and *Riksdag*. But some of Gustavus' most turbulent days lay still ahead. In 1788 he launched a sudden attack on Russia, thus beginning a war that nearly led to national humiliation but finally ended in a remarkably favorable treaty of peace and alliance (October 1791), by which Catherine the Great promised to pay her new ally an annual subsidy of 300,000 rubles.

By this time, all Europe was distracted by the growing virulence of the French Revolution. "The king of France has lost his throne, perhaps his life," Gustavus exclaimed in 1789 when he heard that Louis XVI had convoked the Estates General. Later Gustavus seriously considered invading Normandy with thirty thousand Swedish troops to save the Bourbon throne. But in 1792 the other great powers were disinclined to support such action, and by that time Sweden no longer had sufficient men and resources to act on its own.

Poland in the eighteenth century had an even more turbulent history than Sweden and an even more striking decline. At the beginning of the century it was the third largest country in Europe, outranked in size only by Sweden and Russia, its territory of about 280,000 square miles reaching from the Baltic to the Black Sea; its population of over eleven million people was the fourth largest in Europe. Politically, however, it was much less impressive.

Its last important ruler had been John III Sobieski (1674–1696), whose relief of the Turkish siege of Vienna in 1683 was one of the most dramatic events of the seventeenth century. After his death the Polish cause rapidly ebbed. The next four rulers — beginning with Augustus II (1696–1697) — were imposed on the country from the outside, and that fact, when added to the already fragile structure of Polish constitutional politics, prepared the way for the successive partitions of Poland and its ultimate extinction as an independent state at the end of the eighteenth century.

The decisive weakness of the Polish monarchy lay in the fact that political authority resided ultimately in the hands of a grossly myopic, self-aggrandizing nobility — a nobility which at the opening of the eighteenth century still held five sixths of the peasants in subjugation. Authority was so diffused that the vote of a single nobleman was sufficient to block — or to adjourn — the Polish Diet, and capricious use of this *liberum veto* markedly accelerated the decline of Poland at a time when its neighbors to the east and west, Russia and Prussia, were steadily growing in military power. It was this same aristocratic Diet that, after 1717, interfered increasingly with the religious and political rights of Polish Protestants, thus furnishing the Russian and Prussian governments with useful pretexts for interfering in Poland's internal affairs.

In Spain and Austria the position of the monarch was complicated by the diversity of the territories under his control. Although the Bourbon dynasty eventually created in Spain a more unified and modern state than had ever been possible under the Habsburgs, in 1713 Philip V faced a long uphill struggle against the venerable tradition of Spanish particularism. The different parts of the Iberian peninsula had been added one by one to the inheritance of the Spanish Crown, and each had taken care to guarantee its own autonomy. Consequently, in order to implement any policy, the king had to go through the long and difficult process of gaining the adherence of each part of the kingdom.

Philip V was far from a great king; in fact, after the first few years of his reign, he was hardly a king at all. He abdicated the throne for a brief period in 1724 but was forced to come out of retirement upon the death of his son and continued to rule until 1746. Philip apparently suffered from rather serious mental problems, manifested in ways ranging from his refusal to cut his toenails to a perpetual state of depression which prevented him from taking action. For most of the reign, his wife and the first minister, Jan Willem Ripperdá, governed the kingdom. Both were ambitious and scheming and followed an aggressive foreign policy. In addition, they began the gradual war of attrition against local autonomy which was to be the most important contribution of the Bourbons to Spanish government. Because Catalonia had allied itself with the enemy in the recent war, its privileges were taken away. The Cortes (parliament) in Aragon ceased to meet during Philip's reign, and those in Castille and Navarre lost all their power to obstruct the royal will.

Few of these changes came about through dramatic confrontations; instead, they were small adjustments which gradually altered the relationship of the different areas to the Crown. That was probably one of the main reasons for their success.

The position of the Crown in Austria was similar to that in Spain. The Habsburgs ruled not a kingdom but a group of separate kingdoms, duchies, and other political entities, each with its own institutions and privileges. Unlike Philip v, however, Charles vi of Austria made practically no progress in diminishing the autonomy of his different possessions. Instead, he devoted a tremendous amount of time and energy to getting their acceptance of his daughter, Maria Theresa, as heir to the throne. In addition to profligate spending on the imperial court and army, which very nearly reduced his state to bankruptcy, and largely unsuccessful attempts to develop the ports of Fiume and Trieste on the Adriatic Sea, Charles' reign was largely dominated by his determination to leave his imperial possessions undivided to his heir. This purpose dominated both his relationship with his kingdom and his diplomatic policies.

Extinction of the male line in the Spanish branch of the Habsburg family had set off a costly international war of succession that lasted nearly twenty years. Hoping to avoid any similar conflagration, Charles now made liberal concessions to the other powers of Europe, all of which—including Britain, France, Holland, Russia, Poland, Spain, Sardinia, *and* Prussia—pledged their word and honor to the Pragmatic Sanction, a guarantee of Austria's boundaries after Maria Theresa's accession. It should be added that Charles was much less successful in developing any effective leadership in his capacity as Holy Roman emperor, with the result that during his reign the fortunes of the Empire continued to deteriorate and the prestige of Austria in Germany, already low in the seventeenth century, declined still further.

When Charles died in October 1740, he left his twenty-three-year-old daughter a firm legal position but a poorly administered, impoverished state and a disorganized army. These problems turned out to be much more serious in the long run than her legal right to the throne. Lack of an efficient and centralized administration and inability to persuade the Hungarian Diet to authorize additional taxes left Austria at a disadvantage in the struggle with Prussia which was to begin within a few months.

British and Prussian Solutions

Only two countries in Europe, Great Britain and Prussia, successfully solved the most pressing problems of the early eighteenth century: how to make the nobility a useful ally of the centralized power of the state, and how to tap sources of revenue adequate to support the state's expanding needs. Although the constitutional structures of the two countries were almost diametrically opposed, both were able to integrate the aristocracy into the government, assuring its members of power and leaving them social superiority. At the same time, both the English and the Prussian aristocracies were open-ended and fluid, continually absorbing the upper bourgeoisie into their ranks and thereby avoiding the social rigidity that helped bring down the French monarchy in the latter part of the eighteenth century. It is also true that unlike the aristocracies in most of the rest of Europe, the Prussian and English aristocracies were dynamic groups capable of exercising power; they did not become vestigial organisms isolated from socially useful pursuits.

In England the Glorious Revolution of 1688 had assured both the constitutional position of Parliament and the political dominance of the landed gentry. In the eighteenth century, members of this relatively homogeneous class played an ever increasing role in government through their position in Parliament and their control of local government. The accession of George I, the elector of Hanover, was fully in accord with that trend. Selected by Parliament from several candidates, he could not govern without its cooperation. This did not mean that the king became a creature of Parliament—in fact he was careful to guard his prerogatives, especially in foreign affairs. But Parliament voted taxes and could thus presumably veto almost any royal policy. The king was able to formulate policy, but he had to concern himself constantly with retaining a parliamentary majority.

The development of the cabinet and the office of prime minister in the eighteenth century provided the means through which the king could deal with Parliament. Under George I, however, the cabinet was far from the formal committee which it later became. In fact, it met infrequently and was far less important as a group than the "king's closet," an informal group of advisers and favorites with much more influence on the royal policies. The ministers were chosen by the king to carry out his policies and to gain their acceptance in Parliament, and a minister's power extended only so far as he had the confidence of the king.

Sir Robert Walpole has been called the first prime minister of England, a ranking that is largely justified by the nature and the duration of his position in British government. He was one of four ministers most powerful during the first years of the reign of George I, but he was gradually pushed out of the inner circle of George's advisers and went into opposition. Walpole returned to power in April 1721 (as chancellor of the exchequer and first lord of the treasury) after the South Sea Bubble fiasco left the government in disrepute and the national finances in jeopardy. He used his opportunity well, protecting those whose disgrace would have jeopardized the monarchy itself. (George I and his mistresses, along with many prominent members of the government, had been involved in the scheme.)

Walpole soon proved himself a political genius. Openly hungry for power and riches, he protected his relationship with George I and carefully built up his support in Parliament—a delicate task. In that period a parliamentary majority had little to do with public opinion as such; instead, it required the support of men who controlled parliamentary seats. The government could rely upon the support of members who sat for boroughs where the government had great influence, such as port cities. In addition, those who had pensions or offices from the Crown or had received favors for their families and friends could be counted upon for support. A powerful lord, like Walpole's ally, the duke of Newcastle, could often secure many votes from his followers; but it was also necessary to gain votes from the bloc of country gentlemen – independent of any such influence – who made up the largest single group in the House of Commons. Although the terms Whig and Tory were still in use, there were no political parties in Commons in the early eighteenth century. Instead, there was a complicated system of antagonisms and alliances, and Walpole's genius at manipulating the system was the real source of his long term of power under George I and George II.

For all the widespread idealization of the British political system, it would be a mistake to think of eighteenth-century members of Parliament as public servants. Their parliamentary interests were extensions of their private interests in low taxes and in the power and profit to be gained by involvement in public life. They were usually divided less by issues than by personal considerations. At the same time, however, Parliament did represent those in British society who possessed economic and political power, and the government functioned effectively in their interest. The Whig magnates and ministers who set the parliamentary tone and the style of national politics were not at all concerned with what is now called social progress. The governmental and legal institutions of early eighteenth-century Britain blatantly favored the rich and the powerful, while the workers and the poor were treated with brutal injustice.

If in Great Britain the refinements of parliamentary government served to obscure the more ugly aspects of daily living, no such cover existed in the Hohenzollern monarchy. There was to begin with no such thing as a Prussian parliament. Although provincial estates still existed in various parts of the state, the king of Prussia was, for all practical purposes, an autocrat. But while successive Prussian rulers since the Great Elector had carefully eliminated all institutional opposition to monarchical rule, this is not to say that the kings of Prussia, even the most powerful of them, could do entirely as they pleased. The fact of the matter is that the Prussian aristocracy – like the British – had found ways and means to continue to play a substantial role in the direction of politics and society.

The Prussian landed aristocracy owed this opportunity in large measure to the territorial structure of the Prussian state. Since the fifteenth century the Hohenzollerns had ruled an inheritance of widely scattered territories, and though the size of their holdings had been increasing almost continuously since that time, they still lacked anything resembling a contiguous territorial unity. Given the geographical realities of the Prussian state, the Hohenzol-

THE GROWTH OF PRUSSIA, 1648-1795

- Prussia in 1648
- Acquired 1648-1688
- Acquired 1688-1740
- Acquired 1740-1786
- Acquired 1786-1795

SWEDEN

BALTIC SEA

NORTH SEA

• Copenhagen

• Memel

• Königsberg EAST PRUSSIA

LEBORK

• Danzig

BÜTOW

• Tannenburg NEW EAST PRUSSIA

HOLSTEIN

EASTERN POMERANIA

WEST PRUSSIA

• Hamburg

Emden • EAST FRISIA

MECKLENBERG

WESTERN POMERANIA

• Bremen

NETHERLANDS

• Amsterdam

TECKLENBURG

MINDEN

RAVENSBURG

• Hanover

MITTELMARK (BRANDENBURG)

ALTMARK

Potsdam • • Berlin

MAGDEBURG

• Halberstadt

NEUMARK

SWIEBODZIN

• Posen

Warsaw •

SOUTH PRUSSIA

POLAND

CLEVES

GELDERS

MARK

Crefeld •

• Brussels

Cologne •

NORDHAUSEN •

MANSFELD

HALLE

COTTBUS

• Leipzig

LOWER SILESIA

• Breslau

UPPER SILESIA

• Beuthen

• Ratibor

FRANCE

• Frankfurt

Mainz •

BAYREUTH

• Prague

AUSTRIAN

EMPIRE

ANSBACH

LIMBURG

Danube

Meuse R.

Rhine R.

Elbe R.

Main R.

Vistula R.

Spree R.

The Peace of Westphalia added eastern Pomerania to the Hohenzollern lands. Later gains were small and scattered, until Frederick the Great secured Silesia by war and West Prussia by diplomacy, linking Brandenburg and East Prussia. His successor added another large block of land in the east at Polish expense. Though small compared to gains in the east, where Prussia stretched from the Elbe to Lithuania, Prussia's western holdings would be important to later expansion in the Rhineland.

lerns had learned early that to maintain and possibly expand their frontiers they must establish a powerful army and an effective bureaucratic government. The army and the bureaucracy became the primary means by which the Hohenzollerns worked toward the creation of a reasonably homogeneous state. They overcame the problem of regionalism by governing through bureaucrats and soldiers drawn from all their territories.

Furthermore, the Hohenzollerns were shrewd enough to realize that, in the development of this sort of state, the assistance—indeed, the positive and willing cooperation—of the landed aristocracy and nobility was absolutely indispensable. Hence the important compromise, dating from the 1650's, by which the powers of the landed aristocracy in local government, its judicial rights, and its authority over the peasantry were specifically affirmed by the Great Elector in return for the readiness of the nobles to accord the Hohenzollern rulers virtual independence on most other matters of domestic and —especially important—foreign policy. It was from that time on that the Prussian nobility gladly and proudly manned the leading military and bureaucratic posts in the Prussian government.

The king of Prussia, then, was an autocrat whose predecessors had carefully eliminated all institutional opposition to the power of the monarchy. But the aristocracy in Prussia, as in Britain, found avenues to power and wealth through participation in the government.

Frederick William I (1713–1740) was unusually well suited to carry on the work of building up the power of the Prussian monarchy. He was a rigid but intelligent disciplinarian who refused to indulge in the ceremonial which pervaded the other European courts. He had bad manners, told dirty jokes, smoked tobacco, used his cane to beat those who angered him, and was unpopular even with his own family. At the same time, however, he had Walpole's ability to handle men, and he brought the Prussian bureaucracy and army to a new level of effectiveness, leaving his son a very powerful inheritance.

Frederick William I helped to fashion the values which characterized the Prussian state throughout the eighteenth and nineteenth centuries. Much enamored of his army, he searched all Europe for men over six feet tall to make up his special regiment. Not only his militarism but his penchant for efficiency were to become enduring characteristics of the Prussian state. During his twenty-seven-year reign, he more than doubled the size of the Prussian army, to over eighty thousand men, spending between four and five times as much on his army as on all other government business, so that, while Prussia ranked twelfth in population among European states, its army ranked only behind those of France, Russia, and Austria. He also made a concerted attempt to wipe out inefficiency in the bureaucracy and the army by giving positions and promotions for ability rather than family connections. Although his determined efforts, which often bordered on the brutal and tyrannical, did not eradicate inefficiency, they brought great improvements. More important, it was increasingly possible for men from outside the aristocracy to rise through the ranks of the bureaucracy. While they themselves were often snubbed by those with better social credentials, their sons and grandsons were easily absorbed into the nobility and became an indistinguishable part of the landowning aristocracy that provided the basis of Prussian power down to the twentieth century.

II THE STRUGGLE FOR EMPIRE

Social Conservatism in the Mid-Eighteenth Century

In spite of profound constitutional and social differences among the various European states, Europe in the mid-eighteenth century was more homogeneous than it has been since. More than at any later time it was possible then to think in terms of a single European ruling class, made up of aristocrats who shared a common ideology and etiquette and whose status transcended national boundaries. Thus, for example, a German-speaking elector of Hanover was able to become king of England. His dynastic and religious (Protestant) connections with the English monarchy were more important than what a later age would call his nationality. If he spoke no English and his ministers no German, they could all converse in French—the universal language of the European aristocracy—and sometimes in Latin as well. Although international intrigue and espionage were at an all-time high, the relations between nations nevertheless reflected something of the club-like atmosphere that existed among the ruling elements of European society.

The sanctity of the territorial state was not so far developed that the map of Europe could not be redrawn fairly easily at a peace conference. In the War of the Polish Succession (1733–1735), for instance, the French candidate for the Polish throne, Stanislas Leszczyński, was ultimately indemnified for the loss of his claim by being given the crown of Lorraine. In the ensuing War of the Austrian Succession (1740–1748), the transfer of Silesia from Austrian to Prussian control was likewise a purely dynastic matter—the inhabitants of Silesia were neither consulted nor heard from.

In 1740 the devastating religious wars of the sixteenth and seventeenth centuries were things of the past. Armies were professional forces in the pay of the state. Mercenary troops became increasingly common; both France and Holland, for instance, had regiments partly or entirely composed of foreigners. Most of the officers came from the gentry, which could be depended upon for nobility and courage; common soldiers came from the dregs of society. Pressed into service for long periods of time, soldiers became efficient cogs in the complex mechanism of the eighteenth-century army. As a result, they were far too valuable and difficult to replace to be squandered in last-ditch battles. On the other hand, soldiers were drilled to obey blindly, and discipline was brutal beyond belief.

Eighteenth-century wars depended as much upon strategy and supply as upon bloody clashes of flesh and steel. If these wars now seem trivial in comparison with modern holocausts, they were at least effective in protecting dynastic interests with a minimum of expense—a vital factor, since every king's military power rested upon the limited financial resources of the eighteenth-century state. Wars aimed not at annihilating the enemy but at specific political goals such as territorial concessions, trading rights, or dynastic changes. In these struggles the civilian population was largely ignored. Although they were taxed to support the war—and Prussian towns, for instance, had to pay board and lodging for their garrisons even in time of peace—invading armies were generally fed by an elaborate system of supply magazines rather than by local plunder, and army recruiters usually did not bother the "respectable" elements of the population. The freedom of the civilian population from the worst ravages of war was, in point of fact, a symbol of their political impotence. Public opinion, as it is now understood, was not a factor in early eighteenth-century politics.

Imperialism and Colonial Wars

The period from 1740 to 1763 saw no breakdown in the social conservatism of the *ancien régime*, but in international affairs it was an era of dramatic upheavals and shifts in the balance of power. During the preceding twenty years, two great first ministers—Fleury in France and Walpole in England—had been firmly committed to peace. Their programs encouraged accommodation in international affairs while emphasizing the return to financial solvency at home. The collapse of the general European peace brought about the defeat of the policies of Fleury and Walpole. France and Britain embarked on more than two decades of warfare which left Britain the victor and laid the groundwork for the demise of the *ancien régime* in France and elsewhere in Europe. At the same time that France and Great Britain returned to their old rivalry, the balance of power in eastern Europe was overturned by a struggle between Austria and Prussia which was to dominate Continental politics for the next two decades.

It is not surprising that the first major break in the peace came in a colonial war. A great deal had happened to European imperialism since the age of exploration in the sixteenth and seventeenth centuries. At first, colonial interests were no more than a supplement to national economies. Trade with new colonial areas was largely geared to supplying old demands in new ways, circumventing and ultimately nearly replacing the old Mediterranean trade which had hitherto linked East and West. The change in colonialism in the late seventeenth and the eighteenth century was partly the natural maturing of the old imperialism. That is, the diversity of the colonial world created new demands within Europe for goods such as tea and sugar, which had been nearly unknown before. There were also, however, far-reaching changes in both European and colonial society that helped to make colonial affairs more and more an integral part of national affairs. It was no accident that European wars became world wars in the mid-eighteenth century.

One source of growing involvement in colonial affairs, especially in Britain, was the growth of colonial investments. After the collapse of the South Sea Bubble, merchants and financiers settled down to a more mundane but very profitable trade with the colonial world. For both Britain and France this trade began with the acquisition of slaves on the coast of western Africa. Along with other goods needed by the colonists in the West Indies and the Americas, the slaves were exchanged for valuable agricultural products and natural resources which found ever larger markets in Europe. In addition, there were the fish and furs of North America and the many products of India.

Mercantilist economic theories helped to reinforce the importance of the colonies in the national economic structure. Mercantilism operated on the assumption that a limited amount of trade and wealth was available in the world at any one time. Thus the expansion of the trade of one country necessarily implied a worsening economic position for the others. It was therefore in

ARCTIC   OCEAN

GREENLAN

RUSSIA

ALASKA

BERING
SEA

BERING
STRAIT

Yukon R.

Mackenzie R.

NORTHWEST
TERRITORY

HUDSON
BAY

BAFFIN

Den

Petropavlovsk 1703

Kamchatsk
1740

ALEUTIAN IS.
Russ. 1741

KODIAK I.
Russ. 1784

New Archangel
(Sitka) Russ. 1799

Ft. Simpson 1804

CANADA

Ft. Churchill 173

Hudson's Bay Co.

RUPERT'S
LAND

Ft. Rupert 1668

St. Johns 1713

Halifax 1749

VANCOUVER I.

OREGON
COUNTRY
Claimed by
Sp., Br.,
Russ. and
U.S.

Saskatchewan R.

Ft. Garry 1811
(Winnipeg)

Quebec

Astoria 1811

Missouri R.

LOUISIANA
Fr. Sp. 1762,
Fr. 1800,
U.S. 1803

Detroit 1701

St. Louis
1764

Santa Fe

UNITED

STATES

New York

Washington 1791
Richmond 1733

San Francisco 1776

Los Angeles 1780

Rio Grande R.

Mississippi R.

San
Antonio
1718

Savannah 1733

PACIFIC

NEW

SPAIN

New Orleans 1718
FLORIDA

BERMUDA Br.

ATLANTI

BAHAMA IS. Br.

SANDWICH IS.
(HAWAII)
1778

Mexico

CUBA
Sp.

JAMAICA
Br.

HAITI
Sp.

PUERTO RICO Sp.

GUADELOUPE
MARTINIQUE Br.

BR.
HONDURAS
1786

MARSHALL IS.

GILBERT IS. 1764

OCEAN

Panama

Caracas

TRINIDAD Br.
BR. GUIANA
NETH. GUIANA
FR. GUIANA (Port. 1808

GALAPAGOS IS.

Bogotá

Quito

NEW

GRANADA

SOLOMON IS.

NAVIGATORS' IS.
(SAMOA) 1722

MARQUESAS IS.

Lima

BRAZIL

Ba

SOCIETY IS. 1767

FIJI IS.

TUAMOTU IS.

La Paz

NEW
CALEDONIA
Br. 1774

FRIENDLY IS.
(TONGA)

COOK IS. 1773

P
E
R
U

L
A

P
L
A
T
A

Asunción

Rio de Ja

NEW
ZEALAND

CHATHAM
IS. 1791

Santiago

Montevideo 1726
Buenos Aires

The period 1700–1815 saw great changes in imperial fortunes, colonies
usually being the spoils that changed hands after what were primarily European wars. At the start, Spain, France and England had interests in North
America, Spain and Portugal in South America; India was the scene of
Anglo-French rivalry; Africa remained, except for scattered settlements
along the coasts, the Dark Continent. After the Seven Years' War England
was free to build an Indian empire; likewise it held both Canada and the
area east of the Mississippi River; Spain remained predominant in Latin
America and gained the area west of the Mississippi. England then lost
the American colonies which became the independent United States. During the Napoleonic era, England gained the Cape Colony (South Africa)
from the Dutch, while France regained the area west of the Mississippi only
to be forced to negotiate the Louisiana Purchase with the United States.

FALKLAND IS.

CAPE HORN

DRAKE PASSAGE

ARCTIC OCEAN

EAST SIBERIAN SEA

BARENTS SEA

NOVAYA ZEMLYA

ICELAND Den.

FEROE IS. Den.

SHETLAND IS. Br.

GREAT BRITAIN

DENMARK

NETH.

GERMAN STATES

AUSTRIAN EMPIRE

FRANCE

PORTUGAL SPAIN

MEDITERRANEAN SEA

MADEIRA Port.

ARY

NORWAY

SWEDEN

OTTOMAN EMPIRE

RUSSIA

Moscow

Volga R.

Ob R.

Yenisey R.

Lena R.

Amur R.

CHINA

Ho R.

Huang

Huang R.

Yangtze R.

JAPAN

PERSIA

AFGHANISTAN

Indus R.

MARATHA STATES

Calcutta

Goa Port.

Cochin Br.

LACCADIVE IS. Br.

MALDIVE IS. Br.

ANDAMAN IS. Br.

Pondicherry Fr.

CEYLON Br.

FORMOSA

Macao Port.

PACIFIC OCEAN

MARIANA IS. Sp.

PHILIPPINE IS.

CAROLINE IS. Sp

SENEGAL Fr.
St. Louis

GAMBIA Br.

town 1788

SIERRA LEONE Br.

GOLD COAST Br.

Niger R.

Congo R.

Nile R.

Aden

INDIAN OCEAN

Mombasa Arab 1730
ZANZIBAR Arab 1698
Kilwa Arab. 1698

SEYCHELLES Br.

CHAGOS Br.

SUMATRA

BORNEO

CELEBES

Malacca Br.

Palembang Br. 1812

JAVA Br. 1811-1816

Port. TIMOR Neth.

MOLUCCAS Br. 1810

NEW GUINEA

ASCENSION Br.

OCEAN

ST. HELENA Br. 1815

Luanda

ANGOLA

BENGUELA

Mozambique

Sofala

MADAGASCAR

MAURITIUS Br.
RÉUNION Fr.

NEW SOUTH WALES Br.

Sydney 1788

CAPE COLONY

Capetown Br.

CAPE OF GOOD HOPE

TRISTAN da CUNHA Br. 1815

VAN DIEMAN'S LAND (TASMANIA) Br.

EUROPEAN COLONIAL EMPIRES 1700–1815

	Spain		France
	Portugal		Netherlands
	Great Britain		Russia 1689/1825

Dates after cities, island, etc. indicate year of founding, claim or discovery.

the national interest of every country to increase its own world trade, since by doing so it would reduce that of its rivals.

The involvement of Europe in the non-European world was political as well as economic; economic involvement usually could be secured only by political control. This principle proved itself in eighteenth-century India, where Great Britain and France struggled to gain control through the creation of native puppet rulers. In those areas where the core of colonial involvement was a group of European settlers—as in North America and the West Indies—imperialism was even more politically oriented. The colonists of such areas not only had lobbyists in the government of the mother country but also mirrored European conflicts in their competition with the colonists of other countries. And never far in the background was the sensitive issue of national pride and prestige, which provided an emotional underpinning of the material disputes which embroiled the colonial powers.

By the mid-eighteenth century many shifts had occurred in the relative positions of the original colonial powers. For instance, though Portugal retained title to Brazil and a few other areas, it was no longer a real factor in the world power struggle. The same could be said of the Netherlands. Once the queen of European commerce, the Netherlands had become a second-rate power by 1740. Internally, the government—a narrow oligarchy—was torn by dissension; and Dutch sea power had long been on the wane, leaving predominance on the sea a matter of issue primarily between Great Britain and France. Even the hegemony of the Bank of Amsterdam and the Amsterdam bourse had passed to the Bank of England and other British commercial and financial institutions, and much of the commerce that nominally remained to the Netherlands was really in British hands. The only important remnants of Dutch world power were the spice trade of the Netherlands East Indies and the Netherlands' share of the African slave trade.

By the eighteenth century, Britain was well on the way to becoming the greatest sea power in the world. British commerce possessed those strong foundations so lacking in the Netherlands, in Spain, and, to a lesser degree, even in France. The first stirrings of the Industrial Revolution were increasing Britain's productivity, and the agricultural revolution of the early eighteenth century was producing higher living standards and a rapidly growing population. British shipping increased its capacity, taking an ever larger share of the world's carrying trade. British ships also carried the countless British emigrants who provided the foundation for the European population of North America. The thirteen colonies proved to be only a gateway for continuing expansion into the American hinterland.

Britain's American colonies prospered in the eighteenth century in consequence of steady immigration from the mother country and flourishing trade and agriculture. The theory which the British government professed to follow was the old mercantilist assumption that the colonies existed to supply the homeland with needed raw materials and to provide a market for its industrial goods; but the colonists looked upon themselves as members of new, distinct societies, and in their economic activities they aimed to serve their own interests, not the mother country's. During the heyday of the Whig supremacy, from 1714 down to about 1760, the royal administration was extremely easygoing and often lax in implementing colonial economic regulations, and the colonists prospered with little interference from the representatives of imperial authority. The British governors in the colonies during this period were occasionally involved in disputes with the colonial legislatures, but more often they represented the Crown without making a determined effort to control the development of the new societies.

Away from the coast in the frontier hinterlands, hard-working farmers and craftsmen experienced little or no imperial control and became accustomed to an independent political and social life. Into these frontier regions came new waves of immigrants from Scotland and Scotch-Irish from northern Ireland, and these groups were consciously opposed to interference by London or by aristocratic representatives of the king in the colonies. While this experience of extensive autonomy and this attitude of independence were in the long run dangerous to imperial authority, in the mid-eighteenth century they were an important source of British strength in colonial conflicts with France and Spain. The colonists, not being heavily reliant on the mother country, were capable of organizing for their own defense and frequently did so with marked success.

The French had been somewhat late in committing themselves to a policy of colonial involvement, and empire never took that primary place in French national interests that it did in Britain's. Inescapably embroiled in Continental politics, France could never give undivided attention to colonial affairs. And though the French found the trade in slaves, sugar, furs, fish, and the many goods of the Orient a lucrative undertaking, colonial trade never assumed overwhelming economic importance in France. The British did without a large army and concentrated on building and protecting a large merchant fleet, but the French army always took precedence over the navy. In wartime the French navy possessed a temporary advantage while the British armed their much larger merchant fleet, but in the long run Britain could not be denied control of the seas, a fundamental advantage for the British colonial system. French colonial administration was highly centralized, with French troops at its disposal—another temporary advantage of France—but, again, Britain's more numerous colonists and its superiority at sea were unbeatable in a protracted conflict.

French and British colonies and trading stations faced each other in Africa, the West Indies, North America, and India, and colonial wars were therefore to be expected. It was with Spain, however, that Britain first went to war over colonial interests. Although the stature of Spain as a world power had diminished greatly since the 1500's, in the middle of the eighteenth century Spain still held on to a large part of its colonial empire, especially in South

America and the Philippines. In these areas of plantation and mine a well-established European elite managed Spanish interests and lived a life fabled for its luxury and brilliance. In addition, Spanish colonial power was maintained by a highly centralized, relatively efficient system of colonial administration. The philosophy that governed the Spanish colonial administration defined the colonies as distant but integral parts of Spain. Their primary function was to provide specie and the products of the plantations to the home country as well as to serve as a market for the goods brought annually by the Spanish fleet. Spanish industry had long proved incapable of filling the demand of the colonies, so the goods brought by the Spanish ships were primarily French-made. Thus, for centuries, while the Spanish monopoly of trade with its own colonies brought an annual influx of gold to Spanish ports, the wealth was then transferred into the hands of French merchants and Belgian bankers. In the eighteenth century Spain was no longer a rich country; even Spanish sea power had slowly evaporated.

As Spain declined, its hold on its colonies naturally weakened, allowing Britain and other countries to violate Spain's trading monopoly. Through the years sporadic smuggling had grown into regular and systematic illegal trade covered by only the thinnest veil of deception. A few well-placed bribes and some transparent subterfuge opened the colonies to whoever would supply them; and the Spanish fleet arrived to find the market glutted with smuggled goods. An attempt to enforce the old limitations on trade led to the outbreak of war between Spain and Great Britain.

The issue that touched off the war was rather insignificant; a trader named Robert Jenkins lost his ear as a penalty for violating Spain's exclusive trading rights. The Spanish government seemed willing to avoid a rupture by a reasonable compromise on punishment of other violators; but the British were not so disposed. Those in Parliament who opposed Walpole and his peace policy forced him to make Jenkins' ear a *cause célèbre* and to go to war in 1739. Stuck with responsibility for a war he did not want, for which England was not prepared, and which did not go well, Walpole would not long remain as first minister. The future in English politics rested with William Pitt the Elder (1708–1778), a commoner who represented the aggressive colonial interests of the London merchants.

The War of the Austrian Succession

Despite its repercussions on Britain's domestic politics, the War of Jenkins' Ear was far from a general European conflict. In the next year, however, came the outbreak of a genuine Continental war. Within a few weeks of each other in the year 1740, the crowns of Prussia and Austria passed to a new generation of rulers. The rivalry of the two new sovereigns, Frederick II of Prussia and Maria Theresa of Austria, dominated European politics for the next generation.

When Maria Theresa succeeded to the Austrian throne in October of 1740, she did not have to face the insurrection that her father had feared. Instead, the young and ambitious Frederick II seized the Austrian province of Silesia, plunging Europe into a general war in which Maria Theresa was forced to fight all comers for the very existence of the Habsburg empire. France, Spain, Sweden, Germany, and Bavaria (whose ruler, Charles VII, had designs on the imperial dignity) soon joined the Prussians, and the War of the Austrian Succession began. Austria was backed by its old allies, Russia and Great Britain.

Maria Theresa found the support she needed not in the armies of her allies but in the reconstruction of the Habsburg empire. In an empire where centralized administration was almost totally precluded by intense localism, she had inherited a disorganized army and insufficient sources of revenue. With Bohemia and Silesia out of her grasp, she turned in desperation to Hungary. Historically the most rebellious of all her subjects, the Hungarian nobles were transformed by the tender persuasion of Maria Theresa into a titled, office-holding, German-speaking bulwark of the empire. Maria Theresa was also fortunate enough to find exceptionally able servants of the Crown, such as her chancellor, Count Wenzel Anton von Kaunitz (1711–1794). Her advisers proved to be able diplomats and administrators, and they provided her with men and money to fight off her enemies. In the course of saving the empire, the Habsburg regime also gave the Austrian lands their first centralized and effective government. Thus began the long-delayed molding of an Austrian state.

Maria Theresa was able to secure her throne, but she could not win back Silesia. Under pressure from the British, she ceded it to Frederick II in 1742 in return for Prussian withdrawal from the conflict. His objective achieved, and having no desire to crush Austria, which was probably beyond his means in any case, Frederick II withdrew, earning the reputation of unreliable ally as well as aggressor. It was not the last time that Frederick was the first to declare war and the first to make peace, but in the process he lifted Prussia to the front rank of European powers and exhibited the qualities of military leadership that earned him the appellation of Frederick the Great. (It should be noted that, fearing that Austria might seek to regain Silesia, Frederick reopened the war with an invasion of Bohemia in 1744, only to withdraw the following year after winning another series of victories.)

It would be difficult to exaggerate the importance of Silesia for the future course of Prussian history. By adding one of Austria's richest provinces to his realm, Frederick had gained nearly fourteen thousand square miles of territory and nearly a million and a half people. With Silesia as part of the Prussian state, a much larger army could be supported. Prussia was transformed from a powerful German state into a powerful European state.

In other areas, the outcome of the war was not so decisive. Britain had protected Hanover and had gained ground in the colonies, where it had clashed with both France and Spain, but the territorial adjustments made at the peace conference were of minor importance. In reality, the Peace of Aix-la-Chapelle in 1748 returned Europe to the *status quo ante bellum* and left the British-French colonial rivalry, the expansion of Prussia, and the dissatisfaction of Maria Theresa over the loss of Silesia as unsolved and festering issues.

The early 1750's saw renewed strife in virtually every area of the globe where French and British interests conflicted. In India, the French administrator Joseph François Dupleix (1697–1763) had illustrated two fundamental principles of colonial rule. First, he showed that the necessary political control could be gained by alliance with local leaders. With the support of sepoy (native Indian) forces provided by such allies, a few European troops could defeat a native army even if that army possessed an overwhelming numerical advantage. Second, Dupleix' ultimate defeat proved that political control depended upon control of the seas. British sea power defeated Dupleix despite his victories on land, simply by preventing reinforcements and supplies from reaching him.

In North America, disputed fishing rights and a struggle for control of the Ohio River Valley brought the colonial rivalry to a head. The British colonists saw the Ohio Valley as the logical extension of Virginia, while the French considered it an essential part of the fur trapping lands of the upper St. Lawrence. In the West Indies, Britain opposed the occupation of neutral islands by the French. Finally, in Africa, French and British interests armed rival tribes, and fighting broke out there as elsewhere.

The Diplomatic Revolution and the Seven Years' War

In 1756, as in 1740, a *de facto* state of war in the colonies was widened into another general war by developments in Europe. The reopening of Austro-Prussian hostilities was preceded by what is rightly called the diplomatic revolution of 1756; nothing quite like it had occurred in the history of modern Europe. A dramatic reversal of alliances wrote *finis* to the Habsburg-Bourbon rivalry dating back to the end of the fifteenth century and placed the two great powers on the same side. This momentous development had been many years in the making, and the reasons for it were extremely complex.

The diplomatic revolution began in January 1756 with the signing of an Anglo-Prussian agreement, the Convention of Westminster, based on a variety of British fears and resentments—fears for Hanover, fear of a possible Franco-Austrian alliance (which might leave Britain defenseless), fear of a possible French invasion of Britain, and considerable frustration at the long series of incidents and minor clashes between British and French forces in the New World. In May 1756 France and Austria signed the Treaty of Versailles. The French, for their part, wanted to change partners because the

War of the Austrian Succession had brought them no benefits whatever. Nevertheless, the Franco-Austrian treaty was a half-hearted affair. France merely agreed to pay Austria an annual subsidy. Only if Prussia attacked Austria again would France send an army to assist Maria Theresa, and then only 24,000 men.

Austria and Russia had not been idly sitting by. Early in 1756 they had agreed to convert their alliance of 1726 into an agreement to crush Frederick II, whom the Russian Empress Elizabeth (1741–1762) detested with a passion, not least perhaps because the Prussian monarch had once referred to her as "la Catin du Nord" (the Slut of the North). Finally, Frederick learned that the elector of Saxony had made an agreement with Kaunitz by which, once Prussia had been disposed of, Austria was to recover Silesia, Russia was to acquire East Prussia, and Saxony would get the strategic cities of Magdeburg and Halberstadt.

Frederick knew that time was not on his side. In August 1756 he invaded Saxony. Two weeks later he was in Dresden, where — in a fashion popularized by German forces in the twentieth century — he promptly ransacked the local archives and announced that he had discovered factual evidence to support his charge of an "encirclement plot," thereby justifying his preventive war. Whether Frederick's discovery — if such indeed it was — was a case of a self-fulfilling prophecy is difficult to say. At any rate, his invasion of Saxony gave several of his potential enemies an excuse to attempt to do what they may have had in mind all along — namely, wipe Prussia off the map or, at the very least, reduce it to the third- or fourth-rate power it had been before the seventeenth century. In January 1757 the Diet of the Holy Roman Empire voted to condemn Frederick's action. In February and March, Russia and Sweden joined the Austrian cause, and in May France entered, promising to furnish 120,000 men and to pay Austria a substantial subsidy until Frederick was finally crushed.

It seemed impossible that Prussia, with a population of only five million, could long resist three great Continental powers, with a combined population more than ten times its own. But nothing about the Seven Years' War was to go according to orthodox calculation. Against his enemies' overwhelming resources, Frederick had only the element of surprise, the superbly trained Prussian army, and his own masterful generalship. For some time it was to be a close thing. In June 1757 Frederick suffered the first military disaster of his career at Kolín; the Russians invaded East Prussia and set out on the road to Berlin.

The turn of the tide began with the appointment of William Pitt as prime minister of Great Britain in July 1757. It was the second time within a year that Pitt had headed a British cabinet — his first ministry lasted only four months, from December 1756 to April 1757 — but he left no doubt of his self-confidence. "I know," so went his often quoted remark, "that I can save this nation and that nobody else can." And events were to prove him right. Pitt understood the international situation perfectly; in particular, he realized that, if Prussia went down, France would be able to concentrate all its energies on the struggle against Britain in the New World. So he quickly tightened the sagging Anglo-Prussian alliance, and within a short time its fortunes had taken a marked turn for the better. In November 1757 Frederick won a smashing victory over his massed enemies near Rossbach. Britain went wild with joy; Parliament doubled Frederick's subsidy; and the Prussians went on to score still another smashing victory over Austria at the Battle of Leuthen in December 1757.

But Pitt's finest hours were still to come. In early 1758 George II's speech to Parliament—in effect Pitt's address to the British nation—announced that "the main business of the war is the succour and preservation of America," and before long British victories in Canada began to spell the end of France's empire in North America. The fortress of Louisbourg on Cape Breton Island fell to British forces in June 1758. A British general, with fifty thousand troops, fought his way from Philadelphia to Fort Duquesne (promptly renamed Fort Pitt, now Pittsburgh); and though French forces in Canada managed, for the time being, to fend off final defeat, the strategic Ohio Valley was opened to British expansion.

Even so, the French were not yet prepared to give up the worldwide struggle. In March 1759 they negotiated still another treaty with Austria—this one cutting the Austrian subsidy in half, terminating the plan of sending a large French force into central Europe, and, above all, putting an end to all talk of partitioning Prussia. Instead, the French government now proposed to concentrate all its efforts on an all-out cross-channel attack on Britain. But once again French plans met with disaster. Most of the French naval forces were destroyed at Quiberon Bay (November 1759), and with them went all hope for a successful seaborne attack. In December 1759 British forces under General Wolfe captured the Canadian fortress city of Quebec, which the French had thought to be impregnable. Small wonder the British referred to 1759 as their wonderful year of triumph.

It was one of the ironies of this protracted struggle that in November 1759, just as Britain was beginning to score its decisive victories over France on land and on sea, Frederick's enemies derived fresh comfort from a significant victory over the Prussian forces at Kunersdorf, near Frankfort. By this time, of the original Prussian force of 1756 less than a quarter remained; and a substantial part consisted, for the first time, of poorly trained soldiers, a large proportion of them non-Prussian. But Frederick's enemies were as divided as he was weary, and Count Daun, the Austrian field marshal, was nowhere his equal in strategy or tactics.

For all its high drama, the Seven Years' War drew to an end not because there had been a final decision on the field of battle but because certain developments took place behind the lines of the opposing forces. In October 1760 George II died, and at his first privy council meeting, his grandson and successor, George III, described the war as "bloody and expensive." It soon became clear that the new king wanted to be rid of Pitt, and the prime minister's cabinet were likewise tired of his strong-willed—if brilliantly successful—leadership. In October 1761 Pitt resigned.

The fall of Pitt and the accession of Lord Bute led to a significant reduction of British subsidies for Frederick's steadily thinning ranks, and there can be little doubt that, for all his stirring military victories, the position of the Prussian monarch remained precarious. But just at that moment, when his British ally seemed to be abandoning him, Frederick was saved by another miraculous development—the death of the empress Elizabeth of Russia in January 1762 and the accession of her thirty-four-year-old nephew Peter of Holstein. Peter, a fanatical admirer of Frederick, rapidly moved toward the conclusion of a peace settlement between Prussia and Russia.

The peace settlement of May 1762, it should be noted, earned the new czar no laurels at home, only contempt and hatred for his alleged capitulation to Russia's "mortal enemy." Indeed, it became one more charge against Peter, whose dissolute life and alleged plans to "Protestantize" the country and perhaps lead it into a new war—this time with Denmark over Schleswig—made him increasingly unpopular at his own court. In early July his wife, the German-born Catherine, who had reason to fear for her own future, led a conspiracy to overthrow Peter. The czar abdicated and a week later died under highly suspicious circumstances at a country residence.

But the Russian coup did not alter basic international realities. Both England and France wanted peace badly; and, whatever their own desires, both Austria and Prussia—which had been largely responsible for the outbreak of war in the first place—found that they were too exhausted to carry on the struggle much longer. The treaties of Hubertusburg and Paris (1763) were anything but satisfying for the Franco-Austrian alliance. Prussia was finally confirmed in its possession of Silesia, Frederick II promising only to support Maria Theresa's son, Joseph, for election as imperial heir apparent. French losses were far more humiliating, though thanks in large part to the ineptitude of the British ministry that had succeeded Pitt's, France did not fare quite as badly as might have been expected considering its military debacle. Britain gained all of Canada and all other disputed lands east of the Mississippi, while France ceded Louisiana to Spain. France was thus excluded from the North American mainland, but Britain returned to French control two sugar-rich islands in the West Indies that had been seized during the war. France also lost Senegal, the leading slave-trading post in Africa, and most of its power in India. Spain (which had joined France near the end of the war) ceded Florida to Britain.

Thus the Seven Years' War turned into a dramatic triumph for Great Britain. But that was not its sole historical significance. Prussia was now incontrovertibly certified as one of the great powers of Europe, and Austria's position (and influence) in Germany was correspondingly diminished. The hollowness of the Holy Roman Empire had been shown beyond all question. Yet for both Britain and France the war had fateful consequences that could scarcely have been foreseen in 1763. These consequences were to prove even more momentous than the struggle that produced them.

III REFORM AND CRISIS IN THE *ANCIEN RÉGIME*

Enlightened Despotism

The wars of the 1740's and 1750's had a great impact upon the internal affairs of European states as well as upon the international balance of power. France, Britain, Prussia, and Austria were once again forced to mobilize for war. As usual, heavy taxes and growing deficits strained relations between governments and their tax-paying subjects. As had been the case fifty years earlier, the coming of peace in 1763 brought demands for reform and reconstruction of the power of the state. In the period from 1763 to 1786, the voices of those who demanded change became more and more insistent. Against a background of recurrent economic and financial crises, lines were drawn between these champions of change and conservative defenders of aristocracy and privilege.

It was also a period of paradox in which substantial increases in agricultural production and numbers of inhabitants led not to well-being and expansion but to growing rural unrest and unprecedented fears of overpopulation. Eighteenth-century statistics are a chancy business—in 1753 the House of Commons rejected the idea of a national census on the ground that the results might be useful to a potential enemy—but there can be little doubt that the laboring class was beginning to grow rapidly and that this development was of outstanding importance not only for the coming of the Industrial Revolution but for the future of British and Continental politics.

Throughout most of Europe, the early part of the eighteenth century had been a period of aristocratic resurgence. In eastern Europe rulers secured the nobles' cooperation in the modernization of the state by reaffirming or even increasing their power over the lower classes and local affairs. In France the aristocracy solidified its hold over the offices of the Crown; in the second half of the eighteenth century, it became increasingly difficult for a wealthy commoner to gain entrance into the ranks of the aristocracy.

Since that time, however, important changes had occurred. Pressing problems faced the state in many parts of Europe, and the social and political ideas of the philosophers of the Enlightenment (see Chapter 2) gave ammunition and direction to the forces of change. These philosophers began by asserting that man and society were perfectible. Their optimistic view of human potentialities led them to attack the obvious abuses and contradictions of eighteenth-century society. Torture in the examination of accused criminals, the huge income of the Church and the power of the Jesuits, serfdom, and similar sources of injustice provided easy targets for their invective and satire. From biting criticism it was not far to the proposal of solutions for contemporary social ills.

The ideas of the Enlightenment were not, however, inherently democratic. Intellectuals like Voltaire — who eulogized Louis xiv in a justly famous biography — tended to turn to the benevolent philosopher-king who would use his absolute power with the love and wisdom of a father looking after his children. Thus, the power of the state was to be centralized and rationalized in the interests of society. The king, guided by reason and compassion, should use his power to wipe out inequities and injustices in order to bring prosperity and stability to the state. It was in this form that the ideas of the Enlightenment made their first major impact upon the political structure of Europe. In the latter part of the eighteenth century, several European monarchs entered the struggle against reactionary elements in society armed with the coherent and persuasive ideology of the Enlightenment and spurred on by the impelling crises that agonized this age of transition.

The first and perhaps the greatest monarch to become a practitioner of the principles of enlightened despotism was Frederick the Great of Prussia. His accession to the throne in 1740 had been followed by more than two decades of war and preparation for war. In 1763 Frederick returned from the Seven Years' War to turn his attention to reform and economic improvement in his greatly augmented dominions. He approached domestic affairs with the same energy and ability that had gained him the reputation of a great general on the battlefield. In many ways he embodied the ideals of the Enlightenment. He not only patronized its exponents, such as Voltaire, but himself engaged in the writing of poetry and the composition of music. A true humanist in his outlook, Frederick the Great saw himself as the first servant of the state and the guardian of the welfare of the people entrusted to his care.

Like all other "enlightened" rulers, Frederick continued many of the traditional policies of his predecessors. He, too, was deeply concerned with bureaucratic efficiency and with the growing Prussian army. And he was very much aware that the power of the state ultimately rests upon the health and vigor of the society that supports it. Therefore, his concern for the army found its complement in his energetic promotion of the economic well-being of his people. State-supported industries, aid and advice to farmers, and manuals written by Frederick himself to instruct his generals in the art of warfare were all part of one overriding purpose. There is a story to the effect that, after the Seven Years' War, the Turkish sultan despatched a delegation to his friend, the Prussian monarch, asking for three of the astrologers whose assistance had made Frederick so singularly successful. Frederick replied that his three astrologers were diplomacy, the army, and the treasury.

To be sure, admiration of Frederick was far from unanimous. The formidable system of administration which Frederick did so much to develop led to an extreme centralization that did a great deal to destroy personal initiative and even, on occasion, honesty. "Of all the kings in Europe," wrote Mirabeau, who spent several years at the Prussian court, Frederick "was the most deceived." And though there was a surprising amount of freedom of speech and press in Prussia, the famous writer and critic Lessing once remarked contemptuously that the only real freedom in Prussia was the right to denounce religion.

At a time when the judicial system of the European states left almost everything to be desired, Frederick labored diligently and successfully to make the Prussian judicial system and criminal law models of their kind. Thus he abolished the use of torture save in cases involving murder or treason. On the other hand, the Prussian general code, as promulgated by Frederick in 1784, seemed typical of his conservative view of society: the middle class must not acquire lands of the nobility; the peasant must remain on the land; privileges of the nobility must remain inviolate. If Frederican Prussia was widely admired, this was probably because Frederick's practice tended to be rather more flexible than his formal pronouncements, and because—for the enormous price Prussia paid in the process—he had affected his kingdom as it had never been affected in all its history.

One of Frederick's most ardent admirers was Joseph II of Austria (1765–1790), who spent fifteen years as coruler with his pious, conservative mother before her death in 1780 left him as sole ruler. Maria Theresa, through her able advisers, did much to improve the efficiency and cohesion of the Habsburg state, but she had no sympathy at all with the radical, anticlerical ideas of the Enlightenment. Joseph II, on the other hand, was perhaps the most radical of all the enlightened despots. He was also one of the least effective, lacking both the intellectual capabilities and the qualities of leadership which marked Frederick's happy blend of idealism and realism. Joseph frightened many of his subjects with his unbending dedication to basic social and political changes, and his cold personality left him isolated from those who might otherwise have welcomed his leadership.

Joseph understood the problems of modernizing a state remarkably well. Thus he had shocked his mother by arguing that the whole social caste system should be abolished and that the sons of peasants should be allowed to enter the universities and the civil service. Although a devout Catholic, he also abolished what he believed to be useless monasteries and dangerous clerical censorship of the press.

Joseph's abrupt denial of the traditional autonomy of Hungary, his attempts to abolish serfdom on hereditary lands, and his demand for a universal and rational system of taxation did nothing to moderate his unpopularity; in one short decade he alienated most of the important groups within his empire. He ended his reign embittered and frustrated by the failure of his attempts to bring social justice and effective government to his lands. Yet, though virtually all his new laws save those involving religious toleration and the peasantry were wiped out within a short time of his death in 1790, Joseph became and remained a symbol of energetic reform, and therein may lie his chief historical significance.

Of all the enlightened despots, Catherine II (1762–1796) of Russia is the most difficult to understand. Her enthusiastic espousal of the ideas of the Enlightenment seems to have been tempered in practice by a full measure of opportunism and social conservatism. Part of this enigma is explained by her own clever, ruthless personality. Catherine became empress in July 1762 after the forced abdication and mysterious death of her husband, Peter III. She had at least twenty lovers during her long reign and was one of the most colorful figures in the long history of monarchy.

About Catherine's desire to achieve a reputation for liberalism, especially among the Western intelligentsia, there can be little doubt. Thus for years she carried on a serious correspondence with those paragons of Enlightenment culture, Voltaire and Diderot, and though Voltaire declined Catherine's invitation to come to Russia, Diderot agreed, traveled there in September 1773, and stayed until February 1774, during which time he had frequent discussions with the empress on philosophical and political issues; and when, later on, Diderot found himself in serious financial straits, Catherine quickly agreed to purchase his substantial library. But such gestures had little permanent significance. Catherine, like many subsequent Russian rulers, carefully built up a beneficent image that deceived Western liberals as to the real character of her policy.

Her ambivalent attitude toward the Enlightenment was further evident in the fate of the legislative commission she called in 1767. Although her "Instruction" to that commission was considerably toned down from its original version, it was still so radical that its publication was banned in France, but the commission itself accomplished little except to reveal the enormity of Russia's domestic problems and further inflame class antagonisms. In 1775 Catherine introduced a new system of local government, but she never ventured in the direction of social change. On the contrary, the conditions of the peasantry worsened rapidly in Catherine's reign and at the close of the eighteenth century were probably at their lowest ebb.

Catherine's aversion to social reform may have been caused, in part, by a prudent regard for the deep class antagonisms first revealed during the deliberations of the legislative commission, but it was no doubt greatly intensified by the outbreak of the Pugachev Rebellion of 1773–1775. Misery and disappointed hopes increasingly inflamed the long-suffering Russian peasantry, who rallied around the banner of the Cossack rebel, Emilian Pugachev. With the support of perpetually dissident Don Cossack elements, Pugachev and his troops cut a wide swath across southern Russia and Siberia, leaving a trail of burned and pillaged villages and murdered nobles. Like the legislative commission, however, Pugachev lasted only a few years. He was captured, brought to Moscow in an iron cage, and there publicly executed in a manner

Although Poland was the largest country in eighteenth-century Europe (excluding Russia), it was too weak to withstand its rivals' territorial ambitions. In 1772 Russia, Austria, and Prussia carved off areas in the northeast, south, and west, respectively. During the general European war precipitated by the French Revolution, these same three powers seized the opportunity to carve up the remainder (in 1793 and 1795), and Poland disappeared from the map totally—albeit temporarily.

dramatic enough to discourage any potential emulators. Pugachev's rebellion was the last of its kind in Russian history, and it produced no visible results. Catherine's social conservatism was formalized in the Charter to the Nobility of 1785, which strengthened both the regional autonomy of the aristocrats and their hold over the serfs (who were literally chattels).

Catherine resembled Peter the Great in many ways. Her desire for the westernization of Russian society, as well as her attention to building up effective governmental institutions, can be seen as continuations of his work. The same can be said of her foreign policy. Under Catherine, as under Peter, Russia pushed toward the Black Sea in the south and the Baltic Sea in the north. Two successful wars with Turkey (1768–1774 and 1787–1792) moved the Russian frontier to the Black Sea, and Russian ships were based at Sevastopol and other ports along its northern shore.

Russia was also a major beneficiary of the partitions of Poland. That beleaguered state found itself in a hopeless position at the end of the Seven Years' War. Greatly strengthened, Austria and Prussia found that they could bury their former differences and cooperate in a profitable adventure in Poland while simultaneously easing their tensions with Russia. Unable to act together even to collect taxes, the Polish nobles were incapable of effective resistance.

Foreign interference in the internal affairs of Poland was hardly a new development, but in the 1760's this interference took an even more menacing turn. When King Augustus III died in October 1763, Catherine, posing as the defender of the rights of the Polish nobility, sent Russian troops into the country and secured the election of one of her favorites as the new Polish king. Soon thereafter she concluded an agreement with Frederick the Great providing for the maintenance of the elective monarchy and the *liberum veto* in the Polish Diet, thus making doubly sure that Poland could not put its house in order and resist possible future partition by its powerful neighbors. The end of the independent Polish state was not far off. The first partition took place in August 1772, and similar acts of blatant despoliation in January 1793 and October 1795 completely dismembered the venerable state. In the process, Russia once again expanded its western borders and improved its position on the Baltic Sea. Swedish opposition proved futile, and Russia was firmly established as an important European power.

Outside of Britain, enlightened despotism gained wide adherence in the late eighteenth century as an ideal of government. Gustavus III of Sweden (1771–1792), like Catherine the Great of Russia, took power by a coup d'état. Determined to end corruption and particularism in Sweden, he brought to his task an unusual ability and dedication. The new-found efficiency of the Swedish government, the king's winsome personality, and his achievements in foreign affairs endeared him to his people until he was dramatically cut down by an assassin's bullet at a masked ball at the Stockholm Opera House in March 1792.

In Spain, Charles III (1759–1788) brought both the principles of enlightened government and an unusual amount of ability (for a Spanish king) to the throne. Like other enlightened monarchs, he broke a long tradition of royal dissipation and inattention to affairs of state by his industry and dedication. His attempts to rationalize the law and the operations of government soon brought him into conflict with the Church. Not the least significant development of Charles' reign was that by the time of his death the Inquisition had become largely defunct. He was one of several European monarchs who banned the Society of Jesus from their kingdoms (1767).

In Portugal, the indifference of Joseph I (1750–1777) allowed his chief minister, the ambitious and unscrupulous Marques de Pombal, to dominate the government from 1750 until the king's death in February 1777, when Pombal quickly lost his power. Pombal, a greatly talented and energetic man, often seemed far more interested in establishing his own personal power in an efficient and despotic government than in carrying out the philosophy of the Enlightenment; but even for this limited end it was necessary to break the power of the Roman Catholic Church (especially of the Jesuits) and the nobility, and this Pombal proceeded to do with great effectiveness, if also with often unspeakable brutality. All the same, Pombal must rank among the leading ministers of the eighteenth century. Among his outstanding achievements were his rescue work in Lisbon following the catastrophic earthquake in November 1775, a notable advancement of public education, the systematic development of overseas commerce and trading companies, and the reconstruction of the Portuguese army on the Prussian model.

Perhaps the most successful and beloved of all the enlightened despots was Archduke Leopold of Tuscany (1747–1792). The son-in-law of Charles III and the brother of Joseph II of Austria, he ruled his minor duchy from 1765 to 1790, when he inherited the throne of Austria. Tuscany was a small state, and that fact, along with Leopold's ability, explains the extraordinary degree to which he was able to apply the principles of enlightened government. Leopold went beyond the abolition of torture, the improvement of the economy, and the suppression of the Jesuits. He set out to abolish capital punishment itself and to substitute the concept of crime prevention for that of punishment. He abolished the Inquisition in his lands and even toyed with the idea of some sort of representative government on the British model. These were considerable achievements, but it seems only fair to note that, in the eyes of many of his Italian subjects, Leopold never ceased to be a foreign ruler, and this disability, together with the not inconsiderable conservatism of the local populace, impeded the progress of his reform efforts.

When Leopold became emperor of Austria in February 1790, he found the huge and complicated empire very poor soil for his programs. In addition to the growing menace posed by the revolution in France, Austria itself was in a state of incipient revolution. As a result, he had to concentrate mainly on the reestablishment of the Crown's power and authority until his death in 1792.

There can be little doubt that, despite its considerable achievements, enlightened despotism did not provide a lasting solution to the problems facing European governments. Even the most adventurous reforms left an impoverished peasantry, an overprivileged, undertaxed nobility, a middle class inadequately integrated into government and society, and a central administration too small to meet the demands placed upon it and too large to achieve financial security on its constricted revenue base. In the last analysis it must be said that while enlightened despotism began to face questions that could no longer be ignored, it could provide no real solutions within the political and economic realities of the era. The problems of Great Britain and France, the two most "advanced" states of Europe, illustrate the underlying factors that would soon turn reform to revolution.

Colonial and Constitutional Problems in Great Britain

British government was proclaimed by many observers as the best approximation to the ideal. A model of stability, its separation of powers had impressed political thinkers like Montesquieu as a sure defense against the dangers of despotism. The lack of fundamental divisions in program among the different factions in eighteenth-century British politics has led some historians to see their struggles as little more than an endless competition for personal and family power. The ink was hardly dry on the treaty that closed the war between Britain and France in 1763, however, when a new conflict began between the home government and the American colonies. Within the next two decades Great Britain was faced with the American Revolution, extensive discontent in Ireland, a growing movement for democratization and rationalization of the system of parliamentary representation, and a crisis in the relationship between king and Commons. Clearly, the "balance" of the British constitution was not sufficient to guarantee public tranquility in the troubled waters of the late eighteenth century.

The year 1759 was decisive for Britain. On every major battlefield British armies were victorious. The end of the Seven Years' War seemed to be imminent, but over the concerted opposition of the frugal country gentlemen who chafed under the burden of paying for the war, Pitt insisted upon prolonging the struggle in pursuit of decisive victory. Pitt accurately foresaw that a great deal might have to be traded back to France at the conference table, and he wished to have a surplus of territories at his disposal when the time for negotiation arrived. Most important, Pitt wanted to put an end to France's colonial challenge once and for all. Such an expensive, if far-sighted, policy gradually alienated his followers in Commons, and, as already noted, the death of George II in 1760 led to Pitt's resignation the following year.

The signing of the Peace of Paris in February 1763 did not put an end to political discontent in Britain but added to it the issue of who should pay for the war and the military establishment needed to safeguard the peace. In 1765 the hard-pressed British taxpayers sought to reduce the cost of military protection by imposing a stamp tax on the American colonies. The tax was a recognized part of the British revenue system, and those who sought to extend it to the colonies were greatly surprised when it met with opposition. The colonists, however, saw things very differently. The growing prosperity of American business and industry in the eighteenth century had been accompanied by steadily increasing independence from Britain. Although the protection of the British army was both welcome and necessary, the colonial merchant was often a potential competitor of British trading interests. In addition, the colonial government was only very tenuously connected with Britain. Governors represented the Crown, but they usually cooperated with the local assemblies.

There were few impediments to the decentralization the colonists found so comfortable. Although George Grenville, the British chancellor of the exchequer, had tried to stop violations of the Navigation Acts that controlled colonial commerce, even the collection of customs duties by British revenue agents involved an informal arrangement acceptable to both sides: in return for a moderate bribe at a standardized rate, customs officials ignored the higher duties required by law. The fact that customs collection actually operated at a loss in the colonies did not bother either the officials or the colonists.

The Stamp Tax of 1765, which taxed not only legal documents but bills of lading, notes, bonds, and newspapers, was seen by the American colonists as the first step toward a taxation which might know no limits. The opposition that appeared as soon as the intentions of Parliament became known set the tone for the next decade of British-American relations. First of all, opposition to the new tax legislation centered around the cry of "No taxation without representation." British statesmen could argue that Americans had the same "virtual representation" as any Englishmen, but the colonists had a very real fear that a distant body over which they had no control might actually establish its right to spend American money. As Benjamin Franklin put it: "British subjects, by removing to America, do not thereby lose their native rights." Second, the colonists reacted with near-hysteria and rendered the tax unenforceable even before it had been formally imposed. Potential collectors were intimidated by the public outrage. Once the tax actually went into effect, it went largely unused. Third, the ensuing negotiations were extremely confused. Each side misunderstood the intentions of the other, and misunderstandings were compounded by the lengthy delays and limitations inherent in transatlantic negotiations in the eighteenth century.

In London as the spokesman for the American colonies, Benjamin Franklin led Parliament to believe that the colonists denied only Parliament's right to impose internal taxation. By distinguishing between taxation and legislation, Franklin and his allies in the House of Commons established grounds for abolishing the Stamp Tax while leaving the door open to collecting revenue from the colonies through customs duties. Such duties, it was held, were upon external and not internal trade, and were therefore within the competence of the British Parliament. As it turned out, however, the colonists were opposed to any increase in taxation, whether by internal taxes or by the imposition of import duties.

The British reacted with what seemed to them to be the ultimate in reasonableness and moderation. In March 1766 Parliament repealed the Stamp Tax, replacing it in 1767 with the Townshend Acts (so named after the new chancellor of the exchequer), which placed duties on many of the goods the colonies imported. Colonial opposition was inflamed anew and an embryonic revolutionary organization was formed. Parliament thereupon withdrew all of the duties save the small tax on tea, but even this mere formality of taxation was unacceptable to the colonists. When the British East India Company, finding itself in serious financial troubles, was given the right to dump its surplus tea on the American colonies, most of its ships were turned back with their cargoes; and when British authorities in Boston would not allow three ships to leave without unloading their tea, the tea was thrown into the harbor by colonists disguised as Indians.

Parliamentary revenge was swift; it took the form of the so-called Intolerable Acts, which virtually closed the port of Boston and revised the colonial charter of Massachusetts to increase royal control. This action against one colony did not intimidate the others. Instead, colonial representatives joined in the First Continental Congress, which met at Philadelphia in September 1774. At the same time, arms were gathered and local militias trained to resist coercion. In April 1775 the attempt of the British to seize arms stored at Concord led to the outbreak of hostilities, and in May 1775 a second Continental Congress gathered in Philadelphia. It was doubtless more radical than the first Congress had been, but the mood was still hardly one of secession. In October 1774 George Washington had said, "I am satisfied that no such thing as independence is desired by any thinking man in North America," and early in 1776 John Adams wrote that he doubted there was "public Virtue enough to support a Republic."

But changing circumstances stilled such doubts. An army was organized under George Washington, and peace efforts rapidly collapsed. When Edmund Burke submitted a proposal on conciliation with the colonies to the House of Commons in November 1775, it failed by a ratio of two to one. The following month Parliament passed an act prohibiting "all manner of trade and commerce" with the thirteen colonies. Almost irresistibly, the colonies now seemed to be moving toward a formal break with Britain, and nothing did more to hasten this development than the publication in January 1776 of a stirring pamphlet, *Common Sense*, by Thomas Paine, an English Quaker who had been living in the colonies only a short time. Paine's pamphlet, which had an enormous circulation in British North America during the next six months, articulated the growing belief that America was a new and distinct civilization, a new departure in world history that broke with monarchy and aristocracy and offered men everywhere the hope of a new era of human freedom. "The cause of America," Paine said, "is in a great measure the cause of all mankind." European intellectuals in the eighteenth century were fascinated with America as offering a different culture and way of life from that which prevailed under the *ancien régime*. This sense of American uniqueness now became the basis for proclaiming a revolution against British authority.

On June 7, Richard Henry Lee, speaking for the Virginia delegation, moved in the Congress at Philadelphia that "these United Colonies are, and of right ought to be, free and independent States." After extended debate, on July 2 the motion passed. Thomas Jefferson, whose literary powers were widely known, was asked to prepare the declaration implementing the decision, and his imperishable draft, the Declaration of Independence — with some alterations suggested by John Adams and Benjamin Franklin and some revisions made during the debate in Congress — was adopted on July 4, 1776. Beginning with a Lockean statement of the good society, it passed on to an extended and damning indictment of British policy toward the colonies and concluded "that all political connection between [these united colonies] & the state of Great Britain is, & ought to be totally dissolved . . . . And for the support of this declaration, with a firm reliance on the protection of divine providence we mutually pledge to each other our lives, our fortunes, & our sacred honor."

The outbreak of the American Revolution may have been almost accidental, but by the mid-1770's the American colonists had begun to represent a new kind of intellectual and political community, holding beliefs on domestic and international issues increasingly at variance with—and generally far in advance of—the beliefs espoused in England and France. It was in the American colonies that the best of Enlightenment rationality and sensibility found political expression.

But if the war for American independence began with an eloquent statement of belief, it was brought to a successful conclusion only after six long years of hard and bitter fighting. More than once—for instance, in the bleak winter of 1776–1777—the prospects of the Americans looked dark indeed. But when the limited resources of the colonists were strained to the breaking point, they were pulled through by strong leadership, by British uncertainty and division at home, and by the alliance with France, which came at the very moment—February 1778—when American morale was at its lowest.

Even allowing for colonial leadership and resilience and French aid, it must be admitted that Great Britain in large measure defeated itself. Parliament and the ministers of George III consistently underestimated the ability of the colonists and misjudged their intentions. Too few troops were sent in too many directions, allowing the colonists, for instance, to force the surrender of Burgoyne's army at Saratoga in October 1777. In addition, the British were always far behind in their assessment of the situation. Although American independence soon became virtually inevitable, the British did not realize it until the Franco-American siege of Yorktown forced Cornwallis' surrender in October 1781. "It is all over," Lord North exclaimed when he got the news, and he was right, though a peace treaty was not signed for two years.

Once the American Revolution was an accomplished fact and the British conceded their inability to defeat it, the task of creating a new political unity among the former colonies began. It was a difficult task, involved considerable trial and error, and consumed the better part of a decade. From March 1781 to March 1789 the former colonies organized themselves under the Articles of Confederation in a rather loose, highly decentralized arrangement. But immediate political and economic needs, as well as the existence of a common American political consciousness, led in early 1787 to the calling of a Constitutional Convention in Philadelphia. Presided over by George Washington, that Convention brought together a brilliant galaxy of American political talent and leadership. Thomas Jefferson, then in Paris as American minister to France, was among the few leading Americans not present.

After arduous secret debates lasting from May until September of 1787, a new constitution emerged, and in another nine months most of the American states formally ratified it. More conservative in design and tone than the Declaration of Independence, the Constitution sought to strike a balance between the demonstrated inadequacy of the Articles of Confederation and the European-style centralism supported by conservatives like Alexander Hamilton. Shortly after it was ratified, the Constitution was provided with perhaps its most notable feature — a series of ten amendments collectively called the Bill of Rights. First suggested by James Madison, these amendments spelled out as no constitution of a leading state had ever done before the civil and political rights of all free citizens.

The Constitution did not at once bring political stability and harmony to the new United States, and it left a number of important problems — notably slavery — unresolved. But under the patient leadership of George Washington, who was unanimously elected President in 1789 (and reelected in 1792), the new union was successfully launched just as the Old World was about to be swept by the violence of the French Revolution and the Napoleonic era.

The collapse of the old order in America inspired a radical attack upon privilege and corruption in the British government at home. A widespread demand for "economical reform" — that is, reduction of corruption in the civil service by elimination of the lavish grant of sinecures to government supporters — produced some modest reforms. Much more controversial was the call for reform of the House of Commons itself through abolition of "rotten" or "pocket" boroughs controlled by aristocratic patrons and through extension of the suffrage. The reform program found its adherents among the urban middle class, which was underrepresented in Parliament, among Protestant dissenters, who were still largely excluded from the House of Commons by discriminatory laws of the 1660's, and by some aristocratic Whig politicians, such as the marquis of Rockingham. These Whigs had been driven from office by George III after his accession in 1760, and they looked upon participation in the reform movement as a means of winning popular support.

Democratic agitation began in 1763 when the radical journalist John Wilkes was tried for seditious libel for his biting attack on the government. In the 1770's the reformers coalesced in the Association movement, under the leadership of a Yorkshire gentleman, Chrystopher Wyvill. The Association threatened to set up an extraparliamentary legislature if the Commons would not reform itself. Thomas Paine was a hero to the British radicals as he had been to the American rebels and as he later became to the French revolutionaries. Popular agitation finally resulted in protracted rioting in London in 1780; this frightened the middle class, and the democratic movement rapidly disintegrated.

The underlying turbulence of British politics exhibited in the reform movement was accompanied by persistent instability in the ministry of George III. The king's liking for Lord Bute, who headed the government in the mid-1760's, caused him to rely upon a man who was a political liability, and when George turned to coalitions among the different factions, he could suit neither himself nor his ministers. Lord North came to power in January 1770. A man perpetually unhappy in his work and anxious to resign, he remained in office for lack of a viable alternative rather than because his ministry had firm support. It was not until 1783 that the peace following the American Revolution and the rise of William Pitt the Younger brought a stable and capable ministry to power once again.

Pitt, who became prime minister at the age of twenty-four, had the support of both the king (now half mad) and the vestiges of the radical Association movement. He introduced legislation for reform of parliamentary representation, but it failed in the House of Commons. Pitt reduced corruption in the civil service and greatly improved government efficiency. A brilliant and dedicated leader, he had plans for extensive political and social reform, but before he could do much to implement these ideas, ominous developments in France began to distract the attention not only of Britain but of all Europe.

Incompetence and Intransigence in France

If the year 1784 marked the end of an era of turbulence in Great Britain, it introduced France to critical domestic difficulties. The most immediately pressing of these were financial, for the finances of the French government had still not recovered from the Seven Years' War when France went to the support of the American colonies in 1778. France emerged from that conflict with a treasury depleted beyond hope of repair, and this financial plight greatly exacerbated other social and political troubles.

In the late eighteenth century the French monarchy faced two problems which it never solved, problems which in fact grew worse instead of better as the century wore on. First and foremost was the problem of finances. Even in an era of prosperity the French Crown was unable to tap sufficient revenues to pay the annual expenses of the state. Both the Church and the nobility, the wealthiest elements in society, went virtually untaxed. Moreover, the collection of taxes in France was complicated, notoriously expensive, and corrupt; the abuses were almost legendary. At the same time, the demands on the French state required ever greater expenditures. If corruption and venality in offices were to be controlled, for instance, it would be necessary to pay adequate salaries to trained and able men. Instead, administrative inefficiency and corruption continued to grow, even if the sale of offices did not.

The second major problem of the French Crown was closely related to the first. The greatest enemies of the French state were the privileges of class and region, which blocked every attempt at reform in the eighteenth century. And both the privileged classes and such entities as towns and guilds found their chief guardian in the *parlements*. There was a *parlement* in every part of France, each serving as a kind of judicial supreme court but also possessing certain police powers, the authority to enforce its decisions, and—this is where the *parlements* were to become involved in direct confrontations with the monarchy—the self-assumed right of registering royal edicts before they became law. The members of the *parlements*, moreover, were neither elected nor appointed by the Crown. Most seats were inherited; the rest were purchased from heirs or owners. It was not surprising then that, in an age of aristocratic resurgence, the *parlements* soon became the center of resistance to state authority. After the 1760's it was the *parlements*, more than any other institution, that blocked effective government reform and finally forced the Crown to resort to the desperate expedient of convoking something like a national assembly.

The difficulties inherent in the situation which faced the French Crown between 1763 and 1786 were compounded by the lack of outstanding, or even competent, leadership. Louis XIV had proved that a king who possessed an iron will, boundless energy, and an acute sense of the politically possible could reduce the chaos of the French state to manageable dimensions. Neither of his two successors in the eighteenth century met those requirements.

To be sure, Louis XV was not without intelligence and powers of perception, but he was also indolent, indecisive, and far too pleasure-loving. At a time when Frederick the Great was building up his army and his state, Louis' main preoccuption—once he emerged from Fleury's shadow in the 1740's—seemed to be a long string of mistresses, headed by that illustrious pair, the Comtesse Du Barry and the Marquise de Pompadour. The king's role in the follies of French foreign policy after 1740 remains unclear, but about his vacillation and ineffectiveness when it came to dealing with important questions of domestic reform there can be no doubt.

From 1745 to 1754, for example, he had as chief financial officer Marchault d'Arnouville, an extremely able former *intendant*, who thought that the only way to finance the French war effort was to levy a 5 per cent income tax on everyone, clergy and nobility included. But when the latter protested furiously, Louis dropped both Marchault and his policy. A decade later the king reversed his course once more. In 1763–1764 he first retreated before the *parlements'* refusal to accept the income taxes required by the Seven Years' War, only to announce, at the hastily convened Paris *parlement* of March 1766, "To me alone belongs legislative power without dependence or division."

As if to prove that he finally meant business, Louis in 1770 appointed a new government headed by Chancellor Maupeou, formerly head of the Paris *parlement*. Soon after, Maupeou moved against all the *parlements*, disbanding them and setting up a whole new legal system in their place. The king also appointed a new controller general, who embarked on a large-scale fiscal reform program, based upon but going beyond the abortive 1763 decrees. These changes produced an enormous outcry from the privileged classes. Even the intellectuals, except for Voltaire and a few others, defended the old institution. In May 1774 Louis XV died, unlamented. His reforms did not long outlive him. His grandson and successor, Louis XVI, craved popularity and sought to achieve it by restoring the old *parlements*.

But the longer reform was delayed, the more difficult and dangerous the situation would become. This is not to say that Louis XVI did not make an effort to put his financial house in order. Beginning with Jacques Turgot (1725–1781), whom he appointed as his leading minister in August 1774, Louis called in a series of highly knowledgeable, well-intentioned officials to put France back on its financial feet. None succeeded. Turgot was a member of the new school of "physiocrats," whose liberalizing economic doctrines contrasted sharply with the traditional restrictionist policy made familiar by Colbert in the seventeenth century. The physiocrats believed that only land was capable of producing a real profit, and they wanted as much economic freedom as possible. Turgot elaborated this school of thought in his Six Edicts, which included the establishment of internal free trade in grains, abolition of the craft guilds, and commutation of the *corvée royale*, the labor service peasants owed on nearby royal roads a few days a year, into a tax to be paid by all landowners. But the *parlement* of Paris would have none of the Six Edicts. In March 1776 it bitterly denounced Turgot's program, and Turgot was dismissed soon after.

He was succeeded by the Swiss banker, Jacques Necker, who served from June 1776 to May 1781. Necker's two-part program was to borrow large additional sums of money (mostly to finance the American war) and to present to the country, for the first time, something like a comprehensive statement of French finances. Though grossly optimistic (and misleading because it omitted military spending), Necker's *compte rendu* was a revelation – and a shock. His successor, Charles Calonne, appointed in November 1783, presented a still more comprehensive program involving tax equalization, freer internal trade, and cooperation with new provincial assemblies elected by all taxpayers. Calonne also urged Louis to call the Assembly of Notables in order to win its support. The king agreed to do so in February 1787.

The French historian Jacques Godechot is of the opinion that the French Revolution began with the Assembly of Notables. It certainly ushered in the last effort at piecemeal reform. The Notables rejected Calonne's program, and soon thereafter, in April 1787, the king dismissed him also. As his successor, Louis appointed Loménie de Brienne, the liberal archbishop of Toulouse. But Loménie got nowhere; the *parlements*, in Paris and elsewhere, now declared that only a new Estates General – the first since 1614 – could levy the new taxes he proposed. In May 1788 Louis XVI did almost what his grandfather had done in 1763. He reduced the *parlements* to purely judicial bodies.

But it was too late. In the months that followed, hundreds of pamphlets appeared in the new battle between king and *parlement*, nine tenths of them against the Crown. What was the king to do now? In August 1788 he restored the *parlements*, dismissed Loménie, and recalled Necker. A month later the *parlement* of Paris returned in triumph and registered a royal decree convening a new Estates General for May 1, 1789. The French monarchy was now living on borrowed time.

2

Enlightenment Culture

I THE NATURE OF THE ENLIGHTENMENT

The Critical Spirit

The term *Enlightenment* is used to characterize the spirit of intellectual life and opinion in western Europe during the period from about 1715 to 1789. The leading thinkers of the time firmly believed that theirs was an age of enlightenment, that it held great promise for improving man's life on earth through the exercise of human reason. The felicitous image of a shaft of light turned upon what had previously been dark and unexplored areas of nature and society captured the imagination of these men; it seemed to be the most fitting emblem of their age.

These thinkers also liked to describe their time as an age of criticism, and it is this critical spirit, whereby men would rationally examine natural events and solve chronic human problems, that marks the unique climate of eighteenth-century thought. What was the "critical spirit" that the men of the Enlightenment purposefully cultivated and consciously chose as the symbol of their intellectual movement? They believed in man's unlimited ability to analyze and explain every aspect of his own nature and the world about him. The critical spirit went hand in hand with a new faith in the power and efficacy of the human understanding, or reason. It meant an unfettered freedom of inquiry and examination, no matter how sacrosanct the subject or how bold the investigation. "Dare to know"—thus the German philosopher Kant, writing toward the end of the eighteenth century, defined the critical spirit. "Have the courage to use your own understanding," he said. "This is the motto of the Enlightenment."

The exercise of the critical spirit often did require a kind of intellectual bravery, because men who allowed their minds to range freely inevitably were forced to challenge the power of traditional authorities and accepted beliefs, particularly in religion and politics. Not only were nature's works to be studied and explained, but human phenomena as well were to be scrutinized in the light of rational principles and judged by their concordance with the fundamental laws of nature. No longer were men satisfied with the traditional theological justifications for the suffering and injustice of human existence. Man's reward — the good life — would be achieved not in heaven but only on earth. "Miracles are good," wrote Voltaire, "but to aid one's fellow, to free one's friend from the bosom of misery, to pardon the virtues of one's enemies, this is a greater miracle, and one which is no longer performed." The age-old dogmas of the Church were examined, discredited, and finally rejected.

The legacy of Newton was clear and simple. All nature, it was assumed, was ruled by rational, comprehensible laws. Man had been given reason in order to perceive not the greater glory of God but the natural order of the world — in science, in history, in law, and in all the varied institutions and customs of society. Eighteenth-century morality had a secular emphasis that contrasts dramatically with the older belief in divine Providence and the modern feeling that man's fate is dictated by irrational forces he cannot control.

The critical spirit inspired what the men of the Enlightenment thought of as a new way to philosophize about every area of life and thought. In eighteenth-century parlance, *philosophy* meant much more than the abstract theoretical speculation of the scholastic philosophers; it embraced a vast intellectual movement. D'Alembert, who was a competent and respected mathematician as well as a philosopher, described the movement as "a lively fermentation of minds." It spread in all directions, he wrote, "like a river which has burst its dams." No authority was allowed to rest unchallenged. To this day it is a matter of historical debate as to which traditional beliefs remained and which were swept away.

The Philosophes

Historians have also argued, and probably always will, about the stature of the Enlightenment thinkers — the *philosophes* — who believed their main work lay in clearing away the rubbish of outworn ideas and archaic traditions. The inclusive and virtually untranslatable French term *philosophes* is applied to the protean men of talent who epitomized the Enlightenment. Although they regarded themselves as an extremely cosmopolitan group, and although the group did include such diverse figures as the Scottish empiricist David Hume, the German metaphysician Kant, and the Italian legal reformer Beccaria, the largest and most articulate contingent was composed of Frenchmen, or of men who lived in France or whose language was French. Furthermore, the dates commonly accepted as marking the Age of the Enlightenment, 1715 and 1789, are peculiarly French in historical significance. Louis XIV died in 1715. His death weakened rigid authority in French society, marked the beginning of a kind of thaw in French literary life, and opened the way to a new social criticism. The year 1789 saw the outbreak of the French Revolution, the beginning of the upheavals that characterize the modern world.

The years 1715 and 1789 are, of course, arbitrary dates; the development of the ideas immortalized by the Enlightenment cannot be strictly compressed in time. The great impetus to eighteenth-century thought was the work of men like Locke and Newton, which was completed before 1715, and it can be argued that Enlightenment ideas reach their fruition after 1789 — in the philosophy of Kant, for example, or Thomas Jefferson. Still, these two dates do serve a practical purpose, for they define the period during which the *philosophes* flourished and did most of their work.

The prototype of the *philosophe* formulated ideas and propagated them as well. Strictly speaking, he was neither a philosopher nor a literary man, though he interested himself in the latest philosophical speculation and usually wrote prolifically and well. His style was simple and pungent, and his published work was usually intended for the general reader. He cultivated many and far-ranging interests; Montesquieu literally tended his vineyards, and Rousseau composed an opera. Although most of the *philosophes* were not primarily scientists, they prided themselves on understanding and keeping up with the newest developments in theoretical and applied science. Many of them — Diderot, for example, and Benjamin Franklin — conducted experiments of their own. Others, like Buffon, were scientists who wrote about their own work for the general public. Even Voltaire, who had no particular aptitude for mathematics, published a popular exposition of Newton's theories of light.

The *philosophes* regarded themselves as an international community of like-minded men engaged in a collective intellectual adventure. They were a small, closely knit group like a talented, argumentative family. They kept up a tremendous stream of correspondence among themselves and were seldom stinting of criticism, praise, or gossip. Their role, they believed, was to be the vanguard of the best, most critical, most rational thought of the age. They intended to bear the torch kindled by the great scientific minds of the seventeenth century.

The *philosophes* hoped to accomplish great things. Hostile historians have accused them of indulging in a shallow and self-defeating optimism, but most of them were not so naive. In the course of the eighteenth century the *philosophes* embraced with less and less confidence the Newtonian maxim that "Nature is always in harmony with itself." Harmony might be a fundamental law of nature, but human institutions were not ordered according to rational principles. Nor were hate, intolerance, and superstition dissolved by the exercise of reason, for men clung to outworn traditions. Old and unjust authorities—in government and religion—stubbornly resisted change. The *philosophes* grew steadily angrier, more radical, and more dubious about the prospects of reforming recalcitrant institutions and rehabilitating human nature. "The stupidity of men, barbarous and uninstructed," as Hume put it, proved to be the greatest obstacle to the spread of enlightenment.

Nevertheless, the *philosophes'* crusade to expose irrationality and ameliorate injustices left its own legacy. By their intense analysis of social and political institutions, the *philosophes* incidentally developed the methodological tools that serve as the foundation of modern social science. Their assertion of the autonomy of the human mind and spirit, coupled with their special regard for the growth of the individual in society, fostered a belief in the natural equality of all men and gave rise to a new conception of civil rights. Their demands that the critical spirit be freely exercised led to the formulation of principles of freedom of speech, writing, and conscience that have been enshrined as the basic tenets of liberal doctrine. Finally, the *philosophes'* tender regard for all human beings helped to create a new kind of social consciousness that led eventually to a revolutionary attack on the social order itself.

II PHILOSOPHY AND THEOLOGY

The Philosophy of Man

Eighteenth-century philosophers preferred to think of themselves as empiricists rather than metaphysicians. Like the Newtonian scientists who rejected scholasticism, they turned against the system-building that characterized the work of the great seventeenth-century philosophers, Descartes, Spinoza, and Leibniz. The Enlightenment philosophers hoped to apply the critical spirit in philosophy instead of dabbling with abstract speculation that had little connection with the worldly concerns of active men.

What was the proper subject of philosophy? Newton had suggested that "if natural philosophy . . . shall at length be perfected, the bounds of moral philosophy will also be enlarged"; and the philosophers of the Enlightenment, inspired by the great strides the scientists had made in perceiving the principles underlying natural phenomena, believed that they in turn could uncover the principles governing human conduct and guiding ethical behavior. For the first time since the classical era, philosophy was entirely divorced from theology; once again it concerned itself primarily with secular life. Philosophical principles—whether in metaphysics, epistemology, or ethics—were now to be formulated on a scientific basis.

The special province of the new philosophy of the eighteenth century was not the metaphysical order of the universe but the hitherto uncharted terrain of human behavior. Eighteenth-century philosophers were not concerned with theological justification of the world order; they even questioned the utility of the traditional language of philosophy. They attempted to strike out on a fresh track by using the methods of empirical science to examine the workings of the human mind and the operations of human nature.

The eighteenth-century philosophers believed that philosophy, like science, could be the vehicle of enlightenment. They disparaged metaphysics not only because it was abstruse but because it did not seem to help in answering fundamental questions about man. "Our business here is not to know all things, but those which concern our conduct," Locke had written in his introduction to *An Essay Concerning Human Understanding*, a work taken as the fundamental text of eighteenth-century empirical thought. Locke's suggestion that the proper task of philosophy is to establish the limits of human knowledge itself was eagerly grasped by his successors. "It is of great use to the sailor to know the length of his line, though he cannot with it fathom all the depths of the ocean," he said. "It is well he knows that it is long enough to reach the bottom at such places as are necessary to direct his voyage, and caution him against running upon shoals that may ruin him."

Locke's nautical image aptly sums up the goal of the eighteenth-century philosophers, who almost without exception attempted to make philosophical speculation a useful part of natural philosophy. Man's secular concerns were the proper subjects of philosophy. Philosophy should help man to comprehend his own mind and his emotions and teach him how to chart his dealings with the external world. Thus the main contributions of Enlightenment philosophers were in epistemology, or the philosophy of knowledge, rather than in metaphysics, the philosophy of being and existence.

The focal point of eighteenth-century philosophy was the observation of man himself. The titles of some of the most important philosophical works published during the century reveal the new concern with the operations of the mind and the wellsprings of human behavior. The first great work, of course, was Locke's *Essay*, which, though published in 1690, set the tone that prevailed throughout most of the Enlightenment period. George Berkeley, an English clergyman who eventually became a bishop, published his *Principles of Human Knowledge* in 1710. In 1749 Diderot published his *Letter on the Blind*, an essay treating the problem of how sense impressions (or, in the case of blind people, the absence of them) might affect moral judgment. In 1754 Étienne de Condillac published the *Treatise on Sensations*, which closely followed Locke in analyzing all mental functions as a response to sense impressions. The subtitle for David Hume's *Treatise of Human Nature*, published in 1739, is probably the best description of the new methodology of eighteenth-century philosophy. It was, he declared, "an Attempt to Introduce the Experimental Method of Reasoning into Moral Sciences."

These thinkers were sketching the outlines of an entirely new science, one that we now call psychology. Locke may be thought of as the precursor of modern association psychology, and David Hartley, one of his eighteenth-century disciples, was the first writer to use the term "psychology." Hartley was an early theorist of the association of ideas. If all thoughts and emotions are triggered by sensations impinging on the mind, he said, then physical sense impressions ultimately account for all our ideas, including moral beliefs and judgments. But though the Enlightenment philosophers were confident that morals could be treated scientifically, they were not simpleminded rationalists in their approach to the complexities of the human mind. They did not expect that the science of mind would establish the indisputable principles yielded by other branches of natural science. The operations of the mind would always remain partially obscured, and the intricate patterns of human behavior would never be fully revealed. For "the Characters of Men," Hume readily admitted, "are to a certain Degree inconstant and irregular."

The two most important philosophers of the Enlightenment were the Scotsman David Hume (1711–1776) and the German Immanuel Kant (1724–1804). Neither was typical of the *philosophes*, but both made significant contributions to the new philosophy which was based not on revelation but on observation and reason. Kant had a profound influence on nineteenth-century philosophy, but Hume's major influence was not felt until the twentieth century, when his epistemological ideas were rediscovered by Bertrand Russell and the logical positivists who followed him. Locke, whose theories were modified and improved upon by both Hume and Kant, remained the best-known English philosopher during most of the Enlightenment period.

David Hume

Hume was undoubtedly the most amiable of the *philosophes*. He seems to have been the only one who managed to remain on good terms with his colleagues; in fact, there is no record of his ever being angry with anyone. He was born in Edinburgh to a family of middling gentry, but his father died when he was a child, and Hume's patrimony was, as he put it, "very slender." He was meant to become a lawyer but was soon repelled by the professional legal life of eighteenth-century Scotland. Eventually Hume liberated himself from his narrow Presbyterian upbringing. After emerging from a period of profound depression in late adolescence, he was able to formulate the principles that first appeared in the *Treatise on Human Nature*, which he published anonymously at the age of twenty-seven. The *Treatise* fell flat, but during the 1740's Hume began to make a name for himself through his essays, whose diversity is indicated in such titles as "The Populousness of Ancient Nations," "Liberty of the Press," and "The Dignity and Meanness of Human Nature." In 1748 his revised version of the *Treatise* was published as the *Essay Concerning Human Understanding*, which at first was hardly more successful than its predecessor.

Like Locke, Hume was fully engaged with the social and political life of his day. He never held an academic position, though he did serve in a minor diplomatic post in Paris. The lucidity of his prose has rarely been matched in English, certainly never by a philosopher. Almost everything he wrote is a delight to read. "Where a man of Sense mistakes my Meaning," Hume once said, "I own I am angry: But it is only at myself, for having Exprest my Meaning so ill as to have given Occasion to the Mistake."

Hume's philosophy has been labeled scepticism, but his was not the annihilating scepticism of some of the ancient Greeks, who believed that real knowledge of anything was impossible. For Hume, to be a sceptic was simply to recognize, without bitterness, those things that are unknowable. "So narrow are the Bounds of human Understanding," he wrote, that abstract ideas are only tenuous constructions of the imagination. They can never be verified, nor can the hidden principles of cause and effect ever be known authentically. But although the philosopher may be frustrated, and natural phenomena cannot be fully explained, men nevertheless can do science and achieve a working understanding of nature. Nature instructs that "your Science be human, and such as may have a direct Reference to Action and Society." Men must realize that philosophy is not an end in itself: the goal is humanity. "Be a Philosopher," says Hume, "but amidst all your Philosophy be still a Man."

All our thoughts, Hume believed, are formed in response to sense impressions. It is very difficult to distinguish impressions from thoughts, because impressions always give rise to ideas; and though ideas seem to possess an "unbounded liberty," this is a delusion. The creative powers of the mind are not autonomous; the understanding is capable only of "compounding, augmenting, or diminishing" data from the senses or experience. Thus, while the natural world is palpable, ideas are fragile and elusive. The mind exerts a slender hold on its own processes — and therefore on reason itself.

How are data from the external world translated into ideas? We arrive at all our conclusions about nature, says Hume, solely on the basis of habit and experience. We assume that the sun will rise tomorrow, but we cannot know absolutely that it will, because reason cannot establish an indissoluble link between causes and effects. "From Causes, which *appear* Similar, we expect similar Effects. This is the Sum of all our Experimental Conclusions." Men need not — indeed cannot — refrain from drawing conclusions and making future judgments, but they should realize that these are merely statements of probability. Custom and habit teach us that we can gamble on the operations of cause and effect, but we cannot begin to understand the principles of causality. Thus Hume neatly dispenses with teleology — the philosophical doctrine that there is a design and final purpose to be found in nature. "Who will assert," he asks, "that he can give the ultimate Reason, why Milk or Bread is proper Nourishment for a Man, not for a Lyon or a Tyger?"

The cutting edge of Hume's scepticism is sharpest when he questions the truths of Christianity. Almost all the *philosophes* gleefully debunked miracles, but Hume derided the notion dear to the hearts of eighteenth-century deists such as Voltaire and Rousseau that religious belief could be founded on reason. Religion, Hume claimed, was a response to man's need to bolster his hopes and placate his fears. The idea of God is a mental invention with which men try to account for the otherwise inexplicable principle of causality. But the existence of God, says Hume, can be neither proved nor refuted. Religious belief, therefore, is nothing more than a very strong feeling of the imagination, a total emotional commitment to one probability.

Hume himself was extremely dubious about the existence of a Deity — so much so that he was accused of atheism, to which he never quite admitted. "A wise man," he wrote, "proportions his Belief to the Evidence." The evidence does not permit us to entertain the abstract idea of an omnipresent being like God. If we cannot know how our own minds work, Hume wondered, how can we speculate about God's? Miraculous events, the only justification for the doctrines of Christianity, cannot be accepted by any rational man. All our knowledge of miracles is based on extremely fallible human testimony — and even if it were more reliable, the essential nature of a miracle is its inherent improbability.

Just as Hume did not believe there could be any valid abstract principles of religion, so there were no abstract rules of conduct. Virtue, of course, is admirable but not very difficult to explain: "According to the past Experience of Mankind, Friendship is the chief Joy of human life, and Moderation the only Source of Tranquillity and Happiness." Beyond this, however, there was little to say. The philosophy of Hume and other eighteenth-century empiricists has been severely criticized on the score that its precepts are nothing but a plea for common sense and that its most profound metaphysical and epistemological teachings amount to little more than a bookmaker's analysis of the odds.

Immanuel Kant

The first serious attack on this easygoing empiricism came from Immanuel Kant, who may himself be considered a *philosophe*. Kant's work stands at the pinnacle of Enlightenment thought even while it repudiates some of the fundamental assumptions of Enlightenment philosophy. In metaphysics, Kant said, it is absurd "to think of grounding our judgements upon probability and conjecture." And "to appeal to common sense when insight and science fail . . . is one of the subtle discoveries of modern times, by means of which the most superficial ranter can safely enter the lists with the most thorough thinker and hold his own."

Kant was born in Königsberg, a town in East Prussia that is now part of Russia. He came from a lower-middle-class family; his parents belonged to the Pietists, a Protestant sect whose members resembled Quakers in the plainness of their lives and their concern with conscience. His career was strictly academic: he studied at the University of Königsberg, served as a tutor in several aristocratic families, became an instructor at the university, and in 1770 was appointed professor of logic and metaphysics. He began to publish his major work when he was entering his sixties: *The Critique of Pure Reason* in 1781, the *Prolegomena to any Future Metaphysics* in 1783, the *Fundamental Principles of the Metaphysics of Morals* in 1785, the *Critique of Practical Reason* in 1788. In contrast to the typical *philosophe*, who traveled widely and savored the joys of city life, Kant spent his entire life in Königsberg, a small provincial capital.

Kant belonged to the last, transitional generation of Enlightenment thinkers. These men, whose work dates from the 1760's through the 1780's, were breaking away from the positions held by the older generation of *philosophes*. Kant's work, for example, is not only an enormous synthesis of Enlightenment ideas; it is also the first of the great nineteenth-century philosophical systems.

Kant wrote for a small, specialized audience. His ideas were first presented in the form of university lectures, and his writing made no concessions to popular taste. His prose is opaque and baffling to the ordinary reader even in the original German; in translation it is often impenetrable.

Kant believed in the objective reality of *a priori* ideas whose existence is independent of empirical data. Because he described these ideas as concepts of pure — or transcendental — reason, his philosophy is known as transcendentalism. Metaphysics, he said, is like mathematics — entirely an *a priori* science, an autonomous, rational "system based on no data except reason itself." Metaphysics and mathematics alike deal with concepts "whose truth or falsity cannot be discovered or confirmed by any experience."

Unlike Descartes, however, Kant did not deny the validity of sense experience or the usefulness of empirical science. Sense perceptions and the results of scientific experimentation were reliable, but only so far as they described appearances. Pure reason alone could formulate concepts, and real knowledge of the world was to be found only in these concepts of the mind. "We must not seek the universal laws of nature in nature by means of experience, but conversely must seek nature . . . in the conditions . . . which lie in our understanding." The mind could rise above the indeterminacy of natural events by imposing its own laws of pure reason on the world. Kant reasserted the primacy of human reason. Man himself was to be the lawgiver; "the highest legislation of nature must lie in ourselves, that is, in our understanding." Thus, for Kant, metaphysics was the highest, freest, and most pristine form of rational speculation; and as he divorced metaphysics from empiricism, so his ethical system was also liberated from all ties with experience and common sense.

Kant's ethics is founded on his belief that the rational concepts which formulate laws of nature can dictate laws of ethical behavior as well. Hume had said that morality was essentially a matter of common sense. Earlier eighteenth-century moralists like Shaftesbury and Mandeville had identified virtue with happiness; a good act was simple to know, they said, because it made you feel good. Kant tried to cut morality loose from this easygoing brand of utilitarianism. Experience, he thought, only served to show how men actually do act; it was not sufficient to tell them how they ought to act. Good actions were not good because they were useful or decent, nor could they be justified by their motivations or results. Actions that spring from feelings of love, honor, or affection are devoid of real moral value. Like metaphysical concepts, ethical norms must have a conceptual, objective validity; their truth cannot be tested by any worldly standards. The principles that govern ethical judgment and behavior are known *a priori*. For Kant, the highest principle of morality is duty, and his fundamental ethical precept is "Do your duty."

But how is an individual to know what his duty is in any particular instance? To answer this question, Kant formulated the categorical imperative, a concept of duty which prescribes the laws of ethical behavior. The categorical imperative may be seen as a restatement of the golden rule. For Kant, "Do unto others . . ." merely provided a personal, empirical standard of conduct. Men must act, said Kant, not in accordance with how they might wish others to treat them but rather as if they were legislating for all mankind. For moral actions, like natural phenomena, are ruled by inner principles of reason, and these principles cannot be revealed by studying individual cases, nor can they be influenced by worldly considerations. Kant sets up one standard against which all moral acts are to be measured: they must be judged by their congruence with the moral law, whose principles are known *a priori*. The idea of duty impels the individual to act in the light of those rational concepts of universal law which ought to govern all men. Duty, or "the necessity to act out of reverence for the law," and the inviolable precept that ends can never be cited to justify means are the twin pillars of Kant's ethical system. "Man is the end," he wrote. He did not mean the individual man, with his desires for personal gratification, but man as a transcendental idea, the concept of mankind as a whole.

At bottom, Kant's ethical teaching is extremely simple. The categorical imperative seems, finally, to be nothing but the voice of conscience. The eighteenth-century empiricists had treated the human conscience as a bundle of emotions in which affections, inhibitions, ambitions, and fears were tied together in an ever changing combination. Kant rejected this psychological explanation of human behavior. In any case, he was less interested in what men did than in what they ought to do. He treated conscience as an abstract idea of pure reason.

Whatever one's opinion of Kant's ideas and his way of expressing them, his place in Western philosophy must be acknowledged. He belongs firmly within the tradition of philosophic idealism that stretches back to Plato and forward to the nineteenth-century German, Friedrich Hegel. Kant's role in the German cultural efflorescence of the late eighteenth century was as significant as his contribution to Enlightenment thought. His ideas had a profound influence on the Romantic movement of the early nineteenth century.

Deism

Hume asserted that the existence of God was an unverifiable hypothesis. In the late nineteenth century the term *agnosticism* was coined to describe this attitude of disbelief, but in the eighteenth century agnosticism was so rare that there was no need for a word for it. Hume's contemporaries often called him an atheist, a term of opprobrium casually applied to anyone whose religious thought seemed outrageous or impious to respectable members of society. In fact, only a very few Enlightenment figures were outright atheists, and their position, even in the latter part of the eighteenth century, was considered extreme and unworthy of serious consideration. The most commonly held religious belief of the *philosophes* was deism or, as its proponents often called it, natural religion.

Deism may be seen as a compromise arrived at by men who rejected the centuries-old authority of the Church, the dogmas of Christianity, and the claims of sectarianism on the one hand and scepticism and atheism on the other. It provided a comfortable middle ground where common sense prevailed over superstition, tolerance over self-righteousness, and an informal, humanistic morality over the teaching that sin in this life leads to punishment in the next. Deism was congenial with the Newtonian view of the world, in which revelation and miracles were superfluous remnants of a priest-ridden, unscientific age. The Deity Himself was a remote and inchoate Supreme Being, who did not interfere very much with the minute operations of the world or the petty concerns of mankind. The growth and spread of deism was contemporary with the burgeoning Newtonian revolution in science. The movement began in England late in the seventeenth century, reached its peak there early in the eighteenth century, and had somewhat diminished by the 1750's. By that time it had spread to the Continent, where it was of major importance. The most articulate and persuasive deists on the Continent were *philosophes* of the stature of Voltaire and Rousseau.

Because deism was a belief without formal content or teaching, even its most fervent adherents found it hard to define. But the fuzzy, doctrineless character of deism also explains its popularity. Every man was left to gauge the depth and nature of his belief and was granted the ability to judge his own actions according to reason and common sense. Deists sought to strip superstition and mystery from religious devotion and expression. They believed that atheism was an error born of despair but that the authoritarian structure of the Catholic Church and the rigidity and intolerance of its doctrines were even more deplorable. Since all nature was an expression of God's will and spirit, there was no need for the petty, constricting dogmas imposed by a corrupt and self-serving church hierarchy. The worship of God must be sought in the hearts of men; it has nothing to do with ceremony, with meaningless genuflections and empty words.

The essence of deism was its capacity to embrace virtually any form of religious worship, so long as it came from the heart and was free from dogmatism and irrational authority. One of the most explicit statements of a deist credo was written by Tom Paine in his *Age of Reason*, published toward the end of the eighteenth century. "I believe in one God, and no more; and I hope for happiness beyond this life." This was its sole doctrinal content; the rest of the deist creed was simply a matter of secular morality.

"The best of all religion," wrote Rousseau in the *Profession of Faith of a Savoyard Vicar*, the classic explanation of deist belief, "is undoubtedly the clearest." All men, said the deists, would, by virtue of their natural reason, acknowledge the presence and power of God. However, reverence and worship had nothing to do with an institutionalized church or with any prescribed tenets of belief. "We have set aside all human authority," says Rousseau, speaking for the Enlightenment movement as a whole. "I cannot see how one man can convince another by preaching to him an unreasonable doctrine." For the deists among the *philosophes*, the end of religion, as of all rational thought, was to serve not God but humanity.

III SOCIAL CRITICISM

The Philosophes *and Society*

The *philosophes* found much to criticize in the social and political institutions of the *ancien régime*, but they did not want to restructure their society or uproot its institutions. Their zeal was directed at clearing away the rubble of prejudice, superstition, and irrationality. They meant to liberate the human spirit and lay bare the natural order of things—in government, in religion, in the administration of justice. They envisaged themselves as rational reformers, not revolutionaries. They did not believe revolution was either desirable or necessary.

The *philosophes* were true conservatives. They spoke much of the "natural" equality of all men, but they stopped far short of advocating real egalitarianism. They raged against the inequities of an economic system that allowed the poor to starve, a legal system that produced blatant miscarriages of justice, and the prejudices that inhibited freedom of thought; but they shied away from radical change. It was dangerous, they realized, to tamper with the body politic. "How far does policy allow us to go in destroying superstition?" Voltaire asks in the *Philosophical Dictionary*. "This question is extremely thorny," he admits. "It is like asking how far we should go in tapping a man with dropsy, for he might die in the course of the operation. It depends on the prudence of the physician." However, as the century wore on and the diseases of society did not yield to mild treatment, the *philosophes* grew impatient. The later generation of *philosophes* prescribed stronger medicine and more drastic cures.

Most of the *philosophes* belonged to the relatively small, elite group of educated men in eighteenth-century European society. They were cultivated; most of them were men of leisure. Some were wellborn, and all had powerful connections among their friends and patrons, if not in their own families. Yet most of them remained on the fringes of power. They might be asked to advise governments or even to draw up programs of reform, but they were seldom given any real responsibility. Their talents as publicists were always recognized, but except in England and, for a time, in Prussia, they wrote in constant fear of arbitrary, erratic, and inconsistent censorship by government and church. Their only real weapons were their pens and their ability to appeal to the common sense and conscience of their readers, and in this they were remarkably skilled. It is hard to find another era when so many social critics were also accomplished and prolific popular writers.

The most successful works of the *philosophes* had a circulation comparable proportionately to today's best-selling novels or sensational exposés. Their books were short and readable and, in spite of censorship, were often available in cheap editions. In 1765 Voltaire observed that "twenty-folio volumes will never make a revolution; it's the small portable books at 30 sous that are dangerous. If the Gospel had cost 1200 sesterces, the Christian religion would never have been established." To his enemies, Voltaire's own small, portable books seemed the most dangerous of all, for he was one of the most popular writers in French literary history.

Voltaire

The Enlightenment is often called the Age of Voltaire; in a sense his career was a distillation of the style and thought of the whole era. Voltaire (1694–1778) was born as François Marie Arouet (at the age of twenty-three he added the more aristocratic sounding "de Voltaire"). His father was a Paris notary, a solid bourgeois citizen who intended that his talented son become a successful lawyer. Voltaire was educated at a fashionable Jesuit college, where he was supposed to acquire social polish and useful connections among the rich and wellborn. But instead he nurtured a passion for poetry and a taste for the heady atmosphere of Parisian salons. At the age of twenty-one, he was imprisoned in the Bastille for a year, on a charge of writing libelous verse about the regent. It was his first encounter with the strict censorship against which he battled for the rest of his life. Literary fame came early in his career; poems and plays which no one but scholars read today were the main source of his reputation. It was only as an old man in the 1760's and

1770's that he built a new reputation as a violent anticlerical crusader and humanitarian reformer.

In 1726 Voltaire was again imprisoned in the Bastille, this time for having insulted a great noble, whose servants summoned him from a dinner party and gave him a public beating. He never forgot this lesson in the realities of power in an aristocratic society. After his release from prison Voltaire spent two years in England and returned to France a devout admirer of English institutions, English science, and English religious toleration. His *Letters on the English (Lettres Philosophiques)*, with its enthusiastic praise of the openness of English life, was published in Paris in 1734 and promptly burned by the public hangman because of its subversive and irreligious nature.

The implied criticism of French society in Voltaire's praise of England caused a furor that led to Voltaire's semiexile from Paris. He spent most of the next decade at the chateau of his mistress and intellectual colleague, the Marquise du Châtelet, who encouraged him to work in science and mathematics and started him on *The Age of Louis* xiv, one of the first attempts at social history. He also continued to turn out a cascade of verse dramas and long poems and published a popularization of Newton. "You will find that my explanations are quite clear," he wrote to a friend in the Academy of Sciences. "I am like those little brooks which are clear and transparent because they are not very deep." It was an apt description of his lucid style and a fair appraisal of the quality of his thought, which was never exceptionally original or profound but always incisive, simple, and easily understood.

In the 1740's and early 1750's Voltaire was attracted to the orbit of Frederick the Great of Prussia, who fancied himself a philosopher-king. The relationship between Frederick and Voltaire was always difficult. Frederick appointed his pet intellectual a court chamberlain and gave him a handsome pension, but both men were too prickly and self-centered to remain friends. During his association with Frederick, however, Voltaire perfected the literary techniques that made his later works masterpieces of polemic and satirical wit. These were the *conte* (the short story or tale), the brief dialogue—the form in which he cast much of the *Philosophical Dictionary*—and the *facétie* (the sharp joke which proved a point by making the reader laugh). Voltaire's most telling social criticism appeared in these light literary forms, which he manipulated with a skill no other writer in French has ever quite equaled.

In 1758 Voltaire settled down on his lavish estate, conveniently near the Swiss border. For the next twenty years he bombarded the public and the French authorities with his little books. Virtually everything he wrote from this point on was to expose an injustice, to attack an abuse, or to propose a reform. Although he was a hypochondriac throughout his life and was always certain that he was on the verge of death, he lived to be eighty-four. Until the end of his life he wrote with the fervor and energy of a young man.

Voltaire was not a theorist. His mind was always captured by the concrete, just as his style focused on the earthy detail, the picturesque joke or description, the lewd suggestion. He always upheld a few fundamental principles: freedom of person, of speech, of conscience, of religion, and of the press. His motto against the Church was *écrasez l'infâme* (crush the infamous) but he never totally renounced his religious beliefs, and he abhorred atheism. He meant to reform the archaisms and injustices which deformed the French Church; he called for secular control of the Church's legal functions and for the taxation of church property by the state; he believed secular authorities should be responsible for establishing the legality of marriage and divorce and for overseeing the censorship of publications. But in spite of his lifelong attack, he believed Catholicism should remain the state religion in France.

Voltaire was an ardent proponent of the abolition of feudal taxes and dues and the outmoded regulations imposed by the guilds, but like most of his contemporaries, he had little sense of the problems of industrial workers and did not perceive the significance of the changes in industrial technology that were occurring in England. He called for a thoroughgoing reform of French criminal law and an overhaul of the judicial system. As he grew older, his crusading zeal intensified, and his efforts on behalf of toleration and civil rights for Protestants eventually allowed him to assume the mantle of a respected elder statesman.

In 1764, when Voltaire was seventy, one of his most important books appeared. This was the *Philosophical Dictionary*. The first edition was a pocket-sized volume of 344 pages containing just seventy-three entries. It was published anonymously in Geneva, with a false London imprint. Voltaire strenuously denied that he was the author, although it was obvious to everyone that the book was his. Prudence, not modesty, inspired his disclaimers; within a year the book had been ordered burned by the government of Geneva, the Paris *parlement*, and The Hague and had been condemned by the Holy Office of the Vatican. But it was wildly popular, and new, enlarged editions kept appearing until, by 1769, the *Dictionary*—no longer "*portatif*"—comprised 120 articles in two large volumes. The ideas in the *Dictionary* were not new or startling, but its style was so captivating that it soon was recognized as one of the most significant vehicles of Enlightenment social criticism.

The topics covered in the *Dictionary* include Priest, Love, Great Chain of Being, Circumcision, Divinity of Jesus, Equality, Fanaticism, Inquisition, Freedom of Thought, Pride, Original Sin, Tyranny, and Virtue. Techniques vary from subject to subject, but Voltaire leaned heavily on the dialogue, the anecdote, the ironic tale, and—perhaps most successfully of all—the matter-of-fact narrative with tongue firmly in cheek. The absurdity of church doctrine, the hypocrisy of the clergy and the magistrates, the inhumanity of men, the irrationality of legal and religious institutions, the wickedness of kings—all these are illustrated in a series of short pungent lessons.

The haphazard form of the *Dictionary* allowed Voltaire to indulge freely in irreverence. One of his favorite tactics was to make the protagonists of Biblical stories look ridiculous. The profession of a prophet, he notes, "is a wretched one," and he leaves the reader with little respect for any of the prophets. In another article he demolishes the dietary restrictions of Lent by asking, "Did the first men to think of fasting put themselves on this regimen on their physicians' order, because they had indigestion?"

A sample scarcely does justice to the masterful fashion in which Voltaire bends his lucidity, anger, and sheer exuberant wit to the serious questions tackled in the *Dictionary*. Here all the principles of Voltaire's humanitarian philosophy are, as his French biographer noted, "condensed into a light and nourishing consommé."

The Encyclopedia

If the *Philosophical Dictionary* was a stimulating first course in Enlightenment social thought, heartier nourishment could be found in the multivolume encyclopedia shepherded through the press between 1751 and 1772 by Denis Diderot (1713–1784). In 1750 Diderot announced the publication of an encyclopedia that would be the repository of all current knowledge. *L'Encyclopédie* was described as a systematic dictionary of science, art, and crafts. It was undertaken as a commercial venture on the model of a popular English encyclopedia. The French publisher asked Diderot, a free-lance journalist who was then known only as a competent translator, to supervise the publication. The choice could not have been better. The French encyclopedia far outstripped its English model. There was nothing else like it in France or in all Europe. Seventeen volumes were published between 1751 and 1772, and by 1780 six more, consisting of addenda, data, and tables, had appeared. The illustrations alone were a vast source of information. They show every aspect of contemporary craftsmanship and are still a magnificent guide to eighteenth-century technology. The encyclopedia was astonishingly popular, considering its price.

Diderot belonged by birth to the class of small craftsmen. He received a traditional Jesuit education and at one time thought of becoming a priest, but he soon embraced deism and later in his life even flirted with atheism. Modern historians have come to see Diderot as the most supple and perhaps the most original of all the *philosophes*. He was a scientist; he wrote moral and philosophical essays; he was the first modern art critic; and in *Rameau's Nephew* he produced an imaginative psychological novel. His most significant contribution in his own day was his role in shaping the encyclopedia and the catalytic influence he appeared to have on his colleagues. His training in science was solid, and he had a more professional understanding of scientific rationalism than such literary figures as Voltaire. The characteristic tone of the encyclopedia—the disavowal of any kind of superstition, the attempt to give a clear, rational account of all natural phenomena—reflects Diderot's own cast of mind.

Diderot chose as his general editor the mathematician d'Alembert, who, as secretary of the Academy of Sciences, was able to organize academicians and prominent intellectuals in support of the new venture. The roster of *philosophes* who contributed to the encyclopedia looks impressive, but in fact the bulk of the text was written (or compiled—plagiarism was not considered a sin, and eighteenth-century authors copied freely from one another) by second-rate hack writers. Still, the backing of the more illustrious *philosophes* was good publicity, and their moral support was invaluable.

The purpose of the encyclopedia was announced in Diderot's article, "Encyclopedia." It was designed, he wrote,

to assemble the knowledge scattered over the surface of the Earth; to explain its general plan to the men with whom we live and to transmit it to the men who come after us; in order that the labors of centuries past may not be in vain in centuries to come; that our descendants, by becoming better instructed, may as a consequence be more virtuous and happier, and that we may not die without having deserved well of the human race.

The editors believed they could convey to the literate layman all the new learning of the age. "The truth is simple and can always be made accessible to everyone," d'Alembert wrote.

The presentation of useful knowledge was not the editors' sole aim, however. A good dictionary or encyclopedia, said Diderot, must be able to change "the general way of thinking." The enormous collection of scientific data, he rightly thought, would necessarily encourage readers to cultivate a new, rational attitude toward every aspect of their society. It did not matter that the science in the encyclopedia was soon outmoded; the critical spirit still informed nearly every article.

The implicit ethical teaching of the *Encyclopédie* was utilitarianism. Useful knowledge of nature was more valuable than abstract speculation about God and the universe—by definition, useful knowledge was secular. It was assumed that rational understanding of the scientific world would uplift mankind far more than moral preachings. Although old superstitions were debunked, the men who wrote for the encyclopedia did not attempt to attack the Church explicitly. Religion was undermined simply by being ignored. By their choice of subjects, the editors made it clear that religion was not one of the things men needed to know. There was scarcely any mention of Biblical figures, though many articles dealt with the ethnography of primitive tribes. Subjects like creeds, religious controversies, and church history were dismissed in a few words. The article on the stocking-knitting frame was about ten times as long as the one on cathedrals.

How effective was the encyclopedia? Undoubtedly it reflected and reinforced a sense that common and menial pursuits were dignified and important. It may have contributed to the increasing democratic consciousness and

self-respect of the small artisans and shopkeepers who were the popular democrats of the French Revolution. The encyclopedia has been described as the
Trojan Horse of the *ancien régime*, and perhaps it did help to subvert the old
order from within. Although the editors had set out to teach and instruct, not
to destroy, their work was a very successful instrument of propaganda for the
new, rational style of thought. The religious establishment—the Jesuits in
particular—understood this very well.

Every new volume, it was feared, might provoke the censor and incur ecclesiastical condemnation. The Church still had considerable power to suppress
teachings it disliked or found threatening. The encyclopedia was condemned
and suppressed in 1752 and again in 1758. It was, however, relatively free
from censorship, thanks mainly to the laxity of the French government.
Louis xv's mistress, Madame de Pompadour, was an intelligent, cultivated
woman with ties to the *philosophes* and the Paris literary establishment. She
approved of the encyclopedia and probably intervened on its behalf.

If the *Encyclopédie* had powerful friends, it also made some ferocious enemies. One was the bishop of Montauban, who complained that "Today there are
torrents of errors and impieties which tend towards nothing less than the
submerging of Faith, Religion, Virtues, the Church, Subordination, the Laws,
and Reason." D'Alembert and Diderot might have agreed with him—although they would no doubt have insisted that reason and virtue belonged on
their side. They claimed that the encyclopedia was meant only to aid and instruct, but it was designed to convert as well. As the historian of science
C. C. Gillispie points out, ideology was presented in the guise of technology. It
was not the wit of the *philosophes* but science itself that revealed the institutions of the *ancien régime* as unreasonable, immoral, and unnatural.

Physiocrats and Utilitarians

The *philosophes*, who exercised the critical spirit in examining the economic
relations of their society as well as its political, religious, and social institutions, inaugurated a new discipline—political economy. In the 1750's a group
known as *physiocrats* launched a concerted attack on mercantile theory. This
was by no means the first attack on mercantilism, but it was the first one
undertaken in a scientific spirit. François Quesnay (the royal physician), the
Marquis d'Argenson, and the statesman Turgot were the leaders of the group.
They thought of themselves as "naturalists" whose goal was to discover and
implement the natural principles of economic life.

The physiocrats believed that only agriculture was truly productive and
that land was the most important source of wealth. France was the major
agricultural nation of Europe in the eighteenth century, and the overriding
interests of the landholding class were taken for granted. The physiocrats
insisted upon free trade in agricultural products. There should be no barriers,

they said, and no frontiers, monopolies (for instance, those of retail dealers) should be abolished, and large government contractors whose operations inhibited a free market should be suppressed. Since land was the primary source of national wealth and land taxes the most reliable form of state revenue, capital should be applied to agriculture to increase the productivity of the land.

The physiocrats' program was a rational, attractive attempt to solve the vexatious fiscal problems facing the French government. Their plan to develop a class of rich, large-scale farmers by diverting the flow of capital from banking and commerce to agriculture appealed to landholders throughout western Europe. The physiocratic doctrine appeared first in Quesnay's article "Farmers" in the 1756 edition of the *Encyclopédie*, and during the 1760's the group had an important if short-lived influence on European economic thought. But despite its rationality, the vision of a free agricultural market never became a reality. The system was too naive and simplistic to survive, and by the middle of the 1770's the physiocratic doctrine was supplanted by the teachings of the Scottish political economist Adam Smith.

Adam Smith (1723–1790) was a tough-minded reformer with an austere, middle-class background similar to that of his friend David Hume. He was educated at the University of Glasgow, where he became a professor of moral philosophy. His contacts with the *philosophes* were frequent, and he was familiar with the doctrines of the physiocrats, which he rejected. Smith believed that any meaningful economic analysis had to focus on commerce and on the means of production. Like many members of the eighteenth-century intellectual community, he was revolted by the militarism and unreasonably restrictive legislation that buttressed the old mercantile system. In 1776 he published *The Wealth of Nations*, probably the most influential book on economics ever written. It was a devastating critique of contemporary economic policy and a demand for immediate reform. Smith presented a vast amount of data in a lucid, elegant fashion, and though there is hardly a statistical table in the entire text, it is still an important source of information about eighteenth-century economic life.

Smith was by no means an apologist for private enterprise, but he was a fierce critic of economic nationalism, and he railed against the restrictions of ancient guilds and obsolete monopolies. Like all the *philosophes*, he yearned for freedom—in trade as well as in government—and believed that an individual has the right to choose his occupation and gain autonomy over his economic life. Contemporary government, it must be remembered, was inefficient and unwieldy, the preserve of aristocratic interests; any rational program of economic reform was bound to demand an end to governmental interference. Smith never claimed that free trade would function perfectly, but he preferred the natural operations of a free economy to government controls. He did not ascribe any inherent virtues to the profit motive, nor did he believe that businessmen were especially benevolent. While he perceived that psychological motivation was a prime factor in economic development, he knew that the desire for profit must be curbed by moral restraint.

Adam Smith's thought had a far-reaching influence on English commercial legislation of the early nineteenth century. In the crusade for legal reform, his counterpart was Jeremy Bentham (1748–1832). Smith preached free trade, cheap and efficient government, and the abolition of monopolies; Bentham's formulation of the principle of utility provided an empirical tool for measuring the rationality and effectiveness of legal and political institutions.

Jeremy Bentham was a precocious child who was sent by his ambitious father to an elite preparatory school, to Queen's College, Oxford, and to one of the Inns of Court for legal training. As Bentham immersed himself in the archaic irrationality of the law, he began to search for a principle that would establish a clear path through the maze that was English common law in the eighteenth century. He never did practice law, but he spent his life in attempts to reform it. His spirit never flagged; near his death at the age of eighty-two he was still "codifying like a dragon."

The foundations of utilitarianism had been laid down by Locke and Hobbes, and Bentham's fundamental assumption that man is ruled by "two sovereign masters, pain and pleasure," was not new. It was his attempt to back up the doctrine that was significant. Taking Francis Bacon as his model, he hoped to establish the principle of utility as the basis for nothing less than a complete science of human behavior. There was only one standard, he said, for judging institutions: did they bring about the greatest possible public happiness? This happiness, he believed, could be quantitatively measured by calculating individual sums of pain and pleasure.

In his later years, when he worked out specific calculations in minute detail, Bentham's thought became abstruse and his writing opaque. But his early works, the *Fragment on Government* (1776) and the *Introduction to Principles of Morals and Legislation* (1789), are simple and trenchant; they are read and studied even today. The practical legislative effects of Bentham's crusade became apparent in the early nineteenth century. He created a link between eighteenth-century rationalism and the liberal reform movement in Victorian England.

Montesquieu

Montesquieu, perhaps the most profound and original of all the *philosophes*, was a dispassionate observer of society and its institutions rather than an ardent reformer. He belonged to the magistrate class, the *noblesse de la robe*, and favored the traditional intermediary role of the *parlements* (which stood for the interests of his class) between the authority of the Crown and the pressures of the people. Charles de Secondat, Baron de La Brède et de Montesquieu (1689–1755), was born in a chateau near Bordeaux. As was customary, a passing beggar was made his godfather, to remind the child of his obligations to the poor. He received the usual classical education, with its emphasis on Latin literature and Roman history, and then studied law in Paris. In his early twenties he inherited his lands and wealth and, on the death of an uncle, the family judicial property, the office of president of the Guyenne *parlement*. The young Montesquieu took his judicial responsibilities very seriously even though they were uncongenial. He consoled himself by cultivating other interests: he studied literature, history, and science and became an active member of the Bordeaux Academy.

Until he was twenty-seven, Montesquieu led a respectable, uneventful life. But in 1721 his *Persian Letters*, an incisive attack on French regency society in the guise of an epistolary novel, was published anonymously in Amsterdam and became an instant literary success. Although antecedents could be found in the work of Bayle in the late seventeenth century, the book inaugurated a new French literary form. In the episodic *Letters*, Montesquieu assumes the personae of two Persians who comment freely and irreverently on the strange customs they encounter in their European travels. The description of French society by these alien and supposedly objective observers is comic, pungent, and devastating. In a lighthearted way, Montesquieu's relativistic treatment of institutions and social values foreshadowed the technique he would develop more thoroughly and systematically in his great treatise on government and law.

Beneath its sparkling surface the book makes a fervent plea for liberty. The playful anecdotes narrated by the Persians reveal the hypocrisies of a society that claims to be rational and just but is, in fact, perverse, authoritarian, and cruel. Montesquieu was deadly serious and evenhanded in his criticism. Implicit throughout the book is his belief that man can recognize and liberate himself from the bonds of prejudice and injustice by exercising his reason.

In style as well as substance, the *Persian Letters* was a significant, liberating work of art. Its racy, free-flowing, almost colloquial language was a marked departure from the formal, heavily latinized French considered appropriate for serious literature. At once recognized as a masterpiece, the book was so popular that in Paris it "sold like bread."

Soon after the stunning success of the *Persian Letters*, Montesquieu sold his judicial office. He traveled widely in Europe and spent two particularly fruitful years in England, where he was elected a fellow of the Royal Society. In 1734 he published a history of Rome in which he expounded the theory that societies, like individuals, pass through stages of health and sickness. A whole society decays, he said, when its internal structural principles crumble.

In 1728 Montesquieu began to accumulate data on government and law from all over the world for his most important work—one of the enduring monuments of Enlightenment thought. *The Spirit of the Laws*, published in 1748, was nothing less than an outline of the fundamental principles that order human government, law, and society. Human institutions are intelligible, Montesquieu believed; they can be reduced to simple principles if they are studied like biological organisms and examined according to their natural development. But in his search for scientific principles, he never lost sight of the tenacity of human instincts. The book is informed by one piercing vision — that men do not rationally establish governments or make laws. Rather, these take their shape irrevocably from conditions of society and in response to deep-rooted human needs. Institutions reflect the structure of society and cannot be treated as though they exist in a vacuum. "Men are influenced by various causes, by the climate, the religion, the laws, the maxims of government, by precedents, morals, customs, from whence is formed a general spirit which takes its rise from these." Nor could this "general spirit" be reduced to a simple rubric. It is a gross error, Montesquieu wrote in his *Pensées*, to wish to reduce the sentiments of men to a system.

Nevertheless, in the thirty-one episodic sections that comprise *The Spirit of the Laws*, Montesquieu describes the "general spirit" as a series of responses to two kinds of factors: moral causes, which include religion, law, and custom, and physical causes — climate, population, geography — which were unalterable. In a country where the morals of the people are sound (*bonnes moeurs*), it is hardly necessary, he said, to have laws at all. This conception of the functional relationship between the needs and pressures of society and the development of its legal institutions is Montesquieu's unique contribution to what would become the disciplines of social science. The great French social theorists of the nineteenth century, Comte and Durkheim, claimed him as the precursor of sociology.

What captivated Montesquieu's contemporaries, however, was his simple, elegant prose and some of his more superficial observations. They eagerly grasped his breakdown of governments into three simple categories — monarchy, despotism, and republic. They welcomed his attack on slavery, his condemnation of all forms of tyranny, and his distaste for religious intolerance and harsh penal codes, and they seconded his praise of commerce as a vehicle of civilization.

Although he never failed to laud the true spirit of liberty in the few places where it seemed to flourish, Montesquieu did not try to formulate any proposals for reform. It was more important, he believed, to analyze, to comprehend, to be aware of differences among peoples and societies, than to rush into rapid changes based on ill-formed principles. He was a fervent advocate of limited constitutional monarchy and pleaded for peace and for the protection of the rule of law against despotism; he believed in gradualism above all. "Politics are like a smooth file," he wrote, "which cuts slowly and attains its end by a gradual and tedious progression." Balance is hard to achieve, easy to disrupt. Sometimes the very imprecision of the law allows for the exercise of liberty.

Montesquieu's concept of evolutionary jurisprudence could be interpreted in two conflicting ways. One was extremely conservative—indeed, as expounded by late eighteenth-century writers like Edmund Burke and some post-Revolutionary legal historians, it sounded very much like reaction. If laws are the outgrowth of deeply rooted social and cultural traditions, these men felt, it is not given to individual men, no matter how rational or well meaning, to change them. The other view was taken by utilitarian reformers like Jeremy Bentham and by nineteenth-century liberals and is still the doctrine of many legal sociologists. Since laws are not absolute but must be judged in accordance with their social value, this school teaches, they must be changed in response to new social realities.

Law

Less patient *philosophes* could not accept Montesquieu's cautious attitude toward reforming the legal systems of the *ancien régime*, whose cumbersome, cruel, and irrational procedures were an appalling anachronism in an age when men prided themselves on their humanity and civilization. It was perfectly clear to anyone who looked that the medieval structures no longer functioned properly. The multiplicity of law that so fascinated the scholar in Montesquieu enraged Voltaire. The customary law was rigid and absurd; the relics of the feudal past, utterly nonsensical. Worst of all, the burden of the law fell most heavily on the poor and ignorant. Was it too much to ask, Voltaire wryly wondered, that law be in accord with, if not justice, then at least common sense and humanity? The rottenness of the legal system seemed just one more sign of the decadence of the *ancien régime*.

The *philosophes* might rail, but they failed to come up with a rational program of legal reform. A short tract by a Milanese aristocrat, Cesare Bonesana, Marquis of Beccaria (1738–1794), did make some practical suggestions and thereby laid the foundations of modern penal theory. A less likely candidate for the most influential writer on legal reform in western Europe could hardly have been imagined. Beccaria was an intelligent but somewhat indolent young man who admired the ideas of the *philosophes* and joined a reading and discussion group formed by some young Milanese. Everyone in the group was assigned a topic to read up and report on, and Beccaria happened to get criminal law. The result of his study was a brief, simply written book published in 1764, *An Essay on Crimes and Punishments*. Within six months this work by a young man with no legal background and no experience in the administration of criminal justice went through seven editions of a French translation. Voltaire wrote a commentary, which helped to popularize it all over Europe. Catherine the Great invited Beccaria to come to Russia to codify the criminal law, and by the time he was thirty, he was appointed to a professorship in political economy at Milan. He never again produced anything of importance.

Beccaria did not have to preach. Enlightened opinion was ripe for his recommendations. Everyone loathed the confusing and arbitrary procedures that disfigured the European criminal codes, and Beccaria offered sensible remedies in an elegant, concise, and rational manner. One overriding principle, he said, ought to pervade the administration of criminal justice. Rather than satisfying private vengeance, punishment should be meted out according to the good of the greatest number of people. The aim of all punishment must be prevention. Penalties should be determined by their usefulness in deterring crime; anything beyond that was inhumane. The most effective punishments are prompt, unambiguous, and certain.

Beccaria's utilitarian analysis was the sharpest stroke of all against the shoddy legal system of the *ancien régime*, in which secret accusations, torture, the imposition of harsh statutory penalties for minor offenses against property, imprisonment for debt, and promiscuous recourse to capital punishment were long-established practices. Against this ramshackle irrationality, Beccaria set up a viable system of alternatives. Crimes against property were to be punished by fines or, if the criminal was unable to pay, by imprisonment. Political crimes would incur banishment—this being far more healthy for the state than the imprisonment of dissidents. Capital punishment would be abolished outright; the severity of a sentence would be measured by its duration. Beccaria also proposed a reform of the prison system. Prisoners should be classified according to the nature of their offenses and separated according to their categories.

Beccaria's ideas captured the minds of a generation brought up on the writings of the *philosophes*. However, except for one important achievement—the abolition of torture in most European countries by the end of the eighteenth century—his proposals were honored more in theory than in practice. Even in England, where his influence was felt most strongly, his ideas were not implemented until the first part of the nineteenth century.

History

The critical spirit which led the *philosophes* to probe the nature of men in society also gave rise to a new attitude toward the writing of history. The conviction that theirs was the most enlightened age of all led to a belief, often simplistic and self-serving, in the idea of human progress. Still, the new spirit of rationality also influenced a small group of historians whose perceptiveness and clear-mindedness can justly serve as models for historians today. In assiduous scholarship alone, the eighteenth-century historians never matched the seventeenth-century clerics whose collections of documents and compilations of charters they eagerly used. But they were liberated from the theological framework that limited the historical vision of their predecessors even while it intensified their scholarly dedication. The Enlightenment historians no longer had to account, as the seventeenth-century writers had been obliged to do, for the unfolding of God's plan for the destiny of men and nations.

History in the eighteenth century was rapidly becoming a popular form of literature—"the most popular species of writing, since it can adapt itself to the highest and lowest capacity," as Edward Gibbon remarked. The works of Voltaire, Montesquieu, and the Scottish school represented by Hume and his meticulous colleague William Robertson (1721–1793) sold extremely well. The average layman read much more history than he does today and no doubt enjoyed it more. "A historian has many duties," Voltaire wrote. "The first is not to slander; the second is not to bore." These writers had a new confidence both in their own mastery of their material and in the receptivity of their audiences. Edward Gibbon (1737–1794), the greatest historian of the century, undertook a lifetime of work on his *Decline and Fall of the Roman Empire* in the belief that "an age of light and liberty would receive, without scandal, an inquiry into the *human* causes of the progress and establishment of Christianity."

Descartes had dismissed history as a tissue of gossip. While it was possible to comprehend nature rationally, he believed, human nature and the development of human institutions were irrational, refractory, and beyond the knowledge of men. It was exactly the perplexing tangle of human motives, actions, and accidental events that fascinated the historical writers of the eighteenth century. True history, they said, must delve beneath the surface network of contradictory events. They discarded the Renaissance assumption that history is shaped by the action and character of great men, recognizing that the causes of events must be sought, as Montesquieu believed, in the whole structure of a society. His important work on the decline of Rome grappled with the crucial problem of the flowering and decay of civilizations. "It is not fortune that rules the world," he wrote. Rather, history was ordered by "general causes, whether moral or physical, which act upon every monarchy, which create, maintain, or ruin it." Events may seem accidental, but they are shaped by unseen forces, "and if the chance loss of a battle . . . ruins a state, there is a general cause that created the situation whereby this state could perish by the loss of a single battle." This fundamental canon of modern historiography was a new and fresh concept in the eighteenth century.

True history was not merely the study of politics and kings. "I would like to discover what human society was like," Voltaire wrote in his *Essay on Manners*, published in 1754, "how people lived in the intimacy of the family, and what arts were cultivated, rather than repeat the story of so many misfortunes and military combats—the dreary subject matter of history and the common currency of human perversity." This, of course, is exactly what the modern scholar who thinks of himself as a social historian wants to discover.

Voltaire was often blinded by his own belief in the inevitability of progress, and he could seldom resist writing history as propaganda. He liked to cheer the forces of light and civilization as they overcame the gloomy dark ages and emerged triumphantly in the enlightenment of his own time. The new kind of social history, it soon appeared, could be just as biased as the old school that told of the glory of kings and the workings of divine Providence. As Montesquieu observed, "Voltaire will never write a good history. He is like the monks who do not write for the sake of the subject they treat but for the glory of their order." Still, in his most successful history, *The Age of Louis* XIV, Voltaire set a standard still respected by historians.

With the exception of Gibbon's study of the decline of the Roman Empire, the histories that were the product of Enlightenment culture are virtually unread today. Contemporary scholars are far more interested in the work of the Neapolitan scholar Giambattista Vico (1668–1744), who wrote in almost total obscurity during his lifetime. Vico, the son of a bookseller, was poor and largely self-educated. His first interest was law, but when he failed to win a competition for a university chair in civil law, he turned to historical studies. Eventually he did receive a professorship—in rhetoric. His researches in philology, jurisprudence, and ancient history were undertaken in solitude and carried on without renown. Not until his works were rediscovered in the nineteenth century by the French historian Michelet and in the twentieth by scholars and critics interested in the philosophy of history was Vico recognized as an important historical theorist.

The *philosophes*, with their confident belief in the linear progress of history, did not share Vico's concern with the function of the unconscious in historical development. Nor were they interested in Vico's concept of the cycle (*corso*) through which all societies passed in their evolution from primitive to organized civilization. The theory was presented in Vico's one great book, the *New Science*, first published in 1725. The *New Science* was a strange brew, distilled from such divergent sources as Homer, Plato, Tacitus, Bacon, and the jurist Grotius. Vico, reacting against what he saw as the aridity of Cartesian rationalism, coined a counter slogan—"we know only what we do."

The *New Science* was to be nothing less than the history of human consciousness. Vico examined primitive language, song, and myth—the Homeric legends in particular—for clues to the imagination and thought of men in the early stage of civilization. There were three main cycles, he believed, through which each civilization had to pass. First came a primitive, preliterate age, where "men first feel without observing." Then came the heroic age, the era of epic poetry—"then they observe with a troubled and agitated spirit." The last stage of the cycle was represented by western European civilization, in which language and institutions were developed to a high degree—finally they reflect with a clear mind." When they reached this last stage, societies were bound to decay from within, although Vico did not predict precisely how or when this would happen.

Vico's work was fragmentary, often obscure, and sometimes based on specious evidence. The *New Science* is not a widely read book even though Vico's visionary grasp of the evolution of whole civilizations and his concern for the history of the inarticulate and the irrational assure his reputation today.

IV THE IMPACT OF SCIENCE AND LEARNING

Natural Philosophy

Just as the word *philosophy* in eighteenth-century usage embraced all forms of intellectual speculation, so *natural philosophy* was an omnibus term that covered almost all branches of scientific inquiry. Except for pure mathematics, which had long been recognized as a unique and peculiarly abstract discipline, every aspect of scientific thought, theoretical or experimental, was encompassed by the broad designation, "natural philosophy." Commonplace scientific instruments such as the telescope were called "philosophical apparatus," and men who held university chairs in science (many of which were established during the course of the century) were often known simply as professors of natural philosophy.

For the *philosophes*, it was inconceivable that the study of man and the study of nature could be treated as separate activities undertaken in isolation from each other. Their belief that human behavior and institutions could be explained according to fundamental principles of reason was shaped by what they took as the primary teaching of Newtonian science—the idea that the physical world could be described in terms of mathematical laws. One of the main goals of their educational crusade was to instill this teaching in the minds of the unenlightened; of their many self-imposed tasks, this was perhaps the most successfully realized. During the eighteenth century a popularized version of the Newtonian world view was adopted by the growing body of men who comprised the literate lay public.

Scholars and laymen alike recognized the work of Newton as the dawn of a new era in scientific advancement. Although his mathematics might be inaccessible to laymen and abstruse even to amateur scientists, Newton's underlying concept—that natural phenomena could be reduced to clear and comprehensible laws—was an idea that nearly everyone could grasp. Ambitious hack writers were quick to capitalize on the popular craze for science, and Newton's principles were sometimes simplified to the point of absurdity. In a remarkably short time his name was virtually a household word, and for the first time in European history a scientist—indeed, a physicist whose theories had only recently been accepted by his colleagues—was transformed into a popular idol.

The enshrinement of Newton was mainly the result of a literary movement which in itself signified a new development in the social history of science. This movement is notable because it was fostered and propelled by the *philosophes*, whose vocation was social criticism rather than science. Nevertheless, they were vitally concerned with scientific progress, and their efforts to explain and publicize new advances as well as Newton's original principles were largely responsible for the popular acceptance of a world view based on scientific ideas.

The Community of Scientists

In the great movement disseminating the principles of Newtonian science, the rapidly expanding international network of scientists also played an important role. The scientific societies that had been launched in the seventeenth century soon proliferated throughout almost every country in western Europe, and during the eighteenth century they became an effective means of transmitting scientific information. Members could keep abreast of the latest theories and discoveries, learn how to conduct new experiments, and hear about the development of new techniques. In an age when governments and universities did not sponsor vast research projects, when there were no established scholarly journals, when the various scientific fields were not yet differentiated, these societies served as the main channel of communications among individual scientists, who worked on their own or in laboratories that were primitive by modern standards.

The English Royal Society and the French Academy of Sciences were the most renowned, but they were supplemented by a host of corresponding societies and local associations of learned men. Like the *philosophes*, the scientists felt that they were part of a cosmopolitan community. They were in steady communication with their peers; they compared the results of experiments, exchanged data, appraised new methods, and acclaimed and countered theories put forward by théir counterparts all over western Europe.

The character and organization of the scientific societies varied from place to place. Some were more open and freewheeling than others. Amateurs were not welcomed into the French Academy, but in England, as Voltaire approvingly observed, "any man . . . who declares himself a lover of the mathematics and natural philosophy, and expresses an inclination to be a member of the Royal Society, is immediately elected into it." This was probably an overstatement. Still, the liberal nature of the Royal Society may be seen in its response to Cotton Mather, the Massachusetts Puritan divine, when he sent in a paper containing his descriptions of rainbows, rattlesnakes, and American plants, as well as some notes on variations in the magnetic needle. On the basis of this conglomeration of data he was promptly elected a fellow. The more rigid and formal French Academy was devoted to investigations of a purely scientific nature. At the opposite end of the spectrum was the American Philosophical Society, founded by Benjamin Franklin in Philadelphia in 1744. Its avowed purpose was "the promotion of useful knowledge," which might be taken to include almost anything.

While eighteenth-century scientists worshiped Newton and his principles, in practice most of them followed in the footsteps of Francis Bacon. They inherited the Newtonian breakthrough in theoretical physics, but they also belonged firmly within the Baconian tradition that gave first place to the empirical observation of nature. Voltaire called Bacon the "father of experimental philosophy," which did not mean that he had perceived the crystalline order of nature, as Newton later did. Eighteenth-century scientists adhered closely to Baconian methods of empirical experimentation and data collection. And though they were awed by Newton's revelations of the ordered structure of the universe, their faith in the utility of science and their assurance that science would improve man's estate were more in keeping with Bacon's precepts.

Physics

By applying Baconian methods, eighteenth-century scientists built on the theoretical foundation laid down by Newton and, in some fields, branched out on their own. Newton's great creative hypotheses were tested, supplemented, and refined. Present-day historians of science tell us that the eighteenth century was an age of consolidation. None of the eighteenth-century physicists matched Newton's genius; they devoted themselves to tying together the threads of his vast theoretical statements. But if it was not an age of great discovery, it was a period of significant refinement. The most talented Continental mathematicians—d'Alembert, Laplace, Clairaut, Euler, Bernoulli—followed up Newton's work. They polished some very fine mathematical points and solved some technical problems; some of the mathematics they produced was technically superior to Newton's, though their work was mainly derivative.

Newton's work was also the impetus for eighteenth-century innovations in techniques and instruments. Important experiments were conducted in fields—mechanics, pneumatics, hydraulics, and optics—that were in their infancy at the time of Newton's death. Eighteenth-century scientists improved the design and operation of such commonplace but essential instruments as the balance, the thermometer, and the barometer. Notable advances in the art of exact measurement came about through the work on graduated scales done by Réaumur and Fahrenheit.

In geophysics, ambitious experiments were undertaken to test and refine Newton's hypotheses. During the winter of 1736–1737, for example, the mathematicians Clairaut and Maupertuis, sponsored by Louis xv, made the journey from France up to the Gulf of Bothnia (the northern arm of the Baltic Sea that lies between Sweden and Finland), where they measured the length of one degree of latitude. They then compared their reading with one that had already been obtained in France. This was a very important experiment, for if Newton's theory that the earth was flattened at the poles was true, a degree of latitude would be longer in the Far North. A similar expedition was made to Peru. These journeys were ambitious undertakings for men whose usual milieu was the salons of Paris or the country estates of rich and amiable patrons.

Maupertuis, a Frenchman, eventually became president of the Berlin Academy, one illustration of the cosmopolitan character of eighteenth-century science. Another is the story of the first fumbling experiments with electricity. During the eighteenth century, scientists became intrigued with the potential of what had hitherto been an unknown form of energy and was still a very mysterious one. The main significance of Benjamin Franklin's sensational (and dangerous) experiment with the kite was the impetus it gave to the quantitative study of electricity. Soon scientists all over Europe were trying to measure atmospheric electricity.

If little progress was made in understanding and harnessing electrical energy in the eighteenth century, it was partly because no one yet realized that the study of electricity was itself a distinct field for which new theoretical formulations were required. Thus Luigi Galvani (1737–1798), the Italian physiologist whose famous experiments with frogs are still repeated in elementary science courses, failed to pursue his work on electricity. It was his compatriot, Alessandro Volta, who in 1792 developed—on the basis of Galvani's work—a new theory to account for the phenomenon Galvani had observed. There was no such thing as "animal electricity," Volta explained; the frog was simply acting as a conductor of electricity.

Natural History

Galvani was not to blame for straddling several very different scientific fields, for he did not even know that he was doing so. The eighteenth century had little sense of the breakdown of science into specialized disciplines or, in fact, of science itself as a special profession. Eighteenth-century men were well aware that extraordinary mathematical aptitude was a special gift, but every educated man assumed that he was capable of keeping up with the most advanced intellectual currents of the age. Home laboratories, where men of leisure could conduct their own experiments, were probably as commonplace as basement workshops are today.

Natural history was the area most accessible to laymen. Anyone who could afford a telescope could study the stars; certainly anyone at all could collect plants and rocks or observe the behavior of animals. It was routine for a gentleman to dabble in mineralogy or botany, and in the virtual absence of any accepted standard of professional accreditation, it was difficult to draw the line between the dilettante who wanted to keep in fashion and the talented amateur whose work might make a real contribution to natural history.

In biology the eighteenth century built on the work initiated by Malpighi and Leuwenhoek in the seventeenth century. The seventeenth-century breakthrough in microscopy enabled eighteenth-century scientists to enlarge greatly man's knowledge of plant structure, insects, and spermatozoa. The notable advances in these areas were carried out in line with the Baconian spirit: they came about through the massive accumulation of data, the fruit of empirical observation and description. The body of new information had increased enormously by the last quarter of the century, but the science of natural history still lacked the kind of theoretical framework Newton had bequeathed to physics and mathematics and remained in a haphazard, disorganized state. The theoretical concepts necessary to delineate a scientific discipline had not yet been developed. As A. R. Hall, the distinguished modern historian of science, has noted, it is one thing to study fossils and meticulously describe bones, but unless the bones are evaluated within the framework of a concept of evolution, no real contribution to science will be made. Still, dedicated eighteenth-century natural historians were doing work which led to the differentiation of scientific fields in the nineteenth century. They amassed an enormous body of quantitative data upon which unifying theories eventually were built.

There was one important exception to the general tendency of eighteenth-century natural historians to engage in the haphazard collection of empirical data. The Swedish botanist Carolus Linnaeus (1707–1778) managed to transform natural history into a formal scientific discipline. Linnaeus' system of classification, according to which plants are still labeled, was worked out after he had made a trip through Lapland and was published in 1735 under the ambitious title, *System of Nature*. To elucidate the orderly arrangement of all living things was an exciting idea, and Linnaeus' work captured the imagination of a whole generation.

The beauty of the Linnaean system lay in the way it coupled clarity with universality. It set forth a methodology that everyone could grasp and provided a pattern into which everything could be fitted. The system was designed to include the animal, vegetable, and mineral kingdoms and even diseases, but Linnaeus' contribution to the study of the plant world was by far the most important. No branch of science can become a distinct and formal discipline unless it develops a clear, universally understood system of nomenclature, and this is exactly what Linnaeus provided for botany. He also formulated a concept of individual species that went unchallenged until Darwin. The Linnaean system is extremely simple since it is based on a logical hierarchy of subdivisions. At the top are twenty-four classes into which plants are first separated according to the arrangement of their stamens and styles. After this they are further separated into orders and then into genera, until each one is finally identified as a unique species.

Linnaeus never sought to extend his principles. He believed that species were fixed and immutable, and the question of how the various species had developed did not perplex him. The French naturalist Buffon (1707–1788), who published forty-four volumes in his monumental series, *Natural History*, did grasp the idea that species must evolve, but evolutionary theories were scarcely considered, much less debated, during most of the eighteenth century. The enormous task of describing and identifying individual species absorbed the energies of the natural historians.

Chemistry

The most significant scientific contributions of the eighteenth century were made in chemistry. Antoine Lavoisier (1743–1794), the first great theoretical chemist, established the fundamental principles of modern chemistry.

Until Lavoisier began his work on gases in the 1770's, chemistry was mainly an empirical science. Although considerable advances had been made in chemical technology, there was no conceptual framework within which the basic nature of chemical substances could be understood. The composition of air and water, the primordial substances, was still a mystery, as was the process of combustion. The phlogiston theory, which postulated an element — phlogiston — supposedly released during combustion, was generally accepted by eighteenth-century chemists and by Lavoisier himself before Joseph Priestley's experiments with oxygen (called "dephlogisticated air") in 1774. Lavoisier described combustion as the combination of the burning substance with oxygen, and he went on to show that matter is not destroyed by burning; it is simply changed from one form into another.

The new techniques and apparatus devised by eighteenth-century chemists helped lay the groundwork for Lavoisier's theoretical synthesis. At the beginning of the century chemists were not even aware that there were important distinctions between the various gases; but as satisfactory instruments were devised for collecting and weighing gases, chemists came to see that different gases could be identified by their weight. Before 1720 Stephen Hales had worked out a method for collecting gases over water, and the delicate balance scale was steadily refined. But it was only in the 1750's that the experimenters fully grasped the importance of accurate measurements of weight in chemical research.

Although some eighteenth-century chemists carried out experiments more brilliant and original than Lavoisier's, he was the first to realize the theoretical implications of the work done by men like Priestley, Joseph Black, and Henry Cavendish. His perception of the nature of chemical elements was a breakthrough as decisive in its field as the formulation of the concepts of motion had been in physics, the rotation of the earth in astronomy, and the circulation of the blood in physiology.

Lavoisier finally established a chemical nomenclature. He and his disciples invented a whole new terminology according to which chemical substances could be classified and identified. This was published in 1789 in his *Traité Élémentaire de Chimie*, the first chemistry textbook. The old sloppy descriptions were discarded in favor of logical, unambiguous names. "Inflammable air" became hydrogen (a derivation from the Greek for "water-former"); "eminently respirable air" became oxygen (or "acid-former"). A system of naming chemical compounds was set forth: a compound of any element with oxygen would henceforth be known as an oxide, one with sulfur as a sulfide. This was the ultimate step in establishing the formal outline of the new discipline, and Lavoisier's terminology became the lingua franca of modern chemistry.

V THE ARTS

Art and Society

Eighteenth-century taste was astonishingly eclectic. While Austrian princes were trying to duplicate the grandeur of the court of Louis xiv, English aristocrats sought to emulate the classic simplicity of the sixteenth-century Italian architect Palladio. The music of Haydn and Mozart, generally assumed to be "neoclassical," was commissioned by people who were happily decorating their houses in the extravagant "Rococo" style, collecting porcelain copied from the Chinese, and devouring novels now labeled "Gothic" or "pre-Romantic."

Tastes differed according to age, nationality, religion, and class, but these distinctions were often blurred. Although art and literature were still the special preserve of the rich and leisured, in the eighteenth century this group was expanding rapidly. The more prosperous members of the middle class constituted a new kind of audience. They bought the engravings, prints, and reproductions that were turned out in unprecedented quantities; their wives and daughters read the latest sentimental novels and took lessons on a new instrument—the pianoforte—that was becoming as popular for performances and accompaniments in the home as the lute had been. They bought the popular journals, where they could read about buildings, gardens, art, artists, and the theater. By the 1760's every good-sized western European city had a magazine, modeled on Addison and Steele's *Spectator*, which could enlighten its readers about the current canons of good taste.

These eighteenth-century bourgeoisie were not patrons of art on a grand scale. Only princes and the richest aristocrats or bankers could build up great collections and construct buildings suitable for housing and maintaining them. A middle-class connoisseur who lived in London or Paris, however, had access to exhibitions of important works at the Royal Academy and the Paris Salon. An English gentleman was expected to make the Grand Tour, which included as a matter of course the study of architecture and painting in Italy. The Italians also turned out delightful paintings and engravings of views of ruins and landscapes which foreign visitors loved to take home.

If the rich bourgeois did commission a painting, it was likely to be a portrait of himself or the women of his family; the eighteenth century was one of the great ages of portrait painting. Elegant Frenchwomen in the first half of the century wanted to be portrayed as elaborately garbed mythological heroines and goddesses. Later in the century French artists treated their subjects more realistically, and the English style of portraiture was even more natural and unstudied. Reynolds, Romney, and Gainsborough placed their models in familiar, everyday settings, so that their portraits seem unposed.

The men and women who decorated their houses with likenesses of themselves also yearned to be surrounded with paintings that illustrated, in minute detail, the diversions and activities that were so much a part of their life style. Sporting pictures were extremely popular. French painters often depicted the royal chase, while English hunting scenes were faithful to the more robust pursuits of a rustic gentry class. Dogs and horses (the dogs often shown with a pile of retrieved birds) were favorite subjects.

While the tastes of the middle class were being expanded and enriched by the new prosperity and the new sensibility, the princes and high nobility of central Europe perpetuated the ceremonial courtly style of Louis XIV. Every prince, elector, bishop, and important abbot built himself a palace and modeled his way of life at first on the style of the great French king and eventually on that of the imperial court of Vienna. The German and Austrian phase of the Baroque—particularly as it was interpreted by the petty rulers of the eighteenth century—dictated an entire way of life. The Baroque palace required suitable accessories. It had to be set in a manicured park lined with statues and decorated with fountains. Enormous staircases were called for: exterior ones leading from park to palace set off the vast, ornamented front of the building; interior ones were fit for the grand entrance of an archduke or the emperor. Ceiling paintings, by Italian masters or by German artists trained in the Italian tradition, seemed to lead the eye up to heaven. Churches, in which frescoes covered the entire domed ceiling of the nave, were often more sumptuous than the palaces.

The nobles also built court theaters and decorated them lavishly. A private theater called for an orchestra, a troupe of players, and a company able to present the music, ballet, and opera worthy of the patronage of a great magnate. Painters, architects, performers, and composers were imported—mostly from Italy—to satisfy the ambitions and grandiose tastes of the master.

The Rococo and Neoclassicism

The so-called Rococo style appeared in France early in the eighteenth century, and though it spread through Europe, in its purest form it was always French. Rococo artists delighted and excelled in the decorative arts. Perhaps the highest achievements of the Rococo style are in such minor forms as furniture, silver, and porcelain—the small, costly luxuries that graced the life of the elite. Madame de Pompadour, whose commissions supported a regiment of French artists, was one of the most indefatigable collectors of beautiful, unnecessary things. Her rooms were filled with paintings, gorgeously bound books, gold and crystal boxes, scented bouquets of Meissen china flowers, and semiprecious jewels engraved with portraits and historical scenes. The king made her the patroness of the Vincennes factory, which was soon transferred to a more famous location at Sèvres. After her death, it took two notaries a year merely to make an inventory of her possessions.

Some of the decorative objects—clocks, for example—were also very useful. The new furniture was comfortable as well as beautiful and was available in all shapes and sizes, from chairs and couches to writing desks and coffee tables. The treatise published in 1754 by the English furniture-maker Thomas Chippendale, *The Gentleman and Cabinet-Maker's Director*, circulated widely and helped to popularize the delicate, curving style subsequently given his name. The ability to indulge in the current styles was no longer confined to the very rich or aristocratic. In England a new technique for printing designs on pottery made it possible to cut prices considerably. The technique of silver plating was developed in Sheffield, and this meant that a prosperous middle-class family could dine in relative splendor. In fact, middle-class standards of taste, comfort, and luxury were rising throughout the eighteenth century.

In domestic architecture, the imposing style of the late seventeenth century gave way to a smaller, more human scale. Whether the dwellings were manor houses built in the countryside by English gentry or the town houses (*hôtels*) of urban Frenchmen in the new suburbs (*faubourgs*) of Paris, the progression of vast, showy reception rooms which gave such an awesome dignity to the Baroque palace was replaced by a series of small, intimate rooms designed for special human functions. Rooms were planned to be used as boudoirs, libraries, dining rooms, reception rooms, studies. In place of the marble columns and huge paintings of the seventeenth century, there was ornamental paneling edged with designs in gold. These designs take the characteristic Rococo form: curved and elaborate yet dainty, rich but not heavy. The rooms they adorned were made for people to live in, not for striking splendid poses.

On the elaborately paneled and mirrored walls there was no room for big, dramatic paintings. Only the rounded spaces between the panels and the ceiling were left, and small, intimate pictures were required to fill them. These were provided by artists like Watteau (1684–1721) and Boucher (1703–1770), the favorite painter of Madame de Pompadour, in the style that came to be called *galant*. They depicted a world where flawlessly beautiful people floated about in an ethereal, delicately colored haze. Life was envisioned as a *fête galante*—an elegant picnic. All the women are lovely, all the men handsome and lithe; everyone is dressed in flowing satin; and a mood of exquisite sensitivity hangs over everything, including the landscape. Still, a kind of classical restraint, almost a somberness, is found in the best of the *fêtes galantes*.

Eventually the Rococo style was supplanted by a second strain in eighteenth-century artistic taste: neoclassicism. The works of the German scholar J. J. Winckelmann, who settled in Rome to study classical antiquity, helped to focus the growing interest in all forms of Greek art. Winckelmann laid down a new concept of scholarly inquiry for which he invented a new word—*Kunstgeschichte*, or art history. Excavations at Pompeii and Herculaneum captured the imagination of eighteenth-century connoisseurs who eagerly collected the engravings of Piranesi (1720–1778) depicting classical buildings and ruins. The classical aesthetic theory that the role of art was to convey order and explore human nature was quickly grasped by the writers and artists who figure in the eighteenth-century neoclassical revival. The simple and the dignified were prized above the original and the bizarre, in town planning and interior decoration as well as in poetry. The measured symmetry of classical architecture finds its counterpart in the great open space of the Place de la Concorde in Paris, the restrained elegance of the English resort town of Bath, and the Brandenberg Gate in Berlin, copied from the entrance to the Acropolis. Rococo ornamentation gave way to the cool Grecian decor designed by Robert Adam in England, Wedgwood's porcelain reproductions of Greek vases, and the simplicity of Louis XVI furniture.

The Flowering of European Music

In the charming rooms of French town houses, the music of Couperin and Rameau was meant to be played. François Couperin (1668–1733) was a genius of keyboard music; his style was influenced by the lute, and even today his music sounds more natural on a lute than on a piano, which blurs the clarity of the delicate ornamentation, almost like filigree, which overlays his melodies. His keyboard pieces were much admired throughout Europe, and German composers struggled with little success to imitate what was apparently a unique French style.

Jean Philippe Rameau (1683–1764) is best known for his operas—actually opera-ballets, which virtually re-created Watteau's pastoral scenes. The lovers sing of passions and sorrows, but nothing really tragic ever happens. Rameau's tone painting also evokes the pictures; leaves can be heard rustling, and birds twitter. Rameau always believed that the music counted for everything, and as a result many of the librettos he agreed to work with are extremely silly. He was also a musical theoretician who believed in the systematic analysis of fundamental principles of harmony. His treatises, which deal with such topics as the laws of acoustics and the science of tonality, were not much appreciated in his own day, but late in the nineteenth century they were acknowledged as the foundation of modern musical theory. To would-be reformers of music like Rousseau, Rameau stood for an archaic, artificial style that had corrupted French music. Rousseau's cry that music be brought "back to nature" was a symptom of the mid-eighteenth century's outright rejection of the Rococo style.

In musical genius and creativity, the eighteenth century was not a time of great innovation but rather of slow, natural development. The last flowering of Baroque music overlapped the finest compositions in the Rococo style; the strong contrapuntalism of Bach gradually gives way to homophonic music with its emphasis on a melodic line; and by the end of the century the elaborate *galant* style of Rameau's operas had been transformed into the classicism of Mozart and the delicious lyrical comedy of his *Marriage of Figaro*. An old form, the cathedral mass, reached its heights in the works of Bach, and an entirely new one, the symphony — which emerged from the embryonic sonata form explored in the harpsichord compositions of Domenico Scarlatti (1685 – 1757) — was carried by Haydn and Mozart to a peak that has never been surpassed, even by the great orchestral writers of the nineteenth century.

Johann Sebastian Bach (1685 – 1750) and George Frederick Handel (1685 – 1759) were exact contemporaries who shared similar backgrounds — North German, Protestant, middle-class. Like all the great eighteenth-century composers, they were amazingly prolific. They invented no new forms but rather exhausted the possibilities of an established tradition. Their work marks the end of the era of Baroque music.

In his own day Bach was known mainly as a virtuoso organist. Although respected, he was not recognized as an outstanding composer until his works were rediscovered in the nineteenth century. He never left his native environment, and his most illustrious position was the relatively minor one of municipal music director in Leipzig, a cultural backwater in eastern Germany. Bach was primarily a composer of religious music in a day when secular music was becoming ever more popular. Provincial, isolated by his own genius from the fashionable currents of his time, he was considered conservative and a bit old-fashioned. In the dense polyphony and deep religiosity that characterize all his music, Bach is closer to the spirit of the German Protestant Reformation than to the Gallic rationality of the Enlightenment.

Handel, however, did achieve fame during his lifetime. He was the Hanoverian court conductor, and since the kings of England were also princes of Hanover, he naturally made the transition to England, where he served first as court musician to the duke of Chandos. In England, where aristocratic life flourished in country houses rather than at court, this kind of patronage was rare. (The notable decline of English music in the eighteenth century was partly due to the absence of the kind of private and noble patronage that inspired so much great music on the Continent.) Before long, Handel became virtually a national composer. Eighteenth-century Englishmen treated him as though he were a national monument, and ever since he has been hailed as the most lustrous ornament in the history of English music. In fact, Handel was a German who came to England to practice a style that was specifically Italian, though it rapidly took on certain English trappings. His great oratorios — *The Messiah, Israel in Egypt, Judas Maccabeus, Saul* — were nominally religious works, but Handel's robust, straightforward music transformed the Biblical texts into a form, more congenial to the prevailing English taste, that resembled national epic drama.

Late in the eighteenth century, Austrian aristocrats allowed the public to attend performances by their court musicians upon payment of a fee. The origin of the public concert goes back to the seventeenth century, but the first real concert organization dates from 1725, when the *Concerts Spirituels* began in Paris. It was growing fashionable for middle-class citizens to know about music and even to take sides in the musical controversies of the day. Technical treatises for the professional performer had long been commonplace, but during the eighteenth century a new kind of musical criticism written for the layman appeared, first in the new popular journals, then in books like Charles Burney's four-volume *History of Music*, which was simple, informative, and entertaining.

Although instrumental music was rapidly coming into its own, at least in the first half of the eighteenth century the most popular musical form was still opera. Nearly every provincial city on the Continent had its own opera house, and where there was no resident troupe, traveling companies paid frequent visits. In Italy, opera was a real national pastime, easily accessible to almost everyone. Standards of musical performance were extremely high; even amateurs were expected to attain a level of technical ability that by twentieth-century standards seems extraordinarily demanding. Virtuosity in singers was especially prized. The first half of the eighteenth century was the heyday of the *castrato*, who far outshone the normal female soprano in range, power, and agility. People paid to hear vocal pyrotechnics; the music was less important than the star. Plots were absurd frameworks for the set pieces in which singers could show off their dazzling style.

But just as the demand for classical restraint led to a new simplicity in architecture, so musical taste after the middle of the century called for operas that were simple and more "natural." One response was the development of a new, comic form — *opera buffa*. John Gay's libretto for *The Beggar's Opera* (1728), which depicted the life of the London underworld, spoofed the stilted heroes and heroines of Italian opera. The catchy music (by the Prussian composer John Christoph Pepusch) was based on popular songs and dance tunes. The *Beggar's Opera* was an instant success, but the typical *opera buffa* style was not established until the performance in 1733 of Pergolesi's *La Serva Padrona*, also a rollicking comedy with simple tunes. The *opera buffa* was the musical counterpart of those contemporary novels that dealt with the problems of middle-class life.

The most serious reform of the old Italian *opera seria* was undertaken by Christoph Willibald Gluck (1714–1787), a German from the Palatinate who studied in Prague and eventually settled in Vienna, the undisputed musical capital of late eighteenth-century Europe. His two great operas, *Orfeo ed Euridice* (1762) and *Alceste* (1767), make a conscious return to pure classicism. The simple, austere musical line was meant to enhance the drama and emotion of the libretto. His chief aim, said Gluck, was to "attain a grand simplicity, and consequently I have avoided making a parade of difficulties at the cost of clarity." This might have been the manifesto of the new classical revival that influenced all forms of art in the later eighteenth century. Music was to be made more "expressive" of real feeling; audiences were supposed to listen attentively and be moved.

Gluck's operas are rarely performed today, but the "expressive" music he sought to write reached a pinnacle of beauty in the symphonies and string quartets of Haydn and the operas and piano concertos of Mozart, which are still standard works of the modern repertoire. The music of Haydn and Mozart—two Austrians who were ignorant of German scholarship and oblivious to contemporary cultural trends and fashions—heralds an era of German and central European musical hegemony that prevailed throughout the nineteenth century.

Joseph Haydn (1732–1809), whose music embodies the melodic simplicity and balance of the neoclassic era, was regarded in his own day as an ultramodern composer. Contrary to popular myth, however, he was not a self-conscious experimentalist and did not single-handedly invent the symphony or the string quartet. His meticulous work did, however, fix the symphony and the string quartet in forms that remained almost unchanged until the late nineteenth century. In his maturity, Haydn firmly established the symphonic principle—the exhaustive development and elaboration of an abstract musical idea, or theme. He was the first real master of the architecture of symphonic form.

Haydn's career illustrates the influence on music of the aristocratic patronage system of central Europe. His father was a peasant farmer in a small Austrian village; his mother had been a cook in the household of the local count. Haydn was chosen to be a choir boy at St. Stephen's Cathedral in Vienna, where his life was rigorous and his musical education haphazard. After his voice changed, he was dismissed from the choir and left on his own. He gave lessons, performed when and where he could, and studied in his spare time. After this youthful period of real poverty he became musical director on the estate of Count von Fürnberg, an aristocrat of modest means. The count could not afford to underwrite the most popular and prestigious musical form of the day—the opera; he could not even support a whole orchestra. Of necessity, Haydn wrote his first string quartet. IIe became so intrigued with the possibilities of the pure and abstract quartet form that he produced seventeen quartets within a few years.

In 1759 Haydn went to a more prosperous patron, Count Ferdinand Morzin, who could at least afford a small orchestra. At the age of twenty-seven, he composed his first symphony. Soon afterward he went to work for the Esterhazy family, Hungarians of princely rank, with whom he remained for thirty years. The Esterhazy palace, with its garden and private theater, was one of the musical centers of the Habsburg empire. Haydn's opportunities were great, but so were his responsibilities. He was business manager and administrator of an enormous musical establishment; he conducted the orchestra, ran the library, directed operas, and performed chamber music—all in addition to his composing.

Haydn wrote more than a hundred symphonies, more than eighty quartets, and an array of choral music that includes operas, masses, and the great oratorios of his last years. Some of his freshest and loveliest work was composed when he was in his sixties and seventies. Loyalty and inclination kept Haydn tied to the Esterhazy estate during most of his career, but he gradually acquired a European reputation. Mozart dedicated his six most mature and profound string quartets to Haydn, who was one of the few who appreciated *Don Giovanni*—considered a dissonant and difficult work when it was first performed in 1787.

Wolfgang Amadeus Mozart (1756–1791) was a unique musical genius; musicians and scholars marvel at his inexhaustible creativity and invention. The quantity of his compositions was staggering even in an age when prodigious production was commonplace. The official catalogue of Mozart's compositions has more than six hundred entries, and many of these are major works: more than forty symphonies, nearly thirty piano concertos, and a series of operas—at least five of which are still part of the standard repertory. After Mozart reached his early twenties, he wrote virtually nothing that was not first-rate. His masterpieces defy explanation.

Mozart was born in Salzburg. His father was a violinist and a competent composer with a talent for exploiting the musical aptitudes of his children. Mozart's early life as a prodigy is well known—he began composing at five, was a violin and piano virtuoso at eight, and performed amazing feats of memory and musicianship before delighted aristocratic audiences all over Europe. He became less adorable at adolescence, however, and the rest of his short career was plagued by financial difficulties. When he died at thirty-five, he was buried in a pauper's grave. Unlike Haydn, Mozart was not able to secure a solid court position, and his relationship with an early patron, the archbishop of Salzburg, was bitter and frustrating.

The special iridescence of Mozart's music makes it identifiable even to a novice. No matter what the form—song, symphony, sonata—the characteristic musical texture, simple yet richly elegant, is unmistakable. Mozart was generally content to perfect the musical forms he knew; only in opera did he strike out in a new direction. He wrote nineteen works for the stage, from his first opera as a boy of eleven to *The Magic Flute*, completed three months before his death. In the great operas of his maturity the characters are delineated through the music as real, fully rounded individuals; they are as lifelike as the vibrant figures in eighteenth-century novels. Perhaps no other composer has so fulfilled the dramatic potential of the operatic form.

Literature and Social Criticism

The "natural," the "fit," and the "correct" were the most admired modes of style in the eighteenth century. Jonathan Swift, whose controlled rage made *Gulliver's Travels* (ostensibly a comic travel story) a pungent indictment of his society, defined style as "proper words in proper places." The aim of the great writers of the Enlightenment was to portray the fundamental and enduring characteristics of human nature. It was not necessary to say anything new, but it was essential to convey old truths elegantly and well.

> True wit is Nature to advantage dressed,
> What oft was thought, but ne'er so well expressed.

None of his contemporaries would have quarreled with Pope's dictum.

Eighteenth-century writers also obeyed Pope's injunction in his *Essay on Man* that "the proper study of mankind is man."

> Created half to rise, and half to fall;
> Great lord of all things, yet a prey to all;
> Sole judge of truth, in endless error hurled:
> The glory, jest, and riddle of the world!

With the possible exception of Pope's work, the Enlightenment was barren of great poetry, but it was one of the richest ages of prose in Western literary history. While the lyric impulse was inhibited by the demand for clarity and reason and a meticulous concern for the niceties of diction, the realistic novel was invented and brought to quick maturity. The novel dealt with human nature in the round, offering an unshrinking psychological portrayal of ordinary people. The heroine of Defoe's great novel *Moll Flanders* is a pickpocket; Samuel Richardson's Pamela is a poor (but remarkably literate) servant girl; in *Manon Lescaut*, the Abbé Prévost describes the sordid, humiliating aspects of love—a rather different vision of grand passion than the exalted sentiment of Racine. Henry Fielding's earthy, robust characters are never idealized, but with all their warts and human frailties, they are as irrepressible and unforgettable as Voltaire's Candide.

The novels of Fielding, who liked to think of himself as a "comic history painter," have their counterparts in the paintings and engravings of his friend William Hogarth (1697–1764), who achieved a level of social satire unmatched until Goya. In Hogarth, the critical spirit and a liberal humanitarianism were fired by genius. His dramatic cycles—on marriage, prostitution, cruelty, the madhouse, the law courts — are mordant, realistic, shocking, and often very funny. Hogarth took the whole city of London, and the seamy underside of Enlightenment culture and civilization, as his subject.

While painters (with the exception of Hogarth, whose etchings always sold by the thousands) and musicians in the eighteenth century required private commissions in order to survive, writers began to live on the income from the public sale of their work and became less dependent on pensions, sinecures, and commissions. Perhaps this is why the critical spirit that informs Enlightenment thought is expressed more directly in literature than in the other art forms, which were shaped by the tastes of a small, wealthy group of patrons. Eighteenth-century writers were remarkably free to criticize society and to experiment with new forms and styles.

VI EMOTION AND UNREASON

Religious Revival

Beneath the reasoned clarity of Enlightenment thought ran a dark stream of emotion, unreason, and anti-intellectualism. It emerged full-blown in three astonishing books published by Jean Jacques Rousseau in the early 1760's, but it existed throughout the era and can be discerned earlier in the century in literature and in religion.

Deism, the doctrine most congenial to Enlightenment thinkers, was only one (and in some ways the least interesting) form of Enlightenment religious expression. The undoctrinaire, rational worship of a Newtonian Deity was primarily the religion of the articulate, the enlightened, and the wealthy. Because eighteenth-century deists wrote and spoke a great deal about their beliefs — in part because these represented a minority view — historians until fairly recently accepted the *philosophes'* own judgment that deism was the most significant religious sentiment of the age. But at the same time that the cultured elite in almost every country subscribed to the rational tenets of deist doctrine, a wave of evangelical religious fervor was sweeping through Europe.

The most successful and enduring popular religion was found in the teachings of John Wesley (1703–1791). As a student at Oxford, Wesley decided that the dry platitudes of the Church of England provided no food for the soul. Other men who sought an emotional experience and an opportunity for communion with God in religious worship also rejected the bland and worldly style of the established Church, but few of them were imbued with Wesley's messianic spirit. In place of what he considered to be the lukewarm services and casual sacraments of the Church of England, Wesley turned to preaching, exhortation, and a new "method" of spiritual devotion. After experiencing a mystical conversion at the age of thirty-five, he devoted the rest of his life to teaching through the Methodist society that all men, despite their inherent sinfulness, could also achieve salvation.

The *philosophes*, who found life on earth sufficiently rewarding, could never understand the concern of the lower orders of society for salvation. Their own belief in man's fundamental reason and benevolence was utterly incompatible with Wesley's teaching that man was basically wicked and depraved. The elite sneered (after all, Wesley's religion appealed to the poor and ill-educated), but the preaching of Wesley and his disciples grew more and more popular. Wesley was an organizational genius; though he formally broke with the Church of England only near the end of his life, the lines of authority he had established put the new Methodist Church on a solid structural foundation.

Wesley's "method" combined moral puritanism with uncontrolled emotional abandon. The response he evoked was, literally, wild. In his diary Wesley notes that his preaching led to many cases of what we would call hysterical reaction, manifested by trembling, groaning, weeping, and even convulsions. This was the "enthusiasm" that the *philosophes* found so baffling and repugnant.

The great revival movement of the eighteenth century spread through western Europe and the United States, where the impact of the camp meetings led by the powerful preacher George Whitefield is well documented. In Germany the form of evangelicalism known as Pietism flourished. Although the movement went underground to some extent after 1740, the Pietist strain reappeared toward the end of the century and fed the mysticism of Romantic writers. In America, where a large proportion of the German immigrants belonged to Pietist sects like the Moravian Brethren, evangelicalism was a significant religious current throughout the eighteenth century. The religious revival even touched eastern Europe. In Poland, a small sect of Jews —the Hasidim—turned away from the traditional authority and book-learning that had been the preserve of the rabbinate. The Hasidim encouraged dancing and singing as the expression of religious mysticism and joy. Indeed, music played an important role throughout the religious revival. Wesley's hymns were strong, simple, and very moving, and some of the simple religious poems set to music by the Moravian Brethren are small masterpieces, similar in spirit to the work of Bach.

Rousseau

The vein of anti-intellectualism implicit in evangelical religion went relatively unnoticed, since the new emotional piety was generally restricted to the lower orders, who were not expected to read books or indulge in rational thought. But when expounded by Rousseau, the cult of emotion and the explicit mistrust of civilized reason could no longer be disregarded. The immediate response of the intellectual community to this neurotic, rough-hewn man, who wrote in praise of undisciplined nature as persuasively as the great *philosophes* had of cool rationality, was shock and dismay. Just as Wesley and his followers, who sought spiritual satisfaction in communion with God, were alienated from the established denominations, so Rousseau, who yearned to bring men back in touch with the wellsprings of nature and their own instincts, was alienated, if not from the literary culture of his day, at least from the worldly life style of the *philosophes*.

Jean Jacques Rousseau (1712–1778) was born in Geneva. His mother died at his birth, and the child was rejected by his father, a jeweler. According to his own account, the boy who tortured himself with guilt for his mother's death became a man whose relationships with women were always abnormal and frustrating. Although he was the apostle of the loving education of children, he allowed his own offspring, whom he fathered with a servant girl, to be brought up in an orphanage. His battles with society, with life, and with himself were never resolved. As contrasted with the amusing eccentricity that marked the conduct of so many of the *philosophes*, Rousseau's behavior — often pathological — reveals the torments of a seriously disturbed psyche. He was always difficult to deal with, even at his best, and at his worst he was subject to fits of paranoia.

Rousseau's education was haphazard, his early career aimless and unsuccessful. His first interest was music, but his new system of notation was a complete failure, and in 1749 he entered an essay contest sponsored by the Dijon Academy on the question: Have scientific advances improved morals? He won the prize by asserting that progress had, in fact, corrupted morality. It was the first enunciation of his favorite theme: that civilization oppressed, degraded, and finally destroyed the natural values of mankind. In the late 1750's he cloistered himself at the country retreat of one of his patronesses, where he proceeded to turn out the works that established his fame and notoriety. His sentimental novel of lost virtue, *La Nouvelle Héloïse*, his treatise on education, *Émile*, and his political manifesto, *The Social Contract*, appeared between 1760 and 1762. *Héloïse* was tremendously popular. Historians, seeing in *The Social Contract* a theoretical blueprint for the French Revolution and the authoritarianism of the modern state, take it more seriously than did Rousseau's contemporaries; but *Émile* was one of the most explosive works on education ever to appear in the Western world. It was condemned in both France and Geneva, and for a time Rousseau was forced into hiding. Not until the 1780's, when the seeds of Romanticism were taking root, were Rousseau's ideas widely accepted. But *Émile* so enchanted Kant that he is reported to have broken the habit of a lifetime by forgoing his afternoon walk to pore over the book. Kant hailed Rousseau as "the restorer of the rights of humanity" and called him the "Newton of the moral world."

What did Rousseau preach in *Émile* to stir such controversy? He went much further than the *philosophes*, who managed to enjoy the pleasures of life under the *ancien régime* even while they criticized its irrational institutions. Rousseau rejected the hierarchical society of aristocrats, merchants, and cities, claiming that the good life was possible only for men who liberated themselves from all its bonds. The unequal society of eighteenth-century Europe was corrupt and degrading. "Everything is good as it comes from the hands of the Maker of the World but degenerates once it gets into the hands of man." This, the first sentence of *Émile,* is exactly parallel to the resounding opening of *The Social Contract:* "Man is born free, and yet we see him everywhere in chains." In *The Social Contract* Rousseau sought to guard the individual against the tyranny of the state; *Émile* is a guide by which man can obtain his emotional freedom and spiritual autonomy in the face of the overwhelming tyranny of the social order. Just as authentic freedom is the goal of Rousseau's ideal state, so the liberation of the individual is the aim of the educational program he lays down for his pliant pupil.

Émile's education from birth to marriage is thoroughly described in the book, which blends the novel and the memoir. The adult Émile is nothing less than the model for the good citizen of the state Rousseau envisions in *The Social Contract*—a state where men, subject only to the collective authority of the general will, are able to live according to the pure dictates of nature. "Civilized man is a slave," Rousseau laments. "At birth he is sewn up in swaddling bands, and in death nailed down in a coffin. All through he is fettered by social institutions." Émile leads a carefree, healthful existence out in the country away from the immoral influence of society. He plays (always with his tutor), roams through the woods, and learns the principles of science through his own simple experiments (although these are elaborately organized by the tutor). He learns about the sanctity of property the hard way, when his own little garden is uprooted.

Émile has no formal lessons, since the only real teachers are "experience and feeling." His natural instincts are always the right ones, and they must be left untouched. He is taught a trade—carpentry—because manual labor is the closest approximation to what man does in the state of nature. He is not bothered by lessons in literature or philosophy. Rousseau despised Locke's dictum that children should be reasoned with. Reasoning, Rousseau believes, comes after education. "Nature wants children to be children before they are men." Thus Émile remains a happy illiterate. "If he is not as good a reader in books as other children, he reads better in the books of nature." When he reaches adulthood Émile is, no doubt, a well-adjusted individual—but he is also a bit of a dolt. He may be liberated from society, but his dependence on his tutor lingers—though this does not seem to bother Rousseau. Émile escapes corruption by the simple expedient of having been brought up in total ignorance of society.

Émile can be viewed as Rousseau's own fantasy of wish-fulfillment, a compensation for his terrible childhood. Many of his ideas have been incorporated into the fundamental canons of progressive education, though Freudian psychology has called into question Rousseau's belief in the pristine goodness and purity of all childish instinct. Rousseau's revulsion at the inhibiting effects of traditional child-rearing and his impassioned plea for a return to nature stunned his first readers, but his ideas were embraced, at times to an exaggerated degree, during the ensuing Romantic era.

In his fear of the influence of society on natural man and his obsession with the unbridled expression of natural emotions, Rousseau anticipated Romanticism. By refusing to recognize the benevolence of reason, he turned against a cherished pillar of Enlightenment thought. Nevertheless, while Rousseau hated society as it existed—the ancient hierarchy of church, class, and state that distorted natural man—he did believe that it could be shaped by human reason to serve man, and thus he shared in the Enlightenment spirit. Like his contemporaries, he hoped to transform society to fit human nature and human needs, but his emphasis was unlike theirs. To Rousseau, nature could not be ordered and tamed; it must be worshiped as a wild and uncontrollable force. It is easy enough now to admire Rousseau as a prophetic figure, but we may also sympathize with those contemporaries who shuddered at the blows he struck against their ordered and rational society.

The Enlightenment, which was centered in France, but which made itself felt in virtually every part of Europe, reached its climax with the important writings of Voltaire, Diderot, and Rousseau. It had taken upon itself the task of examining critically almost all aspects of the human condition. It remained only to be seen whether this kind of Enlightenment could be translated into significant and lasting political reform. The answer was not long in coming —and it came first of all in France.

HERITAGE
ESSAY

THE HERITAGE OF THE ENLIGHTENMENT

The eighteenth-century cultural movement was many-sided, and its contribution to the development of Western civilization extremely complex. By emphasizing some aspects of the Enlightenment at the expense of others, it is possible to portray the thought of the *philosophes* as narrow and superficial, and this denigration has been attempted by many later theorists and historians. It is true that the experiences of modern industrial society and the knowledge gained from post-eighteenth-century science have given us insights into human nature that the *philosophes* lacked. But demonstrations of the limits of Enlightenment thought do not detract from the essential role of eighteenth-century culture in Western civilization: the Enlightenment represents the great turning point at which the assumptions about man, society, and nature that had prevailed since ancient times were at last consciously rejected and a new set of attitudes came to prevail.

The *philosophes* emphasized the most radical implications of Renaissance humanism, of Baconian meliorism, of Lockean empiricism, and of Newtonian science. The Enlightenment brought to fruition the secular attitude implicit in the Renaissance. The fifteenth-century humanists had delighted in man's experience and potential, but they could not refrain from integrating this secular spirit within a traditional Christian framework. The *philosophes* boldly concentrated on human experience and achievement and refused to compromise their secular approach. They regarded Locke's thesis that understanding is the product of experience—the impress of environment upon the individual mind—as a liberating doctrine: men were not limited by a cast of mind or set of ideas they had been born with, as claimed by Plato and Descartes. Men could know anything and be conditioned in any direction by the circumstances of environment, education, and experience. Consequently, there was nothing inevitable about the ideas and institutions that currently prevailed—these ideas and institutions could, and should, be superseded. Man's future was unlimited. The *philosophes* believed that Newton's discovery of the laws of physics had at once demonstrated the infinite capacity of the human mind, given men the key to the mastery of nature, and opened up

the possibility of applying natural laws to the functioning of society and politics, thereby greatly improving the circumstances of social and individual life.

The radical philosophy of the Enlightenment represented the first clear and self-conscious attack upon the doctrine of the great chain of being, of the fixed, immutable hierarchy of the universe, that had been the dominant world view in Europe from the fifth century B.C. and that still gave intellectual respectability to the *ancien régime* in the seventeenth century. God, King, Church, Lord, and People were held to be the fixed order of the world; the ideas in the human mind were regarded as innate, needing only to be discovered, and there was no alternative system of government. Voltaire saw, with astonishing insight, that the empirical movement in philosophy, begun with Locke, had inaugurated a direct challenge to the old order, opening up the possibility of an intellectual revolution:

From Plato to Locke there is indeed nothing; no one in that interval developed the operations of the human mind, and a man who knew the whole of Plato and only Plato, would know little and that not well. . . . Locke alone has developed the *human understanding* in a book where there is naught but truths, a book made perfect by the fact that these truths are stated clearly.[1]

David Hume's analysis of the nature of human understanding stands at the opposite epistemological pole from Platonic idealism:

. . . This creative power of the mind amounts to no more than the faculty of compounding,

1. Voltaire, *The Age of Louis* XIV, in I. Schneider, ed., *The Enlightenment*. New York: Braziller, 1965, p. 208.

Science and Human Progress. The eighteenth century marked a turning point in the development of modern science because the contributions science could make to the improvement of life were universally recognized. The art of the century proclaims this widespread faith in progress through scientific discovery. Facing page, top: plan drawn in 1784 for a proposed Newton cenotaph. Newton was idolized in France, where it was felt that he should have the kind of memorial previous eras had accorded kings and saints. Facing page, bottom: flask used by Lavoisier to separate oxygen and hydrogen, lovingly preserved in the *Conservatoire des Arts et Métiers*, Paris. Above: forty-foot reflecting telescope constructed by Sir William Herschel in 1789 to observe the satellites of Saturn. Right: "Experiment with an Air Pump" (1768) by the British artist Joseph Wright evokes the contemporary adoration of the wonders revealed by natural science.

transposing, augmenting, or diminishing the materials afforded us by the senses and experience.[2]

Far from expressing a lack of faith in the power of the human intellect, Hume celebrated the unlimited grandeur of human thought: none could predict its achievements; none would dare question its potential to rise above the best ideas of the past. Taking what can be learned by the internal and external senses, the mind has "unlimited power of mixing, compounding, separating and dividing these ideas."[3]

The epistemological revolution of the eighteenth century paralleled, and in part inspired, the greatest change in the fundamentals of political thought in

2. David Hume, *An Enquiry Concerning Human Understanding,* in S. Commins and R. N. Linscott, eds., *The Speculative Philosophers.* New York: Random House, 1947, p. 353.
3. Hume, *Human Understanding,* in *The Speculative Philosophers,* p. 375.

Rococo and Neoclassicism. In the eighteenth century the grandiose inclination of Baroque style slowly gave way to the precious delicacy of Rococo art and the refinement and restraint of neoclassicism. The aristocracy still had a penchant for majestic and imposing views, as in Belotti's "Riding School" (right); but the best art was concerned with more limited subjects. Above: Watteau's "Judgment of Paris." Watteau was the most accomplished and most profound of the French Rococo artists. His graceful depiction of the body signals a return to classical ideals. Watteau's painting captures the essence of the Rococo style—a never ending quest for beauty exhibited in shimmering perfection and delicate detail. The delicacy of Rococo style was further refined by self-conscious neoclassicism in the work of Robert and James Adam. Facing page: doorway of Northumberland House by Robert Adam. His light and graceful interiors impart a sense of Greek coolness and restraint.

REPRODUCED BY COURTESY OF THE TRUSTEES, THE NATIONAL GALLERY

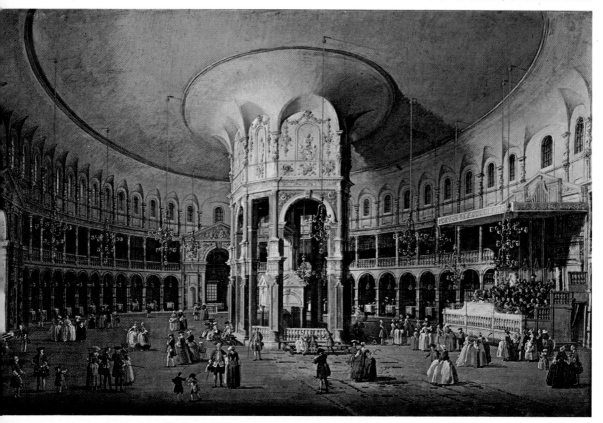

The New Elegance. The most assiduously cultivated art in the eighteenth century was the art of living. In the Indian summer of the preindustrial world, in a relatively stable society in which the state demanded little and the masses still knew their place of subjection, the European aristocracy and upper middle class were free to lavish their vast landed and mercantile wealth on a grossly self-indulgent but elegant and fastidious life style. Facing page: "Lieutenant General Philip Honywood" by Thomas Gainsborough (1727–1788) is a realistic portrayal of the typical aristocrat of this world—self-confident, intelligent, and fastidious in dress and appearance. Above: the rotunda built in his gardens by the earl of Ranelagh to house the concerts and other festivities that occupied the time of an eighteenth-century lord. Its opulent classicism suited aristocratic taste. Left: "The Dutton Family" by Zoffany shows the comforts enjoyed by the upper middle class. The paintings, rich carpet, carved mantelpiece, and inlaid card table were inevitable accoutrements of high bourgeois living, in imitation of aristocratic elegance.

three thousand years. This new doctrine asserted that political and social institutions were no more inflexible and eternal than the ideas of the human mind. Just as human understanding is molded by the impress of experience, so should forms of government be related to human need. The laws of a society are not to be derived from a heavenly pattern; they are to be adapted functionally to environmental and social conditions. The discovery of alternative ways of government and social behavior overseas demonstrated that there was nothing *per se* rational or legitimate about the institutions of monarchical and aristocratic Europe. Montesquieu's *The Spirit of the Laws* decisively affirmed radical functionalism in political theory:

. . . Only by the merest accident will the laws of one nation be suitable for another. . . . They [the laws] should be related to the physical character of the country; to its climate, whether frigid, torrid or temperate; to the way of life of the people, whether farmers, hunters or herdsmen. They should be related to the extent of liberty compatible with the constitution; to the religion of the inhabitants, to their propensities, wealth, number, trade, to their morals and manners.[4]

4. Montesquieu, *The Spirit of the Laws*, trans. H. H. Rowen, in H. H. Rowen, *From Absolutism to Revolution*, 2nd ed. New York: Macmillan, 1968, p. 118.

The Diversions of Great Wealth. Many of the institutionalized forms of play that still prevail among the very wealthy became fashionable in the eighteenth century. They were then (as they are today) signs of economic and social status. Above: gambling at Devonshire House, one of the most prestigious aristocratic establishments, as depicted by Thomas Rowlandson in 1791. The lords who dominated the British political parties transacted important political and state business at their favorite gambling clubs. Facing page: eighteenth-century capitalists at play. This scene in Garroway's popular coffeehouse shows London businessmen studying the "Stock Exchange Gazette Extraordinary" and discussing their investments. Coffeehouses became the meeting place of the upper middle class, where important decisions were made in politics, business, and journalism.

From the new functionalist political theory, Rousseau extrapolated revolutionary implications. There is nothing natural and inevitable, he argued in *The Social Contract*, about prevailing political institutions which foment inequality and injustice; they are artificial constructs which can and should be changed:

. . . Society offers to us only an assembly of artificial men and factitious passions, which are . . . without any real foundation in nature. . . . It is plainly contrary to the laws of nature, however defined, that children should command old men, fools

wise men, and that the privileged few should gorge themselves with superfluities, while the starving multitude are in want of the bare necessities of life.[5]

Enlightenment thinkers did more than formulate a new set of assumptions for political and social thought. They accorded the economic aspects of social life a distinct set of operative rules, free from traditional theological and moral claims. Adam Smith developed a theory of the right ordering of economic life, which would add to the general welfare of mankind. Following Locke's denial of external authority and in imitation of the laws of the physical universe that Newton had discovered, Smith advocated that each man be free to pursue his self-interest in the economic market. This individual self-interest would coincide, as by the actions of an "invisible hand," with what was most agreeable to society:

5. Rousseau, *The Social Contract,* in S. Commins and R. N. Linscott, eds., *The Political Philosophers.* New York: Random House, 1947, pp. 292–293.

Every individual is continually exerting himself to find the most advantageous employment for whatever capital he can command. It is his own advantage, indeed, and not that of his society, which he has in view. But the study of his own advantage naturally, or rather necessarily leads him to prefer that employment which is most advantageous to the society.[6]

For the welfare of society, and to the general advantage of every individual, it followed from Smith's economic theory, the operation of the market should flow according to the natural law of supply and demand, unimpeded by government grants of special privilege to particular persons or groups. The *ancien régime* stood condemned in economic policy as it had been in its general political structure.

It was characteristic of Enlightenment culture

6. Adam Smith, *Works*. London: Cadell, 1811, III, p. 177.

Salon Culture. At the same time that it pursued a lavishly expensive way of life, the aristocracy, particularly in France, was assiduous in its patronage of arts and letters. This support of intellectual and artistic achievement was in part another expression of social status—an aristocrat, being by definition a person of superior mind and tastes, had to show enthusiasm for higher culture. But many eighteenth-century lords and ladies were genuinely devoted to ideas, art, and music and themselves made important intellectual contributions. Many of the *philosophes* were scions of at least the middling and petty nobility. Facing page: Madame Geoffrin's salon in Paris was typical of the aristocratic salons that served as centers of Enlightenment culture and brought aristocrats together with leading thinkers of the age. In this scene, an actor is reading one of Voltaire's tragedies. Above: Zoffany's "The Tribuna of the Uffizi" depicts the art gallery of a great aristocratic collector, Earl Cowper, who in the bottom right of the picture shows his friends a painting by Raphael; in the middle left another group of sophisticated gentlemen admire a painting by Titian.

The New Sensibility. The common
identification of the eighteenth century
as the Age of Reason ignores the deep
appreciation of the value of private
human feeling that was central to Enlightenment culture. A prime form of
this new sensibility was a significant
advance in recognition of the distinctive quality of childhood. Rousseau's
Émile developed an appreciation of
childhood's intuitions into an elaborate
theory, but the purity and beauty of
children was also recognized in art, as
in "Miss Bowles" (facing page) by Sir
Joshua Reynolds. At the other end of
the human spectrum, kings and queens
were portrayed more as distinctive individuals than as symbols of authority.
Marie Antoinette (above, left) was
depicted as a beautiful and gracious
woman rather than as queen of France.
And though Louis XVI (above, right)
was painted in his regal robes, the impression is that of a pleasant gentleman
dressed up for the occasion. The grandeur of monarchy imparted by the portraits of Louis XIV had faded; it was the
human qualities of Louis XVI that received most emphasis.

that the attack upon the old order was not left on
an abstract, theoretical plane. The standards of
rationality and humanity were applied to just about
every aspect of political, social, economic, and legal
life. This spirit of social criticism and political
protest turned out to be the most persistent and
pervasive aspect of the Enlightenment heritage.
The essential message of the *philosophes* was: We
shall not respect authority, privilege, and tradition;
we shall bring everything and everyone to account
before the tribunal of reason and humanity. This remains the fundamental progressive creed in the
Western world.

The first specific corollary of Enlightenment
doctrine was a tremendous diminution in respect
for monarchy. The traditional aura of royal majesty
faded when kingship was judged by utilitarian
standards. As Tom Paine said:

The British Constitution. The attitude of radical intellectuals and political activists toward the British constitution underwent a fundamental and highly significant change during the eighteenth century. In the period of stability from about 1722 to 1760, British institutions were regarded as a model for mankind by English theorists and French *philosophes* alike. But the trend of opinion changed drastically after 1760—first in the American colonies, then in Britain itself, and finally in France. British government was denounced as oligarchic, corrupt, and irrational. By 1782 Edmund Burke was lamenting, "The English Constitution . . . used to be the admiration and the envy of the world . . . . Now all its excellencies are forgot, its faults are now forcibly dragged into day, exaggerated by every artifice of representation." The change reflected the advancing tide of democratic ideology, one of the main consequences of Enlightenment culture. Below: the House of Commons in 1793.

There is something exceedingly ridiculous in the composition of monarchy; it first excludes a man from the means of information, yet empowers him to act in cases where the highest judgment is required. The state of a king shuts him from the world, yet the business of a king requires him to know it thoroughly; wherefore the different parts, by unnaturally opposing and destroying each other, prove the whole character to be absurd and useless.[7]

Henceforth, kings would have to justify their status by the beneficial consequences of their rule, an exceedingly rigorous criterion.

Similarly, the *philosophes* — although many were nobles themselves — demanded that aristocrats justify their privileges and explain why they should have power and status denied to the bourgeoisie. By the standard of social utility, Voltaire said, the merchants were not in any way inferior to the nobility:

I do not know . . . which is most useful to his country, a powdered lord, who knows to a minute when the king rises or goes to bed, perhaps to stool, and who gives himself airs of importance in playing the part of a slave in the antechamber of some minister; or a merchant, who enriches his country, and from his office sends his orders to Surat or Cairo, thereby contributing to the happiness of the world.[8]

When judged by Enlightenment standards of rationality and social utility, nothing seemed more "infamous" than the Church's demands that the state impose religious doctrine upon society. The ideal of religious freedom was enacted into law in Virginia; Thomas Jefferson was the author of the statute:

We, the General Assembly of Virginia, do enact that no man shall be compelled to frequent or support any religious worship, place, or ministry whatsoever, nor shall be enforced, restrained, molested, or burdened in his body or goods, nor shall otherwise suffer on account of his religious opinions or belief; but that all men shall be free to profess, and by argument to maintain, their opinions in matters of religion, and that the same shall in no wise diminish, enlarge, or affect their civil capacities.[9]

The Enlightenment favored a free trade in ideas, which, like Adam Smith's free market, would allow truth to find its proper level and redound to the welfare of mankind.

Enlightenment intellectuals taught that, instead of looking to God, the Church, and tradition, men had to take care of themselves and organize political, social, and economic institutions in a way that would best contribute to the greatest happiness of mankind. They believed that human life was an end in itself and that all the resources of society and of human intellect

7. Thomas Paine, *Common Sense*, in I. Schneider, ed., *The Enlightenment*. New York: Braziller, 1965, p. 85.
8. Voltaire, *On Commerce*, in *The Enlightenment*, p. 259.
9. *Statute of Virginia for Religious Freedom*, in *The Enlightenment*, p. 316.

should be applied to making it as happy and beautiful as possible. This belief has been the dominant view of Western civilization in the twentieth century. It has inspired many ambitious attempts to reform government and the social order, if necessary by means of armed revolution. It has also motivated the application of science to technology, causing tremendous alteration of the circumstances of everyday life. Although the *philosophes* lived in the preindustrial, preponderantly aristocratic world, their faith has been the foundation of modern industrial, democratic society.

Herein lies the paradox of Enlightenment culture. The intellectual leaders of the eighteenth century propounded a belief in material and social progress and in man's capacity to achieve it. This became the prime article of Western faith and spread throughout the world. Yet upon close examination these eighteenth-century men seem fundamentally to be products of the old aristocratic culture of preindustrial Europe, in some respects closer to the humanists of the Renaissance than to ourselves. The *philosophes* vehemently reasserted the value of classical style in art and literature and were blind to the achievements of medieval culture and (before Rousseau) to the irrational and violent aspects of human nature. Like the Florentines of the fifteenth century, they tried to make life into a work of art; nothing was more important to them than the cultivation of elegance and good taste.

We admire this elegance and taste, but we see it as part of a distinctly aristocratic and elitist culture that was achieved at the expense of the masses. The salon and coffeehouse world of the eighteenth century certainly appears to us to have been a delightful one, but from our point of view this privileged little world was almost as alien to the political and economic upheavals that were to follow as was the court of Louis xv.

The Enlightenment's legacy was the liberal and humanitarian ideals that have inspired repeated attempts to improve the circumstances of life of ordinary people. What separates us from the *philosophes* is primarily our realization of the enormous difficulty involved in the implementation of the progressive and meliorist doctrines of the eighteenth century.

3

The
Political
Revolution

I THE EVE OF THE REVOLUTION

The French Revolution in Historical Thought

The French Revolution was one of the most dramatic events in all history. No other single happening in modern times has inspired and horrified so many men or evoked so many pages of polemic and scholarship as the upheaval that brought down the venerable French monarchy. Yet in spite of the innumerable words spent in describing, praising, and condemning it, the French Revolution remains a disputed subject. Historical judgment has been made especially difficult because the questions raised by the Revolution have remained burning political issues: revolutionary versus antirevolutionary, egalitarian versus elitist, liberal versus totalitarian. Both the nineteenth and the twentieth century have been punctuated by revolutions whose ideas and events have continued to echo those of the French Revolution of 1789. Not surprisingly, then, most historians of the French Revolution have found it necessary either to praise or to condemn the subject of their researches, at least implicitly.

The real starting point of modern scholarship on the French Revolution was the work of two French historians who published major studies in the first years of the twentieth century. François Aulard produced a multivolume political history of the Revolution based upon exhaustive critical study of the available documents, pamphlets, letters, and speeches. He divided the Revolution into four phases: (1) the period from 1789 to 1792, when the bourgeoisie came to power and began to grapple with the problems of democracy and national sovereignty; (2) the period from 1792 to 1795, when the adherents of democracy wrested control of the Revolution from the bourgeoisie; (3) the period from 1795 to 1799, when the bourgeoisie ruled in triumph over both the aristocracy and the lower classes; and (4) the despotism of Napoleon. Jean

Jaurès, Aulard's contemporary, wrote the first extensive socialist study of the Revolution, placing it in the general context of the class struggle.

Both Albert Mathiez and Georges Lefebvre, the two greatest twentieth-century French historians of the Revolution, built upon the foundation laid by Aulard and Jaurès. Mathiez and Lefebvre were professional historians who contributed specialized studies of particular aspects of the Revolution (Lefebvre, for example, studied the peasantry) and also greatly advanced general understanding of the Revolution by producing masterly syntheses representing the fruits of a century and a half of historical scholarship. Mathiez was particularly noted for his rehabilitation of the reputation of the left-wing revolutionary leader, Maximilien Robespierre. In Mathiez's view, Robespierre was an idealist but not a blind fanatic, whose genius as a leader saved the Revolution when it was on the point of disaster.

Lefebvre's analysis of the early phases of the Revolution, published in an English translation as *The Coming of the French Revolution*, is a classic study of the dynamics of the conflict. In the bewildering concatenation of events between 1787 and 1792, Lefebvre discerned a pattern of development in which each major social group—nobility, bourgeoisie, and working class—attacked the old regime in its own way and for its own reasons. The interaction of these conflicts pushed the Revolution forward until aristocratic privilege, monarchy, and the old regime itself were brought down.

Historians remain divided on the utility and long-range significance of the Revolution. Thus J. L. Talmon finds in it the origins of totalitarian democracy. He sees the demand that all citizens accept the revolutionary program and the equation of that program with the state as the transformation of the political ideas of the *philosophes* into a totalitarian ideology which the radical revolutionaries sought to impose first upon the French nation and then upon all of Europe. Other historians question the social significance of the Revolution. Alfred Cobban asserts that "the revolution was a triumph for the conservative, propertied, land-owning classes, large and small";[1] far from promoting liberty and equality, it merely strengthened the political power of the already dominant economic groups and may have actually retarded the forces of economic and social change.

The most important recent issue in revolutionary historiography has been raised by R. R. Palmer, an American historian, and his French colleague, Jacques Godechot. Palmer and Godechot have reopened the question of the place of the French Revolution in the general development of the Western world in the late eighteenth century. They see it as only the most dramatic of a whole series of popular disturbances that shook Britain's North American colonies as well as almost every country in Europe between 1770 and 1800. Palmer and Godechot regard the American Revolution as the beginning of the democratic attack upon the privileged aristocracy of the old order.

1. Alfred Cobban, *The Social Interpretation of the French Revolution*. Cambridge: Cambridge University Press, 1964, p. 170.

The Three Estates

To understand why revolution came to France in the late 1780's, we must first of all take a closer look at the condition of French society at that time. Legally, French society was divided into the three estates, an institutional survival from the Middle Ages. The First Estate, the clergy, was far from being a homogeneous social group. The bishops and higher ranks were predominantly drawn from the nobility and lived like nobles. The Church had retained much of its wealth—it was still the single greatest landowner in the kingdom—and also much of the power which had accrued to it as the ally of the state. Below the bishops and abbots ranged the other ranks of the clergy. As the beneficiaries of generations of generous donors, the monasteries had retained a great deal of their earlier splendor, but the parish priests were as humble as their peasant parishioners and often just as poor. Frequently very close to those whose souls were in their charge, they possessed great influence with the rural peasantry. More than once during the Revolution, their weight would bear heavily on the course of events.

The Second Estate, the nobility, was even more complex. There were several formal divisions. The nobles of the sword had the purest blue blood, claiming their rank on the basis of the quality and duration of their noble heritage. The nobles of the robe, on the other hand, were those who owed their position to their service to the state. Throughout the early eighteenth century it had been possible for a wealthy and ambitious member of the bourgeoisie to purchase an office and thereby to join the nobility; but during the latter half of the century the nobility became increasingly aggressive in defense of its hereditary rights. After 1750 it became virtually impossible for a man of common birth to enter the upper echelons of the army or the civil service.

It is likely that this development had a profound effect on the attitudes of the wealthier members of the Third Estate—the commoners. In the mid-eighteenth century the French bourgeoisie was not a self-conscious social class with a sense of common identity. The successful banker, merchant, or lawyer identified with the nobility, emulating the nobles' style of living and frequently striving to enter their ranks. These wealthy bourgeois sought office for themselves, married their daughters to impecunious sons of noblemen, and sent their sons into the officer corps. Many rich members of the Third Estate built mansions in Paris and dressed like noblemen. Often, even without the prestige of a title, they achieved positions of great power as creditors of the government and officers of the Crown.

In composition, the Third Estate was more complex than the other two. While the clergy included both rich prelates and starving parish priests and the nobility included aristocrats as poor as common peasants, the Third Estate—over 90 per cent of the population—was little more than a legal distinction, certainly not a social class. Only a small percentage of the population was involved in the kind of massive enterprise that could be called industrial capitalism. Most Frenchmen were small proprietors, or employees of small proprietors, whose income level ranged from bare subsistence to very substantial. Included in this group were the small peasants, who generally worked a piece of land which they owned or rented; the artisans, craftsmen, and shopkeepers, who would form the bulk of the *sans-culottes* (men who did not wear the breeches fashionable among the well-to-do) during the Revolution; and the more highly educated lawyers, doctors, teachers, and civil servants, who would play a very significant role in the political struggles of the Revolution. There was wide variation in income within all these occupational groups, but a substantial part of each was vulnerable in an era of economic instability, when wages fell further and further behind rising prices and bad harvests repeatedly resulted in a scarcity of grain and other staples. It was they who were repeatedly caught in the vise of a government which demanded taxes but could provide no relief for their distress.

The Governmental Crisis

The French Revolution began as a governmental crisis and then escalated into a general attack on the economic and social institutions of the old regime. It came at the end of the long series of Continental and colonial wars fought between 1740 and 1783. Louis xiv had left the French state virtually bankrupt in 1715 after a similar series of conflicts, and despite subsequent attempts to solve its financial problems, no really effective change in tax structure had been made. French intervention in the American Revolution pushed the French state from financial crisis to bankruptcy.

Corporate privilege exacerbated the financial plight of the state. Each of the three estates was a corporate group with its own duties and privileges. The Church paid no taxes but merely presented the government with a gift, which was very small in comparison with its income; and with few exceptions the nobility, too, was exempt from taxation. Other kinds of corporate privilege limited the power of the state. Guilds had long been corporate entities that could regulate prices, production techniques, and the right to practice a trade. And there were numerous regional variations in the administration of law, the collection of taxes, and the selection of royal officials. Some regions had retained the right to hold local meetings of the Estates General, and others had long-standing exemptions from certain taxes. Every attempt to provide national uniformity in governmental administration meant an unending battle against corporate privilege in all its manifold forms. For the *ancien régime* it was a hopeless struggle.

The prelude to the Revolution was a prolonged conflict between the monarchy and the *parlements,* which played the role of champions of the people. Throughout the reign of Louis xvi, the *parlements* had the advantage of facing an exceedingly weak adversary. Even in the midst of imminent national bankruptcy, the Crown continued the lavish court ceremonial; the king's

FRENCH ADMINISTRATIVE DIVISIONS
UNDER THE ANCIEN RÉGIME

■ Pays d'états
● Seats of Parlements or Sovereign Courts
—— Boundaries of their jurisdiction

Pre-Revolutionary France was a melange of administrative units, many claiming some degree of independence from the Crown. Even under Louis XIV, provincial parliaments had continued to function in some provinces — the *pays d'états*, which were notably on the periphery of the country. And after his death, the aristocratic courts (*parlements*) — particularly the one in Paris — reasserted their power and stymied the Crown's efforts to reform the system of taxation.

household expenses and the pensions that often rewarded his courtiers consumed a major part of the national budget (although they were dwarfed by military expenses). Louis himself was well intentioned but little qualified for the arduous task of governing a nation in turmoil. His wife — Marie Antoinette, daughter of Maria Theresa — was extravagant, unfaithful, and unpopular, increasingly a source of scandal and embarrassment. Louis was the kind of king who could have reigned successfully only under the tutelage of a great minister, a Richelieu or a Fleury. Each of his ministers was driven to propose reforms but lacked the power to impose them over the objections of the *parlements*. The king, whose worst quality was his indecisiveness, was each time forced to withdraw his support and seek a new man who might have the magic to solve the crisis.

The Crown's floundering efforts to resolve its most pressing financial problems led in 1787 to the convocation of the Assembly of Notables. This act of desperation was followed a few months later by the government's agreement to convene the Estates General for the first time in over a hundred and fifty years. Escalating conflict during the two years before the Estates General assembled caused the discerning English traveler Arthur Young to predict that a revolution of the nobility against the king would soon take place. France was flooded with rumors and pamphlets as the monarchy and the *parlements* continued their maneuvering. The *parlements* were not alone in protesting what they called "monarchical despotism." Riots and disorders began to break out in widely scattered parts of France, from Brittany in the northwest to Toulouse and Dijon in the south and southeast.

In the developing controversy all sides resorted to the ideas and language of the *philosophes*. Voltaire, for one, had looked to enlightened despotism to provide an alternative to the inequities and anachronisms of the old regime; and the system of regional and corporate privileges, the archaic judicial system, and the obvious injustice of the taxation system had been common targets for attacks by many *philosophes*. Government propaganda sought to show that these were indeed the causes of the nation's miseries. The *parlements*, on the other hand, found the ideas of Montesquieu on the separation of powers in the state a compelling argument in their favor. They also argued, in the popular phrases of the American Revolution, that legislation could not be enacted without the consent of the governed and that there should be no taxation without representation.

To this crisis of political rhetoric and philosophy was soon added an economic crisis of monumental proportions. Despite the government's growing financial difficulties in the 1770's and 1780's, these years had been, for the general public at least, years of financial and commercial expansion and growth. In 1787, however, this cycle came abruptly to an end, and France was confronted not only with the specter of bankruptcy but with a great decline in business activity and a leap in unemployment. And, as if all this were not enough, a failure of the grain harvest sent the price of bread soaring (when bread could be obtained at all). Under these conditions, most workers had to pay more than half their salaries just to obtain their daily bread. Millions more had to seek some sort of public relief. The problems of the government were thus compounded by the outbreak of popular disturbances—primarily food riots—throughout the kingdom.

II 1789

The Summoning of the Estates General

It was in this feverish atmosphere that the meeting of the Estates General in 1789 was called and the preliminary discussions carried out. Facing a country that was becoming increasingly difficult to govern, the king and his ministers reacted by, in effect, turning the problems over to the people. Not only were the delegates to the Estates General to be elected by virtually universal (though indirect) manhood suffrage, but every significant region and corporate group was invited to draw up a list of grievances to guide their representatives. Such a move was really without precedent in French history. The Estates General had not met since 1614–1615, and it had never functioned as a popularly elected parliament.

This radical departure from tradition created widely differing expectations. The king and his ministers hoped to get the consent of the Estates General to the reform of the tax system, thereby circumventing the *parlements* in a way that could not be questioned. The nobility, on the other hand, hoped to control the Estates General by virtue of the fact that voting would be conducted by order: the first two estates—the clergy and the nobles—could always combine to outvote the third. To the extent that they considered the matter at all, the nobles seem to have expected the Estates General to sit only a brief period of time and, in return for consent to certain additional taxes, to gain royal affirmation of the existing state of political and social organization. Events were soon to prove these expectations illusory.

The clergy was considerably more representative of the diverse social composition and philosophy of the country than the nobility, and its vote would be controlled by the parish priests, who far outnumbered the aristocratic bishops and whose personal interests and sympathies were overwhelmingly with the Third Estate. As for the latter, it is difficult to generalize about the wishes of the great mass of Frenchmen at this turbulent time, except to say that they wanted an end to the most egregious social privileges of the nobility and to the most onerous and burdensome state and feudal dues. Most important, perhaps, was the fact that, while the electoral process was running its course, the French people were expressing their wants and desires in a long list of highly detailed grievances. There were forty thousand of these complaints—called *cahiers de doléances*—and no one who looked at even a small fraction of these could possibly believe that the forthcoming meeting of the Estates General would be either brief or placid.

The direction in which popular feeling was moving among the articulate elements in the Third Estate is illustrated by the arguments of Abbé Sieyès (1748–1836) in his famous pamphlet *What Is the Third Estate?*, which appeared in January 1789. Published about the time that Louis XVI issued his summons of the Estates General, it became an immediate sensation, selling (according to one reliable estimate) something like thirty thousand copies in the first three weeks after its publication. The reasons for this instant fame are not far to seek. As Georges Lefebvre has said, there was in France, on the eve of the Revolution, a distinct sense of national unity, and no one expressed this spirit better than did Sieyès. The prime importance of his tract lay in the fact that it described the state of politics and society in a completely frank and unvarnished way. Uninhibited by stale convention, Sieyès—who was far more reformer and philosopher than priest—answered the principal question posed by his tract: "What Is the Third Estate? Everything." "What," he went on to ask, "has the Third Estate been heretofore in the political order? Nothing. What does it demand? To become something."

Asserting that the first two orders represented about 200,000 people in a population of 26,000,000, Sieyès argued that only the Third Estate could represent the nation. He charged that the first two orders were vestigial organs which served no productive function in the political and economic life of France. Each represented only a particular interest, which had nothing to do with the general interest of the nation. Sieyès was only the most famous of many writers who presented the same arguments and drew the conclusion that the two privileged orders had no right to speak for France. To be sure, such pamphleteers did not challenge the monarchical institutions — no one, not even in the most bitterly critical *cahiers*, did that. But the old regime had been steadily on the intellectual retreat since the middle of the eighteenth century, and tracts like that of Sieyès, especially when taken together with thousands of *cahiers*, augured poorly indeed for the preservation of the status quo.

The National Assembly

The Estates General was solemnly opened on May 5, 1789, and no sooner had it commenced its sessions than the members became embroiled in a bitter dispute. Though on the surface the controversy seemed concerned with a procedural matter, in reality it went to the heart of the questions — what kind of assembly was this to be, and what kind of work was it to do?

The Third Estate refused to take up any business unless voting would be by head, a condition the other estates refused to accept. Most of the reformist nobles and the parish priests agreed with the overwhelming majority of the Third Estate that voting should be by head, but the higher clergy and most of the nobles insisted that the traditional three-estate system be preserved. By June 12 several parish priests had gone over to the Third Estate, and on June 17 the latter, declaring that it represented 98 per cent of the nation, proclaimed itself the National Assembly. Moreover, the Third Estate now went on to claim the right to pass on all taxes, suggesting that if the king refused to agree it might well proclaim a moratorium on taxes.

At this point Louis began to make the first of a series of bad mistakes. On June 20 he had the Assembly locked out of its usual meeting place, whereupon the delegates adjourned to a neighboring tennis court and took the famous oath "not to separate, and to reassemble wherever circumstances require, until the constitution of the kingdom is established and consolidated upon firm foundations." On June 23 the king called the three orders before him to settle the problem. A Louis xiv would have awed them with his majesty, but Louis xvi only succeeded in offending the Third Estate.

The events that followed the formation of the National Assembly were a bewildering jumble for contemporaries. The National Assembly was in revolt but had only the vaguest ideas about what direction its revolt would take. Several factors tended to push the Revolution further to the Left. The king's vacillation and indecision produced first confusion and then mistrust on the part of the people. Once faced with the conflict between the Third Estate and the privileged orders, he tended to forget the recent royal attack on those very privileges. He could not bring himself to give the kind of support to the Third Estate which would have forced the nobility and clergy to capitulate. At the same time, however, he proved to be unable to refuse the demands of the Third Estate. Four days after the royal session of June 23, popular unrest forced him to instruct the two privileged orders to join the Third Estate in the National Assembly. This pattern was to be repeated again and again.

Popular agitation also exerted a strong influence upon the National Assembly. In the beginning the representatives of the Third Estate were far from being militant radicals. Although election of these representatives had been carried out with a very broad suffrage, the National Assembly was composed almost completely of the substantial members of the community. The largest single group was the lawyers, who were joined by other occupational groups of similar social, economic, and educational status. They did not come to Paris with the intention of making a revolution but only to demand an end to certain abuses and a part in the political life of the state. As time went by, however, the obstinacy of the nobility and the pressure of popular agitation escalated their demands.

The Advent of Revolution

If Louis' instruction to the nobility and clergy to join the Third Estate in the new National Assembly led many people to believe that the king was now prepared to accept the new national tide, the king's real intentions soon became unmistakable. Royal troops began to be stationed around Paris and Versailles, where the Assembly was meeting. Fear and anxiety were growing everywhere. There was serious apprehension that the king was plotting some kind of coup—a sentiment strongly reinforced by the dismissal of the popular minister Necker on July 11 and his replacement by a strong royalist.

The storming of the Bastille on July 14, 1789, was only the most dramatic of a series of popular disturbances that now shook Paris and the French countryside. They were inspired in part by a great deal of organized agitation among the Parisian populace. Probably more important, however, were the shortage of food and the rumors that swept through the crowded streets. Rumor of an "aristocratic conspiracy" was most persistent. At first unfounded, it became increasingly credible with the growing opposition of the aristocracy and the king. The desire to get arms and ammunition for protection against a possible counterrevolution led the crowd to assault the Bastille. The *sans-culottes* also hanged individual offenders against "the people" from the street lanterns of Paris or carried their heads about on pikes. At the same time, mobs forced bakers and grain sellers to lower their prices and attacked the toll stations around Paris, whose charges increased the cost of grain.

The attack on the Bastille was a profoundly political act, for that aging citadel was far more important as a feared symbol of royal oppression – having been for many years a prison for political offenders – than it was as an arsenal for the local authorities. Finding the prison virtually deserted, the enraged citizens slaughtered some members of its hapless garrison and dragged off others. The following day Louis withdrew his troops from the city; the day after that he recalled Necker. He followed up these concessions by returning to Paris himself and sanctioning the new Paris municipal government and the new National Guard under the command of the Marquis de Lafayette, a liberal aristocrat who had fought for the colonists in the American Revolution.

The storming of the Bastille did not slow the course of the Revolution but seemed only to institutionalize it. It certainly did not quiet the population in Paris; and elsewhere in the country, reported the British ambassador, "execration of the nobility is universal among the lower order of people." These "July Days" had far-reaching consequences. For the time being they intimidated the king and the nobility while strengthening the position of the National Assembly. They also produced some of the most important institutions of the Revolution. The electoral assembly of Paris, followed by other electoral assemblies throughout France, began to hold meetings in order to discuss the issues of the day and to give instructions to its deputies in the National Assembly. The National Guard, a citizen militia, broke the king's monopoly of military power. The Revolution was no longer merely confined to the few hundred men who sat in the National Assembly. Instead, it now had its own army and elements of organization throughout France.

During the summer of 1789 the "Great Fear" spread from village to village and resulted in widespread violence, directed primarily at the manifestations of the feudal system which were still a part of rural life. The outbreaks were inspired by rumors of an aristocratic conspiracy to unleash bands of brigands upon the country villages. Although the brigands were a myth, the existence of feudal dues was not, and the peasants who went out looking for brigands usually wound up attacking the home of the landlord and destroying his records. What the peasants wanted from the Revolution was the abolition of feudal dues, of the *corvée* (the requirement that peasants work a number of days each year maintaining the roads), and of other institutions that oppressed them.

Like the riots in Paris, the eruption of the countryside moved the Assembly to undertake reforms it had not originally considered. On the night of August 4, several members – including Lafayette, leader of the liberal nobles – rose to move that all feudal rights and privileges be abolished. As the session wore on, the deputies stripped away the remnants of the old feudal system – both the legal and social rights of the nobility so galling to the middle class and the seigneurial dues hated by the peasantry. But events of that night also illustrated the limits of the social egalitarianism of the Assembly. The deputies made a clear and careful distinction between feudal rights and the rights of property. The latter were made by contract and were therefore inviolable, unlike the rights based merely on heredity. As a result, the many large, middle-class landowners in France were left secure in their rents. Furthermore, the holders of seigneurial rights were to be indemnified for their loss. But the peasants were unable to understand such fine legal distinctions and merely stopped paying the burdensome dues and rents.

The Declaration of the Rights of Man and the Citizen

While the Revolution in the streets of Paris and in the French countryside was dissolving the traditional governmental structure, the National Assembly was hard at work registering the "will of the nation." The deputies stated the general principles which would guide them in the Declaration of the Rights of Man and the Citizen. Modeled on the American Declaration of Independence, it differed primarily in being a more abstract enunciation of the basic principles of government. The French Declaration was basically a statement of the relationship between the citizen and the nation. It envisioned a nation of law based upon the general will and respecting the "natural and imprescriptible rights of man"—that is, "liberty, property, security, and resistance to oppression." It affirmed the career open to virtues and talents, guaranteed due process of law in judicial proceedings, allowed the citizen freedom to speak, write, and believe anything not injurious to the nation, and endorsed the separation of powers as a fundamental principle of government. Although not intended to be an attack upon monarchy as such, it did assert the right of all citizens "to take part personally or by their representatives" in the formation of the law. Introduced into a state which had hitherto been governed on the principle that the will of the king was law, it was a truly revolutionary document.

If the Declaration of the Rights of Man and the Citizen was the most liberal statement of its kind ever adopted by a European state up to that time, this is not to say that it was intended to mark the beginning of the end of all old political institutions of France. On the contrary, the radicalism of the Revolution continued to be limited in a number of ways. Perhaps the most telling was the attitude of the revolutionaries toward the king. Even after the events of July and August there were few republicans in France and none in the Assembly. Those drawing up a constitution favored a constitutional monarchy. The king was still personally popular and was generally believed to favor the Revolution. When he acted badly, it was thought to be only because he had been deceived by the fomenters of the "aristocratic plot," who were seeking to destroy the Revolution. Many of those who fought in the streets to wipe out the last vestiges of feudalism felt that they were doing the will of the king, whose desire for the abolition of injustice had been thwarted by the subversion and obstinacy of the aristocrats.

REVOLUTIONARY FRANCE

Acquired 1715-1789
Acquired 1790-1802
Boundaries of Department

NORTH SEA

ENGLAND

- Norwich
- Oxford
- London
- Bristol
- Southampton
- Plymouth

Thames R.

ENGLISH CHANNEL

CHANNEL IS.

BAY

OF

BISCAY

NETHERLANDS

- Amsterdam
- Antwerp
- Cologne
- Aix-La-Chapelle
- Mainz
- Cherbourg

DEUX NETHES
MEUSE INFÉRIEURE
RUR
LYS
ESCAUT
DYLE
PAS-DE-CALAIS
JEMAPPES
OURTHE
RHIN-ET-MOSELLE
SOMME
SAMBRE-ET-MEUSE
FORÊTS
SARRE
MONT-TONNERRE
- Amiens
AISNE
ARDENNES
MANCHE
CALVADOS
EURE
OISE
MARNE
MEUSE
MOSELLE
BAS-RHIN
- Strasbourg
- Valmy
- Varennes
MEURTHE-ET-MOSELLE
- Brest
FINISTÈRE
CÔTES-DU-NORD
ORNE
SEINE-ET-OISE
SEINE-ET-MARNE
AUBE
HAUTE-MARNE
VOSGES
HAUT-RHIN
- Basel
SEINE INFÉRIEURE
Paris
ILLE-ET-VILAINE
MAYENNE
EURE-ET-LOIRE
LOIRET
YONNE
HAUTE-SAÔNE
MORBIHAN
SARTHE
DOUBS
LOIRE INFÉRIEURE
MAINE-ET-LOIRE
INDRE-ET-LOIRE
LOIR-ET-CHER
NIÈVRE
CÔTE-D'OR
- Nantes
- Bourges
CHER
JURA
SWITZERLAND
L. Geneva
VENDÉE
DEUX-SÈVRES
VIENNE
INDRE
ALLIER
SAÔNE-ET-LOIRE
AIN
LEMAN
CHARENTE-INFÉRIEURE
HAUTE-VIENNE
CREUSE
MT. BLANC
DOIRE
CHARENTE
PUY-DE-DÔME
LOIRE
ISÈRE
- Lyons
- Bordeaux
CORRÈZE
- Valence
PO
GIRONDE
DORDOGNE
CANTAL
HAUTE-LOIRE
ARDÈCHE
DRÔME
HAUTES-ALPES
STURA
LOT-ET-GARONNE
LOT
AVEYRON
LOZÈRE
BASSES-ALPES
ALPES-MARITIMES
- Nice
LANDES
GERS
TARN
GARD
VANCLUSE
- Avignon
VAR
- Toulouse
HÉRAULT
BOUCHES-DU-RHÔNE
- Marseilles
BASSES-PYRÈNES
HAUTES-PYRÈNNES
HAUTE-GARONNE
ARIÈGE
AUDE
PYRÈNES-ORIENTALES

Ebro R.
Segre R.

SPAIN

MEDITERRANEAN SEA

CORSICA
GOLO
- Ajaccio
LIAMONE

TANARO

The events of early October 1789 illustrate both this continued admiration for the king and the nature of the forces that continued to animate the Revolution. Louis, residing with the court at Versailles, where the National Assembly was meeting, had indicated his opposition to the abolition of feudal rights and privileges and to the Declaration of the Rights of Man and the Citizen, which the Assembly had proclaimed. In addition, the palace guard at Versailles had been reinforced. These events happened to coincide with yet another food crisis in Paris, the center of revolutionary agitation. On the afternoon of October 5 the Paris crowd, including many women in search of bread, set out for nearby Versailles under the leadership of the reluctant Marquis de Lafayette. There, during an uneasy night, the National Guard joined the palace guard in an uncertain truce, the king tried to make a decision, and the thousands of Parisians outside the palace waited impatiently. Next day they brought the king (wearing the revolutionary cockade) and the royal family back to Paris, the spirits of the crowd fortified by Louis' acceptance of the enactments of the National Assembly and the steps taken to provide food for the French capital. Although Louis was determined never to surrender his royal prerogatives, on October 6 he was hailed as the hero of the Revolution.

Henceforth, both the National Assembly and the king were literally surrounded by the Revolution. That circumstance was to bear on the course of events with ever increasing urgency.

III THE RADICALIZATION OF THE REVOLUTION

The Bourgeois Revolution

By the fall of 1789 much of the old order had been torn down, either abolished by the National Assembly or dissolved by popular disorders or the threat thereof. In its place the Assembly had to build a new government based on the conception of the state as it appeared in the Declaration of the Rights of Man and the Citizen. The muddled internal divisions of the old France were replaced by eighty-three *départements*, each named after its most striking geographic feature. Each *département* was then broken down into districts, and these, in turn, into cantons. As before 1789, the basic administrative unit in France remained the parish, now renamed the commune. Each of these new political units was headed by an elective council; even the central government's representative was elected rather than, as heretofore, appointed from Paris. The Assembly, it seemed clear, was bent on reversing

Under the National Assembly the organs of the administration of the Old Regime were swept away, including the *parlements* and the provinces. Smaller, equal departments took the place of the latter and have remained to this day. And as the Revolutionary armies extended French boundaries to Louis XIV's "natural frontiers," the Rhine and the Alps, the new territory was also divided into departments under the control of Paris.

the whole process of centralization that had characterized French govern-ment since the seventeenth century. The Assembly also abolished a large number of old offices and indemnified their holders (many of whom sat in the Assembly).

The economic policies of the Assembly were more contradictory. On the one hand, it voted to abolish all internal tariffs and duties, favoring free trade in all important commodities including grains. It also abolished the old guilds, which were charged with being intolerably restrictive. On the other hand, workers were denied the right to organize in unions and to strike, protective tariffs were maintained, and commerce with the French colonies continued to be closely regulated. The new legislation best served middle-class interests.

Some of the Assembly's most important acts concerned the judicial system, the object of bitter complaints in many *cahiers*. Thus the *parlements* were finally abolished; along with seigneurial courts and the royal system of jus-tice, they were replaced by a new judicial system with equal laws and punish-ments for everyone. But the Assembly was much less successful in military affairs. Although it recognized the militia that had sprung up spontaneously in 1789 and accorded it the status of "National Guard," the Guard's duties were rigidly limited to the preservation of domestic order. For the larger pur-pose of national defense the Assembly decided to retain the old royal army, stipulating only that henceforth promotion should be open to all, irrespective of social background. This particular action proved to have serious repercus-sions. Many of the army officers remained loyal to the old regime; not a few found themselves with rebellious soldiers; still others fled abroad. Thus the army's fighting strength was decidedly impaired, and its political reli-ability seemed doubtful. Here lay the source of much future difficulty for the Revolution.

The most intractable problem the Assembly faced was the chronic one of collection of revenue. It began by abolishing all the taxes of the old regime, save the stamp tax, and began to reform the tax structure, again in accord-ance with the demands set forth in the *cahiers*. Most important of the new taxes was the land tax; others were taxes on personal property and on income from industry and commerce. But the new direct taxes were not paid or were paid only after much protest and delay. Meanwhile, the fiscal condition of the government was steadily deteriorating — the ordinary expenses of govern-ment and interest on the national debt alone came to around 600 million francs a year.

The desperate need for a new source of revenue was largely responsible for the government's decision in November 1789 to nationalize church lands and put them up for sale. Since the Church owned a very substantial part of the land of the kingdom — its total wealth was estimated to be between two and five billion francs — this was a tremendous asset upon which the Assembly was able to draw. Actually the idea of expropriation was by no means new; it had been suggested by Calonne before the coming of the Revolution, and confiscation of church lands had been urged by a number of *cahiers*. Even so, the proposal to seize these lands and to use them as chattel for new government obligations—introduced by Talleyrand in October 1789—produced lengthy and bitter debate, foreshadowing the emergence of the Church's position as one of the crucial issues of the Revolution.

By early November, however, the Assembly had approved the new policy, and by mid-December 1789 it began to be put into effect. Eventually the *assignats*—bonds issued by the state and secured by the church lands—became the predominant form of currency in France, and the nationalization was generally accepted by the clergy (most of whom would be far more generously provided for on a state salary). Unfortunately, the *assignats* proved to be a highly unsatisfactory method of dealing with France's fiscal problems. They depreciated rapidly and in so doing brought down the fortunes of the men who had created them. By the end of 1791 they had fallen over 20 per cent, and by the spring of 1792 they had lost 40 per cent of their value. They made a partial recovery in 1793 but in 1796 were finally repudiated and replaced.

The Assembly rapidly went beyond the seizure of church lands. It outraged a large number of clergy by rigidly applying the abolition of special privileges and corporations to the Church itself. In July of 1790 the Civil Constitution of the Clergy was enacted, requiring a loyalty oath to the French state. There can be little doubt that passage of the Civil Constitution was one of the most fateful decisions of the Revolution. Although the new arrangement, which in effect made the Church a department of the government, was not passed in any antireligious spirit, bishops and parish priests were henceforth to be elected much like local government officials. It seemed to many ranking members of the Church—not to mention the pope—that ecclesiastical discipline and the integral character of the Church would be increasingly difficult to maintain in an institution thus democratized. While uneasy negotiations with Pope Pius VI dragged on, most members of the clergy refused to take the oath. Finally, the Assembly grew impatient with the pope and instituted the Civil Constitution without his formal consent.

It seems highly unlikely that the pope would ever have given the Civil Constitution his formal approval. He had already secretly denounced the suppression of monastic orders, and in March and April 1791 he denounced not only the Civil Constitution but various other reforms and all the principles underlying the Revolution. A large part of the French clergy was thus alienated. Eventually many were exiled or self-exiled, but thousands of "nonjuring" priests—that is, priests who refused to take the loyalty oath—stayed on in France, either in hiding or tacitly tolerated by the local authorities. In their places were put new, state-appointed clergymen, who were never able to gain the confidence of the people or fill the gap left by their predecessors in local parish life. From this point on, the Church became one of the bulwarks of the counterrevolution.

The dilemma of what to do about the Church was not the only one that the government found itself unable to resolve. Ever since the summer of 1789, France had been living in a kind of constitutional twilight zone, and this weakness became ever more serious as the months went on. One of the principal problems of the new constitution—which the Constituent Assembly (as the National Assembly is generally referred to after 1790) finally completed and Louis XVI formally approved in September 1791—was that it had taken nearly two years to complete. When it finally went into effect, it was hardly adequate to stand up to the extraordinary pressures and strains to which France was being increasingly subjected at home and abroad. The Constitution of 1791 provided a system of national government that was simply too weak and too decentralized to prevent subversion on both the Left and the Right. When the relative domestic and foreign peace of 1790 began to break down in 1791, both the Crown and the legislature lacked adequate power to deal with the threatening chaos.

It is easy enough to observe the shortcomings of the new constitution, but its importance, actual and symbolic, should not be overlooked. To begin with, it was the first written constitution in the history of France and one of the first such documents in the history of modern Europe. Second, it was no doubt a reasonable reflection of political thought in eighteenth-century Europe—and the best and most respectable thought at that. The electoral system it stipulated, first suggested by Sieyès, divided all citizens into two categories—active and passive—on the basis of property, with only the former—about 4,300,000 out of a population of 25 million—having the right to vote, and only a smaller number still—about 50,000—having the right to be elected. Adhering to Montesquieu's principle of separation of powers, the government had independent executive and judicial branches. The king had the right to appoint his own ministers, who could not be members of the Assembly, and he possessed a limited veto of legislation.

This system was to prove a constant source of trouble. Secretly and sometimes even openly opposed to the actions of the Assembly but having no effective way of influencing its decisions, the king resorted to duplicity and secret subversion in both foreign and domestic affairs. It seems perfectly clear, for instance, that Louis never intended to accept the Civil Constitution of the Clergy, and though the new national constitution formally proclaimed that "the King alone may maintain political relations abroad," there can be no doubt that Louis interpreted this freedom to conduct French foreign policy in a very different light than did the Constituent Assembly that voted him the power or the Legislative Assembly that came into office in October 1791. Moreover, while formally free to choose his own ministers, he was in fact forced to avoid alienating the majority of the Assembly in his selections. If a minister were sufficiently unpopular, he had to be removed. Thus relations between the executive and legislative branches could hardly be friendly, and the executive could hardly be truly independent.

Relations between Crown and Legislative Assembly were to be further inflamed by the king's interpretation and use of the veto power bestowed upon him by the new constitution. For while that document gave the monarch only a suspensive veto, which could be overridden by three successive assemblies, Louis did not hesitate to use this authority to defeat whatever measures he opposed. Thus conflict between the letter and the spirit of the constitution continued to envenom political relations between the king and the representatives of the people.

These were serious enough structural defects, but the power of the Assembly was further vitiated by the considerable regional decentralization which was firmly built into the new constitution. This decentralization might have provided adequate government in more tranquil times, but the belief of many deputies that the Revolution had been completed was to prove no more than wishful thinking. Indeed, perhaps nothing was more dangerous than the apparent belief of the members of the Constituent Assembly that they had either resolved France's outstanding difficulties or prepared the way for their constitutional resolution. During 1790–1791 France had to face a steadily mounting economic, political, and military crisis in which both the counterrevolution and the democratic revolution would rise to challenge the constitution that had been so recently established.

Although the king's publicly expressed attitude was ambiguous, he never really accepted the Revolution. By the summer of 1790 the incipient opposition to the Revolution among the aristocracy, the nonjuring clergy (which remained loyal to Rome) and its followers, and those surrounding the king and the royal family rapidly hardened into broad-scale antirevolutionary activity. By that time it was evident to the forces of conservatism and reaction that the Revolution would not collapse of its own accord, and the earlier myth of an "aristocratic plot" seemed on the way to becoming reality.

As a result by the end of 1790 events in France were increasingly determined by what transpired outside French borders, especially by the activities of the *émigrés* who were fleeing abroad in growing numbers, either to seek political refuge or to obtain military assistance for a concerted effort to overthrow the revolutionary order from without. One of the first members of the royal family to leave the country was the highly conservative count of Artois, the younger brother of Louis XVI. (The count returned to France in 1814 and reigned as Charles X from 1824 to 1830.) He was soon followed by several other Bourbon princes and great lords. These exiles were not only losing their cherished economic and social privileges; midst growing public disorder in France, many of them were becoming fearful of losing their lives.

In the beginning, most revolutionaries were delighted to see their conservative or reactionary adversaries go abroad, and before long the presence of the *émigrés* just across the French frontier provided the more radical revolutionaries with a powerful argument for still more drastic change at home. In June 1791 there occurred the flight of the king, his wife, and their two children. What Louis planned to achieve by going abroad remains unclear, as does the complicity of other European governments in his attempted escape, though it is known that it was arranged in part by the Swedish ambassador in Paris. But the scheme was poorly conceived from the start. Louis and his family were recognized and halted in their carriage near Varennes, close to the French border, and returned to Paris flanked by the National Guard. Henceforth, Louis was literally a prisoner of the Revolution, retained as king because he was now a hostage against the plots of the counterrevolutionaries.

From this time forward, republican sentiments grew daily, strengthened by the course of events. Louis gave public support to the Revolution and all its manifestations, but it was widely believed that he was secretly working with his supporters on foreign soil to make the invasion of France a reality. Needless to say, the capture and return of Louis and his family only increased the alarm of other European governments, and within a few months they began to move toward a more active policy against the Revolution.

The attempted defection of Louis XVI and the continued rumors of an aristocratic plot also had a profoundly unsettling effect on the political situation among the revolutionaries at home. While the middle-class leadership sought increasingly to "shut down" the Revolution, events increasingly got out of hand. The predilection of the constitution-makers of 1791 for elections and individual liberties had not made them democrats. In economic policy, for instance, they practiced a *de facto* laissez faire which mainly benefited the bourgeoisie; and in electoral politics they made a clear distinction between representative government and "mob rule" by dividing the citizenry into active and passive categories. It is also indicative of the position of the majority of the National (or Constituent) Assembly in 1790–1791 that they used the National Guard (from which "passive citizens" were specifically excluded) to put down popular disturbances and strikes, which were forbidden throughout the Revolution.

Advance of the Left

In spite of the fact that a large majority of the male adults of France were excluded by the property requirement from active political life, France was now much more democratic than England. In fact, after centuries of political impotence, a broad spectrum of the French populace was plunged into the political decision-making process. Political activism soon advanced far beyond the mere election of representatives and even beyond the electoral bodies themselves. The primary local assemblies began to meet regularly and often for the discussion of current political issues. Those who frequented them received political sustenance from the debates of the National Assembly in Paris, an ample diet of newspapers and pamphlets, and a growing number of political clubs, frequently descended from the "literary societies" of the old regime, which formed around the more important leaders and political factions of the Revolution. The fact that only a small minority of Frenchmen took a sustained interest in these avenues of political influence is irrelevant in assessing their impact—all political movements have been begun by minorities. The fact is that the crowds of Bastille Day and the other great *journées* throughout France never really retired from the political scene. The bourgeois revolution left them largely unsatisfied, and the year that followed the flight of the king was to bring repeated cause for anxiety and outrage.

By late summer 1791 the Revolution entered a new phase. On September 30 the National (or Constituent) Assembly, which had begun as the Estates General and had been in continuous session since May 1789, at last adjourned. Its place was taken, the following day, by the newly elected Legislative Assembly. The new body had 745 members, the great majority of them middle-class, many of them lawyers who had already served in the local courts and assemblies formed after May 1789. When the Legislative Assembly met, most of its members believed that the Revolution had about run its course and that, if anything, the function of the Legislative Assembly was simply to revise and refine the work already done by its predecessor. This view, however, was based on a serious misconception of the state of France. Within six months the country was plunged into a foreign war which was to last, with brief interruptions, for over twenty years—a war which led first to the overthrow of the monarchy, later to the rise of a military dictator, and finally to the most radical reconstruction of Europe since the seventeenth century.

If the new assembly opened with pious expressions of hope, its institutional problems and defects were soon revealed. To be sure, the Legislative Assembly did not seem like a radical body. Of its members, 264 declared themselves to be moderates or conservatives (*Feuillants*), who sat on the right, while only 136 announced themselves as radicals (*Cordeliers* or *Jacobins*—so named after the radical Paris clubs) and sat on the left, and 350 members remained uncommitted. But even the most radical representatives still supported the monarchy, and, on the surface at least, there was little indication of the vast changes soon to come. The principal reason why these changes could not be long delayed was that the political and social system fashioned by the middle-class revolution was, for a variety of reasons, unacceptable to large numbers of Frenchmen, and the most determined opponents of the new status quo—especially the radical Jacobins—managed before long to persuade, or to coerce, a majority of their fellow citizens to demand revolutionary policies unimaginable in 1789.

Because of the problems of the National Assembly, it had been decided almost at the last moment that none of its members should sit in the Legislative Assembly. Thus the new body, whatever its virtues, was almost completely inexperienced in dealing with national and foreign affairs, which were beginning to take an increasingly dangerous turn. Old factional groupings and chains of influence disappeared, and new ones had to be fashioned. More important, the Legislative Assembly was deprived of the able, responsible, yet forward-looking leadership of the Abbé Sieyès and other experienced politicians. Mirabeau, the leading orator of the National Assembly, had died in April 1791, thus depriving the monarchy of its most effective voice. Such ambitious radicals as Maximilien Robespierre (1758–1794), who had been an influential member of the National Assembly, now found themselves unemployed revolutionaries. But Robespierre did not retire to his provincial home and abandon politics. Instead, he remained mostly in Paris, publishing a weekly newspaper called *The Defender of the Constitution* and speaking frequently at the Jacobin Club.

These revolutionary clubs and newspapers became steadily more important as time went on; indeed, it seemed symbolic of the disintegrating political system that, before long, the clubs came to overshadow the debates of the Legislative Assembly itself. Some of the organizations were dubious about the growing radicalism—for instance, the Society of 1789, whose intellectual guide was Lafayette. But most of the clubs were strongly radical in character.

On July 12, 1789, news that the king had dismissed the popular reforming minister Necker precipitated demonstrations in Paris. Crowds gathered in the gardens of the Palais Royal to listen to radical orators. The commander of the Paris garrison withdrew his troops to the Champ de Mars on the outskirts of the city, leaving the capital in the hands of the populace. The Paris electors of the Third Estate formed a provisional city government at the Hôtel de Ville. On July 14 the Parisians, fearing royal reprisals, removed 30,000 muskets from the Hôtel des Invalides and then marched on the Bastille, the ancient fortress that overlooked the crowded Faubourg St. Antoine.

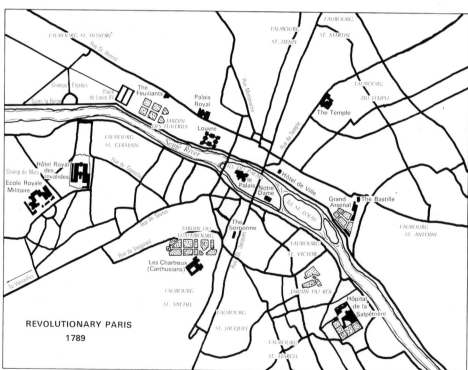

REVOLUTIONARY PARIS
1789

Most important were the Cordeliers and the Jacobins. The Society of the Friends of the Rights of Man and the Citizen was popularly known as the Cordelier Club because it met in an abandoned convent of the Cordeliers. Opened in the spring of 1790, it had as leading members Georges Jacques Danton (1759–1794), Camille Desmoulins (1760–1794), and Jacques René Hébert (1755–1794). The Society of Friends of the Constitution was known as the Jacobin Club because it met in the former convent of the Jacobins. Founded in 1789, the Jacobin Club—with a predominantly middle-class membership—was for a time fairly moderate in tone, its chief purpose being to keep a close watch on the activities of the National Assembly. In late 1790 and 1791, however, its membership grew increasingly radical, and the Jacobins became not only a national correspondence society of great effectiveness but the strongest political organization outside the government in Paris —some would say even more powerful than the government itself.

With the rise of the Cordelier and Jacobin clubs came a whole new generation of revolutionary leaders, who quickly made their mark. The most important of these was Robespierre, but hardly less important were the top members of the Cordelier Club, mentioned above, and others like Jacques Pierre Brissot (1754–1793), who rapidly became leader of the Legislative Assembly, and the Swiss-born physician Jean Paul Marat (1743–1793), founder and editor of *The Friend of the People*. Brissot and the Marquis de Condorcet (1743–1794), the famous mathematician and philosopher, were prominent among the leaders of the *Girondist* faction of the Assembly, so named because they were all from the *département* of the Gironde on the Atlantic coast.

The rise of the Cordeliers and Jacobins symbolized a steady increase in domestic radicalism and violence, actual and rhetorical. Marat's favorite remedy for every problem that ailed the country was the guillotine, invented as the latest thing in humane execution devices by a Dr. Guillotin in early 1792. For the time being, the Legislative Assembly, under Girondist leadership, proved more moderate. In late October 1791 the Assembly gave the count of Provence, younger brother of Louis XVI and later king of France as Louis XVIII (1815–1824), two months to return home on pain of forfeiting his right of succession; and in early March 1791 it demanded the immediate return of all the *émigrés*, on pain of being suspected—and presumably treated—as counterrevolutionaries. At the end of November the Assembly voted to give all nonjuring priests one week to swear allegiance to the new constitution. Louis approved the Assembly's action in regard to his brother, but he vetoed the other proposals, and this, needless to say, further inflamed the political atmosphere in Paris both inside and outside the Assembly. As the situation grew more tense, the clubs and the Parisian populace became the watchdogs of the Assembly. Eventually they would impose their will upon it.

All these developments—and especially the abortive flight of the royal family in June 1791—gave France's conservative neighbors considerable pause, and their concern was heightened by the appearance of prorevolutionary factions in a number of German cities. Although the British still pursued a policy of strict neutrality toward the Revolution, by April 1792, France was at war with Austria and Prussia. The origins of the war have long been debated, and responsibility for the conflict must doubtless be apportioned among all its participants. The Prussians and Austrians believed that the French army, demoralized by events at home, would easily be beaten. In the end, however, the war came because both Left and Right in France—most Jacobins (Robespierre and his followers conspicuously excepted) as well as the king's party—believed that they would profit from it, the radicals because they thought that a war would discredit and possibly lead to the overthrow of the monarchy, the royalists because they thought a war might well regain for Louis something like his old authority.

The war quickly brought France military defeat, rampant inflation and food shortages, the discrediting of the right wing in the Assembly, open proof of the king's treason, and a kind of national hysteria in the face of imminent disaster. In the midst of this crisis the extreme Jacobins in Paris began to import reinforcements from outside the capital—five hundred men came from Marseilles, singing what was to become the battle hymn of the French Republic, "The Marseillaise"—and on August 10 they set up the Revolutionary Commune in an insurrection that had long been carefully planned by such leaders as Danton and Desmoulins.

The creation of the Revolutionary Commune marked the beginning of the end of the monarchy. Louis had now lost control of Paris. The insurrectionists invaded the Tuileries Palace; and the king and his family took refuge with the Legislative Assembly, which—with only a third of its members present —suspended Louis from all his royal functions and called for the election of a new assembly to draw up a new constitution.

The overthrow of the monarchy was only part of the Jacobin seizure of power. An interim revolutionary government was appointed by the Assembly (with Danton as minister of justice) as Paris was swept by reports of approaching enemy armies and of uprisings by conservative peasants in the Vendée. On September 2 the revolutionary forces began the indiscriminate slaughter of political prisoners, a five-day orgy in which untold hundreds were killed. In late September, at Valmy, the French forces scored their first significant triumph over the European powers, which comprised the forces of the First Coalition, but this dramatic turn of events was not to signify a moderation of the Revolution at home. On the contrary, in the weeks and months to come, it became steadily more arbitrary, violent, and bloody.

The new assembly, called the National Convention, met for the first time on September 21, the day after the Battle of Valmy. The Convention had not been elected by anything like direct, universal manhood suffrage. Although property qualifications had been abandoned, the age limit of twenty-five had been maintained, as had the disbarment of domestic servants and the system of primary and secondary (runoff) elections. In Paris, Robespierre had arranged that the runoff elections should be public and should be held at the Jacobin Club. He, Danton, and Marat were elected members of the Convention and quickly assumed leadership of the extreme Left, known as the Mountain because the leftist delegates sat together high up in the back of the hall. The Girondists were now on the extreme Right—a good indication of how far the political balance had shifted to the Left. But for the moment the balance of power was held, at least nominally, by the so-called Plain, or Marsh—a number of independent members led by the ubiquitous Sieyès. At first inclined to support the Girondists, these center delegates moved, or were forced, increasingly to support the Mountain. The Revolution now entered its most violent phase.

The Convention lost no time in showing its true colors. On September 21, without serious debate, it abolished the monarchy; the following day was declared the first day of the new Republic. This act was only the beginning of still more dramatic things to come—the trial and execution of the king, the development of a grandly expansionist foreign policy, aggressive domestic reforms, and a death struggle between Girondists and the Mountain over control of the government and the machinery of the Terror, which was soon to dominate the country.

The first and perhaps most urgent problem was what to do with the king. Whatever his responsibility for the events of the past few years, Louis by this time had virtually no public support. Nevertheless, the Convention feared, perhaps rightly, that if he were freed, Louis might become the center of an effective counterrevolutionary movement. On December 3, therefore, the king—now called Louis Capet—was brought to trial before the Convention, and a long list of charges was presented. On January 16–17, in a twenty-four-hour session with public voting, the Convention decided by a small majority for the death penalty, which was carried out on January 21, 1793. The queen, Marie Antoinette, was executed almost nine months later, on October 16, 1793.

Although the conviction and execution of Louis XVI did not signify any immediate turning point in domestic affairs, taken together with certain other policies of the Revolution, it gravely complicated France's relations with the outside world. The most serious complication resulted from Britain's entry into the war on the side of Austria and Prussia. In 1790–1792, Britain had resisted all such involvement. But a number of developments now led to a change in this policy. One of these was the execution of the king, which caused tremendous outrage in Britain. Second were the announcements, on November 19 and December 15, 1792, that the French revolutionary regime was now prepared to "grant fraternity and aid to all peoples who wish to recover their liberty" and that "the French nation . . . will treat as an enemy of the people anyone who, refusing liberty and equality, or renouncing them, might wish to preserve, recall, or treat with the prince and the privileged castes." And just in case Britain, for one, was in any doubt as to what such decrees meant in practice, in late November 1792, France annexed both Nice and Savoy and, having meanwhile conquered the Austrian Netherlands (Belgium) and occupied Brussels, opened the Scheldt River, a serious blow to British commercial interests. War between Britain and France was now only a matter of time, and on February 1 the Convention issued the formal declaration. On March 7 the Convention declared war on Bourbon Spain. By the beginning of 1793 all Europe, save only Denmark, Russia, Sweden, Switzerland, and Turkey, was at war with France.

Now began a new series of French reverses and a further intensification of the revolutionary Terror. The Austrians retook Brussels, and General Dumouriez, perhaps the outstanding French military commander, defected to the enemy, planning to march on Paris and restore the monarchy and the Constitution of 1791. In addition, French forces had lost the Rhineland to the Prussian army and were in full retreat. It was clear that the Revolution had arrived at a great turning point and that, unless the Paris government adopted still harsher and more effective policies, the Revolution was ultimately doomed.

The crucial battleground therefore was the Convention, where in the midst of these dramatic events, at home and abroad, a violent power struggle was being carried on. The Right had been declining in numbers and influence since the beginning of the Revolution, in the country at large as well as in the Assembly meeting in Paris, and by the spring of 1793 the Convention as a whole was considerably more radical than its predecessors. However, though the right wing of the Convention, the Gironde, had often appealed to the Paris *sans-culottes* to overthrow opposition, the Girondists were basically bourgeois in outlook, favoring the retention of the loose federalism of the Constitution of 1791 and drawing their support from the provinces rather than from Paris. In addition, they opposed economic regulations at a time when the *assignats* dipped to 22 per cent of their face value, producing uncontrolled inflation along with the already severe food shortages.

Members of the left wing of the Convention, the Mountain, were closely associated with the Jacobin clubs, which had spread throughout France. The Jacobins, who looked to Paris for their political strength, advocated a far more highly centralized government than the Girondists and were much more willing to accept the economic restrictions demanded by the poor, for whose support they competed with the ultraradical *Enragés* ("madmen") and Cordeliers. Their success laid the foundation for the democratic phase of the Revolution.

The majority of the National Convention, the Plain or Marsh, was committed to neither the Gironde nor the Mountain. Both had to court these independents to achieve a majority. The struggle between the two factions grew steadily for weeks and months and was finally resolved, not by majority vote, but by another Parisian insurrection, which began in late May 1793. Early on the morning of June 2 the revolutionary committee now controlling Paris surrounded the Convention, put forth a sweeping program of political and social change (including restriction of the franchise to *sans-culottes*), and demanded the immediate surrender of all Girondist deputies. Henceforth, the Mountain had a secure majority, but ultimate power was lodged in the Paris mob, whose fanaticism was unappeasable.

The Jacobin Revolution

The most significant difference between the government of the Jacobins and its predecessors was the centralization of decision-making, administrative, and judicial functions, which brought the discipline that had hitherto been lacking. The vehicle for this centralization was the Committee of Public Safety, dominated from July 1793 by Robespierre and the Mountain. There can be no doubt that this emergency government commanded the respect of the Convention. Only such a government could have made the hard decisions necessary to halt the downward plunge of the value of the *assignat*, stop the rise of prices, restore order to the French army, which was being driven ignominiously backwards, and assure the destruction of an effective opposition to the radical Republic.

From July on, the Committee, which was elected and reelected every month by the Convention, also included Louis Saint-Just and Bertrand Barère, a notable orator who was frequently the Committee's spokesman. In August, Lazare Carnot, an able mathematician and army officer (later known as "the organizer of victory"), was elected.

One of the first moves of the Convention, following the May-June insurrection, was to replace the Constitution of 1791. More democratic in outlook and less generous with provincial autonomy than its predecessor, the new constitution never went into effect. It was quickly set aside pending the reestablishment of public order.

The fact of the matter is that the Convention and the Committee of Public Safety had far more pressing concerns than the introduction of still another form of government. The government was under continuous pressure from the *sans-culottes* and the *Enragés*, and parts of France were rising in what seemed like counterrevolutionary rebellion. Twenty Girondist deputies escaped from Paris to Normandy, raised an army, and prepared to march on Paris. An anti-Jacobin revolt broke out in Brittany; Bordeaux, Lyons, and Marseilles revolted against the Paris regime. By June over sixty *départements* had risen against the government. And in mid-July one of the most voluble and bitterly hated Mountain deputies, Jean Paul Marat, was murdered in his bath by a quiet young woman from Normandy, who thought she was helping save her country from further bloodshed. Instead, the assassination merely created a new political legend. Before long, the Mountain was more fully in power than ever, and Maximilien Robespierre was the most powerful man in France.

Robespierre's career as a revolutionary in many ways paralleled the course of the Revolution itself. In 1774, as the best Latin student in his school, he had delivered a welcoming speech to Louis XVI, then on his way to assume the throne at Versailles. In 1789, as a successful lawyer in the provincial town of Arras, he managed to be elected a deputy to the Estates General. In the early days of the Revolution he became one of the leading left-of-center members of the National Assembly, opposing the institution of the death penalty, the property qualification for holding office, and the retention of slavery in the colonies. He also opposed many of the nondemocratic elements of the Constitution of 1791, but he voted for the document as a whole and named his weekly paper *The Defender of the Constitution*. During the year when he was not a member of the Assembly (October 1791 to September 1792), his influence with the Parisian *sans-culottes* and the Jacobin Club steadily increased. His oratorical ability, democratic ideas, incorruptibility, genuine sympathy for the poor, and, above all, his energetic devotion to the politics of the Revolution provided the basis for his growing power in revolutionary circles.

As leader of the Committee of Public Safety, Robespierre supervised all of its operations, and these rapidly expanded to include most of the policy-making and enforcement activities of the government. He was also the Committee's spokesman in the Assembly, where the Mountain and its supporters in the Plain backed its actions, and his incredible schedule allowed for frequent speeches at the Jacobin Club, which had become the center of extraparliamentary political debate. The Committee contributed to the club's influence by restricting the political activities of the revolutionary neighborhood groups in Paris and by instituting strict control of the press. The Cordelier Club survived until the spring of 1794, when it was charged with "insurrectionary activity" and summarily closed down.

Although the brutal methods of the Committee of Public Safety have long obscured other aspects of its rule in modern historical accounts, its positive contribution to the survival of the Revolution was considerable. It took measures to end economic chaos and to quiet the accompanying unrest of the poor. In September 1793 the limited price control on bread, the so-called "law of the Maximum," was extended to virtually all essential commodities. Wages were reduced and frozen. But these economic controls were difficult to enforce and proved generally ineffective. More successful were efforts designed to put more land in the hands of the peasants. The lands of the *émigrés* were put up for auction in lots of two or three acres, and peasants were allowed to pay in small installments. In July 1793 the Committee also formalized what had long been a reality by abolishing whatever debts or obligations the peasants still owed their landlords.

The administrative system was also drastically revised, with the aim of increasing centralized control. The Committee sent out "representatives on mission" to the *départements* and to the army, to oversee the enforcement of its decrees throughout France. The principle of local autonomy had always caused great difficulties. Now, with large parts of the country in open armed revolt, the revolutionary armies and the Committee representatives were used to subdue the countryside.

The enactments of the Convention marked a dramatic and far-reaching break with prerevolutionary society, and the Committee of Public Safety and the Terror were the main agents of that break. Robespierre himself, as well as his colleagues, had undergone a great change in outlook since the early days of the Revolution, when they had been firm defenders of the "imprescriptible rights of man." The French nation was at war for its life, and those who corrupted or subverted it were treated as public enemies, swiftly, mercilessly, and — not infrequently — indiscriminately. The guillotine became the sword of the Revolution, used to strike down those who sought the return of aristocracy, clericalism, or the monarchy, those who vitiated the Revolution by hoarding food or otherwise violating the economic regulations, and those who fought against the power of Robespierre and the Committee of Public Safety. The number actually executed has sometimes been exaggerated, but it is reliably estimated that more than fourteen thousand were convicted by the "courts" of the Terror, and untold thousands more died in prison or were done away with without a semblance of "revolutionary justice." Subsidiary committees of public safety extended the Terror throughout the French countryside. It is generally agreed, however, that the main victims were not aristocrats, nonjuring priests, or other easily marked "enemies of the Republic." On the contrary, as the important work of Donald Greer has shown, 31 per cent were members of the working class, 28 per cent peasants, and only 8 per cent members of the nobility and 7 per cent members of the clergy.

The radical turn taken by the Revolution under the Convention, the Committee of Public Safety, and the Terror had as profound an impact on French society ideologically as it had in the institutions of government. In 1789 the revolutionaries had had no significant republican sentiment, just as they had had no designs on constituted religion. But the course of the Revolution led to the development of a vehement republicanism and anticlericalism to match the egalitarian sentiments of the Mountain. The concepts of nationalism and of citizenship in the modern sense became the ruling passions of the Paris mobs and the revolutionary armies, as well as the guiding principles of the deputies in the Assembly. Their consciousness that a fundamental change was taking place, or their desire that such a change should take place, is exemplified in their rejection of a variety of social and institutional symbols of the old regime. For instance, the traditional form of address, *monsieur* and *madame*, was replaced by *citoyen* and *citoyenne*. Even the Gregorian calendar of the old regime was abolished. The Convention introduced an enormously involved new calendar which began with the birth of the Republic; the months, consisting of ten-day weeks, were renamed after seasonal qualities —for instance, *Germinal* (month of budding), *Brumaire* (month of frost), *Thermidor* (month of heat).

Loyalty to the nation became a requirement for citizenship and legal protection. Conversely, "aristocratic sentiments"—denial of the concept of human equality and fraternity—represented a danger to the nation. The French revolutionary armies went to war to bring liberty to other people, and their struggle became a crusade of liberty, equality, and fraternity against monarchy, aristocracy, and superstition. A few years before, war had been a matter of concern to the king and his professional army and possibly to taxpayers; universal military conscription, the *levée en masse*, symbolized the advent of total war between the French people and the despised old order at home and abroad.

The high point of the attempt to build a revolutionary ideology was the Cult of the Supreme Being, instituted in the spring of 1794 under Robespierre's sponsorship. Faced with a counterrevolutionary Church on the one hand and growing antireligious sentiment at the other extreme, Robespierre and his associates tried to create a new state religion, a "Republic of Virtue" based on the dual foundation of reason and the state, a moral order designed to create the ideal citizen, and sufficient pomp and pageantry to appeal to the masses. Festivals were to be established celebrating the Supreme Being, nature, liberty and equality, the Republic, truth, modesty, patriotism, love, agriculture, industry, old age, happiness, and so on. On June 8, 1794, the Festival of the Supreme Being was celebrated, featuring the crowning of the Goddess of Reason, a parade in which Robespierre had a featured place, and the singing of patriotic hymns.

The new revolutionary religion came as a profound shock to many Frenchmen; it was sacrilege to the faithful and superstition to those who rejected religion altogether. While it is evidence of Robespierre's profound understanding of the nature of the Revolution, it was a political mistake. It heightened popular consciousness of the radicalism of those in power and gave strength to the growing suspicion that Robespierre was a demagogue who intended to become dictator of France.

In early 1794 the Terror entered a new phase. Its domestic enemies, largely divided, without coherent philosophy or effective battle plan, were being systematically and brutally reduced. By September, Bordeaux surrendered; in October the rebels in the Vendée suffered the first of a series of crushing defeats; and in December government forces took over Lyons, renamed it *Ville Affranchie* (Liberated City), and butchered thousands of innocent people. France's foreign enemies, too, were suffering a series of damaging defeats. In December 1793, French troops occupied the important Rhenish towns of Worms and Speyer, and the British were forced to evacuate the naval base at Toulon by French forces that included a rising young Corsican officer named Napoleon Bonaparte.

But the butchery involved in the victories of the Terror — in Nantes alone, recaptured by government forces in October, fifteen thousand people were reportedly executed — led to an increasing revulsion against it. Moreover, if many people benefited by the Terror's economic and social policies, countless others resented the new restrictions and the stringent administrative regimentation, reminiscent of the old regime they had thought was gone forever. It soon became clear that the country was in no mood for permanent revolution.

Yet the most serious threat to the continuance of the Terror stemmed from the fear, anxiety, and suspicion that increasingly gripped the top revolutionary leadership. By the autumn and winter of 1793–1794 the Revolution was steadily devouring its own. In October 1793, Brissot and several Girondist leaders were executed, along with other eminent revolutionaries of the more moderate persuasion. Until early 1794 Robespierre had avoided taking action against other members of the top leadership in the Convention, the Paris Commune (which largely dominated the Convention), and the Committee of Public Safety, but it was in the revolutionary nature of things that such a frontal attack could not be indefinitely delayed. Believing that the greatest menace to his position came from the extreme Left — the Hébertists — he first turned on their leading representatives, including Hébert himself, who was quickly arrested, tried, convicted, and executed along with more than a dozen others. Having thus rid himself of his left-wing opponents, he turned on his moderate adversaries, the Dantonists. Scarcely a week after the execution of the Hébertists, Danton and his leading supporters, including Camille Desmoulins, were arrested on largely trumped-up charges, quickly sentenced to death, and guillotined.

The judicial murder of the Dantonists seemed to leave Robespierre supreme if not secure, especially since the mayor of Paris was now also a Robespierrist and the Revolutionary Tribunal was fully in his hands. But Robespierre had passed the zenith of his power. Following the guillotining of the Hébertists, there was a notable relaxation in the social fervor of the Robespierrist machine, and this, in turn, led to a growing disaffection among the workers, who saw their wages controlled while prices continued to rise. In the end, however, it was not the long-suffering French masses who brought down Robespierre but the leading members of the Mountain and some of his close associates on the Committee of Public Safety, who were, perhaps not unjustifiably, beginning to wonder about their personal safety. In a stormy address to the Convention on July 26, Robespierre demanded still other purges, including one of the Committee of Public Safety itself, but the next day he was arrested at a meeting of the Convention. A Paris rising to save him failed to materialize; he tried unsuccessfully to shoot himself; and on July 28 (10 Thermidor in the Revolutionary calendar), Robespierre was guillotined in the center of Paris along with his brother, Saint-Just, and eighteen others. In the next two days over eighty members of the Commune met the same fate. The climax of the Revolution had come and gone.

IV REACTION AND MODERATION

The Thermidorians

The Convention had finally overthrown Robespierre not to save the Terror but to save itself. Whether the Thermidorians had planned it or not—and all indications are that they had not—the fall of Robespierre soon led to a dismantling of those instruments and policies most characteristic of the Terror. The overthrow of the Jacobin machine came by bits and pieces, but it was none the less decisive. The power of the radical revolution had become centralized in the Committee of Public Safety, and when that center was effectively subordinated to the Convention, the forces of the Left were divided and largely impotent. The Convention was now dominated by middle-class moderates, and a few leaders of the early phase of the Revolution reappeared to take control of the government. Bereft of power, the surviving leaders of 1793 and 1794 did well to stay alive as reaction against the "terrorists" mounted.

During his last months in power, opposition to Robespierre had been focused largely on alleviating the excesses of the Terror, abandoning restrictive economic policies, paying more attention to the rights of property, and reducing the power of the Parisian *sans-culottes*. These remained the distinguishing characteristics of the more moderate, middle-class governments which were to hold sway—albeit largely ineffectively and only with the assistance of military force—until Napoleon's coup d'état in November 1799.

In line with the new policies, price control was first of all drastically watered down in October 1794 and then completely abolished in December. The result was uncontrollable inflation, which soon destroyed the *assignat* altogether. This economic crisis produced extremely acute distress among the poor. Much of the time the urban population, especially in Paris, found it impossible to obtain an adequate supply of food at any price, although attempts were made to provide the capital with rationed food at reasonable prices. Agitation was resumed in Paris for economic controls and lower prices; once more the city tried to exert a direct influence on the Convention in matters of vital interest. This time, however, conditions were very different than they had been in 1793 or even in 1791. With French armies victorious abroad and most enemies of the Revolution either dead, in exile, or still discreetly silent, the Thermidorians were much less vulnerable than their predecessors, even in the face of mounting economic crisis and popular unrest. The political atmosphere of the Paris districts, or sections, had also changed. Many activists of the early days of the Revolution had joined the army or been given government jobs as a reward for their labors; they were no longer available for the continuous sessions of an earlier time. Moreover, the Thermidorians had the army and a large gang of foppish young men, the notorious *jeunesse dorée* (gilded youths), who could be brought to bear in case of any armed resistance.

At the end of March 1795 conditions in the city had become explosive, and on April 1 parts of Paris rose once more in protest. This time, however, when the crowd—consisting largely of women and children—surrounded the Convention and filled the hall with cries for "bread and the Constitution of 1793," they were quickly dispersed without obtaining any relief whatever. By the next day troops had been brought in to prevent a recurrence of the incident.

To complicate matters still further, a new "White Terror" of vengeance on the radicals broke out in Lyons and at Aix, and in late May and early June this violence spread to other cities, including Avignon and Marseilles. The Convention suddenly recognized that it was in renewed danger from both Jacobins and royalists. On May 20 a large mob, including royalists as well as substantial numbers of working men and women, invaded the Convention, killed one deputy, and enabled a disaffected minority to approve the creation of still another "provisional government." By May 23, however, the Convention had called up twenty thousand reserves from the provinces, and the insurrection was finally stamped out. This time government response was much more severe. The leaders of the Parisian *sans-culottes* were proscribed, and the *sans-culottes* were no longer capable of acting as a political force. "The 'popular' phase of the Revolution was over."[2]

The ability of the Convention of Thermidor to handle the new risings in this manner was ample evidence of the shifting balance of power in the country. Along with the radicals purged from the Convention, the radicals of the Parisian sections were progressively displaced by more moderate men. In addition, the sections themselves were reorganized and largely disarmed. In November 1794 the Jacobin Club in Paris was ordered closed by the Convention. As penalties against aristocrats and other *émigrés* were dropped—one decree of the Convention restored the property of the victims of revolutionary tribunals to their surviving relatives—and the Terror abated, many who had been waiting beyond the borders of France returned. It was not long before royalism provided a new threat to the revolutionary government.

Those who had been victimized by the Terror wasted no time in getting their revenge on their former persecutors once that became possible. In Paris and most of the rest of France, executions as such were kept to a minimum, but the former "terrorists" were often subjected to imprisonment and exile. In addition, a reactionary mob rule was often visited against them. The *jeunesse dorée* roamed the streets of Paris, carrying out a revolutionary justice of their own against the radicals. In the countryside similar roving bands often took such names as "Companies of the Son" and "Companies of Jesus."

Murders and seizures of property by reactionaries took a more organized form in those parts of France, especially the south and west, which had a long history of antirevolutionary sentiment. In those areas a massive return of *émigrés* supplemented the large number of people bent on revenge on the

2. George Rudé, *Revolutionary Europe 1783–1815.* New York: Harper, 1964, pp. 166–167.

"terrorists." This "White Terror" often took the form of mass trials and executions on a scale at least equal to the "Red Terror" of the past. The campaign of vengeance lasted for about a year and shocked even the Thermidorians at Paris, although the Convention, many of whose members approved or accepted the counterrevolutionary activity, did nothing to stop it.

If the Convention had ever doubted that the country needed a new constitution, that doubt was removed by the events of the spring of 1795. Accordingly, the Convention set to work to produce still another fundamental law. The government of the Thermidorians was formalized in the Constitution of the Year III, enacted in August 1795. The experience of the last two years had not been lost on its authors, who clearly defined the limits which were to be put upon liberty and equality and carefully buttressed the rights of property. A new Thermidorian Declaration of the Rights of Man and the Citizen stressed the middle-class doctrine that men were equal in the sense that everyone was subject to the same laws. "The obligations of each individual toward Society," it declared, "consist of defending it, serving it, living subject to the laws, and respecting those who are the agents thereof." The constitution also outlined the laissez-faire economic policy which was to persist under the bourgeois government of the Directory.

France under the Directory

The new constitution created yet another electoral system for France, a variation of the Constitution of 1791. In contrast with the outgoing Convention, the new legislature was to have two houses. The upper chamber, appropriately called the Council of Elders, had 250 members, all over forty years old. It had the power to enact legislation proposed by the lower chamber and to elect members of the executive, called the Directory, from those the lower chamber nominated. The lower chamber, called the Council of the Five Hundred, was composed of men over thirty years old. It had the right to initiate legislation and to nominate members of the Directory.

The Directory was a committee of five men, responsible for the administrative functions of the government. A five-member executive would have made effective decision-making difficult under the best of circumstances, but the particular problems of the government of the Directory magnified the inherent difficulties. The government after Thermidor was based on a coalition of all the moderate groups that favored the Revolution, excluding only monarchists and terrorists. Consequently, the membership of the Directory was always the result of a compromise worked out among the different factions, a circumstance that precluded unanimity. In addition, the Directory was prohibited from drawing its ministers from the legislative body, and this restriction prevented it from ever exercising a decisive influence in the legislature. The Directory would never approach the highly efficient administration achieved by the Committee of Public Safety under Robespierre, but, then, the aim of the Constitution of the Year III was to save France from the rule of another Robespierre.

Though the terms of the new constitution were distinctly moderate, the response that it evoked and the results it produced were not. France continued to be deeply divided between royalists and revolutionaries, and a well-founded fear that the next election would produce a strongly royalist majority led the outgoing Convention to vote that about two thirds of its members should also be members of the new legislature. In the end, the country voted to approve the new constitution, but all save one section of Paris voted against it. These areas of the capital were in no mood to accept the new basic law without a fight, and on October 5 (13 Vendémiaire) still another insurrection broke out in Paris, this one largely led by royalists. Though overwhelmingly outnumbered, forces defending the beleaguered assembly managed to beat back the attack, largely because of the skilled use of artillery—the famous "whiff of grapeshot" directed by the second in command, young Napoleon Bonaparte, who had already made his mark at the capture of Toulon. On October 26, 1795, the Convention at last adjourned, having renewed the legislation against both *émigrés* and nonjuring priests, voted amnesty to all save the latest insurrectionists, and—as perhaps its most optimistic gesture—renamed the *Place de la Révolution* the *Place de la Concorde*.

Thus ended one of the most turbulent eras in French and indeed in European and world history. But the quiet and respite that most Frenchmen now doubtless craved were not to follow. With French armies now invading foreign soil instead of defending their own, the Directory faced major problems: the recurrent economic crisis; the growing strength of the royalist supporters of the count of Provence, who assumed the title of Louis XVIII following the death of the imprisoned son of Louis XVI in 1795; and the increasing power of the army, whose successes were creating popular leaders with large numbers of troops at their disposal.

By early 1796 the Directory was confronted with a resurgence of the lower-class unrest that had already done so much to change the history of France. That social discontent should have risen anew at this time is hardly surprising. By February 1796 the *assignat* had become practically worthless, prices had hit new highs, and the squalid displays of the recently enriched, together with the moral debauchery of this period, were bound to outrage impoverished workingmen. In the spring of 1796 François Émile Babeuf, a minor official under the old regime and a revolutionary journalist since, organized the "Society of the Equals," based upon a small, secret, revolutionary group that was to institute a communistic society. Babeuf's conspiracy—which included former "terrorists" of all kinds—was short-lived, though it has since been given an important place in the French revolutionary tradition. It was soon betrayed to the government, and the Directory moved swiftly against it. Babeuf himself was tried and guillotined in May 1797.

Babeuf's death ended the threat to the power of the Directory from the extreme Left—particularly significant because Babeuf advocated socialist principles that were to be very important in the nineteenth and twentieth centuries. But the Directory's position remained precarious. Royalist sentiment ran deep in French society, buttressed by the wounded religious feelings of the peasantry, the loyalties of the growing body of returned *émigrés*, and the military and conspiratorial forces of the counterrevolution within and outside France. Royalists were the principal winners in the spring elections of 1797, and the Directors retained power only by the coup of 18 Fructidor (September 4), carried out with the help of the National Guard, commanded by General Bonaparte's deputy. The seating of the new royalist delegates was barred, and repressive measures against royalists and *émigrés* were renewed. When the Jacobins gained electoral victories in 1798, the government quashed the elections and secured the return of their own candidates.

Throughout these electoral maneuverings and coups, the Directory continued its unspectacular efforts to put the country on a sounder governmental and economic basis. Government spending was sharply reduced, reforms were undertaken in the assessment and collection of taxes, and more than a little dent was made in France's financial problems. The refurbishing of the army was effected by the introduction of the first truly universal conscription system in Europe. The plentiful harvests of 1796–1798 at last put an end to the food shortage and the exorbitant prices that shortage produced. But the Directory still operated upon a very shaky political base, which tended to become increasingly narrow as time went on. Finally, in November 1799, the Directory was replaced by a new political system that essentially consisted of Napoleon's military dictatorship.

The effectiveness of the government of the Directory has been much debated by historians. Whatever its achievements at home or abroad, there can be little doubt that it failed to bring political stability to France. Unable to obtain a genuine electoral mandate for their policies, the Directors even lacked sufficient power of their own to engage in effective repressive measures without the assistance of the army. By the autumn of 1799 the army was the most important single political body in France.

V THE ARMED REVOLUTION: NAPOLEONIC EUROPE

The Nation in Arms

It is often pointed out that one of the products of the French Revolution was nationalism in the modern sense. Citizenship and the concept of the "nation in arms" (the forerunner of what is now referred to as total mobilization) were products of this intense nationalist feeling. The nationalism of the French Revolution had two meanings to contemporaries. In the first place, it implied the nation, or "the people," as opposed to the king, the nobility, the Church, or other special corporate groups. In that sense the defense of the nation meant the defense of the constitution, of legal equality and the rights of citizenship. And from the beginning the nationalism of the Revolution was an exportable commodity which French armies carried with them to neighboring peoples. Thus the cause of the French people became the cause of all people against the forces of reaction and privilege. At the same time, however, the war was a national struggle between France and the rest of Europe, especially between France and England. Thus, this second aspect of the nationalism of the French Revolution contributed to the continuation of the long series of eighteenth-century wars that had preceded it.

When the war between France and the allied powers first broke out in April 1792, the National Assembly had declared that it was merely "the just defense of a free people against the unjust aggression of a king." But it is difficult to believe that the foreign minister, Dumouriez, who had been one of the leading French generals in the Seven Years' War, did not envisage the coming of a new war as a golden opportunity to make up for the catastrophic losses France had suffered in the wars of the 1750's and 1760's by annexing territory on the northern and eastern frontiers. French expansion, occupation, and administration followed roughly the same pattern, whether in Belgium, the Rhineland, or Italy. In each area, the arrival of French troops would be followed by the organization of Jacobin clubs composed of French officers and reliable local representatives; and, in most instances, one of the first requests of the new organization would be for the territory to be incorporated into the French Republic. Sometimes, of course, the French take-over proved short-lived. For instance, the French occupied Belgium in 1792 but were driven out the following year. When they came back in 1794, they made even less pretense of consulting the wishes of the local population. Thus in foreign policy, as in its centralizing tendencies at home, the Revolution seemed more and more an extension of the old regime.

Surface appearances, of course, often gave a rather different impression. For instance, under the Directory the first concept of nationalism was reflected in the formation of a group of sister republics in Belgium, Switzerland, and Italy, where local "patriots" abolished feudal privileges and established centralized states on the model of the French Constitution of 1795. But not even the clever propaganda of the Revolution could completely disguise its ultimate aims. As time went on, its nationalism inspired the demand that France spread out to its "natural frontiers"—the Alps, the Pyrenees, and the Rhine. This nationalism led to the annexation and exploitation of surrounding territories in the interest of the Republic. France was therefore not only ideologically subversive in the eyes of European monarchs; its foreign policies violently upset the balance of power. While in the early 1790's the British government was not greatly concerned about French revolutionary slogans, Britain could never accept the extension of French control to the Low

In 1795—after three years of near-disastrous campaigning—the citizen armies of France could claim to have more than held their own against Austria, Prussia, England, and Holland. Now some of their gains were re-cognized. The Austrian Netherlands (today Belgium) and the left bank of the Rhine remained in French hands; the Batavian Republic (formerly Holland) became the first of many satellite states.

Countries, for both military and economic reasons. Similarly, Austria could not accept French domination of northern Italy, and neither Britain nor Austria would accept French hegemony on the Continent.

It is difficult to see how Britain and its Continental allies could ever have concluded a lasting peace with France until something like the frontiers of 1789 or even 1791 were restored. The accession to power of Napoleon Bonaparte, France's youngest and most brilliantly successful general, in late 1799 dashed any hopes for such a restoration.

The Rise of Napoleon

The internal difficulties of the Directory and the unsatisfactory course of the war, especially on the northern and eastern fronts, in Belgium and the Rhineland, finally produced a military dictatorship in France. While the coup d'état of November 1799 was from one point of view simply the triumph of a rising military genius, Napoleon Bonaparte, in the broader sense it was the logical outcome of the developments within and outside France since 1795. In his *Reflections on the Revolution in France*, published in 1790, Edmund Burke, the English political theorist, had predicted that the French Revolution would wind up as some kind of military dictatorship. It seems quite likely that had not Napoleon been France's man of destiny, his place might have been taken by one of his leading military colleagues.

The career of Napoleon epitomizes in many ways what was a general development between 1792 and 1799. Although French military theorists had long recognized the need for a citizen army to replace the country's largely mercenary forces, it was only after the outbreak of war in 1792 that the French army was reconstructed and molded into the most effective fighting force in Europe. With the coming of the Revolution in 1789, the old professional army based upon an aristocratic officer corps and professional enlisted men gradually disintegrated (by 1792 only a third of the officers still retained their commands). Not surprisingly, many of the noble officers were among the most determined opponents of the revolutionary government; even those who supported it at first, like Lafayette, were eventually alienated from the Revolution.

The establishment of a National Guard changed the structure of the army at its lower levels, with patriotic volunteers serving alongside the old professionals. In its final form the two elements were assimilated into a generally effective and enthusiastic fighting force in the service of the Republic. At one point, the officers were elected, and in the summer of 1793 the Paris Commune even created an *armée révolutionnaire*, composed largely of *sansculottes*, to try to assure an adequate supply of food for the city of Paris. But these radical experiments did not long survive. On the contrary, nineteen of Napoleon's marshals had served in the old Bourbon army—nine as officers, ten as privates or noncommissioned officers—and only a handful had been civilians before the Revolution.

But if the leadership of the French army—the instrument that changed the face of Europe after the 1790's—showed, on the whole, a remarkable continuity, the man who was to direct that army and the fortunes of France from 1799 to early 1815 was an outstanding example of the changes the Revolution had wrought. Before 1789 it would have been unthinkable that a man of Napoleon's background and position should ever have reached the very top of French politics and diplomacy. He had begun his career as one of the rare outsiders allowed to enter officer training under the old regime. Born in Corsica in August 1769, he was the son of a petty nobleman of Genovese birth. Corsica had been annexed by France only a year before Bonaparte was born, and Napoleon only gradually came to think of himself as French. In fact, he was never able to forget his origins completely, even when he had conquered most of Europe.

Napoleon attended various French military academies between 1779 and 1784 (graduating forty-second in a class of fifty-eight) and soon became a lieutenant in the artillery. Like other poor army officers, he welcomed the

Revolution. On June 20, 1792, he witnessed the incident of the Tuileries. When Louis XVI offered no resistance, young Bonaparte is said to have exclaimed: *"Che coglione!"* ("What a fool!"). Actually, his own revolutionary efforts had got nowhere. At Easter 1792 he had made an abortive attempt to seize his native town, and in the spring of 1793 he made similarly unsuccessful efforts.

After that, Napoleon and his family fled to mainland France. In December 1793 he played an important role in the government's recapture of Toulon, and in early October 1795 — after a setback following the overthrow of Robespierre, when Napoleon was suspended and for a time placed under arrest — the head of the Thermidorian army, in a moment of desperation, drafted him to help put down the attempted coup of Vendémiaire in Paris. A week later he was reinstated in the army as a major general, and in late October 1795 he was appointed commander-in-chief of the Army of the Interior. There can be no doubt that Napoleon combined a striking mastery of the latest principles of warfare with a consummate grasp of political maneuvering (in March 1791 he married Josephine de Beauharnais, the widow of a revolutionary general), and it was these skills that made him, before long, a superb general in Italy and, within a few years, master of France itself.

Despite continued turmoil at home, France's international position had been strengthened during the Directory, while that of its principal foreign adversaries — especially Britain and Austria — had become increasingly difficult. This state of affairs aided Napoleon considerably once he began his operations in Italy in April 1796. He was further assisted by the fact that, in the two decades immediately preceding the Revolution, the French had developed improved armaments and a strategy of battle based upon rapid maneuvering and the sudden massing of units to attack with maximum force. Napoleon proved to be a genius at applying this strategy in Italy, with the result that the Austrians, in October 1797, were forced to sign the Treaty of Campo Formio. This treaty was at the same time evidence of Austria's isolation and weakness and of Napoleon's determination to reconstruct the whole conquered area pretty much as he pleased. It went far beyond the limited rearrangements characteristic of most earlier eighteenth-century peace settlements and largely ignored the explicit desires of his government at home.

Napoleon's most important creation in Italy was the Cisalpine Republic, which included such "liberated" cities as Bologna, Ferrara, Modena, and Parma, as well as Lombardy (including Milan) and certain parts of Venetian and papal territory. To be sure, these "revolutionary republics" were by no means fully loyal to Napoleon or to revolutionary France, and it required repeated French intervention before they became fully pliant and assumed the territorial form they held until the fall of the Napoleonic kingdom in Italy in 1814.

The Italian campaign and the Treaty of Campo Formio also illustrate the difficulties that developed in the relations between the Directory at Paris and the generals in the field. The Directory and its civilian representatives favored the use of Italy as a pawn to be traded to Austria for concessions along the Rhine. They were opposed to the establishment of satellite republics in Italy, which was precisely the policy that Napoleon and other military leaders favored.

Napoleon's victories in Italy allowed him not only to flout the wishes of the Directory and to impose his own policies in the areas he conquered but also to wield considerable influence in Paris itself. His victories produced a steady stream of revenue that helped to keep the struggling Directory afloat. At the same time, Napoleon became virtually independent, since he supported his army with the proceeds of his victories. His troops were among the best paid in the French service, and they fully appreciated their dynamic leader. Besides establishing his own policies in the areas he conquered, he even carried on his own negotiations with foreign powers. Indeed, the Treaty of Campo Formio was the result of Napoleon's personal negotiation and the fulfillment of his policies, not those of the Directory. Under these circumstances, it was hardly surprising that Napoleon was able both to impose his views on the civilian government and to build his popularity in France to new heights.

It was after his striking victories in Italy that Napoleon rendered indispensable service to the Directors by using his men to disperse a crowd hostile to the coup d'état of September 1797. While Napoleon often ignored the government he had temporarily saved, he also knew when it was time to cooperate with the Directory. He went out of his way to cultivate a close relationship with certain influential men in the government, and this relationship enabled him to obtain considerable leeway in regard to policies in which he was especially interested. In 1798 the Directory approved his grand strategy for a mortal blow against Britain and its empire. Napoleon decided to strike at the British lifeline to India by launching a massive attack on Egypt.

The Egyptian campaign began spectacularly enough. In addition to an enormous military and naval force, Napoleon brought with him a number of outstanding scholars, scientists, and other experts, for this was to be a cultural expedition almost as much as a military campaign. Eluding the British naval forces under Admiral Nelson, Napoleon captured the British-controlled island of Malta by surprise attack, landed in Egypt on July 1, and took Alexandria the following day. Before the end of the month Cairo had also fallen into his hands. But then disaster struck. On August 1 Nelson caught the French fleet at anchor at Abukir, east of Alexandria, and almost wiped it out. By the following summer Napoleon realized that his Egyptian venture was a hopeless dead end, and in late August 1799 he slipped away in great secrecy to return to France, which was then in the midst of a protracted series of coups and countercoups.

While Napoleon was tasting disaster in Egypt, the forces of the Directory were successfully fighting the armies of the Second Coalition, headed by

Britain and Russia. In October 1799 the Russians, disgusted with the lack of effective cooperation among the allies, withdrew from the coalition altogether. Yet France was desperately tired of war, and the French people wanted a government that promised stability and peace, not one that stood for continued uncertainty at home and adventure abroad, as the Directory appeared to do.

This feeling was a powerful factor in Napoleon's favor. He had been out of the country for fifteen months, and he was greeted as a conquering hero when he landed in France. The people simply did not know what had happened to him in the Near East, and perhaps they would not have cared. His landing coincided with the low point in the fortunes of the Directory. Sieyès, looking for a cooperative general to assist in yet another coup d'état, recognized that the logical candidate was at hand, and within a month Napoleon had his golden opportunity to seize the reins of power.

Perhaps the only thing that was clear when Napoleon returned to France was that the Directory, as then constituted, could not long survive. If the coup d'état that brought Napoleon to power—or at least within striking distance of full and effective power—had a new and different quality from that of previous overturns, it was that this particular change was made at the top and not from below or from the outside. It seems likely that the Directors —especially the most influential ones, Barras and Sieyès—wanted merely to protect themselves and their future, and Sieyès, of course, had long fancied himself as a clever political theorist and intriguer. A moderate in the early phases of the Revolution, he had survived the Terror and now hoped to win further unspecified powers with the help of the army. Instead, Napoleon used Sieyès and the coup d'état to establish himself in power.

The coup of 18 Brumaire, as it is known, was carried out, on November 9–10, 1799, with hardly enough polish to give the new government even the facade of legality. It was presented as an attempt to forestall still another Jacobin plot, making necessary what was by now a familiar solution, a purge of the legislature. Napoleon almost panicked at the crucial moment, but his brother Lucien, who was president of the lower chamber, saved the situation for the plotters with the help of the Paris garrison. Napoleon now took the title of First Consul, but in fact he had all the power. On December 24, 1799, a new constitution was completed. Thereupon, Napoleon held a plebiscite to obtain popular approval for the document. The people did not disappoint him, approving it by a vote of three million for and 1562 against.

Bonapartism

The Constitution of the Year VIII, as it was called, was the fourth and last constitution of the Revolution and the first of the Napoleonic era. It called for an involved system of checks and balances, but it omitted the elaborate declarations of rights and duties incorporated in previous revolutionary constitutions, including instead such revealing articles as one providing that "in case of armed revolt or disturbances threatening the security of the state, the law may suspend the authority of the Constitution wherever and for whatever length of time it determines." In effect, power was vested in three consuls, who formed the executive branch of government. Napoleon made very sure that the consuls did not have equal status; as First Consul he had effective control of essential aspects of policy-making, administration, and justice. In addition, the federalist tendencies of the Directory were replaced by a highly centralized administrative system. Henceforth, elected officials in the provinces and the local assemblies had only advisory power; administration, tax collection, and other government functions were carried out by men appointed by the central government and responsible to it. The Consulate restricted elections to the selection of advisory bodies and to plebiscites in which the electorate as a whole was given an opportunity to say yes or no to questions proposed to it.

Perhaps the French people had had enough of chaos and longed for the kind of public order Napoleon imposed. But in reality they had no choice; they were his prisoners. Yet the First Consul was determined to provide the French people with the kind of government they might learn to enjoy. Given his modest background, his limited (largely military) education, it remains a wonder that he mastered the arts of government as completely as he did. His personal assets, of course, were by no means negligible. His dramatic rise to power at age thirty attested to that, and all Europe was soon to receive regular demonstrations of his talents.

A master psychologist, Napoleon relied upon the exchange of rewards and concessions for loyalty and obedience. For example, Sieyès, whose love of fame and money was notorious, was appropriately rewarded. Throughout his reign, Napoleon created a long series of honors, decorations, and other prizes to reward those who were of use to him. He also understood perfectly the needs and desires of powerful special interest groups. He retained the loyalty of the bourgeoisie and the peasant landowners who had benefited from the Revolution by reaffirming the vast changes in land ownership which had taken place during those years. He rebuilt the shaky financial structure of France, establishing the national Bank of France and maintaining a relatively stable currency. None of the thousands of army officers who had gained their positions as a result of the Revolution had to worry about their new posts. These were clever and sensible policies, effectively used by Napoleon for his own purposes.

In one sense, Napoleon's policies can be seen as the culmination of the Revolution. In his first proclamation to the French people, in December 1799, he declared: "Citizens, the Revolution is established upon the principles which began it! It is ended." He had no sympathy with the democratic sentiments of Robespierre, but his social views had much in common with the aims of the men of 1789. Napoleon did not—indeed, could not—repudiate the Revolution and the changes it had wrought in the social structure of France. He could never forget that the Bourbon heirs to the throne posed the most likely alternative to his own rule and the most serious threat to his power. He was, however, more than willing to accept those aspects of the *ancien régime* which could be useful to him, and he judged the men who served him by the same criterion, according to their usefulness rather than their pedigree or past history. For this reason, he came to an accommodation with many groups and individuals who had hitherto been irrevocably committed to the old order and hostile to the Revolution.

It suited Napoleon's purpose to make peace with one of the most controversial institutions of the old regime, the Roman Catholic Church. He had few if any religious beliefs, but he was firmly convinced of the social utility of religion and of the necessity for a reconciliation, or at least the appearance of a reconciliation, with the pope. Only in this way could he end the opposition of the refractory priests, terminate the revolt that had long raged in the Vendée, and reconcile the many thousands of French peasants who persisted in longing for their ancient religious establishment. Consequently Napoleon and Pius VII engaged in lengthy negotiations that ended with the Concordat of 1801—a clear victory for Napoleon. The pope received his authority and the peasants their priests, but Napoleon retained effective power over the personnel and practices of the French Church. Although he might refer to himself as "Your Holiness' devoted son," the French ecclesiastical establishment remained shorn of its vast lands and bereft even of the title of state church.

Yet, like many modern bourgeois, Napoleon believed that religious piety was a good thing for the masses. Thus French schools were to make the precepts of the Catholic religion the basis of all educational instruction, and, for Napoleon, the Catholic priesthood was "the sacred gendarmerie of the state." It should be added that, while relations between Napoleon and the Church were generally smooth and mutually profitable during his early days in power, after 1805—when Napoleon's overall policy became more and more aggressive and expansionist—their relations became increasingly strained. In the end, the opposition of the Church was a substantial, if not decisive, factor in Napoleon's downfall.

Hardly had Napoleon embarked upon his negotiations with the Church when he commenced what was to become perhaps his most important and lasting domestic achievement—the establishment of a new legal system in France. The result was the Code Napoléon (first titled the Civil Code), which was drawn up by a group of eminent jurists under his supervision. Although the Revolution had begun to make a start on a new legal order by eradicating much of the particularism and regionalism that had characterized French law under the old regime, it had as yet erected no uniform and comprehensive code of law in its place. The Code Napoléon was vital to the completion of the Revolution in the general spirit of the Constitution of 1791, because it worked out the implications of equality before the law, a nonfeudal system of property ownership, and civil jurisdiction in areas formerly under the rule of ecclesiastical courts. Containing five principal sections, the Code Napoléon was not finally completed until 1810. It was by no means a wholly fresh and unprecedented work; on the contrary, it included sections which owed much to Roman law, to certain surviving French customary law, and especially to legislation passed by the Revolution between 1789 and 1795. But the new Code had a distinct character of its own, and before long it began to derive additional importance from the fact that, wherever French troops took over, the Code Napoléon was soon installed. Although it was frequently harsh and paternalistic, its success was striking evidence of how far French society and government had come since 1789. The existence of such a rational and comprehensive exposition of the principles of the French Revolution proved to be a highly exportable commodity (Japan and some Latin American states also adopted the Code on their own), and long after the Napoleonic armies had been defeated, the Code remained a pervasive influence in the civil law of many European states.

If the Code Napoléon showed the First Consul's most progressive side, equally important were his continuing efforts to blend the ancient social practices of the French monarchy and the revolutionary elite that had risen during the previous decade, and to bind firmly to his regime these new (or not so new) men of power whom he had brought, or planned to bring, to the top and whom he expected to carry on his work and traditions after he was gone. There was, in other words, a strongly traditional and hierarchical streak in Napoleon, as his subjects soon discovered. One of the first expressions of this personal characteristic was the Concordat of 1801, and Napoleon followed this up, in May 1802, with the establishment of the Legion of Honor. Designed to recognize special personal merit and achievement, the Legion was bitterly criticized even by Napoleon's fettered press and carefully chosen legislative assemblies. It was, so the complaint went, the first step toward the creation of a bourgeois aristocracy. This was no doubt true. At first limited to six hundred members, the Legion soon grew far beyond its original size, and while many of its members probably retained whatever personal reservations they had held about Napoleon, in the long run the Legion provided a strong reinforcement of the Napoleonic legend.

Nor did Napoleon stop with the creation of this new kind of bourgeois aristocracy. All noble titles had been abolished in 1790, and Napoleon did not attempt to restore them. Instead, he created his own new nobility. In May 1802 Napoleon made himself Consul for Life. Two years later he had the Senate proclaim him Emperor of the French. Naturally, the new emperor needed a court, and Napoleon lost no time conferring grand-sounding, if largely meaningless titles on some of his closest relatives, personal associates, and friends. For instance, his brother Joseph became Grand Elector; his stepson

Eugène de Beauharnais became Arch-Chancellor of State; his brother Louis became Constable. By the end of his regime, Napoleon had managed to create over thirty dukes, four hundred counts, more than a thousand barons, and fifteen hundred knights.

Given such sweeping yet often contradictory policies and pronouncements, not to mention his own complex personality, Napoleon has long been the subject of considerable controversy among historians. He saw himself as a kind of Julius Caesar, a comparison which seemed natural to his contemporaries. He was highly sensitive to critical opinion, and he knew all about the virtues of "managed history" long before that term became popular in the twentieth century. Napoleon subsidized artists and writers who portrayed him and his regime in a favorable light; he directed his minister of police to suppress books that depreciated his achievements. He was also extremely conscious of the heritage of Charlemagne. When he was crowned emperor in December 1804, he created a sensation by emulating his medieval predecessor, taking the crown from the pope's hand and placing it on his own head.

Napoleon was the Man on the White Horse, whose personal dictatorship cut across all established lines of party and heritage. He absolutely rejected the premises of liberal democracy and believed in a sort of benevolent authoritarianism, leading some historians to see him as the last of the enlightened despots. Although he possessed a remarkable gift for giving men what they wanted, he believed in the primacy of force in human relations. Thus, for example, he restored the Roman Catholic Church in France partly to induce the rebels in the Vendée to lay down their arms. He even extended a pardon to those who would do so. But those who did not met with brutal suppression. Time and again, he silenced opposition ruthlessly. He rationalized the Terror of 1793 and 1794, using a secret police force, the army, retaliatory execution of individuals and groups, press censorship, and all the other trappings of the police state. None of his ministers enjoyed a freer hand than Fouché, the notorious head of the police. The primary difference between Robespierre and Napoleon in regard to the theory and practice of the police state was that the latter more nearly understood the limitations within which terror could be socially useful. Furthermore, the machinery of Napoleon's police system was much more efficient and extensive.

Napoleon saw international relations not in traditional diplomatic terms but primarily as an extension of internal affairs. That is, he had no clear concept of nationality; he did not regard the nation-state as the ultimate political entity. Most historians seem agreed that he either did not understand the powerful nationalist sentiment he was instrumental in arousing in areas like Italy and Germany or disregarded it with arrogant contempt. Utterly self-righteous, he believed that there were no inevitable limits to the extension of his power in Europe. The most common criticism of Napoleon and explanation of his ultimate defeat is that his appetite was insatiable, that his policies of conquest seem to have been without limit.

It was, no doubt, only one of the great ironies of Napoleon's career that he came to power, indeed was welcomed to it, because many people in France were sick to death of war and believed that he could bring peace. Indeed, Napoleon himself never tired of his peaceful professions. But France and Europe knew almost nothing but war after he took over as First Consul in November 1799. In 1800 he waged a dramatic series of campaigns, directed largely against Austria, in the course of which French forces reconquered most of northern Italy, including Genoa and Milan, and restored the Cisalpine Republic. A successful drive into Bavaria and Austria itself was followed by the Treaty of Lunéville of February 1801, which not only confirmed the harsh peace terms of 1796 but provided for the cession to France of the entire left bank of the Rhine — a territory of over 25,000 square miles with three and a half million people — and diplomatic recognition of four French puppet states, the Batavian, Cisalpine, Helvetian, and Ligurian republics.

A year later, in March 1802, Britain and France at last made peace at Amiens. The treaty, widely hailed at the time, was a disaster for Britain. It allowed France to remain in control of Holland and Belgium and its recent conquests in Italy and on the Rhine. Britain failed even to get its products admitted once again to France and France's colonies. "In less than two and a half years," Talleyrand, Napoleon's foreign minister, wrote triumphantly, "France [has] climbed from the depths of degradation, into which the Directory had cast it, to the highest position in Europe." It is possible, though only barely so, that had Napoleon genuinely wished permanent peace at this point, he could have had it. But it seems unlikely that that was his desire. Amiens was only an interval, a breathing space. Despite his peaceful protestations, he thirsted for still bigger things at home and abroad.

In retrospect, it seems clear that Napoleon's assumption of the title of emperor in 1804 marked the culmination of his career and revealed his ultimate aim. Shortly afterwards he inaugurated a system of vassal states under the rule of members of his family in the lands he had conquered. His subsequent actions aimed clearly at the establishment of a new Bonapartist dynasty ruling France and large parts of Europe as well. The creation of a new Napoleonic nobility and an elaborate court ceremonial was only the beginning of his attempts to gain acceptance in the ranks of European monarchs. He seemed intent on making himself master of Europe and first of its princes.

Napoleon believed that his security depended upon the fortunes of war. Victory on the battlefield was the support upon which rested the financial solvency and credit of the French government; it would assure his continued popularity with the French people, who faced increasing hardship as his reign wore on, and it would provide him with a more powerful claim than ever to be recognized as a true equal — and superior — by the old rulers of Europe. Such victories became a necessity for Napoleon, who understood that while Louis XIV could lose a war and go home to his kingdom, Bonaparte without a triumphant army would not long remain emperor of the French.

The Struggle for Europe

Although France was principally responsible for the almost unbroken series of wars that racked Europe from 1789 to 1815, it would be a mistake to
see these wars, especially after 1799, wholly as a function of Napoleon's personality and ambitions. The wars of the French Republic and the French
Empire were also a continuation of the wars of the first part of the eighteenth
century, in which France had fought with Britain for colonial predominance
and had sought to retain that preeminence on the Continent bequeathed by
the wars of Louis xiv. It should be recalled that Britain first went to war with
France not because of the latter's revolutionary changes at home (or even
because of the danger that France might export these changes to neighboring
states) but because Britain could not accept the control over the Low Countries which had been one of the first fruits of French victories.

As Napoleon rolled back the armies of the European monarchs, a lasting
settlement of the international conflict became more difficult to achieve, because French victories left Britain, Austria, Prussia, and Russia in vulnerable positions they could never accept. Napoleon sought to restructure the entire European balance of power, but to accomplish this, he found it necessary
to fight an endless war against the European monarchies. For a time the divisions among his adversaries and his own brilliance as a general made it seem
that a solution was not beyond his grasp, but in the last analysis the task
proved to be too great even for Napoleon.

The complexity of the situation is illustrated by the circumstances accompanying the breakdown of the Peace of Amiens of March 1802. On the surface, both Britain and France had good reason to seek more than a temporary
accommodation. Britain had been plagued with increasingly serious internal
difficulties for some years. Although the parliamentary reform movement
had disintegrated in the 1780's, working-class radicals, given new inspiration
by Jacobinism, organized political groups devoted to democratic agitation,
and the repressive measures that Pitt's government employed against radicalism in the 1790's were only moderately effective. In 1797 British sailors
had twice mutinied, and Ireland had been swept by open insurrection, which
the French had sought to reinforce. In 1800 Ireland was joined to Britain in
the "United Kingdom," a development which left the Irish more dissatisfied
than ever and which led to Pitt's resignation as prime minister, in February
1801, when George iii refused to make certain religious concessions to Ireland's Catholic majority.

To the French people, the peace settlement was as welcome as it was to the
British; yet neither Britain nor Napoleon viewed Amiens as a final solution.
Britain did not believe that Napoleon would be content even with the extensive gains included in the treaty, and Napoleon felt that Britain had not genuinely accepted the terms of the agreement but was merely buying time. In
the months that followed, Napoleon violated the spirit of the peace by various

aggressive maneuvers—for example, he refused to withdraw his troops from Holland, as promised in the earlier Treaty of Lunéville (February 1801) —while Britain violated it by refusing to evacuate Malta.

In January 1802 Napoleon had made himself president of the Cisalpine Republic, and in February 1803, French pressure at last brought about a drastic reorganization of Germany. Most free cities and ecclesiastical principalities along the Franco-German border were summarily handed over to various larger German states, which were either already under strong French influence or were being coaxed or bribed or pressured to join Napoleon's political orbit. Meanwhile, the Holy Roman Empire was rapidly expiring. Francis II, the incumbent emperor, seems to have feared that Napoleon, in addition to all his other titles, might wish to assume the German imperial dignity as well. To forestall this, as well as for other dynastic reasons, Francis assumed the title of emperor of Austria in 1804. In August 1806 he abdicated as Holy Roman emperor. The office died, and the Holy Roman Empire with it. Whether Napoleon had ever planned to make himself head of that expiring body remains uncertain. In any case, he had more important tasks immediately at hand.

The war between Britain and France resumed in May 1803. By the summer of 1805 the Third Coalition—Britain, Austria, Russia, Sweden—was a reality, and once more French troops began moving toward the German border. Napoleon himself led the advance to the new battleground, Bavaria, which had already been invaded by the Austrians. In mid-October the French scored a notable victory at Ulm, and on December 2, 1805, Napoleon achieved one of the greatest triumphs of his career at Austerlitz, where he smashed the combined armies of Austria and Russia.

Some French diplomats wanted Napoleon to conclude a conciliatory peace, to detach Austria from Britain, and to return to the close Franco-Austrian diplomatic collaboration of the years 1756–1789. But Napoleon would have none of it. In late December, Austria signed the humiliating Peace of Pressburg, giving up, among other things, Istria, the Tyrol, large parts of Italy, and what remained of Austrian holdings in western Germany. It also agreed to pay France the huge indemnity of forty million francs, eight million to be paid within a week. All the same, the treaty was a political blunder—the first of a series Napoleon was now to commit. The Carthaginian Peace of Pressburg drove Austria "to secret but irreconcilable hatred."

Napoleon was now overlord of Germany, but that country's worst indignities were still to come. Prussia was the next state to be humiliated by Napoleon. The Prussian army and bureaucracy had lost much of their vigor and effectiveness since the death of Frederick the Great in 1786, and Prussian diplomacy had become increasingly wavering and shortsighted. Allowing its formerly close relations with Britain to fall into disrepair, Prussia—though increasingly affronted by Napoleon's German policy—had stood passively by while the French army had smashed Austria the year before. Now a series of

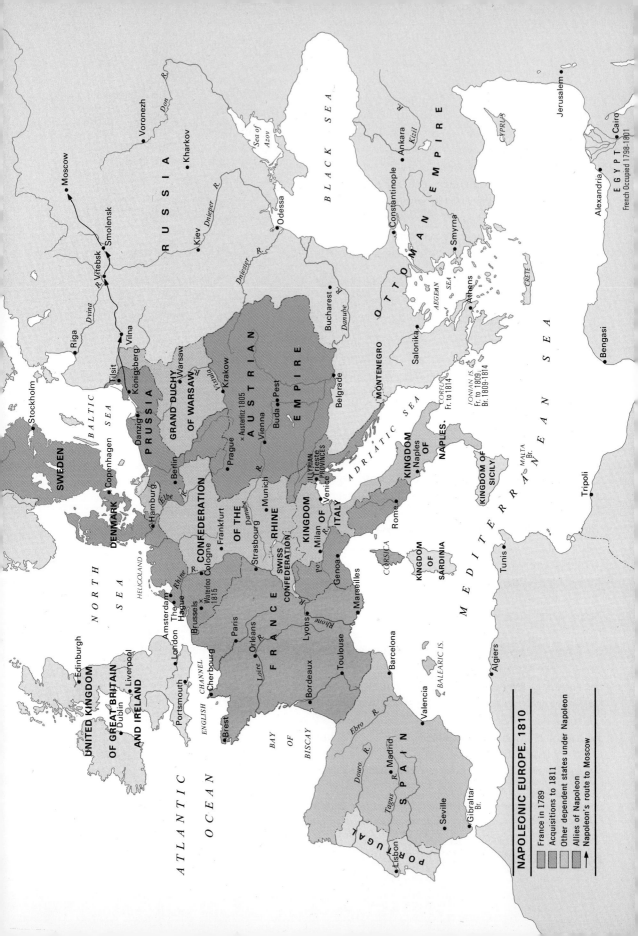

NAPOLEONIC EUROPE, 1810

France in 1789
Acquisitions to 1811
Other dependent states under Napoleon
Allies of Napoleon
Napoleon's route to Moscow

ATLANTIC OCEAN

UNITED KINGDOM OF GREAT BRITAIN AND IRELAND

Edinburgh
Dublin
Liverpool
London
Portsmouth

NORTH SEA

SWEDEN
Stockholm

BALTIC SEA

DENMARK
Copenhagen

HELIGOLAND

RUSSIA
Moscow
Voronezh
Kharkov
Kiev
Smolensk
Vitebsk
Riga
Vilna

Don R.
Dnieper R.
Dvina R.

PRUSSIA
Danzig
Königsberg
Berlin
Hamburg
Tilsit

GRAND DUCHY OF WARSAW
Warsaw
Krakow

Vistula R.

AUSTRIAN EMPIRE
Prague
Vienna
Buda
Pest
x Austerlitz 1805
Belgrade

MONTENEGRO

BLACK SEA

Sea of Azov

OTTOMAN EMPIRE
Constantinople
Ankara
Bucharest
Salonika
Smyrna
Athens

Dniester R.
Danube R.

AEGEAN SEA
CRETE

CYPRUS
Jerusalem
Cairo
Alexandria
EGYPT
French Occupied 1798-1801
Bengasi

CONFEDERATION OF THE RHINE
Frankfurt
Cologne
Munich
Strasbourg

SWISS CONFEDERATION

FRANCE
Paris
Orléans
Brest
Cherbourg
Amsterdam
The Hague
Brussels
x Waterloo 1815
Bordeaux
Lyons
Toulouse

Rhine R.
Loire R.
Rhône R.
Elbe R.

KINGDOM OF ITALY
Milan
Genoa
Venice
Trieste
ILLYRIAN PROVINCES

ADRIATIC SEA

KINGDOM OF NAPLES
Rome
Naples

NAPLES

KINGDOM OF SICILY

MALTA Br.

KINGDOM OF SARDINIA

CORSICA

IONIAN IS.
Fr. to 1809;
Br. 1809-1814
CORFU Fr. to 1809; Br. to 1814

MEDITERRANEAN SEA

Tunis
Tripoli
Algiers

SPAIN
Madrid
Barcelona
Valencia
Seville
Gibraltar Br.

Ebro R.
Douro R.
Tagus R.

PORTUGAL
Lisbon

BALEARIC IS.

BAY OF BISCAY

ENGLISH CHANNEL

petty quarrels between Prussia and Napoleon quickly escalated into war, and within weeks the Prussian army was completely smashed by Napoleon at the great battles of Jena and Auerstädt. Napoleon himself occupied Berlin.

The war was not yet over, for Russia came to Prussia's defense. But in July 1807, Napoleon made peace with both Russia and Prussia at Tilsit. Russia, in return for recognizing Napoleon's conquests and reorganization in western Europe, suffered no loss of territory. Prussia was divested of all its territory west of the Elbe, closed all its ports to British shipping and trade until peace was made with that country, and agreed to being occupied until it had paid an enormous indemnity.

It seems likely that by this time Napoleon had begun to realize that, despite his smashing military triumphs in central Europe, his number one enemy, Britain, remained as unyielding as ever. The day after the great French triumph at Ulm, in October 1805, the combined French and Spanish fleet suffered a crushing defeat at the hands of Admiral Horatio Nelson, who himself died from battle wounds. The Battle of Trafalgar, off the Spanish coast, was one of the greatest naval battles of all time, and the British triumph ended whatever hopes Napoleon still retained of invading Britain. Henceforth he pursued his goal by other means, and some of these led not to Britain's undoing but to Napoleon's.

By the summer of 1807 the Napoleonic empire had reached new heights; only Britain seemed to stand in the way of Napoleon's complete and permanent Continental hegemony. He controlled a vast amount of territory, either directly or through his system of dependent states. The revenue from these lands and their contributions to his armies gave him vast resources upon which to draw. But Britain still had two decisive advantages. One was continuing control of the seas; the other was very substantial economic and financial resources of its own.

Having failed to destroy Britain's mastery of the seas, Napoleon knew he must bring it down economically. It was for this reason that he developed the Continental System. The system had its beginnings in the Berlin Decree of October 1806, by which Napoleon proclaimed a blockade of Britain and banned the importation of British goods into all territories controlled by or allied with him. Not to be outdone, the British responded with successive Orders in Council in January and November 1807, providing, among other things, that neutral ships bound for ports controlled by France should first put in at British harbors and that, if they disregarded warnings to do so, they

In 1810 Napoleonic France dominated European politics, unopposed by any other Continental power. Austria, Prussia, Russia, Denmark, and Sweden were its allies, England its only foe. Napoleon personally ruled France, the former Austrian Netherlands, Holland, the left bank of the Rhine, and—in the quest for a totally effective Continental System—the coasts of Germany and Italy, to the Baltic and Rome respectively. French influence was even more widespread. The rest of the European mainland—save the Balkan peninsula—formed dependent states, which Napoleon controlled, frequently by installing his relatives as their monarchs. Only in Portugal and Spain was resistance continuing: Great Britain used the former as a base for assisting a Spanish national insurrection.

might be seized. Napoleon, in turn, replied with an arrogantly worded series of decrees in November and December 1807, declaring that any ship that had in fact touched a British port or submitted to British search while at sea was subject to confiscation upon arriving at the Continent. In practice, the Continental System involved the extension of the legal and administrative system of France to other parts of Europe, such as Germany, the Netherlands, and Italy. The Continental System thus became both a means of control and a further source of income and materiel for the French army and treasury.

It was one of the oddities of Napoleonic Europe that, while on the whole French control was rigidly and effectively enforced, this was not true in the case of the Continental System. For a time in 1808 it appeared that the ban on British goods might have considerable effect on Britain's trade, even though complete enforcement was always impossible, and in 1810 the threat of famine made Britain vulnerable; but by then the system had begun to break up under the growing pressure of European merchants. Eventually, faced with concerted opposition from the middle classes which had hitherto been among his most valuable supporters, Napoleon was forced to begin a policy of issuing licenses for trade with Britain. In 1810, when he was desperately anxious to achieve full and effective compliance with his Continental System, the French harvest proved so bountiful that it could not possibly be disposed of save by export to Britain, and over a million bushels of wheat were in fact shipped to Britain from France and Flanders, about 25 per cent of all the wheat Britain imported in that embattled year. It is tempting to speculate what would have happened to Britain — and to Napoleon — if he had not sanctioned such trade, which in effect completely undermined the strenuous efforts he was making to bring Britain to its knees.

This new policy, along with the very considerable black market in British goods, soon vitiated the blockade, which became no more than an onerous burden on the Continental economy. In fact, Britain's share of European trade increased rather than decreased during the Napoleonic era. Britain emerged in 1815 clearly predominant in both industry and trade and retained that predominance for several decades.

Other limitations on Napoleon's control over the Continent went beyond the difficulties inherent in governing such a vast extent of territory. Thus in 1808–1809 he became embroiled in two prolonged and seemingly insoluble conflicts which were to exert a steady drain on his political and military resources and were to contribute materially to his ultimate defeat and overthrow. The first of these involved the papacy. Although Pius VII and Napoleon had signed the Concordat of 1801, relations between Paris and Rome remained chilly and were by no means improved by Napoleon's impetuous decision to crown himself in the pope's presence in December 1804. From then on, relations between the two went from bad to worse. In June 1805 Napoleon extended his Code, permitting divorce, to Italy, an act which the pope declared to be contrary to the Italian concordat. Soon after, Napoleon asked Pius to annul his brother Jerome's youthful marriage, and when the pontiff refused to do so, Napoleon decreed the annulment by imperial fiat.

So it went for more than a year. Finally, in February 1808, French forces occupied the papal territories. In May 1809, Napoleon issued a decree annexing Rome to the French Empire, and the following month Pius replied by summarily excommunicating Napoleon and all others involved in that seizure. Needless to say, such conduct was utterly intolerable to Napoleon. In early July, therefore, he had Pius arrested and brought to France as a prisoner, and there the pope remained in captivity until 1814. If Napoleon believed that such a blatant act, unprecedented in modern times, would make the pope more pliable, he was sadly mistaken. He had worked hard to obtain the cooperation of the Church in France and elsewhere in Europe, but his efforts henceforth proved largely unsuccessful. Napoleon's harsh treatment of the pope certainly harmed his image and his moral position.

Even more immediately dangerous to Napoleon, however, was the situation in Spain. Never one for much political subtlety, he used the opportunity provided by a dispute among Bourbon claimants to the Spanish throne to establish his brother Joseph as king. Since he had already established himself as overlord of the Low Countries, most of Germany, and Scandinavia, this particular move should have put the entire Atlantic coast of Europe solidly under Napoleon's control. But it proved a bad blunder. Joseph failed completely to obtain the acceptance of French rule in Catholic Spain, where not only the nobility but, even more so, the peasantry remained irrevocably committed to their priests and their Bourbon king, whom Napoleon had forced to abdicate. The Spanish resistance to Napoleon was not simply another reactionary movement in the Vendéeist model of the 1790's. It consisted, in large part, of liberal nationalists, whose political ideas were closely akin to those of the French Constitution of 1791 but who expressed, above all, that new spirit of national consciousness and will to freedom that Napoleon was increasingly evoking in widely separated parts of Europe. During the next several years, Napoleonic military strategy was repeatedly tested in Spain against determined guerilla resistance, supported by British subsidies and armies operating from bases in Portugal.

In 1812, British forces in Spain, now greatly reinforced and led by Sir Arthur Wellesley, the future duke of Wellington, reconquered Madrid. By then, Napoleon's own fortunes had begun to take a critical turn. But it was in Spain that he first met his match on the battlefield, and his failure there contributed to the growing desperation that led him, in the summer of 1812, to make his ill-fated attack on Russia.

The years that saw the successful Spanish resistance to Napoleon also witnessed important domestic changes within two of the great German powers Napoleon had recently humiliated on the battlefield, Austria and Prussia. In Austria these changes were closely connected with a nationalist revival which led to one last confrontation between Napoleon and Austrian forces, a confrontation that was to end with Napoleon's last and most incomparable military victory. In Prussia the reforms were more significant and permanent, involving an end to hereditary serfdom, revision of the system of taxation, a new degree of self-government for cities and towns, reorganization of the army along the lines of universal military service, and the founding of the University of Berlin.

While Prussian reformers like Baron vom und zum Stein (1757–1831) and Prince von Hardenberg (1750–1822) viewed these policies as largely ends in themselves, in Austria, where comparable changes were far more modest in any case, the government and its ministers viewed political reform primarily as a device to mobilize the population for yet another war with Napoleon. By 1808–1809, Austria was convulsed by a growing patriotic-nationalist movement, the country fired up for a vast rising against the French overlord. But the Austrian design miscarried disastrously. When war with France broke out in April 1809, the archduke Charles' appeal for a national rising throughout Germany went almost totally unheeded. Napoleon rushed back from Spain and quickly overwhelmed the largely isolated Austrians, who in mid-October agreed to the humiliating Treaty of Schönbrunn by which the Habsburgs were divested of vast stretches of territory and Austria agreed to join the Continental System. Efforts at popular resistance in the Habsburg lands were ruthlessly suppressed and in the end came to nothing. Germany was too firmly under Napoleon's heel for a popular rising to have the slightest prospect of success.

Napoleon crowned his astounding triumph over the Austrians with more than a humiliating peace treaty. He had long wanted nothing more than to be accepted as an equal by Europe's great ruling houses. Thus far, all his efforts in that direction had failed, but a suitable marriage would provide such entrée. Napoleon's first marriage to Josephine de Beauharnais had long ago become nothing more than a legal fiction, and in December 1809, after a tearful farewell interview, he finally divorced her. Discouraged from approaching the younger sister of Czar Alexander I of Russia, Napoleon then settled on the eighteen-year-old daughter of the Austrian emperor, the archduchess Marie Louise. The marriage was arranged by Prince Metternich, who had become Austrian foreign minister after the disaster of 1809 and who perhaps saw this marriage as a way for Austria to gain renewed favor in Napoleon's eyes. Napoleon and Marie Louise were married in April 1810, and in March 1811 she bore him a son, whom he modestly named king of Rome.

Napoleon was now at the zenith of his power. Master of virtually all Europe, almost every state his ally, satellite, or tributary, he seemed invincible. But he was not. Britain still held out, the Spanish war dragged on inconclusively, the Russians grumbled increasingly about Napoleon's policies and demands. The religious faithful remained outraged by the pope's continued enforced residence in France. For all his mastery, Napoleon still ruled not by popular approval but by the police spy, the censor, and the fusillade.

Napoleon's Decline and Fall

One of the foundations of the legend that had been building since the early days of his Italian campaign was Napoleon's reputation for invincibility. That image was brilliantly cultivated by Napoleon himself throughout his career, as occasional setbacks or defeats were publicly attributed to the mistakes and incompetence of subordinates while victories redounded to the glory of the emperor. He firmly believed that he was a man of destiny, and before long his complete intolerance of any criticism and opposition became one more significant defect in a seriously flawed personality. Napoleon was more than brutally intolerant; he was completely insensitive even to wholly reasonable complaints and requests. Indeed, it was this imperviousness to the serious economic problems faced by his Russian ally that led, in large part, to their falling out, to Napoleon's attack on Russia in June 1812, and to Napoleon's defeat, overthrow, and exile three years later.

The most serious source of difficulty between Russia and Napoleon was doubtless economic. Russia had joined the Continental System following the conferences of Tilsit and Erfurt in September 1808, but it had done so reluctantly, and the effect of the system on the Russian economy was almost as deleterious as it was on economies in other parts of Europe. By this time, for instance, the Napoleonic economic order had destroyed both the financial power of Amsterdam and the important Dutch carrying trade. There was, however, an important difference. The Dutch were helpless. The Russians were not.

On the last day of 1810, Czar Alexander I issued a decree that in effect opened Russia to British goods and at the same time placed a high protective tariff on France's principal exports to Russia. From then on, both sides made increasingly open preparations for war. In February 1812, Napoleon forced Prussia to sign an onerous treaty of alliance, requiring that state to furnish twenty thousand troops to be commanded by French officers. The following month Napoleon signed a similar treaty with Austria, which was required to furnish thirty thousand men for the Grand Army Napoleon was in the process of assembling. But in April Sweden allied itself with Russia, and so in May 1812 did Turkey.

Was there some way in which the prospective showdown between France and Russia, with all its horrendous losses in men and materiel, could have been avoided? Napoleon apparently believed not. In late June his Grand Army of 600,000 men—the largest military force ever assembled until the outbreak of the First World War—moved across the Russian frontier. But the Russian generals had learned well the lessons of the Spanish war and used delaying tactics and the immense size of the land they were defending to rob him of the decisive engagement he desperately sought. The French army pushed onward thousands of miles, following a phantom army that was content merely to leave the countryside barren behind it.

Napoleon had made another dangerous miscalculation. He believed that the Polish people would rise against their Russian masters and greet him as their long-awaited liberator. But they did not do so. Instead, the Polish peasants were embittered by the Grand Army's widespread pillaging, and Polish nationalists resented Napoleon's evasive statements concerning his future plans for a truly independent Polish state. Nor did Napoleon take advantage of the explosive social situation then existing in Russia, although "Napoleon could conquer Russia only by bringing about a social revolution."[3]

Social revolution was the furthest thing from his authoritarian mind. By August 17 his troops had begun to reach Moscow, but Russian forces had already moved out, and much of the historic city had been burned to the ground. Napoleon waited in Moscow for over two months for a surrender that never came. Then he was forced to march his tattered army back across the vast, barren expanse of western Russia in savage cold and snow. The retreat was one of the greatest disasters in the annals of warfare. By this time he did not dare risk a decisive engagement with the Russian army but had to suffer repeated harassment. The Russian campaign had cost Napoleon half a million men: 250,000 killed; 100,000 taken prisoner; the rest wounded or deserters.

Finally, Napoleon himself was forced to rush on ahead of his decimated forces to quell an attempted coup based on the rumor that the emperor was dead. On returning to Paris he easily regained control of the government, but after 1812 the grand empire was somehow never so grand as it had been before. Napoleon himself had changed, losing most of the incredible physical vigor which had been one of the hallmarks of his early career. The Russian campaign had measurably contributed to the deterioration of his health. In addition, he was no longer as well served as he once had been. By the end of the Russian campaign, his whole political machine was beginning to break down, and some of his closest and most trusted aides were deserting him. By early 1813, for instance, his foreign minister, Talleyrand, was saying openly, "Now is the time to overthrow Napoleon." His minister of police, the notorious Fouché, was caught conspiring with the British and summarily dismissed. Indeed, by this time numerous members of Napoleon's government and entourage were either hoping for or actively moving toward some kind of royalist restoration.

Napoleon had other powerful liabilities, including the relatives and close friends whom, in traditional eighteenth-century fashion, he had appointed to all sorts of important and powerful positions. King of Holland, king of Italy, king of Naples, king of Spain, king of Westphalia—these were some of the titles and high offices he had conferred upon his friends and brothers and which they had filled, on the whole, very badly indeed. Those with ability were too independent to be faithful servants, and those without it were a tremendous burden.

3. George Vernadsky, *A History of Russia*, 5th ed. New Haven: Yale University Press, 1961, pp. 201–202.

And if Napoleon suffered increasingly from the unreliability and inadequacy of his leading associates, subordinates, and representatives, by 1813 his trump card—the once unrivaled French army—had likewise lost much of its superb efficiency, remarkable cohesion, and cumulative striking power. By then Napoleon led not the seasoned veterans of his early campaigns but a new army with a disproportionate number of raw recruits. He missed greatly the services of some of the officers who had so materially contributed to his earlier triumphs on the battlefield. The result was that in 1813 at Leipzig Napoleon suffered his first decisive military defeat at the hands of the newly revived coalition. Before long, French armies were once again fighting to defend the soil of France.

Although by this time the ultimate result was no longer in doubt, the allies did not find administering the final blow an easy matter. One reason was that the German population remained generally passive much longer than might have been expected, perhaps because they had been ground down for so long by the French occupation but also because it was not clear to most of them just what they might gain from the end of the French overlordship. By the end of 1813 the Bavarians had deserted Napoleon, but it was only in Prussia that the semblance of a national rising occurred. Thus the work of the Prussian reformers in the era of Stein and Hardenberg, who had wanted to bring Crown and people closer together, bore significant fruit at last. On the other hand, the Austrians abandoned Napoleon's side with great hesitation and after long delay. Only the entry of allied troops into Paris on March 30, 1814—followed by the triumphant arrival there of Alexander I of Russia and Frederick William III of Prussia the following day—signified that Napoleon was at last finished.

The most pressing question, of course, was what to do with Napoleon. The problem was resolved with almost comic formality. On April 2 the French Senate, acting under the terms of Napoleon's last constitution, formally deposed the emperor, and four days later Napoleon announced his unconditional abdication. But the allies were still faced with the necessity of finding a suitable retirement place for the former ruler of most of Europe. In the end they dealt very liberally with him: by the Treaty of Fontainebleau, which he accepted on April 13, he was exiled to the island of Elba in the Mediterranean, a sovereign with one ship and a domain of a few thousand square miles of territory and a few hundred people but with a munificent annual pension.

Napoleon arrived at the island early in May 1814, but he did not yet accept his defeat and banishment as final. Ten months later he was back in France, where he made a triumphant progress through the countryside toward Paris. The French peasants and the army had always been profoundly loyal to their emperor and they rallied to him one last time.

Both sides now girded for a final showdown. Drawing on all his old political showmanship, Napoleon issued still another constitution, this one a remarkably liberal document, including a responsible ministry, freedom of the press, and broad suffrage. He announced his intention to work for peace and "the fe-licity of mankind." But this time the allies were beyond such rhetorical blan-dishments. They publicly outlawed Napoleon as "an enemy and disturber of the tranquility of the world."

Seeking a decisive victory to reconcile Europe to his return to power, Napo-leon met a combination of German, British, and Dutch troops commanded by the duke of Wellington and the Prussian field marshal, Blücher, near the vil-lage of Waterloo in Belgium on June 17, 1815. Though the battle was brief, the casualties were frightening. Napoleon alone lost thirty thousand men killed and wounded. Wellington's army lost over thirteen thousand, the Prus-sians more than six thousand. But the decisive fact was that Napoleon was beaten; his troops left the battlefield defeated and in disarray. For Napoleon, it was all over. His second regime had lasted a mere "hundred days." On July 15 he surrendered to the British, feeling that of all his enemies, they would treat him most humanely.

This time Napoleon was denied any leeway which might allow him to re-gain power in France. He had hoped to go to England or the United States, but the allies would take no chances. He was sent into captivity on the island of St. Helena in the South Atlantic. He was never happy or comfortable there, often ill and even more often chafing under the tactless observation of his captors. It was on St. Helena that Napoleon dictated the memoirs that con-tributed materially to the Napoleonic legend. And it was there that he died in May 1821.

To his admirers Napoleon has been the man who completed the Revolution and saved the French people from its enemies. To his detractors he has been a man of inordinate ambition whose authoritarianism and extravagant for-eign policies destroyed the liberal republic of the Directory and returned France to monarchical absolutism. Napoleon would have answered that he gave France the two things it wanted and needed most: domestic order after a decade of social and political upheaval, and one of the most glorious episodes in its long history. To have almost conquered all of Europe was, at any rate, enough to earn Napoleon a place alongside Alexander the Great, Caesar, and Charlemagne—and also Hitler.

Napoleon's permanent exile to St. Helena ended an epoch but not its prob-lems. The era of the French Revolution was the great turning point in the development of French government and French society, and it profoundly affected the political and social structure of nearly every other European country. It had witnessed Britain's rise to a position of leadership in European and world affairs and the emergence of a new era of national conscious-ness. Most important of all, though somewhat obscured by the national and international upheavals of the years 1789–1815, Europe and especially Britain had begun to experience an even more radical and permanent trans-formation—the Industrial Revolution.

3

HERITAGE ESSAY

THE HERITAGE OF THE FRENCH REVOLUTION

In the last three decades of the eighteenth century, and most powerfully in the French Revolution, an ideal was asserted and acted upon that became central to Western civilization and that has, beyond any other concept, shaped the modern world. This was the ideal of equality, which fundamentally contradicted the concept of hierarchy that had governed men's political and social relationships since the fourth millennium B.C. The wide acceptance of this democratic ideal marked a historical turning point of unprecedented importance. It was the beginning of the modern era.

There had been partial expressions of the egalitarian ideal earlier—in the Athenian polis, in radical, usually heretical variants of medieval Christianity, in the Leveller movement in early seventeenth-century England, in the political theory of John Locke. The decisive importance of the American Revolution, as R. R. Palmer has written, lay in its effective implementation, through successful armed insurrection, of the concept of equality between colonials and the mother country. The victory of the American colonies undoubtedly provided inspiration for the democratic movement in England, where it produced great controversy but no immediate change, and for the French Revolution.

It is likely, however, that a democratic movement against the *ancien régime* in Europe would have emerged in the later eighteenth century even without the inspiration and example of the American Revolution. There is nothing more powerful than "an idea whose time has come." And the time had come for a decisive assertion of the idea of political equality. The aristocratic governments of Europe were disorganized and inept, and the privileged class, particularly in France, was not only incapable of reforming and rationalizing the institutions of the state but increasingly aggressive and selfish in claiming its privileges. Given the economic and intellectual resources of those just below this elite—the petty nobility, the members of the learned professions, and the bourgeoisie—and given the impact of the *philosophes'* criticism of the *ancien régime*, a great upheaval in one country or another was virtually inevitable. That it came in the nation that was the most heavily

populated, the most literate, and potentially the wealthiest made the impact of the democratic movement all the more powerful. The course of Western civilization was fundamentally altered. The great struggles of the period 1789–1815 inaugurated the modern democratic era.

The basic idea of the French Revolution, as stated in the Declaration of the Rights of Man and the Citizen of August 27, 1789, was that government did not belong to privileged, hereditary, or self-selective elites and power groups in a society but to the people—that is, to the governed:

1. Men are born and remain free and equal in rights; social distinctions may be based only upon general usefulness.

2. The aim of every political association is the natural and inalienable rights of man; these rights are liberty, property, security, and resistance to oppression.

3. The source of all sovereignty resides essentially in the nation; no group, no individual may exercise authority not emanating expressly therefrom.

. . . .

6. Law is the expression of the general will; all citizens have the right to concur personally, or through their representatives, in its formation; it must be the same for all, whether it protects or punishes. All citizens, being equal before it, are equally admissible to all public offices, positions, and employments, according to their capacity, and without other distinction than that of virtues and talents.[1]

This is the antithesis of absolutism.

The democratic ideal of 1789 re-

1. John H. Stewart, ed., *A Documentary Survey of the French Revolution.* New York: Macmillan, 1951, p. 113.

The New Freedom. One of the ways in which the French Revolution set the pattern for all subsequent democratic revolutions was by enlisting art in the service of the popular movement and the national will. Facing page, top: the enslavement of the British people by tyranny. Prime Minister Pitt is shown standing on the crown and holding the people enchained, while the gallows threaten in the background. Facing page, bottom: in vivid contrast, to the revolutionary mind, the happy French people join the democratic army to fight reaction and despotism. Above: democracy at work—a meeting of the Jacobin Club. Right: the newly emancipated and deliriously happy Parisians celebrate the fall of the Bastille.

garded the citizens of a state not as disparate individuals and groups subject to the will of the government but rather as "the nation," a collective entity in which sovereignty resided. Consequently, the concept of political equality had as its corollary a powerful impetus toward nationalism, the feeling that a people are bound together in an indissoluble community with a life of its own apart from the institutions of centralized government. In France, the long war against the enemies of the Republic after 1793 greatly increased the intensity of this national feeling. The fraternity of the people as a collective entity became as central to the revolutionary ideal as the liberty and equality of individual citizens.

VUE DE LA PLACE DE GREVE LE JOUR DE LA PRISE DE LA BASTILLE ∗ NOUS CEDONS A LAMOUR DE LA LIBERTÉ

The Terrible Beauty of Revolutionary Violence. Because violence is often necessary
to destroy the old order, many revolutionaries become fascinated by the techniques of
violence and come to relish the bloody
downfall of their alleged oppressors. In this
way revolutionary violence acquires its own
justification. Again, the French Revolution
set a model. Facing page, bottom: this
crowd of two thousand Parisians gathered
in the Place de Grève after the fall of the
Bastille, overcame the opposition of the
soldiers, and destroyed the houses of two
unpopular manufacturers. Facing page,
top: Robespierre guillotining the enemies
of the Revolution. Above: the execution of
Louis XVI, January 21, 1793, on the *Place
de Louis XV,* henceforth called the *Place
de la Révolution.* Right: Queen Marie Antoinette on her way to execution, as sketched
by David, the greatest artist of the revolutionary era. (Compare with the portrait on
page 114.)

The Face of the People. There was no more important aspect of the French Revolution than its decisive involvement of the *menu peuple*, the common people, in political life. The popular disturbances and riots—*journées* (literally, "days" or, as we would say, "happenings")—of 1789 gave way to organized political movements among the urban *sans-culottes*, consisting of shopkeepers, tradesmen, and artisans. The conscription of a democratic national army further contributed to the political importance of the petty bourgeoisie and workers. Right: a member of the revolutionary Convention with his family, painted by David. The plebeian face and costume accentuate the subject's status as a man of the people. Facing page, top: an engraving of revolutionary types in Paris, 1793–1794. Facing page, bottom: the people's army. An officer reads the order of the day to the battalion of the lower Loire. The wars of revolutionary France proved the superiority of a democratically constituted army, fighting for national freedom, over the mercenary armies of aristocratic Europe.

Thus, from the moment of triumph of the first great democratic movement in Western civilization, a fundamental tension was apparent—the tension between the right of the individual to freedom and equality and the responsibility of the individual to the needs and will of the nation. Democratic equality emancipated citizens from the tyranny of absolute monarchy and aristocratic privilege, but it did not inevitably imply greater freedom for the individual. On the contrary, the democratic state, rationally organized, could make and enforce demands upon the individual far greater than the *ancien régime* was usually capable of implementing. Robespierre and the Jacobin radicals constantly affirmed that the needs of the democratic nation required the subjection of individual interests to the collective good that the revolutionary government sought to foster:

The function of government is to guide the moral and physical energies of the nation toward the goal for which it was established. . . . Revolutionary government . . . rests upon the sanest of all laws—the safety of the people—and the

most indisputable of all rights—necessity. . . . The establishment of the French Republic . . . cannot be the accidental result of the collision of the totality of all the individual purposes and revolutionary forces . . . . When you [the Convention] gave to certain members selected from your midst the redoubtable task of constantly guarding the fate of the fatherland, you accepted the obligation to support them with your strength and your confidence.[2]

The democratic movement of the late eighteenth century proclaimed the principle of popular sovereignty. Beyond this principle, however, its heritage to the modern world was complex and even ambiguous. On the one hand, that heritage asserted the liberal belief that the state should allow individuals to pursue their private interests. On the other hand, it asserted that the private interests of individuals had to be subordinated to the common good, and it gave government the power to see that this was done. Thus the conflict between collectivity and individuality that had existed in ancient and medieval societies was by no means precluded by the implementation of the egalitarian ideal but greatly exacerbated. It has remained a persistent issue in modern political life.

In the thought of the radical wing of the French Revolution there was a cognate motif that became central in Western civilization: the idea of revolution itself. In Jacobin theory, revolution became a rejuvenating force in society, an entity that had its own style. Anyone who resisted the revolu-

The People's Hero. The concluding phase of modern revolutions is usually marked by the accession to supreme power of an adored military and political leader. Napoleon Bonaparte was the prototype of this kind of popular dictator. Although he confirmed the Revolution's modernization of the government and its opening of public careers to middle-class talent, he had no sympathy for political egalitarianism and used the democratized French army to implement an expansionist policy in the Bourbon tradition. Napoleon also set the pattern for all modern dictators in his use of art to advertise his achievements and glamorize his image. Above: Gros' portrait of Napoleon as a young, handsome leader of the people. Facing page, bottom: the triumph of Consul Bonaparte depicted in classical style. Facing page, top: a bronze table made to commemorate the great victory of Austerlitz; the emperor Napoleon is shown in the center porcelain miniature, his generals in the surrounding miniatures.

2. Robespierre, *Discours et Rapports*, trans. H. H. Rowen, in H. H. Rowen, *From Absolutism to Revolution,* 2nd ed. New York: Macmillan, 1967, pp. 208–210.

tion was a "cowardly murderer" who had to be eliminated. The revolutionary
ethos preached the cleansing value of justifiable violence. In the words of
Robespierre: "To the good citizens revolutionary government owes the complete protection of the nation; to the enemies of the people it owes only death."[3]

It was consistent with this view that Robespierre should have tried to found
a new religion of reason and that the revolutionary government should have
established a new calendar. In the Jacobin mind, revolution became not a
mere vehicle for political change but a way of life in itself. Nor was this cleansing of the body politic to be confined to France. Democratic revolution was
regarded as a universal movement which would inaugurate a new era everywhere in Europe. Again, Robespierre expressed with great clarity the universality of revolution:

3. Robespierre, *Discours et Rapports*, in *From Absolutism to Revolution*, p. 208.

The Armed Revolution. While the French Revolution did inspire middle-class rebellions in other countries, it
was the prowess of French arms that was mainly responsible for the establishment of new republics. Under
Napoleon, the democratic significance of this upheaval steadily diminished; the new governments were simply French puppets. Below: proclamation of the Cisalpine Republic in northern Italy. Facing page, bottom:
Napoleon (right) and the British prime minister William Pitt carving up Europe. Finally, the revolutionary ideal
of popular sovereignty found expression in national movements against the Bonapartes. Facing page, top:
Goya's famous painting "And they are like wild beasts," one of his "Disasters of War" series, depicts the ferocity of the Spanish rebellion against French rule.

The Plumb-pudding in danger: — or State Epicures taking un Petit Souper
"the great Globe itself, and all which it inherit, is too small to satisfy such insatiable appetites

The Advent of Modern Warfare. The wars of the French revolutionary government and of Napoleon began a new chapter in military history. In the late seventeenth and the greater part of the eighteenth century, wars had dynastic and strategic causes. Although they were often ferociously fought, the loss of life was largely confined to the armies involved. During the revolutionary and Napoleonic eras, the French people were called upon to fight for moral and ideological motives—freedom and the nation —a throwback to the ideologically based conflicts of the Reformation era. The armies, greatly enlarged and often raised by conscription, were directed with more ruthless and deadly efficiency, and the civilian populations were not spared the brunt of the holocaust. The whole temper of wars fought in the name of revolutionary ideals and national independence was bound to differ radically from that of struggles over frontier towns and dynastic successions. Below: the capture of Saragossa in 1809. Facing page: the burning of Moscow, 1812.

The men of all countries are brothers, and the different peoples should assist each other to the extent of their power, like citizens of the same state. He who oppresses one nation declares himself to be the enemy of all. Those who wage war upon one people in order to halt the progress of freedom and to destroy the rights of man must be hunted down not as ordinary enemies but as assassins and rebellious brigands.[4]

All twentieth-century revolutionary movements — such as the Communist, the Maoist, the Fascist, and the New Left in America today — have perpetuated the Jacobin ethic and aesthetic of revolution: apocalyptic, universal, and beautifully and morally violent. In the modern world, this revolutionary ethic and aesthetic has competed with and challenged Christianity as the prime millennial faith. Like evangelical Christianity, the Jacobin revolutionary

4. Robespierre, *Oeuvres*, in *From Absolutism to Revolution*, p. 207.

ethos offered not merely a program for social reform but a life style, a culture, and an outlet for love and hatred.

It was precisely because the revolution in France became a collective entity with a style and culture of its own that after 1793 it could not be satisfactorily identified with a particular set of constitutional forms or a specific program. When the Revolution became an all-encompassing social force, it was best comprehended by association with one man, or at most a small group of men, rather than with a specific list of demands and expectations. The tendency of the French Revolution — and of all subsequent revolutions — was for the leadership to be taken over by steadily smaller groups and finally to be usurped by an authoritarian figure who proclaimed himself the embodiment of the movement. This was Napoleon's role, and twentieth-century revolutions have spawned similar dictators.

Napoleon's empire was popular with the large middle class in France, which extended from the petty nobility to government functionaries and members of the learned professions, to merchants and industrialists, to prosperous peasants. His regime gave this central group in French society what it had principally wanted from the Revolution — careers open to talent, without the obstacle of aristocratic privilege. These were the people who had been frightened by the specter of the principle of equality being applied to property — by the socialist Babeuf's claim that "stomachs are equal" and even by Robespierre's guarded assertion that the interests of property must be limited by the needs of the general welfare.

The egalitarianism of the French Revolution, except for the assertions of a minute extremist group, stopped far short of socialism. In this sense, it is true that the Revolution served the interests of what might be called the middle class; it did not greatly help the industrial worker and the urban and rural poor. But by committing Western civilization to a democratic attitude, the heritage of the Revolution also opened the way for the socialist movements of the nineteenth century. Writing in the 1830's, Alexis de Tocqueville pointed out this fact with his customary clarity:

The general trend toward equality of conditions is a fact of Providence, of which it bears the principal characteristics: it is universal, it is enduring, it constantly eludes human powers of control; all events and all men contribute to its development.

Would it be wise to think that a social movement of such remote origin can be suspended by the efforts of one generation? Can it be supposed that democracy, after destroying feudalism and overwhelming kings, will yield before the powers of money and business — *devant les bourgeois et les riches?*[5]

5. Alexis de Tocqueville, *Democracy in America*, quoted in R. R. Palmer, *The Age of the Democratic Revolution.* Princeton, N.J.: Princeton University Press, 1964, II, p. 574.

The Economic Revolution

ENVIRONMENT ESSAY

In 1784 a visiting French nobleman described England as "the finest country in Europe for variety and verdure, for beauty and richness, for rural neatness and elegance—a feast for the sight, a charm for the mind."[1] During the previous century, the application of scientific knowledge to agriculture and the modernization of the rural economy that followed completion of the enclosure of the open fields of medieval times had brought the English countryside to a new peak of productivity and beauty. Even London, the political and commercial metropolis, seemed "bright and glittering" to the young poet William Wordsworth in 1802.

In 1815 England was still overwhelmingly rural, with London as its preeminent urban center. But in the north factories were rapidly converting insignificant villages into expanding industrial towns. The pattern of modern industrial society, with all its dynamic economic power and all its ecological and social problems, had emerged in Manchester, Birmingham, and Sheffield. The smoking factory chimneys that loomed on the bleak horizons of northern England heralded a new age as surely as the towers of cathedral and castle rising over the modest houses of medieval burghers had symbolized the power structure and the culture of that earlier era.

With characteristic insight, the poet and mystic William Blake recorded the disturbing presence of "dark satanic mills" in "England's green and pleasant land," and in 1784 a visiting French mineralogist portrayed the demonic fury of the new industrial world:

The night is so filled with fire and light that when from a distance we see, here a glowing mass of coal, there darting flames leaping from the blast furnaces, when we

---

1. Quoted in J. Morris, *The Road to Huddersfield.* New York: Pantheon, 1963, p. 5.

hear the heavy hammers striking the echoing anvils and
the shrill whistling of the air pumps, we do not know
whether we are looking at a volcano in eruption or have
been miraculously transported to Vulcan's cave.[2]

By 1815 the thrust of industrialization and urbanization was transforming the English environment
with each passing year, eating away more and more
of the old England of rural stability and village
community. Not until the middle of the nineteenth
century did half the population of England live in
cities, but already in 1818 nostalgic admirers of the
old order, like the radical journalist William Cobbett,

2. Quoted in P. Mantoux, *The Industrial Revolution in the Eighteenth
Century.* New York: Harcourt, Brace, 1928, p. 313.

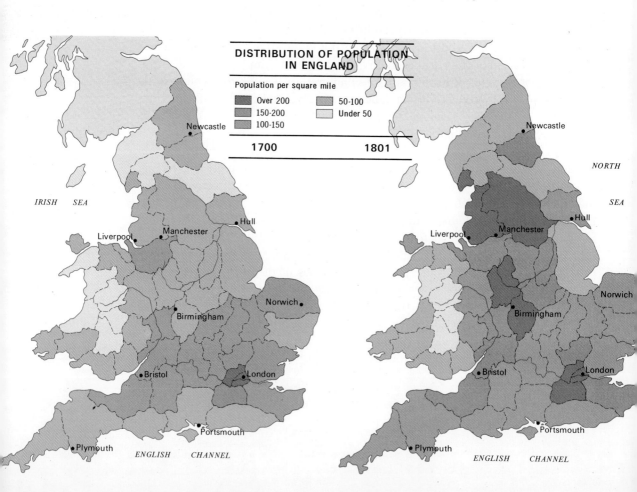

DISTRIBUTION OF POPULATION
IN ENGLAND

Population per square mile

Over 200   50-100
150-200   Under 50
100-150

1700   1801

The Background to Economic Growth. In an agrarian society, the necessary precondition for industrial and urban development is a surplus food supply. Right: "Agriculture" as portrayed in Diderot's *Encyclopédie.* The agricultural surplus conducive to increased longevity produced a rapid rise in the English population in the second half of the eighteenth century. The map on the facing page contrasts England's population in 1700 and a century later and shows the tremendous increase in population density in the new industrial and urban areas. Another precondition for industrial growth is mechanization. Below: loom used in the cotton industry before the application of steam power. It is powered by foot pedals. [Map adapted from page 524 of H. C. Darby, ed., *An Historical Geography of England,* by permission of Cambridge University Press.]

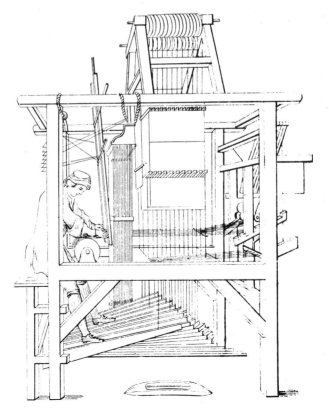

The Transportation Revolution. The expansion of the European economy was inhibited for centuries by a primitive transportation system that kept distribution costs high and limited the mobility of labor. In Britain in the late eighteenth century, road construction and improvement, bridge building, the proliferation of stagecoach lines, and, perhaps most important of all, the development of a network of canals overcame the transportation bottleneck and made industrial expansion possible. Above: Coalbrookdale cast iron bridge, built in 1779 (photograph taken in 1904). Left: coach from Greenwich to Charing Cross, London, 1783. Facing page: the canal aqueduct over the Irwell River at Barton, Lancashire, one of the finest transport engineering achievements of the early Industrial Revolution.

could complain that the urban "wens" were devouring the old small town and village life and imposing the dehumanized standards of ruthless capitalism upon society: "All was looked for at shops. . . . Scarcely anyone thought of providing for his own wants out of his own domestic means."[3]

Aside from a few rich men's houses, a Wesleyan chapel, an occasional public library or Mechanics' Institute (adult education school), there was nothing to alleviate the uniform ugliness of the towns of the early machine age. Factories found their architectural models in military barracks or in the workhouses where the unemployed of preindustrial England had been set to punitive labor. Although there were some entrepreneurs who sought to provide safe and salubrious working conditions and good housing for their workers, the more frequent situation seems to have been that the meanness of unrestrained capitalism, worshiping at the shrine of steam power and hard cash, caused workers to be treated like convicts and slaves. A group of physicians who inspected the Manchester cotton mills in 1784 reported:

The cotton mills are large buildings, but so constructed as to employ the greatest number of persons. That no room may be lost, the several stories are built as low as

3. Quoted in R. J. White, *Life in Regency England.* London: Batsford, 1963, p. 29.

possible . . . . There is a considerable effluvia constantly arising from the bodies of a large number of persons . . . from the oil and cotton dust and from the candles used in the night, without any considerable supply of fresh air.[4]

The extensive employment of women and children, chronic conditions of overcrowding, dreadfully inadequate sanitation, crime, and epidemics gained for the new industrial towns a very bad reputation among contemporaries and among later historians and social theorists. By and large this reputation was deserved. But the conditions in the towns of the early machine age must be considered in the perspective of two important facts. First, the workers themselves were not entirely convinced that they had passed from a rural heaven to an urban hell. Unemployed farm laborers and Irish peasant immigrants were willing to endure bad housing and the other grim aspects of Manchester because they could get jobs in such factory towns. In many in-

4. Quoted in W. Bowden, *Industrial Society in England Towards the End of the Eighteenth Century*, 2nd ed. New York: Barnes & Noble, 1965, p. 267.

The Dawn of Modern Industry. Facing page, top: James Watt's first "sun and planet" steam engine, which provided a new source of power, first in mines and then in factories. Watt applied eighteenth-century physics to industrial technology. He sought the advice of a physicist at Edinburgh, the most science-oriented university in Britain. Facing page, bottom: a steam-driven linen loom, used in northern Ireland. Below: cotton factories on Union Street, Manchester, in the early nineteenth century.

The Triumph of Industrialism. Although many critics condemned the ugly, unhealthful, uncomfortable urban environment created by the growth of industry, the early years of the nineteenth century were hailed by some writers and artists as the beginning of a new beneficent age of human creativity. The engraving above showing the factories at Bradford, Yorkshire, was intended not as a warning against air pollution but as a celebration of the new industrial world. "The Iron Forge" by Joseph Wright (right) is a blatant idealization of the grandeur of industry. As a Manchester writer said in 1791: "These are thy blessings, O Commerce! These are thy rewards, O Industry!"[1]

1. Quoted in W. Bowden, *Industrial Society in England Towards the End of the Eighteenth Century*, 2nd ed. New York: Barnes & Noble, 1965, p. 107.

stances, the industrial laboring families enjoyed a higher standard of living than had been available to them in the picturesque villages of aristocratic rural England. Second, the abysmally inadequate control of the new urban environment was in part the consequence of the failings of the preindustrial old regime itself—its negligent and hostile attitude toward the poor, its chaotic system of local government, its inexperience in dealing with social welfare and public health. England in 1780 did not have the institutions to contend with the impact of the Industrial Revolution.

Even in the twentieth century, newly urbanized societies—and some old industrial centers, too—have continued to experience many of the miseries prevalent in late eighteenth-century Manchester. Social disorganization and slum conditions may be inseparable from the process of industrialization and urbanization, agonizing by-products of social and economic change.

I THE PRECONDITIONS FOR INDUSTRIALIZATION

The Historiographical Problem

While the Western world was preoccupied with the era of upheaval and revolution that began in America in the 1770's and came to an end only with the defeat and overthrow of the Napoleonic tyranny in 1814–1815, Europe —and especially Britain—was beginning to undergo an economic and social transformation that, in time, was to surpass in importance the political and military developments of the previous half-century.

This transformation was called the Industrial Revolution—a term first used in France in the 1820's but popularized only after it became the title of a book by Arnold Toynbee (the Elder), published in the 1880's. In contrast to the intellectual, political, and social movements of the second half of the eighteenth century, which were truly international in scope, the Industrial Revolution came first in Britain, and started the British economy on a path of continuous expansion which extended, with occasional setbacks and interruptions, into the latter decades of the nineteenth century.

Although contemporaries were slow to take note of the transformation of the British economy, its results were clearly visible: a dramatically increasing output of material goods to support a population growing at a rate never before sustained in human history. Increased production required extensive transformation of the methods of production, notably: the application of technology to increase output per unit of input—particularly the use of machines to supplement human labor and make it more productive; the enlargement of the production unit from family to factory, allowing for increased specialization and economies; and urbanization.

Considerable historical controversy still attends attempts to date the Industrial Revolution, to show its causes, and to assess its effect on the British people. The prevalent view is that it began around 1780, when the first great upsurge in production occurred, and that the pattern of continuous growth was established in the first half of the nineteenth century. There are numerous differing views, however: John U. Nef, for example, has traced the growth of massive industrialization back into the sixteenth century, while W. W. Rostow, whose *Stages of Economic Growth* has stimulated worldwide discussion, seeks to limit the time of the actual revolution to the years 1782–1802.

A second area of controversy centers on the role of Britain's colonial empire. Would the revolution have occurred when it did without the stimulus of the colonies' demand for manufactured goods? Were the profits of the domestic and European markets enough to motivate British manufacturers to devote themselves—even at a sacrifice of immediate gain—to the rapid expansion of output? Historians disagree on how large a stimulus was given to industrial expansion in Britain by its empire.

Finally, the most spirited argument over the Industrial Revolution concerns its effects on those who labored in the growing number of factories. For some, the abominable working conditions in the factories is sufficient answer to the question, "What price economic progress?" On the other hand, an influential school of economic historians holds that the populace benefited from the revolution quite early in its course, that the conditions prevailing in the domestic, or cottage, system of industry before the factory system was established were far from ideal, and that industrial wages admittedly increased faster than did the income of farm laborers or peasants. Critics of the social effects of industrialization reply that rising wages were more than offset by rising agricultural prices. Revisionist historians of the Industrial Revolution do not deny its brutal and shocking exploitation of the working masses, whose helpless resentment became a fertile breeding ground for social radicalism of all kinds (including Marxism) for generations. But the revisionist interpretation is inclined to minimize the exploitation, the starvation, the physical and psychological debilitation that were among the most damaging by-products of the new industrial system and to contend that such effects were largely found in marginal or declining enterprises and industries.

There is general agreement, however, that the workers' standard of living did improve in the end, and therefore the controversy really centers around the date *when* it improved significantly. Historians critical of the social consequences of the Industrial Revolution hold that workers' living conditions remained largely unchanged until the 1840's; less critical ones, that conditions began to improve in the 1820's. Both schools would agree that the full political impact of industrialization and urbanization was not felt until after the 1820's.

Population

One of the indispensable prerequisites for the era of economic transformation was a substantial increase in population, and by any previous standards the growth of the population of England in the last half of the eighteenth century and the first two decades of the nineteenth was nothing short of phenomenal. Estimates place England's population in 1500 at approximately three million, and 250 years passed before it crept up to the six million mark. But in the seven decades between 1750 and 1820 it doubled once again to stand at something over twelve million.

Sudden spurts in population were not unknown in medieval times. Usually they occurred in periods of peace and good harvests when food was cheap and people were encouraged to marry young and raise large families. But sooner or later (usually sooner, as English weather, then as now, was not reliable) the population outstripped the food supply. Then famine and disease spread, the death rate caught up with and surpassed the birth rate, and the population dropped back toward its former level. Thus the enormous growth of population in the eighteenth and nineteenth centuries constituted a revolution in itself.

A decrease in the death rate probably was responsible for the initial increase in population in the 1740's. In the earlier decades of the century an unusually high death rate had prevailed, owing partly to an abnormal consumption of cheap gin. More important, a string of good harvests made cheap food plentiful in the years 1730–1755, and a fortuitous drop in the rat population produced an end to the epidemics that had periodically carried off hundreds of thousands. After mid-century, although the run of good harvests was broken, improved methods of transporting goods and more generous administration of poor relief made crop failures less disastrous. At the same time, the birth rate began to rise: first because the good harvests provided more employment, encouraging early marriage and large families, and later because increased opportunities to put young children to work in expanding industries encouraged still larger families.

"The best general test of the industrialization of a nation's life under modern conditions," the eminent British economic historian Sir John Clapham has written, "is the rate and character of its towns,"[1] and on the Continent both the growth of population and the growth of cities were, with some exceptions, slower than in Britain. For instance, the population of Germany in 1800 was perhaps no greater than it was in 1600, and the total population of the twelve cities which in 1914 were to be the largest in all Germany was no more than 750,000 in 1815. The population of Paris alone at that time was about 500,000; but this is not to say that the French population was increas-

1. Sir John Clapham, *The Economic Development of France and Germany 1815–1914*, 4th ed. Cambridge: Cambridge University Press, 1936, p. 53.

ing at anything like the British rate, and France had suffered the dreadful losses of the revolutionary era and the Napoleonic Wars. In Russia, which had the largest population in Europe at the close of the Napoleonic Wars —somewhat over forty million as against France's thirty and England's twelve—the rate of increase was also significantly lower.

Agriculture

No less important for the development of the Industrial Revolution in Britain were basic changes in agriculture. In the first half of the eighteenth century, most Englishmen cultivated the soil under an "open-field" system that had been only slightly modified since medieval times. In a parish or on a lord's estate, there were usually three large fields for crops ("common fields") and some arable lands on which livestock might graze ("common wastes"). Each year, two of the fields were cultivated with various grains (rye, wheat, and the like), and the third lay fallow. Each farmer had at least one plot, or strip, in each of the common fields, on which he grew crops for his family and the local market.

The system was extraordinarily wasteful—the farmer spent much time traveling between his widely separated strips—and it was a positive hindrance to innovation. Effective drainage was impossible without the consent of the whole community, and the common grazing of livestock on the stubble after the harvest prevented the sowing of another crop at that time of year. In short, the whole system bespoke a way of life that had changed very little for centuries and a rural population that accepted a small return for its labors. If output was to increase to feed a rapidly expanding population, it was essential to modify the system so that innovation would be possible and to convince the landholders that improvements in farming techniques would be profitable.

The impetus to modify the system came primarily from the larger landholders—sometimes the nobility, more often the gentry (although some small landholders had tried in the past to consolidate their holdings in the common fields by exchanging strips with their neighbors). From the late seventeenth century, English landlords were increasingly motivated by a capitalist spirit—by a desire to produce for the market and enlarge their incomes. In the eighteenth century, the steady rise in their cost of living forced them to rationalize agricultural production. The nobility and the more ambitious gentry had to meet the costs of the ornate balls and masquerades of a London season, of education for the family heir (several expensive years at Oxford or Cambridge climaxed by a Grand Tour of the Continent), of enlargement of the family house (a veritable epidemic of grandiose building was sweeping the country), and of charity for the parish in which the estate lay.

The landlords' need for additional income and their more rational, capitalist attitude inspired what historians have called the agricultural revolution of the eighteenth century, a substantial improvement in agricultural techniques that was a necessary precondition for industrialization. The agricultural revolution took two forms. First, several landholders tried new methods of cultivation to increase their crops. Jethro Tull devised a seed drill that reduced waste and spaced plants evenly so that the ground between them could be easily hoed. Lord Townshend advocated manuring the soil and growing turnips for fodder. These and similar advances in agrarian technology were adopted by enterprising landlords. More important was the great rush to enclose the common fields and wastes and their transformation into consolidated holdings. The enclosure movement, which had begun in the sixteenth century and slowed down in the seventeenth, was now revived on an unprecedented scale.

After 1750 enclosure became increasingly desirable. The demand for agricultural products rose as the population continued to grow. As prices increased and land became more valuable, landlords were encouraged to enclose the fields and to require their tenants to apply scientific methods of cultivation. It was now particularly worthwhile to go to the expense of securing an act of Parliament to enclose lands cultivated by unprogressive farmers (and after 1801 the General Enclosure Act reduced the cost of procuring such enclosure considerably).

In the late eighteenth and the early nineteenth century, enclosure effected the modernization of English agriculture. Between 1727 and 1760, 75,000 acres had been enclosed. Between 1761 and 1792 enclosure extended over half a million acres, and between 1792 and 1815, partly under the pressure of the wartime boom market, more than a million acres were enclosed.

Under an act of enclosure, commissioners were appointed to reapportion the land equitably among all those with legal claims, and they are credited with having done so in the vast majority of cases. Nonetheless, many small landholders were unable to finance the necessary improvements specified by the law, such as fencing off their holdings. Often they were forced to sell their acres to the large landholder and become his tenants. Those who were able to carry out the initial improvements did well when a rising population and the Napoleonic Wars pushed prices to new heights and made almost any land profitable for cultivation; but for many farmers the enclosure movement spelled dispossession, which in turn forced them to find employment as laborers on large estates. The poor who had used the common wastes by custom and not by legal right were generally dispossessed, although the improvements and the intensified cultivation provided them with more regular work than they had had before.

Enclosures in the late eighteenth century did not cause an immediate mass migration to the rising industrial towns. The extent of migration from rural to urban areas nowhere exceeded the population surplus created by falling death rates and rising birth rates. Only in the depressed years after 1815, when

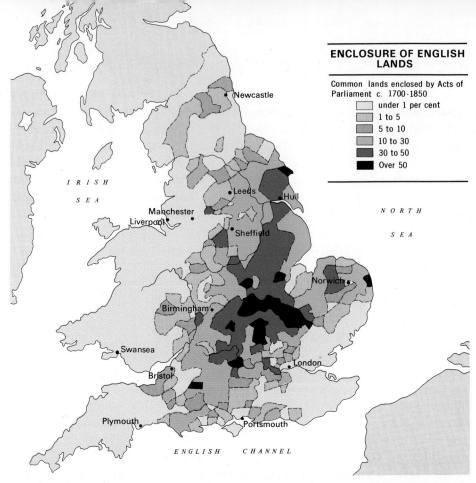

Common lands enclosed by Acts of
Parliament c. 1700-1850

- under 1 per cent
- 1 to 5
- 5 to 10
- 10 to 30
- 30 to 50
- Over 50

Enclosure in the sixteenth century affected no more than 20 per cent of the common lands in any English county, and even this proportion was rare. The extent of enclosure was far greater in the eighteenth and early nineteenth century, as this map demonstrates. Enclosure facilitated the modernization of English agricultural techniques, thereby contributing to an increase in grain production. In the long run, the disintegration of the vestiges of manorialism also forced people off the land and into the labor force of the growing industries in the north and west.

prices for farm products plummeted, that great numbers of small landholders were driven from the land.

The importance of this new rational use of the land in Britain was twofold: first of all, it meant that production of agricultural goods could be increased by a more efficient use of labor, freeing or forcing part of the expanding rural population to move to urban areas to seek employment in the new industrial establishments; and, second, it meant that England—unlike so many under-developed countries today—did not have to buy food abroad but could import raw materials for its developing industries.

On the Continent the pressure on the rural population was, for the most part, rather lower or of a different kind. In France, the Revolution had put much of the church land into the hands of small owners, and there was little or no reason for them to want to migrate to the city. In central Europe, the process of peasant emancipation was rather slower, and because the terms of emancipation—even in Prussia—were generally unfavorable, the peasants found it difficult to leave the land. The lower degree of labor mobility on the Continent—mobility that steadily declined as one went farther east—was one of the principal reasons why the era of industrial transformation occurred first in Britain.

The Expansion of the Market

Another reason why the Industrial Revolution came first in Britain was that country's advantageous position in world trade. Eighteenth-century industry was generally centered in the smallest unit of production possible, the rural cottage. It provided secondary employment for families that could not support themselves by working on the land full time—the majority of the poorer rural population. A merchant usually supplied the family with raw materials, bought their work by the piece, and marketed the product, perhaps at some considerable distance. This has been termed the domestic, or putting-out, system of industry. Naturally, as the demand for particular goods increased and the chances of making a profit correspondingly improved, the merchant wished to expand his business. This was precisely what happened during the seventeenth and eighteenth centuries. In the seventeenth century, while the expansion of the home market was held in check by internal wars and slow population growth, English merchants laid the basis for the great colonial empire of the eighteenth and nineteenth centuries. At first protected from competition by royal charter, enterprising merchants took great risks in sending cargoes to the Far and Near East, Russia, Africa, and the Western Hemisphere. The rewards were impressive, and the success of these voyages encouraged others to vie for the profits that could be won in distant lands.

By the eighteenth century, Britain's trade with other parts of the world was vigorously expanding. The re-export trade (goods imported from one country and subsequently exported to another) grew by 90 per cent in the first half of the eighteenth century; in the second half it almost doubled. British trade with the West Indies was a prime example of re-export. Commodities such as sugar, coffee, tobacco, and indigo were imported from the islands and exported in turn to the Continent (which took from 80 to 90 per cent of Britain's re-exports). The rapid expansion of this trade was in large part due to the Navigation Acts of the seventeenth century, which sought to build up the British merchant marine and enable it to by-pass the thriving Dutch commercial network. The theory behind these acts—mercantilism—subordinated all colonial industry to that of the mother country and contributed to the events leading up to the revolution of the American colonies.

Britain's domestic export trade—consisting in the main of such finished items as woolen cloth, nails, and hats—also expanded in the eighteenth century. In the fifty years between 1750 and 1800, it increased in value by 100 to 150 per cent. Whereas the Continental countries absorbed half of these exports in mid-century, by the turn of the century their share had slipped to one third. Over half went to the West Indies and North America, reflecting the resumption of Anglo-American trade after the end of the Revolutionary War. At the same time, Britain's imports were growing at a rate comparable to that of domestic exports. This increasing contact with other markets created a readily expandable demand for domestic manufactures and was responsible for the amazing growth of British port cities (the population of Liverpool rose from 6000 to 35,000).

Meanwhile, the internal market for British manufactures was also expanding significantly — because the population was growing and because the great expansion of internal transport facilities began to simplify and cheapen the shipment of goods. At the beginning of the eighteenth century, overland transportation in England was abominable; contemporary travelers said so in no uncertain terms. Although the English traveler was spared the numerous tolls and other economic and political obstructions that impeded traffic on the Continent, he was quite likely to find his carriage stuck in a hole at any time. As late as 1760 the coach journey from London to Glasgow took from ten to twelve days; from London to Oxford (fifty miles), two days. For the wagons that transported goods, the situation was even bleaker; frequently they could not move even a single mile in an hour. The most efficient form of overland transport was the horse.

Most of the main roads had originally been laid out by the Romans. Maintenance was the responsibility of each locality rather than the central government, and the result was chaotic disrepair. Sporadic attempts to remedy the situation consisted largely of edicts specifying what traffic was allowed to use the roads. Improvements began only after 1745, when the abominable state of the roads allowed the Young Pretender, Charles Edward Stuart, to lead a small army from Scotland as far south as Derby. Without adequate roads, a large force could not be massed against the invaders, and the situation was alarming enough to convince the central government that the solution lay in fitting the roads to the traffic, not vice versa. In the second half of the century numerous turnpike acts authorized individuals to repair and maintain the roads and charge tolls to those who used them. By 1800 the time for the journey between London and Glasgow had been cut to sixty-two hours. Not until after the Napoleonic Wars, however, were the roads sufficiently improved to make overland freight transport practicable in time and cost.

Yet certain goods had to be shipped around the country. Chief among these was coal, which had taken the place of Britain's dwindling supply of timber as the major source of heat for the growing cities. Because coal was so bulky, land transport was particularly difficult, and until the middle of the eight-

In the early nineteenth century English industrial preeminence depended to a large extent upon a happy combination of water transport and plentiful coal and ore deposits. Several of the largest deposits lay on the coasts, readily accessible to sea transport; a great network of navigable rivers and canals linked the interior fields to the coasts and population centers.

S C O T L A N D

Tweed R.

N O R T H

S E A

Carlisle

Lead
Zinc

Tyne R. Newcastle

Iron

Iron

ISLE OF MAN

Iron

Kendal

Ouse R.

I R I S H

Lancaster

S E A

York

Bradford
Leeds
Halifax

Humber R. Hull

Liverpool

Manchester
Sheffield

Mersey R.

Chester

Salt

R.

Lincoln

Lead

Nantwich

Zinc

Stoke

Lead

Iron

Trent R.

Nottingham

Derby

*The
Wash*

Stafford

Burton
Ashby

Welshpool

Iron

Wolverhampton

Iron

Welland R.

Stamford

Peterborough

Norwich

Birmingham

Thetford

Severn R.

W
A
L
E
S

Leonminster

Worcester

Warwick

Ouse R.
Great

Bury St. Edmunds

Hereford

Avon R.

Stratford

Bedford

Cambridge

Merthyr Tydfil

Gloucester

Iron

Iron

Oxford

Hertford

Cardiff

Bristol

London

BRISTOL CHANNEL

Thames R.

Guildford

Maidstone

ST. GEORGE'S CHANNEL

Salisbury

Portsmouth

Exeter

Tin

Plymouth

Tin

Copper

E N G L I S H

C H A N N E L

FRANCE

eenth century the policy was to ship coal by sea. But the coastal trade was not dependable: sailings could be held up for weeks in bad weather, and in wartime the ships were liable to capture by the enemy. Attention therefore turned to Britain's inland waterways. There were many miles of navigable rivers, and considerable effort was expended at this time to improve and enlarge the system. But by far the most important development was the construction of canals. Their total mileage in 1800 was only half that of the river system, but they linked the various navigable rivers and permitted tremendous savings in time and power. For example, a horse could pull fifty tons of produce along a canal as compared with thirty along a river, eight on a railed track, two on the improved roads. The most common means of land transport, the pack horse, could carry only one eighth of a ton.

The first canal was constructed by the duke of Bridgewater in 1759 to transport coal from his mines at Worsley to Manchester, a distance of less than seven miles. Its success was immediate—haulage costs were halved. The duke led the ensuing boom in canal construction, extending his canal to the mouth of the Mersey. From 1766 to 1777 work progressed on the ninety-three-mile Grand Trunk Canal, which connected the Trent to the Mersey, passing through the pottery area of Staffordshire and the salt-mining area of Cheshire. The project was strongly supported by other far-sighted individuals—great landowners with resources to exploit and rising industrialists who needed raw materials. The boom slowed in the 1770's and 1780's, but between 1790 and 1794 a veritable mania of canal building occurred. By the end of the century England had approximately two thousand miles of navigable waterways, both rivers and canals.

The great improvement in the cost and speed of internal transport had far-reaching effects: it created a larger market for both imported and domestic goods; it reduced the threat of food or fuel famine in the cities; and by making delivery a matter of days rather than weeks, it liberated capital that had hitherto been tied up in transport costs and storage.

Transportation conditions on the Continent varied widely. Holland, for instance, resembled Britain in its great emphasis on waterways, while in Belgium waterways were significantly complemented by paved roads. France witnessed a great road building era under Napoleon, and this program influenced territories immediately adjoining France. Moreover, in those parts of Europe once ruled by the Roman Empire, roads and bridges built centuries before continued to be of service. But in this respect as in many others, the farther east one moved, the more primitive conditions one encountered. This was true even in Prussia. It is said, for instance, that when Prussia took over the famous bishopric of Münster in 1803, a high official sent to preside over a gathering in that newly acquired territory found it easier to walk several miles to the meeting place rather than risk traveling on the only available road. Only after 1815 did Prussia begin to embark on the kind of expansive road building program required of a modern industrialized state.

Capital

Industrial expansion required a rising population to produce goods and growing markets in which to sell them. But equally necessary was a supply of capital to finance the building of factories, the installation of machines, and the hiring of labor. Where did this capital come from? Certainly not from the government, which, as has been seen, left the costly improvements in transportation to private enterprise. Indeed, the government—through its sale of bonds—actually competed with manufacturers for the rather limited funds the public then had available for investment.

The expenses of King William's wars with Louis xiv had brought the British national debt into existence: to support its army, the government had sold bonds paying a fixed sum of interest to the public. Now private borrowers were prohibited by law from offering a return higher than 5 per cent. The government was free from this limitation. In times of peace its interest rate was generally below 5 per cent, and then the public was willing to invest in private ventures that offered a higher return (and carried more risk). But in times of war, when the government needed money quickly to finance armies or subsidize allies, it could offer to pay from 5 to as much as 7 per cent. In such a case, intelligent investors purchased government securities, and private projects languished for want of capital. This happened during the eras of both the American and the French revolutions.

Historians and economists differ in their judgments of how critically government competition for investment capital limited industrial innovation and expansion. Certainly it had more effect on long-term projects such as canals (it has been noted that canal expansion was rapid during the 1760's and early 1790's and slow between 1770 and 1790) than on small enterprises such as textile mills, which could begin to earn a profit almost immediately. Perhaps it was fortunate that so much of the national debt was held by foreign investors (on the eve of the American Revolution three sevenths of the British national debt was held by Dutch investors), for this freed a corresponding amount of domestic capital for investment in more risky private enterprises. The contribution of the government to industrial expansion was mainly indirect: it accustomed the British public to impersonal investment and thereby prepared them to invest millions in the great railroad expansion of the nineteenth century.

If the British government did little to assist in the development of new industrial or commercial enterprises, the country banking system made a direct and important contribution to business expansion. Country banks would extend manufacturers lines of credit—if not to set up a business, at least to expand their operations—with their existing buildings or equipment serving as security. The country banks grew up outside London in the second half of the eighteenth century to fill a significant need of an expanding economy. Their chief functions were to supply capital, facilitate payments of debts in other parts of the country, and accept bills of exchange at a discount in return for currency. At first, any solid citizen through whose hands a volume of currency passed (or who had dealings in London and other parts of the country) might be called upon to perform these functions. Frequently a goldsmith, tax collector, or attorney who received money in trust performed the services unofficially and then set up an actual bank. The country banks (in conjunction with the London banks) were also especially important in transferring funds from one part of the country to another.

Despite the helpful role played by such banks, expansion-minded manufacturers in eighteenth-century England generally found profits from existing businesses were an even more important source of capital than funds loaned by bankers. The eighteenth century witnessed the tremendous success of small family businesses in which every possible cent was plowed back into additional equipment, buildings, or labor, while only a very small portion of the profits was withdrawn to meet personal expenses. Sometimes a partner or two might come in from outside the family, but English law forbade the formation of partnerships of more than six persons unless an expensive charter were secured from Parliament. The success of British manufacturers in this period was in large part a tribute to their energy, capacity for self-sacrifice, and devotion to profit. The expression "a nation of shopkeepers" may sometimes have been applied to Britain as a term of opprobrium, but it also identified an important factor in the rise of modern British business and capitalism.

Although the nature of the British banking system around 1800 left much to be desired, it was infinitely more satisfactory than its Continental counterpart. After the close of the Seven Years' War, Frederick the Great, who understood the economic needs of his ravaged country far better than most other rulers did theirs, set up a series of state banks, and in the 1770's and 1780's similar discount banks were set up in France, Russia, Denmark, Spain, and other countries. But most of these enterprises suffered disaster in the revolutionary era that followed, and, in any case, they never possessed the capital, authority, flexibility, and experience necessary to give the national economies a strong and effective lead. This continued backwardness of Continental banking—a backwardness unaffected by the growing importance of private banking entrepreneurs like those of the Rothschild family—was an additional factor in the continued lag of Continental industrial development.

Intellectual Climate

Certain intangible factors also contributed substantially to the economic progress of eighteenth-century Britain. Doubtless the most important was the prevailing intellectual climate, which was strongly conducive to economic change. The scientific discoveries of the seventeenth and eighteenth centuries encouraged men to believe that they could understand the workings of nature, and the revolutionary teachings of Newton spread confidence in the possibility of achieving progress by observation and experiment. Economics became increasingly an empirical science, and numerous policies — ranging from monopoly to trade restriction and regulations of all kinds — that inhibited economic growth came under increasing public scrutiny and attack.

The strong role of the Nonconformists (those Protestants — Presbyterians and others — who rejected the Church of England) in the growth of industry may be traced not only to their ethic of self-help and hard work but also to the education provided by their schools: the "dissenting academies" were as lively as the English secondary schools were somnolent. Their curriculum included mathematics, bookkeeping, history, and geography in addition to the traditional subjects of religion and rhetoric. And while the education offered by Oxford and Cambridge at this time was a poor joke, the universities at Glasgow and Edinburgh were throbbing with scientific inquiry and bustling with practical application of scientific theory.

Moreover, a new attitude toward human society was being expounded, particularly in the Scottish universities. Known as the "common-sense" or utilitarian school, it stressed empiricism, optimism, and enlightened self-interest as the guidelines for an improving society. The most important contribution to social theory made by the utilitarian school was Adam Smith's *The Wealth of Nations* (1776), which advances the idea that those who pursue enlightened self-interest are simultaneously acting in the best interests of society as a whole.

Adam Smith, a professor of moral philosophy at Glasgow, was no ivory tower theorist. He had read widely (especially the writings of Newton and Hume), traveled extensively abroad, and served the British government for a time as commissioner of taxes. Like the dominant mercantilist school of thought, Smith concerned himself primarily with factors tending to increase national wealth. But whereas mercantilists found the key to such increase to be strictly controlled trade, Smith found the principal factor to be production and advocated the gradual abolition of state restrictions on the freedom of trade. His doctrines rapidly gathered support throughout Europe, though Britain's turn toward freer trade, inaugurated by the Eden Reciprocity Treaty with France in 1786, was long delayed by the French Revolution and the wars that followed. It was not until the 1820's that the ideas of Smith and his disciples began to bear significant fruit in British (and still later Continental) trade policy.

II TECHNICAL AND INDUSTRIAL CHANGE

The Cotton Industry

In the eighteenth and nineteenth centuries British leadership in world affairs was based partly on the widespread popularity of British political and economic doctrines but also on the hard reality of economic power. At the center of that power was the recognized strength of the British textile industry, a key factor in the country's new industrial prominence. In the mid-eighteenth century, Britain's textile industry accounted for well over half its domestic exports. Woolen cloth represented much the largest portion of this trade; in terms of comparative volume the domestic cotton industry was nearly nonexistent. The woolen industry owed its position in good part to protective measures sponsored by the government. When printed cottons (calicoes) from India came into fashion in the first half of the century, the woolen interests persuaded the government to prohibit their importation.

Meanwhile, the British cotton industry (protected from Indian competition by the same legislation for which the woolen interests had argued) grew slowly. Its manufacture was centered in Lancashire, where a suitably damp climate, a good water supply, and a thriving port through which raw cotton could be imported (Liverpool) favored its growth. On the other hand, Lancashire spinners lacked the skills of their Indian counterparts, and the thread they produced was considerably weaker, making it necessary for domestic cotton cloth to be a blend of a cotton woof and a stronger linen warp. Though far inferior to the Indian cloths in texture, the result was eagerly accepted by the domestic market.

The woolen interests were unaware that they were fighting a losing battle with cotton—and so, for that matter, were the cotton manufacturers. But the signs were there: cotton was cheaper to produce than wool, even under the domestic system; the population wanted it (over the centuries there was an irregular but almost uninterrupted trend in favor of lighter fabrics); and the supply of raw material could be increased very quickly through the extension of slavery and the opening of new areas to cultivation. Even more important, cotton manufacture could immediately utilize the technological innovations of the latter half of the century (wool was too fragile for the earliest textile machinery); and simple as they were, these early innovations dramatically increased the output of thread.

The first innovation was the flying shuttle, patented in 1738 by John Kay, a weaver-mechanic in Colchester. This device not only enabled a weaver to produce a broader piece of cloth; it also speeded up the weaving process. But weavers opposed it, manufacturers refused to pay royalties, and court battles impoverished the inventor; and when the flying shuttle finally came into wide use in the 1760's, it made more acute the imbalance between the slow process of spinning thread and the more rapid process of weaving the threads into cloth.

The impetus to remedy this situation was particularly strong in Lancashire, where the people depended to a large extent on their earnings from the domestic textile industry. Many suggestions were put forward, and finally, in 1765, James Hargreaves, a weaver-carpenter, produced the spinning jenny, which enabled a single operator to spin several threads at once. The original model had eight spindles, but by the 1780's this capacity had been increased to eighty spindles or more. In 1769 Richard Arkwright, a barber and wig maker in Preston, took out a patent for another spinning device, the water frame, and in 1771 he and two partners constructed a mill on the Derwent River at Cromford, near Derby, where thread was spun on water-powered frames. The venture succeeded immediately: the water frame not only spun thread much more quickly than the spinning wheel but the thread was much stronger. For the first time it became possible to weave cloth with cotton thread alone. Arkwright and his partners set up workshops at Derby where pure calicoes were woven and printed. In 1785 Arkwright's patent lapsed, and the water frame was made available to all.

In 1779 the spinning mule, an improvement on both the jenny and the frame, was perfected by Samuel Crompton. It produced a thread finer than that of the frame and stronger than that of the jenny. The mule created a whole new branch of the textile industry. With the fine, strong thread it made, British spinners and weavers produced muslins of better quality than those woven in India; and there was an eager market for this lighter, all-cotton fabric. Production centered in Lancashire and in Scotland; as early as 1785 the manufacture of muslin occupied a million looms in Glasgow alone. The first mules were small, wooden devices powered by the spinner and thus suitable to the existing cottage industry; but in 1790 a Scottish manufacturer produced an automatic mule with from three to four hundred spindles, powered (like the frame) by a water wheel. By 1812 the mule had completely superseded the jenny. In petitioning Parliament for a grant, Crompton noted that it was being used in hundreds of factories with a total of four to five million spindles.

The effects of the jenny, water frame, and mule on the output of the cotton industry were revolutionary. In the last two decades of the century, raw cotton imports increased eightfold. The value of exported cotton cloth, a mere £250,000 in the 1760's, rose to £5 million. The balance between spinning and weaving was more than redressed. It was a golden age for the hand loom weavers: the output of spinners throughout Britain kept them oversupplied with work. Wages rose accordingly, and most weavers worked full time at their looms. Fortunately, other stages of manufacture kept up with the weavers: carding was mechanized in the 1770's, and in the 1790's chlorine bleaching replaced the old methods of boiling and sun bleaching and made it possible to achieve in days results which formerly had taken months.

But though early manufacturers could rely on an ever increasing demand for cotton cloth, an adequate supply of workers for their spinning mills was not always immediately available. The mills had to be located out in the country near water, and often there were not enough local workers willing to leave their overcrowded cottages and the small plots on which they scratched out a living. The poor relief system inhibited the mobility of labor in various ways. Parish officials in charge of poor relief were reluctant to allow workers to move to other localities, because the parish would remain responsible for their relief if they became destitute. In addition, potential employees often found the new factories indistinguishable from the workhouses where the unemployed were set to labor, and this feeling created a barrier to recruitment. To solve these problems, early mill owners in rural areas often had to resort to expensive paternalistic care of their workers.

A change of greatest consequence occurred in 1785 when the introduction of steam power made possible the building of mills in urban locations. Labor in the towns was in moderately good supply because of the population boom, but the rapid expansion of the cotton industry soon required new recruits for the work force in northern cities. The need was met by labor migrating from southern towns, by the dispossessed rural poor, and, on an increasing scale, by immigrants from impoverished Ireland. Thereafter, the cotton manufacturers usually could draw upon a more than adequate pool of labor. They could also rely on private contractors to put up jerry-built dwellings for the workers. Operating frequently on small margins of profit themselves, the mill owners were generally neglectful of the working and living conditions the workers had to endure in the mill towns.

One more innovation of the eighteenth century contributed to the cotton industry's great expansion—the power loom, patented in 1785 by Edmund Cartwright. His first factory failed financially, and his second was burned to the ground by hostile weavers. These disasters discouraged other English manufacturers, and the next efforts took place in Scotland. The success of the power loom came slowly: at the beginning of the nineteenth century, there were no more than a few hundred in operation in all Britain (in 1813, only 2400; in 1820, 14,150). But so long as the demand for cotton cloth expanded, its ultimate triumph was assured. The saving in manpower was obvious: a boy watching over two steam-driven looms could produce three-and-a-half times the output of a single adult operating a flying shuttle.

But the opposition of the handloom weavers was undying. Their stubborn refusal to work in the weaving mills despite an inexorable fall in their wages (the piece rate for hand-woven cloth dropped more than 80 per cent between 1814 and 1829) brought them appalling misery. And so long as they would work for near-starvation wages, it was actually cheaper to employ them than to equip a factory with power-driven looms. In addition, the scarcity of capital that prevailed during the wars of the French Revolution and Napoleon probably slowed the building of weaving factories equipped with power looms.

Technical innovations alone did not make increased output of cotton cloth possible. It took resourceful manufacturers to exploit the innovations. Rewards certainly existed for the enterprising: in 1789 Robert Owen borrowed £100 to start a cotton mill; twenty years later he was able to buy out his partners for £84,000 in cash. The greatest spur to expansion was the manufacturer's ability to cut prices and thereby capture—indeed create—new markets. A unique example of the creation of a new market was the systematic destruction of the Indian cotton industry, which continued until India actually became a market for Lancashire cotton goods, importing 11 million yards in 1820 and 145 million in 1840. The volume of British cotton cloth exports in the 1780's was three to four times that of the 1760's, and by 1810 it was ten times that of the 1780's.

Because cutting prices put considerable pressure on profit margins, it was necessary for manufacturers to reduce the costs of production, first with machines that made skilled labor more productive (the mule, for instance, which required a man's strength to operate) and second with machines that replaced expensive labor with cheap labor without reducing output (e.g., the power loom). It was fortunate that the cotton trade was to a large degree self-sustaining: the money spent for raw cotton in the United States and the West Indies returned to the manufacturers when these areas purchased finished cotton cloth.

Though humanitarians had long condemned the use of child labor in domestic industry, the entrepreneurs of the cotton industry soon discovered that women and children were satisfactory workers in the new factories and, for many operations in the mills, the most desirable employees. Not only could they be paid lower wages than male employees but they could more easily be forced to accept harsh factory discipline than adult males. Furthermore, children could crawl under the machines to retrieve fragments of cloth and clean the equipment. But if the cotton industry was a dramatic example of the new industrial Britain, it should be noted that the social abuses of the cotton factories were among the first to be publicized and attacked in Parliament.

On the Continent, too, the cotton industry made some headway around 1800, but that progress was far slower than in Britain. An important reason for the comparative backwardness of France in this regard was the lack of initiative on the part of its manufacturers. Later on, the Napoleonic Wars interrupted the French cotton supply (and produced a corresponding increase in the demand for woolen cloth). The result was that France suffered for decades from serious technological lag in cotton textile manufacture. It was not until after 1815 that this lag began to be overcome, and even then the French cotton industry trailed far behind Britain's.

The Iron Industry

Although technological innovation and the factory system brought spectacular developments in the cotton industry, it would not be true to say that that industry was solely responsible for the revolution that transformed the basic methods of industrial production throughout England. After all, the cotton industry was largely self-contained: its raw material was entirely imported, so that British agriculture was not stimulated; and because the industry was highly localized in Lancashire and Derby and in Scotland, it did not create a spreading demand for transport and building facilities. For the spread of revolutionary production methods throughout the British economy, one must look to the iron industry.

Unlike the cotton industry, the iron industry was already developing along modern lines in the eighteenth century. It was already part of the factory system, in that it required a relatively large physical plant and a large concentration of workers in a single location in both its mining and smelting operations. The mined ore was smelted in a blast furnace to remove impurities. It was then run into molds called "pigs"—hence the name "pig iron" for the product of the blast furnace. The pig iron was remelted and either turned into castings (forming hard and brittle cast iron) or forged into wrought iron (which is malleable and tensile) and then drawn out and cut into rods. Serious problems beset the industry in the early eighteenth century. Pig iron production in the 1720's was actually slightly lower than it had been a hundred years earlier.

The most serious problem involved fuel for the smelting furnaces. At this time the only fuel that could be used with any success was charcoal, and centuries of cutting had depleted the forests of England. Thus smelting had to be carried on in remote wooded areas at some distance from the deposits of iron ore, and the costs of transporting the ore were extremely high. It was not practicable to set up smelting operations near the ore deposits and transport the timber there, because several tons of charcoal were required to smelt a single ton of ore. Moreover, the iron ore found in Britain was of such a low grade that even when expensively smelted with charcoal, it was not suitable for better quality plows, hoes, locks, bolts, and so forth. For these goods, high-quality ore had to be imported from Sweden.

Early in the eighteenth century, Abraham Darby of Coalbrookdale succeeded in smelting iron ore with coke (a coal derivative); but it was not until mid-century that the process produced cast iron of salable quality and spread throughout the countryside. Coke could not yet be used in the forging of wrought iron, however, because it introduced additional impurities into the pig iron. Nonetheless, the use of coke was an important step forward. The new and cheaper cast iron could be substituted for low-quality wrought iron in many cases, so that smelting furnaces were no longer tied to the forests but could be located near iron ore and coal (which were usually found together in Britain). The production of pig iron doubled in the next decade.

The increased supply of pig iron encouraged efforts to find a method of using coke to turn it into high-quality wrought iron. Among the early experimenters who came close to success was John Roebuck of the great Carron ironworks. In 1783 and 1784 Henry Cort, a contractor to the Admiralty, patented "puddling" and "rolling," processes that made possible the production of wrought iron with coke fuel at a price and of a quality that effectively killed both the charcoal industry and the importing of Swedish ore. In the process of puddling and rolling, pig iron was heated with coke and stirred with iron rods until many of its impurities were burned away. Then the white-hot metal passed between rollers which pressed out the remaining molten dross and shaped the iron into rods. The use of rollers in place of extensive hammering made it possible to produce fifteen tons in the time it had previously taken to produce one. Now the smelting and rolling operations could be integrated. Cort's patent lapsed in 1789, and his process became available to the whole industry.

The most ingenious proponent of new uses for iron in the eighteenth century was John Wilkinson, one of the great engineers of the early Industrial Revolution. In addition to his numerous other contributions, including a significantly improved boring engine patented in 1774, he showed that iron could be used effectively for chairs, brewery vats, pipes, bridges, and finally boats. When Wilkinson died in 1805, he was buried, as he had wished, in an iron coffin.

As a result of numerous important technological advances, the output of the British iron industry quadrupled in the early decades of the nineteenth century, spurred on in the first place by the abnormally high demand for naval and military equipment resulting from the wars with France. By 1800 iron had already taken the place of wood in the frames of textile machines (leather simultaneously replaced fiber pulley ropes), and great progress was made in the campaign against factory breakdowns. Britain's share of the world's production of iron rose tremendously, increasing from 19 per cent in 1800 to 40 per cent in 1820 to 52 per cent in 1840—more than all other nations combined.

Whereas in Britain the cotton industry had been the most important expression of the new industrial era, on the Continent it was the coal and iron industry that was in the vanguard—although here, too, the Continent lagged considerably behind Britain. For one thing, coal deposits were too scattered to be effectively utilized without adequate means of transportation (not available before the railroad era that began in the 1830's). French ironworks did not successfully smelt iron with coke until 1785, and it was not until 1818 that the puddling and rolling processes were finally introduced in France. Moreover, both before and after Waterloo, iron imports from Britain tended to retard local production and technological development.

Ever since the 1760's the French government, realizing something of the importance of the iron industry for the continued development of the country's war machine, had sent French scientists and engineers to Britain to study the latest technological developments, and a number of highly knowledgeable and enterprising Britishers had moved to France to assist in the advancement of iron production and machine building, among other enterprises. Yet these efforts were not sufficient to allow France—much less other Continental countries—to overcome Britain's lead in this crucial aspect of industrial development.

Steam Power

No invention was more important to the development of industrial technology than the steam engine. Without a source of power greater than human or animal strength and more dependable than wind or water, the new machines could not have been concentrated on the scale that characterizes the modern factory system.

The history of the steam engine began with Denis Papin's experimental machine in 1690, and about 1702 Thomas Newcomen developed a machine with a cylinder and piston, separate boiler, and hand-operated valves. But it remained for James Watt, a Scottish instrument maker, to produce a workable steam engine in 1769. At the University of Glasgow in the 1760's, Watt became familiar with the Newcomen engine, a rudimentary atmospheric pressure engine used for pumping water from coal mines. Over a period of years, putting to good use scientific advice given him by a physics professor at Edinburgh, Watt developed an engine that used steam as an active motor

In the early nineteenth century the various textile industries were widespread on the Continent, although the introduction of mechanization was a slow process. On the other hand, the growth of national iron industries was hampered by a shortage of domestic coal. France simply lacked extensive deposits; they existed in Germany, but were still largely unworked.

power and consumed considerably less fuel than the Newcomen engine. John Roebuck of the Carron ironworks realized the importance of Watt's machine and entered into partnership with him immediately. The first steam engine, however, worked imperfectly—the Carron works were unable to supply parts accurate enough for Watt's specifications. Shortly, Roebuck transferred his partnership rights to an enterprising friend, Matthew Boulton.

The son of a prosperous Birmingham toy manufacturer and the husband of an heiress, Boulton was the prototype of the freewheeling industrial entrepreneur. Initially, he was interested in Watt's engine because his metal goods factory needed additional motive power. By the end of 1774, Watt's engine had been overhauled by Boulton's skilled workmen; the ironmaster John Wilkinson had supplied parts far more accurate than any hitherto available; and Watt's engine was working effectively. Parliament granted a twenty-five-year extension of his patent, and he and his associates used that time to make additional changes and improvements. In 1781 he took out an additional patent for a device called the "sun and planet," which converted the engine's two-way motion to rotary.

As early as 1775, one of Watt's engines had been put to work pumping water from coal mines, and in the following year Wilkinson ordered an engine for his blast furnaces. Now its uses multiplied; at Boulton's Soho plant the improved steam engine worked bellows, rolling mills, and hammers. All the great ironmasters adopted the new engines, and it became possible to move forges and smelting furnaces from rivers to more centrally located sites. The first steam-powered spinning mill was set up in 1785 (the same year that Arkwright's patent on the frame lapsed). Hereafter it was possible for textile mills to move to urban areas, where the supply of labor was more abundant. By 1800, when the Watt-Boulton patent expired, five hundred steam engines had been constructed. In 1804 another inventor, Arthur Woolf, produced the first commercially successful compound engine, which was more efficient than the Watt model: it saved an enormous amount of energy by reusing the steam that had driven the original cylinder.

Continental experience with the development of steam power was quite similar to Continental experience with other aspects to the Industrial Revolution. A Newcomen engine was set up near Paris in 1726 to pump water, but this remained an isolated event. In 1778 Watt obtained a French patent for his engine; and in 1784 five British steam engines were in operation at the Le Creusot ironworks. But again there was little follow-up. Although France was able to obtain new machines from Britain even during the more than twenty years that the two countries were at war, in 1810 there were only two hundred steam engines in all France as against five thousand in Britain.

The comparative backwardness of France was nothing compared to that of the other European states, and this helps to explain why Britain had such a tremendous head start in the race for industrial leadership and why it was able to maintain its lead throughout the next half-century.

III THE SOCIAL CONSEQUENCES OF INDUSTRIALIZATION

Standards of Living

By modern standards, conditions in British factories during this period — particularly after they relocated in the towns — were close to hellish. The working day was long: twelve to sixteen hours was not uncommon, and after 1792 illumination by coal gas made round-the-clock operations possible. Buildings lacked modern ventilating systems, and the heat was often debilitating. To ensure that the workers kept toiling, many employers instituted systems of financial penalties, which far outweighed the time lost, for lateness or inattention. It is impossible to imagine a child keeping his attention on the same task for twelve to sixteen hours at a stretch, yet over half of the mill workers were between the ages of ten and eighteen. Corporal punishment was not uncommon. It was an accepted maxim of the eighteenth century that the poor would be lazy if they were not forced to work.

Early efforts to improve the treatment of workers achieved some success in 1802, when Parliament passed an act obliging employers to conform to certain rules concerning hygiene (only two children to a bed, proper ventilation, whitewash on factory walls), education, and working hours (a maximum of twelve, excluding meals) for apprentices. Unfortunately, the practical results were slight: factory inspection was a totally new field for government, and the inspectors who were appointed in each county (one a local magistrate, the other an Anglican clergyman) were generally less than conscientious. Effective factory legislation was not achieved until the 1830's.

On the surface, the standard of living in England rose during the period under consideration: the death rate decreased by more than a third in the period from 1730 to 1820. Both agricultural and industrial wages increased by some 75 per cent in the period from the 1760's to the end of the Napoleonic Wars. Such increases, especially when gained by the new industrial working class, became the subject of considerable public discussion and criticism. Even official government reports, compiled for the Board of Agriculture, complained of "the influx of wealth amongst the laboring class," which forced farmers and landlords to pay higher wages to less efficient farm help. But if wages were driven up by full employment in the early war period, so were prices — so much so that real income, measured by the amount of goods wages could buy at any given time, actually declined during this period. When the increased full-time employment of women and children in the factories is taken into account, it seems likely that a family's real wages held their own but did not increase.

The later years of the Napoleonic Wars brought particular distress to the factory workers, as European markets were largely closed t6 British goods and unemployment spread. By the early 1800's, Britain was involved in a murderous trade war. It began in November 1806 with the proclamation of

Napoleon's Continental System, designed to ruin Britain's foreign trade. The British government responded in January-February 1807 by promulgating a series of Orders in Council requiring that all trade with France go through Britain. When the American Embargo Act of 1807 and the Non-Intercourse Act of 1809 closed United States ports to British and French ships, the results for Britain were disastrous: in Birmingham, where half the total volume of the city's output went to the American market, nine thousand people went on relief, and manufacturers were left with huge surpluses in their warehouses. Moreover, bad harvests in 1809 and 1811 forced the price of bread to new heights.

Although the poor were exempt from the income tax that Pitt introduced to help finance the war, the customs duties and excise fell more heavily on the poor than on those who bought luxuries. Nor did the end of the Napoleonic Wars bring noticeable improvement. In the period of deflation that followed, prices declined somewhat more rapidly than wages, but this drop was more than balanced by the rise in unemployment or underemployment that resulted from the addition of some 300,000 demobilized soldiers and seamen to the labor force. As a result, in 1815 many workers were experiencing the condition of sudden unemployment that was to be endemic in nineteenth-century industrialism.

Social Unrest

Considering the widespread political ferment of the decades after 1760 and the unprecedented technological and social changes of those years, it is not surprising that the period during and immediately after the wars with France was marked by a rising tide of unrest among the British working class. Of course, there had been outbreaks of violence in the past — riots when work was scarce or the cost of food too high. But the coming of the French Revolution brought discontent to the surface on a larger scale than ever before.

Initial British reaction to the outbreak of the French Revolution was by no means unfriendly. While the government perhaps secretly welcomed the initial stages of the upheaval because they weakened France as a world power, dissenters and radicals inside and outside Parliament were inspired to join clubs pressing, first of all, for more equal representation of the great mass of the population in Parliament. Poets and intellectuals declared their support. In January 1792 the shoemaker Thomas Hardy founded the London Corresponding Society, a reform group consisting largely of working people, to exchange ideas with similar groups in the provinces. Among the aims of Hardy's group were parliamentary representation for all the people, care for the aged, and a better standard of living for the poor.

The events of the early 1790's — French expansionism and the September massacres in Paris in 1792 — began slowly to alarm the British government, and it embarked on a policy of actively discouraging and, eventually, repressing radical societies, particularly among the working class. Isolated persecutions of reformers took place: in 1794 thirteen members of the leading London reform societies (including Hardy himself) were arrested and tried for treason. When a jury of middle-class citizens found them not guilty, the London mob went wild, but the celebration was premature. In 1795 large public meetings were forbidden without a special permit, and with the Treasonable Practices Act and the Seditious Meetings Act the government banned workers' combinations and the embryonic trade unions, fearful that they would provide cover for political agitation. The government's repressive policy was not based entirely on paranoid fear of Red revolution in Britain; throughout the revolutionary and Napoleonic eras in France, a small but dedicated radical, pro-Jacobin movement was active among British workers.

In years when employment was high, political ideas had little attraction for most workers. But with high prices and rising unemployment, their interest in political action—or any other action designed to protect what they deemed their best interests—increased considerably. Even during the latter years of the Napoleonic Wars, the British working class was beginning to exhibit that conservative hatred of the machine that was to mark many of its struggles against the modern capitalistic system down to our own times. Instead of accepting (much less welcoming) the machine age as a potential liberating force and a social boon that would eventually provide a higher standard of living and a more pleasant, safe, and humane existence, many British workers seemed determined to delay, obstruct, and, if possible, block completely most efforts at economic change. For if their lot was bleak enough before the onset of massive technological change, the social consequences of early industrialization seemed to most British workmen to be even more degrading.

In 1811 and 1812 the "Luddites" rioted and destroyed machines in the industrial areas of Lancashire and Yorkshire to demonstrate solidarity against their employers. The government called out the army to put down the uprising, and at one trial alone more than a dozen "Luddites" were tried and convicted on charges of having violated a 1769 law providing "for the more effectual punishment of such persons as shall demolish or pull down, burn, or otherwise destroy or spoil any mill or mills." That more effectual punishment was death. (Usually, however, the death sentence was commuted to transportation to a penal colony.)

It was hardly surprising, then, that at the opening of the nineteenth century the social gulf between the entrepreneurs and the workers in the factory towns was widening. The workers lived in squalid slums, without running water, lighted streets, or adequate sanitation. Their employers were building substantial homes in the expanding suburbs and driving about in carriages. The industrial bourgeoisie enjoyed the delights of subscription libraries, assemblies (dances), concerts, and theaters. Their sons even went on a modified Grand Tour to see how industry was organized on the Continent. Diversions for the poor were not approved, on the general theory that amusements would distract workers from the job at hand.

Considering the suffering of the British working class during the era of the Napoleonic Wars, it seems remarkable that there was not more popular disaffection—or pro-French revolutionary feeling—during this period. Indeed, it is quite likely that popular agitation might have been considerably stronger, especially in rural districts, had it not been for the implementation of the so-called Speenhamland system of poor relief. In 1795 the plight of rural laborers was severe, and riots and unrest among the hungry populace were spreading. As a result, in that year the justices in Berkshire, who were empowered to fix the level of wages, met in the village of Speenhamland to consider the situation. In their judgment the distress was temporary, and they therefore declined to raise wages. Instead, they decided to supplement wages with poor relief on a scale that varied with the price of bread and the number of people in a family. The Speenhamland plan was adopted all over Britain.

The cost of the program was high: Britain spent £2 million on poor relief in 1785, £4 million in 1801, and £6.5 million in 1812. Some called it useless and self-defeating. The chief spokesman for this point of view was Thomas Malthus, an Anglican clergyman who in 1798 published his controversial treatise, *An Essay on the Principle of Population as It Affects the Future Improvement of Society*. Malthus himself was a generous, outgoing person, yet past history and contemporary social conditions drove him to a position of gloomy pessimism. In brief, Malthus held the working class responsible for its own misery. He put forth the idea that the population of the world naturally tended to outstrip the means of production, that therefore misery and hunger were inevitable (unless the poor mended their ways and practiced sexual continence), and that the current system of poor relief was actually contributing to future suffering by allowing the poor to have far too many children without thinking of the economic consequences.

Criticism notwithstanding, in the short run the justices' decision to implement the Speenhamland plan was a humane one: it kept the workers from starvation. In times of severe depression, poor relief alleviated some of the worst distress and restrained rural discontent. But in the long run, the Speenhamland system operated against the welfare of farm workers by keeping their wages low. So long as wages would be supplemented by poor relief, farmers could continue to pay less than a living wage. Furthermore, by offering a pitifully wretched security, the system tended to keep many people from moving to the cities, and consequently labor was not always available for the manufacturer to hire when he needed it.

On the Continent the problems of the rural and urban masses were rather different. In France after 1791, for instance, the working people operated under the discriminatory *loi Chapelier*, which effectively banned associations of workingmen; and whatever showy concern for the welfare of his subjects

Napoleon displayed from time to time, he neither knew nor cared about the problems produced by the Industrial Revolution or how to alleviate them.

Farther east, the inability of the governments to deal rapidly and effectively with the problems of peasant emancipation stored up still further trouble for the future. Not only was the progress of industrialization retarded by the peasants' continued lack of freedom, but such emancipation policies as were actually instituted—including those in Prussia during the ministries of Stein and Hardenberg in the early 1800's—tended to be protracted, cumbersome, and discriminatory against the peasants.

Two conclusions can be drawn from the study of the beginnings of the Industrial Revolution in Europe. First, Britain set the pace in both economic progress and attendant social problems. Modern industry developed in Britain before it appeared in Continental countries because all the necessary conditions existed there: a surplus food supply, capital for investment, an ample and fluid labor force, and a suitable intellectual climate. Second, while in some areas the Napoleonic Wars contributed significantly to economic and social progress—directly and indirectly—on the whole they tended to distract the attention of European statesmen and politicians who might otherwise have made a start at tackling the gigantic problems created by the incipient technological revolution. What all this meant in practice was that economic, social, political, and national problems would henceforth interact in a new and unprecedented fashion.

4

HERITAGE ESSAY

THE HERITAGE OF THE INDUSTRIAL REVOLUTION

The factory system required a tremendous adjustment in the psychology and daily habits of the working class. Industrial workers had to be taught to subject their daily lives to the authority of the bells that announced the beginning and end of the work shift. The difficulty of teaching workers accustomed to the greater freedom possible in agricultural labor to adjust to industrial schedules was one reason why early factory managers liked to use women and children, who were psychologically more malleable.

Industrial workers also had to be weaned away from the glut-and-famine attitude traditional in rural society. In the old economy, many workers—not only on farms but in cottage industry—were accustomed to labor only until they had earned enough to tide them over for a few weeks or months and then to withdraw and apply themselves to the pleasure of consumption, to drink and leisure. The early industrial entrepreneurs had to educate workers in the advantages of long-term saving and teach them to work for a better future for themselves and their families. In this educational process, the managers were aided by the Wesleyan ethic of independence, thrift, and sobriety. Many early entrepreneurs remarked that their best workers were Methodists; the evangelical morality induced them to stay at their jobs and work hard.

Workers also had to be educated to regard new industrial processes as opportunities to be exploited rather than as threats to be resisted. Many of those who suffered most from unemployment during the early decades of the Industrial Revolution in Britain were engaged in technologically obsolete industries, such as handloom weaving. The natural response of workers faced with competition from new machinery was to riot and destroy the machines—machine-breaking by "Luddites" was common in Britain's embryonic industrial society. As late as the 1830's, violence was a common working-class response to industrial change, and it was not until the 1850's and 1860's that British workers were generally convinced that industrialization could benefit them, given the help and protection of trade union organization.

The Industrial Revolution had another consequence for the workers: it gave them a class consciousness, made them into a community, and induced them to organize. In the early decades of the Industrial Revolution, the for-

221

mation of labor unions was bitterly fought by employers, resisted by the government, and condemned as illegal by the courts. The forming of combinations of workers (and also of employers) was regarded as conspiracy in restraint of trade under the common law. In addition, during the wars with France from 1792 to 1815, the British government was frightened by the persistence of democratic radicalism within the working class, and the landed interests which dominated the government looked upon labor unions as centers of revolutionary Jacobinism. In 1824–1825, however, British workers were finally given the freedom to organize by parliamentary legislation, although legal strictures and impediments to unrestrained trade union activity persisted for several decades.

The New Industrial Order. Factory work imposed discipline that was new to workers who came from the country-side. Facing page, top: "bell-time" in an early nineteenth-century factory. Women and children were easier to subject to this discipline than men; they also could be paid lower wages. Children were also used for work-operations that involved crawling under the machines. Facing page, bottom: women and children at work in a cotton factory in Manchester. Although female and child labor had always been exploited in rural villages, the treatment of women and children in the new factories was unquestionably severe and unjust. "They show their wounds: they accuse." (William Blake) Above: the *Manufacture Nationale,* Paris, 1800, the only French steelworks comparable in size to those in Sheffield. It is significant that much of the power is provided by human labor.

R. *Johnson, del.*   T. *Bewick, sculp.*

THE DEPARTURE.

Published January 1, 1804, by William Bulmer, at the
Shakspeare Printing Office, Cleveland Row.

Social Disorganization. The disinclination of the late eighteenth-century British government, dominated by landed aristocrats and gentry, to intervene in the industrial sector of the economy was a negative but nonetheless important stimulus to the Industrial Revolution. Freed from government restrictions, entrepreneurs and investors could build factories and develop machines entirely in terms of market factors, rather than in accordance with extraneous political considerations. But this economic freedom, beneficial as it was to the capitalists and employers, was disastrous for the British workers. In the early decades of the Machine Age, the government made little effort to protect those in town and country whose lives were disrupted and brutalized by industrialization and urbanization. The agricultural revolution, particularly the enclosure movement, forced rural workers off the land—as shown in the sentimental but basically accurate engraving of the early nineteenth century on the facing page. When these rural emigrants reached the towns, there was no political or legal structure to regulate working conditions. These were especially savage in the mines (above), but in the textile and iron centers the impact of social disorganization was also severe.

The landed class also had to make a painful adjustment to industrialization and urbanization. Although some lords had invested in the new technology —particularly in transportation and mining—it was only very slowly that the aristocracy recognized the great advantages to national wealth and power that the factories represented. Most lords simply ignored the tremendous economic upheaval in the new towns; many regarded the environmental changes as a dreadful departure from the beauty of rural England, and this emphasis on the ugliness of the new society was also a favorite theme of intellectuals and litterateurs. Even more painful for the aristocracy was the recognition of industrial capitalists as political equals; in 1815 the new industrial towns and the entrepreneurs still had no representation in the House of Commons. Acceptance of the lords of industry as social equals by the landed aristocracy was quite unthinkable. Only slowly and grudgingly was that acceptance effected in the second half of the century.

The Industrial Revolution thus inaugurated the most profound transformation in social attitudes that had occurred in many centuries. Partly in response to working-class resistance and aristocratic hostility, the new industrialists developed a distinct ideology that was to have a great influence. This ideology has been variously called "economic liberalism," "laissez-faire philosophy," and "the Manchester school of economics." Since the second half of the nineteenth century it has been generally viewed as a conservative social theory designed to serve the selfish interests of grasping capitalists, but when it was developed, between 1800 and 1820, it was regarded by its proponents as a liberating, indeed radical theory, drawing upon the ideals of the Enlightenment and conducive to the welfare of mankind.

The industrial ideology takes its rise from Adam Smith's *The Wealth of Nations,* published in 1776, before the significance of the new economy was apparent. The liberal economic theory that Smith propounded was further developed by the utilitarian philosopher Jeremy Bentham, an indefatigable critic of privilege and inefficiency in the *ancien régime.* Following Smith's theory of the effective autonomy of the economic system and angered by the extravagant granting of privileges and the irrational economic regulation characteristic of the old aristocratic government, Bentham in 1798 claimed

The Citadel of Capitalism. As Britain assumed its position as the workshop of the world, the commercial and financial importance of London was inevitably enhanced. Its area and population became steadily larger, its streets and buildings ever more imposing, the houses of its high bourgeoisie ever more lavish. Above: Piccadilly Circus and Lower Regent Street in the early nineteenth century. Facing page: the dividend office of the Bank of England, the temple of capitalism, built in 1818. Left: a Methodist chapel in London. The Wesleyan ethic of self-help and hard work appealed to the new industrial bourgeoisie; some capitalists were members of the Methodist Church, others inclined to the evangelical, pro-Wesleyan wing of the Church of England. All of the higher bourgeoisie thought that the Wesleyan ethic was good for the working class, and many of the upper stratum of factory workers did attend Methodist chapels.

The Proletariat. Beginning in the 1830's a series of Factory Acts mitigated the worst abuses of untrammeled capitalism, but the living and employment problems of the working class remained critical in Britain, the modern world's first industrialized society. By mid-century working-class housing in London was somewhat better than it had been earlier in the century, but slum conditions in all industrial centers remained generally horrible. Below: an engraving of a London slum by the French artist Gustav Doré. Mean as the daily life of the worker was, his situation became far worse during chronic periods of economic slump. Unemployment and poverty bore a social stigma—a survival of preindustrial attitudes. The middle class tended to assume that poverty was the workers' own fault—they were alleged to be lazy and shiftless—and the unemployed were accordingly given punitive treatment. The healthy indigent were set to work in prison-like workhouses, whose purpose was to keep the unemployed occupied and under surveillance, lest they riot, and to make unemployment as miserable a condition as possible. Facing page: a workhouse in 1810.

that "security and freedom are all that industry requires" and that "the motto, or watchword of government . . . ought to be—Be quiet."[1]

With the rapid industrial expansion in the new towns, this laissez-faire policy was given a meliorist tone—free enterprise would produce harmony and peace among the nations of the world. David Ricardo, a retired London stockbroker who became the founder of modern economic science, defined the creed of the industrial capitalist as follows:

Under a system of perfectly free commerce, each country naturally devotes its capital and labour to such employments as are most beneficial to each. The pursuit of individual advantage is admirably connected with the universal good of the whole . . . and binds together by one common tie of interest and intercourse, the universal society of nations throughout the civilized world.[2]

According to the new economic theory the wages and employment of the working class were also subject to the operation of the free market and

1. Jeremy Bentham, *A Manual of Political Economy*, in A. Bullock and M. Shock, eds., *The Liberal Tradition.* New York: New York University Press, 1957, pp. 28, 29.
2. David Ricardo, *The Principles of Political Economy and Taxation*, in *The Liberal Tradition*, p. 36.

inflexible economic laws. Thomas Malthus, in 1798, had claimed that when workers are paid more, they produce more children, thereby glutting the labor supply, driving wages down, and causing unemployment. Therefore the workers "are themselves the cause of their own poverty."[3] Ricardo agreed and developed Malthus' gloomy theory into an iron law of wages:

The natural price of labour is that price which is necessary to enable the labourers, one with another, to subsist and to perpetuate their race, without either increase or

3. Thomas Malthus, *Essay on the Principle of Population,* in *The Liberal Tradition,* p. 31.

diminution. . . . When, however, by the encouragement which high wages give to the increase of population, the number of labourers is increased, wages again fall to their natural price, and indeed from a reaction sometimes fall below it.[4]

It is wrong to see Malthus and Ricardo as mere ideological spokesmen for the Manchester capitalists. They were independent and brilliant social theorists, convinced that the Industrial Revolution had brought with it grave economic and social problems. Malthus claimed that in the new industrial society, un-

4. Ricardo, *Principles,* in *The Liberal Tradition,* p. 31.

Violent Protest against Economic Change. Working-class response to the economic changes and social disorganization of the early nineteenth century included rioting and property destruction by bands of militant workers dedicated to mythical symbols of violent protest like Ned Ludd and Captain Swing. Facing page: Ned Ludd disguised as a woman, inciting arsonists and machine-breakers. Above: the established classes prepare to resist working-class violence while insurgents demand "No Machines" and the lowering of parish tithes and proclaim "Swing Forever."

less the workers learned sexual continence, population would increase by geometric progression and the food supply only arithmetically, raising the specter of starvation and social disaster. This, in fact, did not happen in Western civilization, but it may be occurring in the second half of the twentieth century in non-Western societies. Ricardo was pessimistic about the industrial capitalist's prospects: he saw the capitalist squeezed between the "rent" (profit) earned by landlords and the wages demanded by workers. Again, this did not happen, but Ricardo's analysis of the conflict among landlord, capitalist, and worker was a foundation for the Marxist doctrine of the inevitable class struggle

The New Jerusalem. As the Napoleonic Wars drew to a close, more attention was devoted to the social consequences of industrialization. Utopian socialists devised plans for cooperative communities and radical democrats demanded that the workers be enfranchised. Below: Robert Owen's plan for a model agricultural and industrial village of happy workers. Facing page: one of the very few left-wing M.P.'s of the period, Henry "Orator" Hunt, addressing a crowd of militant workers in Manchester. Yet these great expectations for rapid social and political progress were soon disappointed. Owen finally managed to establish a utopian community in the United States, but it failed and disintegrated rapidly. British skilled workers were not enfranchised until 1867 and unskilled workers only gained the vote in 1884.

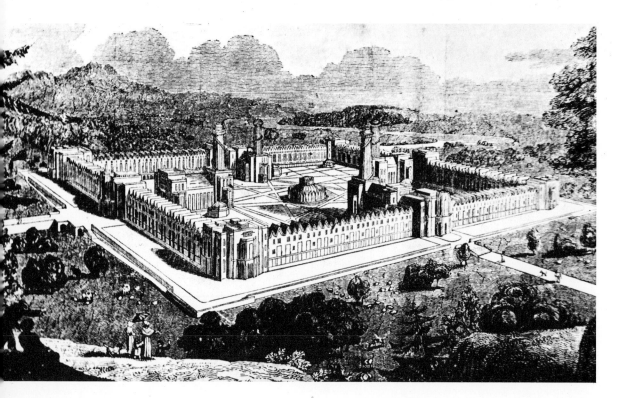

The era of the early Industrial Revolution left not only a heritage of industrial capitalist ideology but various antitheses to it. The simplest, most direct, and yet most futile reaction was the visceral response of some workers in industries rendered technologically obsolescent by the new economic order: they attempted to destroy the machinery that had brought such dislocation and deprivation into their lives. At a trial in Yorkshire in 1813, an angry crown prosecutor described the activities of these "Luddites":

Those mischievous Associations . . . have had for their object merely the destruction of machinery invented for the purpose of saving manual labor in manufactures. . . . Armed bodies of these men, in some instances several hundred in number . . . have attacked the mills, shops, and houses of manufacturers and others, . . . destroyed tools worked by machinery, and in some instances shot at persons whose property they have attacked.[5]

A second response to industrialism—characteristic of working-class leaders and of radical social theorists like William Godwin—drew upon the natural rights doctrine of the eighteenth century, which became unfashionable in middle-class intellectual circles after the Jacobin scare of the 1790's. This view held that the workers had a right to the vote, and furthermore a right to a reasonable share of the world's goods so that they might lead secure and happy lives.

A third response was somewhat more innovative. Robert Owen, himself a successful mill owner in Scotland, contended that "the characters of men are formed chiefly by the circumstances in which they are placed." He himself provided good housing and salubrious working conditions for his employees. But he envisaged something beyond this: the establishment of a workers' community in which the carefully controlled environment would mold men's characters toward cooperation, creativity, and joy. Thus was born—or reborn—the utopian ideal that inspired early nineteenth-century socialism. Owen also participated in yet a fourth response to aggressive industrialism—the appeal to Parliament to legislate a code protecting workers from the selfishness of entrepreneurial capitalism. With the assistance of Robert Peel (another industrialist and the father of the prime minister of that name) Owen persuaded Parliament in 1802 to take the first faltering steps to protect laboring women and children from the impact of the new economy.

Luddism died out for the most part by 1840, but the other responses to the Industrial Revolution would be pressed not only in Britain but in all countries of the Western world in the nineteenth century as ways of emancipating the working class. The improvement of working-class conditions would be one of the main themes of modern history.

5. *Proceedings at York Special Commission, January, 1813*, M. Harris *et al.*, eds., *Introduction to Contemporary Civilization in the West.* New York: Columbia University Press, 1963, II, pp. 254-255.

PART TWO

The

Democratization

of Western

Civilization

**From the Romantic Upheaval
to the Unification of Germany**

Between 1815 and 1871, Western civilization accommodated its institutions to the democratic ideal of the rule of the people. But the process of democratization was slow and painful—often violent—and sharply varied from one country to the next. Generally, the development of democratic political systems was resisted most strongly and effectively in central and eastern Europe; the split between the liberal Western countries and the autocratic societies of eastern Europe, which still prevails, emerged during these decades. But there were other significant trends and problems. Who constituted the people—the nobility and the middle class alone or the working class spawned by the Industrial Revolution as well? Would each ethnic and linguistic group that had attained a national consciousness achieve political independence and form its own state? In a democratic country, what were the limits, if any, to the power of the majority over the minority?

The resolution of these agonizing problems often depended on the skill and energy of particular leaders, the success or failure of revolutions, and the outcome of wars and civil wars. Yet whatever the institutional structure arrived at in particular states, everywhere the driving forces for change were the ideals of liberty and equality and the economic and social changes effected by industrialization. The leaders and theorists of this economic and democratic revolution could draw upon new insights into human nature, social structure, political organization, and historical change provided by the Romantic cultural movement and by scientific doctrines and data. Intellectual advances made educated people more conscious of individual rights and national aspirations and allowed them to conceptualize the significance of political and economic change.

Uncloak one by one the crimes, the injustice,
the infamy of our rulers . . . .
Shout Liberty in the ears of the People.
Revolt is the principle of the century . . . .
The right not to be oppressed, or maimed, or tortured
by the tyranny of the few, or by foreign invasion,
is enshrined in the hearts of all as a sacred imprescriptible right.
Giuseppe Mazzini, *Interests and Principles*

Page 235: a nineteenth-century engraving of Giuseppe Mazzini, Italian nationalist, theorist, and political leader.

The Age
of Romanticism

I THE ROMANTIC REVOLUTION

The Romantic Ethos

During the last decade of the eighteenth century and the first half of the nineteenth, political revolution and economic change were paralleled by simultaneous transformations of great consequence in art, literature, and philosophy. To cultural historians the period between 1790 and 1850 is known as the Age of Romanticism. During these years, artists and intellectuals made a frontal attack on the ordered, rational universe of Locke, Newton, and Voltaire. They proclaimed their rejection of the teachings and style of the Enlightenment, developing new canons for art, for morality, for political thought. Romanticism was a revolution in human sensibility and self-consciousness, and it affected every major European country. Without the great monuments of Romanticism—Berlioz's symphonies, Heine's poems, Stendhal's novels, Turner's paintings—Western culture as we know it is as unimaginable as it would be if the steam engine and the spinning jenny had never been invented.

Romantic writers embarked on a strange, wondrous, often fearful voyage of discovery. The subject of their explorations was the human personality itself, everywhere breaking free of the intellectual straitjacket of classical thought. The Romantic eye was attentive to those aspects of personality that the eighteenth century had scorned, ignored, or branded as illegitimate vestiges from barbaric ages. Like Napoleon, whose supermortal myth dominated the age, the Romantics seemed at times to respect no limits and no laws. They were intoxicated with power—the power of man to create, to conquer, to transcend, to discover, and to experience his own unique self. Romanticism was a response, often inchoate and confused but always creative, to a world in which all the old certainties had vanished, a world in which the received wisdom of centuries suddenly seemed no more than a collection of threadbare clichés.

The Romantics were men seeking to build a new world on the ruins of the old. Severed from the certainties of the Enlightenment and the fixed political and social order of the *ancien régime*, they became rebels perforce, and, making a virtue of necessity, they sometimes inflated their rebellion to cosmic proportions. Prometheus, Don Juan, Faust were all Romantic heroes because they dared to defy the very gods. Yet defying the gods was no easy matter and was certainly not conducive to serenity. When the Romantics were not exulting in their mission, they were racked with doubt, anxiety, and self-recrimination. They suffered from a sense of their own impotence and inadequacy. Romantic writers recorded both their misery and their triumphs in chronicles filled with self-pity and passion.

To the eighteenth century, nature had been the source of stability and law. The nineteenth rediscovered the extravagant, capricious side of nature. The eighteenth century had fixed its gaze on celestial bodies traveling in their prescribed orbits, and the sight had filled the *philosophes* with a kind of detached benevolence mixed with just a little smugness and complacency. The nineteenth century discovered nature awesome, tempestuous, and beautiful. Not planets but mountains, hurricanes, and daffodils thrilled the souls of the Romantics.

To apprehend the lawful, orderly universe, eighteenth-century illuminati had relied on reason as the highest faculty of man. But the world of the Romantics was a world of change, of growth and decay, of flowering and festering; and to confront this new universe, they found reason static, cold, and generally bankrupt. In its place they put the vagaries and inspired flights of the imagination and the urgent promptings of the heart. The Romantics welcomed back into the universe ghosts, spirits, dreams, gods, and ineffable yearnings. Peasants, children, and physical and moral outcasts became fit subjects for literature and painting. The Romantics were not interested, or claimed not to be interested, in mankind in the abstract sense. They were interested in unique, individual, particular men. Men were not uniform; each had his own aspirations, talents, and needs. All men were not suited to live under the same social system, designed by Parisian philosopher-gentlemen, for no single system suited all cultures and all circumstances.

The men of the Romantic era lived through cataclysmic wars and revolutions, which toppled governments once thought to be sacrosanct and which redrew maps and boundaries a dozen times in the space of two decades. They were intensely conscious of mutability in human affairs. Whereas the eighteenth century had enjoyed positing absolute laws to govern human as well as cosmic affairs, the nineteenth century was, of necessity, profoundly relativistic in outlook. Biology came to replace physics as the source of metaphors, concepts, and analogies. Whereas physics emphasized symmetry, balance, and mathematical certitude, biology emphasized process and organic development, mirroring a dynamic rather than a static world.

Deep into the Romantic Age powerful minds continued to hold fast to the Enlightenment creed. Classical liberal economics, for example, and Bentham's utilitarian philosophy remained immune from Romantic attacks. But such thinking was anathema to the Romantics. As a generation, they mistrusted formulas which laid claim to universal validity. They were haunted by the specter of the French Revolution. They had seen "the Rights of Man" lead to unspeakable carnage and suffering. In the name of an abstraction called Liberty, they had seen armies ruthlessly impose the will of a despot on peoples who simply wanted to be left alone to till their fields. The French Revolution and Napoleon had set about ruthlessly extirpating the past. Everywhere laws, constitutions, and social institutions had been standardized, codified, and rationalized. The brutality of this operation made the Romantics feel a new reverence for variety—for the unique, the idiosyncratic, and the mysterious in individual personalities as well as in states.

In England some of the major writers of the neoclassical period had placed a new value on emotion. Laurence Sterne (1713–1768) had written in praise of "dear sensibility"; his novel, *A Sentimental Journey*, published in 1768, had demonstrated that tears and laughter could enrich experience and permit the world to be viewed with fresh eyes. And the eighteenth century produced at least one writer—Jean Jacques Rousseau—who was to become to the next generation the personification of Romantic Man. The Romantics regarded Rousseau's *Émile* as the proclamation of a new philosophy and his *Confessions* as a realistic rendering of their own inner lives. Rousseau had sensed that all men were moved by impulse and emotion and sometimes by perverse desire, and he had been willing to present his own life as a case history. For this, he had been condemned in his own time. The Romantics found in him the archetypal modern man.

Herder and the New History

In 1774 Johann Gottfried Herder (1744–1803), the pastor in the tiny German principality of Schaumburg-Lippe, published a book with the awkward title, *Still Another Philosophy of History*. It was a direct attack on the historical thought of Voltaire and an indirect challenge to the French-dominated "cosmopolitan" culture of Europe. Herder questioned the classicists' dream of reviving the glories of Greece and Rome. All cultures, he maintained, were unique and inimitable, and all were capable of producing beautiful works of art. It was not the philosopher's task to judge past eras, ranking them in some absurd hierarchy of greater or lesser civilization. To understand a people or an era, the first requirement was sympathy on the part of the observer. "Go into the era, into the geography, into the entire history. *Feel* yourself into it," urged Herder.

The discovery of oral tradition among various "primitive" European peoples was not the work of Herder alone. It was going on throughout much of Europe in the middle decades of the eighteenth century. And the ballads, myths, and folk tales unearthed in these years were to play an important role in the evolution of Romanticism. It was discovered that poetry, universally recognized as one of the supreme arts, could be produced by peasants as well as academicians. In 1756 James Macpherson, a Scot, had published his *Fragments of Ancient Poetry Collected in the Highlands of Scotland.* The poetry in this volume Macpherson falsely attributed to the pre-Christian Celtic bard, Ossian, who became a Romantic hero, depicted in innumerable paintings of the early nineteenth century. Alongside the discovery of pseudo-Celtic folklore, there came publication of the mythology of Scandinavia and Germany, introducing the heroes of Valhalla. The epic grandeur of these sagas forced a reevaluation of the "low" literature of the common people.

There was also a reevaluation of two of the titans of Western literature, Homer and Shakespeare. Scholars were beginning to reach the astounding conclusion that Homer himself had been a primitive, recounting his tales in a preliterate society, and that his songs had attained their heroic grandeur not because he had triumphed over his impoverished environment but because he had mirrored it. Herder and other young Germans were pointing out that Shakespeare, the greatest master of drama, had been unashamedly a "popular" writer; so much was evident from the language of the plays, which was earthy as often as it was noble. Language, announced the Shakespeare enthusiasts, had been impoverished since the sixteenth century, and this was the fault of the cultural tyranny exercised by Versailles. In the name of noble simplicity, the idiomatic, the colorful, and the quaint had been expurgated. A monotonous uniformity had replaced rich variety. The popular and provincial in vocabulary and usage had been banished, and, similarly, human experience had been stifled, cramped, and distorted.

Struck by the fact that the Bible itself seemed to be the work of a primitive people, Herder looked upon the Book of Genesis not only as superb poetry but as an early attempt of man to explain the origin of the world. Such attempts, he argued, must be treated with wonder and admiration, not with contempt. The theology, the myths, of primitive, non-Christian people were monuments from which historians and philosophers might learn much. He was grappling his way toward what was eventually to become comparative anthropology. By the time he published his historical works, he had come to believe that the poetry, philosophy, science, and theology of a people had to be understood as a synthetic whole: a common spirit permeated all expressions of a culture. Herder returned again and again to the fact that poetry had its genesis in "the dark regions of the soul," a long way from enlightened Paris. The past was better approached by and more accessible to those who retained the reverent wonder and curiosity of a child than those who belittled, categorized, and depersonalized experience.

Goethe and the New Sensibility

The year 1774 was important in German letters. Besides the publication of Herder's first historical writing, it saw the appearance of a slim novella by Johann Wolfgang von Goethe (1749–1832), a young Frankfurt lawyer. This work, *The Sorrows of the Young Werther*, was to capture the imagination of an entire generation of Goethe's countrymen. Superficially, *Werther* was a simple, even a trite story of frustrated, disappointed love, ending with the tragic suicide of the hero. But overnight this hero became the idol and in not a few cases the model of smitten, pining lovers throughout Europe. Emulation of Goethe's fictional Werther produced a fad of blue frock coats and yellow waistcoats as dreamy, morose young men set off to wander around the countryside, a sketchbook in one hand, a copy of "Ossian's" poems in the other. In Leipzig and Copenhagen the novella had to be banned, as "Wertherfever" propelled young men out of windows or put pistols to their heads. Goethe himself came to deplore the reception of his little book. He had meant Werther to be a tragic symptom, a walking neurosis, not a hero and prophet for his time.

Goethe produced Werther in four weeks' time, "as though in a trance," weaving into it his own grief at an unhappy love affair. The young hero, talented, well-educated, and handsome, with excellent worldly prospects, combines in his person all the characteristics prized by the rebels from the mainstream of eighteenth-century culture. The story of the young man's advance toward extinction takes on the quality of a great psychological drama. His own sensibilities, which alone he cares to cultivate, at last render him wholly unfit for the mundane world. In gradually severing his ties to that world, he finds solace in the tempestuous grandeur of nature, which renders insignificant and paltry all the petty loves and strivings of man. In the end, his grasp on the world is totally loosened, his will to live completely sapped.

Werther thus became the first victim of the enigmatic disease that would plague so many nineteenth-century figures. Variously called spleen, *Weltschmerz*, *mal du siècle*, ennui, and, more recently, alienation, in the Romantic era this peculiar psychological state became a sign of membership in the spiritual elite, the mark of an artist and a sufferer.

II ROMANTIC LITERATURE

National Literature

To speak of Romantic literature is to speak both of variety and of a new abundance. All over Europe, but especially in the most remote and primitive corners, the Romantic ideology led to the collection of works that no one till then had bothered to notice. Myths, ballads, legends, and folk songs were transcribed and anthologized. And this does not exhaust the Romantic accomplishment. The ideas derived from Herder created a new consciousness of the importance of "national" literature, which began to be created at a furious rate.

Countries which had been blank slates so far as literature was concerned suddenly produced poets, and some of them were very fine indeed. A Russian literature of international stature developed within a few decades as Alexander Pushkin and Nikolai Gogol burst upon the world. Hungary produced Sándor Petöfi, who is still regarded as *the* national poet of the country. In Poland appeared Adam Mickiewicz, probably the finest poet of that nation. Hans Christian Andersen was writing in Denmark, Thomas Moore in Ireland, Robert Burns in Scotland. The American Romantic flowering came much later than in Europe — in the 1840's and 1850's.

The three richest patterns of Romanticism as an orientation affecting all aspects of thought were created in Germany, Britain, and France. Romanticism in German literature began with the *Sturm und Drang* (storm and stress) movement of the late eighteenth century, which emphasized the Promethean, demonic qualities of humanity. Its monument was Goethe's *Werther,* and it also influenced the great poet and dramatist Friedrich Schiller (1759–1805). Both Goethe and Schiller, in their more mature work, tended in the direction of classicism and away from the sentimentality and personal intensity of Romanticism. But they remained loyal to central doctrines of the Romantic ethos. In Goethe's *Faust* the hero pursues an endless quest for self-realization, while Mephistopheles represents false and dangerous satisfaction with what has already been achieved in life and culture. Schiller's finest drama, *Wallenstein,* explored the tensions and crises of a transcendent personality within the context of the Greek tragic tradition. His last work, *William Tell*, issued a call for national liberation.

The central figure in German Romantic poetry was Heinrich Heine (1797–1856). His personality, his philosophy, and his mastery of the lyric form all placed him in the front rank of the writers of the Romantic era. Scion of a wealthy German Jewish family, he spent half his life in France, a failure by the standards of bourgeois society. His grail was the union of Hellenic beauty and Judaic-Christian morality in a "third and true New Testament" which would combine spiritual and personal love: "God, too, is in our kisses." Along with this personal quest for God, beauty, and love, Heine was very much involved in the political and social issues of his day and invariably took the radical side. He was an enemy of tyranny in all forms and became a socialist in his later years. The sufferings of the workers seemed to him the shame and disgrace of Germany and of Western culture in general.

Except for Heine himself, the leading minds of German Romanticism in his generation expressed their ideas not through belletristic literature but through social and political theory, philosophy, and history. (They will be discussed under these categories.) Heine was deeply disappointed at this development. He pointed to the lack of integration of philosophy and art with social and political life in Germany—a split of pure intellect from practical affairs which, he prophesied, would have catastrophic implications for the culture of the Fatherland.

English Romanticism

Those who like to date intellectual movements with some precision make 1798 the year when fully self-conscious Romantic poetry first appeared in England. That year saw the publication of the *Lyrical Ballads* of William Wordsworth (1770–1850) and Samuel Taylor Coleridge (1772–1834), the two key figures of the first generation of English Romanticism. Published anonymously, the volume was greeted with a resounding silence. This reception prompted Wordsworth to provide a preface to the second edition, published in 1800, explaining to the public some of the intentions and assumptions of the new poetry.

The preface to the *Lyrical Ballads* was the first and most influential manifesto of the new literature in Britain. The poems took their subject matter from the incidents and situations of humble and rustic life because in such scenes the "essential passions of the heart find a better soil." The poet, Wordsworth asserted, was a man like all others, but with a difference. A special sensibility, a deeper knowledge of human nature, a heart more tender, more moved by enthusiasm and passion, equipped him to bring to his subject matter "a certain coloring of imagination, whereby ordinary things should be presented to the mind in an unusual aspect." Poetry is both sublime and immortal. Its object is truth itself—not the remote and impersonal truths of science but intimate, affective truths of the human heart.

Bitter disillusionment with the course of events in revolutionary France had moved Wordsworth to a profound reconsideration of what constituted the good society and the good life, and indirectly this reconsideration had led him to a new view of poetry. Returning from a year in France, he had looked back on his childhood in the beautiful Lake District of northwestern England, and the wisdom of the country folk there seemed to him superior to the wisdom of the ideologues of the French National Assembly. Close to the soil, to the seasons, to the customs of their fathers, these men pursued their timeless round of activities undisturbed and unpolluted by the frenzy across the channel. Living in intimate communion with nature, they lived in intimate communion with God as well, and thus with their own souls.

In confronting nature, Wordsworth believed, we confront ourselves. Nature is a catalyst for the human mind: a sudden encounter with a natural phenomenon—a mountain stream, a field of waving flowers—reveals harmonies and discords in our own souls to which we have long been oblivious. The process of self-discovery recorded in Wordsworth's greatest poem, *The Prelude*, comes about when the imagination, stirred by nature, becomes fruitful. From the meeting of the reflective mind and the sensuous world, there ensues creation. The separation between man and the natural world is erased; each becomes the measure and mirror of the other.

Unlike Wordsworth, who painted the inner significance of common scenes, Samuel Taylor Coleridge in his best-known poems, *The Rime of the Ancient Mariner* and *Kubla Khan*, evoked exotic, surreal realms—symbolic rather than naturalistic worlds. *The Ancient Mariner*, a parable of guilt and regeneration, was written in imitation of the folk ballads collected by antiquarians of the mid-eighteenth century. Coleridge at his best was a prophet and seer deliberately speaking a language of mystery that called upon the reader to provide "that willing suspension of disbelief . . . which constitutes poetic faith." Coleridge insisted that his poetry was not allegorical, that no single key would unlock its secrets. For him, poetry was a dynamic figment of the imagination, whole in and of itself, not reducible to paraphrase or moral. Coleridge was conscious of the magical properties of words: his *Kubla Khan* has been described as the most musical poem in the English language.

Although Coleridge's poetic output was small, he was also a philosopher and social critic and one of the seminal minds of nineteenth-century Britain. Instinctively distrusting the new world of finance and industry, he made sensitive comment on the brutal competitiveness of early industrial Great Britain. No rights existed, he asserted, without duties and responsibilities, else the communal principle would be lost and the world would be ruled by egotism gone wild. In practice, the emphasis on duties and responsibilities placed Coleridge on the side of institutional authorities.

Unlike Coleridge and Wordsworth, the second generation of English Romantic poets—particularly Percy Bysshe Shelley (1792–1822) and George Gordon, Lord Byron (1788–1824)—was defiantly radical. Shelley was variously a proponent of women's emancipation, nudity, vegetarianism, atheism, and democracy, and Byron was vilified and ostracized by the Tory establishment as a traitor to the political and private morality of his aristocratic social milieu. His death in 1824 in the Greek war for liberation made him a hero and martyr to nationalist movements across all of western Europe. Whereas Wordsworth and Coleridge had favored duty and authority, Byron and Shelley sang in praise of liberty—intellectual, moral, and political.

Alone among the major English Romantics, John Keats (1795–1821) stayed aloof from political and social questions in his poetry. Though he struggled all his life trying to work out some satisfactory relationship between art and life, it was to art itself that his mind constantly reverted: it was the highest reality, the only claim man could make to immortality. His belief in the absolute primacy of art (" 'Beauty is truth, truth beauty,' that is all / Ye know on earth, and all ye need to know") made him a forerunner of the later nineteenth-century aesthetes who enshrined the doctrine of "Art for Art's sake." Perhaps because he sensed the fragility of his own health, Keats was painfully and ecstatically conscious of the perishability of all sensuous beauty. He wrote poetry that combined acute passion with exquisite delicacy of detail, seeking to capture in art the quintessence of life. To Keats, sensation and thought became, at least in art, equivalent; his poetry is meditation on the significance of beauty.

By temperament an anarchist, Shelley loathed institutional authority as a drag on the soul. He shared with the Enlightenment a passionate belief in the goodness of human nature and a vision of a golden age yet to come when mankind would be happy, prosperous, and fully emancipated. His greatest literary creation was *Prometheus Unbound*, a lyrical drama based on the story of the god in the Greek pantheon who had loved mankind so much that he had defied Zeus in order to proffer the gift of fire to men. For this, Prometheus had been consigned to chains, but the chains were destined one day to be broken, for Prometheus' love for man and for liberty was no impotent yearning. He could endure struggle forever, and his ultimate triumph was assured.

In Shelley's *Ode to the West Wind*, destruction and ruin are but a prelude to regeneration and new life, not only for the poet but for all men. Yet poetry had a special mission in the pilgrimage of mankind: it alone, not the language of calculating logical discourse, could animate men's hearts to those altruistic impulses which would usher in the golden age to come. Art led man from the prison of the egotistical self to sympathy with all humanity and all beauty of thought and action. The imagination of the artist thus became the chief agent of moral good in the universe. It was the artist who built toward the reign of love that man was destined one day to achieve, despite tyrants and the inhibitions created by society.

While Shelley never lost touch with the practical steps by which the new world was to be built, Lord Byron quickly abandoned politics after making a few speeches in the House of Lords; and following an incestuous love affair with his half-sister and an unhappy marriage, he abandoned England as well, to spend the last eight years of his life as a wandering exile and a living legend. Byron's heroes—Childe Harold, Manfred, Cain, Don Juan—are, like him, archrebels, isolated from both nature and man. Damned and tormented, they are also irresistibly attractive pilgrims and soldiers of liberty, standing outside society and its constraints. Although their transgressions—particularly of sexual taboos—eventually bring about their ruin, they are men who hurl themselves against all barriers, willing to pay the price of extinction in order to realize personal freedom. Byron himself tried to escape from the nihilistic implications of his heroes' lives, but he could find no faith, no anchor. Unlike Wordsworth, he found no solace in nature. He could not, like Keats, posit art as the highest reality and the great reconciler of all contradictions, and he was not blessed with the surging optimism of Shelley. The contradictions between what men desired and what society and nature permitted seemed to him irreconcilable.

The world inhabited by the English Romantics was changing with unprecedented speed. Their lifetimes coincide with the first herculean stages of the Industrial Revolution, which permanently altered the material and social basis of life for all time to come. Even as Wordsworth idealized the self-sufficient, isolated, rural communities of England, these communities were vanishing forever. The growth of factories and large urban conglomerates was radically altering the most elemental relationships of human life. Traditional class and family structure was breaking down to be replaced by—no one knew precisely what.

All the English Romantics agreed in idealizing the artist and in exalting his special faculty, the imagination, as a vehicle of personal and social regeneration. It was a creative response to the advent of the modern world but also an ambiguous and somewhat pitiful one. Even as they wrote, the advent of industrial mass society, of which they were so acutely conscious, was utterly transforming the social role of the artist. They were living on the threshold of an era in which art and ideas were to become commodities to be sold in the open marketplace, when, for the first time in history, artists were in danger of becoming lost in the crowd. Shelley raised the cry that poets were to be "the legislators for mankind." When "art" and "culture" seemed threatened, when the artists' social function was no longer clear, literature and art were exalted as a special, higher branch of ethics.

The complacent bourgeois, as well as the wage slave whom he had brought into being, was feared and detested by the Romantic artist, who saw in the routinization and mechanization of society his own nemesis. Byron felt that he had better die young, else he would surely settle into conformity and respectability. To escape this fate before dying, he discovered and dramatized alienation as the special plight (and badge of distinction) of the artist. The violent, satanic rebelliousness of the Byronic hero was, psychologically speaking, the bravado of the individual haunted by the fear that he was doomed to be homeless and superfluous in mass industrial society.

The tremendous impact Byron had on the European Romantic movement was matched by one other British author. Sir Walter Scott (1771–1832) was virtually the creator of a new literary genre, the historical novel. Already an established poet, in 1814 with the publication of his first novel he achieved a popularity with the middle-class reading public that never diminished in his lifetime. And in his own time his influence on the writing of history was as important as his influence on the novel. In his fiction, the ideas of Herder were given flesh and blood. Through sympathetic imagination, he brought to life societies long dead and depicted their customs, their dress, their speech, and their manners as unique and wondrous. Reading Scott, one felt and saw what a medieval abbot or a seventeenth-century Scottish laird had been like.

Scott's wide appeal is a significant indication that Romanticism was not the special preserve of creative, first-class minds. Scott satisfied on a popular level the desire to feel and experience a life wholly different from one's own. Exoticism had been a strain of the Romantic movement since the eighteenth century; it was part of the appeal of the old ballads that had been collected and anthologized. Scott made it respectable as literature and smuggled in between the lines a plea for the preservation of old mores and institutions, confident that the heart of man would find room to accommodate them.

Continuing in the same vein, English Romanticism tended increasingly in the direction of emotionalism and sentimentality. In the novels of the Brontë sisters — particularly Charlotte Brontë's *Jane Eyre* and Emily Brontë's *Wuthering Heights* — this tendency was combined with great dramatic power and skill in the portrayal of turbulent passions. Popular Romanticism was skilfully exploited by Charles Dickens (1812 – 1870), who loaded his novels with weepy scenes of beaten, neglected, and brutalized orphans. The 1840's saw a rash of novels decrying the new industrial system, levying many of the same charges that Coleridge had made many years earlier. Novels such as *Sybil*, by Benjamin Disraeli, the future prime minister, described the "two nations" of rich and poor, living side by side in mutual misunderstanding, and caused many a tear to be shed over the plight of poor but honest factory hands. This popular Romanticism significantly shaped the ambience of nineteenth-century England. Pity and compassion became respectable and permeated mid-nineteenth-century British life. Sentimentality, one of the prime offshoots of Romanticism, mobilized many of those who passed the first factory acts, fought to abolish the slave trade and slavery, and founded schools for the instruction of the poor.

Charles Dickens' passion for social justice and his sentimental evocations of the goodness of the suffering poor helped to win him an enormous audience. But these are not the qualities that place his finest work — such as *David Copperfield* and *Great Expectations* — in the front rank of Western literature. Dickens' greatness lay in his delineation of character, his ability to capture the facets of human personality. His people are recognizable social types, but at the same time they are real individuals whom we can never forget. From the experiences of a miserable childhood and youth and a hectic early career as a journalist, Dickens was able to create, with loving care and unsurpassed skill, a gallery of early nineteenth-century humanity.

American Romanticism

The Romantic movement in American literature originated in the Boston area in the late 1830's as a direct offshoot of English Romantic thought. Ralph Waldo Emerson (1803 – 1882) was very influential in disseminating transcendental, individualistic, and antimechanistic doctrines. But the development of American Romanticism was shaped by indigenous aspects of American society: by the ambition of native, particularly New England writers to gain a place in world literature, by a humanistic and evangelical reaction against the early stages of industrialization, by a radical democratic faith in the virtue of the common man, and by a grandiose sense of the capacity of individuals, as exemplified in the phenomenal achievements of America's westward expansion. Emerson, a rhetorician of some power, was only a second-rate philosopher. More important as an original thinker was Henry David Thoreau (1817–1862), whose *Walden* is one of the most sensitive and persuasive statements of the Romantic belief that the individual can live without mechanistic civilization and can realize the union of self and nature. A Romantic but no transcendentalist, Edgar Allan Poe (1809–1849) explored the occult and the beauty of terror in his poems and tales.

The flowering of the American Romantic sensibility came in the 1850's in the novels of Nathaniel Hawthorne (1804–1864) and Herman Melville (1819–1891) and the poetry of Walt Whitman (1819–1892). Hawthorne made excellent use of the seventeenth-century historical setting to explore, with unusual psychological insight, problems of guilt and mental anguish. Whitman's poems expound a rampant democratic individualism at the same time that they communicate, in free verse, an entirely personal vision. Melville's *Moby Dick*, although not widely appreciated until the twentieth century, is now recognized as one of the great works of Romantic literature, an enormously powerful and intricate examination of the grandeur of the individual in conflict, and at the same time in symbiotic union, with nature and fate.

Romanticism in France

The full flowering of Romanticism in France, the home of neoclassicism and the Enlightenment, was not achieved until the 1830's and 1840's, by which time it was already something of a spent force in England. It first appeared on the extreme Right, flourishing as a kind of diseased sentimentality among ruined aristocrats and unregenerate royalists. François René, Vicomte de Chateaubriand (1768–1848), was the first French Romantic writer of note to appear in the nineteenth century. Chateaubriand came from an old provincial aristocratic family whose life had been completely overturned by the Revolution. While exiled in England, he was beset by poverty and loneliness, which, coupled with a naturally melancholic temperament, produced a sudden, mystical religious experience—a common phenomenon among the exiled, demoralized nobility whose world had gone all topsy-turvy. In the eighteenth century French aristocrats had been notoriously atheistic, cynical, and worldly, and the disasters that befell them in the 1790's seemed to many to be divine punishment for their former frivolities. By 1800, when Napoleon had consolidated his position and many *émigré* noblemen were returning, France was ripe for a religious revival.

In 1802 Chateaubriand, who had been appointed to a diplomatic position by Napoleon, published *The Genius of Christianity*, subtitled *Poetic and Moral Beauties of the Christian Religion*. Two sections of this work, *Atala* and *René*, very quickly became widely celebrated. Set in a fantastic American landscape of green serpents, pink flamingos, tulips, pines, and magnolias, *Atala* is the bittersweet love story of two ill-starred Indian lovers who attain not each other but the ecstatic solace of a kind of primitive Christianity. *René* is the tale of the progressive dissolution of another dreamy, listless, insatiably dissatisfied Werther, who has the misfortune of being consumed by a hopeless — though highly spiritual — love for his sister. Chateaubriand's kind of sentimental Christianity was an avenue to God particularly suited to aristocratic sensibilities, and it remained important through the entire nineteenth century, capturing several egotistical and rebellious intellects.

The first generation of French Romanticism appeared to be firmly wed to reaction. Alfred de Vigny, Victor Hugo, Alphonse de Lamartine — young poets who first made their impact in the 1820's — were all inclined toward monarchy. Delicately lyrical, painting soft, muted word-pictures, sensuous and religious at the same time, the new poetry provoked both puzzlement and irritation among the still strongly entrenched academicians, who were neoclassicists fighting a grand last-ditch battle to preserve the culture of Corneille and Racine. Excluded from the major literary organs, the young writers gathered in small, informal groups to propagate the new artistic ideas. One of the bibles of the new movement was *De l'Allemagne*, an appreciation of the literature of Germany written by Madame de Staël (1766–1817), the formidable daughter of an ill-starred minister of finance of the old regime. A salon patroness of considerable talent, she wrote several influential works proselytizing for a new literature, which was to be national, popular, and Christian. Sir Walter Scott was also producing an impact: the 1820's and 1830's saw the publication of a spate of historical novels, of which the swashbuckling adventure tales of Alexandre Dumas (1802–1870) were the most popular.

At first, the young writers pleaded only for cultural tolerance — freedom in arts and letters — but as the restrictions on civil liberties and freedom of the press were multiplied, the battle became politicized, and French Romanticism underwent a complete ideological turnabout. In 1830 Victor Hugo (1802–1885), who was fast emerging as the leader of the new movement, published a manifesto that identified Romanticism with liberalism and advocated the double goal of freedom in art and freedom in society. A great many French Romantics became intoxicated with a fervent, naive love for "the people." Both Hugo and Lamartine saw themselves as writers who had a special rapport with the working class of Paris. It was their divine mission to lead the people, whose instincts were good but whose education was unsound, to a love of art and poetry, just as the people would in their turn infuse the poets' art with their own vitality and fresh vision. The Romantics envisioned the people, simple and good, in huge, surging crowds, manning the barricades that toppled the Bourbons, singing "The Marseillaise," moved by a divine spark of freedom. Lamartine liked to see himself standing on Parisian balconies exhorting the people to take up the torch of Liberty.

This alliance of liberalism and Romanticism was a generous, impulsive, exultant creed that aimed at nothing less than the regeneration of all mankind, the freeing of oppressed peoples such as Poles and Italians by a new triumphant march of French armies, the striking down and confounding of censors, police spies, and princes everywhere. Moreover, this idealistic espousal of "the people" was not confined to France alone. Throughout Europe it affected young writers who, while remaining ignorant of actual class interests and aspirations, championed and extolled the eternal, suffering people who would one day rise like a great ocean wave and sweep away tyranny and oppression.

Perhaps the greatest literary monument of this discovery of the Parisian proletariat was Victor Hugo's *Les Misérables* (1862), a kind of literary symphony to the eternally oppressed but unvanquished people. *Les Misérables* is a voyage through the sewers, prisons, and hovels of the great metropolis, filled with passion, crime, evil, faith, and unsuspected sublimity. In Hugo's masterpiece of subterranean Paris, beauty and redemption are found in misery and squalor.

Hugo remained a democrat for the rest of his life, but democracy as an ideal and as a social reality was receiving a negative reaction among many Romantics unable to share his optimistic, messianic faith in redemption through suffering. The trouble was that democracy was inexorably bound up with the ascendancy of the middle class, and toward the middle class the later French Romantics almost to a man felt the most profound disgust, fear, and loathing. The Romantics, particularly in France, were the first generation of artists to perceive that the bourgeois had now become the measure of man. The new culture was his culture, and writers such as Stendhal, Balzac, and Baudelaire found it appalling. The philistine bourgeois obsessed the late Romantics; to subvert and finally destroy his commodity-ridden world was their dearest wish. The rest of mankind, including the aristocracy and "the people," was surrendering to the soulless materialism of the bourgeois, the implacable enemy of all talent and sensitivity. The artist alone was left as custodian of the higher values. It was his sacred duty to wage unremitting war against modernity, which he equated with machinery, technology, material progress, the profit motive, and spiritual paralysis.

The social reaction to the ubiquitous bourgeois was the creation of "bohemia" as a separate community wherein the artist dwelt. Paris in the middle years of the nineteenth century was the first city to develop the artists' quarter—today a feature of most metropolises—as a distinct, ongoing oasis for those who chose to live outside the pale of respectable society. Here the Left Bank developed as a refuge for real and would-be painters, writers, and students. And as Parisian bohemianism developed, it elaborated its own dress codes and styles of behavior. Young France in the 1840's lived in garrets and cultivated outlandish hairdos and foppish dress to distinguish itself from the ordinary denizens of the city.

Behind the garish ostentation there was a method and a rationale. Young Romantics were carving out their own empire in the midst of a hostile society. The values they chose to cultivate and display were those perceived to be inimical and threatening to the bourgeois. The bohemians developed the cult of youth as a virtue and a style. Youth and creativity, youth and originality, youth and courageous flamboyance became ideals because bourgeois society collectively was a kind of geriatrics ward of the dying in spirit. Similarly, the cult of joblessness — while in part, of course, a cruel necessity — was also a point of pride, since pursuit of a career and a remunerative job was held to be deadening to all instincts but the acquisitive, the grasping, the social-climbing. Along with a career, it was felt, came a household, an establishment, and a routinization of life which was fatal to the imagination. Thus marriage — which, of course, entailed the necessity of a career — was often treated rather like a funeral. The ultimate step in the renunciation of what the middle-class world had to offer to the talented and sensitive was taken by those who proclaimed as their great ambition, "To be a great poet and to die."

The most significant artistic response to the unfriendly environment encountered by the artist was the development of the aesthetic ideal summarized as "Art for Art's sake." Vastly influential in the dissemination of this philosophy was the poet Théophile Gautier (1811–1872), who sported red waistcoats and acted as a kind of spiritual mentor to Parisian intellectuals of the 1830's and 1840's. Gautier saw it as his task to rescue young writers from a misguided meddling in political and social problems. Art served neither freedom, nor liberalism, nor morality; it served only itself. The present world was to be rejected outright on the grounds that it was aesthetically and morally repulsive and beyond salvation. In these circumstances the artist had to look out for himself alone, lest he and his work as well became contaminated by the general poison. The doctrine of "Art for Art's sake" led inevitably to the creation of poetry that could be appreciated only by the artists themselves. This trend was a complete about-face from the position of the early Romantics, who had pleaded for a popularization and democratization of literature.

Gautier's most famous pupil was the poet Charles Baudelaire (1821–1867), who displayed most of the chief characteristics of late, embittered, disillusioned Romanticism. Baudelaire created in his person the dandy as the spiritual aristocrat pitted against all the grossness of the modern age. His dress, his walk, his habits of eating and conversation all had to be sculpted with elaborate self-control. The ideal of the traditional bohemian had been the natural play of instincts and impulsive spontaneity, but Baudelaire scorned this lack of restraint and artistry. He aimed at total mastery of the self — the perfectly composed outward demeanor as a reflection of exacting internal standards of behavior and thought. This self-imposed discipline gave the dandy a heroic dimension. He was a sojourner in this vile world, but he was not of it; it did not touch him.

Baudelaire was much taken with the aesthetic possibilities of depravity, partly because depravity was so useful a means of shocking the somnolent bourgeois. He entitled his great collection of poems published in 1857 *The Flowers of Evil*. The artistic point of this magnificent collection was that beauty could be made out of any material whatever, even the most sordid and ugly. Thus he took for his subjects prostitutes, beggars, criminals, lesbians, and other social lepers, constructing nevertheless the most delicate, lyrical tone poems imaginable from this unlikely subject matter. By resting his case on the moral depravity of man, Baudelaire made another radical departure from early Romantics like Wordsworth and Shelley, who retained faith in the natural goodness of man. But it was not horror as such that attracted Baudelaire; it was the beauty that could be extracted even from horror—could be fashioned despite the conspiracy of the social and natural order to destroy it.

Two great French novelists—Stendhal and Balzac—shared many of Baudelaire's antipathies. Stendhal (1783–1842) set out to study the problem of how best to survive in an epoch he considered almost wholly damned. The world in which Julien Sorel moves in *The Red and the Black* (1830) is petrified into mutually hostile classes, within which individuals wage a relentless battle of one-upmanship. But it is also littered with ambitious young men like Julien Sorel, who are rootless outsiders, compulsively on the make. The time of grandeur that was the Napoleonic era is past. The Revolution has reached a state of total exhaustion; all combatants have been discredited; society is in a kind of paralysis. Julien Sorel, consumed by drives which once could have been expressed in great political deeds, is doomed to war against an era that oppresses him by its mean dimensions. The clever Sorel is forced to assume the role of bandit, operating by stealth and ruse to outwit a society that is instinctively hostile to talent, ambition, and intelligence. He is the perpetual opportunist caught in his own game and finally destroyed.

Stendhal shared Sorel's hunger for an age when heroes were not automatically outcasts. He idealized the classical world, the *ancien régime*, Renaissance Italy—any era, in fact, which allowed unbridled energy to master human events and human destinies. Having despaired of substance, he staked all on style. He had an abounding admiration for splendid gestures. Thus revolutions pleased him aesthetically, for they occasioned grand outbursts of passion, magnificent spectacles which dispelled for a moment the triviality and boredom of the daily round. Stendhal was an unashamed worshiper of the great man—like Napoleon—who alone could give drama to the mundane and petty which made up modern life.

The same disenchantment with postrevolutionary bourgeois society is reflected in the novels of Honoré de Balzac (1799–1850). He was obsessed with depicting every niche and crevice of contemporary France, with subjecting every class and every occupation to pitiless scrutiny. His *The Human Comedy* was to consist of some one hundred and twenty separate novels. He worked with such prodigious energy—indeed, monomania—that more than ninety were actually completed at the time of his death in 1850. Balzac was much influenced by Sir Walter Scott, but whereas Scott had labored to bring the past to life, Balzac turned his attention to the present. Scott had the sensibilities of a historian; Balzac, those of a sociologist. He sought to observe and record every detail in the lives of his protagonists, down to the special jargon of their jobs.

With Balzac, and to a certain extent even with Stendhal, we begin to move away from the great Romantic tradition. These writers did not seek to transfigure reality; this was all too plainly beyond the artist's capabilities. Their task was to document, to report the facts. It was the beginning of the shift to realism and the science of society.

III THE ROMANTIC INSIGHT INTO HUMAN EXPERIENCE

The Impact of the French Revolution

The Romantic reconstruction was not confined to literature and the arts; it affected every area of human thought and experience and none more profoundly than social and political theory. The Church and the monarchy were the chief victims of the Republic of Reason. It was only natural that after the Revolution had done its worst, the old order should mount an intellectual as well as a political counteroffensive. But Romantic political thought was not merely propaganda for the old order. The disruption wrought by the French Revolution had been so traumatic that thoughtful men everywhere were led to reexamine not only the principles of stable and just government but the fabric of society within which governments operated. The relationship of government to society, family, and Church received new attention. Continuity was discovered as one of the first principles of a sane society. The violent rupture with the past which the French Revolution had attempted produced a new respect, even a reverence, for a different kind of change – the change accomplished by slow growth and maturation, the imperceptible modifications that habits and customs make on institutions. Edmund Burke found in this principle the glory and longevity of the British constitution. A generation later, Alexis de Tocqueville discovered that continuity persisted beneath the most cataclysmic upheavals and that the *ancien régime* and the revolutionary Republic had had more in common than the revolutionaries had realized. Not only was it undesirable to wipe the historical slate clean; it was not even possible.

The ungovernable momentum of the French Revolution made men wonder how far history and the tide of human events were amenable to management and direction by individuals. Was national destiny shaped by men, or was it the product of vast, blind, impersonal forces? If the latter, what was the nature of these forces? The answers offered were various. Race and nationality were put forth as anterior to political development, as great animating powers that conditioned or even determined the march of historical events. The early socialists saw economic and technological revolutions as antecedent and primary, politics as no more than superstructure. The German philosopher Hegel suggested that history was governed by an inner logic of its own, a dialectic which assured that each stage of historical development would be a unique higher synthesis of the thesis and antithesis of previous eras. Hegel, as well as the English philosopher and historian Thomas Carlyle, focused on Napoleon and decided that individual men could on occasion rise to the level of vast impersonal forces and become "world historical individuals" beyond the understanding or judgment of ordinary mortals. The power of crowds in the French Revolution left an indelible impression on sensitive minds of the postrevolutionary generation. The French historian Jules Michelet was the first to suspect that the anonymous multitudes which the ancient world and the eighteenth century had treated only as "rabble" might themselves be one of those great, mysterious forces that moved the world.

Reflection on and analysis of the French Revolution enlarged historical consciousness throughout Europe. Men could not help but see that they were living in a new era, one such as mankind had never before experienced. The probing of the past was undertaken from a variety of motives: it might provide a guide to present action, a justification for this or that political regime, but it also provided consolation—reassurance that the old order and the old certainties had not been utterly destroyed. The historical past was an anchor which enabled men to ride out present tempests.

The dethronement of reason after the French Revolution, coupled with the personal agonies men experienced in a world in which stability seemed permanently undermined, pushed some of the most sensitive to a new exploration of the meaning of religious truth. The early nineteenth century is generally cited as the period during which the mass of Europeans became firmly secular in their outlook. But this was also the period when the search for God became for many a personal hunger. By and large, the new departures in religious thought came from outside the established churches and had very little concern for dogma or theology. Chateaubriand, Schleiermacher, and Kierkegaard rested their case for religion on their own emotional, aesthetic, and psychological needs. The new mass movements—Methodism, Evangelicalism, Pietism—were similarly based on direct, personal appeal to the intimate demands of the heart.

Political and Social Thought

Edmund Burke (1729–1797) has long been called the father of modern conservative thought—a somewhat bizarre accolade to bestow on a man who championed the American Revolution and was part of a progressive, reformist faction in his own country. Burke's *Reflections on the Revolution in France* was published in 1790, well before the French Revolution had entered its bloodiest phase. It very quickly became the catechism for all those to whom the revolutionary doctrines were anathema. The book was endlessly praised and elaborated on by publicists in *émigré* circles in France and Germany, striving to erect dikes to protect absolutism. It was translated into German by Friedrich Gentz, personal adviser to Metternich, the conservative Austrian statesman. Gentz went on to produce a comparison of the American and French revolutions that found the two great conflagrations entirely dissimilar—the one preserving, the other destroying liberty. In France after 1815, Count Joseph de Maistre (1754–1821) drew on Burke's inspiration to rehabilitate and vindicate entirely the government of prerevolutionary France. Maistre, who was witty and incisive, became the mouthpiece of intransigence, stating baldly that social order was based on Providence and that to tamper with constitutions or with sovereignty in the name of reform was to tamper with the ordinances of God. Maistre's argument shored up the postrevolutionary alliance between Church, monarchy, and aristocracy.

Burke's *Reflections* was far more profound and searching. Burke took his stand against those who, spouting fine words on social contracts and inalienable rights, thought that constitutions could be fashioned by a flourish of the pen. The essence of his argument lay in the assertion that governments were not fortuitous constructs but part and parcel of a social fabric which included customs, habits, other forms of association, religious sympathies, and all manner of prejudices. Governments represented the habits and wisdom a people accumulated over centuries. All "rights" were historic rights, products of the circumstances that had called them forth. Burke asserted the priority of the community versus the form of government. No political system, he felt, could be severed from the community that had produced it.

In Burke's organic view of society, men were creatures whose sympathies extended naturally from their families to their neighborhoods, to their towns, and finally and last to their governments. To jostle one set of loyalties and affections was to disturb them all. A constitution, like a tree, sprang up differently in different soils; it was nourished and watered naturally by the community, and it grew and changed eternally. Burke's view, unlike Gentz's and Maistre's extrapolations, was profoundly relativistic. Reform and conservation of the past were not opposites but complementary processes, going on all the time spontaneously and often unconsciously. Burke was a conservative, not a reactionary. He saw in the French Revolution the ruinous dissolution of all specific, traditional loyalties, and he feared an atomized society. The separation of the individual from the community, estate, town, guild, family, and class into which he had been born was inimical to the Romantic conservatives' idea of freedom, for freedom was inconceivable without variety and individual peculiarity. All leveling and equalizing doctrines tended toward despotism.

Burke was essentially a practical man, whose political philosophy never lost touch with actual conditions in England. It was in Germany that his ideas received their most extreme expression. The German Romantics did not always understand Burke, but they made a cult of worshiping him. Adam Müller (1779–1829), the chief German philosopher of political Romanticism, transferred Burke's theory into mysticism. His lectures, delivered at a period when Germany was politically prostrate before the armies of Napoleon and later published as *Elements of Politics*, had a profound effect on the development of German political thought. For Müller, the state represented "the totality of all human concerns." Adulation of the Middle Ages led him to advocate that the nobility should be entrusted with the direction of the state and also to subordinate the values of the present to those of the past. Human happiness and welfare in the here and now counted but little against the immortal community. Individual life had no meaning apart from the state, which alone put paltry men in touch with eternity.

Müller was led by his theories to a new discovery of the virtues of war. War was preferable to peace because the tears, the shared grief, it produced made the state in time of war a powerful emotional reality, while in times of peace and prosperity men tended to take the state for granted. Later in the century Karl Marx commented that Germany had experienced and reacted to the French Revolution on a purely philosophical plane—hence the extremism and the peculiar unreality of the German response. In their adulation of Burke, the Germans forgot that he had defined government as "a contrivance of human wisdom to provide for human wants."

In Great Britain, where the Industrial Revolution had advanced further and faster than elsewhere, the vitality of Romantic thought was rapidly channeled into an attack on industrialism and the resulting mechanization of the human spirit. Thomas Carlyle (1795–1881), essayist, historian, and impassioned social critic, expressed the frustration that many of the most sensitive mid-century minds felt in confronting the new society. Along with Coleridge, he was the chief disseminator of German Romantic thought in Britain. It was Carlyle who first spoke of the industrial age as the era when "the cash-nexus" supplanted all other relationships and values. Carlyle, in fact, was lamenting the same dissolution of the social ties of family and community that Burke before him and Marx after him saw as the chief characteristic of the new age.

The present epoch, wrote Carlyle in *Signs of the Times*, an essay published in 1829, was not a heroical, devotional, moral, or philosophical age but "the Mechanical Age." And the mechanization of life was not confined to external and physical phenomena—men were becoming mechanized in thought and feeling. Carlyle detested the liberal utilitarians, who, he felt, were attempting to comprehend and manage life and experience by the computing principle. He showed himself a true disciple of Burke by lashing out against those who sought to cure social and spiritual ills by tinkering with "mere political arrangements." The modern propensity to putter with the structure of governments (of which the French Revolution was a symptom, not a cause) was a result of the development of the new trade of "code-making" as a panacea for all discontents. The Romantic bent of Carlyle's thought is obvious in his stress on the primacy of inward experience, ethics, and spirit.

Carlyle was not content merely to denounce. He wanted regeneration. He struggled incessantly with the problem of how to combat spiritual emptiness. In *Past and Present* he held up a glorious (if unreal) picture of medieval England as a society that had not lost its veneration for spiritual values. Modern laissez-faire government he loathed for its "Donothingism," which he saw simply as an abdication of social responsibility, a symptom of the drying up of compassion and fellow-feeling. He sought frantically for a class of men to free society from the moral atrophy in which it was sunk. For a time he pinned his hopes on the great new industrialists themselves, the captains of industry who might be educated to their social responsibilities; but as he grew older, he turned more and more to the veneration of great men — heroes — as the saviors of men's souls. He wrote biographies of Cromwell and Frederick the Great and a set of essays on heroes and hero worship. It was a familiar pitfall for disillusioned Romantics. Beset by a sense of impotence in the face of the relentless impersonal forces of the age, they pinned their hopes on charisma, on some mighty personage who would transfigure the world by his personal example. Ultimately, this hope was an admission of despair.

The changing nature of political power, of which the French Revolution had provided such an unforgettable example, haunted nineteenth-century Europeans. It was gradually becoming clear that power was passing to new classes of men — to the much-despised bourgeois and perhaps ultimately to the mob. Alexis de Tocqueville (1805–1859), the French political analyst, was one of the first European thinkers to set out to study with scientific detachment the transformation of political and social life under the impact of democracy. He chose for his case study the United States, the country where democracy had achieved its fullest development. *Democracy in America*, published in 1835, still stands as one of the pioneering works of sociology as well as an immensely incisive analysis of the character of American life. For Tocqueville, America was the land of equality, which had been achieved by the erasure of those distinctions of rank and status that characterized traditional societies. He regarded the drive for equality as the great tendency of the modern age. He saw it operating in the monarchies of the *ancien régime* long before the coming of the French Revolution.

Tocqueville was the first modern political analyst to perceive clearly that liberty and equality, far from being essentially the same thing, might in fact be inimical and incompatible. No governments, he said, were so powerful or potentially so despotic as democratic ones. Democracy, by dissolving time-honored social identities, leads to a greater and greater reliance on government; all authority now devolves on the state, which the people have no reason to mistrust since it represents themselves and is shaped in their own image. As each man becomes more and more the replica of his neighbor, his individuality is lost.

On the whole, Tocqueville feared popular despotism less than the permanent degradation of culture, which seemed to him sadly but inevitably bound up with the progress of democracy. Equality distrusted and was frightfully jealous of all distinction; it was the implacable enemy of distinguished talent, intelligence, wealth, and social privilege. Tocqueville saw much that was admirable and exciting in American life, but he feared that the progress of democracy—particularly its advent in Europe—would turn mankind into "a flock of industrious animals, of which the government is the shepherd." He decided that, emancipated from the fetters of class and tradition, the individual, far from coming into his own, was impoverished, diminished, and circumscribed. Coleridge, Burke, and Carlyle had all had forebodings of this fundamental modern dilemma.

Philosophy and History

If Tocqueville surveyed the future with apprehension, the greatest German philosopher of the age, Georg Wilhelm Friedrich Hegel (1770–1831), must be classed with the optimists. Marx excepted, Hegel was the last nineteenth-century thinker to attempt to include all the contradictions that rent modern philosophy in a single, coherent, all-embracing system. The world, Hegel believed, embodies God's rationality, and human history must therefore be similarly rational. History is purposeful and amenable to human understanding. It is, moreover, progressive, continuously moving to higher stages of development. But in human affairs progress is not tranquil and linear. The universe—and here Hegel's debt to the Romantics again becomes apparent—is dynamic and organic. All is in a state of flux, strife, and contradiction.

Hegel capitalized, so to speak, on chaos, by making conflict and the clash of ideas and cultures the very mechanism of progress. This is the heart of his famous dialectic. Consciousness comes about through the seeing of opposites, then through their integration. This, in turn, leads to the seeing of new opposites. The dialectic led Hegel to the conclusion that there is no finality in any structures, be they moral, metaphysical, or social. Truths of one age are superseded by the new-found knowledge of the next, though the old is always conserved in the new synthesis. Since the resolution of one conflict automatically engenders another, the world is constantly evolving.

Like his fellow Germans and like most Romantics, Hegel made the community rather than the individual his starting point. He recognized that men everywhere are nurtured and determined as cultural and moral beings by their societies. It is in products of communal life—art, religion, philosophy, and the state—that man finds his fullest expression. The discords that beset human life can ultimately be resolved only within a community. The great antithesis between freedom and necessity, for example – the bugaboo of philosophers and theologians since time began – can be reconciled only in the state. Hegel's choice of the state as the center of his moral universe, itself an actual embodiment of the highest morality attained in any age, was to have enormous consequences in the future development of all German political thought and, quite likely, in the actions of the men who shaped modern German history. Not all states, of course, are equally rational or free. Like ideas, states are in constant competition. The highest development of "the world historical spirit" is found in different peoples in different historical epochs. As one nation's mission is fulfilled, it yields the center of the stage to another. The dynamic creativity passes to another people, another land.

If Hegel impressed anything on his followers, it was that history moves according to a grand, providential design, that it obeys laws and follows patterns that can be discerned, at least in retrospect. But if societies are shaped by the ineluctable working-out of great ideas, then it follows that individual actions and volitions do not count for very much. In fact, Hegel's grand conceptual scheme renders the role of the individual highly precarious and problematic. Individual responsibility for controlling political events becomes illusory or at any rate dubious. Immanuel Kant's great concern for the individual as moral agent is abandoned. In the Hegelian view, individuals can attain significance only if they are moving with the trend of the times, only if they conform to the prevailing world-spirit. To talk of opposing history is nonsense. Insofar as men try to do so, they are relegated to insignificance – moral as well as historical.

The state embodies the highest development of morality at any given time, and every stage of historical development is a necessary one. These two propositions, when combined, reduce all too easily to the postulate that whatever is, is necessary and is therefore as it ought to be – that "Whatever is, is right." In the next century this vulgarized extrapolation from Hegel became the rationalization for acquiescence to some of the greatest tyrannies the world has ever seen.

In Hegel, one of the paradoxes that threads its way through so many aspects of Romantic thought – the painful opposition between man perceived as petty, wretched, and impotent and man perceived as heroic, magnificent, and godlike – finds a curious resolution. Caught in the ebb and backwash of history, man is utterly insignificant. On the other hand, a man or a nation marching in tune with the spirit of the age is invincible. In rare instances such a man may even become a "world historical figure," advancing the destiny of mankind – an Alexander, a Caesar, a Napoleon. Hegel remained a fan of Napoleon to the end of his days, even after Bonaparte's armies had vanquished the philosopher's homeland. World historical figures were exempt from ordinary standards of moral judgment. They could be selfish adventurers or scoundrels satisfying their own whims if, however unwittingly, these private pleasures served history. The heroes of Carlyle, Byron, and Stendhal had retained certain recognizable ethical dimensions. For Hegel, these ceased to matter.

While Hegel was reshaping the foundations of the philosophy of history, western Europe was experiencing an epidemic of books that laid the foundations for history as a formal academic discipline. The influence of Herder and Scott and the need to understand the French Revolution precipitated a great spate of historical studies in the early decades of the nineteenth century. Of the many tomes that were produced, the works of a German, Leopold von Ranke (1795–1886), and a Frenchman, Jules Michelet (1798–1874), established new standards for historical research, a new sense of how the past should be approached and understood.

The year 1824, when Ranke published his first book (he was to produce dozens over a period of sixty years), is generally regarded as beginning the critical, scientific study of the past. Ranke announced in his preface that he intended simply to "show how things really were," leaving it to others to draw lessons from history. This seemingly modest pronouncement was to reverberate down the halls of academia for generations. It was the debut of allegedly value-free history: the facts, all the facts, and nothing but the facts. History was no longer to be a great morality play or a statesman's manual of conduct. Ranke said that he wanted history to be objective, to be science. His influence was vast; in the decades that followed, dozens of his students were appointed to university chairs throughout Germany. Yet Ranke was more influenced by Hegel than he cared to admit, or perhaps realized, for he tended to see history as a series of epochs, each one carrying to fruition the germ of some great idea—for example, Protestantism. For Ranke as well as for Hegel, history came to be the inevitable working-out of great ideas in no particular ethical context.

Michelet's work was utterly different. He was an unashamed partisan. His multivolume *History of France*, produced over a period of more than thirty years (1833–1867), was shot through with values. Deeply influenced by Vico, the eighteenth-century philosopher who first suggested that civilization was the collective product of humanity, Michelet saw humanity as the great inarticulate multitudes, the anonymous peasantry, the riotous urban crowds; he wanted to become the tribune of the voiceless people who had been cheated of access to history by illiteracy, poverty, and servitude. In his *History of the French Revolution*, the people are the only hero. *The History of France* is the story of the progressive development of the masses to ever greater self-consciousness and self-assertiveness.

Michelet was moved to tell the story of "the people" by his own passionately democratic temperament. His political prejudices led him to a view of history that was ultimately much richer and deeper than that of Ranke, his conservative German peer. Frustrated in his attempts to find the voice of the common man in diplomatic charters and government records, he looked elsewhere—to medieval cathedrals, oral traditions, and other monuments of the collective mind of an epoch. Michelet had read Herder and, with him, believed that all knowledge is one: human culture can and must be understood as a totality. This Romantic desire to apprehend and encompass all facets of human experience, to embrace together man, God, and nature, inspired the enormous creativity of the first half of the nineteenth century.

Religion: The Search for a New Faith

The social and psychological dislocation produced by the tempests of the French Revolution, combined with evangelical and pietistic subversion of the comfortable, commonsensical deism of the eighteenth century, produced a sudden quest for faith. Homeless and estranged from the bewildering new social order, men sought new grounds for certainty, a new basis for conduct, an explanation for their despair and loneliness. Chateaubriand was typical of the sizable group of aristocrats who sought solace in a return to the Catholic Church. For him and other aristocrats, Catholicism was a sensuous bath in splendid music, magnificent cathedrals, statues of Madonnas, candlelight, and incense. Ultraconservative Catholicism became something of an affectation among the European aristocracy following the French Revolution.

A more serious manifestation of the prevailing mood of repentance was the sudden flowering of High Church Anglicanism in England after a century and a half of easygoing, unaggressive latitudinarianism. Because the movement centered around a group of Oxford University intellectuals, it came to be called the Oxford movement. It produced at least one great theologian in the person of John Henry Newman (1801–1890). The Oxford movement was a return to the doctrinal conservatism of Anglicanism as it had existed in the seventeenth century under Archbishop Laud. Its leaders brought a new austerity and solemnity to the established Church and, by emphasizing the importance of ritual, liturgy, music, and prayer, satisfied the new taste for awe and beauty. Some of its adherents, notably Newman, were led the whole way back to the Catholic Church. The 1830's marked the beginning of periodic outbursts of conversion to Rome, which continued in England well into the twentieth century. While some of these were certainly the fashionable affectations of young aesthetes, many others must be seen as symptoms of the new need for authority and mystery which developed in an increasingly secular and strife-torn world.

In Germany the longing for the lost unity and harmony of universal Christendom found its highest expression in the poetry and prose of Novalis (1772–1801). Like many Europeans of his day, Novalis (Friedrich Leopold von Hardenberg) saw the Protestant Reformation as the birth of Europe's nemesis, the intellectual seedbed of the social and political anarchy that led straight to the disaster of the French Revolution. His writing mingled aspirations for a new European oneness with a mystical faith in the special destiny of Germany as the vehicle of mankind's deliverance. But he conceived of Germany as an ethos rather than a political construct. The state was a divine work of art, a poetic creation.

On Religion: Speeches to Its Cultural Despisers, by the celebrated preacher Friedrich Schleiermacher (1768–1834), was far more important in the development of religious thought than Novalis' lyrical outpourings. Deeply affected by Rousseau, Schleiermacher saw religious faith as one of the primary instincts and impulses of man. He argued simply: "I *feel* there is a God. That is proof of his existence." Religion and piety had nothing to do with dogma and theology—these were products of the reflective critical intellect that transcribed (and falsified) the religious experience, which was intimate, personal, and not communicable in words. Piety alone, said Schleiermacher, could restore to man a sense of his own wholeness; without it, he was a creature torn by antagonistic faculties and desires.

Schleiermacher made the individual personality the point of departure for all religious sentiment. Everything men experienced as holy *was* holy. Religion was both the supreme expression and fulfillment of the human personality and the means by which the individual was united with the natural order, attaining extinction of the private self in the great mystery of the One and the All. Grounded in psychology, in the primitive instincts of man, it could not be undermined by logic or reason; it became inviolate to all onslaughts of modern scepticism.

It was only a few steps from the pious affirmation of Schleiermacher to the bitterness of Sören Kierkegaard (1813–1855), the Dane who is generally regarded as the founder of modern existentialism. Whereas Schleiermacher had made faith independent of reason, Kierkegaard insisted that faith existed only when reason was defied and violated. The test and sign of faith was the ability to believe with perfect serenity that which was a paradox, ridiculous and absurd. Kierkegaard was an isolated figure in his own day, and it is difficult to find characteristically Romantic elements in his thought. He shared with his age only an acute apprehension of the wretchedness of the human being severed from all traditional authority, compelled to strike out on his own in a lonely, terrifying voyage of discovery. His influence was to come much later.

Other religious explorers began in profound pessimism and ended in triumphant affirmation. Such a man was Félicité Robert de Lamennais (1782–1854), a priest who became an embarrassment to the Church by gradually reviving the long dormant Christian social gospel. Christianity, he reminded the world, had once been the religion of the poor and the oppressed. He wanted the clergy to become missionaries in the modern world, getting their hands dirty in the slums and hovels of Paris. Lamennais advocated the solidarity of all the lowly against the tyrants and usurpers of liberty, the parasites who fed on their fellowman. It was an old message but one which neither the conservative French Church nor the papacy was particularly anxious to hear expounded. Lamennais' views were condemned by a papal encyclical. He became more and more mistrustful of authority and, after the publication of *Words of a Believer* in 1830, broke with the Church entirely and became the apostle of a humanistic, militant Christianity with communistic overtones. Lamennais was one of a small group of Catholic intellectuals who tried to push the Church toward a creative confrontation with the new industrial urban masses. He feared that popular atheism would be the inevitable result of the perpetuation of the alliance between the Church and political reactionaries.

The philosophical justification for the demythologizing of Christianity was provided by Ludwig Feuerbach (1804–1872), a disciple of Hegel. In *The Essence of Christianity*, published in 1841, Feuerbach announced that God had been created by man and that it was now time for mankind to reclaim its own. Mankind, he argued, had taken its own highest nature, its most sublime aspirations and ethical ideas, and set them up as a transcendental autonomous power. Actually the sublime was human. The Divine Being was nothing more than a symbol of man's own highest potentials; while no individual possessed these magnificent capacities, the human species did. But having created God, man had impoverished himself and denied his own latent perfections. When he set God up as his antithesis, he split his own personality. The Christian God—or any other god—was an anthropological construct. Once understood as such, He would lose his mystery, and man would become truly free. Until such time, Christian ethical precepts must always seem coercive —the impositions of an alien being. A turning point in history would come when man recognized that consciousness of God was nothing more than consciousness of the human species.

Feuerbach's fusion of anthropological and psychological arguments to explain the origins of religion had a great influence on the development of ethical and religious thought. Karl Marx was profoundly impressed by his work. The idea that man had at some time in the distant past alienated a part of himself for the benefit of some phantom or illegitimate master was applied by Marx not to morality but to labor. The plea to expropriate the usurper and thus become fully human and free remained the same.

IV NATIONALISM: MYTHS AND MYTH-MAKERS

The Variety and Complexity of Nationalism

The development of nationalism as an articulate, self-conscious ideology during the Napoleonic era was to have enormous consequences for the history of nineteenth-century Europe. A force that grew more potent as the century advanced, it signaled the doom of old territorial, dynastic states like Austria and Turkey and acted as a constant menace to the equilibrium of the European state system. In post-Napoleonic Europe there loomed the specter of an entirely new political order, one in which popular passions for the first time impinged on the policies of diplomats and foreign offices.

Even in authoritarian states, nationalism was an inherently democratic concept insofar as it invoked every citizen down to the lowest peasant. Yet its first appearance was far from a spontaneous surge of popular feelings. On the contrary, it can be argued that nationalism was everywhere instilled by the propaganda of poets, prophets, and paid publicists. No ground swell of popular resistance, for example, greeted the Napoleonic armies marching through Germany in the first decade of the nineteenth century. The French soldiery were often welcomed, more often simply ignored, by the great masses of people, who felt that one set of masters was as good as another. It was a decade and more after the Prussian defeat at the Battle of Jena (1806) that the exhortations of German intellectuals to a national awakening began to produce some stirrings among the masses.

The ideology of nationalism was not everywhere the same. The new mystique of the nation-state developed in Germany, Italy, Ireland, and eastern Europe. And even in these areas the doctrines differed. The faith that informed the Italian national awakening was not at all the same as that which was propagated in the German universities. Yet everywhere the nationalist struggle was intensely emotional and intoxicating. For much of Europe it was the chief outlet of messianic impulses in the nineteenth century.

German nationalism had begun as a cultural movement in the 1770's with the work of Herder. Most of the early German nationalists could also lay claim to being poets or theologians — Novalis, Schleiermacher, and Müller are all counted as founders of German nationalism, though in their principal works the state may be only a marginal concern. Early German nationalism tended on the whole toward an exaltation of Germany's literary, philosophical, and religious heritage, but a great deal was heard about the distinctive character of the German mind. Also, the pious Romanticism of Novalis and Schleiermacher had produced a distinctly German conception of the state. It was regarded as an ethical body, and its relationships were patriarchal rather than contractual. It was divine and beautiful, and it served some higher end than mere pragmatic convenience. Men belonged to the German state the way they belonged to a family, not to a club or a business association; it served and nourished their highest spiritual needs. Here and there a voice was raised to the effect that Germany — the Germany of the spirit — would be the vehicle for the regeneration of Europe.

The German cultural mission to the world was expounded in 1807 by Johann Gottlieb Fichte (1762–1814) in a series of lectures subsequently entitled *Addresses to the German Nation*. The lectures were delivered in a Berlin amphitheater while that city was under occupation by French troops, but they were barely noticed at the time. They were delivered by a philosopher who in his youth had drafted plans for a league of nations, who only a few years earlier had championed the French Revolution, and who clung to a residual cosmopolitanism to the end of his life. Although Fichte's chief distinction lies in his development of Kantian philosophy, he has gone down in history as the first great voice of German nationalism.

Leaning heavily on Herder, Fichte rested his case for the originality of the German people on an intricate argument about linguistics. He had discovered that, alone among European peoples, the Germans had a living, original language. This remarkable situation arose from the fact that German had never been bastardized by the admixture of other dialects. Germans had never migrated; they had remained in the dwelling place of their ancestral stock. Therefore their speech at all times arose out of direct experience, containing no "dead" elements. Vitality of language ensured nobility of thought. Thus the Germans alone were equipped for great cultural feats. The linguistic theory was dubious, but the underlying point was clear enough. A people infused with a national heritage is a people infused with a mystical strength. Every time Fritz the German peasant uttered a sentence, Frederick Barbarossa, Luther, and Goethe spoke in his mouth.

Fichte felt acutely the political prostration of Germany. A national regeneration was necessary. He urged a new educational system to train young boys in patriotism and citizenship. Education would create a new Germany, and Germany a new world. Fichte was somewhat vague as to what exactly a German was, suggesting at one point that anyone who believed in freedom and spontaneity qualified and was "of our blood"; but he was the first of the German nationalists to put forward something approximating a political program. In later years he was credited with having inspired the Prussian government to administrative and political reforms effected in the following decade. Fichte stood somewhere in between those who continued to proselytize a purely spiritual German state and those who wanted Germany to become a political power.

After Fichte, German nationalist thought degenerated into shrill, coarse boastfulness. In the writings of Ernst Arndt (1769–1860) and particularly Ludwig Jahn (1778–1852), non-German peoples first began to be referred to as "mongrels." Germans began to be defined by blood and race rather than history and poetry. Myths about joyous Teutons romping around the primeval German forest proliferated. Arndt composed battle songs and war poems and urged Prussia to carry on a long war of national liberation against the French in order to arouse dormant patriotism. Jahn urged the celebration of national festivals to commemorate great days in Prussian history and the erection of monuments to military heroes. He lamented the Peace of Westphalia, which had robbed Germany of Switzerland and the Netherlands.

In eastern Europe the rhetoric of nationhood had not become political ideology. The nation was still the pious hope or the fond memory of isolated poets and intellectuals. In Russia, nationalism during the Romantic era took the form of establishing a distinctive cultural identity, as in Germany in Fichte's time. This purpose inspired Alexander Pushkin (1799–1837), whom Russians regard as their greatest poet and the founder of their national literature. The descendant of an old noble family, Pushkin subtly blended in his voluminous writings a cosmopolitan humanitarianism, Byronic heroic themes, and an intense devotion to the Russian past and the beauty of the Russian language. His first major poem, *Ruslan and Ludmilla*, drew upon folklore traditions. The heroine of his masterpiece *Eugene Onegin*, a novel in verse, came to be viewed as the ideal of Russian womanhood. Pushkin's drama, *Boris Godunov*, was based on the tempestuous career of an early seventeenth-century czar. Pushkin's early work was influenced by French models, but in his later poems he consciously tried to develop a distinctive Russian literary style, characterized, he said, by "roughness and simplicity."

The great voice of Polish nationalism in the age was Adam Mickiewicz (1798–1885), who spent most of his adult life in Moscow and Paris as a political exile, Poland having been partitioned off the map in 1795. Mickiewicz's nationalist creed was little more than a nostalgic, sentimental longing for the cornfields of his native village. His songs praised the simple virtues of the humble peasantry—their oneness with God and nature, their instinctive piety, and their ability to endure the eternal suffering that was their lot.

Mickiewicz was one of the writers whose works were important in the development of that racial and cultural creed called Slavophilism—the collection of romantic, mystical ideas that set up Slavic eastern Europe as the antithesis of the materialist, egotistical West. Slavophilism became an important intellectual orientation later in the century, particularly in Russia, where it polarized intellectuals into those who wished to emulate Western institutions and economic organization and those who clung tenaciously to indigenous customs and institutions. Since it tended to make the eternal Russian peasant its hero, it proved in the main to be highly conservative, even reactionary—as when it supported the argument that the Russian soul needed and loved the autocracy of the "little father," the czar. The naive, charming peasants of Mickiewicz's poems thus had important political consequences.

Giuseppe Mazzini

Giuseppe Mazzini (1805–1872), the Italian patriot and nationalist, captured the imagination of all Europe. Around him there grew up the popular myth of the professional revolutionary which has persisted to this day. A man of absolute dedication, handsome, with burning eyes (they made aristocratic English ladies swoon) and unfailing courage and energy, he is surely one of the most attractive figures of the nineteenth century. The nationalism of which he was a prophet and an apostle strikes us today as remarkably naive; but it was at all times humane, generous, and liberal, showing none of those exclusive, aggressive tendencies that appeared early in Germany.

Mazzini was as much a religious as a political thinker. He believed that religious faith must inform all social and political considerations, though he considered Christianity a spent force that had fulfilled its mission when it produced the liberal rights-of-man ideas of the Enlightenment. Humanity was ready for a new dispensation, and with it would come a new social order. The doctrine of individual rights had been valuable as a weapon in the overthrow of old despotisms, but to Mazzini it could never be more than a negative doctrine. From it derived selfish individualism and competition that pitted one man, one class, one state, against another. Some liberty and even equality could be derived from individual rights but not fraternity, and it was fraternity above all that Mazzini sought. He saw all men as part of a single human family and looked forward to the day when the word *foreigner* would disappear from every tongue—when men from every corner of the earth would greet each other as "brother."

For Mazzini, nationalism—the creation of a united Italy or a restored Poland—was not a denial of cosmopolitanism but a precondition for it. The pact of humanity, the great federation of nations, could only be signed by free and equal states. Each man must have a *patria*, as each man has a family. Each is endowed with special talents and aptitudes; each has a unique contribution to make to civilization and the collective destiny of mankind. Although Mazzini cherished the Italian language and the great art of the Renaissance, he advanced no special claims of superiority for the Italian cultural heritage. For Mazzini—and his thinking was characteristic of the tone of Italian nationalism—the state was an object of simple piety and affection, like one's family and one's home town. It was never cloaked in mystical, metaphysical garb. Man's first duty was to humanity; his country and family were like two circles within the greater circle that contained them both.

Mazzini gave first place to duty and sacrifice for one's fellowman. The new religion was yet another variant of the religion of humanity to which Lamennais was devoted. Mazzini believed in the continuous progress and betterment of the human race but at the same time retained a direct, childlike belief in God. The man who could deny Him on a starry night, or beside the graves of his dearest ones, or in the presence of martyrdom, must indeed be very unhappy or very wicked, Mazzini once wrote. Wordsworth would have understood him perfectly. There is a great deal of simple, even simplistic optimism in his thought but no obfuscation. He is one of the heroic figures of the first half of the nineteenth century—the era when burgeoning liberal, nationalist, and socialist aspirations had not yet hardened into exclusive, antagonistic dogmas.

V ROMANTIC ART AND MUSIC

The Spirit of Liberation

Romanticism in the arts was blatantly, vociferously, a movement for emancipation, a struggle to break away from the tyrannies of the past. Here the influence of literature seems to have been paramount. A great many of the painters and musicians of the age openly acknowledged their debt to Goethe, to the rediscovery of Shakespeare with his freedom from neoclassical norms. The French composer Berlioz paid his homage to Scott, Shakespeare, and Byron in naming his early compositions: *Waverley*, *King Lear*, *Harold in Italy*. Many other artists were similarly affected.

Romanticism was a self-conscious quest for liberation — at times too self-conscious, for at its worst it could produce the novel, the grotesque, and the disharmonious simply for their own sake. The worst Romantic art exhibits a didactic posturing, but the style and sensibility of a culture cannot be finally evaluated by its third-rate products. In painting, the Romantic Age produced Blake, Delacroix, Turner, Constable, Friedrich, Goya, and a host of other artists of the first rank. In music, it did more. Mozart, Haydn, and Bach excepted, what we call classical music is almost synonymous with the nineteenth century. Almost all the great names fall within the Romantic era: Beethoven, Berlioz, Schubert, Mendelssohn, Schumann, Liszt, Chopin — the list is long. This was the heroic age of modern music.

The emancipation of art and music in the Romantic Age was accomplished in a variety of ways. One was purely negative. The composer or painter lost his patron and, with his patron, his assured if circumscribed public, with its clear expectations and tastes. Bach had been a court composer, creating his passions and cantatas to please the congregations and the princes who hired him. The same was true of Haydn. One very important reason why portraits and historical paintings flourished in the eighteenth century was that aristocrats were eager to pay to see themselves idealized on canvas. All this changed rather abruptly at the end of the century. Beethoven disdained his aristocratic patrons — he would compose what he pleased and be no one's servant. This was one reason why he was worshiped by the rebels of the following generation: he had the proper conception of the splendor and dignity of his art. Though the young artists were often bitter at having to rely on the vagaries of public taste, in the long run the new freedom proved salubrious. The criteria aristocratic patronage had imposed on art gave way to a myriad of new possibilities.

In painting, the Romantics' preoccupation with feeling and imagination resulted in new freedom in dealing with color and light. Color, above all else, evoked sensation and created mood. Both the exotic lushness of Ingres and the intense tones of Delacroix were appropriate to an age in which men investigated the full range of sensation from the subtlest nuances of the

affections to the most violent emotions. Light was a source of fascination because it could alter color – alter reality – from minute to minute. Spontaneity,
sudden intense apprehension of meaning in nature, is one of the leitmotifs of
Romanticism, the theme of much of Wordsworth's and Keats's poetry. Light is
by its very nature evanescent – the perfect visual symbol for the transitory,
the ephemeral, the unexpected.

Since the Middle Ages, artists had observed certain conventions in the use
of color. Colors were automatically identified with particular subjects and
particular states of mind, and certain colors were not juxtaposed for fear of
producing a jarring or unpleasant sensation. The Romantics took decisive
steps toward freeing color from these traditions and limitations. Eugène Delacroix (1799 – 1863) was the first to break the rules. His brilliant, clashing
colors staggered his viewers, producing an aesthetic shock like a wrong note
in a musical composition.

The Romantic era saw the sudden enormous expansion of subject matter in
pictorial art. As in literature, a wealth of new themes appeared. For the first
time it became legitimate to paint landscapes devoid of human beings. John
Constable (1776 – 1837) and J. M. Turner (1775 – 1851) in England, followed
by Camille Corot (1796 – 1875) and J. F. Millet (1814 – 1875) in France,
brought nature into art not as a stage setting or decoration but as a source of
instruction and pleasure in itself. A vitalism – a sense that the natural order
is alive and dynamic – floods the canvases of Constable and Turner. A grum-
bling critic complained of Constable's paintings that not an inch of repose could
be found there. Every element – plants, trees, sky – cried out for attention.

In the eighteenth century the presumed function of landscape was to
soothe, to lull, and to prettify. Constable's landscapes seemed to many critics
to be too assertive, too intense. The intensity came from the freshness of vision, like that of a child or of a man long blind seeing – really seeing – a scene
for the first time. But for the new public, Constable's scenes from nature at
least had the virtue of being recognizable – as a matter of fact, he depicted
them in all their uniqueness. Turner's later paintings, "Steamer in a Snow-
storm" and "Rain, Steam, and Speed," seemed to be no more than a riotous
assault of color – great swirls and streaks blazing across the canvas. Turner
portrayed nature frenzied and riotous; forms and shapes dissolved in the elements gone mad. His canvases obliterated commonsensical apprehensions.
They were monuments to the power of the imagination to transfigure reality,
and hence to the power of the artist, whose special endowment is imagination. The artist could remake the world and triumph over material existence.
Turner was carrying out Shelley's program on canvas.

Ludwig van Beethoven

Ludwig van Beethoven (1770 – 1827), born in Bonn, Germany, inaugurated
a shattering of conventions in music that paralleled the developments in early

nineteenth-century painting. Even as a child, he showed obvious evidence of great talent, which his father, a poor musician, was not above exploiting. The boy gave his first public concert at the age of eight and made a concert tour three years later. He received little proper education and never lost the traces of his humble background. Throughout his life, he remained a strangely disorderly, unkempt individual. His portraits show a face of tremendous intensity and volcanic strength.

Beethoven's lack of education did not stop him from gaining access to the court in Vienna in 1792. His brilliance as a pianist quickly gained him a reputation, and it was the aristocracy that courted him. But though he became the favorite of court society, he was to remain totally independent, never having much to do with the artificial, overrefined world of the nobility. He used the wealthy, but he never submitted to them. From the beginning he asserted his own freedom. This assertion was to be of crucial importance to other Romantic composers, who saw in Beethoven the symbol of the musician whose art was an extension of his inner self. Beethoven's whole attitude was determined by his belief "that music was a higher revelation than all wisdom and philosophy."

Beethoven was to struggle all his life to achieve mastery of his art. He was his own most violent critic, and his chronic dissatisfaction gives his music a force very different from the serenity of the purely classical composition. Although his own music was basically classical in form, his supreme individuality and his belief in the ability of music to express man's deepest emotions made his compositions radically different from those of the eighteenth century.

Beethoven was essentially the child of the chaos and disruption of the last quarter of that century. Through his music, he gave utterance to his belief in man's humanity. As early as 1801 he turned his attention to the heroic in mankind, composing a ballet on the legend of Prometheus, who symbolized for him (and other Romantics) man's will to survive despite fate's cruelest blows. Beethoven was himself Prometheus, chained to a barren rock of deafness, and his refusal to be defeated by his affliction added a dimension of nobility to his character. Surely there is no other example in all of music of such courage and inexhaustible determination.

Beethoven's Third Symphony in E Flat Major (1803–1804) revolutionized all symphonic composition: he made of the symphony a musical poem, an expression of his own feeling, a portrayal of his own personality. Originally the work was to be dedicated to Napoleon: "The title of the Symphony is really Bonaparte." But Beethoven's grief when Napoleon the liberator became Napoleon the despot made him alter both the dedication and title. He simply called his work the *Sinfonia Eroica* (the Heroic Symphony) and added a few words: "To the memory of a great man."

Yet another of Beethoven's works must be examined in order to understand why he had such appeal for other Romantic composers. He called his Sixth Symphony, written during the years 1807–1808, the "Pastoral Symphony or

Recollection of Country Life, an expression of feeling rather than a description." Beethoven, the tempestuous, tortured individual at variance with others and with himself, sought all his life to find inner peace but was never to enjoy the serenity of an ordinary man. And perhaps his music might have suffered had he gained calm. It was an outpouring of his agonies, a torrential storm filled with the wild forces of his inner world. Through the uncorrupt perfection of nature, however, Beethoven gained a kind of peace both in himself and in his art. The Sixth Symphony is Beethoven's most beautiful expression of his love for nature.

The last darkening years of Beethoven's life brought no diminution of his genius. During the years 1822–1824 he produced his magnificent Choral Symphony in D Minor, Opus 125, the last and perhaps the greatest of his nine symphonies. On May 7, 1824, by now completely deaf, he conducted its first performance. He had to be turned around to see the audience's applause. Yet the last movement of the Ninth Symphony includes a choral setting for Schiller's *Ode to Joy*. Even in his complete isolation, Beethoven could create sounds that celebrated man's greatness. The work is a personal testament to the composer's own sense of his destiny.

The string quartets of Beethoven's last years took what appeared to be extravagant liberties with the structure deemed essential to the genre. They no longer proceeded along neatly from melody to melody with brief variations between. Instead, the variations were elaborated in infinite directions—the listener was in danger of becoming lost. Beethoven, like the later Romantic artists and composers, sought to destroy predictability, to jolt the viewer or listener into an unhackneyed response, to destroy his passivity before the work of art—to disturb him, to astound him, to force him to struggle for interpretation and meaning, and thus to demonstrate to him that the world is full of the most astounding possibilities.

The Absolute

The Romantics were interested in extremes—in ascertaining and if possible defying the limits of the human mind, of permissible behavior, of power over the cosmic and the social order. Romantic poetry is shot through with superlatives—the highest mountain, the deepest stream, even the briefest moment. Romantic painting and music show this same aspiration to plumb the depths and soar to the heights—to penetrate to the absolute—in a word, to attain omnipotence. Goya's brutal scenes from the Peninsula War have never been surpassed in evoking war's horror. They reach the zenith of the macabre, of pain and violence. Similarly, Turner's canvases capture the extreme moment when the swirling snow annihilates everything else, when fire consumes all in its path. The new attention paid by artists to lunatics—they were a favorite subject of Théodore Géricault (1791–1824)—was part of the same desire to go beyond the boundaries of normal life.

The ambition of the Romantic painter to penetrate to the absolute—to an intimation of the ultimate human experience—was expressed in a variety of ways. The angels, gods, and devils in the paintings of the poet-mystic William Blake (1757–1827) communicate a personal vision; they evoke an internal world of the liberated imagination. Romantic artists also sought to portray the ultimate moment of social experience. A painting such as Delacroix's "Liberty on the Barricades," depicting a scene from the Revolution of 1830, portrays humanity—the crowd—in the act of revolution, animated by an extreme passion, destroying all barriers. Daumier's "The Uprising" captures the proletariat at the height of its fury and despair.

The Romantic striving for omnipotence can be seen clearly in music in the works of Hector Berlioz (1803–1869). Berlioz wrote for orchestras so vast that his music was often impractical to stage. He used instruments in utterly new combinations, mixing, blending, contrasting sounds with a daring not even Beethoven had displayed. The exploration of the multitude of acoustic possibilities latent in a full orchestra was further evidence of the Romantics' desire to discover, master, and transcend every possible permutation of experience.

The trend towards greater intimacy in music, which was going on at the same time, was the reverse side of the same impulse. The compositions for piano by Chopin, Schumann, and Liszt are works for the solitary artist that can be performed in a drawing room before a small audience. This was art made absolutely personal. A single personality—a great virtuoso—exercised total control over the music produced by the most versatile of all instruments.

Why among the Romantics was music considered the most perfect, the only perfect art? Simply because music, more than any other art, created something out of nothing—the prerogative of God. Poetry or painting was always a representation of something else, embellished, glamorized, recast, but still at bottom a transcription of extrinsic reality. Not so music. No images or concepts are attached to music. It copies nothing—it is pure creation. Therefore the Romantics saw it as the most spiritual of all the arts, bound by no laws but those of its own making.

HERITAGE ESSAY

THE ROMANTIC HERITAGE

While the modern world derived the essentials of its liberal, meliorist credo from Enlightenment culture, the contribution of the Romantic era to modern thought was no less important. Through their exploration of the relationship between self and nature and between self and society, Romantic philosophy, literature, and art opened up new perspectives on the meaning of individual experience. All subsequent probings of how the individual relates to the external world have been extrapolations from the revolution of the human spirit that Romanticism proclaimed. From Romanticism, later nineteenth- and twentieth-century culture derived the doctrines, assumptions, and attitudes that created modern sensibility and that fundamentally conditioned the way in which Western civilization has understood human experience.

The Romantic heritage inculcated a set of values that still inspires both individual and communal action and a distinctive life style that remains extremely attractive, particularly to intellectuals, artists, and the young. The implications of the Romantic ethos for political and social theory tended in several directions, some mutually contradictory. But all who wish to act in society today must continually work within the context of the Romantic heritage — to perpetuate, to modify, or to oppose it.

The Enlightenment had established the belief that the authority of government resided in the consent of the governed. But in eighteenth-century thought "the people" was still a lifeless abstraction. The Romantics gave it life and individuality. Rejecting the elitism of eighteenth-century culture, the Romantics attributed the values of purity, wisdom, and beauty to the thoughts and mores of the common man with an intensity that went far beyond the democratic intimations of any previous era. Romantics relished the idea that the honest laborer — particularly the rural laborer — was the bearer of the primordial wisdom and sense of justice of mankind. In 1786 Robert Burns, in "A Man's a Man for A' That," announced

> The honest man, though e'er sae poor,
> Is king o' men for a' that.

Similarly, William Wordsworth discovered unsurpassed beauty in the song of "Yon solitary Highland Lass/Reaping and singing by herself" and professed the highest admiration for "the confident and cheerful thoughts" of an obscure shepherd.[1]

In general, the Romantics adored those who were excluded from power in society—not only the workers and the poor but also women, old men, and children. As most powerless and defenseless, children and youth were accorded a special value in the Romantic vision and invested with the most profound wisdom. "The Child is father of the Man," said Wordsworth:

> Heaven lies about us in our infancy!
> Shades of the prison-house begin to close
> Upon the growing Boy,
> But he beholds the light, and whence it flows,
> He sees it in his joy;
> The Youth, who daily farther from the east
> Must travel, still is Nature's priest . . . .[2]

1. William Wordsworth, *The Solitary Reaper* and *Michael*, in R. Sharrock, ed., *Selected Poems of William Wordsworth.* New York: Macmillan, 1958, p. 95, p. 81.
2. Wordsworth, *Ode on Intimations of Immortality from Recollections of Early Childhood,* in *Selected Poems,* p. 105.

The Common Man. The Romantic concept of "the people" as the font of wisdom and virtue was a central theme in early nineteenth-century art. The underprivileged and the powerless—workers, children, and the old, particularly those bound to the soil—were portrayed sympathetically, often sentimentally. Facing page: Samuel Palmer's "Coming from Evening Church" (1830) enshrines the Wordsworthian doctrine—veneration of the common man combined with the intimations of nature that were communicated to the rural working class. John Ruskin regarded Palmer as an important Romantic "renovator" of English art. The workers' integrity, strength, and purity remained a favorite subject of nineteenth-century artists. Left: Gustave Courbet eschewed the impressionistic style of some Romantic artists in favor of more realism, but his "The Stone Breakers" (1849) perpetuated the Romantic theme of the uncorrupted virtue of the rural worker.

The adoration of childhood and youth as a time of pure vision and uncontaminated integrity has been a recurring theme in modern thought, with mixed social consequences. The Romantics arrived at this perception partly out of their anti-establishment bias and partly out of sheer sentimentality. But the youth creed was also a corollary of the main philosophical movement of the Romantic era, usually called idealism or transcendentalism. This philosophy claimed to find in each man an innate intellectual power and life force that transcended the physical world and imposed on it whatever order, beauty, and justice it contained. An adherent of transcendental phi-

The Union of Self and Nature. Faith in a transcendental Spirit in which self and nature participate and unite in the Absolute was a leading theme of Romantic painting. At its most sentimental level, this attitude merely engendered a host of depictions of nature as mysterious and appealing. Facing page, bottom: John Martin's "Sadak in Search of the Waters of Oblivion" (1812). In its most ambitious aspect it inspired the use of color to communicate boldly impressionistic evocations of the individual experience of Spirit in the universe. Two of the finest examples of Romantic perception of the Absolute in nature are Caspar David Friedrich's "Man and Woman Gazing at the Moon" (1819), facing page, top, and Joseph Turner's "Rain, Steam, and Speed" (1844), below.

REPRODUCED BY COURTESY OF THE TRUSTEES, THE NATIONAL GALLERY

losophy could well believe that human creativity and virtue existed in children in a particularly pure and uncorrupted form.

In the perspective of the long-range development of Western thought, Romantic transcendentalism marked a revolt against eighteenth-century empiricism and a partial reversion to Platonism. Immanuel Kant showed the Romantic thinkers the road back to philosophical idealism. Kant concluded that the human mind could never penetrate to knowledge of the ultimate reality—the noumenon, or thing-in-itself. Instead, the mind imposed order and coherence on the phenomenal world of experience by applying its own categories of space, time, and causality. Although Kant's metaphysic still fell within the Enlightenment tradition, his German disciples used his theory as the starting point for a philosophy of transcendental idealism.

The Medieval Mystique. In their rebellion against the Enlightenment, the Romantics developed a veneration for the Middle Ages, which they viewed as an age of faith, mysticism, and lyrical sensuousness. Right: Gothic churches were considered the monuments of this sublime culture, as in Karl Friedrich Schinkel's "Medieval Town on a River" (1815). The medieval mystique became a prime Romantic vehicle for expressing a vision of a world of holiness, love, and purity. Facing page: "The Cross and the Cathedral in the Mountains" (1819) by Caspar David Friedrich is the finest depiction of this vision, which represents a rebellion against the rationalism and secularism of the eighteenth century and the mechanization and brutality of contemporary society. It was also intended to give Germans a sense of national identity by evoking the glories of medieval German culture. Below: in the works of William Blake, such as "Beatrice Addressing Dante from the Car" (1824), symbolism drawn from medieval literature was used to communicate the intensely private, apocalyptic experience of this poet-mystic.

One of the more effective exponents of this extremely influential intellectual movement was Arthur Schopenhauer (1788–1860). He took the simple but audacious step of effacing the distinction between Kant's phenomenal world of human experience and the noumenal world of ultimate reality. By so doing, Schopenhauer reached the conclusion that human thought and feeling gave value and meaning to all reality and that the world was the product of the human mind. "Will . . . is properly the *thing-in-itself*."[3] Romantic transcendentalism thus abolished the dichotomy between self and nature, between the individual mind and the external world. Since the mind imposes order and beauty on the world, self and reality are one.

Schopenhauer was a confused and rather slipshod philosopher, but his metaphysic articulated the assumption of Romantic painters, writers, and composers: the intuitions of the artist are reality itself. "What kind of knowledge . . . is really essential to the world, the true content of its phenomena, that which is subject to no change . . . ?" asked Schopenhauer. "We answer, *Art*, the work of genius."[4]

German idealism got a very mixed reception from succeeding generations of philosophers. It

3. Arthur Schopenhauer, *The World as Will and Idea*, in Irwin Edman, ed., *The Philosophy of Schopenhauer*. New York: Random House, 1928, p. 131.
4. Schopenhauer, *The World as Will and Idea*, in *The Philosophy of Schopenhauer*, p. 155.

Romantic Heroism. The Romantics believed in the philosophy of act—in the theory that salvation and self-realization are to be found in the perilous quest for fulfillment, in the passionate striving for attainment of the ideal. Liberation was therefore equivalent to the heroic life. The image of Don Quixote—as in Honoré Daumier's painting (facing page, bottom)—was especially appealing to the Romantic mind: Don Quixote's quest served no useful purpose; it was in his striving for an ideal that he achieved greatness. Any struggle against authority was admired by the Romantics, not only because they adored "the people" and venerated the underprivileged, but also because struggle itself was the process by which the human spirit was ennobled. Consequently, the Greek rebellion against Turkish tyranny in the 1820's fired the imagination of poets and painters alike. Right: "Greece Expiring on the Ruins of Missolongi" by Eugène Delacroix. Perhaps inevitably, the Romantic heroic ideal was debased into blatant adulation of the warrior, inspiring a hysterical militarism. Typical of this Romantic militarism (which was to be endlessly repeated in nineteenth- and twentieth-century popular art) are Rude's "Hymn of Departure for War" (facing page, top) and Girodet's "Ossian Receiving Napoleon's Generals" (above).

had many adherents until the end of the nineteenth century and very few after that time: the trend of twentieth-century philosophy has been decidedly away from metaphysics. But as Schopenhauer clearly perceived, Romantic transcendentalism had great significance for the arts: nearly all of the painting, literature, and music of the twentieth century, insofar as it professes a theory, assumes the validity of the artist's imposition of meaning on experience.

A leading aspect of the Romantic heritage in Western culture is the belief that history is extremely important and that historical writing is one of the major art forms. This concern with history was in part simply another manifestation of Romantic sentimentality. At a higher level, it was part of the Romantic devotion to truth in art — the past was another area of experience that could be given coherence and beauty by the artist. At its most abstract level, the Romantic devotion to history was a product of the idealist philosophy. For if reality is to be found in the meaning that mind imposes on phenomena, the history of *all* experience, of *all* phenomena — world history — should

The Revolutionary Temperament. The Romantics, particularly in France, were fascinated by and enthusiastically predisposed toward revolution, not only as a means of emancipating "the people" but as a supreme act of personal liberation. Through revolutionary action, the individual could experience the heroic life and achieve union with the spirit of history. French painters worshiped at the shrine of the liberal republic. Right: in Honoré Daumier's "The Republic" (1848), the democratic state is the new secular goddess. Distinctively Romantic was the celebration of the liberating moment of rebellion and upheaval itself. Eugène Delacroix's "Liberty Leading the People" (1831), below, and Daumier's "The Uprising" (1848), on the facing page, are the finest examples of the revolutionary mode in French Romantic art.

reveal a pattern of the ultimate reality. This is the starting point for Hegel's philosophy. In the total experience of the past we can discern an objective, rational pattern that reveals the form of "Reason," of "Spirit"—the Absolute, the truth about reality:

The history of the World . . . has been a rational process; . . . the history . . . has constituted the rational necessary course of the World-Spirit—that Spirit whose nature is always one and the same, but which unfolds this its one nature in the phenomena of the World's existence.[5]

5. Friedrich Hegel, *The Philosophy of History*, in S. Commins and R. N. Linscott, eds., *The Political Philosophers*. New York: Random House, 1947, p. 407.

Exoticism. In its reaction against the Enlightenment, Romanticism favored any culture that departed significantly from neoclassical traditions. Right: the Royal Pavilion at Brighton, designed in 1815–1821 by the British prince regent's favorite architect, John Nash, reflects the Romantic fascination with the exotic East. Below: this oriental mystique inspires Delacroix's "Massacre at Scio" (1824); although the ostensible subject matter is an event in the Greeks' struggle against the Turks, Delacroix's main concern is to depict his vision of the colorful Levantine world. Facing page: the sensuousness of the East is the theme of Ingres' "Odalisque with Slave" (1840). Ingres adopted the eighteenth-century neoclassical style while expressing blatantly Romantic themes and attitudes.

In the twentieth century both right-wing and left-wing disciples of Hegel have claimed universal truth for their reading of the Spirit of History and have sought to impose their vision of the "necessary course" of the World-Spirit on unbelievers. Perhaps half of mankind today believes in the "phenomena of the World's existence" as expostulated by a left-wing Hegelian, Karl Marx. Hegel and his disciples transformed the Romantic fascination with history into the *historicist* worship of history as the only source of objective truth. Whatever terror and torment this philosophy has left in its wake, Hegel must be given his due as the preeminent philosopher of history in Western civilization.

Romanticism not only stimulated new insights into both individual and

Vulgarized Romanticism. The great weakness of a cultural movement devoted to the expression of feeling is that it has nothing to fall back on when the modes of fragile sensibility become routinized. A vast amount of nineteenth-century art depicts Romantic themes in a mannered and banal way. This kind of vulgarized Romantic art was immensely popular with the ever growing middle-class public, which relished sentimentality. Above: there can be little worse in art than contrived Romanticism, as in Henry Fuseli's "Lady Macbeth Seizing the Daggers" (1801). The same defect is to be found in the work of the group of mid-nineteenth-century British artists who called themselves the Pre-Raphaelite Brotherhood. They announced they were going back to the religious and artistic traditions that prevailed before the Renaissance, but the result was mostly bourgeois sentimentalism. Facing page, bottom: John Everett Millais' "Ophelia" (1851). Facing page, top: Dante Gabriel Rossetti's "The Wedding of St. George and Princess Sabra" (1851).

social experience that are still vital in the culture of the world today; it propounded a philosophy of life that evolved into a distinctive life style. Romanticism put the greatest value on action; it taught that ideals must be lived from day to day and that freedom and redemption lie in the experience of struggle itself. This doctrine is the message of Goethe's *Faust*:

> He only earns his freedom and his life
> Who takes them every day by storm.[6]

And the same ethic is preached by the hero of Byron's *Manfred*, who aspired

> To make my own mind the mind of other men,
> The enlightener of nations; and to rise
> I knew not whither—it might be to fall;
> But fall, even as the mountain-cataract . . .
> Lies low but mighty still.[7]

Goethe played a Faustian role, and Byron was himself the supreme example of the Byronic hero: both men fulfilled the Romantic philosophy of act, the equation of the ideal with a heroic life style. Thomas Carlyle perceived that the philosophy of act was but another form of transcendentalism, and in *Sartor Resartus* he skillfully combined Goethe's and Schopenhauer's teachings and vulgarized them for the English-speaking world:

The Ideal is in thyself, the impediment too is in thyself: thy Condition is but the stuff thou art to shape that same Ideal out of: what matters such stuff be of this sort or that, so the Form thou give it be heroic, be poetic?[8]

The ramifications of transcendental heroism were varied and far-reaching. It led to admiration for the activists of history, for the self-sustaining, self-fulfilling heroes. Carlyle adored Oliver Cromwell and Frederick the Great, and Stendhal said of himself, "He respected a single man, Napoleon." It inspired Romantic enthusiasm for revolution—not only to achieve the liberation of the poor and downtrodden, not only to overthrow despotism, but also to provide the stormy, perilous quality of the revolutionary's life style. To make the grand gesture for freedom, risking life itself, to mount the barricades, to direct the onsurging, vital force of humanity at the moment of crisis—this was the apotheosis of the Romantic vision.

Similarly, the Faustian-Byronic ideal of life as act inspired other, less violent, but totally integrated life styles. The Man on Horseback, the complete revolutionary, the antisocial artist, the Bohemian (or hippie), the single-minded aesthete—these variants of the Faustian-Byronic Romantic hero have been ever recurring types in Western culture and society—assuredly, as much as statesmen and entrepreneurs, the makers of the modern world.

6. Johann Wolfgang von Goethe, *Faust*, trans. Louis MacNeice, in M. Peckham, ed., *Romanticism*. New York: Braziller, 1965, p. 75.
7. George Gordon, Lord Byron, *Manfred*, in *Romanticism*, p. 49.
8. Thomas Carlyle, *Sartor Resartus*, in *Romanticism*, pp. 184–185.

6

The Impact
of Liberalism
and Industrialism

ENVIRONMENT ESSAY

The period between 1815 and 1848 can rightly be described as the adolescence of the Industrial Revolution, a deeply troubled era in which probably as many men suffered severe deprivation as a result of technological change as benefited from it. The urban working class, created by the needs of the new factory system and the rapid growth of consumer demands, became a symbol of human degradation — a mass of badly fed, poorly housed, largely illiterate slum-dwellers, who frightened both property owners and the more thoughtful elements of society. The lot of those workers who were gradually displaced by the new machines was frequently even more wretched. Nor was the peasantry exempt from the effects of the Industrial Revolution; in western Europe the increasing mechanization and capitalization of agriculture produced larger farms requiring fewer laborers and drove the excess to the city factories, while in central Europe the adverse effects of peasant emancipation threatened to create a new class of impoverished and largely landless farmers. In sum, the early nineteenth century was a period of unprecedented technological and environmental change, and it was this upheaval — as much as the unresponsiveness of the upper classes — that produced the suffering and the popular resentment that was to harden, in the years to come, into various radical political movements, particularly socialism of one sort or another.

The malaise of European society during this second phase of the Industrial Revolution was in part the consequence of the uneven and unplanned progress of mechanization in industry. The Industrial Revolution could proceed only as fast as the invention and production of the necessary machines permitted. These were slow processes, and it is not surprising that Professor Clapham, in his studies of British industry between 1820 and 1850, found, for example, that no single British industry passed through a complete technical

EUROPEAN RAILROADS

——— 1840   ——— 1850

revolution before 1830. Even after that date, progress was often slow and halting.

One reason was that the production of steam engines, reapers, locomotives, and the factory equipment needed for mechanization was a risky and expensive business, involving a great gamble for investors and many hazards for entrepreneurs and managers. Another factor contributing to the disorderly progress of industrialization was that improvement in transportation and

The Entrenchment of the Industrial Revolution. Britain continued to hold an overwhelming lead in industrialization between 1815 and the middle of the century. The economic and technological expansion was marked by uneven industrial growth, by business slumps and crop failures, and by chaotic social conditions; but significant progress toward an industrial economy was achieved. First of all, there was extensive growth in heavy industry—in iron and steel and machine tools. Above: razor-grinding in a Sheffield steel mill. Second, there was improvement in both intracity and (especially in the 1840's) intercity transportation. Right: a horse-drawn London omnibus around 1850. Facing page: one of the first railroad trains, built by George Stephenson for the Liverpool-Manchester line, which opened in 1830. By 1850 Britain had more than six thousand miles of track. The expansion of the European railroad network is shown on the map on the facing page.

communication came slowly. Railroads, which revolutionized the transportation of raw materials and the marketing of goods, existed as early as 1830 but became important only during the 1840's and did not begin to realize their full potential until the second half of the nineteenth century.

Precisely because the progress of mechanization was both hesitant and unplanned, the social dislocations of the early nineteenth century were frequently severe. Moreover, the rise of the middle class and the growth of an urban working class during the first half of the century were complicated by serious crises resulting from periodic crop failures and drastic fluctuations in the industrial economy. Resultant failures in the market for industrial goods brought financial ruin for the entrepreneur and starvation for the worker and his family. The most serious of these economic crises occurred in the 1840's, culminating in widespread famine toward the end of the decade and the revolutions of 1848, which engulfed nearly every European country. Possibly this crisis would not have resulted in revolution had the governments in France and Germany, for instance, been willing and able to take effective measures against it. But this was something they felt themselves incapable of doing — because of either administrative uncertainty or moral and ideological blindness or both. It is significant that the one country in which the government responded to the crisis with some alacrity — Great Britain — was also the one

Monuments of Industrial Power. The economic and technological achievements of the industrial bourgeoisie were served by engineering marvels and memorialized by grandiose buildings. Facing page, bottom: one of the great engineering feats of the 1830's, I. K. Brunel's suspension bridge spanning Clifton Gorge. The bourgeoisie did not develop a distinctive architectural style but copied classical, medieval, and Renaissance models. Facing page, top: the opulent Paris Bourse. Sensitive critics denounced this kind of imitation as "philistinism" — a showy display of wealth and power, a crude borrowing from previous cultures to demonstrate the success of the middle-class *arrivistes*. Right: Euston Railway Station in London. Here a Doric facade covers the functional part of the station, as if expressing embarrassment over the material and technological aspects of the age of steam and steel.

country largely untouched by industrial and agricultural disorder in 1848. Elsewhere, governments remained immobile in the face of economic disaster and made no effort to mitigate the hardships of workers and peasants.

The purely physical changes in the first half of the nineteenth century—aside from the attendant political and social problems—were dramatic in themselves. The population of London increased from 958,000 to 2,362,000 and there was prodigious growth in the industrial cities of northern England. Perhaps even more significant in the long run was the transformation of social class relationships. While the commercial revolution of the seventeenth century had produced a growing number of merchants, financiers, and industrial

The Universality of Human Misery. The "hungry 40's" with their depression and famines seemed to promise increasing impoverishment and maltreatment for urban and rural workers (although, in fact, very rapid improvement came in the 1850's). The impact of all the widespread suffering on men of deep moral consciousness can be gauged from Dickens' novels and from Marx and Engels' *Communist Manifesto*, characteristic products of this bleak decade. Many contemporary drawings and paintings also recall the anguish and despair. Facing page, bottom: a Quaker soup kitchen for the unemployed in Manchester. Facing page, top: a school for poor boys in London. The horrors of this kind of institution are depicted in Dickens' *Nicholas Nickleby*. Above: Irish emigrants leaving their famine-ridden country for America. These emigrant ships were usually floating hells.

workers, the tendency of the merchant class to blend into the country gentry and the diversity that existed in the working class (artisans, putting-out workers, etc.) made class lines indistinct and inhibited class consciousness. By 1848, on the other hand, the existence of a distinct, self-conscious middle class was an inescapable fact. It was largely the genius of mid-nineteenth-century British politics that these classes never came to confront each other in revolutionary fashion, as they did on the Continent. Indeed, it was one of the ironies of British history in the post-Napoleonic years that at a time when the relations of upper, middle, and lower classes seemed most precarious, the basis was laid for lasting, orderly, peaceful change. No other great power in Europe could boast of the same achievement between 1815 and 1848.

I FOUNDATIONS OF NINETEENTH-CENTURY POLITICS

The Aftermath of the Napoleonic Era

In the post-Napoleonic era Europe was largely concerned with three general problems: the extension of the political reforms of the preceding half-century, the transformation of social relationships by industrialism, and the reorganization of Europe along national rather than dynastic lines. After 1815 the issue was joined between those who wished to restore the *ancien régime* and those who were liberal in outlook. The latter favored the legal equality promised by the American and French revolutions, the constitutionalism that had become a symbol of revolution in France, and the nationalism that had emerged in parts of the Napoleonic empire. The defeat of Napoleon signified a victory for conservative and reactionary forces in European society. Internationally, it favored the dynastic state structure that had stood unchallenged before 1789.

It was perhaps no accident that the kingdom that had the most to lose from the spread of liberalism and nationalism after 1815 soon became the spearhead of the drive to defeat those ideas that had become closely associated with the revolutions of the late eighteenth century and Napoleon. This kingdom was Austria, ruled by its Habsburg emperor, Francis I, who in 1804 had given up his title as the last Holy Roman emperor to devote himself entirely to his own state. In purely nationalist terms, the Habsburg empire made no sense whatsoever. It was the accumulation of centuries of Habsburg marriages, military victories, and diplomatic gains, passed on from generation to generation. Each of the disparate elements, such as Bohemia and Hungary, fought for as much autonomy and as little taxation as possible. For the Habsburgs, the question was never how to create a modern centralized state but how to keep the stresses and strains of nationalism and particularism from breaking the empire apart altogether.

In Prince Klemens von Metternich (1773–1859), the Austrian minister of foreign affairs, Francis I had a man well suited to the task of preserving the empire. Metternich was in many ways the embodiment of the *ancien régime.* Clever rather than profound, with little understanding and less appreciation of constitutionalism or liberalism, he was a conservative by temperament as well as by policy and a master diplomat whose abilities were surpassed only by his own opinion of them. He fully understood that the survival of the Habsburg monarchy depended upon stopping the clock, not only in the Habsburg domains but throughout all of Europe. That realization became the cornerstone of his program throughout the four decades (1809–1848) during which he largely controlled Austrian foreign policy. Metternich was not so naive as to believe that social and political change could be avoided forever, but he left the problems of the future to his successors.

Metternich's inaction—or worse—proved a disaster for European conservatism. For if Europe's political, social, and intellectual problems were difficult enough around 1815, they became considerably more complicated and inflamed in the generation or two that followed, and the longer a solution to these problems was delayed, the greater the menace to European peace and stability. Thus Metternich's brand of conservatism only set the stage for much greater violence and disorder.

The Concert of Europe

The Age of Metternich began with the Congress of Vienna. That resplendent international conference, convened in October 1814, was the instrument whereby Metternich reaped the diplomatic fruits of allied military victory. The Congress met for eight months, during which Europe—further disrupted by Napoleon's dramatic return from St. Helena—was to be rearranged largely for the benefit of the victors. The Congress itself was almost never officially in session. The main evidence of its existence was the endless succession of social events designed to occupy the time of the numerous diplomats who had come to Vienna. Meanwhile, the four great powers—Austria, Britain, Russia, and Prussia—(and sometimes France as well) worked out the general postwar settlement.

Metternich dominated the policy of Prussia almost as much as that of Austria. The other statesmen at the Congress were the British foreign secretary Lord Castlereagh, Czar Alexander I of Russia, and Talleyrand, the foreign minister of France. It was Metternich's task to play them off against one another to achieve his principal diplomatic goals—a European political and social order made safe against a renewal of revolution in any form. On the surface, the problems of the Congress seemed not insoluble. Castlereagh had achieved most of Britain's diplomatic objectives before the Congress opened; Britain protected its colonial interests and assured the preservation of the

Low Countries from undue French influence. Moreover, the long-standing British goal of restoring the Bourbons to the throne of France was entirely compatible with Metternich's principle of a return to legitimacy throughout monarchical Europe.

Oddly enough it was Alexander I—a relatively liberal monarch who liked to consider himself the liberator of Europe and had even promised a constitutional government to a reconstituted Polish state—who gave Metternich his greatest problems. At one point, Russian territorial ambitions brought the Congress very nearly to dissolution and the allies to war among themselves. In these circumstances, it was Castlereagh who proved to be Metternich's most valuable ally in curbing the dangerous territorial ambitions of the Russian czar. Furthermore, Talleyrand (who at one time or another had been on almost every side in the French Revolution) had deserted Napoleon early enough to become the first foreign minister of the restored Bourbons, and he now employed his considerable diplomatic skills to preserve peace among the powers and—most significantly for France—moderate the harshness of the allies' terms.

Since it was Napoleon and French armies that had tyrannized Europe for nearly two decades, these peace terms were, everything considered, remarkably mild. Actually, there were two sets of peace terms, the first agreed on before Napoleon's sudden return, the second after the "hundred days." In the former, France was allowed its frontiers of 1792; but after seeing the enthusiasm with which many Frenchmen responded to the return of their former master, the allies decided that France should be restricted to its frontiers of 1790, that an indemnity of 500 million francs should be imposed, that an occupation army should remain on French soil for five years, and that France should restore the art treasures Napoleon and his legions had looted all over Europe. There was, however, no attempt to decimate French power, a course that would probably have aroused bitter longings for the days of Napoleon. As it was, Bourbon France soon took its place with the conservative bloc of states that constituted the foundation of Metternich's diplomatic system.

Probably the most far-reaching achievement of the Congress of Vienna was the "Concert of Europe" system, which emerged as the guardian of the interests of monarchy, aristocracy, and legitimacy. The Quadruple Alliance —Austria, Prussia, Russia, and Britain—was designed to extend the Congress indefinitely by providing for regular meetings of the great powers to oversee the carrying out of the terms of the settlement. Both Metternich and Alexander I considered this Concert of Europe to be far more than a watchdog over the French. They felt that the agreement could be applied to all of Europe, empowering the allies to intervene in the interests of the status quo whenever and wherever governments were not able to restrain their own radicals.

This principle was also implicit in the Holy Alliance, which was formed by Austria, Prussia, and Russia. The Holy Alliance owed its origins to Czar Alexander's mystical predilections. What Alexander seems to have had in

EUROPE IN 1815 AFTER THE TREATY OF VIENNA

— Boundary of the German Confederation

The Congress of Vienna set up a balance of power to prevent any one state from dominating Continental affairs. Britain, whose role in containing the French Revolution and ultimately overthrowing Napoleon had been crucial, acquired only Heligoland, Malta, and the Ionian Islands. Austria received the Venetian Republic and the duchy of Milan, as well as Polish Galicia and partial control over the free city of Krakow. Russia gained over half of Poland—which Alexander turned into the satellite kingdom called "Congress Poland" —and also Finland and Bessarabia. Prussia received substantial sections of Saxony and the Rhineland, presumably to allow the Hohenzollern monarchy to guard against French expansion.

mind was a formal agreement among the great powers to base their future policies on a higher spiritual basis, and something of this, indeed, emerged in the final text of the Holy Alliance, signed in September 1815.

Nevertheless, the settlement which emerged from the Congress of Vienna was more remarkable for its specific results than for its underlying conservative principles. No general European war broke out for nearly four decades. In that period the internal problems of the European powers were more than enough to occupy their attention. The Congress of Vienna produced a settlement that left none of the major powers in an intolerable position yet did not reward any of them so lavishly as to upset the balance of power.

All the same, the territorial settlement agreed upon at Vienna contained the seed of much future trouble. Above all, the Congress denied Germany's and Italy's quest for national unity. Leaving Italy largely under the influence of Austria, the Congress created a new German Confederation to take the place of the defunct Holy Roman Empire. Neither the Hohenzollerns nor the other German princes were satisfied with the settlement, nor were the Poles and other nationalities (the Belgians and Dutch, for instance, who were combined in still another anti-French buffer state). Thus, while the political settlement agreed on at Vienna lasted about a half century, the Congress missed a great opportunity to fulfill the true longings of many European peoples. At worst, it created a system that could only be changed—as indeed it was—by a new era of international violence.

Political and Social Unrest and Repression

If the Concert of Europe was a successful diplomatic policy for Austria and other major European powers, its political conservatism was anachronistic in view of the profound changes that were taking place in European society. As in all periods of social change, the defense of "legitimate" governments and institutions was an attempt to prevent those institutions from succumbing to new demands and expectations. As a result, the period from 1815 to 1848 was not one of wars but of revolutions. It was relatively easy for men like Metternich, Talleyrand, Castlereagh, Francis I, and even Alexander I to agree on the absurdity and iniquity of liberal ideas such as constitutionalism, but even the consensus of the reigning monarchs of Europe could not possibly convince the rising middle class of the relevance or efficacy of monarchical absolutism. Nor could the Holy Alliance provide for the hungry masses, increasingly subject now to the dual perils of the business cycle and recurrent failures of the food supply. Between 1815 and 1848 the *ancien régime* in its reconstituted form was increasingly confronted by a rising middle class and a dramatically growing urban working class. The ambition of the first and the vexation of the second could be neither ignored nor effectively repressed, although—save in Britain—European conservatives generally sought to do one or both.

Almost everywhere in Europe the defeat of Napoleon was celebrated by an orgy of repression aimed at the liberals and nationalists who had risen in his shadow. In Great Britain the outbreak of the French Revolution in 1789 had soon led to the discouragement, and at times actual repression, of the nascent movement for parliamentary reform; indeed, it seems fair to say that the French Revolution and Napoleon set back the cause of liberalism and parliamentary reform in Britain more than a generation. Even after 1815, fear of political agitation led to various hard measures designed to limit the rights of those considered to harbor dangerous thoughts and political plans. If such reactionary policies were possible in Britain, it was hardly surprising that in Germany the enthusiastic student celebration of Luther's tercentenary and the murder of a noted reactionary playwright by a radical student led to the so-called Carlsbad Decrees, the embodiment of post-Napoleonic anti-intellectual reaction. Based on Metternich's proposals, presented to the leading German rulers at the Bohemian spa of Carlsbad in August 1819, and formally adopted by the German Confederation the following month, they decreased civil liberties and introduced more rigid control of the universities, which were seen as hotbeds of radicalism.

Before long the Concert of Europe had to deal with more serious problems than mere student agitation. Revolutions in Italy and Spain against "legitimate" rulers soon brought foreign armies to effect their restoration. France intervened in Spain and Austria in Italy, both with the general approval of their allies. Britain, on the other hand, stood aside, refusing to endorse any such reactionary moves but unable to prevent them. The troubles of the reactionary Ferdinand VII in Spain had important consequences across the Atlantic as well as within Europe, since most of the Latin American colonies from Mexico to Argentina and Chile, under the direction of Simón Bolívar and other national leaders, took the occasion of the disorders in Spain to move toward independence. Not only was the possibility of effective Spanish intervention against the Latin American liberation movement precluded by the benevolent neutrality of the dominant sea power, Great Britain, but official United States government policy, as set forth in the Monroe Doctrine (December 1823), now arrayed the moral and political authority of the United States on the side of national independence. The result was that, save for the islands of Cuba and Puerto Rico, the immense Spanish empire in the Western Hemisphere came to an end by 1825, to be replaced by several independent states.

Probably the most severe test of Europe's equilibrium was the Greek revolution against the decaying Ottoman Empire. Alexander I had always blended his rather fragile liberalism with a healthy portion of expansionism, maintaining traditional Russian designs upon the Balkans, Constantinople, and the Straits. At the same time, Britain's growing interest in Egypt and the Mediterranean route to India heightened its concern over the state of affairs in southeastern Europe. In view of this situation, it is remarkable that the Greek revolution, which raged intermittently between 1821 and 1829, did not destroy the general European peace. Metternich, for example, was furious —"the insurrection in Greece," he wrote in the late 1820's, "was . . . provoked by the crowd of Sophists and self-seekers"—but he was baffled as to what to do. Britain and Russia, on the other hand, were torn between an impulse toward unilateral intervention in their own interests and a policy of nonintervention designed to prevent the other side from gaining ground.

In the end, Russia received certain ports on the Black Sea, and Greece was recognized as an independent country, owing formal obedience to the Turkish sultan but none to the Russian czar. In view of the irrevocable decline of the Ottoman Empire and the growth of Russian power, this solution of the Greek problem could hardly be considered a definitive settlement of Anglo-Russian relations in the eastern Mediterranean; but it served to postpone the confrontation between Russia and Britain for almost another thirty years.

It was not possible, however, to postpone the consequences of the French Revolution and the Industrial Revolution by international agreement. The nationalism of the Greek rebels, the liberalism of the European middle class, and the demands of a growing number of radical thinkers and agitators reflected profound changes in the very foundations of European society, and even Metternich never really believed he could eradicate them. The seeming immutability of the restored regimes served only to create a temporary alliance of the politically ambitious middle class and the voteless working class, an alliance that bore fruit in many of the revolutionary confrontations of the early post-Napoleonic decades.

II THE PROBLEMS AND ACHIEVEMENTS OF MIDDLE-CLASS LIBERALISM

Early Nineteenth-Century Government

The problems faced by all European governments between the end of the Napoleonic Wars and the mid-century revolutions were, in many ways, remarkably similar. Moreover, these governments faced the changes brought about by industrialization—the growth of cities and attendant urban social problems, the increase in the speed and frequency of communications, and the shift in the balance of power from landed to industrial wealth—with institutions and concepts that were at best antiquated and inefficient and at worst completely inappropriate. In the period between 1815 and 1850, therefore, much of the institutional structure of European governments was reformed not only to reflect the shifting composition of the economic and social elite that held real political power but also to deal with the increased scope and complexity of the problems that government alone was competent to solve.

In a subtle sense, the transformation of nineteenth-century government involved a change in the relationship between the citizen and the state: by the end of the nineteenth century, most Europeans assumed that governments were somehow responsible for whatever went on within their nations' borders. Evidence of the development of the role of government as a social-economic-political institution can best be found not in the dramatic conflicts of the century but in the quiet evolution of subsidiary governmental institutions—the maturation of the civil service, the reform of local government, the creation of effective police forces—and in the steady growth of the machinery of government and of the proportion of the citizenry involved with it in one way or another. Gradually, in spite of the laissez-faire theories of many of the political leaders of the nineteenth century, the regulations and services of the state became indispensable to the industrial society it served, an integral part of the day-to-day life of its citizens.

It was this gradual expansion of public affairs that gave special urgency to the question of who should participate in the decision-making processes of government. Throughout the nineteenth century, one of the most pressing demands of reformers was for the establishment of some form of parliamentary government, in which essential legislative decisions would be made by elected representatives of the citizenry. A small but growing minority advocated universal manhood suffrage.

Reform in Britain

Throughout Europe the development of industrial society in the nineteenth century was punctuated with political and social revolutions. Britain's history is unique in that there the issue of broadened political participation was resolved by peaceful means. By the middle of the century, both radical theories like socialism and antitechnological violence (the Luddites' attempts to reverse the trend of industrialization by destroying machines) were overshadowed by the successful movement for political reform.

In an age such as ours when political democracy is taken for granted, it is easy to overlook, or to minimize, the British achievement. Britain not only moved steadily toward universal male suffrage; it also made the most progress in democratizing the decision-making process of government. Although other countries had broader electorates, in Britain extension of the right to vote was accompanied by an increase in the power of the House of Commons and by the development of relatively effective means of organizing and expressing political opinions and of calling elected representatives to account for their actions. The democratization of the political process was inseparable from the growth of political parties and the appearance of daily newspapers with a mass circulation. Still, it is important to remember that the House of Commons remained the preserve of the upper classes throughout the nineteenth century. Only occasionally was it possible for public opinion to promote an issue so effectively that a majority of the members of Parliament could be turned from opposition to support of radical measures.

The road to political democracy, therefore, even in Britain, was anything but smooth. The British government in 1815 was still, for the most part, an aristocratic oligarchy with a constitutional monarch. Although the king no longer possessed the power to act independently of Parliament or in opposition to the wishes of a substantial majority of its members, he could still exert considerable pressure through his power to select ministers. The major development in the constitution in the eighteenth century was the diminution of the governing power of the monarch and the increase in the combined power of the House of Lords and the House of Commons. The growth of the cabinet system, with the various phases of governmental activity directed by ministers appointed by the king but responsible to Parliament, had helped to increase the power of the legislative branch of government. The great issue of the nineteenth century was who was to be represented in that legislature.

The British electoral process in 1815 was almost as venerable as the constitution itself. Most members of Parliament were landed aristocrats chosen by a system of election whose contradictions and inequities could be explained only by its very considerable age. Two basic types of constituency existed in Britain: counties (with 188 seats), where "forty-shilling freeholders" (moderately prosperous landowners) had the franchise; and boroughs (with 465 seats), where the system of election varied according to the terms of the borough charter. Some boroughs had corporations whose members had the hereditary right to vote; in a few others, the franchise was a very broad one. In many boroughs a small handful of men selected the parliamentary representatives. In most boroughs and many counties, members of Parliament were in fact selected by the great landowning families.

Elections in early nineteenth-century Britain were conducted under conditions that illustrate the profound difference between the traditional British concept of representation and the more recent idea of representative democracy. For one thing, seats in Parliament represented not numbers of constituents but different types of constituencies. For another, the rights of the boroughs were justified on historical, not rational, grounds. A wealthy man holding property in several constituencies could vote several times and in addition, if he was an Oxford or Cambridge graduate, cast a vote to elect a representative from one of these universities. But the most obvious difference was the system of public voting, which brought the electors to the polling place over a period of several days. Electors usually voted under the eyes of representatives of all the candidates. The secret ballot (not introduced until 1872) was deplored on the grounds that it would cover up irresponsibility on the part of the voter—no man who voted according to his conscience should be afraid to acknowledge his choice publicly.

The abuses that characterized such a system are obvious to any modern democrat. The public voter was vulnerable to the influence of his landlord, or creditor, or richest customer; and if he could not be reached by intimidation, there were many ways to buy his vote. Most voters, however, got neither a chance to make a profit—nor an opportunity to turn out an unsatisfactory representative—because few seats were contested in any given election. When they were, the voter's choice was limited almost exclusively to men of considerable means. Running for office could be very expensive, and until 1911 British M.P.'s received no salaries. It is no wonder that even a man in comfortable financial circumstances might pass up the chance to stand for Parliament.

In yet another way the electoral system of Great Britain was inequitable by modern standards. England had 489 seats in the House of Commons, Ireland 100, Scotland 45, and Wales 24. And not only were the non-English components of the United Kingdom underrepresented; religious disabilities narrowed the franchise and frequently made it unrepresentative of the constituency involved. Protestant dissenters (non-Anglicans) and Roman Catholics were prohibited from voting, holding office, or even attending the universities at Oxford and Cambridge. These disabilities were not removed from the majority of the Scottish and Irish or from an important minority of Englishmen until 1828–1829. Even then, the vast majority of the representatives in Parliament came from the Anglican landed aristocracy.

Within Parliament itself, the essentially agricultural and aristocratic interests of the majority were reflected in the repeal of the income tax and the passage of the Corn Laws (which placed a protective tariff on grain) in 1815, whereby the members celebrated the defeat of Napoleon. There was as yet little evidence of party organization in either the election of members of Parliament or in their votes. The real division in parliamentary debates was between the "government" and the "opposition," and that division was usually determined by lines of personal and family connection which operated like an invisible web in parliamentary affairs. There were always, however, a large number of country squires, secure in their own constituencies but not prominent enough to aspire to the pinnacles of power, who provided a bloc independent of any influence. It was these men especially who responded freely to the issues of the day, less concerned about support or opposition to the government than with whether or not a proposal would raise taxes or lower Britain's prestige.

Beneath the complex buttress of party, family, connections, and issues, the structure of power was supported by a vast system of patronage at the disposal of the group in power at any given time. Before the days of mass politics, when an electorate still consisted of only a few hundred thousand people, the patronage system was an effective whip in the hands of party leaders. Although some of the worst abuses of the system had been removed by reforms in the eighteenth century, in 1815 a great number of government jobs were available to the family, friends, and political allies of a loyal and successful member of Parliament.

It would not have been surprising if a Parliament thus constituted had turned a deaf ear to all demands for political and social change and reform. But the reaction of Parliament to the crises of domestic politics in the nineteenth century has always delighted and amazed liberal historians. Contrary to what might be expected, the country gentlemen of the British Parliament responded to the political consequences of the Industrial Revolution by gradually abolishing their monopoly of political power—though they surrendered it much more quickly in law than in practice, thereby cushioning the blow. Indeed, perhaps the greatest political discovery of the nineteenth century was the fact that the inherent conservatism of political institutions greatly softens the impact of reform.

Those conservatives who maintained that one reform would lead to another proved to be correct, but the horrible specter of drunken, illiterate workers running Parliament and ruining the rich never materialized, and the disgusting if less frightening prospect of sitting next to one of the gaudy *nouveaux riches* of Manchester or Birmingham turned out to be much worse than the reality. Despite the inclusion of some middle-class radicals and Roman Catholics (such as Ireland's Daniel O'Connell) in Parliament, the social standing of M.P.'s did not decrease noticeably, because the British aristocracy lost little of its prestige. Even working-class voters usually preferred a sympathetic member of the upper classes to a social equal, and Parliament remained staid as well as stable well beyond the end of the nineteenth century.

The process of reform itself was neither automatic nor easy. Each revision of the franchise was preceded by a considerable period of public and parliamentary agitation which impressed the inevitability of reform upon those who had opposed it. The movement for parliamentary reform had been an important, if unsuccessful, political cause in the late eighteenth century. During the French Revolution it was associated in many minds with "Jacobinism." After 1815 popular discontent growing out of the economic slump that followed the Congress of Vienna led to rioting, and rioting led to government repression. In 1819 a mass demonstration at St. Peter's Field near Manchester had to be dispersed by troops, who fired into the crowd, killing nearly a dozen people and wounding four hundred. The "Peterloo Massacre," as it was called, became a rallying point for the discontented but also for the forces of repression in Parliament, which passed the "Six Acts" limiting many of the civil liberties that were believed to be conducive to such disturbances.

The antagonism aroused among various groups by Tory repression was not immediately channeled into political or economic reform. With the return of prosperity in the 1820's, the agitation subsided, and with less unrest to frighten the landed classes, "liberal Toryism" began to characterize the government headed by Lord Liverpool. Sir Robert Peel, the home secretary, strengthened and humanized the home office and the criminal code—cutting in half the more than two hundred offenses that were then punishable by death—reduced waste and corruption in the courts, and inaugurated the Metropolitan Police Force. At the same time, the conservative Castlereagh was succeeded at the foreign office by the liberal George Canning, who supported nationalism and constitutional government abroad—notably in the newly proclaimed independent nations of Latin America.

Prosperity collapsed again in 1825, however, and the resultant economic and industrial distress was blamed by many on the system of government and its implementation. Under the influence of Jeremy Bentham, the philosopher of utilitarianism, the criterion of majority welfare—the "greatest happiness of the greatest number"—was applied to the constitution. Bentham and his followers believed in the "scientific" scrutiny of institutions and in their reform in the interest of the majority, and Benthamite ideas were adopted by radicals who believed that parliamentary reform would bring economic improvement.

In the spring of 1827 Lord Liverpool, who had been prime minister since 1812, became ill and resigned, and the British government entered a period of short-lived cabinets. Canning formed a liberal Tory government scorned by extreme conservatives like the duke of Wellington but backed by leading Whigs and popular enthusiasm. However, Canning died in August 1827, his promising government fell apart, and Wellington became prime minister in January 1828. Although he has long had the reputation of having been an inflexible conservative, his administration was by no means a complete failure. In the face of severe food shortages, for instance, he secured a significant reduction in the tariff on corn (grain), and in the spring of 1829 he forced through a bitterly hostile Parliament a repeal of the Test Act of 1673, which prohibited Catholics from holding political office. In addition, both British and Irish Catholics were now granted the right to vote.

These were important achievements, pointing the way to even more significant reforms, but Wellington got little credit for what he had achieved. In June 1830, George IV died, and in the general election that soon followed, the proponents of electoral reforms gained nearly fifty seats in the House of Commons. In November 1830, therefore, Wellington was forced to resign, and the new monarch, William IV, asked the leader of the Whigs, Earl Grey, to form a cabinet. Drastic political reform was now only a matter of time.

The reforms under consideration in 1830 centered around two basic issues: elimination of the inequities of a system of representation that was centuries old and extension of the suffrage, hitherto largely the preserve of the landed aristocracy. The first issue involved the abolition of boroughs that had no real claim to representation—some boroughs were totally uninhabited and others had only a few voters—and the enfranchisement of the new cities of the north such as Birmingham and Manchester, which had no parliamentary representation at all. The second issue revolved around the demand that all the "respectable" members of society be allowed to vote. (No one in Parliament favored the enfranchisement of ignorant rabble.)

Conservatives argued that the British constitution was a permanent and sufficient political system and that Parliament represented neither numbers nor interests but the kingdom as a whole. They insisted that any changes, no matter how minor, would implicitly acknowledge that numbers or interests were the basis of representation; and they warned that once changed, the constitution would never be safe from further alteration. Liberals argued that the constitution had become anachronistic but that, once moderately adjusted in the interests of justice, it would stand permanently.

The Whigs themselves were far from a unified party; they represented the shifting alliances of the old landed aristocracy, commercial and industrial interests, and religious dissenters. Most Whigs were far from radical; they promoted reform to avoid revolution, not to foster it. They were as respectful of property rights as any Tory, and they had the support of various more or less conservative elements throughout the country. Although no other program than reform was possible, it met with a series of obstacles on its two-year journey through Parliament.

The first Reform Bill passed a first reading in the House of Commons in March 1831 with a majority of one vote, but it was rejected in committee, and the government persuaded the king to dissolve Parliament and put the question to the voters. The electorate (still unreformed) voted overwhelmingly for reform, and the government submitted a new bill. It was passed by a large majority in the Commons, and its rejection in the House of Lords caused a tremendous popular outcry against the peers. The government brought in a third bill, slightly modified, and Grey asked the king to create enough new peers to assure its passage in the House of Lords. The king at first refused; Grey resigned; and there was a growing threat of disorder throughout the country. Wellington was asked to form a new government, but he failed, and William IV reluctantly recalled Grey. The king then persuaded sufficient numbers of conservative peers not to oppose the bill, and it passed in the House of Lords in June 1832.

The Reform Bill of 1832 did not itself revolutionize the electoral system of the United Kingdom, but it did enfranchise the upper half of the middle class, and it made a beginning in the rationalization of electoral districts. Fifty-six "rotten" boroughs were abolished, and a number of new boroughs were added in their place—particularly in the industrial north of England. Additional seats were also given to the counties and to Ireland, Scotland, and Wales. Many remaining boroughs were considerably enlarged. The franchise itself was made more rational by the establishment of uniform property requirements in the boroughs as well as in the counties, although there were still fewer than a million qualified voters in the entire United Kingdom. One reform whose full effects became apparent only with time was the institution of a formal system of voter registration, which made it possible to organize the electorate along party lines.

The Practical Politics of Reform

It was probably no accident that the first extraparliamentary party organizations appeared almost immediately after passage of the Reform Bill. The conservative Carlton Club, founded in 1832, provided members of Parliament with the finest company and food and the party with a permanent center where meetings could be held and records kept. Before long, the countryside was dotted with local branches of the Conservative party, as the old Tory party came to be called. The Reform Club, founded in 1836, was less splendid in its outward trapping and in the social standing of its membership, but it proved no less effective as a center of party organization. Probably the most important innovation which accompanied the establishment of physical centers of Tory and Whig activity was the appearance of party managers, who spent their time readying the parties for the next elections. Efforts to register as many voters as possible and to find candidates for constituencies and constituencies for candidates became important and complicated tasks, necessary in order to hold and build party strength. It must be noted, however, that party organization was still weak and frequently did not go beyond the effort to register favorable voters.

While the Reform Bill of 1832 produced no immediate drastic changes in the nature of British elections or the men who were selected, the years that followed brought profound changes in the nature of British politics. The slow development of party organization inside and outside Parliament was only one manifestation. The public—that vague entity to which Parliament had ultimately to answer—gained power through the development of coherent parties and awareness through the proliferation of newspapers. Public meetings and petitions began to affect Parliament as much as the quiet manipulation of businessmen and landlords. The effect of these tools of public pressure was steadily heightened as the working class moved toward political maturity.

The struggle for the Reform Bill itself had helped the growth of extraparliamentary political agitation, but it was the success of the Anti-Corn-Law League that signaled the maturation of public opinion and political organization—those indispensable parts of the modern system of representative government. The Anti-Corn-Law League was based upon that combination of public agitation and organization of the electorate around a crucial issue which is the stuff of mass politics. Even in a restricted electorate, the preponderant weight of public opinion opposing the Corn Laws could not be ignored. The great proponents of tariff reform and free trade, Richard Cobden (1804 –1865) and John Bright (1811–1889)—liberal Manchester businessmen— provided the necessary personification of the issue; the League's success in putting forward candidates and getting them elected and the bad harvests of the early 1840's rendered the reform of the British tariff system not only necessary but perhaps inevitable.

The way in which the Corn Laws were repealed reveals another essential element of the British parliamentary system—the very broad base of consensus that made it possible for opposing sides to keep their competition within acceptable limits. (The principle of majority rule cannot work where the minority is not willing to accept the consequences of losing an election.) The stability of the British system can be partially explained by the essential homogeneity of the articulate and "respectable" part of the British population. In fact, it was the great conservative leader of the first half of the nineteenth century, Sir Robert Peel, who was responsible for instituting many of the reforms demanded by the liberals. Time and again the Tory party, or Conservative party, fought against reforms demanded by the Whigs (and later the

Liberals) until it became apparent that reform was inevitable; then, recognizing necessity, the Tories repeatedly instituted the reform themselves and won the popular credit for it. That an opposition party could take such a course clearly indicates the narrow ideological gap between the two major parties. This has become one of the distinguishing characteristics of the modern two-party system, in which both parties appeal to essentially the same electorate.

The career of Sir Robert Peel (1788–1850) provides a classic example of the conservative reformer in British politics. He began his career in Ireland as one of the few successful English administrators in the history of that troubled country. From 1818 to 1822 he was an ordinary member of Parliament, and it was during this period that he wrote, in a famous letter to a friend, "Do you not think that the tone of England is more liberal than the government?" In 1822 he became home secretary. Convinced of the necessity for reform of the judicial and penal system, Peel rationalized and speeded its procedures. One of the great impediments to moderating the extremely harsh penalties imposed on criminals was the fear of crime in a society without adequate means of law enforcement. But the severity of the penalties for minor crimes—even pickpockets faced the death penalty—made it difficult to get juries to return a verdict of guilty. Robert Peel's answer was to accompany revision of the penal code with establishment of an effective domestic police force. The "bobbies" were introduced first in London, then throughout England, as their success in preventing crime transformed early suspicions that they would violate age-old British freedoms into enthusiastic public endorsement.

The most difficult problem Peel faced as prime minister (1841–1846) was the economic crisis of the early 1840's, which coincided with, indeed helped to produce, the climax of the Anti-Corn-Law agitation. The Anti-Corn-Law League was organized around the principle of free trade in grain as a means to lower the price of the main staple of the British diet. The movement found its greatest support among the urban middle class and in the working class, where the price of bread was of critical importance. The fight against the abolition of tariffs on grain was carried on mainly by the agricultural interests, whose position was vulnerable because grain production in the United Kingdom was less efficient than in France and other Continental countries. They, too, appealed to the working class, on the grounds that since wages tended to represent the minimum subsistence level, lowering the price of grain would result in lower wages.

This latter argument had a certain validity under existing conditions, but the demand for lower prices on vital food commodities had great emotional appeal. The Anti-Corn-Law League capitalized on the popularity of its issue to wage a contracted campaign to elect free-trade advocates to Parliament, an enterprise that required sophisticated use of the techniques of registration of favorable voters. The public appeals of eloquent liberal spokesmen like Cobden and Bright paved the way by creating favorable public opinion.

It was not necessary, however, for the League to wait for a parliamentary majority created by its own efforts. The conversion of Robert Peel to a position favorable to free trade gave the repeal of the Corn Laws the support it needed to pass through Parliament in the mid-1840's. Peel was persuaded mainly by the failure of the Irish potato crop, which caused a horrible famine in that country. In 1846 Peel reduced the tariff on almost all food imports to a nominal rate that allowed them to compete freely with domestic agricultural products. Although the repeal of the Corn Laws produced neither the immediate ruin of British agriculture feared by its opponents nor the era of plentiful cheap food heralded by its supporters, it had a profound effect upon British economic policy; it signaled the beginning of a general free-trade policy that would predominate in Britain for more than half a century. Perhaps its greatest immediate effect was the break-up of the Tory party into a Conservative and a Liberal Peelite faction, a split which moved British politics toward a clearer demarcation of the parties along ideological lines.

Peel was an administrator above all, and his efforts at constructive reform centered on matters of governmental efficiency like the police force. The reform of the machinery of government had already made a dramatic advance in 1835 with the reorganization of local government. Hitherto, local governments had been organized along the most casual lines and had frequently been run by a handful of men whose only qualification was the inherited status of members of the urban corporation. As the functions of local government became more important, the old structure was neither appropriate nor adequate to its new tasks. The reform of 1835 standardized the franchise in local elections and centralized the administration of such matters as sanitation, public health, education, and care for the indigent and insane, which had previously been under the haphazard care of local authorities.

Twenty years later this administrative reform was followed by another even more essential and significant: the creation of a civil service in which hiring and promotion were governed by a standardized examination system. The reform of 1855 was only partial, but it set the stage for the full-blown policy of hiring and promoting according to ability and performance that took effect in the 1870's. This was the last great blow to the patronage system of earlier days, since it took control of the vast majority of the jobs that had long been used as rewards for loyal supporters of the victorious party. At the same time, it established a basis for a much more efficient and respected British civil service.

The utilitarian standard of efficiency and rationality was also applied to the Poor Law system. The new Poor Law of 1834 abolished the Speenhamland practice by which workers on low wages had been subsidized by relief granted by parish authorities. The government was convinced that this was a wasteful system which contributed to the pauperization of the working class. Poor relief was now brought under closer central control in larger territorial units; the unemployed were set to work in rigidly supervised workhouses.

The poor did not appreciate this advance in administrative efficiency, regarding the workhouses as horrible "bastilles."

Working-class agitation had assisted middle-class liberals in securing the passage of the Reform Bill of 1832, by which a substantial number of the middle class had been enfranchised; and the new Poor Law seemed to working-class leaders to represent middle-class betrayal. During the late 1830's various working-class political organizations coalesced into the Chartist movement, which drew up a charter of political democracy and presented petitions to Parliament demanding universal male suffrage. During the hard times of the 40's, Chartism steadily gained support, and a militant "physical force" wing engaged in strikes and rioting which the government countered by repressive police action and imprisonment of Chartist leaders. In 1848, a new Chartist petition, claiming three million signatures, was presented to the House of Commons, and rejected overwhelmingly. The consequence was not revolution like that currently raging on the Continent but the rapid disintegration of the Chartist movement.

The failure of Chartism either to gain immediate acceptance of its democratic demands or to transform itself into an effective revolutionary movement can be attributed to several factors: lack of support from middle-class liberals, incompetent leadership, skillful resistance by Peel's government, the return of prosperity at the end of the 1840's, and the expectation that the repeal of the Corn Laws would materially improve the life of the working class. Another reason for the impotence of working-class radicalism is that the British Parliament showed itself increasingly responsive to the need for government intervention to meliorate the worst ravages of the Industrial Revolution. Agitation by humanitarians and evangelical Protestants led to the abolition of the slave trade in the British Empire in 1807, and the royal navy was effective in enforcing this law by preventing further transportation of blacks to the Americas. In 1833 Parliament emancipated all slaves in the British Empire, an act which particularly affected the British West Indies. In the 1830's Tories like Lord Shaftesbury directed humanitarian efforts to improve the condition of industrial wage slaves. The Factory Act of 1802, designed to protect child and woman labor, had been rendered ineffective by a lack of diligent inspection. This deficiency was corrected in the more ambitious Factory Act of 1833, which shortened hours and improved conditions for children and women employed in all textile industries. The Ten Hours Bill of 1847 was concerned with all industrial workers, while the Mines Act of 1842 prohibited the employment of women and children in mines and established safety standards. The Factory Act of 1844 prescribed safety procedures in the textile industry.

This legislation left untouched many of the dehumanizing consequences of industrialization and urbanization, but it effected some real improvement in working conditions, and it demonstrated the beneficent attitude of the classes represented in Parliament, helping to detract from the appeal of Chartism.

Laissez-faire doctrinaires vociferously opposed state interference with the economic market. But, at the very same time that Britain was moving toward free trade, the government inaugurated the regulation and supervision of working conditions in industry. The establishing of this "inspection state" — the nineteenth-century antecedent of the welfare state — lessened the alienation of the British working class from the ruling classes. In the 1850's, British workers abandoned political radicalism in favor of labor unions which negotiated for better conditions within the prevailing political and social system. And the Chartist demand for universal adult suffrage was eventually achieved in the second and third parliamentary reform bills of 1867 and 1884.

The era of change and reform that began before 1830 made it possible for Britain to avoid the kind of recurrent violent revolution that harassed Continental government in the first half of the nineteenth century. In Britain, as in no other European country, the conflicts produced by the evolution of industrial society were fought out within the political system rather than in opposition to it. The willingness of the British Parliament to respond to crises with concessions repeatedly drained away the strength of British radicalism. The admission of the middle class to parliamentary representation brought the struggle between the landed and manufacturing interests of the kingdom within the walls of Parliament, and the working class was sufficiently placated to preclude the success of a proletarian revolutionary movement. Throughout the rest of Europe, the established order repeatedly rejected such a policy of gradualism, and the result of such intransigence was the revolutions of 1830 and 1848.

Liberalism in Continental Western Europe

On the Continent the story of reform after the Congress of Vienna was not a happy one. This is not to say that the post-Napoleonic reaction managed to eradicate all or even most liberal hopes and expectations but rather that local and national circumstances made it very difficult to translate these hopes and expectations into substantial reforms by peaceful means.

The gaining of independence by Belgium and the establishment of a liberal constitution there was the most unequivocal victory won by liberalism and nationalism in Continental Europe. Belgium was made part of the Netherlands under the Dutch king William I in 1815, after liberation from Napoleonic rule. Arranged largely to create a buffer state against renewed French expansion, the political marriage did not prove to be a happy one, despite the fact that Belgium and Holland were among the most advanced countries in Europe. Although they had once been joined in the Spanish Netherlands, nearly two centuries of separation had produced not only commercial antagonisms but deep-seated religious and political divergences as well. Catholic Belgium and the Calvinist Netherlands could not comfortably blend. In addition, Belgium followed closely on the heels of the British in the development of the factory system, of heavy industry, and, later, of the most extensive railroad network in Europe. Dominated politically by the more conservative Dutch, the Belgians soon found grievances enough to drive them to revolution and the establishment of an independent state.

The Belgian revolution of 1830 was fortunate in several ways. It was brief and comparatively nonviolent. Both Austria and Russia would no doubt have wished to interfere to crush the liberal revolt, but neither was able to do so. The British also managed to keep King William from using force to reconquer his Belgian territory. In the end, the Belgians chose as their monarch a minor German prince—Leopold of Saxe-Coburg-Gotha, who had been living for some time in Great Britain—and adopted what was doubtless the most liberal constitution in Europe at that time. For many years, the Belgian Charter of 1831 was the constitution upon which liberals all over the Continent modeled their own demands. It was one of the tragedies of European liberalism that efforts to transplant the Belgian constitution to other states proved either short-lived or unsuccessful.

By contrast, French history, from the overthrow of Napoleon to the revolution of 1848, centered around a long series of unsuccessful attempts to establish some kind of political equilibrium. The Bourbon restoration in the person of Louis XVIII (Louis XVI's brother) in June 1814 coincided with the beginnings of large-scale industrialism in France. From the latter date until 1848, French political history resembled the swinging of a pendulum. The adherents of the old regime were divided into the *Ultras*, who wished simply to erase the preceding twenty-five years of French history, and the more moderate conservatives, who were willing to accept the past quarter of a century as a *fait accompli* upon which to build a rejuvenated French monarchy. The liberals, on the other hand, thought in terms of a constitutional monarchy, with real power vested in a legislature based on a fairly restricted suffrage. It is possible that if the charter issued by Louis XVIII upon his return to France had been fulfilled, a real measure of stability might have come to the country. But neither the king nor his closest supporters apparently intended to live up to the new constitution. All this strengthened the radicals—few in number and barely represented within the restricted suffrage of the political system —many of whom blended socialist ideas with Jacobin tactics as the basis of their political program.

It was one of the deplorable features of post-Napoleonic French history that the political moderates remained largely isolated and powerless. They never succeeded in developing an effective political program that would allow them to make significant inroads into either the Left or the Right. Although briefly in power after the revolution of 1830, they never were able to establish a strong political base. The result was that the revolution of 1848 led not to the emergence of constitutional government but to the rise of another dictatorship, this time under Napoleon's nephew.

During the 1820's liberal and national revolts against oppressive governments took place in many European states. The great powers (excepting England) did not scruple to intervene and put down these alleged threats to European peace when they occurred in such smaller powers as Spain, Italy, and Poland. Belgium managed a successful revolt only because the powers were embroiled elsewhere. Their intervention to secure Greek independence was prompted by self-interest. Of the major powers, only France had a successful revolution. In the July Revolution of 1830 the bourgeoisie and working class drove Charles X from the throne and replaced him with the more liberal Louis Philippe. Prussia and Austria remained calm, and in England revolution was forestalled in 1832 by the First Reform Bill. In Russia Nicholas I easily crushed the Decembrist revolt of 1825 which centered in the army officer corps.

That Bonaparte's defeat in 1815 would not lead to reconciliation in France became clear as soon as he was himself out of the way. The Ultras celebrated his downfall by instituting a "White Terror" against his supporters as well as other former revolutionaries, a purge conducted by both legal and illegal means. Indeed, the first elections were so completely dominated by the Ultras that Louis XVIII was forced to dissolve the legislature in order to avert the passage of the more extreme aspects of their program. In the ensuing years there was a slow drift to the Left until the Duc de Berry was assassinated in February 1820. This violent act by an obscure fanatic lent fresh strength to reactionary elements in the country, and the accession in 1824 of Charles X, another brother of Louis XVI, coincided with the apex of another rise in the fortunes of the Ultras. Charles X was even less attuned to the demands of the liberals than his predecessor had been. He cooperated with the Ultras in the passage of antiliberal legislation, including tight restrictions on the press, severe punishment for sacrilege, indemnities for nobles who had lost property in the Revolution, and the restoration of aristocratic primogeniture in the inheritance of landed property.

The reign of Charles x was characterized by the growing discontent of the moderates and the Left in the face of the continuing predominance of the Ultras. Charles seems not to have fully understood the intensity of the dissatisfaction. In August 1829 he appointed the prince of Polignac, perhaps the most unpopular man in the kingdom, to form a new government. When repeated elections resulted in legislative chambers dominated overwhelmingly by the liberal opposition, Charles proclaimed what came to be known as the July Ordinances. These dissolved the legislature, narrowed the suffrage to disfranchise even the upper middle class, and effectively removed the last vestiges of freedom of the press.

A few days later Charles was forced to abdicate in the face of the successful "July Revolution," based upon a temporary alliance of the lower classes with the bourgeoisie. His successor was the choice of the bourgeoisie, the first French monarch to identify with their interests. Louis Philippe (1830–1848), the duke of Orléans and a member of a branch of the Bourbon family, had remained aloof from partisan strife during the Napoleonic era. The new monarch liked to appear in the black business suit of the bourgeoisie and cultivated the friendship of members of that class; he had even sent his sons to the public *lycées* (secondary schools). Formally proclaimed as "King of the French, by the Grace of God, and the will of the Nation," Louis Philippe reinstituted the military organization of the bourgeoisie, the National Guard. His government was supported by (and later included) such notable liberal intellectuals as François Guizot and Adolphe Thiers, and the middle class regained its voting rights.

Despite its promising beginning, the government of Louis Philippe was soon confronted by a number of crucial problems which denied it lasting popularity and stability. In the first place, it soon became clear that Louis Philippe did not take his political alliance with the middle class so seriously that he was willing to accept the bourgeois concept of the role of the monarch—a figurehead in a basically parliamentary form of government. By the middle 1830's, he left no doubt that he intended to rule as well as reign, and this soon led to open conflict between king and legislature.

The alliance between the bourgeoisie and the Parisian working class also lasted only a short time. The bourgeoisie had no intention of acquiescing in the democratization of the government, or of using the powers of government to moderate the harsh social effects of the Industrial Revolution. The middle class rebuffed the demands of radicals that substantial reforms be instituted to improve working conditions and halt the decline of real wages. As a result, much of Louis Philippe's reign, especially between 1831 and 1834, was characterized by serious popular disorders. These frequently took the form of mass riots like the Lyons insurrection of 1831, when a clash between fifteen thousand silk workers and the National Guard caused more than six hundred casualties.

To these violent outbursts the government of Louis Philippe responded with the so-called September Laws of 1835, which sharply reduced the existing freedom of the press and otherwise sought to array the machinery of the state against the workers. In the short run, these laws did indeed succeed in the purpose for which they were designed; the disorders began to decline. But the evils that had produced the riots scarcely abated, and, as the years went on, neither did political and intellectual disaffection with the "July monarchy" diminish. As early as 1817–1818, the Comte de Saint-Simon had published his important multivolume study of modern industry, its nature and consequences, in which he called for the adaptation of industry to the needs of the people rather than the other way around. Saint-Simon's treatise was followed by several other works pointing to the evils and irrationality of modern capitalism. Yet Louis Philippe and his ministers were prepared to do very little to alleviate these evils.

In spite of significant advances in industry, the planning of a railroad network, and the political predominance of the upper bourgeoisie, France remained predominantly agricultural far into the nineteenth century. Even slower to industrialize was its southern neighbor, Spain, which emerged from Napoleonic domination in 1814 with the restoration of King Ferdinand VII. Although Spanish liberalism was only a pale reflection of its French counterpart, the constitutional and political conflict that characterized the ensuing decades of Spanish history paralleled in many ways the conflicts that occurred in France in the same period. The situation in Spain was complicated by the intervention of foreign powers, especially France, which intervened in the early 1820's to overthrow a liberal government.

The conflict in Spain was never simply a struggle between Crown, bourgeoisie, and proletariat, because industrialism had hardly touched the Spanish economy. Town-dwellers, disappointed office seekers (a numerous class), and disenchanted army officers gave the liberals their impetus. Although their demands were rather mild in comparison with those of other European liberals—restriction of the power of the clergy, especially the Inquisition; creation of a parliament; relaxation of censorship—Spanish conservatives resisted change with a passion.

The conservatives derived much of their strength from the rural areas, where king and clergy were venerated and provincial autonomy demanded almost as an article of faith, where repressive government was deemed the best assurance of the status quo and protective import duties were essential to keeping up the price of wool. The restoration of Ferdinand VII in March 1814 represented victory for the conservative countryside. Although the king had promised to honor the liberal constitution of 1812, it soon became clear that he had no intention of doing so. The ensuing repression of liberal forces and liberal ideas served for a time to silence the opposition to Ferdinand's rule, but it also precluded the possibility of liberal reconciliation to the restored monarchy.

Even harsh repression was insufficient to put down the revolutionary movement, however. Before long, the government of Ferdinand VII was faced with the dual problems of bankruptcy at home and widespread revolt in Spain's Latin American possessions. It proved incapable of solving either one, and in 1820 the two problems combined to bring about its downfall as disgruntled officers and underpaid soldiers (about to be shipped to America) joined a number of Spanish cities in rebellion.

By this time the members of the Holy Alliance had become so concerned that they met at Verona, in October 1822. Although the British foreign minister, Castlereagh, committed suicide on the eve of the conference and his successor, George Canning, refused to cooperate with its decisions, the allies agreed once more upon foreign intervention to bank the fires of revolutionary discontent. Accordingly, in early 1823 French troops entered Spain, liberated the king, and dealt the revolution a fatal blow. The French sought to persuade Ferdinand to follow a more moderate course henceforth, but the king spurned such advice, and until his death in September 1833, Spain was in the iron grip of counterrevolution. Thus began still another round in the long cycle of revolution and counterrevolution that was to beset Spain until well into the twentieth century.

The Western Hemisphere

Soon after order was restored in Spain, the question of Latin American independence became critical. Actually, the quest of the Spanish colonies for autonomy and independence dated back to the eighteenth century and had been fed by many of the same ideas and circumstances that had led to the revolt of Britain's American colonies in the 1770's. Moreover, in the revolutionary era that followed, many parts of the Spanish Empire had refused to recognize the French usurper, Joseph Bonaparte, when he was placed on the throne of Spain by his brother, Napoleon. These rebellions tended to swing to the Left and continue after the restoration in Spain, partly because of the shift of control in Spanish America from the Spanish aristocracy to Creoles (Americans born of Spanish parentage), mestizos (of mixed Spanish-Indian parentage), and native Indians. It was also due in part to an unwillingness to submit, even in name only, to the economic disadvantages imposed by Spanish rule.

Mexico and Paraguay achieved independence even before the end of the Napoleonic Wars. Between 1817 and 1825 two famous generals led virtually all of South America to independence. Simón Bolívar (1783–1830) centered his efforts in the northern part of the continent, hoping to found a large, unified state to be called *Gran Colombia*. He succeeded instead in laying the groundwork for the appearance of a number of smaller countries. In the south, José de San Martín (1778–1850) organized an army in what is now Argentina, liberated the southeastern part of South America, then crossed over the Andes and defeated the Spanish in Chile. Finally in 1822 he marched north to Peru, the economic and political center of Spanish rule. In 1824 Bolívar completed the destruction of Spanish power in the Americas.

Brazil achieved independence from Portugal under the leadership of Pedro I, son of King John VI of Portugal and first emperor of Brazil (1822–1831). The Portuguese royal family, forced to flee their country during the French occupation of Portugal, had taken refuge in their largest colonial possession. Although the Portuguese parliament sought to reestablish the mother country's prewar status, Brazil, like the other parts of Latin America, was unwilling to return to the rank of colony and became an independent constitutional state in October 1822. Even the Holy Alliance did not think of interfering.

By 1824 almost all of the Latin American states had become independent. Their independence was supported in part by Britain, which had developed important trading interests in South America despite Spanish laws against colonial trade with foreign nations. Britain disapproved of the Continental policy of intervention against liberal revolutions. It was consistent with British policy to stand aloof while the Latin American republics asserted their independence and then to let it be known that the mighty British navy would brook no attempts to restore Spanish or Portuguese rule.

The United States joined Britain in protecting Latin American independence movements and nascent republics from possible reprisal by Spain and other reactionary forces. This confluence of American and British interests marked a sharp reversal from the unfortunate War of 1812, when the United States had engaged in a desultory armed conflict with Britain. British men-of-war had been stopping and searching American ships on the high seas in an effort to block American shipments to Napoleonic Europe, and the United States, under James Madison's presidency, reluctantly declared war. Enthusiasm for the war in Washington—there was none in London—came from some western Senators who hoped that war would provide opportunity for American expansion. Little glory was gained on either side, however. An American invasion of Canada was turned back with heavy losses, a marauding British expedition needlessly sacked and burned Washington, and the great American victory at New Orleans under General Andrew Jackson actually occurred a couple of weeks after the peace treaty had been signed.

Although the United States in the 1820's had hardly any navy at all, its government insisted on playing a strongly anticolonial role in Latin America. That it should have played such a role is hardly surprising. Even before the outbreak of the American Revolution, American thinking had generally favored movements of national independence and the "new diplomacy" being advocated by the most advanced European thinkers. Predictably, these tend-

In 1800 Spain and Portugal controlled the affairs of Latin America, although France, Great Britain, and the Netherlands had small, rich holdings in the area. Revolutionary sentiment developed in the Iberian colonies because they were denied even a semblance of self-government: viceroys and other high secular and religious leaders were sent out from Europe and generally subordinated the interests of the native-born population to those of the mother country. After the Napoleonic Wars, internal dissension in Spain, British interest in

LATIN AMERICA BEFORE INDEPENDENCE

encies had become much stronger after 1776; Jefferson himself was one of their principal exponents. The result of this kind of thinking was the Monroe Doctrine, which was enunciated by President Monroe in his annual message to Congress in December 1823, soon after the United States had recognized the new Latin American republics.

Monroe had been approached by the British about the possibility of issuing a joint statement prohibiting European intervention in the Latin American revolutions. Not wishing to appear to be riding on British coattails and determined to preserve America's freedom of action, Monroe issued his own statement. He warned European nations to accept the revolutions in Latin America as a *fait accompli* because the United States would not tolerate European colonization in the Western Hemisphere. Although the United States at this time lacked the naval power to enforce its will upon the European states, the latter were never tempted to reassert mastery over their former colonies, and it seems highly likely that if they had sought to do so, they would have met with decisive opposition from Great Britain. The Monroe Doctrine became a permanent part of American foreign policy and was used later in the nine-

LATIN AMERICA AFTER THE WARS OF INDEPENDENCE, 1825

the independence of Spain's Latin American colonies, and growing American determination to keep the European powers out of the Western Hemisphere combined to aid the colonies' struggle for freedom. Mexico and Paraguay secured their independence first; other colonies soon followed suit. Brazil had considered itself independent since the Portuguese king moved there in 1808; after his return to Europe in 1821 it formally declared its independence, retaining his son as its monarch.

teenth century as the basis for intervention in disputes among Latin American republics as well as in disputes between those republics and European nations. Its pronouncement marked one of the first times that the United States had given concrete expression to its own philosophy of international affairs.

Although the United States was now beginning to interject an important new note in world affairs, in its domestic politics it soon found itself subjected to pressures not unfamiliar to the Old World. By the early nineteenth century, the predominance of European-born families along the eastern seaboard was gradually giving way to the first generation of American-born leaders, while the adoption of virtually universal adult manhood suffrage (except for slaves) as the nation expanded westward opened participation in the political process to the ordinary citizen.

The growing democratization of American politics led to renewed attention to the issue of Negro slavery, which had been generally in abeyance since the formation of the United States, and began to make increasingly precarious the political situation of the one region of the country — the South — where slavery was deemed by many whites to be an economic necessity. For a time the rising sectional conflict, which grew out of other issues as well, was papered over by a series of temporary settlements. The most notable was the Missouri Compromise of 1820, under which Missouri was admitted to the Union without restriction as to slavery within its borders but all remaining parts of the former Louisiana Territory north of 36° 30′ were to be forever free of slavery. Although the Missouri Compromise put an end to the first great national crisis over slavery, the whole issue was reopened, much more explosively, following the annexation of Texas and the war with Mexico in the middle 1840's.

Meanwhile, the South and the West frequently found common interests. For instance, both generally favored states' rights and low tariffs, as well as rapid westward expansion. In the Northeast, powerful manufacturing interests fought to maintain a high tariff to keep prices up and looked with little favor upon westward expansion, which made factory labor scarce and therefore much more expensive than it would have been if men had not had the alternative of moving westward to settle upon new land.

One of the most disputed issues was the national bank. The first Bank of the United States had originally been proposed by Alexander Hamilton and was approved in 1791 by President Washington over the objections of Thomas Jefferson, at that time secretary of state. Located in Philadelphia, it was chartered for twenty years. In one of his last important acts before leaving office, President Madison refused to approve an extension of that charter, whereupon the first bank expired. In 1816 the second Bank of the United States was chartered. Its management was accused of dabbling in politics and became the target for bitter opposition from Jeffersonians and debtor elements supporting the administration of Andrew Jackson (1829–1837).

Jackson was the first President who really represented the South and the West. The son of Scotch-Irish immigrants from Northern Ireland, he educated himself, gained admittance to the bar in 1787, helped to draft Tennessee's constitution, and served as that state's first representative in Congress. As an Indian fighter and a successful commander in the War of 1812, he became a military hero, and in the presidential election of 1824 he polled the largest popular vote, only to be defeated in the House of Representatives by John Quincy Adams. Jackson's election in 1828 marked the triumph of a new democratic spirit in American politics. But in constitutional and economic matters, Jackson was essentially conservative. In his first inaugural address, he declared, "The Federal Constitution must be obeyed, states' rights preserved, our national debt must be paid, direct taxes and loans avoided, and the Federal Union preserved." Jackson was especially determined to destroy the second Bank of the United States, and fighting the campaign of 1832 largely on this issue, he was overwhelmingly reelected. In 1836 the Bank's charter finally expired, but Jackson's victory—and the victory of those who thought like him—was not an unmixed blessing. The resultant period of easy credit led to inflation and currency speculation and contributed to the Panic of 1837, when the economy of the United States faced one of its first major crises.

Although Jackson was a strong advocate of states' rights, he did not seriously attempt to undermine the power of the federal government. In fact, during his term in office the Supreme Court, under the leadership of Chief Justice John Marshall (1755–1835), took an expansionist view of the Constitution which considerably strengthened the power of the federal government in relation to that of the states. In numerous cases dating over three decades—he served as Chief Justice from 1801 to 1835—Marshall established the principle of judicial review, created legal barriers to attacks on private property, and generally favored centralization at the expense of the states. But the Marshall Court did not confront the problem of slavery, and this further helped to postpone—and additionally inflame—this explosive issue.

Economically, the development of the United States during its first half century compared favorably with that of western Europe. Although still largely agricultural and subject to intermittent setbacks as a result of the international situation (especially during the Napoleonic Wars), the United States developed steadily into a major industrial power. Save for permitting the continued existence of slavery—which some indeed believed adaptable to industrialization—the United States placed fewer obstacles in the way of industry than did European countries like France and Germany. American manufacturers had a large and growing market shielded from possible European competitors by the Atlantic Ocean and, after 1816, by increasingly steep tariff barriers. Moreover, the United States was meeting the need for efficient transportation over long distances with a comprehensive system of turnpikes and canals, which brought further economic advance and served to knit the country together more closely. By 1834, for instance, the Great Lakes had been linked with the Mississippi River, and by the 1840's over three thousand miles of canals had been constructed. The Baltimore and Ohio, America's first railroad, was chartered in 1830, and by 1840 railroad construction was under way at a furious pace. It contributed significantly to America's rapid rise to leadership among the industrial powers of the world. Furthermore, the United States had begun to assert itself as a technological leader by the end of the eighteenth century. Eli Whitney's invention of interchangeable parts in 1798 was perhaps the most revolutionary development in the history of American industry, paving the way for mass production.

While the Latin American peoples were gaining their independence and Jacksonian democracy was transforming political life in the United States, liberal principles were inspiring rebellion in Canada. After coming under British rule during the Seven Years' War, the Canadian colonies were governed by the same awkward system by which the British had ruled the thirteen colonies farther to the south before the American Revolution. By the 1830's this system was no more successful in Canada than it had been in the colonies that formed the United States. A governor sent out by the British colonial office ruled with the advice of a group of wealthy gentlemen in his council, while the middle-class representatives in the legislature chronically quarreled with the governor and resented the political privileges of the patrician families. In 1837 the gross incompetence of particularly mindless aristocrats whom the colonial office had sent to govern Lower and Upper Canada (later Quebec and Ontario) and the spread of liberal ideology inspired rebellions. These were easily suppressed, but the alarmed Whig government in Britain, sensing a possible repetition of the American Revolution, sent out a radical aristocrat, Lord Durham, to investigate. Durham's major proposal was simple: let the colonists govern their own domestic affairs, and give the governor the same constitutional role in the colonies that Queen Victoria played at home. Although the nervous Whigs never officially accepted the recommendation, in the following decades a series of instructions from the colonial secretary to the governors in Canada in effect established what Canadian liberals called "responsible government."

In the 1850's and 1860's, the same rights of self-government were extended to the other British colonies with overwhelming or at least sizable proportions of Europeans in their populations — Australia, New Zealand, and South Africa. This enlightened policy was inspired by liberal attitudes on the part of British statesmen; but the decision was also conditioned by the belief that these countries were more expensive to govern than they were economically useful to Britain. In non-European-populated colonies, such as India, where imperial rule was profitable to the British upper classes, the granting of self-government was not seriously considered, although some liberal civil servants like Thomas Macaulay foresaw the day when even the Indian people would be allowed to govern themselves.

Nationalism and Conservatism in Central and Eastern Europe

The rapid development of industrialism in the United States illustrates the importance of the political and social structure of a country in a period of economic transition. In Germany, the Austrian Empire, Russia, and the other areas of eastern Europe, landed aristocracies and absolutists, separately and together, often blocked or otherwise delayed economic development and social change, which they regarded as menacing to the existing political order.

During the first half of the nineteenth century, the economic development of Germany was retarded considerably by its political division. German particularism, of course, was a long-standing phenomenon; Napoleon had taken advantage of it to conquer and occupy most of Germany. Since he had also reorganized large parts of the country, the Congress of Vienna was confronted with the task of unscrambling the Napoleonic settlement and giving a new form to the German political system. It did not, however, completely erase the changes — territorial, political, and social — brought about during the previous twenty-five years. In particular, the simplified political division of the country was retained, and there was a vague suggestion that the various German states would or might grant constitutions to their citizens (a promise only as good as the intention of the individual ruler). All thirty-eight German states and the German part of Austria were brought together in the new German Confederation. This new body was to be the successor to the Holy Roman Empire—that is, it was to provide at least a minimum bond for the post-Napoleonic German states. The conservative statesmen who agreed on the establishment of the Confederation had no desire to satisfy the liberal and national longings of the German people, and in practice it proved impossible to get the Confederation to exercise even those limited powers that had been granted to it by the Congress of Vienna. The Diet of the Confederation lacked the authority to collect taxes or raise an army of its own, and it was vitiated from the beginning by the requirement of unanimity (or at least a two-thirds majority) on all important matters.

Austria was the dominant member of the Confederation, a fact that assured its continued strong influence in German affairs. This situation seemed to satisfy Metternich's basic objective, which was to prevent any significant change in the Habsburg empire by preventing it in Austria's neighbors. Among the earliest expressions of Metternich's dominant influence were the Carlsbad Decrees of 1819, which reintroduced censorship of the press and control of the universities to prevent the spread of liberalism and nationalism. The result of the Confederation's inaction (save to crack down on any liberal or national movements) was that the dream of national unification soon began to fade, and so also did the hope for internal reform in most German states. This was especially true in the 1820's, though after the July Revolution in France, the 1830's saw the beginnings of a new liberal and national movement that led first to the revolutions of 1848 and later—though in rather drastically changed form—to the unification of Germany in the era of Bismarck.

Although Austria was at first predominant in German affairs, several factors soon favored the rise of Prussian influence. Prussia had acquired a reputation in Germany for liberal and progressive government as a result of the political and social reforms that Baron vom Stein and Prince Hardenberg had implemented in that state after its devastating defeat by Napoleon at Jena in 1806. First of all, the bourgeoisie were emancipated—they were allowed to acquire land, to become army officers, and to choose their occupation freely. Second, an effective system of municipal government was instituted. Third, the peasantry was freed from the legal bond of serfdom and permitted to leave the land, if they could afford to. The army was also modernized, a good school system was established, and the University of Berlin, which rapidly became a formidable center of humanistic learning and scientific research, was founded.

Prussian development after 1815 presents something of a paradox. On the one hand, the monarchy dispensed with many of the liberal changes and ignored many of the promises made during the Napoleonic era. On the other hand, the reputation of Prussia as the most advanced of the large German states persisted, and by the 1830's many German liberals were again looking to Prussia to lead the German unity movement. Meanwhile, Austria was doing almost nothing to satisfy the needs and aspirations of its subjects, and before long nationalism would begin to present an increasing threat to the continued existence of the Austrian Empire. More important, the peace settlement of 1815 provided for substantial Prussian expansion to the west, and the territory Prussia acquired in the Rhineland not only proved to be of outstanding economic importance, but also became one of Prussia's most liberal and influential provinces.

It was hardly surprising, then, that it was Prussia, not Austria, that began to pave the way for the effective economic union of the country. Until the establishment of the Prussian-sponsored and Prussian-led *Zollverein* (customs union) in January 1834 — its beginnings dated back as early as 1819 — the German states had been separated by a variety of customs barriers that severely hindered the free flow of trade. The abolition of these barriers and the resultant economic unification of much of Germany were important steps toward later political unification.

While nationalism in Prussia and the rest of Germany was directed toward political unification, in Austria nationalism was inherently a disintegrating force. The Austrian Empire was a mass of national groups united primarily by their subjection to Habsburg rule. Emperor Francis I (1804–1835) believed that the only answer to the threat of disintegration was a rigid adherence to the status quo, both socially and politically. Relying upon an antiquated and inefficient Austrian bureaucracy, Francis was unwilling to listen even to Metternich's modest proposals for reforms that were designed to make absolutism more tolerable. The dominant symbols of Francis' reign were the secret police, an unreformed Church, and the powerful local landed nobility, whose interests were tied to the government in Vienna. Metternich considered freedom of the press and political freedom highly dangerous; the principal purpose of government seemed to be a kind of all-pervasive surveillance of society to root out any plots, or even radical tendencies, within Austria and the rest of the Habsburg empire.

The most immediate victims of such repressive tendencies were the middle-class liberals, and in view of their fate after the Congress of Vienna, it was hardly surprising that the position of the peasant throughout much of central and eastern Europe was even more wretched. In Prussia, the formal abolition of serfdom merely introduced the peasant to a new form of servitude. Unable with his meager resources to buy enough land to farm successfully, the former serf found himself depressed to the condition of landless laborer, working for pitiful wages with little or no social mobility or independence. Although doubtless not the intention of the great Prussian reformers of the Stein-

Hardenberg era, the abolition of serfdom allowed the Prussian Junkers to increase the size of their holdings considerably, while at the same time maintaining the political and social mastery of the countryside they had enjoyed for several centuries. Nor was the situation of the peasantry any better in Austria, where Francis I would never consider the abolition of serfdom, even if it guaranteed results favorable to the landed aristocracy. Instead, serfdom was rigidly enforced, with the peasant commonly owing two thirds of his crop and one half of his time to the lord. The accession of the feeble-minded Ferdinand I to the emperorship in 1835 offered no prospect of improvement and further reduced the government's ability to deal with the economic crisis of the 1840's.

The system of autocratic government supported by landed aristocracy that characterized the nations of eastern Europe reached its most absolute form in Russia. For the most part, Russia was still a land of lords and serfs; there was

The Habsburgs ruled an empire that encompassed a bewildering welter of peoples, and consequently in the post-Napoleonic era they had to contend with a staggering number of nationalist demands. Most of the empire's ethnic groups—with their individual languages, cultures, and traditions—lived in historic homelands (Czechs in Bohemia, Germans in Austria, Italians in the Tyrol, Magyars in Hungary, and so on), but enough internal migration had taken place to scatter minorities throughout the various provinces. The existence of so many national groups doomed the revolution of 1848; their intransigence meant that the empire was never able to satisfy the demands of one group without alienating a second.

THE AUSTRIAN EMPIRE 1848

only a small and struggling middle class. Factory production was very limited. The trade that found its outlet at the Baltic Sea dealt largely in natural products such as lumber, furs, flax, and hemp and was usually controlled by nobles.

Alexander I, who came to the throne in 1801, seemed to promise some liberalization of Russian society and government, but he never completed any plan before being distracted by something else. It was typical of Alexander that, on the one hand, he promised a constitution to Polish liberals and, on the other, he advocated intervention in the Spanish revolution to prevent liberals from forcing a constitution on their monarch. A generally repressive atmosphere existed in Russia as in the rest of Europe after the Napoleonic Wars. The Russian peasants, who had shared in the glorious victories of their country, profited not at all from their part in the conflict. In 1803 the government went so far as to issue an edict providing for the emancipation of serfs by owners who wished to take that step; but though Alexander made a number of other efforts to make the Russian government less autocratic and more responsive to popular needs, he was never prepared to go very far in this direction, resisting, for instance, all suggestions that he move toward some sort of constitutional government.

As Alexander grew older, he became more and more frightened of revolutionary conspiracies at home and abroad. When he died in December 1825, he left behind a series of repressive measures, a disputed succession to the throne, and a growing underground revolutionary movement centered among army officers. The revolutionaries were young noblemen familiar with European philosophy and literature; many had seen something of the world outside Russia during the Napoleonic Wars. They all agreed on two things. There had to be an end to serfdom, and the slowly rising Russian middle class had to be given a larger and more important role in the government. Shortly after Alexander's death, various military groups—first in the north, then the south—mutinied against the new czar, Nicholas I (1825–1855). Unorganized, without coherent goals or widespread popular sympathy, they were easily and severely crushed; yet these "Decembrists" wrote an important chapter of the Russian revolutionary tradition.

Nicholas never forgot the circumstances of his accession. Not only did he suppress the Decembrists—whose ties and connections were in many instances with the highest and most impeccable social circles—but his reign was one of the most repressive in Russian history. This is not to say that he was unaware of what ailed his country and what needed to be done to improve it. For instance, he appointed a commission to examine all his predecessor's reform plans and proposals, but almost nothing came of this detailed inquiry, save for a new Code of Laws, which was published in 1833 and which, with some changes, remained in effect until the revolution of 1917. For the rest, the secret police—now called the Third Section—kept all suspected intellectuals, teachers, students, and other potential revolutionaries under constant surveillance. Education as a whole regressed, not only through restrictions on what could be taught, but through the discouragement of education of the lower classes.

The government also sought to make it difficult for Russian students to go abroad, where they might come into contact with dangerous ideas, but the radicalization of the Russian intelligentsia proceeded apace after the 1830's. There was a deep division between the so-called "Westernizers" and the "Slavophiles," who believed that Russia could and should have its own tradition of reform. It was not, however, until Russia experienced an international disaster that these reform-minded factions could at least begin to acquire real influence at home.

This disaster finally came in the form of the Crimean War in the mid-1850's. Nicholas had long combined repression at home with an active policy of expansion to the south, and some of his early efforts in this direction were fairly successful. For example, his intervention in the Greek revolution against the Ottoman Empire established good relations with Greece and achieved both important territorial concessions – notably the principal mouth of the Danube River – and growing influence upon Turkish foreign policy, including a secret treaty provision (July 1833) providing that Turkey close the Straits to all foreign warships. In central Europe, Russia allied itself with Austria and Prussia to defend the principle of legitimate dynasties and, especially important, to keep Poland partitioned and dependent. When Poland rose against Russian rule in November 1830, Nicholas's forces were able to crush the rebellion so thoroughly that Russian Poland did not join effectively in the widespread revolutions of 1848. There was no revolution in Russia in 1848, and this fact contributed to its prestige.

From 1815 until the middle 1850's, Russia considered itself, and was considered by the other European powers, to be the greatest land power on the Continent. But beneath this surface appearance of triumphant conservatism, the Russian state and Russian society were steadily decaying, to the point where – when Russia suffered humiliating defeat at Sebastopol, in September 1855 – a leading Russian conservative declared that the war had been lost so that "God might reveal all the decadence of the government system."

III THE CRISIS OF THE 1840'S

Economic and Intellectual Problems

Only the most naive and narrow-minded of autocrats regarded the ability of European states to dismantle or delay interminably the reforms begun during the previous half century as a permanent settlement of the questions posed by liberalism and nationalism. By the 1840's most Europeans had some intimation of a new and perhaps more ominous crisis. To be sure, in no Continental country had the urban working class begun to constitute anything like a majority of the population, and nowhere had the struggle for political power between the landed aristocracy and the bourgeoisie been finally decided. Yet in spite of the gradualness of industrialization, by the 1840's it was clear that important changes in the social and political structure were inevitable products of this economic transformation. Even in cities and towns where the urban proletariat numbered only a few thousand, their pitiful living quarters, clustered together beneath the shadow and smoke of factories, were beginning to transform the face of Europe. At the same time, the rhythm of prosperity and depression depended increasingly upon an economy based on capital investment. Few men pretended to understand the mysteries of the business cycle, whose uncertainties added greatly to the existing discontent.

Between 1844 and 1847 a general European economic crisis compounded the hardships produced by the uneven development of industry. Dependent upon expanding markets, industry entered a period of business failures and growing unemployment at the same time that a blight was destroying the potatoes—the most basic food of the working class—from Ireland all across the Continent. Thousands of peasants, artisans, and factory workers were reduced to starvation as prices spiraled upward. The result of this crisis was growing political and social disaffection climaxed by the revolutions of 1848—a general European upheaval which broke out in countless places from Ireland to Hungary and from Sicily to Berlin.

These revolutions were more than acts of desperation. Invariably spontaneous and in no sense the products of a general conspiracy, they pursued goals and objectives that had been articulated for some time by middle-class spokesmen and leading members of the intelligentsia. In that sense they were the culmination of a debate which had been going on since the middle of the eighteenth century. In a very real sense the Enlightenment had been an intellectual revolution of hope, and that intellectual revolution had been both expanded and complicated by the Industrial Revolution. Industrialism presented new possibilities which seemed to promise almost unlimited improvement in living conditions. The ultimate justification for the changes it brought about was progress, and one of the most important aspects of the idea of progress was the belief that both industry and society should be freed from all possible restraints.

The policy of laissez faire, according to Adam Smith and his successors, would produce a constant increase in the quantity and quality of available goods as businessmen were forced by competition to produce cheaply and well. Political liberals and radicals—the English Chartists, for example—applied this theory of free competition to politics. Thus it was argued, for instance, that the extension of the suffrage to all men would guarantee governments open to change and responsive to the common good rather than to the desires of narrow, selfish interests. Freedom of speech and the press was nec-

In 1848 revolutions broke out all over Europe. Of the great powers, only England and Russia were spared; the regimes in France, Austria, and Prussia were hard pressed. In France the Second Republic was declared but foundered on the gulf between the interests of the workers and those of the middle class. In the face of mounting disorder in Berlin, Frederick William agreed to call a Prussian parliament to draft a constitution but easily regained control within a few months. After violence flared in Vienna, Metternich fled the country, but the conflicting interests of the national minorities worked in the emperor's favor. Russian troops sealed Hungary's doom, and an Austrian army was successful in putting down the Italian national revolts. The Frankfurt Assembly—called by German revolutionaries to create a unified German state that would enact liberal reforms—made little headway, and its last remnants were driven into exile by Austrian troops.

essary for that free competition of ideas that was a precondition of democracy. Although some demands varied from country to country according to local circumstances, need, and tradition, some form of constitutional government, the rationalization of the legal system (as Jeremy Bentham proposed in England), and the abolition of all remaining social and legal disabilities—for instance, against Catholics and Jews—were usually considered indispensable prerequisites for the fashioning of the liberal state.

This is not to say that most liberals and radicals agreed about the details of the free society they were seeking to create. Even liberals disagreed greatly about desirable limitations on suffrage; only the most radical advocated giving the vote to all adult males. Most feared the lower classes and wished to use educational or property qualifications to exclude from the voting lists the most ignorant, whose brutish existence did not allow them the means or the leisure to acquaint themselves adequately with public affairs. These differences may have seemed comparatively minor in the early and middle 1840's, but as the time for political action approached, they became increasingly important and divisive.

Moreover, the assertions of liberalism were severely tested by the evident inability of the new industrial system to provide anything like the good life for the majority of people. Workers who lived on a bare subsistence wage often faced starvation when they were laid off during a slump in business. Their only alternative was to take jobs that drove them to complete physical exhaustion—and sometimes beyond it. Nor were such deplorable conditions limited to backward areas and declining industries and enterprises. The living and working conditions of the working class shocked the more comfortable elements of society. The question was, What could society and the workers themselves do to improve the situation? The process that reduced countless workers to the status of marginal wage laborers and brought them together in huge slum communities laid the groundwork for the development of attitudes that bore fruit in the workers' brotherhoods, unions, and radical mass organizations that became the particular tools of the urban working class in dealing with industrialism.

In the 1820's and 1830's, unions in Britain and on the Continent boldly pressed for better conditions. In England, legal restrictions against unions were considerably eased in 1824; in France the silk workers in Lyons had formed several unions of their own by the 1830's. About the same time, Robert Owen formed the Grand National Consolidated Trades Union. These were important steps forward but they remained fairly isolated, and when economic conflict broke out between capital and labor, the governments—in Britain, France, and elsewhere—were almost invariably on the side of capital.

Those who felt that the conditions of the working class were intolerable were forced to seek an alternative to the system of wage labor in which employer and employee faced each other as individuals. The alternative most often put forward by the upper classes was a system of paternalism in which the state established minimum working conditions and wages and maximum hours and insured the worker against sickness and unemployment. Both the British aristocracy and the Prussian government of the later nineteenth century favored this course. Indeed, especially in Prussia, there were enlightened conservatives and aristocrats who saw early in the 1840's that the government had to do something to help the working class—and that there were substantial political dividends in such a course. But it was extremely difficult to enact effective protection for the worker because of the expense to the state and because of the concerted opposition of the bourgeoisie. By 1848 no state in Europe had anything that remotely resembled an adequate system of protection for the rights and health of the working class.

Another alternative was fundamental change in the conditions of ownership of business. The French theorist Henri de Rouvroy, Comte de Saint-Simon (1760–1825), advocated a planned economy, a sort of technocracy in which experts could regulate the economy for maximum efficiency. Napoleon Bonaparte's nephew Louis, who became head of the French state in late 1848, was one of many influential members of the French government who were disciples of Saint-Simon. More than any other country on the Continent, France was willing to have the state direct the economy and even engage in various enterprises. Thus, for example, France's system of railroads was constructed in accordance with state planning and largely through state funds.

This is not to say, however, that the French government and influential Frenchmen generally were prepared to go very far in using public resources to assist the working class. When Louis Blanc (1811–1882), the distinguished socialist who was to play a leading role during the revolutions of 1848, proposed in his most important work, *The Organization of Labor* (1838), the establishment of "social workshops" supported by government funds, he received, like most social critics of the July monarchy, a respectful hearing – and then was promptly forgotten.

Still another appealing alternative was a change in the system of property ownership. For the British industrialist Robert Owen, this meant the formation of a community in which all men shared equally in the profits of industry. Owen led a group of followers to the United States and in 1824 founded New Harmony in Indiana, one of many such utopian communities in the nineteenth century. Like most of the others, it failed through internal dissension. The proposal by the French social theorist Charles Fourier (1772–1837) for the establishment of large socialist communities called *phalanstères*, to be devoted to both agricultural and industrial production, received no support from either capitalist investors or workers.

More attractive to the masses was the demand for the abolition of private property through a revolution of the proletariat, as proposed by theorists like Karl Marx (1818–1883) and Pierre Joseph Proudhon (1809–1865). Actually Proudhon – best known for his aphorism "property is theft" – was one of the few important social critics of the time who did not put his faith in the state. Indeed, he viewed socialism and communism as equally oppressive and believed instead (somewhat like Owen) that society should be based on voluntary cooperation among individuals living together in small communities. But Proudhon's plans were no more realistic than those of Owen, and perhaps it is not surprising that the regimentation of modern industrialism spawned as its most powerful critic and adversary Marxian socialism.

At first glance, Karl Marx was a highly unlikely candidate for founder (or co-founder) of perhaps the most important theoretical and social revolutionary movement of modern times. Born into a Jewish bourgeois family in the Prussian Rhineland, at a time when the Jews in that state were just beginning to become fully emancipated politically (his father was a lawyer), he had his hopes for an academic career rudely dashed when he was refused a university appointment at Bonn because of his atheistic views. Following a brief career as editor of a bourgeois-radical newspaper, which was suppressed by the authorities as anti-Russian, Marx fled to Paris, from there to Brussels, and finally to London, where—save for a few months during the revolutions of 1848—he was to spend the remainder of his life.

A facile and prolific writer with a trenchant, biting style, Marx was economic historian, social critic, and political philosopher all in one. In 1844 he began his lifelong collaboration with Friedrich Engels (1820–1895), another discerning young German observer of the times, who in 1845 made his own mark by publishing an explosive, somewhat overdrawn account, *The Condition of the Working Class in England, 1844*. Working with Engels in Brussels, Marx formulated the theory of proletarian revolution that was powerfully expressed in the *Communist Manifesto* of early 1848 and later defended in his multivolume study of the principles of economics, *Das Kapital* (1867–1894). Marx began his intellectual life as a leftist Hegelian, and in his early writings, many of them discovered only after the First World War, he was concerned not only with the physical deprivation caused by the system of wage labor but also with its reduction of men to a subhuman state in which they could respond only to their animal instincts. He attacked the capitalist system because it degraded a man by substituting money for true human values and by alienating him from his labor (since the capitalist, not the worker, owns what the worker produces) and from other men (since he must compete with other men rather than cooperate with them).

In the *Communist Manifesto*, Marx (and Engels) asserted baldly, "The history of all hitherto existing society is the history of class struggles." The capitalist phase, however, was unique, because it would see mankind divided into two classes. The bourgeoisie—the owners of the means of production—would constantly increase in wealth and decrease in numbers as other men—the workers, who do not own the means of production but are forced to sell their labor to the owners, who keep the profits—were degraded into the proletariat. Eventually the proletariat would comprise all but a small minority of men; then, pushed forward by desperate deprivation, it would rise up and overthrow the bourgeoisie.

"The theory of the Communists," Marx and Engels declared in the *Manifesto*, "may be summed up in the single sentence: Abolition of private property." This act presumably would eradicate class conflict for the first time in history and create a classless society through the establishment of a Communist state. Although Marx was relatively unknown in 1848, the disappointment of the working class with the results of their revolutions and the disenchantment of the workers with the performance of the middle class during those revolutions made his ideas increasingly attractive to radical reformers.

The Revolutions of 1848

Despite the growing radicalization of politics and social thought throughout the 1840's, the revolutions of 1848 were not, in the first instance, the result of this renewed intellectual ferment but of the weakness and corruption of most European governments – in short, of their inability to deal with, much less resolve, their peoples' most pressing needs. The revolutions had their beginning in France, where the remarkably ineffective government of Louis Philippe had become more and more unpopular. The French uprising was touched off in late February of 1848 when, following growing public disaffection, meetings, and fairly restrained demonstrations, government troops fired into a large crowd gathering in Paris. Within hours, barricades were up throughout the capital. Bourgeois republicans, disgusted with the July monarchy, joined in an effective (if short-lived) alliance with radicals and socialists of all persuasions. Louis Philippe abdicated and fled to England, and the Second Republic was proclaimed. Its leaders included the socialist Louis Blanc and a Paris workingman, and the new government set off with an advanced – if confused – social program.

The revolution in France produced political turmoil throughout Europe. Though the revolts that followed varied widely from place to place, there was nevertheless something of a pattern to them all. They usually began with a flurry of increasingly acrimonious speeches and public discussions; then crowds of students, workers, and ordinary citizens would gather in the streets to learn the news, discuss the latest events, and perhaps add a few demands of their own. At this point, the authorities attempted to disperse the crowds. These efforts were followed in turn by the beginning of concerted resistance and, before long, by the capitulation of the government to the major demands of the crowds, which were supported by the bourgeoisie and intelligentsia, who had their own share of resentments to set forth.

While in France dramatic political issues were almost solely responsible for the outbreak of revolution, in Germany, Austria, and Italy nationalism was an important ingredient in the ideology of the revolutions. The German revolutionaries were, for the most part, educated men whose grievances against their local rulers and governments had accumulated for many years. In almost every German state, middle-class reformers and revolutionaries – temporarily joining ranks – demanded the calling of a national parliament to draw up a constitution for a unified Germany. For a time, the German revolution seemed to be progressing well. The first nationally elected assembly met at Frankfurt in May 1848 and immediately plunged into arduous and lengthy – some said far too lengthy – debate about the myriad problems of the country and how to solve them. The leaders of the Frankfurt Parliament, who believed that reactionary German governments had blocked the development of liberal, constitutional reforms, looked to a unified state as the great hope for political and social improvement. It soon became clear, however, that the Frankfurt Parliament had very little power of its own and was able to mobilize even less direct support from the great mass of the people. If the German revolution was to succeed, therefore, it first of all had to triumph in the principal German states, notably Prussia and Austria. In view of the political and social conditions prevailing in those states—and in view of Austria's almost unbelievably complex nationality problems—this was hardly a promising prospect.

The revolution in Austria had several aspects. In Vienna, workers and students took to the streets while their leaders sought concessions limiting Habsburg absolutism. The Austrian government was intellectually and politically bankrupt and faction-ridden to boot; despite oppressive censorship, its weaknesses were sufficiently obvious to unite most elements in opposition. After the violent uprising in Vienna on March 13, Metternich fled from the city in disguise, and the emperor Ferdinand promised his people a constitution. But the troubles of the Habsburg government were not limited to its German-speaking lands. Both in Hungary and in Bohemia nationalists were calling for independence or at the least for considerable autonomy within the empire. The eloquent Hungarian revolutionary Louis Kossuth (1802–1894), who helped to incite the Viennese revolution, successfully demanded the convening of a Hungarian parliament to draw up a constitution. Although the Bohemian revolution appeared to have solid popular support, it had hardly got under way when dangerous divisions began to appear between the Czech and German inhabitants of Bohemia.

In Italy the revolutionaries had needed no signal from Paris or anywhere else. Revolution had broken out in Sicily as early as January 1848, and before long virtually the entire Italian peninsula had risen up. Changes came thick and fast. The king of Naples was forced to grant his subjects a moderate constitution, and the same thing happened in Tuscany, in Piedmont, even in the Papal States headed up by the liberal Pius IX (elected in 1846). Giuseppe Mazzini, the leader of the Italian nationalist society known as the *Carbonari*, became the president of a Roman republic emancipated from papal control. In northern Italy, controlled by Austria, powerful independence movements appeared, inspired by the revolution in Austria itself. For example, both Venetia and Lombardy drove out the Austrian troops and proclaimed their independence before the end of March. By early May, Italy seemed well on the way to a sound solution of its national and internal problems.

There was a successful revolution even in Prussia, widely (if wrongly) considered central Europe's bastion of absolutism. In rapid order Frederick William IV was forced to promise both to agree to a constitution and to convene a Prussian parliament, whose function it would be to prepare, debate, and approve such a constitution. Perhaps the romantic Frederick William IV, frightened by the initial disorders and the threat of still greater violence in Berlin, conceded more than he had to. For one thing, the monarchy never really lost control of the army, and the Prussian National Assembly, though probably even more liberal and radical than the Frankfurt Parliament, was too slow in getting around to dealing with that state's accumulated and pressing economic and social problems. The result was that the Prussian revolution soon lost much of its popular support, and the Crown, supported by emerging new conservatives such as the thirty-three-year-old Otto von Bismarck, could begin to lay plans for a successful counterrevolution.

Unfortunately, the Prussian experience was all too representative of what went on elsewhere in Europe. The revolutions of 1848 shared common ideologies; they also shared defeat. Unable to marshal adequate support among the real sources of political power, they found it difficult to institute the reforms for which they had fought. Furthermore, the groups that combined to make the revolutions a reality in the first place soon began to discover that they had in common only their dissatisfactions. Once they achieved even limited success, their basic differences in opinion and emphasis began to emerge and tear them apart.

The first crucial defeat of the revolutions came in France. The republican government had established "national workshops" in Paris and elsewhere in the country where a man could receive help in finding employment and subsistence payments if existing business could not get him a job. These "national workshops," a pale imitation of Louis Blanc's original idea, never really got off the ground. Within a few months the bourgeois leaders of the government (who were opposed to real social or economic reform) abolished them and cruelly suppressed the workers' protests that broke out in May and June 1848. During these "June Days" democratic ideas were discredited by the violence of the workers' uprising and the bloody repression thereof.

There had never been such fighting in any European city as during those "June Days," when the guns of General Cavaignac finally reduced the revolutionary working class in the French capital. It was perfectly clear that a majority of French bourgeois and French peasants had turned against the Paris workmen who had triumphed in February. The form of the republic was modified. As late as November 1848 the Constituent Assembly, which had been sitting since late spring, drafted a constitution that was fairly democratic; but by this time the French people wanted stability more than they desired liberal or social democracy. The result was that, in the first presidential elections under the new constitution, the overwhelming victor proved to be Prince Louis Napoleon Bonaparte (1808–1873). It was not long before Bonaparte's nephew set about converting the Second Republic—or what was left of it—into an empire on the original Napoleonic model.

The "June Days" had a shattering effect on German liberals and a correspondingly encouraging one upon their enemies. Nowhere was the impact of events in France felt more keenly than in Prussia, where the conservative and reactionary tide seemed to flow ever more strongly after midsummer. By November 9, Frederick William adjourned the Prussian National Assembly and moved it to the small town of Brandenburg, and on December 5 he dissolved it entirely, while at the same time decreeing a moderate constitution, further amended in a conservative sense in the next few years, which remained in effect until the overthrow of the Hohenzollern dynasty in November 1918.

The German situation as a whole was faring little better. After nearly nine months of discussion and debate the Frankfurt Assembly finally completed a constitution, but the deputies failed to provide any concrete economic and social program for the German masses—either peasants or workers—and in March 1849 they offered the German crown to Frederick William of Prussia. In defense of the principle of legitimacy and in contempt of the Assembly, Frederick William—having already dealt a near deathblow to Prussian liberalism—turned it down.

In fairness to the Frankfurt Assembly, it should be pointed out that it faced some virtually insoluble dilemmas. Though seeking to bring about some kind of unification of Germany, it was puzzled and uncertain about whether to assist nationalism in neighboring territories that had risen up against the Habsburgs. The fact of the matter is that the Frankfurt Assembly knew much too little about, say, conditions in Bohemia to act upon them effectively. While Frankfurt waited and debated, the Habsburgs gradually regained control of their territories.

In Austria itself, the peasants—frightened by the continuing unrest in the cities—became enemies of the revolution, thus joining forces with the Austrian army and with conservatives who detested both nationalistic and liberal ideas. In June 1848, General Windisch-Graetz reached Vienna and shelled the Austrian rebels into submission.

It was not long before the revival of Habsburg power threatened the newly acquired independence of the Italian states. The Austrian general Joseph Radetzky used the increasing weakness and dissension of the Italian nationalists to restore the *status quo ante bellum*. From July 1848, when they smashed the Piedmontese at the Battle of Custozza, to March 1849, when they again decisively defeated Piedmontese troops at the Battle of Novara, Austrian forces were almost continuously on the offensive. The result was that the Bourbon king of Naples, the pope, and the Habsburgs together confined the ephemeral "independence" of Italy to a tiny section of central Italy and Piedmont. And what the Habsburg troops were unable to take care of—such as the subjection of Hungary—was put in the hands of imperial Russian troops only too happy to be of help.

Thus the revolutions of 1848 failed all over Europe to establish the liberal and national principles for which they were fought. The appearance of serious dissension within the ranks of the revolutionaries was a cruel blow to the aspirations of the liberals who had led the uprisings and now found nationhood and constitutionalism once more beyond their grasp. It was equally disenchanting to the peasants and the workers, whose hopes and expectations had, by and large, also been ignored or frustrated. Nevertheless, most of the aims of the revolutionary leaders of 1848 were eventually achieved, and this suggests that the significance of the revolutions can be found not in their immediate tangible results but in the precedents they set and in the problems they raised and left unsolved for succeeding generations.

HERITAGE ESSAY

THE LIBERAL HERITAGE

Early nineteenth-century liberalism was not only a political doctrine. It was an integrated view of man and society that synthesized ideas stemming from most of the finest values in the Western tradition. From classical culture, liberalism obtained its faith in human rationality; from Christianity, it derived its acceptance of the right and duty of conscience; from the Renaissance, its optimism concerning the prospects of human life in this world; from the Enlightenment, the egalitarian principle; and from the Romantic ethos — and the Protestant heritage of the Reformation — the inspiration for a life of endless quest and endless improvement. Liberalism tended to ignore the underlying conflicts among these principles, intuitions, and aspirations, and this was a potential weakness in the liberal world view. But in the first half of the nineteenth century, the synthesis of values was successfully achieved, and liberalism, particularly in England, became the faith of intellectuals and reformers and exercised a great influence toward the melioration of political and social institutions. Although the foundations of the liberal creed were partly eroded in the late nineteenth and the twentieth century by new perceptions of the nature of man and society, the liberal philosophy remains synonymous with the spirit of Western civilization and continues to dominate the political life of the Western world. Whatever its inner contradictions, whatever the limitations of its basic assumptions about human nature, liberalism remains the last best hope of mankind.

Liberalism sought the fulfillment of the reform of government that the American and French revolutions had proclaimed; its adherents believed passionately in the justice and utility of representative institutions, of parliamentary government. Bitterly resisted on the Continent by the embattled vestiges of the *ancien régime*, democratization of government was most readily implemented in Britain. The Reform Bill of 1832 was passed and revolution avoided because a group of aristocratic Whigs saw the absolute need for constitutional reform and carried the bill through Parliament. The Whigs, with Lord John Russell serving as their spokesman in the House of Commons,

The Fortunes of Liberalism. In Britain, the Reform Bill of 1832 signaled the aristocracy's acceptance of the main political tenet of middle-class liberalism—reform of parliamentary representation so as to enfranchise the industrial bourgeoisie and the new factory towns. Above: an engraving in *Bell's Weekly Messenger* in the issue of April 15, 1832, shows the Whig cabinet led by Lord Grey surrounding the king at the top of the picture, while the Tories at the bottom left flee before the wrath of the British lion. Liberalism did not achieve such a clear and easy victory on the Continent. Facing page, top: the German National Assembly at Frankfurt in 1848 is shown in characteristic activity—speech-making. Facing page, bottom: a sardonic view of the French legislature by the brilliant satirical artist Honoré Daumier.

accepted the basic political tenet of liberalism:

To establish the constitution on a firm basis, you [the members of Parliament] must show that you are determined not to be the representatives of a small class or a particular interest, but to form a body who, representing the people, springing from the people, and sympathizing with the people, can fairly call upon the people to support the future burdens of the country. . . .[1]

For middle-class British liberals (often called radicals in the early nineteenth century), the Reform Bill was only the beginning of vast political and economic changes that would inaugurate a golden age. For men like

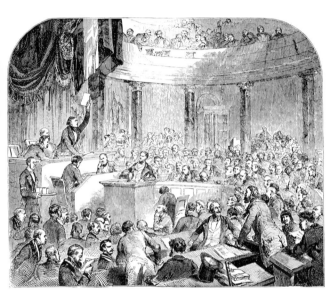

1. *Debates on the Reform Bill*, in F. Marcham and C. Stephenson, eds., *Sources of English Constitutional History.* New York: Harper, 1937, p. 758.

Japanische Tändeleien nach Kappo,

wie die Lasten des Staates gleichmäßig vertheilt sind, um die Krone balanciren zu könn

The Class Struggle in Germany and France. Preventing the realization of liberal ideals on the Continent was the inability of the aristocracy, middle class, and working class to agree on a program of political reform, such as Britain had achieved in 1832. The German situation was quite truthfully depicted by a cartoonist in 1849 (right). The bourgeoisie stand on the prostrate working class; the intransigent Prussian aristocracy and the military lord it over the middle class; and Frederick William IV retains his position at the top of the political and social pyramid. Facing page: Daumier's satirical portrait of Parisian lawyers captures the arrogance and smugness of the French professional middle class. This group had come into its own during the Napoleonic era and continued to flourish in the nineteenth century, as governments rose and fell. Middle-class intellectuals in France detested the bourgeoisie from which they came; Daumier's paintings—and the contemporary novels of Gustave Flaubert and other writers—express this hostility.

Richard Cobden, the Manchester industrialist and politician, free trade —which was instituted in the late 1840's—would not only liberate the industrial skills of middle-class entrepreneurs and bring greater prosperity to the working class but also launch an era of international harmony and peace. Nineteenth-century liberals hated war and militarism, which they looked upon as the agency of the now superseded *ancien régime*. There was a very prominent utopian strain in the liberal ethos as formulated by Cobden in 1846:

I believe that the effect [of free trade] will be to change the face of the world, so as to introduce a system of government entirely distinct from that which now prevails. I believe that the desire and the motive for large and mighty empires; for gigantic armies and great navies—for those materials which are used for the destruction of life and the desolation of the rewards of labour—will die away; I believe that such things will cease to be necessary, or to be used, when man becomes one family, and freely exchanges the fruits of his labour with his brother man.[2]

The liberals believed that the new era of human freedom demanded the abolition of religious privilege along with political and economic privilege. They

2. *Speeches by Richard Cobden, M. P.*, in A. Bullock and M. Schock, eds., *The Liberal Tradition*. New York: New York University Press, 1957, p. 53.

THE RAILWAY—FIRST CLASS.

SECOND CLASS.

THIRD CLASS.

called for an end to the religious test for public office and for entry into the universities and for the disestablishment of the Church of England—in this respect following the example of the authors of the American Constitution. The disassociation of politics and religion was largely achieved in England by 1830; free entry into the universities came in 1871; the disestablishment of the Anglican Church has not yet occurred. But the liberals kept up a constant

A PETERLOO MEDAL.

Q. " Am I not a man and a brother ?"
J. " No !—you are a poor weaver !!!"

battle on this issue and gradually gained wide acceptance of their view that the modern state must be secular, that it must allow equal rights to all religious groups. John Bright, a Manchester political leader and a devout Nonconformist, was one of the most vociferous exponents of this liberal principle: "England with her free press, her advancing civilization, her daily and hourly progress in the arts, sciences, industry, and morals, will withstand any priestly attempt to subjugate the mind . . . ."[3] This anticlerical attitude was central to nineteenth-century liberalism and was

3. *Speeches by John Bright, M. P.*, ed. J. Rogers, in *The Liberal Tradition*, pp. 74-75.

The Class Struggle in Britain. The Industrial Revolution modified the British class structure, but centuries-old habits of authority and deference were often intensified by the advent of modern society. The earliest British railroads offered three classes of carriages corresponding to the threefold division of society. Facing page: first, second, and third class on a British railroad in 1847; lords, bourgeoisie, and proletariat are headed for a day at the Epsom Races. The upper bourgeoisie sent their children to the venerable, aristocratic "public" schools, which trained the new generation in the style of life and speech of the landed class and facilitated intermarriage between the landed and the industrial baronage in the late nineteenth century. British workers, meanwhile, tried to improve their condition by political and trade union action. Above: a cartoon depicting the gentry massacring working-class political activists at "Peterloo," Manchester, in 1819. Right: a trade union protest meeting in 1834.

Europe at the Barricades. The failure of Continental countries to solve the problems raised by nationalism and industrial society resulted in resorts to armed insurrection, on the tempting model of the French Revolution. In 1830 the French bourgeoisie drove out the reactionary Bourbons, and in 1848–1849 there were national, middle-class, proletarian, and peasant risings all over Continental Europe. Facing page, bottom: the July Revolution of 1830 in Paris. Right: government troops storming the barricades erected by insurgent workers during the Paris rising of June 1848. Tocqueville remarked that this insurrection differed from previous rebellions in France in that "it did not aim at changing the form of government, but at altering the order of society. It was a struggle of class against class." The insurgents' slogans were "Abolition of the exploitation of man by man" and "Bread and work, or death." Facing page, top: the peasant rising in Moravia, 1849.

even more important in French and German liberalism than it was in the British liberal tradition, because of the more intransigent hostility of the Catholic Church and many of the Protestant churches on the Continent to the idea of the secular state.

At the heart of the liberal creed was the belief that the individual should be free not only from oppression but also from government and society itself. Early nineteenth-century liberalism was synonymous with individualism; it brought together all those radical affirmations of the emancipation of the individual from tradition, authority, and society that were imbedded in Renaissance humanism, in Protestantism, in the philosophy of the Enlightenment, and in Romanticism. The most eloquent spokesman for liberal individualism was John Stuart Mill. A logician, economist, and political theorist of a very high order, Mill played an important role in most of the reform movements of his era. Mill's treatise *On Liberty* (1859) was to be the classic formulation of liberal individualism, but his views were already clearly enunciated in 1848 in *Principles of Political Economy:*

No society in which eccentricity is a matter of reproach can be in a wholesome state . . . . There is a circle around every individual human being which no government, be it that of the one, of a few, or of the many, ought to be permitted to overstep . . . . There was never more necessity for surrounding individual independence of thought, speech, and conduct, with the most powerful defenses, in order to maintain that originality of mind and individuality of character, which are the only source of any real progress, and of most of the qualities which make the human race much superior to any herd of animals.[4]

It was in connection with this principle of individualism that liberalism began to encounter problems and contradictions that would later in the century challenge its claim to be the liberating and progressive philosophy in European culture. In the 1830's and the 1840's there was a persistent demand by humanitarians and working-class leaders that the British government interfere with the free operation of the economic market so as to protect the workers from the worst ravages of the Industrial Revolution—in other words, that it control the untrammeled individualism of business entrepreneurs. An additional cloud on the horizon, which Mill (and Tocqueville in France) clearly saw, was that a democracy was not necessarily more conducive to freedom of thought and expression than an autocracy and that the tyranny of the majority could well replace the tyranny exercised by the privileged few.

Liberalism slowly accommodated itself to the need for state limitation of laissez faire in the interests of the working class. In 1848 Mill condemned "communism," but later he became a moderate socialist. As to the tension between the masses and the intellectual elite—this problem liberalism never clearly resolved. Liberals hoped that the masses could be educated to respect and appreciate what Mill called "eccentricity"—that is, nonconformity in speech, manner, and thought—and this is still the liberal faith.

In the ultimate moment of crisis, such as the occasion of a popular war which he nevertheless deemed unjust and irrational, the liberal stood firm and insisted that the right of individual conscience took precedence over the will of the majority. This was the stand that John Bright took in 1854, when the outbreak of the Crimean War vitiated the liberal dream of an era of permanent peace and international brotherhood. His statement expresses the courage and glory of nineteenth-century liberalism:

No respect for men who form a Government, no regard I have for "going with the stream," and no fear of being deemed wanting in patriotism, shall influence me in favor of a policy which, in my conscience, I believe to be as criminal before God as it is destructive of the true interest of my country.[5]

4. John Stuart Mill, *Principles of Political Economy*, in *The Liberal Tradition*, pp. 62-64.
5. *Speeches by John Bright, M. P.*, in *The Liberal Tradition*, p. 83.

CHAPTER 7

Realism and Scientism

I THE WORSHIP OF SCIENCE AND TECHNOLOGY

The Crystal Palace

The disintegration of the Romantic movement, the failure of the revolutions of 1848, and the steady pace of industrialization and urbanization all contributed to a significant change in higher culture and thought in the years between 1848 and 1870. The period was characterized by widespread enthusiasm for the methods and the accomplishments of science, technology, mechanics, and organized research. The leading European thinkers of the 1850's and 1860's abandoned the Romantic quest for the absolute in favor of critical analysis and scientism.

Scientism can be defined as the desire or the effort to apply the techniques used in the natural sciences to all aspects of life. Since scientists had been remarkably successful in discovering the physical laws of the natural universe and predicting the behavior of natural phenomena, Europeans at mid-century asked why scientific methods could not be applied to man himself in order to achieve a "realistic" understanding of his biological and psychological nature, his society, and his economic and political systems.

Science was firmly joined to technology in the second half of the nineteenth century, and the fruits of the union were everywhere apparent: railroads were stretching across Europe and North America, iron and steel were replacing wood and brick, and complicated machines were enriching their owners and producing a variety of new and exciting products for consumption by the affluent, growing middle class. The Suez Canal, built between 1856 and 1869, was more than a political and commercial achievement; it was a feat of engineering that would not have been possible fifty years before. In the Victorian Age it was difficult *not* to believe that hard work and scientific techniques could solve all problems, human as well as material.

The Crystal Palace, a towering structure of iron and glass built for the Great Exhibition of 1851, seemed to represent the very spirit of the Victorian Age, for here the common elements of the earth were translated by study, work, and human ingenuity into a monument to science and prosperity. It was built, within a few short months, of prefabricated, interchangeable parts. Its chief designer, Sir Joseph Paxton, had once been a gardener. His rise to eminence through intelligence and hard work made him the very prototype of the middle-class hero, the self-made man.

The Palace was the focal point of the Great Exhibition, which was intended to bring together the finest examples of scientific and manufacturing achievement. This it accomplished, leaving little doubt that Britain led the world in material progress. More than six million people visited the exhibition, including large numbers of British workingmen, but it remained a peaceful festival at which capitalist and worker alike could congratulate themselves on their accomplishments and speculate on the glorious future.

The exhibition had the enthusiastic support of the royal family—the prince consort was its chief sponsor—and this relationship was entirely appropriate, for the dominant industrial bourgeois class found its natural leaders in Victoria and Albert, whose court was an upper-middle-class household on a royal scale. The virtues of the royal couple were those most admired by the middle class: decency, hard work, and devotion to duty. Neither aristocratic idlers nor wild-eyed radicals were encouraged by the queen, and the prince's deep attachment to learning and science was entirely characteristic of the educated bourgeois.

The success of the British international fair encouraged imitation, and within the next decades there were similar expositions in almost every Western country. The United States built its own Crystal Palace in New York in 1853—most unsuccessfully; the roof leaked and the investors lost money. France had an important exposition in 1855 and another in 1867, but though these were successful and stimulated international competition in manufactures and technology, none attained the symbolic stature of the Great Exhibition, which had seemed to inaugurate the new era of scientific attainment and progress.

The Second Scientific Revolution

The accomplishments of science between 1848 and 1870 amply justified its public image. Both the theoretical advances and their application to industrial and human problems were so notable that the period has been described as a second scientific revolution, comparable to that of the seventeenth century. The intellectual process by which natural science had been divided into several distinct disciplines—such as physics, chemistry, biology, and geology — was intensified in the first half of the nineteenth century. But now advances in one science influenced others; international exchange of information was extensive, thanks to the growth of scientific journals and the rapid communication for which science itself was responsible. Improvements in instruments and techniques kept pace with progress in ideas, and in Germany, at least, the development of the universities provided scientists with professional training as well as with laboratories and equipment.

In physics and mechanics, nineteenth-century scientists took a giant theoretical step away from the Newtonian system, and in these same fields they formed the closest and most fruitful alliance with industry. In England, experiments by Michael Faraday (1791 – 1867) established the concept of lines of magnetic force and proved that electricity and magnetism are "convertible into each other." James Clerk Maxwell (1831 – 1879) built on Faraday's experiments to provide the theoretical basis for the electromagnetic theory of light and accounted for the attraction and repulsion of magnetic bodies in terms of forces produced by the action of a field, departing from the "hard, massy particles" of Newton's universe. Maxwell did not attempt to say what electricity *is*; he described how it worked, using physical and mathematical analogy.

The basic principles of thermodynamics had been established in the 1830's, but scientists of the 1850's and 1860's were able to make significant advances in the field. Newly discovered laws governing the relationship between heat energy and mechanical energy were basic to modern physics and engineering and crucial to the provision of power for industry and engines for transportation and manufacture. The study of organic chemistry was also particularly well suited to a materialistic era. Scientists' attempts to separate matter into its chemical components resulted in the development of such new products as artificial fertilizers, dyes, rubber, and explosives. Biochemistry was developed as a scientific specialty during these years, while biology itself became the revolutionary science of the century with the work of Charles Darwin. Even before Darwin, biology and geology had captured the attention of a broad segment of the educated public — amateur naturalists and fossil hunters were fascinated by speculation about the age of the earth and the development of plant, animal, and human life.

Louis Pasteur (1822 – 1895), the French chemist, did most of his important work in the third quarter of the century, even though some of his basic principles were not accepted until later. Studying yeasts, he traced the process of fermentation to the presence of microscopic "germs' and went on to prove experimentally that these same microorganisms are present in ordinary air as well. The English surgeon Joseph Lister (1827 – 1912) carried Pasteur's principles into the operating room when he insisted upon antiseptic surgical procedures, with dramatic implications for medical practice and hospital mortality rates. Pasteur rescued the French silk industry by isolating the bacilli of various diseases of the silkworm and then joined his efforts to those of Robert Koch (1843–1910) of Germany to isolate the anthrax bacillus and produce a workable vaccine against the disease. Pasteur's work on rabies and the first successful inoculation of a child who had been infected by a rabid dog assured the acceptance of the germ theory of disease, with incalculable results for human life expectancy.

Education and Scholarship

The mid-nineteenth century was the great age of university organization. Though the major impulse for this movement came from science, scholarship in every branch of knowledge benefited. Old universities were expanded and reformed, and new kinds of schools and new fields of study began to develop.

In science, particularly on the Continent, the gifted amateur was giving way to the trained professional. As scientific apparatus became more sophisticated and more expensive, as research techniques were developed and the body of existing knowledge expanded, it was no longer possible for a gentleman to become a scientist through self-education at home in his leisure time; formal instruction and well-equipped laboratories were essential. In addition, industry required trained technicians to understand its new machines, as well as skilled workmen to operate them.

Germany was preeminent in providing education to meet the needs of science. There, eminent scientists and scholars were almost always attached to universities, and university teaching was improved by the development of the seminar system. Due in part to the intimate involvement of the state in the educational process at every level, German libraries and laboratories were the best in the world. New universities—particularly in the United States—were modeled on the German universities, and German became the language of scientific and scholarly communication. Between the 1840's and the 1870's, Germany rose to the top rank in industry and manufacture primarily through the excellence of its technical education.

In Great Britain the government stayed out of education until after 1870, and only a few iconoclasts like the prince consort (a German) challenged the traditional preeminence of classical education. The objective of the best British education remained the training of cultured gentlemen. In the 1850's the British civil service was reformed, and admission to the bureaucracy began to be determined by competitive examination; but the nature of the examinations was such that the best preparation for them was the classical and philosophical training provided by Oxford and Cambridge. Thus the formal education of the men who governed the British Empire remained focused on Plato and Cicero. France had an uneven educational system, with a few outstanding schools (such as the *École Polytechnique*); overall, it was in no way comparable to the German system.

Germany led the world in scholarship of all kinds, not in science alone. This period, for example, saw the founding of the great German schools of

During the eighteenth century the old medieval universities were generally moribund and played only a small role in intellectual life. But by the late nineteenth century, universities were becoming the main centers of scientific research, humanistic learning, and training for the professions and the civil service. Germany took the lead in this academicization of thought, and after the middle of the century the French universities also underwent a renaissance, followed by the English universities after 1870. Many new universities were founded, usually with government support, and professors were accorded a high social status.

Biblical history and criticism. In the so-called higher criticism of the 1850's scholars applied the "scientific" methods of philological and textual criticism to the Scriptures, assuming in the spirit of the age that theological questions could be answered by extensive research and a scientific approach. Earlier, in 1835, David Friedrich Strauss had analyzed the various Gospels as if the Bible were any ancient text, and the popular furor that his work aroused was echoed in 1863 with the publication of Ernest Renan's *Life of Jesus*. Although much less scholarly, Renan's work was widely read and attracted public attention to the school of higher criticism.

Biblical studies and textual criticism helped stimulate the expansion in historical scholarship in the 1850's. An increasing interest in modern history produced discussion among historians as to the definition of historical periods, particularly the dividing line between the medieval period and the modern. The concept of the Renaissance was first fully expressed in 1860 by the Swiss historian Jacob Burckhardt in his *Civilization of the Renaissance in Italy*. This was no dry collection of data but an exciting, interpretative work which defined the Renaissance as a political, social, and cultural phenomenon that began in Italy during the fourteenth century. Through such studies in the past, nineteenth-century scholars hoped to find the sources of their remarkable present.

The search for a usable past was conducted by scholars armed with the critical methods developed by the early nineteenth-century German school of historians; it was supported by governments wishing to foster national sentiment. In Britain, France, and Germany, governments subsidized scholars who edited medieval documents, and chairs were founded in the universities to reward and maintain historians who would write imposing accounts of the national past and train young scholars in scientific methods and nationalist interpretations. In Germany a host of historians expounded the glories of the medieval Holy Roman Empire and, going further back, analyzed the institutions of the barbarian German tribes. Since many of these historians were middle-class liberals, their discovery that the inhabitants of the primeval German forests were freemen who made communal decisions in pristine parliaments is not surprising. The greatest of the French scholars, Fustel de Coulanges, demonstrated to the satisfaction of his countrymen that the origins of French institutions lay in the late Roman Empire, rather than in Germany. At Oxford, William Stubbs propounded a Germanic origin for cherished English institutions. In a magisterial three-volume work, he portrayed the whole constitutional development of medieval England. Thomas Macaulay, a liberal civil servant and man of letters, described in colorful manner the struggle for liberty against Stuart despotism in the late seventeenth century, and George Bancroft similarly recounted the rise of freedom in the United States. Never before, and perhaps never since, did the work of historians have such a wide audience as in the 1850's and 1860's. In leading Western countries, historians gave to nationalist and liberal dogmas an impressive and apparently secure scientific foundation in the experience of the past.

II THE SOCIAL SCIENCES

Positivism

The general term *positivism* can be used to describe any philosophy that concerns itself with observable phenomena rather than metaphysical speculation. Since the laws of physical nature can be ascertained by research and rational thought, some men reasoned, these methods should be efficacious in determining the laws that govern human nature, psychological or social. The founder of the special doctrine of positivism, in the sense of a specific philosophy, was Auguste Comte (1798–1857), a French philosopher. Once the laws of human association had been established, Comte believed, it would be possible to adjust social, political, and economic systems to conform to human capabilities and requirements. Comte himself aspired to participate in the adjustment.

Although Comte relied heavily on the work of earlier thinkers, including his mentor Saint-Simon, he is known as the founder of sociology and gave the discipline its name. His special contributions were his law of three stages and his classification of the sciences. He believed that all human societies develop through three stages: the theological, based on primitive anthropomorphism; the philosophical, based on metaphysical abstraction; and the scientific, based on natural laws. The sciences can be classified from the simplest and most general to the most complex: mathematics, astronomy, physics, chemistry, biology, and sociology. Western man, having attained mastery of the first four, had reached the scientific stage of biology in the mid-nineteenth century. Comte believed that he himself had appeared just in time to initiate the last of the sciences—sociology. Despite endless quarrels over his more extreme ideas, Comte exerted a significant influence on contemporary philosophy. His eagerness to apply the scientific method to social problems appealed to many thinkers of the 1850's.

One of Comte's adherents was Herbert Spencer (1820–1903), an outstanding champion of the individual over society and of science over religion. Spencer accepted theories of the early nineteenth-century French naturalist Lamarck, who claimed that organisms adapt to environmental changes. Spencer s *Principles of Psychology* (1855) expressed the belief that human psychology was part of evolutionary biology and that the human nervous system had developed in response to environmental pressures. Spencer began as a railroad engineer, and his sociological opinions reflect the practical approach. In the tradition of Bentham and the British utilitarians, he believed that social institutions exist to be useful to man and that a government that interferes with the liberty of its citizens is worse than no government at all. He also thought that a society became increasingly complex and diverse as it progressed, and he welcomed the professional and scientific specialization that eventually would make careers like his own (from engineer to philosopher) improbable or impossible.

The thought and writings of John Stuart Mill (1806–1873) can be described as positivist in a general sense, but the label is inadequate. Son of the utilitarian James Mill, an influential philosophical radical who struggled against the tide of Romanticism in his own time, John Stuart had a sound classical education before he was twelve and went on to study history, political economy, and utilitarian philosophy. He shared the contemporary passion for system and science; whether he wrote on philosophy, economics, or politics, he strove to achieve a synthesis of human knowledge and to offer "scientific proof" of social and moral theories.

Mill was a great logician, but he is remembered best for the essay *On Liberty*, a lucid exposition of the doctrine of individual freedom. He believed that progress is always accomplished by individuals rather than groups and that men must be free to experiment with progressive ideas if society is to move forward. The free competition of ideas is as essential to a healthy society as the free competition of goods to a healthy economy. Having inherited classical economic theory and utilitarian radicalism from his father's generation, Mill turned them to account in a passionate defense of the rights of individuals and minorities. Fearing the tyranny of the majority, he believed that variety gave life its meaning. Yet Mill could not accept the logical extension of his own position—if man is to be free, he must be free to do evil—and he has been criticized for inconsistency. Mill departed significantly from the principles of utilitarianism and classical economics in his later works. He introduced qualitative and moral considerations into utilitarian philosophy, and favored state action to improve social conditions.

The French historian, critic, and philosopher Hippolyte Adolphe Taine (1823–1893) attempted to apply the strict methods of the natural sciences to historical, psychological, artistic, and metaphysical studies. In the introduction to his *History of English Literature*, Taine emphasized the search for the abstract psychological causes that make history more than a series of events and that should be as accessible to the historian as chemical components are to the chemist: "Vice and virtue are products, like vitriol and sugar; and every complex phenomenon arises from other more simple phenomena on which it depends." By "products," Taine meant the qualities produced by the specific circumstances of race, environment, and time—"*la race, le milieu, le moment*"—which could be computed for any group of people at any point in history. Given sufficient knowledge of these factors, the behavior of a people could be predicted, history being a deterministic process analogous to the computation and prediction of the behavior of objects responding to physical forces in a laboratory. Taine emphasized the historical importance of literary and artistic evidence, claiming that "a great poem, a fine novel, the confessions of a superior man are more instructive than a heap of historians with their histories."

In art and literature as in history, Taine believed, race, time, and environment encourage certain styles and discourage others. The artistic forms of an industrial, democratic society must differ from those of a Christian, feudal society, because an artist expresses the spirit of his own age. A founder of the historical school of art criticism, Taine supported his views with studies of the art of Renaissance Italy, of the early modern Netherlands, and of classical Greece, pointing out the distinctive features produced by physical and psychological circumstances. Pessimistic about the nature of man but hopeful for the future of science, Taine had enormous influence on contemporaries and on later historians and art critics.

Walter Bagehot (1826–1877), an English economist, did not attempt to formulate laws or create a vast system, but he was a careful observer, and his philosophical and political theories grew out of his perceptions of existing social and political circumstances. In one of his major works, *The English*

Constitution (1867), Bagehot emphasized the "deference"—the quiet recognition of social differences—that made the English system work. Like Mill, he prized individual liberty as the only hope for constructive change. Profoundly influenced by Darwin's theories of evolution, Bagehot attempted in *Physics and Politics* (1875) to apply the theory of natural selection to human history, arguing that primitive societies were strengthened by imposed unity and strict law and advanced societies by free competition.

Like Bagehot, Thomas Henry Buckle (1821–1862) believed that English civilization was the finest flower of human history. In the *History of Civilization in England* (1857, 1861), he tried to demonstrate that human progress is governed by principles as regular as those that underlie the physical universe, principles he hoped to establish by inductive reasoning. Buckle equated the progress of civilization with scientific advance. He died too soon to incorporate Darwin's theories of evolution, and his work was soon cast aside for more up-to-date interpretations.

Karl Marx

All the social, economic, and political theorists of the 1850's and 1860's appear as minor thinkers in comparison with Karl Marx, the German philosopher and economist who became the master system-builder of the scientific age. Marx's early career has been discussed in the previous chapter. After the *Communist Manifesto* by Marx and Friedrich Engels appeared in 1848, Marx was expelled from Brussels, where he had been living since 1845. He visited Paris and Germany during the abortive revolutions of that year and witnessed the defeat of the radical idealists. Realizing that the intellectual elite of the revolution had failed to attract and hold mass support, he focused his attention more closely on the education and indoctrination of the working class. After the collapse of the revolutions, Marx found refuge in England and stayed for the rest of his life, in poverty and relative obscurity. Supporting his growing family by free-lance journalism and with contributions from friends and disciples (chiefly Engels), he concentrated on the painstaking, exhaustive studies of society and economics that supported his mature theories. In the Reading Room of the British Museum and in a series of crowded, substandard lodging houses, Marx put together the colossal body of doctrine that bears his name.

The ideas of the early nineteenth-century utopian socialists were denounced by Marx, but many of them survive in Marxist doctrine. Saint-Simon had perceived that a society can be defined by its economic forms; he anticipated Comte's belief that society can be studied with the intellectual tools of science and Marx's concept of class war. Marx's contemporaries and associates in Paris, the French revolutionaries Barbès and Blanqui, advocated violent revolution and the abolition of private property, and their ideas were very influential during the years just before 1848, when the *Communist*

Manifesto was taking shape. Equally influential was Ludwig Feuerbach, whose writings on religion contain the materialistic view of human thought that is intrinsic to Marxist doctrines. Marx was also greatly indebted to British economic theorists — particularly David Ricardo, who had stressed the conflict between the interests of landlords, capitalists, and labor. Marx's system incorporated many of the prevailing ideas of his century.

Toward the end of his life, Marx became well known in European socialist circles, if not to his neighbors in London. He was active in the First International Workingmen's Association, or First International, founded in 1864, and saw it come to grief through internal philosophical and political dissension. Marx died before Marxists achieved a position of power in any country. He spent the latter part of his life arguing against earlier forms of socialism, anarchism, and political opportunism within the workers' movement. His was a crabbed, difficult nature made bitter by poverty and arrogant through conviction of the rightness of his cause. His ideas are among the most dynamic in Western intellectual history.

Historical Materialism

Marx departed radically from romantic or utopian socialism in many respects but most particularly in the assertion that human history is determined by economic development. He regarded himself as the first "scientific" socialist; like several other social thinkers of the period, he believed that philosophical ideas and social structures are governed by natural laws as regular and inexorable as those of the physical universe. The social, political, and ethical institutions and values of a society are determined by the changing relationship of its members to the means of production and distribution. Out of that relationship arise all the complex institutions and creeds that make a society what it is.

Unlike earlier socialists, Marx — in his mature years — did not urge reform out of humanitarianism or democratic idealism. He appealed instead to reason. Through the study of social and economic forces, he believed, one could predict the future, and a reasonable man would cast in his lot with history because (in Hegelian fashion) its course is inevitable — not because he wished to do good. Detesting sentiment and democratic idealism, Marx cast aside the doctrine of the natural rights of man as merely a philosophical disguise for the class interest of the rising bourgeoisie in removing the legal obstacles to its power. He avoided moral argument in his writings after 1848. Instead of appealing to man's better nature or conscience, he sought proof in the objective facts of economics and history. Marx was convinced that the economic interests of the various social groups are incompatible, and he considered the belief that well-intentioned men of different classes may agree a harmful delusion.

To Marx, history revealed the pattern of class conflict: one class gains control and exploits others; in time, oppressed groups rise up and take possession on the basis of new techniques of production and distribution. Just as the capitalistic bourgeoisie displaced the feudal aristocracy, the communistic industrial proletariat will displace the bourgeoisie. When the proletariat achieves full control and imposes its will on the rest of society, a new era of history will begin — in a classless society. The transition from the dictatorship of the proletariat to the classless society was not very clearly described by Marx, who was more interested in the achievement of the penultimate stage, and it remains a source of ambiguity and dissension in Communist thought. What is essential to Marxist theory is the doctrine of inevitability: the class war has followed and will follow its prescribed course, and all a man can do is develop proletarian class-consciousness, the indispensable preliminary to the proletarian revolution.

Although Marx attacked the industrial bourgeoisie and laissez-faire capitalism at the very height of their power, he thought that he could perceive the potential weakness of the capitalist system. Capital accumulates and concentrates, he believed, until society is completely and intolerably polarized. Like fallen systems of the past, capitalism held the seeds of its own destruction. From Hegelian philosophy, Marx derived an underlying idea of violent, creative change through continual conflict. To Hegel, the nation, or the national idea, operated as the creative force in history; to Marx, creative forces were entirely material; the sources of conflict and change should be sought in economic relationships. Marx was convinced that his study of social data proved that capitalism would inevitably collapse as a result of economic forces already at work. Conflicts between employers and workers would increase with the growth of capital, as would the relative number of workers, who would explode capitalism at its apogee by expropriating their expropriators, collectively seizing the means of production and distribution.

Marxist Economic Theories

The first volume of Marx's major work, *Das Kapital* (Capital), appeared in 1867. He made extensive notes for the remainder, and these were edited and completed by Engels and others after his death. Marx wrote *Das Kapital* to provide the factual basis for his economic and social theories. Throughout his life he emphasized study, research, and learning; his passion for fact made him a true representative of his time. Accurate information about the actual working of economic laws in society was essential to Marxist doctrine, which in intention was not romantic speculation but a scientific exposition of things as they were. According to Marx, earlier economists had assumed that economic laws, like physical laws, remain the same in all circumstances. Marx perceived that economic laws evolve with the state of technology and the mode of production at any given moment in history. In *Das Kapital*, he focused on the economic and social conditions produced by the Industrial Revolution, which had created new economic relationships and new classes to engage in the inevitable class war. He pointed up the connection between the development of technological means of production and the appearance of the proletariat, and he discussed in detail the periodic economic crises of capitalism—inevitable forerunners of the self-destruction of the system.

Marx's basic economic theories build upon those of classical economists such as David Ricardo and Adam Smith. He accepted their labor theory of value, which states that the commercial value of any commodity is established by the number of man-hours required to produce it. Under capitalism, the worker himself becomes a commodity; he—that is, his productive capacity—can be bought and sold like any material object. The political and religious institutions of capitalist society are organized to permit the capitalist class to profit from the surplus created by the workers, and this legalized exploitation of labor is the foundation—the root relationship—of contemporary industrial society.

Various elements of Marxist theory have provided generations of Communists and socialists with the stuff of debate and argument. Marx was not always clear, nor did he prove to be right about the subsequent development of industrial society. His social and historical doctrine awkwardly combines scientific analysis with apocalyptic myth. The Communist revolution finally came, not in the most advanced (i.e., decadent) capitalist society, but in underdeveloped czarist Russia, a country Marx considered helplessly retrograde. Nevertheless, *Das Kapital* is a watershed in the history of economic and social thought.

III DARWINISM

Charles Darwin and The Origin of Species

While Marx was working out his monumental analysis of capitalism in the British Museum, not far away Charles Darwin was formulating the most important new theory in natural science since the Newtonian era. Marx and Darwin were the two great system-makers who laid the foundation for the intellectual history of the later nineteenth century. While Marxism did not command wide attention until the 1880's, Darwin achieved enormous renown immediately upon the publication of his major work.

Charles Darwin (1809–1882) was born to a middle-class English family of agnostic and Nonconforming intelligentsia. His grandfather, Erasmus Darwin, had been a well-known physician with a profound interest in biology and in theories of evolution. Charles grew up in the atmosphere of free thought and scientific curiosity that was fairly common in prosperous middle-class households in the early nineteenth century. He was sent first to

Edinburgh to be trained in medicine—for which he had neither aptitude nor enthusiasm—and then to Cambridge to prepare for the ministry, which was considered a suitable career for a young man without special talent or ambition. In both universities he attached himself to groups of students and professors who shared the intense interest in geology and fossil hunting that was a current fad among affluent amateur scientists.

Before Darwin could settle down in a country parsonage, as he planned to do, he was invited to attach himself as an unpaid naturalist to a round-the-world scientific expedition on H.M.S. *Beagle*. The voyage, which began in 1831 and lasted for five years, transformed an enthusiastic amateur into a scientist and laid the factual groundwork for the theory of natural selection. The young naturalist was "much struck with certain facts in the distribution of the organic beings inhabiting South America, and in the geological relations of the present to the past inhabitants of that continent." He observed the differences and similarities of related plant and animal forms in different latitudes; he witnessed an earthquake and its dramatic effect on the crust of the earth; he visited the Galápagos Islands and found the indigenous fauna dominated by reptile forms distinct from yet related to mainland forms and to reptile forms on other islands in the Pacific. He collected fossils wherever he went, but it was not until he got them home and identified them that he began to relate them to living animals.

When Darwin returned to England in 1836, he prepared his extensive notes and journal for publication and won the attention and assistance of the English scientific community. He became the secretary of the Geological Society and a close friend of Sir Charles Lyell, the leading geologist of the period, who had delineated a theory of the evolution of the earth. With notebooks crammed with objective data and a mind filled with wonder at the variety of life, and with the benefit of hypotheses propounded by Lyell and by his grandfather, Darwin began to work his material into a scientific theory. He did so primarily by study and discussion with practical men—gardeners and animal breeders whose business was selection and alteration in plant and animal species.

In 1838 Darwin read Malthus' *Essay on the Principle of Population* and was struck by its description of the "struggle for existence" that controlled potentially explosive human populations. Within the next few years, he transformed the Malthusian struggle into a great systematic natural law that explained both the similarity and the diversity of plant and animal species. The concept of evolution itself was widely accepted in scientific circles long before Darwin. Geology revealed the development of species as well as the age of the earth. But it did not explain how or why changes occurred. Lamarck, among others, had defied the traditional religious view of fixed species (created once and for all by the Lord when the earth began), but Lamarck had believed that animal species changed—almost purposively—in direct response to environmental conditions and transmitted the changes to their offspring. Darwin did not object to this inheritance of acquired characteristics, but he saw that purposive adaptation to environmental changes was not sufficient to explain variation of species, particularly in plants.

By 1842 Darwin had made a sketch or outline of his theory of evolution through natural selection. He was in no hurry to publish it. Plagued by poor health, he spent the next sixteen years gathering and studying facts to support and fill out his hypothesis. He trained himself in zoology (including an eight-year digression into the study of barnacles), anatomy, botany, and animal breeding. His friends kept urging him to publish his ideas, but Darwin would not be hurried. In 1858 he received a manuscript from a young naturalist then on an expedition to Malaya. The author, Alfred Russel Wallace, had arrived independently at the theory of natural selection. Honorably, Darwin forwarded the manuscript to the Linnaean Society, where it was read together with an abstract of Darwin's 1842 outline. The joint reading attracted little attention, but Darwin was spurred to finish his book. In November 1859 he published *On the Origin of Species by Means of Natural Selection, or the Preservation of Favoured Races in the Struggle for Life*

Since evolutionary theories were well accepted before Darwin wrote, what is the significance of his work? Natural selection is the key. In Darwin's theory, favorable variations that arise at random in plant or animal forms tend to be preserved because they confer on their owners an advantage in the struggle for existence—the continual competition within a species for sustenance and survival. Lamarck had claimed that a giraffe elongated its neck by stretching to reach the leaves at the top of the tree and passed on that acquired characteristic to its offspring; Darwin believed that those giraffes which had longer necks than their fellows tended to survive and thus to reproduce that characteristic in their offspring. Less-favored strains tended to die out, and thus competition shaped a species. Darwin borrowed from Herbert Spencer the phrase "survival of the fittest" to characterize the process; he saw "no evidence of beneficent design, or indeed of design of any kind, in the details."

Darwin perceived that the struggle which forms a species takes place primarily within that species—its members in competition with one another. While Lamarck believed that adaptation was a function of response to environment, Darwin made competition the forming agent. This seemed to answer the questions posed by the existence of similar forms in very different environments and different forms in very similar environments—for example, animal forms isolated on separate islands. Darwin had observed what growers and breeders could do with domestic plants and animals by artificial selection for one chosen (favored) characteristic. Natural selection does the same thing on a much larger scale, and it has almost all of geologic time in which to work.

Darwin's view of the process of inheritance did not go much beyond that of Lamarck. Like most of his contemporaries, he believed that characteristics were inherited through "blending"—for example, a tall parent and a short parent produce a medium-size offspring. Knowing nothing of mutations, he made no attempt to explain why variations arise in the first place, leaving an enormous gap in his theory. (Religious fundamentalists often filled it by asserting divine interference.) Although Darwin never knew it, the problem of heredity was solved in his own lifetime. While the fight over natural selection raged in England, an Austrian monk named Gregor Mendel (1822–1884) was performing experiments with garden peas that eventually became the basis of modern genetics. Mendel discovered the basic principles of heredity on which evolution depends, refuting the theory of the "blending" of parental characteristics. He realized that discrete characteristics are inherited in units (now known as genes) and that this process occurs according to mathematically describable laws. Although the results of Mendel's experiments were published in 1865, they attracted no attention until the beginning of the twentieth century.

The Darwinian Controversy

The first edition of *The Origin of Species* sold out at once, and it soon became obvious that its publication was a major scientific and philosophical event. It was a solid, well-reasoned work that appealed to the growing educated class, many of them amateur scientists. Materialistic philosophy had cleared the way for an evolutionary theory based on the impersonal interplay of matter and natural forces, and positivism demanded that biology reach its definitive, scientific stage so that sociology could progress in its wake. It could be said, in fact, that many thinkers were already prejudiced in favor of natural selection. Further, even in 1859 the Victorians had a well-publicized record of religious doubt; a large number of educated people were ready and willing to cast off revelation and follow science wherever it led.

Yet Darwin did not have it all his own way. A tremendous protest arose along with the applause. Even though the *Origin* itself dealt with plant and animal species and not with man, Darwin's supporters and adversaries alike applied the theory at once to human evolution. The opposition to Darwin was of two quite different varieties, but both were concerned with the evolution of man.

Official and unofficial representatives of organized religion, particularly those of the Protestant faith, opposed Darwin singly and collectively. Many believing Christians feared the loss of man's unique position on the earth as profoundly as their counterparts in the sixteenth century had feared the loss of earth's unique position in the heavens. While not every believer insisted that the day and hour of Creation could be named, there were many who resisted the idea of man's origin in the primal ooze. Notable among the religious opponents of Darwinism was Samuel Wilberforce, bishop of Oxford, whose scathing review of the *Origin* provoked the biologist T. H. Huxley,

Darwin's self-appointed defender, to reply in a famous debate. With supposedly crushing sarcasm, Wilberforce asked Huxley whether it was through his grandfather or his grandmother that he was descended from monkeys, and this attitude survived in many parts of the world long after natural selection was accepted by the scientific community.

Despite its vehemence and persistence, the fundamentalist opposition to Darwin was intellectually and philosophically less significant than the opposition that arose among those who resisted what they considered to be the degradation of man. Romantics and philosophical idealists resented the denial of man's unique soul. Within the scientific community, Darwinism became a kind of generation symbol, with younger men acclaiming the new theory and older men skeptical of its novelty and concerned about the security of entrenched ideas. Whatever the opposition, however, natural selection was widely accepted within one decade. After all, there was little to challenge it (except revealed Creation). No other scientific theory approached *The Origin of Species* in scope, factual backing, or reasoned argument.

Most of the arguments over natural selection turned on the origin of *homo sapiens*, although no theory of human evolution was put forward in the *Origin*. Darwin's adherents took up the subject because that was the issue raised by the Church, by representatives of the intellectual community, and by the general public. Huxley and Wallace propounded theories of human evolution, concentrating at first on man's body rather than his mind. Huxley wrote of the "missing link" between man and his distant ancestors that he hoped to establish. Wallace declared that man's development had been controlled by natural selection until his brain reached a certain critical size, at which time he was freed by reason to take charge of his own progress; physical change ended when natural selection ceased to operate. The "most favored races," he felt, assured human progress by competing successfully with the weaker and less fit.

Darwin joined the argument in 1871 with the publication of *Descent of Man and Selection in Relation to Sex*. The new book was less forceful than the *Origin*, not as thoroughly documented and well reasoned. Darwin hoped to put social science on a biological basis, but he wrote very cautiously in order to avoid offending religious believers (and discovered that the climate of opinion had changed so much since 1859 that he could have been more daring). Darwin believed that human morality had developed through social institutions favorable to survival. Characteristics like loyalty and altruism helped a tribe or a community to maintain its existence in the face of competition. Darwin assumed that moral and cultural progress had always accompanied the advance of technology and always would—that the race would grow better as it grew more sophisticated. He never gave up his belief in progress. He did not accept Wallace's ideas of racial superiority (at least he did not believe in the necessary *moral* superiority of those who survived), but he could not shake off the vision of Sydney Harbor in Australia—a bustling, progressive port in a continent peopled with dying aborigines. Darwin perceived a danger in removing through social progress the spur of competition that had made Western man such a complex and successful creature.

In Darwin's later works the concept of sexual selection played an increasingly important role. He explained the apparently useless tail feathers of certain male birds as variations that tended to attract the female and thus assure reproduction, and he extended this concept to human and racial differentiation. He began to rely more and more on Lamarck's ideas of adaptation through use, departing considerably from the theory of natural selection—but by then that theory had permeated almost every field of scientific and social philosophy.

Science and Religion

Although Darwin's theory of evolution clearly confronted theologians and religious leaders with a new problem, it would be a mistake to imagine that widespread conflict between science and religion racked the Western world. The cataclysmic effect the *Origin* is supposed to have had on Christianity was much exaggerated by late nineteenth-century controversialists and early twentieth-century historians. Once the initial shock wave had passed, many believers—theologians and clergy as well as laymen of most Protestant denominations—sought to reconcile Darwinism and religion wherever they appeared to collide. Some found the theory of evolution a marvelous confirmation of the glory of God manifest in nature, and many were willing to accept a Divinity who had created a few simple forms and left them to evolve into an incredible variety of complex species. Men who still wanted to believe could look for God in natural laws instead of in unnatural miracles. Although some of its spokesmen initially launched vigorous attacks on the new science, the Church of England came to realize that there was no irreconcilable conflict between Darwinism and Christianity, and Darwin was buried in Westminster Abbey.

The relationship between Darwinism and Christianity must be understood in a broad context. From the early decades of the nineteenth century, all traditional religious groups were threatened by the spread of liberal, secular culture. An even greater challenge than Darwinian science had been posed by the higher criticism of the Bible, which called into question the historicity of the Old and New Testaments. Furthermore, the advance of industrialization and urbanization had so expanded the possibilities for material accomplishment and enjoyment that many people had simply lost interest in a life directed by traditional dogma. In both Europe and America a significant decline in the churches' influence had occurred by the 1860's. At the same time, various religious groups were beginning to disagree about the response believers should make to the new liberal, scientific culture.

The Church of England and most Protestant groups slowly but steadily accommodated themselves to intellectual and social change. If they were tardy and inconsistent in confronting the social injustice caused by the Industrial Revolution, they were generally quick to seek a reconciliation of science and theism. But there were exceptions: a small group in the Church of England, taking its inspiration from the Oxford movement of the 1830's, continued to express hostility toward contemporary scientific and secularized culture, and the Baptists and some Methodists and Lutherans remained fundamentalist, rejecting both the higher criticism of the Bible and the new science in favor of a simple faith in the literal text of the Bible. In western Europe and the United States, a split gradually developed between Orthodox (traditional) Judaism and Liberal or Reform Judaism, which eagerly accommodated itself to new social and scientific ideas. Significantly, Liberal Judaism gained its adherents among wealthy Jews who felt emancipated from ghetto culture and moved freely in society.

It was in the Roman Catholic Church that the issue of the relationship between modern thought and traditional faith became most crucial. In the post-Napoleonic period, the Church had tended to ally itself with the forces of reaction. In 1832 the papacy condemned liberty of conscience, freedom of the press, and revolution against authority. Early in the pontificate of Pius IX (1846–1878), it appeared that the Roman Church was moving toward an accommodation with the new political and intellectual trends; but Pius was driven from Rome in 1848 by republican radicals, and in the 1860's the Papal States were lost to the newly united Italian state. Following these indignities, Pius became extremely hostile to the whole thrust of European political and intellectual life. Not only Darwinism but nearly every other aspect of modern liberal and rational thought was condemned by the pope's *Syllabus of Errors* in 1864. At the same time, the papacy sought to harden belief in medieval Catholic tradition as a bulwark against the growing secularism of the age. The Immaculate Conception of the Virgin Mary was made a dogma in 1854, and papal infallibility became an absolute article of faith by ruling of the Vatican Council in 1870. This latter decision was designed to remove any doubt that the pope could legislate for every Catholic on moral, social, and political issues.

This extremely conservative stance of the papacy was by no means universally favored by Catholics. Especially in Britain and Germany, many liberal Catholic intellectuals—such as the eminent historian Lord Acton—fought vigorously against the reactionary policies and particularly the doctrine of papal infallibility. Pius IX's intransigent hostility to liberalism and science greatly enhanced the influence of ultramontane (conservative) groups within the Church in each country. The ultramontanes were invariably political reactionaries, often monarchists and intellectual obscurantists. Thus the Roman Church not only cut itself off from modern thought and science but came to appear to liberals everywhere as their implacable enemy. In Germany and Austria, papal support of the ultramontanes encouraged Catholics who flirted with racist myths and anti-Semitic doctrines in the late nineteenth century.

In the thirteenth century—the age of Thomas Aquinas—the Church had readily accommodated itself to a new science; in the nineteenth century the papacy adopted just the opposite course, although Thomism was still the Church's official philosophy. Actually, the rejection of materialism and secularism by the Roman Church could have had a salutary effect on nineteenth-century culture. But most Catholic scholars today recognize that Pius's rejection of liberalism and science as well was an unfortunate policy.

The Darwinian Impact on Moral and Social Thought

For the Darwinists who believed that the support of revealed religion had been removed from traditional morality, there was a real problem. How could they justify traditional ethics without Christian revelation? Herbert Spencer's solution was utilitarian: he declared that morality was useful, that right behavior brought individual happiness and public good. Man would behave better as society progressed—as it inevitably would, since evolution and progress were identical. Most of the Darwinists, including Darwin himself, were strictly conventional in their standards of public and private morality. Vice and social disorganization—crime, prostitution, alcoholism—cause misery and suffering here and now; a wise man is good and therefore happy.

But Darwinism had ethical implications that could not be resolved by utilitarian morality. Even Huxley, as he grew older, realized that nature was not a suitable model for human behavior, that the savage struggle for existence was unacceptable to a civilized man. He advocated religious education and grew to appreciate the value of the Church in the battle *against* the natural man. It became increasingly obvious that natural selection in human society had little connection with the ethical system of the Sermon on the Mount. Although a Darwinist might appreciate the beauty of humanitarian ideals, he would have to admit that they were of little value—and might even be damaging—to the evolutionary progress of the human race.

Darwinism had social and political implications of which its amiable founder never dreamed. The term "social Darwinism" has been used to explain or justify an amazingly diverse collection of theories. In Germany, social Darwinists tended to be democrats and socialists; in England, social Darwinists were likely to be conservatives. Social Darwinism was offered by nationalists as a justification for a strong state and by individualists as justification for a weak one. In the United States social Darwinism was used to justify the depredations of industrial robber barons. It was claimed as a basis for both militarism and pacifism, for socialism and capitalism, for racism, Pan-Slavism, and abolitionism. Although Darwinism itself was certainly distorted, in most of these "isms" there was some thread of connection with natural selection.

A major connecting link in the varieties of social Darwinism was the idea of progress through struggle. This was particularly evident in the ideas of those who believed in a superman or a superstate that would demonstrate (in fact, create) superiority through competition and war. Some Darwinists disliked violence but acknowledged its place in progressive evolution; others — in the latter part of the nineteenth century, a great many others — glorified war. Violence and war were the mechanisms by which the fittest were enabled to survive and superior men and superior races to dominate their inferiors.

The concept of struggle figured prominently in the ideas of economic Darwinians. Those who favored laissez faire argued that since the "natural order" tended to bring the best to the top, businesses and businessmen should be left alone to flourish or fail. If a large business swallowed up smaller ones, if weak or incompetent workmen lost their jobs, starved, and died, it might be unfortunate, but it was an inescapable aspect of progress. Social and economic reforms interfered with nature by protecting the weak at the cost of impeding the strong. Weak plants and animals could not appeal to ideals of equality and brotherhood to defend themselves against predators, and the weaker members of society should not be protected by government interference, which might result in the weakening of all of society.

Scientific socialists, too, appreciated the unsentimental view of life reflected in *The Origin of Species*. In Marxism as in Darwinism, history progressed by means of natural, inevitable laws which were not subject to divine or human interference. Marx believed in struggle and in progressive evolution, though to him the struggle was nearing its historic end and evolution had to develop at certain periods into revolution. In Darwinism, the inevitable struggle took place between individuals in the same species, while Marx envisioned the development of proletarian solidarity to replace intraclass proletarian rivalry. Like other social Darwinists, Marx took what he needed from the theory and ignored the rest.

Not all socialists appreciated social Darwinism. Many emphasized cooperation rather than struggle and refused to accept the ruling class in human society as the "fittest" simply because it ruled. These socialists were dedicated to progress through reform. They wanted the state to interfere actively to improve man by improving his environment.

In order to give their theories the appearance of scientific legitimacy, many late nineteenth-century writers used the terminology of social Darwinism, including fomentors of racist myths and totalitarian ideologies. Certainly Darwin cannot be held responsible for all the inferences drawn from his theories. He was not a social philosopher but a scientist, and his main contribution to science was an orderly, lucid scheme of evolution — the greatest achievement of science in the nineteenth century. In evolution through natural selection, the mid-Victorians had a system to satisfy their urge to understand themselves and the world. Its flaws appeared later on. For the moment, it supplied yet another reason to worship science and keep faith in human progress.

IV THE ARTS

Literature

The achievements of science and technology and the efforts of social theorists to analyze the functioning of economic and social institutions were bound to inspire creative writers to portray the world as it actually existed in their time. By the end of the 1840's, Romanticism as an intellectual movement was exhausted and divided; many of the more imaginative and sensitive writers of the 1850's and 1860's consciously adhered to the principle of literary realism, depicting individuals and social groups precisely and often critically. Balzac's *Human Comedy* had pointed the way before this period, and many of the later novels of Charles Dickens, with their mordant renditions of cruelty and injustice in contemporary society, followed in it.

Like all terms in the history of the arts and letters, *realism* is artificial and ambiguous. All movements in higher culture are realistic in the sense that they aim to communicate a perception of the truth about the nature of man and the world. In this sense, classicism and Romanticism were as realistic as the dominant mode of literature and art in the 1850's and 1860's. It is furthermore characteristic of any self-consciously new movement in higher culture to claim that it is more realistic—that is, more truthful in its perception—than the style of thought and expression against which it is rebelling. What distinguished the movement in the 1850's and 1860's was the conviction held by writers and artists that natural science and social theory had, by dispassionate inquiry, penetrated to a much fuller understanding of the physical world and of society and that they could do the same.

In Germany, a realist strain had appeared before 1850 in the works of playwrights Georg Büchner and Johann Nestroy. Büchner depicted the political world from a radical point of view in *Danton's Death*; the comedies of the Austrian Nestroy mirrored contemporary society. During this period, the only major novelist with some realist leanings was the Swiss Gottfried Keller. By and large, German literature was still heavily under the sway of Romantic traditions, and an important realist school did not emerge in German-speaking countries in the 1850's and 1860's.

Nor was it easy for the British writers of the period to put aside Romantic attitudes. Alfred Tennyson (1809–1892), the favorite poet of the Victorian middle class—he was Poet Laureate for the last four decades of his life—exhibited in his early poems an awareness of the corrupting effect of materialism and a faith in science, industrial progress, and liberalism. But most of his work, although distinguished by great metrical skill, was infected by contrived sentimentality, heavy-handed learning, and a shallow view of the great economic and social upheavals of his era.

Another paragon of the Victorian literary world, Matthew Arnold (1822–1888), saw more deeply than Tennyson into the problems of the mid-nineteenth century. His poems, written when he was young, reflect the growing doubt about revealed religion and exhibit a distinctive pessimism about the future of a society in which "ignorant armies clash by night." His influential essays express Arnold's distaste for the middle class's shallow "philistinism" and suffocating puritanism. His elitist prescription for overcoming these defects was a more comprehensive and intensive literary culture, appreciative of the classical tradition.

The prolific poet Robert Browning (1812–1889) was, like Tennyson and Arnold, much admired in his day. He was an indefatigable experimenter with poetical forms, and his dramatic monologues are important not only for their elaborate craftsmanship but also for the author's attempts to lay bare facets of human psychology. But because of Browning's characteristic Victorian reticence about sexual drives, his psychological insight now seems to have been quite limited.

At the beginning of the nineteenth century, in the midst of the Romantic efflorescence, Britain had one novelist who was a superb observer and commentator on society, somewhat in the vein that later realism professed. This was Jane Austen (1775–1817), the spinster daughter of a country parson. Miss Austen's novels—such as *Pride and Prejudice* and *Sense and Sensibility*—focus only on her genteel little world of marriages, family, and minor scandals (she totally ignored the French Revolution and the Industrial Revolution); but they rise above their environment: they are precise, marvelously skillful etchings of a limited, perhaps unimportant, but very real world. The day-to-day trivia of gentry and middle-class families are treated sympathetically but with remarkable insight into the petty triumphs and tragedies of this kind of people.

Charles Dickens' novels (see Chapter 5) cannot be classified—they combine bitter portraits of middle-class materialism with gross sentimentality. More consciously in the vein of mid-century realism was the novelist and satirist William Thackeray (1811–1863) who set out to describe "greedy, pompous men." His finest work, *Vanity Fair*, creates a great middle-class character, the hard, competitive, clever, self-seeking woman. In the work of Anthony Trollope (1815–1882), realism is mixed with genteel sentimentalism. Trollope believed that "a novel should give a picture of common life enlivened by humor and sweetened by pathos." His "Barsetshire" series portrays small-town and clerical life precisely along these lines, and his other novels set in a political world illuminate some of the corruption and confusion of parliamentary politics. But Trollope was too sympathetic to the way of life of the established classes to offer a realistic portrayal of common life.

Of all the English Victorian novelists, the one most in tune with the era of scientism was Mary Ann Evans (1819–1880), who wrote under the pen name of George Eliot. Independent and unconventional (she never married the man she lived with), George Eliot lived in the very center of British political religious radicalism; she was an associate of Herbert Spencer and a follower of

Comte and Darwin. Her first novel, *Adam Bede* (1859), was still somewhat in the Romantic tradition, but the theme of male aggression and cruelty toward women, which became central in her more mature work, was already apparent. Her greatest novel, *Middlemarch* (1871–1872), is a profound study of character corrupted by greed in a competitive industrial world, of the misery of modern marriage, and of the struggle of an intelligent woman against the selfish masculine values and institutions of contemporary society. The psychological insight and social realism of George Eliot's best novels have slowly gained for her recognition as one of the founders of modern literature.

Realism was much more of an integrated, self-conscious literary movement in France than in Britain. During the 1850's and 1860's a large number of novelists depicted contemporary society; they were particularly eager to expose the materialism and selfishness of the bourgeoisie. Of these writers the Goncourt brothers (Edmond, 1822–1896, and Jules, 1830–1870) and Gustave Flaubert (1821–1880) were preeminent. The Goncourt brothers aimed at the documentary novel—they sought to reveal family life, to analyze artistic creation, and to describe some of the darker side of contemporary life, such as prostitution and hospital conditions. They worked at their material in a disciplined, scientific way, keeping detailed journals and personally observing the institutions they described. Much the same aim and the same method was employed by Flaubert. "I am an eye," Flaubert said of himself, and his novels were also slowly built up out of journal entries and several drafts.

What distinguishes Flaubert is that his realistic purpose was combined with penetrating psychological insight and a brilliantly precise style. He spent five years in the writing of his greatest novel, *Madame Bovary* (1856), searching assiduously for *le mot juste*, the exact word that could communicate precisely and unforgettably his picture of provincial middle-class life. The heroine is the most convincing portrait of a bourgeois woman in French fiction; she is depicted without sentiment on the one hand or moral judgment on the other. A bitter and obsessive hostility toward middle-class life and attitudes inspires Flaubert's work. He remarked that a riot was the only public event that he could look upon with any pleasure; otherwise he could find only banality and boredom in contemporary society.

The novel reached its high point not only in France but also in Russia, whose contributions to European literature had begun only in the 1820's. In a society where intellectuals were engaged in an agonizing appraisal of the relevance and value of Western culture, where the response to an ever growing need for social and political reform was repression by the czarist government and the aristocracy, the novel became the prime vehicle for social analysis and political criticism.

Dead Souls (1842) by Nikolai Gogol (1809–1852) inaugurated the great era of the Russian novel; it stirred a vast public controversy and exercised a profound influence on the rising generation of Russian writers. *Dead Souls* portrays a marvelous collection of stupid, greedy officials and selfish, ineffectual aristocrats. A subtle blend of grotesque comedy and bitter realism, it laid bare the savagery, corruption, and the social disintegration characteristic of crumbling feudalism. *Oblomov* (1859), by Ivan Goncharov (1812–1891), pursues the same theme by concentrating on one representative of the faltering landholding class. Well-meaning but confused, lazy, incompetent, selfish, and finally immobile, Oblomov became a symbol of the nineteenth-century Russian nobility.

The first Russian novelist to be widely appreciated in western Europe was Ivan Turgenev (1818–1883), who came from a wealthy family and was educated at the University of Berlin. Often involved in radical groups, he spent half of his adult life in western Europe, much of the time in pursuit of a French singer. Turgenev's early work, *A Sportsman's Sketches* (1852), was strongly influenced by Gogol's *Dead Souls*; he offered an iconoclastic view of country life in which serfs were regarded as human beings, perhaps even better ones than their masters. Turgenev's stormy and quite unhappy experience in radical movements in St. Petersburg led to his masterpiece, *Fathers and Sons* (1862). In this work, he portrayed one of the great characters in modern literature, an alienated radical who emerges as neither hero nor monster but as a genuinely complex human being. Turgenev's subtle portrait remains the most convincing study ever made of the revolutionary personality. His later work, *Smoke* (1867), aroused bitter criticism in Russia because of its negative attitude toward the ambiguities in Russian society and Russian culture. Russia's hope, Turgenev believed, lay in further westernization of its culture and society.

Painting and Architecture

The best Russian, French, and British novelists applied realist criteria in order to expose the flaws in their societies. With the exception of French painting—and even there to a limited degree—the other arts revealed no parallel development during the 1850's and 1860's. In part, this failure to develop schools of realist criticism in the visual arts and music was due to the nature of the media. It was relatively easy to turn the novel into an analysis of society but harder to do in painting and immensely difficult in music. Furthermore, the novelist could turn scientism against its admirers by using it to dissect the materialism and philistinism of the bourgeoisie: a middle-class fetish was made a weapon against middle-class culture. But when painters set out to depict the contemporary scene realistically, the results were usually banal and uninspired. In any case, by the 1860's the invention of photography had established a powerful competitor for merely representational art. Another fatal weakness of the realist mode in the nonliterary arts was that painting, architecture, and music were much more dependent than the novel on the patronage and commissions of the high bourgeoisie, who naturally

Realism in French Painting. Realism in art was manifested in three ways: first, an effort to depict the life of the common man, as in Millet's "The Bleaching Tub" (1861), top, left; second, an attempt at photographic representationalism, as in Courbet's "Encounter" (1854), top, right; third, a concern with the natural environment, as in Corot's "Mur (Côtes du Norde)" above (1850–1855). But the social, stylistic, and environmental types of realism were not integrated into a coherent or self-conscious artistic school.

would not support works of art and music that attacked their mores and status.

The artist whose intent most closely paralleled that of the literary realists was Honoré Daumier (1800–1879), who used exaggeration and caricature in scathing comment upon contemporary life. His washerwomen and lawyers are recognizable social types as well as individuals, and his work preserves the underside of Parisian prosperity and elegance in the 1850's and 1860's. In technique and subject matter, the work of Gustave Courbet (1819–1877) and Jean François Millet (1814–1875) often reflects the attitudes that prevailed in literary realism. To Courbet, human subjects were aspects of nature—not necessarily heroic or beautiful—that should be depicted realistically. The women in his "Bathers," which caused a public scandal, are not idealized nymphs but heavy, realistic nudes. In his paintings of Ornans, the provincial town in which he grew up, Courbet showed the lined, homely faces of real people. Millet also chose simple people for his subjects, but his paintings of peasants—like "The Sower" and "The Man with the Hoe"—are invested with humanitarian and social feeling; they are not simply objective depictions of the social world.

The work of Camille Corot (1796–1875) is not easy to characterize. His portraiture shows an intent to capture the inner personal qualities of his subjects; this approach is Romantic as much as it is realist. Corot's insistence on painting landscapes, at that time unfashionable in France, reveals a desire to turn away from the oppressive bourgeois environment and come to terms with the simplicity and profundity of nature. Although this attitude can be termed antibourgeois, it can scarcely be regarded as realist in the literary sense.

By the 1860's there was a great restlessness and experimentation in French art, and the French painters, before other leaders of higher culture, seem to have sensed that the rebellion against middle-class values would have to go beyond realism and develop new insights into human experience. Corot belonged to a group of artists called the Barbizon school, which sought to liberate art from the limitations of the studio, to take it out of doors into new vistas. Corot's interest in light and color made him a forerunner of the Impressionist movement of the 1870's and 1880's. Indeed, he was the first artist to use the term "impression."

With Édouard Manet (1832–1883) we have arrived at the beginning of a new era in French, and Western, art, one that in many ways still prevails. Manet's "Déjeuner sur l'Herbe" (1863), which shows two nude women breakfasting on the grass with two fully clad gentlemen, scandalized middle-class sensibilities, not as much because of the subject matter as because of the prosaic, everyday character of the casual pose and the setting. Manet was less interested in the ambiguous situation of his subjects than in the representation of shadow and depth by flat solid patches of color. The new school of French painters was developing its new understanding of the meaning and focus of art itself, not simply scandalizing middle-class feelings.

The year 1863, when Manet and Edgar Degas (1834–1917) showed works in the *Salon des Refusés*, the gallery for anti-establishment painting, marked the beginning of a new era in European art. Degas, still very young, was interested in exploring the mechanics of human and animal anatomy; his studies of dancers and racehorses owe something to the spirit of mid-century scientism. Although his "Woman with Chrysanthemums" (1865) is vividly and carefully realistic, the painter is chiefly concerned with new patterns of composition — with an uncontrived, asymmetrical arrangement of contemporary scenes. Thus by the 1860's a search for new modes of expression was the main tendency in the best French art. This experimental spirit would carry French painting to unprecedented greatness in subsequent decades.

In the era of the Crystal Palace, John Stuart Mill, and George Eliot, British painting lost its eminence in European culture; henceforth it would languish very far behind French art. In part, this can be attributed to the eagerness with which the Victorian middle class took up art as a necessary house furnishing. A huge market developed, and the results were overblown tributes to the achievements of the Industrial Revolution, endless shallow repetitions of Romantic motifs, and the heroic stags of Edward Landseer and similar academic clichés. In British art the rebellion against convention, which characterized the Parisian Left Bank, was lacking.

The decline of British art was also due in part to the baleful persuasions of the extremely influential critic John Ruskin (1819–1900). Early in his long career, Ruskin championed the work of Turner, but as he developed his mature philosophy, he decided that the only great art was that which imparted religious and moral ideas of the noblest kind. Ruskin thought he saw this ideal in medieval and early Renaissance art, but efforts by the Pre-Raphaelite brotherhood — a group championed by Ruskin — to recapture the spirit of that period failed almost totally from the aesthetic point of view. Confusing ethics with beauty, Pre-Raphaelites like Dante Gabriel Rossetti and John Millais improved little upon the crushing sentimentality and didacticism that ruined Victorian painting. Ruskin and his friends were trenchant critics of scientism and materialism, and Ruskin's socialist doctrines played an important role in late Victorian thought; but he and the Pre-Raphaelites could not extricate themselves from the compulsion to judge art by irrelevant moral standards.

The finest artistic achievements of Victorian England lay in the iron and glass of the Crystal Palace and the massive railroad stations of the Age of Steam — all repugnant to aesthetes like Ruskin. In such functional buildings and in the great boulevards of Paris designed by Baron Georges Haussmann in the 1850's and 1860's, there was a ready acceptance of the power and prosperity of the bourgeois era. But in the age of realism and scientism, there never developed a clear understanding that architecture should serve a society and directly reflect the contemporary ethos; architecture never emancipated itself from the neoclassical and Romantic penchant for imitating the styles of previous eras. The eclecticism of the early nineteenth century continued, with a confusion of styles and lack of discrimination that precluded any effort to create a new style of architecture that would express the spirit of the capitalist era. Banks were built in the form of Byzantine cathedrals, and government offices were disguised as Renaissance palazzos. Pretentiousness, academicism, and giganticism were the hallmarks of the 1850's and 1860's, whether in tortured and ungainly buildings like the Albert Memorial in London or more skillful ones like the Paris *Opéra*. In their gigantic proportions and their conspicuous display of prosperity, the buildings of the 1850's and 1860's caught some of the middle-class ethos, but not its best.

Music

European music was dominated at mid-century by Romantic composers like Hector Berlioz and Franz Liszt. The works of Giuseppe Verdi (1813–1901) maintained the Romantic mood as well as the traditions of grand opera. *Rigoletto*, *Il Trovatore*, and *La Traviata* are peculiarly Italian in style; the libretto takes second place to the music. *Aïda*, composed in 1871 to celebrate the opening of the Suez Canal, is more cosmopolitan, but with its arias, ensembles, and other set pieces it, too, is squarely in the Romantic operatic tradition.

The work of Johannes Brahms (1833–1897) seems to restore some of the classical restraint of an earlier period. Disliking grandeur and extravagant emotionalism and having less interest in the "music-of-the-future" than in Germany's great classical heritage, Brahms confined himself to traditional forms and helped to restore the symphony and chamber music to the center of Western music.

The controversial figure of Richard Wagner (1813–1883) bestrode the cultural world of the latter half of the nineteenth century. Unlike Brahms, Wagner was passionately interested in experimenting with new musical form, and like Marx and Darwin, he was a great system-maker. Wagner's theories about music were as influential as the music itself, and his tempestuous personality and tumultuous life guaranteed public attention. Wagner can be described, with some justification, either as the last Romantic or as the first modern musician.

Rejecting history as a subject for opera, Wagner turned instead to Norse and German legend and myth. His stories unfold psychological conflict more than physical action. *Tristan und Isolde* (1859) has been regarded as the culmination of the Romantic movement in music, but the love it celebrates is not romantic love. With its emphasis on sexual passion and death, the opera may also be called the first psychoanalytic drama. The lovers in *Tristan* fall prey to the blind forces of nature—an echo of *Origin of Species*, which was published in the same year.

It was not until the mid-1870's that Wagner completed his masterpieces, the four music-dramas (as he liked to call them) that comprise *Der Ring des Nibelungen*. It was at this point that Wagner revealed that he had gone beyond both Romanticism and the system-building of the age of Marx and Darwin and that, like Manet, he was one of the harbingers of a new consciousness.

7

HERITAGE
ESSAY

THE MIDDLE-CLASS ETHOS

In the 1850's and 1860's the middle class fully came into its own, emerging as the dominant class in Western civilization. This fulfillment of the potential of the political and economic revolutions of the late eighteenth century shaped all aspects of European life. Although in most countries the aristocracy still provided leadership in government, the middle class gained a substantial share of power, and the main course of political development followed the bourgeois ideals of liberalism and nationalism. Economic growth was now almost entirely the consequence of middle-class enterprise. Most pervasive of all, the culture and ethic of Western civilization became essentially bourgeois. By the 1860's, the thought, feeling, and style of life in western Europe were determined by the middle-class ethos. Very little was left of the monarchical and aristocratic ideals and attitudes of previous eras. The greatest transvaluation of standards in many centuries had been effected. The bourgeois revolution, which had been launched economically by the advent of steam power and the factory system and politically by the French Revolution, had now reached the decisive state in which middle-class mores, ideals, and expectations were the hallmark of Western civilization.

The term *middle class* covered all members of European society who were neither landed aristocrats nor peasants and industrial workers. The size of the middle class, which had increased rapidly through the first half of the nineteenth century, varied markedly from country to country; it was 20 to 30 per cent of the population in Britain and France and not more than 5 per cent in Russia. Within the middle class, there was enormous variation in wealth. At mid-century the bourgeoisie could be divided into five distinct groups: the shopkeepers and small tradesmen; the professionals, such as lawyers, physicians, and civil servants; the prosperous, independent farmers; the intellectuals, students, and artists; and the industrial, mercantile, and financial magnates. The last group, the capitalist entrepreneurs, was regarded as the bourgeoisie proper because the great wealth of its members gave them power and influence over society as a whole.

The first category of middle-class values was a somewhat naive, quite materialistic, but nevertheless dedicated rationality. The bourgeoisie could be

The Shrine of Progress. The Crystal Palace Exhibition of 1851 expressed the mid-nineteenth-century middle-class faith in the beneficence of science, technology, and capitalism and also reflected both the most enterprising and the most stultifying aspects of bourgeois culture. Above: the finest part of the Exhibition was Joseph Paxton's Crystal Palace itself, a building fifty years ahead of its time in architectural perception. While contemporary architects enclosed space with structures as ponderous as medieval fortresses, Paxton used glass and iron to provide a transparent cover that opened the interior to the rapidly changing outer world. His building was made up of portable units that could be disassembled and reassembled, an eminently practical arrangement suggesting the vibrant character of the new industrial economy.

It was what was presented inside the Crystal Palace (facing page) that demonstrated the banality and vulgarity of the middle-class mind. The vast number of machines and articles of furniture that crowded the interior were elaborately decorated with florid, neo-Baroque ornamentation designed to disguise their natural lines. This fear of revealing the functional structure of machinery and manufactured furniture contrasted markedly with the eager acceptance of the new technology in Paxton's design. It indicated a deep-seated middle-class reluctance to come to terms with the ultimate cultural significance of the Industrial Revolution.

extremely sentimental about personal and family matters, but they were clear-headed pragmatists about making a living and "getting on" in the world—about economic enterprise. They were not prepared to allow tradition and sentiment to stand in the way of business success and social progress. They believed in a realistic appraisal of the economic market and a shrewd analysis of what was necessary for commercial success. For the middle class, knowledge was a functional instrument for personal gain and social improvement. At the level of higher culture, this attitude was reflected in the realism and scientism of the 1850's and 1860's. At the level of everyday experience —which was essentially the middle-class level of thought—this pragmatic rationality was clearly expressed by the bourgeois moralist Samuel Smiles, a British engineer. His *Self-Help* was a collection of middle-class truisms: "It is not . . . how much a man may know that is of importance, but the end and purpose for which he knows it."[1] Charles Dickens, who had a fine ear for middle-class speech, put this bourgeois philosophy into the mouth of one of his characters in *Hard Times*: "Now what I want is Facts. . . . Facts alone are wanted in life. Plant nothing else, and root out everything else. . . . Stick to Facts, Sir!"

1. Samuel Smiles, *Self-Help*. London: John Murray, 1950, XI, p. 313.

The Worship of Science and Technology. The faith of the educated public of the 1850's and 1860's that science and technology would transform the world and greatly improve the condition of human society was inspired by advances in physics, chemistry, biology, and medicine, as well as in transportation and communication. Above: Michael Faraday in his laboratory. Pictures of scientific wizards at work were middle-class favorites. Right: a sentimentalized view of a surgery class before an operation. The great advances in surgery made possible during this period by the use of antiseptics and anesthetics greatly enhanced the social status of medical doctors, who henceforth were bourgeois idols. Facing page: the Atlantic cable, ready for shipment. In 1851 a cable was laid between England and France, and in 1865, after a decade of experiments and breakdowns, the cable between Ireland and Newfoundland was opened. This was the most radical improvement in international communication in human history.

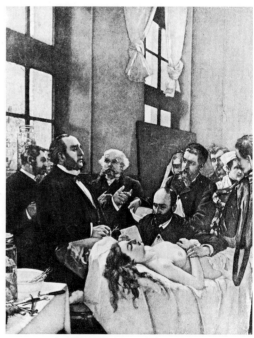

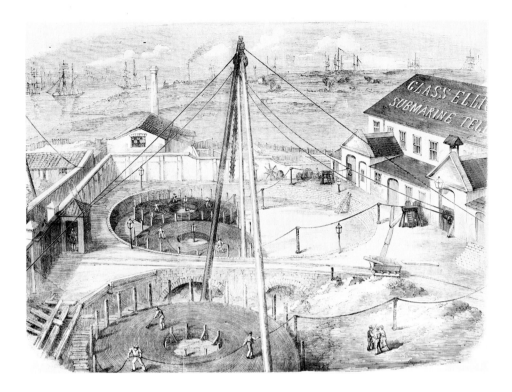

In the middle-class ethos, this harsh realism, this vulgarized Baconian attitude toward knowledge, was put at the service of the second and most basic bourgeois tenet, the gospel of work. Unceasing labor in one's business, profession, or craft was more than the road to personal and social advancement. Work was virtually identified with human happiness itself; it was man's highest good. Samuel Smiles stated this prime middle-class dogma succinctly:

The career of industry which the nation has pursued, has also proved its best education. As steady application to work is the healthiest training for every individual, so is it the best discipline of a state. Honorable industry travels the same road with duty; and Providence has closely linked both with human happiness.[2]

In part, the gospel of work was important to the middle-class ethos because it represented the antithesis of aristocratic and clerical privilege. The bourgeoisie claimed that a man should be given his due for what he achieved; he should *earn* material reward, not receive it as a gift through noble birth or clerical status. Thus the gospel of work was inextricably bound up with economic liberalism, the laissez-faire doctrine of the free market, and with the radical individualism of the early nineteenth century. Self-help, said Samuel Smiles, brings out the best in individuals and redounds to the welfare of society:

The spirit of self-help is the root of all genuine growth in the individual; and exhibited in the lives of many, it constitutes the true source of national vigor and strength. Help from without is often enfeebling in its effects, but help from within invariably invigorates.[3]

2. Smiles, *Self-Help*, II, p. 58.
3. Smiles, *Self-Help*, I, p. 35.

The middle-class doctrine of work and self-help has so often been condemned as a mere facade for greed that it is necessary to stress that the nineteenth-century middle class did work hard, that its pursuit of individual advancement was of great importance in expanding the Industrial Revolution, in transforming European technology, and, in the long run, in improving the circumstances of daily life for all mankind. There is much to be said for a doctrine that calls for men to be judged by the fruits of their labors rather than by traditional prejudices and the whims of kings and lords. Whatever the defects of the middle-class ethos, it represented a liberating attitude in European culture. The middle-class faith that a man should be judged by the results of his work played a powerful role in removing political disabilities from religious minorities. This attitude could allow the Rothschild family not only to achieve great wealth but also to become socially prominent and could permit a scion of this Jewish banking family to take a seat in Parliament.

Those who have only a sneer for the bourgeois philosophy should ponder the speech delivered in the House of Commons in 1833 by the middle-class

The Scientific Treatment of Social Expendables. By mid-century, the utilitarian and scientific spirit of the age was hard at work on social problems, particularly those that threatened the stability of bourgeois order. There can be no doubt that imprisoned criminals and the unemployed were dealt with more efficiently, but it is questionable whether bourgeois society treated them any more humanely or wisely than had the disorganized *ancien régime*. Facing page: a dormitory in Marylebone workhouse for the unemployed in London. The inscriptions invoke a kind of gimcrack piety to keep the poor contented and subservient. Above: female convicts at work in Brixton Prison in England. The solution to all social ills was deemed to be hard labor; the similarity between the workhouse and the prison was not accidental.

historian and civil servant, Thomas Macaulay, during the debate on the civil disabilities of the Jews:

The honourable member for Oldham tells us that the Jews are naturally a mean race, a sordid race, a money-getting race. . . . Such, Sir, has in every age been the reasoning of bigots. They never fail to plead in justification of persecution the vices which persecution has engendered. . . . Let us do justice to [the Jews]. Let us open to them every career in which ability and energy can be displayed.[4]

Another bourgeois value was devotion to family. The bourgeoisie adopted the aristocracy's view of the family as the most immediate and important unit of society. They also inherited the puritanical belief that sexual relations

4. Quoted in A. Bullock and M. Schock, eds., *The Liberal Tradition.* New York: New York University Press, 1957, pp. 71-72.

Bourgeois Realism. Favorite themes of middle-class art were the achievements of industry and sexless, excrutiatingly sentimental love. The former theme celebrated the gospel of work and the latter a degenerate Romanticism that was eagerly embraced by the educated middle class. Pictures like the ones on these two pages were painted, reproduced, and sold by the thousands. This kind of mindless realism remained extremely popular for the next century—in the 1950's similar banalities flourished weekly on the covers of mass circulation American magazines. Above: "Work" by Ford Madox Brown; left: "Newcastle Quayside" by William Bell Scott. Facing page: a classic Victorian monstrosity, "The Long Engagement" by Alfred Hughes. A remark by the immensely successful Victorian artist Edwin Landseer epitomizes both contemporary taste and the cynicism of the fashionable middle-class artist: "If people only knew as much about painting as I do, they would never buy my pictures."

were moral only between husband and wife and were justified only by the need to procreate children. Much has been written—in a pejorative vein—about the suffocating tightness of the middle-class family and its moral code. This does not seem to have been more than a perpetuation of traditional aristocratic devotion to progeny and of Christian puritanism. But because the middle-class man, in his competitive world, had only his immediate family to rely on, and because the gospel of work made sexual promiscuity seem reckless and improvident, the age-old familial ideal and sexual puritanism assumed a particular emphasis in middle-class culture.

But devotion to family often contradicted the doctrine of self-help and individual achievement. The bourgeois father fiercely inculcated work habits in his children, but he was as prejudiced in their favor as any noble of the *ancien régime*. Privilege of birth to high bourgeois families was as advantageous as birth into the landed families. Although the gospel of work and self-help seemed a good argument against aristocracy, inherited status continued to count for a great deal in the supposedly emancipated society of individual achievement. The bourgeoisie tended to blame poverty on personal unworthiness—the poor were held to be lazy, drunken, and sexually promiscuous. In fact, the nineteenth-century poor were usually born poor, and the self-righteous man of property often gained his affluence not by merit but by inheritance.

PUBLISHED BY PERMISSION OF THE BIRMINGHAM MUSEUM AND ART GALLERY

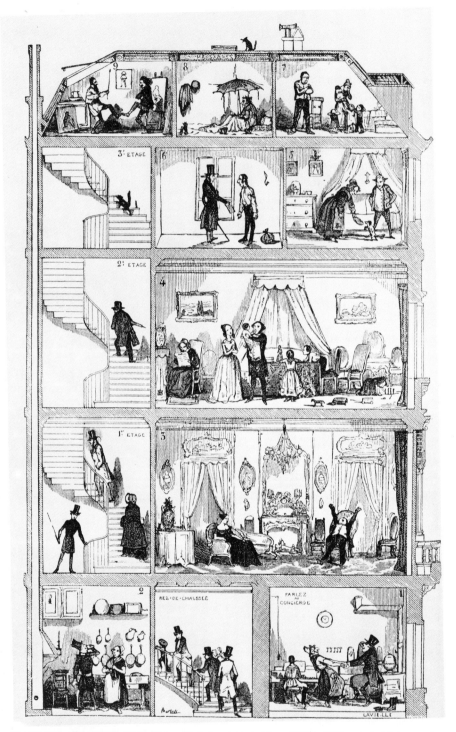

The Triumph of the Middle Class. Queen Victoria, who ruled from 1837 to 1901, was the high priestess of middle-class mores and taste. An extremely opinionated woman of limited education and modest intelligence, she prescribed a stern moral code for the British upper classes. The sitting room of Osborne House, Victoria's personal residence (facing page), enshrines high bourgeois taste—the sentimental painting over the mantelpiece, the dozens of family pictures, the clutter of heavy furniture. Above: a French cartoon of 1852 showing the tenants of a Paris apartment house floor by floor. The high bourgeoisie, occupying the first and second floors, bask in familial bliss and opulent if boring comfort, while the lesser orders in the basement, on the third floor, and in the attic, exhibit their customary squalor, improvidence, anxiety, and misery.

Middle-class intellectuals sensed this self-serving quality in the middle-class ethos. It was—and still is—the greatest weakness of the Western bourgeoisie that its most sensitive spirits have turned against their class (and often their families) with hatred and contempt. Almost from the start of the industrial era, the alienation of intellectuals, artists, and students was the Achilles' heel of bourgeois power. What incensed the intellectuals most was the materialism of the middle class. "Finance," remarks a character in Balzac's novel *Cousin Bette*, "is just another name for organized self-seeking. . . . The law makes money the standard to measure everything." To artists and writers, bourgeois values seemed the nadir of the human spirit. Flaubert described middle-class culture as "a permanent conspiracy against originality."

The infamy of the bourgeoisie has been the article of faith most persistently subscribed to by middle-class intellectuals, from the Paris bohemian of the mid-nineteenth century to left-wing American professors and students today. The special appeal of Marxism for such intellectuals has always lain in Marx's ability to transform their contempt for their fathers' attitudes and mores into a philosophy of history and a "scientific" economic and social doctrine which claims to demonstrate that the bourgeoisie will be transcended. Ironically, however, no one was ever more appreciative of the achievements of the middle class than Karl Marx:

The bourgeoisie, historically, has played a most revolutionary part. . . . It has pitilessly torn asunder the motley feudal ties that bound man to his "natural superiors." . . . The bourgeoisie has through its exploitation of the world-market given a cosmopolitan character to production and consumption in every country. . . . The bourgeoisie, by the rapid improvement of all instruments of production, by the im-

mensely facilitated means of communication, draws all, even the most barbarian nations, into civilization. . . . It has created enormous cities, has greatly increased the urban population as compared with the rural, and has thus rescued a considerable part of the population from the idiocy of rural life.[5]

This brilliant tribute to the dynamism of the middle class raises the question: What, then, is wrong with the bourgeoisie from the Marxist point of view? Marx replies that the triumphs of the bourgeoisie have been won at a terrible price. He agrees with the bitter complaints of Balzac and Flaubert and British anticapitalist humanitarians like Coleridge and Carlyle:

[The bourgeoisie] has resolved personal worth into exchange value. . . . The bourgeoisie has converted the physician, the lawyer, the priest, the poet, the man of science, into its paid wage laborers. . . . [It] has reduced the family relation to a mere money relation.[6]

But the greatest crime of the bourgeoisie, according to Marx, is its dehumanization of the working man:

For exploitation, veiled by religious and political illusions, the bourgeoisie has substituted naked, shameless, direct, brutal exploitation. . . . Owing to the extensive use of machinery and to division of labor, the work of the proletarians has lost all individual character and consequently all charm for the workman. He becomes an appendage of the machine . . . .[7]

Accumulation of wealth at one pole is, therefore, at the same time accumulation of misery, agony of toil, slavery, ignorance, brutality, moral degradation, at the opposite pole.[8]

Marx spent the last thirty years of his life trying to prove that the capitalist system would undergo a series of crises and disintegrate, that somehow a proletarian revolution would inaugurate "the Communist society" which in its "higher phase" would eliminate "the enslaving subordination of the individual to the division of labor . . . and with it the antagonisms between intellectual and manual labor." Then will come "the development of the individual in every sense . . . and all the springs of collective wealth will flow with abundance."[9]

The world is still waiting for the dawn of this blissful post-bourgeois era.

5. Marx and Engels, *The Communist Manifesto*, in S. Commins and R. N. Linscott, eds., *The Political Philosophers*. New York: Random House, 1947, pp. 490-493.
6. Marx and Engels, *The Communist Manifesto*, in *The Political Philosophers*, p. 491.
7. Marx and Engels, *The Communist Manifesto*, in *The Political Philosophers*, pp. 491, 495.
8. Karl Marx, *Capital*, in M. Eastman, ed., *Capital*. New York: Modern Library, 1932, p. 182.
9. Karl Marx, *The German Ideology*, in *Capital*, p. 7.

Democracy and Autocracy

I MID-VICTORIAN LIBERALISM

Between Reaction and Reform

The intellectual upheavals of the 1850's and 1860's—climaxed by the appearance of Darwin's *The Origin of Species*—had their counterpart in politics and society. The surface calm that characterized Europe in the early 1850's was very deceptive. The defeat of the revolutions of 1848 had been more apparent than real; it had set back but not destroyed the powerful forces clamoring for liberal and national reforms all over Europe.

At first glance, the revolutions of 1848 seemed to accomplish very little. Germany and Italy remained almost as disunited as they had been before, and the cause of political and social reform in those countries had made only limited progress. In France the revolution of 1848 had ended—as the revolution of 1789 had ultimately done—with a Napoleonic coup. Russia had been touched only a little by the revolutions in central and western Europe, although the Russian government was more fearful of internal disorders than it was prepared to admit. Slavic and national minorities in east-central and southern Europe were not much closer to autonomy or independence in the 1850's and 1860's than they had been before early 1848.

But this was only one side of the story. Most of the reforms of that year —the quest for some kind of constitutional government in Prussia and Austria and the end of all legal dependency for the peasantry—could not be permanently undone. Efforts to restore something of the old political authoritarianism led to much greater difficulties in the years to follow. The two states that came through the 1850's most creditably were those that sought, in one way or another, to meet the demands and expectations of the revolutionary era

—namely, Britain and Prussia. The tide of liberalism and nationalism now flowed too powerfully for any government sensibly to resist or wholly ignore these forces for change.

The Age of Palmerston

In the years preceding the French Revolution, France was the center of Europe. In the years immediately preceding and following the revolutions of 1848, the center was Great Britain. The repeal of the Corn Laws precipitated the fall of Peel's cabinet in June 1846, and his death in 1850 left British politics somewhat adrift. In the next fifteen years no party was able to gain a clear majority and establish strong and stable government. However, it is the stability and not the chaos in Britain in the third quarter of the nineteenth century that impresses historians. Although there were many problems —such as working conditions and wages, the need for further reform of the franchise, and the status of Ireland—it was impossible to organize even enough public interest to bring the issues effectively before Parliament. In the years after 1850, most Britishers thought more about national prestige in foreign affairs, the Empire, Queen Victoria, and the state of public and private morality than they did about economic, social, and political reform. This does not mean that the mid-Victorians were free from anxieties; it means that, at that time, their anxieties were not expressed in a general desire for change.

The two greatest personalities of the period, Queen Victoria (who ruled from 1837 to 1901) and Lord Palmerston (1784–1865), personified various aspects of its spirit. They were both anachronisms in a way: Victoria was the last British monarch to exercise any real controlling authority in governmental affairs, and Palmerston was the last minister whose government transcended party affiliations. Victoria, who succeeded her uncle, William IV, in June 1837 at the age of eighteen, was a distinct contrast to her immediate predecessors, particularly in her determination to enforce high standards of moral behavior and decorum upon her court. She was an appropriate symbol of Britain in an era of missionary societies, temperance leagues, and books like Samuel Smiles' *Self-Help*. Victoria's husband—her first cousin, Prince Albert of Saxe-Coburg, whom she married in February 1840 despite strong opposition from conservative elements in Britain—was an ideal consort. He shared most of her views and was both intelligent and hard-working, an indispensable ally for the queen in the masculine political world of the nineteenth century. Victoria never quite recovered from his death in December 1861, but her popularity continued to grow throughout the nineteenth century.

The Great Exhibition of 1851 was only one of many visible and dramatic manifestations of the maturation of the Industrial Revolution in Britain. For example, the development of the Bessemer converter, which made it possible to manufacture steel quickly and economically, the growth of a network of rail lines across Britain, the appearance of standardized machinery, the invention of the telegraph, and the spread of the factory system were all parts of a new period of industrial expansion. By 1850 half the population of Britain was urban. Far ahead of its Continental rivals for the time being, Britain was unaware that the new age of steel would narrow that gap and eventually put an end to its industrial predominance.

The optimism that characterized the British middle class was perhaps most clearly manifest in its confidence in free trade — an economic theory which presumed that Britain and the rest of the world as well could develop most fully in an atmosphere of open economic competition. Applications of the free-trade ideology ranged from the repeal of the Corn Laws and other tariffs in the 1840's to the Opium War in China (1839–1842), in which Britain demanded the right to trade freely with the Chinese. Palmerston initially opposed the war on the ground that the British government should not assist its merchants to violate the laws of areas where they were trading. The conflict concluded, after the Treaty of Nanking (October 1842), with Britain gaining Hong Kong and numerous other concessions.

At home as much as abroad, British liberalism suffered from internal conflicts and contradictions. In the long run, liberal doctrine would have to face the question of how much the freedom of businessmen should be limited by the state in the interests of the welfare of the working class. The growing literacy and political involvement of workers made them ever more effective agitators on their own behalf. But in the 1850's and 1860's, anxieties about the social effects of the Industrial Revolution were only a peripheral concern in British politics. The factory acts of the 1830's and 1840's had corrected the most blatant social evils attendant upon the Industrial Revolution, and the benefits to workers that followed from the prosperity of the 1850's and 1860's deflated the militancy of British trade unionism.

Foreign affairs occupied most of the attention of Lord Palmerston, the greatest politician of the age, and of the British public. The three main concerns were the political situation in the eastern Mediterranean, the nature and status of the British Empire, and that rather intangible concept — the "national prestige." Palmerston was recalled to power in February 1855 during the crisis produced by government mismanagement of the Crimean War. This war, which began in 1853, was at first a continuation of the centuries-old conflict between Russia and Turkey, with the crucial difference that both Britain and France intervened in 1854 on behalf of the Turks.

By the time of the peace settlement in 1856, there was ample evidence of the need for the reform of the British army in personnel, equipment, and tactics. The early military disasters for Britain were due at least in part to incompetence — the commanding officer, who had last seen action against Napoleon at Waterloo, often referred to the enemy as "the French." During the war Florence Nightingale pioneered in the development of medical care for the

The Crisis of the British Raj. The Indian Mutiny of 1857 unleashed racial tensions that had lain just beneath the surface in the relations between the British sahibs and their Indian subjects. The mutiny was marked by cruelty and atrocities on both sides. Above: M. S. Morgan's painting of the storming of the Kashmir Gate, Delhi. After the mutiny British rule tended to become more conservative and arrogant in character.

wounded, and afterward some improvements were made in the conditions of service. But loosening of the aristocracy's stranglehold on the officer corps was slow in coming, and indeed not until the first administration of William Gladstone in the 1870's did the British military establishment begin to undergo significant change and reform.

No sooner was the Crimean War over than Palmerston and his government had to deal with a crisis in the relationship between Britain and India. The Indian Mutiny of 1857 pointed up a fundamental difference between the two kinds of British colonies. In Canada, Australia, New Zealand, and South Africa, the colonial population was composed of white men of European descent. The Durham Report of 1839 had set forth a formula which was followed by the British government in these colonies. Durham's argument that the common background and interests of Britain and its colonies would allow them to operate in harmony as free partners turned out to be largely correct, and his report soon became one of the most important documents in the devolution of the British Empire.

In India, however, the basic situation was very different. The advance of British control there had been due largely to the activities of the East India Company, which had long followed a policy of expanding its own authority and the domain under its control while also undertaking a limited "Europeanization" of Indian society. This policy did not work out well, especially because of the increasing corruption within the company, but the efforts of the British government to take over complete direct control of the vast peninsula were slow and half-hearted. The result, not surprisingly, was growing unrest, which—following the spread of the false rumor that religious conversion was to be forced on the native troops, or sepoys—finally burst into open rebellion in 1857. The sepoys became convinced that animal fat had been used to grease their new cartridges (the ends of which had to be bitten off for loading). Since the Hindus considered cattle sacred and the Muslims were forbidden to touch pigs, members of both religions mutinied.

The rebellion was put down—after carnage on both sides—but it signaled the end of the East India Company. The British Parliament speedily moved to bring India within the jurisdiction of a special government department. The Sepoy Mutiny served to reveal the widespread and deep-seated discontent existing in India. It marked a turning point in Anglo-Indian relations, involving abandonment of the assumption that Indian society and culture could possibly be remolded along European lines. After 1857, British statesmen refrained from making optimistic prophecies about the day when the Indians would be allowed self-government. A constant suspicion and underlying hostility henceforth conditioned relations between the British rulers and the native populace in India.

It was one of the many paradoxes of Victorian England that mid-century liberals characterized the colonial system as an unnecessary burden at the same time that some politicians and government officials were coming to regard Asian and African colonies as an increasingly vital foundation of British power and prosperity. The late 1860's saw both the low point in British imperial ambition and a revival of imperialist sentiment. It is not easy to explain this sudden change. Perhaps it took place because the British people, like so many Europeans in the 1860's, turned from liberalism to aggressive nationalism. The change was foreshadowed by Palmerston himself, who in a famous address in Parliament in 1850 enunciated the principle that a British citizen—like a Roman in the heyday of the Roman Empire—had the privilege of protection by his government wherever he went in the world.

Yet essentially Palmerston was a vestige of the early nineteenth century, and his death in October 1865 marked a turning point in British politics. His personal position had far transcended party loyalties and had cut across ideological lines. He had refused to acquiesce in the demands of his own party for reform of the franchise and had instead forced it to accept a frequently expansionist foreign policy. Between the fall of Peel in June 1846 and the first Disraeli government (February–December 1869), Conservative governments had been in power for a total of less than five years (at three different intervals), and no party had long been able to maintain a stable majority. Both the Conservatives and the Whigs had been forced to rely upon votes from radicals and from the Irish M. P.'s, a situation that had produced frequent cabinet changes, usually with Palmerston in a dominant position.

Gladstone and Disraeli

The death of Palmerston opened leadership of Parliament to the two foremost British political figures of the third quarter of the nineteenth century: William E. Gladstone (1809–1898), the leader of the Liberal party (formed from an alliance of Whigs, middle-class liberals, and Peelite Conservatives), and Benjamin Disraeli (1804–1881), the leader of the Conservatives. Both had served long political apprenticeships (including service under Palmerston), developing their faculties of leadership, their connections, and parliamentary experience. Both were rather indefinite about party affiliation or loyalty throughout their careers—Gladstone began his career in Parliament as a Tory; Disraeli, first one of the Tory Radicals of the 1830's, broke with Peel and opposed repeal of the Corn Laws—and eventually both made a choice dictated partly by personal political advantage as well as by deep-seated ideological conviction.

The first major political change following Palmerston's death was the passage of the Second Reform Bill in August 1867. The progress of the bill was in many ways similar to the repeal of the Corn Laws in the mid-1840's. The demand for expansion of the suffrage, as well as a redistribution of seats as a result of population changes since the 1830's, had long been a favorite issue of radicals and of many liberals, but Palmerston's opposition and the placid mood of the public in the 1850's had been distinctly unfavorable for an important revision in the electoral system. It was Gladstone who emerged as the leading proponent of moderate reform in the suffrage—only to have his bill defeated in March 1866.

It remained for the Conservative leader, Disraeli, to push through a much more radical reform measure in 1867. The reasons for Disraeli's acquiescence in such a radical measure are somewhat obscure, but in general he seems to have believed that the Conservatives would gain the confidence and support of the middle and lower classes by giving them what the Liberals had been unable to give them. In other words, finding reform unavoidable (as had Peel in 1846), Disraeli preferred to steal the issue from the Liberals and thus salvage what political advantage he and his party could from the change.

The Second Reform Bill was regarded by many members of Parliament as a great gamble—Lord Derby, the former Conservative prime minister, described it, in a memorable phrase, as "a leap in the dark." A leap it certainly was, for not only were the seats in the House of Commons increased and re-apportioned, but the electorate was roughly doubled, from about one to about two million voters. In effect, the Second Reform Bill enfranchised not only all of the middle class but many prosperous skilled workers as well.

As in 1832, the British soon discovered that extension of the suffrage did not lead to a revolution in the personnel or policies of government. But the reform of 1867 did act as a catalyst to further change. Many opponents of the Reform Bill, including John Stuart Mill, had argued that the lack of education and the animal-like existence of the working class had to be corrected before its members could become responsible voters. When the Second Reform Bill passed, Parliament began to take steps to correct the conditions to which Mill and others referred. Like the 1830's, the late 1860's and early 1870's were to be one of the great reform eras in British history. Broadening of educational opportunity, reform of the army and civil service, fundamental changes in Irish landholding and ecclesiastical affairs, introduction of the secret ballot, and an end to religious tests at Oxford and Cambridge—these were some of the outstanding changes brought about by the first Gladstone ministry (December 1868–February 1874). In 1870 the democratic principle that the government was responsible to the people, that it was in effect a microcosm of the nation itself, had been indelibly written into the British constitution. In Britain, the liberal solution of crucial social issues through peaceful, democratic reform had been tried and had proved itself. It was one of the great accomplishments in European political history, but unfortunately the avoidance of force as a means of resolving domestic problems was not widely emulated on the Continent—or, for that matter, across the sea in the United States.

II THE CRISIS IN THE UNITED STATES

Industrial Growth and Westward Expansion

Although at mid-century the suffrage in the United States was much broader than it was in Britain, the American republic was still confronted by dangerous and divisive political and constitutional questions. The United States faced a conflict over the balance of power among the states and sections of the country that brought into question the nature and, indeed, the continued existence of the federal union.

At the end of the Jackson administration in early 1837 the problems of American government still seemed comparatively clear and simple. The principal purpose of government, so the Jeffersonians and Jacksonians believed, was to serve the people, not to dominate them. In particular, there were distinct limits to what the government could and could not do. But after the mid-1830's, the economic and political condition of the country began to change rapidly, and it was the problems growing out of these changes that brought on rising sectional conflict and, finally, civil war.

The economic background of the growing conflict lay primarily in the expansion of American industry and agriculture. In the South, where cotton was the major product of the plantation system, production rose from 1.5 million bales in 1840 to well over 5 million in 1860. While this remarkable increase in production seemed, at first glance, to be an economic blessing, it proved to be a social curse, for it established Negro slavery — an essential ingredient of the "cotton kingdom" — in the Southern (and some Southwestern) states more firmly than ever. In the North, on the other hand, the expansion of industrial production and of the transportation system that was indispensable to it was even more rapid. Although the textile industry in the North and the importance of cotton as an export commodity gave the North a stake in the Southern economic system, by and large the two regions moved further and further apart economically.

Meanwhile, both North and South, for reasons of their own, looked to the new West as a necessary avenue of expansion. The Southern planter along the Atlantic coast, whose soil was slowly becoming exhausted after generations of raising the same crop, began more and more to supply slaves to farmers who were expanding the plantation system westward to the Mississippi and beyond. Thus, after the 1830's and 1840's, Negro slavery seemed in fact to be expanding, and it was not long before the very institution became the center of bitter political controversy.

Perhaps the single most important development in the emerging struggle over slavery was the opening up of the Southwest in the 1830's, followed by the Mexican War a decade later. Texas, in particular, acted as a powerful magnet for thousands of colonists, who migrated there to seek the opportunities they had been unable to find in older, more fully settled areas. It seems extremely doubtful that the Mexican authorities — Texas had become part of Mexico after it won independence from Spain in 1821 — had any idea what they were letting themselves in for when they granted permission for this influx of settlers. Within a decade, powerful opposition to Mexican rule had developed. In 1836 Texas revolted and was soon recognized by the United States as an independent republic.

By the middle 1840's the United States was embroiled in bitter controversy with Mexico, and in 1846 war broke out between the two countries. The origins of that fateful war — which, like the War of 1812, was very unpopular in certain parts of the Northeast — were extremely complex; but they centered partly around the American annexation of Texas in 1845, and there is no doubt that Southern planters, anxious for new lands to cultivate still more cotton, were strongly behind the war. President James K. Polk (1845–1849), one of the stronger chief executives in American history, would have much preferred to acquire the vast and largely unsettled California and New Mexico territories by peaceful means, but when offers to purchase these lands proved unsuccessful, he accepted war as an alternative method.

The Mexican War was destined to alter the course of American history beyond anyone's hopes and fears. Despite considerable military and diplomatic ineptitude, the United States was finally able to achieve its objective by force of superior numbers, and by the Treaty of Guadalupe Hidalgo in 1848 it acquired all the lands later to become the states of California, Utah, and Nevada, most of Arizona and New Mexico, and parts of Wyoming and Colorado. Taken together with the peaceful acquisition of the Oregon territory from Britain in 1846 and the purchase of nearly thirty thousand square miles from Mexico in 1853 – the Gadsden Purchase – the United States had now rounded out its continental frontiers. But its political future – and especially the outcome of the growing struggle between slavery and abolition – was increasingly in doubt.

Peace had not yet been concluded with Mexico when gold was discovered in California in January 1848. Within weeks the so-called California gold rush

During the first half of the nineteenth century the United States extended its boundaries west to the shores of the Pacific, south to the Gulf of Mexico and the Rio Grande, and north to the 49th parallel. The Louisiana territory was purchased in 1803 while France was embroiled in war; Spain, helpless to withstand American pressure, ceded Florida in 1819. Texas, independent from Mexico since 1836, was finally taken into the Union in 1845. Three months later Mexico was provoked into war, defeated, and forced to deed the territory west of Texas to the United States. Supporters of a southern route for the transcontinental railroad arranged the Gadsden Purchase in 1853. In the northwest the United States and Great Britain had rival claims to the Oregon territory; in 1846 both parties accepted the 49th parallel as the American-Canadian border.

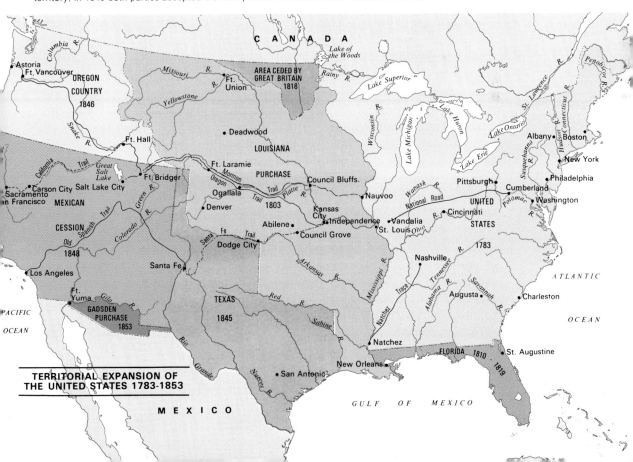

TERRITORIAL EXPANSION OF
THE UNITED STATES 1783-1853

was on in full swing; San Francisco, for example, became a city of twenty thousand inhabitants within a matter of months. But if the settlement of California soon became one of the great American success stories, its prospective admission to the Union was to touch off one of the bitterest debates in the history of Congress and open a tragic decade of sectional confrontation that ended in civil war.

One reason why the admission of states became such a hotly disputed issue was that the political control, if not the economic interests, of the various sections of the United States had passed increasingly into mutually hostile hands. Thus, in the Northern states, political power tended more and more to reside in the hands of friends of the industrial interests. As a result, it was increasingly believed in the North that high tariffs to protect newly developing industries and the involvement of the government in such matters as the building of railroads and canals were absolutely essential to the sound development of that region. To the South, on the other hand, whose agricultural society was a major market for Northern industrial goods, high tariffs were anathema. The result was that, from the War of 1812 on, the tariff issue was the subject of chronic and extremely bitter sectional controversy, which was not abated until the tariff act of 1857 put the United States in the forefront of the free-trading nations.

The long struggle over the tariff taught the South how precarious was its position in national economic affairs, but this uncertainty was modest compared with the growing anxiety of the South on the subject of slavery. By the 1840's there was a notable revival of antislavery sentiment in large parts of the North, making the South acutely aware of its minority position within the nation. The Northern states with their substantially larger population dominated the House of Representatives; the attack upon slavery was blunted primarily by the equal division of slave and nonslave states in the Senate.

The antislavery movement in the United States had a long history. The first antislavery society had been formed in Philadelphia as early as 1775, and Congress had outlawed the importation of slaves in 1808. Nevertheless, slavery remained largely a muted issue—save for the isolated crisis over the admission of Missouri in 1820—for a quarter of a century. The abolitionist movement revived with the founding of the New England Anti-Slavery Society in 1832 and the American Anti-Slavery Society in 1833. By 1840 there were about two thousand antislavery organizations, with a combined membership of approximately 200,000. Mounting opposition to slavery was expressed in the North by aid to the growing number of fugitive slaves, by attacks on the interstate sale of slaves, and by a swelling literary outcry against the "peculiar institution" itself.

The longer this estrangement between North and South persisted, the greater was the danger to the continued existence of the Union. In early 1850, Senator Henry Clay of Kentucky averted a serious crisis by proposing what became known as the Compromise of 1850. As finally passed in November of that year, the compromise provided for the admission of California as a free state, the organization of Utah and New Mexico as territories without restriction as to slavery, and the abolition of slavery in the District of Columbia, along with a more stringent fugitive slave law—this last a concession to the South.

If the Compromise of 1850 had been fully complied with, the sectional controversy might possibly have begun to abate, but radical elements in the North—including prominent citizens appalled by slavery—immediately announced plans to disobey or violate the new Fugitive Slave Act. By 1854 the pacifying effects of the Compromise of 1850 were largely nullified, and a new furor developed over the prospective admission of Kansas and Nebraska into the Union. The settlement and organization of these territories was vitally important both to the Northerners who were planning to build a transcontinental railroad across the central United States and to the Southerners who were seeking to maintain the balance of slave and free states in the Senate. If Kansas and Nebraska entered the Union as free states, in accordance with the provisions of the Missouri Compromise of 1820, their admission would decisively unbalance the Senate in favor of the North; and this the South was determined to prevent. The result was another bitter congressional debate, lasting from January to May 1854. In the end Senator Stephen Douglas of Illinois, who was deeply interested in railroad expansion, managed to secure the passage of the Kansas-Nebraska Act, which established the principle of "popular sovereignty" for states admitted to the Union from west of the Mississippi. According to the Kansas-Nebraska Act, the citizens of each new state could now decide for themselves whether or not they wanted slavery in their state.

If Douglas believed that removing the slavery issue from the halls of Congress would help to cool the ever growing sectional passions, ensuing developments soon proved him grievously mistaken. Disputed elections and bloody battles between "free soilers" and proslavery elements kept the issue very much alive in Kansas. James Buchanan, a Democrat elected President in 1856, pursued a cautious and vacillating policy in regard to the Kansas situation and was unable to resolve it.

Hardly had Buchanan been inaugurated when in March 1857 the Supreme Court delivered its momentous decision in the Dred Scott case. By holding that, as a Negro and hence not a citizen, Scott could not sue in federal court, that his temporary residence in free territory had not made him free, and that the Missouri Compromise (including its prohibition of slavery in Western territories) was unconstitutional, the Supreme Court greatly intensified national rancor over the slavery issue. The decision marked the first time in over fifty years that the Court had declared an act of Congress unconstitutional, and it outraged Northern abolitionists and further confused the whole issue. The violent and impatient temper of the times was further exacerbated by the business "panic" (depression) of 1857. Coming at the end of a decade of gross speculation and other unsound practices, the panic caused bank and business failures and unemployment, particularly in the North.

Other influences were meanwhile at work heating moral and political passions. As early as 1851 Harriet Beecher Stowe (1811–1896), the daughter of a Connecticut clergyman, began the publication of *Uncle Tom's Cabin, or Life Among the Lowly*, which soon became a powerful weapon in the hands of abolitionists. No less important perhaps was Hinton Rowman Helper's *The Impending Crisis of the South*, first published in the summer of 1857, which sought to prove that slavery was the curse of the South, and the cause of its white people's degradation. Helper was violently abolitionist, even though he had no liking whatever for Negroes. In the South his work—along with much other liberal and abolitionist writing—was speedily proscribed.

The Civil War and Reconstruction

By early 1860 the life of the Union was hanging by a thread. The nominating conventions and national election of that year severed that thread and began the tragic era of secession, civil war, and reconstruction. In late April 1860 the Democratic convention met at Charleston, South Carolina. When Southern intransigents demanded that the party platform support slavery in the territories while the majority—led by Stephen Douglas—stood by the 1856 platform pledge of nonintervention, the convention broke up. The Northern delegates thereupon adjourned to Baltimore, where they nominated Douglas; the Southerners chose their own candidate. The Republican party, which had been formed in 1854 out of a fusion of Free-Soil Democrats and Northern Whigs and whose presidential candidate in 1856 had carried eleven states, met in Chicago and chose Abraham Lincoln of Illinois. Lincoln had served only one term in the House of Representatives but his losing campaign for the Senate in 1858 against Douglas had drawn widespread attention.

Lincoln's election in November 1860—made possible by the split in the Democratic vote—was not an immediate threat to slavery, but it did signify an end to its expansion. "My paramount object," Lincoln had said, "is to save the Union, and not either to save or destroy slavery." Southerners, however, believed that unless slavery could continue to expand, it was ultimately doomed, and with a Republican in the White House, they feared that their influence in national affairs would henceforth be severely reduced. Under those circumstances, desperate and radical counsels were increasingly dominant in the South.

The doctrine that a state could nullify federal legislation which it found repugnant and if necessary secede from the Union had been popular in the South, particularly in South Carolina, since the 1830's. A month after Lincoln's election, South Carolina formally seceded from the Union, to be followed in a few months by the other states of the Deep South—Mississippi,

Florida, Alabama, Georgia, Louisiana, and Texas—and, after the outbreak of hostilities at Fort Sumter in April 1861, by Virginia, Arkansas, Tennessee, and North Carolina. It must not be supposed, however, that secession was a course easily embarked upon or that there were not many staunch advocates of the Union even in the Deep South.

The secession of the Southern states was followed, in February 1861, by the establishment, at Montgomery, Alabama, of a rival Confederate States of America. In early February the Confederacy elected as its president Jefferson Davis (1808–1889), a native Kentuckian who had twice served in the United States Senate, and who had been secretary of war in the 1850's under President Franklin K. Pierce. The Confederate constitution was emphatic in its concern for states' rights, yet, as the Civil War progressed, Davis himself was accused of the kind of centralizing tendencies against which the South had gone to war in the first place.

The war that began in April 1861 was as devastating and exhausting as it was protracted. The North had an overwhelming advantage in industry, transportation, wealth, education, and population. The Southern economy, moreover, depended largely upon one major crop—cotton—and was soon severely affected by the combined effects of the Northern naval blockade and increasing devastation by Northern armies. Furthermore, the Confederate government was in serious financial straits almost from the beginning, finding it even more difficult to levy and collect sufficient taxes than to procure enough men for the army. Confederate losses in manpower were so serious that, although over 800,000 men saw military service during the course of the war, fewer than 200,000 were under arms when the war finally ended in April 1865.

Why did the war drag on for almost exactly four years, despite the North's overwhelming advantages? The reasons included not only the vast territorial extent of the Confederacy but its adequate internal lines of communications, its remarkably high morale, and especially its outstanding military leadership, headed by a native Virginian, General Robert E. Lee (1807–1870). Sought as well by President Lincoln, who offered him the command of the Union army, Lee—who loved the Union and was personally opposed to both slavery and secession—finally agreed to accept a Confederate command and in April 1862 took over the Army of Northern Virginia.

Against Lee—who lost only one battle, the climactic one at Gettysburg in July 1863—and other excellent Southern commanders, the North could only offer a series of ineffective or blundering mediocrities, until in a moment of political desperation, in March 1864, President Lincoln appointed as general-in-chief of the Union forces, Ulysses S. Grant (1822–1885)—whose distinguished military career had once been all but terminated by immoderate drinking. It was Grant who devised the grand strategy that led to the final military defeat of the Confederacy in early 1865.

If the military conquest of the South proved almost more than the North could manage, the political aspect of the war was no less divisive, trouble-some, and dangerous for the North. The conflict was never popular there, and became progressively less so as time went on and casualties mounted. Not until March 1863 did the Congress pass a conscription act, and even then the law allowed a draftee to avoid serving by hiring a substitute or paying the government $300, which only the better-off could afford. In July 1863 there were bloody draft riots in New York City, and the large number of "peace Democrats"—called Copperheads (after the snake that strikes without warn-ing)—nearly brought Lincoln down in the presidential election of 1864. (To enhance the President's chances, a Southern Democrat—Andrew Johnson —was chosen as his running mate.)

Lincoln, then, had good reason to be aware of the precariousness of his po-sition, both military and political. In addition, he was by nature a rather cautious statesman. Originally, he had carefully limited the issues to a straightforward defense of the principle of national sovereignty. In his debate with Douglas in 1858 he had stated, "A house divided cannot stand," to which he had immediately and significantly added, "I believe this government can-not endure permanently half-slave and half-free." But even after Fort Sum-ter, Lincoln was long reluctant to move toward the abolition of slavery. By 1862, however, he had become aware also of the great international impor-tance of the issues and of the fact that the sentiments of European liberals, in particular, were aroused against the South because of the slavery issue.

Nevertheless, Lincoln would have preferred emancipation which compen-sated slave owners, and it was only after long study and much soul-searching that he issued the Emancipation Proclamation of September 22, 1862. That preliminary proclamation applied only to areas under effective Union control; but it went on to say that slaves in states "in rebellion against the United States" would be free as of January 1, 1863, and on that day a final proclama-tion to that effect was issued.

The end of the war resolved only the question of whether the South would return to the Union; it left unsolved all the ramifications of that question. What would be the status of the freed slaves? What would be done with the former rebels— in fact, with a whole society whose opposition had been hard-ened rather than weakened by defeat? How would the Northern economy adjust to the return of an army of jobless soldiers and an end to the expendi-tures of war? Would the significantly increased powers exercised by the federal government during the war be temporary or become permanent?

Of these, the first two questions were the most pressing and the most con-troversial. Two major positions emerged in the North. President Lincoln and Vice-President Johnson both favored a moderate position which would permit the reconstruction of the Southern enonomic and social system somewhat along prewar lines, with the abolition of slavery the only decisive and perma-nent change. On the other hand, the so-called Radical Republicans in Con-gress—led by Thaddeus Stevens and Charles Sumner—were supporters of abolition who regarded Lincoln's policy as intolerably lenient and wanted in effect to revolutionize Southern society and to use the Negro for that purpose. Lincoln's policy survived his assassination in April 1865, but by 1867 the Radicals were in control.

The history of Reconstruction has been debated over the past half-century. Older scholars like William A. Dunning saw it largely as a mistake which did great harm to both North and South; more recent historians, like Kenneth P. Stampp, have argued that, while it doubtless involved certain excesses, it produced the beginning of important and long overdue social changes and may have been too soon abandoned. Perhaps either the moderate or the harsh policy could have proved successful if it had been applied consistently. It was the tragedy of the Reconstruction era that the switch from the first to the second vitiated the effects of both and left Southerners for many decades a backward and dissident minority in the national political and intellectual structure.

In the decade after 1867, Radical Reconstruction worked to break the monopoly of economic and political power held by the planter aristocracy. It sought, for instance, to revolutionize Southern society by establishing the full political rights of Negroes. This was the purpose of the most important so-called Reconstruction amendments to the Constitution—the Fourteenth (1868) and Fifteenth (1870)—which provided for Negro citizenship, denied the states the right to abridge this citizenship, and provided further that no citizen should be denied the right to vote "on account of race, color, or previous condition of servitude." The Reconstruction governments in the Southern states also made an effort to educate both Negroes and poor whites alike through a system of public schools. These were necessary and long overdue beginnings. But it seems clear that Radical Reconstruction was frequently characterized by inefficiency, graft, and corruption, and these flaws increasingly discredited the whole policy in the eyes of moderate Northerners.

Beyond that, it soon became fairly apparent that the resistance of the white population could not be overcome even by stern military rule. Within a few years, Negro political activity in the South had been thwarted—first by such semilegal measures as the "black codes," then by the terror and intimidation practiced by groups like the Ku Klux Klan, and finally by the establishment of new discriminatory laws—so-called Jim Crow laws—which were eventually approved by the Supreme Court. Within a few years, the New South looked increasingly like the Old South. To be sure, slavery was gone, but, for the rest, little or nothing about the position of either Negroes or poor whites had been permanently improved. Outwardly, in the most formal sense, the South seemed to have accepted the changes wrought by the Civil War. But many decades were to go by before the promise of freedom would become reality to the Negro in the South—or, for that matter, in the North, where the late 1870's and the 1880's were characterized by economic expansion and a sharp decline in political idealism.

Democracy, the will of the majority, had prevailed in the United States, but the price had been high, and the follow-through and the end results were confused and disappointing. The failure to resolve the critical issue of slavery without force and then the failure to complete the social and economic emancipation of the Negro were an American tragedy. As events were soon to show, that tragedy was not without its European counterpart.

III FRANCE—FROM SECOND REPUBLIC TO SECOND EMPIRE

Louis Napoleon and the Second Empire

While the mid-century crisis of the American democracy built slowly to a shattering climax, the trial of French democracy followed almost a reverse course. It began with the blood bath of the "June Days" of 1848, when France was initiated into the hideousness of class warfare (of which even the French Revolution of 1789 had known comparatively little), and proceeded to a more covert but hardly less serious conflict extending over the next twenty years. The course of French history led from the "June Days" to another Napoleonic coup and another Napoleonic dictatorship and in 1871 to still another terrible blood bath, the Paris Commune.

If the most striking quality of the modern British parliamentary system has been the essential consensus among significant political groups, the opposite condition has been notably true in French political life. It has been the particular malaise of parliamentary politics in France that the country lacked almost completely the kind of political consensus that had existed in England for generations. What this has meant in practice is that in France most major parties or factions sought not only office but the transformation of the constitution to suit their own particular ideology or prejudice. In French politics, the middle ground was little more than the eye of the storm that intermittently threatened the stability of the French state. That was true before the outbreak of the revolution of 1848, it remained true in the generation after that revolution, and it has been disconcertingly true of French politics in the twentieth century.

It is difficult to say whether the Second Republic, which began in February 1848, was fated to go the way of the First in the 1790's. As in the 1790's, no effective middle-class individuals or groups emerged who could lead France through its new travails. As a result, by the closing months of 1848, the Second Republic faced a formidable challenge from Louis Napoleon (1809–1873), Bonaparte's nephew. The emergence of Louis Napoleon was due to a number of factors: the power of the Napoleonic legend, the political impotence of the moderate republicans who headed the government, his own persistent aspirations, and the electoral system of the Second Republic, whose constitution provided for a strong chief executive elected by popular vote. In such a vote, who—and what—could match the new Napoleon?

It is but one of the oddities of nineteenth-century French history that the Orléanist monarch, Louis Philippe, had consciously revived the Napoleonic legend for his own political reasons and thus helped to set the stage for the political ascendancy of the first emperor's nephew. Less than twenty years after Napoleon's death in 1821, his last remains had been brought back to France from St. Helena and given informal canonization by a government and people whose dissatisfaction with the post-Napoleonic present markedly enhanced their recollection of past splendors. To a largely disaffected peasantry and working class, a frustrated bourgeoisie, a dissatisfied army, and many other Frenchmen in the 1840's, Napoleon ɪ appeared—retrospectively—as the friend and protector of the masses, the source of glory, placement, and promotion for the middle class, and the embodiment of the power of the French nation, which lay idle under the quiescent or ineffective diplomacy of Louis Philippe and his timid counselors.

Young Louis Napoleon was very much aware of the magic of the Bonapartist legend, and of the grand opportunity that legend presented him. "I am sure," he wrote in the 1840's, "the shade of the Emperor protects and blesses me . . . . I have sacrificed my youth, my future, my life to the triumph of the cause which we cannot desert without dishonor." Although his prosaic appearance and scant charisma made him an improbable successor to his powerful uncle, it was perhaps these factors that led many to underestimate him, and he remained at liberty to pursue his goal. Twice he attempted a coup d'état—first at Strasbourg in 1836, then at Boulogne in 1840—relying upon the magic of his name and the loyalty of a motley band of followers. But the coups failed, and the second was serious enough to earn him a sentence of life imprisonment. In 1845, after five years of relatively comfortable confinement, he escaped to England. There he proved himself a master at propaganda, a device he had exploited in prison and earlier, while pursuing something of a literary career. In 1839 he had published an apologia for his uncle's dictatorship, which did much to keep alive the Napoleonic legend.

In 1848 Louis entered formal political life as a representative in the National Assembly. The first time he was elected, the Assembly refused to lift the ban upon members of the Bonaparte family, but when he was victorious again in several by-elections, it was decided that he would be an innocuous addition to French politics. Even if Louis had had no higher political ambitions when he first entered the National Assembly, they would quickly have been aroused by that body's hapless course and by the frightening social confrontation of the summer of 1848 and the resulting open split among various revolutionary groups. Louis knew when to seize his opportunity, and the constitution of the Second Republic—providing for popular election of the president—was tailor-made for him. In November 1848 he became a candidate for the highest office, and the following month he was overwhelmingly elected.

While campaigning for office Napoleon avowed his loyalty to the Second Republic. But once installed, he lost no time in undermining and, before long, overthrowing the Republic he was sworn to protect. For more than a year, Louis sought to advance his objectives by making systematic concessions to the Right—for example, approving the Falloux Law of March 1850, which gave the Catholic Church considerable powers over French education. Liberal and radical elements throughout the country were hounded and harassed. A new electoral law tended to disenfranchise many working men.

But Louis wanted more than a conservative reorganization of the country. Like his uncle, he thirsted for full and unlimited power; and after the French Assembly refused to repeal the existing ban on successive four-year presidential terms, he prepared a coup d'état, which was carried through on December 2, 1851, the forty-sixth anniversary of Bonaparte's smashing victory over the Austrians at Austerlitz. A plebiscite confirmed Napoleon's coup and empowered him to draft a new constitution, which bore a strong resemblance to that of the Year VIII (1800). Highly authoritarian, the new constitution gave Napoleon wide-ranging legislative and police powers, both of which he used without hesitation. It soon became clear that Napoleon had in mind nothing less than the restoration of the Empire, and the results of a second plebiscite were favorable. Accordingly, the Second Empire was proclaimed on December 2, 1852, the first anniversary of his coup d'état.

Thus once again an embryonic attempt at parliamentary government in France gave way to personal absolutism in the familiar Bonapartist tradition. Despite his evident shortcomings, Louis Napoleon was not unaware of the ideas and needs of his time. As a result, the liberal preference for freedom of press and assembly under a fairly broad electorate was abandoned in favor of a centralized bureaucratic absolutism that sought to vitiate the appeal of liberalism and socialism by combining careful attention to the health of business and industry with a paternalistic concern for the welfare of peasants and workers. Louis Napoleon, now called Napoleon III, operated under the assumption that the interests of business and the workers were, in the long run, identical or at least compatible. In the provinces, he relied upon the traditionally dominant role of the upper class and the overwhelming affection of the peasants for the name of Napoleon.

The institutions of the Second Empire echoed those of the first; both were more authoritarian than those of the liberals and more democratic than those of the monarchists. The government was firmly based on a centralized bureaucracy which, in traditional French fashion, saw to it that official policy was effectively carried out. On the surface the electoral system was democratic in its provision for universal manhood suffrage, but in fact it was weighted in favor of official candidates, who normally undertook in writing to support the government before receiving its endorsement. In addition the use of plebiscites—"the President of the Republic is responsible to the French people, to whom he always has the right to appeal," declared the new constitution—allowed Louis to circumvent the normal processes of government by asking the population at large to endorse his policies. The plebiscite was used to legitimize the constitution of January 1852 as well as most of the subsequent major changes in governmental structure.

These not so subtle means of influencing the electoral process were reinforced by other frankly authoritarian aspects of the government. Although the new constitution declared that "legislative authority is exercised collectively by the President of the Republic, the Senate, and the Legislative Body," in practice the legislature, once elected, could only approve or veto proposals submitted to it. It could not initiate legislation or call ministers to account. Political discussion and even public scrutiny of the government were carefully limited by restrictions on the freedom of speech, press, and assembly.

The history of the Second Empire falls into two parts—the first, the more conservative period, extending from 1852 to the late 1860's; the second, the so-called Liberal Empire, from the late 1860's until the Franco-Prussian War and the overthrow of the Empire in September 1870. The first period was marked by an extension of those essentially conservative, pro-business policies Napoleon had pursued between his election as president in December 1848

The Paris *Opéra* reflected the ideals of Napoleon III's empire and the architectural tastes of the European ruling class in the 1860's. The *Opéra* was one of the prime achievements of Napoleon's program for beautifying Paris. But its Baroque style symbolized Napoleon's emphasis on recreating the grandeur of the past rather than realistically facing the problems of modern society. The most obvious defect of nineteenth-century culture was its failure to develop a new architectural style suitable to an age of industrialism, capitalism, and democracy.

and his coup in December 1851. Thus French newspapers continued to be under strict government control, the Catholic Church gained additional power over the educational system, and banks and industries were granted concessions and support of all kinds. But even during those years, Napoleon initiated a more active social policy. He appointed Baron Georges Haussmann prefect of the Seine and put him in charge of the vast rebuilding program that was to give the French capital much of the character it retains to the present day.

By the late 1850's, however, such policies were clearly insufficient to sustain the Napoleonic regime, and the emperor now began to move toward what is usually referred to as the Liberal Empire, marked by further reforms. The mounting dissatisfaction with Napoleon III stemmed more immediately from his foreign than from his domestic policies. Seeking to reassure his countrymen and the rest of Europe, he had declared (upon taking the imperial title), *"L'Empire, c'est la paix."* But this was a policy Napoleon found difficult — indeed impossible — to follow. In March 1854 France plunged into the Crimean War with Russia, largely over the control of the holy places in Palestine. The peace settlement at the Congress of Paris in 1856 seemed to satisfy France's diplomatic objectives in the Middle East. But the prestige that Napoleon thereby gained was short-lived. Domestic dissension continued to mount, and before long Napoleon began to intervene in Italian affairs, with considerable benefit to the cause of Italian unity but very little to himself or France. Napoleon's Italian adventure began in January 1858 when an Italian nationalist made an unsuccessful attempt to assassinate the emperor and his wife. The result was that Napoleon III became interested in Italian affairs as never before. But unlike his illustrious uncle, whose Italian triumphs in the mid-1790's had been the prelude to much greater conquests, Napoleon III launched his own downfall with his intervention in Italy.

It all began with a highly secret, eight-hour meeting between Napoleon and Camillo di Cavour, the prime minister of Piedmont-Sardinia, at the French village of Plombières. The two reached a closely guarded agreement providing for France to join Piedmont, the leader of a revived Italian unity movement, in a war against Austria, the purpose being to drive Austria completely out of Italy. While the agreement fell short of providing for effective Italian unity once the war was over, it was doubtless intended to reinforce Napoleon's image as a champion of the principle of nationality. And as the price of French assistance, it provided for the transfer of Nice and Savoy to France and for the marriage of Napoleon's cousin to the daughter of the King of Piedmont.

In late April 1859 war between Austria and Piedmont began, and in mid-May the French entered the war. But Napoleon's policy outraged conservative Catholic elements in France, the emperor himself disliked the sight of blood, and for these and other reasons (including unfounded fear of a possible Prussian attack), Napoleon concluded an armistice with Austria in mid-July.

Napoleon's flip-flop outraged the Piedmontese—especially since he now agreed to Austria's retaining the vital Italian province of Venetia—and provided further evidence of his lack of personal steadfastness.

After the Italian venture it was almost all downhill for Napoleon, though he was to remain in power for a decade, and his last years were not without their positive aspects. In 1860–1861, for instance, he broadened the powers of the French parliament, which now received some additional authority in budgetary matters. In 1863 he came out, futilely, in favor of the Polish insurrection of that year, and in 1864—on the promise of the new Italian government not to occupy Rome itself—he agreed to withdraw French troops which he had sent to Rome in 1849 as protectors of the papacy.

But these moves did not arrest the steady decline in Napoleon's political prestige. Adolphe Thiers, one of the founders of the July monarchy, demanded that the majority of the French lower house "direct the actions of the government." Léon Gambetta, spokesman for Republican sentiment, called for a return to the "principles of the French Revolution." Napoleon was further discredited by the humiliating failure of his reckless attempt, between 1863 and 1867, to create a French imperial satellite in Mexico under the rule of the Austrian archduke Maximilian. Strong protests by the United States government in 1865 forced Napoleon to withdraw French troops from Mexico, and Maximilian was tried and executed by Mexican republicans.

Public discontent was soon reflected in election returns. In May 1869 the government survived the parliamentary elections by a fairly close vote. During the next year Napoleon made repeated efforts to adapt his faltering regime to the steadily growing demands for genuine liberalization. In May 1870 a referendum was held on numerous changes, and they were approved by a vote of about 7,300,000 to 1,500,000.

It is difficult to say whether the reforms represented Napoleon III's own attitudes or political expediency. It is worth recalling that, as a member of a liberal secret society, the *Carbonari*, in his younger days in Italy, he had taken part in a revolution against papal authority and had been expelled as a result. Such youthful involvement in liberal causes and his occasional reference to himself as a socialist suggest that perhaps there was, after all, another side to him than that presented by the brutal and reactionary policies of the 1850's. In any case, it is unclear whether the liberal reforms of 1869–1870 could possibly have transformed the Empire into a more democratic form of government, for they were variously implemented and abandoned in an atmosphere of increasing political uncertainty.

The country's delicate situation was transformed into a desperate crisis by a series of disastrous failures in foreign policy which brought about the end of the Second Empire. These failures grew out of Napoleon's relations with Bismarck and Prussia, both of which he consistently underrated. Although he had come to know Bismarck when the latter served as Prussian minister to France just before becoming prime minister of Prussia in 1862, Napoleon

The Second Napoleonic Empire. Daumier's cartoon "History of a Reign" (above left) reflects the opinion of republican democrats on how France fared under the rule of Napoleon III. The destruction of the Second Republic by Napoleon's coup in 1851 was followed in 1870 by France's devastating defeat at the hands of the Prussian army at Sedan. Napoleon III liked to have himself portrayed (above right) in the trappings of royal grandeur and traditional glory, but these were of little practical value in solving France's many domestic and foreign problems.

seemed to have no comprehension of his objectives or his intelligence or, above all, of the power of the Prussian army. One result was that he did nothing to support Austria in the dramatic Seven Weeks' War (June–August 1866), by which Prussia established itself in a dominant political-military position in Germany. Then, with the French army largely unprepared and with France diplomatically isolated, he allowed himself to be goaded into a disastrous war with Prussia in July 1870, a war which he believed the French people wanted and would support.

Napoleon, who prided himself on his network of political intelligence, proved badly mistaken. In early September, following a crushing French defeat at Sedan, he was himself captured by the Prussians, and the following day a republic was once again proclaimed in Paris. But the agony of France was far from over. For the lost war brought to the surface all the political and social conflict of 1848, and while Napoleon headed for exile in England, where he died in 1873, France was plunged into a desperate internal crisis, centering largely on a revolutionary upheaval in beleaguered Paris—known as the Paris Commune.

IV THE OLD EMPIRES AND SMALLER POWERS

Austria in Decline

If the forces of liberal reform made steady progress in mid-Victorian England and rather less in France under Napoleon III, the cause of political and social change encountered mighty obstacles in the old eastern empires, Austria and Russia. Even in those states the years between the revolutions of 1848 and the late 1860's were not wholly devoid of progress. But it was slow and halting, usually far too late, and not infrequently counterproductive. The result was that even worthwhile political and social reforms — for instance, those in Russia in the 1860's — produced either strong conservative counter-movements or — as in the Habsburg monarchy — were of a kind that made further reforms far more difficult. In neither state was there an effective national legislature or a farsighted monarch. After the 1850's both Austria and Russia entered a period of troubled decline that ended only with the overthrow of the Habsburg and Romanov dynasties in 1917–1918.

The Austrian Empire had been most clearly put on notice during the mid-century revolutions; but once it had finally suppressed all liberal and national elements — with Russian help — the Habsburg regime believed that it could relapse into the kind of unenlightened policies it had followed before 1848. With Metternich at the helm, Austria had dominated European politics both at the Congress of Vienna and during the thirty years that followed, but by the late 1860's it was diplomatically isolated, shorn of its power in Italy and Germany, and increasingly threatened by Russian expansionism. For the emperors of Austria the nineteenth century became the era of a long and painful holding action — a holding action that might postpone disaster but could not permanently prevent it.

In one sense, the Habsburg monarchy was a victim of time and circumstance, for the very structure of the Empire pitted the imperial government against the two most dynamic forces in nineteenth-century politics: liberalism and nationalism. Given the Empire's multinational character, nationalism there was bound to be a force for disunity, and any significant concession to representative government was likely to afford various national groups a powerful new tool with which to press their growing claims for autonomy. To be sure, the continued survival of the Empire was due almost as much to the inability of the various nationalities to agree on a replacement (or even to its dissolution) as to the innate strength of the imperial system. Thus, in various parts of the Empire, Magyars (or Hungarians) were struggling with Croats, and Czechs with Bohemian Germans. The result from the late 1840's was growing political deadlock. National particularism not only prevented the Empire from functioning; it prevented any viable government from replacing it, while for various reasons — including conservatism and lassitude

—the Habsburg monarchy eschewed the kind of strong liberal centralism that alone might have given the Empire a longer lease on life.

The revolution of 1848 revealed to Europe the tenuous nature of Austrian control over the various elements in the Empire; the events of 1848–1849 also made clear that neither Britain nor France would intervene either to help the various nationalities in the Austrian Empire attain autonomy or to check the Russian forces that were called in by the Austrian government to put an end to the revolt in Hungary. Their hands-off attitude was a powerful factor in the Habsburg's favor. The ruling elements in Vienna believed that if they replaced the weak-minded Emperor Ferdinand I with his eighteen-year-old nephew, Francis Joseph, they could then disavow all the constitutional promises and arrangements agreed to since the spring of 1848. This change in rulers was brought about in December 1848, and in early March 1849 the Austrian government dissolved the promising imperial parliament and replaced the constitution that the assembly had just finished drafting with a highly conservative one of its own.

This perfidy was neither the first nor the last of its kind: even the conservative constitution was summarily suspended in 1851. But for its temporary victory, which German liberal elements as well as the non-German nationalities were powerless to prevent, the Habsburg monarchy ultimately paid a very high price.

Even more than elsewhere in Germany, the 1850's in Austria were years of myopic reaction and repression. Once again the German bureaucracy provided the unifying and centralizing force that held together various parts of the empire and supported the authoritarian system of government upon which the imperial power was based. The Bach system, named after Alexander Bach, the minister of the interior, was characterized by renewed censorship as well as by a revival of the police state mentality that viewed all tendencies toward reform as a threat to the government. In addition, Habsburg educational policy seemed increasingly to estrange Austria from the rest of Germany; the Austrian universities in particular suffered from ideological and religious restrictions. In economic development, Austria lagged increasingly behind Prussia and other German states. Its currency remained unstable, its government bonds weak, its industrial and technological development seriously backward. The result was that Austria was unable to force its way into the *Zollverein*, the German customs union, and Prussian leadership in that important organization gave Prussia a powerful advantage in the struggle for economic, intellectual, and political leadership in Germany.

Austrian foreign policy throughout the 1850's was equally unwise and shortsighted. Having benefited handsomely from Russian military intervention against the Hungarian revolution in June 1849, the Austrians demonstrated their ingratitude by taking the Anglo-French-Turkish side in the Crimean War (1853–1856), thereby outraging the Russian government and permanently rupturing the conservative alliance that had survived all vicissitudes since 1815. Furthermore, Austria paid dearly for its role in that war. For though it never actually entered the conflict, its armies were fully mobilized for a long period of time, at a cost that the already heavily burdened Austrian treasury could hardly bear.

In the late 1850's and 1860's the combined result of these failures in domestic and foreign affairs produced a crisis that shook the foundations of the Empire. This crisis began with the war with France and Italy. It is true that the war would have been highly unlikely but for the scheming of Napoleon III, and but for French intervention Piedmont's fate would almost certainly have been rather different. But it was a good indication of Austria's rapidly slipping international prestige that Napoleon felt it safe to embark on this adventure, and it was further evidence of the Habsburg monarchy's diplomatic isolation that neither the German Confederation nor Russia moved to its support.

The disaster in Italy seemed momentarily to open a new era of reform in Austria. But the Crown's effort to hand down new political institutions from above was largely unsuccessful. Only the German middle class seemed at all pleased; all the other nationalities in the Empire were becoming more and more disenchanted. The political failure of the early 1860's was all the more serious since it roughly coincided with the failure of Austria's last attempt to force its way into the *Zollverein*. By the middle 1860's Austria's position in the German Confederation had clearly reached a new low.

Some political and military leaders in Austria viewed the situation realistically and strongly favored either a policy of reasonable cooperation with Prussia or a policy of serious domestic reform. But these men were not in the majority, and those who were sent the Empire plunging toward a dangerous confrontation. The result was Austria's humiliating defeat by Prussia in the Seven Weeks' War of June–August 1866. That defeat not only marked Austria's loss of predominance in central Europe to Prussia but also provided an opportunity for the Magyars and other constituent nationalities to question again the fundamental structure of the Empire. The Habsburg response was, if anything, even more dangerous than the insincere schemes and proposals with which earlier crises had been met. In 1848–1849 the Habsburgs had ended by cheating all nationalities. In the agreement reached in 1867 they favored the Magyars at the expense of the rest.

The result of the *Ausgleich* of that year was to set up the dualism that lasted, with certain changes, down to the First World War and the dissolution of the Habsburg monarchy itself. Under the new constitutional arrangements, Austria and Hungary were joined by a personal union—that is, they shared the same ruler, who was simultaneously emperor of Austria and king of Hungary; they were also to have joint ministries of war and foreign affairs and finance. But beyond this, Austria and Hungary became constitutionally separate kingdoms, each with its own diet and bureaucracy. The most damaging—and potentially explosive—part of the Compromise of 1867 was that it in effect handed over the smaller nationalities in the eastern half of the Empire to the Magyars, who comprised less than half the population of Hungary. The nature of the settlement made further decentralization of the Empire virtually impossible. Thus the Habsburg state was now in a worse straitjacket than before, as events over the next half-century were to prove.

Reaction and Reform in Russia

In the middle of the nineteenth century the Russian system of government and many of its problems bore a definite resemblance to those of Austria. Both countries retained an autocratic system under leaders who largely refused to make the concessions to liberalism and democracy offered by other authoritarian systems, such as Prussia and the Second Empire in France. Both came ultimately to believe that their survival depended on nearly complete opposition to all significant change. In Austria, successive governments were convinced that any concessions to nationalism or parliamentarianism could be suicidal. The Russian czars and their governments also saw liberalism and democracy as a direct threat; indeed, especially in the reign of Nicholas I (1825–1855), almost any change came to be regarded as inimical to the security of the state. Thus the reforms made in Russia in the middle of the nineteenth century were undertaken only with the greatest hesitation and trepidation. At best they were only half measures; to open the door fully to reform, the czars believed, might start a flood that could not be stopped before their own authority was called into question.

The attitude of Nicholas I toward Russian society and government is well illustrated by the doctrine of "Official Nationality," which was first proclaimed by his minister of education in 1833 and soon became the theme of governmental ideology. Official Nationality was centered around three concepts: autocracy, the Russian Orthodox Church, and nationalism, or the unique culture and traditional structure of Russian society.

Given this philosophy of politics, it is not difficult to see why intelligent and farsighted Russians began increasingly to despair about the future of their country and why in central and western Europe the very word "Russia" began to conjure up increasingly ominous overtones. This is not to say that even Nicholas was wholly oblivious to the domestic needs of his sprawling Empire. He knew fairly well that his people were growing restless, but it was one thing to be aware of this condition and quite another to do something about the sources of popular discontent. Thus he agonized for most of his reign over the position of the serfs and repeatedly looked for a way to end serfdom; but though he truly sought reforms that would make the government more efficient, he remained steadfastly committed to the conservative ideology implicit in the doctrine of Official Nationality and for that reason was basically opposed to any significant change. "There is no question," Nich-

The Russian Nobility. The view of the mid-nineteenth-century Russian aristocracy held by west European liberals is typified in this caricature by the French artist, Gustave Doré. He shows Russian lords using serfs as stakes in a card game. The Russian nobility's reputation for reaction, selfishness, and brutal treatment of the peasantry was richly deserved. Even those Russian aristocrats who were concerned about the condition of their society and government lacked the courage and energy to effect the necessary fundamental reforms.

olas told his council of state in March 1842, "that serfdom, as it now exists among us, is an evil, palpable and evident to everyone, but to touch it now would be even more disastrous."[1]

Indeed, Nicholas I moved the Russian government further into autocracy than it had been under his predecessors. The essence of his government was personal rule. He established a pattern of bypassing the normal bureaucracy by expanding the chancery, which was under his personal control. Furthermore, he preferred to do almost everything of importance in secret. The infamous "Third Department" of his chancery was a secret police force with virtually unlimited powers. In seeking to ferret out subversion and other threats to the security of the state, it censored all publications printed in or imported into Russia. These were carefully scrutinized not only for evident subversive tendencies but for anything that might be in the least offensive to the view of the world put forth in the doctrine of Official Nationality.

Nicholas's problems are revealed in his suspicion of the Russian educational, system. He saw in education a twofold danger. First, it opened the door to critical thought and subversive ideas which could undermine the authority of

1. Quoted in Jerome Blum, *Lord and Peasant in Russia from the Ninth to the Nineteenth Century*. Princeton, N.J.: Princeton University Press, 1961, p. 547.

the government, particularly the teaching of western European liberalism. Second, it opened the door to social advancement to the lower classes, thereby threatening the class structure. Not only was the system closely supervised, so that teachers relayed only prescribed material to their students, but care was taken to see that each class of the population received only the education the czar considered appropriate to its place in society. It was very difficult for children of the lower classes to attend secondary schools or (especially) the universities, but the education of children of the aristocracy was subsidized. Nicholas hated even the language and terminology of liberalism and reform. When a minister closed a report with the word *progress*, Nicholas angrily commented on the document, "Progress? What progress? This word must be deleted from official terminology!"

But within the apparently stable political and social structure of Russia changes were taking place that Nicholas was powerless to stop. With its population growing rapidly, with serfdom becoming a political issue, and with the rudiments of an industrial working class beginning to appear, Russia was slowly entering the modern age. Although Nicholas's economic policies were for the most part vacillating and capricious, the economic advance of Russia during his reign should not be underestimated. In the late 1830's the first Russian railroad was constructed. Vast regions in the north and in Siberia were brought into the economic and social fabric of the country, and Russia steadily extended its effective power eastward to the Pacific and in the Black Sea region. In part this was the natural result of the growth of the Russian population and economy, but it was also the product of an aggressive foreign policy that involved Nicholas in the affairs of the decaying Ottoman Empire and led him to intervene in western European affairs in 1848 on the side of autocracy.

Russian interest in southeastern Europe was based primarily upon its long cherished desire to gain access, through the Bosporus, to the Mediterranean. This goal was buttressed by Nicholas's desire to protect his Orthodox co-religionists in the Ottoman Empire and by the Pan-Slavism which was slowly becoming a significant element in Russian nationalism. These cultural and religious ties served to strengthen the natural Russian interest in the unsettled politics of the Balkans and the Ottoman Empire. Faced with increasing internal unrest, the Turkish sultan was seldom able to resist foreign influence, and during the first half of the nineteenth century the Russian government repeatedly won concessions allowing it to intervene in Turkish affairs. As a result of the Russo-Turkish war of 1828–1829, Russia gained the right to protect Christian citizens of the Ottoman Empire, as well as control of the mouth of the Danube and the eastern Black Sea coast.

In the mid-nineteenth century Russia was not yet a highly industrialized nation. Agriculture and light industry predominated; heavy industry, particularly iron and steel manufacturing, was handicapped by an inferior transportation system. Also a hindrance to industrial development was the fact that serfdom tied a large proportion of the population—centered in the heavily populated western part of the Empire—to the land. This situation could not, and in fact did not, last for many more years.

NORWAY

SWEDEN

FINLAND

Gulf of Bothnia

White
Sea

Lake
Ladoga

Lake
Onega

• Arkhangelsk

N. Dvina R.

Ob R.

Pechora R.

Iron
and
Steel

Gulf of Finland

Iron
and
Steel

• St. Petersburg
Leather

Iron
and
Steel

Perm
Copper
Coal
Leather

Iron
and
Steel

BALTIC SEA

Wool

• Riga
Iron
and
Steel

Wool

W. Dvina R.

• Novgorod

• Pskov
Leather

Leather

Leather

Leather

Linen

Leather

• Yaroslavl
Linen

Iron and
Steel
Leather

• Viatka

Iron
and
Steel

Iron
and
Steel

Perm

• Kazan

Kama R.

• Ufa
Copper

Iron
and
Steel

• Kovno
• Vilna

Cotton
Linen
Wool

Smolensk •

• Minsk

Cotton
Linen
Wool

Linen
Silk

• Moscow
Cotton
Wool

Iron
and
Steel

Iron
and
Steel

Linen

• Nizhni
Novgorod

RUSSIA

Warsaw
Cotton

POLAND

Vistula R.

Zhitomir •

• Orel

• Chernigov

• Kiev
Linen

• Kharkov

Sugar

Dniester R.

Dnieper R.

AUSTRIA-
HUNGARY

Odessa •

• Cherson

Danube R.

Sevastopol •

Linen
Cotton
Wool

Iron and
Steel

Iron
and
Steel

Linen

• Tambov

• Voronezh

Volga R.

Saratov •

• Penza

Volga R.

Samara

• Chkalov

Ural R.

Uralsk

Iron
and
Steel

Rostov •

Coal Don

Don R.

Coal

Sea of
Azov

BLACK SEA

Astrakhan •

CASPIAN
SEA

OTTOMAN EMPIRE

Constantinople •

AEGEAN
SEA

CE

• Tiflis

Baku •
Oil

Araks R.

OTTOMAN EMPIRE

PERSIA

RUSSIAN ECONOMY AND
SOCIETY ABOUT 1860

Percentage of serfs in total population

Up to 15

16-35

36-55

Over 55

No data

• Large cities

• Other important cities

Nicholas was zealous in his desire to protect the Orthodox in the Ottoman Empire. But he showed no such zeal when it came to protecting the liberties of the Polish people, who had been returned to the Russian sphere of influence, if not to full and complete Russian control, by the Congress of Vienna. Thus in 1830–1831 the Russian government finally smashed the Polish revolution that had broken out in the spring of 1830. Nicholas abrogated the existing Polish constitution and dashed the hopes of Polish nationalists by annexing Poland, making it virtually a part of the Russian Empire under the direct authority of the czar. This action was followed by an attack upon Polish nationalism that was representative of Nicholas's attitude toward all dissenting religious and cultural groups. The Polish language was no longer taught in the schools, and other vestiges of a distinct Polish nationality were suppressed as far as possible.

Russia's treatment of Poland earned it the hatred and contempt of enlightened and liberal people throughout Europe, but there was nothing the European governments would do to stop the Russians. What Russia did in Poland and what it had in mind in regard to Turkey and the Straits were two different matters, however. The Crimean War of 1853–1856 that closed out Nicholas's reign revealed that Russia's stature in Europe was much more fragile than its earlier behavior seemed to indicate. The war, which pitted Russia against the Ottoman Empire, Britain, and France—later joined by Piedmont—with Austria as a cobelligerent, was in a sense a historical accident, an unfortunate occurrence that neither side wanted. Militarily it was a disaster, a conflict that showed both sides—especially the Russians and the British—that their military forces were totally unprepared for modern war. The climax was reached with the allied siege and capture of the Russian fortress of Sevastopol in 1854–1855.

The Treaty of Paris of March 1856 was a humiliating expression of the Russian defeat; the Russians were forced to abandon their original objectives, to accept the neutralization of the Black Sea, to give up the mouth of the Danube and part of Bessarabia, and to allow the Danubian principalities (Moldavia and Wallachia) to be placed under an international guarantee. To assure Russian compliance, Britain, France, and Austria signed a supplementary treaty stipulating that renewed Russian attack on Turkey would constitute a *casus belli* and that they would take concerted action to meet such an attack. The war put a temporary halt to Russia's southern expansion and made clear the Western powers' vital interest in the future of the Ottoman Empire. The decadent Empire itself survived the war—an anachronism preserved only because no satisfactory alternative could be found. The Western powers could not accept the vastly improved position in the eastern Mediterranean that Russia would surely achieve if the Empire was partitioned, and Russia could not abide the emergence of a powerful and effective state on its vital southern border.

Although Nicholas, who died in March 1855, was spared the embarrassing outcome of the conflict, he seems to have become aware before his death that politics and society in Russia could not go on indefinitely as they were. It remained for his son and successor, Alexander II (1855–1881), to liquidate the war and to make a major effort to remedy some of Russia's most gnawing problems. For the rest of his reign Alexander was engaged in the task of regaining Russia's lost position in the south. Perhaps the most momentous developments in foreign policy, however, were Russia's tacit acceptance of the aggressive policies of Bismarck toward Austria and France and, finally, Russia's acquiescence in the formation of a powerful, united German Empire.

Alexander II is remembered not for his foreign policy but for his domestic reforms. The most dramatic change was the abolition of serfdom, which stands out in Russian history as a rare example of both decisive and meaningful reform. It also marks the beginning of a cyclical pattern—tolerance of new ideas, reform, radical demands, reaction, and repression—that was to characterize Russian history until 1917. By 1861 serfdom stood out as one of the anachronisms that distinguished archaic Russia from the more progressive countries in western Europe. Furthermore, serfdom was becoming less practical, less profitable for the landowner, and more frequently a source of social turbulence. When he became czar, Alexander made it clear that serfdom would soon be abolished. The emancipation edict of March 1861 finally ended centuries of servitude for the mass of Russian peasants two years before the abolition of slavery in the United States.

While the abolition of serfdom was doubtless a marked step forward in Russian history, it was by no means an unmixed blessing. Under the new law, former serfs could buy part of the land they had worked as serfs through their village community or *mir*. The landlords, in turn, received at least partial compensation for the loss of the services and dues which had formerly been theirs, and the newly freed peasants were not cut off from the land. But the rather high redemption payments demanded from the peasantry—to be paid over fifty years—were clearly beyond their means; and as a result, though a tremendous amount of money was paid by the peasantry in the ensuing decades, the debt of the former serfs was finally liquidated only by governmental decree in 1917. Besides beginning his existence as a free farmer deeply, even hopelessly, in debt, the Russian peasant was further circumscribed by compulsory membership in the *mir*. The village community was responsible for dividing up the land, for paying the debt owed on the land, and for providing conscripts for the army. It was hardly surprising, then, that the emancipation edict bitterly disappointed the peasants and led, before long, to numerous disturbances throughout rural Russia.

Alexander also addressed himself to the long overdue reform of local government. In a vast country largely devoid of effective public services, the creation of elected governmental agencies on the local and district level with power to raise taxes and to concern themselves with (among other things) schools, roads, and public health was a truly revolutionary improvement. The process of election was indirect, and voting was proportional to land owner-ship, but nobility, townsmen, and peasants were all represented—a radical change in the thoroughgoing Russian autocracy. In 1870 a series of munici-pal reforms provided that cities and towns enjoy much the same kind of in-creased local self-government, with the franchise regulated by the amount of taxes paid. At one stroke, a new and more effective form of local government was created, largely independent of the centralized Russian bureaucracy.

Alexander also sought to reform Russia's desperately antiquated legal sys-tem and its military establishment. In 1864 the czar began to move toward an independent judiciary on the Western model. The judicial reforms pro-vided for public trials with adequate legal representation, trial by jury in seri-ous cases, and—most important—equality before the law. While other features of the system left much to be desired, and these reforms were not all applied in Poland, for instance, Alexander nevertheless had brought Russia much closer to the judicial standards prevailing in the great Western powers. The same was true of his military reforms, which provided for universal military service and did away with the exemption the privileged classes had enjoyed for centuries.

The reign of Alexander represents a genuine attempt to reform the Russian government, but it also illustrates the dilemma from which the czars seemed unwilling or unable to escape. Throughout his reign, Alexander was con-cerned with the entrenched conservatism of the Russian government, with the ponderous immobility of an inefficient and frequently ineffective bureau-cracy which represented one of the most important sources of livelihood and social status—and political power—available to the Russian nobility. But as time went on he also became aware that any modification of the repressive aspects of the government was bound to ease the restrictions upon those who questioned the authoritarian structure of Russian government and society. Time and again, Alexander (like his predecessors and successor) drew back when his own reforms seemed about to produce significant changes in the structure and practice of government. Action was too often followed by inac-tion or reaction. If a jury freed the assassin of a leading official, trial by jury could be eliminated from cases involving subversion. If the *zemstvos*, or local assemblies, could use their power to make real changes in the level of educa-tion in the countryside, conservatives could act through other channels of government to restrict their power of taxation. When reform brought demands for further reform, criticism was silenced by rigid censorship, the closing of universities, and exile for troublemakers. In his attempts to reform but to stop reforms from going too far, Alexander alienated both conservatives and radicals and prevented the real changes that might have produced the compro-mise which would allow Russia to continue under autocracy.

The result of Alexander's reforms, therefore, was not the pacification of the country but the steady rise of extremism, especially of a revolutionary sort. Some of these extremists, to be sure, were of the Right, but far more were of the radical, social revolutionary variety. One of the radical groups was the

Populist movement, composed of young intellectuals who sought to stir up the peasantry. The peasants did not give them a warm response, but this did not keep the more extreme Populists from becoming advocates of out-and-out political terrorism.

Even in the late 1860's, it was difficult to believe that the fraternization of intellectuals with the peasantry, or terrorism, could possibly produce the kind of political and social reforms Russia so badly needed. How then could Russia be transformed into a modern and humane society? Russian intellectuals had struggled with that question ever since the 1830's and 1840's, and none considered it longer and more seriously than did the writer Alexander Herzen (1812–1870). The son of a prosperous Russian landowner and his German wife, Herzen had had a French tutor and was early introduced to the writings of such leading social critics as Saint-Simon. Arrested for singing revolutionary songs as part of a university graduation celebration, he suffered brief administrative exile in the mid-thirties and went abroad of his own volition in 1847.

Herzen lived the rest of his life mostly outside Russia. He witnessed the rise of industrialism in western Europe and the unsuccessful revolutions of 1848, both of which deeply disconcerted him. From 1858 to 1867 Herzen published in London his famous journal *Kolokol* (The Bell), which despite the strict censorship in Russia soon began to enjoy considerable circulation there. At first Herzen welcomed the emancipation of the peasantry, but later he bitterly criticized it. In 1863 he supported the cause of the Polish revolutionaries, which lost him many friends and a good deal of his immediate influence in Russia.

It is not easy to assess Herzen's influence nor that of the other Russian intellectuals. Their sententious alienation from contemporary life—especially when there seemed at least some prospect that Russia might finally be headed in the right direction—contributed little or nothing toward making the existence of their fellow men more tolerable or even hopeful. Under the circumstances, the Russian people had to look for guidance not to their intellectual leaders but to Alexander II and his government. But Alexander failed to provide peace and stability; instead he laid the foundation for an era of reaction and repression.

The Smaller Powers

Fortunately, the pattern of growing decay and extremism that marked the history of Austria and Russia in the middle decades of the nineteenth century did not apply to all the states in Europe; indeed, in addition to Great Britain, there were a number of states in which slow but steady progress toward greater democracy and parliamentary government was being achieved by peaceful means. The Low Countries, Switzerland, and the Scandinavian states (Finland, still under Russian rule, excepted) were generally fortunate in this regard. Spain, on the other hand, remained, as it had been for centuries, a deeply troubled country; its instability finally helped to plunge two major powers — France and Prussia — into a war that was to change the course of European history.

The separation of Holland and Belgium in 1830 had led many people to fear more trouble in northwest Europe and possible French intervention to boot, but this gloomy possibility did not come about. Belgium, indeed, seemed destined to lead the way in responsible, constitutional government. The German-born Leopold I (1831–1865) proved to be one of the ablest monarchs of the nineteenth century. By 1847–1848 Belgium had achieved ministerial responsibility and enjoyed a much broadened system of suffrage. As a result, Belgium was one of the few European countries to escape serious revolutionary disorders — or the fear thereof — during those years.

Holland, under William I (1815–1840), an able but hard-headed ruler, had been slow to adjust to the independence of Belgium, which it did not formally recognize until 1839. Though Holland continued to enjoy prosperity, William himself grew more and more unpopular; he had the foresight to abdicate of his own volition in October 1840. He was succeeded by his son William II (1840–1849), who, though married to a Russian princess, had the good sense to make substantial political concessions early in 1848 and thus managed to avoid serious disorders in his country. Holland, like Belgium, now enjoyed a system of ministerial responsibility. In 1849 William was succeeded by his son William III (1849–1870), under whose enlightened rule Holland greatly increased its prosperity. Though the country continued to be divided on such issues as religion in the schools and further extension of the suffrage, it entered the last quarter of the nineteenth century a fairly sound and stable state with a thriving upper middle class.

In Switzerland — whose independence had been reaffirmed by the Congress of Vienna — democracy spread more rapidly during the middle decades of the century. By 1830 most of Switzerland enjoyed equality before the law, freedom of the press, and universal suffrage. But this is not to say that racial and religious differences did not make for some continued strife, which indeed became so serious for a time in the mid-1840's that the seven predominantly Catholic provinces gathered together for the purpose of protecting their own interests. The fifteen Protestant cantons (as the Swiss provinces were called) demanded that the Catholic *Sonderbund* dissolve; and when it refused to do so, a brief civil war ensued in November 1847. The Catholic forces were quickly and overwhelmingly defeated. The result was a new constitution, agreed on in September 1848, which provided for somewhat greater centralization, although the annually elected president of the Swiss Confederation had little or no power.

The political and social experiences of the Scandinavian states during these years were very similar. Denmark, which had been made to pay for its lack of judgment in siding with Napoleon by losing Norway to Sweden, recovered fairly rapidly from the serious economic dislocation produced by the Napoleonic era. Governed by a series of moderate rulers, Denmark achieved steady expansion of local self-government as well as the development of limited monarchy on the British and Belgian models. But the Danes were unable to resolve satisfactorily the situation of the substantial German population in the provinces of Schleswig and Holstein, and in 1864 Denmark was forced to yield these territories to Austria and Prussia. Oddly enough, such foreign disaster did not lead to a radicalization of Danish politics. On the contrary, after 1866 there was a strong conservative countermovement, in which the upper house of the Danish parliament received additional powers, a trend that lasted for nearly twenty years.

The Swedish-Norwegian union, consummated by the Congress of Vienna, suffered from no such foreign complications, and the rise of Norwegian nationalism, which was to lead to that country's independence in 1905, did not begin in earnest until the 1860's. In the nearly fifty years before that, Sweden and Norway moved—the former less easily, the latter more so—toward parliamentary government and liberal democracy. Though King Charles XIV (1818–1844) had rather autocratic tendencies, strong legislative opposition, notably in Norway, continued to check them throughout his reign. From the mid-1840's on, liberalism grew steadily in both countries. There were additional monarchial concessions under Charles's son Oscar I (1844–1859), and in 1864 a thoroughly new and liberal constitution was agreed to, by which the lower house was elected by a quite extensive democratic suffrage.

Although the Low Countries, Switzerland, and the Scandinavian states had been by no means free from internal conflict, they had all shown a significant sense of political community that kept them from going to pieces even at moments of fairly serious tension. But Spain—whose troubled history dated back as far as anyone could remember—was much less fortunate. As suggested earlier, in Chapter 6, it was in Spain that one of the most flagrantly counterrevolutionary monarchs, Ferdinand VII (1814–1833), succeeded to the throne at the end of the Napoleonic era, and it was to support him against domestic insurrection that the Holy Alliance intervened in Spain in 1823. Ferdinand's daughter Isabella, who occupied the throne from 1833 to 1868, was much less autocratically inclined, and after the mid-1830's substantial decentralization of the government was undertaken. But the result was a civil war—the so-called Carlist War (1834–1839)—in which supporters of Ferdinand's brother, Don Carlos, sought still further decentralization. In 1836 there was a liberal revolt, and from then until the middle 1870's Spain was swept by a long series of revolts and counterrevolts. Some of these were ideologically motivated; others were aimed at Queen Isabella and her several unpopular husbands and favorites. No faction could command sustained national support, and the army—to say nothing of the Catholic Church—exerted an influence it had nowhere else in Europe.

Conditions in Spain became steadily more unsettled until none save a trusted and respected ruler could have brought the country to anything like political and social soundness. In 1868 it was racked by still another revolution, and in September 1869 Isabella fled to France and was declared deposed. Thus Spain, like smaller European states in similar need, went shopping for a king. Several candidates declined. Finally, Prince Leopold von Hohenzollern-Sigmaringen, a distant relative of both Napoleon III and King William I of Prussia, accepted. But his acceptance became the signal for a military showdown between France and Prussia. Leopold finally withdrew, and Spain's misfortunes continued.

What was the reason for the differences between the fate of Spain and that of the other small powers? Perhaps the key factor in the comparative success of the latter was their more advanced economic status and the greater power of their middle class. Certainly Spain seemed the most backward of all these countries, and the dominant role repeatedly assumed by the Spanish army was representative of a much more primitive kind of state and society.

V UNIFICATION: THE NEW NATIONS

Italy

While Russia and Austria were struggling in the 1850's and 1860's to master their internal problems, the Italians and Germans were searching for the kind of national unity long achieved by the Western democracies. Their quests for freedom and union had been an integral part of the revolutions of 1848, and the failure of those revolutions had, in both countries, been due largely to the same causes. Particularism was too firmly entrenched, the leading states (Prussia in Germany and Piedmont in Italy) could not or would not provide effective direction, and economic and social problems created serious obstacles. The result was that by early 1849, in both areas, the national unity movements seemed to have been defeated. But their death was more apparent than real. Within a dozen years both Italy and Germany were well on the way to political unification. The price they were eventually to pay for this achievement was high indeed, however; the liberal elements that had given both countries their finest hours in the mid-century revolutions and that contributed significantly to their unification were greatly weakened in the process.

It was one of the ironies of Italian history that just as it was Napoleon Bonaparte who had done so much to arouse national consciousness in Italy, so it was his nephew who played a well-nigh indispensable role in bringing about the political union of the Italian states. The allied victory in 1815 had led to a return to something like the *status quo ante bellum* and denied Italian aspirations for closer national association. Once again, Austria and France held the balance of power south of the Alps. Napoleon III was well aware of Italian resentment of this new condition. By the later 1850's, he viewed intervention as a chance to restore some of the glory of the First Empire to French foreign affairs, as well as an opportunity to undermine Austrian influence in Europe generally.

For the Italians, French intervention was an absolute necessity; by themselves they simply lacked the strength to expel the Austrians from Italian soil. Even if economic and social conditions in the Austrian-occupied provinces were rather better than was widely believed outside of Italy, the Italians still wanted to control their own lives and destiny. But several attempts—most notably in 1848–1849—had come to nothing precisely because the Italians were unable to obtain the necessary foreign assistance. There is no doubt that one reason for this protracted failure lay in the inability or unwillingness of most Italian states or governments to work together for the common good. The result was that when unification finally came, it was effected not by cooperation among the states but by the combined force of a popular nationalist movement, the political and military leadership of the government of the kingdom of Piedmont-Sardinia, and the decisive intervention of France at the crucial moment.

The hero of the early development of Italian nationalism was Giuseppe Mazzini (1805–1872), who in 1831 had founded the secret organization known as Young Italy. Mazzini's virtues as a leader came from his inspirational qualities rather than from his abilities as a politician. Although he spent much of his life exiled from Italy, his writings provided an eloquent ideological base for Italian nationalism. Mazzini (see Chapter 5) viewed the state as the natural and divine means by which mankind was organized for the benefit of all. The state was, in effect, an association of brothers for the common good. A liberal as well as a nationalist, Mazzini believed that all men should participate in the processes of government.

This deeply idealistic man caught the imagination of reformers all over Europe, but his efforts to lead a successful revolution against overwhelming foreign intervention failed dramatically in 1848. In that year revolutionaries all over Italy sought to bring down the old system, and Mazzini himself was called to head up the newly established Roman Republic. But the attempt proved as premature as it was heroic. Beleaguered by Austrian, French, and Spanish forces, Mazzini's Roman Republic held out from late April to early July 1849. Then Mazzini himself had to flee once more, and King Charles Albert of Sardinia, who had assisted Mazzini's efforts, was forced to abdicate. The biggest disappointment to Italian liberals proved to be Pope Pius IX, who, when he first became Supreme Pontiff, had been widely regarded as a liberal nationalist but who was forced to flee from Rome in 1849 and thereafter became, as noted in Chapter 7, an inveterate foe of all secular, liberal, and national movements.

During the next year, the disastrous defeat of the revolution was partly allayed by developments in Piedmont, where a mediocre but benevolent king—Victor Emmanuel II (1849–1878)—joined forces with a progressive and highly determined nobleman, Count Camillo di Cavour (1810–1861). Cavour, who had wide interests in such fields as agriculture and transportation and who had founded the liberal newspaper *Il Risorgimento* in 1847, entered the Piedmontese government in 1850. An admirer of the British form of government, he began by drafting important legislation to reduce the secular power of the Church. In November 1852 he became prime minister. Although highly authoritarian in some ways, Cavour now embarked on a detailed program of domestic reform designed to make Piedmont the most effective and progressive government in Italy.

Having achieved numerous advances, especially in commercial and industrial policy, Cavour was ready for bigger things—notably Austria. Giving his

After provoking a war with Austria in 1859, Sardinia-Piedmont was deserted by its French ally but nevertheless gained several northern territories. Nationalist uprisings spread throughout the peninsula, and Garibaldi raised an army that conquered Sicily and moved north to threaten Rome. In 1861 Victor Emmanuel, the king of Piedmont, became head of a new Italian state that included all but Venetia and the Papal States. Italy received Venetia as a prize for being Prussia's ally in the Austro-Prussian War of 1866; and the Papal States were annexed after France's defeat in the Franco-Prussian War of 1870.

THE UNIFICATION OF
ITALY 1859–1870

- Kingdom of Sardinia to 1859
- To Sardinia, 1859
- To Sardinia, 1860, to form Kingdom of Italy
- To Kingdom of Italy 1866
- To Kingdom of Italy 1870

covert support to various nationalist groups, he now combined the baiting of Austria with a careful diplomacy designed to bring Italy's case to the attention of Europe, to obtain the support of international public opinion, and to gain the sympathy and, if possible, the assistance of Napoleon III. Before long, good fortune began to favor Italian nationalism. Napoleon gained new interest in Italian affairs as the result of an attempt on his life by an Italian nationalist in January 1858. In July he met secretly with Count Cavour at Plombières, and in December of that year France and Piedmont signed a treaty by which France in effect promised to support Piedmont in a war against Austria and to agree to the establishment of four Italian states in return for (among other things) the cession of Nice and Savoy.

At their secret meeting in July 1858 at Plombières, Napoleon and Cavour had plotted to goad Austria into war, and a treaty between France and Piedmont was signed that December. In April 1859 Austria took Cavour's bait and attacked Piedmont; France came to Piedmont's aid; and Austrian armies suffered a series of defeats. Piedmont gained Lombardy, annexed Parma, Modena, Tuscany, and Romagna by plebiscite, and ceded Nice and Savoy to France. But Napoleon III soon double-crossed Cavour, agreeing now with Austria that Venetia was not to be handed over to Italy as Cavour had been promised. When he learned of the new arrangement, Cavour resigned in a rage, but he returned to office in January 1860.

By now, northern Italy was largely united, but the Papal States in central Italy and the kingdom of the two Sicilies in the south still stood in the way. It remained for the third great hero of Italian unification, Giuseppe Garibaldi (1807–1882), to break the stalemate. Garibaldi was a sometime revolutionary and soldier of fortune, particularly good at guerrilla warfare. In May 1860 he and a few thousand of his famed Red Shirts landed in Sicily, liberated that island from its pro-Austrian ruler, and proceeded to the mainland to conquer Naples in September. In the meantime, the armies of Piedmont occupied the Papal States on the pretext of protecting them. In late October both Naples and Sicily voted to join the Italian union, and plebiscites — all favorable to national unity — were held elsewhere in Italy. The result was that in March 1861 the kingdom of Italy was proclaimed — with Victor Emmanuel as its first king and the Piedmontese consititution as the basis for the new government. In July 1866 Italy at last acquired the province of Venetia, and in September 1870 Italian forces took over Rome, which became the Italian capital the following month.

Although the unification of Italy — like that of Germany — was regarded by contemporaries as a great advance (and no doubt was), the history of Italy after unification was to prove disappointing in many ways. The profound differences among the sections of the newly unified state were a great obstacle to governmental stability and effectiveness. The division between the northern and southern sections of the country transcended those of language and custom; in fact, differences were so deeply ingrained in the social and economic configuration of the regions that the two have seldom been in harmony. The agrarian and rural south frequently felt victimized in the interests of the industrial society of the more heavily populated north.

Faced with such problems, the government of Italy eschewed liberal institutions that might have ameliorated at least some of its difficulties and established instead a political structure based on the model of the Second Empire. With Victor Emmanuel ii as king, it relied on a highly centralized bureaucracy to enforce its decisions and to influence elections. The franchise itself was limited to less than 2 per cent of the population and was not increased substantially for many years. So organized, the Italian state successfully established control over its territory, but it made only very slow headway against the profound economic and social problems of Italian society. It was the unsatisfied needs of the Italian people that provided fertile soil for imperialist adventures and — in the twentieth century — for the demagoguery and dictatorship of Mussolini.

Germany

Even after 1870 the role of the Italian government in international affairs was restricted by its limited resources and comparative economic backwardness. While France, and certainly Austria, would have preferred to deal with an Italy less fully united, the existence of Italy was not in itself a direct threat to the European balance of power. The unification of Germany was quite another matter. The appearance of a powerful state in central Europe completely altered the balance of power. The new Germany was an unsettling factor in European politics, first of all because the unification of the country had been brought about partly at the expense of France, Austria, and various other small German states and also because Germany soon threatened to predominate in European affairs.

The creation of the German Empire in January 1871 represented much more than the unification of a number of small states; it was the political integration of the most dynamic economic area in Europe. The unification of Germany was all the more striking and upsetting because it ran completely counter to that country's place and role in European history over many centuries. It will be recalled, for instance, that during the commercial revolution at the end of the Middle Ages the German cities had fallen far behind their competitors in France, the Low Countries, and England. Even the early stages of the Industrial Revolution had had comparatively little effect on most of the German economy. The German revolution of 1848 was not the result of mass urban unrest; rather, it rose out of the increasing disaffection of peasants, artisans, and a slowly emerging middle class. In the second half of the nineteenth century, however, Germany proved to be ideally suited to heavy industry, and by the 1870's it was the greatest industrial and military power on the Continent, threatening even to challenge British predominance in world shipping and trade.

Germany's role in late nineteenth-century European politics was in part the consequence of its available resources, but it was also profoundly shaped by the circumstances that surrounded German unification. As in Italy, the rivalries among the separate states were rooted in a venerable tradition of competition and hostility. Before 1800 the desire for unification had been primarily a rather vague longing based on the tradition of the Holy Roman Empire and the consciousness of the common cultural tradition of all German-speaking people. In the nineteenth century that rather vague national consciousness was given force and direction by political liberalism. Still another reason why national unification became increasingly attractive after the middle of the century was that it seemed to open opportunities to economic growth and development not attainable in any other way.

Awareness of the economic advantages of national unification was stimulated by the success of the economic union of northern German states known as the *Zollverein*, which was organized under Prussian sponsorship that dated back to October 1819 and which began full-scale operations as a free-trade area in 1834. The *Zollverein* was important because it showed what could be done by the cooperation of the various German states to advance their individual interests and those of Germany as a whole. "It is by their *Zollverein* that the German peoples now enjoy one of the most important attributes of nationality," wrote the German economist Friedrich List in 1841. List was both a fervent liberal and a nationalist. He envisaged further great benefits when Germany achieved a "national economy" at the time when "the state of confederation embraces the whole nation."

The *Zollverein* could not, of course, satisfy the political aspirations of the German people. The result of the unsuccessful revolution of 1848 and the failure of the Frankfurt Parliament of that year to unite Germany was that the German Confederation, which had been established by the Congress of Vienna in 1815, was officially revived and became once more the sole political institution binding together the thirty-odd German states. It remained what it had been before 1848—primarily a diplomatic organization with each state having equal representation; it had no power to enforce its will upon a recalcitrant member. Dominated by Austria, whose internal problems led it to oppose all forms of nationalism, the Confederation became less and less relevant to the struggle for unification in the face of growing Prussian predominance in German affairs.

The decisive factor in shaping the ultimate nature of a new German state was Prussia. Even in the middle of the nineteenth century, the Prussian system of government was basically absolutist, with power vested in the hands of the king and with a bureaucracy and an army responsible, in the end, only to the king. One reason for the effectiveness of that structure lay in the fact that it was traditionally based upon cooperation between the Hohenzollern monarchs, the Junker class—a landed aristocracy that also predominated in the upper levels of the bureaucracy—and the army. While far from flawless, Prussia's bureaucracy was known as the most efficient and incorruptible in Europe; and though badly beaten by Napoleon in 1806, the Prussian army subsequently defeated the emperor's forces and was again one of Europe's most effective fighting machines. Based upon a system of universal conscription, it owed much of its effectiveness to the recognized professionalism of its officer corps.

But, as in the eighteenth century, Prussia's strength and reputation were based not on its army and its bureaucracy alone. At the end of the Napoleonic Wars, Prussia had gained control of most of the Rhineland, whose enormous industrial and other economic resources and potential were only slowly becoming apparent and being exploited. The Rhineland, moreover, was one of the centers of Prussian liberalism, and the rising middle class in that area sought not only the liberalization of Prussia but the unification of the whole country, if at all possible on liberal and constitutional terms. Prussia also benefited significantly from its increasingly important educational institutions, such as the University of Berlin. Prussia was especially attractive in this regard since—whatever the reactionary political spirit of its government—there were no religious tests, and men of promise and talent—both Catholics and Protestants—found there the opportunities frequently denied them in such intolerant (and backward) states as Austria.

Although the revolution of 1848—which was especially important and effective in Prussia—forced Frederick William IV to agree to various liberal reforms, including a parliament and a constitution, the early 1850's were an era of reaction, dominated by the conservative Prussian aristocracy. By the late 1850's, however, the liberals had once more gained a majority in the Chamber of Deputies, and they were soon engaged in a struggle with the new Prussian king, William I (1861–1888). William was even more conservative than his brother had been. After a brief period of conciliation, when it seemed that the king and Parliament might be able to cooperate, he precipitated a bitter struggle by proposing to lengthen the term of conscription from two to three years, doubling the size of the regular army. Although the Crown's case was by no means without merit, the conflict soon became a dangerous stalemate in which neither side would budge. It was clear that the Prussian liberals were trying to use the issue of military reform as a way of bringing about something like responsible constitutional government in Prussia, and despite all William's efforts to break their opposition, they persisted, pushing the king to the verge of abdication. Thus the stage was set for the emergence of Otto von Bismarck (1815–1898) at the center of Prussian politics.

Bismarck, who came from an old aristocratic family and who had made a considerable name for himself as an extreme conservative before, during, and after the revolution of 1848, spent most of the 1850's as the unhappy Prussian delegate to the Diet of the German Confederation and as minister to

Bismarck and German Militarism. In the early nineteenth century, Germany was regarded as the land of poets, philosophers, and artists. After the humiliation of Austria in 1866 and of France in 1870, aggressive militarism and ruthless efficiency seemed the dominant characteristics of German *Kultur.* Below: a Prussian regiment returning triumphantly from the Franco-Prussian War. Bismarck (left), an able conservative nationalist, was primarily responsible for the defeat of liberalism in Germany and for the ascendancy of Prussia and the new German Empire.

Russia. His personal dislike of a subordinate role and his disagreement with the quiescence of Prussian foreign policy clouded his relations with his immediate superiors. On the other hand, his assignment in Russia, where he witnessed the era of peasant emancipation, and a few months as Prussian minister to France in the spring and summer of 1862 had not only taught him the perils of intransigent conservatism but had given him an opportunity to size up Napoleon III and his strengths and weaknesses. Although there is some reason to believe that William would have preferred not to appoint Bismarck as head of his government, by September 1862 he found that he had nowhere else to turn.

Bismarck's appointment created a sensation. He began his career as the obdurate opponent of the liberals, the man who chose to govern in defiance of Parliament when it refused to enact the necessary changes in the conscription law and the budget. Worse, Bismarck almost seemed to mock everything that Prussian and other German liberals stood for. "The great questions of the day," he told the budget commission of the Prussian Chamber of Deputies soon after he took over, "will not be decided by speeches or by majority decisions—that was the mistake of 1848 and 1849—but by blood and iron." But he was far more than an intransigent conservative and a militarist. In the next decade he solidified the position of the monarchy within Prussia and engineered the unification of Germany under Prussian leadership.

Beginning as the supporter of Prussian autocracy, Bismarck proceeded to ignore Parliament and strengthen the army. But he was aware that the forces of liberal nationalism were very strong throughout the country, and it was his burden and opportunity to use these forces, too, for his own purposes. Thus he lost little time in taking command of Prussian foreign policy, long notoriously cautious and ineffective, and embarking upon a carefully conceived contest with Austria for predominance in German affairs. This contest took two forms. In the first place, Bismarck continued the highly successful policy followed by Prussia since the early 1850's of keeping the Austrians out of the *Zollverein*, for continued Prussian leadership in the all-important realm of economic politics was bound to strengthen Prussia's hand in the contest for national political leadership. Second, he used to superb advantage the war with Denmark over Schleswig and Holstein that broke out in February 1864. This conflict grew out of the attempt of Denmark, in March 1863, to annex the two provinces, which had been under the personal rule of the king of Denmark but were not legally part of that state. The Danes were easily and quickly vanquished by Austro-Prussian forces, and the war ended in October 1864 with Austria exercising jurisdiction over Holstein and Prussia over Schleswig, a situation that provided convenient pretexts for numerous incidents between the two states over the next twenty months.

What Bismarck had in mind at this point—in 1865 and early 1866—is still debated by historians. But whatever his precise intentions, it seems fairly clear that he was carefully laying the groundwork for a successful war with

Austria. If nothing else, his diplomatic experience had taught him that he must keep Russia and France out of any such conflict and, if possible, gain support in Austria's rear. Thus as early as February 1863 he had won Alexander II's friendship and gratitude by promising Russia assistance in putting down the new Polish rebellion that had just broken out. Later, in 1865, he gained the neutrality of Napoleon III with hints of Prussian approval of possible French acquisitions along the Rhine. In April 1866 he signed a short-term alliance with Italy, providing for Italian assistance against Austria if war broke out within three months, with Venetia as Italy's reward. Austria was thus faced with potential enemies along its northern and southern frontiers.

Finally, Bismarck provoked Austria in such a way that it was the first to mobilize for war and the rest of Europe believed that it was the real aggressor against an innocent Prussia. The genius of Bismarck's political maneuvering is further illustrated by his success in arranging the Austrian war in the service of a king who believed that such a policy was unthinkable, indeed morally reprehensible. In the face of that opposition, Bismarck proceeded with the utmost caution, never giving away his ultimate aim and always standing ready to alter his policy if it proved unsuccessful at any stage. In the end, even William I believed that Austria was an aggressor against which he had no choice but to defend himself.

The Seven Weeks' War that broke out in mid-June 1866 was a disaster for the Austrians and an almost unimaginable triumph for Prussia. Though the Austrians managed to defeat the hapless Italians, the stronger and better equipped Prussians, armed with the most modern weapons of the day—the "needle gun" that allowed firing from a prone position—smashed the Austrians at Königgrätz on July 3. Seven weeks later the Treaty of Prague was signed.

The decisive Prussian victory and the terms of the Treaty of Prague marked the effectual elimination of Austria from German affairs. Henceforth the Austrian Empire was merely a southeastern European power. Prussia obtained considerable territory—annexing, among other lands, Holstein and the kingdom of Hanover—and a degree of power over the southern German states that had participated in the war on Austria's side. In 1867 all states north of the River Main were organized as the North German Confederation, which, despite an appearance of considerable autonomy and equality among its members, was in fact largely under Prussian domination.

The year 1866 represents a turning point both in Bismarck's personal career and in the whole course of modern German history. In the course of a few months Bismarck the unpopular reactionary became a public hero who received cheers in the streets and whose power in the inner circles of the government was almost unchallengeable. Furthermore, new parliamentary elections, held just as Prussian forces were triumphing at Königgrätz, had the dual result of greatly increasing the power of the conservatives in the Prussian Chamber of Deputies and of splitting the liberal opposition into two factions, one of which now accepted what Bismarck had wrought and the means he had used in the process. Henceforth known as the National Liberals, its members supported the goal of national unification while maintaining a rather weak opposition to Bismarck on some domestic issues.

The division of the liberals as a result of the war of 1866 proved disastrous to the cause of political and social progress in Germany. Many of the country's leading intellectuals, who had for months and years bitterly denounced Bismarck, now became reconciled to him. They contended that it was time for the liberals to accept Bismarck's leadership, and this a majority proceeded to do.

Bismarck made certain efforts to ease the liberal pangs of conscience. He obeyed, for example, his own dictum against dogmatism by proving to be much more amenable to certain liberal and even democratic ideas than most of his conservative supporters. In the first place, he incurred the wrath of the army by refusing to be drawn into an all-out war against Austria. Faced with

The German settlement reached at the Congress of Vienna endured until 1866. In that year Bismarck took the first step toward bringing the whole of Germany under Prussian control. He provoked a war with Austria and annexed several states in northern Germany. The following year he set up a North German Confederation, headed by the Prussian king. To secure the allegiance of the south German states, Bismarck engineered a war with France in 1870. At the conclusion of the Franco-Prussian War, Alsace-Lorraine and the south German states joined the North German Confederation to form the German Empire. Its boundaries remained unchanged until Germany's defeat in World War I.

**THE UNIFICATION OF GERMANY
1815–1871**

- Prussia 1815-1866
- Annexed by Prussia 1866
- Joined Prussia in forming the North German Confederation 1867
- Joined with Prussia to form the German Empire 1871
- Alsace-Lorraine ceded to German Empire by France 1871
- German Confederation 1815-1866

the utter collapse of Austrian resistance, he chose to stop when his original aims had been met rather than risk upsetting the general European peace. Thus he rejected William I's demands for large-scale territorial acquisitions. This policy was in keeping with Bismarck's view of war as an acceptable extension of diplomacy but not as an end in itself. In the second place, Bismarck was evidently impressed with the example of electoral politics provided by the Second Empire in France. Democracy, properly used, need not be a threat to authoritarian government: in universal suffrage he saw an effective defense against the rising power of the middle-class liberals who were his most insistent enemies. A basic fear of the masses remained one of his most consistent ideas, however, and led him to establish extensive safeguards against their influencing the processes of government in any decisive way.

In the years following 1866, Bismarck's greatest achievement was his amalgamation of nationalist sentiment and an authoritarian concept of government which maximized his personal power. He exploited the diplomatic weaknesses of the other European states to bring about what many of them strongly opposed: the unification of Germany under Prussian leadership. Politically, he first separated nationalism from the liberal groups with which it had historically been associated and then converted the conservatives who were his natural supporters to a nationalist position. The product was the nationalist ideology which was henceforth associated with the German state.

The nationalist ideology became an increasingly potent factor in German politics in the period after 1866, but it was not enough to effect unification by itself. Opinions on national unification were increasingly polarized, particularly in such southern and southwestern German states as Bavaria and Baden. Although national feelings ran fairly high in both, their proximity to France and Austria made pressure by Prussia dangerous and difficult to apply; it would not be possible to incorporate them into an expanded version of the North German Confederation without provoking the French into war. Furthermore, Bismarck felt it very important to place the southern states in a position where they would voluntarily join a new German state rather than enter unwillingly or under protest.

As in his policy toward Austria before the summer of 1866, Bismarck resolved the problem by a series of brilliant diplomatic maneuvers that hid his ultimate intentions until the last moment and forced France to become the aggressor in a war it was not militarily prepared to fight. He prepared the way by first maneuvering Napoleon III into neutrality in the struggle with Austria; at his famous meeting with the French emperor at Biarritz in October 1865, for example, he suggested that Prussian gains in the south might be accompanied by certain territorial concessions to France. Napoleon seems to have fallen for this approach, but by leaving his erstwhile ally, Austria, prey to Prussian armies in the summer of 1866, he succeeded only in isolating himself. He aided the cause of Prussian expansion and received nothing in return. Meanwhile, as Bismarck doubtless knew, Napoleon's domestic situation was steadily worsening, and Napoleon rashly decided that he must recoup his domestic fortunes by foreign success. Bismarck correctly concluded that the French emperor would be more reckless than ever.

In the atmosphere of growing hostility between the two countries, Bismarck found the proper provocative incident in a crisis over the succession to the Spanish throne. As we have seen, the Spanish revolutionaries of 1868, seeking a suitable candidate for the throne, found one in Prince Leopold von Hohenzollern-Sigmaringen, a nephew of King William I of Prussia. French outrage was immediate and, coupled with Leopold's own reluctance to accept the throne, resulted after considerable diplomatic activity in the withdrawal of the Hohenzollern candidature. Bismarck was almost thwarted by this removal of what had promised to be the essential catalyst for war with France, but circumstances once more turned in his favor. When, at a meeting with the Prussian king at Ems on July 13, 1870, the French ambassador demanded William's promise that the candidature would never be revived, the king refused. Bismarck edited the telegraphed description of the meeting so that each participant seemed to have insulted the other and had his version printed in the newspapers. By morning, war between France and Prussia could no longer be avoided.

The Hohenzollern Triumph. While the German army besieged Paris, Bismarck arranged for the proclamation of the Second German Empire at Versailles on January 18, 1871, in the same Hall of Mirrors where Louis XIV had lorded over Europe. The elevation of the king of Prussia to emperor of a unified German state (excluding Austria) was acceded to by the rulers of the principalities; their people were not asked whether they wished to be subjects of the Hohenzollerns.

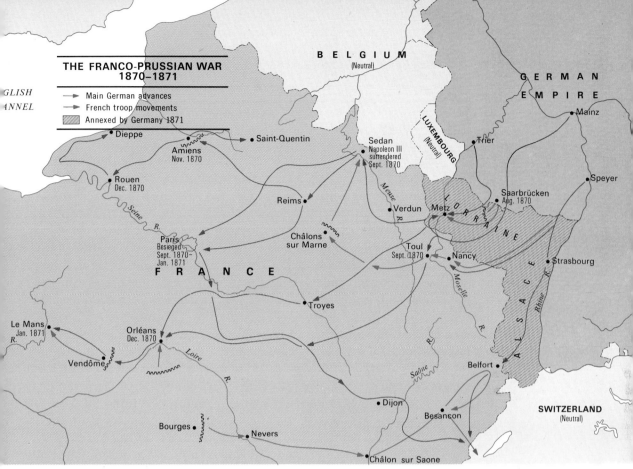

The Prussian army's efficient use of transport facilities (particularly railroads) was crucial to the course of the Franco-Prussian War. Within eighteen days (half the time necessary in 1866) 380,000 men were ready to invade France, which could muster only 200,000 men in so short a time and was unable to get all of them into position. Hostilities commenced on July 19; on September 2 the French army capitulated at Sedan and Napoleon III was taken prisoner. Two days later the Third Republic was proclaimed in Paris, and new armies began forming in the provinces. But resistance could be no more than feeble without foreign support. After a siege of four months the capital capitulated; by that time the provincial forces had been defeated. As its prize Germany claimed a huge indemnity and annexed Alsace and most of Lorraine.

Although it was by no means obvious before the beginning of the war, Prussia far outclassed France as a military power. The size of the Prussian army, coupled with the superior preparation of its officer corps and the efficiency of its supply system, contrasted in every detail with the inept anachronism that was the French army. The Franco-Prussian War, like the Austro-Prussian War, was decided in a few weeks. On September 2 the French suffered a decisive defeat at Sedan; Napoleon himself was taken prisoner; and the following day his army capitulated. But the French were not only humiliated by the swift and easy Prussian victory; they were appalled and outraged by the harsh peace terms that were now imposed upon them. Abandoning the comparative moderation that had stood him in good stead in 1866, Bismarck demanded a war indemnity of one billion dollars—an unheard-of sum for its day—and, far worse, the cession of Alsace and most of Lorraine. The loss of these provinces materially damaged the French economy, because they represented a sizable part of the most productive mining and industrial area in Europe, and became the source of bitter revanchist feeling that did much to poison Franco-German relations and set the stage for another war.

For Germany the Franco-Prussian War was more than a military victory. The southern German states declared war against France almost immediately after the fighting began and—perhaps as Bismarck had expected all along—soon moved toward closer union with the North German Confederation. This closer union, of course, could be nothing else than some kind of national state. To be sure, the final negotiations that led to the creation of the new German Empire were anything but smooth and rapid. Several states, notably Bavaria, wanted all sorts of special privileges in the new Empire, and some of these Bismarck found it necessary to concede. Bismarck also had to agree to a highly secret lifetime retainer for the Bavarian king, so that the latter could continue to engage in his elaborate and highly expensive building projects and other undertakings. Nevertheless, the proclamation of the Empire at Versailles, on January 18, 1871, was decisive proof of the success of Bismarck's policies. In the end the states outside the North German Confederation had voluntarily entered the Empire, and in accepting the king of Prussia as the German emperor, they also accepted the authoritarian form of government that gave effective control of the new state to the men and classes who had been leading Prussia and the North German Confederation. Bismarck thus entered the wider field of the German imperial government with his powers virtually unimpaired. In many ways it seemed as if Prussia had merely grown until it swallowed up the rest of Germany.

It was not liberal nationalism that carried the day in Germany in 1870–1871. Instead, the conservative Prussian monarchy, its army and bureaucracy, and its largely authoritarian form of government placed their permanent stamp on German domestic and international politics. Although many enlightened people in Europe and America overlooked the fact at the time, the triumph of Bismarck and what he stood for was a turning point in history. For the tide of political liberalism that had seemed ultimately invincible in central Europe had in fact been halted and reversed. The forces of conservatism and conformist nationalism were now in control in the heart of Europe. It was an ominous augury for the decades to come.

PART THREE

The Hegemony of Western Civilization

**From the New Imperialism
to the First World War**

In the late nineteenth century the scientific and technological superiority of Western civilization over other civilizations reached its zenith. The great powers took advantage of this superiority to expand their colonial possessions in Asia and Africa, often in a manner that ignored the moral traditions of the West. Yet at the very moment of hegemony abroad, Western leadership was threatened by severe problems at home. The autocratic governments of Austria-Hungary and Russia were incapable of reforming themselves and dealing with critical domestic issues. The great powers became involved in a series of international crises, leading to a dangerous arms race and the polarization of states into competing alliance systems. The volatile question of nationalism in the Balkans was not resolved.

There were perhaps even more fundamental problems facing Western civilization at the beginning of the twentieth century. The tremendous industrial expansion of the preceding decades had brought about increasing working-class solidarity behind demands for a more equitable distribution of the wealth, and socialist movements pressed for far-reaching economic and social reorganization. While new insights into human consciousness inspired the efflorescence of art and literature and the advance of the social and behavioral sciences, they also undermined the liberal, rational doctrines of the mid-nineteenth century. By 1910 the stability of Western civilization was threatened by violence and anarchy at all levels of action and thought. The crisis culminated in the unprecedented holocaust of the First World War and the triumph of communism in Russia.

The very groundless and unjust feeling against England in Germany
is beginning to arouse great indignation here . . . .
I consider the danger great and serious that the two great nations
should become so far irritated against one another
as to be unable to put things right again. . . .
I said it was so important that Russia and England should
go well together, as they were the most powerful Empires,
for then the world must be at peace.

Queen Victoria

Page 427: the official portrait of Queen Victoria taken in 1897 by W. D. Downey on the occasion of the Jubilee commemorating the sixtieth year of her reign.

Nationalism and Imperialism

ENVIRONMENT ESSAY

The late nineteenth century was a white man's world. European science, technology, military force, and governmental expertise seemed so vastly superior to anything that nonwhite peoples could offer that they both assured the steady expansion of European hegemony and at the same time provided the justification for imperial rule and colonial exploitation. It followed from the competitive, social Darwinist assumptions of the era that the strong ("advanced" or "civilized") Western nations should rule the weak ("primitive" or "decadent") non-Western countries and should — it was claimed — bring the benefits of Western civilization to the Asian and African continents.

The ideology of Western imperialism has been so decisively repudiated in the twentieth century, almost as thoroughly in the West as in the non-West, that it is not easy to imagine how central the doctrine of the superiority of Western civilization and the righteousness of its subjugation of Africa and Asia was to the ambience of the late nineteenth century. In 1876, King Leopold of Belgium — whose colony in the Congo became notorious for vicious treatment of the native population — summarized the civilizing purpose of European imperialism: "To open up to civilization the sole portion of the globe to which it has not yet penetrated, to pierce the darkness which still envelops whole populations, is . . . a crusade worthy of progress."[1]

In 1878 a British government official wrote that British power in India "is like a vast bridge over which an enormous multitude of human beings are passing . . . from a dreary land."[2] Such statements were commonplace and were frequently accompanied by expressions of the innate superiority of the white race. The composer Richard Wagner wrote in 1881:

1. Quoted in William Woodruff, *Impact of Western Man*. New York: St. Martin's Press, 1967, p. 49.
2. Quoted in A. P. Thornton, *Doctrines of Imperialism*. New York: Wiley, 1965, p. 217.

It has been made quite clear that we should have no History of Man at all, had there been no movements, creations, and achievements of the white men; and we may fitly take world-history as the consequence of these white men mixing with the black and yellow, and bringing them so far into history as that mixture altered them and made them less unlike the white.[3]

3. H. Kohn, ed., *The Modern World*, 2nd ed. New York: Macmillan, 1968, p. 112.

The Good Life. The period from 1875–1910 was the halcyon era of the European upper classes. Never before or since have they enjoyed such comfort, power, and security. Facing page: the interior of the *Bon Marché* department store, Paris, 1876. Designed and decorated in the finest tradition of bourgeois Baroque, this and similar stores of the period catered to the propensity of the prosperous middle class for conspicuous consumption. Left: Cambridge University undergraduates in 1892. These confident young gentlemen could look forward to exciting careers as governors of the Empire, like the Roman aristocrats they were taught to emulate. Below: the Cunard liner *Lusitania* docking in New York. The great passenger steamships were symbols of the age: its bold technology, its love of the grandiose and ornate, and —in the ship's three distinct classes of passenger accommodation —its rigid class attitudes.

The British imperialist poet, Rudyard Kipling, born and raised in India, was one of the few who sensed the transitory character of the British Empire:

> Far-called, our navies melt away;
>> On dune and headland sinks the fire:
> Lo, all our pomp of yesterday
>> Is one with Nineveh and Tyre!

But Kipling was as contemptuous as Wagner when he considered what the African and Asian peoples could do on their own. Civilization was the white man's monopoly; the non-Westerners were "lesser breeds without the Law":

> Take up the White Man's Burden . . .
> And when your goal is nearest
> The end for others sought,
> Watch Sloth and heathen Folly
> Bring all your hopes to nought.
>
> . . . .
>
> Take up the White Man's Burden—
> And reap his old reward:
> The blame of those ye better,
> The hate of those ye guard . . . .[4]

4. Rudyard Kipling, *Rudyard Kipling's Verse*. New York: Doubleday, 1940, p. 322.

Power and Pomposity. Central to the late nineteenth-century ambience was the widespread belief in the benefits of national military power and the adulation of statesmen as wise and virtuous preservers of peace and national prestige. Below: machine works in a Krupp munitions plant, harbinger of the age of blood and iron. Right: Anton Romako's "Admiral Tegetthoff at Lissa," a typical expression of the flamboyant militarism of the period. Europe had experienced no long, debilitating armed conflict since 1815, and the lessons that might have been learned from the Crimean War, the Franco-Prussian War, and particularly the American Civil War were largely ignored. The upper classes still thought war an occasion for heroic gestures. Facing page: proud and elegant statesmen preserving the peace of Europe at the Congress of Berlin of 1878. The skill and beneficence of the leaders of government was thought to be demonstrated in the alliances and conferences by which they maintained the balance of power.

Imperial Power. In the last quarter of the nineteenth century there seemed no reason to doubt the infinite duration of the Western empires in underdeveloped countries. Right: working-class crowds in London cheer colonial troops gathered at the heart of the British Empire to celebrate Queen Victoria's Diamond Jubilee in 1897. Facing page, bottom: the Yellow Man's Burden—Chinese families in Tien-Tsin flee from bombardment by European gunboats dispatched to put down the Boxer Rebellion in 1899. Facing page, top: the rise of the American empire. A Roughrider poses proudly with the American eagle, which has spread its wings and is about to strike down the degenerate Spaniards in aid of "the little brown brothers" in Cuba. The Roughriders were a cavalry contingent that served during the Spanish-American War of 1898 under the leadership of Colonel (later President) Theodore Roosevelt.

In the closing decades of the nineteenth century, the common man in the great cities of Europe had these imperialist and racist sentiments drummed into his consciousness daily. Ever expanding factories (including munitions plants) proclaimed European economic and technological power. Vast, ornate government offices symbolized the solidity—indeed eternity—of Western authority. Corpulent, magnificiently dressed monarchs and statesmen rode by in elaborate carriages, accompanied by mounted, splendidly uniformed guards. In concert halls and from rotundas in public parks the clanging strains of "land of Hope and Glory . . . Wider still and Wider shall thy bounds be set" and similar jingoistic anthems stirred enthusiastic audiences. Newspaper headlines shrieked of new triumphs over the black and yellow races, while paintings and lithographs depicting the virtue of the European conquerors and the savagery of the lesser breeds flooded from artists' studios and printing presses. Europe in 1890 was the "proud tower" from which the civilized looked down on the rest of mankind, congratulating themselves on their culture, wealth, and power, convinced that this was not only the climax but the culmination of human history.

Intertwined with and inspiring the imperialist tone that dominated the European environment in the late nineteenth century was an ever more aggressive nationalism. Each nation-state considered its values and way of life superior to those of all others. The purpose of education and culture, it was widely believed in every Western country, was to instill this sense of national identity and superiority. The sentiment of Maurice Barrès, a French right-wing writer in 1899, was echoed in every country: "Our need

Imperial Sentiment. This painting by George Harcourt was shown at the citadel of British establishment art, the Royal Academy, in 1900. It depicts the Grenadier Guards departing from Waterloo Station to serve in the Boer War in South Africa. The painting illustrates the popular sentiment that, at least in Britain, served as a necessary foundation for late nineteenth-century imperialism. The Guards, in resplendent uniforms, are heroic and handsome as they wave farewell to beautiful, chaste British womanhood. A paragon of British femininity bestows a pure kiss on her noble fiancé. There were political and economic factors involved in imperial expansion, but the whole venture would have been impossible without the simple-minded militarism and sentimentality that inspired this painting. Imperialism was regarded as an opportunity for British valor; the feelings of the subjugated people were not taken into account.

is for men firmly rooted in our soil, in our history, in our national conscience, and adapted to the French necessities of this day and date."[5]

The drums rolled, the armies marched, the navies put out to sea, and aggressive nationalism became fierce militarism, nowhere more vehemently than in Germany. This aggressiveness seriously threatened the liberal dream of universal peace and brotherhood. Soon it would destroy it. In 1870, during the Franco-Prussian War, the English statesman William Gladstone had foreseen this tragedy with prophetic clarity:

Amidst the many additions which this age has contributed to the comfort and happiness of man, it has made some also to his miseries. And among these last is the deplorable discovery of methods by which we can environ peace with many of the worst attributes of war; as, for instance, with . . . the influence of great standing armies, and the prevalence of military ideas; . . . with the jealous and angry temper which it kindles between nations; and lastly, with the almost certainty of war itself, as the issue of that state of highly armed preparation, which, we are affectedly told, is the true security for the avoidance of quarrels among men.[6]

I EUROPE AND THE WORLD AFTER 1871

The unification of Germany in January 1871 marked a watershed in modern European history. Yet it brought about no immediate change in European problems and leadership. Statesmen like Bismarck and Gladstone, rulers like Francis Joseph of Austria and Alexander II of Russia still dominated European politics and diplomacy as they had done for some time. The processes of political consolidation and rationalization, described in the previous chapter, continued in the decades after 1871.

Yet some things were different after the 1870's. In particular, a new feeling of violence was in the air. Suffused with the spirit of aggressive nationalism, the major world powers began to engage in intense competition for political, economic, and military superiority. Each nation wished to demonstrate its strength, its military and industrial prowess, its status as a great power. At the same time each nation feared losing to the other powers what it had so laboriously gained itself. This mixture of arrogance and fear, of superiority and insecurity, served to create further aggressive and expansionist tendencies. Imperialism, the outstanding phenomenon of the period, was the principal product of those explosive national energies. Imperialism was nationalism run riot.

European civilization had long had a tendency to expand beyond its immediate borders. But after the American Revolution, the European powers lost much of their enthusiasm for colonies, regarding them for a time as an un-

5. Quoted in P. Pulzer, *The Rise of Political Anti-Semitism in Germany and Austria.* New York: Wiley, 1964, p. 57.
6. William E. Gladstone, *Gleanings of Past Years*, Vol. IV. New York: Scribner's, 1898, p. 243.

warranted administrative and financial burden, and valuing only those overseas possessions with commercial or strategic advantages.

Interest in further expansion overseas, which reached its nadir between Waterloo and the Franco-Prussian War, revived dramatically in the 1870's and hit a new peak around the turn of the century. Visions of overseas glory fired the public imagination, and arguments for imperialism were heard at all levels of society. Throughout most of Europe, and even in the United States, it became fashionable to believe that the possession of an empire was important to a nation's prestige, an almost indispensable prerequisite for "greatness." Europeans, it was widely said, had a special obligation to carry their superior culture to "uncivilized" regions.

Of course, not all of the imperialist arguments were on this idealistic plane. Some proponents of imperial expansion argued that the development of overseas territories would open up new markets for goods and provide sources of raw materials—both of which were essential to industrial economies eager to keep ahead of competitors. It was contended, too, that new Europes could be planted overseas—colonies to serve as receptacles for some of Europe's "surplus population."

The result was that between the 1870's and the turn of the century there developed a "new imperialism" (called "new" in order to distinguish it from previous colonial development) which resulted in the establishment of global European hegemony. Imperial control expressed itself in a variety of ways: some places were annexed outright and became "colonies"; others were "protectorates," in which the imperial powers ruled through traditional native authorities; still others constituted rather vaguely defined "spheres of influence." By the turn of the century, most of the world was controlled in one form or another by Western imperial powers.

During this period, European imperialistic attitudes were not directed only toward the so-called backward peoples overseas. They also found expression in extremist nationalizing tendencies and policies. At mid-century, it had seemed for a brief time that the various nations of Europe had found, or would find, new ways and means of living peacefully together. But after the abortive revolutions of 1848 those expectations rapidly declined. Respect between nations increasingly gave way to condescension, hatred, and (where possible) suppression. What the Germans had demanded for themselves, they were clearly not prepared to yield to the Poles. The Habsburg monarchy showed no signs of significantly greater responsiveness to its constituent nationalities, and in Britain Gladstone's heroic struggle to obtain a substantial measure of home rule for Ireland was largely unsuccessful.

Thus the years between 1871 and the end of the century presented a notable paradox: vast technological progress and territorial expansion promised much, while at the same time growing national intolerance and international anxiety made the prospects for a dangerous confrontation more likely with every passing decade.

II THE WESTERN DEMOCRACIES

Britain and the Empire

In the late Victorian era (from the 1870's through 1901, the date of Queen Victoria's death) Great Britain underwent two distinctive developments: a continued trend toward political liberalism and egalitarian democracy on the one hand and an enormous expansion of overseas empire on the other. Though not concurrent, democratic reform at home and colonial expansion abroad were the alternating motifs of late nineteenth-century England.

None of the deep political cleavages which characterized France, Germany, and Russia were apparent in Britain. Virtually all important political factions were agreed in affirming the legitimacy, or at least the desirability, of the constitutional monarchy and parliamentary government. Even the most reactionary conservatives did not dream of restoring the royal prerogatives of the seventeenth century; nor did the slowly emerging socialist movement yearn for violent revolution. The two major parties—the Liberals and the Conservatives—succeeded each other peacefully in office throughout the period. The Liberals never genuinely aroused Conservative fears that established institutions were about to be utterly destroyed, and when the Conservatives were in power, they did not attempt to repeal existing Liberal legislation.

Nevertheless, the differences between the Conservative and Liberal parties in the 1870's were significant. For the most part, the Liberals represented the interests of the commercial classes and of those who were not communicants of the Church of England. The Conservatives, on the other hand, spoke in large part for the interests of the landed aristocracy and the established Church while they often took the lead in legislation designed to protect the working man. With no strong ties to the industrial capitalists, the Conservatives often enjoyed more freedom than the Liberals in matters of labor legislation.

As already noted in Chapter 8, the outstanding example of middle-class liberalism in late Victorian England was Gladstone's first Liberal ministry (1868–1874). One of the great reforming ministries in British history, it initiated important changes in education, local government, civil service, and the military. Perhaps the most significant piece of legislation was the Ballot Act of 1872, which allowed the British voter to exercise his franchise in private. This Act was almost as important as the more spectacular Reform Bills, for it ended a system by which voters could be subtly or not so subtly coerced.

A Conservative ministry headed by Benjamin Disraeli replaced the Gladstone government in February 1874 and remained in office until April 1880. Although primarily concerned with foreign affairs and imperial expansion, Disraeli and his lieutenants expanded the role of the state in protecting certain vital interests of laboring men and the poorer elements generally. To improve public health, they codified legislation which formed the basis of

British sanitation law, and they made the first serious attempt to deal with the complex problem of low-income housing. But the Disraeli government moved too slowly for British tastes. In a spectacular election campaign in 1879–1880, Gladstone denounced the government for neglecting domestic reform in favor of foreign adventures, and he was overwhelmingly returned to office in March 1880.

The second Gladstone ministry, which served until June 1885, enacted the highly significant Third Reform Bill of 1884. Building upon the Reform Bills of 1832 and 1867, this legislative landmark now extended the franchise — which had been given to industrial workers in 1867 — to those who lived and worked in rural areas. Nearly two million people were thus made eligible to vote, twice as many as had been enfranchised by the Second Reform Bill in 1867. Except for certain specified groups — such as domestic servants who were not granted the vote until 1918 — all male inhabitants of the United Kingdom now enjoyed the franchise. Following closely upon the Third Reform Bill, Parliament approved an important Redistribution Bill in June 1885, which gave greater and fairer representation to urban areas — London for instance received thirty-seven more seats in the House of Commons — and made representation in the House strictly dependent upon population.

The development of democracy in Britain was slow, but it was sure. Gradually but perceptibly the privileges of the landed aristocracy and the established Church were chipped away. The goals of liberalism were realized, and the working class slowly gained a share of political power: its demands for social legislation were being heard and, in some cases, granted. All the same, the full effect of the Third Reform Bill did not begin to be felt for a number of years, and the British working class did not really come into its own as a political force until the first decade of the twentieth century.

The late Victorian era also witnessed a strong resurgence of imperial feeling, which reached its zenith during the Salisbury ministry (1895–1902) and culminated in the Boer War. This new enthusiasm for empire was not, however, shared by all Englishmen. In general, the Conservatives were the party of imperialism; Disraeli established this policy with a flamboyant speech at the Crystal Palace in 1872. The Liberals, more interested in democratic reforms, tended to oppose the acquisition of new colonies. Gladstone himself was strenuously anti-imperialist. Perhaps the finest embodiment of nineteenth-century liberalism, he took seriously the principles of humanitarianism and of apostolic Christianity. He had enormous sympathy for oppressed nationality groups and for those tribal peoples described by Rudyard Kipling as "lesser breeds without the Law." Gladstone had fought the election campaign of 1879–1880 on the principle of anti-imperialism, and although he was later forced to become involved in Egypt, he never ceased to preach the gospel of anti-imperialism, the dangers of militarism and foreign adventure.

The cornerstone of the British Empire, of course, continued to be India. Its very name fired the public imagination. Disraeli cleverly arranged to invest

Queen Victoria with the title of Empress of India in 1877, and thus further inflated popular enthusiasm for British rule in the subcontinent. Moreover, India provided an opportunity for the sons of the landed aristocracy, which had not entirely lost its original martial character, to win fame as military heroes. The protection of India was the key to the expansion of the British Empire after 1870. The Suez Canal, built by the Frenchman Ferdinand de Lesseps and finally opened in November 1869, greatly shortened the distance from Britain to India and became "the lifeline of Empire." The desire to protect Suez and the sea lanes to India led Britain to expand into Africa. In the early 1870's the British had limited interests on the west coast and around the Cape of Good Hope; by the end of the nineteenth century they had "painted the map red" from the Cape to Cairo. The British Empire at its height was the largest empire the world has ever known.

The British ruled their subject peoples with a firm hand, believing them generally unfit to rule themselves. Nevertheless, British colonial administrators were usually conscientious and efficient royal servants, often men of generous principles, who introduced needed reforms and ruled in accordance with what they took to be the best interests of the native peoples. A good example of this type was Lord Cromer, the British governor general in Egypt from 1883 to 1907. Under "proconsuls" like Cromer, the British built roads, ended the corruption of local native governments, reformed the educational system along British lines, and even sent talented colonial subjects off to Oxford and Cambridge. Yet however enlightened British rule may have been by Western standards, it inevitably gave rise to nationalist stirrings. In India, for example, imperial rule created a class of educated, Westernized, English-speaking Indians to run the civil service. Members of this class founded the Indian National Congress in 1885 and the All-India Muslim League in 1905, both of which soon began to agitate for more native control over Indian affairs.

Paradoxically, while Britain was extending imperial rule over much of the nonwhite world, it was steadily yielding to nationalistic sentiments in its older, white-controlled "settlement colonies." Canada in 1867, Australia in 1901, New Zealand in 1907, and South Africa in 1909 achieved dominion status and thus gained full control over their domestic affairs. Each of these self-governing colonies developed political institutions similar to those of Britain. The export of parliamentary government to the ends of the earth was a lasting monument to the most progressive aspects of the British imperial impulse.

Somewhere on the boundary between foreign and domestic affairs was the problem of Ireland, which had sorely plagued every British government since the end of the eighteenth century. Occupied during the Middle Ages, ruthlessly crushed by Cromwell's army in the mid-seventeenth century, Ireland was incorporated into the United Kingdom in 1801. Most of the Irish people were peasants who lived in abject poverty. They bore a heavy burden: the system of land tenure gave them no defense against their Anglo-Irish landlords. By the late nineteenth century, Britain began to harvest the fruit of centuries of neglect and oppression. Discontent spread rapidly, and peasant risings became more frequent. Increasingly, Irish members of the House of Commons employed obstructionist tactics to call attention to the grievances of their constituents.

The Irish problem weighed heavily upon the conscience of Gladstone, who even before taking office for the first time declared "My mission is to pacify Ireland." By a series of legislative measures, Gladstone set about correcting conditions responsible for Irish discontent. The Church of Ireland was disestablished in 1869, freeing the predominantly Catholic country from the obligation to support an alien state church. The Irish Land Act of 1870 was the first in a series of agrarian reforms aimed at securing for the Irish tenant the "three F's"—fair rent, fixity of tenure, and free sale.

Gladstone gradually recognized, however, that piecemeal measures would never solve the Irish problem. Irish nationalism, fortified by religious sentiments, would be satisfied only by sweeping reforms. In April 1886, therefore, he proposed his first home rule bill for Ireland, which included a provision for an Irish legislature in which the Catholic majority would dominate. But Gladstone was ahead of his time. To the Liberals who favored the union with Ireland, Irish home rule seriously compromised the integrity of the British Empire. When Gladstone refused to yield, these Unionists—including Joseph Chamberlain, the radical mayor of Birmingham, hitherto leader of the left wing of the party—broke with the Liberal party. Thus Gladstone's stern adherence to conscience and strict moral principle shattered the unity of the Liberal party. Defeated in the House of Commons, he appealed to the country. But he was once more defeated, and in July 1886 the Conservatives under Lord Salisbury returned to power.

The Conservative government sought to deal with Irish disaffection largely by trying to suppress it. The effort was unsuccessful, and demands for further Irish reform grew. In August 1892, Gladstone returned to office for the last time. His second attempt at Irish home rule passed the Commons, after eighty-five sittings, in September 1893, but was almost at once thrown out by the House of Lords. At odds with his cabinet on numerous issues, Gladstone retired from office in March 1894, and in June 1895 the Conservatives, under Salisbury, returned to power. The issue of home rule for Ireland was forgotten for a time, only to be revived in the tumultuous decade before the First World War.

On the eve of World War I the Dark Continent had submitted to European domination. Great Britain enjoyed the lion's share of the spoils: scattered areas on the west coast, solid blocks south from Egypt to Kenya and north from the Cape to Rhodesia. France held vast expanses in West and Equatorial Africa and along the Mediterranean. Ethiopia remained stubbornly independent in defiance of Italian ambitions. German holdings in the west were separated by Portuguese Angola and the Belgian Congo. Quarrels were not infrequent: France and England locked horns at Fashoda in 1898; England and the Boer Republics went to war in 1899; in 1911 German and French claims to Morocco were adjudicated by an international conference, and in 1912 Italy seized Libya from Turkey.

EUROPE

AZORES
Port.
1480

ADEIRA IS.
Port.
1419

ANARY IS.
Sp.
1478

MEDITERRANEAN SEA

Algiers   Tunis   Tripoli
SPANISH MOROCCO
1912
Casablanca

TUNISIA
1881

ASIA

MOROCCO
Fr. Prot.1912

IFNI
1860

ALGERIA
1830

LIBYA
Ital.
1912

Benghazi   Alexandria
Suez
Canal
Cairo

EGYPT
Occupied by Britain 1882
Br. Prot. 1914
Indep. 1922
Aswan

RED SEA

RIO DE ORO
1885

MAURITANIA

SAHARA

FRENCH WEST AFRICA
1895

CHAD

ANGLO-EGYPTIAN
SUDAN
1899

Port Sudan

Khartoum

ERITREA
Ital. 1889

nt-Louis
Senegal R.
SENEGAL
1815
kar
IBIA
07
RT. GUINEA
1886

Timbuktu

NIGER

L. Chad

WADAI

DARFUR

Mahdi Revolt 1882
Reconquered by British 1898

Djibouti
FRENCH
SOMALILAND
1884
Berbera
BRITISH
SOMALILAND
1884

FRENCH
GUINEA
1881

UPPER
VOLTA

Bamako

Kano
Chari R.

BAHR EL
GHAZAL

Addis
Ababa

ETHIOPIA
Ital. Prot. 1889
Indep. 1896

Freetown
SIERRA LEONE
1807
Monrovia
LIBERIA
Indep. 1847

IVORY
COAST
1893

GOLD
COAST
1874

TOGO
Ger. 1885

DAHOMEY
1894

NIGERIA
1886

Benue R.

Lagos

CAMEROONS
Ger. 1884

UBANGI-SHARI

UGANDA
1890

KENYA
1886

Mogadishu

FRENCH EQUATORIAL AFRICA

GULF OF
GUINEA

FERNANDO POO
1778
SPANISH GUINEA
PRINCIPE
Port.
SÃO TOMÉ
Port.
ANNOBÓN
Sp.
1778

Douala

1843

Libreville

Congo R.

Stanleyville

L. Rudolf

ITALIAN SOMALILAND
1889

Juba R.

L.
Victoria

Entebbe

Nairobi

Mombasa

FRENCH EQUATORIAL AFRICA
(FRENCH CONGO)
1887

Brazzaville
Léopoldville

BELGIAN CONGO
(CONGO-FREE STATE)
Under personal sovereignty
of Léopold II 1885
Belgian colony 1908

Lake
Tanganyika

TANGANYIKA
(GERMAN EAST
AFRICA)
1885

Tabora

ZANZIBAR 1890
Dar Es Salaam

CABINDA
1886

Kasai R.

ASCENSION
Br.
1815

Luanda

ALDABRA IS.
Br.
1810

Benguela

ANGOLA
1886

NYASALAND
1891

Lake
Nyasa

COMORO IS.
Fr.
1843

ATLANTIC

ST. HELENA
Br.
1651

OCEAN

NORTHERN RHODESIA
1889

Victoria
Falls

Zambezi R.

Salisbury

MOZAMBIQUE

Tamatave

Antananarivo

MADAGASCAR
1896

SOUTH-WEST

Cunene R.

Kubango R.

SOUTHERN
RHODESIA
1889

Beira

MOZAMBIQUE CHANNEL

Walvis Bay
1778

AFRICA
Ger.1884

BECHUANALAND
1885

Limpopo R.

TRANSVAAL
1902

SWAZILAND
1894

Lüderitz

Pretoria
Johannesburg
1885

UNION OF

ORANGE FREE
STATE
1902

NATAL
1844

Orange R.

1885

BASUTOLAND
1868

Durban

SOUTH AFRICA
CAPE COLONY
1906

1878

Cape Town

Port Elizabeth

INDIAN

EUROPEAN IMPERIALISM IN AFRICA

British   Portuguese
French   Spanish

OCEAN

In the case of Ireland Gladstone had been unable to carry through his announced objective; in the case of Egypt he was forced to adopt a policy of intervention which he had long and vigorously denounced. British involvement in Egypt began in earnest in November 1875, when Disraeli, always enthusiastic for almost any sort of imperial undertaking, purchased from the impoverished *khedive* (or ruler) of Egypt a 44 per cent interest in the Suez Canal. In the following year Britain and France joined in a condominium to reform Egyptian finances and satisfy Egypt's creditors.

Financial involvement soon led to political and military involvement. Trouble began a few years later when the new khedive came under growing attack from Egyptian nationalists. In June 1882 the leader of the nationalist revolt began to mount guns in the Alexandria harbor, threatening Royal Navy vessels, and, after a British bombardment of Alexandria in mid-July, Gladstone was obliged to order British forces to move into the Canal Zone and to occupy Cairo. Gladstone always regarded the occupation as a temporary measure, but instead of strengthening the authority of the khedive, the British presence accelerated its erosion, and before long the British, whether they wished it or not, had to take effective command of the government.

Although the British occupation of Egypt may well have benefited Egypt substantially, it caused Gladstone no end of personal agony and political difficulties. In 1883–1884 the British moved their thinly spread troops deeper into the Sudan, where they tried, for a time, to reach some kind of accommodation with local nationalist elements. In January 1885, Gladstone's appointee, General Gordon, failed in his pacifying mission, and he and his garrison were besieged and massacred by native forces at Khartoum. Gladstone was excoriated throughout England for not having sought to relieve Gordon earlier and more effectively. It was supremely ironic that the anti-imperial Gladstone was forced by circumstance to play so major a role in the development of imperialism, but it is also enormously suggestive of the strange exigencies of international politics and imperial power.

The heyday of British imperialism occurred during the Salisbury ministry (1895–1902). Salisbury took personal charge of foreign affairs and entrusted the colonial office to the enthusiastic hands of Joseph Chamberlain. During Salisbury's administration, Britain finally defeated the Sudanese rebels, but this victory was only the prelude to a dangerous confrontation with the French, who had their own designs on this part of Africa. Salisbury also dabbled dangerously in Near Eastern politics, frankly suggesting the dismemberment of the Ottoman Empire; and he became embroiled in an explosive dispute with the United States over the boundary of Venezuela.

The outstanding crisis of the Salisbury government was the Boer War (1899–1902) in South Africa, which represented the high-water mark of British imperialism. The Dutch East India Company had first used Africa's Cape of Good Hope as a way station on the route to the Indies in 1652, and the region was settled by Dutch Calvinists. These white settlers, the Boers, tilled the soil, feared the Lord, and developed a set of democratic institutions. They also found it useful to enslave the native Africans. After Britain acquired the Cape Colony in the Napoleonic Wars, British settlers began to arrive. To escape from British customs and policies, including the abolition of slavery, the Boers in the 1840's undertook the "Great Trek" to the lands north and east of the Orange River, and founded the Orange Free State and the Transvaal as Boer republics.

The discovery of gold in the Transvaal in 1886 brought enormous changes to South Africa. People rushed to the Transvaal from all over the world, and within a few years Johannesburg grew into a major city. These developments tipped the South African balance of power in favor of the Boers and against the British in the Cape Colony. Economic and political rivalry mounted; there was a long series of incidents and provocations, and in October 1899 the Boers declared war on the British.

The Boer War is a classic case study in motives for imperial expansion. In part, the war came about to protect the economic interests of Englishmen like Cecil Rhodes (1853–1902), an empire builder, financier, and Cape politician who had invested heavily in the Transvaal, and whose fondest dream—a railroad from the Cape to Cairo—was effectively blocked by the Boer government. The British were upset, too, over the denial of traditional British political rights to the *Uitlanders*, recent immigrants to the Transvaal, many of whom were British subjects. Then, in December 1895, Rhodes, the prime minister of the Cape Colony, exacerbated the situation by dispatching Leander Storr Jameson, the administrator of Rhodesia, on an abortive raid into the Transvaal for the purpose of assisting an *Uitlander* rebellion. In October 1899, the British rejected a Boer ultimatum and went to war because they feared that aggressive Boer nationalism would finally drive them from the Cape and destroy their invaluable investments, including all prospects for the Cape-to-Cairo railroad Rhodes had dreamed of.

Though the Boers had the best of it when the war broke out, in a few months British reinforcements arrived, and the major Boer cities were occupied. Yet for two more years Boer commandos continued to harass the British army, which gained no glory during the conflict. In the end, overwhelming British resources forced the Boers to surrender, and as Paul Kruger, the president of the Transvaal, had feared, his country and the Orange Free State were annexed to the British Empire.

The domestic and international repercussions of the Boer War were far-reaching. World opinion generally condemned the British as brutal aggressors against a peaceful, freedom-loving people. The war, moreover, served to expose both Britain's military weakness and its diplomatic isolation. Despite the Gladstonian army reforms of a generation before, the British were not ready to fight, and when at the time of the Jameson raid the German emperor, William II, sent a telegram to President Kruger congratulating him on his success in crushing foreign subversion, the British became painfully aware of their international weakness. Although the war was popular at first, domestic reaction soon turned sour. The Conservative party won a new mandate in October 1902 and clung to power until December 1905, but the growth of antiwar sentiment in Britain strengthened the forces of liberalism and humanitarianism and brought about a kind of national soul-searching about Britain's role in the world.

During the first years of the twentieth century, the late Victorian world of middle-class liberalism and imperial expansion gave way to new political currents. The urban working class began slowly to emerge as a political force with the founding of the Labour party. Moderate and non-Marxist, the British Labour party stood in distinct contrast to most European socialist parties. Marxism failed in England because the two main groups within the Labour party—middle-class intellectuals and trade unionists—were dedicated to parliamentary, evolutionary socialism instead of to violent revolution.

The main focus of socialist activity among English intellectuals was the Fabian Society. Founded in 1883, the Fabians included such rising literary figures as George Bernard Shaw and H. G. Wells and such leading social critics as Graham Wallas and Beatrice and Sidney Webb. Thoroughly British and intensely pragmatic, the Fabians believed that socialism was the economic counterpart of democracy. More influenced by Bentham than by Marx, they were convinced that socialism would evolve gradually as the inevitable result of universal suffrage and representative institutions; hence to the Fabians, class conflict of a Marxian type was neither inherent in the social order nor necessary for social progress. Their belief in the inevitability of socialism led the Fabians to concentrate their efforts on the achievement of specific solutions to social problems. They advocated publicly owned utilities and increased state regulation of working conditions and carried out important political and sociological research that provided a basis for subsequent legislation. The Fabians also helped to found the Labour party.

British political institutions worked their special magic on intellectuals and trade union members alike. The craft unions of the 1850's and 1860's, which included only skilled workers in a given trade, were often explicitly apolitical. In the 1880's, with the growth of industrial unions to which all workers in the same industry could belong, a new militancy developed, culminating in the London dock strike of August–September 1889, the first major successful work stoppage by unskilled workers. By 1900 about two million laboring men belonged to trade unions. Even then Marxism failed to gain a substantial following among the working classes, mainly because British trade unions were rather successful in winning concessions from employers and because—as in the London dockers' strike—the workers were able to win considerable middle-class support. In 1884 Henry M. Hyndman attempted to found a Social Democratic Federation based on a Marxist program, but he soon discovered that British workingmen simply were not interested.

In the last years of the nineteenth century, a handful of "Lib-Labs" (that is,

Liberals enjoying the support of the new Independent Labour party) represented the interests of the workingman in the House of Commons. The Independent Labour party, founded in 1893, remained of little political importance; and no further serious efforts to form a strong workingman's party were made until after 1901, when the House of Lords, sitting as court of ultimate appeal, ruled that unions could be sued for damage resulting from a strike. This decision in the Taff-Vale case produced a dramatic spurt in the membership of the Labour Representation Committee, a joint organization of socialist groups, including the Fabians, and labor unions and the immediate forerunner of the modern Labour party. Headed by Keir Hardie (1856–1915), a former Scottish coal miner, this new party espoused state welfare measures, and, in the elections of October 1902, it succeeded in electing two candidates to the House of Commons. But meanwhile the Liberal party itself was moving away from laissez-faire and toward a collectivist, state-welfare attitude. The political tide in Britain was now running to the left, and in the election of 1906 the forces of radical reform were to score a dramatic victory.

The Emergence of the Third Republic

While political reform was advancing steadily and peacefully in late Victorian Britain, across the English Channel in France the progress of democracy was both slow and painful. No sooner had the Prussian-led German forces defeated France in the autumn of 1870 than the Second Empire collapsed, a republic was at once proclaimed in its place, and elections for a new National Assembly were held. But when this democratically elected body assembled at Bordeaux in mid-February 1871, it soon became clear that a majority of its members were actually monarchists. Discontent with the Assembly spread rapidly in radical Paris, and the deep political chasm between the capital and the provinces—a longstanding feature of French politics—reappeared almost immediately.

At this point there were two principal areas of disagreement between Paris and the new National Assembly. First, the latter had agreed to make peace with Germany, while Paris wanted to fight on. The Parisians, no doubt, were also incensed at the harsh peace terms which Bismarck was demanding and which included not only the then unheard-of indemnity of one billion dollars but also the cession of the rich provinces of Alsace and Lorraine. Second, the composition of the new Assembly was predominantly conservative, and the radical Parisians had good reason to fear that France was in for a new era of political and social stagnation. The result was an insurrection, which broke out in mid-March 1871. The government sent troops to Paris to quell the uprising, but they joined the radicals, and in late March Paris elected a new city government called the Commune.

Thus began one of the darkest episodes in modern French history. The leaders of the Commune were of various political leanings—radical republicans in the Jacobin tradition, members of the First (Marxist) International, anarchists, and other leftists. Their differences made it difficult for the *Communards* (as they were called) to agree on common political goals. For the most part, however, they favored the decentralization of power, the substitution of the national guard for a standing army, and the separation of church and state.

It was not surprising that an armed conflict soon developed between the Assembly and the Commune. Paris was devastated by indiscriminate slaughter: in the last week of the struggle (May 21–28) more than 15,000 people were killed. The Communards executed several generals as well as the archbishop of Paris; once victorious, the government punished the revolutionaries with court-martials, lengthy prison sentences, deportation, and execution. Some of these sentences were later reduced or commuted, but it was many years before France recovered from the Paris Commune.

For a brief time the Commune episode aroused sensational fears and expectations in Europe. Karl Marx, for example, hoped—and Bismarck feared—that the Paris Commune presaged the dictatorship of the proletariat. It

The Extinction of the Paris Commune. This early photograph shows some of the devastation of Paris during the fighting that marked the last days of the Commune in May of 1871. The Communards, who for the most part espoused a radical Jacobinism, were suppressed with a ferocity unprecedented in French history. More than 15,000 Communards were summarily executed, 7500 deported to penal colonies. To many of the French bourgeoisie and peasantry, the Commune seemed to threaten Red revolution—a misconception to which Karl Marx also adhered.

seems clear now, however, that both men seriously overestimated the historical importance of the Commune. It was an episode of the dying rather than the dawning day. It was a vestige of the old Parisian revolutionary tradition of the 1790's, not the inauguration of a new proletarian uprising. The Commune's failure did, however, leave French socialism and labor unions weak and disorganized for the next two decades.

The Paris Commune was a most ominous beginning for the infant Third Republic. Too conservative for Paris and too radical for the rest of the country, the Third Republic emerged in an atmosphere of political divisiveness and class hatred. Throughout the last three decades of the nineteenth century, the French Republic was distinctly unstable. Thus while late Victorian Britain debated liberal and social legislation, the great debates in France concerned the very form of government itself.

From its uncertain beginnings, the Third Republic never developed anything like a viable two-party system. Instead, the country was divided into a variety of monarchists (principally Bourbons and Orleanists), conservatives of various kinds, republicans, and socialists. The fragmentation of French politics, moreover, made it difficult for any party to form a ministry which could enjoy the confidence of a majority of the members of the Chamber of Deputies for any long period of time. Ministries were constantly coming and going. Some lasted only a few weeks or months. From the outset, therefore, the strength of the Third Republic lay in the stability of its administrative institutions, which lent remarkable continuity to a country which suffered from interminable cabinet changes.

The political problems of the Third Republic were exacerbated by economic and social difficulties. The French surprised the Germans by rapidly paying the billion dollar indemnity. But French economic development after the 1870's fell increasingly behind that of Great Britain and the United States, and in a few years it fell behind that of the new German Empire as well. Yet French economic growth was sufficient to present the Third Republic with the social problems of an emerging laboring class. One of the themes of subsequent French political history gained acute significance during the latter decades of the nineteenth century: the alienation of the French working class from the traditional political process. Socialism spread rapidly among the workers, as did radical political activity of a violent character. Considering its lagging response to the serious social needs of the time, the Third Republic was extremely fortunate in avoiding further revolutionary confrontations.

The establishment of the Third Republic as the generally accepted government of the French people was doubtless the outstanding French achievement of the decades after 1871. It was especially notable since distrust of republicanism continued to be widespread in French society, particularly among the upper classes, royalists of all sorts, the Catholic clergy and devout Catholic laymen, and the army officer corps. Those who wished to destroy the Republic and replace it with a monarchy had every opportunity to do so.

Between 1871 and 1873, monarchists were a majority in the National Assembly. But the fragmentation that characterized French politics as a whole also applied to the monarchist camp. Thus the Legitimists, for instance, supported the Count of Chambord, the Bourbon pretender; Orleanists supported the Count of Paris, the grandson of Louis Philippe; and there were Bonapartists as well. After considerable discussion, the monarchists finally reached a compromise, but it fell through because the Count of Chambord refused to ascend the throne unless he could rule under the white Bourbon flag of the *ancien régime*. But for this disagreement, France might well have reverted to monarchy.

Before 1875 France was a republic in name only. In that year the Assembly agreed on a new form of government providing for a president with limited powers, a Chamber of Deputies to be elected on the basis of universal manhood suffrage, and a Senate to be chosen by indirect vote for a period of nine years. The new constitutional arrangements left much to be desired, but the Republic was now fairly solidly established. By 1877 the principle of ministerial responsibility was in effect accepted, and by 1879 Republicans were in control of the Third Republic for the first time. Nevertheless, the Republic was not yet out of danger. During the following two decades, a series of crises almost destroyed the Third Republic, and in most instances the chief threat came from the Right.

The first of these constitutional crises came during the years 1886–1889, when France was preoccupied with a dangerous situation centering around a leading general, Georges Boulanger. By attempting to steer a moderate course, the conservative Republicans (who controlled the government most of the time between 1879 and the turn of the century) had alienated large sections of the Right and the Left, and by the 1880's both nationalism and social discontent were once more on the rise. Boulanger had several things going for him. He had achieved something of a reputation as a military reformer; orthodox Republicans believed him to be one of their own; his violently anti-German remarks were music to the ears of conservative nationalists; and many other people believed that his political triumph might usher in a new era of social reform, an area in which the Third Republic had been notably lagging. Boulanger himself was suitably vague, but he was handsome and appealing, he drew support from both the Right and Left, and by 1887 he emerged as a powerful national figure. It was widely feared that Boulanger was sufficiently popular to make himself dictator of France—but he missed his chance, his popularity waned, he was forced to flee the country, and he finally committed suicide in Brussels in September 1891.

Hardly had the Boulanger crisis faded away when a new series of scandals in high places weakened public confidence in the Third Republic. The most important of these revelations of official corruption were the Panama Scandals of 1892–1893. The Panama Company (headed by Ferdinand de Lesseps, who had built the Suez Canal) attracted thousands of large and small French investors who wished to profit from the construction of a canal through the Isthmus of Panama. The company suddenly collapsed, and the investments were wiped out. When it became known that numerous government officials—including members of the French parliament—were implicated, there was an enormous public outcry. Instead of moving swiftly and effectively against the corrupt officials, the government first denied any connection with the collapse of the company and then, for a time, tried to cover up the whole affair. Eventually, however, most of the sordid story came out into the open, and the government's prestige was correspondingly impaired.

By far the most serious crisis faced by the Third Republic, however, was the complicated Dreyfus affair, which began in the fall of 1894 and lasted until 1906. The case began when Captain Alfred Dreyfus, a Jewish officer assigned to the French general staff, was arrested and convicted by an army court-martial of giving military intelligence to a foreign power (Germany) and was sent off to prison on Devil's Island in French Guiana. Eventually, the full details of the case came to light. Treason had in fact been committed, but Dreyfus was in no way involved. Public opinion had been inflamed against the government during the Panama affair, and in the new crisis that threatened, Dreyfus was a convenient scapegoat because he was a Jew, intensely disliked by his royalist, anti-Semitic colleagues and superiors. As early as the spring of 1896 the government had good reason to doubt Dreyfus's guilt, but it decided not to reopen the case. In 1898 the novelist Émile Zola published an open letter—*J'accuse*—which denounced the general staff and listed the officers who had framed Dreyfus. Zola himself was promptly arrested, convicted, and sentenced to one year in prison. Virtually all of France split into two hostile camps: Dreyfusards (who supported Dreyfus and demanded a new trial) and anti-Dreyfusards (who wished to let the decision of the court-martial stand).

Republicans of all shades rallied to the cause of Dreyfus, while various factions of the Right generally supported the army and the government. The conflict intensified further in 1899 when a second court-martial found Dreyfus guilty once again, although this time with "extenuating circumstances." The army had clearly misused its authority, and there was widespread fear of a rightist coup. Under growing pressure from the Center and the Left, the government finally moved against the clearly prejudiced and untenable verdict. In July 1906 the French supreme court set aside both court-martials, whereupon the government at once promoted Dreyfus to the rank of major and decorated him with the Legion of Honor. The Dreyfus affair brought all the conflicts of French society into the open; it forced people to take a stand for or against Dreyfus and, by implication, for or against the Third Republic. In the end, Dreyfus's acquittal turned the crisis into a great victory for the forces of republicanism.

An important aspect of the consolidation of the Third Republic after 1880 lay in the restriction of the power and privileges of the Catholic Church. French anticlericalism was, of course, not a new phenomenon, but this latest expression of it arose from a variety of causes. Radical Republicans and Socialists wished to curtail the influence of the Church for largely ideological reasons. Even conservative Republicans resented the political activities of the Church, for the papacy's claims to temporal and spiritual power had been growing steadily since the 1860's. But perhaps the prime cause of the new anticlericalism was the known hostility of the Church toward the Republic. To this the conservative Republicans responded increasingly with retaliatory legislation. Under the leadership of Jules Ferry, they enacted a series of measures to expel the Jesuits, to make primary education totally secular, and to legalize divorce for the first time since the days of Napoleon. After the Dreyfus affair, in which the Church came out clearly against the liberal, secular Dreyfusards, there developed a growing feeling that its influence had to be more effectively controlled. Beginning in 1901, anticlericalism scored another series of legislative victories, when the French government passed and vigorously enforced a new Law of Associations, designed to bring the Church, and especially its congregations and teaching orders, under strict state regulation. Even this policy, however, did not go far enough to suit the secular-minded Republicans, who finally decided that the only answer to the continuing problem of church-state relations lay not in further governmental control but in the complete separation of church and state. This was finally accomplished in December 1905.

While a bourgeois, anticlerical Republic was slowly being consolidated at home, the French were building an enormous empire abroad. There was, indeed, a connection between these two developments—both represented the rising spirit of nationalism that dominated French politics after the late 1880's. Not all sections of French society were enthusiastic about their country's joining the new imperialism. In general, monarchists and conservative Republicans favored imperial expansion, while liberal Republicans and Socialists opposed it. If until the 1880's the French seemed considerably less vigorous imperialists than the British, that may be partly explained by the fragmentation and instability of domestic French politics. Yet once the French appetite was whetted, their imperial endeavors became substantial indeed. They were in large measure the work of Jules Ferry, the conservative Republican premier, whose fervent nationalism had already found expression in the anticlerical legislation of the early 1880's.

French imperialism in Africa, of course, was no novelty. The French had been active in Algeria since 1830, and following their disastrous defeat in the war of 1870, Bismarck, for one, had encouraged them to renew their interest in Africa. After a period of intense economic and political rivalry with Italy, France occupied Tunis in the spring of 1881 and eventually added the whole area known as Tunisia to its empire. Like the British in Egypt, the French discovered that their presence strengthened native nationalist movements;

throughout this period, they had to suppress risings in Algeria and Tunisia. But they continued to expand into the Sahara and even beyond.

By the end of the nineteenth century, much of northern, western, and equatorial Africa belonged to France. Imperialists like Ferry hoped to build a solid block of French territory from Senegal straight across Africa to French Somaliland, which became a French protectorate in 1884. This dream never materialized. Indeed, it led in 1898 to an explosive confrontation between British and French forces at Fashoda in the Sudan. For a time, it appeared that the two countries might be plunged into hostilities over their conflicting ambitions in eastern Africa, but the French, sensing that they were in a distinctly weak position, finally withdrew. After 1900 the French concentrated their efforts in Morocco. But strong German opposition before long precipitated several international crises of major proportions.

Ferry's sights were set on more than Africa. He also plunged headlong into imperialist ventures in the Far East, although these were eventually to bring about his downfall. Actually, French involvement in that part of the world was not wholly unprecedented (French Catholic missionaries had been active in Indochina since 1615), but it was only in the nineteenth century that the French began to intervene directly. Properly speaking, French imperialism in this region began in the late 1850's, and by the Treaty of Saigon in 1862, Cochin China became a French protectorate. In the following year Cambodia accepted the same status. In the 1870's French influence in Indochina continued to grow, and by 1888 Cochin China, Cambodia, Annam, Tonkin, and Laos were united in the Indochinese Union.

During these years of bourgeois republicanism and imperial expansion, powerful forces were at work among the French laboring classes. Legalized in 1884, unionism grew rapidly and took on a more radical character than it had in England. An important socialist movement also developed: by the 1890's, around fifty socialists sat in the Chamber of Deputies. Like everything else in French politics, the socialists were deeply divided. Some followed the Marxist Jules Guesde (1845–1922), who preached that no compromise with the bourgeois order was acceptable. Others called themselves "Possibilists" and believed that socialism could be achieved by constitutional and parliamentary means. The Guesdist and Possibilist factions did not finally unite until April 1905. Despite the diversity of socialist opinion, the dominant tone of French socialism was "revisionist" (reformist) rather than revolutionary. One such revisionist, Jean Jaurès (1859–1914), eventually emerged as the leader of French socialism.

Labor and social problems became increasingly acute. France had long lagged behind in the area of social reform, nor did social reform come easily after the 1870's. The conservative Republican governments were not noted for sympathy for the workingman, and—except for a few measures regulating child labor—they did nothing to alleviate the grievances of the industrial proletariat. As a result of official indifference, outbreaks of violence by workers became frequent. Anarchistic acts such as dynamiting and assassination grew commonplace, and on one occasion a bomb was exploded in the Chamber of Deputies. When the government resorted to repression, increasing numbers of workingmen turned to the syndicalist movement. Enunciated by Georges Sorel (1847–1922), the doctrines of syndicalism derided all hopes of peaceful change or of cooperation with other progressive elements in the population and stressed instead systematic violence on the part of the workers in preparation for the destruction of capitalism by a general strike.

By 1900 imperialist victories no longer papered over deep domestic divisions: revisionist socialism, revolutionary socialism, anarchism, and syndicalism were growing at a steady pace, and the French unions were becoming increasingly powerful.

The United States in the Age of Big Business and Imperialism

In the late 1860's, American history began to enter a new phase—the age of big business. During the next three decades, a period marked by rather conservative Presidents, largely undistinguished political leaders, and frequently corrupt officials, the United States experienced remarkable economic growth, which in turn was accompanied by social changes of great import. Although the problems America encountered in the decades after the Civil War were in some ways distinctly similar to those faced by the European powers, there were also significant differences. The United States was spared bitter struggles over universal manhood suffrage, anticlerical legislation, and the kind of social and intellectual alienation that marked the history of the Continental European states during this period.

It was not surprising that the first President elected after the Civil War was the greatest Northern general in that conflict—Ulysses S. Grant. Although himself a man of intelligence and probity, Grant's two administrations were largely filled with impropriety and scandal, public and private. This was the Gilded Age of easy self-enrichment, and too many members of the Grant administration had either improperly enriched themselves, or had helped their friends and associates to do so. This corruption—together with the strong American distaste for effective government regulation of business—set the stage for systematic depredation of the nation's wealth and resources over the next thirty years.

The most important development of this period, however, was the emergence of the United States as the leading industrial nation in the world, surpassing both Great Britain and the new German Empire in industrial growth. One striking example of this remarkable growth was the rise of major urban and industrial centers along the Eastern seaboard and in the Middle West. By the end of the century, New York, Philadelphia, and Chicago all had populations exceeding one million. Urbanization was a direct result of

The Rise of American Industry. The Industrial Revolution was well under way in the northeastern United States before the Civil War. After 1865, however, American industry made enormous and rapid strides, and industrialization moved westward from the Atlantic seaboard. This engraving shows iron works in Pittsburgh around 1880. A packet boat passes the blast furnaces on its way to the South. By the end of the century, the pace of American industrial growth exceeded that of any other country.

the rapidly spreading industrialization of the country, which in turn was immensely stimulated by a large and steady flood of immigrants from the Old World, who formed the bulk of the working force required by the burgeoning industrialism of the country. Europe also provided much of the capital used in financing American industrial growth. American railroads, for example, were built in large part with British capital. But perhaps the major reason for the phenomenal growth of American industrial power lay in the exploitation of the nation's own vast natural resources — especially in the West.

In one sense, all American history has been the history of westward movement; even before the end of the Civil War a new wave of migration had started toward the trans-Mississippi West. This migration was considerably facilitated by the construction of railroads; by 1893 there existed five transcontinental railroads and many smaller lines, which carried settlers to the West and brought back raw materials for use in the industrial mills of the East. As a result the social character of the West began increasingly to resemble that of the East and Midwest.

An important part of the settlement of the West — and one of the unloveliest chapters of American history — was the treatment of the aboriginal Americans, the Indians. Following a long series of clashes, they were brought under federal control and eventually confined to a number of large reservations. The Indian Wars of the post-Civil War era, in particular, were marked by brutality on both sides. An Indian Bureau had been established to handle relations between the tribes and the United States government, but its employees systematically robbed and cheated the Indians of the money and supplies promised them by various treaties with the government.

As the trans-Mississippi region became economically developed and grew more populous, the remaining Western territories were, one by one, incorporated into the federal union. Already in April 1891 a bulletin of the superintendent of the U.S. Census for 1890 had announced that "at present . . . there can hardly be said to be a frontier line." In effect, the American frontier was closed. Thus, the American people had brought under their political control a country of continental dimensions, which they were rapidly settling and whose rich resources they were vigorously exploiting.

But the expansive drive of a nation frequently spills beyond its own borders. When their western frontier was formally declared closed in 1890, the American people began to look for new frontiers in Latin America and the Far East. The 1890's, the decade of greatest imperial fervor in the other major powers, was also the period in which the United States itself became something of an imperial power.

American involvement in Latin America was nothing new. But in the quarter-century following the 1890's the role of the United States in Latin American affairs became bolder, more aggressive, and certainly less subtle than at any time before or since. The Monroe Doctrine was now interpreted to signify that the entire Western Hemisphere was America's sphere of influence. The first specific expression of this interpretation came in 1895 when Britain refused to submit to arbitration the frontier dispute between Venezuela and British Guiana, leading Richard Olney, secretary of state in the second Cleveland administration, tartly to inform the British that "today the United States is practically sovereign on this continent, and its fiat is law upon the subjects to which it confines its interposition."

The Spanish-American War of April–December 1898 ushered in the climactic period of American intervention in Latin America. The origins of the war went back some years and were a mixture of idealism and interventionism. In 1895 a group of Cuban nationalists revolted against Spanish rule. At first the United States, under the leadership of the strongly anti-imperialist President Grover Cleveland, kept strictly "hands off." As time went on, however, the Spaniards' undeniable barbarity and cruelty aroused strong feelings throughout the United States. Stirred up by the circulation-conscious "Yellow Press," war fever swept the country. In addition to genuine sympathy for the Cubans, public interest was no doubt increased by American investments in Cuba. When the American battleship *Maine* blew up mysteriously in Havana Harbor in February 1898 with the loss of 260 members of her crew, newspapers at once blamed Spain. A month later President William Mc-

Kinley demanded that the Spanish government put an end to its concentration camps and accept an armistice between its troops and the Cuban rebels. After a brief delay, the Spanish government agreed to the American demands, but it was too late. Popular clamor for war was irresistible, and on April 11 the President asked the Congress for authority to intervene with force, a request approved nine days later. But Congress was careful to disclaim through the Teller Amendment any "disposition or intention to exercise sovereignty, jurisdiction or control" over Cuba and asserted "its determination, when [the pacification of the island] is accomplished, to leave the government and the control of the Island to its people."

In the war that followed the United States won easily, and by the Treaty of Paris of December 1898 it gained control of Cuba, Puerto Rico, and Guam and acquired the Philippines as well for a sum of $20,000,000. The Senate did not consent to the peace treaty without a bitter struggle; a vocal and powerful group of anti-imperialists was opposed to its terms. Finally, however, the Senate approved the treaty by a two-vote margin, and the United States emerged as a full-fledged world power. Despite the Teller Amendment, it did not grant immediate independence to Cuba. In 1902 American forces left Cuba, but Cuba was meanwhile required to agree that it would make no treaty with a third power impairing its independence, that the United States had the right to intervene to preserve the independence of Cuba, and that certain Cuban territory be leased to the United States as a naval station. These provisions were finally abrogated in 1934, but even after that date the United States retained the naval base at Guantánamo Bay.

United States influence and power in Latin America expanded dramatically during the administration of Theodore Roosevelt (1901–1909). The outstanding example of Roosevelt's imperial way of doing things concerned the issue of an isthmian canal. The United States had for some time been interested in building a waterway connecting the Atlantic and Pacific oceans. The most desirable route was through Colombia, but the Colombian government was anything but cooperative. In early November 1903 the Colombian province of Panama revolted; less than a week later, the United States recognized its independence, and soon after it concluded a treaty with Panama providing for the building of an isthmian canal. In 1911 Roosevelt boasted: "I took the Canal Zone." The Panama Canal was opened in August 1914.

Hardly less important than the Panamanian affair was the so-called Roosevelt Corollary to the Monroe Doctrine. In 1905 Roosevelt declared that under certain conditions the United States might be forced to exercise what he termed "international police power" in the Americas. Specifically, Roosevelt's policy reserved to the United States the right to intervene if a Latin American nation could not meet its financial obligations to European creditors; and it was under the Roosevelt Corollary that the United States proceeded, first, to take over customs in the Dominican Republic in 1905, and later to intervene in Haiti, Nicaragua, and, once more, in Cuba. In defense of Roosevelt's policy, it should be said that even he looked upon such intervention only as a last resort and that the Roosevelt Corollary kept Latin America from being partitioned by the European powers—from becoming another Africa.

While the United States was beginning to play a dominant role in Latin America, it also became considerably more active in the Pacific and the Far East. After a long and bitter congressional struggle, Hawaii was annexed in July 1898. The Americans were welcomed in Hawaii, but they were not welcomed in the Philippines. In 1899 the Senate had declared that the occupation of the Philippines was not to be permanent, but this did not put an end to local insurrections, which went on until 1901. Within a few years, however, the progressive administration directed by William Howard Taft had brought about notable reforms. Beginning in 1907 the Filipinos elected the lower house of their legislature, while the United States continued to appoint the upper house.

Given its involvement in the Philippines, it was not surprising that, along with the other imperial powers, the United States soon became drawn into Chinese affairs. American policy toward China had long favored full sovereignty and independence for that troubled country, and around the turn of the century that position was reasserted in the so-called "Open Door Policy," which, in the words of Secretary of State John Hay, also sought to "safeguard for the world the principle of equal and impartial trade with all parts of the Chinese Empire." The Open Door Policy was inspired as much by a genuine sympathy and compassion which many Americans had long held for the Chinese people as by an eagerness for American trade and investment in China, which in fact were still very limited. As if to demonstrate anew that the American attitude toward Chinese nationalism was different from that of the European powers, when the United States joined those powers, in 1900, in a punitive expedition against rampaging Chinese nationalists (called Boxers), the United States first returned most of the $25,000,000 indemnity it received and later applied the remainder to a scholarship program for Chinese students in America.

There was little compassion, however, in the practices and attitudes of American industrial capitalism in the decades after the Civil War. These were the years when enormous corporations developed, and huge fortunes were amassed by businessmen like Andrew Carnegie and John D. Rockefeller. Though American corporations often produced technological and economic miracles, much of the spectacular growth of American capitalism came at the expense of the general public. American farmers were frequently charged exorbitant rates by the railroads for the shipment of their products—indeed, no segment of the economy was totally immune from the depredation of largely unregulated corporations.

Such widespread economic grievances produced serious unrest, which was greatly intensified by periodic financial panics in 1873, 1884, and 1893.

Against such dislocations the federal government seemed all but powerless, its economic policy a matter of simply letting nature — and the market — take its course. The abuses of big business — stock manipulation and various monopolistic practices — finally impelled Congress in 1890 to pass the regulatory Sherman Antitrust Act. All the same, trusts and other forms of monopoly continued to flourish.

The greatest domestic problems of the post-Civil War decades arose from the growth of an industrial working class. A strong trade union movement was long years — and many false starts — in the making. Founded in 1881 and led by the hard-headed Samuel Gompers, the American Federation of Labor (AFL) was not the first labor movement of national significance. Many smaller and larger unions had struggled courageously against brutally insensitive employers, indifferent public officials, and frequently hostile courts.

Slowly but steadily, national movements were forming in the closing years of the century to protest the brutality of laissez faire. For decades the Negro, the farmer, and the worker had been abandoned or neglected. By the 1890's the Populists, organized in 1892 as the People's party, were demanding, among other things, a graduated income tax and government ownership of railroads, telephone, and telegraph. Failing to achieve national political power, the Populists rapidly disintegrated, and in the presidential election of 1896, the Democratic candidate, William Jennings Bryan, running on a reform platform, was defeated. But at the turn of the century a protest movement against unrestrained capitalism was gradually forming in the United States.

III THE CONSERVATIVE POWERS

Bismarckian Germany

For all their difficulties in the last decades of the nineteenth century, the political institutions of the Western democracies probably emerged strengthened in the end. It was otherwise in the conservative states of central and eastern Europe, where the accumulation of political and social problems not only taxed the powers of the governments but contributed to undermining their popular support.

As in the French Third Republic, the most important domestic problem facing the new German Empire was the task of national consolidation. The new state was essentially a federation of princes, with the king of Prussia as the German emperor and the Prussian army, aristocracy, and bureaucracy as dominating forces. On the surface, conservative Prussia should have had no difficulty in maintaining the political, constitutional, military, and economic mastery it had finally achieved. But in practice, things worked out rather differently, and almost from the founding of the Empire, Bismarck, who served as chancellor in the new Reich, faced two major challenges to imperial authority: first, the power of the Catholic Church and, later, the growing threat of liberalism and, especially, socialism. Furthermore, the international system of alliances that he sought to construct after 1871 broke down repeatedly and dangerously.

Hardly had Germany been unified in 1870–1871 when Bismarck virtually declared war upon the Catholic Church. In Bismarck's view, a powerful, independent Church and a united German nation were almost certainly incompatible. Bismarck's fears were not wholly unjustified: in 1864 Pius IX declared in the *Syllabus of Errors* that the modern state could in no way interfere with ecclesiastical powers and prerogatives, and in 1870 the First Vatican Council declared the pope infallible in matters of faith and morals. These events had an immediate effect upon German politics: in March 1871, the Center party was formed in the Reichstag to defend the Church and the southern German states (which were largely Catholic) against Protestant Prussia and the imperial government.

Bismarck was appalled by what he regarded as the intolerable spiritual and temporal meddling of the Catholic Church, and although he was by no means antireligious, within a few months he launched his campaign against it—the so-called *Kulturkampf* ("the battle for civilization"). For support in the anticlerical struggle, Bismarck formed a temporary alliance with the National Liberal party. Bismarck had alienated many of his natural allies in the Conservative party, which was Prussian, Protestant, and Junker in outlook, by what they believed was a dangerously democratic policy, including holding national elections on the basis of universal manhood suffrage. But the National Liberals proved to be enthusiastic allies, for liberals throughout nineteenth-century Europe regarded the Church as an enemy of progress.

Bismarck and the National Liberals waged the *Kulturkampf* with such bitter intensity that it seemed as if the Reich itself were at stake. In June 1872 the Jesuits were expelled from Germany, and in the following year a series of drastic measures known as the Falk Laws (after Dr. Falk, the Prussian minister of public worship) brought the Church under strict government regulation. The Falk Laws resulted in the removal of over half of the German Catholic bishops, many of whom fled the country, and the imprisonment of hundreds of the clergy. In time, every Catholic religious order was disbanded. Moreover, the government decreed that all marriages be performed as civil ceremonies rather than religious sacraments.

All this caused extreme tension between the Reich and the Vatican. But even while these anticlerical measures were being rigorously enforced, Bismarck gradually became aware that his policy was not destroying the Catholic Center party as an effective political force in the country. More importantly, he began to dislike the political company he was having to keep, and he grew somewhat concerned over his continued estrangement from his conservative friends. William I, also a deeply religious man, opposed the whole policy from its inception. Bismarck then began to persuade himself that he had somewhat overestimated the political threat posed by the Church, especially after 1878 when Pius IX was succeeded by the more moderate Pope Leo XIII. By the late 1870's Bismarck began to feel that he was face to face with even more serious domestic problems and enemies. The result was that, within a short time, the enforcement of the anti-Catholic legislation was considerably relaxed, and the crucial paragraphs of the Falk Laws were finally repealed. By 1879 the *Kulturkampf* was, for practical purposes, at an end.

Bismarck's principal domestic task, after 1871, was quite simply to create a new national government. In this building task, Bismarck was once again able to obtain the assistance of the National Liberals, for as the party of big business and finance, they had the most immediate interest in establishing a uniform currency, a system of civil and criminal law, and such laws as would facilitate the further growth of business and industry. The National Liberals also had some favorite policies of their own which they persuaded Bismarck to accept. Perhaps the most notable of these was free trade, which the Prussian agrarians—whose interest lay in securing an export market for their grain—had also long favored.

By the middle and late 1870's, however, the German economic climate had considerably changed. The panic of 1873 ushered in a period of falling prices, and American and Russian produce was increasingly competing with Prussian grain even at home. Bismarck abandoned free trade and, with the support of the Conservatives and the Center party, enacted a protective tariff of enormous consequence in 1879. It is difficult to say whether this step set the stage for the period of substantial urban and industrial growth that followed. But it is certain that by the opening of the twentieth century Germany did rank as one of the leading industrial powers of the world. It surpassed Britain and France in the production of iron and steel and was second only to the United States. German railroad mileage had expanded rapidly, and foreign trade showed a substantial increase. As the nation exploited its rich deposits of iron and coal, the Ruhr Valley became a densely populated urban and industrial sprawl, similar to the English Midlands.

Industrialization made Germany the dominant power in Europe, but it also steadily increased the size and power of the business and laboring classes and led to demands for political change and social reform. In concrete political terms, industrialization strengthened the Progressives and the Marxist Social Democrats, as well as the National Liberals, and both of the former demanded additional democratic reforms. But democracy was totally alien to the character of the Empire and the men who made it. Despite Bismarck's occasional sops to democratic opinion, the new German state remained at bottom a conservative monarchy of the old Prussian type. Bismarck generally found it necessary to obtain the support of a majority in the Reichstag, but he acknowledged no principle of ministerial responsibility. Political power remained largely in the hands of the kaiser and his chancellor.

If Bismarck and the kaiser regarded democracy as an enemy of the German state, they viewed the development of socialism with absolute horror. Industrialized Germany proved to be fertile soil for socialism; Germans had been active in the First International in the 1860's, and, before long, socialist activity in the country was notably on the rise. German socialism consisted of two strains—one was descended from orthodox Marxism; the other took its inspiration largely from Ferdinand Lassalle, a moderate socialist who had eschewed violence. In 1871 the socialists won two seats in the Reichstag; in 1874 they won nine. In May 1875, at Gotha, the two factions merged temporarily and agreed to a Lassallean program. This compromise outraged Marx in London, but it helped the party at home. As more Social Democrats were elected to the Reichstag, Bismarck became increasingly alarmed; and in 1878, when radicals attempted to assassinate the kaiser, Bismarck resolved once and for all to remove the cancer of socialism from the German body politic.

As a result Bismarck launched an intense campaign aimed at exterminating socialism in the Reich. The first phase may be characterized as political repression. The Anti-Socialist Law of October 1878 severely restricted or banned socialist meetings, socialist publications, and the raising of funds for socialist causes. The government enforced these laws with the bureaucratic efficiency for which Germans were now renowned. But Bismarck quickly discovered the difficulty of killing ideas. Socialists continued to be elected to the Reichstag, which—following constitutional procedure—stoutly refused to restrict its members' freedom of expression.

Sensing that his policy was producing only limited successes, Bismarck soon decided to combine repression with a far-reaching program of social legislation. Like other eastern European landowners, Bismarck was familiar with the patriarchal treatment of the poor. Though never a great believer in government-sponsored social programs, he hoped that if workers' burdens were lightened by government action, the German laboring man would place his faith in his imperial benefactor and forget the treasonous siren song of socialism. Thus Bismarck initiated a substantial program of welfare legislation: a sickness insurance law in 1883, an accident insurance law in 1884, and a law providing insurance for invalids and the aged in 1889. These laws passed only after long debates, arousing opposition from many laissez-faire liberals. With regard to certain highly objectionable practices—such as Sunday labor—Bismarck refused to undertake corrective action. Despite these limits and Bismarck's rather cynical motives, the German system of social legislation was, for a time, the most advanced in Europe. Nevertheless Bismarck's two-pronged attack upon socialism proved, in the end, to be a dismal failure. More socialist deputies sat in the Reichstag in 1890 than in 1878. At best, Bismarck merely drove socialist activity underground. Socialism and the desire for political democracy continued to grow with industrialism.

In the realm of foreign affairs, Bismarck exhibited, after 1871, much the same curious combination of tactical skill and ideological myopia that was his stock-in-trade at home. His foreign policy was governed by the sensible twin notions of keeping defeated France isolated, and, as far as possible, preserving the status quo elsewhere, especially in the Balkans. The diplomatic arrangement that would satisfy both requirements was some sort of German-Austro-Russian alliance or *entente,* and this was the goal Bismarck pursued, with some success, in the early and middle 1870's. In the end, however, circumstances and nationalistic ambitions were too much for his fragile system. In 1872–1873 Bismarck managed to establish a fairly solid Three Emperors' League (Germany, Austria, Russia), but in the spring of 1875 the League was seriously shaken by the threat of a new German-French confrontation, and it came apart completely soon after, when Bismarck opposed Russia's efforts to take over a substantial part of the disintegrating Ottoman Empire.

These efforts reached a climax in the Russo-Turkish War of 1877–1878. At the Congress of Berlin that followed in June and July 1878, Bismarck is often considered to have played his role as European diplomat and "honest broker" with greatest success. But in fact, the Russians were enraged by the results of the Berlin conference, and Bismarck faced the international situation with more trepidation than ease. Consequently, despite his theoretical aversion to a system of alliances, Bismarck felt compelled to sign a military alliance with Austria-Hungary in October 1879. He was fearful that the Balkan problem might eventually lead to a general war, and he felt obliged to choose between the great powers competing in the Balkans. Concerned that the more powerful Russians might prove intractable, Bismarck formed the so-called Dual Alliance with the Austro-Hungarians. This was a purely defensive alliance: Austria and Germany would come to each other's aid only in the event of Russian aggression. In 1882 Italy joined Germany and Austria in a defensive pact known as the Triple Alliance. Building upon the Austro-German Dual Alliance of 1879, the Triple Alliance provided that all three powers would unite in the event of an attack by two powers—presumably France and Russia—upon any member. Designed as a pillar of the Bismarckian alliance system, the Triple Alliance lasted until the First World War, but Italy proved to be both a weak and doubtfully loyal partner.

Having secured Germany against the possibility of attack by Russia or France, Bismarck sought to discourage the Russians and the French from forming a military alliance of their own. From the mid-1870's to the mid-1880's, there was a kind of Franco-German rapprochement. One of the reasons for Bismarck's support of French colonial ambitions, especially in North Africa, was his hope that France would become so obsessed with overseas glory that it would tend to forget about the loss of Alsace-Lorraine and take only a limited role in European politics.

Although Bismarck sought to discourage Russian ambitions in the Balkans, he nevertheless cultivated reasonably good relations with Russia, hoping thereby to prevent a Franco-Russian alliance. After the second Three

Emperors' League, formed in 1881, broke up over still another explosive Balkan crisis in 1885–1886, Bismarck negotiated a highly secret Russian-German Reinsurance Treaty. Since Russia and Germany remained potential enemies, such a treaty could only have been achieved by the utmost diplomatic finesse. The Reinsurance Treaty of 1887 was Bismarck's last important diplomatic triumph. A wonderful feat of political legerdemain, it reflected his growing desperation to preserve peace and also the increasing pressures upon him caused by political problems at home. The treaty clearly contradicted the Triple Alliance. Yet Bismarck apparently felt that such inconsistency was a small price to pay for peace. While Bismarck remained in office, his alliance system and his diplomatic expertise prevented war – a great achievement in such a competitive and aggressive age – but his system of alliances was more a palliative than a permanent solution.

In the realm of colonial affairs Bismarckian Germany exhibited many of the same imperial impulses that were at work in England and France. Together with the other major powers, Germany continued to be deeply involved in the "Eastern Question," wishing to preserve for itself at least an area of special influence in the decaying Ottoman Empire. After the Russo-Turkish War of 1877–1878, Bismarck supported a vigorous policy in the Middle East. Substantial amounts of German capital were sunk into the Turkish sands, resulting in widespread German influence in that politically sensitive area of the world. Before long, German imperial planners began work on the great Berlin-to-Baghdad railroad, which was almost completed when World War I broke out in 1914.

On the other hand, the Germans entered the race for African colonies rather late. Agitation for colonial expansion developed in Germany in the mid-70's, and the influential German Colonial Society was founded in 1887. For a time, Bismarck resisted the pressures of various imperial-minded groups, although not so vigorously as to discourage them completely or to suggest that he could not change his mind. Unlike Britain and France, the new German Empire had no long-standing interests in Africa, and Bismarck did not seem anxious to acquire any African territory. He had more important things to do at home – fighting first the Church and then the socialists. Yet Bismarck was also a practical politician; in the end, it was a matter of German national prestige – and the chancellor would not allow the Reich to be left behind by the British and French.

Bismarck was a reluctant imperialist, but once he had decided to become involved in overseas affairs, he steered Germany into a colonial course with characteristic skill, cunning, and thoroughness. German colonial development in Africa between 1883 and 1885 generally followed the pattern set by other European powers in that part of the world. First, an area was explored, then taken over by a private German company; in the next phase it became a German protectorate; finally it was integrated into the colonial empire itself. The first such German colony was a barren desert known as

Perfidious Albion—a German view. Although the British saw themselves as the liberal and humane disseminators of Western civilization, this view was not always shared. On the Continent Britain was often regarded as greedy, treacherous, and hypocritical. This cartoon represents a German view of British imperialism in the 1890's. England is viewed as trying to dominate three continents—an ambition which some German leaders themselves held by this time. The cartoon illustrates the national hostilities exacerbated by aggressive imperialism.

German Southwest Africa. Next came Togoland and the German Cameroons in West Africa. In 1885 Bismarck added the final and most valuable jewel to the colonial diadem—German East Africa (Tanganyika).

To this group of territories, Bismarck hoped eventually to add Portuguese East Africa and Angola. By defending these Portuguese colonies against encroachment by other powers, Bismarck planned to win by restraint what he knew he could not achieve by naked aggression. When the expected collapse of the Portuguese colonial empire occurred, with some judicious exchanges of territory not unknown even to hard-headed imperialist governments, the Germans might someday find themselves with a solid band of African territories.

Bismarck's interest in colonies rose as his difficulties mounted at home. If he had expected to distract his dissatisfied countrymen with foreign exploits, he soon learned better. In 1884 Bismarck suffered a serious defeat in the national elections, and although he recovered his losses in 1887, the elections of early 1890 marked another, and more serious, setback.

This setback was ominous because by the spring of 1890 Bismarck's relations with his emperor were anything but satisfactory. William I, who had brought Bismarck to office in September 1862 and had stuck with him through good and foul times, had died in March 1888. His son and successor, Frederick III, was already mortally ill, and his death in June brought to the throne Frederick's twenty-nine-year-old son William II. Though he was the grandson of Queen Victoria, there was nothing British about William's political outlook or sympathies. Young, modestly intelligent, and alternately extremely self-confident and unsure of himself, the new kaiser wished to rule Germany by himself in the old Hohenzollern manner, and he resented the enormous powers wielded by Chancellor Bismarck. The impulsive young monarch and the elder statesman soon began to clash, and following a long series of disputes over domestic and foreign policies, William II forced Bismarck to resign in March 1890.

The political and social structure of Bismarckian Germany remained largely unchanged after his dismissal. Industrialization and urbanization continued at a quickened pace. There was a surface change in the style of German politics. The kaiser pretended to be a great friend of the workingman; he abandoned Bismarck's ineffectual antisocialist legislation, and he saw to it that existing schemes of social welfare were enlarged and expanded. But despite limited additional social legislation, the policy of killing socialism with kindness continued to fail, and, before long, William's relations with his working-class subjects turned increasingly sour.

In 1890 thirty-five socialist deputies sat in the Reichstag, and thereafter the Social Democratic party grew steadily more powerful. Under the influence of Eduard Bernstein (1850–1932), the German Socialist movement continued its tendency toward moderate "revisionism," turning away from orthodox Marxist revolutionary theory, toward parliamentary methods and gradualism. The continued growth of German trade unionism was partly responsible for the moderate, nonviolent, pragmatic direction the Social Democrats followed until the early 1900's.

In one sense, the future of Germany's Social Democrats was tied to the overriding if largely unspoken issue of contemporary German political life: Would the kaiser finally begin to yield, however slowly, to demands for the meaningful democratization of the government by choosing his ministers from the majority party in the Reichstag? If so, the future of moderate socialism in Germany was rather promising, as indeed it was in Britain. But what if the kaiser decided to stand pat?

Perhaps William II himself did not know the direction in which he was headed. Certainly his foreign and colonial policy was one of bluster, bluff, and bullying. Intentionally or not, it took on an increasingly aggressive complexion after Bismarck's fall. Bismarck's successors were unable to maintain his delicate balance of aggression and restraint; the Bismarckian system was clearly too intricate for men of lesser powers of mind, and it gave way at the turn of the century to a new and dangerous era of international expansion and confrontation in the Far East, the Near East, and North Africa.

From a deeply divided country, the Germans had become in less than half a century one of the great powers of the world. More and more they felt that they were striving, no longer for equality, but for supremacy. It was a dangerous game for which the Germans were ill-equipped, and, as the next two decades were to show, they were heading for disaster.

The Decline of the Habsburg Monarchy

Given Austria's political history over the previous century, it would have been too much to hope that the Habsburgs would finally take effective steps to put their house in order after 1870. Instead, the Compromise of 1867 created a political structure unprecedented in European history. In the Dual Monarchy, as it was to be called, Francis Joseph I (1848–1916) ruled an empire composed of Germans, Magyars, and various Slavic peoples. In theory, the Habsburg monarch governed through responsible ministries in the two parliamentary, constitutional states (Austria and Hungary) which comprised his empire; in fact, he enjoyed virtually complete control over foreign and military affairs and had considerable power to rule by personal decree. A conservative, clerical monarch of the old style, Francis Joseph had no sympathy whatever for the nationalistic aspirations of his subject peoples or of ethnic groups just beyond the borders of the Empire in the Balkan peninsula. Moreover, while the Austrian constitution guaranteed the individual the right to express his opinions and declared that there should be no censorship of the press, statutory regulations provided that printing could not be carried on without a license and that all periodicals had to be submitted to the police before publication so that they could be confiscated if they contained anything contrary to law.

The problems of the Austro-Hungarian Empire, however, were not caused by the personality or political outlook of the emperor alone or by the ambivalence of the fundamental law but by the national composition and constitutional structure of the Empire. In fact if not in intent, the Compromise of 1867 perpetuated the rule of minority groups over the vast Slavic majority within the empire. In Austria the Slavs were dominated by the Germans, in Hungary by the Magyars. Indeed, the desire to maintain their political superiority over the Slavic peoples formed the main bond between the ruling Germans and Magyars. In an age of rising nationalism, the official energies of the Empire were largely absorbed in preserving its very existence.

Austria was somewhat more industrialized at this time than Hungary, but even after the 1870's its economy suffered from the same weaknesses that had burdened Austria in its struggle for economic-political leadership in Germany before 1866 — lagging railroad construction, a seriously adverse balance of trade, and generally inadequate technical education. In almost all industrial enterprise, the stifling hand of the powerful Austrian bureaucracy asserted itself.

Attention that should have been given to economic planning was taken up by the labyrinthine nationalities question. Although only about one third of the total population of Austria was German-speaking, the Germans continued to enjoy a distinct economic, social, linguistic, and cultural hegemony over the Slavic peoples — such as Czechs, Slovenes, and Poles. The Magyars, who comprised less than half the population of Hungary, vigorously asserted their supremacy there and in 1867 were able to force the Vienna government to agree that Hungarian should be the only language spoken in the Hungarian parliament.

The growing nationalism of the other racial and linguistic groups manifested itself politically in efforts to decentralize the empire and achieve a kind of home-rule status for various nationalities. This movement was particularly pronounced among the Czechs, who boycotted the parliamentary elections and demanded a triple monarchy (Austria, Hungary, and a Czech state in Bohemia) to replace the dual system. But the emperor rejected this proposal in 1871, after the Magyars protested that it would endanger imperial unity (and incidentally set a bad example for Hungary's own subject peoples). Germans in Bohemia, unwilling to be dominated by Czechs, were also strongly opposed, and even the Czechs themselves were divided on the issue: older men boycotted the Vienna parliament while the young Czechs thought that policy self-defeating and favored participation and stronger agitation.

The ministry of Count Taaffe (1879–1893) made some concessions to the forces of Slavic nationalism, but the piecemeal and inadequate reforms outraged the Germans without satisfying the other groups, and tensions grew on both sides. When the non-German languages received official recognition in the local courts and administrative offices for the first time in 1897, the Germans in Bohemia protested violently, and a constitutional crisis of the first order resulted. The monarchy was shaken, and for a number of years orderly parliamentary government was impossible. Moreover, the uncertainty at the center of government was compounded by administrative fragmentation and frequent paralysis on the local and provincial level.

The kingdom of Hungary was unlike Austria in one important respect: it remained a predominantly agricultural region. As late as 1900 less than 13 per cent of the population was employed in industry. The considerable economic burdens of the peasant class merged with a growing consciousness of Slavic national identity to create an explosive social and political compound. But the Magyar landowners stood their ground. In contrast to the confused liberals of Austria, the Magyars refused to make any significant concessions to the majority. As late as the end of the nineteenth century, only those men who could speak Hungarian were eligible to vote; some property requirements remained, and so did other local prerequisites. Except for the Croats, who were allowed to use their own language in the Hungarian Parliament, all other members could speak only in Hungarian. For the rest, the Hungarians promulgated a series of regulations aimed at "Magyarizing" the realm which served only to affront and exacerbate Slavic nationalism.

Although the Habsburg monarchy was technically one state, even after 1867 its internal structure was significantly different from a federal union like the United States. Thus there was no such thing as common citizenship; Hungarians were foreigners in Austria, and vice versa. Though such integral features of a national state as a common currency and basic legislation on commerce and communication did exist, they rested not—as in the German Empire—on a permanent constitutional foundation, but on formal international treaties, renewable or terminable every ten years. The result, not surprisingly, was a series of bitter battles between the two halves of the Empire. In 1878, after a long and acrimonious dispute, the Hungarians forced the Austrians to transform the Austrian National Bank into an Austro-Hungarian National Bank, without offering to contribute any capital stock of their own. Still another conflict arose right after the turn of the century over the control and administration of the army. The Magyars insisted that Hungarian units be permitted to display the traditional Magyar insignia and that Hungarian replace German as the sole language of command. But this matter encroached upon the imperial prerogative, and Francis Joseph—who grew more stubborn and inflexible with the years—refused to retreat. When he threatened to destroy Magyar domination over the Slavs by instituting universal suffrage in Hungary, the Magyars quickly decided that German domination of the army was a lesser evil than Slavic voting privileges.

While the Magyars and Germans were continuing to struggle for power and position at the top, the attitude of the other nationalities was slowly becoming more radical and hostile. Until the 1880's, the Czechs, in particular, were, on the whole, reconciled to their continued membership in the Austrian Empire. After that date, as new Czech leadership began to arise, this attitude began slowly but significantly to change. How long the Hungarians particularly could successfully persist in their policy of national repression, no one could possibly predict in 1900.

An empire with such pronounced internal problems was distinctly ill-prepared to play an important international role in an age of growing nationalism and imperialism. Nevertheless, despite these domestic difficulties, Austria-Hungary continued to conduct its foreign policy in an unwise and dangerous manner. The Habsburg empire, of course, had long-standing interests in the Balkan peninsula and, almost in spite of itself, continued to expand into that uneasy part of Europe. At the end of the Russo-Turkish War of 1877–1878, Austria-Hungary received the right to occupy and administer the provinces of Bosnia and Herzegovina, though these two Balkan provinces were to remain nominal parts of the Ottoman Empire. The occupation exacerbated existing tensions in Austria-Hungary where the Slavs were outraged at the extension of imperial authority over additional members of their race. Austria's continued expansion into the Balkans also increased friction between the Habsburg monarchy and Russia, which liked to think of itself as the protector of Slavic interests. After the late 1870's Austro-Russian conflict in the Balkans consequently had an important influence upon international relations. None probably understood this better than did Bismarck, and from the Congress of Berlin in 1878 to his own dismissal in 1890, he labored hard to stabilize that turbulent region. Yet Bismarck failed. It is possible that the rivalries in the Balkans could not have been resolved without a great war. But it cannot be said that the Austrians tried very hard.

Imperial Russia from Reform to Revolution

In the late nineteenth century, the condition of both the Austrian and Russian empires was such as to demand extreme care and caution from their governments. There were important differences in the problems confronting these two empires: in the case of Austria the principal source of anxiety at this time was undoubtedly the nationality problem, while in Russia it was the peasantry. Yet the Russian government—even more than the Austrian

—indulged in reaction at home and adventure abroad. This policy was to prove a one-way ticket to disaster.

A decade after the emancipation of the serfs in 1861, it was clear that Czar Alexander II had failed to solve the most serious social and economic issue of all. Simply stated, the peasants needed more land. The emancipated serfs became a depressed rural class which made up four fifths of the population and suffered chronic land hunger. Living in wretched poverty, the Russian peasants were weighed down by heavy taxes and steep repayments for redemption of their feudal obligations. A full-scale redistribution of land was needed to complement the legal freedom they had to purchase.

The tragedy of Russia in these years lay in the czar's renewed reliance upon various forms of repression to solve the peasant problem and numerous other political and social grievances. Even the reforms of the 1860's had fallen short of bringing Russia into the mainstream of European political development, and the gap between Russia and the West widened again after 1870, when the "Czar Liberator" and his successors reverted to more traditional autocratic practices of Russian statecraft. It was not surprising that the new policy of repression soon gave rise to even greater dissatisfaction, and that the dominant tone of much of this opposition was increasingly violent and revolutionary. Many intellectuals, in particular, came to feel that reform would come only after the czarist regime had been overthrown by force. In the 1870's and 1880's, there were some revolutionaries who adhered to the anarchist doctrine of Mikhail Bakunin, who wished to liberate mankind from the tyranny of the state; others described themselves as nihilists (a phrase first used in Turgenev's novel *Fathers and Sons,* published in 1862), and advocated the destruction not only of the state but of civilization and social order; still others, beginning in the late 1880's and 1890's, were Marxists who placed their faith in the nascent Russian industrial proletariat as the agent of eventual revolution.

Within this broad spectrum of ideas and tactics, the main thrust of revolutionary activity in the 1870's centered in the Populist movement, which drew its inspiration from the traditions of peasant violence that had characterized much of the Russian past. Agrarian Populism stressed the ability of the oppressed peasant class to topple the czar and erect in his place a native peasant socialism based upon existing communal institutions like the *mir.* In the late 1870's, a new and still more radical wing of the Populist movement, known as the "Will of the People," was founded, dedicated to the fine art of assassination. Its targets were not closely circumscribed. Almost any ranking member of the government was fair game. Alexander may not have been intimidated by this movement, but by 1880 he had decided to take another major step toward the political modernization of Russia. He agreed, at last, to some sort of national assembly. But on the same day in March 1881 that he was formally to approve the plan he was assassinated by "Will of the People" terrorists.

Revolutionary Violence in Russia. This drawing from a German weekly magazine depicts the death of Czar Alexander II in March 1881, after his carriage was bombed by terrorists belonging to the "Will of the People," an extreme wing of the Populist movement. The terrorists had made no less than seven previous attempts on the czar's life. The Russian government was characteristically inept in its efforts to suppress the revolutionaries, who at one point even infiltrated the czar's police.

The assassination of Alexander II ushered in an era of even more intense repression under his son Alexander III (1881–1894). The new czar lost no time attempting to restore the style and substance of old Russia, hoping that the Orthodox Church and the state could act together to suppress dissent and revolution. To accomplish this, he relied upon his reactionary friend Konstantin P. Pobedonostsev, whom he made procurator of the Holy Synod (or lay head of the Russian Orthodox Church). Pobedonostsev was no empty-headed reactionary. He had begun his career as a scholar and bureaucrat and was an authority on serfdom and Russian civil law, a Slavophile, and later a pan-Slav. But above all he was a dedicated conservative.

Alexander and Pobedonostsev worked relentlessly to restore the nobility to something like its former status, although this was difficult even in late nineteenth-century Russia. They also branched out into persecuting non-Orthodox religious groups (especially the large and highly vulnerable Jewish population), and they initiated a new policy of official discrimination against various groups in the multinational Russian empire. Alexander's reign saw the first attempt to "Russify" peoples as diverse as Asian Muslims and Baltic Germans.

While Alexander feverishly strove to strengthen czarist autocracy and the Orthodox Church, he had at the same time no compunction about reaching diplomatic understandings with the liberal, anticlerical French Third Republic. The Russians resented what they considered Germany's condescending and discriminatory treatment, especially in economic matters. Therefore, after Bismarck was dismissed and the German-Russian Reinsurance Treaty lapsed in 1890, the Russians and French soon moved closer together. By early 1894 the two countries had concluded a fateful military agreement, providing for French assistance if Russia was attacked by Germany—or by Austria supported by Germany—and for Russian assistance if France was attacked by Germany—or by Italy supported by Germany. If the Triple Alliance (Germany, Austria, Italy) or any of its members mobilized, France and Russia would mobilize without delay. Mobilization, it went without saying, meant war. In 1894 no one could foresee the circumstances under which such an occasion might arise, but both France and Russia were evidently much pleased with the new agreement, which they held in strictest secrecy until August 1914.

Whatever their shortcomings, these policies did serve to strengthen Russia and to keep the lid on for a while longer. At least Alexander III died peacefully in his bed in October 1894. His son and successor, the ill-fated Nicholas II (1894–1917), sought to continue his father's reactionary policies during the first decade of his own reign—divine-right autocracy, the inordinate influence of the Church, and the refusal to grant a constitution or to establish national representative government.

Despite the extreme political conservatism of Alexander III and Nicholas II, Russia began to enter the age of industrial revolution in the last years of the century. No spontaneous development, it began in the 1880's as the result of the enlightened economic policies of Count Sergei Witte (1849–1915), who was successively minister of communications and minister of finance under Alexander III and Nicholas II and, in October 1905, became the first prime minister in Russian history. Under Witte's strong-willed leadership, Russia adopted a high protective tariff in order to encourage and protect the development of domestic industry, much of which was owned and operated by the government itself. To finance the development of industry, Witte borrowed heavily abroad and encouraged the investment of foreign capital in Russia. In all, about $4 billion of European capital, much of it French, flowed into Russia.

The results of such high-pressure industrialization were remarkable. Between 1896 and 1906 iron and steel production nearly doubled, coal production increased over 200 per cent, and the population rose from about 129,000,000 to more than 149,000,000. In 1891 work began on the Trans-Siberian Railroad (St. Petersburg to Vladivostok), which opened up Asian Russia to settlement and to the further development of natural resources. Although Russia remained basically agricultural, industrialization ushered in a revolution in communication, transportation, demographic patterns, and economic and social relationships. It resulted in rapid urbanization; by the early 1900's both St. Petersburg and Moscow had populations of well over one million. And there was a great eastward migration of millions of people, which resulted in the conquest and settlement of Asian Russia. This internal expansion and development of resources constituted a kind of continental filling-out similar to the American westward movement in the nineteenth century. At the same time Siberia was also serving another important purpose. It was to

Siberian prisons that the Russian government dispatched its opponents or victims, where they suffered unbelievable misery and brutality.

Czarist repression of dissenters and potential revolutionaries could not prevent the erosion of traditional political beliefs. Industrialization was steadily changing the Russian class structure and social conditions, and this change inevitably had a profound influence on Russian political life. The new class of industrialists, managers, and technicians favored political liberalization, while many in the new working class were attracted to various forms of socialism. In the 1890's extremely bad working conditions led to bitter labor conflict, and inequitable taxation exacerbated the misery of the Russian working class. Thus by bringing industrialism to Russia, Witte also brought all its attendant political and social problems, familiar from the history of early Victorian England. Both the liberal bourgeoisie and the restless proletariat were fundamentally inimical to the czarist state, which was rooted in the ancient landlord-serf society. Industrialization created explosive social conditions and new political forces to magnify and complicate the grievances of the peasants and the violent, revolutionary attitudes of the intellectuals, and demand for new political forms arose precisely when the czars were trying to discourage or suppress all dissent and to preserve as much of the old order as possible.

Despite serious domestic problems, Russia was able to compete remarkably well in the international arena with far more modernized nations. Russian imperialism arose essentially not from any strong class or financial interest in Russian society but rather from political motives. It was the almost natural expression of a largely landlocked, partially icebound empire's quest for power and prestige. As a result, Russia's long-standing need for warm-water ports drove it into the "soft" border regions on its frontiers. Before long, Russians began to put increased pressure not only on the Ottoman Empire, but on the vast reaches of central Asia and the Far East as well.

Russian interest in the Ottoman Empire went back many centuries and stemmed from several imperial motives. Perhaps the purest of these was the deeply felt desire of many Russian Orthodox Christians to lead a great crusade against the heathen Turk in order to free Constantinople, the Rome of the Eastern Church. Such an annexation would also have been of commercial value; but the main benefit would have been the strategic one of establishing the Russian Empire on the shores of the Bosporus.

Directly on the Russian route to Constantinople lay the Balkan peninsula, whose Slavic peoples were regarded as brothers by members of the Russian pan-Slavic movement, which included a strange assortment of liberals and conservatives. According to pan-Slav rhetoric, the Balkans were to be "liberated" by the Russian Empire; in the reality of power politics this meant that Russia would gain control of part of the Ottoman Empire and, as the Austrians and Germans were well aware, a good deal of territory besides. As far as the Balkan peoples were concerned, the doctrines of pan-Slavism were largely rhetorical devices to be used against their Turkish masters (later against the Austrians). What they really wanted was not Russian conquest but a number of fully independent national states.

In 1875 some Balkan groups invoked pan-Slav arguments and revolted against Turkey. Russia came to their defense in 1877, bringing on another Russo-Turkish war. As a result of the war, Serbia, Rumania, and Montenegro gained their independence, and Russia expanded into Bessarabia, northwest of the Black Sea. But the Congress of Berlin in 1878 gave Russia far less than it wished, and its appetite was anything but satisfied. Russia's interest in achieving greater influence and control over the Ottoman Empire and the Balkan peninsula continued to grow after the turn of the century.

While they expanded into the Ottoman Empire, the Russians also pressed into central Asia. Russians had been in northern Asia in the eighteenth century, but the process of expansion accelerated in the last half of the nineteenth century, and by 1881 Russia had annexed most of the vast area between the Caspian Sea and the Chinese Empire. It continued its advance to the southeast until it pressed on Afghanistan, arousing British concern for the security of India, and pushed down on Persia from both sides of the Caspian, seeking an ice-free port—this time on the Persian Gulf.

Internal expansion eastward further encouraged Russia to assume an aggressive, imperial role in the Far East. Nor was intellectual support lacking for such expansion. In Europe, argued the famous novelist Dostoevski, the Russians were condemned to be "hangers-on and slaves, whereas we shall go to Asia as masters." Asia, Dostoevski contended, was a new world that would regenerate the old. Russia completed its push to the Pacific in 1860 with the founding of Vladivostok, "the Lord of the East," a port on the Sea of Japan.

Russia's eastward movement precipitated intense rivalry with the rising imperial power of Japan. The Russian occupation of Manchuria (through which the Trans-Siberian Railroad system was scheduled to pass) and extensive penetration into northern Korea resulted in the dramatic Russo-Japanese War of 1904–1905. In that war—which began with a sneak attack on the Russian naval base at Port Arthur—Japan quickly defeated Russia's Far Eastern fleet and then won a series of major battles in Manchuria. Finally, to the surprise of the entire world, the Japanese navy destroyed the Russian European fleet sent halfway around the world from its base in the Baltic Sea. Russia agreed to the humbling provisions of the Treaty of Portsmouth (1905), yielding most of its east Asian gains to Japan, and accepting that country's protectorate over Korea. Like the Crimean War half a century before, the Russo-Japanese War strikingly revealed the grave backwardness of czarist Russia and helped to bring on the revolution that began in Russia in October 1905.

The lost war was not solely responsible for the revolution. Dissatisfaction with the repressive regime of Czar Nicholas II had been growing for many years before 1905. It crystallized in the formation of various political factions, though these were not parties in the traditional European sense. These groups nominated no candidates, for there were no elections above the *zemstvo* level; and the central government had taken to interfering with, and even annulling, local elections. Russia was still without a national parliament. The new factions operated as surreptitious information agencies and centers of discontent. Around the turn of the century, there were three fairly distinct factions: the agrarian Social Revolutionaries, the Marxist Social Democrats, and the liberal Union of Liberation.

At the time, the czarist government regarded the Social Revolutionary party with its terrorist tactics as far more dangerous than the Social Democrats. Founded in 1901, the Social Revolutionaries were descended from the earlier Populist movement. They sought to adapt Marxism to the social conditions of an agricultural society, hoping to bring about the dictatorship of the peasantry rather than of the proletariat. As Slavophiles, who believed Russian society and culture to be distinctive and separate from western European civilization, they felt that Russia could achieve peasant socialism without passing through the stages of capitalism and industrialism. Social Revolutionaries planned to nationalize all land and to build the new society around peasant institutions like the *mir*. Their ideas spread rapidly among the intellectuals and students who formed the bulk of the party membership. Around the turn of the century, Social Revolutionaries were riding through the Russian countryside in an attempt to stir the oppressed but still quiescent rural masses to violent political action.

The foundation of the Marxist Social Democratic party is important in retrospect because Russian communism developed from this party. Since revolutionary activity was proscribed in Russia, early Russian Marxists often lived abroad and their influence was obscured by exile. A crucial issue that soon began to divide them was whether their country would have to go through the capitalist stage of history before "advancing" to socialism. On this point the Marxists began to quarrel among themselves, and so factionalism was added to obscurity. In 1898 a handful of intellectuals met at Minsk for what they called the First Congress of the Russian Social Democratic Labor party, but almost all were quickly arrested, and it was not until the so-called Second Congress in 1903 that the Social Democratic party really got under way.

It was at this point that Vladimir Ilich Ulyanov (1870–1924)—known in history as Vladimir Lenin—began to emerge to prominence. One of the outstanding figures of the twentieth century, Lenin was the son of a middle-class school inspector and had trained to become a lawyer, but was forced to terminate his legal studies when his older brother was implicated in a plot to kill the czar. The doors to a bourgeois career were thus closed to him, and Lenin plunged into full-time revolutionary activity for which he eventually spent two years in exile in Siberia. After that, save for a few brief and highly secret visits to Russia, Lenin spent the years before 1917 abroad. He possessed a quick and powerful mind, if not an original one.

In 1903, under Lenin's leadership, the radical faction of the Social Democratic party challenged the moderate leadership at the party congress which began in Brussels but was forced to finish in London. The Leninist faction won, causing a deep cleavage which lasted until the Russian Revolution of 1917; indeed, its scars remained long beyond that date. The issue in 1903 was quite simple. The *Menshevik*, or minority, faction wanted the party to cooperate with the liberal and democratic elements in Russia; the Mensheviks favored a party open to a range of leftist viewpoints. This position was flatly rejected by the majority, or *Bolshevik*, faction led by Lenin: the Bolsheviks were totally unwilling to compromise with non-Marxists and insisted that the party remain a small, elite, highly centralized cadre of revolutionary intellectuals.

The Social Democratic party departed in several major respects from the Russian revolutionary tradition. Westerners rather than Slavophiles, the Marxists despised the peasants and their folkways and looked to the emerging proletariat as the truly revolutionary class. In contrast to the Populists, most of them believed that Russia had to pass through the detestable capitalist industrial phase before historical inevitability produced the socialist commonwealth. Because they saw the dictatorship of the proletariat only on the distant horizon, Social Democrats were not taken very seriously in the period before 1905. But even in 1905, the slow spread of Marxism among the workers was a further ominous indication of growing discontent.

If the Social Democrats were destined to shape Russia's future in ways that could not possibly be foreseen around the turn of the century, the most immediately important of the newly formed political factions to come on the political scene at that time was the moderate Union of Liberation. Meeting on Russian soil (St. Petersburg) for the first time in January 1904, the new Union represented radical intellectuals, including socialists, as well as more conservative *zemstvo* leaders. It wanted a constitution, a parliament, and civil liberties, but it wanted them by peaceful and, if at all possible, legal and constitutional means. The question was whether thoroughgoing reform in Russia could be achieved under such circumstances.

The testing time of Russian liberalism — and the older order as well — was not long in coming. Russia's disastrous defeat at the hands of the Japanese in 1904 – 1905 cruelly exposed the inefficiency of the czarist regime and made it all but certain that the existing system could not much longer be maintained. Discontent spread rapidly, and political factions stepped up their activities. In 1904 the able but utterly ruthless minister of the interior, V. K. Plehve, was assassinated, and though the government hoped for some kind of peaceful change, revolution was now clearly in the air.

The revolution of 1905 began under middle-class auspices, with the Union of Liberation holding a series of banquets to stir up public opinion. But things soon got out of hand. On January 22, 1905, known as Bloody Sunday, the workers emerged as an important force in the movement. Led by a priest, Father Gapon, and accompanied by their families, a large number of workers marched with a petition to the czar's Winter Palace in St. Petersburg but were quickly fired upon by the troops. More than a hundred people were killed and several hundred were wounded. In the following months, all the accumulated grievances of Russian society surfaced in a series of industrial strikes, peasant risings, nationalist revolts in the provinces, and even mutinies in the army and navy.

Hoping to stop (or at least slow) the revolution, the czar, in early March, announced his intention of convening an imperial assembly, or Duma, which was to be elected on a narrow franchise and to have no real legislative power. Once more, as in so many nineteenth-century European revolutions, royal action was too little and too late. This inadequate concession only quickened the pace of the revolution. In mid-August Nicholas finally issued a decree convening such an assembly, but the edict had no effect whatsoever. In October a wave of strikes swept the country. In St. Petersburg, workers formed the first *soviet*, or council, to direct strategy there, but the work stoppage soon took on the character of a spontaneous, nationwide general strike. The country was paralyzed, and Count Witte advised the czar to yield to some of the revolutionaries' demands.

In the October Manifesto, the czar guaranteed civil liberties, granted a more representative Duma with the power to legislate, and appointed Witte the first prime minister of the new Russian government. A shrewd piece of statecraft, the October Manifesto divided the liberal opposition: the Union of Liberation split into a moderate faction (which rallied to the government and became the Octobrist party) and a progressive wing, whose members called themselves Constitutional Democrats (abbreviated to K. D.'s or "Kadets"). More radical groups were not at all satisfied; the Social Democrats rejected the October Manifesto, and the St. Petersburg soviet attempted to organize another general strike. Upon learning that members of the soviet had been arrested, the workers of Moscow revolted against the czarist state. Bloody street fighting broke out. The army eventually crushed the insurrection, and in the provinces the czar's troops restored imperial authority with indiscriminate brutality.

In the meantime, Count Witte and the czar were preparing for a representative Russian national assembly. They took no chances: to insure that the czar would not become financially dependent upon the Duma, Witte floated an enormous loan in Britain and France to cover the expenses of running the country. But Witte had miscalculated. The czar had no intention of going through with any serious political or social changes. In May 1906 Witte himself was dismissed and succeeded by a conservative bureaucrat. The government then issued what it called Fundamental Laws, designed to clarify certain matters which the October Manifesto had failed to define. The czar remained autocrat of all Russia; he retained absolute control over its military and foreign policy; no changes could be made in the constitution without the czar's consent; and the powers of the Duma were severely restricted.

But the revolution of 1905 had not yet run its course. On May 10 the first Duma met, and though fairly conservative, it became highly critical of the government and was dismissed after less than ten weeks. In early March 1907 a second Duma convened. It was more radical but was not dissolved until mid-June. Thereupon the government decided to take no further chances. They decreed a new electoral law giving the propertied classes an overwhelming majority; the representation of the workers, peasants, and national minorities was comparably reduced. In October 1907 the third Duma met. As planned, it proved more conservative, yet it was far from servile. To head the government, Nicholas in June 1906 sensibly picked Peter Stolypin, a moderate conservative who believed in reform from above.

If Russia could enjoy a protracted era of peace, a lasting new order might emerge. The future of Russia — like that of Austria — would be decided not at home but abroad.

IV IMPERIALISM AND WORLD POLITICS

The Origins of the New Imperialism

While the dominant force within the European states in the latter decades of the nineteenth century was nationalism, the most explosive ingredient added to the international scene was the new imperialism. For after the 1870's the unified centralized nation-states — "hard" political organisms — began to expand as never before into the "soft," decentralized, economically underdeveloped areas of the world. At first the new imperialism of the European powers led to little conflict among them. But, before long, the competition for empire led to numerous armed confrontations, or threats of confrontations, greatly increasing existing tensions in European politics. Thus the European balance of power was extended outward to include most of the rest of the world. Of all the developments at the end of the nineteenth century, none was more dangerous.

The underlying causes of imperial expansion — and especially the new imperialism of the late nineteenth century — have been debated for many years. To most of the world, "imperialism" is today synonymous with economic exploitation and political repression. A denunciation of imperialism is now an important category of radical political analysis, and thus the scholarly debate over imperialism merges imperceptibly into the ideological struggles of our time.

The most influential and controversial interpretations of imperialism stress economic motivations as fundamental to imperial expansion. This view was set forth by John Hobson, an English socialist, in his influential book *Impe-*

rialism (1902) and by Vladimir Lenin in his important Marxist tract *Imperialism — The Highest Stage of Capitalism* (1917). Though differing on numerous details, Hobson and Lenin (who was much influenced by Hobson) agreed that imperialism came about largely as a result of the desire of industrial capitalists to make a profit. When the industrial development of a country is essentially complete, surplus capital becomes available for overseas investment. In order to protect these investments, the investors persuade their governments to expand into territory overseas. As Lenin put it, "imperialism must be characterized as capitalism in transition, or, more precisely, as dying capitalism."

Of course, there was nothing new about powerful economic interests using the state for their own purposes. Moreover, the scale of economic activity in the late nineteenth century was beyond the wildest dreams of earlier times, and Lenin and Hobson were right to note the importance of the investment of surplus capital. Nevertheless, there are serious weaknesses in the Hobson-Lenin analysis. For one thing, they were mistaken in associating the new imperialism largely with the bourgeois financiers. The investment of surplus capital involved countless people of modest means — it was not at all a class phenomenon. But most important, Hobson and Lenin failed to explain satisfactorily the mechanism by which financiers turned private wishes into public policy. During the period 1870 to 1914, as the French historian Raymond Aron has pointed out, it was "not that foreign ministers were manipulated by capitalists, but they felt there were valid reasons for defending certain economic positions. The fact is that under the system of private ownership, the ambitions of certain corporations are genuinely identical with national interests."[1]

The economic interpretation is simply not a generally satisfactory explanation of imperial expansion. Some colonies — for example the Belgian Congo or the Dutch East Indies — were fairly or highly profitable. But many areas which came under imperial rule, such as the German colonies in Africa, were of little or no value and were, in fact, clearly an economic burden; the cost of their administration alone exceeded the economic advantages derived from their exploitation. When the cost of acquiring, governing, and defending colonies is considered, no one can say for certain whether the balance sheet would show a profit for the European colonial powers.

In reaction to the economic interpretation, alternative explanations for imperialism have been set forth. It has been pointed out that the missionary and "civilizing" impulse was doubtless of substantial importance to imperial development. Defenders of imperialism stress the genuine uplifting purpose demonstrated by outstanding colonial administrations — for example, Lord Cromer's in Egypt. On the other hand, it has been suggested that the desire to dominate other peoples has deep, primordial psychological roots.

1. Raymond Aron, *The Century of Total War.* London: Derek Verschoyle, 1954, p. 59.

Yet the fundamental cause of imperial expansion probably lies in the competitive—the aggressive and arrogant—nature of the European state system itself. If one major power expanded, others felt obliged to follow suit. In the 1880's and after, Germany developed a largely worthless African empire mainly out of fear of being left behind in the race for national greatness and prestige. The competition for markets, emphasized by Lenin, was part of the more general pattern of industrial and political rivalry among the great powers. A nation's fear of aggression on the part of other great powers, moreover, caused concern for the military security of its colonial possessions. This in turn often led to what might be called "preventive" expansion. For example, Britain's increasing involvement in the Near East and in Africa—especially its concern over Egypt and the Suez Canal—stemmed from its anxiety that some great power would threaten its empire in India. Needless to say, this compensatory aggression had a way of feeding on itself and becoming more intense with every passing year. Not the least dangerous by-product of the new imperialism was the volatile Anglo-German naval race that developed at the turn of the century. Hobson was not altogether wrong when he wrote that "Imperialism . . . implies militarism now and ruinous wars in the future."

Imperialism and International Rivalry

In the closing decades of the nineteenth century the main areas of imperial competition and conflict were the Ottoman Empire, Africa, and Asia. Perhaps the most explosive of these areas was the Ottoman Empire, which was really not a nation but a collection of religious communities ruled by ecclesiastics who, in turn, were responsible to the sultan of Turkey. In the nineteenth century, Turkey lost all of North Africa to the British, French, and Italians and considerable territory in the Balkans to the Russians and the Austrians. New Balkan nations like Serbia achieved their independence at the expense of the Turks. Turkey was indeed "the sick man of Europe."

The gradual erosion of the Ottoman Empire stimulated attempts to reorganize the area along Western lines. After the Crimean War in the mid-1850's the British and French forced the Turkish government to adopt a reform edict known as the *Hatt-i Humayun,* which aimed at transforming the empire into an efficient, secular, liberal national state. Since there was little enthusiasm for reform in Turkey itself, the *Hatt-i Humayun* failed. In 1876 efforts at reform revived, a palace revolution took place, and Turkey received a constitution and a parliament. But the new sultan, Abdul Hamid II, soon repudiated these innovations and spent the rest of the century restoring absolutism by political repression. This led to a quickening of radical nationalist efforts in the Balkans and on the Anatolian peninsula.

The Ottoman crisis soon merged into an even more dangerous crisis centering in the Balkans. It is not too much to say that the Balkan problem—an explosive compound of nationalism, dying empires, and aggressive imperialism—was the key to international relations between 1870 and 1914. Balkan nationality groups were rising against the repressive Turks. Austria, beset by its own Slavic problems (many of the south Slavs wanted to establish their own national state), was expanding into the Balkan peninsula, while the Russian Empire, posing as the friend of Slavic nationalism, was pushing toward Constantinople. To this Austro-Russian conflict was added an Anglo-Russian one; fearing for the security of Suez and India, the British were opposed to any further Russian advance.

In the mid-1870's the Balkan problem brought Europe to the brink of general war. In 1875 and 1876 Herzegovina, Bosnia, and Bulgaria, with the help of Serbia and Montenegro, rose against their Turkish masters. When the Turks smashed the rebellious Balkan nationals, the Russians came to their defense. Advancing easily to the gates of Constantinople, the Russians created much anxiety in Austria and Great Britain. War fever spread rapidly in Britain, and the British fleet was dispatched to the Straits. When the Russians forced upon the Turks a treaty which would have greatly expanded Russian influence in the Balkans, Bismarck feared that war was near. In 1878 he called for a conference of interested powers to meet at Berlin for the purpose of resolving the Eastern Question.

At the Congress of Berlin, in June–July 1878, Bismarck prevented a European war by what he thought was shrewd diplomacy. He preserved the balance of power by seeing to it that each of the main contenders received a piece of the Ottoman Empire: Austria-Hungary was allowed to occupy and administer Bosnia and Herzegovina; the Russians received territories at the far end of the Black Sea; the British received Cyprus. Typical of the diplomacy of the age, the Treaty of Berlin sought to resolve conflict between the great powers by satisfying them at the expense of lesser powers. But it did not solve the problems of Balkan nationalism, Russian pan-Slavism, or Turkish weakness. While Disraeli returned from Berlin proclaiming he had brought back "peace with honour," the Balkans continued to be the powder keg of Europe.

Other serious imperial rivalries developed in various parts of Africa. Beginning with the establishment of a French protectorate over Tunisia in 1881 and British occupation of Egypt in 1882, a scramble for African territories developed in which all the major European powers except Russia and Austria participated. Yet the history of the imperial powers in Africa was not simply one long chronicle of aggressive competition. There were notable examples of cooperation among the great powers, the most important of which was the Berlin Conference on African affairs (1884–1885). Conceived by Bismarck and Jules Ferry, the Berlin Conference was attended by fourteen nations, including the United States, and attempted to set up rules governing the exploitation and partition of Africa. While the Congress reached a number of important agreements—for example, in regard to ending the African slave trade—the attempt at cooperation failed in the long run, because

EUROPEAN IMPERIALISM IN ASIA 1820-1914

| | Great Britain | | Netherlands |
| | France | | Russia 1815/1914 |

Nineteenth-century Asia was still a prey to European imperial ambitions. In the Far East, Russia's expansion southward in search of an ice-free port brought it into conflict with Japan over Manchuria and Korea. Russian penetration both west of the Caspian and into Turkestan posed a threat to Persia and Afghanistan, which the British considered vital to overland contact with their Indian empire. Both France and Britain controlled large portions of Indochina; Siam served as an independent buffer between their interests. Despite rivalry from stronger powers, the Dutch Empire in the East Indies underwent considerable expansion. In the last years of the century, the Chinese Empire was forced to open "treaty ports" to various European powers, while the United States became a factor in Far Eastern affairs, particularly after taking over the Philippines from Spain.

Lena R.

Lake Baikal

• Chita

• Ulan-Ude

Ulan Bator •

MON GOLIA

• Tsitsihar

Sungari R. Harbin •

GOBI DESERT

Taiyuan •

Peking • Tientsin •

• Sian

Huang Ho Kaifeng •

C H I N A

•ngtu

Yangtze Chungking • Changsha •

• Yunnan

Hsi R. Canton •

TONKIN 1884 • Hanoi

ANNAM 1885 • Hué

LAOS 1893

SIAM

FRENCH INDO-CHINA

ngkok

CAMBODIA 1863 Phnom Penh •

• Saigon

COCHIN CHINA 1863

Gulf of Siam

KARAFUTO Jap. 1905

SAKHALIN

KURIL ISLANDS Jap. 1875

• Khabarovsk

Amur R.

MANCHURIA Occupied by Russia 1900-1905

• Mukden

Vladivostok •

SEA OF JAPAN

HOKKAIDO • Sapporo

• Sendai

KOREA

Port Arthur • Russ. 1898-Jap. 1905 Seoul •

Weihaiwei • Br. 1898

Kiaochow • Ger. 1898

YELLOW SEA

Fusan •

Niigata •

Osaka •

HONSHU

• Tokyo

Hiroshima • *SHIKOKU*

KYUSHU

Nanking • Shanghai •

Wuhu •

Hangchow •

Ichang •

Wenchow •

Foochow •

• Taipei

FORMOSA Jap. 1895

Amoy •

Swatow •

EAST CHINA SEA

RYUKYU ISLANDS Jap. 1879

OKINAWA

P A C I F I C

O C E A N

BONIN IS. Jap. 1875

MARIANA IS. Ger. 1899

GUAM U.S. 1898

HONG KONG Br. 1842 Macao Port. Kwangchow • Fr. 1898

HAINAN

LUZON

Manila •

PHILIPPINE

ISLANDS Sp.; U.S. 1898

Iloilo •

Penang • MALAY STATES Br. Prot. 1895

Malacca •

Singapore •

ang SUMATRA

• Palembang

Jesselton • NORTH BORNEO Br. 1888

BRUNEI Br. 1888

SARAWAK Br. 1888

Kuching •

BORNEO

N E T H E R L A N D S

Batavia •

J A V A

PALAWAN

SULU SEA

MINDANAO

Davao •

CELEBES SEA

HALMAHERA

Hollandia •

NORTHEAST NEW GUINEA Ger. 1884

NEW GUINEA Neth. 1828

PAPUA Br. 1884; Austl. 1906

MOLUCCA (SPICE) IS.

CELEBES

CERAM

E A S T   I N D I E S

Bandjermasin • Makassar •

BALI

LOMBOK

JAVA SEA

FLORES

SOEMBAWA

SUMBA

BANDA SEA

ARAFURA SEA

Dili • Port. 1859 *TIMOR*

Darwin •

SOUTH CHINA SEA

A U S T R A L I A

there was no effective international machinery to enforce the rules that had been agreed upon.

By the late 1890's, however, most of Africa had been divided, and some serious tensions developed. In 1896 Germany gave moral support to the Boer republics, which were vigorously resisting a British takeover. Following the abortive Jameson raid, William II sent a telegram to Paul Kruger, president of the Transvaal, congratulating him on his victory and implying that Germany might come to the defense of the Boers. Although no armed Anglo-German conflict occurred, the telegram stirred up war fever in Germany and England and, for a time, made for extremely strained relations. Shortly after this confrontation, Britain became involved in an even more serious clash with France. The British and the French converged upon the Sudan, a largely unoccupied area, from different directions. Since the Sudan was essential to both the French and the British plans for African empire, both sides refused to yield and war seemed imminent. But the pressures of internal politics, particularly the Dreyfus affair, finally forced France to retreat.

In addition to opposing the French and the Germans in Africa, the British also resisted Russian colonial expansion into the Middle East and central Asia. Russia's drive for a warm-water port at once stirred Britain's concern for the security of India. The Russian advance resulted in a series of localized conflicts in the 1870's. Disraeli, in particular, had resisted Russian expansion. In 1885 Russia invaded Afghanistan, and a full-scale Anglo-Russian conflict threatened to develop. Although a timely compromise prevented open war, Anglo-Russian relations remained considerably strained.

Comparatively speaking, the most amicable relations among various imperial powers existed in the Far East. Instead of competing for large territorial acquisitions in China, the European powers limited themselves to certain port cities and spheres of influence. When Chinese nationalists called Boxers rose in violent rebellion against the intruding Europeans in 1899, the revolt was ferociously suppressed by collaborative efforts of the great powers' gunboats.

The Development of Alliances

The tensions growing out of imperialistic expansion should have made the European powers more cautious in dealing with each other. But this was hardly the case. Instead, threats of war dominated the diplomatic history of the period after 1870. As a result of advances in industrial technology, the weapons of warfare were potentially more destructive than ever before. Everyone feared that Europe was moving inexorably toward a war that no one wanted. This belief led nations to train large standing armies, develop huge stockpiles of arms, and negotiate a wide variety of military agreements, defensive alliances, secret protocols, and ententes (literally, "understandings") with other powers. But this activity only increased the fears, the tensions, the insecurities, and even the aggressiveness of the great powers, so that in the end the belief that war was inevitable turned into a self-fulfilling prophecy.

International relations in the last decades of the century were dominated by the powerful new German Empire. We have seen that Bismarck's policy was generally to keep the French in diplomatic isolation, to maintain as far as possible the unity of the conservative powers—Germany, Austria, and Russia—and hope for the best. Though Bismarck the diplomatist has enjoyed extravagant praise from generations of historians, his alliances were, for the most part, ill-fated and short-lived. The first Three Emperors' League, founded in 1872, lasted less than a half-dozen years; the second, founded in 1881, did not survive the Balkan crisis of 1885. The Triple Alliance (with Austria and Italy) of 1882 never meant much. His Reinsurance Treaty with Russia, of June 1887, was allowed to lapse as soon as he was out of office. The Dual Alliance of 1879 with Austria did survive him, but eventually helped to drag Germany into the First World War. It is quite true, of course, that Germany's diplomatic position deteriorated further after Bismarck's dismissal, but it is not at all clear that he could have prevented such a situation. The Russo-German rift, which led to the crucial Franco-Russian alliance of 1891–1894, was already evident in Bismarck's time and indeed was partly his responsibility.

By the 1890's, then, Europe was divided (though not yet rigidly) into the Triple Alliance and the Franco-Russian alliance. The only nonaligned great power was Britain, a most unlikely candidate for membership in either of the rival alliances. Shunning involvement in Continental politics, Britain clung to a policy of "splendid isolation," save for its participation in the Mediterranean Pact of 1887, with Austria and Italy, designed to preserve the status quo in that area. But Britain's diplomatic position was not an enviable one. Its relations with France and Russia were strained for long periods of time, due partly to Anglo-French rivalry in Africa and to Anglo-Russian conflict in Asia and the Middle East. By the late 1890's the British recognized that "splendid isolation" was no longer tolerable, and they began to look around for possible allies. Conversations were held with the Germans, but the latter demanded too much—especially British support against France and Russia —and the talks finally collapsed. In January 1902 Britain concluded an alliance with Japan, providing for neutrality in case either became involved in war with a third party, but for mutual assistance in case either signatory found itself at war with two or more powers. The Japanese alliance, which the British government momentarily believed would be the only diplomatic agreement it would need to protect its worldwide interests, soon proved less than satisfactory for British needs.

Before long, Britain put aside long-standing rivalries and signed diplomatic agreements with France in 1904 and with Russia in 1907. The Anglo-French *Entente Cordiale* completely settled colonial disputes. France recognized British preponderance in Egypt in return for British support of French

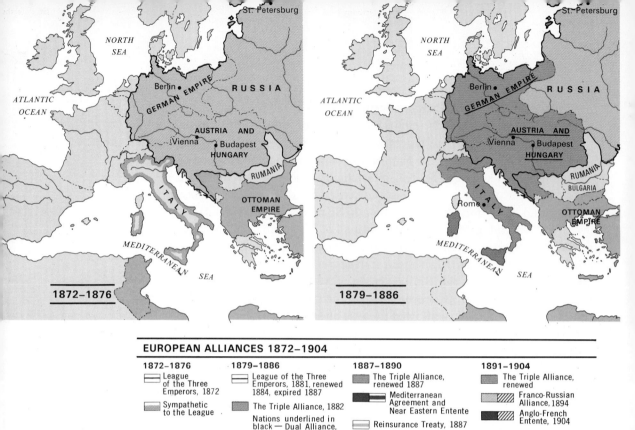

EUROPEAN ALLIANCES 1872–1904

1872–1876	1879–1886	1887–1890	1891–1904
League of the Three Emperors, 1872	League of the Three Emperors, 1881, renewed 1884, expired 1887	The Triple Alliance, renewed 1887	The Triple Alliance, renewed
Sympathetic to the League	The Triple Alliance, 1882	Mediterranean Agreement and Near Eastern Entente	Franco-Russian Alliance, 1894
	Nations underlined in black — Dual Alliance, 1879	Reinsurance Treaty, 1887	Anglo-French Entente, 1904

interests in Morocco. Upon the conclusion of this agreement, France attempted to promote good relations between Britain and Russia. The fruit of this diplomatic initiative was the Anglo-Russian entente of 1907, which composed differences in Persia by establishing Russian and British spheres of influence. Taken together, these "understandings" constituted the Triple Entente. Although Britain was reluctant to make military commitments like those of the Franco-Russian alliance, the Triple Entente gradually hardened into an alliance system.

The development of rival alliances in Europe—even those of a defensive nature—tended to heighten international tensions and to increase the possibility of war. Like nation-states, rival power blocs competed for military and political superiority. Moreover, the system of interlocking alliances was likely to transform localized crises into matters of general concern. The first such crisis occurred in 1905–1906 in Morocco, where French influence had been increasing for some time. The crisis was precipitated by the kaiser, who made a spectacular visit to Tangier in March 1905, and portentously proclaimed the sovereignty of the sultan. By stirring up Moroccan nationalism, William II clearly hoped to embarrass France and to test, if not disrupt or destroy, the new Anglo-French entente. But the plan miscarried. In January 1906 a great international conference gathered at Algeciras to deal with the Moroccan problem. Though the conference nominally agreed to affirm the territorial integrity of Morocco—a German victory—the French gained important police and

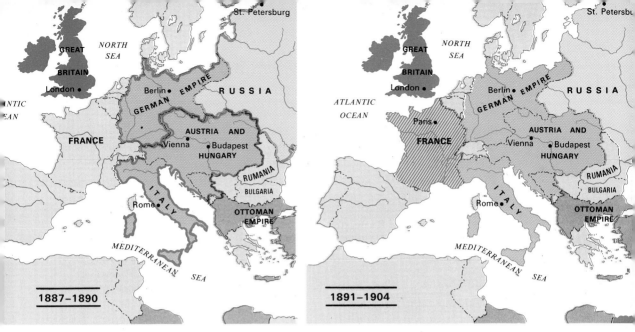

The proliferation of European alliances between 1870 and 1890 can be attributed mainly to Bismarck's efforts to prevent any war that might destroy the new German Empire. His strategy was to isolate France, the empire's natural enemy. In the Three Emperors' League (1872) he hoped to relieve the tension between Russia and Austria over the Balkans. The secret Dual Alliance (1879) drew Germany and Austria together against Russia, which felt cheated by the Congress of Berlin. Three years later Italy joined them in the Triple Alliance. When new Balkan disputes caused Russia to refuse to renew the Three Emperors' League in the mid-1880's, Bismarck signed the secret Reinsurance Treaty with the czarist government. For its part, Austria found in Britain and Italy allies against Russia's threat to the Ottoman Empire. After Bismarck's dismissal, the German government allowed the Reinsurance Treaty to lapse, causing Russia to begin to look favorably on France (hitherto hated as a center of revolution and liberalism). The Franco-Russian Alliance became a reality in 1894. The division of Europe into two camps was complete when Germany's construction of a great fleet caused enough alarm in British government circles to bring about the Anglo-French Entente in 1904.

financial powers, and the Anglo-French entente stood firm. The first Moroccan crisis thus turned out to be a major German setback, although the kaiser did not see it that way.

The Algeciras Conference did not bring lasting peace to Morocco. Nevertheless, for a brief time the prospects of international peace were better than they had been for many years. With Anglo-French differences largely reconciled and Anglo-Russian relations improving, with England, France, and Germany turning increasingly to internal affairs, and with Austria and Russia preoccupied with overwhelming domestic problems, it was not inconceivable that Europe was about to enter a prolonged period of diplomatic and social stability. In June–October 1907 a conference on international peace met at The Hague, and although little concrete progress was made on disarmament or on binding arbitration agreements, the delegates came away with high hopes for a peaceful international situation in the foreseeable future.

The Legacy of Imperialism

The debate on the merits and demerits of imperial rule, the purity or baseness of the imperial motive, continues today in academic and other circles. The immediate effect of imperial rule upon village and tribal societies was destructive. Local political institutions were eroded by highly centralized colonial administrations. In addition, European economic exploitation and contro often destroyed local industries, which were suited only to nontechnologi cal societies. Imperialism also disrupted primitive social structures by creat ing new classes and groups — workers, civil servants, lawyers, businessmen. But perhaps most important, imperial rule destroyed traditional folkways and culture. The introduction of European economic, political, social, and cultural standards tore apart the very fabric of non-Western societies.

Yet imperialism was creative as well as destructive. It introduced Western science, medicine, and technology into many parts of Asia and Africa. In many places, it fashioned new political entities. Colonial rule turned geographical expressions like India, Kenya, and Algeria into nation-states of the European type. The leaders of these new nations, when they gained independence during the two decades after 1945, were a Westernized class; many of them had been educated at Oxford or the University of Paris and exposed to the European intellectual and cultural heritage. They learned about socialism, democracy, liberalism, and national independence, and hoped to put these ideas into practice at home.

Thus, in the end, imperialism was its own undoing, for it inspired a sense of national oppression, and it provided leaders for the nationalist movements. After 1900 strong nationalist movements developed sooner or later in almost all colonial possessions in Asia and Africa. In most cases, nationalist leaders wished to rid their countries of both the imperial presence and the native rulers who had proved themselves willing to cooperate with European domination. Imperial rule created colonial nationalism, and colonial nationalism spelled the doom of imperialism.

At the beginning of the twentieth century nationalist feeling and a desire for *de facto* independence even dominated the attitudes of those British dominions, collectively called the British Commonwealth of Nations, where there was a large or even preponderant population of British extraction. By 1900 the dominions had autonomy in domestic matters, with the British government still retaining some voice in these countries' foreign relations. In the decade after 1895 the Conservative statesman Joseph Chamberlain held conferences of dominion prime ministers in London with an aim of working toward a more centralized, federal empire. But these imperialist schemes were strongly resisted by the dominion leaders, particularly by the Canadian prime minister Sir Wilfrid Laurier, an astute French-Canadian Liberal, who envisioned Canada's future as lying in industrial expansion and in close economic ties with the United States. By 1914, the dominions were chafing under the moderate vestiges of British control, and in the 1920's, at the urging of the Canadian prime minister William Lyon Mackenzie King and the South African leader Jan Smuts (who had fought the British in the Boer War), Britain allowed the dominions to become, in effect, fully sovereign nations, with the term British Commonwealth henceforth having mainly symbolic and emotional significance.

The Dimensions of Industrial Economy and Society

I THE REVOLUTION IN TRANSPORTATION AND COMMUNICATION

Overland and Marine Transport

By the middle of the nineteenth century the Industrial Revolution had begun to exert a profound influence on Europe and North America. By 1900 the contours of modern industrial society had been clearly established, and the impact—both for good and for evil—was worldwide. The Industrial Revolution before 1850 had transformed society in western Europe; but in terms of the area affected and the number of people involved, the impact of industrialization and urbanization in the second half of the nineteenth century—what has been called the Second Industrial Revolution—was even more profound and far-reaching.

The railroad system that spread throughout western Europe was both a symbol of the new society and a prime agency of its diffusion. The steam-powered locomotive revolutionized overland transport, offering both superior speed and lower costs for the shipment of goods. So while turnpikes and canals languished, iron rails and "iron horses" crossed and crisscrossed Europe and North America. And the trickle of goods and passengers crossing the continents swelled to a torrent.

Railroad transport began in England, the first country to experience the Industrial Revolution. By the mid-1820's, transportation between the port of Liverpool and the manufacturing center of Manchester had degenerated into chaos, hampering the growth of the textile industry. Accordingly, plans for a railroad line were mooted among the businessmen of the two cities; shares were sold; a survey was begun. Canal owners stirred up opposition with dire warnings and ridicule, and Parliament scoffed when the line's engineer,

George Stephenson, maintained that a speed of thirty miles an hour was practicable; but the line had its important supporters, and the bill authorizing it was finally passed. On September 15, 1830, the Manchester-Liverpool line was officially opened; the engine hit a top speed of over thirty miles an hour, bearing out Stephenson's predictions.

Most important for its success, the railroad captured the imagination of the investing public. Investors saw the effect it had on both commerce and passenger travel, and its future seemed boundless. Profit possibilities were good, too—the Manchester-Liverpool line was soon earning a 10 per cent return. By 1838 some 500 miles of track were in operation; at mid-century, 6621 miles; and in 1886, a total of 16,708 miles. The amount of capital investment this represented was truly astounding. Funds came from private sources rather than from the government, which participated only in determining routes and, later, in controlling rates. The legalization of joint-stock companies in 1825, when an act of Parliament permitted stockholders limited liability, simplified the financial organization of railroads.

Given the overwhelming role of private enterprise in railroad development, one might have expected chaos. And it is true that during the great railroad building sprees of 1836 and 1845–1847 ridiculous schemes were propounded. But in the main the British lines were well laid out. Furthermore, integration took place early; short lines began to be consolidated in the 1840's, and in 1846 Parliament required a standard gauge for track.

After England had taken the initial steps, railroad construction was taken up posthaste both in North America and on the Continent. The chart below shows how rapidly and extensively.

Railroad Route Mileage: 1840–1900

	1840	1870	1900
Europe	1818	65,192	176,179
North America	2954	56,106	223,454
World	4772	130,361	490,974

England could claim considerable credit for this worldwide boom. Free trade was becoming that nation's avowed economic policy, and Englishmen were eager to invest in foreign railroads and to export their equipment and knowledge—both for the immediate profits to be gained and in the hope of opening up new markets for British goods.

The spectacular breakthrough in American railroading came in 1869 when the first transcontinental line was opened. By the 1850's a network of canals and railroads effectively linked principal industrial and commercial centers in the Northeast and Midwest, and steamers sailed up and down the Mississippi and its tributaries. But men of vision saw the possibilities of profit in a transcontinental railroad line, if government aid could be obtained. Since the area west of the Mississippi was only sparsely settled, there would not be enough business to defray construction costs immediately. But if the government would subsidize the initial construction, with land grants and loans, the line would open the West to a flood of settlers, and they in turn would support the road. The first transcontinental line was completed in 1869. Despite the business crisis of 1873, work continued on other lines, and by 1884 seven routes reached westward to the Rockies. Two years later passengers could ride from Montreal to Vancouver on the Canadian Pacific.

On the European continent, the various governments took much more active roles in promoting railroad construction. Most enterprising was the Belgian government, which in 1834 made the decision to construct a comprehensive and national railroad. In a decade the work was almost complete; though not large, the Belgian system was notably efficient. In Germany the existence of many sovereign states prevented the construction of a coordinated system over the whole of the country. While Prussia and Saxony encouraged private construction in the 1840's, the states in southern and western Germany used public funds to finance construction. Nevertheless, the results were generally excellent—and at a per-mile cost of only one third that spent in England. Under Bismarck's influence, the unified German state began constructing new lines and buying out the private ones until in 1910 only 6 per cent of the country's 36,600 miles of track was in private hands. Under state control, strategic rather than purely economic lines were laid out, and low rates encouraged both exports and important industries.

French railways were built by a combination of public and private funds. A compromise worked out in 1842 provided that the government would own the land, roadbeds, tunnels, and bridges and control rate and routes; private interests would own the rolling stock, stations, and rails. Throughout the 1850's, construction proceeded rapidly, but the disaster of the Franco-Prussian War woke the government to the need for more lines. Those it built, however, were not economically sound, and in 1883 private capital had to come to the rescue. Lines were swapped so that the state ended up with a small network in the southwest and guaranteed a return to investors on all lines. It was an expensive solution.

Czarist Russia was a latecomer to the railroad age, but the Crimean defeat spurred construction. Private capital built the lines, and, as in France, the state guaranteed a certain return. By 1882 some fifteen thousand miles were in service. But if the total mileage was impressive, its deployment was highly uneven. Under the leadership of the czarist minister Sergei Witte, the Russian government bought up the private lines and embarked on its own construction. On the eve of the First World War 47,000 miles were in operation. Witte's special project, the Trans-Siberian Railroad, was completed in 1905 and opened up a vast, rich territory to which some five million people emigrated in the ten years prior to World War I.

Even the vast proliferation of railroad lines on the Continent failed to exhaust the available capital; European investors built railroads all over the world, often before their own networks were completed. Part of the impetus

The Russian Railroad Expansion. Czarist Russia's participation in the railroad boom came relatively late, but in the last decade of the nineteenth century Russian railroad mileage grew more rapidly than that of any other country. The most significant achievement was the building of the Trans-Siberian Railroad (above), which was begun in 1891 under the direction of Sergei Witte, himself a former stationmaster, and which eventually brought the Pacific within eight days' travel of Moscow.

was to cement together the colonial holdings that were being acquired during this, the heyday of imperialism, but the desire for profits was even more compelling. Naturally enough, Britain—the great power whose railroad system was completed earliest—was the leader. In Africa the Cape-to-Cairo line was begun in the last decade of the century, and by 1914 almost five sixths of that continent's railway mileage lay in British possessions. In South America, Argentina led in construction before the war, and the bulk of railroad mileage there was in the hands of British-controlled companies. In Asia more than half the total railroad mileage was in British India. German ambitions in the Balkans prompted the beginning of construction on the Berlin-Baghdad line in 1902. And French investors—though cautious at home—subscribed to loan after loan floated on the Bourse (the Paris stock exchange), financing a large part of the Russian railroad system.

Another revolutionary land vehicle appeared on the scene in the years just before the First World War—the automobile. In 1914 a million motor vehicles were registered in the United States. Yet down to 1914 the railroad was virtually unchallenged as the chief means of overland transport.

During the second half of the nineteenth century, steam power also revolutionized ocean transport. Earlier, steam engines had provided so little power and required so much coal that steamships were limited to inland and coastal traffic. Moreover, the appearance in 1845 of fast clipper ships that could cross the Atlantic in twelve to fourteen days postponed the supremacy of steam. But improvements in steamers in the 1850's and 1860's spelled the end of the sailing era. When iron was substituted for wood in ship construction, making larger ships feasible, sails could not be enlarged enough to power the iron vessels. Finally, the compound steam engine delivered more power with half the coal consumption. Now steamships could make longer voyages, stop less often for fuel, and provide more space for paying cargo. By the end of the century their speed had nearly doubled, so that an Atlantic crossing normally took six days. And when the Suez Canal opened in 1869, ships found their route to the Far East shortened by some four thousand miles. In consequence of these advantages, steam tonnage rose from 12.5 per cent of total tonnage (among the chief maritime nations) in 1850 to 63.9 per cent in 1900. In the 1880's, steel — lighter and more durable than iron — began to replace it in ship construction.

Greater speed and lower charges (by the end of the century the latter had been halved) made it profitable to ship a whole range of new products overseas — and passenger traffic rose sharply, too. Expansion was further stimulated by national governments. The old-time mercantilist, protectionist navigation acts were repealed in Great Britain in 1849 and subsequently in France. Now the state offered lucrative mail contracts, subsidies for building and carrying, and loans at low interest. The result was a fourfold increase in merchant tonnage — accompanied by a radical expansion of port facilities — in the second half of the century. Britain was the leader in the transition from sail to steam, and on the eve of the First World War some 42 per cent of the world's shipping tonnage was registered in the United Kingdom — and the British merchant fleet carried more than 50 per cent of the world's seaborne trade.

Communication

The second half of the nineteenth century saw the birth of instant communication with the development of the telegraph, the telephone, and the wireless. The telegraph was first developed in the 1830's by an American inventor and artist, Samuel F. B. Morse. In 1844 the first line was opened, between Baltimore and Washington, D.C. By 1861 some fifty thousand miles of line were in use, and the following year a transcontinental line was opened. Europe was slow to follow America's lead, but by 1865 London was linked with Calcutta. In the next year a transatlantic submarine cable was successfully operated. Early in the twentieth century, transpacific cables were laid.

In 1876 another American inventor, Alexander Graham Bell, unveiled the telephone to the public at Philadelphia's Centennial Exposition. But the new device came into general use slowly. At the turn of the century the American Telephone and Telegraph Company controlled some 855,000 phones, but not until 1915 was it possible to telephone across the continent.

The potential of the wireless was spectacularly demonstrated in 1901 when its inventor, the Italian physicist Guglielmo Marconi, picked up a signal sent from England to Newfoundland. But its prime use in prewar years was to communicate with ships at sea. Not until the 1930's did radio become an instrument of mass information and popular entertainment.

Consequences of the Transportation and Communication Revolution

The construction of the great railroad networks and merchant fleets and the development of the telegraph and telephone stimulated both commerce and industry to revolutionary growth. Because the cost of shipping goods and the time involved in shipment were reduced, more and different kinds of products could be profitably shipped, and new markets could be opened for goods that had previously been marketed only near their place of origin.

As mentioned earlier, by the end of the century the speed of steamers had doubled, while their fuel consumption had been halved. Railroads, too, reaped the benefits of compound steam engines. By 1900 sixty miles an hour was not an unusual running speed for passenger trains on the better systems, though heavy freight trains averaged only between fifteen and thirty. At the same time, both comfort and safety were improved: dining cars, sleeping cars, steam and electric heating, and gas and electric lighting were added to passenger trains. Safety improved with the introduction of Westinghouse air brakes and automatic couplings.

The commercial result of the development of the railroad and the steamship was a great expansion of both interregional and overseas traffic. In England the railroads meant, for instance, that the poor of East Anglia could now afford coal, that Norfolk livestock could be shipped to market without a high weight loss, and that grain farmers could meet the challenge of free trade. On a worldwide scale, the railroad allowed industrialized European countries to import increasing supplies of foodstuffs and other primary products with the proceeds from sales of manufactured goods to the producers of primary goods. International specialization was on the rise.

The new methods of transport and communication also made industrial growth possible. First of all, they made resources more readily available and enabled manufacturers to build factories where there was an adequate supply of labor. And the savings in time and money freed capital hitherto tied up in overhead for investment in permanent plant. By making international dealings less risky, instantaneous communication encouraged overseas expansion.

Not only did the services offered by railroads, merchant fleets, and the telegraph make expansion possible; their construction created a demand for iron, steel, timber, and other industrial products. In less developed areas, such as Latin America and India, the effects of railway building were particularly important. The initial construction materials and rolling stock would often be imported from Europe; but once the line was actually running, repairs and maintenance had to be carried out locally. The works established to fulfill this need often served as the nucleus for a more general engineering industry.

The Great Migration

There is a further way in which the new modes of transport gave impetus to industrial expansion: by making human resources available. During the second half of the nineteenth century, people traveled from country to country and from continent to continent on an unprecedented scale. Business depressions and unemployment, recruitment by railroad companies and inducements provided by governments of countries that needed labor, political upheavals, and racial persecution were special factors encouraging migration.

The greatest movement was from Europe and Asia into the Americas, where in 1850 one twentieth of the world's population inhabited one third of its land area. Figures reveal that in the period 1820–1930 some 62 million individuals migrated, almost three fourths of them during the fifty years preceding the First World War. The availability of cheap transport was a contributing factor; relaxation of legal restraints on emigration was another; population pressure on available resources was a third. The great bulk of intercontinental migration was directed to seven countries: the United States (61.4 per cent), Canada (11.5 per cent), Argentina (10.1 per cent), Brazil (7.3 per cent), Australia (4.5 per cent), New Zealand (3 per cent), and South Africa (2.2 per cent).

Among those countries from which significant emigration occurred were Ireland, Germany, Italy, Spain, and Portugal. During the half-century after the great famine of 1846, no less than 1 per cent of Ireland's total population emigrated *each year.* In 1840–1859 Ireland sent more immigrants to the United States than any other country. Emigration from Sweden and Norway to the United States was also heavy. In terms of sheer numbers, however, Germany took the lead from 1859 until 1890, after which the southern European states – particularly Italy and Austria-Hungary – predominated. Nearly seventeen million emigrated from Italy in the quarter-century before 1914, mostly from the acutely overpopulated agrarian south. Italy was second only to Germany in numbers of immigrants to the United States for the entire period, and it provided the largest immigration to Argentina and Brazil. Spain sent the majority of its 2.5 million emigrants to Argentina, while most of Portugal's emigrants went to Brazil. In the main, Chinese and Indian emigrants went to other parts of Asia; after 1885 (when emigration was legalized) Japan sent significant numbers to Hawaii, the United States, and Manchuria and Korea.

Aside from its magnitude, the real importance of this migration of labor lay in the directions it took. Generally, the emigrants came from countries where population was pressing on available resources and where per capita income remained very low. They moved to areas that had more natural resources than their populations could adequately exploit. Thus, in general, immigrants became more productive in their new homes – an obvious example is the agricultural workers who migrated from southern Europe to the

United States. Often, immigrants went into new occupations, becoming part of the urban labor force serving mechanized industry. Then their productivity increased geometrically.

II THE SECOND INDUSTRIAL REVOLUTION

Technology

In the second half of the nineteenth century, the world's productive capacity registered an unprecedented increase. In the years 1870–1913 alone, it rose fourfold. Traditional industries expanded—textiles, coal, iron and steel; new industries came into being—electricity, chemicals, petroleum. Enlarged output depended sometimes on the discovery of new resources, sometimes on an enlarged labor force, sometimes on a technical breakthrough. But the most important factor was the progress of mechanization. Increasingly powerful, complex machines were supplementing and replacing handwork, making a unit of labor considerably more productive. The modern factory system was becoming the rule, not the exception.

In 1870 four nations—Britain, France, Germany, and the United States—accounted for 79 per cent of the world's manufactures; in 1913 the figure was still 72 per cent. In other countries industrialization was progressing, but only in piecemeal fashion. The preeminence of these four countries in mechanization and manufacturing output depended largely on their advanced position in a few fields.

Vital to the expansion of production was an increase in power to run the machines of industry. It is estimated that between 1870 and 1913 world production of sources of commercial energy increased by close to 600 per cent. Throughout the period, steam engines remained the main source of power, and they grew larger and more efficient as time passed. In compound steam engines, a second engine would be powered by the first, and so on. Whereas industry depended on 10–20 horsepower engines in the early decades of the century, at its close there were 3000 h.p. giants. Still, a great deal of power was going to waste. Then in 1884 Sir Charles Parsons invented the steam turbine, which turned force directly into rotary motion—as with a pinwheel—eliminating the waste of turning it first into reciprocating motion.

The internal combustion engine was a contemporaneous development, but until the oil field discoveries of the twentieth century, the cost of petroleum—on which it depended for fuel—remained high. Nevertheless, by 1914 automobiles were being mass-produced in both the United States and Britain.

Electricity, a transmitter rather than a source of power, was crucial to industrial expansion. No more than a laboratory curiosity at the beginning of the nineteenth century, it soon became useful in communication, and the invention of the dynamo in 1867 made it possible to generate enough electricity for industry. The Parsons generator, built to complement his steam turbine, was another major step along the route to a large-scale electric power industry. The market for electricity was greatly expanded in 1879 by Thomas A. Edison's invention of a bulb that made electric light a practicable means of factory and household illumination. In the same year the first electric railroad was demonstrated at the Berlin Industrial Exposition. Then came the electric furnace for metallurgy and electrochemistry. The invention of the transformer in 1883 made it possible to transmit electric current over long distances without significant loss. Now a new source of power—falling water—could be utilized. From hydroelectric power stations, current could be transmitted to distant cities and factories. The resulting addition to the world's output of power was enormous.

The coal industry illustrates the magnitude of industrial expansion. In the period 1860–1864 the average annual production of coal for the four most industrialized countries was some 127 million tons; in 1900–1904 the comparable figure was four times greater. In part this was due to the exploitation of new coal beds, but it also reflected the effects of new, more efficient production methods. Electric locomotives and electrically powered conveyers had replaced ponies for carrying coal from the seam to the mouth of the mine. Above ground, machinery both sorted out the coal and loaded it into freight cars. New discoveries cut down on waste; for example, in the transformation of coal dust into gas to be used in metallurgy and to power gas engines, valuable by-products were manufactured.

Another fuel, petroleum, made a strong beginning during this period. In 1859 the first commercial well was introduced in Pennsylvania, and kerosene (a product of petroleum) became widely used for lighting. After 1890 the internal combustion engine began to create a small demand. More important, however, oil sprayed into a firebox under pressure was used to power steam engines. Per pound, this new fuel did twice the work of coal but took only half the space. It could also be fed into the engine cleanly and automatically and thus was particularly useful at sea, where stokers generally accounted for more than half the crew. Due to its high price, however, in 1900 petroleum supplied only 5 per cent of the world's commercial energy.

The late nineteenth century has been called the age of steel. World production of this superior form of iron was a mere 419,000 metric tons in 1865; in 1910 it had climbed to 58,656,000 metric tons. Three specific technological advances spurred this expansion. In 1856 the Bessemer process was unveiled: heat was blown through molten iron, rather than on its periphery, and steel was produced in a very short time (half an hour or less, as opposed to twenty-four hours). The very speed of the process was to necessitate increased mechanization: continuous conveyers, traveling cranes, suspended railways, tiltable furnaces, the three-high mill (where the metal was rolled in one direction on one level and then passed up to another level to be rolled the other way, without stopping the mill and wasting power). The Bessemer process made the price of steel competitive with that of wrought iron. Unfortunately, however, the process would not work with the phosphoric iron ores that predominated on the Continent. Even Great Britain, which had extensive deposits of hematite ore, had to import additional quantities from Spain.

The Siemens-Martin open-hearth process took longer than the Bessemer process (from six to eighteen hours) but could be more precisely controlled and therefore produced steel of higher quality. Moreover, it utilized scrap iron. But like the Bessemer process it was unsuccessful with phosphoric ores. Finally, in 1878, yet a third method developed in Britain, the Thomas Gilchrist process (also called the "basic" process), provided the means for drawing off the troublesome phosphorous. Commerical manufacture of steel by the Thomas Gilchrist process started in 1879. The demand for cheap steel and its alloys steadily increased, as it proved a superior material for rails, steamships, cables, and larger, stronger, more efficient machines. Together with cement, it was to revolutionize the building industry.

In the textile industry — everywhere a leading sector in industrialization — there was still scope for mechanization. Improvements in machine construction, power, and lubrication during the second half of the nineteenth century made it generally possible for a single worker to tend twice as much equipment. Spindles in use in the cotton industries of the four leading countries more than tripled between 1852 and 1913.

Chemistry revolutionized some industries and created others. The coal-tar dye industry — a development of the last half of the century, resulting from the researches of German scientists — produced synthetic colors that were fast to light, washing, and perspiration. Considerable improvement was made in producing alkalis — substances that are used to make glass and soaps and that change the tint of vegetable coloring matter. The need for such products was increasing, as soap and textile production expanded. In 1863 a young Belgian, Ernest Solvay, devised a way to produce soda ash, one of the common alkalis, without losing expensive ammonia (as had been the case in the generally used Leblanc process). In the 1870's the Solvay process was perfected, and by the end of the century it was in widespread use.

Chemists also used electricity to their advantage. By electrolysis it became possible to produce from a rare metal, bauxite, an inexpensive multipurpose metal, aluminum. In the 1890's an electrolytic means of preparing chlorine was discovered. All of these achievements in applied chemistry were immediately turned into new consumer products. This meant not only the establishment of new industries but a great improvement in the well-being of the masses who used these new, cheap products in daily life.

Business Organization

The vast technological changes of the late nineteenth century were paralleled by an increasing tendency to industrial concentration — that is, large industrial enterprises became steadily larger. Technological advance was one impetus to industrial concentration. Improved processes and new machines made it financially advantageous to construct large complexes, where work could be performed in an unbroken chain. Industrial concentration effected economies and facilitated production. For example, by-products could be utilized rather than wasted, and metal could be transported from furnace to mill while molten, with no costly delays for cooling and reheating.

Meanwhile, economic pressure also stimulated concentration. Railroads and steamships brought competition to producers whom distance had previously protected. Supply was outstripping demand, and as a result prices had to be cut, subjecting profit margins to an uncomfortable squeeze. While many smaller firms simply went under, larger ones put up a fight.

Monopolies were the most common answer to an industrialist's problems. Whether pools or cartels, the principle was the same: a group of producers representing a practical monopoly of production of a commodity would agree to charge a certain price. Frequently, production quotas were fixed and sales territory divided. But such agreements did nothing to lower production costs. The answer to this problem was business integration, which allowed economies in production, contributed to efficiency in management, and created savings in financing. The most common means of integration was to form a holding company (a trust or combine) or to merge one firm with another completely. Generally, in the nineteenth century, horizontal integration of various sorts was most common: that is, companies producing a commodity in a given stage would be combined. In the years from 1900 to 1914, however, vertical integration made an appearance: all or a good part of the production of an article would be overseen by a single concern — everything, perhaps, from the mining of ore to the sale of the finished product.

The extent of concentration was staggering. In the United States alone in 1914, 318 industrial combines were capitalized at more than $7 billion; of those, 236 (accounting for $6 billion) had been formed since 1897. Both the United States government and European governments favored and assisted efforts by industry to maximize profits. Throughout the world, except in Great Britain, tariff walls were erected. The German government favored cartels, and in the first decade of the twentieth century close to four hundred existed in that country alone. In addition, over one hundred international cartels made an appearance in the years prior to 1914, while a smaller number of international combines controlled such industries as oil, margarine, rayon, and armaments.

European governments, of whatever political complexion, took no action against the trusts; industrial monopolies and combines were regarded as an inevitable part of modern economic life, conducive in any case to efficiency in production and distribution. Both left-wing and extreme right-wing politicians might complain of the baleful influence of industrial magnates on government policy, and doctrinaire socialists envision an alternative economic and social system; but the institutional forms that capitalism was adopting were considered an inevitable consequence of the operation of the economic market. Only in the United States was there a popular outcry against industrial concentration and the abuses of monopoly power. Consequently the Interstate Commerce Act of 1887 and the Sherman Antitrust Act of 1890 provided the legal bases for government action against the trusts, but very little was done by the federal government to implement this legislation until the Roosevelt and Taft administrations (1901–1913).

Transition in Industrial Leadership

During the late nineteenth century, the combined industrial production of Great Britain, France, Germany, and the United States continued to surpass the output of the rest of the world. At the same time, American industry consistently outperformed British industry, while Germany managed so meteoric a rise that in 1914 its production in several industries also overtook that of Great Britain. French output generally lagged behind that of the other three countries.

The emergence of the United States as the most industrialized nation in the world can be attributed to several factors. At the outbreak of the Civil War, it was the second largest manufacturing nation. American manufacturing was efficient, specialized, and centralized—71 per cent of the country's industrial work force was located in the Northeast. Natural resources of a magnitude unknown to the other industrial powers were still to be exploited. A large and expanding domestic market—the population rose from 31 million to 91 million between 1860 and 1910—further encouraged industrial expansion. While plentiful, labor was more expensive than in Britain, and this encouraged entrepreneurs to organize their operations in the most efficient manner possible. At mid-century, British investigators were impressed by the readiness with which America adopted new production techniques.

Statistics reveal that Great Britain simply could not keep the pace set by its former colonies. In the period 1870–1907 the annual percentage increase in physical output per worker was 0.6 per cent for the United Kingdom, 1.4 per cent for the United States. Letting each country's stock of capital equipment for the year 1896 equal 100, by 1907 the United Kingdom's had grown to 159.7, that of the United States to 210.3. In the years between 1860 and 1913, the gross national product was also growing faster in the United States than in either Germany or Great Britain.

France's record in economic expansion was a mixed one. During the first half of the century, the nation faced the task of recovering the industrial rhythm destroyed in the Napoleonic Wars. Capital, skilled labor, and raw materials were all in short supply, and even with legislative and administrative support for industry, recovery was slow. In the second half of the century, however, steam power used in industry rose from 67,000 h.p. in 1850 to 863,000 h.p. in 1890, and after 1900 there was a further rapid rise.

Until the turn of the century when water power was harnessed, the cost of electricity in France remained high. Even in 1913, the capital invested in French electrical industries was only one third that invested similarly in Germany. France was not supplying its own technological needs: despite a high tariff, imports of electric generating plant amounted to almost one seventh the domestically produced equipment. Similarly, France's coal supply never came close to meeting the country's industrial needs, which consistently ran 50 per cent higher than domestic production. At the same time, French coal was both inferior to the better British and German grades and more expensive. Moreover, in several important industrial areas inconveniently far from the coast, coal deposits were altogether lacking, and the cost of transporting coal to these regions was high.

The lack of coal and coke within France made it cheaper to ship iron ore to the German coal fields for smelting. In 1913 France was the world's greatest exporter of iron ore, exporting fully half of the ore it mined. Not surprisingly, it then had to import a large percentage of its textile machinery, locomotives, and steel ships.

On the eve of the First World War, French textile production compared favorably with Germany's, but its showing in the new chemical industries was particularly poor. Earlier, it had led Europe in the application of science to manufactures. Now its lack of physical resources—such as coal, and consequently coal-tar products, and the materials necessary to the production of soda and chlorine—was critical. In the twenty-five years prior to World War I, France was a growing buyer of foreign chemicals.

Germany's industrial expansion in the late nineteenth century was second only to that of the United States. German industry's use of mechanical power increased from 1,056,000 h.p. in 1875 to 3,357,000 h.p. twenty years later, to 8,008,000 h.p. in 1907. By far the greatest source of power was the steam engine; electricity supplied only 11 per cent of the total in 1911. But it was in the generation of electric power and the production of electrical equipment that Germany outstripped its near rivals. Spurred on by the American example, Germany's electrical industry underwent rapid expansion, beginning in the 1880's. Installations to generate power for lighting were established earliest, followed closely by factories to produce electrical equipment. After 1891 electrification of streetcars went forward with a rush. In the early years of the new century electricity drove furnaces, railroads, and agricultural machinery. By 1914 Germany was producing one third of the world output of electrical products and nearly half of all electrical exports.

While the German states started out in the 1840's with a smaller production of coal than either France or Belgium, by 1860 the exploitation of new fields (made possible by the railroads) had already pushed their production ahead of either neighbor's. After the great Silesian field was opened in the

1870's, Germany gained steadily. German geography was used to economic advantage: while large amounts of German coal were exported to various Continental countries, British coal was imported into northern Germany, where there were no great coal deposits but excellent water transport. Just before World War I, the Reich emerged as Britain's very serious rival in the coal industry.

Germany was blessed with excellent iron ore deposits along the lower Rhine, located conveniently close to its Ruhr coal fields (whose mines produced good coal for coke). By 1845 a start had been made at exploitation, but fifteen years later Germany was producing little over one half France's output and less than one seventh of Great Britain's. Then the Franco-Prussian War left the Lorraine mines and ironworks in German hands. Five years later the Reich was outproducing France in pig iron. When duties on imported iron were removed, British competition broke the German boom, but by 1880 the tariff barrier was revived, and the "basic" process for smelting steel had been devised. A new wave of exploitation could begin. During the 1880's, Germany was the only European nation to increase its output of both pig iron and steel substantially. By 1900 German steel production exceeded Great Britain's, and by 1910 Germany stood second only to the United States in both steel and pig iron production.

German progress in heavy industry was especially striking in the new chemical industry. The Reich's natural resources enabled it to draw ahead of the United Kingdom in this field. Plentiful deposits of iron pyrites yielded sodium chloride, potassium salts, and sulfur, and there were large supplies of coal and coal tar. While in 1878 the whole world's output of sulfuric acid was a little over one million tons, in 1907 German output alone was 1.4 million tons.

The long industrial lead over other countries which Britain enjoyed in the first half of the nineteenth century was steadily dissipated after 1870 as American and German industrial expansion surpassed British growth. What were the causes of this erosion of British industrial leadership? Certainly Great Britain's domestic supplies of petroleum and of water to generate hydroelectric power were inferior to those of the United States and Germany. On the other hand, the United Kingdom was rich in coal, and its superior commercial position significantly reduced the disadvantage of having no domestic supply of petroleum and many raw materials. Therefore Britain's industrial slowdown cannot be attributed primarily to a lack of resources. Similarly, although from 1875 to 1914 British management faced the strongest trade union movement in the world in number of members and sophistication of organization, and although the suspicious attitude of the union leaders was not conducive to technological innovation, the unions were not principally to blame for the decline in the pace of British economic growth.

In the end, the brunt of the responsibility rests with British entrepreneurs, who failed to move with the times. Where and why did British industrialists fail? They were both slow and late in introducing mass production techniques; this has been explained by the smaller size of the British domestic market as compared with the American. While in the 1850's and 1860's the disparity between the two was not large, it grew as the century progressed. Britain was in a most favorable position to secure foreign markets: the Continent was at its very doorstep, and indeed the United Kingdom was the world's greatest trading nation. But this fact actually worked against standardization of production, for overseas markets demanded a variety of goods. Consequently it was usual for a British ironworks to turn out many different types and sizes of products, while an American mill could often turn out a single standardized item and reap the advantages of uninterrupted, efficient production. Not until the First World War created a demand for tremendous quantities of standardized items (such as shells) did standardized work become common in Great Britain.

The "handicap of an early start" also contributed to the United Kingdom's relative decline. By pioneering in mechanization, British industry in the third quarter of the century found itself saddled with plant that was outmoded by technological innovations. The majority of British industrial leaders simply chose not to scrap expensive plant until it had worn out. A prime example occurred in the chemical industry, where the changeover from the Leblanc to the Solvay soda process was very slow. In the steel industry the Thomas

The greater part of Germany's domestic coal supplies has come consistently from the Ruhr district. Not surprisingly, then, German output lagged far behind that of Great Britain in the early nineteenth century, when less than one half of the Ruhr coal field was being exploited. Although working costs were high there (because its coal lay in thin seams), exploitation rapidly expanded after 1840, since the Ruhr district was crossed by natural waterways, canals, and some of the country's earliest railways.

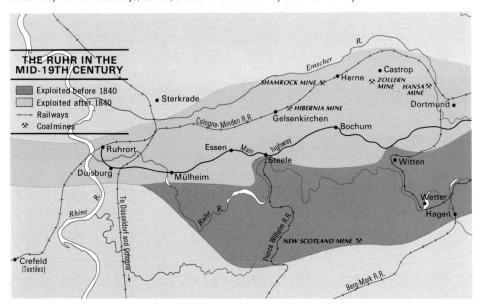

Gilchrist or "basic" process, originally a British discovery, was adopted much more slowly in Britain than on the Continent.

Another handicap of an early start was the existence of a great many small-scale production units in Britain. In Germany, by contrast, the late start of the coal and metallurgical industries had allowed the establishment of large-scale enterprises. Despite the trend to concentration—which was considerably stronger in Germany than in the United Kingdom in any case—there were still relatively few integrated operations in British industry. Hence it was often the case in Britain that when a decision to renew one segment of the production process required changes in another phase, it would cut across ownership lines and run into opposition not found in Germany.

Finally, the charge must be leveled that British captains of industry were essentially conservative businessmen. Their country had gained its industrial preeminence by diligence and sacrifice on the part of their ancestors, with only limited aid from science or special training. Much confidence was therefore placed in the amateur innovator; much suspicion was exhibited toward the professional scientist. Compared to those in Germany, British facilities for training business leaders were inadequate in both quantity and quality. Whereas in Germany the government subsidized chemical research by individual companies, in Great Britain the few scientists employed by industry were not long-term researchers in laboratories but day-to-day testers and analysts.

On the eve of the First World War, the traditional staples—coal and textiles—still comprised 62 per cent of British exports, but only 35 per cent of the German total. At the same time, a significant share (14–18 per cent) of German exports was in chemicals and machinery, reflecting the Reich's superior utilization of science and technological expertise.

III FINANCE CAPITALISM

Financing Industrial Expansion

In the late nineteenth century, a manufacturer planning to expand his firm's production faced a financial problem. In the early days of industrialization, he could have financed expansion by plowing back his day-to-day profits. This was called "industrial capitalism." Now, however, larger and larger sums had to be put into physical plant as well as into raw material and labor costs, and it took too long for the business itself to generate sums of this magnitude—too many opportunities for profit would be lost. So ambitious entrepreneurs turned to outside sources, and the era of "finance capitalism" opened.

The commercial banks that had financed business in the short term in a variety of ways could still be called on to provide working capital. But by their very nature they could not afford to tie up their capital for long periods of time. To finance long-term projects—such as railroads and large industrial undertakings—investment banks came into increasing prominence on the Continent. These companies raised capital—frequently by the sale of stock—which was in turn invested in long-term projects that promised a high return in recompense for the risk involved. The most ambitious of the early investment banks was the French *Crédit Mobilier*, founded in 1852. For some fourteen years it financed railroads, shipping, and real estate improvement schemes on a vast scale, paying huge dividends. In the tight money crisis of 1866, however, it was unable to call in its loans and abruptly collapsed. Not surprisingly, French banks subsequently followed a more prudent course of mixed banking, engaging in both commercial and investment functions. In Germany, investment banks played much the largest role in the financing of industrial expansion. They kept exceptionally close watch over their investments, and this careful analysis was undoubtedly responsible for their unusual success.

To augment what he could expect from investment banks, the entrepreneur approached the investing public directly. First he had to offer them profit, then some degree of security and liquidity. Incorporation of a business into a joint-stock company filled these requirements. In return for buying shares in such a company, investors were entitled to receive a portion of its profits—without participation in the daily management of the enterprise and with limited liability. In every European country earlier misuse of this type of organization had prompted governments to regulate such companies—a charter usually had to be secured from the state in every separate case—but around mid-century, the demand of the investing public caused this restriction to be swept away. In Britain limited liability had been legalized in 1825, and in the United States limited liability could be obtained quite easily by mid-century. In France and Germany limited liability became generally available in the late 1860's and 1870's. Until the turn of the century, joint-stock enterprise was most common in transport and banking. In other fields, the high cost of making a stock offering postponed the boom in joint-stock enterprise until about 1900.

Not only did investors demand a chance to invest in the future of various enterprises without excessive risk; they also required a mechanism by which their investments could be liquidated—stock exchanges. A number of new exchanges were founded in the second half of the century, while existing exchanges rapidly increased the volume of transactions they handled. Government securities continued to make up the bulk of their listings, but a significant change was in progress. For example, on the London stock exchange government securities represented 80 per cent of the total listings (reckoned on the basis of value) in 1843; by 1875 they represented only 68 per cent.

The growth of industrial firms was accompanied by the development of a truly international economy, characterized by specialization, multilateral trade patterns, fluidity of capital and labor, and consequently more interdependence among nations. Certainly foreign trade was no new phenomenon, and limited amounts of capital had moved across borders in the past. But the volume of investment and trade and the ease with which transactions now took place were unprecedented. The third quarter of the nineteenth century witnessed the fastest growth of international trade—400 per cent between 1840 and 1872. Thereafter the pace slowed, though in absolute terms the increase was even larger. The value of total world trade rose 300 per cent between 1880 and 1913.

World trade was facilitated by the increasing sophistication of the mechanisms of international exchange. A first step was taken when various governments followed Britain's lead and established national currencies, giving a specific bank the sole right of issue. Then gold came to be adopted as the standard for most of the world's currencies. With an established value in relation to gold, the world's currencies had a fixed relationship to one another.

While the gold standard offered the prospect of convertibility, it did not provide stable prices. Indeed, gold became scarce as the century wore on, and this contributed substantially to the price decline of 1873–1896. Only when the mines of South Africa and the Yukon began to be worked did gold become significantly more plentiful and prices begin to rise once again.

The swift flow of information that the telegraph made possible—and the lure of huge profits to be made in foreign lands—stimulated a boom in overseas investment. For example, British investors, who had made foreign investments at the rate of £1.7 million ($8.5 million) annually in the period 1875–1879, were investing some £185 million ($925 million) annually during the years 1910–1913. Although no other country came close to matching this performance, in 1914 France had some 45 billion francs ($8.9 billion) tied up in foreign investments; Germany 25 billion marks ($6.1 billion); the United States some $2.6 billion. This investment played a major role in building railroads overseas and in settling and exploiting thinly populated areas.

The direction of this foreign investment was also important. Before 1870 it was largely contained within Europe. After that date, however, adequate capital was available on the Continent, and Continental entrepreneurs were no longer willing to pay interest as high as that being offered overseas. Capital then began to flow abroad. British funds were invested particularly in the United States, the countries within the Empire, and South America. Over a quarter of France's foreign investments were in Russia. Germany's were more evenly distributed, but over a quarter went to the Western Hemisphere. Thus in a large measure European investments abroad coincided with the flow of immigration. The combined effect of these two factors was to give the new areas of European settlement dynamic roles in the world economy within a very short period of time.

The earnings from Great Britain's foreign investments represented 20 per cent of its total foreign earnings in the years immediately preceding 1914. They reinforced the profits made from trading and assured Britain of a surplus in its balance of payments. The pound sterling was, consequently, a "hard" currency. Moreover, more than any other currency it was available throughout the world: Britain was still the world's largest trading nation on the eve of the First World War (its share amounted to 14 per cent of the world's total volume in 1911–1913, down from 19 per cent in 1880–1883). Thus the pound was, in practice, something of an international currency. In fact, the large expansion of international trade depended a great deal on the stability of the pound.

An indication of the growing economic interdependence was the heightened effect that an economic crisis occurring in one nation had on others. From the start, the business cycle had been a characteristic of capitalism. According to elementary economic theory, when the demand for goods is expanding (or at least larger than the supply), prices naturally rise, and producers are encouraged to expand output. Eventually, however, costs rise also, and profit margins shrink. Then, as production is curtailed, recession occurs. Unemployment follows, demand falls off, and prices and interest rates decline. As production contracts, management practices greater efficiency, and low prices stimulate consumption. Then expansion is encouraged, investment picks up, production increases, employment rises, and prices move upwards once more. The cycle has returned to prosperity.

In the early nineteenth century, timing of these cycles often varied widely from one country to another. Between 1790 and 1857 in Britain and the United States the phases of the cycles were diametrically opposed almost as often as they coincided, and between 1840 and 1882 Britain and France were "in phase" only 28 per cent of the time. On the other hand, during the period 1857–1925 America and Great Britain were directly opposed only 21 per cent of the time, and between 1882 and 1925 Britain and France were in agreement 65 per cent of the time. Falling prices were almost universal during the period 1873–1896; after that, prices were generally rising until the outbreak of the First World War. Contemporaries considered the earlier period to be one of general depression (of prices and profits, not of output).

Several international business crises occurred in the second half of the nineteenth century. In 1857 over fifteen hundred banks and five thousand businesses collapsed in the United States in a panic that began with the failure of an Ohio insurance company. A fortnight later the news reached Great Britain, where firms with American connections were faced with demands to repay loans and deposits. Numerous banks and businesses closed, and severe unemployment and economic distress ensued. The crisis also spread to France and Germany, where it was the first major capitalist crisis, earlier ones having been caused by war or other nonbusiness catastrophes.

Similar phenomena occurred in 1873 and in 1890. The crisis of 1873 was speeded by bank failures in both Europe and the United States, the crisis of 1892 by a French scandal involving shares in the Panama Canal and the near failure of the British banking house of Baring Brothers. These "panics" or "crashes" ruined many entrepreneurs, wiped out the savings of middle-class people who had invested in stock, and caused widespread, though temporary, unemployment. The cyclical boom-and-depression tendency of late nineteenth-century capitalism gave plausibility to the Marxist claim that the capitalist system was doomed to suffer increasing crises.

IV CHANGING LIVING CONDITIONS

Population Growth and Urbanization

In Europe, the second half of the nineteenth century was an era of rapid population growth. In 1850 the total population stood at some 266 million. By 1900 it had reached some 400 million, and by 1914, some 463 million. Even after taking into account an unprecedented emigration rate (40 per cent of the natural increase), Europe's population still rose some 30 per cent in the thirty years after 1870.

Significant reductions in national mortality rates can be credited with having the greatest effect. Great strides were made in medicine: anesthetics and antiseptics made operations considerably safer, and the bacteria causing cholera, tuberculosis, diphtheria, typhoid fever, and plague were identified. Improvements in diet and hygiene were conducive not only to a longer life span but also to a physical change: in 1800 the average height for men was five feet; at the end of the century it was five feet six inches.

Had the birth rate remained high, the reduction in mortality rates would have caused phenomenal population growth—perhaps the catastrophe that Thomas Malthus feared. Fortunately, the size of families was being limited. Malthus had called for sexual self-restraint by the working class; contraceptive methods achieved the same result. The birth rate actually began to decline in Britain and Germany soon after mid-century and in France the decline in the birth rate so closely paralleled the decline in the mortality rate that the population remained practically stationary throughout the period.

Even more striking than the general ascent of the demographic curve was the rise in urban population. In every European country urban centers were expanding more rapidly than the overall rate. In France four fifths of the population increase between 1830 and 1851 centered in the cities; from 1850 to 1871 the ratio was eleven twelfths. In the decade of the 1860's, German cities absorbed the amount of the entire population increase. Scandinavia and the Low Countries reached that point at about the same time, and Austria experienced the phenomenon by the 1880's. England was more than half urban by mid-century, Germany by 1900, and the United States by 1920.

The cities grew faster than the general population mainly because of the vast migration from rural areas. Since the development of railroads made it possible for industries to be established at a distance from natural resources, urban centers could offer mass employment in factories—in addition to jobs in trade and government—that was unavailable in the countryside. The railroads could also carry enough food to support concentrated masses of people and provide cheap transport to the cities from the countryside. Yet it was not so much that cities *drew* people to them as that economic pressures *drove* people from the land.

The most dramatic change in rural life was the abolition of serfdom everywhere in Europe by the 1860's. But this and other changes brought many problems for the agricultural workers. Paying even subsistence wages meant that landed proprietors had to produce increasingly for the market. In the market they faced competition, and to compete successfully they had to make more rational use of their land. Rational use meant not only raising root crops and using fertilizers to eliminate wasteful fallow; it also meant using new, more productive equipment. With new equipment, output per unit of manpower increased, and fewer (or at least no additional) laborers were needed.

While changes in rural life freed the peasant from onerous personal servitude, it did not usually give him the land necessary to maintain his independence. (France was an outstanding exception.) Often the land distributed to the peasant was insufficient to support a family: few large estates were broken up, and in any case the aristocrats kept the best lands for themselves. Now that the peasant or small farmer everywhere was free to sell his few acres, he was often subjected to considerable pressure to do so by neighboring large landlords. He also found his obligations to government to be extremely onerous. In England the cost of required enclosure in the early nineteenth century was beyond the resources of small farmers. In Russia the emancipated serfs owed both taxes and redemption payments to the state. And in southern Italy peasants were expected to pay both taxes to the state (in accordance with relatively high northern Italian standards) and sharecroppers' dues to their landlords. The need for cash to meet these new obligations pushed the peasant into growing crops for the market. The peasants' economic and social advancement was impeded by lack of education and by inadequate credit facilities. In Russia there was another barrier: the village made communal decisions, and peasants found it difficult to leave the village.

Unrest was an obvious barometer of peasant discontent. In Ireland peasant crime increased fivefold late in the century. The rural poor in Spain and Italy likewise resorted to sporadic violence. When prices were high, merchants became the target of peasant resentment. Frequent demonstrations at gov-

EUROPEAN POPULATION DENSITY ABOUT 1870

Approximate number of inhabitants per square mile

- 50 or fewer
- 50-130
- 130-260
- 260-520
- More than 520
- ■ Cities with populations over one million

The population of Europe was expanding rapidly during the nineteenth century. By 1870 only Spain, Russia, and the Scandinavian countries had vast expanses of territory which might be called sparsely populated. There were many large urban centers, headed by London with a population of over 2.5 million and Paris with about 1.5 million. The proliferation of such mammoth cities was still, however, a development of the future.

ernment offices protested tax collection and redemption payments, and sometimes peasants assuaged their hunger for land by attempting to seize part of a large estate. In 1905 the Russian peasantry—stirred by bad harvests and Russia's defeat in the war with Japan—pillaged estates, refused to pay rents, and burned records of indebtedness.

City and Farm Life

The most memorable qualities of mid-nineteenth-century cities were their horrific ones. The growing class of landless rural laborers, whose lot was becoming more and more desperate, poured in from the countryside and created unbelievable problems. The housing shortage was critical: new, flimsy structures were thrown up in a rush (often "back to back" with no through ventilation); old buildings were divided and redivided; cellars and attics housed whole families. Sewers were woefully lacking, and refuse was often heaped up inside the city itself; swamps drained into water supplies. Many streets were unpaved, and street lighting was all but unknown. Police and fire protection was grossly inadequate: Berlin with two hundred policemen for a population of 400,000 was one of the best-policed cities in western Europe in 1848.

As time went on, these deplorable conditions were significantly mitigated. There was a general betterment of the economic status of the urban masses, and urban governments concerned themselves more and more with the problems posed by the slums. The outbreak of epidemics in the slums generally captured the authorities' first attention, if only because it threatened the rest of the population. In Britain the cholera epidemic of 1831 spurred a great

New York in 1890. This view of Broadway and John Street in lower Manhattan illustrates environmental problems common to the late-nineteenth-century city in western Europe and the United States. A dangerous and unsightly maze of telegraph and telephone wires covered the streets. The slow speed and limited capacity of the main mode of public transportation—horse-drawn streetcars—forced most people to live close to their place of work. In the lower East Side of Manhattan, population density was 250,000 people per square mile. After 1900, the quality of urban life improved: in large cities, wires were placed underground, and the building of rapid-transit electric subway systems allowed many workers to move out of the congested district.

movement to enforce rules to improve public health on both national and local levels. Everywhere, large cities embarked on efforts to filter their water supplies. Quarantine regulations were tightened and vaccination required. Drainage systems were expanded and improved. The effect of these advances was to lower the urban death rate, and cities now began to expand from within. Toward the end of the nineteenth century, London owed only 15 per cent of its annual growth to immigration. Between 1880 and 1900, street lighting — first gas, then electricity — was gradually introduced, police forces were expanded, municipal fire departments were set up, and streets were broadened and paved. Late in the century electric streetcars appeared, along with subways, and it became possible for workers to get away from the cities to the countryside for excursions, especially as fares and services came under government regulation. At the turn of the century municipal governments, particularly in London and some German cities, were making tentative and piecemeal efforts to remedy the chronically substandard and overcrowded conditions of working-class housing, but ambitious schemes for slum clearance and city planning were developed only in the 1920's and 1930's.

Life for urban workers also improved in terms of real wages and better working conditions. Real wages — workers' income in relation to prices — rose between 25 per cent and 50 per cent from 1870 to 1900. The length of the average work week was reduced during the second half of the nineteenth cen-

The growth of London in the nineteenth and the early twentieth century is a classic example — in some ways a model — of urban expansion. As the capital's population grew rapidly, both middle- and working-class people moved to the open land on the city's outskirts to escape filth, noise, and overcrowding. How far they could move from the center depended largely on the quality and direction of the public transportation lines, and in the 1860's London began to build its excellent subway system, making possible unprecedented suburban

tury—in England from sixty to fifty-four hours. Factory conditions improved due to government inspection and the dawning recognition that better conditions could mean better production. Child labor was declining at the same time that elementary education was made compulsory and brought under government supervision. After 1907 English schoolchildren were given medical examinations. An important index of working-class leisure and literacy was the growth of popular newspapers—some could count circulations of over a million by 1900.

The comforts of a worker's life were still modest. His diet consisted mainly of starches (bread or potatoes), a bit of meat once or twice a week, a few milk products and vegetables, some coffee and sugar, and occasionally beer. With the revolution in transport, new items of better quality were available, and the worker had more money with which to make purchases. The general depression of the 1880's and early 1890's worked in his favor (as long as he was fully employed), for wages fell more slowly than did prices and the result was higher real wages. In addition, workers' consumer cooperatives became common in the last quarter of the century. Through them, workers could purchase commodities at less than the general retail price, thereby increasing the value of their wages. After 1896, however, prices again began to climb, and from 1900 to the outbreak of the First World War real wages were practically stationary.

growth in the last four decades of the century. In 1890, improved deep-cut lines were opened, with electric locomotives instead of the steam engines that had previously been used. The suburban sprawl raised complex administrative problems. Before 1888 London was made up of several municipal governments, but in that year, metropolitan government was vested in the London County Council, leading to extensive improvement in the quantity and quality of public services.

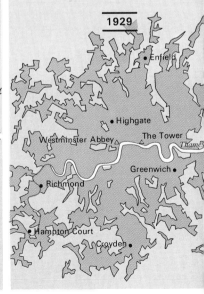

The effect of rising real income on the factory worker's standard of living was reflected in the consumption habits of the nation as a whole. For the United Kingdom, per capita consumption of such staples as tea, coffee, cocoa, sugar, meat, beer, and tobacco increased an average of 20 per cent from the early 1880's to the turn of the century. In Germany, sugar, spices, tea, and cocoa became a larger part of the urban worker's diet, and annual per capita consumption of meat rose from sixty-five pounds to ninety-five pounds (still far below that in Great Britain) between 1873 and 1912. In France consumption of these items more than doubled during the forty years from 1871 to 1910. Testimony of contemporary observers speaks of an improvement in the quality and style of cheap clothing that made it harder to distinguish between urban workers and middle-class citizens. Certainly most workers had a change of clothing and shoes for Sunday and holiday wear.

The rural laborer was hard hit by falling wages during the agricultural crisis of the 1870's (when imports of grain from America drastically reduced agricultural prices, profits, and wages in Europe), but his position began to improve during the 1890's. This recovery was due in part to price rises (promoted by tariffs to a large extent) and also to considerable changes both in production methods and in goods produced. There was significant change-over to livestock raising; Danish peasants, for example, turned increasingly to dairy farming. To finance these changes, farmers' cooperatives came into existence. Credit cooperatives reduced rates on loans and made funds available where there had formerly been none; purchasing cooperatives bought expensive supplies and heavy machinery to be used in common. Finally, there were even cooperatives with storage and processing facilities that acted as sales agents for their members. Yet despite these improvements, conditions for rural workers generally lagged behind those for their urban counterparts. Their diet remained noticeably inferior; their clothing was simpler; and they received less schooling; and while their homes might be less crowded, they lacked conveniences enjoyed by many city workers.

If living conditions had improved for the majority of both urban and rural workers during this period, there still remained the desperately poor. Studies conducted in Great Britain around the turn of the century revealed that an appreciable segment of the urban working-class population lived in appalling poverty. *Life and Labour of the People in London,* a series of volumes issued between 1889 and 1907 as the result of an investigation organized by a wealthy shipowner, Charles Booth, showed that a third of the London population was living in continuous poverty, while a tenth was perpetually on the brink of starvation. Seebohm Rowntree's *Poverty: A Study of Town Life* (1901) showed that in York, a relatively prosperous town where railway works were the main industry, 28 per cent of the population earned less than the minimum necessary to provide the bare physical needs of a household. It should be remembered that these conditions existed in the most advanced industrial country in the world.

Advance of the Left

The Industrial Revolution had from its early stages engendered protest against the conditions of urban misery that accompanied industrialization. Should the working class have to pay the social price for economic and technological advances in production, distribution, and transportation? This was a continual issue in the nineteenth century — as it still is. Many people, not only workers but also middle-class intellectuals and humanitarians, advocated changes in the economic and social system by which the benefits of industrialization would accrue to society as a whole. They wanted limitations on the operation of the capitalist free market, or its total abolition, in accordance with some ideal of distributive justice.

Various means for attaining these goals were attempted in the early nineteenth century. Socialist theorists like Robert Owen, Henri de Saint-Simon, Charles Fourier, and Louis Blanc proposed cooperative systems or communes which would make conditions of labor and living salubrious for workers. Others, particularly Karl Marx, advocated proletarian solidarity in a revolutionary movement. In the 1830's and 1840's, working-class political organizations joined with bourgeois liberals to press for political democracy. Particularly in Britain, workers formed labor unions to demand improved wages and working conditions; the most important was the Grand National Consolidated Union in Britain in the 1830's, led by Robert Owen. None of these efforts met with much success. Experiments in utopian socialist communes invariably failed; the bourgeois liberals, having gained their goals, cared little for working-class interests; the unions of the 1830's and 1840's disintegrated in times of unemployment and government repression.

During the second half of the nineteenth century, the movement to reform the conditions of industrial society at last made significant headway. As the industrial system matured and became much more highly organized and more prosperous, working-class and socialist movements underwent a parallel process of organization and achievement. Generally speaking, the more advanced a country was industrially in 1900, the stronger were its labor and socialist movements. But the movement for social justice was an extremely complex one: it was divided by many kinds of organizations and a great variety of ideals, and the pattern varied from country to country and also from decade to decade. A very substantial part of the working class never joined a union or voted for a socialist party; many workers pursued entirely private goals. Furthermore, there was an imprecise but real division of purpose between the greater part of the union movement on the one side and the socialist groups on the other.

The unionized workers were mainly interested in securing higher wages and better working and living conditions. The socialist groups were dominated by alienated middle-class intellectuals who wanted major changes in economic and social organization. The unions also differed among themselves on aims, tactics, and the kind of workers they recruited. The socialists encompassed a very broad spectrum from essentially middle-class radicals to extreme revolutionaries. Even the Marxists were deeply divided between those who were prepared to work within parliamentary institutions and those who would tolerate no cooperation with the bourgeoisie and its political processes. Earnest efforts were made to bridge the deep divisions among labor unions and socialists, but these often amounted to not much more than rhetorical affirmations of left-wing solidarity. Similarly, the founding of national and international associations and congresses of socialist groups and unions often had little or no practical consequence.

The most moderate and, in terms of its limited aims, the most successful movement to mitigate the harsh effects of industrialism was the formation of producers' and consumers' cooperatives. By 1900 they had millions of members in the advanced industrial countries. But their aim was to help the workers through mutual benefit and insurance; they were not engaged in a confrontation with capitalism. The most important single development leading to melioration of working-class conditions was the growth of labor unions. Legal proscription or severe restriction on union organization had been lifted in western European countries in the late nineteenth century, and by 1900 there were two million union members in Britain, 850,000 in Germany, a quarter-million in France, and more than a million in the United States; in the following decade union membership increased rapidly in all countries. (Unions were finally legalized in Russia in 1906, but the right to strike was still denied.)

The main causes for the great increase in union membership are obvious: the spread of the factory system produced working-class solidarity, and the improvement in real wages in the second half of the nineteenth century increased the workers' expectations, which they sought to realize through union agitation, collective bargaining, and strikes. In addition, effective and sometimes heroic leadership was instrumental in the expansion of union membership, as were also—particularly in Germany, Austria, and France—the inspiration of socialist ideas and the assistance of socialist leaders.

There were three distinct types of unions: craft, industrial, and revolutionary or syndicalist. The craft unions, initiated during the 1850's and 1860's, were organizations of skilled workers—the artisan "aristocracy of labor," particularly machinists. They engaged in peaceful collective bargaining, undertook few strikes and then only as a last resort, and were assiduous in providing medical, insurance, and educational benefits for their members. The craft unions were similar in spirit to the old guilds: they were politically inert; they accepted capitalism, often with enthusiasm; and they did little or nothing for the far more numerous unskilled workers in mining, transportation, textile manufacture, and the construction trades.

It was only in the last two decades of the nineteenth century, particularly in Britain and Germany, that unskilled workers were organized in industrial unions, which brought all the workers in an industry, both skilled and unskilled, into a single union and also formed national unions of workers drawn from a variety of trades. The industrial unions were far more militant than the craft unions, partly because their leaders were more hostile to prevailing capitalism but mostly because they had to be—their efforts at organizing and improving wages and working conditions were often bitterly resisted. It was one thing to give raises to a few skilled machinists in a craft union; it was a very different thing when demands were made by masses of miners, railroad workers, or textile workers. The industrial unions regarded strikes as a necessary weapon to be used frequently. Particularly in the first decade of the twentieth century, when the increase in real wages stopped and unemployment rose, there were thousands of strikes annually in every European country.

Because of this increasing confrontation between capital and labor, some of the leaders of industrial unions in France, and to a lesser degree in Britain, were influenced by the ideals of revolutionary or syndicalist (from the French word for union, *syndicat*) unionism at the turn of the century. Syndicalist unionism envisioned the use of a general strike and, in its most extreme form, violence to bring the capitalist system crashing down, to be replaced by workers' communes. It received its theoretical formulation from the French philosopher Georges Sorel. Even in France, only a minority of union members subscribed to full-fledged syndicalist programs, and these were mainly in industries that were becoming technologically obsolescent. But in countries where industrialization was only beginning and where the governments were repressive, revolutionary unionism—syndicalist in Italy and Spain, Marxist in Russia—became the dominant form. Although French and a few British industrial union leaders might speculate on the usefulness of the general strike, they were not fully committed to the revolutionary or syndicalist program. It is the opinion of some historians, however, that if the First World War had not intervened, revolutionary and syndicalist unionism would have gained mass working-class support in the more advanced industrial countries.

The pattern of late nineteenth-century socialism was even more varied than the pattern of unionism. Certainly the most popular socialist ideology was Marxism. In the 1870's, 1880's, and 1890's, it gained millions of supporters in Germany, France, and Austria—or at least political parties led by Marxists attracted millions of voters. By the 1890's, Marxism was also winning strong support among Russian radicals and revolutionaries. It never achieved any significant support in Britain; socialism in that country was of the Fabian variety, a perpetuation of radical, humanitarian, and utilitarian traditions, emphatically nonrevolutionary.

In the countries where Marxism was strong, a great controversy raged among Marxists from the 1890's until 1914. On the one side were the reformist or "revisionist" groups, led by Jean Jaurès in France and Eduard Bernstein in Germany. The revisionists wanted the socialists not only to participate in parliamentary politics but also, if necessary, to join in governments with bourgeois liberals and serve as cabinet ministers. They pointed out that the polarization of society predicted by Marx was not occurring, and they wished to abandon the revolutionary aspect of Marxist doctrine. On the other side, revolutionary, antirevisionist Marxism was reasserted in the first decade of the twentieth century by the German socialist Karl Kautsky and the Russian Marxist theoretician and leader, Lenin. Marxist political parties, whose members often took the name Social Democrats, did well at the polls — in the German Reichstag the Social Democrats became the largest single party — but Marxist socialists were split over whether to become a left-wing political reform party or revert to revolutionary ideology and activity.

There were socialist groups to both the left and the right of the Marxists. To the left were varieties of anarchism, which rejected the state altogether as a vehicle for social reform. The Frenchman Pierre Joseph Proudhon, who came — unlike Marx and Engels — from a working-class background, attacked not only economic exploitation but also government, which he viewed as a terrible kind of tyranny. The second great name in anarchist annals was Mikhail Bakunin. A former Russian army officer who spent his later years in Paris and Geneva, Bakunin (1814–1876) favored common ownership of land and other means of production and vehemently opposed the regulating force of government. In general, the anarchists perpetuated the belief, common among the earlier utopian socialists, that the innate goodness of human nature would lead to the spontaneous formation of egalitarian communities once the evil institutions of capitalism and the state were abolished.

Although both Marxists and anarchists looked to revolution to usher in the socialist economic system, there was a great disparity in the tactics they advocated. Anarchists stressed the efficacy of spontaneous armed revolt, for every rising was a further step in the revolutionary education of the masses. After 1848, however, Marx recognized that violence with no hope of success only gave the capitalist enemy an unnecessary opportunity to destroy the strength of the proletariat's revolutionary organization. He stressed the need for a well-organized working-class movement engaged in a day-to-day struggle for reform, and he wanted the workers to organize to attain some degree of political power. Consequently, Marxist thought recognized the role of trade unions as instruments for creating the new order; anarchism, in its hostility to organization and its faith that the new order would be wrought spontaneously, had no place for trade union activities. Marx believed that voluntary cooperation would be insufficient and that socialism would have to be inaugurated by governmental control. He opposed the bourgeois state; Bakunin, any state. Finally, though both factions posited a dictatorship of the proletariat, anarchism stressed that it would be a spontaneous dictatorship of the entire working class, not one exercised, in Marxist fashion, by a closely knit group of leaders. In the anarchist view, such a group would be, by its very nature, no more than a new instrument of tyranny over the workers.

Marx and Bakunin quarreled incessantly, and Marx secured Bakunin's expulsion from the First International. Nevertheless anarchism remained a main current in late nineteenth-century Russian socialism, and in the theories of Georges Sorel and the syndicalist union movement in France, Italy, and Spain at the beginning of the twentieth century there was also a prominent anarchist strain.

To the right of Marxism, and still within the socialist spectrum, was a variety of groups. In Britain the Fabian Society advocated state regulation of the economy to protect the worker and various welfare measures. At mid-century there had been a British Christian socialist group of some influence, including the novelist Charles Kingsley and the theologian F. D. Maurice. Christian socialists believed that the lives of the workers would improve when an altruistic Christian spirit pervaded the relationships between employers and workers. The Fabians absorbed the British Christian socialist movement, and in the early twentieth century its ablest theoretician, the historian R. H. Tawney, continued to speak for the evangelical Christian conscience. In the United States in the 1890's a pallid Christian socialist group preached the "Social Gospel."

On the Continent, Christian socialism and labor unions sponsored by the clergy were inspired by the encyclical *Rerum Novarum* (Modern Things) issued by Pope Leo XIII in 1891. Leo made the first tentative effort of the Roman Church to come to terms with modern society. While upholding the right of private property, he criticized capitalism for its exploitation and degradation of the worker. He condemned godless Marxism but favored Catholic unions, Christian Socialist parties, and cooperative and meliorist ventures. By 1900, Catholic unions were strong in Germany, Austria, Belgium, and France, though in membership they were a distant second to the industrial unions and their existence further divided organized labor. Christian socialism was never more than a hesitant and tardy response by Christianity to the problems of industrial society. By 1900 a great many workers both in Britain and on the Continent had committed themselves either to private material goals or to secular socialism, and church membership—and, even more, regular church attendance—had declined substantially.

National Labor Movements

Nowhere in the first half of the nineteenth century were labor organizations strong. In Great Britain the Combination Acts that outlawed unions were repealed in 1824, but a rash of strikes the following year prompted a reaction that imposed new restraining measures. Unions had little more than a bare existence, and many of their activities were proscribed. During the next two decades efforts to gain a political voice to transform the state were largely abortive. Agitation for the Reform Act of 1832 supported a measure that benefited only the upper middle class, and though the working-class Chartist agitators of 1838–1848 collected millions of signatures, their three huge petitions were ignored by the government. In the early 1830's, Robert Owen founded the Grand National Consolidated Trades Union of skilled and unskilled male and female workers. Its membership grew quickly to more than 500,000, and Owen envisioned a surrender of industry to workers, who would then form a cooperative system. But within two years Owen's union had foundered on the rocks of employer opposition, government repression, and internal dissension.

During the decades of the 1850's and 1860's the British craft unions turned away from visionary leaders. At the same time, they remained immune to Marxist doctrines, even though Marx himself was living and writing in London. Unfortunately for Marxism, the British upper classes had met workers' demands to remedy the worst factory abuses: the Factory Acts of 1833 and 1844, the Mines Act (1842), and the Ten-Hour Act (1847) had improved working conditions, and in 1867 the Disraeli government extended the franchise so that almost all the old Chartist demands were met. Union organization went forward apace, but it was conservatively concerned with organizing skilled workers and making the best of the capitalist system. In 1867 leaders of the Society of Amalgamated Engineers pronounced strikes a waste of money for both employers and workers.

New labor leaders emerging in the 1870's and 1880's were critical of this conservative attitude and turned their attention to organizing unskilled workers—three fourths of the British laboring class was still outside any organization. Having gained greater legal freedom for strike activity in 1875, British unions became increasingly militant. In 1889 John Burns, Tom Mann, and Ben Tillet organized the unskilled, miserably paid London dock workers and waged a successful strike—a landmark in the history of British unionism. In the following years, industrial strikes grew more common and more prolonged. At the same time, other workers' movements were developing, and the ideas of socialism were spreading.

In Britain, however, the most influential strain of socialism was Fabian. Founded in 1883, the Fabian Society proposed to extend socialism throughout the country by gradualist, parliamentary methods, and their activity was directed mainly to educating the middle class. The workers needed a political party to represent their views in Parliament. Already a few independent working-class representatives had been elected to that body. In 1893 the Independent Labour party was founded, but its socialist policies failed to win the support of the Trades Union Congress (which had been founded in 1868, and to which a significant number of British unions belonged). In 1900, however, the Fabians helped to bring the TUC and the ILP together to form the Labour Representation Committee, which became the Labour party in 1906.

The Labour party in its early years was not socialist; it merely wanted welfare legislation. It approved the social reforms of Liberal governments: the Old Age Pensions Act (1908), the National Health Insurance Act (1911), and the National Unemployment Insurance Act (1911). But the trade unions continued to meet upper-class resistance. In 1901 the Taff Vale decision made unions liable for strike damages, and not until 1906 did the Trade Disputes Act wipe that decision from the books. In 1909 the Osborne decision prohibited payments by unions to political candidates; four years later the Trade Union Act removed that impediment to Labour party growth.

A powerful, organized working-class movement developed later in France because industrialization there was slower and less sweeping than in Britain. The government during the French Revolution had banned combinations of either workingmen or employers, but as in Britain this restraint worked primarily against the former. Early French laws to regulate factory conditions were less effective than contemporary British measures. During the 1830's, French unions had to operate in secrecy; the workers' support for Louis Blanc's experiment with national workshops ended in bloody repression in 1848.

Napoleon III made a few halting attempts to win over the working class in the hope of balancing its support against rising bourgeois opposition, and most working-class leaders took advantage of the concessions by organizing openly without renouncing their opposition to the regime. By the late 1860's, working-class leadership had moved to a group favoring a French version of collectivism whereby land would be owned by local communes, not the state.

Militant Unionism in Britain. The organization of unskilled British workers in large industrial unions during the 1880's marked a turning point in the history of British labor. After the turn of the century, rising unemployment and declining real wages made these unions steadily more militant, and in the decade before 1914 there were thousands of strikes each year in Britain. The struggle between employers and organized labor in the coal industry was particularly bitter. Left: a union leader addressing striking coal miners in 1912.

The experience of the Commune of 1871, however, left the working-class movement in a shambles, though the Communards were not generally members of the working class.

Under the Third Republic, labor organization slowly recovered. In 1882 a congress at Marseilles, attended by delegates from the *syndicats* and cooperatives, voted itself the title Socialist Labor Congress and organized the first French socialist party. Factional strife between anarchists, Marxists, and moderates played havoc both with the party and with the trade unions, which were sought as prizes and used as training grounds by the rival socialist groups. Nonetheless, after the government extended full recognition to the unions in 1884, expansion went forward. In 1886 the National Federation of Unions was organized and came under the control of the Marxist French Workers' party; it fell apart on the issue of the general strike, which was gaining much influence in the 1880's.

In 1887 the first *bourse du travail* (an employment exchange offering benefit activities, education, and propaganda services) was established by labor leaders in Paris. Five years later, fourteen were in existence, and ten of them formed a national organization, the *Fédération des Bourses du Travail*. As they grew in prestige, their organizers conceived of them as more than relief and reform bodies—indeed, as bases for a new social order. In 1902 the federation merged with the *Confédération Générale du Travail* (CGT), the successor organization to the National Federation of Unions, which had declared its independence of political organizations and approved the general strike as the ultimate weapon. The new CGT represented some 600,000 workers. Some of its leaders and part of its rank and file subscribed to revolutionary syndicalist doctrine. Meanwhile, in 1905, the various socialist political groups had formed a united front. But an attempt to unite the party and the CGT in support of social reform was unsuccessful.

In the years before 1914, strikes in France were on the increase. The poverty of the unions meant that extended strikes were impracticable, and thus the strategy was to compel government intervention in labor disputes. Despite occasional repression of strikes, French union membership reached more than a million in 1914.

In Germany industrialization came late; until the 1860's, laws kept workers' organizations weak, local, and ineffective. In 1863 Ferdinand Lassalle (1825–1864) founded the country's first political organization representing the interests of the laboring class, the Universal Workingman's Association. In doing so, Lassalle was repudiating the theory of the adequacy of individualism and self-help. He considered the greatest enemy of the working class to be, not the German state, but the middle-class Progressive party, which emphasized the doctrine of laissez faire; and his letters to Bismarck indicate that he would have allied the workers with the monarchy against the bourgeoisie.

This position was, of course, distinctly contrary to Marxism. So, too, was

Lassalle's view of trade unions. Believing in Ricardo's iron law of wages — that a wage rise would inevitably be followed by a rise in population that would cancel out its benefits — he held that trade unions were of no use. Lassalle believed that labor's success lay in achieving universal manhood suffrage and then having the state supply credit to cooperative associations for production. It was very much the same idea that Louis Blanc had put forward in France during the 1840's. In a rapidly industrializing economy, however, unionism had great appeal, and after Lassalle's romantic death in a duel in 1864, his followers quickly set up a union organization.

In 1869 the Marxist socialists, led by Wilhelm Liebknecht and August Bebel, organized both the Social Democratic Labor party and a trade union movement. The new Marxist party chose to side with the more progressive elements of the bourgeoisie for the time being, and consequently it was a rival of the Lassalle group. But the refusal of the Social Democratic leaders to vote war credits during the Franco-Prussian War and the experience of the Commune in France turned Bismarck against all socialists, and government opposition pressured the two groups to merge. In 1875 a successful unity conference was held at Gotha. Out of the Gotha program emerged the United Social Democratic Workers party (usually called the Social Democrats) and a single trade union organization (the so-called "free" unions).

During these same years a Christian socialist movement had gained prominence in Germany. Under the leadership of the Catholic Bishop von Ketteler, it opposed the "materialist atheism" of the other socialist parties. In 1878 the (Protestant) Christian Socialist Labor party was formed under the leadership of Pastor Adolf Stöcker; its distinguishing feature was fervent anti-Semitism.

Following Bismarck's antisocialist legislation of 1878, the Social Democratic party was forced underground; its trade unions also disappeared from view. At the same time, in an attempt to wean the workers away from socialism, Bismarck sought to tie their interest to the existing order through insurance schemes. After Bismarck's dismissal in 1890, his antisocialist measures soon lapsed, and it immediately became apparent that the Social Democrats had actually flourished under repression: they polled some 1.5 million votes and secured thirty-five seats in the Reichstag elections of that year. The following year — with the Marxists fully in control — the party met at Erfurt to draft a new program which emphasized the need to gain political power and to strengthen workers' organizations.

The Social Democrats emerged from the Bismarckian era stronger than ever, but they were divided into the revisionist and more orthodox wings. Although the revisionist position was formally rejected at a party congress in 1903, it remained an important force in German socialist circles. Union membership had substantially declined under Bismarck, and the revival of the unions in the 1890's was marked by an increasing tendency to assert union independence from the party. (At the same time, the tactic of the general strike was rejected on the grounds that it could push the government to new repression.) In 1906 the Social Democratic party recognized the autonomous position of the unions. Out of a total union membership of 3.25 million on the eve of the First World War, 2.5 million belonged to these "free" unions. The Christian unions constituted by far the largest other group. Originating in the 1880's under the influence of local Catholic clergy, they became interdenominational. Unlike their competitors, they denied the existence of a class struggle. Disputes were to be settled in accordance with Christian ideals, and strikes were a weapon of last resort.

The Italian and Spanish labor movements were both characterized by strong anarchist tendencies. In Italy there was no organized labor movement until the last quarter of the century: until then Italian governments considered combination illegal and strikes rebellious. In southern and central Italy, where peasant poverty was severe, anarchism had a particularly strong appeal; in the north, where industry was developing, the labor movement came under Marxist as well as anarchist and syndicalist influence.

Italy's modern Socialist party was founded in 1892 and elected six deputies to the Chamber in the same year. Factional disputes among the right wing, which favored gradual reform, the Marxist center, and left-wing anarcho-syndicalist groups were frequent. The party was often subjected to government repression, and the trade union movement was likewise prone to government harassment, although its growth was more seriously inhibited by the relatively slight development of large-scale industry.

In Spain the Socialist party and a trade union movement—the General Union of Workers (UGT)—did their best to follow a moderate course, using constitutional action and collective bargaining to further their goals. But the left wing of the working-class movement was committed to anarchist and syndicalist ideals. Shortly before the First World War, the Spanish Socialist party gained a substantial following. The UGT also expanded greatly, becoming more independent of the Socialist party and more militant, but at the same time, the larger labor movements outside the UGT united to form the National Confederation of Labor (CNT). This body soon came under anarchist leadership.

The socialist movement in the Russian Empire was forced in a revolutionary direction by government repression and the absence of liberal institutions. This development, crucial for Russia's future, has been examined in the previous chapter. Despite the presence of numerous exiled European socialists in the United States after 1848, America's working-class movement was largely nonrevolutionary. The government, at both federal and state levels, was considerably more democratic than its European counterparts, and the tremendous expansion of the American economy provided so many opportunities for workers that working-class radicalism was inevitably muted. At the same time, the influx of immigrants divided the laboring class into widely disparate skilled and unskilled groups, thus making any concerted action difficult.

Nevertheless, the rapid industrialization of the country induced a considerable degree of working-class solidarity, and the example of successful union organization in western Europe was imitated in the United States. In the 1850's and 1860's many craft unions were established, and by the early 1870's these organizations had a membership of three million. An attempt to establish an effective national federation of craft unions was aborted when the National Labor Union, as the federation was called, turned itself into a political organization, failed to gain any support at the election of 1872, and was thereby discredited. Temporarily far more successful was the Knights of Labor, founded in 1869, which attained a membership of 729,000 by the early 1880's. The Knights of Labor at first operated as a secret guild, but in 1879 it came into the open and began to organize workers at a furious pace along large-scale industrial union lines. It disintegrated rapidly in the late 1880's after it had organized a series of unsuccessful strikes and after it was falsely implicated in the Haymarket Square riot of 1886 in Chicago, where seven policemen were killed when they tried to break up an anarchist meeting.

The Knights of Labor's place as the largest American union was taken by Samuel Gompers' American Federation of Labor, which by 1901 had a million members. Gompers adhered to the traditions of British craft unions, aiming to secure the best possible terms from employers without in any way attacking or even questioning the prevailing economic system. Gompers successfully pursued his cautious policy, but in the 1890's there occurred explosive confrontations between capital and labor unions, including some AFL affiliates. The main reason for these violent struggles was the intention of some industrial magnates to destroy the unions – which they identified with communism – with the help of the federal government and the courts. In 1892 a strike at Andrew Carnegie's Homestead steel plant near Pittsburgh was suppressed through the use of strikebreakers and armed guards, and the steel workers' union, an AFL affiliate, suffered a fatal blow. In 1894 a strike against the Pullman Company, manufacturer of railroad cars in Chicago, was suppressed with the help of government troops. The leader of the union, Eugene V. Debs, was jailed for a short time. Debs thereupon became a socialist (of the moderate revisionist variety) and united various minuscule socialist factions into the American Socialist party. In 1912 Debs received 900,000 votes for the presidency, but socialism in the United States always remained a marginal movement, with little political significance.

Similarly, revolutionary syndicalist unionism made only modest gains in the United States. It developed only in the Far West, where employers engaged in savage repression of working-class militance. In 1905 the Industrial Workers of the World – the IWW or "Wobblies" – was founded in Chicago with a membership that was primarily Western. Though it won a great deal of fame (and infamy), it remained very small as compared with the AFL. In sum, the steady growth of American prosperity served to limit the spread of militant unionism and socialism.

In the years before World War I an international trade union movement was founded. The International Secretariat of National Trade Union Centers (later the International Federation of Trade Unions) was established in 1901, and the International Secretariat of Christian Trade Unions in 1908. Of far greater consequence to the labor movement—in that it frightened conservative forces everywhere—was the International Workingmen's Association. Karl Marx was the moving power behind the IWMA (the First International). In 1862 British and French trade union representatives met at the London International Exhibition and agreed that an international body was necessary to reflect the solidarity of organized workers in the various countries. Marx looked on it as a means for guiding workers' movements throughout Europe along Marxist channels, and from the start he and other German exiles living in London played a large part in formulating its policies. The First International held nine congresses in various western European cities between 1864 and 1872. These meetings were dominated by the struggle of Marx and his supporters against other groups—at first the followers of Proudhon and then Bakunin and his anarchist supporters. The congress of the First International at The Hague in 1872 was so badly split that the Marxist majority voted to remove the International to New York. Bakunin and other non-Marxists then established a rival congress at Zurich, but for all practical purposes, the First International was now extinct.

The Second International was organized by Marxian socialists in Paris in 1889. At its height it included representatives from socialist parties in thirty-three countries. At its first meeting four objectives were listed: the eight-hour work day, universal manhood suffrage, citizens' militias in place of armies, and May Day observances as a show of working-class strength. The old dispute with the anarchist faction once again emerged, and at the Zurich congress in 1893 the anarchists were expelled. Revisionism then became an issue, and controversy followed over whether socialist leaders could take part in bourgeois governments, as had occurred in France. At Karl Kautsky's urging, such participation was condemned at the Amsterdam congress of 1904.

As the likelihood of war grew, the congresses of the Second International addressed themselves to the problem of preventing its outbreak. Even on this vital point, the members were divided, for while some favored a general strike for peace, others opposed it. The International's tenth congress was scheduled to meet in August 1914 in Vienna. Before that, war had broken out, and in the patriotic stampede that ensued, the international solidarity of the workers was an early casualty.

HERITAGE
ESSAY

THE INDUSTRIAL AND SOCIALIST HERITAGE

From an agency of social change in various parts of Europe, the Industrial Revolution became synonymous in the later nineteenth century with the common experience of Western civilization: from a torrent that inundated the old agricultural and hierarchical order, industrialization became a vast ocean that engulfed the Western world and then significantly penetrated traditional societies in the non-Western world. We are still trying to come to terms with the heritage of the climactic stage of the Industrial Revolution in the later nineteenth century, still trying to adjust our political institutions and reformulate our perception of the meaning of human life relative to the material and technological conditions of our modern world.

The technology that we have learned to take for granted is a product of the late nineteenth century, and it is not easy for us to realize how much the material things it produced altered the quality of social and personal life. Not the least of the consequences of the revolution in transport and communication was the advent of democratic politics on a national scale. Politicians went out from their capitals to address huge crowds in every corner of the nation, and the populace was informed — or misinformed — about current events and issues by papers that printed news of yesterday's happenings from telegraphic reports. By 1900 a global economy, and also a global politics, was emerging. But war has its victories no less than peace. The integration of the world greatly increased the probability that international incidents in Asia and Africa would engender confrontations in Europe and that struggles among European powers would precipitate global warfare.

The life style and daily expectations of the common man were transformed. It was not until the later nineteenth century that a sick person stood a better chance of survival within a hospital than outside it. The advent of the gaslight, and then the electric light, altered the quality of life in all cities; no longer did nightfall plunge the world into terrifying darkness. Proliferation of the forms of mass entertainment — the popular press, theaters and music halls, spectator sports, and then motion pictures — enormously increased the variety of leisure enjoyment available to the common man, who was now educated in state-supported schools. By competing with religion for the work-

ingman's free time, politics, labor union activity, and popular entertainment contributed to the decline of church attendance, particularly in Protestant countries. At the same time, moral condemnation of drunkenness and prostitution could gain a hearing because there were now suitable alternatives to alcohol and promiscuity as popular diversions.

The entrenchment of an industrial economy and mass culture brought social ills as well as human benefits. It was the tragic irony of the late nineteenth century that material and technological progress in some respects exacerbated economic crises, the poverty and misery of part of society, and the hatred of various social and national groups for one another. Mass literacy and ease of communication did not necessarily foster public commitment to liberal ideals; on the contrary, the masses were often enthusiastic supporters of aggressive nationalism, militarism, and racism. Democracy did not necessarily augur an era of human brotherhood; indeed, by 1900 there were indications that it might well usher in an age of fanaticism and violence.

Among the many indices of this menacing trend was the sharp rise in anti-Semitism in all Western countries in the late nineteenth century. This virus had been relatively inert in Western society since the sixteenth century, and early nineteenth-century liberalism had strongly condemned such prejudice as unworthy of a civilized society. By 1900 it was evident that many people at all levels of society, particularly among the petite bourgeoisie and the working class, were making Jewish minorities scapegoats for their personal frustrations and national disappointments.

Throughout the Western world, as the second Industrial Revolution moved

The Perils from Within. For all their political and economic achievements, the democratic capitalist societies of western Europe encountered grave domestic problems at the close of the nineteenth century. The masses were susceptible to both right-wing and left-wing agitation and could be indoctrinated with a variety of hateful myths. The Dreyfus affair in France stirred the passions of the mob, as extreme right-wing leaders tried to turn popular feeling against liberals and Jews. Left: Théophile Steinlen's drawing of the frenzied Paris mob during the trial of Émile Zola, who had attacked the army for convicting Captain Dreyfus on the basis of forged documents. Facing page: an example of anti-Semitic propaganda in the 1890's—the caricature of Rothschild is supposed to reveal the menace of Jewish bankers. Along with the spread of popular fanaticism, the capitalist order was threatened by periodic business crises that caused middle-class ruin and working-class unemployment. Below: crash on the Berlin Bourse, 1873.

The Wretched of the Earth. The capitalist economy made tremendous progress, and many of the working class participated in the increasing prosperity of the nineteenth century. But a substantial proportion of the population still lived in horrible misery and poverty; scenes of human degradation, visible in every European city, were portrayed by the photographers and artists of the period. Facing page, top: scene in a slum in Newcastle, England, in the 1870's. Dreadfully inadequate housing for the poor remained a universal blight. Facing page, bottom: an illustration of the morally debilitating method of public assistance to the poor—"Applicants to a Casual Ward" by Sir Luke Fildes. The unemployed are lined up to secure admittance to a poorhouse. Above: the consequence of employers' hostility to union organization—Théophile Steinlen's "Lockout."

toward its climax, vast numbers of people still were mired in squalor and hereditary poverty. Few workers were satisfied with their wages or their working and living conditions. They joined militant—and in some cases revolutionary—unions, and they voted for socialist political parties, usually led by middle-class intellectuals more or less hostile to the capitalist system.

In the closing decades of the nineteenth century the merits of the prevailing economic and social system were the subject of vociferous debate by social theorists—a debate that continues to the present day. First of all, a few respectable thinkers and many industrial and financial magnates used (or perhaps misused) social Darwinism to advocate unrestrained power for capitalists. Society was viewed as a primordial jungle in which the strong justifiably ruled and exploited the weak. But the great majority of European intellectuals agreed with the English economist and historian Arnold Toynbee (the Elder) in unequivocally condemning this variant of the doctrine of the struggle for existence. "The whole meaning of civilisation," Toynbee wrote in 1884, "is interference with this brute struggle. We intend to modify the violence of the fight, and to prevent the weak being trampled under foot."[1] Among men of good will in all countries and in all classes, there was an urge for social justice, of the kind expressed by William Morris, the English poet and artist:

1. Arnold Toynbee, *Lectures on the Industrial Revolution in England.* London: Rivingtons, 1884, p. 86.

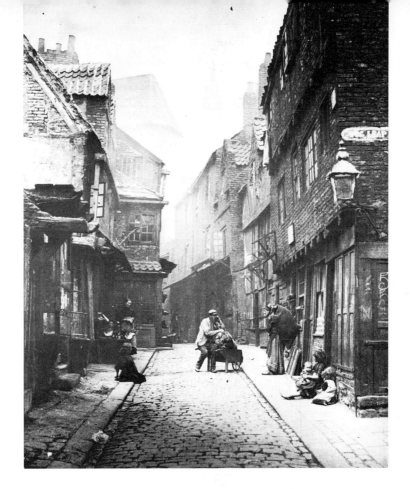

Men in that time a'coming shall work and have no fear
For to-morrow's lack of earning and the hunger-wolf anear.

Yea, the voiceless wrath of the wretched, and their unlearned discontent,
We must give it voice and wisdom till the waiting-tide be spent.[2]

But what should be done to prevent the weak from being trampled under-
foot? How should the voiceless wrath of the wretched be answered? This was
the central issue in the domestic life of most Western states, and social theorists offered a great variety of solutions. Some, particularly in Britain and
the United States, still held fast to the principles of early nineteenth-century
economic liberalism. The most effective spokesman for this point of view was
the eminent Cambridge economist Alfred Marshall, who continued to celebrate the effectiveness of the capitalist free market as the font of technological progress that would eventually abolish poverty. He believed that continued increase in "material resources will make about equal additions to the
fulness of human life, and the true progress of the human race."[3]

But even Marshall was concerned about the implications of monopolies and
trusts; big business might vitiate the free market that had fostered capital-

2. William Morris, *Chants for Socialism*, in H. Kohn, ed., *The Modern World*, 2nd ed. New York: Macmillan,
1968, pp. 132-133.
3. Alfred Marshall, *The Principles of Economics*, in R. Leckachman, ed., *The Varieties of Economics*. Cleveland:
Meridian, 1962, II, p. 163.

Cures for Poverty. At the turn of the century, churches and humanitarian organizations offered food, shelter, and clothing while dispensing religious lessons and moral advice to the unfortunate. Facing page: a Salvation Army hostel in London. The state slowly moved toward programs of public welfare. Above: dinner in a workhouse in London in 1900. Below: the salvation of the wretched—emigration to America, where millions of Europeans sought and often found a better life. This group of Italian immigrants has just landed at Ellis Island, New York City.

The Perils from Without. At the turn of the century intensive union activity and socialist agitation pressed employers to improve wages and working conditions and governments to undertake more effective programs of public welfare. Industrial unions became more militant; in some countries revolutionary syndicalist unionism gained adherents; and in all democratic countries socialist parties made significant gains at the polls. Facing page: "Strike of the Miners" by Henry Luyten. Below: "Strike" by Théophile Steinlen. Union confrontations with employers and socialist political successes, as well as a general increase in concern for social justice, pushed governments into taking more effective measures to alleviate misery and degradation. Left: collecting the first old-age pensions in Britain, January 1, 1909. The pensions were not munificent; they provided five shillings a week (equivalent to about $4.00 today) at age seventy, seven shillings for a married couple. Anyone earning ten shillings a week was disqualified as being too prosperous for state assistance. No other country's welfare program matched Germany's, which Bismarck had introduced in the 1880's in an attempt to stem the socialist tide.

ism's fantastic productivity in the nineteenth century. And another economic theorist of the period, the American Thorstein Veblen, pointed to an even greater defect in the capitalist ethos. As they became a ruling leisure class, he argued, businessmen were no longer interested in technological advance but simply in preserving their own power and status. The business enterprise of his day, Veblen contended, was actually an obstacle to progress.

Whatever the future prospects of laissez-faire capitalism might be, many intellectuals and political leaders at the end of the nineteenth century did not intend to await them; they wanted immediate state interference to improve the conditions of the workers and the poor. "It lies in the power of a ruler to benefit every class in the State, and amongst the rest to promote to the utmost the interests of the poor,"[4] declared Pope Leo XIII in 1891. Politicians everywhere agreed. "We are all socialists now," remarked a leading British Liberal in the mid-1890's, meaning that politicians of all idological shades were increasingly inclined toward state action on behalf of the worker, the weak, and the poor. In the United States, scene of brazen depredations by capitalist robber barons, President Theodore Roosevelt in the early years of the twen-

4. Leo XIII, *Rerum Novarum,* in A. Fremantle, ed., *The Papal Encyclicals in their Historical Context.* New York: Putnam, 1956, p. 181.

tieth century raged against "the malefactors of great wealth." Philosophers quickly sensed the shift in political attitudes; in the late nineteenth century, social theorists looked back beyond liberal individualism and recalled Greek, medieval, and Hegelian traditions of the primacy of the community over the interests of the individual. The pronouncement of the Oxford philosopher T. H. Green was typical of this statist revival in political thought: "Legislation . . . with reference to labour, and education, and health . . . is justified on the ground that it is the business of the state . . . to maintain the conditions without which a free exercise of the human faculties is impossible."[5]

The increasing acceptance of the collectivist principle of state welfare posed a great dilemma for Marxist theorists. The beginnings of the melioration of the ravages of capitalism seemed to Marxist revisionists and moderates like Jean Jaurès in France and Eduard Bernstein in Germany to belie Marx's prophecy that the working class under capitalism was doomed to increasing poverty and misery. Jaurès and Bernstein envisioned the triumph of socialism by democratic political processes and, for the present, approved of the participation of socialist ministers in middle-class liberal governments. Jaurès repudiated Marxist materialism; essentially he was a humanist who wished to make available to the working class the finest traditions of Western, and particularly French, culture. "Constitutional legislation," rather than revolutionary violence, Bernstein wrote in 1899, "is best adapted to positive social-political work and the creation of permanent economic arrangements capable of lasting."[6] But the left wing of the Marxist movement would not accept this proposed alliance of socialism and liberalism. "The class antagonisms between the proletariat and the possessing class," Karl Kautsky insisted in 1909, "are so great that the proletariat can never share governmental power with any possessing class."[7]

At the extreme Left of the intellectual spectrum stood the anarchists, at once the most violently revolutionary and the most romantically optimistic of social critics. Mikhail Bakunin condemned the state itself, whether bourgeois or socialist, as a "voracious abstraction." Take away the state, contended Bakunin's disciple Prince Peter Kropotkin, and man's innate love will be liberated; people will spontaneously draw together in "mutual aid." In the syndicalist doctrine of Georges Sorel in the first decade of the twentieth century, the general strike and revolutionary violence were relished not only for the emancipation they would bring but for their own sake, as life-enhancing acts. Revolution is spiritual redemption, Sorel claimed—a release from the repressions of civilization. Such rebellion, not just against capitalism but against reason itself, was common in Sorel's generation and again became attractive to young rebels in the late 1960's.

5. T. H. Green, *Liberal Legislation and Freedom of Contract*, in R. L. Nettleship, ed., *The Works of Thomas Hill Green*. London: Longmans, 1911, III, p. 374.
6. Eduard Bernstein, *Evolutionary Socialism*, in A. Fried and R. Sanders, eds., *Socialist Thought*. New York: Doubleday, 1964, pp. 430-431.
7. Karl Kautsky, *The Road to Power*, in A. Fried and R. Sanders, eds., *Socialist Thought*, p. 439.

The New Consciousness

I THE REVOLT AGAINST REASON

The New View of Man

The intellectual and cultural development of Europe and America between 1870 and 1918 was dominated by a reaction against the salient characteristic of the preceding decades — an almost naive faith in the powers of human reason and the methods of objective science. After 1870 the foundations of this liberal, rational self-confidence began to crumble. During the next twenty years, objective science and rationalism seemed played out, spent forces, and the formulas they prescribed for human happiness and progress increasingly sterile and inadequate. The new restlessness was particularly apparent among those engaged in the creative arts; both in Europe and America, the last decade of the nineteenth century saw frantic experimentation and innovation in literature and painting. There was much talk of the decadence of old forms and techniques. It was fashionable to speak of a kind of jaded world-weariness supposedly characteristic of the end of a century. Artists gathered in little coteries whose avowed purpose it was to shock respectable society by mocking ideas which solid citizens looked upon as eternal verities.

The desire of many artists to shock and provoke by being as outlandish as possible was more than just a fad or a pose. It was symptomatic of the attempt to escape from a number of intellectual straitjackets. Although European economic and political power stood at its zenith, many perceptive and original minds detected sickness, misery, and boredom beneath the glittering facade of affluence. It was becoming apparent that the human personality was more complex and ambiguous than the men of mid-century had realized. Scientific objectivity as the cure-all for social and personal ills itself became suspect. The new generation insisted that since all knowledge was human knowledge, it was imperfect and subjective, lacking any absolute or transcendent validity. Instead of deluding himself by credulously clinging to objectivity, man should frankly and joyfully explore the subjective. The focus of intellectual and cultural activity shifted to the inner world of human self-consciousness. A new view of man emerged.

The central motif of the new consciousness was the inner world of imagination, dreams, and recollections. The human mind was discovered to be less emancipated from ghosts, myths, superstitions, and dimly apprehended desires than the older generation had realized. Something called the unconscious was discovered. The unconscious was fecund and powerful; it disrupted and subverted the workings of the rational intellect and insured that the order of personal and social life decreed by the system-builders was volatile and transient. But the unconscious was also the source of great creativity and vitality. It affirmed a myriad of bizarre, sometimes sinister, but always exciting human possibilities. Friedrich Nietzsche, the greatest philosopher of the age, spoke for many when he said, "Unless you have chaos within you cannot give birth to a dancing star."

Forerunners of the New Consciousness

In the development of the new consciousness there were two important figures whose creative activity took place wholly or partially before 1870. Forerunners of the new age, both men lived outside the European heartland, and the full impact of their ideas was delayed. The first, the Danish religious philosopher Sören Kierkegaard (1813–1855), continues to have an important influence upon theological speculation in the twentieth century. A devout Lutheran, he was concerned primarily with the spiritual development of the individual Christian. Kierkegaard believed that the inner spiritual life was hindered by institutionalized Christianity, rationalistic theology, and the many secular gods of European civilization—progress, materialism, reason, objectivity, and the like. In clearly written but highly unsystematic works, Kierkegaard unveiled his vision of the inner world of religious sensibility. He attempted to persuade the reader to share this world with him, to face the "existential" predicament of the human race, and to find true salvation. His chief philosophical writings are *Either/Or, Fear and Trembling,* and *The Sickness unto Death.*

Kierkegaard maintained that reason cannot understand the ultimate reality of inward, conscious life. Intuition, or the subjective reflection upon consciousness itself, is the only way of apprehending that reality. Truth is inward and subjective. In contrast to Hegel's dialectic of reason, Kierkegaard's intuition follows a "qualitative" dialectic or "psycho-logic" and leads to nonrational, nonobjective ends. Intuition exhibits the human predicament, revealing the true meaning of life itself. Kierkegaard was morbidly obsessed with what most people would regard as abnormal psychological states. The fear of death was for him a necessary precondition for understanding the meaning of life and the possibility of salvation. Rather than merely thinking about religious matters, one must make a personal commitment of faith.

The second great forerunner of the new consciousness was the Russian novelist Fëdor Dostoevski (1821–1881), who shared Kierkegaard's belief in subjective truth. A Russian landowner, Russian nationalist, Russian Orthodox Christian, and Slavophile, Dostoevski intensely despised European civilization. He rejected reason, science, industrialism, liberalism, positivism, and all the other Western "isms" of the nineteenth century. He regarded reason as an inadequate guide for the ordering of individual life or the life of society. Dostoevski had a profound, intuitive understanding of the human mind and spirit. He himself suffered recurrent epileptic fits, and his mind was exceedingly disturbed, reflecting the tension created by a deeply felt contradiction between reason and religious faith. Dostoevski suspected that the Orthodox Christian message was probably not true—but he longed to believe, to lose his self in something greater. Tormented by a profound sense of guilt and sin, he felt he could be saved only by following the example of Christ. Dostoevski spent four years at hard labor in Siberia for socialist activities and there came to believe in the redemptive efficacy of suffering.

In Dostoevski's novels the major characters struggle with the conflict between faith and reason. Significantly, all the major novels deal with crime, reflecting the author's belief that crime, or sin, is the basic fact of human nature. *Crime and Punishment* (1866) is a study of the evil consequences of the attempt to embrace reason as one's sole guide; its central character, Raskolnikov, is a man of reason who decides that he is above the moral laws that ordinary human beings must follow. To demonstrate his moral and intellectual superiority, he murders an ordinary pawnbroker. It is a perfect crime, but the isolation from humanity that the crime produces forces Raskolnikov to confess to the murder and to embrace suffering in order to expiate his sin. These same general themes are found in *The Possessed* (1871), a study of Russian anarchists. In *The Brothers Karamazov* (1879–1880), Dostoevski developed the theme that all men are brothers—because all are equally guilty of sin. Many critics believe that Dostoevski's insight into the human mind and personality has never been surpassed.

II PHILOSOPHY

The Moral Vision of Nietzsche

Many philosophers of the late nineteenth century reacted against the belief in reason and objectivity that had distinguished the thought of their immediate predecessors. This doubting of accepted values was an important part of the general self-scrutiny occurring throughout Western culture. Philosophers, wondering whether man was indeed a rational animal, came to believe that irrational forces played an important role in his nature. They rejected the claim that science could ultimately explain all aspects of the real world because they questioned the ability of the human mind to apprehend the real world. Indeed, they questioned the very existence of the real world.

In many ways the leading figure of this period was the German philosopher Friedrich Wilhelm Nietzsche (1844–1900). The son of a Protestant minister, Nietzsche spent much of his life in quasi-adolescent rebellion against Christian values, and in his last years he suffered from mental illness. His writings —such as *Thus Spake Zarathustra* and *Beyond Good and Evil*—are informal, somewhat racy, full of rich metaphor. More a moralist than a systematic philosopher, Nietzsche remains one of the foremost critics of traditional Western values.

With persuasive eloquence, Nietzsche pictured man as an irrational creature. The epitome of irrationality himself, he contended that reason plays little role in human life. All ideas are rooted in emotion, and every great philosophy is no more than "a species of involuntary and unconscious autobiography." Nietzsche believed that man is at the mercy of irrational life forces, and rather than being disturbed by this fact he rejoiced in it. In the *Birth of Tragedy*, he celebrated the Dionysian passions that he saw as the mainsprings of human actions and ideas and that found musical expression in the orgiastic music of Richard Wagner. Nietzsche identified these vital forces as the true source of individual creativity and denounced social and religious constraints upon the individual as the attempt of the majority, "the herd," to smash the creative impulses of the gifted few. Antiliberal, antidemocratic, and anticollectivistic, Nietzsche damned the common man as "a herd animal, a creature compounded of good will, sickliness, and mediocrity." At bottom, he despised the ordinary person for lacking will, intelligence, power. The vital, irrational impulses of strong-willed and creative people are repressed by a code of Christian ethics which stresses humility, charity, self-sacrifice; this is the morality of slaves, the ethics of the weak and the mediocre. The notion of a God controlling human affairs was repugnant to Nietzsche, who believed in unbridled individual freedom.

Nietzsche wanted man to be his own God, to work out his own salvation; his writing was a call to ethical action. He urged a thoroughgoing "transvaluation of values" and sought a kind of aristocratic elite of the spirit, who would rise above the herd to be creative and free. Nietzsche spoke in glowing terms of the "Will to Power"—the fundamental drive of life, strength itself. By the exercise of this will to power—this innate life force—a few individuals may rise above the masses and become "superior men," truly creative, free, and life-affirming persons.

Nietzsche's worship of the will to power and the superior man allowed the Fascists and Nazis later to distort his philosophy for propaganda purposes, but Nietzsche himself would have rejected Fascism and National Socialism as vehemently as he rejected Christianity. The significance of Nietzsche's work lies in his disenchantment with liberal Western culture, his stress upon the irrational, and his view of the totally subjective nature of ethics and of truth itself. If reason and objectivity were the gods of European thought, then it may truly be said that Nietzsche ushered in the *Götterdämmerung* of Western philosophy — "the twilight of the gods."

The Continuing Influence of Kant and Hegel

But the old gods were not dead yet — nor were all the old philosophers. Various schools of late nineteenth-century philosophy reformulated the ideas of men like Hegel and Kant. The leading figure of the German neo-Kantian school was Wilhelm Dilthey (1833–1911). Dilthey wrote mostly for learned journals, but his work is central to an understanding of thought in this period. He wished to protect history and the other humanities from the claims of metaphysics on the one hand and the exact sciences on the other. His most important work, *Introduction to the Intellectual Sciences*, successfully defends the autonomy of the humanities as disciplines distinct from science. He is also credited with founding intellectual history as an academic discipline.

In contrast to most earlier philosophers, Dilthey declared that man has no nature or essence but only a history. Each culture has a certain world vision — a constantly changing psychological state containing answers to "the riddles of life." There are no final answers to the riddles of life — no final or correct world view — for that would violate the very nature of history itself. Dilthey's philosophical position is termed "relativistic": he believed that answers to questions concerning the nature of man and the nature of truth are relative to environment, not absolute, final, or unconditional.

Dilthey is credited with the founding of modern relativism, a leading trend in subsequent intellectual development. Yet he would agree that his own ideas were relative to his own intellectual environment. His stress upon consciousness as the stuff of history was typical of the enormous contemporary interest in psychology. And, like Nietzsche, he was a vitalist; that is, he felt that life was prior to reason or knowledge. Moreover, he distrusted science, contending that the historian must rely upon "sympathetic intuition" rather than the methods of the sciences and must attempt to enter fully into the consciousness or world vision of other ages.

The relativism espoused by Dilthey and others was rejected by F. H. Bradley (1846–1924), the commanding figure in the English neo-Hegelian school of philosophy. The son of an Evangelical preacher, Bradley was associated with Oxford University during most of his life. As a young man, he was deeply influenced by Hegelian idealism, which he used to combat the prevailing doctrines of utilitarianism and empiricism as enunciated by John Stuart Mill. Bradley contended that the only reality is spiritual and that the spiritual world constitutes a harmonious system of experience. In some ways, his emphasis upon the ideal or spiritual world as the only reality distinguished him from other philosophers of his day. Yet, like many of them, he was deeply suspicious of reason and thought and declared that, though his philosophy of absolute idealism was true, it was beyond the power of the human intellect to prove or disprove it. A man can understand the reality of the spiritual world only by using his spiritual capacities. In other words, metaphysics as an intellectual discipline is an impossibility. Other philosophers, most of them rejecting Bradley's absolute spiritual idealism, eventually came to the same conclusion.

The leading Italian neo-Hegelian, Benedetto Croce (1866–1952), remained much truer to Hegel's original doctrine than Bradley. A leading historian and philosopher of history as well as a literary critic and aesthetician, Croce was the most influential intellectual figure in twentieth-century Italy. He took seriously Hegel's equation of reason and reality, declaring that the subject matter of thought was the mind, life, or spirit, all of which he took to be identical. In true Hegelian fashion, Croce declared that "All philosophy . . . shows that there is nothing outside the mind." The only reality, the only thing we can know with certainty, is human mental or spiritual activity. In his four-volume *Philosophy of Spirit*, Croce revealed that his conception of mental and spiritual activity included intuition and abstraction as well as economics and ethics. And, since mental and spiritual activity is the subject matter of philosophy, the study of philosophy must involve all these diverse activities. Yet history also embraces the consideration of all these activities. Thus Croce arrived at a truly revolutionary statement: history and philosophy are identical.

Croce was indeed a rationalist in the Hegelian tradition, but his identification of history with philosophy arose from a desire to protect the discipline of history from the claims of the exact sciences. In his insistence that the so-called scientific method was inappropriate to historical research, Croce expressed the antirationalist spirit of late nineteenth- and early twentieth-century thought. In reaction to historians who claimed that the application of the scientific method to history could produce an objective, ultimate, or universal history, Croce declared that all history is "contemporary history." By this he meant that the writing of history took place within the stream of history itself and that therefore it was motivated by contemporary concerns. History was conditioned by history: the writing of history was relative to the historical environment itself. Somewhat paradoxically, Croce was at once a rationalist and an opponent of scientism, a philosophical idealist and a historical relativist.

Henri Bergson

The most thoroughgoing attack upon the claims of science came from the French philosopher Henri Bergson (1859–1941), the most popular and influential philosopher of the early twentieth century. His doctrines were much in vogue among writers and artists and much discussed in the fashionable salons of Paris. Bergson believed that the task of the philosopher was to turn his mind inward upon the data of consciousness. He stressed intuition, rather than reason, as a means of knowing reality, and believed that reason was incapable of understanding the true character of human life, since life consisted less in knowing than in willing, feeling, intuiting. Intuition reveals that the inner psychological life is a world of constant change and everlasting becoming. Intuition thus reveals the nature of inner psychological time and assures us of our freedom as moral beings.

Because Bergson was rather unsystematic, the substance of his philosophy consisted less in his arguments than in the meaning of a few key words and phrases. The central Bergsonian concepts were "intuition," "*élan vital*," "duration," and "creative evolution." He called the fundamental reality of human nature the *élan vital*, or "vital impetus," a mixture of all of the nonrational faculties. In other words, Bergson was a voluntarist (one who stresses the will) and a vitalist (one who stresses life itself) rather than a rationalist. Bergson believed that life itself was psychological consciousness; it was a unified flow of impulse and experience, a kind of stream of consciousness. The artificial, objective concept of time employed by the physicist cannot be used to understand life and change. Intuition, on the other hand, reveals the nature of real time, or "duration," as purely subjective — as found in the human consciousness. The central task of philosophy is the understanding of time or "duration."

Concerned with the threat to human freedom posed by the popularized doctrines of evolution, Bergson offered his own idea of evolutionary development in *Creative Evolution* (1906), an immediate success. In it, he rejected the mechanistic, deterministic scheme of evolution for one in which the course of evolution was determined by human will. "To exist is to change," he declared, "to change is to mature, to mature is to go on creating oneself endlessly." It is easy to understand how Bergson's concept of "creative evolution" appealed to a generation troubled by the problem of evolution and moral freedom.

American Philosophy

In the last decades of the nineteenth century the United States produced several important thinkers. George Santayana (1863–1952) was born in Spain and eventually became a professor of philosophy at Harvard. A fine literary stylist, he is known best for his *Life of Reason* (1905–1906). Santayana is important chiefly as a moral philosopher. He criticized religion for seeking to "arrogate to itself literal truth and moral authority, neither of which it possesses," and preferred to consider theology as a body of myth. Far from being a literal account of truth, religion for him was a mythical, allegorical, metaphorical, or poetic rendering of a purely moral truth. Therefore, it should be judged not by rational and scientific standards but by mythical and allegorical ones. A religion may be considered good, though not strictly speaking "true," if its mythology is pleasing to the worshiper.

This concept enabled Santayana to consider himself both an ardent atheist and a devout Catholic; it also had a great influence on twentieth-century philosophers, poets, and novelists, who have been fascinated with the idea of myth. By making the subjective effect of religion upon the devout the criterion of religious truth, Santayana displayed the pragmatic or practical emphasis of American philosophy.

But the true father of American pragmatism was Santayana's Harvard colleague, Charles Sanders Peirce (1839–1914). Little known in his own time, Peirce never got around to writing a book; but he was a brilliant thinker, perhaps the greatest philosopher America has ever produced. His famous paper of 1878, entitled "How to Make Our Ideas Clear," enunciated the pragmatic theory of meaning. Essentially, Peirce prescribed certain linguistic tests to determine the precise meaning of general terms and concepts. He emphasized the practical or pragmatic results of ideas as their definition: "What a thing means is simply what habits it involves." Simply put, ideas are what they do or, better, what can be done with them. This was a truly revolutionary way of looking at ideas; it implied that most theological and metaphysical ideas were meaningless from a pragmatic point of view. Ideas like "God," "ultimate reality," and "the secret of the universe" could not pass the necessary pragmatic tests.

If Peirce was the spiritual father of American pragmatism, William James (1842–1910) was its most eloquent spokesman. An eminent psychologist and philosopher, James sought a philosophy that would allow him to be what seemed impossible at the time: an empiricist and a religious man. Beginning in 1898, he revived the ideas of Peirce, transforming them into a philosophy that attempted to mediate between science and absolute idealism and thus to resolve his own inner spiritual difficulties. His book *Pragmatism*, published in 1907, gave classic expression to that distinctively American philosophy.

Whereas Peirce's pragmatic theory concerned itself only with the meaning of concepts, James was interested in the more difficult matter of the truth or falsehood of ideas. He expanded Peirce's theory into the pragmatic theory of truth, according to which an idea is true if it produces good results and false if it does not. To find out if an idea is true, believe in it and see if you get satisfactory results. By declaring those ideas to be true that are personally satisfying, James opened the door to the possibility that many of the theological and philosophical ideas that Peirce declared to be meaningless might actually be true nevertheless.

William James radically transformed the idea of truth as it had existed for centuries in Western philosophy. Since he stressed the practical results of ideas as the criterion for truth, his pragmatism appeared to be empirical and scientific in character. As James himself said, "Pragmatism is uncomfortable away from the facts." But in fact pragmatism was highly subjective, for the determination of truth rested upon highly individual personal judgment. In the main, pragmatism lacked the substance of prior philosophies; in James's hands philosophy became little more than a technique or, as James put it, "a method only."

III SOCIAL, PSYCHOLOGICAL, AND SCIENTIFIC THEORY

Political and Social Thought

Two distinct trends characterized the political and social thought of the period 1870–1918: 1) reinterpretations of earlier thinkers such as Hegel, Kant, and Darwin, and 2) original thought arising from the newly established "social sciences." Anthropology, sociology, and psychology emerged as academic disciplines, and their rise was both a cause and an effect of the new consciousness. The state, society, and the human mind itself became objects of empirical, "scientific" study. While this emphasis upon science may seem to be at odds with the rather antiscientific spirit of the new philosophy, it is clear that social science functioned as a powerful solvent of traditional Western values. The emergence of modern relativism in anthropology, sociology, and psychology created a crisis in the mind of Western men that continues to the present day. From the field of psychology, moreover, came a revolutionary system of thought which profoundly altered man's view of his nature.

In political theory, one of the most influential developments was the growth of *statism*. The early and middle years of the nineteenth century had witnessed the development of individualistic "classical" or "bourgeois" liberalism. Essentially a negative conception of the state, this philosophy viewed society as a loose collection of individuals. The proper function of the state was to maximize the freedom of action of its constituent parts. Later, under the influence of Kantian and Hegelian political philosophy, some philosophers began to enunciate a more positive conception of the state: the state was coterminous with society, not a mere superstructure atop the social pyramid. Called statism, this view had two main schools. Some thinkers glorified the state and stressed the duty of the individual to it; others stressed the moral obligation of the state to ensure the well-being of individuals. One representative figure from the latter school was T. H. Green (1836–1882). A professor of philosophy at Oxford, Green reformulated English liberalism in terms of the positive, organic conception of the state. The resulting new or collectivistic liberalism became the theoretical basis of the welfare state.

But the most important political ideology in this age of industrial turmoil was socialism. While traditional conservatism was on the decline and liberals like Green were seeking to develop a new collectivist brand of liberalism, the doctrines of Karl Marx were permeating European society. This was also the period when Marx's ideas were being critically examined by leading academicians and his tactics were being modified by leading socialists. This debate among socialist thinkers has been examined in the previous chapter.

While Marxism was being reexamined, the social implications of Darwinian evolutionary theory were also being explored. Social Darwinists, intoxicated by what they took to be implications of the ideas of Darwin and Spencer, declared that the fittest races not only *did* survive but deserved to survive by reason of their natural superiority. This vulgarization of evolutionary theory degenerated into wild notions of racial superiority, which were used to justify the least savory aspects of imperialism. Perhaps the most pernicious result of these racist theories was the growth of political anti-Semitism. Politicians in all countries discovered that they could manipulate popular resentment of Jews to political advantage. Anti-Semitic leagues sprang up all over Europe, and there developed an enormous literature of hate. In the hands of the ignorant, the cynical, and the prejudiced, evolutionary theory was made to rationalize the dark side of the human spirit. Nor was anti-Semitism confined to the discontented masses. It became fashionable in elite social circles and was given intellectual respectability by some scholars and professors.

Darwinian evolutionary theory also gave birth to the new academic discipline of anthropology. Part natural science and part social science, anthropology involved a naturalistic interpretation of man and human culture. Stated simply, anthropology is the scientific study of human and cultural evolution. Sir Edward Burnett Taylor, an Englishman, wrote the seminal work in this discipline, *Primitive Culture*, in 1871. In a few years there developed a vast literature of anthropology, much of it concerned with aboriginal men and primitive cultures. Very early in its development the science divided into two rather distinct areas of scholarly concern: physical anthropology, which dealt with the evolution of man's physiological characteristics, and cultural anthropology, which treated cultural or social evolution.

In addition to its impact on academic scholarship, anthropology exerted at least two discernible influences on European thought and culture. On the one hand, the findings of the physical anthropologists were used by social Darwinists, racial theorists, and pedestrian anti-Semites to bolster their fanciful ideas about "fittest" and superior races. In general, physical anthropology contributed to that arrogant race consciousness that characterized the mind of Europe and America during this period. On the other hand, the cultural anthropologist contributed to the atmosphere of relativism and skepticism concerning traditional values. Once again, moral values seemed to be little more than adaptations to the environment. The cultural anthropologists pointed out that mores were indeed relative, in the sense that they were constantly evolving to meet the demands of changing social and cultural environments. The study of primitive religions posed an especially serious threat to Christianity. In his seminal work *The Golden Bough* (1890), Sir James Frazer (1854–1941) demonstrated that the practices and beliefs of the Christian religion could be found in many of the "heathen" religions of the world. The findings of anthropology accelerated Europeans' loss of their sense of uniqueness.

The discipline of sociology also contributed to the trend toward relativism. In a general way, sociology may be said to descend from Auguste Comte, who had argued for a science of man and his social institutions. Nineteenth-century thinkers had been deeply concerned with expounding social and political doctrines, but sociology was truly revolutionary in that it treated social institutions as purely natural phenomena, as objects of scientific inquiry. Although perhaps the least mature and the most controversial of academic disciplines, it included among its practitioners some of the most prominent intellectual figures of the late nineteenth century.

Vilfredo Pareto (1848–1923), the leading Italian sociologist, published an important mathematical analysis of economic and sociological problems in 1916. One of his major contributions to sociological thought was his distinction between fundamental human motivations and the ideas men employ as rationalizations for those motivations. The leading sociologist in France was Émile Durkheim (1858–1917). The son of a Jewish rabbi in Alsace, he was trained at French and German universities before succeeding Auguste Comte at the University of Paris. Both sociologist and philosopher, Durkheim combined the precision of an empiricist with the boldness of a theoretician. His most important works deal with suicide, the division of labor, and primitive religion. *The Elementary Forms of the Religious Life* (1912) was a highly influential book. One of his most notable contributions to sociology was his concept of collective representation, which concerned the effect of the total societal consciousness upon the individual. Durkheim's study of this phenomenon led him to conclude that stability in a society depends upon the existence of a generally accepted system of values.

In intellectual stature the German sociologist Max Weber (1864–1920) towered over Pareto, Durkheim, and others. It is no exaggeration to suggest that Weber's was the most powerful analytic mind of his time. An invalid during much of his most creative period, Weber was little known outside the academic community, but his work had a profound impact there. Controversial in his own day and since, it remains enormously influential.

Weber was the founder of the sociology of religion. He was also profoundly interested in capitalism, which he believed to be unique to Western civilization. In his most famous work, *The Protestant Ethic and the Spirit of Capitalism* (1904–1905), he declared that Protestantism and capitalism were closely related. The key to this affinity of religion and economics lay in the doctrine of predestination, which encouraged a work ethic in the devout Calvinist. Protestantism thus created a frame of mind conducive to the development of capitalism. From these ideas Weber built a monumental analysis of the relationship between religion and work ethics in the major cultures of the world.

Arguing for a radical separation of science and values, Weber wanted sociology to become a pure, empirical science—relativistic and, above all, absolutely dispassionate. Weber was almost ruthless in his effort to be scientific:

he ripped away the cant, the pious rhetoric, the cynical euphemisms, and the sweet illusions that legitimize human institutions. He defined the state baldly as "the human community that successfully claims the monopoly of the legitimate use of physical force within a given territory." But while he wanted sociology to be scientific, he did not believe that it could formulate laws like those of the physical sciences. Rather than trying to establish laws, sociology should concern itself with ideal types—with general concepts like "nationalism" or "the Protestant ethic"—which serve as tools for analyzing empirical data. All twentieth-century Western social science is heavily indebted to Weber's methodology.

Like Hegel, by whom he was influenced, Weber was fascinated by power. He devoted much effort to the scientific analysis of the bases of power in society, producing important studies of bureaucracy and charisma—two antithetical means by which power is obtained and consolidated. To Weber, notions of justice, the common weal, and the like had no place in political analysis. Politics was power, nothing more and nothing less. One could choose to place his faith in one form of government or another, but from a sociological viewpoint no political system enjoyed any special value. "I do not give a damn about the forms of the state," Weber declared. "Forms of state are for me techniques like any other machinery." For Weber, politics was the study of the techniques of power. No amount of wishful thinking could erase the fact that every human institution embodied the will to power.

Psychology and Psychoanalysis

The third academic discipline that developed in the late nineteenth century was psychology. It is an open question whether this field should be classified as a natural science or as a social science. Of all the new disciplines, psychology had the most profound impact upon the general public. Psychology radically altered man's view of himself.

Modern psychology may be said to date from 1879, when the German Wilhelm Wundt (1832–1900) established the first psychological laboratory. Like many later psychologists, Wundt conducted experiments involving animals. In a few years, psychologists all over Europe and the United States were conducting similar experiments and writing articles for learned journals. The dominant trend or "school" of psychology in these years was known as behaviorism. Behaviorist psychologists felt that behavior was the proper object of psychological research. Experimenting with animals and humans, they sought to establish how and why their subjects responded to certain stimuli.

One of the most important early behaviorists was Ivan Pavlov (1849–1936), a Russian who conducted a series of famous experiments in which he "conditioned" dogs to salivate upon hearing a bell. The work of Pavlov and other behaviorists raised the age-old problem of freedom and determinism. Psychological research implied that men, like dogs, had no freedom of choice at all. All human behavior could be explained scientifically in terms of conditioning or training. Our choices were determined, our responses were conditioned, and therefore we were not free. The conception of man as a rational, responsible, free moral agent was in great peril.

Yet it was a decidedly nonbehaviorist Viennese physician, Sigmund Freud (1856–1939), whose work was most influential in changing Western man's conception of his own nature. Freud was born into a humble Austrian Jewish family. It is said that he was a precocious child of rather more than normal sexual curiosity, deeply attached to his mother. As a young doctor, he specialized in the treatment of nervous disorders called neuroses. He became interested in psychology when he discovered that the traditional ways of treating neuroses did not work. The need for a new method led him to investigate the inner world of mental processes. What emerged from this work was not only a new treatment for neuroses but a new theory of the mind, a new vision of man, and a new interpretation of man's culture.

From talking with his neurotic patients, Freud concluded that the causes of nervous disorders lay in painful past events that were forcibly forgotten, or "repressed" into the subconscious, that part of the human mind that lies below consciousness. The discovery that there were "powerful mental processes . . . hidden from the consciousness of men" was truly revolutionary. Freud went on to declare that the subconscious was more powerful than the rational realm of consciousness. The subconscious knows no ethical restrictions. It maximizes vital human needs, the most important of which is sex. Freud believed that human motivation was basically irrational and that the sexual drive was the main component of that irrationality.

Freud's theory of the subconscious became the basis of psychoanalysis, the method he devised for the treatment of neuroses. While the body of Freud's work remained extremely controversial within and beyond the field of psychology, the main outlines of his technique were widely accepted in the 1920's and 1930's. The major element in psychoanalysis is "free association," whereby the patient speaks freely of his thoughts and dreams, enabling the doctor to descend into the depths of the patient's subconscious. The doctor helps the patient to remember repressed episodes by interpreting the patient's dreams, which Freud regarded as products of the subconscious. Freud was quick to admit that psychoanalysis was as much an art as a science, since it depended on the skill of the doctor and the cooperation of the patient.

By far the most controversial and unscientific aspect of Freud's work was his interpretation of human culture. He viewed man's conscious or rational life as the result of repressed instinct, especially sexual instinct. Freud declared everything conscious—all knowledge, art, music, religion—to be the product of repression and sexual frustration. On one occasion he spoke of "that repression of instinct upon which what is most valuable in human culture is built." So all-encompassing was the Freudian "system" that Freud felt he could explain all of human history in psychoanalytic terms. In *Totem and*

Tabu (1918) he interpreted religion, morality, and social life itself as products of the "Oedipus complex."

Whatever one may think of the Freudian system, it can probably be said that Freud has been the most influential intellectual figure of the twentieth century. His impact on Western culture has been as great as that of Marx or Darwin or even Newton. During his own lifetime he attracted a host of disciples, some of whom—like Alfred Adler (1870–1937) and Carl Jung (1875–1961)—eventually broke with the master and founded their own schools. He has been criticized severely within the field of psychology for the vagueness of his concepts, but it is surely a mark of his greatness that many of them —"repression," "ego," and the like—have become so much a part of our thinking that they are virtual clichés. Finally, it is easy to do Freud an injustice by emphasizing certain aspects of his thought to the exclusion of others. His *Civilization and its Discontents* indicates that he was basically a moralist who wanted to help people accommodate themselves to society's repressive regimen.

Under the impact of the relativistic conclusions of the cultural anthropologists, the sociologists, and the behaviorist psychologists, the traditional values, received ideas, and moral homilies of Western man were seriously eroded. After Sigmund Freud, the whole structure of easy, liberal, rational confidence was critically weakened.

The Exact Sciences

Between 1870 and 1918 numerous important discoveries in the exact sciences were made; our chief concern is with their impact upon Western culture. Thus far, we have observed on the one hand a general reaction against science in the field of philosophy and on the other the application of scientific methods to the new social sciences. Yet the philosophers who decried the scientific method and the social scientists who embraced it were almost totally unaware of what was actually going on in the physical sciences. For during these years there occurred a veritable revolution that eventually changed the scientists' own conception of the nature and function of their work and profoundly altered Western man's view of the material world. It is fair to speculate that if the philosophers and social scientists had known of these developments, the philosophers would have been less hostile, the social scientists more humble.

Basic to these changes in the exact sciences were some important developments in mathematics. Between 1910 and 1913 two Englishmen who later became eminent philosophers—Alfred North Whitehead (1861–1947) and Bertrand Russell (b. 1872)—published their *Principia Mathematica*, a systematic derivation of mathematics from pure logic. The significance of the work lay in the fact that it set forth a symbolic logic quite different from traditional Aristotelian logic. Symbolic logic became the analytical tool of important movements in later twentieth-century philosophy.

Among the many important discoveries in the biological sciences, the most significant was in genetics. The origin, nature, and frequency of observable hereditary traits were explained for the first time, in physiological as well as quantitative and statistical terms. The father of genetic theory was Gregor Mendel (1822–1884), an Augustinian monk who conducted a series of important experiments involving the crossbreeding of peas. Mendel hypothesized that inheritance was particulate in character—that is, that hereditary traits were produced by certain tiny particles known as *genes*. These discrete conveyors of inheritable traits, Mendel continued, combine in certain statistically predictable ways, generating hereditary traits that are similarly predictable. In short, heredity was both explicable and predictable.

Mendel's experimental results fully confirmed his hypothesis, but his revolutionary work went largely unnoticed for three decades. The real breakthrough in genetics came in 1903, when Walter S. Sutton (1876–1916) demonstrated that Mendel's results could be explained in terms of the cytological behavior of chromosomes. In a few years it became clear to biologists that genes were linked to chromosomes. Mendel and the other formulators of genetic theory had opened up a whole new field of scientific research.

But the true revolution in science and scientific theory occurred in physics. Since the days of Newton, most educated people had made certain assumptions about the material world, including the following: (1) that certain material causes produced certain material effects; (2) that these causes and effects could be explained in terms of laws which were valid at all times and in all places; (3) that an objective knowledge of these laws was possible, at least in theory; and (4) that space, time, matter, energy, and motion were distinct and absolute. All the previous scientific discoveries of the nineteenth century both accepted these assumptions and confirmed them. Further, it was universally accepted that the basic unit of matter was the atom—one, indivisible, and indestructible. Roughly speaking, these ideas constituted the Newtonian world picture.

The old view began to break down as a result of studies in the field of radiation: certain experimental results in radiation research could not be explained within the framework of the Newtonian system. Out of radiation research there developed an enormously complicated "new physics," which was concerned with the problems of energy and atomic structure. With each fresh discovery in this new field of scientific endeavor, the crisis in scientific thinking became more acute.

Before 1900 it was thought that energy existed in constantly flowing streams or showers, but in that year Max Planck (1858–1947) of Germany enunciated the famous quantum theory, in which energy was said to exist in small bits or packages called *quanta*. The quantum theory implied that the atom itself was a unit of energy rather than a tangible, continuous piece of matter. This idea was carried one step further in 1911 by Ernest Rutherford (1871–1937) of Great Britain, who compared the structure of the atom to the solar system, and again in 1913 by Niels Bohr (1885–1962) of Denmark, who constructed a nuclear model of the atom.

The leading figure in the new physics was Albert Einstein (1879–1955), who almost single-handedly brought about a fundamental revision of accepted Newtonian concepts. Born to a middle-class German Jewish family, Einstein had a checkered career at school and university. He finally found a job in the Swiss patent office, which gave him plenty of leisure time to pursue his scientific speculations. It soon transpired that Einstein had not impressed his teachers favorably because he was so original a thinker. In 1905 he announced his "special theory of relativity," in which he challenged traditional concepts of space, time, and motion. Far from being absolute and measurable, observed space, time, and motion are relative to the space, time, and motion of the measurer or observer. Moreover, Einstein rejected the separateness of space and time by positing the existence of a four-dimensional space-time continuum. Nor was mass discrete, since it increased with an increase in velocity. Finally, in his famous equation $E = mc^2$, Einstein declared that matter and energy were interchangeable: energy equals mass times the square of the speed of light.

The implications of Einstein's theory were startling to the scientific community and to the world of thought beyond the laboratory. The concept of a relativity of space, time, and motion bore an obvious similarity to moral relativism, and in a general way Einstein's theory of relativity speeded the development of relativism in the other disciplines. The supposedly universal laws of Newton were not valid in the physical world, and as a consequence, thinkers questioned whether universal laws of any sort could or should be formulated. Einstein had remarked at one point that objective knowledge of cause and effect might not be possible even in the exact sciences. In atomic research, he said, the most one could hope for was a high degree of statistical probability. Stimulated by his thoughts, men in other disciplines began to wonder if an objective knowledge of anything was possible—perhaps they, too, would have to settle for a high statistical probability.

Whether the discoveries in physics have disproved the accepted notions of "causality" and "objectivity" remains questionable, but it is clear that the work of Einstein and other physicists has contributed to the steady decline of these concepts. And it is also clear that the substitution of statistical probability for absolute knowledge as a goal for science profoundly changed the character of scientific thought.

IV UPHEAVAL IN THE ARTS

Literature

Most of the leading literary figures of the late nineteenth century struggled with the question: What relationship, if any, exists—or should exist—between the arts and the "real" world? Two distinct literary movements emerged with answers: for convenience sake we may loosely characterize them as the Naturalists and the Symbolists. The Naturalists presumed that man could be explained in the terms used by scientists to explain the natural world and by sociologists to analyze human society. In the main, they believed that man was the product of heredity and environment and that literature should concern itself with this indisputable fact. Accepting the material world as real, the Naturalists felt that literature must be realistic. It should concern itself with problems of men living in society. Thus the world of art and the wider world beyond were one and indivisible. The artist need not be happy with the world, but he should address himself to its problems. The Naturalists believed that the artist could participate in, and contribute to, an objective understanding of the world.

The Naturalist school in literature was essentially a continuation of earlier realism, but Naturalism was inevitably affected by the scientific and philosophical developments of the late nineteenth century. Hence Naturalism lacked the underlying note of liberal optimism about man and society that was still prevalent in the 1850's. The Naturalists tended to be deeply pessimistic.

The Symbolists believed that objective knowledge of the world was impossible or simply uninteresting for purposes of art. For most of them the external world was not real at all but only a collection of symbols reflecting the true reality of the individual human mind. The proper study of literature was the inner working of this mind. The world of imagination and the arts was a subjective realm where infinite beauty was possible, in contrast to the hopelessly ugly material world. Rather then serving society, criticizing it, or seeking to understand it, art should function for its own sake. The name "Symbolist" was originally applied to a rather small group of esoteric French writers who gathered around the poet Stéphane Mallarmé in Paris in the 1870's and 1880's. But the Symbolist orientation—away from any involvement with mundane matters—was far more general.

As in all ages, the greatest literary masters transcended the prevailing antipodes. Whereas most literary figures concentrated on society or on self, the greatest novelist of the period, Count Leo Tolstoi (1828–1910), was equally at home in both worlds. A wealthy Russian landowner, he survived a period of youthful dissipation and a term of military service in the Crimea to become extremely concerned with the problem of the peasantry. He personally established a strikingly modern education system for peasants under his control. At the same time he pursued a busy literary career, publishing many moral pamphlets and short stories as well as his brilliant novels.

Considered by many to be the finest novel ever written, *War and Peace* (1865–1872) is a panoramic history of five Russian families during the Napoleonic period. The book exhibits all the richness and variety of human life, portraying Frenchmen and Russians, rural folk and urban dwellers, army officers and civilians, aristocrats and peasants, and, of course, war and peace. In his mammoth work Tolstoi showed himself to be a profound observer of human society as well as of the very depths of the human mind and personality. Revealing deep moral concerns, the book poses the question: Should one live for oneself or for others? This unresolved conflict, which was Tolstoi's own spiritual predicament, continues in *Anna Karenina* (1875–1876). Set in Russia in the 1860's, this rather pessimistic novel deals with the hypocrisies of society and the tragedy of human life. Tolstoi implicitly condemns Russian aristocratic society for punishing the heroine, whose only crime is her honesty in confessing to a love affair.

Tolstoi was rapidly approaching a spiritual crisis when he finished *Anna Karenina*. After several attempts at suicide, he found meaning for his life in the person, message, and example of Christ. Believing that obedience to Christ involved living for others in simple, apostolic poverty, he wrote books and articles on his faith and engaged in a range of philanthropic activities. In time he became an anarchist, condemning the czarist state and the institution of private property. The conflict between his political-religious ideas and his status as an aristocratic landowner grew too great, and shortly before his death he left his family and his property to lead the simple life of a religious hermit. Throughout his life, Tolstoi felt that personal salvation and the problems of the world were intimately linked.

The Norwegian-born dramatist Henrik Ibsen (1828–1906) began his career firmly rooted in the Naturalist school. His early plays dealt with the contemporary problems of European society. A good bourgeois himself, Ibsen felt both guilt and responsibility for his class. Set in Norwegian middle-class society of the 1870's, his plays—*Ghosts, A Doll's House,* and *The Pillars of Society*—bitterly attack the hypocrisy and "respectability" of the bourgeoisie. They express Ibsen's passionate devotion to truth by exposing the raw facts about middle-class lives. Their frank treatment of such "delicate" topics as marital discord, venereal disease, and women's rights has established Ibsen as a champion of modernity. But he was interested in the problems of the inner life as well. His later works are full of tragic characters who ask questions for which they can find no satisfactory answers. And despite his passion for truth, in *The Wild Duck* the playwright suggests that people need lies in order to bear the burdens of life; human beings may be too weak to live with the truth after all.

Commensurate with Ibsen in stature as one of the founders of modern drama was the Swede, August Strindberg (1849–1912). More markedly than Ibsen, Strindberg moved steadily away from Naturalism as he grew older, and his later works, *The Ghost Sonata* and *A Dream Play*, prefigure the mid-twentieth-century Theater of the Absurd. Strindberg's early plays, *The Father* and *Miss Julie*, are masterpieces of Naturalism. *Miss Julie* is a brutal play about class struggle acted out as sexual conflict between an aristocratic girl and a valet. A few years later Strindberg departed radically from real-

ism. He now wrote that it was his aim to "reproduce the detached and disunited—although apparently logical—form of dreams." Not only his style but
his sensibilities had altered. *A Dream Play* suggests that it is not society but
the mind itself which is the agent of human frustration. Our vision, idealism, and imagination, far from being blessings, doom us to eternal pain. Our
deepest desires can never be attained.

This stark and tragic tone was sounded in theaters across Europe at the
turn of the century. This was a period of extraordinary vitality in the theater.
But the messages of the new playwrights tended to be very gloomy indeed.
Gerhard Hauptmann (1862–1946), a German Naturalist, produced powerful
but gruesome studies of alcoholism, domestic disorder, and class struggle. *The
Weavers*, a play about exploited Silesian textile workers, is one of the earliest
and best examples of "proletarian drama." *Spring's Awakening*, by Frank
Wedekind (1864–1918), brought the unheard-of subject of childhood sexuality
to the stage at a time when the European middle class was still ignorant of
Freud and utterly unprepared to discuss such matters in public. The great
Russian dramatist and short-story writer Anton Chekhov (1860–1904) wrote
about the decadence of the Russian gentry. *The Cherry Orchard*, *The Three
Sisters*, and *Uncle Vanya* depict with loving irony the vacuous lives of the
emotionally and economically bankrupt upper classes. Chekhov's characters
are charming but impotent and pathetic. They struggle lethargically with
forces they cannot quite comprehend or control. One senses about them what
the Russian Revolution later confirmed: that they were doomed to perish.
Futility characterizes their lives; it was Chekhov's abiding theme.

The foremost British dramatist of the day was George Bernard Shaw
(1856–1950). Born in Ireland, Shaw lived most of his life in London, where
he was a leader of the Fabians. Like the Continental playwrights, he took a
hard, unsentimental look at hypocrisy and snobbery in society. The biting
mockery of his dramas gained him a reputation as an uncompromising social
critic and an unabashed iconoclast. Unlike many self-styled reformers, however, he possessed a delightful, trenchant wit that exposed the sham of conventional attitudes in plays like *Major Barbara*, *St. Joan*, and *Pygmalion*. In
his masterpiece, *Man and Superman*, Shaw established himself as a vitalist
and an irrationalist in the tradition of Nietzsche and Bergson by celebrating
what he called the "Life-Force."

Vitalism and irrationalism also pervade the writings of the greatest English novelist of the age, D. H. Lawrence (1885–1930). Lawrence is most
famous for treating erotic themes with great beauty and frankness, but,
while sex dominates almost all his novels, he was passionately concerned
with society as well. His first novel, *Sons and Lovers* (1913), powerfully
evoked life in the small mining community where he was reared.

Lawrence could never reconcile himself to the indignities perpetrated on the
human spirit by industrialism. The industrial society which he saw around
him frustrated man's deepest feelings for beauty, spontaneity, and community

and stifled all human instincts save the desire for material gain. He celebrated sex as the last area of human life where these instincts could still be affirmed. Lawrence saw himself as fighting a rearguard action against modernity, which, he felt, threatened to denature man. He was a fierce individualist who hated all modern forms of government. Socialism, democracy, liberalism, conservatism—all were oppressive; all were dehumanizing men. Lawrence arrived at the paradoxical conclusion that man had to assert his animal, instinctual nature in order to retain his humanity.

Lawrence was not the only literary figure to quarrel violently with the society around him. The French novelist Émile Zola (1840–1902) was sentenced to a year in prison for his role in the defense of Captain Dreyfus. Zola saw his literary work as an important part of his activity as social critic and social reformer. Much impressed by science, he sought to apply scientific techniques to literature and became a complete Naturalist. In an attempt to present a full, scientific picture of the influence of heredity and environment upon bourgeois society, he wrote some twenty novels on the Rougon-Macquart family. Although highly popular in his day, Zola's works are very uneven and most critics would dispute his claim that he explained bourgeois society completely.

In England the most distinguished Naturalist to appear was Thomas Hardy (1840–1928). Hardy's novels, *The Return of the Native, Tess of the d'Urbevilles*, and *Jude the Obscure*, are set in Wessex, a remote part of England where the customs and superstitions of the peasantry still linger. But Hardy was anything but nostalgic for the old order. One of the characters in *Jude* speaks for her creator when she laments that "the social moulds civilization fits us into have no more relation to our actual shapes than the conventional shapes of the constellations have to the real star-patterns." Yet Hardy's quarrel ultimately was not with society but with an absent God. Hardy belonged to the generation which had read and digested Darwin and Huxley, but he could derive no comfort from their conclusions. Darwin had taught him that man and nature were constantly at war. Without God as mediator, man in his struggle for happiness was at the mercy of blind chance. In fact, chance or fate is not so much blind in Hardy's works as downright malevolent. His heroes never attain happiness. The most sensitive and idealistic among them fare the worst. Hardy was not a profound philosopher; his great reliance on chance and accident as destroyers of human happiness was a kind of literary shorthand for psychological and social contradictions which he sensed acutely but could not always clearly conceptualize.

In American literature, Naturalism emerged as a current in the immensely popular work of Mark Twain (Samuel L. Clemens, 1835–1910). Mixed in with homespun frontier humor and Romantic sentimentality, a sharply critical view of American social institutions distinguished Twain's novels. In his finest work, *Huckleberry Finn* (1885), Twain dealt in deceptively lighthearted fashion with highly serious issues: the universality of humanity as against racial division; individual ideals in conflict with social mores; and the repressive tendencies of civilized society.

Naturalism in America reached its full flowering in the works of Theodore Dreiser (1871–1945). After leaving school Dreiser spent several years working at odd jobs, struggling to break into the world of power and money. His novels, *Sister Carrie, The Financier, The Tycoon,* and *An American Tragedy,* are all concerned with people who are "on the make." He studied with the cold-bloodedness of a scientist the lives of those who had imbibed the American dream and spent their days trying to live by the values of self-help, initiative, and enterprise. He concluded that the strong survived and the weak perished and nobody was very happy. His favorite hero was the American businessman caught in the rat race of success, always pursued by nagging unhappiness. Dreiser was not one of the muckrakers who attacked big business: it fascinated him. He knew that he himself shared the values of his heroes; he too was hungry for prestige, power, and money even though he recognized the disastrous moral consequences they produced.

Of the many studies of middle-class family life, the most distinguished were those of Thomas Mann and John Galsworthy. Himself a member of the upper middle class, the English novelist Galsworthy (1867–1933) was able to write critically yet sympathetically of the problems of this sector of society. His *Forsyte Saga* is a probing analysis of the virtues and vices of a typical Edwardian bourgeois family. The German novelist Thomas Mann (1875–1955), whom many regard as the finest German writer since Goethe, was a bourgeois like Galsworthy, and he wrote of the middle class with the same subtle mixture of affection and contempt but with greater insight and stylistic grace. In his classic novel *Buddenbrooks* (1901), Mann showed acute sensitivity to the standard middle-class characteristics—respectability, crassness, devotion to family and property—but he also captured the pathos of this segment of human kind. In *Buddenbrooks* the bourgeois family is in a state of grave crisis, and it is not capable of meeting the challenge. Mann believed that, whatever else one might think of bourgeois society, there was no use denying its decadence. He and Galsworthy both concluded that the so-called values of the middle class served only to dull its artistic and moral potential.

Thus far we have discussed novelists and dramatists who were interested in the problems of society and who used literature as a vehicle of social analysis and criticism. The most popular British poet of the period, Rudyard Kipling (1865–1936), was less interested in criticizing society than in celebrating and encouraging Britain's self-styled imperial mission. He was a marvelous storyteller; many of his best tales deal with India, where he was born and where he was later a journalist. Kipling's real significance lies not in the literary merit of his work, which was uneven, but in the major role he played in the development of imperial sentiment in England.

The sheer quantity and variety of the short stories, literary criticism, novels, biographies, and reminiscences by the eminent French man of letters, Anatole France (1844–1924), defies adequate capsule description. He dominated French literature for over a generation and enjoyed the greatest reputation of any French writer since the days of Voltaire. France is an interesting transitional figure. His early ideas were similar to those of the Symbolists. Aloof, even indifferent to the everyday world, he felt that beauty and art alone were worthwhile. But the Dreyfus affair changed all that, and after 1900 France became deeply involved in politics and wrote a number of novels which were politically revolutionary in tone. His greatest work, *Mr. Bergeret in Paris*, is a study of French society before and during the Dreyfus affair.

Symbolists—or authors who were more interested in the workings of the mind than in social problems—reacted against Naturalists like Ibsen, Dreiser, and Zola. In the main, Naturalism was the prevailing tendency of the late nineteenth century, and Symbolism was more characteristic of the early twentieth century. In general, too, Naturalism was strongest in the drama and the novel, whereas poetry was the special province of the Symbolists.

The greatest lyric poet of the age, William Butler Yeats (1865–1939), was an Irishman and the son of a Romantic painter. As a young man he participated in the general turn-of-the-century revolt against the excesses and the pretensions of Naturalism. His early poetry shows the influence of the French Symbolists and the English visionary Romantic, William Blake. Yeats also drew on Celtic mythology to create a delightful pagan fairyland in his verse. But he soon became dissatisfied with this misty romanticism. Against his natural instincts, which told him to dwell in the world of feeling and imagination, he was drawn into the fierce struggles of the Irish nationalists of his day. His sense of duty and responsibility was too strong for him to ignore the demands of the world. He both loved and despised his countrymen, who intruded their virulent politics into his art. This painful tension with society lasted throughout his entire life and produced some of his greatest poems, including *Easter 1916* and *Sailing to Byzantium*. His later poetry had an austerity and tragic grandeur which most Symbolist poetry lacked.

Yeats affirmed the glory and dignity of the human condition, for all its pain. But the verse of Rainer Rilke (1875–1926), the most famous modern German poet, concentrated upon the darker aspects of human experience. After a most abnormal childhood, Rilke was troubled by internal tensions and contradictions when he came under the intoxicating influence of the Symbolists in Paris, where he lived from 1902 until the First World War. One of the poet's early creations, *The Book of Hours*, revealed his highly developed subjectivity in characteristically delightful rhythms and rich imagery. Rilke's own mind and spirit were beset with anguish; he was keenly aware of man's loneliness, weakness, and frailty, and he was obsessed with the idea of death.

The Austrian lyric poet Hugo von Hofmannsthal (1874–1929) played a major role in the "Art for Art's sake" movement. A confirmed aesthete in his early years, Hofmannsthal sensed a great gulf between the inner life and ordinary life in the material world. But in time the poet came to feel that there should be no gulf and that its existence was the fault of the artist. *Death and the Fool* is a picture of his own spiritual crisis. The poet has gone through life as a spectator. He has never been a part of the world, nor has he ever known the world in any meaningful sense; and as a consequence he does not even know himself. He does know that to be aloof from the world is not only harmful but positively evil. Sensing his human and moral isolation, Hofmannsthal broke with the "Art for Art's sake" poets at the age of twenty-five. Like Rilke, he was preoccupied with death. His spiritual saga was similar to that of many artists and intellectuals in prewar Europe.

Although it would be misleading to label Joseph Conrad (1857–1924) a Symbolist, he was far more interested in problems of the self than in those of society. Polish by birth, Conrad became devoted to England, his adopted country, and is considered one of the masters of English prose. His early life was spent at sea, the setting of many of his novels and short stories. But Conrad was no mere teller of exotic tales. The sea became a backdrop against which the facts of human nature and human existence could be seen most starkly. One of Conrad's most famous works, *Heart of Darkness* (which was based upon his own trip up the Congo River), is the chilling story of an idealistic European's reversion to savagery in the African jungle. Conrad was deeply pessimistic about human nature. He felt that men's lawless, destructive instincts could never be eradicated. By implication, European civilization was a fragile structure; the primordial chaos was very close.

Chaos was also the concern of Franz Kafka (1883–1924), a German novelist whose work has greatly influenced twentieth-century literature. Kafka's chaos was not the jungle but the lucid, apparently logical chaos of bureaucracies. The heroes of *The Castle* and *The Trial*, Kafka's most famous novels, dwell in a world that is clear, ordered, and utterly mad. Inaccessible public authorities give them an endless run-around. No questions are ever satisfactorily answered, no keys can be found to unlock doors. His works have the awful clarity of nightmares. They have been praised as brilliant depictions of the human mind struggling to come to grips with a vicious totalitarianism. But Kafka was no social critic; the ordered madness was not the fault of a political regime—it was endemic in the universe itself. His overriding concern was the anguish of the human mind trying to find meaning in a universe where man's fate is never explained and everyone is doomed to live in fearful spiritual isolation.

The greatest literary master of psychology was the French novelist Marcel Proust (1871–1922). The spoiled child of rich parents, Proust was extremely self-indulgent and perpetually dissatisfied. The first major figure to apply Symbolist ideas to the novel, Proust felt no need to relate to social problems. Moreover, he was heavily influenced by Henri Bergson's concept of the consciousness of time in the human mind, and this idea became an important element in his multivolume novel, *Remembrance of Things Past* (1913–1927). On the surface a study of the frivolity and decadence of the middle and upper classes of French society, on a deeper level it is perhaps the classic exposition of Symbolist ideas. The theme of this extremely subtle, pessimistic work is that it is impossible to achieve any measure of knowledge of the external world, to master its inscrutable ways, or to find fulfillment in it. One cannot find happiness in relationships with other people. If happiness and knowledge are possible at all, they will be realized only when the mind concerns itself with its own inner workings. Only the inner world is real, knowable, and desirable. The genius of Proust lay in his intimate understanding of conscious and unconscious mental processes, of that inner universe of dreams, memories, wishes, perceptions, forgotten memories, and pure imagination. Proust dissected the essence of the human psyche.

Like Proust, the American novelist Henry James (1843–1916) was a master of psychological insight. The brother of the distinguished Harvard psychologist and philosopher William James, he left America as a young man to live as an expatriate in England. James felt that Europe alone could provide him with the refined civilization and the refined sensibilities he sought. He needed to be surrounded by an aristocracy, an established Church, country houses, and beautiful works of art. He peered at European society like a cultivated, highly appreciative voyeur. His characters are drawn from the international set of the 1880's and 1890's. They consist chiefly of rich American heiresses, English aristocrats, and Continental adventurers. Many of his works (such as *The Portrait of a Lady* and *The Ambassadors*) have as their theme the initiation of high-spirited, innocent Americans into the sophistication and corruption of an older civilization. James was an aesthete for whom truth was to be found in the subtle sensibilities of his highly cultivated heroes and heroines. Though he set his stories in various parts of Europe and America, his range was really very narrow. He was interested exclusively in fine shades of feeling and somewhat tenuous moral distinctions.

Painting

The period from 1870 to 1918 was one of the most fertile in the history of art. It was distinguished by a number of important schools and movements, some of which arose in reaction to others but all of which shared certain characteristics. In the first place, no major artist of this period attempted to copy nature—this could now be left to the camera. Some artists painted what they felt; others tried to represent the unorganized data of the visual senses; still others attempted to impose the rational concepts of the human mind upon nature. Moreover, each artist aimed at eliciting a certain response from the viewer. Thus, the purpose of painting was to create a visual experience by means of color, shape, feeling, and atmosphere.

Modern art begins with the movement called Impressionism, which may be dated from 1874, when Claude Monet's "Impression—Sunrise" was first exhibited in Paris. Although at first *Impressionism* was a term of derision, it is actually quite appropriate in that it suggests art which appears rather unfinished or incomplete. Impressionist art was based upon a new theory, in which light and color took precedence over everything else in the raw data of visual sensation. In fact, the Impressionist painters believed that form, space, perspective, and the like, were artificial concepts imposed on the unorganized data of sense experience by the rational mind. It was the immediacy of visual sensation—the momentary experience of human vision—that the Impressionists hoped to capture. Since the artists believed light and color to be the primary stuff of visual experience, Impressionist paintings are extremely colorful; detail is suggested with broad patches of color instead of being reproduced as in a photograph, and color is used to achieve perspective. Thus we may characterize Impressionism as the art of sensation rather than of reason.

Yet Impressionism was also objective in that the Impressionists intended their canvases to be exact records of visual experience. There were no messages or morals in Impressionist paintings. Nor was there any emotional involvement on the part of the artist or of the viewer. Feeling and psychological depth were utterly lacking. Virtually indifferent to the content of their artistic creation, the Impressionists often painted casual, fleeting, random scenes from everyday urban life, working out of doors in order to capture the immediacy of visual experience. Their one goal was to create a color experience in the eye of the viewer.

The Impressionist school centered in Paris during the years 1874–1886 and was composed largely of French artists, led by Claude Monet (1840–1926). Monet is noted for capturing the effect of light playing on water and for conveying that intangible quality known as atmosphere. He often painted the same subject many times, recording the changes caused by variations in light, weather, and atmosphere. One such series of paintings dealt with Rouen Cathedral. Besides Monet, Auguste Renoir (1841–1919) and Édouard Manet (1832–1883) were major figures in the Impressionist school. All were often accused of hasty work and faulty craftsmanship. But these charges reflected a failure to understand Impressionist art, which required careful and painstaking work and displayed astonishing skill in the use of color.

Like all similar styles, Impressionism had definite limits and reached them in the mid-1880's. The next generation of painters, known as the Postimpressionists, retained the emphasis upon light and color but paid attention to more formal aspects of painting which the Impressionists had scorned. Georges Seurat (1859–1891), for example, replaced the broad patches of color characteristic of Impressionism with thousands of tiny dots of color—a painstaking technique known as pointillism. This logical, scientific method brought Impressionism to an almost mathematical conclusion.

The Postimpressionist movement in painting begins with the work of Paul

Cézanne (1839–1906). Cézanne considered the colorful Impressionist paintings too superficial and advocated more stability in art, more distinct line and form. In short, Cézanne wanted painting to become an activity of the mind and heart as well as the eye; he wished for an emotional and psychological dimension that was lacking in Impressionism. Cézanne's own paintings are ordered, stable, and deep. They must be studied; their structure is never immediately obvious. Cézanne was also influential as an art theorist. Wishing to unite the mind with the world of nature, he suggested that all of the natural could be reduced to the pure geometrical shapes of the cone, the cylinder, and the sphere. Later this notion served as a kind of bridge between Postimpressionism and nonrepresentational painting, and for this reason Cézanne is often considered the true father of modern art.

The Postimpressionist movement was carried further by Vincent van Gogh (1853–1890) and Paul Gauguin (1848–1903), who thought Cézanne was too much involved in the architecture of form. They wanted to use color and line to express inner feelings. "With green and red, I have tried to express those terrible things, men's passions," van Gogh said. Born in Holland, he spent his creative life in France. After bouts of madness, he committed suicide. In his brilliant landscapes van Gogh succeeded in uniting the material with the spiritual and in joining the medium of color with the subject matter. Gauguin was a prosperous stockbroker until a slump in the market gave him an opportunity to leave the financial world and devote himself exclusively to painting. Deserting his bourgeois family, he moved to Tahiti where he spent his later years and did his best work. Gauguin was fascinated by primitive art because he sensed that preliterate people used painting for expression of their private feelings. Gauguin's purpose was "to clothe the idea in visual form," to use form and color to express "beautiful thoughts." Gauguin's work, like van Gogh's, represents a transition from Impressionism to Expressionism and beyond to twentieth-century abstract art.

The school of Expressionism was formed in reaction against the dispassion of the Impressionists, against their lack of personal involvement with their subject matter. By contrast, Expressionist paintings were highly emotional; they represented a conscious expression of the psychological makeup of the painter and were designed to elicit emotion from the observer. Turning away from the objective world, the Expressionists concentrated upon feeling; to create emotional depth, they exaggerated color and distorted outlines and shapes. Expressionist art is highly subjective and frequently emphasizes the dark, the horrible, and the evil.

Expressionism flourished in the decade before World War I. In France, the Expressionist painters were known as the *Fauves* (Wild Beasts)—a term of derision which reminds us that all the great artistic innovations of the age experienced an initial period of public hostility. The most important of these "Wild Beasts" was the eminently sophisticated Henri Matisse (1869–1954). Expressionism was also very strong in Germany, where important schools were centered in Dresden and Munich. The leading Munich Expressionist was Wassily Kandinsky (1866–1944), a Russian whose paintings were distinguished by undulating, pulsating curves. Kandinsky began by painting the usual objects from the natural world, but in 1913 he abandoned nature entirely and turned to the purely abstract. Significantly, Kandinsky believed that the content of his paintings lay not in what was represented on the canvas (for nothing was "represented," properly speaking) but in what the viewer felt as a result of the artist's arrangement of form and color.

The first sustained movement of pure abstract art was known as Cubism; it developed from Cézanne's famous remark that all nature could be reduced to the forms of the cylinder, the sphere, and the cone. In the years before World War I, Georges Braque (1882–1963) and Pablo Picasso (b. 1881), working together in Paris, formulated the theoretical foundations of Cubist art. According to their theories, painting should in no way attempt to imitate nature but rather should impose upon nature the geometrical forms contained in the human mind. Cubism represented the artistic victory of intellectual order over matter.

In its early stages, Cubist art was highly theoretical, rational, and abstract; the paintings were cold, unemotional studies. Eschewing the orgy of color in which the Impressionists had indulged, Cubist painters preferred bland, neutral tones and an emphasis upon shapes, lines, and angles. In some cases they suggested the shape of natural objects; in others they played with pure geometrical designs. Cubism was famous for radical experiments with perspective: many paintings represented objects from several points of view simultaneously. If Impressionism was the art of the eye and Expressionism the art of the heart, Cubism was the art of the mind.

Shortly before and during the First World War, the avenue to nonrepresentational art opened up by Expressionism and Cubism ran off in several experimental directions. Self-conscious rebellion, the shattering of order and coherence, and the perverse beauty of the macabre and the absurd spawned avant-garde artistic movements that adopted provocative titles like Futurism and Dadaism. Futurism was centered in Italy; its aim was to celebrate the exuberance of action, of movement and speed, particularly in the technological world. Dadaism centered originally in Switzerland but became international; Dadaists sought to express the anarchism and nihilism that was central to the culture of the era.

Architecture

Throughout most of the nineteenth century, public and private architecture was overwhelmingly imitative, producing numerous Greco-Roman and Gothic post offices, libraries, and railroad stations that offended the sophisticated and artistic. The first reaction to this unimaginative style was *Art Nouveau*, a movement that originated among a group of Belgian architects and eventually spread throughout Europe. *Art Nouveau* signified both a style of architecture and an ornamental technique for vases, jewelry, and similar private effects. Extremely ornate and elaborate, its characteristic continuous flow of curved lines on the model of flowers and peacock fans became fashionable in the decoration of homes, shops, restaurants, and public buildings. In a way this style was a perfect artistic expression of the frivolous prosperity of the European middle class during the years before 1914. Behind the obvious frivolity, however, there was a high seriousness. *Art Nouveau* broke with traditional styles in decoration and architecture and expressed a personal vision, thereby heralding an architectural revolution.

The architectural revolution achieved its first triumphs in the United States, where Louis Sullivan (1856–1924) led the movement known as functionalism. According to this school, the form of a building ought to be determined by the function it is to serve, which should be frankly revealed in its lines. Functionalism honestly recognized the advent of the industrial age and no longer tried to disguise the purpose of an office or factory building. The new attitude inspired the office buildings in the American Midwest that Sullivan designed in 1891–1895. Although inclined to the use of heavy ornamentation in the *Art Nouveau* style, Sullivan revealed the linear and rectangular shape of his structures and forcefully exhibited their commercial and financial function. Sullivan's leading disciple, Frank Lloyd Wright (1869–1959), transformed functionalism into the broader concept of "organic" architecture. According to Wright, all architecture should be organic in the sense that it should harmonize both with its uses and with its physical setting. Although the bulk of his work was accomplished after 1918, he designed a number of skyscrapers, homes, and churches in the earlier period.

Meanwhile, at the turn of the century, several western European architects were engaged in similar efforts to develop a style relevant to the industrial age and free from the dead hand of classical and medieval traditions. In Scotland, the work of Charles R. Mackintosh (1868–1928) exhibits an intriguing transition from *Art Nouveau* to simplifying functionalism, but Mackintosh was ahead of his time; he gained few commissions. The origins of twentieth-century building style are to be found mostly in Germany just before and during the First World War in the work of Walter Gropius (1883–1969) and Ludwig Mies van der Rohe (1886–1969). Their plans for factories and skyscrapers with plain facades of glass and concrete established the style that was to become the international functional design of the 1920's and 1930's.

Music

In music as in other fields of art, there was a tendency at the end of the nineteenth century to break with classical or traditional forms. Once this had been accomplished, composers were free to go off in revolutionary directions.

At the same time, the great innovations in music in this period produced a reaction that resulted in a kind of musical neo-orthodoxy. Any attempt to understand late nineteenth- and early twentieth-century music must begin with a consideration of the contribution of Richard Wagner (1813–1883), the German dramatic composer. Wagner's rather undisciplined private life and his participation in the abortive revolution of 1848 forced him to spend much of his life in exile in Paris, Vienna, and elsewhere. During these years, Wagner produced such important operas as *Tannhäuser, Lohengrin, Tristan and Isolde,* and *The Mastersingers of Nuremberg.* The turning point in his life came in 1864, when Louis ii of Bavaria agreed to support him in his attempt to produce a radically new art form.

Wagner was unique among composers of his age in that he valued music less for its own sake than as a means to emotional and psychological expression. Ever since 1852 he had dreamed of breaking with the old forms of the opera and of replacing them with the "music-drama." Instead of catering to the shallow tastes of opera-going aristocrats, the music-dramatist, according to Wagner, should compose his works for the nation as a whole. With the aid of music to create dramatic intensity, the music-drama should celebrate human and social aspirations by the reenactment of national myths. Moreover, it should be a complete work of art, with one man creating and coordinating the drama, music, and verse.

Wagner's new form of dramatic and musical expression demanded a new kind of theater, and Louis ii was only too eager to build one to Wagner's specifications at Bayreuth in Bavaria. In 1876 there occurred at Bayreuth one of the key events in the history of music—the first performance of Wagner's epic *The Ring of the Nibelungs.* This remarkable tetralogy, comprised of *Rhinegold, The Valkyrie, Siegfried,* and *The Twilight of the Gods,* is based upon ancient German legends. Layer upon layer of symbolic meaning make *The Ring* a work of incredible artistic complexity. With penetrating psychological insight, Wagner created an irrational, almost orgiastic compound of intense emotion, sex, and lust for power. To achieve these dizzy emotional heights, Wagner's music broke with classical forms. In fact, from a traditional point of view *The Ring* was essentially formless.

The Ring was a great work of art for intrinsic reasons, and it had an immense influence upon the future of music. It has been said that all music after Wagner is either a reaction against him or a logical extension of the musical principles implicit in his work. On the one hand, music became emotional, irrational, symbolic, formless, even atonal; on the other, there was a reversion to classical formalities.

Three outstanding composers were contemporaries of Wagner in his later years. One was Giuseppe Verdi (1813–1901), whose list of important operas composed after 1871 includes his two masterpieces, *Otello* and *Falstaff,* both based on Shakespearean themes, as well as his *Requiem Mass* and *Te Deum.* Another, Peter Ilich Tchaikovsky (1840–1893), worked in a variety of musical forms, composing several outstanding symphonies (especially his Fourth, Fifth, and Sixth, the last known as *Pathétique*), a number of superb ballet scores (*Swan Lake, Sleeping Beauty,* and the *Nutcracker*), virtuoso concertos for violin and piano, and hauntingly beautiful operas (including *Eugene Onegin*), all of which are justly famous and popular. Wagner's third eminent contemporary was Johannes Brahms, who wrote several of his finest symphonies and concertos, as well as many of his songs and much of his chamber music, in the 1880's and 1890's.

The center of German music in the decades after Wagner was Vienna, and the leading Austrian-German composers around the turn of the century included Anton Bruckner (1824–1896), Gustav Mahler (1860–1911), and the Bavarian Richard Strauss (1864–1949), all of whom—especially Bruckner and Strauss—strongly reflected Wagner's influence.

While Bruckner, a devout Catholic, composed a series of massive symphonies as well as shorter choral and organ works, Strauss devoted himself mainly to the writing of shorter tone poems (including *Don Juan, Till Eulenspiegel's Merry Pranks*, and *Death and Transfiguration*) by which he attempted to convey visual impressions in sound. Strauss also wrote a number of operas, of which the most exciting and important were his early works, *Salome, Elektra*, and *Der Rosenkavalier* (with text by Hugo von Hofmannsthal).

Bruckner and Strauss, particularly the latter, built upon and expanded the new harmonic combinations developed by Wagner. But far more radical in its tonal, structural, and emotional character was the work of Gustav Mahler. Mahler composed both a series of lovely songs and a number of imposing symphonies, whose completely original sound and technical complexities were a long time gaining popularity, but which have now become standard works on both sides of the Atlantic. Far more than Bruckner's or Strauss's work, Mahler's compositions are permeated by the subject of death and by an almost desperate striving to transcend the limits of personal experience and mortal sensibility.

While Bruckner, Strauss, and Mahler were extending the limits of form and tonality in a post-Wagnerian idiom, in France Claude Debussy (1862–1918) represented the zenith of the Impressionist school in music. Eschewing the philosophical overtones and aspirations of Mahler, Debussy devoted himself in the main to the writing of a series of tone pictures for orchestra, piano, and other combinations of instruments, including such widely performed pieces as *Prelude to the Afternoon of a Faun, Iberia*, and *The Sea*. Less important, though still highly popular, is the work of Maurice Ravel (1875–1937), whose most famous compositions include the ballet *Daphnis and Chloe* and the orgiastic *Bolero*.

The turn of the century saw the emergence of several other composers destined to enjoy great popularity and influence. The Italian Giacomo Puccini (1858–1924) wrote a number of highly successful operas which blended appealing melodic invention with post-Verdian naturalism. Among his works are *La Bohème, Tosca,* and *Madame Butterfly.* One of the most original and influential composers in the twentieth century has been Igor Stravinsky (b. 1882), whose outstanding success with a series of brilliant scores, including *The Firebird, Petrushka,* and *Rite of Spring,* ushered in a remarkable career that has now spanned more than six decades.

The most radical innovations in music in this period, however, were made by Arnold Schoenberg (1874–1951). Schoenberg's early compositions were little more than variations on late Romantic styles. Vienna, his home, was still under the heavy influence of Wagner in the 1890's. After composing an opera that equaled or surpassed those of Wagner in monumentality, Schoenberg apparently became convinced that further development in this art form was no longer possible. In the early 1900's he began to move toward a radically new kind of tonality. His *Pierrot Lunaire* and other works of this period abandoned rhythmic conventions and defied the age-old assumption that consonance and harmony were beautiful and dissonance ugly. Schoenberg propounded a theory of tonal relativity which suggested that there was nothing absolute about musical intervals. What one age thought of as discordant, another might find smooth and pleasing. To his contemporaries he seemed a musical atheist rejecting all established values. Yet he continued his daring experimentations for the rest of his life and profoundly influenced the development of twentieth-century music.

The Cultural Capitals of the West

The intellectual and cultural activity of these years flourished in Vienna and Paris. The city of Freud, Hofmannsthal, Richard Strauss, and numerous lesser lights, the Habsburg capital was a place of surpassing grace and charm. The period after 1860 witnessed the building of a new university, a fine museum, a famous opera house, and many other cultural institutions. Music, theater, and poetry were the cultural specialties of Vienna in these years. The Viennese middle class was renowned throughout Europe for its refinement and artistic sensitivity. Yet the tone of Viennese culture was traditional and almost aristocratic in flavor; Viennese thought and literature showed little interest in realism, naturalism, or social criticism, but it was much concerned with psychological exploration.

A radical, innovative attitude distinguished the cultural life of Paris, the great international center of art and literature. Due perhaps to the instability of the Third Republic, Parisian intellectuals tended to be alienated from bourgeois civilization. An extreme expression of this alienation was bohemianism, a movement which carried the ideas of the Symbolists to their logical conclusion. Bohemians withdrew from society, led unconventional personal lives, and produced art for its own sake, or for the sake of other bohemians.

Paris was an extremely exciting place during these years, and creative people flocked there from all over the world. The newly constructed *Biblio-*

thèque Nationale and the Eiffel Tower were visible expressions of cultural and intellectual vitality. Many important figures lived in Paris at the height of their productivity, including Impressionists, Postimpressionists, Fauves, and Cubists; Émile Zola, Anatole France, and Marcel Proust; Debussy, Ravel, and Igor Stravinsky; Émile Durkheim and Henri Bergson. Seldom in history has so much sheer genius existed in one place at one time. Justifiably, the French still look back upon the prewar period in Paris as *la belle époque.*

Maturity and Decay: A Bourgeois Culture

The period 1870–1914 marked the zenith of European power and influence in the world. An era of aggressive nationalism and imperial expansion, it was characterized by peace at home and conquest abroad. Germany, Great Britain, and the United States were the leading political and industrial powers. The sociological aspect of European hegemony was the ascendancy of the European middle class. This was the era of "bourgeois civilization" *par excellence*. But beneath the peaceful facade of prosperity, progress, and power, there were abrasive inner tensions and contradictions. Russia underwent a revolution in 1905, Slavic nationalism was ripping apart the fabric of Austria-Hungary, and the Third French Republic was suffering repeated attacks from the Right. The European state system was extremely unstable, and it finally reached a point of crisis in 1914. Moreover, the rapid development of socialism among the industrial proletariat posed a serious threat to the dominance of the middle class. Europe presented two faces near the turn of the century: it was a culture at its height and simultaneously a culture in decay.

The intellectual and cultural history of the period bears a very curious relationship to this combination of maturity and decay. The new consciousness may be considered the flowering of a high civilization: in quantitative and qualitative terms, it resulted in monumental intellectual, scientific, and artistic activity. Yet the signs of decadence were unmistakable. Intellectual and cultural creativity, particularly in literature, art, and music, was centered less in the stronger powers—Britain, America, and Germany—than in the troubled Third French Republic and the decaying Austro-Hungarian Empire. The main trends in late nineteenth-century culture eroded faith in rationalism, humanism, and liberalism, which had hitherto been the most progressive and influential ideals in modern civilization.

Most of the thinkers, scholars, novelists, poets, artists, composers, and scientists were drawn from the bourgeoisie, and their activities may be regarded as the cultural flowering of bourgeois civilization. Yet the critical and creative powers of these men were often turned against the class of their origin. Still, one could argue that the prosperity and life style of the middle class stimulated intellectual rebellion and thus indirectly contributed to the cultural achievements of the age.

CHAPTER 11

HERITAGE
ESSAY

THE CONTRIBUTION OF *FIN-DE-SIÈCLE* CULTURE TO WESTERN CIVILIZATION

In the cultural history of Western civilization, there are many eras of high attainment in philosophy, literature, and the arts. But the shaping of the Western consciousness has been primarily determined by those moments of great upheaval in thought and feeling when men of transcendent insight and sensibility rebel against the reigning ethos, proclaim anew the freedom of the human spirit, and penetrate undiscovered countries of the mind. The closing years of the nineteenth century were such an era of rebellion, spiritual liberation, and intellectual discovery. We are still trying to come to terms, as it were, with the new consciousness of 1900. We are still working out the implications of *fin-de-siècle* culture. In every phase of human thought—the natural and biological sciences, the behaviorial sciences, literature, the arts, philosophy, theology—our conditioning assumptions are in most instances still derived from the great upheaval fomented by the intellectual giants of the years 1880–1918.

Nietzsche was the prophet of the new ethos. He wanted Western man to transcend himself, to become an *Übermensch* (literally a "superior man") who would go far beyond what liberal rationalism and Christian culture had achieved. He affirmed a "yes-saying to life, born of an abundance and superabundance of life." Throwing aside the bonds of guilt and repressive morality and religion—"Gods, too, putrefy. God is dead. God will remain dead" —Nietzsche proclaimed the liberation of "the creative mind" and its penetration of

a country still undiscovered, the frontiers of which no one has yet seen, a country beyond every existing country and every existing refuge of the ideal that man has ever known, a world so overflowing with beauty, strangeness, doubt, terror and divinity, that our curiosity and our lust for possession can never be satisfied by anything else.[1]

In a world in which science and technology had achieved so much, Nietzsche announced the perilous yet joyful quest for still greater triumphs,

1. Friedrich Nietzsche, *Ecce Homo*, in H. Kohn, ed., *The Modern World*, 2nd ed. New York: Macmillan, 1968, p. 173.

not mechanistic but human, spiritual, aesthetic, and moral: "There are a thousand paths that have never yet been trodden—a thousand heaths and a thousand islands of life." The new culture that will emerge from this quest, said Nietzsche, will transcend the stultifying canons of morality that prevail in contemporary, "decadent" culture. The creative man will develop a new morality: "No one knows yet what is good or evil, unless it be the creative man, the man who sets man's goal and gives the earth its meaning and its future."[2]

Seldom has a philosopher so perfectly articulated the feelings of liberation and innovation not only of his own generation but of the succeeding century as well. In addition to representing the subjectivist and relativist rebels of the late nineteenth century, Nietzsche anticipated the avant-garde of the 1920's and the 1960's.

If Nietzsche was the Prince Henry the Navigator of the undiscovered country of the human mind, Freud was its Columbus. Like Columbus's discovery, the new country that Freud revealed may not have been entirely what had been anticipated, but it was a marvelous new world nonetheless. Although the discovery of the unconscious had been anticipated by all manner of creative people—philosophers, painters, poets, novelists and musicians—Freud's was a fourfold achievement. First, he gave scientific authority to the intimations of philosophers and artists. Second, he demonstrated the importance of sex in the unconscious, thereby discrediting Victorian reluctance to consider the implications of sexual drives for morality and personal conduct:

Psychoanalytic investigations trace back the symptoms of disease with really surprising regularity to impressions from the sexual life [and] show us that pathogenic wishes are of the nature of erotic-impulse components. . . . This holds true of both sexes.[3]

Although Freud's conclusions were bitterly condemned by many in his day, he was responsible, before all others, for the gradual extinction of the nineteenth-century image of pure, sexless ladies and gentlemen and for the serious consideration of sexual motivations and mores, as well as for the increasingly major role that eroticism came to play in modern literature and art. His third achievement was his elaborate map of the world of consciousness and unconsciousness, focused on the id, the ego, and the superego. If, like the efforts of the pioneering mapmakers of the sixteenth century, the contours of his plan were challenged by later researchers, his principle that "in the unconscious the suppressed wish still exists" revealed the inlets of the human psyche that had to be explored.

2. Nietzsche, *The Gay Science, Thus Spake Zarathustra*, in Kohn, *The Modern World*, pp. 179, 183.
3. Sigmund Freud, *The Origin and Development of Psychoanalysis*, in Kohn, *The Modern World*, p. 189.

The Autonomy of Art. The modern era in painting begins with the work of Paul Cézanne. Facing page: "Landscape near Aix-en-Provence" (1887). While he developed the approach inaugurated by the Impressionists, he was also, as he said, "the primitive of the way I have discovered." For Cézanne, the union of nature and form was realized in color, and a painting was not a representation but an entity with its own language and meaning: "A picture should first of all represent nothing but color." While "art is a harmony parallel to nature," it is a harmony that exists in and for itself. This is the main principle of twentieth-century painting.

La Belle Époque. Not since Renaissance Florence had there been such a gathering of artists, writers, and musicians in one city as in Paris in the closing years of the nineteenth century. Constantly meeting, discussing, collaborating, influencing each other, they sought new intuitions into society and personality, into art and nature. Parisian life, with its wealth, vibrancy, vitality, and corruption, created an intoxicating ambience and provided a constant source of inspiration. Edgar Degas' "Boulevard Montmartre" (facing page, top) captures this ambience, combining the spectrum of color with the easy arrogance of the *demi-monde.* This painting is typical of Degas' unique style, bridging realism and Impressionism. The culture hero of the hour was the Symbolist poet Stéphane Mallarmé, who found poetic truth in "the image distilled from the dreams called forth by things." This, too, was the Impressionist attitude in art, as in Édouard Manet's portrait of Mallarmé (facing page, bottom). The subject becomes the occasion for the distilled image realized in color. Paul Gauguin consciously tried to achieve in painting what Mallarmé prescribed for poetry. Gauguin thought he could find in "the grandeur, profundity, and mystery of Tahiti" (right) the simplicity and universality of primitivism and sought to create in his paintings the abstract, immediate truth that was the counterpart of the pure mythic imagery of primitive culture.

Freud's fourth contribution was to reveal the ambiguity and the tenuousness of polarities and antinomies that had heretofore been taken for granted. The Romantics had claimed that the child is the father of the man, but they had never doubted that the child inhabited a world of innocence and that only as he grew up did "the prison-house begin to close / Upon the growing boy," as Wordsworth said. But Freudian psychology questioned whether anyone really grows up and denied the innocence of childhood: "The child has his sexual impulses and activities from the beginning." And if dreams reflect repressed wishes, where lies the difference between the world of fantasy and the world of conscious reality?

The discovery of the unconscious at the end of the nineteenth century, particularly as it was given scientific respectability and decisive form by Freudian psychology, marks one of the most important turning points in the intellec-

The Modernism of Decadence. The *Art Nouveau* movement flourished briefly in several countries at the turn of the century, principally in painting, drawing, book illustrations, and house decoration and furnishing. "The Mysterious Rose Garden" (1895) by the British illustrator Aubrey Beardsley (right) and "The Three Ages of Woman" (1908) by the eclectic Viennese painter Gustav Klimt (below) are typical of the *Art Nouveau* style. *Art Nouveau* transformed the conceits of late Romanticism into the expression of personal sensibility by carrying decadence to the point of exoticism. In interior decoration, such as Victor Horta's staircase at the Hotel Solvay in Brussels (facing page), *Art Nouveau* paradoxically represented a step toward the new, simple functionalism of the early twentieth century, because the *Art Nouveau* decorators departed from traditional forms and freely used any available material to express personal taste.

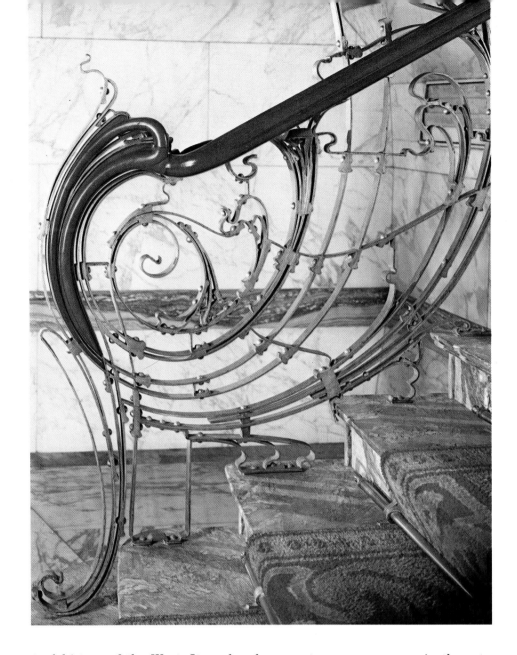

tual history of the West. It produced momentous consequences in the arts, where attempts to evoke the inner realities of the heart and mind led to the proliferation of nonrepresentational painting and sculpture and stream-of-consciousness literature. But the impact of the discovery of subterranean aspects of the human personality went far beyond the arts. It crippled and eroded the faith of modern man in the linear, progressive development of institutions and the moral growth of mankind. The power and tenacity of dreams, myths, and memories shattered the idea of time as a progressive continuum. If it was true that the child continued to live in the man, if the "primitive" could not be expunged from the civilized, many lines that had seemed sharp and clear became blurred. What were the borders between child and adult, between past and present, between human and animal, between sleep and waking?

The Sick Society. Between 1890 and 1918 many artists—particularly in Germany, Belgium, and Italy—shared the conviction of novelists and social theorists that European civilization was rotten, immoral, and brutal. Hostility toward prevailing institutions and political leaders became a prime theme in the art of the period. The horrors of war and the hypocrisy of the bourgeoisie were favorite targets. Left: "War" (1896) by Arnold Böcklin, a member of the German school of *Naturlyrismus,* which expressed Romantic themes in conventional realist style. Bottom: "Intrigue" (1890) by the Belgian Expressionist master James Ensor. The faces of the men and women in Ensor's world are ugly masks. "These express the individual's extreme alienation from his environment: he can see his fellow man only as phantoms, as ghosts eroded by death."[1] Facing page: "Armored Train" (1915) by the Italian Futurist Gino Severini. Here warfare dehumanizes the individual, making him part of a machine that fractures civilization.

1. W. Haftmann, *Painting in the Twentieth Century.* New York: Praeger, 1965, I, p. 63.

The rise of the social sciences at the turn of the century was prime evidence that the old conceptual framework for understanding society was disintegrating and badly in need of revision and reconstruction. The new kind of social theorist was consciously relativistic and pluralistic in his approach. Whereas liberal rationalists of the older generation had believed they could reach conclusions that could be termed scientifically certain, Max Weber and his colleagues were satisfied with probability. Weber contended that

the cultural problems which move men form themselves ever anew and in different colors, and the boundaries of that area in the infinite stream of concrete events which

The Dream World. Artists joined poets and Freudian psychologists at the turn of the century in exploring the world of dream, fantasy, and myth—the psychic experience where a more profound truth and reality lay. The Norwegian-born Expressionist Edvard Munch followed his Scandinavian countrymen Kierkegaard and Strindberg in examining the inner world of morbidity and psychosis. He aimed to paint "living men, who suffer and love." Above: Munch's "Jealousy." Similarly, the French Expressionist Odilon Redon, much under the influence of the Symbolist poets, subjected himself "to the coming of the unconscious" and sought to ascend to "the Olympus of our dreams." His concentration on the world of fantasy and myth makes Redon a forerunner of Surrealism. Right: Redon's "Cyclops." At the same time in Paris, Henri Rousseau, a completely self-taught genuine "primitive" artist, was exploring the private, lyrical realm of exotic fantasy. Facing page: Rousseau's "The Dream."

acquires meaning and significance for us ... are constantly subject to change. ... A systematic science of culture, even only in the sense of a definitive, objectively valid, systematic fixation of the problems which it should treat, would be senseless in itself.[4]

This new relativism, which was built into the social sciences from their inception, was intimately bound up with the new subjectivity which insisted that the vantage point of the observer conditioned all perception and experience. The concepts that the historian and social scientist employ in their analyses are only "ideal analytical constructs," Weber assumed, subject to "the inevitable shift of guiding value-ideas." Mid-nineteenth-century liberal thinkers had believed that absolute truths about government and society could be predicated. But Weber and the new academic social scientists believed that all concepts, including their own, were socially and culturally conditioned. Thus one view of society could be more sophisticated, more useful, and, for the moment, more probable than another, but no social theory could claim the legitimacy of objective truth.

The rise of the social sciences — sociology, anthropology, and psychology — as

4. Quoted in J. Freund, *The Sociology of Max Weber* New York: Pantheon, 1968, p. 67.

MUSEUM OF MODERN ART, NEW YORK

The Aesthetic of Form. In an era dominated by relativism, subjectivism, and the exploration of the unconscious, the artist's own feelings and perceptions were bound to become the primary focus of art. From the 1870's down into the second decade of the twentieth century, the direction of art was toward greater and greater concentration on the artist's own emotions, as the stylistic progression, in general, moved from Impressionism to Expressionism to Cubism and Abstract Expressionism. Around 1910, artistic representations of physical objects became more and more distorted. The visible external world provided only the initial stimulus; it was the categories of his own mind that the artist now imposed on canvas or stone. Left: stone head (1915) by Amedeo Modigliani; bottom: "Improvisation #35" (1914) by Wassily Kandinsky; facing page: "Le Portugais" (1911) by Georges Braque.

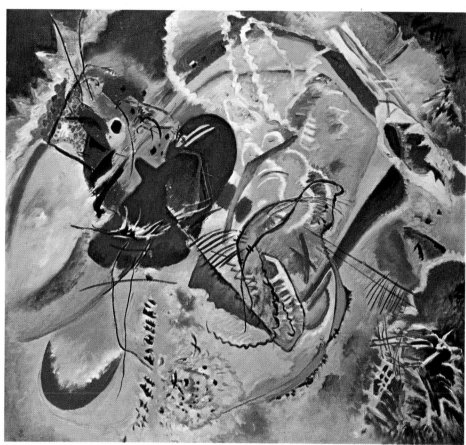

The Architectural Revolution. Not until the early years of the twentieth century did a building style functionally suitable to an industrial, technological culture finally emerge. The work of the Americans Louis Sullivan and Frank Lloyd Wright had an immediate, widespread influence in Europe, but in the designs of the much neglected Scottish architect and decorator Charles Rennie Mackintosh—such as the entrance to Hill House, Glasgow (above)—the liberating but excessively flamboyant experiments of the *Art Nouveau* were also modulated and refined into a recognizable twentieth-century style. In Germany, the transition was effected by Walter Gropius and Ludwig Mies van der Rohe, who simplified the earlier, self-conscious "romanticization of the Machine." Facing page, left: Gropius's Fagus factory (1910); facing page, right: Mies van der Rohe's model of a skyscraper (1919).

MUSEUM OF MODERN ART, NEW YORK

formal, academic disciplines marked a new, ambitious attempt to comprehend both individual and collective human experience. But their advent also signaled the erosion of the old-style Western humanism which had sought to understand human life in all its integrity and totality. The social sciences fragmented the old humanist ideal by apportioning the study of man among a variety of experts and specialists. With the rise of the social sciences came a great deal of new knowledge of human behavior. The price of the new knowledge was the compartmentalizing of the intellect.

The excitement generated by the discovery of the inner world raised again the old question of the proper relationship between the artist and society. Does the life of the mind, however conceived, have any responsibility to the life of the world?

Many thinking people answered in the negative, rejecting the world and choosing to dwell in the inner realm of heightened sensibility. But the new consciousness led others to return to the world with increased sensitivity to social problems; a number of intellectuals and artists adopted the role of social critic. In some cases the new consciousness merged with the new relativism of the natural and social sciences to produce a kind of detachment that differed radically from the easy, self-confident objectivity of the previous period. Sober, disenchanted, acutely conscious of its own limitations, this new clinical attitude involved a cold, hard look at man and society. The social scientist could now offer no concessions to the sentiments of the common man. While people may complain about the evils of bureaucracy, Weber remarked,

it would be sheer illusion to think for a moment that continuous administrative work can be carried out in any field except by officials working in offices. The choice is only between bureaucracy and dilettantism in the field of administration. It makes no difference whether the economic system is organized on a capitalistic or socialistic basis.[5]

The benefits we have derived from Nietzsche's liberating philosophy, from Freudian insight into human nature, and from the analyses of Weber and other social scientists are immeasurable; they have become central not only to our value system but to our institutionalized way of life. Yet the heritage of *fin-de-siècle* culture has not been an unmixed blessing. The denial of the validity of traditional Christian ethics and the parallel enthronement of a new elite that fashions its own morality; the breakdown of the distinction between child and adult, between primitive and civilized man, and the revelation of the primacy of erotic impulses in human nature; the undermining of the liberal humanist faith in absolute principles of social and political science, and the substitution of a relativistic attitude toward social values, along with a clinical detachment from the sentiments of the common man — it is not unfair to attribute these currents in twentieth-century culture, if not directly to the genius of Nietzsche, Freud, and Weber, at least to logical extrapolations from their doctrines. Taken together, these extrapolations deprive us of the humanity of the Enlightenment, the moral fervor of the Romantics, and the conscience of liberalism and provide a theoretical basis for totalitarian and terrorist systems beside which the tyrannies of the past pale into insignificance.

5. Quoted in Freund, *The Sociology of Max Weber*, p. 238.

12

The Apogee
of Western Hegemony

ENVIRONMENT ESSAY

The Greek poets had a word for it—*hubris*. So did the medieval theologians—*superbia*. The Greek and Latin words mean substantially the same thing: the arrogant pride by which men puff themselves up and convince themselves that they are rulers of nature and masters of their own destiny. To the Greeks, pride was the ultimate corruption that brings down on men the wrath of the gods. To medieval (and later Protestant) Christians, pride was equivalent to sinful rebellion against God, the stance of Lucifer, who rebelled against the Lord and was cast down into hell.

By the first decade of the twentieth century the European elite of power and money had cast aside the restraints of classical and Christian traditions. The distinguishing feature of the European scene in the decade before 1914 was an arrogant, ostentatious display of enormous authority and fabulous wealth. Never before in human history had so few ruled so many and controlled so much. No one who observed the members of the elite at work or play could envisage any serious threat to the perpetuation of their mastery or foresee the shattering of their security. Their hegemony—not only in their own society but over the rest of the world as well—seemed as impregnable as the neoclassical and Baroque banks, stock exchanges, and chancelleries within whose marble halls they determined the fate of mankind.

Before 1914 the old aristocracy was rapidly intermarrying with the families of industrial and financial tycoons, and the members of this ruling class regarded themselves as the invincible lords of creation. They possessed incredible wealth, which was taxed at trivial rates or not at all; they dominated, or at least exerted tremendous influence on, the government in nearly every country; they stood behind Europe's sway over Asia and Africa; the working class labored to satisfy their unquenchable avarice and their every

capricious whim—it is no wonder that the pride of the European social and political
elite was boundless. And the common man was infected with pride as well—pride in
nation, which he considered superior to all other nations. The rich man, exulting in his
possessions and his personal power, joined the common man in relishing membership

The Pinnacle of European Power. Photographs have preserved many reminders of the reckless arrogance of European ruling groups just before the First World War. Below: Financial Power—the Bank of England and the Royal Exchange, decorated for the coronation of George V in 1910. Traffic jams had become everyday problems in metropolitan centers. Facing page, top: Political Power—the new emperor receiving homage from native princes at the coronation durbar at Delhi, India, in 1911. Left: George Curzon, viceroy of India, appropriately attired in lordly robes. Raised to the peerage as Lord Curzon of Kedleston, he became a Conservative leader in the House of Lords. A vain and pompous man, he was famous before the war for his elegant dinner parties and his liaison with the novelist Elinor Glyn. Facing page, bottom: Military Power—Britain's H.M.S. Dreadnought and Germany's zeppelin, an effective aircraft for military observation and the bombing of civilian centers.

in a glorious national community, despising foreign peoples, and looking forward to the day when competing nations would be struck down.

The captains of finance and industry were driven in magnificent new automobiles from country villas or town mansions to "the City," the business center of the nation and the world. And here they speculated, organized yet greater combines, planned their domination of still more overseas markets, and summoned police and soldiers, gangs of private detectives and scabs to smash the strikes undertaken by desperate workers. Meanwhile, other members of the power elite, often with fine aristocratic names, met to sign new alliances that would both keep the peace and gain some additional imperial territory. In country fields starched officers watched army maneuvers through binoculars,

The Overstuffed World. The ethos of the ruling groups in Europe and America in the early twentieth century was reflected in their attitude toward food and women, which was summed up in Thorstein Veblen's phrase, "conspicuous consumption." Women were supposed to be buxom, voluptuous instruments for the satisfaction of male aggression. Facing page, top: "the Gibson girl" style, the erotic ideal of the period. Women subjected themselves to heavy corsets and bustles in order to protrude in appropriate places. Above: gentlemen celebrating a win at the races in the company of ladies of the *demimonde*. While unemployment rose and real wages declined, the rich and powerful gorged themselves. Facing page, bottom: Harrison G. Fiske's dinner in 1901 for eminent New York bankers, who wear vine leaves in their hair in emulation of Roman aristocrats. Obesity was characteristic of the ruling class, dieting as yet unheard of. Right: a fish, game, and poultry shop in London in 1909. Grand ladies search for new delicacies for their husbands and paramours.

admiring the precision of troop movements and the firepower of their cannon, and elegant admirals were ceremoniously piped aboard floating fortresses to pose boldly beneath their mighty guns.

In the evening the masters of the human race sat down to twenty-course dinner parties with their corseted wives, after which, over brandy and cigars, the gentlemen cursed socialist agitators and speculated on the intentions of foreign powers. Then the lords of mankind repaired to the Rococo boudoirs of their mistresses for suitable relaxation before facing the duties of another day.

At the other end of the social spectrum, the urban workers, if they were strong and able and were not on strike or subject to a lockout, trudged from mean houses and starchy breakfasts to another day of labor at the machines, taking their assigned places at the ever growing assembly lines, and then gathered in the dusk at pub or beer garden to exchange their dim comprehensions of international crises, cursing the foreigner and venting their contempt for the black man and yellow man. If the worker was not young and strong, he could anticipate another day of degradation and terror forestalling starvation, perhaps with some help from a public dole.

This proud world was not peaceful, but caught up in their impenetrable self-satisfaction, the leaders of the European states could find no way to calm the alarms of war. Radical union leaders fomented strikes, spokesmen for submerged nationalities plotted revolution, anarchists threw bombs — and in Britain dotty ladies marched, agitating for women's suffrage. A dank mist of violence and extremism was rising, and menacing rumbles of protest, rebellion, and nationalism warned of approaching storm. But these signs went unheeded by the masters of power and capital; they did not interrupt the gay dance of the beautiful people. The rulers transmuted the snarls of hatred into a patriotic tocsin for summoning the masses into gargantuan armies that went marching off to their doom in the mad August days of 1914.

The Second Transportation Revolution. Around 1910 the beginnings of mass production in the United States and Britain brought the price of the automobile down to a level at which it could be used extensively for public and private transportation. Pioneers in the assembly-line production of automobiles were Henry Ford in Detroit and William Morris in Oxford, England. Below: Morris's factory in 1913. Morris's success and the steady expansion of his business slowly transformed Oxford from an academic community into an industrial center. Raised to the peerage as Lord Nuffield, Morris compensated Oxford by generous gifts to the university. Meanwhile, in 1903, two bicycle mechanics from Dayton, Ohio, had invented the first successful heavier-than-air flying machine. It looked like a combination of a bicycle and a box kite. Facing page: Orville Wright preparing for take-off at Belmont Park, New York, in 1910. Before the war, airplanes had no practical use; they were mere curiosities. Substantially improved for military purposes during the war, they began to be used commercially in the 1920's to transport mail, passengers, and cargo.

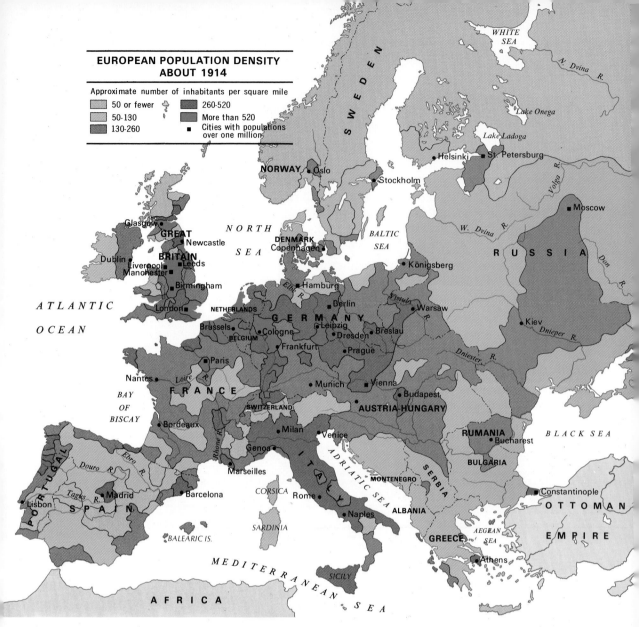

EUROPEAN POPULATION DENSITY ABOUT 1914

Approximate number of inhabitants per square mile

- 50 or fewer
- 50-130
- 130-260
- 260-520
- More than 520
- ■ Cities with populations over one million

WHITE SEA

N. Dvina R.

Lake Onega

Lake Ladoga

■ St. Petersburg

■ Moscow

■ Helsinki

S W E D E N

Volga R.

W. Dvina R.

R U S S I A

Don R.

NORWAY

• Oslo

• Stockholm

N O R T H
S E A

*BALTIC
SEA*

• Königsberg

■ Berlin

• Warsaw

Vistula R.

• Kiev

Dnieper R.

DENMARK
Copenhagen •

Glasgow

GREAT

Newcastle

BRITAIN

Dublin

Liverpool
Manchester

Leeds

Birmingham

London ■

Elbe R.

• Hamburg

NETHERLANDS

G E R M A N Y

Brussels •

BELGIUM

• Cologne

• Leipzig

• Dresden

• Breslau

• Frankfurt

• Prague

A T L A N T I C

O C E A N

■ Paris

Nantes •

Loire R.

F R A N C E

Dniester R.

• Munich

• Vienna

AUSTRIA-HUNGARY

• Budapest

*BAY
OF
BISCAY*

• Bordeaux

SWITZERLAND

• Milan

• Venice

Rhône R.

Genoa •

I T A L Y

RUMANIA

• Bucharest

BLACK SEA

Marseilles •

CORSICA

Rome •

A D R I A T I C   S E A

MONTENEGRO

SERBIA

BULGARIA

• Constantinople

O T T O M A N

PORTUGAL

Douro R.

Ebro R.

• Madrid

SPAIN

Tagus R.

• Barcelona

ALBANIA

E M P I R E

Lisbon •

BALEARIC IS.

SARDINIA

• Naples

GREECE

*AEGEAN
SEA*

• Athens

M E D I T E R R A N E A N   S E A

SICILY

A F R I C A

European Population Density about 1914. From the mid-nineteenth century to the outbreak of the First World War, Europe's population continued to grow rapidly and became increasingly urbanized. In 1914 more than 150 cities had populations exceeding 100,000; Berlin, Moscow, St. Petersburg, and Vienna joined London and Paris in having more than a million inhabitants. Toward the end of the century, however, the rest of the world was growing faster than the Continent, as the birthrate in various European states began to decline. Outside Europe in 1914, New York, Chicago, Philadelphia, Rio de Janeiro, Buenos Aires, Calcutta, Tokyo, and Osaka had populations that exceeded one million.

I. THE WORLD BEFORE THE WAR

The Great Watershed

In the years before 1914, frequent and regular summit conferences (the name had not yet been invented) took place between the rulers of the leading European states. But whatever their theoretical or actual constitutional prerogatives, these monarchs were increasingly incapable of stemming the "international anarchy"—repeated confrontations between the great powers—that was the besetting curse of European politics in the early twentieth century. Probably all the crowned heads of Europe, and their ministers and diplomats too, knew that since the late eighteenth century war had bred revolution. So it was in their immediate interest to see that peace was preserved. But they failed, and after a long series of international crises and after desperate efforts to head it off, the Great War (as it was first called) broke out in 1914.

The First World War (as it was later called) was a watershed in Western history. Before 1914 the domestic and foreign policies of European governments were determined and largely administered by a specific social class whose members were expected to rule and were trained for political leadership. It is true that pressures from outside and beneath had begun to produce cracks in the social and political systems of the nations of Europe, but before the Great War the fissures were few and narrow.

Dramatic change occurred only after the mass slaughter of World War I. Then it began to be widely felt that the old system had brought disaster; the old leaders were discredited; the old diplomacy was outdated. Furthermore, many of the natural heirs of the old regime died in the trenches. As a result of the devastation of the war, changes that had seemed unattainable at the beginning of the twentieth century became serious possibilities or concrete realities.

The Atlantic Democracies

In Great Britain, various out-groups sought political power and social change during the decade preceding the war. At the opening of the twentieth century, the Unionist party (composed of Conservatives joined with former Liberals who had left their party out of opposition to Irish home rule) still commanded a strong, but weakening, majority in the House of Commons. The Unionists were led first by Lord Salisbury and after his retirement in July 1902 by his nephew, Arthur James Balfour. Of necessity, the government concentrated first on bringing the unpopular Boer War to a satisfactory conclusion. When that was accomplished in 1902, it began to attend to long deferred and pressing domestic matters.

The last years of Unionist rule have—justifiably—not enjoyed a good historical reputation, but they were not wholly devoid of accomplishment. The most successful legislation was the Education Act of 1902, which enabled the state to ensure proper pay for teachers and a standardized level of secondary as well as primary education. But by the early 1900's the government was very obviously suffering from political fatigue and intraparty conflict. Joseph Chamberlain, a prominent party leader who in the 1880's had helped to split the Liberals with his conservative stand on the Irish question, now began to split the Unionists by advocating a system of tariffs based on imperial preference. But by that time too many acts or omissions stamped the Conservative party as indifferent to social problems. In December 1905 the Liberals came to power under the leadership of Sir Henry Campbell-Bannerman, and at the national elections of January 1906 they won an absolute majority of 357, an overwhelming triumph unequalled since the first election following the Reform Bill of 1832.

The Liberal party in the House of Commons proved a strange yet remarkably effective combination of small businessmen, middle-class lawyers, Nonconformist preachers, journalists, trade union leaders, and radical intellectuals. The first three years of the Liberal government were marked by a determined attempt at significant social reform. In December 1906 the Liberal government repealed the Taff Vale decision by providing that the unions could not be held liable for the illegal acts of their members, and it also passed an important Workman's Compensation Act making employers almost fully liable for accidents suffered by their lower paid employees.

Out of power, the Conservatives still attempted to run the country through the veto power of the extremely conservative House of Lords. Time after time the hereditary upper house killed government bills. In April 1908 Campbell-Bannerman died, and he was succeeded as prime minister by Herbert H. Asquith (1852–1928), chancellor of the exchequer. Asquith appointed David Lloyd George (1863–1945), a fiery Welsh radical and indefatigable demagogue, to replace him at the exchequer. At the urging of Lloyd George and of Winston Churchill (1874–1965), an aristocrat with somewhat leftist inclinations, the government tried to proceed with its welfare program. In 1908 Parliament passed the noncontributory Old Age Pensions Act, which made an important beginning in the practice of mitigating poverty by direct state payments. The House of Lords was inclined at first to tamper with the bill but finally desisted in response to pressure from the Commons.

Before long, the first of several scares over German naval building badly upset the country's financial priorities; £15 million in additional revenue now had to be found to finance both the old age pensions and extra naval armaments. Lloyd George, who had recently visited Germany to study that country's welfare policies, seized the opportunity to submit his "People's Budget," some proposals of which were clearly a direct counteroffensive aimed at the House of Lords. To raise revenue, Lloyd George proposed to increase death duties and to levy a duty on undeveloped land and on coal and mineral royalties. It was the tradition of the British Parliament that while the Lords could reject ordinary legislation, they could not veto a money bill. The Lords now claimed that Lloyd George's budget involved social reform legislation and that consequently they were entitled to reject it. Lloyd George and the Liberal cabinet denounced the Conservative majority in the Lords as selfish rich men who wished to avoid paying their fair share to the nation. A major constitutional crisis was brewing, and although both Balfour in the Commons and the Marquess of Lansdowne, the Conservative leader in the Lords, wanted to let the budget pass, the peers were in an intransigent mood and in November 1909 defeated the budget by an overwhelming margin.

In January 1910 the Liberals went to the electorate for a mandate on this issue. They were returned to power, but with sharply reduced representation; they now had to depend on Labour and Irish support for their majority. On April 27 the budget passed the Commons again, and on the following day the Lords let it through without a murmur. But the issue of their veto power was far from dead.

Edward VII, the merry monarch who had ruled since 1901, died unexpectedly in May, and in the political truce that allowed George V (1910–1935) to accustom himself to the throne, Liberals and Conservatives met to try to reach a compromise. The Lords were willing to yield on money bills, but they insisted on their right to veto bills for Irish home rule. Compromise was impossible, because the government had struck a bargain with the Irish members in return for their support on the budget. Guarantees for the creation of new peers to swamp the Conservative majority were secured from the king, and once again elections were called to demonstrate the country's support. In December, the Liberals were returned with an almost identical majority.

In 1911 the government's Parliament Bill—designed to put an end to the Lords' misuse of their power—reached the upper house. It provided, first of all, that money bills should become law without the consent of the House of Lords (the Speaker of the Commons would decide what bills qualified as such); second, that other bills should become law without the Lords' approval if they were passed by the Commons in three successive sessions and if more than two years had elapsed since their original introduction; and, finally, that the duration of Parliament should be reduced from seven to five years. Not until the actual vote on August 10 could either side be sure of the outcome. Knowing that George V was prepared to create sufficient peers to pass the bill, the Lords approved it by a vote of 131 to 114, and the British political system was transformed as it had not been since 1832.

Though defeated in their effort to prevent significant social change through their domination of the House of Lords, the Conservatives remained determined to break the Liberal government over the question of Irish home rule. In 1912 their tactic was to accept home rule so long as Ulster, the predominantly Protestant counties of northeastern Ireland, remained outside the projected Irish state. This made home rule unacceptable to militant Irish nationalists. Since the elections of January 1910, the Ulster Protestants had been preparing to oppose the plans of the Liberal-Irish coalition. In January 1912 a volunteer force of Ulstermen began drilling, and in April the new leader of the Conservative party, Andrew Bonar Law (1858–1923), promised "to support to the end" this loyal minority. Two days before the government was to present its Home Rule Bill, Bonar Law reviewed eighty thousand Ulster volunteers. On April 11 the government bill came before the Commons. Far from extreme, it proposed home rule on purely Irish matters while preserving to the British Parliament all matters involving foreign affairs. In late July, Bonar Law told an audience of fifteen thousand that he could not imagine any action that Ulster might take that his party and the public would not support. That autumn, almost half a million Ulstermen signed an oath opposing home rule.

Britain was now getting a taste of the hatreds and passions that were increasingly tearing apart the Habsburg monarchy, as it became obvious that the Northern Protestants would fight to avoid Catholic dominance. The government and the British army were badly divided on the question of coercion. In early 1914, when ordered to move to Ulster as a precautionary measure, a significant number of the officer corps in the army base at the Curragh refused to march against the Protestant loyalists and resigned their commissions. With the threat of a major European war increasing, the prime minister dared not purge the army. For a time it looked as though nothing could prevent armed conflict in Ireland; but shortly thereafter, in August 1914, war broke out on the Continent. For the moment, most Irishmen, both in Ulster and in the south, supported the British war effort. The third Home Rule Bill finally passed both houses in September 1914, but Asquith announced that home rule was shelved for the duration and that, before it should finally go into effect, separate legislation would be passed to protect Ulster. Here lay the seed of much future bitterness and strife.

It was the budgetary and constitutional crises together with the Irish issue that brought Britain dangerously close to political chaos and civil war before August 1914. But these were not the only serious problems. Less immediately dangerous, but no less vexing, was the determination of British women to win the right to vote. Civil disobedience was their stock-in-trade. There was little these suffragettes would not do. In 1912 thousands of windows were smashed in London and untold property damage done. By 1914 Asquith knew that he would have to surrender on this issue. Only the outbreak of war delayed the introduction of women's suffrage.

The government's third great problem stemmed from the tide of industrial unrest that was spreading through the country, threatening a general strike. The Liberal government had been more than moderately responsive to the needs of the working class. The National Insurance Act of 1911 protected the entire working population against sickness, and some against unemployment. Nevertheless, wages had not risen significantly, prices were climbing, and workers in other countries had set an example of militant strikes. The

British labor unions were increasingly inspired by syndicalist attitudes. In any case, worsening economic conditions impelled them toward strike agitation.

The first great wave of strikes occurred in 1910, as workers in the coal, railroad, textile, and shipbuilding industries walked off their jobs in quick succession. The most dramatic dispute occurred in South Wales, where a confrontation between coal miners — on strike against the advice of their leaders and the Miners' Federation of Great Britain — and local police protecting the mines erupted into bloody street fighting. The following year, 1911, a railroad strike paralyzed the country, and only the acute international situation induced the railroad companies to recognize the unions. In all, over 10 million working days were lost in the course of the year, and almost a million workers were involved.

The record in 1912 was worse yet. Over 1,200,000 men were involved in work stoppages costing over 38 million working days. In 1913 the dissatisfied miners and transport workers, together with the National Union of Railwaymen, formed a "triple alliance" in preparation for a general strike to establish a national minimum wage. As they worked to build up their strength, British strikes changed in character from prolonged, large strikes to small, short-lived ones. Between January and July 1914 there were 937 strikes, and as autumn approached the country was very close to a general strike. Just as the tension was becoming unbearable the First World War broke out, sweeping aside all considerations save those of national defense.

Britain in the Edwardian period — as the years from 1901 to 1914 are generally called — presented a very mixed picture of significant political progress and social turbulence. Unquestionably, the political and social changes of the decade preceding the war were of the utmost significance. In the realm of fiscal and constitutional policy they set the stage for the growing democratization of Britain in the years to come. All the same, as time went on, the Asquith government was repeatedly challenged by the Left, and the rise of the Labour party — which elected forty-two members to the House of Commons in 1911 — was but one indication that the pattern of British politics might be on the verge of a permanent change. It also became clear that the foreign policy promises that the Liberal party had made upon taking office in 1905 had proved impossible of realization. Instead of less foreign involvement, there was now much more; instead of being checked, the Anglo-German naval race was now more accelerated than ever. The Liberal party, which had aimed at reform at home and tranquility abroad, had been forced off its intended course. In the face of labor, Irish, and suffragette agitation, it had become confused, hesitant, and generally impotent. Indeed, it is plausible that the outbreak of war saved Britain from some great upheaval in 1914, possibly civil war or revolution.

Had the liberal ethos, which had dominated Britain since the 1830's and which had reached its climax in the age of Gladstone, arrived at its limits? Had Britain entered a period of economic decline and class bitterness, not unlike that long known on the Continent? Could Britain continue to play for much longer the part of the leading Western democracy? These were crucial questions troubling Englishmen in the summer of 1914.

Whereas Britain had entered the twentieth century relatively united on fundamental political philosophy and practice, France remained bitterly divided by the Dreyfus affair. Most of French society had chosen up sides on the issue, and even when Dreyfus was finally vindicated, French politics did not acquire any real sense of political community. The army was condemned by the more liberal elements in the country for misusing its power and prestige to convict an innocent man and to maintain his guilt when his innocence had become clearly evident. Those of the Catholic clergy who had thrown all their weight into proving that the Jewish captain was a traitor had jeopardized the accomplishments of the *Ralliement*, the progressive and pro-Republic movement sponsored by Pope Leo XIII in the 1890's.

The elections of 1899 had put the government in the hands of a moderate liberal coalition led by René Waldeck-Rousseau. For the first time a French cabinet included a socialist. On the surface this augured well for social reform. But passions aroused by the Dreyfus affair still ran high, and the government was committed first to destroy the power of the "enemies of the Republic"—the Church and the army. The new minister of war, General André, set out to purge the officer corps of its monarchist, Catholic elements. He set up a private spy system, and officers were encouraged to inform on one another. In the end, an employee betrayed the system to the Right, and the ensuing uproar in the French parliament led to André's fall.

Undaunted, the Dreyfusard majority continued to demand the destruction of the political power of the Church, and in July 1901 a new Law on Associations dissolved all religious orders except those specifically authorized by the government. Actually, Waldeck-Rousseau's aim had been to exile only those orders that had gone to extreme lengths during the Dreyfus affair, but the elections of 1901 produced a chamber that was intransigent in its demands that unauthorized orders be dissolved, and in June 1902 he resigned. His successor, Émile Combes, was violently anticlerical: in the next two years a sweeping attack upon Catholic institutions effected the closing of nearly three thousand schools and numerous teaching orders. Indeed, in July 1904 the government went still further and banned all religious teaching orders. Finally, in December 1905, France denounced the Concordat of 1801 and severed all ties between the state and the Catholic Church. Complete freedom of religion now became official policy; title to Church property passed either to local authorities or to private associations.

The year 1905 also marked the end of socialist participation in middle-class governments. All the extraordinary persuasive powers of Jean Jaurès had been required to keep the French socialists behind the Waldeck-Rousseau and Combes cabinets. For five years Jaurès had argued that when the radicals had accomplished their anticlerical goals, they would turn to social reform. But he had to accept the Second International's prohibition of socialist participation in bourgeois ministries. This move to the left did not harm the party's political fortunes. In the national elections of 1914, Socialists won 102 seats in the Chamber of Deputies.

At the same time, the largest trade union, the *Confédération Générale du Travail* (CGT), was also becoming more militant. Its leaders were angry because successive governments had done comparatively little for the laboring class. The result was a wave of ever more explosive strikes and other labor stoppages in the postal service and certain railroads, strikes which the government met with great severity. In 1909 Aristide Briand, then prime minister, put an end to the railroad strikes by the simple expedient of drafting the strikers.

Parallel to a rising tide of violence on the Left, the French Right inclined more and more toward force and extraparliamentary pressure on the government. The fortnightly journal *L'Action Française* was founded to fight the Dreyfusards, and after 1900 a whole movement—nationalistic, anti-Semitic, antiparliamentarian, and antirepublican—swirled around its founder, Charles Maurras. Maurras preached the "degeneracy" of the governing politicians, who had failed to restore France to its position of natural greatness. *L' Action Française* became the focus of an extreme right-wing movement that claimed, "the Republic of France is the regime of the foreigner." Maurras gained some Catholic support, but in January 1914 his extreme rightist movement and his writings were condemned by the papacy.

The radicalization of the Left and Right after 1900 was both a reflection and a source of the growing nationalism and extremism in French politics. For some years the unifying bond of the parties governing France was nationalism and anticlericalism; after 1909–1910 it was, with brief exceptions, nationalism and militarism. Georges Clemenceau (1841–1929), premier from 1906 to 1909, was an authoritarian and an extreme Germanophobe. He introduced few significant social reforms and severely repressed a wave of strikes. On the other hand, Joseph Caillaux, premier in 1911–1912, was an avowed moderate who hoped to bring about a rapprochement with Germany. But increasing international tension sparked a revival of nationalist fervor, and in January 1912 Caillaux was replaced by the passionate Lorraine patriot Raymond Poincaré, who headed a government somewhat concerned with labor problems but especially devoted to a strong national defense and foreign policy. In January 1913 Poincaré was elected president of France.

The overriding issue in French politics in 1913–1914 was the enactment, in July 1913, of a new army bill, lengthening the term of military service from two to three years. The debate about this bill was extremely bitter and it hardly lessened once the bill had become law. The Socialist party opposed the law, thus contributing further to the polarization of French politics, which came to a dramatic climax with the assassination of Jaurès by a patriotic fanatic in August 1914.

By that date, the Third Republic had been in existence over forty years, longer than any form of government in France since the revolution of 1789, although it had failed to gain the passionate loyalty of its citizens. While foreign setbacks—such as the Indochinese crisis of 1885 or the Moroccan crises of the early 1900's—could still topple governments, by 1914 France had long escaped the diplomatic isolation which Bismarck had imposed during the years 1870–1890. With a strong alliance with Russia and a growing entente with Britain, France could face the international future with fair assurance and confidence.

While Britain and France experienced years of economic and social turmoil after 1900, the history of the United States before the First World War was one of striking economic growth, the rise of a powerful reform movement, and the triumph of that movement in the administrations of Theodore Roosevelt (1901–1909) and Woodrow Wilson (1913–1921).

American wealth and power did not exempt the country from manifold serious problems, some of them similar to those besetting the principal governments of Europe. Britain and France were unitary states in which existing political subdivisions allowed for no significant autonomy—or corruption. On the other hand, the federal system of the United States made for both greater diversity and, all too often, laxity, mismanagement, and worse. At the end of the nineteenth century, entrenched and corrupt politicians controlled numerous city and state governments.

But around the turn of the century America entered a new age of political reform and concern for social justice. The Progressive movement of the early 1900's was a more respectable and broader movement than the predominantly agrarian Populism of preceding decades. In a sense, the Progressive movement was largely a middle-class or even a patrician movement, and it was much concerned with reform of municipal and state administration. It sought first of all honest and impartial government and more responsiveness to the needs of the working class. Such vital improvements were effectively inaugurated in many cities struggling against established political machines. Moreover, the reformers also brought about the adoption of the direct primary, direct election of senators, and—what was at the time considered a great political advance in many states—popular initiative, referendum, and recall, all measures by which government could be made, presumably, both more honest and responsive to the people.

Theodore Roosevelt's accession to the presidency after the assassination of McKinley in September 1901 brought a strong champion of reform to the White House for the first time. An activist in everything, Roosevelt believed that a bold and positive program of federal intervention in economic and social affairs was absolutely necessary. He advanced the regulation of interstate commerce, began a notable campaign for conservation, reactivated the Sherman Antitrust Act, established the Bureau of Corporations to investigate business practices, and secured passage of the Pure Food and Drug Act. Roosevelt sometimes spoke more vigorously than he acted; his most significant achievement was that he greatly revitalized the presidency and thus set the stage for an enormous expansion of federal authority later in the century.

In 1908 Roosevelt put forward as his successor his secretary of war, William Howard Taft, who ran on a platform that included tariff reform and an improved banking system. Roosevelt made an unfortunate choice, for Taft did not have the necessary drive to push much progressive legislation through the Senate. The Payne-Aldrich Tariff Act of 1909, for example, was really a triumph for Eastern manufacturers—as amended by the Senate it actually raised duties on many commodities.

Taft's indifferent performance disgusted progressive Republicans, and in 1912 they turned back to Roosevelt. Denied the nomination at the party's national convention, Roosevelt and his supporters formed a third party, the Progressive or "Bull Moose" party. Its "New Nationalism" called on reformers to abandon laissez faire and use the federal government as a regulator and protector of both labor and business.

The Democratic party chose as its candidate Woodrow Wilson (1856–1924), a historian, former president of Princeton University, and governor of New Jersey. Wilson was a classical liberal in the tradition of J. S. Mill and Gladstone. His "New Freedom" was a laissez-faire variety of progressivism that viewed government as a destroyer of artificial barriers rather than as a protector of traditional vested interests. Roosevelt's campaign split his own party, and Wilson was elected with less than a majority of the popular vote. Nevertheless, Wilson's position when he assumed office in March 1913 was unusually favorable. The country was clearly in the mood for new leadership and new departures in policy, and it did not have to wait long for either. Within six months, a new tariff act was passed which, while it did not introduce free trade, significantly reduced existing rates and forced American manufacturers to compete with European producers in the home market. It was followed soon after by the Federal Reserve Act, which established a new system of banking and currency.

Before long Wilson began to depart from the New Freedom doctrine of limited government intervention and to move closer to Roosevelt's New Nationalism. In 1914 he established the Federal Trade Commission, with authority to investigate and regulate numerous business practices; on its heels came the Clayton Antitrust Act, which significantly expanded the original Sherman Act of 1890 and specifically exempted labor organizations from the antitrust laws.

With the possibility that a reunited Republican party might defeat the Democrats in the 1916 elections, Wilson began to move further in the direction of the New Nationalism. He now sponsored in quick succession bills that regulated child labor and provided for federal workmen's compensation, a substantial increase in the federal income tax, the establishment of a federal inheritance tax, an eight-hour day for interstate railroad workers, and similar measures. In no other country — except perhaps Britain — was the government so responsive to the needs and spirit of the times.

In foreign affairs, also, Wilson sought to apply liberal and moral ideals. In this area his problems were, from the beginning, highly sensitive. His predecessor, President Taft, had inherited all the ill feeling growing out of the construction of the Panama Canal and the policy of Caribbean intervention that accompanied it, and had attempted to strengthen American influence in Central and South America with his policy of "dollar diplomacy," by which American funds and fiscal know-how were to stabilize and direct financial affairs in the Caribbean area. This policy had seemingly worked well in 1910 in Haiti, but in Nicaragua in 1912 popular opposition to an American-backed regime forced the United States government to send marines to suppress an uprising.

Under Woodrow Wilson and his secretary of state, William Jennings Bryan — an arch anti-imperialist — a new era of morality and idealism was introduced into America's policy toward its southern neighbors. "We must prove ourselves their friends and champions," Wilson said, "upon terms of equality and honor." To show that these were not empty phrases, in April 1914 the President signed a treaty agreeing to pay Colombia $25 million for the loss of Panama and expressing "sincere regret" for the incidents which had caused a rupture between the two states, but Theodore Roosevelt (and his senatorial friends) rose up to denounce the treaty in violent language, and it was not ratified until after Roosevelt had died and Wilson left office in 1921.

Yet at the same time that Wilson gave every indication of abandoning the expansionist features of recent American diplomacy, he felt compelled to intervene in the affairs of Caribbean nations. American marines continued to occupy Nicaragua and support an unpopular dictatorship, and in 1915–1916 the American navy set up a military government to preserve order in the strife-torn Dominican Republic and Haiti. Although they were later severely criticized, these moves did bring order to the occupied countries, and they were not used directly to further American financial interests at the expense of native populations. Wilson clung to his promise that "the United States will never again seek one additional foot of territory by conquest."

No doubt the most humbling episode of early Wilsonian diplomacy concerned the Mexican revolution of 1911–1917. Bandit raids by an insurgent Mexican general along the border led the President to send troops into Mexico in pursuit. Several unfortunate clashes between American troops and Mexican forces increased the demands of American war hawks for a full-scale invasion of Mexico, until it became known that the Americans had on one occasion been the aggressors. Wilson thereupon agreed to a mediation of the whole dispute. During the extended and ultimately unsuccessful mediation process of 1916–1917, the United States became increasingly involved in the First World War, and in January 1917 Wilson withdrew the American punitive expedition from Mexico. Although he aimed to apply the principles of liberal idealism in his dealings with all countries, his response to the Mexican revolution showed how difficult it was to conduct foreign policy along these lines.

The Conservative Powers

At the opening of the twentieth century, the economic growth and gradual social democratization of the liberal nation-states appeared on the whole to strengthen the existing institutions in those countries, whereas in the conservative powers of Europe — above all, Germany, Austria, and Russia — economic development and attempts at reform only served to expose and intensify internal weakness.

About 1900, the German Empire was a strong, vital state. Despite a falling birth rate, the German population was increasing faster than the English or French. Its educational system was acclaimed as the best in the whole world. Urbanization was proceeding rapidly; coal and steel production exceeded that of Britain or France; the German share of international trade was expanding as that of the other great European nations shrank. Germany produced a third of the world's electrical goods.

But such striking material advances were accompanied by critical political problems. The Reichstag, the lower house of the German parliament, was elected by universal manhood suffrage, candidates could and did campaign freely, and a broad spectrum of political thought was represented in the Reichstag. Yet beneath this appearance of democracy lay the hard facts of German political life — namely, that after Bismarck's fall Germany remained as ideologically divided as it had been during the nearly thirty years that he presided over the course of Prussian and German history. The German Constitution of 1871 provided for a balance between Crown and Parliament that was bound to lead — if indeed it was not intended to lead — to political stalemate and paralysis. And this increasingly intolerable condition was further accelerated by the fragmentation of the German party system that — like other odious features of German public life — dated back to the tragic defeat of Prussian-German liberalism in the 1860's.

By 1900 the Reichstag was marked by divisive splintering almost as bewildering as that in France. There was, first of all, the Conservative party — which derived most of its power from the landowning aristocracy in the older parts of Prussia. The party of "authority rather than majority," it was the political faction closest to the Prussian-German throne, and it also furnished most of the high officials of the army and bureaucracy. Next to it stood the Free Conservative party — also known as the Bismarck party because of the willingness it had shown to support the chancellor on all important issues — which included substantial landowners outside old Prussia, as well as big capitalists and industrialists. Slightly to the left was the National Liberal party, a strange amalgam which included genuine liberals, bankers, and industrialists, as well as strong nationalists such as the historian Heinrich von Treitschke, but which, as time went on, became increasingly conservative and imperialist. Perhaps the most truly national party was the Center party, which included both conservative and liberal elements and drew much of its support from Catholic peasants and workers. The Center party was the chief support of the government from 1895 to 1907, and after that there was never a government majority without it. In other words, the Center party became precisely what Bismarck had feared—it became the arbiter, if the somewhat uncertain and unpredictable one, of German politics.

On the Left stood the Progressives, who derived most of their support from urban areas, artisans, small businessmen, lower government officials, and intellectuals. Traditional liberals, the Progressives strongly opposed militarism, protectionism, and statism in all its forms. They also opposed the Social Democrats. The most radical party in the country and the fastest growing, by 1912 the Social Democrats had won 110 seats in the Reichstag (the next largest party was the Center, with 90 seats). While the Social Democrats were basically a working-class party, they became more bourgeois as time went on, and this changing character eventually led to a deep split within the party. As it grew in number and importance, the party moved steadily to the Right under the influence of the revisionists, led by Eduard Bernstein. The orthodox Marxists in the party were now led by Karl Liebknecht and Rosa Luxemburg.

Universal suffrage in national elections made it possible for the Social Democrats to become the largest party in the country, but it did not mean that the German government policy was in the hands of the people. The conservative, militarist, expansionist elements asserted control through the Bundesrat, the upper house of the imperial parliament. Each state in the empire sent representatives to the Bundesrat. Since the size of the delegation was determined by the population of each state, seventeen out of its fifty-eight members came from Prussia, the center of the agrarian and military interests, and since delegates to the Bundesrat were named by their state governments, this arrangement meant—as Bismarck had carefully designed it—that no legislation opposed by the Prussian Crown could ever pass. The most the Reichstag could do, then, was to block, to harass, and to object. The kaiser was constitutionally independent of the Reichstag. He appointed the chancellor, who was responsible to him and not to the parliament. Although it was necessary for the chancellor to seek the support of the parties of the Reichstag, their votes could often be disregarded.

The acquisition of great economic, political, and military power had not led the Germans to use that power with restraint and responsibility. The cry for an active "world policy," for "a place in the sun"—alongside or ahead of Britain—entranced large segments of the German population and was responsible, among other things, for the widespread demands for a powerful navy.

German intellectuals—historians included—also caught this nationalist, imperialist, and militarist spirit. It would be unfair, therefore, to place the blame for the growing German militarism entirely on the army or the uniform-enchanted kaiser. The German Empire had been created by force; it grew mightier and wealthier as the years passed. The majority of Germans gloried in their country's power and grandeur. There were, in those heady days before 1914, only a few Germans who questioned the means used to achieve international success and who would have agreed with the industrialist Walther Rathenau, who wrote in 1911, "I see shadows rising wherever I turn. I see them in the evening when I walk through the noisy streets of Berlin; when I perceive the insolence of our wealth gone mad."[1]

The problems of the German Empire, however serious, were nothing compared to those of the Habsburg monarchy. Above and beyond the bewildering and seemingly insoluble conflicts of class, race, and nationality—conflicts which were continuing to grow with every passing year—the real power in the monarchy was centered in the person of Francis Joseph, the aging emperor of Austria and king of Hungary. An inflexible conservative, he had for years controlled the Reichsrath, the imperial parliament, in the Crown's interest. But around the turn of the century the growing unrest of the subject nationalities was making even that impossible. From 1897 to 1904 there was no parliamentary majority, and the government was run by emergency ordinances. In addition to the parties representing the diverse interests of component nationalities, important new groups were beginning to make themselves significantly felt—the Christian Socialist party led by Karl Lueger, the golden-voiced Viennese politician and sometime mayor, openly hostile to Jews and big business; and the Austrian Social Democrats, who pressed for social reform along Marxist lines.

Despite the outward placidity of the Empire, the turn of the century found Austria in the midst of an age of personal despair, cultural revolution, and incipient political disintegration. The rigid political and social caste system, maintained for centuries by court and Church, was slowly but painfully breaking down. No longer was the emperor's word fiat in his own house, but those who inhabited it—whether they were members of his immediate family or the gloomy and distraught Slavic minorities—were far from sure how to proceed. This uncertainty was symbolized by the sensational suicide of the archduke Rudolf, the heir to the Habsburg throne, and his beautiful young friend Maria Vetsera at Mayerling in January 1889; by the assassination of the Emperor's wife by an anarchist in Geneva; by the violent outbursts provoked by Francis Joseph's announcement of the so-called Badeni Ordinances in 1897, equalizing the German and Czech languages in Bohemia; but, above all, by mounting intellectual and cultural disaffection. While this

---

1. Quoted in Koppel S. Pinson, *Modern Germany—Its History and Civilization.* New York: 1954, p. 291.

cultural revolution was going on beneath Francis Joseph's uncomprehending eyes, rising young Czech intellectuals—for example, young Thomas Masaryk and Eduard Benes—were beginning to publish works that showed the Slavic cultural and political consciousness was moving from a quest for autonomy to a desire for complete political independence.

The latter decades of Francis Joseph's reign were not wholly without significant achievements. In the 1880's social legislation based on the German model had been passed, trade unions were legalized, and railroads—so important to the lagging industrial development of the empire—were increasingly nationalized. But this progress was, for the most part, limited to Austria; in Hungary bitter battles were still being fought over far more elementary political questions. As late as 1910 the complicated and discriminatory electoral laws ensured that, in a population of more than 20 million, no more than one million were qualified to vote. This repressive situation led more than a million people to emigrate from Hungary between 1896 and 1910.

The arrogance of the Magyars seemed to grow with the years, and the Dual Monarchy was further shaken in 1902 when a separatist Independence party led by the son of Louis Kossuth demanded Magyarization of the Hungarian regiments that served in the imperial army. The emperor refused—he may well have seen this issue as the harbinger of more dangerous demands to come—but after an acrimonious dispute, a compromise was worked out.

The compromise between the Magyars and Francis Joseph was followed by renewed repression in Croatia, as the Magyars did away with Croat schools and made Magyar the language of the Croatian railroad administration. Those Slavs who had hoped for autonomy within the Dual Monarchy were discouraged, and, before long, they began to turn to Serbia, itself fairly recently independent, as their possible future leader. The emergence of Serbia as leader of a new South Slav unity movement was an ominous development for the Habsburg monarchy, for, in June 1903, there had been a palace revolt in Serbia and the old pro-Austrian Obrenovitch dynasty had been replaced by the strongly pro-Russian Karageorgevitch line. The Viennese government, sensing that a peaceful solution to the problem was virtually impossible and that Serbia might well become a South Slav Piedmont, sought to prevent Serbia from becoming a dangerous threat. The result was that in October 1908 Austria-Hungary formally annexed the provinces of Bosnia and Herzegovina to frustrate Serb aspirations in that direction. In the following year, further actions of the Austrian government—including the use of forged evidence to convict Serbo-Croat leaders of treasonable negotiations with Serbia—helped to drive its Slav subjects deeper into the arms of the Serbs. The nationalists were eventually acquitted, but the damage had been done.

Even when the emperor instituted a liberal measure, the results were unfortunate. The granting of universal manhood suffrage in Austria in 1907 had disappointing consequences. The Christian Socialists and Social Democrats, who won the most seats in the Reichsrath, turned to bitter quarreling.

The national budget could not be passed, and the government continued to operate largely by emergency decree. At the same time, Czech-German rivalry in Bohemia was no closer to a solution.

Of all the conservative monarchies, Russia in the early twentieth century had by far the most turbulent history. Following the Revolution of 1905 it remained to be seen whether the ensuing conservative "revolution from above" would succeed in restoring a measure of social tranquility and at the same time help Russia to catch up in the race for industrial modernization. Whatever its other excuses for lack of achievement after 1906, the Russian government could not blame its troubles—as the Austro-Hungarian government might well have done—on an unmanageable constitution or on continuing deadlock among its various political parties or factions. For within a few years after the revolution, the government had managed to revise the country's fundamental law so that both the rights of its people and the effectiveness of their representation were held to an absolute minimum. Between 1906 and 1909 nearly 2500 political offenders were executed and uncounted thousands sent into exile. This harsh policy did not, however, put an end either to popular disaffection or to the readiness of terrorists and other revolutionary agitators to remove as many of their political oppressors as possible. Repressive police measures succeeded finally in reducing the terrorist attacks—of which there had been thousands in the years 1906–1908—but in September 1911 Stolypin, prime minister since 1906, was assassinated in Kiev.

The death of Stolypin came at a time when the Third Duma, elected in February 1907, had begun to show significant legislative results. Stolypin, moreover, had become aware that the emancipation policy of 1861 was a dead end and that, unless the individual peasant could gain his freedom from the commune or consolidate his scattered holdings into an economically rewarding unit, peasant unrest would continue to mount and burst forth anew, with what results no one could foretell. The Stolypin policy thus at last gave a real chance to the country's hard-working and ambitious peasants, and, as available statistics clearly show, the policy was notably successful. There was a marked increase in production, and mechanization proceeded apace. The consumption of farm machinery, valued at 27.9 million rubles in 1900, had by 1908 risen to 61.3 million and by 1913 to 109.2 million—though such increases affected mostly the largest and most prosperous farms. Substantial progress was also achieved in other fields, particularly education. Despite continuing autocratic control after 1905, notable improvements were to be found at all levels of the educational system.

Yet progress in a variety of important areas of Russian life did not significantly reduce political opposition and social tension. On the contrary, the familiar "revolution of rising expectations" was at work; the years immediately preceding the outbreak of the First World War saw intensified confrontation between government and people, between different classes and nationalities. At the top of the Russian government there was little or no appreciation of the achievements recorded. When she heard that Stolypin had been assassinated, the czarina reportedly said, "He is gone: let us hear no more of him." There was no letup in the repression—or attempted repression—of various minorities and subject people, including the Jews and the Finns, both of whom were hated for their alleged liberal tendencies. Student radicalism and nihilism, too, increased; among many of the young there was a feeling of vast indifference and alienation, dangerously combined with self-pity and aggressive resentment—the characteristic ambience of a revolutionary situation.

Like the other conservative states, imperial Russia would have been best served by a period of diplomatic retrenchment, a reduction in its foreign commitments, and the cessation of its aggressive reconnoitering of explosive opportunities, especially in the Balkans. But the last of the Romanov czars lacked the determination to implement such a wise policy. Although he was no aggressive expansionist, he was too weak willed to put a stop to the dreams and schemes of his over-ambitious generals and diplomats. The crisis of 1905 and the auguries of another upheaval ought to have taught Nicholas II and his advisers a stern lesson. The czarist empire needed beneficent and effective leadership and above all a long period of peace and stability to absorb the far-reaching economic and social changes attendant upon industrialization. Instead, Russia—like the other conservative powers—was slowly but steadily moving toward involvement in another war, whose only harvest would prove to be the overthrow of the dynasty itself.

The Latin World and the Smaller States

In the two generations between the unification of Germany in 1871 and the outbreak of the First World War in 1914, seven great powers dominated world politics—the United States, Britain, France, Germany, Austria-Hungary, Russia, and Japan. In an age which measured most things in terms of sheer size or physical power, these were the states that mattered most. But these powers were far from being able to determine the shape of world affairs wholly as they pleased. At least one other European power—Italy—soon rose to play a substantial role in international politics; and what occurred in the expiring Spanish and Turkish empires, to say nothing of the Scandinavian states and various Latin American countries, was of more than passing interest to the seven leading powers.

Of all the states ranking immediately below the great powers, Italy was the most significant. Territorially united by 1870, Italy with its proud ancient, medieval, and Renaissance past, combined with its courageous struggle for national unity in the nineteenth century, had long enjoyed the sympathetic interest of the international community. So long, so nobly, and so eloquently had the Italians struggled for national unity that it seemed difficult to believe that the triumph of Cavour and the liberation of Rome had not brought Italy

close to the millennium. But they had not. On the contrary, Italian governments after 1870 were far too often characterized by weakness, inefficiency,
and corruption. North and South grew increasingly apart, and though industry
made rapid strides in northern Italy after the 1880's, the government
was hardly up to dealing effectively with the demands and problems of
industrialism.

To be sure, the Italian government made a stab at it. It sought to expand
compulsory elementary education; it built highways and railroads; it encouraged and assisted the spread of manufacturing; it improved rivers and harbors. But most of these improvements came in the North. In the South many
people were saying that things were not much better under the house of Savoy than under the Bourbons. Although the South had more than a third of
the country's population, in 1877 it had only about 7.1 per cent of the savings
accounts and in 1887, 12 per cent of the capital in corporations. This sectional
lag was both vexing and, in the long run, dangerous. Italy's political institutions were also defective. Under its new constitution, Italy was highly centralized, but it had a disturbingly divisive multiparty system, an appointed, highly
conservative upper house, and until 1912 a remarkably narrow franchise.

A political and social order of this sort was headed for considerable trouble,
and this trouble was brought nearer still by the strong anticlericalism that
marked most of the liberal governments after the 1870's. Oddly enough, this
anticlericalism did not lead, as it had in France, to a complete separation of
Church and state; on the contrary, it meant that the state continued both to
pay the salaries of the clergy and to pass on the appointments of bishops and
other important church officials. Dissatisfied with the "law of papal guarantee" of May 1871, which he regarded as grossly inconsiderate of his needs and
power, Pius ix denounced it and forbade any good Catholic to rule or accept
office under the new government, a ban that remained in effect until modified
by Pius x in 1905.

During the years 1870 to 1876, Italy was in the hands of the conservatives
who had presided over, or assisted in, the unification of the country. Then, for
over a decade after 1876, it was the turn of the moderate Left, under the leadership of Agostino Depretis, which proceeded to extend the franchise somewhat and to introduce the first significant social legislation. But such policies
did not change the fundamental structure and problems of Italian society.

During the next decade, Italy's grave economic and social problems were
ignored in favor of dangerous and largely unsuccessful ventures in imperialism. In the summer of 1887 Francesco Crispi, one of Garibaldi's followers,
came to power and soon initiated a vigorous African policy. Before long, Italy
went to war with Ethiopia and won some successes. In the middle 1890's,
when Crispi returned to office, Italy went to war a second time but suffered
an overwhelming and humiliating defeat in March 1896 at Aduwa and was
forced to recognize the continued independence of Ethiopia. Crispi fell almost
immediately.

The 1880's had not been without diplomatic successes—in 1882 Italy had joined the Triple Alliance with Germany and Austria, and in 1887 it signed the Mediterranean Agreement with Austria and Britain. In the late 1890's Italy began a rapprochement with France; in 1898 a treaty was signed ending a damaging tariff war between the two that had been going on for a dozen years. In December 1900 Italy and France signed another agreement by which Italy gave France a free hand in Morocco in return for French support in Tripoli, which Italy had long wished to take over.

Unlike France, where foreign and imperial successes had strengthened the Third Republic, Italy did not gain greater domestic tranquility from its diplomatic achievements. From the early 1890's there were increasing domestic disorders, including a long series of bitter labor disputes and several general strikes. Political and social radicalism was rampant, and in July 1900 King Umberto was assassinated by an anarchist. Nevertheless, the Socialists continued to gain. In 1890 four Socialists were elected to the Italian parliament; in 1913, after the establishment of universal manhood suffrage, their number rose to 77. But like Socialists all over the Continent, the Italian Marxists were fighting bitterly among themselves. Thus some Socialists favored the extension of the suffrage because they thought it would help them; others were opposed because they thought it would involve them too deeply in bourgeois politics. Similarly, orthodox and reformist Socialists quarreled over whether to support social reforms sponsored by middle-class leaders, and they were especially divided over the Tripolitanian War of 1911–1912 with Turkey. The reformers supported this war, but they were in the minority and found themselves purged from the Socialist party.

While the Italian Socialists quarreled among themselves, the government through almost the entire period from 1903 to 1914 was in the hands of a coalition of center factions led by Giovanni Giolitti as prime minister. Giolitti wanted to revitalize Italy. He instituted a few social welfare measures and greatly extended the suffrage. But he was so embroiled in the machinations of party politics that he was never able to make more than a small dent in Italy's enormous economic and social problems. Nor did he reduce the gross corruption that infected all levels of the government. Giolitti's singular achievement was his shrewd handling of the extreme Left. His prescription for government response to the calling of a general strike by syndicalist unions was to do nothing, and the strikes collapsed of their own accord after a few days.

The instability of Italian politics and society was relatively modest compared to the situation in Spain, which between 1871 and 1914 experienced a long series of constitutional upheavals, military coups, and a variety of bitter labor disputes and anarchist risings. In 1874 Spain was formally proclaimed a Republic; this was followed by a period of civil strife, a decade of reasonable stability under King Alfonso XII (1875–1885), and after 1890—especially after the outbreak of the Cuban revolution of 1895—another decade of conflict. In 1902 Alfonso XIII, who was to rule until 1931, became king. Alfonso attempted to befriend the anticlerical liberals, but the country remained bitterly divided. In 1909 there were widespread radical attacks against the Church; in 1912 the anticlerical and highly liberal prime minister, José Caralegas, was assassinated.

The political situation was somewhat more stable in Portugal under King Louis I (1861–1889). But his son, Carlos I, who ruled until he too was assassinated in 1908, was a wastrel and scoundrel. Political discontent grew, and in 1906 Carlos sought to put an end to opposition by the traditional expedient of suppressing parliament and muzzling the press. His son and successor, Manuel II, knew better and brought about a return to constitutional government. But he too was outrageously spendthrift and was forced to abdicate in 1910 after a revolution. The new Republic did not, however, have an easy time. It affronted the Church by anticlerical legislation on the French model, and its lack of effective economic and social policy aroused the working class, which vented its displeasure in a series of labor disputes and violent strikes.

The political instability and social and economic backwardness of Spain and Portugal were paralleled in the development of the Latin American countries which had gained their independence in the early nineteenth century. In some Latin American societies promising economic advances had occurred, but these new states still had not resolved many of the pressing problems acquired along with independence from colonial rule. All of them struggled with political, social, and economic difficulties produced by their status as underdeveloped countries in an increasingly complex technological world.

It is difficult to generalize about Latin America because each country has had a distinct character and history of its own. All of the new republics, however, lacked a tradition of representative democratic government. Government had been imported, and there was no indigenous class trained in civil service or administration. The small elite group of wealthy landowners was markedly selfish and irresponsible, and no urban middle class or sizable number of small landowners existed to oppose their monopoly of power and wealth. The large plantations of coastal Latin America—worked by Negro slaves or Indians—resembled the feudal holdings of medieval Europe rather than the nineteenth-century Western world. The Roman Catholic Church owned vast amounts of land and unfortunately chose to cast its great weight against reform or change of any kind. The Church (in South America particularly and to a lesser extent in Mexico and Central America) was often more powerful than the civil government.

The heterogeneous population of Latin America provided both tinder and spark for racial unrest. In 1823 the population was about twenty million, of which about one fifth were Negro slaves, three fifths Indians and *mestizos* (mixed bloods), and one fifth white—the latter steadily augmented by immigration from Europe during the nineteenth century. Without a well-established educational system, the growing Indian population was not easily assimilated by the European upper class and presented a perpetual threat of radical revolution along racial lines—a contributing factor to the fear of change which characterized the conservative classes.

These fundamental obstacles to viable government in the new independent states had their inevitable consequences, of which the most important was political instability. The new nations were not really governable units, and dissatisfaction with existing regimes was endemic. Coup followed coup, but the supposedly "revolutionary" new governments were not essentially different from the old; until the Mexican revolution of 1910 the endless shifts in political power produced no genuine social or economic reform. The army became the great vehicle of political change and advancement, and mestizos who could not ordinarily compete with whites achieved education and political power within the military establishment. The army remains a center of power in Latin America to this day.

The economic penetration of Latin America by European and, after 1900, by North American capital accelerated after independence. Opportunities for investment, especially in the richer countries (Argentina, Brazil, Chile, and Venezuela), were enormous; European money and technology moved into Latin American mining, railroad-building, and agriculture. The result was a limited kind of prosperity, but one which was more helpful to landowners than to peasants and Indians. Foreign capitalism encouraged restriction to a few staple products—notably meat in Argentina, coffee in Brazil, and copper and tin in various mining countries—leaving the Latin American economy on a dangerously narrow base which was largely dependent on the fluctuations of the world market. On the whole the effects of economic penetration from Europe in the nineteenth century and from the United States in the twentieth were exploitative and harmful.

Immigration continued too; it has been estimated that more than ten million Europeans moved to Latin America between 1825 and 1940. This contributed to the development of a few large cities (such as Rio de Janeiro and Buenos Aires) and thus to the beginning of an urban middle class, but it also added to social problems.

The only genuine revolution in Latin America in the period before the First World War began in Mexico in 1910. By then, the dictator Porfirio Díaz had been in and out of power for nearly thirty-five years. Mexico had grown prosperous at the beginning of the century, thanks to railroad-building and United States investment, but the resulting inflation had made the lot of the *peons* (debt-slaves on plantations) more miserable than ever. Village communal land had been lost under the constitution of 1857, when large estates were allowed to absorb not only Church holdings but land which had traditionally been used by Indians and mestizos. Further, the foreign capital which made some Mexicans prosperous had produced a wave of resentment against foreigners and their enterprises. Díaz was an old man in 1910, and the country was ripe for rebellion.

The revolution of 1910 seemed at first like any other Latin American coup—a struggle for power among generals. Francisco Madero, who became president when Díaz was ousted in 1911, was an ineffective leader who offered no real reform. However, the peasants and Indians began to fight for their own rights against the landowners under such local leaders as Emiliano Zapata and Francisco Villa, and for the first time their struggles were effective. After a counterrevolution and several years of civil war, Venustiano Carranza established himself as president and called a constitutional convention in 1917.

The most important achievement of the convention was the adoption of a radical program of land reform. During the chaotic years of the revolution the peasants had seized lands which they believed to be theirs by right. The convention not only ratified their actions but accepted the responsibility of

Although the Congress of Berlin (1878) recognized Bulgarian autonomy and the independence of Serbia, Montenegro, and Rumania, the Balkan peninsula remained in the throes of nationalist turmoil. The independent states were jealous of one another, hated the Ottoman Empire, which still controlled Macedonia, and feared Russian and Austrian interference in Balkan affairs. The two wars fought in 1912 and 1913 changed boundaries but did little to alleviate the tension. Turkey lost all but a small corner of its European holdings; Bulgaria felt cheated when Rumania gained territory on the Black Sea at its expense and when Serbia and Greece took the lion's share of Macedonia; Serbia resented the creation of Albania by Austria and Italy, which cut the Serbs off from the Adriatic.

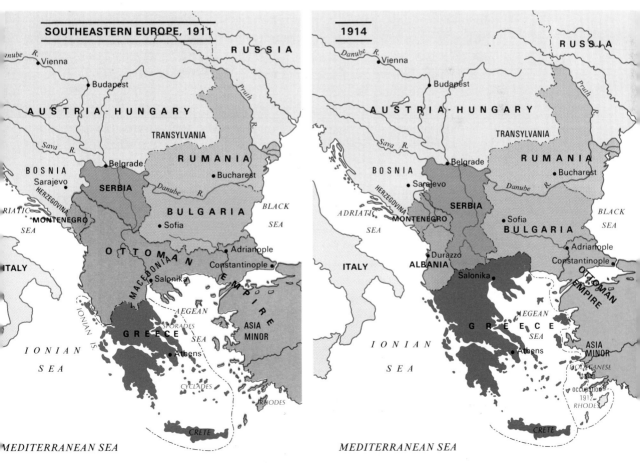

expropriating and apportioning large estates. Further, the nation claimed ownership of mineral and subsoil deposits — a blow at foreign oil interests. The constitution promulgated an advanced program of social and labor legislation, including the guarantee of the right to strike; it abolished peonage; it severely limited the rights and perquisites of the Church.

The Mexican constitution of 1917 represented the introduction of modern democratic government to Latin America. It aimed at nothing less than restructuring the national institutions, and the revolution which preceded it was achieved through the efforts and determination of the oppressed classes themselves. The medieval structure of landlord, peasant, and priest was shattered by the first genuine reforms in a hundred years of independence.

While the Latin states in both Europe and America were caught up in continuing political and social strife, the Scandinavian countries were demonstrating that peaceful change could resolve significant national and international problems. Not only were the decades before 1914 years of economic progress and social advance in the northern region, but in 1905 the Norwegian-Swedish Union, which had been in effect since the Congress of Vienna, was peacefully dissolved. The growth of modern Norwegian nationalism was not a sudden development, though it had been considerably accelerated after the introduction of universal manhood suffrage in Norway in 1898. The Scandinavian states managed to resolve smoothly the kind of problem that, farther south, had led time and again to wars or domestic upheaval. In the northern states, the practice of political accommodation and compromise that had developed in the nineteenth century culminated in the separation of 1905. And this separation was followed by friendship and cooperation between Sweden and Norway.

The Norwegian-Swedish relationship contrasts most sharply with the increasingly violent and dangerous developments in the Ottoman Empire and the Balkans. The corruption and oppression of the regime of Abdul-Hamid II (1876–1909) — against which Bosnia and Herzegovina had revolted in 1875 — had ended only with his overthrow by the so-called "Young Turks" in April 1909. But that revolution did not mark the opening of a new era of constitutional government and peaceful change. On the contrary, plot and counterplot, insurrection and repression, followed in rapid order. In Baghdad, Damascus, Beirut, and other cities Arab nationalist factions were springing up; in European Turkey, various constituent nationalities (mostly South Slav) were moving toward independence. This quest for independence made for further conflict and military confrontation. In October 1912 the first Balkan War — between Bulgaria, Greece, and Serbia on the one hand and Turkey on the other — broke out; it was ended by the Treaty of London in May 1913, with Bulgaria the chief beneficiary. In June 1913 came a second Balkan war; this time Serbia, Greece, Rumania, and Turkey joined forces against Bulgaria. Within a month, Bulgaria was overwhelmed and yielded most of its earlier gains.

The Balkan Wars were ominous evidence that aggressive nationalism had affected southeastern Europe in a critical manner. The great powers knew it, and had moved quietly to damp down the new conflagration. But by 1913 Turkey was not the only "sick man of Europe"; Austria-Hungary was on the danger list as well. Before long, Slavic nationalism and Habsburg power collided, and the result was World War I.

II THE APPROACH TO WAR

Rivalries and Alliances among the Great Powers

By the opening of the twentieth century, the system of diplomacy inaugurated by the Concert of Europe was showing distinct signs of wear. In its heyday, the Concert had successfully maintained the Continental peace. On numerous occasions, collective action by the several great European states had prevented a single state from gaining so powerful an influence as to threaten the security of its neighbors. But in the late nineteenth century, as the various powers began to polarize into two camps—the Triple Alliance of Germany, Austria, and Italy and the Dual Alliance of France and Russia —such concerted action became increasingly difficult.

At the same time, the areas of potential conflict grew more numerous. The two driving forces behind expanding rivalries were nationalism and the closely related phenomenon of imperialism. On the Continent the areas of international tension included the provinces of Alsace and Lorraine, which Germany had annexed from France at the close of the Franco-Prussian War, and Turkey's Balkan provinces, where Russia had long sought to expand and was now increasingly supporting Slavic nationalist forces against Austria-Hungary. Outside the Continent, the force of imperialist expansion that had erupted in the last three decades of the nineteenth century brought virtually every one of the great European powers into overseas conflict with its neighbors. The most acute colonial rivalries were between the British and French in Africa, the British and Russians in Persia, Afghanistan, and the Far East, and the Russians and the Japanese in the Far East. In the late nineteenth century preoccupation with imperial expansion tended to center European rivalries outside the Continent, and it temporarily diverted Europe's attention away from the explosive Balkan situation.

Particularly dangerous was Germany's desire for overseas colonies. With the accession of William II to the throne of the German Empire in 1888 and the dismissal of Bismarck in 1890, Germany's expansionist aims took on an openly threatening tone. The kaiser's personality was no small factor in the growing tension that pervaded diplomatic affairs in the years before the world war. He was twenty-nine when he came to the throne, determined to match

Germany's growing wealth at home with an "appropriate" influence in world affairs. Unfortunately, the kaiser's style of diplomacy was crude, impatient, and histrionic—hardly the best combination for lulling the suspicions of Germany's imperial rivals.

Anglo-German relations had seemed to improve for a time after Bismarck's dismissal. In 1890 Germany had ceded to Britain certain large East African claims in return for the island of Heligoland in the North Sea, and this was followed up, almost at once, by a highly successful state visit by William II to his grandmother, Queen Victoria, in London. In 1895 Lord Salisbury had hinted that the time to partition the Ottoman Empire might have arrived, but William misunderstood Salisbury, and relations between the two countries soon took a turn for the worse. They deteriorated further when the kaiser sent his congratulatory telegram to the Boer leader, Paul Kruger, in 1896.

Germany's moves in the Near and Far East were not so flagrantly provocative. In 1897 Germany seized the Chinese port of Kiaochow, but the other powers had done the same sort of thing, and in any case the British government was much more worried about Russian expansion in the Far East. In 1898 German financial interests had obtained a concession from the Ottoman Empire to construct a Berlin-to-Baghdad railroad, but for the time being at least that alarmed only the Russians, who were powerless to block it.

From the British point of view, the most threatening challenge was the buildup of the German fleet. It had its start in 1897 when Admiral Alfred von Tirpitz became minister of marine and at once launched a program designed to whip up support for a large, high seas fleet. One of the first to catch the fever was the kaiser. A series of German naval bills passed in 1898 and 1900 projected a force of no fewer than thirty-eight battleships, fourteen battle cruisers, and thirty-eight light cruisers to be launched by 1920.

For all that has been written on the subject, it remains unclear just what use the Germans envisaged for their new fleet. If they ever expected a navy large enough to challenge Britain's, that was a dangerous illusion, although no more so than some of the others that the kaiser and many of his officials and countrymen entertained. One of these illusions was that Britain was so overcommitted internationally that it would soon have to pay the price the Germans were demanding for an alliance, and another was that the Anglo-Japanese alliance of 1902, the Anglo-French entente of 1904, and the Anglo-Russian agreement of 1907 all amounted to very little. It was this miscalculation that led the Germans to one diplomatic blunder after another and finally to a world war in 1914.

More than three years had elapsed between the Anglo-French entente of 1904 and the Anglo-Russian agreement of 1907. Germany did not, diplomatically speaking, spend that interval very profitably. In early 1905 the kaiser had paid a visit to Tangier, and German demands for the "independence" of Morocco, which was rapidly passing into French hands, led to the Algeciras Conference (January–April 1906), which indeed affirmed the nominal independence of the country, but also gave the French additional, highly valuable financial and police powers.

While the first Moroccan crisis, as it came to be known, was still in progress, William II and Nicholas II met at Björkö, Finland, in July 1905, where the kaiser cleverly persuaded the czar to sign an agreement providing among other things that "In case one of the two Empires shall be attacked by a European Power, its ally will aid it in Europe with all its military and naval forces." It was a diplomatic coup of the first order—a Continental alliance against France or Britain. But it did not last. When Nicholas returned home, his foreign minister explained to him the full meaning of what he had signed and how contrary to the Franco-Russian alliance it really was. The agreement never went into effect.

While the collapse of the Björkö agreement was a serious blow for Germany, the Balkan situation was rapidly turning against Austria. Despite Russia's long-standing support of pan-Slavist movements, the Dual Monarchy had always been able to count on one South Slav state, Serbia, to resist Russian blandishments. But in 1903, as already noted, a bloody palace revolution in Serbia had replaced the pro-Austrian dynasty with an openly pro-Russian line, and relations between Austria and Serbia soon began to deteriorate.

By the summer of 1908 the Austrians had decided that something had to be done to curb the ever growing South Slav agitation—whose principal object was doubtless the creation of a large South Slav state under Serbian leadership. There was only one way to check such ambition at the moment—namely, to annex Bosnia and Herzegovina. At about the same time, expansionist pressure and domestic turmoil were once more leading the Russian government to cast covetous glances toward the Straits. In September 1908, Isvolsky, the Russian foreign minister, visited his Austrian opposite, Count von Aehrenthal, at Buchlau Castle, Moravia, to discuss both subjects. What passed between the two diplomats has never been satisfactorily explained. But Isvolsky thought he had reached an agreement by which Russia would support the annexation in return for Austrian support for revision of existing Straits agreements. Isvolsky made plans to visit Rome, Paris, London, and Berlin to organize further backing for his claims. But the Austrians did not wait for the other powers. In early October they annexed the provinces.

Russian public opinion was outraged. It appeared that Isvolsky had been outmaneuvered by the Austrians. The existing conventions governing the Straits were not revised, for England insisted that if the Straits were to be opened to Russian vessels, they also be opened to British vessels. This, of course, was completely unacceptable to Russia. Needless to say, Serbia viewed the annexation of Bosnia and Herzegovina as tantamount to an act of war. Supported by bellicose elements in Russia, Serbia demanded compensation in the strongest possible terms and built its military strength to a level of near-mobilization. Austria was determined to stand firm, and for a time in early 1909 a European war over Bosnia-Herzegovina appeared likely.

Under the circumstances, the key to the crisis lay in Berlin. When word of the Austrian-Russian agreement first reached Berlin, the German government itself was highly indignant. The kaiser felt that he had been kept in the dark much too long, and he regarded the agreement as an unwarranted attack on Turkey. In the end, however, Chancellor Prince Bernhard von Bülow persuaded the kaiser to stand by Austria. He informed Vienna that "in case difficulties or complications arise, our ally can count upon us," and the Germans then devised a face-saving formula under which the other powers — including Russia — would recognize the Austrian annexation. In late March 1909 the German government informed St. Petersburg: "We expect an answer — yes or no; we must regard any evasive, conditional, or unclear answer as a refusal. We should then draw back and let things take their course." The Russians backed down. German intervention had carried the day, but Germany had also succeeded in offending everyone, particularly Russia, which began to arm in earnest. In a separate note to Austria, the chastened Serbs promised to stop anti-Austrian propaganda on their territory and to live on

Although the crises that occurred from 1905 to 1914 were settled peaceably, they hardened the rival alliance systems and increased the tension between them. The Tangier crisis (1905) and ensuing Algeciras Conference demonstrated that Germany could depend only on Austria. The *Panther* incident at Agadir (1911) also backfired, leading to closer Anglo-French cooperation. After Austria precipitately annexed Bosnia and Herzogovina in 1908, Russia became more determined to resist further Austrian designs on the Balkans.

DIPLOMATIC CRISES 1905-1914

good terms with the Dual Monarchy. It was a worthless promise and meant nothing.

No sooner had the Bosnian crisis blown over than, in October 1909, the kaiser granted an interview to the London *Daily Telegraph* in which he foolishly remarked, "The prevailing sentiment amongst my own people is not friendly to England. I am in a minority in my own land." At once, international tension revived. Over the next few months some progress in reducing existing Franco-German friction and improving Austro-Turkish relations seems to have been made. But the air of distrust remained, and a revolution in naval construction—begun with Britain's launching of the H.M.S. *Dreadnought*—soon led to further intensification of the naval race. Britain's naval expenditures rose sharply and were justified on the grounds that Germany was becoming increasingly bellicose.

International tension was further inflamed by another Moroccan crisis in the summer of 1911. Earlier that year, heightened discontent and disorders in Morocco led the French to consider sending in additional force to protect the lives of Europeans. At first, the German government—including the kaiser—did not object. But soon the Germans began to fish in troubled waters. In July the German gunboat *Panther* arrived at Agadir on the pretext of protecting German nationals in that city. But in fact the Germans had already given up on Morocco. What they really wanted was compensation for their prospective loss. The German performance puzzled and alarmed the English cabinet, even those members who had hitherto hoped for an Anglo-German alliance. In late July, Lloyd George declared that Great Britain would prefer war to a settlement achieved at the cost of its national honor.

The French government strove to reach a peaceful agreement with Germany, and by the end of 1911 the crisis passed; France obtained German recognition of a protectorate over Morocco, and Germany received 100,000 square miles of the French Congo. Inside France, however, German belligerence had provoked a virulent outbreak of nationalist feeling, and in the next year the moderate government of Joseph Caillaux was replaced by that of the more militant Raymond Poincaré. Other effects of the second Moroccan crisis were even more ominous. The day before Lloyd George's address, a leading member of the British general staff, Sir Henry Wilson, met with the French chief of staff, General Dubail, at the ministry of war in Paris, "to determine the new conditions for the participation of an English army in the operations of the French armies in the North-East in case of a war with Germany." The war clouds were now gathering.

The second Moroccan crisis also led to the last and climactic effort to head off an all-out Anglo-German naval race and military showdown by diplomatic negotiation. In 1912 the British secretary of war, Lord Haldane, was dispatched to Berlin to see what kind of agreement the Germans would accept. Haldane remained in Berlin nearly a week, but the conversations came to nothing. Britain rejected all attempts to limit its right to come to France's assistance; Germany would make no significant reductions in the latest Supplementary Naval Law, shortly to be put before the Reichstag. The British, in brief, had demanded concrete naval concessions; the Germans, political concessions. Neither would budge.

As it turned out, the Haldane mission was the prelude to the last years of peace. The Balkan Wars of 1912–1913 greatly strengthened Serbia, but in October 1913 the Serbs were outraged by the Austrian demand that they evacuate Albania, which they had recently occupied, within eight days. The Austrians in turn became increasingly frantic because of what—ever since their annexation of Bosnia—they had regarded as the wavering and uncertain course of Berlin. On July 6, 1913, the German chancellor Theobald von Bethmann-Hollweg tried to calm the Habsburg government: "I can only express the hope that the people in Vienna will not let themselves be upset by the nightmare of a Great Serbia, but will await further developments. . . . Only insistently can I warn against the idea of wanting to gobble up Serbia, for that would simply weaken Austria."[2] There the matter still rested in June 1914.

Sarajevo and the Outbreak of the Great War

In late 1913 and early 1914 there was a relaxation of international tensions, and in mid-June 1914 Britain and Germany signed an agreement apparently resolving most of their long-standing differences over the Near East and German plans for a Berlin-to-Baghdad railroad. It was against this encouraging background that a shocked and astounded world learned of the assassination of the heir to the Habsburg throne. On Sunday, June 28, 1914, Archduke Francis Ferdinand and his wife, while on a state visit to Sarajevo, capital of the recently annexed province of Bosnia, were shot by a young Serbian nationalist.

Political assassination was not exactly uncommon during the prewar years, but this particular assassination had tremendous repercussions. All Europe joined in condemning the murders. It was immediately assumed that Serbia had a hand in the plot, but there was a delay in discovering just what role the Serbian government had played, and that delay allowed the first wave of anti-Serbian feeling to ebb. In Russia, sentiment was aroused against an expected Austrian assault on Serbian independence.

Oddly enough, Russian expectations were not to be fulfilled for several weeks. The archduke was reputedly quite liberal and was anything but popular at the Viennese court; the Habsburg government was at first undecided what to do. In early July, however, it decided to seek German support, as

---

2. Quoted in Sidney B. Fay, *The Origins of the World War.* New York: Macmillan, 1928, I, p. 454.

The End of the Old Order. Soon after Archduke Francis Ferdinand and his wife arrived in Sarajevo, a bomb was thrown at their car as it made its way to the town hall. Only a few bystanders and an officer in the royal party were wounded. But a number of Serbian nationalists with orders to kill the archduke were in Sarajevo. Before going on to an official luncheon, the Habsburg heir insisted on visiting the wounded officer in the hospital, and it was on the way there that a young man waiting in the crowd shot and killed Francis Ferdinand and his consort. Above: the archduke (center) saying good-bye to the mayor at the town hall a few minutes before the assassination.

assurance against the possibility of Russian intervention on Serbia's behalf. The German government — which detested the South Slav movement but had little notion what it was letting itself in for — gave this assurance almost at once. Nevertheless, Vienna still held back from the next step, because the Hungarians, who wanted no more South Slavs in the empire, were generally opposed to war, and because the Austrian government itself lacked firm evidence of official Serb complicity. Finally, on July 23, Austria issued an ultimatum the terms of which amounted to the establishment of a virtual Austrian protectorate over Serbia. Surprisingly, two days later Serbia accepted most of the Austrian demands. Nevertheless the Austrian government at once declared the reply unsatisfactory and on July 28 declared war on Serbia.

Austria's declaration of war did not by itself mean that a great war was about to begin, and for the next few days frantic efforts were made to head off this conflict. The origins of the war — and the diplomacy that led up to it — have been the subject of an enormously detailed body of historical literature.

Essentially, two general interpretations have developed. The first one, formalized by the Allies at the end of the war in the so-called war guilt clause of the Treaty of Versailles, holds that Austria and Germany—but especially Germany—were principally responsible for the war. This was the position of scholars like the American Bernadotte E. Schmitt, whose *The Coming of the War, 1914,* was published in 1930; the Italian Luigi Albertini, whose *Origins of the War of 1914* appeared during the Second World War; and, more recently, the German historian Fritz Fischer, whose *Germany's War Aims in the First World War* (1961) also views the war as the climax of German efforts to dominate Europe. As against this school, there are the works of the American Sidney B. Fay, who published his carefully reasoned *Origins of the World War* in 1928, and the British scholar G. P. Gooch; they view the responsibility for the war as considerably more widespread.

"The verdict . . . that Germany and her allies were responsible for the war," Fay wrote at the end of his work, "in view of the evidence now available, is historically unsound." There is much to be said for this point of view. It is true that the Germans had foolishly given the Austrians in early July what has been called " a blank check," but when the kaiser, ever militant and excitable, heard the details of the conciliatory Serb reply to the Austrian ultimatum, he remarked: "This is more than one could have expected! A great moral success for Vienna; but with it every reason for war drops away." The Austrians, however, did not see it that way. They ignored British pleas for an international conference, which the Germans also rejected, partly out of fear of another diplomatic disaster such as Morocco. The Austrians also spurned British suggestions for Anglo-German mediation; they decided to confront both Germany and the Triple Entente with a *fait accompli.*

This was a dangerous game which was to have perilous consequences. For the Russians, fearing that the Austrians would soon overrun and defeat Serbia, began to move toward mobilization, despite German warnings that such a step meant war. On July 30 Nicholas II, after long debate and with grave reservations, approved full Russian mobilization. "Think of the responsibility which you are advising me to take!" he told his foreign minister. "Think of the thousands and thousands of men who will be sent to their deaths!" Once the news of Russian mobilization arrived in Berlin, Germany sent a twelve-hour ultimatum demanding that Russia cease mobilizing forthwith, and inquired of the French government what its position would be in view of a Russian-German conflict. There is, in the French diplomatic documents, no evidence to show that the French ever actively sought to restrain the Russians. About 3:45 on the afternoon of August 1, the French government decreed general mobilization; almost simultaneously Germany did the same; at seven o'clock that evening Germany declared war on Russia.

Even at this point, a great war was not yet certain, but it became so in the next forty-eight hours when, at seven o'clock on the evening of August 2, the German minister at Brussels handed the Belgian government a twelve-hour ultimatum demanding "benevolent neutrality toward Germany " and permission for German troops to pass through Belgium on the way to attack France. The Belgian ultimatum ushered in the last phase of the hurried events of those fateful days. At 6:00 P.M. on August 3 Germany declared war on France, and this made the position of Britain all the more crucial. British diplomacy in those hectic days and weeks, and especially the policy of the British foreign secretary Sir Edward Grey, has been much criticized. It is true that British diplomacy had long been vague and—almost deliberately—obscure. One reason was that the British cabinet itself was divided on the issue of going to war. Britain had made some worthwhile and significant efforts to save the peace, especially its proposal for mediation between Austria and Serbia and between Austria and Russia.

On the other hand, Britain had long made it clear that it would come to the defense of Belgium—whose neutrality had been guaranteed by an international treaty in 1839. And it was Belgium that was in Germany's immediate path. The reason for this was that the German high command's Schlieffen Plan—named for its inventor, Alfred von Schlieffen, the German chief of staff from 1891 to 1905—envisioned that any future war would necessarily be a two-front war for Germany. But since the German army could not wage such a war successfully, one adversary would have to be knocked out as quickly as possible. Russia, with its immense army and enormous territory, would be impossible to conquer speedily. The only alternative was to knock France out of the war while Russia was slowly mobilizing. Because the border between France and Germany was heavily fortified, the Schlieffen Plan called for an initial invasion of Belgium to the north, outflanking the French armies and driving them from the field within six weeks.

Unfortunately for Germany, an invasion that violated Belgian neutrality gave those members of the British cabinet who favored war an argument with which to rally most of their colleagues and the nation. When German troops crossed the Belgian frontier early on August 4, and when the German government rejected a British ultimatum that their demands on Belgium be withdrawn, a British declaration of war followed that night.

The question remains: Why should this particular crisis have launched the World War? In earlier crises, one power had always backed down when confronted by the specter of war, and it seems very likely that, conditioned by what had gone before, each of the powers believed that its threatening gestures would result in a diplomatic victory. Certainly a good deal of blame must rest with those men in each government who encouraged the snowballing arms race. In Germany, particularly, the army was in a fighting condition never before attained. If Germany had to go to war, 1914 probably was the best time for it.

Instead of relieving tension, the system of alliances actually contributed to the likelihood of war. Without German support, Austria-Hungary probably would not have pressed the conflict with Serbia and Russia. It is also probable that Russia, though certainly on the lookout for diplomatic coups, would not have stood up to the combined threat of Germany and Austria-Hungary without some assurances from France. Why did France give such assurances? Probably because French leaders were afraid of losing their Russian ally. There is no telling what might have happened—to the Franco-Russian alliance, the Triple Entente, and the peace of Europe—had not France assured Russia, in late July 1914, that "it would enter the war if Germany intervened with arms in an eventual Austro-Russian war".

In the perspective of more than half a century, it is difficult to avoid the conclusion that responsibility for the coming of the war must be spread around very liberally. Certainly British diplomacy had been considerably less forthright and independent than Sir Edward Grey sought to make it appear. Ironically—and not for the last time in a great international confrontation—the original culprit, Serbia, escaped with comparatively little criticism, even though the assassination of the archduke almost certainly had the tacit approval of the Serbian government.

In his important study of international relations from 1871 to 1914, the French historian Pierre Renouvin has written that the ultimate impulse to war "came from national feeling and from passionate emotion." Until the very last moment, the leading governments and their ministers had done little to avert the catastrophe or to warn their people of its likely consequences. It had remained for the socialists throughout Europe to preach that war meant the end of the old order, and they alone were to be proved very nearly correct. But even the socialists—including those in France and Germany—rallied to their country's side, forgetting all their talk about the international solidarity of the working class. Most of Europe, then, went to war with a sense of exhilaration, even joy. Before long, such sentiments were to prove tragically unfounded.

III THE FIRST WORLD WAR AND THE RUSSIAN REVOLUTION

The War on Land and Sea

As the German high command had foreseen, hostilities opened immediately on both eastern and western fronts. In the west the German army ran into unexpectedly stiff opposition from the Belgians in its attempt to take Liège and the surrounding fortresses. By August 16 it had penetrated only ten miles into Belgium. On August 18, however, the right wing of the German army was able to start its major drive. Within two days Brussels fell, and on September 2 the French government retreated from Paris to Bordeaux.

The French army launched a counterassault from the south (into Alsace and Lorraine), fighting several hard battles but gaining no victories. Meanwhile, the French army in the north was retreating steadily before powerful German forces, estimated at nearly a million and a half men. The French retreated to the east of Paris, and instead of swinging west and enveloping the French capital, the German army followed the retreating French forces. The Germans had made a tactical blunder: French troops left outside the German right wing were able to counterattack and hold the advancing German armies on September 5 in the first Battle of the Marne. The Germans then attempted to return to the original Schlieffen Plan; they swung north again to outflank the armies of the French and British Allies. On October 9 the Germans took the Belgian port of Antwerp. There followed a running battle that spread northward. When neither succeeded in outflanking the other, both sides dug in. By the end of 1914, the trench warfare that was to characterize the western front for the greater part of the war had begun.

Meanwhile, in the east, the Russian offensive against Galicia and East Prussia had been stopped by massive defeats at Tannenburg (August 26–30) and the Masurian Lakes (September 6–15). The Russians were considerably more successful against the Austrians, but a decisive victory was lost when the Austrians intercepted the Russian plan of attack. (The Russian general staff followed the peculiar practice of sending orders to its field commanders in plain language instead of code.) Although the Russians failed to score any lasting victories, against either the Germans or the Austrians, they nevertheless accomplished one crucial objective—they forced the Germans to divide their armies between east and west, and by doing so, they probably kept the Germans from knocking out France in the early weeks of the war. The Austrians were not successful in their Serbian offensives. By December they had been repulsed with heavy casualties.

The year ended in a virtual stalemate. No offensive had succeeded in crippling the opposing force, though battle losses had been unexpectedly high. Some of the best-trained units of the various armies had been decimated, and younger, less experienced troops had to be rushed into the trenches. None of the commanders understood that trench warfare made traditional offensive tactics obsolete, and the next three years saw an astonishing number of massive assaults on equally massive troop concentrations that resulted only in terrible loss of life.

World War I was, first and foremost, a war of men. Airplanes, still in their infancy, were used mainly for scouting enemy positions. Tanks were not widely used until almost the end of the war. Although trains played a major part in transport and some troops were rushed to the front lines at the Battle of the Marne by Parisian cabs, the movement of armies depended primarily on horse and foot.

With the war in the west stalemated for the time being, at the end of 1914 attention turned once more to the eastern and Balkan fronts. In January 1915 Turkey, which had joined the Central Powers—as Germany and its allies were called—suffered a crushing defeat at the hands of the Russian army at Sarikamis. More important, in mid-February the British began a campaign to seize the Dardanelles and Constantinople. If the attempt had been adequately planned and consistently supplied, it would probably have been successful. Instead, the undertaking—conceived by Winston Churchill, then the forty-one-year-old First Lord of the Admiralty—had led to bitter interservice rivalry, and the plans had been very poorly worked out. As a result, the British army did not land until the end of April, after the Turks had had a chance to scrape together a defending force. A long and bloody campaign developed that lasted for a year; Britain's 250,000 casualties were matched by those of the Turkish and German forces. The failure of the campaign was more than a tactical disaster. It ended hope of Allied-Russian contact through the Straits, perhaps lengthened the war by as much as two or three years, and quite possibly helped to bring on the Russian Revolution of 1917. For an Allied victory in the Black Sea area would not only have substantially improved Russian morale; it would also have made it much easier for the western Allies to supply Russian military forces.

By early 1915, the western front began to stir once more. In February the French attempted to breach the German trenches in Champagne. For small gains they suffered ninety thousand casualties. The British offensive further north was pushed back to Ypres. In that battle the Germans used poison gas for the first time. In May, at Artois, the French launched a larger attack and scored some limited gains. In both cases the Germans missed a major victory because they were short of reserves to pour into the fighting and because the use of gas was purely experimental and they were unprepared to follow it up.

Meanwhile, in addition to extending the conflict to the Dardanelles, the Allies sought to break the stalemate by bringing in new supporters. By a highly secret treaty signed at London in late April 1915, Italy—which had declared its neutrality as soon as war broke out—joined the Allied camp. It was not a selfless move. In outbidding the Germans for Italy's services, the Allies were obliged to promise Italy Tyrol, Trieste, a share of Asia Minor, and other territory in the Balkans and North Africa. Thus began the long series of secret treaties and promises that were to prove so dangerous and troublesome at the end of the war. On May 23, 1915, Italy declared war on Austria-Hungary, but not until August 1916 was it to declare war on Germany. Italy was anything but prepared; it suffered from shortages of funds and factories, and its store of war materiel had been seriously depleted during the war with Turkey three years earlier. Such weakness, however, only seemed to feed national arrogance and ambition.

The war was going even better for the Central Powers in the east. Beginning in May 1915, a great Austro-German offensive shattered the Russian line, and by September the Central Powers had advanced three hundred miles and captured Warsaw, taking 300,000 prisoners and 3000 guns. Russia was saved only by a campaign in Serbia that diverted the Central Powers. On September 6 the Bulgarians entered the war on the side of the Central Powers, hoping to gain Macedonia, and launched an offensive against Serbia. In early October, the Allies landed a small force at Salonika in neutral Greece, but King Constantine (whose wife was the kaiser's sister) opposed Allied operations within his country. Consequently, the Allies never went forward in support of Serbia, and the remnants of that country's army were forced to retreat to the island of Corfu. Bulgarian troops overran Montenegro and Albania in quick succession, and the Allies were left bottled up in Salonika. Meanwhile, four Italian offensives against the Austrians in the area of the Isonzo River met with little success, despite Italian numerical superiority, and cost the Italian army frightful casualties.

In September 1915, the Allies in the west began another major offensive under the direction of General Joffre. Once again they penetrated the German lines (this time for several miles), but in the end the Anglo-French forces were unable to force the Germans into a pincers as planned. The toll was enormous on both sides.

As the western front turned into a deadlock, the war at sea became more critical. The British navy had driven German warships from the Atlantic trade routes by the end of 1914, and the primary threat to the English fleet came not from the numerically inferior German surface fleet but from mines and submarines lurking in England's home waters. On February 4, 1915, Germany announced a policy of unrestricted submarine warfare, refusing to respect the neutrality of ships from nonbelligerent nations. Protests were immediate, but Germany ignored them. In early May the liner *Lusitania* was sunk with a loss of approximately 1200 passengers, including more than a hundred Americans. Widely hailed as a success in Germany, the sinking outraged the United States. Further sinkings made the situation worse, and after a series of increasingly stiff American notes, Germany abandoned the policy on September 1.

At the beginning of 1916 both sides were planning offensives, but because the Russian army had not recovered from its crushing defeats and would be useless until summer, the Central Powers struck first. Their objective was the famous French fortress of Verdun. A victory there would not have given the Germans a strategic advantage, but it would have been a shattering blow to French morale. The fortress was not prepared for the attack that began on February 21 — the fall of the Belgian fortresses had convinced General Joffre, the head of the French army, that fortresses were useless. But General Henri Philippe Pétain, one of the few supporters of a defensive strategy, was placed in command. He effected a rapid reinforcement; the result was that the German drive made imperceptible headway, but casualties on both sides were beyond belief, the French losing about 350,000, the Germans somewhat fewer.

In June 1916 a long-planned Allied offensive (predominantly British) was launched at the Somme, relieving some of the pressure on Verdun. But the Germans were extraordinarily well dug in, and when they were quickly relieved, trench warfare ensued once more. In September the Allies used tanks for the first time, but while the lumbering machines lifted the morale of the soldiers, they were ineptly directed by the Allied generals and they gained little territorial advantage. In November the weather broke, and conditions on the battlefield became intolerable—the mud was so bad that it often took an hour to dig a man out. In the Somme offensive the Allies lost 614,000 men; the Germans, 650,000. Meanwhile, there had been a major shake-up of the German army high command. In late August Paul von Hindenburg, who had mastered the Russians in the autumn of 1914, took command with Erich von Ludendorff in the important post of quartermaster-general.

For the time being, stalemate remained the keynote also on the eastern front. In mid-March 1916, the Russians massed an offensive against Germany. Although Russian forces outnumbered the Germans five to two, they made no progress, and their casualties were high. In May the Austrians launched a successful offensive in the Trentino that led to the fall of the Italian government. About that time, Russia came to its embattled ally's aid. Begun in early June, the Russian attack eventually broke through the Austrian defenses, taking about 500,000 prisoners. In the end, however, it proved little more than an enormous exercise in bloodletting. By late summer, the German high command—whose relations with the Austrians were anything but close or comfortable—had brought fifteen divisions from the western front to relieve the pressure on the Austrians. In late September the Russian offensive came to a halt, it had cost about one million in dead, wounded, or imprisoned, and perhaps its chief significance was that it brought revolution in Russia that much closer.

While the attention of the world seemed riveted on the Battle of Verdun and the Russian offensive, the one full-scale naval battle of the war took place on May 31, 1916, off the coast of Jutland, in the waters between Denmark and Norway. The affair was accidental, brief, and indecisive. The British, despite their distinct superiority in ships and men, behaved with great caution, fearing that a serious naval defeat might lead to the most dangerous sort of consequences. Though British losses somewhat exceeded those of the Germans, who had shown themselves to be superb tacticians and marksmen, the end result was a victory for the British, for Jutland discouraged the German fleet from venturing onto the high seas again. Thereafter, Germany was to concentrate on building up its fleet of U-boats.

By the end of 1916, it was certain that the Allies—however embattled their own position—would not make peace with the existing German government, and that the United States, which had followed a policy of neutrality since the outbreak of the war, was edging closer to the Anglo-French position. Wilson's closest political adviser, Colonel E. M. House, had made several visits to Europe, and the highly secret House-Grey memorandum of 1916 suggested that if the Germans refused a reasonable peace offer by the United States, America would probably join the Allied war effort. Consequently, the

WORLD WAR I

- Triple Entente
- Central Powers
- Allies of Triple Entente
- Neutral nations
- → Allied thrust
- → Central Powers' thrust

Battles:
- × Allied victory
- ⊗ Central Powers' victory

The military history of World War I is one of attrition and stalemate. Little more than a month after its outbreak, the Germans had been held at the Marne and the western front had stabilized. The eastern front was more fluid, but the Russian army held on stubbornly in spite of severe losses until the outbreak of internal revolution in 1917. Anglo-French campaigns against the Dardanelles and the Balkans were unsuccessful. Taking advantage of Arab nationalist aspirations, and supplying their forces from Egypt, the British finally made substantial gains against the Turks in 1917. Control of the sea was decided by the defeat of the German U-boat campaign rather than by a confrontation between great fleets of warships.

Allies believed that, despite all their hardships, time was on their side.

The German high command seems to have come to the same conclusion. In February 1917, Germany resumed unrestricted submarine warfare in hopes of effectively blockading Britain and gaining an advantageous peace settlement. The submarines had great initial success, sinking 335 ships in April alone; and though the United States broke off diplomatic relations with Germany immediately, it still declined to enter the war. But renewed sinkings of American ships—three were sunk without warning on March 18—angered the American government. The revelation of the Zimmermann telegram—a cable from Berlin to the German minister in Mexico City, asking him to propose an alliance with Mexico in the event of war between the United States and Germany and to promise Texas, New Mexico, and Arizona to Mexico—also persuaded President Wilson in April 1917 to ask the Congress for a declaration of war on the German Empire.

There was, moreover, one other reason why such a declaration seemed highly opportune to the President. Only a few days before, revolution had broken out in Russia, and it seemed to Wilson, who welcomed the revolution, that the prospects for peace and democracy were now better than ever. "The world," he told the Congress in his dramatic, personally delivered war message, "must be made safe for democracy." A brief and bitter debate followed Wilson's request, but Congress approved the declaration. Immediately President Wilson offered loans, troops, and ships to the Allied cause.

By mid-1917 the Allies had perfected the convoy system to protect their own and neutral merchant ships. The system was immediately successful, reducing the casualty rate of ships from 25 per cent to 1 per cent. The Allies were winning the war at sea, and before too many months had passed, the arrival of the young and fresh American troops would begin to turn the tide in France as well.

The War and the Home Fronts

When war broke out in August 1914, every belligerent government had reason to worry about the response of its citizens. In most states, a vocal socialist minority seemed committed to class rather than national solidarity. In addition, the Dual Monarchy had reason to fear the reaction of its subject minorities. Initially, at least, these concerns proved groundless. In France and Germany, a kind of political truce was arranged; in Great Britain, the Liberal government continued in office with support from Conservatives, Labour, and the Irish. In Austria-Hungary, the subject nationalities reported for service in the Austrian army (though nationalist agitation, particularly among the Czechs, continued to mount). In Russia, only the Bolsheviks called for revolution.

No country was prepared for a long war. Consequently, when the fighting went on and on, every country felt the pinch of shortages and was obliged to institute rationing of basic commodities. Everywhere women were called upon to do the work of men conscripted into the army. As the battles raged the early enthusiasm for the war began to wane. In many countries radical elements became more powerful as the public grew disillusioned with the governments in office at the outbreak of war. These governments found it difficult or impossible to remedy conditions at home, because all the nations' resources were being mobilized to meet the needs of the war.

Wartime Britain provides fairly typical examples of the unfamiliar problems which governments had to meet and the improvised ways in which they sought to meet them. For one thing, the demands of a war economy were at variance with free trade and free enterprise, which were all but sacred principles in the prewar years. The Liberal government had put through welfare legislation, but it had never conceived of a planned economy and state control over industry. Nonetheless, the necessity of supporting the war effort soon forced politicians and businessmen to accept collectivist measures.

At first the government's only infringements of laissez-faire occurred in spheres that were clearly related to national defense—particularly shipping and railroads—and even in these areas government control was modest. But in May 1915 a battle over the conduct of the unsuccessful Dardanelles campaign, coupled with the exposure of a critical shortage of shells at the front, forced Asquith to form a coalition cabinet of Liberals, Conservatives, and the first Labour minister. One of the first acts of the new government was to prohibit all industrial stoppages and to make arbitration compulsory. The coalition introduced diverse elements into the cabinet, enabling the government to deal more forcefully with its manifold domestic problems without outwardly compromising its principles. The new ministry also established national factories. By August, sixteen had been built; by the end of the war, 250 (most of them in 1915–1916). Price controls were instituted on coal, but there was no move toward nationalization. All in all, the government ran considerably behind intelligent public opinion regarding state intervention in production and distribution.

The failure of the Dardanelles campaign strengthened critics of the way the war was being managed, and in December 1916, Lloyd George—with the support of Bonar Law and the Conservatives—formed a new government that mobilized the national resources more effectively. The most pressing matter was the threat of food and fuel shortages: sugar, potatoes, margarine, and coal were in particularly short supply. Sugar rationing was finally introduced in 1917, while a government subsidy helped keep down the price of bread and potatoes. By early 1918, grave food shortages led to the introduction of rationing for meat, tea, and butter.

Labor troubles in South Wales had necessitated the extension of government control over (but not nationalization of) coal mines there. The government also found itself assuming a large amount of control over the textile industry: the Cotton Control Board rationed the dwindling supply of raw material to prevent total disruption. The new Ministry of Shipping took control of almost every British ship and determined what vessels should be built to expedite transportation of materials. The government also took an active role in making plans for "social reconstruction" at the end of the war. In 1917 and 1918 top priorities were placed on housing, education, and health.

Thus war-induced collectivism made large inroads in the laissez-faire state. When the war ended, private enterprise, silent during the years of the war, once again attacked state interference in British economic life. But what had been achieved by government leadership and planning would not be soon forgotten, and it strengthened the advocates of central planning and reform socialism for years to come.

Lloyd George's achievements were particularly impressive when compared with those of the civilian governments in France and Germany, to say nothing of Austria and Russia. Continued political (and especially parliamentary) instability added no end to French domestic and military problems throughout the war. One especially awesome problem was that of military discipline. This required a commander who could lead and a government the soldiers had confidence in. Both were long in coming. A crisis began in late April 1917, when a full-fledged mutiny occurred within a battalion recently reduced by casualties from six hundred to two hundred men. The remnant now refused to follow orders to march to the front. A score of ringleaders were tried and condemned to death or to prison in penal colonies. But the rebellion did not end there. In the next few months mutinies spread through the army. There was no planned conspiracy; though fed by the pacifist leaflets that were flooding the camps from behind the lines, the revolts were spontaneous, and most of the participants had no idea of the extent (or precise origins) of the phenomenon.

A decisive step forward came with the appointment in May 1917 of General Henri Philippe Pétain, whose main task was to rebuild the army's fighting spirit before the Germans could learn of the trouble and launch another attack. Most of his remedies were based on good common sense, such as instituting a reasonable system of leave and rest for front-line troops. Above all, Pétain understood the wisdom and necessity of abstaining from another general offensive until American reinforcements had begun to arrive in substantial numbers.

Pétain's problems were complicated by the government's long-standing unwillingness to stop the flow of pacifist literature to the front lines. One weekly leftist newspaper, the leading exponent of defeatism, enjoyed a government subsidy for a time, and then was supported by German money in a shadowy way. Its subtly worded, antiwar articles confounded the censors. The paper had no small effect on the country's morale. After Georges Clemenceau took over as premier in November 1917, he quickly put an end to such dangerous activities. "The Tiger" imposed ruthless censorship on defeatist newspapers and pamphlets, and Pétain was given the backing he needed to restore the spirit of the troops.

In the realm of economic and social policy France's wartime experience was on the whole very much the same as Britain's, although France's smaller resources and continuing political difficulties made the domestic situation much more difficult. The planning, rationing, and related policies that were finally adopted in Britain were either later coming to France or came there in a less effective form. Because of increasing labor problems, growing out of mounting inflation, in January 1917 the minister of munitions established minimum wage rates in those industries where the government had contracts. But the government's efforts to impose an effective fiscal policy, to raise taxes to a point where they paid for a substantial part of the war, were completely unsuccessful. The result was a vaulting national debt and a serious inflation of the currency. Both were to haunt France for some years after the war.

The domestic problems of Britain and France were modest compared with those of Germany and Russia, and—lost war aside—it was not surprising that the monarchies in both countries were overthrown in 1917–1918. In the matter of war economy the Germans commenced with several serious disadvantages. First, despite a long tradition of state paternalism and control, the imposition of new wartime curbs produced excessive friction and resentment. Second, not since the Napoleonic Wars had Germany fought a long war, and it was neither psychologically nor economically ready for a protracted conflict. Woefully unprepared for an exhausting war of attrition, the Germans responded with alacrity and imagination but also with rigid controls and regimentation which led to much evasion and disaffection. Most serious of all was the kaiser's refusal to support any significant political and social reforms during the war. As a result, not even the odious Prussian three-class system of weighted voting according to wealth and tax rating was done away with; it simply disappeared in November 1918—along with William and his Hohenzollern empire.

Revolution in Russia

In Russia the military campaigns on the eastern front destroyed both civilian and military morale as men were sacrificed on a horrifying scale. Economic dislocation was acute, for the government took no steps to control production. War-related industries did moderately well, but consumer goods very nearly disappeared, and when that happened the peasants lost their incentive to produce much more than their own needs. Food supplies in urban areas were dangerously low by the autumn of 1916.

In this atmosphere of devastation and dislocation, even conservative Russians were increasingly appalled and disgusted by the devious influence on the government of the Siberian peasant-monk Grigori Rasputin. Rasputin had won the intense loyalty of the empress Alexandra, who believed that the monk could control the illness of her only son, the czarevitch Alexis, who suffered from hemophilia. Alexandra had complete faith in Rasputin's healing and prophetic powers. She convinced her well-meaning but weak husband, Nicholas II, to follow the monk's directions in all matters, and at the height of the war, ministers were appointed and dismissed on a word from Rasputin. When Nicholas took command of the armies at the front in September 1916, the government was largely handed over to the empress and her detested adviser. Rasputin, universally loathed, was finally assassinated in December 1916 by a conspiracy of noblemen led by a member of the royal family.

The Duma persistently criticized the conduct of the war, the government, and Rasputin, but the czar continued to view all criticism, however moderate, as sedition. In mid-February 1917 he decided to dismiss the Duma, but a pro-gressive bloc composed mainly of Kadets and Octobrists appointed a per-manent committee which remained active during the worsening riots and disturbances that plagued St. Petersburg in March. Food shortages set off dem-onstrations, and the soldiers sent to quiet the demonstrators joined them in-stead. The permanent committee of the Duma assumed leadership; Nicholas abdicated in April; and a Provisional Government was formed, initially headed by the liberal aristocrat Prince Lvov.

The Provisional Government was widely acclaimed at home and abroad; it brought to Russia a modicum of free speech, free religion, and a free press. But it failed to achieve the two goals foremost in the minds of the soldiers, workers, and peasants of Russia: peace and land reform. Instead it decided to continue the war, thinking that defeat and German occupation would en-danger the revolution. Pursuit of the war precluded immediate land reform as well as concessions to the protesting subject peoples within the Russian Em-pire, and war itself meant continued shortages and suffering. Nor could the Provisional Government's progressive labor legislation check the decline of the Russian economy, which could no more sustain an enormous war machine under a liberal government than under a czar. The socialist Alexander Kerensky, first as minister of justice and later as prime minister, lacked the authority and toughness to force his decisions on the nation. As a result the Provisional Government was under constant pressure from the Social Revolu-tionaries and the Bolsheviks, by whom it was eventually superseded.

In April 1917, Vladimir Lenin returned to Russia from exile in Switzerland on a train thoughtfully provided by the German government. Arriving at the Finland Station in St. Petersburg, he at once announced the need for imme-diate peace, land reform, and self-determination, discounting the German threat on the grounds that the German proletariat was sure to save Russia by revolting against its own leaders. His first goal, however, was to win sup-port for his program, and at this time only a minority of the Russian Social Democratic party or the populace agreed with him.

The instruments Lenin utilized to gain control of the revolution were the soviets (councils) of workers' deputies, self-created bodies representing the proletariat and at least a part of the military, which became first shadow governments and eventually were to take over complete power. The most strategically located soviet, the one in St. Petersburg, did not aspire to challenge the Provisional Government immediately, for it subscribed to the doctrine that Russia was ready only for a bourgeois revolution. Yet by its very existence the soviet was a potential challenge to the government, and Lenin maintained that the "dual power" of the two bodies could only be transitional. On April 24 a conference representing soviets throughout Russia came over to his view. The slogan it adopted was "all power to the soviets." Russian politics began clearly to move to the left.

In mid-May, a new Provisional Government was formed, with ten non-socialists but with the Mensheviks, Social Revolutionaries, and Independent Socialists each holding two portfolios. The new government aimed to establish some sort of control over the St. Petersburg soviet. But when the government could not conclude a peace, its members lost standing in the eyes of those soldiers and workers who wanted to end the war.

The summer of 1917 was alive with conferences. At the First All-Russian Congress of Soviets in June, there were 105 Bolsheviks, 248 Mensheviks, and 285 Social Revolutionaries. Accordingly, the Congress passed a vote of confidence in the Provisional Government. But the tide was turning against the government and in favor of the Bolsheviks. In July, when the Provisional Government was pressing the offensive in Galicia, demonstrations in St. Petersburg were so menacing that it recalled loyal troops to the capital and Lenin had to flee to Finland. When the offensive failed shortly after, the Provisional Government moved further left, and Kerensky became its head, but more Bolsheviks were arrested.

Bolshevik fortunes were improving, however, especially in rural areas, where the Social Revolutionaries had failed to give land to the peasants as promised. Yet the central committee of the Bolshevik party still hesitated to seize power by force. In September the Provisional Government defeated a counterrevolutionary movement headed by General Kornilov, whom Kerensky had appointed commander-in-chief of the army. But this episode showed how vulnerable the Provisional Government was. The way was now open for a coup from the Left; in October Lenin came to St. Petersburg in disguise to shake the Bolshevik central committee out of its lethargy. By this time, the Provisional Government had largely lost control over the capital. The St. Petersburg soviet (of which Leon Trotsky was the new president) now began military preparations for revolution, and on November 7 Bolshevik forces occupied the key points in St. Petersburg with little resistance. That evening the newly elected Second All-Russian Congress of Soviets — now composed of 390 Bosheviks and 260 others — approved the first "Workers' and Peasants' Government," the Council of People's Commissars. Peace negotiations with Germany began at once, for it seemed possible that the peasants would overthrow the revolution if they were forced to continue the war. At this point, Lenin and the Council of People's Commissars had a choice between trying for peace or further and immediate international revolution. They decided for the former, and in early March 1918 the Bolsheviks signed the harsh, punitive Treaty of Brest-Litovsk with Germany and the other Central Powers. Russia lost Poland, Finland, the Ukraine, the Baltic provinces, and Transcaucasia.

Thus ended the first part of the Bolshevik revolution, which in retrospect appears as a momentous turning point in modern history. But at the time, the significance of the revolution was not clear. Europe's main concern was still the Great War, and it remained to be concluded.

Toward Allied Victory

In the spring of 1918 the Allied prospects were mixed. Allied war efforts and peace plans had been progressing apace during the winter. American troops had been arriving in Europe at a steadily increasing rate; the demand for men was soon superseded by the need for ships. On the other hand, the revolution in Russia threatened to take that country out of the war. Such a development would permit Germany to redeploy most of its troops in the east to the western front, with serious consequences for the western democracies. Despite the devastating effects of the Allied blockade on the German military and civilian economy, the power of the Hohenzollern empire remained considerable. The previous summer, at Ypres, the British had launched a major attack against the German forces. Though the terrain looked attractive on the map, it was not good territory for a frontal assault against strongly reinforced lines, for the ground was heavy, wet clay that bombardment churned into deep mud. The attack literally bogged down. Men, guns, and tanks disappeared into the mud. Ypres became a slaughterhouse, each side losing at least a quarter of a million men.

In November 1917 the British had tried another offensive on the western front, on hard ground at Cambrai. This time the tank corps succeeded in breaking through the German lines for five miles, but the infantry could not keep up with them, and the cavalry was easily destroyed by German machine guns. The Germans were able to bring up reinforcements and recover the lost ground.

The final test came in March 1918 when the Germans launched a massive attack mainly against British forces. Germany's time was clearly running out; its manpower position could henceforth only deteriorate, for although Russia had just about left the war, American troops were starting to make up for the Russian defection. With large numerical superiority, the Germans attacked at the Somme and progressed some forty miles within a few days. By the end of May another German offensive to the south had broken through and penetrated to the Marne, only thirty-seven miles from Paris, when a combined French and American force was at last able to hold the line. For a

The Allied Triumph. The loss to the Allied military effort resulting from Russia's withdrawal from the war was more than compensated for by the participation of the American Expeditionary Force beginning in the spring of 1918. By September, the United States had 1.2 million soldiers in the field. This was enough to turn the tide of victory in favor of the Allies. Above: an American machine-gun crew on the western front, 1918.

brief moment, it appeared that what had eluded the Germans for four bitter years was now within their grasp. In July another German offensive struck across the Marne, but it was a decisive failure as the Allies had guessed where it would be launched. A French counteroffensive broke through the German lines but was unable to keep the Germans from re-forming.

Now the Allies began to launch their own attacks. Happily, they had learned something from the past years: massed troops were not thrown against the bulk of the German army. Instead, a series of sharp, short attacks beginning in early August drove the Germans back from their gains of the previous spring and winter. By this time large numbers of fresh American troops were in the field, giving the Allies superiority in numbers and fire power. In September a huge Allied force assembled on the front, and the Germans feared a breakthrough.

As the autumn of 1918 approached, the German army was steadily on the defensive, but at least it was still intact. Austria was in a far worse predicament. Since early July Vienna had been near the end of its food supplies. The Austrians had begged the Reich for help, but Germany could provide none. The emperor, Charles I, who had succeeded Francis Joseph in November 1916, declared that his empire must have peace within the year.

Since it was no longer possible for Germany to achieve a settlement by military means, military and civilian elements in the government had to work together. As early as July 1917 the Reichstag had voted a resolution which declared its desire for "a peace of understanding and lasting reconciliation . . . . Such a peace is not in keeping with forcible annexations of territory or forcible measures of a political, economic, or financial character."

By the summer of 1918 the military leadership of the country realized the indispensable need for diplomacy.

As September passed, however, the German high command became more and more anxious. Although the Allies had not achieved a breakthrough, they were pressing hard, while the Bulgarian army was known to be on the verge of surrender in the Balkans, foreshadowing the exit of Turkey and Austria from the war effort. Still the high command kept reassuring the civilian government that collapse was not to be feared.

Suddenly, however, General von Ludendorff seemed to lose his nerve. In a series of meetings at the end of September, he and Field Marshal von Hindenburg announced to the kaiser and his ministers that an armistice "without delay" was an absolute necessity. This abrupt reversal stunned the government, but it was impressed by the insistence of the high command. Hindenburg and Ludendorff further suggested that a change in government was necessary to assure the Allies of Germany's sincerity and to gain popular support so that a last struggle could be waged in the event that a satisfactory armistice could not be negotiated.

The resignation of Chancellor Hertling was announced on September 30, and in the next few days continued pressure from the high command led to the formation of a coalition government under Prince Max of Baden, one of the more liberal members of the southern German aristocracy. On October 3 Hindenburg wrote Prince Max that "the supreme command continues to hold to its demand expressed on September 29 of this year that a request for an armistice should be sent to our enemies immediately." The moderate Social Democrats rallied to the new government. Prince Max was not eager to send a note asking for an armistice, for he believed that the Allies' terms would be more lenient if there were a possibility that the war would be continued; but the army command was adamant, and the kaiser backed it up. On the night of October 3 Prince Max sent his note, making the action public in a speech to the Reichstag on the following day.

The German note was addressed to President Wilson. This was understandable enough. Wilson was the head of the most powerful democratic state, and it was the intervention of the United States that had sealed Germany's fate. Above all, however, Wilson had by 1918 emerged as the preeminent leader of liberal international opinion, having set forth his views in a series of eloquent statements and addresses, climaxed by his Fourteen Points in January 1918. This program, which at once captured the imagination and support of liberals in Europe and America, called for "open covenants openly arrived at," the adjustment of frontiers "along clearly recognizable lines of nationality," the right of all nations "to the freest opportunity for autonomous development," and the establishment of an international organization to keep the peace and arbitrate disputes between nations. Although Wilson had spoken only for himself and the United States, the German government seized upon the Fourteen Points as a program for a moderate peace. They accepted the Fourteen Points as a basis for peace negotiations and requested an immediate armistice.

Wilson replied that the Germans must evacuate all invaded territory before an armistice could be promoted, and on October 12 the Germans agreed to comply with Wilson's note. Meanwhile, in response to demands from the Social Democrats, the Reichstag passed a series of measures to make the monarchy truly constitutional. On October 16 Wilson addressed a second note to the German government, stating that "conditions of an armistice are matters which must be left to the judgment and advice of the military advisers of the Government of the United States and the Allied Governments . . . ." In his note, Wilson also made a thinly-veiled suggestion that the kaiser must abdicate before peace could come. The disappointment in Germany was enormous. For a brief moment, Ludendorff, evidently changing his mind, suggested that the fighting could go on. But Prince Max could see no change in conditions in the field, and he resolved to push for an armistice. On October 20 a note informed the United States that Germany accepted its conditions. On October 23, Wilson called on Germany to rid itself of its "monarchical autocrats" or face complete defeat.

The feeling was increasing in Germany that the kaiser was holding up the armistice and peace negotiations, and now that they had been told the truth about the war, there was nothing the German people wanted more than peace. On October 30 the German fleet at Kiel rebelled at the order to put to sea. The men wanted peace and were determined that their officers should not jeopardize it. Revolution spread from Kiel through northern and western Germany, alarming the government in Berlin. The moderate Social Democrats believed that the monarchy could be retained if the kaiser would abdicate at once. By November 7, Prince Max had also become convinced that the kaiser had to abdicate to save Germany from civil war. A republic was proclaimed in Bavaria that night. The revolutionary socialists—Independent Socialists and Spartacists (German Communists)—planned a major strike for November 9, and the moderate Social Democrats were forced to support it so as not to lose the faith of the masses.

At noon on November 9 the kaiser's abdication was announced by Prince Max, who turned over his own position to Friedrich Ebert, the Social Democrat leader; under increasing pressure by the revolutionary Left, a German republic was declared within two hours. The same day the kaiser crossed the German frontier into Holland, where he was to spend the rest of his days—he died in 1941—in exile.

On November 11 the armistice ending the Great War was signed at Compiègne in the name of the new German Republic. This fact was, in later years, to prove highly useful to those German elements who wished to discredit the Republic—particularly since, on November 11, 1918, the German army had not yet suffered the kind of real defeat it was to experience in the spring of 1945.

By the time the Hohenzollern empire ceased to be, the Habsburg monarchy, too, had disappeared. The last phase, beginning in the summer of 1914, had been a sad one in every way. The Dual Monarchy's declaration of war against Serbia in July 1914 had been intended to reassert its own independence and stature as a great power. Instead, it sealed its doom. When the war broke out in 1914, most of the subject nationalities rallied to the cause of the Dual Monarchy, but before long, dissident nationalist movements gathered strength. In particular, a Czech underground movement soon sprang up. The Czech leader Thomas Masaryk escaped to Paris in December 1914 and in 1915 founded a Czech national committee there. This committee worked to gain Allied support for Czech independence from the Habsburgs.

By the summer of 1918 the future of the Habsburg dynasty was extremely perilous. The Empire was breaking up into rival nationalities, and Austria could no longer remain at war. On October 4 the Austrian government joined with the Reich in seeking an armistice, and twelve days later, the emperor Charles I issued a manifesto reorganizing the non-Hungarian part of the Dual Monarchy into a federal state in which the subject nationalities would enjoy complete self-government.

On October 21, Charles received a reply from President Wilson, stating that the subject nationalities were to decide for themselves what system of government they wished to be under. On the same day Masaryk proclaimed Czechoslovakian independence. The southern Slavs and Poles followed suit. The Magyars sought to preserve Hungary in the guise of a revolutionary republic under Count Karolyi (whose unenviable task was to convince the Allies that the Magyars had not been the oppressors but an oppressed nationality themselves). Lastly, at the end of October, "German-Austria" was proclaimed, a state without boundaries or definition, including all German subjects of the Habsburgs. On November 3, Austria and the Allies signed an armistice, and on November 11, Charles resigned his imperial functions. After hundreds of years, the Habsburg empire was no more.

Thus, on November 11, 1918, World War I came to an end. But it was one thing to declare a cease-fire, another to make a lasting peace. For several weeks, the Allies had been laying plans for a great peace conference. President Wilson would have preferred it to be held in Switzerland but finally agreed to Paris and announced that he would go to Paris himself. On a cold but sunny day in early December 1918, Woodrow Wilson, Mrs. Wilson, and his top advisers embarked on the S.S. *Washington* bound for Europe. Tens of thousands gathered on shore and gave the President a tumultuous send-off. The future of mankind was in the balance.

12

HERITAGE
ESSAY

THE LEGACY OF WAR AND REVOLUTION

The First World War was a calamity of unprecedented magnitude for Western civilization. Not since the Black Death of the mid-fourteenth century had such a significant proportion of Europe's population been lost in such a short space of time; and the mortality during the war was probably an even greater blow to the stability and progress of society than the Black Death had been. The ten million killed in World War I included many of the most vigorous and idealistic of a whole generation, which suddenly vanished from the face of history. Among these fallen soldiers were those who would have become the leaders of their era, men who would have done great things in the world. Now their corpses rotted in Flanders fields and other battlegrounds, and those who were left to take their places as leaders of society were almost entirely the old, the weak, and the vicious. The primary explanation for the incompetence (at best) and the bestiality (in many cases) of the leadership of the European states in the 1920's and 1930's lies in the loss of an entire generation in the military holocaust.

By 1917 the war had ceased to have any meaning, purpose, or value for sensitive and liberal men.

> What passing-bells for those who die as cattle?
> Only the monstrous anger of the guns.[1]

Thus wrote the English poet Wilfred Owen in the trenches; he was killed in battle shortly before the Armistice. The war, H. G. Wells had concluded by 1917, "has become a mere incoherent fighting and destruction, a demonstration in vast and tragic terms of the stupidity and ineffectiveness of our species."[2] The war afflicted the European soul with a cancerous malaise, a pessimism and sense of guilt and futility that accelerated the trend to irrationality and extremism and further vitiated the moral heritage of liberal rational-

---

1. Wilfred Owen, *Anthem for Doomed Youth*, in A. Quiller-Couch, ed., *The Oxford Book of English Verse.* Oxford: Clarendon Press, 1943, p. 1137.
2. Quoted in A. F. Havighurst, *Twentieth Century Britain.* Evanston, Ill.: Row, Peterson, 1962, p. 138.

ism and humanism. The older generation was completely discredited in everything — its politics, its dress, its sexual mores — and there emerged a new insistence on the righteousness of youth, a theme that was to recur again and again in twentieth-century culture.

Everywhere, the standards of social behavior — already in decline — were devastated. If the politicians and generals had treated the millions under their care like animals dispatched to slaughter, then what canons of religion or ethics could any longer inhibit men from treating each other with the ferocity of jungle beasts? Before asking how Hitler and Stalin could have murdered millions with scarcely a murmur of protest from their followers, we must first recognize that the slaughter of the First World War thoroughly debased the value of human life. Men are conditioned by their experience; the butchery of the war prepared the way for butchery by totalitarianism.

The demoralization of the Western conscience and the decimation of liberal and humane values were perceived and described with force and clarity by intellectuals and artists. After the war those politicians who thought they could return to "normalcy" and those capitalists who expected to resume "business as usual," must be judged among the worst fools and dupes in all recorded history. Paul Valéry, the French poet, spoke for the more sensitive of his generation when he described the ineradicable scars of war:

The Emancipation of Women. The British suffragette movement was launched in 1905 by a middle-class widow, Mrs. Emmeline Pankhurst, and her daughters. By 1912 Mrs. Pankhurst was addressing large groups of women in London: "Be militant each in his own way. Those of you who can break windows break them . . . . I incite this meeting to rebellion." The suffragettes handcuffed themselves to railings outside the House of Commons, threw matches into mailboxes, and flung themselves on startled cabinet ministers in their carriages. Facing page: a suffragette dressed as Joan of Arc marching in a women's parade for the vote. Left: police brutality against a suffragette. Women gained the vote in Britain in 1918 partly in consequence of prewar suffragette agitation but mostly because of their meritorious service as replacements for the men in the trenches. Below: middle-class ladies making packages for the troops in France. Note the change in women's clothes since the era of the "Gibson Girl."

You know how greatly the general economic situation has been disturbed, and the policy of states, and the very life of the individual; you are familiar with the universal discomfort, hesitation, apprehension. But among all these injured things is the Mind. The Mind has indeed been cruelly wounded; its complaint is heard in the hearts of intellectual men; it passes a mournful judgment on itself. It doubts itself profoundly.[3]

The Irish poet William Butler Yeats foresaw in 1919 the whole pattern of what was to come in the twentieth century:

3. Paul Valéry, *Variety*, trans. Malcolm Cowley. New York: Harcourt, Brace, 1927, p. 28.

The Irish Revolt. The Irish demonstrated that no Western democratic government could sustain a repressive war against a national independence movement; liberal outcry in the imperial country and the government's own guilt feelings would force it to give in. Above: the Dublin General Post Office, headquarters of the abortive 1916 rebellion, after the rebels' surrender. Right: British troops firing at the rebels down Abbey Street, Dublin, in 1916.

Left: ruins of an Irish home in Balbriggan, twenty miles north of Dublin, destroyed by the "Black and Tans" (mercenaries recruited into the Royal Irish Constabulary) in reprisal for the murder of a police officer. Below: Cork burning in 1920, another atrocity committed by the Black and Tans, which aroused indignation in Britain.

"It's a Long, Long Way to Tipperary." So went a British marching song popular at the beginning of World War I. It turned out to be a very long way indeed to the Armistice. In the first two years of the war, there was great public enthusiasm in the belligerent countries. Facing page: young men flocking to enlist in London in 1915. "Now God be thanked Who has matched us with His hour, and caught our youth, and wakened us from sleeping," sang the patriotic poet Rupert Brooke when the war began. Brooke was dead by 1916. As the holocaust mounted, the common man became less enthusiastic, although he never quite lost his faith in the national cause. Below: King Albert of Belgium, President Poincaré of France, and General Joffe (second from right) look at the distant German lines before Metz in 1915. Although historians disagree as to just how incompetent the Allied generals were in the First World War, it seems clear that at best they were stubbornly unimaginative. For example, until late in the war they rejected the use of tanks in favor of suicidal mass infantry assaults and insane cavalry attacks. The ablest Allied leaders were British statesmen David Lloyd George and Winston Churchill (left), who had some sense of the need for new tactics. Churchill was politically ruined by the ill-fated Dardanelles expedition of 1915, which he had planned; it failed because of bad military and naval direction.

Things fall apart; the centre cannot hold;
Mere anarchy is loosed upon the world,
The blood-dimmed tide is loosed, and everywhere
The ceremony of innocence is drowned;
The best lack all conviction, while the worst
Are full of passionate intensity.[4]

The war discredited Europe's elite of money and power and crippled its self-confidence. The bastions of masculinity, imperial rule, aristocracy, and capitalism that had seemed so impregnable in 1914 were disintegrating by 1920. During and shortly after the war several groups in European society that had been subjected to exploitation and rigid control claimed the rights and privileges of free citizens and, in their methods and slogans, established a pattern of emancipation for the downtrodden all over the world. The First World War inaugurated a new era of social change and egalitarian rebellion as far-reaching in its impact as the French Revolution.

The largest group to benefit from emancipation constituted half of Western society—women. Until the first decade of the twentieth century, the tide of

4. William Butler Yeats, *The Second Coming,* in *The Collected Poems of W. B. Yeats.* New York: Macmillan, 1966, pp. 184–185.

enfranchisement seemed to have stopped at universal manhood suffrage. Only a few humanitarian and liberal men, like John Stuart Mill, and a handful of bold women even dared raise the issue of women's suffrage, and they were greeted with, at best, amused contempt.

Even middle-class women in the nineteenth century were treated by their husbands as household serfs. It is probably true that in Victorian bourgeois society women were less accepted as intellectual equals than they had been during the Enlightenment. Bourgeois reticence about sex kept secret the sadistic aggression of husbands against wives. The double standard flourished: in London of the 1850's one out of every sixteen women was a prostitute. The women's suffrage movement that developed in prewar London was inspired not only by democratic ideals but by deep resentment of male domination—as indicated by its slogan, "Votes for Women and Purity for Men."

The suffragettes developed techniques that are still much in use: they marched and petitioned; they disrupted political assemblies; they held sit-ins at the House of Commons; they engaged in hunger strikes; they resorted to occasional violence (including arson) and even martyrdom. These respectable middle-class women were denounced and jailed, but the need for women

Into the Maelstrom. From September 1914 to October 1918 the contending armies faced each other along a thousand miles of trenches on the western front. Neither side could advance more than a few miles. The Allied generals, safely ensconced well behind the lines, sent millions of men to their deaths in repeated attacks on the German positions, vainly hoping that somehow the soldiers could overcome machine-gun nests, howitzers, barbed wire, and—the worst threat—mud. Amazingly, only once did Allied troops rebel against this massacre: there was a serious but short-lived mutiny in the French army in 1917. Above: the soldiers' home for four years, a typical trench on the western front. Facing page: cannon fodder.

The Russian Revolutions. In the first revolution of 1917, the czarist regime was overthrown and replaced by the Provisional Government eventually headed by Alexander Kerensky. Facing page, top: rebellious soldiers firing on czarist forces in Petrograd in February 1917. Facing page, bottom: a crowd dispersed by gunfire during the February conflict. The Kerensky government continued the war, and the consequent misery and confusion gave Lenin and the Bolsheviks their opportunity. Above: Red rally in Admiralty Square, Petrograd, in April 1917. Below: Bolshevik march on the Winter Palace, headquarters of the Provisional Government on November 7, 1917. The Bolsheviks finally entered by a side door and took over.

in offices and munitions plants and on farms during the war added force to their claims for equality. In 1918 the British Parliament gave the vote to women who had reached the responsible age of thirty, and enfranchisement of women followed rapidly in almost every Western country.

Having gained the vote, women showed their inclination toward conservative parties at the polls. But the war brought them more than political emancipation, and conservatism was hardly the rule: they cut their hair,

threw away their corsets and crinolines, raised their skirts, smoked, and drank. Some intrepid protagonists of flaming youth even asserted their right to equal promiscuity with men. There is no doubt that women made greater strides toward political and personal freedom in the decade after 1914 than in all the previous centuries of mankind put together.

On Easter Monday of 1916 another submerged group—the Irish—rose in rebellion. Tired of waiting for the British to make home rule effective, a few dozen Dublin poets, teachers, and clerks rose against the world's greatest empire. Their rebellion had all the elements of a comic opera, except for its shocking denouement: the British government proceeded to execute the rebel leaders. Yet these nationalist idealists knew from the start they were doomed. Padraic Pearse, president of the short-lived republic, wrote:

> I have squandered the splendid years
>> That the Lord God gave to my youth
> In attempting impossible things
>> Deeming them alone worth the toil.[5]

Fired by the example of the martyrs' heroism, a widespread revolution began in 1918, and the British could not stomach for long the measures used to suppress it. By 1922 most of Ireland was a self-governing republic. Its long-time political leader was Eamon de Valera, who as one of the Easter rebels of 1916 had been spared the death penalty because he happened to be an American citizen. Ireland started the fire of colonial rebellion that was to sweep over Asia and Africa in the next four decades, destroying European empires that in 1914 had seemed eternal.

The most important single consequence of the First World War was the replacement of the rotting czarist government of Russia by Lenin's Bolshevik regime. The Bolshevik success was by no means inevitable; it was the consequence of the ineptitude of Russian liberals and moderate socialists and the skill, cunning, and fierce courage of Lenin himself. Amid all the socialist groups in Europe in 1914, some of which had the support of millions of voters, a small revolutionary cadre on the extreme left had seized control of a great power and henceforth commanded its resources. No single event so powerfully affected the destiny of mankind in the next half-century as the Bolshevik take-over in Russia. The humanism of Jaurès and the revisionist liberal socialism of Bernstein were unequivocally rejected by Lenin:

The substitution of a proletarian for the capitalist State is impossible without a violent revolution. . . . We must crush the [exploiters and capitalists] in order to free humanity from wage-slavery; their resistance must be broken by force. It is clear that where there is suppression there must also be violence, and there cannot be liberty and democracy.[6]

5. Padraic Pearse, *The Fool,* in *Collected Works.* Dublin: Phoenix Press, 1917, p. 334.
6. V. I. Lenin, *The State and Revolution,* in S. Hook, *Marx and the Marxists.* Princeton, N.J.: Van Nostrand, 1955, pp. 182–184.

PART FOUR

The
Crisis
of Western
Civilization

**From the Versailles Peace Settlement
to the Present Day**

The series of crises threatening the integrity and stability of Western civilization that began with the First World War and the Russian Revolution continued through the next half-century. The political and economic reconstruction of Europe inaugurated in 1918 brought only a decade of prosperity and relative calm. In the 1930's the whole Western world was racked by a catastrophic depression, and in the demoralizing situation that resulted, Nazi Germany launched its drive for world conquest, seeking to destroy the moral foundations of Western civilization. The defeat of Germany and its allies in the Second World War was accompanied by the devastation of western Europe; world leadership passed to the United States and the Soviet Union. In the next quarter of a century these two superpowers, and the ideologies they espoused, competed for the allegiance of the rest of the world and confronted each other, directly or indirectly, on every inhabited continent.

Yet the period since 1918 has not been without its significant achievements: the remarkable economic recovery of western Europe after 1945; tremendous advances in science and technology, particularly the discovery of new forms of energy and great developments in communication and transportation; a marked improvement in the well-being of the working class; new directions in higher culture and the arts; and the dissolution of the European overseas empires, providing an opportunity for non-Western people to develop their own political and social systems while utilizing Western science and technology. The challenge facing mankind at the end of the 1960's was whether a developing world society would be able to live in peace and work more or less harmoniously for the advancement of human welfare.

This noble continent . . . is the origin of most
of the culture, art, philosophy, and science
of both ancient and modern times.
If Europe were once united in the sharing of its common inheritance,
there would be no limit to the happiness, to the prosperity and glory
which its three to four hundred million people would enjoy.

Winston S. Churchill

Page 641: Sir Jacob Epstein's bronze bust of Winston Churchill, 1946.

Reconstruction and Depression

ENVIRONMENT ESSAY

The weary soldiers who returned from the trenches in 1918 had been promised "homes fit for heroes" and "a world made safe for democracy." Within months of the war's end, they found themselves facing housing shortages, galloping inflation, unemployment, and sometimes the breadline. These were chronic problems of the interwar period. The political leaders of western Europe and America in the 1920's and the early 1930's faced the new world with stale ideas left over from the pre-1914 era. Caution, retrenchment, isolation, a stubborn adherence to the mental habits of a vanished past characterized the age. Everywhere there was a desperate longing for "normalcy"—for the stable, the familiar, the comfortable. Far-sighted reformers were looked upon suspiciously as adventurers better excluded from high office.

In the Western democracies, the political leaders of the period were at best affable, well-meaning, and not overly bright; at worst they were lazy, selfish, and dishonest. Newsreels and photographs in the press daily revealed the leaders' comings and goings; they were forever making speeches, contesting elections, negotiating international problems, conferring on national crises. They turned their faces boldly to the cameras and exuded an air of confidence. But they accomplished little or nothing. The archetypal political figure of the age was Stanley Baldwin, prime minister of Britain; cartoonists commonly caricatured him as a tadpole. Another giant on the political horizon was Ramsay MacDonald, celebrated as Britain's first Labour prime minister. But it transpired that what he yearned for was not the New Jerusalem of the socialist commonwealth but merely the rare privilege of wearing a tuxedo and taking tea with duchesses. American Presidents in the twenties were solid representatives of middle-class culture: Harding had the tastes —and the ethics—of a traveling salesman; Coolidge the wit of a small-town alderman; and Hoover the understanding of economics and sociology perfectly suitable for the "great engineer," as his many admirers called him.

THE WORLD IN THE 1920'S

ARCTIC   OCEAN

*East Siberian
Sea*

WRANGEL I.

*BANKS
ISLAND*

QUEEN ELIZABETH
ISLANDS

*ELLESMERE
ISLAND*

G R E E N L A N

Den.

*Baffin
Bay*

*VICTORIA
ISLAND*

*BAFFIN
ISLAND*

Godhavn

Davis Strait

**S O V I E T
U N I O N**

Yukon R.

Nome   Fairbanks

A L A S K A
U.S.

Mackenzie R.

*Great Bear
Lake*
Fort Norman

Great Slave Lake
Fort Resolution

Churchill

*Hudson
Bay*

Bering Sea

*Gulf
of
Alaska*

Juneau

ALEUTIAN IS.

Seattle

C A N A D A

Edmonton

Vancouver

Winnipeg

NEWFOUNDLAND
Br.
St. Johns

*Sea
of
Okhotsk*

KURIL IS.
Jap.

*Great
Lakes*

Montreal
Toronto
Boston
New York

U N I T E D

San Francisco

Denver

Chicago   Detroit

Missouri R.

St. Louis *Ohio R.*

Washington

S T A T E S

Los Angeles

Atlanta

Mississippi R.

New Orleans

*BERMUDA
Br.*

A T L A N T I

MIDWAY IS.
U.S.

HAWAIIAN ISLANDS

*Gulf
of
Mexico*

MEXICO

*BAHAMA IS.
Br.*

Havana
CUBA

DOM. REP.

WAKE I.
U.S.

JOHNSTON I.
U.S.

Mexico City

JAMAICA Br.
BR. HOND.
HONDURAS
GUATEMALA
EL SALVADOR
NICARAGUA
COSTA RICA
PANAMA

HAITI

PUERTO RICO
U.S.

CAPE VE

CANAL ZONE
U.S.

TRINIDAD
Br.

Caracas

VENEZUELA

BR. GUIANA

SURINAM Neth.

FR. GUIANA

P A C I F I C

MARSHALL IS.
Jap.

LINE IS.
Br.-U.S.

Bogotá

COLOMBIA

ECUADOR

*GALAPAGOS IS.
Ec.*

Amazon   *R.*
Manaus

CAROLINE IS.
Jap.

GILBERT IS.
Br.

PHOENIX IS.
Br.

MARQUESAS IS.
Fr.

PERU

Recife

B R A Z I L

Sa

SOLOMON IS.
Br.

ELLIS IS.
Br.

SAMOA IS.
N.Z.-U.S.

SOCIETY IS.
Fr.

TUAMOTU ARCHIPELAGO

Lima

La Paz

BOLIVIA

Rio de Ja

*Coral
Sea*

NEW HEBRIDES
Br.-Fr.

FIJI IS.
Br.

TONGA IS.
Br.

COOK IS.
Br.

AUSTRAL IS.
Fr.

PITCAIRN I.
Br.

PARAGUAY

São Paulo

NEW CALEDONIA
Fr.

*EASTER I.
Chile*

R.

URUGUAY

AUSTRALIA

KERMADEC IS.
N.Z.

O C E A N

Santiago

ARGENTINA

Buenos Aires

*Tasman
Sea*

Wellington

**NEW
ZEALAND**

*FALKLAND IS.
Br.*

*SOUTH GEORGIA
Br.*

Drake   Passage

After the First World War, Turkish territories in the Middle East and German colonies in southwest Africa and East Asia came under the control of France, Britain, or British dominions, either through outright acquisition or through the League of Nations mandate system. The 1920's, therefore, can be said to mark the high tide of West European imperialism. But the gaining of dominion status by Ireland and the emergence of a strong national independence movement in India had already set in motion the forces that would lead to the dismantling of the European overseas empires in the 1950's and 1960's.

Leninism and Stalinism. In the space of a few years in the 1920's and 1930's the Soviet regime lost its revolutionary ardor and settled into a bureaucratized police state. Facing page: Lenin addressing a street rally in November 1917, during the days when Bolshevism had not yet atrophied and idealists saw the events in Russia as a harbinger of worldwide revolution. The spontaneity and improvised creativity of those early days rapidly waned. Right: Lenin with Joseph Stalin, his successor. Stalin's provincial background and lack of intellectual distinction made him a figure very different from the cosmopolitan professional revolutionary and Marxist theoretician who led the Bolsheviks in their moment of victory. Below: "The Shining Light," by the Russian artist M. Mariasch, illustrates the abysmal artistic results of the Stalin period, when the cult of personality and "socialist realism" produced endless canvases glamorizing the Soviet regime. Here Stalin, a squat, pragmatic Georgian, is transformed into a handsome, romantic idealist.

The middle class everywhere in Europe felt itself financially and psychologically threatened. Class lines hardened despite the advent of socialist parties to power all over Europe. It was remarkable how little ostensibly radical working-class champions did. Elected representatives of the German Social Democrats and the British Labour party proved to be nothing but stodgy politicians concerned in the first instance with keeping themselves securely in office. The General Strike, that apocalyptic day when all workers would simultaneously lay down tools, actually came to Britain in 1926, but the syndicalist dawn of freedom proved a desultory affair that created bad traffic snarls.

Ordinary men and women saved their enthusiasm for nonpolitical matters.

Italian Fascism. Passion, charisma, and energy sometimes seemed the monopoly of the new fascist regimes during the interwar period. Above: Benito Mussolini making a fiery appeal to his followers in the early days when the fascist experiment was looked upon as promising by many Europeans. Mussolini had begun life as a militant socialist, a left-wing demagogue who imagined himself particularly close to the common people. Italian fascism retained a radical aura throughout the twenties, although its social program served big business and its social policies embodied very middle-class values and aspirations. Facing page: Mussolini reviewing a parade of children in May 1935, when Italy was celebrating the twentieth anniversary of its entrance into World War I. Fascist regimes all over Europe carefully cultivated the minds of the young, who were pressed into various militaristic youth movements. Marching, drilling, singing songs of martial valor, these were a new and sinister type of boy scout.

The world breathlessly followed the exploits of the first aviators who attempted daredevil transatlantic flights in rickety one-engine planes. This was the age when going to the movies on a Saturday night became a popular habit—a cheap way to live briefly and vicariously among beautiful, affluent, and glamorous people. American jazz and such dances as the fox trot, the shimmy, and the vampire caught the fancy of the young.

A common sight in Paris cafés, along with expatriate American intellectuals, was the displaced person, the political refugee from Bolshevism or fanatical nationalism. No longer could these people be syphoned off to America. In the early twenties, as restrictive immigration quotas were introduced, the United States ceased to be the haven of European exiles. This was part of a resurgent American isolationism which preferred to leave Europe to its own dubious destiny while self-righteously exacting vast sums in war debts from near-bankrupt European states.

Even in Russia a staid conservatism was taking hold. After the death of Lenin in 1924, power passed into the hands of Joseph Stalin, a harsh party bureaucrat who had no use for the ardent idealism of the early Bolsheviks. Freedom of discussion, even within party circles, was replaced by a monolithic conformity ruthlessly imposed from above. Intellectually, Stalin's Russia was a stultifying place. All art and thought was forced to follow the party line.

The German Sickness. A combination of terror and mass hypnosis brought the National Socialist party to power in 1933. Facing page: militant young Hitler supporters during an election campaign in 1931. They claimed that the Nazis alone remained uncontaminated by decadence, corruption, and the shame of the Versailles Treaty. Above: Hitler immediately after he was made chancellor, arriving at Nuremberg to address 520,000 of his followers. Though Hitler himself had no religious sentiments, he took care to placate the Church, here represented by the Reichsbishop Ludwig Müller, as a bulwark of German middle-class domestic virtues. Right: the famous fire which destroyed the Reichstag and with it the last vestiges of Weimar liberal institutions. The fire, attributed to Bolsheviks but probably set by the Nazis themselves, became the official pretext for a ruthless crackdown on all dissident elements a few months after the Nazis came to power.

In the prewar years the centers of European culture had been Paris and Vienna. Now, paradoxically, the most vibrant center was Berlin, capital of defeated Germany. In Berlin, artists, dramatists, and philosophers penetrated yet further into the reaches of consciousness, the motion picture was transmuted into an art form, and scientific and humanistic learning attained new heights. This German renaissance flourished in an atmosphere sodden with decadence, absurdity, and violence. While the feeble liberals of Germany's first democratic republic stumbled along, inflation rocketed to incredible heights, industrialists and financiers acquired new fortunes, disgruntled militarists conspired against the Republic, left- and right-wing extremists battled in the streets. Hitler mesmerized street-corner crowds of anxious petit bourgeois and incited young toughs to assault Jews. Berlin in the 1920's offered the intense, febrile quality of life that came from pushing too far, from taking too great a risk, from standing on the edge of the precipice. And the brilliant art and literature reflected this quality: it relished the grotesque and the absurd; it mutilated its own beauty with the rough edge of sadistic mockery and self-hatred.

Much that was dynamic and vital in Europe seemed to belong to the fascist regimes that came to power in Italy in 1922 and in Germany in 1933. It was the fascists with their flashy uniforms, their torchlight parades, their gigantic outdoor rallies, and their ritualistic incantation of the glories of patriotism,

The Great Depression. The hopelessness and misery of the early 1930's, when millions were thrown out of work, helped persuade many that capitalism and liberal democracy were doomed. Right: unemployed men in London line up for the relief "dole." Although statistics showed that England was hit less hard than America by the economic debacle, it did not seem so to the demoralized men who experienced the ignominy of public relief for the first time. Apathy, frustration, and bewilderment were the characteristic reactions to the Depression. Below: shacks in New York City's Central Park during the economic collapse. The squalor to which the families shown here were reduced contrasts sharply with the backdrop of expensive town houses on Fifth Avenue.

of blood, of sacrifice and war who won the ardent young. Nazi ideology was the garbage pail of nineteenth-century culture. All the antiliberal, anti-humanist, authoritarian, hypernationalist, racist, nihilist, and paranoid delusions of late ninteenth-century society were drawn upon by Hitler and his gang. It was not only the disgruntled petite bourgeoisie who responded eagerly; men of high social status, vast wealth, even academic reputation in a few instances, found in Hitler's ravings an echo of something valuable, if only the opportunity for their own advancement. Even in staunchly democratic countries like England, Hitler and Mussolini were much admired in their early days: at least they were not drab party hacks. That Hitler and Mussolini were able to trample on democratic institutions with such ease was a measure of the disrespect accorded these institutions all over Europe. The erosion of democracy, of civil liberties, was regretted in a perfunctory manner until the mid-1930's, when intellectuals and a few statesmen in the Western democracies awoke from their somnolence to discover that new barbarians were pounding at the gates of civilization.

I THE PEACE SETTLEMENT

Background of the Paris Conference

In January 1919, two months after the armistice, Allied statesmen met in Paris to draft a peace treaty. Except for the United States, the major belligerents—both the victorious and the defeated—had been drained of men and material resources during four years of war. Among the Allies the overwhelming desire was to construct a peace that would preclude any recurrence of the holocaust. They had no common blueprint for a settlement, however; its final shape was determined by the personal convictions, objectives, and strength (or intransigence) of the negotiators. Although nearly thirty nations sent delegates to the peace conference and commissions of experts carried out studies and made recommendations, the real decisions were made by Wilson, Lloyd George, and Clemenceau.

Wilson's opponents cited the Republican victory in the congressional elections of November 1918 as proof that he lacked a mandate, but the President was personally committed to establishing a peace that would incorporate the Fourteen Points he had enunciated before Congress on January 8, 1918. He believed that a lasting peace demanded a territorial settlement based as far as possible on self-determination, and he opposed the exaction of punitive damages from the defeated powers. Knowing the reluctance of the other Allies to establish the peace on the basis of the Fourteen Points, Wilson bent his greatest efforts to securing a league of nations, which he believed would right any injustices included in the peace treaties.

The other Allied powers were less idealistic. Having suffered far more from the war than the Americans, the French were concerned with insuring their own future security and justifying their great wartime sacrifices by imposing harsh conditions on a defeated Germany. In particular, they were determined to make Germany pay the full cost of the war — not just the cost of damage to civilians and their property, as specified in a prearmistice agreement among the victors. The British, too, sought to reestablish their security in Europe; and Lloyd George, though he realized the political and economic dangers of attempting to exact enormous reparations from Germany, gradually came to side with the French on this issue under the pressure of British public opinion and American unwillingness to agree to British proposals for a settlement of inter-Allied war debts.

The idea of a league of nations to secure peace was eventually approved, but there was considerable disagreement as to how it should work. Wilson and Lloyd George envisioned a league of sovereign nations wielding power through moral force; Clemenceau was set upon a league with supranational powers to police the world and to guarantee French security against the ever present German threat. The French also sought to weaken Germany as much as possible and urged the creation of an independent state in the Rhineland under French influence.

The Peace Treaties

The peace conference was in session for six months before the first treaty with Germany was ready for signing. The settlement was entirely the work of the Allies; it was a "dictated," rather than a negotiated, peace. German representatives were simply presented with the Allied terms and allowed to submit a single set of counterproposals. These were considered, and then the Germans were handed the final terms. If they rejected these, the Allies were prepared to reimpose the blockade and mount an invasion. The Germans signed the treaty on June 28, 1919, in the Hall of Mirrors at Versailles.

The territorial settlement of the Treaty of Versailles was neither wholly punitive nor wholly based on the principle of self-determination. Germany remained politically united, notwithstanding French efforts to create an independent Rhineland and to encourage a separatist movement in the south. The east bank of the Rhine was demilitarized to a depth of fifty kilometers, and the Allies were to occupy the Rhineland for fifteen years, but its civilian administration was left in German hands. The Saar Basin was put under international administration for fifteen years, after which a plebiscite was to decide its fate; its coal mines were transferred to France in compensation for those Germany had destroyed in northeastern France.

Germany lost more than 25,000 square miles of territory in Europe and nearly seven million inhabitants. In the west, Alsace-Lorraine was returned to France; in the east, most of the territories seized by Prussia during the eighteenth-century partitions of Poland were given to the reconstituted Polish Republic (although some of this territory was now predominantly German as a result of a concerted policy of "colonization" undertaken in the years before the war). Poland's need for access to the sea resulted in the internationalization of the port of Danzig (a wholly German city) and the detaching of East Prussia from the rest of Germany by the ceding of a "corridor" to the Poles. The future of disputed Upper Silesia and Schleswig was left to plebiscites.

The conference failed to agree upon the total of Germany's debt. The United States pressed for a sum covering civilian damage based on Germany's ability to pay, but Lloyd George and Clemenceau responded to their vocal electorates' cry for "full war costs." The maximum American estimate was $30 billion; the French figures ran as high as $200 billion; the British calculated the sum of $120 billion. It was agreed to call the debt "reparations," though (at the insistence of Lloyd George) the cost of war pensions was also to be included. Since it was still impossible to agree on a sum, a reparations commission was charged with totaling the bill and settling on methods of payment before May 1, 1921. In the meantime, Germany was required to pay the Allies $5 billion in gold or kind. To justify the reparations demands, Article 231 of the treaty declared that "the aggression of Germany and her allies" was responsible for the war.

The peace also imposed permanent restrictions on German military strength: the army was limited to 100,000 volunteers, the navy to six battleships and a few smaller ships. Germany was to possess no submarines, no military aircraft, and no heavy guns and was to construct no fortifications. War materiel was restricted and factories capable of producing it limited in number and size, and Allied naval, military, and air commissions were stationed in Germany to see that these provisions were obeyed. Germany was also required to hand over many of its merchant ships to the Allies and to make large deliveries of coal to France, Belgium, and Italy for ten years. Finally, union with Austria (*Anschluss*) was forbidden, despite the fact that there was strong sentiment in both countries for such a step.

On September 10, 1919, Austria accepted Allied terms in the Treaty of St. Germain. The once-great empire was reduced to a quarter of its former area and a fifth of its prewar population. The treaty recognized the existence of the new states of Czechoslovakia and Yugoslavia. To the former, Austria ceded Bohemia, Moravia, Austrian Silesia, and parts of Lower Austria; to the latter went Bosnia, Herzegovina, and Dalmatia. Italy received Trieste, Istria, and the South Tyrol up to the strategic frontier of the Brenner Pass. Austria was limited to an army of 30,000 men and a navy consisting of three police boats on the Danube, and it also undertook to pay reparations.

On November 27, the Treaty of Neuilly confirmed Bulgaria's losses after the second Balkan War, though guaranteeing it "economic outlets to the Aegean Sea." But the harshest peace was reserved for Hungary. By the Treaty of Trianon (June 4, 1920), Hungary lost three fourths of its population, ceded large areas to Yugoslavia, Czechoslovakia, and Rumania, and saw three million Magyars placed under foreign rule.

Finally, on July 23, 1923, the Turks came to terms with the Allies in the Treaty of Lausanne. Unlike the other treaties, this document was negotiated after long bargaining. In 1920 the Allies had signed the Treaty of Sèvres with representatives of the sultan in Constantinople. But a group of army officers led by Mustafa Kemal opposed key provisions of the treaty, overthrew the sultan, and in 1922 proclaimed a republic. Kemal (who later styled himself Ataturk – "Father of the Turks") aimed to modernize Turkey's government and economy. The Turks supported Kemal in his efforts to expel the Greeks, who had occupied Smyrna with Allied support. When King Constantine was recalled to the Greek throne, Allied sympathies toward Greece were alienated (the king had been expelled during the war for his pro-German sentiments), and the Allies began to come to terms with the Kemal government. Soon, only the British government supported the Greeks, and the Turks drove the Greek army from Asia Minor, advancing until blocked by British forces in the Straits zone.

In the Treaty of Lausanne, the new Turkish republic renounced its claims to all territories with Arab majorities. Following the lines of the Sèvres agreement, the former Ottoman province of Syria came under French mandate, and Iraq, incorporating oil-rich Mosul, was mandated to Great Britain. Palestine also became a British mandate, and the Balfour Declaration of 1917 (which stated that "His Majesty's Government views with favour the establishment in Palestine of a national home for the Jewish people") was to be applied there. European Turkey was extended beyond Adrianople at the expense of Greece; demilitarized zones were set up in Thrace and in the area of the Straits; and Italy received the Dodecanese Islands.

The Covenant of the League of Nations was included in the Treaty of Versailles. It provided for an organization set up according to Anglo-American wishes: its power rested not on an international police force that could intervene to subdue an aggressor but on the diplomatic and moral pressure it could exert to bring warring nations to the negotiating table. From the beginning the League was not a truly global body; Germany was not yet allowed to join, and Soviet Russia was treated as a pariah nation, "unfit" for membership. Every member state was represented in the Assembly, where each had an equal vote. Except in the case of procedural matters and the admission of new members, complete unanimity of the Assembly was required before action could be taken. The League Council had no power of independent action; it could only hear disputes and make recommendations to the Assembly.

The whole edifice rested on Article 10 of the Covenant, which bound the members of the League to respect and preserve the territorial and political independence of every member against external aggression. Article 12 bound them to submit any dispute likely to lead to war to arbitration, judicial settlement, or inquiry by the Council. Article 16 called on them to break off diplomatic and financial relations with any Covenant-breaking state and gave the Council the power to *recommend* what armed forces they were to con-

THE PEACE SETTLEMENT
IN EUROPE

Newly Created States
Ceded Territories

The map of Europe was radically altered after the First World War. In central Europe the Habsburg Empire gave way to a number of states created to satisfy the national aspirations of its former subject peoples. On the Baltic the subject nationalities of the Russian Empire also gained their independence. Germany lost Alsace-Lorraine and its Saar coalfield to France. Recreated Poland claimed Upper Silesia and was in the perilous position of dividing East Prussia from the rest of Germany. Italy gained the South Tyrol and bit of the Dalmatian coast. In the Balkans, Yugoslavia was created as the home of the South Slavs, and Bulgaria lost its Aegean coastline to Greece and more territory to Yugoslavia.

tribute to protect the Covenant. The mandate system was instituted, placing the colonies of the Central Powers under the control of various "advanced nations," which were required to submit annual reports to a League commission. (The mandatory nations were those in possession of the colonies at war's end, particularly Japan and the British dominions of Australia, New Zealand, and the Union of South Africa.) The Permanent Court of International Justice (also known as the World Court) was to be set up to hear disputes, and the League was to take an active role in economic, social, and humanitarian concerns.

The weakness of the League in the postwar years can be attributed in part to the determination of the European states to act independently in international affairs, and in part to the absence of the United States and (until the 1930's) the Soviet Union from the international body. The fear of involvement in European disputes that did not affect any vital American interests aroused opposition to the League in the United States Senate, and in 1920 the Versailles Treaty failed to achieve the two-thirds majority necessary for ratification. Without the power and prestige of the United States, the League of Nations appeared to be stillborn.

Evaluation of the Peace Settlement

Woodrow Wilson arrived in Paris with the idealistic assumption that a natural harmony of interests existed among the nations of the world and that by dint of good will and intelligence it was possible to embody the principles upon which this harmony rested in a peace treaty which would provide both for justice and for security against war. Yet Wilson's conception of a natural harmony was ill-adapted to the realities of postwar Europe. For the self-interest of Britain, or France, or Poland, or the inhabitants of Danzig did not necessarily coincide with the good of all; on the contrary, these interests were continually in conflict, and the good of all varied according to the nationality of the individual defining it.

Thus, instead of embodying in the peace treaties the immutable verities of international brotherhood (which were in any case a mirage), the peacemakers acted in the manner in which diplomats usually act: they bargained, they horse-traded, they argued, they threatened, they made concessions. The problem was that Wilson (and to a degree Lloyd George as well) was loathe to admit this fact, especially to a public accustomed to the notion that the war had been fought to "make the world safe for democracy" and "to end all wars." The peace conference became trapped in its own rhetoric, and when the world discovered the inevitable disparity between the conditions of the treaties and the announced principles of the peacemakers, many people overreacted and denounced the peace settlement.

The best illustration of all this was the much-heralded principle of self-determination (or, as it was sometimes called, the "ethnographic principle"). Proclaimed in Wilson's Fourteen Points and given lip service even by the crusty old pragmatist Clemenceau, this principle was to form the basis of the postwar territorial settlement. But what, after all, did it mean? And how could it be realized? Presumably frontiers were now to be drawn in accordance with local ethnic composition and the wishes of the populace, usually assumed to be identical. But it was obviously both impossible and undesirable to grant independence to every one of Europe's many nationalities. In the first place, the ethnic map of Europe was not neatly constructed. Rather than forming homogeneous blocs, nationalities usually formed concentrated pockets separated by other such pockets. In the second place, even when ethnic frontiers were reasonably clear, they rarely coincided with geographical, strategic, or traditional frontiers. Thus, for example, *ethnographic* Poland would lack both a port and a militarily defensible frontier in the east. Finally, a proliferation of states in central and eastern Europe was not necessarily conducive either to the security of the great powers or to individual national interests.

As a result, the ethnographic principle came to be invoked selectively and only insofar as it coincided with the interests of one or another of the great powers, particularly Britain and France. Taken as a whole, the peace settlement represented a giant step toward the realization of nationalist aspirations in south-central and eastern Europe. Serious anomalies remained, however, and these were all the more apparent now that the peacemakers had formally committed themselves to the principle of self-determination. For example, Rumania now contained 1.5 million Magyars; Yugoslavia included 1.7 million Rumanians, Albanians, Magyars, and Germans in its population of 12 million; Czechoslovakia's population of 14.3 million included 4.6 million Poles, Ruthenes, Magyars, and Germans; and in Poland less than two thirds of the population spoke Polish as their mother tongue. These anomalies generated a host of animosities and created an instability that was hardly conducive to lasting peace in Europe.

The leaders in Paris assumed that they had the right, the responsibility, and the power to redraw frontiers and impose conditions throughout Europe. Unlike the Congress of Vienna in 1815, however, the Paris Conference failed to include one of the most important and powerful nations of Europe—Russia. Any European peace made without the approval of both Germany and Russia was bound to be a tenuous one at best, and by excluding them from the deliberations, the Allies created a situation in which these two great powers had a common, vested interest in revising the settlement and a common hostility toward Britain and France. Moreover, the absence of Russia meant that the frontiers which the Allies attempted to establish in eastern Europe were not ratified by the Soviets and were unenforceable except by recourse to arms.

In evaluating the peace settlement, it has often been argued that the cardinal error of the Allies was their failure to impose either a truly harsh peace on the defeated Central Powers or a truly lenient one. But this formulation of the problem assumes that the Allies were sufficiently united in their aspirations and interests to put forward a completely consistent policy. This was not the case, and therein lay the difficulty. "Security" meant one thing to Britain, another thing to France, and still another thing to the United States; and it meant something altogether different for—say—Poland. As a result, compromise was necessary.

The Aftermath of the Peace Settlement

Reaction to the peace treaties was mostly unfavorable. Italy came away from the conference without the gains it had sought in Asia Minor and Africa. Moreover, its ambition to dominate the Adriatic had been thwarted: not until 1924 was it able to secure most of the disputed territory of Fiume. A year earlier, Benito Mussolini – newly come to power as prime minister and eager to prove himself a man of action and Italy a power in the Balkans – ordered Italian forces to shell and occupy the island of Corfu after some Italian members of an international commission in Greece were killed. When Greece appealed to the League, Mussolini threatened to take Italy out of the organization. In the end, Greece agreed to pay an indemnity, and the Italian force was withdrawn. But the League had failed to halt Italian aggression, and the inviolability of the peace settlement had been challenged.

France was also disappointed by the terms of the settlement. The League of Nations lacked supranational authority; the Rhineland had not been detached from Germany; and while Britain had guaranteed to come to the aid of France in the event of any unprovoked aggression by Germany, the American Senate refused even to consider such a guarantee. Believing itself inadequately protected from the German menace, France concluded an alliance with Poland and reached military understandings with Yugoslavia, Czechoslovakia, and Rumania, known as the Little Entente.

France also exerted its influence on the Reparations Commission to extract the largest possible sum from Germany. On April 27, 1921, the German debt to the Allied powers was fixed at $33 billion (it had been decided earlier that France was to take 52 per cent, Britain 22 per cent, Italy 10 per cent, and Belgium 8 per cent, the remainder to be divided among minor Allies). Germany was to make annual payments of $500 million plus 25 per cent of the value of its exports. These terms were accepted only after the Allies threatened to occupy the Ruhr Valley, where Germany's metallurgical industries were centered. Even though the French wished to reinforce the peace settlement by peaceful means, their intransigence toward Germany did much to discredit the justice of the peace settlement in the eyes of the world.

Not surprisingly, the country with the strongest sense of grievance and the greatest desire for revision of the settlement was Germany. The cries emanating from postwar German nationalist circles about the "shameful peace" were disingenuous and self-serving in view of what is known about the Carthaginian peace that Germany would have imposed if it had emerged the victor. Generals and politicians who only a short time before had spoken of German world hegemony now attempted to obscure their own past follies and defeat by heaping abuse on the Allies and on the German statesmen who had signed the treaty. Though Germany had some reason to complain, the peace was not nearly so harsh as its critics liked to make out.

Except for internationalizing Danzig and incorporating some predominantly

German areas into Poland, the territorial settlement for Germany con-
formed relatively closely to the ethnographic principle (unless one counts the
failure to include the Germans of Austria and of the Sudetenland – who had
never previously been part of the Reich – in the new German state). Part of
Schleswig was returned to Germany through a plebiscite. A plebiscite in
Upper Silesia was less conclusive, and eventually the Council of the League
arrived at a compromise somewhat in Poland's favor. Allied occupation of the
Rhineland, though bitterly resented, was to be only temporary; the region
was not taken away from Germany. Resented, too, were the commissions enforcing disarmament, which, almost from the beginning, the German government tried to circumvent.

German opinion seized at once on Article 231, which, though included in
the treaty mainly to provide a legal basis for the collection of reparations,
was now taken as a moral condemnation of Germany's "war guilt." Needless
to say, such guilt was vehemently denied by the Germans, who published
prewar diplomatic documents to support their case. The reparations demanded
from Germany were hotly denounced – by Germans and non-Germans
alike – as unjust and completely unrealistic. Further criticism came from the
brilliant English economist John Maynard Keynes, who had officially represented the British treasury at the Paris Peace Conference until June 7, 1919.
In *The Economic Consequences of the Peace*, published in December 1919,
Keynes denounced the reparations section of the Versailles Treaty. He argued that the amount of reparations proposed at the conference was counterproductive – that Germany could not possibly pay such a large sum without a
favorable balance of trade. Although Keynes attacked only the reparations
section of the Versailles Treaty, his arguments did much to discredit the
whole of the peace settlement.

Whatever the merits of Keynes' arguments, by the end of 1921 the German
mark had begun a drastic decline in value. Before the war an American dollar could be exchanged for four marks; now a dollar bought 160 marks. Although reparations played an important part in this inflation, they were not
its sole cause: deficit wartime finance contributed to the initial decline in the
value of the mark; and inflation was at least in part self-induced, in order to
prove that reparations payments were unworkable. The incumbent German
government, weak and divided, made no attempt to limit this inflation by
increasing taxes but instead printed more paper money.

In May 1922 a partial moratorium was granted on cash payment of reparations. But the French government believed (in part, correctly) that the depreciation of the mark was fostered by Germany in order to escape paying. In
December, Germany failed to make a required delivery of timber and was
declared to be in voluntary default by the Reparations Commission, over the
opposition of the British member. The declaration was repeated in January
when Germany failed to make required coal deliveries. Thereupon, French and
Belgian troops occupied the Ruhr Valley. The German government encour-

aged passive resistance to the occupation and subsidized both employers and striking workers by printing vast quantities of paper money. This move proved disastrous to the value of the mark — by the end of 1923 a single dollar could be exchanged for 4.2 billion marks.

Many German industrialists made fortunes out of this calamity, paying off their debts and purchasing new equipment with worthless money. But the working class soon found its wages hopelessly inadequate, and lower-middle-class Germans, especially those on fixed incomes, lost all their savings in a single blow and found themselves reduced to the level of the proletariat. More than any other social group, it was this petit bourgeois class that bitterly condemned the Versailles Treaty and the government of the new Republic, which had done nothing to control the inflation.

Sending troops into the Ruhr was not the answer to French needs, either. The coal seized from the Ruhr mines did not even pay for the occupation, and it became obvious that the reparations problem could not be settled by force. At the end of 1923 a committee of experts from France, Belgium, Italy, Great Britain, and the United States was set up under the leadership of Charles G. Dawes of the United States to investigate ways to put German finances in order so that reparations payments could be resumed.

This protracted crisis in Allied-German relations was not the only problem left over from the peace settlements. The Paris peace settlement failed notably to establish cordial relations between the western Allies and the Bolshevik government in Russia. On the Russian side, there was more than adequate ground for suspicion. After the revolution in 1917 the Allies had been concerned with maintaining an eastern front against Germany and keeping Allied supplies in Russia out of German hands; but the intervention of British, French, American, and Japanese troops, which had begun in June 1918, soon took on ominous dimensions. When the war ended, the troops stayed on in Russia, and the Allies at Versailles gave open support and encouragement to the counterrevolutionary "White" armies.

On the Allied side, distrust was no less natural. The Bolshevik government had repudiated the debts of the czarist regime. In March 1919 the Third International, or Comintern, was founded in Moscow. The Comintern, which consisted of Communist parties all over the world, viewed its purpose as one of aiding revolutionary movements wherever they arose. It damned the League of Nations (from which Russia was excluded) as a "stinking corpse" and helped spread anti-British propaganda throughout Britain's colonial empire. Though the Soviets had granted independence to the Baltic states and Finland in 1918, they soon made it clear that they hoped to export communism wherever possible and were prepared to use force to do so.

These developments undercut the attempts of the Russian foreign office to establish normal relations with the rest of the world. Although Russia and Britain signed a commercial agreement in 1921, the first diplomatic recognition accorded the Bolshevik government by a major power did not come until

April 1922, when the Treaty of Rapallo was signed by Russia and Germany. Driven together by French intransigence over reparations and prewar debts and by common opposition to the existence of Poland, the two countries agreed to renounce claims against each other and set up preferential tariffs.

Thus in the immediate postwar years the various shortcomings, real or imagined, of the peace settlements generated resentment and instability throughout Europe. The growing belief that certain revisions should be allowed encouraged those who hoped to overthrow the entire settlement. As it turned out, allowance of some revision by peaceful means was to encourage further revision by violence.

II THE WESTERN DEMOCRACIES IN THE TWENTIES

Weak Leadership in Britain

The victorious Allies — Britain, France, and the United States — had a splendid opportunity after 1918 to confirm the claim that their victory had been a triumph for liberal democracy by presenting to the world models of effective reforming governments. This opportunity was lost, with dire consequences for mankind. The complex postwar economic problems and the reaction against idealism that inevitably followed a long and costly war required great political skill combined with a firm commitment to progressive principles on the part of the leaders of the Western democracies in the 1920's. In neither Britain, France, nor the United States were these qualities abundantly demonstrated by the men who held power. In general, their record in foreign policy and international relations was somewhat better than their record in domestic matters. In the latter area, their performance fell far short of the level necessary to convince the rest of the world that liberal democracy was the political system clearly most conducive to the welfare of the common man.

The British elections of December 1918 returned to power the coalition government led by Lloyd George. It was immediately confronted by a multitude of problems, including negotiation of the peace settlement, the future of wartime collectivism, and rebellion in Ireland.

In July 1917 a Ministry of Reconstruction had been established to supervise the transition from war to peace. Implicit in the planning reports issued by the ministry was the assumption that the various wartime controls which the government had exercised over industry should, in some form or other, be carried over into the postwar period. But despite the lip service he occasionally paid to reconstruction and nationalization, at war's end Lloyd George succumbed almost immediately to the clamor of private enterprise for the removal of wartime controls. The hopes of all those who believed that the experience of wartime could prove useful in rationalizing and democratizing British society were cruelly dashed.

In 1919 prices rose at twice the rate of the worst war year, and optimism ran high in industry in expectation of increased sales in markets cut off during the war. But inflation and the prospect of decontrol also rekindled trade union militancy, and in the winter of 1920–1921 the postwar boom abruptly collapsed. The expected overseas markets had not materialized, foreign competition depressed British shipping, and between December 1920 and March 1921 unemployment doubled. In June 1921 it reached a peak of over one million. Thinking that the situation was only temporary, the government extended unemployment insurance benefits and met the mounting deficits out of the treasury. The benefits became a form of poor relief known as the dole.

Heavy taxation and public expenditure were believed to be the root of all evil, and the government seized upon the old remedy of reducing expenses to relieve depression. In the process, it abandoned once and for all any plans it had for nationalizing the coal industry and the railroads and reorganizing the electric power industry. Moreover, the mine owners now embarked on a plan for reducing their costs, in order to compete in the world market, by cutting wages. In late March a national miners' strike began, but at the last minute the leaders of the railroad and transport workers' unions repealed their decision for a turnout in sympathy with the miners. By July the miners had been forced back to work on onerous terms.

In Ireland, the Easter Rebellion of 1916 and its repressive aftermath were followed in 1918 by an ill-timed British attempt to introduce conscription (which was averted by the Armistice). By 1920 the situation had degenerated so badly that former prime minister, Herbert Asquith, observed, "Things are being done in Ireland which would disgrace the blackest annals of the lowest despotism in Europe." After achieving great success in the general election of 1918, the Irish republicans of the Sinn Fein party set up their own parliament, the *Dáil Éireann*, proclaimed the Irish Republic, and unsuccessfully sought recognition at the Paris Peace Conference. The Irish Republican Army soon launched a guerrilla war against British authority. For their part, the British recruited the hated "Black and Tans" (mainly ex-soldiers) and "Auxies" (mainly ex-officers) to serve in the Royal Irish Constabulary and encouraged them to terrorize the countryside. In July 1921 a truce was finally arranged, and on December 6 a treaty was signed according dominion status to the twenty-six southern counties as the Irish Free State, while the six northeastern counties remained part of the United Kingdom. This ended the problem for Britain, but in Ireland a bloody civil war between die-hard republicans, who opposed the treaty, and the government of the Free State continued until 1923.

Though Lloyd George was still prime minister, his position was precarious: the Conservatives—who dominated the coalition established in wartime—no longer needed him, and he had failed to end the economic depression. He met with even less success abroad, where his attempts to solve the reparations quandary ran into French intransigence and his policy against Turkey threatened to plunge Britain into war. When in 1922 he called for new elections, hoping to gain a popular mandate, the Conservatives—led by Bonar Law and Stanley Baldwin, who both originally entered politics from the business world—decided to break up the coalition and campaign as an independent party.

In the election of November 1922 the Conservatives won 347 seats; Labour, 142; the Liberals, 117 (divided approximately evenly between those who followed Asquith and those who followed Lloyd George). The Labour vote had grown from fifty-nine in the last election, due in part to the fact that it ran more candidates and in part to the large gains it made in the working-class districts of London, northern England, and Scotland. Bonar Law, as the new prime minister, had to form a cabinet of mediocrities, for the important leaders (Arthur Balfour and Austen Chamberlain) stayed loyal to the coalition. Stanley Baldwin became chancellor of the exchequer, and Neville Chamberlain (Austen's younger half-brother), postmaster general.

Unemployment continued at an unprecedented rate under the new government, and very little was accomplished except for Neville Chamberlain's Housing Act, which subsidized homes built by private enterprise to be sold to the public. In May, Baldwin succeeded the dying Bonar Law. In October he announced without warning that he could not combat unemployment without protection—that is, without turning from free trade to protective tariffs. (Baldwin explained much later that he did this to reunite his party permanently.) As a result, the Conservatives lost their absolute majority in the elections of December 1923, although they remained the largest single party. The Liberals' dislike of protection proved stronger than their dislike of socialism, and in January 1924 they voted with Labour to bring down the government. A minority Labour government was sworn in, with Ramsay MacDonald (1866-1937), a sometime union leader, as its prime minister.

The advent of the first Labour government, pledged as it was to instituting socialism in Britain, produced great consternation among the conservative middle class and great enthusiasm among the workers and their allies; but its brief tenure in office quieted the fears of its critics and dampened the enthusiasm of its supporters. With only a minority in the House of Commons, MacDonald decided that his most prudent course would be to prove that Labour was "fit" to govern the nation, and this meant not rocking the boat. As a result, MacDonald and his chancellor of the exchequer, Philip Snowden, acted timidly or not at all. Snowden, an avowed socialist, ran the exchequer in a manner that would have warmed the heart of a nineteenth-century Liberal: he had a positive mania for balancing budgets and reducing expenditures. In domestic policy the only important accomplishment of the Labour government was the passage of the Wheatley Housing Act, which increased the state subsidy for low-income housing. In foreign affairs MacDonald was bolder and more successful. An ardent advocate of the League of Nations, he was the first foreign minister to attend its sessions. He also helped to secure the adoption of the Dawes Plan for German reparations, made Britain the first of the great powers to recognize the Bolshevik government of Russia, and helped to prepare the Geneva Protocol of 1924, providing for effective settlement of international disputes.

The French occupation of the Ruhr in 1923 temporarily increased the market for British coal, and miners' wages rose somewhat. Although industrial unrest continued among the dockers and streetcar men, crisis was avoided. But Snowden's fiscal policy failed altogether to relieve unemployment, and in August 1924 the government fell.

The election of October 1924 returned the Conservatives to power, partly as a result of the forged "Zinoviev Letter" allegedly showing Bolshevik intrigue in Britain. Austen Chamberlain became foreign secretary, his half brother returned to the ministry of health, and Winston Churchill became chancellor of the exchequer. For the next five years the British government was led by Stanley Baldwin, who wanted above all a quiet life for himself and the country. In the main, he was successful. The international scene appeared to justify optimism, and under the Dawes Plan, Germany was making regular reparations payments. But though industries producing for the home market had recovered, industries producing for export lagged behind, and unemployment remained at more than one million. High wages were blamed for sluggish export sales and unemployment, and in July 1925 Baldwin called upon all workers in the country to take wage reductions. This attitude caused the single greatest crisis of the Baldwin government – the general strike, which was in fact a national sympathy strike without clear political objectives.

Trouble began – inevitably – in the coal industry, recently hurt by the resumption of German coal production. In June 1925 the owners proposed sharp pay cuts, and a strike was averted only when the government agreed to subsidize wages and profits for the next nine months while the Samuel Commission investigated the industry. Meanwhile the government prudently began to organize the public to keep vital services functioning in the event of a strike. Neither owners nor miners accepted the commission's report (advocating first wage reduction, then reorganization), and on May 1, 1926, a lockout began. A nationwide strike, called by the Trades Union Congress, went into effect at midnight, May 3.

The response to the strike call was phenomenal. To a man, union members ceased work. For nine remarkable days the work of Britain came to a halt. But as a result the strike became a struggle between the government (whose duty it was to maintain order and services) and the labor movement, rather than between labor and management. The leaders of the TUC, shunning the revolutionary implications of the tactic they had so long been advocating, finally backed down. On the strength of a memorandum by the head of the Samuel Commission, promising to hold off wage reductions until the reorganization of the coal industry was effected, they called off the strike on May 12. Unfortunately, neither the miners' union nor the mine owners (nor even the

Class War in Britain. The British general strike of 1926 was an ugly episode that demonstrated deep class divisions and inept leadership on all sides. The TUC leaders stumbled unwillingly into the strike and called it off at the first pretext. The government did nothing to oppose the reactionary intransigence of the mine owners, which ultimately brought on the strike. Middle-class people became hysterical and acted as though a Communist takeover was imminent. Above: armored cars stationed in London to suppress riots that never occurred.

government) had accepted the memorandum, and in its haste to call off the strike, the TUC had not set up safeguards for the returning strikers, who suffered wage reductions and dismissals. The miners suffered worst of all. Rejecting the TUC's decision, they continued their strike for six months until, wholly defeated, they were compelled to accept lower wages and longer hours.

Baldwin's failure to avert the general strike and his complacency over the fate of the miners in the months that followed represented the nadir of his generally undistinguished regime. But his government did score some achievements: imperial relations were tidied up; Neville Chamberlain reorganized, simplified, and much improved local government; all women over twenty-one were given the vote (1928); and the Widows, Orphans, and Old Age Contributory Pensions Bill was passed. A bill that increased benefits somewhat for the unemployed was also passed, but the Baldwin government could not solve the nation's chief problem — unemployment. Popular support for the Conservatives began to melt away, and when elections were held in May 1929, Labour emerged as the largest single party, with 287 seats. As in 1924, however, they did not command a majority in Parliament. The return of a minority government did not bode well for the solution of Britain's problems.

Stalemate in France

In France, the decade after World War I was characterized by social stagnation and political stalemate. Successive governments strove to restore prewar conditions of economic stability and military security. There was little impetus toward radical social change. In 1919 the threat of a wave of strikes led Clemenceau to establish the eight-hour work day, but the next great victory for social legislation was not won until 1930, when a national system of old age and sickness insurance was inaugurated.

Although its popular mandate grew throughout the twenties, the far Left was so badly divided that the center parties — the Radicals and Moderates — formed the governments. In a party congress at Tours in December 1920, a large majority of the Socialist party voted to join the Comintern and renamed itself the *Parti Communiste Français* (PCF). During the next few years, Moscow's attempts to dictate party policy had a disastrous effect on membership, driving away an estimated two thirds by 1923. But even at the nadir of its numerical strength, its militants gave the party formidable potential. Meanwhile the Socialists, under the leadership of Léon Blum (1872–1950), remained aloof from moderate leftist governments and committed to revolutionary change. In preventing his party from becoming an adjunct of the Radicals, Blum allowed it to remain a haven for disillusioned Communists and proletarian idealists, and by 1936 it had become France's largest party.

Small rightist pressure groups were also active: *L'Action Française* suffered after it was disavowed by the Vatican, but the *Croix de Feu* (an organization of decorated veterans) joined an authoritarian temper with a growing tendency to political action, and the *Jeunesses Patriotes* was modeled on Mussolini's Fascist movement in Italy.

Clemenceau was defeated for the presidency in the election of 1919, which brought to power an alliance of the center and rightist parties in a *Bloc National*. The government devoted itself to establishing security for France and to rebuilding the war-ravaged northeastern *départements*. The wartime policy of meeting current expenses by borrowing at home and abroad and by printing paper money was continued. Government expenditures which could not be paid for out of tax revenues were simply put into a separate budget, to be balanced by the expected receipt of reparations from Germany. This satisfied both the wealthier classes, who resisted any increase in direct taxation, and the parties of the Left, which opposed increases in indirect taxation. The result was inflation and continued depreciation in the value of the franc. The Poincaré government in 1923 seized the Ruhr to force the payment of reparations, but the occupation cost more than was collected, and taxes finally had to be raised by 20 per cent.

In the following year the electorate — alarmed by international opposition to the seizure of the Ruhr and aroused by new taxes — voted in a *Cartel des Gauches*, or leftist coalition, and a Radical government was formed with strong Socialist support. Foreign affairs came under the direction of Aristide Briand (1862–1932) and remained there for the next seven years. Still the franc declined in value. Rather than support the Socialists' plan for a levy on capital holdings and a lower rate of interest on government bonds, the Radicals

—mindful of their support from peasants and small businessmen and concerned over the growing economic crisis—abdicated power to the moderate
Right. In July 1926, Poincaré formed a government of "National Union,"
promising to halt the fall of the franc and to avoid the dreaded capital levy.
Capital began to return to the country; taxes were increased sharply; and
drastic cuts in government spending were instituted. The franc was stabilized
at 20 per cent of its prewar level, and most Frenchmen were relieved not to
have lost everything. Yet the long inflation left a legacy of fear and fiscal conservatism that was to hamper the government during greater economic crises.

By the end of the decade, the reconstruction of the northeast had succeeded,
and modernized industry and agriculture predominated there. But in the
rest of the country, little progress was made. Agricultural stagnation—initially reflecting worldwide conditions—increased rural dissatisfaction and
forced a continuing exodus to urban centers. The failure of a succession of
governments to act decisively to halt postwar inflation had alarmed investors
and deprived industry of capital for expansion and modernization. Industrial
production was up only moderately—considering France's gains in territory
—while industrial wages lagged behind. Prosperity was tenuous, and new
forces waited in the wings to take advantage of economic crises.

Prosperity in the United States

At the war's end, the United States was uneasy in its new position as an
arbiter of European and world affairs. Its insecurity was made evident by the
failure of President Wilson's efforts to secure ratification of the Versailles
Treaty and American membership in the League of Nations. Ratification was
opposed not only by conservative groups but also by some liberals who believed that the settlement and the format of the League betrayed Wilson's own
peace programs and promises. Nevertheless, the treaty could have been
ratified if Wilson had been willing to accept the changes proposed by the
"moderate reservationists" in the Senate, who wanted major revisions to safeguard American interests. But having been forced to compromise in Europe,
he would not do so at home. When the treaty, with reservations, came to a
vote on March 19, 1920, twenty-three Democrats voted against it on his orders, and it failed by seven votes to gain the necessary two-thirds majority.

At the same time, the country was alarmed by a rising tide of violence.
With controls removed, prices immediately shot up, touching off a wave of
strikes by workers seeking higher wages. Employers charged many strikes to
"Bolsheviks," and during the "Red scare" that ensued, Attorney General A.
Mitchell Palmer rounded up and prosecuted all those suspected of radical activities, deporting them if they were aliens. Civil liberties went by the board.
In July 1921 two admitted anarchists, Nicola Sacco and Bartolomeo Vanzetti,
were sentenced to death for murder by a Massachusetts court. In 1927 they
were executed. Critics then and now contend that the court was convinced of

their guilt more by their anarchist beliefs and foreign origins than by the evidence presented.

Anxious for a respite from the turbulence of the Wilson years, the American electorate voted in a landslide for the Republican presidential candidate, Warren G. Harding, a senator from Ohio who campaigned from his porch and urged a return to "normalcy." The Harding administration is best remembered for the malfeasance of the President's cronies and the scandals that came to light in later years. Together with the succeeding administration of Calvin Coolidge, it returned to power "Old Guard" Republicans who halted social welfare legislation and gave business interests as free a hand as possible. The secretary of the treasury, Andrew Mellon, successfully introduced bills reducing corporation, estate, and income taxes so as to reverse almost completely the progressive tax policies of the Wilson administration.

The prosperity that characterized the Coolidge era for most Americans — although farmers generally did not participate in the boom — was mainly the consequence of remarkable strides in industrial technology and output. Never had the people of the United States been offered so much to buy; by autumn of 1925 a complete Model T Ford rolled off the assembly line every ten seconds. And never before had consumption been so conspicuous. Topping it all was the speculative mania in the stock market, which claimed the attention of the entire country.

III EXTREMISM AND DICTATORSHIP

The Antiliberal Tide

In the 1920's, inept leadership in Britain and the United States and political instability in France dimmed the prospects of liberalism elsewhere and encouraged extremism of the Left and Right. In countries where democratic traditions were weak, such as Germany, liberal, republican institutions came under constant attack. In states which had virtually no liberal tradition, such as the Soviet Union and most of the eastern European nations, governmental systems almost invariably took the form of dictatorships of one kind or another.

The largest gains in the twenties were made by right-wing extremist parties and movements. By the end of the decade the extreme Right in each European country was coming to be labeled "fascist," at least by its enemies. The term was derived from Mussolini's party in Italy, the first extreme rightist group to gain power in a major country. Fascist parties throughout Europe were inspired by a common set of factors: the pessimism and anguish that followed the First World War, the ambitions of officer groups, the discontent of the masses, virulent nationalism, and middle-class fears of Red revolution. Right-wing leaders generally sought to institute dictatorial regimes and professed a doctrinaire belief in a strongly centralized, corporative kind of government.

On this point, the extreme Right and the extreme Left coincided, for the Communists also advocated a collectivist state run by the so-called dictatorship of the proletariat, which actually became the dictatorship of the Communist party, just as in the fascist state corporatism meant in practice the dictatorship of a fascist party.

The fascist and Communist regimes of the 1920's and 1930's have been called totalitarian because they were antiliberal systems that subordinated all groups and institutions to the will and power of the dictator and his party. The term *totalitarian* is a useful one for post-1918 extremist movements, as is also the generic designation *fascist*. But just as a wide spectrum of attitudes and systems falls under the rubric of *socialist* (as was pointed out in Chapter 10), so it must be recognized that fascist movements and regimes also differ from each other in significant ways, and that the degree and structure of central control exercised by governments that can be labeled totalitarian also vary substantially.

The Transition from Lenin to Stalin in Russia

The Bolshevik coup against the Kerensky government in November 1917 was intended to usher in the dictatorship of the proletariat – a socialist democracy of workers and peasants. The leading revolutionaries appreciated the difficulties of creating such a government for the most autocratic – and industrially nearly the most backward – country in Europe, especially as the new regime was vulnerable to both civil war and foreign intervention.

Nevertheless, the Bolsheviks tried to achieve this goal when they came to power. By a series of decrees that had enormous propaganda value abroad, industry was thoroughly nationalized (including all enterprises employing more than ten workers), land was expropriated from the landlords, and the government appealed for peace negotiations. Yet when elections were held for a constituent assembly, the Bolsheviks were in a minority, winning only 225 seats out of a total of 707. Democracy was not allowed to stand in Lenin's way. The assembly met just once – in January 1918 – expressed anti-Bolshevik sentiments, and was dissolved by force. The Bolsheviks decided immediately not to tolerate any threats to the progress of the revolution.

During 1918 and 1919 the exigencies of civil war between the "Red" Bolsheviks and the "White" anti-Bolsheviks caused great hardship throughout the country, and the Bolsheviks alienated much of their rural support by requisitioning food for the starving urban population. The urban population in turn was demoralized by unemployment, hunger, and worthless currency. The easing of tensions resulting from the conclusion of hostilities with Poland and the end of the civil war in the fall of 1920 served to exacerbate these discontents. The system of extreme concentration of economic authority and of ruthless requisitioning (known as "War Communism") had perhaps been justified during the crisis years; but now that a measure of stability was returning, workers and peasants alike protested against its severity and the famine it had produced. As Lenin himself admitted, "tens of hundreds of thousands of disbanded soldiers" were turning to banditry. These disorders finally culminated in March 1921 is the sailors' rising at the Kronstadt naval base, a former Bolshevik stronghold.

Faced with the danger of losing the support of both peasants and workers, Lenin announced the "New Economic Policy" (NEP), which continued from 1921 to 1927. The NEP abolished "War Communism," whose hardships it was designed to reduce. The major problem was to restore internal trade between the cities and the country. The peasants were to pay a heavy tax in kind to the state but were free to sell their remaining crops on the open market. The result of the NEP was to enhance the wealth of the large farmers producing for the market (the *kulaks*) and to call into being a class of middlemen who bought and sold for private profit. In industry, the NEP tended to decentralize economic control, expand small-scale production, and stimulate light or consumer industries at the expense of heavy industry. Thus the NEP as a whole represented a new emphasis on consumption, distribution, and exchange rather than on production and rapid industrialization, the traditional cornerstones of Soviet Marxist theory. Even so, by 1926–1927 Russian industrial production had regained the level reached in 1914.

At about the same time the NEP was introduced, the conflict over the Soviet-Polish boundary was finally resolved, both sides reluctantly accepting a compromise line recommended by the British foreign secretary, Lord Curzon. But at the end of 1921 Lenin became ill, and the next years witnessed a power struggle between his likely successors: Trotsky, the commissar of war, who had brought the civil war to a successful close and crushed the Kronstadt mutiny, and Joseph Stalin, the commissar of nationalities. Trotsky was brilliant, idealistic, mercurial; Stalin was skillful, ambitious, and ruthless—in his last years Lenin came to distrust him. Trotsky argued a position which later became known as "left deviationist"; he wished to abolish the NEP and return to more orthodox Soviet Marxist principles at home—rapid industrialization, concentration on heavy industry, state planning, and the subordination of the agricultural sector—and to the support of world revolution abroad. The "right deviationists" (whose chief theoretician was Nikolai Bukharin) favored the extension of the NEP and of the private capital sectors. Stalin—an unprincipled opportunist—eventually took ideas from both, combining industrialization and collectivization of agriculture with the subordination of world revolution to national needs. This policy came to be known as "Socialism in One Country."

In the end it was not doctrine but shrewdness and calculation that determined Stalin's success. He contrived to hold so many offices in the party bureaucracy that he effectively controlled party patronage, and after Lenin's death in January 1924, he established himself as the leader of the emerging cult of Leninism. In 1927 he expelled Trotsky from the party. When Trotsky refused to disavow his beliefs – which included the right of individual Communists to criticize the regime – he was exiled to central Asia. Later he sought refuge in Mexico. In 1928 and 1929 Stalin began to put into practice a policy of rapid industrialization at the expense of the independent peasants, and particularly of the prosperous class of *kulaks*.

The Weimar Republic

The republic proclaimed by the German Social Democratic party (SPD) on November 9, 1918, was threatened from its inception by extraparliamentary agitation. Although an avowedly Marxist party, the SPD was unwilling to capitalize on the revolutionary situation which existed in the fall of 1918 by boldly instituting a socialist program. On the contrary, the party's motto became "peace, security, and order." Unwilling to take any steps that would revolutionize the nation without a mandate from the German electorate, the SPD limited itself to summoning a constituent assembly to write the constitution of a liberal democratic republic. This assembly was opposed by the extreme Left as well as the Right.

In December the Spartacists formed the German Communist Party (KPD). The following month Communist demonstrations precipitated a bloody reprisal by the army and the *Freikorps,* a right-wing volunteer force of discharged soldiers, in which the leaders of the KPD, Rosa Luxemburg and Karl Liebknecht, were foully murdered. Fighting continued sporadically throughout Germany (a Communist republic was temporarily set up in Bavaria). For some weeks the country was governed by a committee of Socialists. The SPD leaders, however, made the portentous decision to seek the support of the military, thus strengthening the forces of the Right and forsaking fundamental social change in favor of protection against left-wing extremists. The January elections failed to give the SPD a majority, and thus it was a coalition of Centrists, Socialists, and Democrats that drafted the Republic's constitution at Weimar and signed the Treaty of Versailles.

The Weimar Republic was identified from the outset with Germany's defeat in the war. From its inception it was viciously attacked by right-wing nationalist groups and conspired against by Communists. In March 1920 certain army forces supported the "Kapp *Putsch,*" which attempted to set up a rival government in Berlin. The Republic was saved – not by the army but by a general strike of the rank and file of the SPD in the capital – but the participants in the *Putsch* were not severely punished, and the unreliability of the army was not remedied.

The following years of economic hardship witnessed a rising tide of violence: Matthias Erzberger, who proposed the 1917 peace resolution, and Walther Rathenau, organizer of German wartime industry, were murdered by right-wing extremists, and abortive Communist risings occurred in many German states. The crisis of the Ruhr occupation and the failure of the government's policy of passive resistance brought much suffering throughout the country. In Bavaria, rightist and nationalist groups which had come to the fore in reaction to the Communist revolution were seething at the Republic's impotence and at its allegedly socialist bent. In November 1923 still another *Putsch* against the Berlin government was attempted in Munich, this one sponsored by the National Socialist German Workers' party and General Ludendorff. Once again, the courts treated the plotters in a kindly way: Ludendorff was acquitted, while the leader of the National Socialists, Adolf Hitler (1889–1945), though found guilty of high treason, was given the minimum sentence – five years in prison. In fact, Hitler spent only nine months in pleasant confinement before he was released. During this time he wrote *Mein Kampf* (My Struggle), describing the program for national and world supremacy from which he never deviated.

The National Socialists (commonly abbreviated to Nazis) originated in the German Workers' party, one of many inconspicuous racist-militarist groups founded in Germany after the war. In 1919 the army hired Hitler, then a young veteran, to investigate it. Instead he joined and rapidly assumed a leading position in the fledgling party. Exposed as a youth in Vienna to the feverish national and racial tensions in that troubled city, Hitler brought to the party a total belief in the efficacy of propaganda and explosive oratory. The Workers' party (which soon changed its name to National Socialist) also made use of a private army, the *Sturmabteilungen* (SA), composed mainly of former *Freikorps* members. In compliance with the terms of the Versailles Treaty, the government had disbanded the *Freikorps* in May 1920, driving its members into clandestine operations. The Nazis used the swastika – hitherto a peace symbol – as their emblem.

The failure of the November 1923 *Putsch* convinced Hitler that he would have to take power by legal means, and the party turned its attention to collecting a mass following. Fortunately for the government, the recovery and relative prosperity of the latter half of the decade deprived the National Socialists of much of their appeal; for the next few years the party languished. Meanwhile, under the leadership of Gustav Stresemann (1878-1929), the moderate and practical leader of the monarchist People's party, a coalition of Social Democrats, Centrists, Democrats, and his own followers pressed for a program of practical cooperation with the victorious powers.

The reparations settlement submitted by the Dawes Committee in 1924 was accepted; and at the same time Germany received a $200 million foreign loan. During the next five years Germany was to indulge in a veritable orgy of borrowing abroad to finance both its reparations payments and reconstruction. Thus the restoration of German prosperity was closely tied to the willingness of American investors to continue to lend their money.

The election of Field Marshal von Hindenburg (1847–1934) to the presidency of the Republic in 1925 was at first hailed as a triumph for the Right, but the new president surprised both his backers and his opponents by supporting the parliamentary government for the rest of the decade. However, the death of Stresemann in October 1929 coincided with the beginning of the Depression and brought the more intransigent wing of the People's party to the fore. This threatened the coalition of moderates that had prevailed in the Reichstag. German economic decline, in response to the American business crash, made more difficult the formation of workable moderate coalitions, opening the way for the formation of governments that were not responsible to the Reichstag and eventually for the Nazi dictatorship.

Fascism in Italy

Like Germany, Italy was troubled by revolutionary unrest after the First World War, inspired by inflation, unemployment, food shortages, and above all by nationalist resentment at having been denied a larger share of the spoils. A wave of industrial strikes swept the country. Giolitti, who returned to power in 1920, played his usual waiting game while the strikes collapsed by themselves. At the same time, peasants were alarming landlords by seizing uncultivated (and cultivated) lands, and landowners and businessmen were disillusioned by the government's failure to reestablish order. Meanwhile, the old-line politicians were being challenged by new parties formed on issues that created mass support among the electorate. One such group was the Catholic *Partito Popolare*, another the Socialist party. From the Right came a new extraparliamentary challenge in the *Fasci di combattimento*, or combat groups, formed by Benito Mussolini (1883–1945). Before the war Mussolini had been the leader of the left wing of the Socialist party and had edited the party newspaper, *Avanti!* When war broke out in 1914, he suddenly reversed his extreme antimilitarist position and became a vehement advocate of interventionism and Italian nationalism. Expelled from the Socialist party, he founded a newspaper of his own, the *Popolo d'Italia* (which seems to have been financed by the British and the French), and agitated for Italy's entrance into the war on the side of the Allies.

The Fascist movement that developed after the war at first combined radical demands (such as the confiscation of 85 per cent of war profits) with extreme anticlericalism and nationalism. The Fascists played on the national sense of disgrace that resulted from the failure of the Paris Peace Conference to allow Italy to annex Fiume and Dalmatia. In the elections of 1919 the Fascists failed dismally, and this strengthened the antiparliamentarian attitude within the movement. The name and emblem of Mussolini's party was derived from the *fasces*, a two-headed axe which was the symbol of consular authority in ancient Rome.

From the outset the Fascists were rabidly anti-Socialist and anti-Communist. Marxism was considered detestable because of its internationalism, its pacifism, and its "soullessness." Thus even when the Fascists were still paying lip service to the radical planks in their program, they insisted on distinguishing between the workers, whose legitimate demands they supported, and the socialist parties and trade unions, who were to be fought. By 1920 Mussolini was concentrating the energies of the movement on exploiting agrarian unrest in order to launch a civil war against the Socialists. In the process the Fascists shed most of their radicalism (and anticlericalism) as they became allied with the "forces of order" — the army (which helped arm them), the police (which protected them), and the landlords, industrialists, and government (which subsidized them).

Fascist toughs roamed the countryside breaking up strikes and interfering with Socialist or Communist municipal governments. In the elections of May 1921, Giolitti, who saw in the Fascists a means to defeat his parliamentary enemies, the *Partito Popolare* and the Socialists, gave them police protection and government support. Though they won only thirty-five out of over five hundred seats, the Fascists now had entered respectable politics.

The liberal parties were unable to form effective governments or to end the violence that was spreading throughout the countryside. In 1921 Giolitti retired, and his successors did no better. The Fascists gained control of Milan by force and felt strong enough to challenge the Chamber of Deputies. On October 26, 1922, Mussolini announced that the Fascists would march on Rome to take over the government. The march was a farce, but unlike Hitler's pathetic *Putsch* of the following year, it succeeded — the Italian military was sympathetic with the Fascists, and the opposition was divided, incompetent, and inert. Though the march could easily have been dispersed by force, King Victor Emmanuel III, on the advice of the army, refused to declare martial law. The dry rot which had long since consumed Italy's parliamentary system now became apparent. When an attempt to form a right-wing cabinet failed, Mussolini was called to take over on October 31.

The government Mussolini formed did not immediately reveal his intentions to overthrow the parliamentary system. It included members of the *Partito Popolare*, and its dictatorial powers to restore law and order were supposed to end on December 31, 1923. But the *Popolari* were ejected from the government in May 1923, and a new electoral law gave the leading party an automatic two thirds of the seats in the Chamber. With his majority thus guaranteed, Mussolini instituted press censorship and banned political meetings by opponents of his regime. There was a brief moment of rebellion among the other parties in 1924, in response to the murder of a Socialist deputy who had spoken out against the terroristic methods of the Fascists; but unfortunately the anti-Fascists dramatized their opposition by withdrawing from the Chamber (the "Aventine secession"), and when they tried to return, Mussolini refused to admit them. In 1925 the premier was designated "head of the government" and made responsible only to the monarch, and in 1928 the Fascist Grand Council was given the power to nominate the head of the government.

Thus the party became an official organ of the state. Instead of free parliamentary elections, the electorate voted for candidates chosen by the Council.

Mussolini's early economic policies were quite orthodox: he tried to preserve the value of the lira by deflationary measures. After 1925, however, state intervention increased. Fascist trade unions supplanted those run by Socialists. In 1926 machinery was set up by which the state negotiated collective contracts between management and labor. The same year Mussolini destroyed the vestiges of free government by making all local offices appointive rather than elective. Mussolini's greatest success was a reconciliation with the Vatican. A new independent state, Vatican City, was set up as an indemnity for papal losses in the nineteenth century, and the end of the temporal power of the pope was acknowledged. The reconciliation was affirmed by the signing of the Lateran Treaty agreements in February 1929.

Toward Civil War in Spain

During the postwar years, powerful segments of Spanish society — trade unions, Catalan separatists, the army, and the Church — became increasingly disaffected from the existing parliamentary government. The dissatisfaction was hardly a new development, for Spain's liberal monarchical constitution of 1875 had been consistently violated by national politicians with the aid of local political bosses. Most Spaniards regarded the parliamentary system as a way of preventing their participation in political life.

One consequence of this sense of exclusion was the emergence of trade unions having a high degree of political consciousness and distinctly radical aims. By the First World War there were two very powerful unions: the anarchist CNT (*Confederación Nacional del Trabajo*) and the Marxian socialist UGT (*Unión General de Trabajadores*). The UGT was largely reform-minded, but the CNT was adamantly opposed to the government and indeed felt that it should be abolished. A serious and continuing problem for the regime was posed by the Catalan nationalists, who aimed at the separation of Catalonia (which differed greatly from the rest of Spain in language and customs) from the nation. Barcelona was the industrial center of Spain, and many of the wealthy bourgeoisie in that city, feeling hampered by the incompetence of the Madrid government, were attracted to the growing cause of Catalan nationalism. This, added to Barcelona's position as the stronghold of Spanish anarchism, made for a scene of constant agitation and frequent violence. At the same time the army blamed the civilian government for allowing it to be defeated under humiliating circumstances by Moroccan rebels in 1921. In the uproar following this defeat, the Left threatened to bring the army under civilian control and to institute radical reforms in its organization. But this show of vigor came too late; disgusted with the government's inability to keep order, the public acquiesced when General Miguel Primo de Rivera carried out a successful coup in September 1923, dissolved the Cortes (parliament), and instituted press censorship.

Initially, the dictator succeeded in establishing industrial peace by repressing the CNT militants and conciliating the UGT. Catalan nationalism was suppressed, and official use of the Catalan language was prohibited, even in churches. A joint French and Spanish action subdued the rebelling Moroccan tribes and ended the long and disastrous war in 1927. Under Primo's nominally civilian government, considerable economic recovery was accomplished. Primo wanted to finance economic growth by an income tax, but the upper and middle classes united in opposition. Instead, an Extraordinary Budget raised loans, with interest to be paid out of ordinary revenues—a feasible plan as the economy and the ordinary revenues expanded. New banks were set up to finance workers' housing and new industry. The oil concessions of Shell and Standard Oil were confiscated in a move that actually hurt Spanish financial interests and discouraged foreign investment in the country.

Resentment was aroused among intellectuals when the dictator purged the judiciary and suspended laws at will. The Church worried about government support of the socialist unions and about the growing strength of the national government (as evidenced, for instance, in its suppression of the Catalans). The army was offended when the government suspended the artillery officer corps—too weak to reform the army by halving the number of officers, the government thus sought to limit the independence of one of its branches. The new constitution proposed in 1928 was opposed by the politicians because it did away with ministerial responsibility and would be instituted by a plebiscite rather than by normal means; and it was opposed by the king, whose royal prerogative of choosing and dismissing ministers was to be put in the hands of a body imitating the Fascist Grand Council. Lacking the support of the king and the army, Primo de Rivera was forced to resign in January 1930 and died shortly thereafter.

Central and Eastern Europe

In most cases, the new (or radically changed) nations that emerged in eastern Europe after the First World War installed democratic governments, complete with carefully drawn constitutions providing for parliaments, bills of rights, and responsible ministries. But despite such careful preparations, most of these governments were unable to survive the turbulence of the postwar years. The new democratic regimes were in most cases called upon to create strong nation-states out of collections of diverse nationalities and territories; and amid the nationalist fervor aroused by the war and the hopes of minority groups, which had been raised by the words of the Allied victors, this task was almost hopeless.

Austria—reduced to a small state of eight million people, a quarter of whom lived in Vienna—was plagued by economic distress through the postwar years. The Social Democrats and the Christian Socialists (a conservative Catholic party) momentarily collaborated to form a democratic republic along federal lines. But here their cooperation stopped, and the resumption of their prewar quarrels produced a parliamentary stalemate. In addition, both parties organized private armies.

In October of 1918, Hungary separated itself from Austria and became a republic under a liberal prime minister; but the continuation of the war, the dissatisfaction of the non-Magyar population, general poverty, and revolutionary agitation brought down the government. In March 1919 a Hungarian Soviet Republic was proclaimed. It was led by a Communist, Bela Kun.

Although Kun socialized about two and a half million acres of land, he failed to soothe the anger of the peasants, who were suffering from heavy food requisitions. Further troubles stemmed from Kun's aggressive foreign policy. In late March Hungary declared war on Czechoslovakia and rapidly conquered Slovakia. But within two weeks the Rumanians (members of the Allies) advanced on Budapest. Kun submitted to the Allied demand to evacuate Slovakia and internal disorders flared again. There were strikes and peasant uprisings, and the ex-Imperial officers who had fought for the Communist regime against the Rumanians joined with the "Whites" – the anti-Bolshevik forces of Hungary. Kun left the country in August, and the "Whites," led by Admiral Horthy, took over the government while an anti-Bolshevik terrorist campaign raged throughout the nation. A kingdom of Hungary was set up, with Horthy as "regent." In 1921 a stable, conservative government was formed which remained in power for the next decade, forwarding the interests of the gentry, making some concessions to the industrial working class, but disenfranchising the peasants.

In November 1918 the union of Montenegro and Serbia created the new nation of Yugoslavia. The union did not change the fact that there were great differences among the Serbs, Croats, and Slovenes. The Serbs were committed to a strong central government and Croats and Slovenes (a minority) to a loose federation. In the parliament, the main political parties were the Serbian Radical party, which was not in the least radical, and the Democratic party, also fairly conservative. The Communist party was suppressed in 1921 after a cabinet minister was murdered by a young Communist. Thus the Left was excluded from the government and forced to go underground. In addition, there existed a small agrarian party representing the interests of the peasants, and the Croatian Peasant party. A crisis came in 1928 when the Croatian Peasant party leader was shot in Parliament. In January 1929, King Alexander initiated a royal dictatorship to halt further political disintegration.

Poland's postwar government was created amidst a host of acrimonious disputes among the many parties. In the Polish parliament substantive issues were often discussed more in terms of personal hatreds than in terms of the problems themselves. In addition, Poland – the battlefield of eastern Europe – was faced with enormous diplomatic, political, and economic difficulties. Finally, in 1926, General Joseph Pilsudski, who had been the figurehead president, staged a successful coup. Once in control of the government, he based his power on the military and the great landowners and industrialists.

The government of Bulgaria was headed by the agrarian leader Alexander Stamboliski, who believed that the state should be run by the peasantry. From 1920 to 1923 he carried out a thorough land reform, but in the latter year Macedonian revolutionaries joined with the army to overthrow the government, and Stamboliski was brutally murdered. Despite the installation of an authoritarian regime, Communist plots and terrorist attacks disrupted political life for the rest of the decade.

Czechoslovakia, on the other hand, adjusted successfully to a democracy under the leadership of Thomas Masaryk, a vigorous and idealistic liberal. The nation benefited from the balance between the bourgeoisie, the working class, and the peasantry, which did much to preclude the social strains that occurred in other eastern European states. Although the large German population felt outraged at its new minority status and refused to participate in the national government until the mid-twenties, no group within the country felt so threatened that it had to resort to violence.

IV THE GREAT DEPRESSION

The Postwar Economy of Europe

The disruption of the European economy caused by the First World War was both physical and psychological. Huge amounts of productive resources were destroyed during the war or—from an economic point of view—misallocated. Consequently capital had to be amassed to finance reconstruction and reconversion of both industry and agriculture. In theory, the way for the European belligerents to raise this capital was to increase their exports while maintaining the volume of their imports, so that purchasers of European goods would be obliged to pay for them by direct capital transactions. But the war had largely disrupted the markets to which the European countries exported. European manufacturers suffered from the competition of American firms, which were protected by a high tariff.

At the same time, stimulated by Europe's increased need for foodstuffs and raw materials, the Americas had greatly expanded their own agricultural output. Thus, after the war, central and eastern European nations that exported farm products had to compete with the Americas for western European markets—and the unfavorable situation of these central and eastern European states was compounded by the implementation of land reform. Large estates were divided among the peasantry, but the new owners did not have enough capital or technical knowledge to modernize their production methods. Costs of food production were high, especially as compared with costs in highly mechanized nations overseas.

In the long run it was also unfortunate that postwar reconstruction was pursued with a purely national outlook. Instead of economic cooperation among states, there was wasteful duplication of industries, and protective tariff barriers were erected to foster the development of these uneconomical enterprises. The basis was thereby laid for future crises of overproduction.

By 1929 considerable progress in reconstruction had been effected throughout Europe. Recovery was slow and uneven but on the whole substantial. In 1925 output had regained its prewar level, and four years later Europe's share of total world production was as great as it had been in 1913. Beginning in the mid-1920's there was a brief movement toward international economic cooperation. In 1927 the League of Nations called a conference to consider tariff reduction, but it accomplished little because many countries had increased their tariffs before the meeting to improve their bargaining position. Later that year, the former archenemies France and Germany concluded a commercial treaty that stabilized, and in some cases reduced, their tariff rates. In 1930 Aristide Briand proposed a European customs union to complement his effort at establishing political reconciliation, but this proposal was not accepted. In general, little was done to reverse the trend to high protective tariffs that fostered a misallocation of resources and hindered economic development.

The Crash in the United States

American prosperity in the 1920's was largely based on the boom in residential construction and the rapid growth of the automobile industry. By the end of the twenties, however, the housing boom had slackened off, and the automobile industry was growing at a much slower rate. In the boom years autos had acted as a stimulus for the entire economy: an increase in car production engendered a "multiplier effect" that benefited the steel, rubber, glass, and other industries. But the automobile manufacturers had expanded too quickly, and when they retrenched, the "multiplier effect" worked in reverse, causing a cutback in production all along the line. Moreover, the widespread assumption that businessmen knew best what was in the national interest only exacerbated the serious underlying weaknesses in the economy.

The great speculative mania that began in 1928 served for a time to conceal these weaknesses. But in October 1929 the Big Bull Market collapsed, and the American business community suddenly lost confidence in itself. In the last four months of the year, stock values declined by $40 billion. Financial institutions that had not invested carefully were hurt, credit was hard to obtain, industrial production slumped, and American purchases and investments abroad dropped sharply. By the end of 1930 industrial production was 26 per cent below the peak 1929 level; by midsummer 1932, 51 per cent. As production was cut back, workers lost their jobs: there were four million unemployed in October 1930; seven million a year later; eleven million after another year; and in early 1933, between twelve and fourteen million. Total labor income dropped from $53 billion in 1929 to $31.5 billion in 1933. Farm income fell by more than 50 per cent.

A classic depression of enormous proportions had occurred. Falling prices caused a cutback in production, which caused unemployment, which caused a decrease in demand, which caused a further production cutback. The origins of the crash were rooted in the mistaken policies of the twenties: the maldistribution of income (encouraged by federal tax policy) had led to excessive saving by the rich while restricting mass demand. Profits had grown so large that their only outlet was the stock market, which was largely unregulated by the government.

Herbert Hoover (1874–1964), a Republican, had been elected President in 1928. Well known for his humanitarian work in international food relief at the end of the war, Hoover was not a strict laissez-faire economist, but he did believe that American prosperity depended essentially upon private initiative. And he firmly believed that any direct relief should come from the cities and the states and not from the federal government. The first efforts of the administration to counter the recession were measures to maintain domestic farm prices. To make marketing of farm products more efficient, the Agricultural Marketing Act created a Federal Farm Board empowered to make loans to agricultural marketing cooperatives and established corporations to buy up surpluses. The Board had no authority to compel farmers to limit production, however, and when prices abroad fell in 1931, they had to fall in America too. Wheat sold for $1.09 per bushel in 1929, for 67¢ in 1930, and for 39¢ in 1931–1932. The Hawley-Smoot Tariff of June 1930 increased agricultural duties from 20 per cent to 34 per cent and all duties from 33 per cent to 40 per cent; but it did not succeed in protecting American farm produce, and it set an unfortunate precedent for the rest of the world.

In an attempt to shore up industrial production, Hoover used his influence to gain labor's promise to refrain from demanding increased wages or striking and management's promise to refrain from cutting wages or employment. He also called on city and state officials to increase expenditures on public works to provide additional employment. For a while this had a steadying effect, but the collapse of the European economy in 1931 (despite an American moratorium for one year on intergovernmental debt payments) tightened credit within the United States; the loss of foreign markets sent agricultural prices still lower; and manufacturers cut production and wages drastically.

In October, Hoover persuaded financial leaders to form an emergency credit pool of $500 million and to agree not to foreclose mortgages when reputable debtors were hard up. In December he proposed a series of measures to Congress designed to counter the Depression, including an expansion of federal public works projects and a system of home-loan banks to prevent foreclosures. In January 1932 the Reconstruction Finance Corporation (RFC) was established to loan funds to banking institutions, life insurance companies, building and loan societies, railroads, and farm mortgage associations. In July it was authorized to lend $300 million to states without further resources and $1.5 billion to states and cities for self-liquidating public works.

Notwithstanding these well-intentioned but inadequate measures, the crisis continued to worsen, and the government lost the confidence of the nation. Although revolution was never a real possibility, there was a notable increase in violence, particularly among the nation's farmers. Sheriffs attempting to foreclose mortgages were turned back by crowds of farmers carrying pitchforks and nooses. Highways were barricaded in an attempt to force up milk prices by preventing milk from getting to market. All over the nation there were hunger marches. In May and June of 1932 the "Bonus Expeditionary Force" of between twelve and fourteen thousand unemployed veterans came to the capital to demand immediate payment of a bonus. The administration refused, and the army dispersed the remaining "bonus marchers" and burned their shantytown outside the capital.

Conditions were getting steadily worse: the nation's banking system was on the verge of total collapse, unemployment was rising, and the administration seemed powerless to cope with—even unable to recognize—the full magnitude of the crisis. In the elections of 1932, Hoover was defeated by a landslide vote for Franklin Delano Roosevelt, the Democratic governor of New York, who carried all but six states. In the same election the Democrats won large majorities in both houses of Congress. It remained to be seen how the new President, who had denounced Hoover's extravagance and campaigned on the promise of a balanced budget, would meet the problems of a shattered economy and a demoralized people.

The World Economic Crisis

The Depression in the United States had immediate worldwide consequences. American industrial production had accounted for 46 per cent of the total output of the world's twenty-four most productive nations, while its consumption of nine important primary products had been 36 per cent of the total of the fifteen leading countries. Consequently, the loss of purchasing power in that single country, the high tariff rates on its imports, the end of the flow of its loans to Europe, and the fall of its prices had serious repercussions. The agricultural countries in central and eastern Europe, no longer able to export their crops profitably to western Europe, had to curtail their own imports drastically. The industrial countries of western Europe were now largely cut off from their American market. In short, most countries quickly suffered from falling production, rising unemployment, and falling prices. By the end of 1932, world industrial production had dropped by 30 per cent and world trade in manufactured goods by 41.5 per cent.

A few countries remained comparatively unshaken by the world economic crisis. In Japan, substantial armament expenditure took up production slack. Thanks to the dynamic policies pursued by the socialist governments of the Scandinavian countries, those nations enjoyed balanced, mixed economies and were able to extend social security services. Elsewhere in Europe, however, the spread of the Depression caused far-reaching unrest and brought down many governments. The government of Greece failed to deal effectively with the Depression and met defeat in the 1932 elections, a prelude to restoration of the monarchy and a military dictatorship. France suffered the rigors of the Depression considerably later than most countries. Its level of industrial production remained high, as tariffs were raised and import quotas extended. When France finally reached the depths of the Depression in the mid-1930's, however, it experienced more social protest than did America or Britain.

In eastern Europe the fall of agricultural prices was all but catastrophic: as prices declined, more and more areas adopted a premonetary economy of subsistence production and barter, and between 60 and 80 per cent of the population ceased to be effective consumers. Another consequence of the Depression was increasing anti-Semitism: Jews became the scapegoats for great numbers of distressed farmers and unemployed workers.

Great Britain During the Depression

As Europe's leading banker and trader, it was not surprising that Britain should have been hit early and very hard by the decline in international trade. Markets for British exports shrank visibly, while the export of services such as shipping and insurance, which had long kept Britain's balance of payments in equilibrium, also declined. British manufacturers cut back production as their markets dwindled, contributing to the sharply rising unemployment, which reached two and a half million by December of 1930.

The Labour government's inertia in the face of rising unemployment, and the fiscal conservatism of MacDonald and Snowden, generated an increasing amount of criticism from within the Labour party. Snowden, once again at the exchequer, was in full agreement with the bankers and businessmen that the nation's best defense against the crisis was a balanced budget. The trade unions and the workers naturally opposed the suggested cuts in unemployment benefits that would be necessary to balance the budget, and the Labour government was fatally divided, with nine ministers preferring to resign rather than accept the cuts. It was replaced in August 1931 by a National Government put together in the hope of avoiding a deeper crisis. The new cabinet was led by MacDonald, with four Conservative, four Labour, and two Liberal ministers. The trade unions were so opposed to the proposed economies that they refused to support their old leader in this new role, and MacDonald was expelled from the Labour party; but he continued to head the government. After a balanced budget was passed in September, it became clear that this alone would not be enough to stop the withdrawal of funds from London banks by foreign investors who doubted that the banks could recover their German loans. On September 21, Britain was forced to go off the gold standard.

Nonetheless, supporters of the National Government won a huge majority in the October elections. Although MacDonald remained prime minister, the Conservatives controlled the government with 473 out of the 554 coalition seats. Free trade was finally abandoned in February 1932 with the passage of Neville Chamberlain's Import Duties Act. An immediate general tariff of 10 per cent was established, and higher duties were soon placed on certain important industrial goods.

There was little left to economize on in the new budget; the government had been forced to bring in the lowest arms estimates of the interwar years. A system whereby certain British goods received a preferential tariff rate within the dominions, and vice versa, was instituted during the summer of 1932 at the Imperial Economic Conference at Ottawa, and trade with the Commonwealth expanded considerably. Elsewhere, British exports had to compete with goods from countries outside the tariff wall. These palliatives did little to improve the situation. In 1932, Britain was economically prostrate and socially and politically divided—extremely adverse conditions for reacting to new and dangerous developments in Berlin.

Disaster in Germany

Germany's amazing economic recovery in the mid-1920's resulted partly from the adoption by German industry of scientific management and efficiency on the American model and partly from the influx of foreign capital and loans, primarily from the United States. Consequently, the stoppage of further loans and the calling of loans already granted had an immediate and deeply depressing effect on the German economy. Unemployment soared from 1.4 million in 1929 to 3.1 million in 1930.

In May 1928, the Social Democrats had taken over the government for the first time since 1920. The chancellor, Hermann Müller, sought to remedy declining production and rising unemployment by balancing the budget and cutting down on social benefits. This, however, his party would not stand, and in March a new government was formed under Heinrich Brüning, leader of the Center party. Strongly religious, believing himself responsible not to the Reichstag but to the nation (as personified in President von Hindenburg), Brüning lacked a Reichstag majority but had no qualms about enacting his proposals by persuading the president to use his emergency powers. (Under Article 48 of the Weimar constitution, the president of the Reich was granted the power to "take such measures as are necessary to restore public safety and order.") Rather than risk devaluation of the mark, however, Brüning pursued deflationary policies which only increased unemployment.

The Reichstag elections of September 1930 showed which political groups were benefiting from the growing economic crisis and the continued impotence of the government: the National Socialists (Nazis) polled some 6,400,000 votes and elected 107 deputies (as compared to twelve elected in 1928); the Communists received 4,587,000 votes and held 77 seats (against 54 previously). Although Brüning continued as chancellor, these elections did nothing to improve domestic stability or to placate foreign investors.

The winter of 1930–1931 saw continued decline in the German economy, and the government looked for new ways to promote recovery. An Austro-German customs union was proposed, which was to coordinate efforts against the Depression. Though there was to be no political or territorial merger, most of the other European powers (especially France) were strongly opposed, and finally the issue was referred to the World Court. Then Austria's greatest banking institution, the Vienna *Kreditanstalt,* collapsed, pulling German banks down with it and starting a flight of capital from Germany.

By 1932 the number of German unemployed had risen to over six million, and Brüning's position was worse than ever. He attempted to achieve a triumph in the cancellation of reparations, but the conference was postponed until the summer. In February he failed to get recognition for Germany's right to equality in armaments. Brüning's government finally fell at the end of May, not so much because it failed to deal with the Depression as because it had alienated the powerful Prussian landlords by proposing to partition some insolvent estates in East Prussia to provide relief for the unemployed.

The new government was headed by Franz von Papen, a Westphalian Catholic aristocrat. Like its predecessors, the Papen government could not compete successfully with the National Socialists for the loyalty of the voters, to whom the Nazis offered a ready-made scapegoat (the Jews), the sense of belonging to a rapidly growing mass movement, and the most successful demagogic orator of modern times. The next elections, in November 1932, showed an appreciable decline in National Socialist strength but also revealed that support was swinging from the moderate leftist parties to the Communists. The Papen government was succeeded in early December by a new right-wing government under General Kurt von Schleicher, which lasted less than two months. Thereupon Papen, with the consent of the army and some big business elements, finally turned to Hitler in the expectation that the responsibility of governing would serve to "domesticate" him. On January 30, 1933, Hitler was offered the chancellorship. This came at a moment when the Nazi movement's morale was at a low ebb. Only two months before, Hitler's trusted assistant Joseph Goebbels had despondently reviewed the Nazis' failure to make any further headway during 1932 and had written in his diary: "This year has brought us eternal ill-luck. . . . The past was sad, and the future looks dark and gloomy; all chances and hopes have quite disappeared." Suddenly, Hitler's fortunes were reversed. The Nazis had at last come to power.

V INTERNATIONAL RELATIONS IN THE POSTWAR ERA

The Optimism of the Twenties

During the period 1923–1933 the Western nations were determined that world war should never be allowed to recur and hopeful that it could be avoided. In the Versailles Treaty it was declared that German disarmament was to be followed by limitation of the armaments of all nations. In November 1920 a commission was appointed to devise disarmament plans, but nothing was accomplished during the immediate postwar years. The only success in disarmament came at the Washington Conference in late 1921 and early 1922. Called by the United States, which was uneasy at the growing power of Japan in the Pacific, the Conference led to the Five-Power Naval Pact. It established naval parity (for capital ships) between Great Britain and the United States and limited Japan's navy to 60 per cent of British or American strength; the French and Italian navies were held to 35 per cent of that maximum. To conform to the formula, the major naval powers scrapped a large number of their old capital ships. But this is as far as the multilateral disarmament envisioned by the Versailles Treaty was carried. The French government made it clear that French security must be guaranteed before any steps toward disarmament could be implemented.

There still was hope, however, that the League of Nations provided (or could be made to provide) the machinery for settling international disputes by peaceful means. In 1924 the Assembly of the League unanimously endorsed the "Geneva Protocol," which defined aggression more precisely than the Covenant, extended the compulsory jurisdiction of the Court of International Justice, and provided for settlement by the League's Council or by mandatory arbitration of disputes that did not come within the Court's new jurisdiction. Both the MacDonald government in Britain and the Radical cabinet that succeeded Poincaré's government in France accepted the Protocol—a move that represented a considerable compromise for the French, since the Protocol failed to make military sanctions obligatory. But the Protocol met with strong opposition from the British overseas dominions, which feared interference in their domestic sovereignty and were strongly averse to becoming involved in the application of sanctions resulting from their connection with Britain. The unwillingness of nations like India, Canada, and South Africa to support the Protocol was an ominous sign. Although the Protocol did not increase the burden of sanctions but simply clarified their application, for many nations such clarity was anathema. Thus when MacDonald's government fell, the Conservative Baldwin regime repudiated the Protocol, which thereupon failed to achieve ratification.

When even this guarantee of their security could not be attained, the French became receptive to a German suggestion that Britain, Belgium, France, and Germany guarantee nonrecourse to war for a generation. It was incorporated in the 1925 Locarno Agreements: Britain and Italy guaranteed the Franco-German frontier against aggression by either nation, as well as the border between Belgium and Germany. Germany would not extend the agreement to its eastern borders, and it was evident that Britain, too, was unwilling to guarantee the peace settlement in eastern Europe. Instead, arbitration treaties were signed between Germany and Poland and between Germany and Czechoslovakia, while France guaranteed their common borders.

In French eyes the Locarno Agreements represented a giant step in the direction of achieving Continental security, not least because of the guarantees Britain had given regarding the Franco-German border. However, in the long run the precedents established at Locarno were also to prove unfortunate, for they undermined the Versailles settlement by implying that it required confirmation by voluntary agreements and by suggesting that revision might be acceptable. Moreover, the distinction made by the British between Germany's eastern and western frontiers suggested that Britain was less concerned with preserving the status quo in east-central Europe than in western Europe. Finally, France took upon itself obligations with respect to eastern Europe which, without British support, it would be unable to fulfill.

Insofar as the Locarno Agreements undermined the peace settlement of 1919, the country that benefited most was Germany. Locarno was a triumph for Germany's foreign minister, Gustav Stresemann; and it was soon followed by another diplomatic success, the admission of Germany to the League of Nations in 1926. Though Stresemann by no means accepted the Versailles settlement as just, and secretly attempted to circumvent it, he was willing publicly to pursue a policy of "fulfillment," i.e., acceding to those terms that could not be avoided without precipitating a crisis, in order to restore Germany to its position as a great power, accepted and recognized as such by the other states of Europe. His willingness to compromise on the international front did much to relieve tension until the end of the decade. Also conducive to flexible treatment for Germany and the maintenance of peace was the control of French foreign affairs by Aristide Briand. Briand was as security-conscious as Poincaré; but he was not in favor of unilateral action, and he believed that lasting peace necessitated some rapprochement with Germany.

In the years immediately following Locarno, there was a prevailing current of optimism among the European states with respect to the peace-keeping capability of the League. The United States and Soviet Russia appeared less important, and the League's prestige rose in the pervasive atmosphere of postwar pacifism. Though the League's mandate system was the source of continual crisis in Syria and incipient crisis in Palestine, its humanitarian activities such as regulating labor conditions and the traffic in drugs were more successful. As for actually keeping the peace, the League was a useful instrument when it was not required to act in a crisis in which the aggressor was a major power, and when conditions allowed moral suasion to be effective.

France and its allies still were not satisfied with the security offered by the League. In 1927 Briand approached the United States with a treaty that assured American neutrality in all European disputes. But a strange combination of conservative and pacifist elements in the United States carried on a successful campaign to transform the treaty into a renunciation of war as an instrument of national policy. This outlawing of war was incorporated into the Kellogg-Briand Pact of August 1928 (Kellogg was the American secretary of state). Instead of remaining a bilateral treaty, it was extended to all other nations for signing (sixty-three did so, including the Soviet Union). But the celebrated pact failed altogether to strengthen collective security. Lacking any machinery for enforcing its ban on war, it left to each signatory the power to decide whether or not it was an aggressor. Moreover, from the beginning the great powers made their acceptance of the pact conditional. The United States regarded any action taken to preserve the Monroe Doctrine as "self-defense" (and thus not subject to the pact's ban on war), and the British took a similar view with respect to "defending" the Empire.

Stresemann took the signing of the Kellogg-Briand Pact as an opportunity to suggest an end to Allied occupation of the Rhineland, and in 1928 the major powers agreed that such a move would be desirable *after* the reparations question had been definitely settled. A committee of financial experts from the main Allied powers (chaired by an American, Owen D. Young) devised a solution known as the "Young Plan"—presumably the final reparations settlement. Under its provisions Germany agreed to make thirty-seven annual payments of $500 million, followed by twenty-two smaller payments to cover the war debts owed by the European Allies to the United States. Foreign controls set up under the Dawes Plan were abolished. In May 1930 the Young Plan came into effect. Six weeks later the last Allied troops were withdrawn from the Rhineland, five years ahead of schedule.

Nevertheless, the world economic crisis made a shambles of the Young Plan. In June 1931 the breakdown of the world's exchange system prompted President Hoover to offer a one-year moratorium on the payment of war debts to the United States if the moratorium would be extended to Germany's reparations payments. This was accepted. In 1932 it was still impossible for Germany to make any payments, and that summer the Lausanne Conference agreed to cancel all reparations claims against Germany in return for a single payment of $750 million. In effect, this was no more than a way for the French government to save face, as the payment was never made. Except for a few token payments, inter-Allied debts fell into permanent abeyance that winter. Only Finland fully discharged its modest debt to the United States.

The Breakdown of the League

In 1929 Stresemann died and Briand and Austen Chamberlain fell from office, thus removing from the international scene the three foreign ministers associated with the "spirit of Locarno." Their removal coincided with the on-set of the world economic crisis and the rise of nationalist and demagogic movements. The governments of the European powers began to turn inward and to preoccupy themselves with domestic problems. Confronted by a major international crisis, the Japanese seizure of Manchuria, the powers revealed themselves to be unwilling to fulfill their responsibility to repel aggression under the Covenant.

Though pledged to respect the integrity of China, the Japanese had through-out the late 1920's opposed the growing strength of the nationalist govern-ment there. Then in September 1931, under the guise of a "police operation," Japan suddenly moved to take control of Manchuria, setting up a puppet republic of Manchukuo administered by Japanese advisers. Japan's action was in clear violation not only of its obligations under the League Cove-nant but also of the Kellogg-Briand Pact and the Nine Power Treaty signed in Washington in 1922. The Chinese government immediately protested, but the League's moral pressure to get Japan to withdraw its forces had no effect.

An investigating commission went to study the situation and in October 1932 published a report which, though sharply critical of Japan, recommended a compromise settlement: Japan's rights and interests in Manchuria were to be respected, Manchuria's autonomy widened, and China's ultimate sover-eignty in the area recognized. Unwilling to apply sanctions under Article 16, the British and French seized on the report, but when it was adopted by the Assembly of the League, Japan announced that it was resigning its member-ship in the world organization, and Japanese aggression went unpunished.

The episode was a great humiliation for the League. Its members clearly would not resist an act of aggression when initiated by a major power. They excused their failure in this instance by pointing out that the distance in-volved was exceptional. It was also noticed that the two powers most interested in the Pacific, Russia and the United States, were not even members of the League. In January 1932 the United States announced that it would not rec-ognize "any situation, treaty, or agreement" brought about by means contrary to the Kellogg-Briand Pact. But this policy of nonrecognition had no effect on the Japanese.

The League's inability to stop aggression in the Far East was watched with great interest by representatives of the leading powers as they met, month after month, at Geneva, trying to agree upon some program of disarmament. In February 1932 still another conference of sixty-nine nations gathered in the Swiss city. France continued to press for "security" while Germany continued to insist on recognition of its right to rearm. No agreement could be reached. In October 1933, after Hitler had come to power, Germany announced its withdrawal from the disarmament conference and from the League of Na-tions as well. Germany's resignation from the League, following Japan's withdrawal, was an ominous sign of the gathering storm.

The Struggle for World Power

ENVIRONMENT ESSAY

By the early 1930's few in the Western world were free from anxiety, fear, violence, and terror. Millions were subjected to these trials in their daily lives; but even those who were relatively safe and secure felt some of the impact of disaster and strife through the media of newsreels and radio broadcasts. The hungry faces of the unemployed as they listlessly lined up to receive food or a meager dole, the vast sea of uniformed Nazis filling the Berlin Sports Palace, shouting "Sieg Heil!" as the Führer shrieked slogans of chauvinism, racism, and hate—these were ever recurring scenes throughout most of the decade. Other images, too, flickered on the screen: in 1932 Japanese bombs devastating Manchurian cities; in 1935 Italian Fascist soldiers massacring helpless Ethiopians; and in 1936 columns of smoke rising from Madrid and Barcelona as the insurgent Spanish generals and their fascist supporters strangled the Spanish Republic. In 1939 it was Czechoslovakia's turn: sandwiched between a Disney cartoon and a Clark Gable movie, the newsreel showed German troops swaggering through the streets of Prague, while the Czech populace stood on the sidewalks and wept. A diversion from these terrifying military scenes was offered by the carefully staged Russian purge trials, in which bedraggled Soviet officials confessed to the world that they were traitors to the Communist party, the state, the revolution, and, above all, to that benign father figure, Joseph Stalin.

Already in 1936, many leftists, liberals, intellectuals, and young people had decided that there could be no compromise or even peace with fascism, that the only recourse was a struggle to the death for human freedom. The cause of republican Spain became a mystique to its champions. To be on the side of the Republic was to be for democracy, enlightenment, freedom, culture, legally constituted government. It was also to be on the side of the poor

Rehearsal for War. In the late thirties the Western democracies tried desperately to avoid war with Germany and Italy, refusing to believe that Hitler intended to conquer Europe. Above: the murderous fury of the Spanish Civil War as the Republicans made a futile last-ditch effort to save Madrid from conquest by General Franco's fascist troops. Below: the appeasers. Britain's Prime Minister Neville Chamberlain is surrounded by his cabinet as he prepares to leave London airport on September 29, 1938, to meet with Hitler at Munich. Here Chamberlain will momentarily preserve "peace in our time" by betraying the Czech democracy.

Festung Europa. The Axis march to conquest between 1938 and 1941 (facing page). Like the arms of an octopus, the Nazi armies sweep invincibly over Europe, to be stopped finally only at the English Channel in the west, and at the gates of Moscow in the north and of Alexandria in the south. All this vast territory became Hitler's "Fortress Europe," which remained virtually impregnable until 1943 and was not completely destroyed until 1945.

THE CREST OF AXIS POWER

- Allies and areas they controlled
- Axis nations
- Area occupied by the Axis
- Neutral nations
- → Allied thrusts
- → Axis thrusts

and oppressed of the earth. To be for General Franco's insurgents was to be for militarism, bigotry, fascism, barbarism, and the rich.

Aid-for-Spain committees sprang up all over Europe and America. Thousands of volunteers—writers, engineers, artists, university professors—came to Spain to fight the first battle against fascism. Russians, Englishmen, Americans, and Frenchmen fought side by side to save Barcelona and Madrid from German tanks. The tragedy of Spain produced poems, novels, and paintings by artists all over the world. It made ideological commitment a necessity among intellectuals and artists. The personal sensibilities of the 1920's were rejected as irresponsible. To be on the side of righteousness, one did not have to be a Communist, but it was assumed that one was at least a fellow traveler who gave money to arm the Republic.

In the mid 1930's all the factions of the Left buried their mutual hostilities

and even gladly joined with hitherto detested bourgeois liberals in a "Popular Front" against fascism. Demonstrations, political rallies, an avalanche of pamphlets and books—left-wing agitation became a way of life that consumed all the energy and capacity of its eager legions.

In September 1939 the outbreak of World War II offered at last the possibility of real armed confrontation with Nazism. Nevertheless, there was little of the naive exultation that had sent jubilant crowds into the streets in August

The March of Conquest. In the year 1940 the Nazi bid for world hegemony seemed irresistible. Facing page: the blackest day in French history—German troops occupying Paris in June, 1940. Immediately after Paris fell, France capitulated and signed an armistice. A quasi-fascist government of defeatists and collaborators was soon after installed at Vichy. Hitler was exultant: the fall of Paris put him ahead of his own timetable. Below: the ruins of Coventry Cathedral, completely gutted by German bombs. Such attacks hit most southern English cities during the summer and fall of 1940, when the "Battle of Britain" raged at its grimmest. Churchill had to depend on a few thousand Royal Air Force pilots to protect England from the German invasion Hitler was planning.

1914. Expectations of an immediate clash with Nazi armies were disappointed. But after a lethargic few months of "phony war," the incredible began to happen. Europe seemed to be crumbling like something decayed before a Nazi *blitzkrieg* that struck out in all directions. Nazi armies paraded in fallen Paris through Napoleon's Arch of Triumph; for months England could barely hold on as the German air force bombed its cities nightly. Londoners grew accustomed to sleeping in subways and cellars. The summer and fall of 1940 were the saddest, the most fearful, in modern history. God, fortune, and reason seemed to have deserted mankind. Members of Hitler's inner circle talked of Hegel's world-historical figures and drew up plans for a New Order in Europe. Nazi Germany was to be master with the other European states subjugated to a greater or lesser degree. There was to be a hierarchy based on race. The Norwegians,

The Allied Triumph. Below: American Fifth Army troops occupy Rome on June 5, 1944, and are greeted by the jubilant citizens. The Allies had been slowly creeping up the Italian peninsula for a year by the time Rome fell. After the liberation of Rome, a new Italian army was trained to fight alongside British, French, and U.S. forces. The day after the fall of Rome (June 6, 1944), there came the long-awaited Allied landing in Normandy, and the liberation of France was under way. Rome was the first European capital to be freed. From then on, the arrival of the Allies was often preceded by the rising of native guerrilla forces. When the Allies reached Florence, they found it had been effectively liberated by its own citizens.

The Holocaust. The Second World War significantly differed from the First in that both sides engaged in the slaughter of civilians, either in fulfillment of racist theories or as a tactic of total war. Right: despite frantic last-minute efforts by the Nazis to hide what they had done, living and dead bodies were found side by side in great pits when Allied soldiers entered German extermination camps. Rudolf Hoess, the commandant of Auschwitz, testified at his postwar trial that about three million people had perished in that camp alone. Above: Hiroshima, August 6, 1945, a few hours after the dropping of the first atomic bomb. The burned and maimed huddle together awaiting first aid. The bomb killed at least eighty thousand people outright, and thousands more died of radiation in the weeks and years that followed.

the Danes, and other "true Nordics" would rank only just below the Germans themselves. The French, people of mixed racial ancestry, ranked lower. Below them were the Slavs, who would do slave labor for the Germans. Finally came the Jews and the Gypsies; they were to be liquidated.

Most European Jews and Gypsies were liquidated, but otherwise the New Order was short-lived. From 1943 to 1945, the inexorable Allied push to victory brought moments of exultation in the Western world. But it was the millions of deaths in frozen Russian snows, the fire bombings, the hopeless resistance of the Warsaw ghetto, the docile submission of most of those who were marched to extermination camps, the piles of gold teeth, the lampshades made of human skin, the burning bodies of Hiroshima that impressed themselved as permanent specters on the Western mind.

The significance of totalitarianism and genocide had somehow to be assimilated and understood. The Nazi death camp at Auschwitz bespoke a human capacity for evil never before realized. As the Second World War drew to a close, theologians, psychologists, social scientists, and novelists began to try to explain what it was in men that made them participate or acquiesce in monstrosity. If the human mind could be so controlled and manipulated as it had been under Nazi rule, if human beings could become so bestial and degraded as they had been in the German death camps, rejoicing in victory was meaningless and indecent.

I THE DICTATORSHIPS

The Approach to the Second World War

The Great Depression that began in the United States in 1929 left no European nation untouched. Unemployment, want, and inflation forced democratic leaders to concentrate on domestic problems. The same conditions allowed dictators to consolidate their power. While Great Britain, France, and the United States struggled with problems of economic recovery and novel ideas about social welfare, Stalin launched Russia on its race to catch up with the industrial nations, and Hitler used economic suffering, social unrest, and widespread dissatisfaction with the Treaty of Versailles to justify the buildup of his military machine. As the worst effects of the Depression were meliorated by government action or by the passage of time, Europe drew closer to war.

In the mid-1930's, the camp to which a nation belonged was determined more by its form of government than by treaties or foreign policies. The dictatorships—Germany and Italy, joined in spirit if not in geography by Japan—were expansionist states whose leaders not only accepted but required war to enhance their power. Although Russia was also a dictatorship and in August 1939 fashioned a short-lived alliance with Germany, the two nations were at opposite ideological poles.

The democratic states, and Russia as well, were threatened by the aggressive policies of Germany, Italy, and Japan, but they avoided the inevitable confrontation as long as possible. The small nations of Europe tended to fall into line with the powers that shared their form of government—Czechoslovakia, the only really successful democratic state in central Europe, was a consistent ally of Britain and France until it was abandoned by them in 1938. On the other hand, Poland, a thinly disguised military dictatorship, wavered between the Anglo-French alliance and Berlin until it was finally attacked by Germany in September 1939. This aggression precipitated another great war between the western Allies and Germany. By the end of 1941, Germany had turned on Russia, and Japan had attacked the United States in the Pacific. In the ensuing world conflict, the Communist dictatorship of Russia was allied with the capitalist democracies against Germany, Italy, and their lesser allies from 1941 on and against Japan in 1945.

Fascism in Italy

After the mid-1920's, Italy was governed by the Fascist dictator Benito Mussolini, a megalomaniac poseur with a penchant for grandiose gestures and military pomp and ceremony. The Duce, as he liked to be called, enjoyed a personal dictatorship within the Fascist party. In 1926 he was empowered to issue decrees that automatically became law. Parliamentary elections ceased to have any meaning after 1928. Candidates were chosen by the Grand Council of the Fascist party, and voters could accept or reject them only as a bloc. Moreover, the party was absorbing the entire governmental apparatus in the provinces, where elected officials were replaced by Fascist bureaucrats. In 1933 a decree made party membership a requisite for any administrative post. In 1938 the Chamber of Deputies was superseded by the Chamber of Fasces and Corporations.

Opposition to the Fascist regime was effectively stifled by force. In October 1926—after the fourth attempt on Mussolini's life in twelve months—a number of laws were passed "for the defense of the state." Antigovernment parties and papers were suppressed. Political offenders faced military judges presiding over a special court of justice from which there was no appeal. A secret police force, OVRA, was also established. (Mussolini gave it its meaningless but ominous name simply to frighten people.) Had this network been efficient, it might have destroyed all opposition, but it included as many as twenty separate police units, often working at cross-purposes.

Italian political expatriates formed a large colony in Paris, publishing antifascist periodicals and working for antifascist causes. But internal divisions seriously hampered their efforts. Inside Italy, very few intellectuals dared to criticize the regime. When in 1931 university professors were required to sign an oath of loyalty to Fascism, only eleven had the courage to refuse.

Neither the Crown nor the military played an effective role against the

Fascists during these years. Victor Emanuel III, though he resented the personal dominance of the Duce, had always been one to swim with the tide. He felt little loyalty to the liberal constitution, which had exposed the monarchy to the pressure of democratic forces, and he was not about to lead a resistance movement against the Fascists. The army still held aloof from the Fascist regime, remaining loyal to the Crown. Mussolini saw that this situation potentially threatened his position, and in January 1923 a "Voluntary Militia for National Security" was created from the former Fascist squads to offset the army's power. Supported by state funds, the militia was under the Duce's personal control. It was given preference in armaments, and in the 1930's it duplicated the activities of the regular army in the field in Spain and Ethiopia. Within the regular army, promotion came to depend on party membership, on family size, and on vocal support of the Fascist regime.

Throughout the Fascist period, the government enjoyed Church support to a degree unprecedented since the occupation of the Papal States by Italy in 1860. The Fascist leader who had called for confiscation of ecclesiastical property in 1919 was hailed as "the man that Providence had placed in Our path" by Pius XI on the occasion of the signing of the Lateran Treaties in February 1929. Yet Mussolini soon made it clear that the treaties were not a papal victory. He refused to surrender "the totalitarian principle of education of the young," and in the spring of 1931 he denounced Catholic Action, a lay organization through which the Church trained the young. In 1931 Pius XI responded with an encyclical that asserted the Church's independence from totalitarian temporal powers (while explaining that the Fascist party was not specifically in question), and a compromise was eventually reached. Although the Church opposed Mussolini's racial laws, which encroached on its sphere of influence—marriage and family relations—in general the pope's appreciation of Mussolini as a powerful bulwark against Bolshevism and socialism outweighed other considerations.

State control of economic and social life slowly grew as the Duce strove to make the national economy strong and self-sufficient. The famous "battles" for wheat (launched in 1925), for a rapidly expanding population (1926), and for land reclamation (1928) were part of this effort. In the first, the government subsidized expanded wheat production, and the Duce gave annual prizes to wheat growers. Superficially this program was highly successful—in ten years imports were cut by 75 per cent—but it was not economical. Domestic wheat cost 50 per cent more than American wheat, and the poor simply had to eat less.

Mussolini's campaign to increase the population 50 per cent by mid-century was based on his conviction that national strength depended largely on numbers. A tax was levied on bachelors, and being unmarried hindered promotion in most careers—in 1939, bachelors in government service lost all chance of promotion. Fathers with unusually large families received higher pay, newlyweds were given government insurance policies offering a prize for fecundity, and particularly prolific couples were honored. But despite these efforts, the birth rate continued to fall.

Land reclamation was more successful: at huge government expense, several hundred thousand acres of the Pontine marshes were drained and hundreds of peasant families resettled there. But the problem of the poverty-stricken south, central in the history of the Italian kingdom since its founding, was avoided and left unsolved.

The Fascist state encouraged industrial production with awards and subsidies. Electric power production was successfully raised fivefold, but gas and oil production did not come close to the self-sufficiency predicted for 1938. In return for high capital levies and compulsory loans, the state permitted cartels, which kept inefficient companies in existence. The worldwide Depression caused many businesses to falter, and in 1933 the *Instituto per la Riconstruzione Industriale* was founded to save these companies and banks which had been too generous with credit. The state thereby took direct control of many of the country's leading firms in the years before the war. But control by Fascist bureaucrats only spread graft and inefficiency.

When Mussolini abandoned orthodox socialism for Fascism, he did not entirely abandon the working class. In the Fascist state the workers' lot was to be improved not by class warfare but by class collaboration. To this end the apparatus of corporativism was established. By 1934 the corporate state was taking positive shape: the labor force was divided along industry lines by twenty-two corporations (national trade councils), which were coordinated by a National Council of Corporations. Each corporation consisted of workers' representatives, employers' representatives, and government officials. The workers' representatives were appointed from above (jobs had to be found for party members); the employers' representatives managed to hold the upper hand in decision-making; and the government supervisors looked on their jobs as rewards for loyalty to the regime. Wages and working conditions actually regressed: in 1930 real wages were lower in Italy than anywhere else in western Europe, including Spain. By 1936, Mussolini was telling the Italian people to expect not prosperity but a lower standard of living.

Under these adverse circumstances, it was all the more necessary to indoctrinate the young. Traditional textbooks were rewritten or replaced, and new courses (Fascist culture or corporative law) were added to the curriculum. Lessons were meant to foster passionate loyalty and a fighting spirit. Physical training was emphasized, and children learned to drill from an early age through their teens in quasi-military units for both boys and girls.

In the late 1930's and particularly after his rapprochement with Hitler, Mussolini concocted preposterous new demands: the salute replaced the handshake; correspondence was dated from *anno primo* (1922); uniforms became *de rigueur*. His most gratuitous move came with the racial laws of 1938. Hitherto, Fascist racial persecution had been directed largely against Germans in the South Tyrol. In interviews held in the spring of 1932, the Duce said, "Anti-Sematism does not exist in Italy. Italians of Jewish birth have shown themselves good citizens . . . ." But in his aping of Hitler, the Duce started an anti-Semitic campaign. Jews (who represented only one per cent of the population) were forbidden to be journalists, teachers, or notaries; recent Jewish immigrants were expelled; Jews could not join the party or attend state schools; special permission from the government was necessary before Jews could marry into the "Italian race." Jewish officers and administrators were dismissed along with ninety or more leading scholars, depriving the state of brain power needed for the war effort — and the Duce had to change his dentist.

Fascist Italy was meant to be a totalitarian dictatorship, but it was sloppily organized, with too much power concentrated in the hands of a single man, and it was bureaucratically stagnant. As a result, it was a good deal more humane and less rigorous, more ridiculous and less frightening, than Nazi Germany. On the other hand, there is no doubt that Hitler learned from Mussolini; the favorable international reputation that Fascist Italy enjoyed in many Western circles in the early 1930's demonstrated to Hitler the flabbiness of the democracies.

National Socialism in Germany

The parties of the Left and Right which acquiesced in Hitler's elevation to the chancellorship in January 1933 had few illusions about the aims of National Socialism, but they badly misjudged their ability to control the new chancellor. Hitler's own powers were broad; but the reactionary petty aristocrat Franz von Papen, who had the special confidence of President Hindenburg, was vice-chancellor, and he was to be present whenever the chancellor made a report to the president. ("That man for chancellor? I'll make him a postmaster and he can lick stamps with my head on them," Hindenburg is reputed to have said after his first meeting with Hitler in August 1932.) Only three of the eleven cabinet posts were in the hands of Nazis, and their powers were thought to be circumscribed. However, they exploited those posts they did hold far beyond anything others in the government thought possible. For example, Hermann Goering, who had been drawn to the party as an unemployed ex-officer after the war and had risen to be president of the Reichstag, was named Prussian minister of the interior. As president of Prussia, Papen thought he could control Goering. And yet it was under Goering that the Secret State Police of Prussia (the Gestapo) was transformed into an agency serving the Nazis.

In March 1933 Hitler forced another parliamentary election. For the first time the Nazi party could campaign with the power of the state behind it. Goering augmented that power by purging the Prussian state service, replacing hundreds of government employees with men whom the Nazis could trust. Late in February he established an auxiliary police force composed mostly of active members of two dreaded Nazi paramilitary organizations, the SA (Storm Troopers) and the SS (Elite Guard), who could now indulge freely in political intimidation. At the same time an attempt was made to discredit the Communists. On February 27 the Reichstag building was mysteriously set afire in an alleged Communist plot. The next day the Reichstag passed a "Decree for the Protection of the People and the State," which suspended civil and personal liberties. Despite this campaign of terror directed at the leadership of the opposing parties, the National Socialists won only 43.9 per cent of the votes. But together with the 8 per cent polled by the Nationalists, these votes gave Hitler an absolute majority.

Thus strengthened, Hitler did away with all constitutional restraints. On March 23 two thirds of the members of the Reichstag (eighty-one Communist deputies were arrested or did not dare take their seats) were persuaded—or forced through fear—to pass an Enabling Act that transferred the legislative function to the Reich cabinet, allowed deviations from the constitution, and provided that laws drafted by the chancellor went into effect automatically and immediately. Only the Social Democrats had the courage to vote against the measure.

The Nazis next moved to put the whole of Germany's organized life under the control of the party by the process of *Gleichschaltung*, or "coordination." By January 1934 the federal states had been subordinated to the central government. A *Reichstatthalter* (Reich governor) was appointed for each state, with the power to dissolve the state diets and to prepare and publish state laws. In January 1935 the state diets were abolished altogether.

When simple physical intimidation failed to force the trade unions to dissolve, the Nazis staged a huge May Day celebration, following which the leaders of the unions were arrested and thrown into concentration camps. Strikes and lockouts had been banned in 1933, and in 1934 the administration of the unions was taken over by the Nazi Labor Front, controlled by the employers. Within a month, collective bargaining had been discarded and government-appointed "labor trustees" were charged with settling disputes.

Next liquidated were the rival political parties. On June 22 the Social Democratic party was dissolved (its funds had already been seized); the Catholic Center party, the Democrats, and the People's parties dissolved themselves. At the end of June even Hitler's erstwhile allies—the Nationalists—had succumbed to the pressure. By the end of the year, the *Stahlhelm*, the major veterans' organization, was incorporated into the SA.

While German institutions were being brought under party control during 1933, Hitler was faced with the problem of keeping his unruly followers from destroying the economic and military strength of the state. The chief threat came from the radical SA, whose violence had contributed much to silencing the party's enemies but whose aspirations to take over the army and effect radical economic experiments would have brought chaos. For the rest of 1933 and into 1934 tension mounted, particularly between the SA and the regular army, which was perfectly willing for the rest of the country to undergo Nazification so long as the military establishment remained untouched.

Hitler was able to control the SA and its leader, the infamous sadist Ernst Roehm, through the winter of 1933–1934, but that was no permanent solution. In the spring, news that Hindenburg did not have long to live made Hitler decide in the generals' favor: he needed the army's support to succeed unchallenged to the presidency. At the end of June a purge of the SA, of Catholic leaders, and of others who might threaten Hitler's position continued for two days. At its end, over a hundred people had been shot, including General von Schleicher, the former chancellor, and the menace of the SA was destroyed. Two weeks later Hitler proclaimed to the Reichstag that he was the "supreme justiciar" of the land. On August 2, 1934, Hindenburg died; Hitler assumed the powers of both president and chancellor under the title *Der Führer* (the Leader), and the army swore him an oath of personal loyalty.

Hitler's support of the military kept the army loyal to his regime during the crucial period when he was consolidating his power. In 1937, when its leaders began to object to his increasingly provocative foreign policy, he no longer had any need of their support. In early 1938 several leading generals were discredited in a series of real and contrived scandals, and Hitler replaced them with officers he could control. The army's belief that it could remain aloof from *Gleichschaltung* proved to be a dangerous delusion.

The Roman Catholic and Protestant churches in Germany were able to remain somewhat independent of the regime, and Hitler's Nazified religion did not have many converts. On the other hand, though there were certainly individual cases of heroism and martyrdom, the churches failed to provide any great rallying point of opposition. Persecution of those who resisted Nazism was more brutal and more effective than persecution of anti-Fascists in Italy. Under the leadership of Heinrich Himmler, who was also head of the SS, the Gestapo became notorious for the tactics it used to silence the Nazis' opponents. Thousands—including well-known public figures—were taken to concentration camps and incarcerated indefinitely under inhuman conditions.

The Nazi regime did not delay in attacking "the Jewish problem." On April 1, 1933, a boycott of all Jewish shops in Germany began. At first Jews were dismissed from political and cultural positions—those in important economic positions were able to hold on a little longer—and allowed to emigrate. In September 1935, in a special session at the party rally in Nuremberg, the Reichstag passed the notorious Nuremberg Laws "for the protection of the racial purity of the state." The first law deprived German Jews (defined as any German having a Jewish grandparent) of citizenship, of their political and civil rights and privileges; the second forbade marriage between Germans and Jews and the employment of Germans as servants to Jews. In November 1938 a carefully planned pogrom was carried out against the Jewish population in revenge for the slaying of a Nazi diplomat by a young Jew in Paris. After this, the means of economic subsistence were denied to the Jews, and their emigration was limited by vigorous restrictions. By the time war broke out in September 1939, the number of Jews in Germany and Austria had been reduced from 500,000 in Germany and 190,000 in Austria to a total of 285,000.

German economic policy during this period was predicated on the increasing likelihood of war. Armaments production had to be expanded rapidly; the country had to be made self-sufficient in many commodities. At the same time, the regime sought to meet the workers' desire for an end to economic insecurity; the industrialists' insistence on further protection from organized labor, profitable (meaning largely government) contracts, and wider markets; and the agriculturists' demands for continued subsidies. The first Four-Year Plan (in imitation of the Soviet Five-Year Plan of 1928) was inaugurated in 1933, with an end to unemployment and an increase in the production of necessities as its goals. Women were discouraged from working, while young Germans were subjected to a mandatory year of agricultural labor (which foreshadowed the reinstitution of military conscription). By the end of 1934 unemployment had dropped from 6 million to 2.6 million. But the creation of the Nazi-controlled *Arbeitsfront* (organization of workers and employers) in place of the free trade unions undermined the workers' power to win concessions from business by collective action; in 1937 the German worker had a standard of living no higher, and perhaps lower, than he had had in 1933. On the other hand, the demoralization and consequent radicalization of the unemployed was considerably lessened.

The state moved to encourage (and compel) agricultural production. Protective tariffs were raised, and subsidies were granted for new plantings (e.g., oil seeds, fruit trees, textile fibers). To utilize every inch of available land, the state ordered that the walls dividing holdings be torn down. Considerable progress was made in increasing the use of chemical fertilizer. The government manipulated consumption to cut down on the demand for imports; and people were required to patronize specified shops, which would facilitate the introduction of wartime rationing. In industry, the state likewise brought pressure to bear to expand the production of capital goods. Actual state investment was mostly limited to public works and the aircraft and motor vehicle industries. A law of 1933 limited business expansion without authorization from the state. At the same time, the state further controlled industrial production through allocation of materials and orders.

Under the leadership of Dr. Hjalmar Schacht (who had stabilized the currency after the disastrous inflation of the mid-1920's), the first Four-Year Plan achieved its goals. Germany's lack of foreign exchange to pay for necessary imports was also overcome, as the small nations of eastern Europe became more dependent on the German market for their exports and more willing to accept German goods in return—goods which were not always needed. Under the second Four-Year Plan, proclaimed by the Führer in 1936, control of the economy was given to Hermann Goering, for Schacht had begun to protest against the huge government expenditures on armaments, which were inflationary and tended to produce state bankruptcy. Emphasis was now placed on producing vast quantities of armaments and substitute materials to take the place of imports unavailable in time of war. Great strides were made in the development of synthetic textiles, oil, and rubber. Because the production of such commodities was often unprofitable, the state guaranteed prices or made loans to private industry to cover capital costs.

Like the Fascists in Italy, the Nazi government set out to indoctrinate youth with the values of the system, to occupy the workers with government sponsored recreation in the "strength through joy" program, to control the arts and sciences, and so on; but in general the Germans were more successful than their Italian counterparts. This was due in part to better planning and in part to greater and more horrifying physical coercion. Yet the Nazis owed some of their success to Germany's scientific, technological, and industrial base, which was substantially superior to Italy's. Without such resources, Hitler's dreams of conquest would have remained just that.

Russia Under Stalin

At the beginning of the 1930's, Russia was in the firm grip of Joseph Stalin, a tireless, single-minded, completely ruthless politician, whose rivals had by this time been eliminated from the scene. In 1929 the Soviet Union celebrated his fiftieth birthday as though it were a historical event. The Five-Year Plan inaugurated in 1928 projected a rapid expansion of heavy industry accompanied by a gradual application of collectivization to agriculture. The plan was optimistic to the point of being revolutionary, and its consequences brought about another great upheaval that transformed Russia from an underdeveloped society to an advanced industrial power. Stalin recognized that for the Soviet Union to maintain itself in a largely hostile world, its industrial production would have to be greatly expanded. This meant that more farm labor had to become industrial labor.

The economic situation became critical in 1928–1929, when the peasants failed to deliver enough grain to feed the townspeople. The solution was to increase production of foodstuffs either by expanding the capitalist section of agriculture to allow the farmers larger profits or by enforcing thoroughgoing collectivization, which would probably drive more rural laborers into the factories. For a time Stalin hesitated to choose between the two: he had previously disclaimed any intention of forcing collectivization on the peasantry, but to allow more free enterprise in agriculture would have enraged the regimented urban workers, who were already paying high prices for their food. Finally, in mid-1929, the decision was made to force the peasants onto centrally controlled collective farms (*kolkhoz*) or state farms (*sovkhoz*), which were expected to be more efficient and responsive to government goals than privately owned farms. A war was proclaimed against the *kulaks*, the relatively prosperous class of peasants who opposed collectivization. To carry out this revolution against the *kulaks*, Stalin appealed to the destitute *muzhiks*, peasants who worked tiny holdings with wooden plows and had no livestock.

Within a very short time the countryside was in pandemonium, as the peasants fought against collectivization. Rebellious villages were surrounded by troops and forced to surrender. *Kulaks* were killed or deported to Siberia; the rest were herded onto collective farms. Within a short period the increase in acreage cultivated on collective as opposed to private farms was phenomenal. On July 1, 1928, collectives accounted for 1.7 per cent of the total sown acreage; on March 1, 1930, 50 per cent.

On that day Stalin put a severe brake on the collectivist drive, so that by the end of the first Five-Year Plan only 60 per cent of all holdings were collectivized. Nonetheless, severe damage had been done to Russian agriculture: peasants, for instance, had slaughtered their livestock instead of bringing it with them to the collectives. Thus an important consequence of Stalin's collectivization drive was the precipitous decline in Russian livestock between 1929 and 1933. Stalin now moderated the impact of collectivization and state ownership by making it possible for members of collectives to own some small plots of land and some livestock privately rather than merely sharing the profits of the collective farms or receiving laborers' wages on the state farms.

Russian agriculture was further hampered during the early 1930's by a lack of the modern equipment needed to make the new collectives more productive and efficient. When the upheaval began, there were only seven thousand tractors in the whole of Russia (thirty thousand more secured by the end of 1929 had but little additional impact). Nor did the *muzhiks* know how to operate these machines. Finally, in the mid-1930's, attempts were made to train the *muzhiks*, and these were fairly successful.

While he pressed the drive to force the peasants onto collectives, Stalin was making impossible demands on heavy industry. Although Russian iron production in 1928 was only 3.5 million tons, the Five-Year Plan demanded 10 million tons for 1933. Then Stalin announced that 17 million tons were to be produced in 1932. Such goals, of course, were patently impossible, but great progress was nonetheless made, at a cost of tremendous sacrifices wrung from the Russian people. The funds to finance this expansion were acquired through a sales tax, which absorbed 64 per cent of a worker's wages in 1935. More than half the proceeds were collected from sales of grain, on which the workers and peasants mainly existed. And considerable quantities of Russian grain never even reached the people but were exported to pay for imports of foreign machinery. Not only was the worker deprived of most of the value of his wages; he was forced to live in the worst of conditions, for the new industrial complexes opening throughout the country often had only rudimentary accommodations. Many of the difficult goals of the Five-Year Plan were accomplished by the forced labor of political foes and of peasants who had tried to resist collectivization.

The demands made by Stalin on the Russian populace brought to the surface a longing for change even among some of his close followers. Famine and starvation, partly attributable to the government's agrarian policies, swept the country, giving rise to considerable discontent. In November 1932, even Stalin's wife protested against the terrible privations. In front of their friends, Stalin burst out in a flood of vulgar abuse, and that evening she committed suicide. Stalin was shaken. A little while later he offered his resignation, but no one at the Politburo (the Communist party executive committee) had the courage to accept it. He soon regained his confidence and proceeded with the hardly less ambitious second Five-Year Plan, which extended the progress of the first.

As Stalin had misjudged the results of the campaign against the *kulaks,* so, too, he badly misjudged the importance of the Nazi rise to power in Germany. This miscalculation had important repercussions in both foreign and domestic policy. In 1928 he had forecast the coming economic crisis in the capitalist countries and had called on Communist parties throughout Europe to launch final offensives. The Comintern ordered these parties to regard the Social Democrats as their most dangerous enemies. The dangers of fascism were not grasped in Russian government circles: it was not foreseen that the fascists would destroy the Social Democrats and construct a monopoly of power. Even after Hitler had destroyed both the Social Democrats and the Communists in Germany, there was still no change in Soviet policy.

The conclusion of a nonaggression pact between Germany and Poland in 1934, however, brought the German threat closer to home, and Stalin began looking for protection. In 1934 the USSR joined the League of Nations; Stalin supported an abortive attempt to create an eastern Locarno; and by the beginning of 1935 Russia was seeking defensive alliances with the West. Late in that year the Comintern did an abrupt about-face: the defense of democracy (the pejorative adjective "bourgeois" was temporarily dropped) became a foremost goal of Communist parties. The result was the creation in Western countries of "popular fronts"—combinations of Communists, socialists, and liberals in a unified opposition to the growing threat of fascism.

The German menace also awoke in Stalin's mind a fear that his position within Russia was not entirely secure. During the years 1933–1935 he reacted to criticism of his regime by deporting some of his potential rivals (many were allowed to return after admitting that his policy was the only correct one) and by expelling hundreds of thousands of party members. In December 1934 the assassination of one of Stalin's closest deputies (probably by the dictator's own secret order) gave him a pretext for further purges. Several secret trials were held, followed by a feverish search for dissidents throughout the party. In the spring of 1935 tens of thousands of suspected opponents ("oppositionists") were deported to northern Siberia. Then, as plans went ahead for a new Soviet constitution and the second Five-Year Plan achieved success, the regime seemed to relax; and when the constitution was eventually promulgated in November 1936, there was much hope that it would end the lawlessness of the secret police, who had been active in the purges and deportations. The constitution fooled innocent Western liberals ready to be duped, but it did little or nothing for the Russian people. It guaranteed individual rights in theory, but when messages were intercepted by the police or when arbitrary arrests were made, there was no redress. The party was still supreme: only its members could be politically active, and in elections only party lists were offered to the voters.

Meanwhile, the purge of the lower echelons of the party continued. And in 1936, when Hitler occupied the Rhineland, Stalin was convinced that it was necessary to get rid of everyone who might conspire to overthrow him in the event of a war with Germany or who might in any other way endanger continued Stalinist rule. Now the purges began in earnest. There were endless trials, both public and secret, climaxed by the prosecution of a group of important generals in June 1937. All the defendants were accused of plotting to assassinate Stalin and restore capitalism and of working as spies for Germany, Japan, France, and Great Britain. Many were tried *in camera* or executed without a trial because they could not be made to admit their guilt. Those who confessed were tried in public, where they praised the Stalinist regime and denounced themselves. The charges were patently false, but brutal physical torture and intolerable moral pressure (relatives were taken as hostages by the political police) extracted confessions from many accused.

The public trials involved very few, however, compared with the secret trials and the summary executions and deportations. Thousands of the followers of suspect leaders were executed, and hundreds of thousands were sent to prison or to concentration camps. One estimate is that some seven million people suffered under the purges.

Thus, while great strides were made in industrialization and Russia was launched on a way of life far different from that lived under the czars, Stalin's totalitarian regime was in several respects as vicious as those in Italy and Germany. He did not scruple to murder his opponents, real or imagined, and he held the political life of the country in a viselike grip.

II THE DEMOCRACIES

Recovery and Gradual Rearmament in Great Britain

From 1931 to 1935 the National Government in Great Britain—consisting of Conservatives and a few exiles from the Labour party, including the prime minister, Ramsay MacDonald—concentrated on two major problems: economic recovery and disarmament. The government's efforts to end the effects of the Depression could hardly be described as dynamic. Its policy generally relied on the operation of "natural factors" within the existing economic system. MacDonald and his colleagues believed that a cutback in government expenditures and reduction of taxes would encourage new enterprise, bringing about lasting recovery. Consequently there were no large expenditures on public works; the housing boom that continued through the 1930's was maintained mostly without government assistance. Construction of new roads stopped altogether and that of new schools plunged sharply. Behind a wall of tariff protection the government used its influence to persuade private companies to undertake programs conducive to economic recovery and stability. Sometimes this entailed subsidies to encourage expansion; in other cases, companies with the same products were allowed to enter into agreements restricting output and raising prices—approaches not unlike those under America's National Recovery Administration.

Nationalization occurred in only two industries during the Depression: in 1933 London's streetcars, subways, and buses were put under coordinated control and government ownership, and in 1939–1940 two competing civil aviation companies which had been receiving subsidies were merged into BOAC, a public corporation. At the same time, in a conspicuous reversal of the trend that had made Britain an industrial nation dependent on other countries for its food supply, the government encouraged increased food production—adding to the international problem of agricultural surpluses. It was hoped that by reducing imports Britain might thereby strengthen its domestic economy through an improved balance of payments.

The National Government was also forced to take steps to remedy the condition of the unemployed. Rather than provide relief work for these millions, its chief policy was to maintain them out of public funds on the dole. When a man was dismissed, he and his family at first had recourse to benefit payments from a fund to which he had contributed while working. After that, he received "transitional payments" subject to a means test. This meant that he had to prove his family's need—and the family could be questioned whenever it showed signs of having been able to save anything.

The government tried somewhat harder to deal with the situation in the "distressed areas"—districts with an unemployment rate considerably higher than that for the rest of the country. For example, of the insured workers in the town of Jarrow on the River Tyne in September 1935, 72.9 per cent were unemployed. To remedy the plight of such areas, the Special Areas Bill was passed in 1934, allocating £2 million to be spent to spur economic recovery. These were small beginnings and barely made a dent in the problem. Full recovery came only with the armaments boom of the late 1930's.

Yet despite the apparent hopelessness of people in the depressed areas and the bitter resentment of the dole by many, British workers did not turn to violence or to radical action. From time to time the Communist-dominated National Unemployed Workers' Movement led hunger marches on the capital, but they were peaceful affairs. Their chief result was to remind the public of the plight of the unemployed.

While Communist-inspired violence remained at a minimum in Britain, Sir Oswald Mosley's British Union of Fascists was looked upon favorably by many conservative people. In 1934 it had a membership of twenty thousand. But its respectable facade was destroyed at a mass meeting on June 7 of that year. At that meeting, attended by fifteen thousand, hecklers who interrupted Mosley's speech were brutally beaten by Fascist stewards while the police were busy arresting Communist and other antifascist demonstrators outside the hall. Several prominent men were present; the affair eventually was debated in Commons, and Mosley lost his respectable support.

The volume of government assistance to the underprivileged was considerably extended in the mid-1930's, but Britain was still far from a welfare state. Unemployment insurance and assistance did not cover independent workers, and family allowances were accompanied by the means test. National health insurance covered only wage earners, not dependents or the self-employed; children too young to go to school were not covered, and those in school were examined but seldom treated. The holes were haphazardly plugged by a vast conglomeration of voluntary social services supported by charity drives of one sort or another.

Nor can one credit the National Government with effectively fostering the recovery of the British economy. Recovery was spurred by the increase of consumption resulting from a fall in world commodity prices combined with a much smaller reduction in the wage level in Britain. British overseas investment declined, providing needed capital for such enterprises as the growing domestic automobile industry, which was superseding dying industries like textiles. Government policies merely reassured the business community by talking of deflation. Government spending stimulated production and employment only very late in the period, when the likelihood of war forced a buildup of the armed forces.

The National Government was caught in something of a bind on the subject of armaments. In the interests of economy, Chancellor of the Exchequer Neville Chamberlain's 1932 budget included the lowest arms estimates since World War I, and the government would have liked to continue this trend. However, professional advisers were sounding the alarm over Japan's invasion of Manchuria and Adolf Hitler's rise to power. Their warnings were reinforced by the failure of the disarmament conference of 1933 and by Germany's withdrawal from the League of Nations. But no matter how good the case for rearmament, the National Government was concerned with public opinion, which seemed as confirmed as ever in its wish for disarmament.

In February 1933 the prestigious debating society, the Oxford Union, resolved that "this House will in no circumstances fight for its King and Country." Disarmament had become a higher loyalty — a loyalty to the welfare of the world. The Labour party and a large segment of the public rejected rearmament as incompatible with faith in the League of Nations. Nowhere was the idea of rearming to support the League — of backing up "collective security" with force—accepted. And so the British government disregarded the warnings of its military advisers. Tentative rearmament plans were drawn up, but the annual arms estimates remained low.

Riots, purges, coups, and assassinations abroad in the following year—coupled with the dire warnings of Winston Churchill—moved the government hesitantly down the path to rearmament. In March 1935 a White Paper was published which—though it contained much mitigating language about the League, collective security, and disarmament—announced that the government was going to rely on armed force to secure the nation's defenses. Ironically, Prime Minister MacDonald, who retired in 1935, signed it as one of his last state papers, after working for peace for so many years. Hitler seized the opportunity to announce the restoration of conscription in Germany and to admit the existence of the German *Luftwaffe* (air force).

With the Conservative Stanley Baldwin as prime minister once again and with this published change in policy, the government might have been expected to back strong League action against Italy's unprovoked attack on Ethiopia in the autumn of 1935. But the results of the so-called Peace Ballot, released a few months earlier, persuaded Baldwin that public opinion favored only nonmilitary sanctions. Then the Labour party, coming around to more pragmatic support of the League, called on the government to enforce stricter sanctions against Italy. In this atmosphere, Baldwin dissolved the government and called a general election in November 1935.

It was a very confusing campaign, ending in a very low turnout of voters. Baldwin first spoke in strong terms of the need for rearmament, then declared: "There will be no great armaments." The National Government was returned to office by a huge majority, but it began to lose prestige dramatically, first over the Hoare-Laval Plan (December 1935) to placate Mussolini in his Ethiopian adventure—which plan had to be replaced with sanctions against Italy more acceptable to British public opinion—and then because of Hitler's reoccupation of the Rhineland (March 1936) and Britain's feeble policy concerning the Spanish Civil War which began four months later. But Baldwin rode out the storm, helped by the scandal caused by the devotion of Edward VIII (who had succeeded his father, George V, in January 1936) to Mrs. Simpson, in which public opinion overwhelmingly sided with the prime minister. Baldwin would not permit the king to marry Mrs. Simpson because she was not only a commoner and an American but also a divorcée. Following Edward's abdication and the coronation of George VI in May 1937, Baldwin retired. He was succeeded by Neville Chamberlain.

Already the move toward rearmament was gaining momentum. In his last budget as chancellor of the exchequer, Chamberlain provided for the costs of additional rearmament for the next five years not by increased taxation but by borrowing £400 million. As the international scene grew more tense and the Commons more preoccupied with foreign affairs, a war economy began to be fashioned. In March 1938 the unions abandoned their pacifist attitudes and agreed to relax restrictions on armament production; in February 1939 aircraft production was authorized "to the limit," without regard to cost. It was an ironic situation for Chamberlain, who was primarily interested in domestic reform projects, saw himself as a man of peace, and consequently resented spending money on arms.

The Popular Front in France

Throughout the 1930's, France was plagued by a series of unstable governments that failed to give the nation strong leadership in foreign or domestic affairs. From Poincaré's resignation in July 1929 to Hitler's rise to the chancellorship in January 1933, there were thirteen changes of government in France and eight different premiers — and the years that followed were not much better. Out of this chaos grew disillusionment that threatened the very existence of French parliamentary government.

Partly to blame were the competing parties. Their sheer irresponsibility and lack of foresight were compounded by the problems of the worldwide Depression, which began to affect France after 1931. The immediate shock of the 1929 stock market crash in the United States was cushioned by the simple fact that the French economy was less dynamic than others. Small agricultural and industrial enterprises could exist without large overseas markets; few of France's conservative bankers had extended credit unwisely; and the urban unemployed could be maintained by relatives with small farms in the country. In the first year or two, then, the government was content with negative policies: a tariff wall and quota system protected the domestic market; cartels were allowed to keep prices at prewar levels; immigration of foreign workers was halted — and 100,000 of them (with their families) were repatriated — so that at no time did official unemployment figures rise much above 500,000.

By 1932, however, France was clearly caught in a spiral of depression, and the programs of the Left began to have increasing appeal. After the elections of May 1932, the successful parties of the Left formed a government with Socialist support (but not participation). It proved no more capable than its predecessors of combatting either the Depression or parliamentary instability, and the succession of six different cabinets in the next twenty months convinced many Frenchmen that some sort of authoritarian regime was needed to keep the country from disintegrating. Thousands joined various extraparliamentary rightist "leagues." When in late 1933 the government was badly compromised by a financial scandal, major riots broke out.

On February 6, 1934, huge mobs of rightist rioters (and a smaller number of Communists) were turned away from the Chamber of Deputies after bloody fighting with the police. One outcome of these riots was the beginning of a coalition of various leftist groups in defense of the Republic. Traditionally, the Communists had worked separately for a Soviet-style revolution and refused to collaborate with other leftists; but in July 1934 they agreed to an embryonic alliance with the Socialists, although the more moderate parties of the Left still held aloof. During 1935 there was some progress toward a leftist coalition, spurred especially by a Franco-Russian alliance signed in May 1935. Late in 1935 the Radicals finally joined the Communists and Socialists to form the so-called Popular Front.

The Front's program fell far short of socialist or Communist ideals. The Radicals and Communists wanted it to include vague generalities against fascism; the Socialists, a precise and sweeping plan for socio-economic reform. But the Front inspired unprecedented enthusiasm from the workers, and its chances of victory in the forthcoming elections were enhanced by the strict deflationary policy of the incumbent Pierre Laval government. In the May 1936 balloting the Popular Front won a narrow but clear-cut victory: the Socialists emerged as the largest group in the Chamber, while the number of Communist deputies increased from ten to seventy-two. The government that took office was made up of Socialists and Radicals; the Communists, taking a leaf from the Socialists' book, gave their support but refused to participate in the cabinet. Léon Blum, a Socialist who had been a noted jurist and literary critic, was the new premier; he dominated the Popular Front government, and its successes and failures were very much a result of his personal views.

In the campaign, the Popular Front had called for the dissolution of various rightist factions, stressed its commitment to the principle of collective security and disarmament, and promised to reverse the deflationary policies of the previous governments. Blum himself greatly admired the New Deal policies of President Roosevelt in the United States and planned to inaugurate such a program himself. He had not planned anything like Roosevelt's hundred-day spate of legislation, but events precipitated a crisis. In the month between the election and the time he took office, a genuine financial panic took place: though the Popular Front program was hardly socialist, it alarmed businessmen. Their fear was heightened when a spontaneous wave of sit-down strikes swept the country. The very fact that the strikes were seldom accompanied by vandalism was all the more alarming: the workers acted as though they already owned the plants. At this point, critics say, management was so much on the defensive that Blum could have taken charge and put through a revolutionary program. But Blum was aware that his party had no mandate for social revolution, and he was determined to demonstrate that it could rule responsibly. He met with the workers and the industrialists, working out a settlement to satisfy the workers' legitimate demands. Wages were raised throughout industry; the forty-hour work week was adopted; the principle of collective bargaining was recognized by management; and paid vacations were to be introduced.

From June to August, legislation was passed making these agreements the law of the land. In addition, the Bank of France was first reorganized and then completely nationalized in order to make its control more democratic (the Popular Front had pledged a war on the "two hundred families" reputed to control the French economy). Twenty billion francs were allocated for public works projects over the next three years; there were to be loans to industries and attempts to raise agricultural prices. The government promised to introduce legislation to establish insurance against unemployment and agricultural disasters.

Though far-reaching, this program did not bring about economic recovery. The forty-hour week actually lowered production, while the wage increases meant rising production costs. Neither workers nor employers cooperated in implementing the reforms: the former remained militant, and the latter tried to evade the new legislation. Moreover, the Popular Front undertook large-scale rearmament, and the cost of this program necessitated a pause in the reforms. The financial crisis continued to mount as capital flowed out of the country at an alarming rate. Finally, in October 1936 the government was forced to devalue the currency, and when the drain of capital still continued, Blum had to ask for special powers to control it. The Senate refused, and in June 1937 Blum chose to resign. Meanwhile, he had lost support from the Left by his policy of nonintervention in the Spanish Civil War.

Blum's immediate successors, the Radicals, allowed the country to drift along for a time. In March 1938, Blum became premier for a second time, but in the face of divisions in the Popular Front and the Senate's intransigent opposition to reform, he could accomplish little and resigned after five weeks. He was succeeded by Édouard Daladier, a conservative member of the Radical party. Daladier modified some of the principal social gains of the first Blum government, to the satisfaction of die-hard conservatives whose slogan was "Better Hitler than Blum." In the late 1930's France was a deeply divided country.

The New Deal

In contrast with Britain and France, the United States in the 1930's benefited from strong central direction and a broad national consensus. By 1932 the American electorate—terribly shaken by the deepening Depression—had lost confidence in Herbert Hoover. Turning from his solemn warnings and cautious leadership, they elected the Democratic candidate, Governor Franklin Delano Roosevelt (1882–1945) of New York, to the presidency by a popular vote of 22.8 to 15.8 million. The programs espoused by the two candidates revealed few if any substantial differences. Nor did Roosevelt's past career indicate that he would be likely to adopt anything other than a moderate economic policy to remedy the nationwide Depression. Nevertheless he waged a shrewd, effective campaign, projecting the confident leadership for which the electorate longed.

When Roosevelt took the oath of office on March 4, 1933, the national economy was in a sorry state. Most pressing of all was the financial panic that had been building since October: in March every state had either shut down or severely restricted banking operations. Though pressed by Hoover, Roosevelt declined to clarify his financial intentions until after the inauguration —because he distrusted Hoover's motives and because he was as yet unaware of the actual dimensions of public misery. Once in office, however, he moved swiftly. Following the advice of economic experts whom he recruited from leading universities, Roosevelt declared a national bank holiday, presented Congress with the Emergency Banking Relief Act, which made liquid funds available to sound banks, and directed treasury officials to supervise the reopening of banks in order to eliminate unsound ones. Then he held the first of many "fireside chats"—radio talks to explain to the nation what was being done.

Subsequent measures were more far-reaching. In June the Banking Act separated investment from commercial banking functions and set up a system to insure small savings accounts (FDIC). Steps were taken to supervise the issue of new securities, and in June 1934 the Securities and Exchange Commission was established to regulate trading practices and margin requirements and to enforce full disclosure of information.

Though the banking crisis could be dealt with swiftly and directly, it was far more difficult to start the entire economy on the road to prosperity. Pushed partly by the silver interests in Congress and partly by his own conviction that devaluation would lead to the recovery of industrial production, Roosevelt persuaded Congress, early in 1933, to pass a resolution declaring that the currency was no longer tied to the gold standard. But the manipulation of currency to influence prices and wages was not a success and was soon abandoned.

In what has become known as the "first hundred days" of the New Deal, the foundation of the administration's efforts to promote recovery was legislated into existence. Congress passed the Agricultural Adjustment Act in June 1933. Farmers were encouraged to cut production, to plant less acreage, and to raise less livestock. Those who agreed to restrict production received subsidies based on parity (i.e., payments from the government that kept agricultural prices on a par with overall prices in the prewar period). By the end of 1935, $1.5 billion had been spent in such subsidies, but the consequent increase in farm prices and income did not stimulate the general economy through any increased demand for industrial products. The effect was a degree of recovery among the farming population—recovery gained at the consumer's expense—but it was not uniformly distributed. Small sharecroppers were forced off the land, and farm laborers had fewer work opportunities.

Another attempt to stimulate recovery was the National Industrial Recovery Act, also passed by Congress in June 1933. An omnibus measure, the NIRA was meant to satisfy business, labor, and government planners. Businessmen were to arrive openly at codes that would end cutthroat competition and limit production to actual needs, thereby allowing prices to rise; the codes would also guarantee minimum wages and maximum working hours. Section 7A of the Act affirmed labor's right to organize and bargain collectively. Expanding a device of the Hoover administration whereby federal funds were channeled through state and local agencies, the NIRA also established the Public Works Administration with an appropriation of $3.3 billion to finance relief work and stimulate recovery.

None of these initial programs ended the Depression. The PWA was so cautiously administered (and its funds so often raided for other programs) that the money spurred no recovery that year. The drafting of industrial codes under the National Recovery Administration (set up by the NIRA) proceeded quickly, but too often the businessmen charged with writing the codes were dominated by representatives of the bigger corporations, who sometimes used their powers to stifle competition, boost prices, and cut back production. And many evaded the provisions designed to protect labor.

Although the Roosevelt administration was bound by its commitment to social justice to extend aid to the unemployed, no one kind of aid was consistently offered. The Federal Emergency Relief Administration, created in May 1933, gave direct assistance to millions. It was supplemented in February 1934 by the Civil Works Administration, which created jobs, paid minimum wages to those it employed, and supplied additional funds for direct relief through FERA. Its high cost caused the program to be closed down in 1935, however, and millions were forced to rely solely on relief. Finally, in early 1935, the Works Progress Administration was established with $5 billion to provide work for 3.5 million unemployed. In addition to building schools, hospitals, post offices, and airports, the WPA funded several projects for the creative arts.

Combining the President's goals of providing work for the unemployed and conserving the nation's resources, the Civilian Conservation Corps (CCC) was authorized in April 1933. Under the direction of the military, 250,000 young men were sent to camps where they worked at reforestation, flood control, and soil conservation. When the program came to an end in 1942, more than 2.5 million men had served in the Corps. A final landmark of the "first hundred days" was the Tennessee Valley Authority. Starting with a single dam and nitrate plant built during World War I, the government set up an independent public corporation that launched a vast, regional program, coordinating conservation, navigation and flood control, the production of power at reasonable cost, and development plans that invigorated the economy of the entire area.

The second spate of legislation (the "second hundred days") occurred during the spring and summer of 1935. It is widely cited as the beginning of the welfare state in the United States. A number of significant measures were passed at this time. The first was the Emergency Relief Appropriation of almost

$5 billion, about a third of which went to the newly created WPA and another large chunk to the new Resettlement Administration. The government was now strongly committed to deficit spending on a large scale to alleviate distress and stimulate recovery. Despite flagrant abuse by local politicians and despite its inability to employ all who needed work, the WPA was fairly successful in relieving the discontent of those who would otherwise have been forced to live on relief. The Resettlement Administration was set up to help exploited and underprivileged rural residents. It fought for equal benefits for Negroes, tried to alleviate the plight of migrant workers, and made loans to small farmers. A good measure of its success was the prompt antagonism of many powerful vested interests.

The Social Security Act of 1935 established a national system of old age insurance, a federal-state program of unemployment insurance, and federal aid on a matching basis for the care of the disabled and for dependent mothers and children. The old age benefits were to be funded by contributions from employers and employees. Though by no means everyone came under the program and though the benefits were not entirely adequate, it was an important step toward the welfare state.

Another important measure passed during the second hundred days was the Wagner-Connery Act (the National Labor Relations Act), which sought to redress the balance between business and labor. Largely the work of an individual senator, Robert F. Wagner of New York, rather than of the administration, the new act defined unfair practices against employees by employers (e.g., blacklisting for union activities); it established a nonpartisan National Labor Relations Board, which, among other duties, was to investigate employers' practices, and it specified conditions under which unions should be recognized by employers. Called "Labor's Magna Carta" by its friends, the Wagner Act gave the American workingman a kind of federal recognition and support he had never before enjoyed.

Recovery was finally stimulated, and it continued to accelerate until 1937, sparked by government spending. National income rose from $42.5 billion to $57.1 billion between 1933 and 1935. By September 1937 employment was higher than the peak figure in 1929 and disposable per capita income a little higher than it had been in 1929. But Roosevelt was uneasy about the mounting deficits. Although he was willing to borrow to meet emergencies, he believed in balanced budgets; and early in 1937 he launched a campaign of relative austerity. Relief spending was slashed — WPA rolls were reduced from 3 million to 1.5 million between January and August. At the same time, the Federal Reserve Board increased reserve requirements, thereby limiting credit. There was no outlay comparable to the soldiers' bonus of $1.7 billion paid in 1936. The results of Roosevelt's retrenchment were not encouraging. A recession, clearly discernible in July, reached serious proportions by autumn.

Once again the federal government had to step into the breach. In April 1938 Roosevelt announced a new spending program, for which Congress voted almost $4 billion. A new Agricultural Adjustment Act prevented a collapse of farm prices, and after a struggle a Fair Labor Standards bill was enacted to counteract wage cutting that had occurred during the early months of the recession. The measure established a minimum hourly wage of 25¢, which was gradually increased to 40¢, limited the work week to forty-four hours, and outlawed the use of child labor by industries engaged in interstate commerce. Credit restrictions were loosened at the same time. Recovery to the levels of 1937 was nearly complete by 1939.

In many countries, the hardships stemming from the Depression of the 1930's caused violent unrest that threatened to force a change in the system of government (and in Germany did so). Similarly, American democracy was attacked by a motley group of right-wing agitators, including Senator Huey Long of Louisiana, Father Charles E. Coughlin (Detroit's "Radio Priest" and an anti-Semitic demagogue), the blatantly pro-Nazi German-American Bund, and the Silver Shirts; but these groups could never coalesce long enough to become a serious threat.

A more powerful and far more respectable challenge to the New Deal came from the Supreme Court. During 1935 and 1936 a majority of the justices upheld decisions that declared unconstitutional the NIRA (a week earlier, Roosevelt had decided to support the Wagner Bill, which supplanted some of the NIRA's most significant elements), the Agricultural Adjustment Act, and state legislation to establish minimum wages. In February 1937, after receiving an overwhelming popular mandate in the 1936 elections, Roosevelt submitted a judicial reorganization bill. Under this measure, a certain number of Supreme Court and other federal judges could be replaced by the President if they did not retire within six months of reaching age seventy. Roosevelt's justification for his proposal was the huge backlog of cases that had developed. Bipartisan opposition at once developed in Congress, and the plan was soon defeated, but a notable change occurred in the decisions of the Court. From March 1937 on, it began to uphold rather than deny the constitutionality of social legislation, including, eventually, the constitutionality of the Wagner Act, the Social Security Act, and the states' right to set minimum wages. Thereupon Roosevelt dropped his efforts to "pack" the Court.

Despite all Roosevelt's efforts at reform, he was still denounced by many radicals as a capitalist temporizer. On the other hand, efforts of the American Communist party to gain a mass following were thoroughly unsuccessful during the early years of the Depression and New Deal. Until 1935 the party eschewed cooperation with labor and with democratic political leaders on Stalin's orders. Its efforts to gain control of the American Federation of Labor failed, and it earned the hatred of AFL leaders when it tried to establish rival unions. In the 1932 presidential election its candidate polled only a little over 100,000 votes. After Stalin's about-face toward "bourgeois" democracy in 1935, the Communists dropped their hard-line slogans and joined "popular front" organizations dedicated to combating fascism. At this time they gained control of several unions; the party enjoyed considerable support from intellectuals sickened by the misery wrought by the Depression; and several Communist sympathizers attained high positions in government. But the purge trials of the late 1930's and the Russo-German pact of 1939 disillusioned many pro-Communists, and the party was reduced to a small nucleus of conspirators.

The Roosevelt administration was also bothered by the growing militancy of organized labor. (Agitation was not directed against the government—on the contrary, Roosevelt received unprecedented union backing and lost some middle-class support for his refusal to put down strikes with force.) One reason for the rise of militancy was labor's disillusionment with the workings of codes drawn up under the NIRA. Contrary to the spirit of that act, management was determined to avoid having to recognize unions as bargaining agents for employees. Employees who worked for unionization were blacklisted, subservient company unions were hurriedly set up, and strikes met with strong resistance. The result was a series of short but extremely violent strikes.

At the same time, organized labor was being split from within. A group of militant leaders such as John L. Lewis of the United Mine Workers demanded that the AFL (a federation of craft unions) take steps to unionize entire industries, both skilled and unskilled workers. In 1935 these militants broke away to form the Committee for Industrial Organization. In the next few years, unions supported by the CIO organized the steel industry (U.S. Steel surrendered without a fight) and the automobile industry (a six-week sit-down strike and pressure from the President compelled General Motors to come to terms, although Ford held out until 1941). By the time the United States entered World War II, 28.2 per cent of the country's nonagricultural workers were unionized, as against 11.5 per cent in 1933. The advance of unionism in the New Deal era was one of the most important of the many social and legislative results of Roosevelt's first two terms, for which the President gained the warm support of liberals at home and abroad and the dislike of conservatives in both America and Europe.

III THE SMALLER POWERS

Eastern and Central Europe

The period between the two world wars saw the disappearance of parliamentary governments in all eastern European countries except Czechoslovakia. It would be convenient to attribute this to the machinations of Mussolini and Hitler, for neither of them scrupled to interfere in the internal affairs of those countries; but several of these antidemocratic, dictatorial regimes opposed the influence of native fascist groups inspired by Italy and Germany.

In Poland a military dictatorship directed by Marshal Pilsudski, a national hero in the post-World War I struggle for independence, was succeeded by a "government of colonels" after Pilsudski's death in 1935. The regime veered from right to left and back again. Germany made no attempt to interfere in these oscillations, for there was no need. Since 1932, Polish foreign policy had been directed by Colonel Josef Beck, who, in trying to play Russia and Germany off against each other, had allowed Hitler to gain significant advantages. Beck and the other colonels hoped to deflect German expansion to the southeast, and to this end the Polish minority in Czechoslovakia was instructed to cooperate with the Sudeten Germans in making trouble for the Prague government. Polish agents worked in Rumania with the Iron Guard, an organization that had terrorized Jews, liberals, and Communists in the 1920's, and Poland expressed sympathy for Hungary's pro-German proposals for revising the Versailles settlement.

In Hungary the Depression heightened traditional anti-Semitism, and the government used its influence to force Jews to leave industry. After 1935 numerous Nazi groups began to appear on the political scene. At the same time Germany had become the best customer for Hungary's exports. Yet though the regime opposed existing democratic parties, it jailed the leader of the Arrow-Cross, a subversive Nazi party formed in late 1938. Ultimately Hungary's interest in the revision of the Versailles settlement bound it to Germany. After the breakup of Czechoslovakia in March 1939, Hungary received Carpatho-Ruthenia and a small portion of southern Slovakia.

Royal dictatorships in Rumania, Bulgaria, and Yugoslavia were in control when the Second World War broke out. When King Carol II assumed the throne of Rumania in 1930, he immediately set out to break up the old political parties, using the services of the fascist Iron Guard. In the midst of a deteriorating economic situation, the Iron Guard gained a mass following by promising land reform and an end to administrative corruption and by disseminating anti-Semitic propaganda. Carol then moved successfully against it. In 1937 he declared a dictatorship "in the interests of the people"; subsequently the head of the Iron Guard was arrested and "shot while trying to escape." In December 1938 the "Front of National Rebirth" was created. Carol's personal dictatorship could thereafter be overthrown only from without.

The government of King Boris III in Bulgaria was powerless to oppose the Macedonian terrorists (IMRO), who murdered any politicians who sought friendly relations with neighboring countries. In May 1934 a military revolution took place; but its leaders, unlike other militarists hitherto mentioned, were not out for personal gain but for reform. IMRO was dispersed; peasant debts were reduced; the credit system was reformed; doctors were encouraged to work among the peasants; trade unions were replaced by unions that refrained from political action and were devoted to the corporative principle of state organization and control. In 1935, however, the king was able to turn the dictatorship into a personal despotism. Though he continued the military's policy of reconciliation with Yugoslavia and never permitted IMRO to regain its power, extreme nationalist organizations were allowed to flourish, and a party modeled on the German Nazis gradually built up. In 1938 there was a return to the forms of parliamentary government, but the elections were managed by bribery and terror, and the opposition groups allowed to sit in parliament offered docile acquiescence to the king's policies.

In Yugoslavia, King Alexander's efforts to create a new "Yugoslav patriotism" foundered on continued rivalries among Serbs, Croats, and Slovenes. In 1934 Alexander was assassinated, and his place was taken by the regent, Prince Paul, who guided the country along a path that would please the fascist powers. Then in 1937 the Serbs and Croats reached an agreement to work for a more democratic government and a solution to Croat grievances. This was strongly supported by the people, who had grown tired of the dictatorship. Paul was spurred into positive action by the Czechoslovak crisis of March 1939, and in August he reached an agreement with the Croat leadership whereby democratic government was revived. The Serbian parties that had sought government reform remained in opposition, however; and the Croatian peasants remained dissatisfied, for the radical reforms they had been promised were not forthcoming.

While both Mussolini and Hitler were more or less content to allow the governments of these eastern European countries to determine their own course, they had active and often conflicting interests in Austrian internal affairs. The Duce looked on an independent Austria as a convenient and necessary buffer between his country and the other great powers; on the other hand, *Anschluss*, or union, between Germany and Austria was a goal of the Nazi government, as it had been of every other nationalist faction in Germany since the end of the First World War.

Mussolini was the first to intervene in Austrian internal politics. In 1930 he began to send secret subsidies to the Christian Socialists, an authoritarian party with a fascist-style auxiliary militia. Two years later a Christian Socialist, Engelbert Dollfuss, became chancellor. The press was strictly censored, political meetings and parades were alternately harassed and banned, and the parties of the Right were formed into a Fatherland Front. At the same time, the regime retained a strong clerical bias. But Dollfuss's policy did not work out well. He soon found himself opposed by the Social Democrats on the left and, on the right, by agitation from a native Nazi party, guided and supported by the German government.

The Duce advised Dollfuss to attack the Social Democrats openly in order to win the loyalty of the Austrian Nazis. The attack was made in February 1934, but its brutality served only to alienate the workers from the regime. And the Austrian Nazis continued to make trouble. Finally in July they attempted a coup; it was put down easily, but Dollfuss himself was murdered during the uprising. Hitler hesitated to send aid to the Austrian Nazis when he learned that Mussolini had mobilized troops on his side of the Austrian border.

The Austrian government was now headed by Kurt von Schuschnigg, an uninspiring lawyer who attempted to maintain his country's independence by relying on Mussolini's support, as his predecessor had. But the growing partnership between the Duce and Hitler deprived him of this backing, and his talk of a possible Habsburg restoration angered the Nazis. More pressure was put on the Austrian government, and in July 1936 an agreement between Germany and Austria was signed that provided for participation in the government by "respectable" leaders of the Austrian Nazis. Although the agreement recognized Austrian independence and foreswore intervention in its internal affairs, German plans for another *Putsch* went ahead, and by May 1938 Austria had been taken over by Nazi Germany.

Czechoslovakia was the only state in central and eastern Europe to maintain a democratic form of government throughout the 1930's. There were obvious reasons for the hardiness of democratic institutions in Czechoslovakia. Unlike their Austrian counterparts, most Czechoslovak parties accepted the workings of democracy, and the authoritarian parties were for the time being too weak to cause serious trouble. The major problem of the Czech democracy was that the Sudeten Germans had never been fully reconciled to the Czechoslovak Republic. Their dissatisfaction was stirred anew, even before Hitler's rise to power, by the world Depression, which severely affected the predominantly industrial area the Sudeten Germans inhabited.

After 1935 these problems were greatly intensified by the increasing power of the Sudeten-German party, which was secretly subsidized by the German foreign office. By 1938 it had strong support among the 3.25 million Czechoslovakian citizens of German descent. At first these German-Czechoslovakians simply insisted that they were not being treated fairly by the Czech government; but in 1937 they were calling for autonomy, and following the annexation of Austria they were instructed to press such demands, which the Czech government could not possibly satisfy. After Czechoslovakia was deserted by its allies at Munich in September 1938, resulting in the loss of the Sudetenland to Germany, popular fury toward the Western powers brought in a government that collaborated with Germany until March 1939, when the remainder of the country was invaded and occupied by German troops.

The Trial of Republican Government in Spain

Primo de Rivera resigned as dictator of Spain in 1930 and was succeeded by an elderly and ailing general who continued the policy of government by decree and censorship, alienating all but the staunchest conservatives, further discrediting the monarchy, and making the idea of a republic increasingly appealing to most Spaniards. In August 1930 the radical Republicans and the Catalan nationalists agreed to a joint effort to overthrow the monarchy and inaugurate a democratic republic. The revolt was easily suppressed; but the government, afraid of making martyrs of the jailed conspirators, allowed their trial to turn into a republican demonstration, and riots by workers and students underlined the government's impotence. Unexpectedly, the municipal elections of April 1931 produced victory for a republican-socialist bloc. Although rural areas had continued to support nonrepublican candidates, the urban centers had voted for Republicans. Faced by rioting in Madrid and the knowledge that it would take a civil war to reimpose the monarchy's control over the provincial capitals, King Alfonso XIII followed the advice of several of his ministers and left the country.

The provisional republican government was headed by Niceto Alcalá Zamora, a Catholic and recent convert to republicanism who had done much to reassure the middle class that the Republic would be bourgeois and Catholic. But the mood of the country as expressed in the June elections to the Cortes was more radical: the parliamentary majority was a coalition of left-wing republicans and socialists. In October, after a democratic new constitution had been put into effect, Zamora resigned, and a coalition headed by the able Manuel Azaña came to power.

The Azaña government instituted an extensive and long-overdue program of labor legislation and welfare measures. The moderate socialists were satisfied with these accomplishments, but the extreme radical groups had been put at a disadvantage. The militants instigated an outbreak of strikes and violence, and when the government was forced to crush such outbreaks, it inspired unfavorable comparisons with previous regimes. The government's attempts to initiate agrarian reform were largely unsuccessful.

The most dangerous step of the Azaña government was its attempt to implement fully the new constitutional provisions for ending the privileged position of the Catholic Church. This policy engendered intense Catholic opposition and created a new Catholic party—the *Acción popular*, led by Gil Robles.

The government also alienated the army with a series of long-overdue reforms that pensioned off superfluous officers and eliminated special privileges enjoyed by the various corps. Those officers who remained began to feel that their dignity came before their loyalty to the state. Nor did it help that many of them were monarchical and Catholic in their sympathies. In 1932 monarchist civilians and pensioned-off officers attempted a coup. They were not strong enough to succeed, but their cause was aided in January 1933 when a radical and syndicalist rising in Barcelona was suppressed by government troops.

In November 1933 the government coalition was so weak that elections were necessary. The Left split badly and went down to defeat, and the next two years—the *bienio negro,* or black years—witnessed a succession of coalition governments firmly devoted to the Republic but dominated by conservatives and antisocialists. Leftist youth groups became increasingly radical, and the working-class parties began to plan a revolution, but disturbances in Barcelona and Madrid in April and October of 1934 were suppressed, and in the Asturian mining region the workers' two-week takeover was also crushed.

Less stable than ever, the government dropped all pretense of support for the "peaceful revolution" attempted by the Azaña cabinet. The campaign against the Church was halted and agrarian reform abandoned. Government expenditure was drastically cut, and wage regulation lapsed—wages dropped by 50 per cent in the agrarian south. In late 1935 government figures were involved in a series of financial scandals, and in February 1936 a general election was called. The Left profited from the lesson of November 1933 and ran a Popular Front coalition of Communists, anarchists, syndicalists, socialists, and radical republicans. This time the coalition of right-wing parties split, and the Popular Front won a victory, though in actual strength the Left and Right were evenly matched in the country.

The new republican regime—liberal and gradualist—became increasingly isolated from the groups of the radical Left that had brought it to power and those of the radical Right that had contested it. Direct action soon replaced political maneuvering, and revolutionary fervor gave rise to street fighting and political assassination, workers' strikes, and land seizures by the peasants. On the right, Primo de Rivera's son had founded a fascist party known as the *Falange*. Although it was designed to appeal to the workers, stressing the revolutionary, authoritarian aspects of the corporate state, it had its greatest following among activist students.

But the determining factor in this prerevolutionary situation was the Spanish army, whose leaders wanted most of all a regime that would keep order and stay out of military affairs. Despite their different objectives, the Falange and the generals cooperated in launching a revolution against the Republic in July 1936. The government was aware of the threat—the plotting generals were transferred shortly before the outbreak—but it was confident that a military revolt would be unsuccessful. When the generals struck, it was caught unprepared.

This kind of turmoil, so familiar in Spanish history, invited foreign intervention. It had done so in the 1860's and helped to bring on the Franco-Prussian War. It did so again in the summer of 1936 and hastened the coming of World War II.

IV THE STEPS TO WAR

The End of the Versailles System

In 1933 the nightmare of the First World War was still so vivid that France and Great Britain were agreed that another war was to be avoided at all costs. They did not agree, however, on the methods that would best achieve this end. The French recognized Germany as the greatest threat to

Continental security and had little faith in the League's ability to restrain German ambitions. Consequently the French foreign office set up a system of alliances with the small states that surrounded the Reich. In Britain, on the other hand, it was widely believed that some German goals were reasonably legitimate and would have to be met: the demands for equality in armaments, eventual return of the Rhineland, an end to reparations. In short, the British government (and public) thought that some parts of the Versailles settlement were unjust and would have to be changed if peace was to be lasting — and that in any case it would be impossible to deny a country of Germany's size and strength a leading role in Continental affairs indefinitely.

There were other significant differences among the great nations that might oppose German policies. Fascist Italy, unlike the democracies, had no commitment to peace; it considered warfare a glorifying and strengthening experience. The democracies' willingness to trust Russia was undermined by the Comintern's incessant propaganda efforts in those countries. Thus there were disagreements and suspicions among Germany's potential enemies that a skillful and daring government could exploit. This is precisely what Hitler set out to do.

Hitler took charge of Germany's military affairs and foreign relations almost as soon as he assumed office. In *Mein Kampf* he had explicitly outlined what Europe was to expect: renunciation of the Treaty of Versailles (including reparations, disarmament, and territorial settlements); the building of Greater Germany, which would include the Sudeten and Austrian German minorities who had been subjects of the Habsburg empire before 1914; and a quest for living space (*Lebensraum*) in eastern Europe to accommodate the surplus population of the Reich. Contemporary statesmen worked to obviate the Führer's willingness to resort to war to gain these ends. Their own horror of war (particularly in the case of the British) was so great that they wanted to believe that Hitler did not mean what he said about the glories of warfare; and the Führer skillfully used propaganda to camouflage the ultimate goals of his aggression and the means he was willing to use to achieve them. While denouncing France and Russia as archenemies, he held out an olive branch of sorts to England and Italy. Only when it was dangerously late — after 1938 — did France and Britain face up to the reality of his ambitions.

By June 1934 the League's Disarmament Conference came to a disappointing end. Since 1930, successive German governments had demanded equal treatment. They insisted that Germany be granted the right to rearm or that Britain and France be obliged to disarm. Hitler, of course, continued this demand, knowing full well that France would never agree to disarmament. The French clearly feared German superiority in manpower and industrial resources and would not permit German rearmament without substantial British guarantees against possible German bad faith. The British government was unwilling to give such guarantees because of the cost involved and the British public's aversion to Continental commitments. Agreement was therefore impossible, and on October 14 Germany withdrew from both the Conference and the League. Hitler announced that the decision had been made in sorrow rather than anger but that it was essential to German self-respect.

The following January, the Führer greatly enhanced Germany's peaceful posture by concluding a nonaggression pact with Poland. The Polish government wished to maintain an independent neutrality between Germany and Russia rather than commit itself to France's system of alliances, both for reasons of prestige and because France had been evasive when Poland suggested preventive action against Hitler. The pact was a clever move, for it made the best of Germany's current inability to bring pressure against Poland, while at the same time it weakened the French system of alliances in eastern Europe.

In June 1934, Hitler made his first trip outside Germany—to Italy. But his meetings with the Duce failed to create any strong bond between the two countries. Mussolini realized that their interests in central and eastern Europe were in conflict: the Duce considered himself a protector of Austrian independence (a weak Austria was much more desirable than a strong Germany on his borders), while the Führer was intent on *Anschluss*. When in July 1934 Austrian Nazis attempted a coup against the Austrian government, Mussolini mobilized forces on his Austrian frontier to make sure that Germany did not interfere.

Disarmament and collective security—discredited earlier when Japan seized and held Manchuria in the face of League disapproval—were thoroughly undermined in 1935. The year opened with Franco-Italian agreements over colonial matters, which seemed to draw Mussolini away from Hitler. In March the British issued their White Paper placing reliance on armed force for defense, and on March 16 Hitler announced that conscription would be reintroduced to bring the German army to a peacetime strength of approximately 550,000. Four days earlier, the French had doubled the term of service and lowered the age of enlistment in their own army to balance the fall of conscripts due to the lower birth rate during 1914–1918. At the Stresa conference in April, Britain, France, and Italy condemned German rearmament moves, agreed to preserve Austrian independence, and pledged loyalty to the spirit of collective security outlined in the 1925 Locarno Pact. In May the French signed a defensive alliance with Russia.

This solidarity of opposition to Germany was only a sham, however. In June 1935 the British dealt it a heavy blow by signing a naval agreement with Germany without informing their allies. The British government did this in the hope of averting the kind of naval race that had brought on World War I. But Hitler knew that he could not possibly surpass Britain in naval construction. While getting the British formally to agree to German naval rearmament (and thereby breaching the Versailles Treaty), Hitler gave up nothing substantial in return.

The Ethiopian War and the Occupation of the Rhineland

In the early 1930's, Mussolini badly needed a diversion from internal problems to unite the country behind the Fascist regime in a great upsurge of patriotism. It was time to prove to the world the much-vaunted virility of the Fascist state; and what better (and less dangerous) way than by expanding Italy's sorry colonial empire? Mussolini's attention naturally centered on Africa—where Italy already had control of a few desert areas and claims to others—and specifically on Ethiopia (Abyssinia). The last African country independent of white rule, Ethiopia bordered conveniently on the Italian colonies of Eritrea and Somaliland.

In 1934 an incident at Wal-Wal, a watering place inside Ethiopia but close to Somaliland, made military intervention seem plausible. The Ethiopian emperor, Haile Selassie, protested to the League of Nations, which began an investigation. Unfortunately for the emperor, France and Great Britain were anxious to keep the Duce's goodwill, particularly so after Germany's reintroduction of conscription and the agreement reached at Stresa. The Ethiopian problem had been carefully avoided at the Stresa conference, and up to the outbreak of hostilities, the British government declined to sell modern weapons to Haile Selassie.

In October 1935, Italy began military operations, and in November the League called for economic sanctions against Italy: Italian goods were not to be imported, and arms and financial embargoes were imposed. This had no effect on the war, because the restrictions did not extend to the strategic commodities oil and coal. While the public—outraged by Italy's use of bombers, tanks, and poison gas against tribesmen armed only with ancient rifles and spears—cried for stiffer sanctions, the British and French governments worked to end hostilities by negotiations outside the League. In December the British foreign secretary, Sir Samuel Hoare, and the French premier, Pierre Laval, reached agreement to have Ethiopia cede two thirds of its territory to Mussolini. When news of their pact became public, however, the outcry in France and Britain against this betrayal of the League was so great that the plan had to be abandoned. Instead, the ineffectual sanctions were continued. Italian forces entered the Ethiopian capital in triumph on May 5, 1936, and the king of Italy was proclaimed emperor of Ethiopia.

The Ethiopian war had crucial significance for future international relations. The League's power to contain aggression by imposing sanctions on the aggressor power was shown to be totally ineffective. Moreover, the ephemeral unity forged at Stresa had been destroyed, and Mussolini, diplomatically isolated by the League's sanction efforts, began to consider Germany as a possible ally.

Meanwhile, on March 7, 1936, Germany had seized the initiative in overthrowing the Versailles settlement by occupying the demilitarized Rhineland. Hitler used as an excuse the recent Franco-Russian pact, in which each party agreed to come to the aid of the other in case of unprovoked attack. (The treaty had become a subject of bitter controversy in French politics; though concluded in May 1935, it was not ratified until February 1936.) Hitler said that the agreement violated the Locarno Pact. More to the point, his actions violated both the Locarno Pact and the Versailles settlement.

It was a daring bluff: Hitler and the German general staff knew well that their troops would have to retreat if France responded with military opposition. But the French army was prepared only for a defensive war, and the French domestic situation was such that the government could not move without a firm British commitment, which Baldwin would not give. After all, the French had been willing to appease Mussolini at Ethiopia's expense, and the British did not understand why they should now oppose Germany's move to regain full control over its own territory. At the same time, Hitler offered new and far-reaching peace proposals, including a new nonaggression pact with France and Belgium, others with Germany's eastern neighbors, and an offer to reenter the League. It was a shrewd tactic that thoroughly befogged essential realities. There was more talk of new opportunities for peace than condemnation of Hitler's aggression.

Germany was thus allowed to begin fortifying its French boundary, which made an alliance with France considerably less attractive to the small eastern states and freed a substantial part of the German army for operations elsewhere. The realization that nothing would come of Germany's new peace proposals was overshadowed by the outbreak of civil war in Spain.

The Spanish Civil War

The first few days after the generals' initial revolt in Morocco on July 18, 1936, were full of confusion throughout Spain. The army was successful where there was little resistance, but it seemed to have little chance in those parts of the country where determined opposition was mounted by the civilian population and local militias. The government in Madrid sought to bargain with the generals. When they refused to negotiate, it was overthrown by public pressure for an administration that would arm the populace. In areas loyal to the Republic, committee and militia rule took over local administration. The most extreme social revolutionaries in some localities began a reign of terror directed against the Church and the rich that confirmed the hostility of the middle class.

The Republican partisans formed what they called an "antifascist front" comprising various left-wing parties, but their war effort was hampered by serious disagreements about the means to be employed. True to their principles, the syndicalist and anarchist militants supported the "revolutionary improvisation" of local committees and militia. In their eyes, military discipline was "an assault on dignity and human personality." On the other hand, the more moderate groups loyal to the Republic, including the socialists and

Communists, took the more practical viewpoint that military success demanded a regular army and a central government.

At first the more extreme militants held the upper hand. They inaugurated a piecemeal program of collectivization to carry out a social revolution in areas they controlled. But the incumbent government of the Republic moved to halt this social and economic revolution, and as part of its coalition, the Communists, paradoxically, were instrumental in accomplishing this goal. In October 1936 the Communist minister of agriculture put an end to the agrarian revolution. Collectivization and workers' control were replaced by centrally controlled nationalization and economic planning. In opposing the local revolutionary spontaneity, the Communists were motivated by more than immediate practical considerations. They planned to control the revolution that would come after the war was successfully concluded.

By November 1936, however, all the radical factions except the non-Communist Marxists and the purist anarcho-syndicalists had been brought into a coalition government headed by Largo Caballero. But the excluded extremists were increasingly alarmed that those in power might oppose the revolutionary efforts they were making in some regions. Unable to reconcile the differences among its members, the coalition government collapsed in May 1937. And the new more moderate ministry, headed by Socialist Juan Negrin, fared no better in its efforts to coalesce the disparate elements supporting the Republic. Already gravely weakened by this internal conflict, the central government also had its war effort further undermined by a revival of the traditional separatist tendencies of the Catalans and the Basques. Distrust and disagreement over economic and political policies became so extreme that Republican army units occasionally withdrew from the field of battle "on political grounds."

In the camp of the Nationalists, as the rebel army and its supporters were soon called, existing internal rivalries were far less serious because the generals asserted their control over the politicians early in the war. Of their various factions, the Traditionalists (or Carlists) were intent on reestablishing the monarchy, the Falange was committed to fascist social reorganization, and the generals were most concerned with installing a stable regime. The leading general was Francisco Franco (b. 1892), whose Spanish Moroccan army was the core of Nationalist strength. Franco, a cunning, corpulent little man without fanatical commitment to any ideology, was able to merge the Traditionalists and the Falangists, who had been weakened by internal factional disputes, into a single party. The idea of restoration of the monarchy was dropped, but the Traditionalists were appeased by a commitment to reverse the Republic's anticlericalism. To this was added the rhetoric of the Falangist movement, which stressed a disciplined paternalism.

Six hundred thousand Spaniards perished in the Civil War. The importance for the rest of Europe, however, lay in the rapid transformation of the conflict into a struggle between the Right and the Left. Both sides were made up of combinations of factions with very different aims. Yet when either side sought help from foreign powers, it was to its advantage to paint its opponents in the blackest of terms. Thus, to the Republicans, Franco's Nationalists were always characterized as "fascists" rather than anti-Republicans; to the Nationalists, the Republicans were "Reds." Consequently, the struggle in Spain hardened the already growing fascist-antifascist lines that divided country from country and party from party.

The rebel Nationalists very quickly secured aid from outside powers. War planes from Italy arrived in Morocco as early as June 30, 1936, and these craft and others from Germany were vital in getting the Moroccan army onto the Iberian peninsula. Mussolini had at least two motives for helping the Nationalists: to create a right-wing government, inspired by semifascist ideas, that would draw French troops from the Italian border; and to provide a second display of Italian fighting prowess. Hitler too had several reasons for aiding the Nationalist cause: to contain communism; to ensure Germany a supply of Spanish iron ore; to provide German submarines with a place to refuel; to test the recently strengthened *Luftwaffe*; and to distract the attention of France and Great Britain from German rearmament.

The Republican government immediately sought aid from France, where the Popular Front government of Léon Blum seemed a likely ally. Blum agreed at once to sell airplanes and ammunition to the Republicans, but when he flew to London late in July at the request of the British government, he was asked by the British foreign secretary, Anthony Eden, to "be cautious." Afraid of alienating either liberal or conservative support, the National Government in Great Britain was not prepared to intervene on either side, and it hoped to persuade Blum to act in the same manner. Blum was also subject to anti-interventionist pressure within France, as news of the arms purchase had leaked into the newspapers.

In August 1936, after a stormy cabinet meeting, the French government proposed to other interested powers a nonintervention plan that would ban all shipments of arms to Spain. Before the month was out, Germany, Italy, France, Great Britain, Russia, and a host of lesser nations had agreed to it. (Although the United States government did not participate in the work of the nonintervention committee, it maintained a strict neutrality with regard to the Spanish conflict.) Thereafter, the fiction of nonintervention was maintained, and the war was contained within Spain's territorial boundaries; but military aid from various countries reached one side or the other. In the autumn of 1936, German forces in Spain numbered about ten thousand—the maximum at any one time. In November, the famed Condor Legion was assembled at Seville to give the *Luftwaffe* experience in combat. Italian forces were at their maximum number in Spain in mid-1937—about fifty thousand. Italian aid to the Nationalists in supplies and material was valued at $400 million; German aid at about half that sum.

Russian aid to the Republican cause was at first of a nonmilitary nature:

food, raw materials, money, and additional Comintern representatives. Stalin believed that a Nationalist victory would surround France on a third side with a potentially hostile country, freeing Germany to attack Russia. On the other hand, a Republican victory followed by extreme social revolution might alarm Britain and France, two countries to which he was looking as antifascist allies. After a meeting with the leader of the French Communists, Stalin finally decided to ship arms to the Republic through the Comintern. At the same time, the Comintern began to recruit and organize groups of volunteers to travel to Spain to fight in International Brigades. A total of forty thousand foreigners served in the International Brigades during the war, though never more than eighteen thousand at one time. They came from France, the United States, Great Britain, Canada, eastern Europe, and Scandinavia. In addition, many refugees from Nazi Germany and Fascist Italy joined the fight against Franco. Fewer than two thousand Russians were sent to Spain in the entire course of the war. The total value of Russian and Comintern aid was estimated at $440 million. This aid saved the Republican side during the early part of the war, but by late 1938 the Soviet Union no longer thought an alliance with France and Britain was likely and started to cut back on aid.

The strategy of the Nationalist forces was to capture Madrid and bring the war to an early end. Surprisingly, the Republicans were able to hold them back. Fierce and bloody fighting took place as the Nationalists advanced into Madrid's suburbs, and in November 1936 the two sides—exhausted—dug in with trenches and fortifications. Thereafter the Nationalists simply wore down the Republicans' power of resistance with constant pressure on the various fronts. In January 1939 the Nationalists entered Barcelona; in March, Madrid fell, and the Republic was dead.

Franco's success had little direct effect on international affairs. After years of fighting, Spain was so weakened as to be militarily negligible. But German and Italian involvement in the war contributed to the creation of the Rome-Berlin Axis that Hitler had sought for so long. For the Western democracies the Civil War created a bitter crisis of political conscience.

The Road to Munich and World War

Soon after the Spanish Civil War broke out, Hitler judged that the time was ripe to draw Italy closer to Germany—especially as the Austro-German agreement of July 1936, in which Germany pledged to respect Austrian independence, seemed to lessen Mussolini's suspicion of Hitler. In October a protocol was signed covering the common interests of the two countries in regard to Austria, Spain, the League, Manchuria, and so on. The Duce now spoke of an axis "round which all those European states which are animated by a desire for collaboration and peace may work together."

The following month Hitler used the spectacle of the Spanish Civil War to emphasize the Bolshevik danger (and to camouflage Germany's rampant militarism) when he fashioned an anti-Comintern pact with Japan. Aimed at defeating the Communist "world conspiracy," the agreement was intended from the first to serve as a basis for a military alliance to which other powers would subscribe. In that regard it was a failure, though it did demonstrate community of interests between Asian and European right-wing dictatorships.

The year 1937 opened with renewed attempts by Great Britain to repair its broken friendship with Italy. An agreement was signed in which each recognized the status quo in the Mediterranean. But this was only a small and temporary crack in the Rome-Berlin Axis, and by the end of the year the Duce was again safely in Hitler's camp. On a visit to Germany in September, the Duce and his entourage were treated to a vast ceremonial parade, witnessed military maneuvers, and visited weapons factories. The Duce was impressed by German might, and returned to Rome convinced that the Reich was militarily the most prepared country in the world. Three weeks later, he added his signature to the anti-Comintern pact. He offered the Führer an added dividend by declaring that Italy was tired of mounting guard over Austria's independence.

This was the signal Hitler had been waiting for. In February 1938 the Austrian president Kurt von Schuschnigg met with Hitler at Berchtesgaden in an attempt to forestall a violent take-over and was bullied into many concessions. Imprisoned Austrian Nazis were to receive amnesty, National Socialism was to be recognized as compatible with loyalty to the Austrian state, and Arthur von Seyss-Inquart (a "respectable" crypto-Nazi) was to be the new minister of the interior, with control of the police. Officers were to be exchanged between the two armies, and a Nazi nominee was to be appointed minister of finance.

Once back in Austria, Schuschnigg attempted to get the jump on the Führer by calling for a plebiscite on the *Anschluss* question. But Hitler was not to be out-maneuvered. On March 11, 1938, after a German ultimatum, Schuschnigg resigned. The following day German troops crossed the border, and on March 13 Seyss-Inquart declared the union of Austria and Germany. In April, Hitler held his own plebiscite in both countries, with 99.08 per cent of the German vote and 99.75 per cent of the Austrian vote ratifying the union. *Anschluss* was complete. The Duce, though hurt that he had not been consulted in advance, nonetheless did nothing.

Nor did the British government make more than a feeble protest. Indeed, the elections of the summer of 1937 had brought something of a revolution to British foreign policy. The new Conservative prime minister, Neville Chamberlain (1864–1940), who had established a good record as the administrator of welfare programs, intended to direct foreign policy himself. Chamberlain was opinionated and arrogant; he put little stock in warnings against the Hitlerian menace given him by British foreign-office experts. He was not a coward by any means, but he sincerely believed that another conflict of the magnitude of the First World War would shatter the civilized world. Although he detested Hitler, he considered some of Germany's claims just, and he thought that the Führer could be persuaded through personal contact that these claims could be peacefully negotiated.

It was essentially an unrealistic belief, for at a secret meeting of his top officials in November 1937 Hitler had declared, "Germany's problem can only be resolved by means of force." While Chamberlain could not know of this meeting, Hitler had said substantially the same thing many years before in *Mein Kampf*. Yet Chamberlain, desperately eager to avoid war, chose to ignore this fundamental fact. His policy of meeting Hitler's demands — in the belief that war could thereby be averted — came to be known as appeasement.

Chamberlain's advisers, however, had been aware for some time that a free hand in Austria was not enough to satisfy Hitler. In 1935 the Führer had begun to subsidize the activities of the Sudeten Germans led by Konrad Henlein, who in 1938 was instructed by Hitler to escalate his demands upon the Czech government. The appeal for fairer treatment for the Sudeten German minority was replaced by the call for full autonomy for the German areas of Czechoslovakia. Neville Chamberlain thought this a reasonable solution to the problem, and he brought pressure to bear on the Prague government to accede. He did not know that at the end of May Hitler had drafted a directive that began: "It is my unalterable decision to smash Czechoslovakia by military action in the near future."

Over the summer, fruitless negotiations between the Czech government and the Sudeten Germans were held. On September 12, Hitler's closing speech at the Nazi party rally at Nuremburg was the signal for a rising in the Sudetenland; but the Prague government had the situation well in hand, and Henlein broke off all negotiations with the government and left for Germany. Chamberlain decided to take the sensational step of flying to Germany to discuss the crisis with Hitler. Accordingly, on September 15 he flew to Berchtesgaden in the Bavarian Alps, where he agreed to the detachment of the Sudeten area from Czechoslovakia, asking only that Hitler gave him time to return home and persuade his cabinet. This Hitler generously agreed to do.

On September 22, Chamberlain met with Hitler again, this time at Godesberg, with a plan to transfer the Sudeten districts to Germany peacefully. The Czech government had been forced to agree to this plan, on pain of being left alone to face the Germans. Now, however, Hitler asked for further concessions from the Czechs: immediate surrender of the Sudeten areas, plebiscites in other areas with large German minorities, and satisfaction of Polish, Hungarian, and Slovak claims. Chamberlain was outraged by Hitler's new demands, and there was much sentiment in the British cabinet that the limit had been reached. At the last minute, however, after frantic Anglo-French discussions, and when it was evident that nothing was to be expected from the United States, Chamberlain appealed to Mussolini to bring Hitler to the conference table again.

The third conference, attended by Hitler, Mussolini, Chamberlain, and

Daladier, was held at Munich on September 29. With the Czechs excluded from the meeting, it was quickly agreed that Germany was to occupy the Sudetenland by October 10 and that plebiscites would be held in certain other heavily German areas; Czech areas populated predominantly by those of Polish and Hungarian extraction also faced annexation. For their part, Germany and Italy promised to guarantee the revised Czechoslovak frontiers once all outstanding territorial claims against Czechoslovakia had been met. (The guarantees were never given.) Again Czechoslovakia accepted the terms after being assured that it would otherwise have to fight Germany alone. Chamberlain flew home, declaring on his arrival, "I believe there will be peace in our time." He referred to the Czech crisis as a "quarrel in a far-away country between people of whom we know nothing." Daladier, expecting to be met at the Paris airport with rotten eggs, was greeted instead by wildly cheering crowds.

This was not the end of the Czechoslovak crisis, despite Chamberlain's optimistic belief that he had assuaged the demands of the Third Reich. The armaments, gold, and potential *Luftwaffe* bases of Czechoslovakia still made the weakened republic a tempting prize. In mid-March 1939, Hitler brought pressure on the rather unwilling Slovak minority in Czechoslovakia to declare its independence, and on this pretext German forces marched into Prague on March 15. Two days later, Chamberlain warned the Führer that if his latest move was a step towards dominating the world by force, Great Britain would resist the challenge. But the British declined to act as Czechoslovakia was joined to the Reich under the pretext that the action of the Slovaks had caused "internal disruption." Nor did Britain or any other power act when Mussolini—not to be left behind—seized Albania in April. However, the British government was made aware of the German threat as never before. For the first time, Hitler had joined non-Germans to Germany, and the British began to look around for the Nazis' next victim, convinced that they would have to give it support.

The British believed that the Germans would next demand a protectorate over Rumania, a country almost impossible to supply and assist, given its geographic position. Hoping to line up an ally bordering Rumania, Britain tried to induce Poland to join a four-power pact including France and Russia. The Poles refused, fearing to provoke Germany by any alliance with the Soviets. But Chamberlain was able to get Polish acceptance of an Anglo-French guarantee of aid in the event of aggression on Poland. The end result of these efforts, ostensibly directed at protecting Rumania and satisfying anti-German public opinion in Great Britain, did not reduce the tensions between Poland and Germany. Having grandly announced his guarantee of Poland in Parliament at the end of March, Chamberlain could not back down as he had in the Sudeten crisis. Thus appeasement had sacrificed a loyal ally in Czechoslovakia, and now efforts to avoid further appeasement were creating a situation where Britain would be forced to support a most reluctant ally—Poland.

Polish-German relations worsened rapidly after the disappearance of Czechoslovakia. In October after Munich, the German foreign minister, Joachim von Ribbentrop, suggested three proposals for Polish consideration: the return of Danzig to the Reich, the construction of a road and railroad across the Polish Corridor to connect East Prussia with the Reich, and Poland's adherence to the anti-Comintern pact. In return, Germany would guarantee Poland's borders. For a time the Poles were allowed to evade an answer, as Hitler was preoccupied with Czechoslovakian affairs. In late March 1939, however, pressure was renewed on the Polish government. Chamberlain's announcement of a guarantee to Poland surprised and angered Hitler, but he ordered his generals to prepare a war plan just the same.

Diplomatic maneuverings continued during the summer of 1939: Hitler hoped to isolate Poland to achieve another Munich, while the French and British tried to negotiate some sort of pact with Russia, for they could do little themselves to protect or assist Poland. But negotiations between Russia and the Western powers made little progress. The Poles had refused to countenance the entry of Russian troops under any agreement, and the British were uneasy about concluding an alliance with the Bolsheviks. They doubted the strength of the Soviet army (the recent purges had thinned the officer corps badly), and they could offer little to Stalin. Hitler could offer him much more—a guarantee that Russia would not find itself fighting Germany and an agreement on respective holdings in eastern Europe. Hitler had no scru-

The Czechoslovak state set up after World War I included a German minority numbering three million in the Sudetenland. When Hitler threatened to go to war to incorporate the Sudetenland into Germany, the French and British governments brought pressure on the Czech government to cede that territory to the Reich. This move in turn encouraged Hungary and Poland to demand their own slices. Finally, in March 1939, the rest of Czechoslovakia was swallowed up as France and Britain stood by. Bohemia-Moravia and Slovakia became German protectorates, while Hungary took over the whole of Ruthenia.

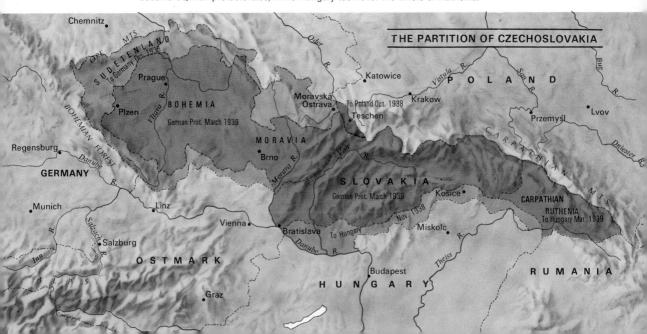

ples about reversing his anti-Bolshevik stand if he could gain so spectacular a diplomatic coup. During the spring and summer, Germany manufactured incidents to provoke and discredit the Poles, signed a military alliance with Italy (the "Pact of Steel"), and in August carried on negotiations with Russia.

On August 23 it was announced that Germany and Russia had concluded a nonaggression pact. Each of the signatories agreed that if the other power became involved in a war, it would not help the other power's enemies (nor would it participate in any grouping aimed against the other power). A secret protocol divided eastern Europe into German and Russian spheres of influence. To Hitler's surprise, the British government reiterated its guarantee to Poland. And an alarmed Mussolini emphasized that Italy still needed three years in which to prepare for war. For the next six days the attack on Poland was postponed, as further German attempts were made to detach the British. In the end the attempts failed; the Chamberlain government would not be bribed by an offer of recognition for the British Empire.

At 8:00 P.M. on August 31 the SS faked a Polish attack on a German radio station. At dawn on September 1, German guns began to fire on Poland. The Chamberlain government delayed sending an ultimatum to Berlin until the morning of September 3. The ultimatum expired that day at 11:00 A.M., and Britain at once declared war on Germany. France declared war on Germany at 5:00 in the afternoon. For the time being, Italy remained neutral.

The military struggle that began with Germany's Polish campaign was to reach a magnitude undreamed of by the diplomats of the interwar era. Tens of millions of men were to be engaged in campaigns in Europe, on the Asian mainland, on scores of Pacific islands, in North Africa, on the oceans, and in the air over much of the world. The amount of strategic materials produced and expended and the number of civilian and military casualties suffered would have seemed absolutely beyond the powers of the nations of the 1930's to survive.

V THE SECOND WORLD WAR

The Axis Advance

Once war was declared, the German military proceeded to rout the Polish army. It had the advantages of larger size, better equipment, better training, and superior mobility. Particularly effective was the *blitzkrieg* (lightning war) of *panzer* (armored) divisions, supported by dive bombers of the *Luftwaffe* and using tactics developed in the Spanish Civil War. By September 17, when the Soviets invaded Poland from the east, the campaign was almost over. Warsaw was defended until September 27. After its fall, Poland was partitioned once again.

What became the blitzkrieg method of warfare had been expounded as early as the 1920's by a British army captain, Liddell Hart. In the 1930's, a French officer, Charles de Gaulle (b. 1890), had tried to persuade the French high command to prepare for rapid attack with tanks and planes. But the French generals, having lost millions of men in reckless infantry offensives in the First World War, had become defense-minded. It was the brilliant German generals who applied the new battle techniques, while the French constructed the Maginot Line, a defensive system designed with the military mobility and firepower of 1914, not 1940, in mind. While Hitler attacked Poland, the French army and a British expeditionary force on the western front—which were both led by timid and thoroughly incompetent generals—did nothing.

The winter of 1939–1940 has been described as the "phony war." In England, precautions were taken for air raids that did not come. Bombing of civilians was renounced by the British, and the Royal Air Force bombarded the Germans with propaganda leaflets. The British blockade of Germany was ineffectual because Germany could get necessary materials from Italy, the Soviet Union, and Sweden. The Germans, again inferior at sea, relied on submarines and a few surface raiders to harass merchant shipping.

The three Baltic states acquiesced to Soviet military control, but Finland refused. At the end of November 1939 the Russian army attacked, but the Finns held. There was talk of raising an Allied expeditionary force, but Norway and Sweden refused to allow it to cross their territory. A second Soviet offensive succeeded, and the Finnish government made peace on March 12, ceding to Russia the important Karelian Isthmus.

On April 9, 1940, Hitler moved against Norway and Denmark, principally to secure his supply of iron ore but also for their strategic value. In Norway, Nazi fifth columnists (a term for traitors coined in the Spanish Civil War) led by Vidkun Quisling helped to deliver the government into German hands. An Allied attempt to open a Norwegian front was entirely insufficient and militarily disastrous. The British blamed their government. Chamberlain attempted to form a coalition cabinet, but the Liberals and Labour refused to serve under him. He was forced to resign, and Winston Churchill became the new prime minister.

Although in retrospect the choice of Churchill as a war leader seems right and inevitable, his career before 1940 had been a chequered one. A member of the reforming Liberal cabinet before World War I, he served in Conservative cabinets in the 1920's and remained in Parliament, though out of power, during the period of the National Government. He was suspect by both parties for his apparent instability and lack of judgment, and his warnings of the Nazi threat were ignored. However, as the thirties continued and the German menace gradually grew obvious, Churchill's admirers became more numerous, and after the outbreak of war, Chamberlain had to take him into the cabinet as First Lord of the Admiralty. In a very short time after he assumed full power in 1940, his energy and dynamism had made him the beloved leader of the nation. His ability to sink old differences made the war cabinet a genuine coalition, and his personal charm and courage made as many friends—including President Roosevelt—as his mistakes had made enemies. The inspiration of Churchill's wartime eloquence contributed immeasurably to the war effort, encouraging the British and Americans alike.

On May 10, 1940, the German westward assault finally began. With a maniacal belief in his invincible destiny, Hitler made a tremendous gamble and won. Some military historians believe that behind his well equipped and superbly led first-line army Hitler's reserves were inadequate in quality and quantity and that if the French could have withstood the initial onslaught, the position of the German army would have been precarious. But the defenses of Belgium, the Netherlands, and Luxembourg were quickly breached, and the main German forces invaded France through the Ardennes forest, which was thought to be militarily impenetrable. The British Expeditionary Force and the French First Army on the French frontier between the Ardennes and the English Channel, were cut off from the south by May 20. They retreated to Dunkirk, where some 335,000 troops were evacuated by sea between May 27 and June 4. Elsewhere the Allies were even less successful: the Maginot Line had been flanked, and on June 14 the unthinkable happened —Paris was occupied. Mussolini had hurried to declare war on France and Britain on June 10.

The French government—which had shown itself divided, defeatist, and corrupt—disintegrated in the face of German victory. Marshal Pétain now headed a new French government whose sole task was to negotiate an armistice. This it did, while General Charles de Gaulle flew to London, where he laid the groundwork for a Free French movement to liberate France. The Germans occupied the northern half of France, and a puppet regime for the rest of the country was established at Vichy. It was headed by Pétain and the devious right-wing politician Pierre Laval. Ostensibly, the regime devoted itself to the moral regeneration of the French people; in practice, this meant that it was a reactionary government that betrayed everything the French Revolution had signified.

The attack on France did not bring the United States into the war—isolationist sentiment there was much too strong. But Roosevelt was able to take other measures to help the Allies as well as protect the United States. Armament production was stepped up. The President called for 50,000 planes, and a huge naval construction program was inaugurated. And after Mussolini abandoned neutrality, the United States became a "nonbelligerent," supplying all the arms it could spare to the British government.

Having reached additional agreements with Russia about the spoils of eastern Europe, Germany now planned to attack the British Isles. Operation Sea Lion was to take place in August 1940, but on July 31 it was postponed to September. The *Luftwaffe* was to be the key to the invasion's success; the relative weakness of the German navy meant that the air force would have to neutralize both the RAF and the British navy. Large-scale raids on British airfields, and on civilian areas as well, began in mid-August. After suffering a thousand-plane attack on several cities on August 15, the British retaliated with raids on Berlin and other German cities. The result was that the Germans—for prestige reasons—now concentrated on bombing the metropolitan area. The London blitz began at the very time when continued attacks on British airfields would probably have eliminated the RAF within a few days. Aided by an effective radar warning system, the RAF fighters were just able to keep the German bombers from controlling the air, and when German air supremacy was not won by September 17, Hitler's invasion plan had to be shelved. In any case, the Germans had not been able to develop effective techniques and equipment for an amphibious landing on the British coast. Britain was now to be worn down gradually by an air and sea war.

German submarines, surface raiders, and bombers sank an enormous tonnage of British merchant shipping, despite extensive use of the convoy system. In early December, Churchill wrote to Roosevelt—who had just been elected to an unprecedented third term—that England was gravely threatened and needed American aircraft and American aid to keep the North Atlantic sea lanes open. Moreover, the British government was running out of money. The following March, Congress passed the Lend-Lease Act, which allowed the President to turn war supplies over to England to be paid for in goods and services at the end of the war. Most immediately useful in Britain's antisubmarine warfare were fifty American destroyers dating from the First World War. Lend-Lease supplies and other American assistance enabled Britain to continue the fight.

Having turned away from the British Isles, Hitler next planned to invade and conquer Russia (Operation Barbarossa) in a campaign scheduled to begin in June 1941 and to be completed within five months. First, however, the Germans had to rescue an Italian army that had launched an attack on Greece in October 1940 and had been checked all winter by a Greek army half its size (aided in the air by the RAF). Hungary, Rumania, and Bulgaria had already been brought into the Axis, and German troops forced both Yugoslavia and Greece to capitulate by April 1941. Also successful that spring and summer (though not decisive because General Erwin Rommel was not given enough troops to drive to the Suez Canal) was the campaign to expel the British from North Africa and thereby dominate the Mediterranean.

For some time Britain and the United States had been warning the USSR that it was to be Hitler's next target, but Stalin had chosen not to cut free from his ally. The purges of the 1930's had decimated the Soviet army officer corp, and he desperately hoped that he would not have to confront the German army for several years. The attack of three million German troops on June 22, 1941, therefore, caught the Russian army largely unprepared. Stalin at the first provided little or no leadership, and the German blitzkrieg advanced rapidly. Churchill offered Stalin an alliance, which was concluded on July 13. Great Britain sent aid to the USSR, and in November, American Lend-Lease was extended to Russia. The Germans launched three massive drives against Moscow, Leningrad, and Kiev, but only Kiev fell. Under Marshal Georgi Zukhov, the Soviet army began to offer stiffer resistance, and drives on Moscow and Leningrad bogged down and became sieges at the end of October. Once again the Russian winter helped stall a foreign invader.

Hitler had seriously underestimated both the size and skill of the Soviet army. In the winter of 1941–1942, he faced a new enemy, whose enormous potential he also discounted. The entrance of the United States into the war as a full belligerent came about as the result of a surprise attack by the Japanese on the American fleet at Pearl Harbor on December 7. Since 1937 Japan had been engaged in large-scale military operations in China—operations for which Japan needed strategic raw materials that could be found in British, Dutch, or French holdings in the Pacific. Having calculated that they would

After disabling the American fleet at Pearl Harbor, the Japanese armed forces could move through the western Pacific at will. In short order they took Singapore, moved on to Burma, and threatened India. One after another, America's Pacific bases surrendered. The last American forces surrendered at Bataan and Corregidor after a prolonged siege. A Japanese naval victory in the Battle of Java Sea cleared the way to the Dutch East Indies, but the Japanese fleet was ultimately turned back by the Allies as it was steaming through the Coral Sea. In June 1942 at Midway the Japanese were intercepted and beaten back by American forces in a four-day air and naval battle. This was the turning point of the war in the Pacific.

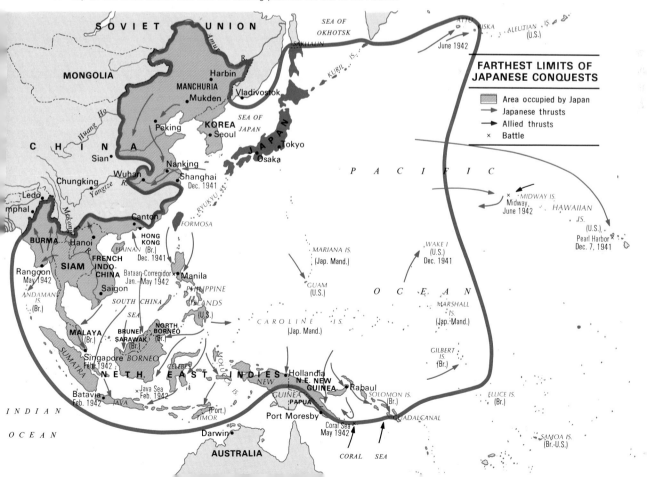

have to seize these areas to succeed on the Chinese mainland and that such a step would mean war with the United States, they resolved to strike first. Germany declared war on the United States a few days later.

After crippling nearly half the American fleet in the raid on Pearl Harbor, the Japanese scored repeated successes in the Pacific. Britain lost several frontline ships immediately after Pearl Harbor, and the Japanese destroyed the American air force in the Philippines while it was still on the ground. Hong Kong and Malaya fell between December and February and the Dutch East Indies in March. At Singapore the British suffered the worst defeat in their history. A large British garrison surrendered with little resistance. The guns of the British fortress there could be pointed only toward the sea; no one had foreseen that the Japanese would come down the Malayan peninsula and attack from the rear. The United States lost Wake Island and Guam before Christmas, and the Philippines fell soon after, although the American strongholds at Bataan and Corregidor held out until April and May of 1942. In early May, however, the Japanese navy was defeated in the Battle of the Coral Sea, and the next month an American victory in a great naval battle at Midway restored the balance of naval power in the Pacific and halted the Japanese drive toward Australia.

The United States and Britain now prepared for counterattack. In a cooperative manner never achieved by the Allies in the First World War, they joined their commands and resources under the direction of the combined chiefs of staff. It was decided for the present to engage in a holding action against the Japanese and to concentrate Allied power against Hitler's *Festung Europa* – "Fortress Europe."

Life in Occupied Countries

The most accurate description of the ruthless treatment of citizens of countries that fell to the Nazis during the first years of the war is found in Hermann Goering's own words: "I intend to plunder and to do it thoroughly." And Nazi "plundering" encompassed oppression, regimentation, slave labor, torture, and murder.

The immediate wartime needs of the German Reich were to be met by mass seizure of the resources of the conquered lands: foodstuffs, machinery, raw materials, workers. This requisitioning was to be effected without regard for the welfare of the subject peoples. In Russia, it was expected that "many tens of millions of people in the industrial areas will become redundant and will either die or have to emigrate to Siberia." Since the Reich needed slave labor to keep its industry functioning while its men were fighting at the front, huge herds of workers were transported into the Reich to work in industry and agriculture. Those in the heavily bombed industrial centers were the worst off, for they lived under primitive conditions, exposed to epidemics, and were ill-fed and frequently beaten. By the end of 1944 some 4,795,000 foreign workers had been "recruited" to work inside Germany, and of those no more than 200,000 came willingly.

As Hitler explained at a conference in July 1941, the captive peoples in eastern and western Europe were to be kept in permanent subjection after the war's end. Part of the population was to provide slave labor for the industries and agriculture of the Third Reich. They would have no rights, receive no education, be at the arbitrary disposal of their German overlords. The "surplus" population—which included those whose superior education or social status might enable them to organize resistance to the Nazi regime—would be exterminated or left to starve. The instrument for carrying out this program was Himmler's SS. As Himmler described the program in October 1943: "Whether nations live in prosperity or starve to death interests me only in so far as we need them as slaves for our *Kultur*. . . ."

A particular duty of the SS elite was the organization of concentration camps. Prior to the outbreak of war, such places had been the prisons for opponents of the regime. After 1939 many millions of Jews and other political or racial prisoners, as well as resistance fighters from occupied countries, were housed in them. In 1942 inmates began to be used as labor in the armaments industry. Certain categories of prisoners were judged "suitable to be worked to death," while many inmates were forced to be subjects of medical experiments performed by SS doctors.

It was in the extermination camps, however, that the worst crimes against humanity were perpetrated. In 1941 the decision was made to exterminate the country's "racial enemies." By the end of the war the Nazis had murdered some 8.5 million human beings, 6 million of whom were Jews. Anti-Semitism was no longer merely a propaganda tool; the "final solution" was an act of genocide of a ferocity and magnitude unprecedented in European history.

Not surprisingly, the atrocities of the Nazi regime fostered resistance movements within the subject populations. In Poland, where about 20 per cent of the population (6.5 million) was murdered during the war, an extraordinary resistance movement kept alive an entire underground "state." The Jews in the Warsaw ghetto rose in hopeless revolt before they were exterminated. The Czechs were unable to put up any organized resistance; Slovakia was an ally of sorts for the Germans. In Yugoslavia, although the resistance forces fought against one another, the Communist partisans, led by Tito, wished to form an allied resistance front against the Nazis. The French were treated better than the conquered Slavs, for they were thought to be more desirable (racially) by the Germans. Pétain and Laval, leaders of the collaborationist French government centered at Vichy, were able to keep German demands within bearable limits until 1942 when the Nazis took over control of the whole country. After that, the French resistance fought Germans all over France. The resistance was nominally under the control of General de Gaulle, although local autonomy was a tactical necessity and at one point the French Communists attempted to gain the leadership. In Russia, Himmler's harsh measures soon destroyed whatever initially friendly reception had been accorded the invading German armies. Many had longed to be free of the Stalinist regime, but they were quickly disillusioned by the treatment meted out by their German liberators. Partisan activity was most prevalent in areas where the Germans demanded new sacrifices from the people and where it became likely that the Soviet army would return.

The nightmare of life for the vanquished under Nazi rule was a bitter fore-taste of the fate awaiting the Allies should they fail to defeat Hitler. This horrible specter gave added incentive and urgency to their war efforts.

Allied Victory

The second half of 1942 saw the beginnings of a reversal of Axis successes. The Battle of Midway, which redressed the balance in the Pacific, was fol-lowed by the Battle of El Alamein in North Africa (October 23), where a superior British force under General Bernard Montgomery drove an Italo-German army under Rommel into retreat. In November, American, British, and Commonwealth armies commanded by General Dwight D. Eisenhower made major landings in North Africa. The Germans responded by occupying previously unoccupied Vichy France. By May of 1943 the North African campaign had ended in a complete Allied triumph. The Axis armies were unable to escape; over a quarter of a million prisoners were taken; and Italy's will to fight was badly shaken.

By 1942 the Soviet army had been reorganized. Now supplied with arms from Soviet industry that had been relocated in the trans-Ural region, the Russians fought the German army to a standstill outside Leningrad and began to push back the Nazi forces on the Moscow front. The Germans, however, were still capable of striking deadly blows. Hitler, who had now taken over supreme command of the German army, launched a drive on the Caucasus, whose oil he desperately needed.

Guarding the northern flank of the entrance to the Caucasus was the city of Stalingrad on the Volga River. The Germans penetrated the city and reduced most of it to rubble. But the Russian army would not abandon the ruins, and as the weeks went by, fighting continued in the streets and from building to building. Then Russian armies surrounded the city, trapping the German Sixth Army. Thinking only of his prestige, Hitler ignored sane military princi-ples and the entreaties of his commanders and ordered the Sixth to hold rather than try to fight its way out. In January 1943 what remained of this entire army was captured, and in the spring a Russian counteroffensive on a wide front was successful. Germany and its allies lost 300,000 men in the Battle of Stalingrad, and Hitler never regained the initiative. By now Germany was beginning to experience manpower and materiel shortages.

In January of 1943, Churchill and Roosevelt met at Casablanca to review Allied strategy, particularly in the Mediterranean. Churchill wished to invade Italy immediately; American military leaders pressed for a later invasion of northern France. A compromise was reached whereby an invasion of Sicily was to be undertaken to secure an additional base for the strategic bombing of Germany in the year to come. Roosevelt announced that unconditional surrender would be demanded from the Axis powers.

Before the invasion of Sicily (Operation Husky) got under way, the Allies, using radar and hunter-killer groups of aircraft carriers and destroyers, managed to stem the tide of shipping losses to the German submarines. The invasion of Sicily on July 10 had immediate repercussions in Italy proper. To prevent discontent arising from the economic hardships of the war from becoming revolution, the king and the army command dismissed Mussolini on July 25, after the Fascist Grand Council had voted no confidence in him. The new government almost immediately dissolved the Fascist party and began secret negotiations for peace.

Churchill had won United States consent to an invasion of the Italian mainland, and the first landings were made in Calabria on September 2. The next day the Italian government concluded an armistice with the Allies and joined their ranks as a "cobelligerent," pledging its fleet to the Allies and further cooperation in establishing Allied administration throughout Italy. But Hitler was not ready to see Italy fall without a fight, and German forces bitterly contested the Allies' advance northward. The Germans rescued Mussolini from detention and set him up in a puppet state in northern Italy. But the Axis' position was becoming steadily more desperate. The Allies' supply of men and weapons was so great that the Germans could do no more than delay the inevitable defeat. Furthermore, continuous Allied bombing—the RAF in night raids and the United States Air Force in daylight attacks—was inflicting a tremendous loss of life and property on German cities, although the massive air raids never achieved their intended purpose of decisively crippling German war production.

In late November of 1943, Roosevelt, Churchill, and Stalin met at Teheran. There the main order of business was strategy for an Allied invasion of France—the second European front that Stalin had been requesting since 1942. Roosevelt was particularly conciliatory to Russian ambitions, believing that Russia was the decisive factor in the European theater and that it would inevitably dominate eastern Europe after the war. After Teheran a plan was implemented to crush the Nazis between Allied forces in the west and Soviet armies in the east. In May, on the eve of the proposed invasion of France, the Russian army was poised to attack Nazi forces in the Baltic states, Poland, and East Prussia. In eastern Europe the Soviet offensive stopped short of Warsaw, allowing the German army to wipe out the resistance fighters who were loyal to the anti-Communist Polish government-in-exile. By October, Russian forces had won control of the Baltic states. Finland requested an armistice at the end of August, and in December a joint operation of Finnish and Russian forces drove the Germans from that country. During September

THE ALLIED TRIUMPH V-E DAY MAY 8, 1945

Allies and areas they controlled November 1942
Areas retaken by Allies
Areas held by Germany on V-E Day
Neutral nations
Allied thrusts
Axis thrusts

ARCTIC
OCEAN

Murmansk

WHITE
SEA
Arkhangelsk

ATLANTIC

OCEAN

Allied supply convoys

FAEROE IS.
Den.

SHETLAND IS.

ORKNEY
IS.
Scapa
Flow

Perm

N. Dvina R.

Trondheim

N O R W A Y

S W E D E N

F I N L A N D

S O V I E T

Lake
Onega

Lake
Ladoga

Bergen

Glasgow

Oslo

Stockholm

Helsinki

Leningrad

Kazan

Gorki

GREAT
Dublin

BRITAIN
Liverpool

IRELAND

Birmingham

London
Southampton

Invasion on D-Day

BALTIC
SEA

Göteborg

DENMARK
Copenhagen

Hamburg

Tallinn
ESTONIA

Pskov

Moscow

Saratov

N O R T H
S E A

NETHERLANDS

BELGIUM
Le Havre

GERMANY
Hanover

Berlin

Danzig

Riga
LATVIA

Dvina

LITHUANIA
Kaunas

Minsk

Smolensk

Voronezh

Don R.

Volga R.

Stalingrad

Stalingrad
Nov. 1942-
Feb. 1943

Cologne

Remagen Mar.1945

Battle of the Bulge
Dec. 1944-Jan. 1945

Frankfurt

Dresden

Prague

Vistula

Warsaw

P O L A N D

Kiev

Kharkov

Dnieper R.

Rostov

Paris

Loire R.

Nantes

F R A N C E

Rhine R.

Munich

CZECHOSLOVAKIA

Vienna

Krakow

Lvov

Dniester R.

Odessa

Sevastopol

Sea of
Azov

Vichy

Lyons

SWITZERLAND

AUSTRIA

HUNGARY
Budapest

RUMANIA

Bordeaux

Milan

Trieste

Venice

Bucharest

Danube

Marseilles

Genoa

A D R I A T I C
S E A

Belgrade

YUGOSLAVIA

BULGARIA
Sofia

B L A C K   S E A

Trabzon

Madrid

Barcelona

CORSICA

Rome ×Anzio Jan.1944

ALBANIA

Istanbul

Ankara

Kizil R.

T U R K E Y

Adana

S P A I N

Valencia

BALEARIC IS.

SARDINIA

TYRRHENIAN

Naples

ITALY

Salerno Sept.
1943

GREECE

Salonika

AEGEAN
SEA

Smyrna

Aleppo

SYRIA

Allied landings Nov. 1942

M

Palermo

SICILY

SEA

IONIAN
SEA

Athens

CRETE

CYPRUS
Br.

Damascus

Beirut

Oran

Algiers

Bône

Tunis

MALTA
Br.

Kasserine Pass
Feb. 1943

TUNISIA

M E D I T E R R A N E A N   S E A

Jerusalem

PALESTINE

TRANSJORDAN

A L G E R I A
Joined Allies Nov. 1942

Tripoli

Bengasi

Alexandria

El Alamein ×
Oct. 1942

Cairo

Suez
Canal

SAUDI
ARABIA

L I B Y A

E G Y P T

Nile R.

RED
SEA

and October the Russian army pressed into Rumania, Bulgaria, and Hungary, setting up pro-Communist regimes as it went. In Greece a pro-Western regime was established as a result of an agreement between Churchill and Stalin; Anglo-American troops landed in Greece and, after liberating it from the Germans, put down the Communist resistance forces.

On the morning of June 6, 1944, the largest amphibious operation in history began the invasion of France with the storming of the Normandy beaches. In the first day the Allies, under General Eisenhower's command, landed 130,000 men, and within a month they had committed a million troops to the battle for France. The Allied forces were obviously superior, but Hitler forbade retreat. He believed that his so-called secret weapons—the V-1 "flying bombs" (unmanned airplanes) and the V-2 ballistic missiles—which had begun to fall on London, could still save him from defeat. But the Allies were now about to overrun the German rocket bases. On July 20 a small group of German generals and aristocrats attempted to assassinate Hitler, in the hope of freeing the army of his fanatical control and ending the war through negotiation—but the attempt accidentally miscarried, and Hitler wrought awful vengeance on thousands of dissidents and uninvolved Germans.

The Allies pushed their way out of Normandy and entered Paris on August 24. To the end, Churchill and Roosevelt hoped to reach an agreement with Vichy, but it became clear that the French people followed de Gaulle, and Gaullist authorities took over the administration of the country as soon as the Germans fled. Shortly after the war the collaborators were punished: Laval was executed and Pétain imprisoned for life.

When the Allies pressed closer to Germany, resistance was much more stubborn. At the end of 1944 the Nazi forces scored a last, temporary success in the savage Battle of the Bulge. By mid-January 1945 the Russians were attacking from the east once again. On January 17 they captured Warsaw and set up a puppet government. In March they entered Austria, and on April 17 they took Vienna. The Allied victory in Italy was completed late in April 1945. Captured by anti-Fascist Italian partisans while trying to escape to Switzerland, Mussolini and his mistress were killed on April 28.

At the Yalta Conference of February 4–12, 1945, Churchill, Roosevelt, and Stalin met for the second and last time. It was decided that Germany should be broken up into separate states (this decision was soon dropped) and should be controlled by the three victorious powers and France. The Russo-Polish border was fixed at the old Curzon Line of 1919. Stalin promised that the new governments in Poland and Yugoslavia would be enlarged to include some

The winter of 1942–1943 marked the turning point of Nazi fortunes. The *Wehrmacht's* siege of Stalingrad ended in a devastating defeat, and in the west the Allies made landings in North Africa and Sicily. By the spring of 1944 the Russian armies controlled the Black Sea region, and in June 1944 the western Allies opened up a second European front after a successful amphibious operation against the Normandy beaches. Though surrounded, the German armies fought doggedly. The Allies pressed slowly north through Italy and more rapidly east through France (stopping a desperate German counteroffensive at the Battle of the Bulge) while the Balkans were falling to the Russian armies. In April 1945 the eastern and western Allied armies began to meet at the Elbe River and in Austria and Bohemia.

non-Communists. And the three powers pledged to assist the newly liberated countries to create democratic governments. (It was soon clear that these promises were open to more than one interpretation.) In March, Churchill proposed that the Western armies should push as far east as possible and that Berlin should not be left to the Russians, even though it fell within the Russian sphere in Germany. This was not done, however, and by April 25 the Russians had encircled Berlin. Hitler committed suicide on April 30. On May 7 the Germans agreed to unconditional surrender.

Meanwhile, in the Pacific theater, American sea, air, and land forces under General Douglas MacArthur and Admiral Chester Nimitz were slowly but steadily winning back many of the islands the Japanese had conquered in 1941. Beginning with Guadalcanal in 1942, the Americans had taken the

The American counterattack, which began in the summer of 1942, involved island-hopping and large sea battles. The slow American conquest of Japanese-held islands brought the American forces steadily closer to Japan, while the Japanese navy was beaten back in the major engagements of Bismarck Sea, the Philippine Sea, and Leyte Gulf. Allied victories in Burma further weakened the Japanese position, and the American conquest of Okinawa in June 1945 left the American forces poised for an invasion of the Japanese mainland. The Japanese surrender on August 14, after atomic bombs had been dropped on Hiroshima and Nagasaki, made the projected invasion unnecessary.

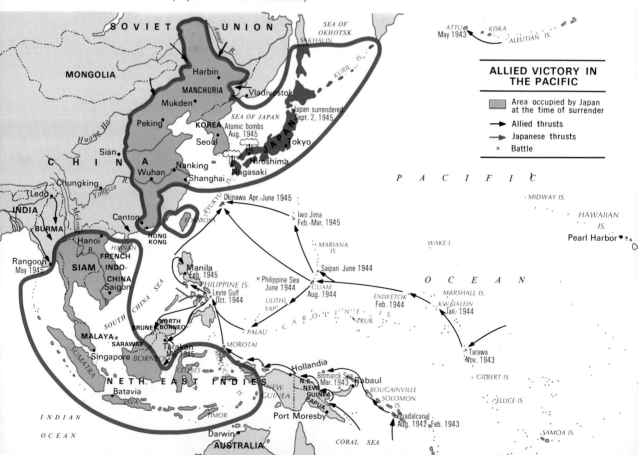

counteroffensive. Japanese troops fought to the death for every inch of rocky and sandy soil, and American losses were heavy. But American successes against the Japanese continued, culminating in the great victory of Leyte Gulf in October 1944. When the war in Europe ended, the Americans had taken Okinawa, just three hundred miles from Japan. From this and other islands a devastating air attack on Japanese cities was launched, and the United States made plans for the invasion of Japan.

Japan's position was now completely hopeless, and the emperor supported a party in the Japanese government that wished to seek a negotiated peace. But the army remained committed to a fight to the finish, and the Allies continued to demand unconditional surrender. On July 16, 1945, President Harry S. Truman (b. 1884) — who had assumed office on Roosevelt's death on April 12 — was informed that an atomic bomb had been successfully tested in New Mexico. His military advisers maintained that unless the awful new weapon was used, only invasion could force Japan to surrender and that invasion would cost thousands of American lives. Truman decided to use the bomb, and it was dropped on the Japanese city of Hiroshima on August 6, 1945. About 80,000 people were killed immediately. Many thousands died later of radiation or were maimed for life. Two days later, on August 8, Russia declared war on Japan and crossed the Manchurian frontier. A second atom bomb was dropped on Nagasaki on August 9. The following day the Japanese government offered to surrender. On August 14, the terms laid down at Potsdam were accepted, and the Second World War was over. It had been the most devastating conflict in the history of mankind, causing fifteen million military deaths and an equal number of civilian fatalities, levelling great cities, and bringing indescribable suffering on whole nations.

Yet if the taking of human life can ever be justified, the Second World War was a just war — it prevented Europe, and perhaps the world, from falling under Nazi control. It must be remembered that in 1940 Hitler's triumph seemed highly likely. If Britain, like France, had betrayed its heritage and made peace with Hitler, the end of Western civilization would have been the result. It is to the eternal credit of the British that, rallied by a great liberal from one of the first families of the British aristocracy, they chose to fight on, alone and against seemingly hopeless odds. As Churchill said, this was his country's "finest hour." What Churchill said of the RAF fighter pilots in the Battle of Britain can be said of Great Britain's role in World War II: Never have so many owed so much to so few.

The main consequence of the Second World War was that it brought to a climax the trend that had begun in the First: western Europe's power and influence in the world declined and global leadership passed to the Soviet Union and the United States. In 1945, Germany was in ashes, Japan thoroughly beaten, Britain exhausted and impoverished, France and Italy confused and demoralized. Victory lay with the United States and the Soviet Union. They were to be the superpowers of the postwar world.

15

Twentieth-Century Culture

I THE NATURAL SCIENCES

The Age of the Scientist

Science has profoundly shaped the intellectual history of the twentieth century. It has been a revolutionary spark, a pervasive cult. Men have looked to science, to technology, and to the scientific method for mastery of the material world and for assistance in their attempts to improve the human condition. If any universal symbol does exist, it is surely scientific in character and mathematical in language. Yet the confidence and admiration that caused so many people to place their trust in scientific progress has been sorely tried since 1945. Whether scientists can master their discoveries for the benefit of mankind has become a critical issue.

The most dramatic and revolutionary discoveries of modern physics were made very early in the century. Max Planck developed the quantum theory in 1900, and Einstein announced his special theory of relativity in 1905, his general theory in 1916. Ernest Rutherford (1871–1937), a New Zealander by birth, joined the famous Cavendish Laboratory at Cambridge University in 1895. At the University of Manchester in 1907 he began the work which led to the discovery in 1911 of the atomic nucleus. There Rutherford worked with the Danish physicist Niels Bohr (1885–1962), then a young student, and thus became the intellectual godfather of Bohr's work on atomic structure.

Niels Bohr was responsible for a large share of the modern understanding of the structure of matter. He applied Planck's quantum theory to Rutherford's nuclear atom, in order to make sense of the observable facts about radioactivity. Bohr used spectrum analysis to probe the atom, relating the chemical properties of an element to its spectographic characteristics and inaugurating the age of nuclear physics. In the 1920's, important discoveries were made with inadequate mathematical tools, quantum mechanics was developed, and Bohr and others contributed to the stockpile of data even while they developed the collateral mathematical theory. Bohr's Institute for Theoretical Physics in Copenhagen attracted young physicists from all over the world.

One of Bohr's associates was the German physicist Werner Heisenberg (b. 1901), whose most notable contribution to quantum mechanics was the revolutionary "uncertainty principle" (1927). Heisenberg was the first to state in mathematical language the relativist principle that, on the atomic scale, observation cannot be made without affecting the object or process observed. Whatever measuring device is used, its presence and activity inevitably alter at least one characteristic of the phenomenon under observation; thus one cannot establish both position *and* velocity (of an electron, for instance) without a definite minimum quantity of uncertainty. This principle is a building stone of modern physics, which (unlike classical physics) accepts the fact that the behavior of an individual particle of matter can never be predicted. However, the behavior of groups of particles can be predicted, and contemporary physics has, in fact, moved forward through the new science of statistics and probability. Scientists can assert with confidence that a certain proportion of a group of electrons will behave in a certain manner, even though no such prediction can be made for any individual electron.

One aspect of Einstein's special theory of relativity, its statement of the convertability of mass and energy, hinted at the enormous forces contained within the atomic nucleus. Rutherford produced the first laboratory nuclear reaction in 1919; after the discovery of the neutron by James Chadwick in 1932, nuclear reactions were produced by the Italian Enrico Fermi (1901–1954) and others, but it seemed impossible at first to apply the liberated energy to any purpose. Not until the Germans Otto Hahn and Fritz Strassmann produced barium by splitting the uranium atom in 1938 was there any real possibility of practical fission.

Their accomplishment was known to Niels Bohr because an associate of Hahn and Strassmann had fled from Nazi persecution to Copenhagen. Bohr took the news to the United States in 1939 and discussed it with Einstein, Fermi, and others who feared the military implications of work with fission in the laboratories of Nazi Germany. Fermi was the first to understand the possibilities of chain reaction and was chiefly responsible for the first nuclear reactor in a squash court at the University of Chicago in 1942. The production of self-sustaining nuclear energy was a scientific triumph of the greatest significance, and it was turned at once to military purposes. Bohr and Einstein knew that Werner Heisenberg was at work in Germany on a uranium pile, and Einstein wrote to President Roosevelt in 1939 to warn him of the German effort. After appeals to the President by other distinguished scientists, the Manhattan Project, whose purpose was to develop the military possibilities of atomic energy, was authorized.

In 1943 the Manhattan Project laboratory at Los Alamos, New Mexico, with J. Robert Oppenheimer as its director, was assigned the task of developing an atomic bomb. The first test at Alamogordo on July 16, 1945, was an outstanding success (the desert sand was fused to glass for hundreds of yards around the site). In August two atom bombs were dropped on Japan.

Hiroshima inaugurated not only a new age of science but a new kind of scientist—the government servant whose knowledge and talent is an important part of the national arsenal. Furthermore, scientists were now much more conscious of their social position and responsibilities. This was true in all advanced industrial countries, but particularly in the United States and the Soviet Union. Presumably, Soviet scientists were satisfied to follow the dictates of government leaders, but after World War II, Oppenheimer and other American scientists entered into a great debate over the human, political, and social implications of atomic science and a profound searching of their own consciences. Oppenheimer resisted the building of the hydrogen bomb—a much more devastating weapon than the bombs used against Japan—in the early 1950's, and he made important enemies. When Oppenheimer's security clearance was withdrawn in 1954, a great outcry from his colleagues expressed more than personal indignation. The Frankenstein myth appeared to be true, and the monster had locked the scientist out of his own laboratory. Certain branches of scientific research are not only secret today; they are expensive

The Conquest of Space. As early as the 1920's, the American scientist Robert Goddard claimed that it was feasible to use rockets to study the upper atmosphere and even to reach the moon. He was ignored or derided by aeronautical experts until just before his death in 1945. In that year the age of modern rocketry began with the development of the German V-2 ballistic missile by a team of scientists headed by Wernher von Braun. After the war, von Braun and several of his colleagues went to work for the United States. But other German rocket experts had entered the service of the Soviet Union. In 1957 the launching of an unmanned Soviet satellite, Sputnik I, produced a panic reaction in the United States; by 1959 the Jupiter C rocket (left), developed by von Braun and his group, was able to launch an American unmanned satellite. In the early 1960's American rocket development moved ahead rapidly, with 1970 as the target date for a moon landing. In 1965, during the Gemini-Titan 4 orbital flight, Edward H. White (right) became the first man to walk in space. The landing on the moon in July 1969 by the space module Eagle, together with the two-hour moon walk by American astronauts Armstrong and Aldrin (far right), was in the words of the former "one giant leap for mankind" in the conquest and exploration of space.

secrets: the cyclotrons and reactors of the 1960's are far beyond the means of any university or other institution without government support.

Rocketry and Space

Although rockets have been used in war since the early nineteenth century, they were never very effective before the days of modern electronics and nuclear warheads. Modern rocketry began in Germany, where the V-2 robot bomb that contributed to the horrors of the Nazi blitz against London during World War II was developed under the direction of Wernher von Braun in the 1930's and early 1940's. The sophisticated rockets of the next quarter-century were used both for long-range ballistic missiles and in the exploration of outer space. Intercontinental missiles could be armed with nuclear or thermonuclear warheads; in fact, they were so expensive to build that the destructive capacity of a conventional warhead would not justify the cost. The development of solid fuels and inertial guidance systems made it possible to devastate a target anywhere on earth with a missile shot from a plane, a surface vessel or submarine, or a silo. The very existence of such weapons, of course, encouraged the development of equally complicated and expensive defensive systems, or antimissile missiles; the possibilities for escalation of weaponry became endless.

As missile-carrying rockets grew more sophisticated during the arms race of the 1950's, it became obvious that it was possible to build a rocket powerful enough to escape the earth's gravitational field. The first artificial satellite (Sputnik I) was put into orbit by the USSR on October 4, 1957. This scientific and engineering triumph produced a panic among government officials and military men in the United States (with repercussions in American education), and the humiliation was shortly compounded by Yuri Gagarin's orbit of the earth in April 1961. The American Mercury, Gemini, and Apollo programs were conceived and put into execution as fast as possible, and the astronaut Alan Shepard went into suborbital flight in May 1961, inaugurating the American manned space program, which caught up with and then surpassed the Russian program shortly thereafter. In 1968 and early 1969, American manned spacecraft circumnavigated the moon, preparatory to a landing on the moon's surface. On July 20, 1969, the American astronauts Neil A. Armstrong and Edwin A. Aldrin, Jr., landed on the moon near the Sea of Tranquility and spent a couple of hours walking on the surface collecting rock samples. In the opinion of many, this feat inaugurated a new era in the history of mankind. It was at least a superb tribute to the achievement of post-World War II science and technology.

Spy satellites permit the major powers to scan one another's terrains, and weather satellites provide a great deal of information to meteorologists. Communications satellites allow instantaneous intercontinental telecasting. But few economic or social assets can be expected from men on the moon, and in space exploration as in nuclear physics, scientists and laymen debate the value and expedience of the programs. Can the enormous cost in money, materials, and brains be justified in a world where so many human needs are not met?

The Biological Sciences

The early twentieth century saw the greatest changes in the physical sciences since the Age of Newton. In the mid-twentieth century, the biological sciences experienced a revolution of comparable importance. The most dramatic discovery was that of the structure of the molecule of DNA (deoxyribonucleic acid) by Francis H. C. Crick and James D. Watson in Cambridge, England, in the early 1950's. DNA is the fundamental genetic material, and the new understanding of its structure was expected ultimately to reveal the working of the genetic code and even permit men to interfere in the process of heredity. The result has been an "explosion in biochemistry which has transformed the science."[1]

Modern medicine has extended human life, chiefly through the incredible

1. Sir Lawrence Bragg, foreword to James D. Watson, *The Double Helix*. New York: Atheneum, 1968, p. vii.

range and variety of new drugs and techniques in chemotherapy and surgery. Sulfanilimide was synthesized from coal tar in the 1930's; it was the first drug to act specifically against streptococcal infections and was used widely in the treatment of wounds during World War II. The effectiveness of penicillin — the first and greatest of the antibiotics — was first noticed by Alexander Fleming (1881 – 1955) in 1928; the strain was isolated during the 1930's, and wartime needs propelled it into production. Penicillin and related drugs have lengthened human life and incidentally added to the burdens of twentieth-century man, one of whose major problems is overpopulation.

Viruses are not as susceptible to drugs as bacteria, but in certain instances they have succumbed to the growing science of immunology. The most important recent advance in this field was the development by the Americans Jonas Salk and Albert Sabin of vaccines that provided immunity to polio. Insulin, discovered by two Canadians, Frederick Banting and Charles Best, has made it possible for diabetics to live normal lives. Rheumatoid arthritis has been ameliorated, though not cured, by cortisone. The discovery and isolation of vitamins has made it possible to eradicate deficiency diseases such as scurvy and rickets. Modern insecticides, beginning with DDT, can rid the world of malaria, but the effects of insecticides upon human life and the planetary ecology are only beginning to be understood. Even while streptomycin reduced TB mortality, cigarette smoking and perhaps air pollution affected the mortality rate, and though modern medical research has been concentrating on cancer for many years, no cure has been found.

Surgical techniques have become immensely more ambitious and complex since the development of anesthesia and asepsis. The first organ transplants in the later 1960's revealed a need for the study of the immune reaction (the body's rejection of foreign materials); since then, transplants of almost every major organ, including the heart, have been accomplished. Here again, technical and scientific achievements have created a new concern over their social and moral implications.

Communications and Transportation

The basic scientific knowledge that lies behind what was first called wireless telegraphy and then radio had largely been attained by the early years of the century. Radio was applied first to ship-to-shore communication and then, in the 1920's, to intercontinental communication and to the development of national radio networks that broadcast information and entertainment. In the 1920's and early 1930's scientists and engineers in both Britain and the United States experimented with television broadcasting; a few stations already were in operation in 1939. After World War II television became a prime source of information and entertainment in all industrialized countries. The development of transistors to take the place of large, cumbersome vacuum tubes allowed radio and television sets to become lighter, less bulky, and much cheaper.

Between 1935 and 1938 a team of British scientists headed by Robert A. Watson Watt (b. 1892) developed radar, which allowed the presence of ships and planes to be detected at long distances. Further research made radar a serviceable military weapon, and after World War II it contributed to an increase in air safety. The most important change in air transportation resulted from the invention of the jet engine, developed almost simultaneously in Germany, the United States, Great Britain, and the Soviet Union at the close of the war. Jet engines greatly increased air speed and made the building of much larger planes feasible.

The three decades after 1940 comprised another era of revolution in transportation and communication, which enormously increased the opportunity for communicating knowledge and providing education and entertainment for the masses. By and large, the new technology was used beneficently, but unquestionably more could have been done in all countries to make television a medium of public enlightenment. This aim was pursued most sincerely in Great Britain, but in the late 1950's British television followed the pattern already set in the United States: its main purpose was popular entertainment. In Communist countries, television, like the press, was mainly an instrument for political indoctrination. Nowhere was television's potential as a vehicle for raising the level of public taste and public understanding of political issues consistently pursued. Once again the twentieth-century pattern was repeated, by which scientists abdicated responsibility for the social applications of their discoveries.

II THE SOCIAL AND BEHAVIORAL SCIENCES

Economics

One of the most significant changes in the pattern of higher culture since the First World War has been the expansion and proliferation of the social and behavioral sciences, their entrenchment in universities as full-fledged academic disciplines, and their substantial influence on public policy.

Economics, the oldest and most firmly established of the social sciences, experienced in the twentieth century a transformation in methodology and doctrine. The direction of this transformation was strongly determined by a charismatic figure, a single individual whose bold ideas changed theory and practice alike. John Maynard Keynes (1883–1946) was one of the rare revolutionaries of the social sciences. His work is a watershed in the history of economics. Keynes, a Cambridge don who was also a member of the Bloomsbury intellectual group of prewar and postwar London, served as Britain's financial representative at the peace conference in 1919. His condemnation of the reparations policy made him unpopular in government circles, and he returned to Cambridge, where his teaching influenced a generation of British economists. At Cambridge he wrote his major work, which, particularly after World War II, revolutionized public policy as well as academic economic theory. *The General Theory of Employment, Interest and Money* (1936) sets forth Keynes's belief that man is not necessarily a helpless victim of the business or industrial cycle, that unemployment and depression can be controlled by reasonable government action. This view departed from classical economics and Marxism as well.

The General Theory is an attack on the old notion that capitalistic systems adjust themselves automatically to the most favorable level of employment and of prices and wages. Keynes denied the nineteenth-century principle that demand follows production—that as businesses spend more on labor, the wages they pay out enable workmen to buy more goods. He also rejected the prevailing belief that any workman can be employed if he will simply accept a lower wage, that unemployment is essentially voluntary.

Keynes explained unemployment by the theory of aggregate demand, which says in effect that although *one* businessman may increase demand for his product by cutting prices (and costs, including wages paid to labor), this does not work when *all* businessmen cut prices and wages. In that situation, demand declines along with wages because workers can then buy fewer goods of any kind. Thus the level of aggregate demand determines the level of employment. How can the level of aggregate demand be raised? Keynes asserted that investment is a major factor in economic expansion. He believed that "investment increases when either interest rates fall or expected profits rise, and of the two, interest rates are firmly within the power of the public agencies."[2]

Keynes was certain that government monetary policy could effect significant changes in the rate of economic growth and employment levels, but that public works (which could be financed by government deficits and which Keynes and most other social theorists hoped could be of social value) were even more effective. Government investment—in a war or in public works—was as effective as, or more effective than, private investment. Tax reduction served a similar purpose by encouraging spending, but it did not, of course, assure that the spending would take socially desirable forms.

Keynes' radical ideas made him a public figure. In the United States, his theories influenced the economic thinkers of the New Deal although President Roosevelt himself was never a convinced Keynesian. It was World War II —not the New Deal—that seemed fully to substantiate Keynesian theory. The economic boom that followed the enormous wartime public spending and deficit financing produced full employment and unheard-of economic expansion. Keynesian analysis of statistics (on employment, prices, wages, interest

---

2. Robert Lekachman, *The Age of Keynes.* New York: Random House, 1966, p. 101.

rates, etc.) became part of the routine work of any modern government financial department, and analysis occupied a large part of the time of theoretical economists as well. Further, the desirability of deficit financing—the ultimate denial of the old Puritan virtue of thrift—was widely accepted. Post-Keynesian economists accept the deficit and believe that government can and should stimulate the economy, but they argue over whether this should be done by tax reform (as most conservatives believe) or by expansion of government into ever larger areas of social welfare. The latter view is held by the influential American economist John Kenneth Galbraith, whose book *The Affluent Society* (1958) expresses the view that economic growth should be redirected from the production and consumption of a surplus of consumer goods into needed public services.

The modern economist deals with quantitative matters and with the mathematical relationships of various economic circumstances. He uses statistical techniques; the subspecialty of econometrics is concerned entirely with statistical measurements. Computers handle the mass of available information, and economics itself is approaching the stage where it can be communicated as well in mathematical symbols as in words, if not better.

Sociology, History, and Anthropology

In the 1920's and 1930's European sociologists—working in the tradition of Marx, Weber, and Durkheim—continued to search for the universal truths that might allow them to understand increasingly complex human institutions. In *Ideology and Utopia* (1921–1931) Karl Mannheim wrote of the "structure" of social reality and the inevitability of social planning in the complicated modern world. American sociologists on the whole avoided the search for comprehensive patterns, but Talcott Parsons (b. 1902) of Harvard developed a universal theory of social action that was intended to transcend differences among specific societies.

In the 1920's and 1930's, however, the main trend of American sociology was in the direction of empirical research, involving the careful accumulation of data. Scholars left their armchairs for field work on the streets of Chicago or in the vineyards of California, and their published work was heavily statistical and nonideological. Simultaneously, statistics itself became a science. Testing methods, demographic surveys, and ultimately computers all became more sophisticated, and sociological data was put to use by insurance companies, advertising agencies, political parties, and government bureaus responsible for the supply of goods and services.

Sociologists in the 1940's and 1950's insisted that their work was a science, that their findings were not speculative theories but verifiable facts, like the findings of physicists. Underlying all their activity was the assumption (analogous to the assumptions of quantum mechanics) that group behavior can be predicted—that, in this instance, a social scientist can predict the behavior of a group of people, if not that of an individual. Just as in physics the measuring process affects the behavior of atomic particles, so in sociology the announcement of a poll or rating may alter the voting pattern or buying habits of the object of study.

By the late 1950's a trend away from amoral, purely descriptive studies was beginning. Sociologists began to return to the reforming spirit and moral commitment of early twentieth-century social science. The Swedish sociologist Gunnar Myrdal (b. 1898) had already provided an arsenal of facts and figures for the American civil rights movement in his study *An American Dilemma: The Negro Problem and Modern Democracy* (1944). David Riesman's *The Lonely Crowd* (1950) used data gained from empirical research to portray contemporary values and life styles. By the 1960's this kind of liberal and critical sociological literature was competing with the novel as a vehicle for providing the educated public with an awareness of its group habits and ideals. In 1968 Myrdal published a detailed analysis of southeast Asian society, *Asian Drama*; his conclusions were tinged with Malthusian pessimism about the viability of efforts made in the postwar period to bring these countries from the agricultural to the industrial stage. C. Wright Mills, a Columbia University professor, contributed to this growing body of sociological critiques with *The Sociological Imagination* (1959), in which he criticized theorists like Parsons as too abstract and general to be meaningful. Mills claimed that most twentieth-century sociology defeated itself by excessive empiricism. The sociological imagination, he believed, should apply itself to building a better society.

Between 1920 and 1950 it was fashionable for academic historians to sneer at sociologists, whom they frequently regarded as arrogant fabricators of unfounded theories. The overwhelming majority of professional historians remained oblivious to the tremendous upheaval in thought that had begun in the late nineteenth century. With passionate and (in retrospect) ignorant conservatism, historians avowed their loyalty to mid-nineteenth-century positivism—if only enough documents were studied and enough facts gathered, somehow a meaningful interpretation of the past would ultimately emerge. Understandably, history steadily lost the interest of the intellectual public.

There were, however, some significant exceptions to academic positivism. A few historians, such as G. M. Trevelyan in Britain and Allan Nevins in the United States, perpetuated the liberal and romantic traditions of nineteenth-century historiography and commanded a wide audience. Some important scholars presented broad interpretations predicated on the Marxist view that the basis of political and social change is economic and that class struggle is inevitable and perpetual. Charles Beard viewed American history in this way, R. H. Tawney perceived the development of sixteenth-century England in this framework, and Michael Rostovtzeff—although an anti-Communist Russian émigré—found this pattern in Roman history. The two celebrated philosophers of history of the interwar era, the German Oswald Spengler, in his *The Decline of the West*, and the omnivorously learned Englishman Arnold Toynbee, in his multivolume *A Study of History*, both revived the cyclic theory of the development of civilizations, to which Greek and Roman thinkers had been devoted—Spengler with the mystical tone of German Romanticism, Toynbee with the analytical acumen of British scholarship.

Meanwhile, in the 1930's, isolated efforts were made to apply ideas derived from the behavioral and social sciences to historical interpretation. Lewis B. Namier, convinced by the Freudian view of human nature, undertook a realistic analysis of the functioning of eighteenth-century British politics. At the same time, the eminent French medievalist Marc Bloch was applying Durkheim's sociology to his analysis of feudal society. Bloch was killed by the Nazis while he was fighting in the resistance, but after the war several of his disciples, notably Ferdinand Braudel, developed a major French school of sociological history. In the late 1950's a similar trend began to emerge in the United States and Britain, and by the late 1960's, far from sneering at sociology, leading historians of the younger generation were applying the insights and theories of all the social and psychological sciences to the understanding of the patterns of historical change.

As was the case with all sciences in their early stage of development, anthropology has had a difficult time deciding what its subject matter and purpose are. Physical anthropology, which was developed mainly in German universities in the early years of the twentieth century, concentrated on human biology and genetics, on the characteristics of various racial groups, and on human evolution. There can be no doubt that this branch of anthropology, when it has confined itself to the subject of prehistory, has been a particularly careful and empirical science. But in their study of racial groups, the physical anthropologists achieved only modest results. They never reached agreement on what constitutes a race or whether the term is valid at all. The pernicious racist doctrines of the Nazis effectively discouraged further inquiry into the subject.

The other branch of anthropology—cultural or social anthropology—set out to establish nothing less than the patterns of human institutions: kinship and family life, political systems, economic practices, religious beliefs and organizations, and language patterns. Partly because of the Darwinist assumption that the laws of social behavior can best be observed among primitive people who had not yet evolved to more sophisticated and complex forms of behavior, and partly because sociologists had already preempted the study of advanced societies, anthropologists during the first two decades of the twentieth century committed themselves to detailed field work among extremely primitive peoples, particularly in Asia and Africa. Essentially, cultural anthropology has never advanced beyond this subject matter.

The founder of scientific analyses of primitive peoples still extant was Franz Boas (1858–1942) of Columbia University, who sent his students to conduct ethnographic studies in the Americas and Asia. Boas was not only hostile to evolutionary doctrines, social Darwinism, and racist theories but also to the effort to establish any patterns or laws in social development. A thorough empiricist, he exercised a very salutary influence on anthropological thought. It is difficult, however, for a science to develop with no general theory. Since 1920 anthropologists have devoted a great deal of time and energy trying to find a substitute for the earlier evolutionary theory. Boas's own students Ruth Benedict (1887–1948) and Margaret Mead (b. 1901) tried to impose an interpretative pattern on their studies, respectively, of Indians of the American Southwest and of Pacific islanders. Their well-written, imaginative books were highly popular but received a decidedly mixed reaction from their anthropological colleagues.

Among the welter of interpretations offered by twentieth-century anthropologists, three schools have gained the widest adherence. The "structural-functional" approach developed in Britain in the 1920's and 1930's by Alfred Radcliffe-Brown and Bronislaw Malinowski tried to show how institutions developed in response to basic human needs. The French school of cultural anthropology has used linguistic analysis and empirical social data to demonstrate that institutions develop in response to mental structures and reflect psychological types. The leading exponent of this school has been Claude Lévi-Strauss. Yet a third school of anthropological interpretation gave precedence to material and environmental factors. In the work of the Australian-born British scholar V. Gordon Childe, an authority on the prehistory of the ancient Near East, this cultural materialism was openly associated with Marxist doctrine. The American school of cultural materialism—to which Julian Steward and Marvin Harris, among others, made important contributions—was more empirical and less schematic in its approach.

Psychology and Psychiatry

Psychologists, particularly in the United States, shared in the general scientism (the emphasis on verifiableness and objectivity) that characterized the social sciences during much of the twentieth century. Even while Freud's disciples were working out new schools in which both consciousness and the unconscious were used in psychoanalysis, American psychologists turned away from consciousness on the grounds that it could be known only by introspection and was therefore unreliable. J. B. Watson (1878–1958) inaugurated psychological behaviorism, which remained dominant in the United States until the late 1940's. Watson defined psychology as an objective, experimental, natural science that should be restricted to the relation of observable, measurable stimuli and responses.

The behaviorists, who based their work on Pavlov's experiments with conditioned responses in animals, believed that environmental forces are crucial in the development of behavior. Watson's was essentially an optimistic view—of child-raising, at least—and thousands of American parents brought up their children in the confidence that they could be trained by stimuli to develop proper patterns of behavior. Later neobehaviorists such as Clark L. Hull (1884–1952) and B. F. Skinner (b. 1904) redefined and extended classical behaviorism.

The Gestalt school of psychology originated in Germany and became active in the United States after most of its leading representatives fled Hitler's regime. Gestalt psychologists were particularly concerned with perception, stressing the organization of sense data by the brain in the Kantian tradition, which held that mind imposes structure upon experience. They provided an alternative to behaviorism, but the psychology laboratories developed during the 1920's and 1930's still flourished in the 1960's. New applications —in industry, in the military, in motivational research, and in educational and vocational testing—required a great deal of complicated apparatus and made psychology a big business.

Even while behaviorism predominated in the United States, European psychologists continued to work out Freud's ideas in new schools. Some of Freud's disciples continued in the strict Freudian tradition; others broke away; but none shed Freud's influence entirely. Alfred Adler (1870–1937), an Austrian psychiatrist, worked with Freud from 1902 until 1911, when he left to found his own school. He differed from Freud in emphasizing the drive for superiority, a sociogenic drive that may be expressed in either productive or antisocial attitudes. For Adler, the crucial determining factor in mental health was not Freud's biological necessity but individual, subjective response to a particular social situation, including the family.

Carl Gustav Jung (1875–1961), a Swiss associate of Freud's between 1907 and 1912, founded an important school of psychological interpretation in Zurich. Jung divided men into introverts and extroverts, depending on the predominance of thought, emotion, sensation, or intuition in the individual personality. He emphasized the immediate conflicts of his neurotic patients instead of concentrating on their childhood histories. Jung's most important contribution was his theory of the "collective unconscious" inherited by all men from primitive ancestors; this theory was both a reflection of, and further inducement to, the great resurgence of interest in myth and legend and in primitive or preliterate societies.

The influential contemporary social psychologist Erik Erikson stresses the importance of interpersonal relationships in creativity and personality. In *Childhood and Society* (1950) Erikson studied the development of the healthy personality, which he described as a series of crises in the concept of self. The reinforcement of traditional social and sexual identification is essential to this process, particularly in the crisis of identity that accompanies adolescence. Much of Erikson's work suggests the desirability of a stable, traditional society in which the "generation gap" is not too large to allow the young to identify with adult models.

Obviously Freud's theories are basic to modern psychological thought, but the practice of psychoanalysis which he inaugurated seems destined to play a reduced role in the treatment of mental illness. Analysis became a quasi-religion among intellectuals of the 1930's and 1940's; it was an inherent part of up-to-date artistic and social theory, and its techniques, assumptions, and jargon were closely bound into the higher culture of the era. However, as medical practice it was simply too expensive, too slow, and too elitist to be very useful. Research in the late 1950's seemed to establish a biochemical basis for schizophrenia, and this discovery has provided the greatest existing hope for the future treatment of mental illness. Group therapy is becoming more and more common, though Freudian analysis is still used in certain cases and Freud's theories have had a permanent influence in all the fields of thought that require insight into the human personality.

Education

Rarely has an eminent philosopher directed his attention to the nature and problems of education – although Plato and Rousseau did. The main issue in the early twentieth century was the continued utility of traditional, humanist, classical education in an industrial and technological society. This was the problem to which John Dewey (1859 – 1952) addressed himself. Dewey, who, with William James and Charles Sanders Peirce, was one of the American pragmatist trinity, established the famous Laboratory School at the University of Chicago. In 1904 he went to Columbia, where he taught philosophy until 1930. His philosophy of education was derived both from his interpretation of the psychology of learning and from his analysis of modern society. Thinking, he believed, is an activity of inquiry undertaken to solve problems and to deal with situations of uncertainty. Learning is a process that occurs when experience provides new situations which our customary responses do not handle satisfactorily. Education, then, must begin with experience – a student must experience (do, see, touch, taste) a problem – actively and tangibly, if possible – in order to reason out and understand its solution. The second plank in Dewey's platform of educational reform was his conviction that an education suitable to the nineteenth century was not adequate in the scientific society of the twentieth.

Dewey was fascinated by methods, by the concept of "instrumentality," believing that art, scientific techniques, and ethical principles are tools with which men impose order on a chaotic universe. Like Peirce and James, he saw philosophy as an active agent in culture and society. Dewey himself was a staunch supporter of personal liberty and social justice; he strongly opposed communism because it repressed human freedom.

These attitudes were combined in the theory that education must be organized around students—or rather their problems—instead of around subjects, that the traditional learning by memorizing and reciting must give way to experience-based learning by thinking and doing in schools which were essentially models of the outside world. Education should pattern itself on scientific investigation; problems should be examined on their merits as they presented themselves to students through experience; there was no good reason to turn to the past for authoritative beliefs, although what former generations have learned and passed on to us is the only resource we have except our own ability to learn from experience. These ideas were enthusiastically received by "progressive" educators, especially in the United States. Education through activity—learning by doing—became a cherished tenet of American educational theory.

In the 1950's progressive theories were blamed for a great many failings of American education. Some of these failings might have been better blamed on the population explosion, or even on the concept of mass education. Dewey's progressive program—by which the school was a reflection of the democratic and industrial society and was itself a quasi-democratic community—was the most important educational innovation of the twentieth century.

In European countries the democratization of the secondary schools was never attempted. Whether public or private, they remained elitist institutions in which the superior intellectual minority was given rigorous training in the traditional literary curriculum, with appropriate mathematical and scientific additions. The same was true of European higher education, which remained an elitist system, both in terms of the rigorous standards required for matriculation and graduation and in terms of the small percentage of the college-age population that had the opportunity and qualifications for university study.

Down to the mid-1960's the main trend in universities throughout the Western world was neither curricular experimentation nor democratization of the institutional structure. Rather, it was the proliferation and expansion of graduate and professional schools and research institutes. In the period after World War II this trend was accelerated everywhere, as governments and business corporations lavishly endowed research in the natural, biological, social, and behavioral sciences. The underside of the coin was the general neglect of the interests of the undergraduate college in favor of the more prestigious and prosperous branches of the university. Many universities, particularly in France and Germany but also to a somewhat lesser degree in Britain and the United States, were notoriously overcrowded. This general neglect of the teaching function of the university, as compared with its scholarly and research functions, provided a seedbed for discontent which, inflamed by left-wing agitation against capitalism and war, exploded into student rebellion all over the Western world in the late 1960's.

III **PHILOSOPHY AND THEOLOGY**

The Great Divide in Twentieth-Century Philosophy

Modern philosophy divides quite naturally into two separate schools of thought. One group, centered in Great Britain and the United States (although some of its original leaders were Germans), concentrates on logic and theory of knowledge; the other—Continental European—on ethics and metaphysics. Anglo-American philosophers, impressed by the achievements and methods of modern science, have disdained what they regard as the intuitive insights of metaphysics, particularly the vestiges of Romantic idealism. They have accordingly turned to mathematicians, physicists, and students of linguistics; they criticize what men believe by analyzing what men say and how they know.

The patriarch of modern American and British philosophy is Bertrand Russell (b.1872). Russell's early work on the foundations of mathematics led him into a philosophy he described as "logical atomism." After his collaboration with Alfred North Whitehead on *Principia Mathematica* (1910–1913), Russell continued to focus on mathematical logic as the instrument of meaningful thought about the world. To Russell, knowable truths were like those of pure mathematics, ascertainable only by rigorous intellectual analysis that owed nothing to experience or experiment. In contrast, beliefs about "the external world" could be probable at best, based on very complicated inferences from our sensations.

Russell's aim was to establish modern science on a firm logical foundation, to achieve complete clarity by choosing a mathematical language that could not mislead us. Much of Russell's confidence in an "ideal" symbolic language has been rejected by later philosophers, but his contribution to the philosophy of mathematics makes him one of the great figures in the history of modern thought.

Russell's work was influential in the development of logical positivism, which appeared as a philosophical school in the "Vienna Circle" of the early 1920's. The chief spokesman for logical positivism was Rudolf Carnap, who left Vienna for the United States in 1935 and taught at the University of Chicago and the University of California. He and his colleagues shifted the emphasis of scientific philosophy from understanding nature to understanding the way we talk about nature. Every meaningful statement must be verifiable, just as a scientific hypothesis must be verifiable—its meaning lies in its verifiableness. The logical positivists hoped to remove all the obscure or irrational elements of science by perfecting and clarifying scientific language. Because all scientific knowledge has the same formal linguistic structure and is advanced by the same experimental and logical methods, the philosophers of the Vienna circle hoped to unify all the sciences in a single encyclopedic system that would easily distinguish real science from the "pseudo-science" of metaphysicians and other "poetic" and "mystical" thinkers.

Ludwig Wittgenstein (1889–1951) also influenced the development of logical positivism although his own work grew beyond it. Wittgenstein was an Austrian by birth, but he was a member in good standing of the modern Anglo-American philosophical tradition. In 1921 he published *Tractatus Logico-Philosophicus,* his own version of logical positivism, which stated that language reflects the real world of fact and experience and cannot express ethical or metaphysical speculation. The world *is,* and can be described, but religion and value systems and most of the important and interesting things do not lend themselves to explicit and meaningful statement.

Since the only meaningful philosophical discussion was confined to mathematical logic and empirical science, philosophy itself—like much of the poetry and painting of the 1920's—rapidly became inaccessible to the layman. Philosophers could not and did not attempt to communicate their ideas except in technical language. Wittgenstein himself, concluding that discourse about important matters was not possible, followed his own logic and retired to Austria to teach kindergarten. Later he accepted a post at Cambridge University. In his *Philosophical Investigations,* published posthumously in 1953, Wittgenstein modified the emphasis of much of his earlier thinking but concentrated again on the place of language in thought. The meaning of words is settled through usage, which reflects "a form of life," he said. It is the philosopher's analysis of the meaning of common terms and his untangling of puzzles that arise when we "stretch" language beyond its limits that make his work useful.

Wittgenstein's later work was essential to the formation of the "new Oxford movement," the contemporary philosophical school whose chief concern is analyzing and understanding the language and concepts we use in ordinary life. Its members departed from their logical positivist teachers after World War II made the older philosophy seem narrow and remote, unable to help solve the desperate problems of human life. No statement, they say, is absolutely verifiable, because there is none that will not change its meaning in altered circumstances. Everything depends on context, and thus neither ethics nor metaphysics in any timeless or absolute form is a suitable subject for philosophical thought. In a discussion of good and evil, it is our varied uses of these concepts that are studied—not any inherent, permanent meaning of the words. These English thinkers, whose chief spokesman was John Austin of Oxford until his death in 1960, have moved a long way from the belief that exact mathematical language is the ultimate goal of philosophy, but their concern is still with knowledge and language.

A figure who bridged the opposed interests of the Anglo-Saxon and Continental schools was Alfred North Whitehead (1861–1947), an Englishman who spent his later years in America. Whitehead had worked with Russell in logic and mathematics and was so well versed in physics that he formulated a distinctive theory of relativity, but he turned to metaphysics during his years at Harvard in the 1920's and 1930's. *Process and Reality* (1929) stated his organic philosophy of "process." Just as the physicists had abolished the empty universe and substituted a field of force and energy, so Whitehead saw man's world of nature and society as alive and continuous. He sought a synthesis of scientific, social, moral, and aesthetic categories, hoping that an organic philosophy could unify and illuminate the interrelated aspects of experience.

Another transitional figure was the German philosopher Edmund Husserl (1859–1938), the founder of phenomenology. Like his French predecessor Henri Bergson, Husserl was neither a pure intuitive idealist in the German tradition nor a complete empiricist. Husserl thought that everyday experience must be reduced to its base elements by subtracting all presuppositions and interpretations of experience (such as scientific laws) from consciousness. The phenomenological philosopher must examine all kinds of experience, subjecting them to his own analyses to reveal elements of pure consciousness or intuition. Husserl's emphasis on intuition was extremely influential in Continental philosophy.

In striking contrast to the Anglo-American school, the Continental philosophies were expressions of moral, historical, and metaphysical understanding, not reflections of preoccupation with science. These philosophers demanded social or political commitment. They regarded the detachment of a linguistic analyst as immoral and in fact impossible in the modern world. Martin Heidegger (b. 1889), a German, was much influenced by Husserl's emphasis on intuition and by Kierkegaard's grounding of philosophy on the fear and certainty of death. In *Being and Nothingness* (1927) Heidegger explored the meaning of Being in relation to its corollary—Death. Being is temporal; it is "becoming"; and man can realize himself only by accepting this basic fact. This kind of tragic humanism makes Heidegger a forerunner of the existentialist school.

Existentialists assert that "existence precedes essence"—that, in other words, man has no determinate nature but creates himself after he comes into the world. He forms his own essence by the choices he makes. Thus men differ from manufactured products, which come into the world according to a preconceived plan in the mind of a creator or designer. In atheistic existentialism there is no Creator; men choose for themselves and for all men, thus contributing to the human essence. Man is doomed to the anguish of responsibility for his choices. God and prescribed value systems have been abandoned in modern secular society, and human life is nothing but the sum of individual actions. Man is condemned to a life of perfect freedom, for which he cannot avoid responsibility by suicide or by yielding to a belief in superhuman values to guide him.

The chief spokesman for existentialism was Jean-Paul Sartre (b. 1905), a novelist, dramatist, journalist, and leader of the French left-wing intelligentsia. Sartre's fictional heroes are antiheroes who know only their own consciousnesses and cannot form meaningful relationships with others. Often their anguish prevents any action except violence, which liberates them from anxiety and doubt. Sartre reconciles existentialism and Marxism on the basis that man must make a choice and do what he can—acting through violence, if necessary, to express his freedom.

On the latter point Sartre differed from Albert Camus (1913–1960), a playwright, novelist, and journalist whose writings have an important place in contemporary religious thought and philosophy. Camus was a French Algerian of working-class origin; as an outsider he could evaluate communism without the predispositions common to French left-wing intellectuals. His major theme was human freedom, which all men have in this absurd, irrational, and meaningless universe. God is dead, and so are absolute values. In the absence of eternity, human life on earth must be cherished. Like Sartre, Camus felt that the artist had a duty to speak out for human rights—to be *engagé* ("involved")—but unlike Sartre, he would not accept any ideology.

In *The Myth of Sisyphus* (1942) Camus attempted to find an individual solution to the problem posed by the death of God: if the universe is irrational, why live at all? He has been described as a nihilist, but in fact his recognition of meaninglessness was only a starting point from which he began to search for positive values. Confessing the terror of mortality from which man cannot escape, Camus hoped to reveal the value of life. In *The Rebel* (1951) Camus described the artist as the perfect rebel who tries to impose order on natural disorder. Because man is not moving toward any utopia, Camus found no reason to accept the Marxist willingness to disregard human life and freedom in order to attain utopian ends. Ends cannot justify means in a world which is not moving anywhere and in which only humanism and aesthetics provide any value.

Theology

Something like existentialism has had a place in Christian theology since St. Augustine, but the Death-of-God attitude appeared only with Nietzsche and achieved wide influence only in the mid-twentieth century. Before atheistic existentialism was clearly formulated after World War II, Christian theology enjoyed a renaissance in the form of a reaffirmation of the Augustinian doctrine of a transcendent God. The Protestant movement was sparked by thinkers like Karl Barth (1886–1968), a Swiss theologian who in the 1920's led a reaction to nineteenth-century liberal theology. Barth rediscovered divine grace and "Christology," claiming that the death and resurrection of Jesus Christ was the only reality. Barth's "theology of crisis" intended to describe God, not men's idea of God. Barth's contemporary, Rudolf Bultmann (b. 1884), attempted to "demythologize" the New Testament. He believed the Gospels to be statements of the Christian message and Jewish tradition, not accurate biographies of Jesus, which were in any case unnecessary. Both Barth and Bultmann were influenced by a Christian existentialism which found in God's grace the source of hope and in the life of Jesus a model for human action. Paul Tillich (1886–1965), who became an important figure in American theology after he was expelled from Germany by Hitler in 1933, believed that new forms and interpretations would arise out of the old, making Protestantism relevant to every age.

Certain French thinkers have maintained the orthodox Roman Catholic position while making significant contributions to contemporary theology. Jacques Maritain (b. 1882) has devoted much of his life to the study of Thomas Aquinas. In the liberal Thomist spirit, Maritain urged the Church to abandon conservatism and concern itself with the needs of industrial society. Pierre Teilhard de Chardin (1881–1955) developed an evolutionary Christ-centered philosophy, contending that all human history would ultimately converge in Christ. An upheaval in Catholic theology, relating traditional doctrine to the problems of contemporary society, began in the late 1950's, particularly in Germany, Austria, and Holland. This trend was greatly accentuated during the pontificate of John XXIII (1958–1963), who favored the reform and renewal of the Roman Church, and by the Second Vatican Council that Pope John summoned. The Council, which opened in 1962, had a mixed record of accomplishment but undeniably sparked Catholic thought on all kinds of subjects. It fostered a renewed emphasis on Scripture, thereby bringing the Roman Church closer to the Protestant, and it inaugurated cooperation with other Christian faiths. Pope John's encouragement of free thought, free speech, and ecumenism opened the Church to a great wave of questioning in all aspects of doctrine and established practice, including the relevance of Christianity to modern society.

IV THE ARTS

Literature

At the end of the First World War there was an outburst of talent and creative energy in arts and letters. The drawn-out horror of the war had its inevitable impact, and the useless, bloody years in the trenches seemed to verify the irrationality in human nature that had been expressed in literature and painting at the turn of the century. Artists and writers turned away from the immediate world to a deepening search for the self, a personal quest for individual understanding.

James Joyce (1882–1941), one of the outstanding writers of the century, left his native Ireland in 1904, oppressed by its religious and social authoritarianism but deeply imbued with its popular folklore and Roman Catholic tradition. Joyce projected the cultural past of Western man through the myths and allegories of his own consciousness. In *Ulysses* (1922), an account of one day in the life of a middle-aged, middle-class Irish Jew became an allegory of all humanity. *Ulysses* is allusive and difficult, requiring of its readers a broad education in the humanities, and *Finnegans Wake* (1939) delves deeply into the obscurities of the author's private world. Using the technique of interior monologue, Joyce entered the consciousness of each character and reported the inmost thoughts that lie below the level of speech. Stream-of-consciousness was adopted by other writers of the 1920's, including Virginia Woolf (1882–1941)—a member of the Bloomsbury group—who also explored the relation of the individual consciousness to the outside world.

On the Continent, many French poets continued to work in the Symbolist tradition established in the late nineteenth century. Paul Valéry (1871–1945) wrote lyric poems that express the music of pure language without necessarily reflecting any aspect of the real world. Confusion about reality is the theme of much of the work of Luigi Pirandello (1867–1936), an Italian dramatist whose plays were enthusiastically received in Europe and the United States in the 1920's. The playwright's domestic life was tragic and disordered, and his plays seem to imply, through a series of questions or paradoxes about reality and personality, that a private, illogical universe offers a possible escape from an ugly world.

The American-born English writer T. S. Eliot (1888–1965) produced a rich and varied body of poetry, drama, and criticism during a long, active career, but in his complex, private sensibility he was a poet of the 1920's. *The Waste Land* (1922) is a powerful statement of postwar disillusion and despair at the ugliness and sterility of industrial society. In the late 1920's, Eliot experienced a religious conversion, and after he accepted the Anglican creed, his poetry was enriched by the faith and symbolism of orthodox Christianity. But he continued to look inward to the individual soul and to search for meaningful personal expression and language.

American writers of the 1920's flocked to Paris in search of personal liberation and intellectual stimulation. Their most typical representative was F. Scott Fitzgerald (1896–1940), whose novels and short stories seemed to sum up the very essence of the Jazz Age. *The Great Gatsby,* recognized as Fitzgerald's most powerful novel, took up the themes that fascinated the author and characterized the United States in the twenties: sudden wealth and violent death. The expatriate Ernest Hemingway (1889–1961), whose terse style disguised a romantic spirit, influenced a whole generation of writers to use short sentences and glorify virility. William Faulkner (1897–1962), on the other hand, stayed in Mississippi and developed a stream-of-consciousness technique with which to record the disintegration of the American South. Faulkner is a transitional figure; he concerned himself with social analysis, but his commitment was to art and to the individual rather than to any program of reform. The plays of the American dramatist Eugene O'Neill (1888–1953) are realistic in style and setting, but his doomed, embittered characters are victims not of a wicked society but of the evil in themselves. A man's psychology is his fate, and O'Neill returned to the principles, plots, and techniques (including the chorus) of classical Greek tragedy to enrich his contemporary dramas.

André Gide (1869–1951), a great French stylist whose major concern was always individual sensibility, anticipated the shift to social commitment that took place in the 1930's. Gide wrote against the oppression of such minorities as Africans and homosexuals, making a plea for tolerance, for ethical relativism. *The Counterfeiters* (1926) is an exercise in style as well as a story of individual rebellion against the family, which was to Gide the most repressive social institution of all.

The careers of three French novelists—Romain Rolland, Colette, and André Malraux—reflect several aspects of French intellectual history. Rolland (1866–1944) wrote his monumental ten-volume novel *Jean Christophe*—a satirical study of contemporary society and its values—before World War I and published in 1914 a collection of essays and articles entitled *Above the Struggle*, which made him very unpopular in France. His pacifist nonviolent views were attacked as "pro-German" or (later) "pro-Russian," and not for some time after the war were his works appreciated for their literary merit. Colette (1873–1954) wrote during two wars and a depression, but her work was almost completely nonideological. She wrote about individuals, about love and human nature, and her stylistic gifts made her books very successful. André Malraux (b. 1901) has been described as a late Romantic; his books concern the grandeur and glory of humanity. Malraux' best-known novel, *Man's Fate* (1933), describes the impact of revolution on a few lucky or heroic individuals who find in revolutionary brotherhood a defense against the loneliness to which men are doomed.

During the Great Depression of the 1930's, concentration on style seemed frivolous in the face of working-class suffering. From Hitler's rise to power in Germany right through the years of World War II, it seemed immoral—and was nearly impossible—for any sensitive man to avoid social and political commitment. The career and writings of Arthur Koestler (b. 1905) are representative of an entire era. Koestler was born in Hungary, worked as a journalist in Germany, and joined the Communist party in 1931. He left Germany in 1933, fought in Spain, and left the party in 1937. Koestler fought with the Allies in World War II and has lived in London since 1945. His wartime novels—notably *Darkness at Noon* (1941) and *Arrival and Departure* (1943)—denounce all dictatorships and express a passionate concern for political freedom. At the same time they reflect the disillusionment with communism which struck the intellectual world after the Soviet purges and still more forcefully after the Nazi-Soviet pact of 1939.

English writers were in the vanguard of the renewal of interest in social justice. George Orwell (1903–1950), for instance, exposed the sordid underside of capitalist society in such books as *Down and Out in Paris and London*

(1933) and *The Road to Wigan Pier* (1937) before he turned his merciless attention to Stalinism in *Animal Farm* (1945). Orwell was one of the few intellectual socialists who ever lived as a member of the working class, and he was disgusted with the dilettantism of the British Labour party. He saw the tyrannous implications of communism during the Spanish Civil War and exposed them in *Homage to Catalonia* (1938), earning the scorn of the radical Left.

In the United States during the 1930's, novelists like John Steinbeck (1902–1968) and John Dos Passos (b. 1896) poured forth anger and protest against social injustice and economic deprivation. Clifford Odets (1906–1963) wrote plays about prize fighters and taxi drivers—polemics of the struggles of the inherently noble working class. The Italian novelist Ignazio Silone (b. 1900) was a Communist as a young man but left the party in 1930 and became a Christian Socialist. His novels, such as *Bread and Wine* (1937), reveal devout Christian faith intertwined with socialist ideals.

The leading German dramatist, Bertolt Brecht (1898–1956), unlike most American and British writers, remained committed to Marxism throughout his career. After spending the war years in the United States, he returned to East Berlin in 1948 to establish and direct the outstanding *Berliner Ensemble*, a state-supported theater. Brecht's plays are in the first rank of contemporary literature, as he never allowed his social theories to force them into the dreary mold of state art. Ironic, deeply perceptive, and experimental in form, such plays as *Mother Courage* (1941), *Galileo* (1943), and the delightful *Threepenny Opera* (1928), with music by Kurt Weill, assure him a permanent place among playwrights who transcend the mood and ideals of an era by individual genius.

The poems of the Russian Boris Pasternak (1890–1960)—apolitical, symbolic, and strongly individualistic—were rejected by Soviet critics and publishers, as was his novel *Dr. Zhivago* (1956), which won much applause in the West. Pasternak was offered the Nobel Prize for Literature in 1958 but refused it, presumably under pressure from the Soviet government. Another Russian-born writer with a large Western following is Vladimir Nabokov (b. 1899), an American citizen since 1945, whose characteristic themes are exile and alienation.

In the 1950's and 1960's, another postwar period of gloom, despondency, and dissatisfaction, there was a new trend toward the individual consciousness and the individual vision. The British playwright Harold Pinter (b. 1920) presents a world which seems at first real and recognizable but reveals below the surface a hornet's nest of terror, betrayal, and mystery. The French novelist Alain Robbe-Grillet has spoken of *"les vieux mythes de la profondeur"*—the old myths of depth—and has chosen to write in static, visual images, ignoring penetration into meaning or character. Without preexisting values, the present is everything, and art should be purified of political, social, or psychological messages. Once again, unreason was hailed as more meaningful than reason or argument. The French novelist and playwright Jean Genêt (b. 1909) chose evil as his theme and wrote—often from prison—of social outcasts, perverts, and prisoners whose gross humanity achieves general significance through Genêt's poetic style and understanding. Playwrights and film-makers experimented with a "theater of the absurd." In the difficult, obscure, almost nonsensical dramas of Eugene Ionesco (b. 1912) and Samuel Beckett (b. 1906) the audience is drawn into the playwright's private world by image and feeling rather than rational exposition or character identification. The theater of the absurd is at the opposite pole from realism. If there is any meaning at all to life, it can be conveyed only in fragmentary glimpses of some private truth.

Painting

The painters of the 1920's shared with writers a conviction that individual consciousness was the source of meaning. The styles of the period were not new; they were a working-out of Expressionism and Cubism developed during the creative outburst at the beginning of the century. Nonrepresentational art was widely accepted in the 1920's (except in the Soviet Union, where socialist realism was demanded by the state), and the leading artists after World War II continued to explore the possibilities of abstraction.

Pure Cubism had reached its peak by 1919, although Georges Braque (1882–1963), Fernand Léger (1881–1955), Juan Gris (1887–1927), and others continued to experiment productively in individual Cubist styles. Pablo Picasso (b. 1881), one of the founders of Cubism, turned in the early 1920's to a neoclassical style best represented by his "Woman In White" (1924). In the mid-1920's he experimented with the double image in which visual meaning is gained through distortion, and he has continued to develop his style ever since. An interest in geometrical abstraction dominated the work of Piet Mondrian (1872–1944), who removed all realistic details from his paintings, reducing nature to the straight lines, squares, and rectangles of plane geometry. Painting became a purely visual experience.

While Cubism was developing into geometric design, Expressionism was also becoming pure abstraction, concentrating on the color material of painting. Wassily Kandinsky (1866–1944) communicated personal emotion in a nonrepresentational style, allowing the intuitive to dominate the intellectual. Postwar Abstract Expressionists conveyed emotion through color and form, enjoying total freedom from limitations of subject matter. The American Jackson Pollock (1912–1956), using a dribbling, spattering technique, titled his various works simply "Improvisation" or "Composition"; William de Kooning (b. 1904), the American artist who has most influenced the younger generation of painters of the 1960's, reintroduced recognizable human figures into his work in the early 1950's but also returned to completely nonobjective paintings in which color expresses the artist's feeling.

Among the influences on twentieth-century art was the rediscovery of the primitive and the exotic. Modern anthropology and easy travel have made African, Indian, and Oriental art forms a source of inspiration to modern painters, designers, and sculptors. The British sculptor Henry Moore (b. 1898) fashioned chunky, monumental human figures—semiabstract, organic forms —which resemble primitive sculptures and make psychological statements about human beings and their relationships.

Freud's insight into the unconscious has had enormous impact on artists as well as on writers and psychologists. Surrealism—the artistic school that places value on symbols, dreams, myths, and unspoken drives—emerged in the mid-1920's. Paul Klee (1879–1940), who was not a Surrealist but was much influenced by their ideas, developed a private symbolic system. His inventive paintings and collages display a highly personal technique that can be appreciated for its charm and design or studied and interpreted as a secret language. The German Expressionist Max Ernst exploited Dadaist and Surrealist ideas in vivid, nightmare landscapes marked by primitive and mythological themes. Emil Nolde, another German Expressionist of the 1920's, painted a private vision of religious passion and exaltation. A leading Surrealist painter, Salvador Dali (b. 1904), aimed to reveal "the phenomena of delirium." Dali's drawing is highly realistic; the familiar limp watches in "Persistence of Memory" (1939) are totally recognizable as watches, whatever they may be in the unconscious of the artist. Dali's representational Surrealism stands in contrast to the abstract Surrealism of Joan Miró (b. 1893), who conveys the swirl of inner consciousness and mythic symbols of nature.

The social commitment of the 1930's did not completely pass by the world of painting. In 1937, Picasso cried out against the meaningless violence of the Spanish Civil War (and all war) in his great painting "Guernica," in which artistic distortion expresses the discordance of modern life. In the 1930's attempts to create a "people's art" largely failed because the proponents were mediocre artists, but the American Ben Shahn (1898–1969) was an exception. Shahn hoped to speak directly to ordinary people through paintings dealing with their lives, activities, and social concerns. In his "Handball" (1939) an ordinary street scene is organized and enhanced by the artist's vision. The Mexicans Diego Rivera (1886–1957) and José Orozco (1883–1949) combined social conviction with heroic figure painting and careful composition in sweeping, declamatory murals.

Abstract sculpture has come to maturity in the twentieth century, and many of its outstanding exponents have worked in the United States. Naum Gabo, born in Russia in 1890, specializes in the mathematical and sculptural use of space as an element of sculpture. Alexander Calder (b. 1898) built sculptural mobiles in which space was continually redefined by motion. The Rumanian-born Constantin Brancusi (1876–1957) worked in Paris, expressing what he called "the real sense of things" through form in which motion was implicit.

In general, twentieth-century art has become less and less representational. A new "pop art" appeared in the early 1960's, when artists began to create pictures out of advertising matter, comic-strip characters, and ordinary objects elevated to pseudo-heroic stature. Sculptors picked up hubcaps and rusted wire and created fabrications that may (or may not) make a statement about the quality of American life.

Architecture

Functionalism was transformed in the 1920's from the creed of a few advanced thinkers to a widely recognized international style. As a movement, it reached its fullest expression in the Bauhaus school of 1925 – 1933, founded by Walter Gropius (1883 – 1969). Under the leadership of Gropius and Ludwig Mies van der Rohe (1886 – 1969), the Bauhaus teachers (including Klee and Kandinsky) preached the unity of the arts and industries. They hoped to reunite the artist and craftsman, separated by modern technology, and to incorporate the revolution in industrial production into architectural theory and practice. The Bauhaus was very influential, particularly when its leaders spread the gospel to other countries after Hitler closed the school in 1933. Gropius worked in partnership with Marcel Breuer (b. 1902) — another leading representative of the Bauhaus school — in Boston in the 1930's and 1940's and he directed the Graduate School of Design at Harvard from 1937 until 1952. The influence of Gropius, Breuer, Mies van der Rohe, and their colleagues has dominated sophisticated urban building in the United States and elsewhere.

The Bauhaus style was eminently rational and severe, but when its principles became popular in the 1930's, they were easily vulgarized by less talented architects and builders into a stark, dull modernism. A relieving influence has been that of Le Corbusier (1887 – 1965), Swiss by birth and French by education, whose imaginative use of abstract geometric forms gave a new vitality to modern architecture based on functional principles. Le Corbusier visited Brazil in 1936, sparking a renaissance in architecture and city planning that has made that country a modern architectural center. On the whole, however, the Bauhaus style succeeded all too well and was absorbed and brutalized by big business. Since modern architecture has generally abandoned traditional symbols and styles, the quality of the individual architect is immensely important. The United States has been fortunate in the continuing influence of Frank Lloyd Wright, whose school for architects at Taliesin West (near Phoenix, Arizona) has been an architectural asset to the country since it opened in 1938.

European architects of the 1930's were much concerned with the contribution they might make to social problems, and it was then that city planning became a profession in its own right. Designers began to worry about total environment and the relationship of new houses to schools, factories, and civic services. Industrial housing was a major interest, and the Scandinavians led the way in planning the setting for a whole way of life for working people. As environmental pollution and urban sprawl create serious problems, architects attempt to find rational solutions, to work for order and control in the midst of chaos.

Music and Popular Culture

The personal quest for individual expression that has marked the arts and letters of much of the twentieth century has been reflected in musical composition. Nonrepresentational music—music that is not lyrical, didactic, or pragmatic, music that does not seek to impart a mood or tell a story—was inaugurated early in the century by Arnold Schoenberg, the Austrian who established a wholly new system of composition to state a new tonality. His twelve-tone scale was taken up successfully by a student—Alban Berg (1885–1935)—whose work has a logic of its own, unsupported by traditional harmonic relationships. However, the twelve-tone scale has not persisted as a significant means of expression.

Folk music was rediscovered in the 1920's, and the primitive rhythms of Balkan folk songs enriched the music of the Hungarian Béla Bartók (1881–1945) and the Russian Igor Stravinsky (b. 1882). Stravinsky has composed in a wide range of traditional and modern styles. Some composers continued to work in the neoclassical tradition, including Paul Hindemith (1895–1963), who emphasized polyphony but widened the tonality of the nineteenth-century masters. Jean Sibelius (1865–1957), the grand national composer of Finland, continued the Romanticism of Tchaikovsky.

Twentieth-century American composers have been much influenced by folk-song traditions, by commercial popular music, and by the discovery of New Orleans jazz in the 1920's. Aaron Copland (b. 1900) and George Gershwin (1898–1937) tried to unite these native traditions with classical forms. Twentieth-century American music has been most inventive in popular forms, particularly jazz and blues, the creation of American Negro culture. Light opera was supplanted by musical comedy in the United States after the success of *Oklahoma!* (1943); some of the best musical comedies combined music, ballet, and drama in an honest and effective popular theater. This vein of musical comedy appeared to be exhausted by the mid-60's, but new versions of old folk songs, new pseudo-folk songs, and rock (again derived from Negro tradition) attracted enormous audiences in Europe as well as the United States, indicating the continuing development of a genuine "people's art" in music.

Along with rock and folk music, the most popular—and most innovative—cultural medium of the 1960's was the motion picture. Film directors in several countries, but particularly in France, transformed the cinema into a distinct art form, with great appeal to the younger generation. By the end of the 1960's, film appeared to be surpassing theatre in the effectiveness and variety of the ways in which it portrayed human experience.

15

HERITAGE ESSAY

THE HERITAGE OF THE TWENTIETH CENTURY

In the twentieth century, most forms of higher thought have been absorbed into the university, and in the 1950's and 1960's, especially in the United States, even many artists and belletristic writers did their work on the campus. Nearly every major thinker after 1920 became, if he did not start out as, a university professor. The university has been called upon to solve every social problem, from management of the business cycle to racial conflict to the development of new technology for both peace and war. Not since 1300 has the university played such a central role in Western culture nor academics taken such a lead in formulating new ideas.

The academicization of thought, which was already under way at the beginning of the century but which was intensified with each passing decade and sharply accentuated in all Western countries after the Second World War, brought with it obvious benefits. Research in the natural and biological sciences was no longer undertaken by isolated geniuses. Rather, it was pursued by teams of scientists at leading universities who commanded vast resources. Their hypotheses and discoveries were immediately reported at academic meetings—often international in character—and subjected at once to scrutiny, testing, and amplification by other scientists. Thus a breakthrough achieved at one university triggered a whole series of additional discoveries in the same field at other research centers in several countries. The development of atomic physics since the early 1900's is a prime example of this phenomenon. In the 1960's similar accelerated progress occurred in the biological sciences.

The social and behavorial sciences likewise benefited. Theories of social action and individual behavior, which until the end of the nineteenth century had been the province of philosophers, theologians, and poets, by the mid-twentieth century were subjected to the rigorous academic scrutiny that had come to prevail in the natural and biological sciences. Anyone who set out to answer the age-old questions "What is human nature?" and "How does society function?" could not gain a hearing in serious intellectual circles unless he could express his theories in the technical vocabulary of sociology,

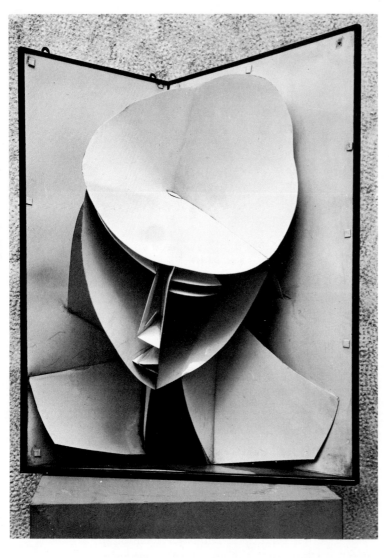

COLLECTION OF THE MUSEUM OF MODERN ART, NEW YORK. PURCHASE.

The Inner Chord. The movement towards abstract painting that had been inaugurated before the First World War flourished in the 1920's. Wassily Kandinsky, one of the founders of the movement, had stated that its purpose was to express the "inner chord" in line and color. Kandinsky's colleague at the great German Bauhaus school of painting and architecture in the 1920's, Paul Klee, had the same philosophy and his work is similar to Kandinsky's, although inclined towards a neo-Romantic lyricism. Klee sought to express "the primordial realm of psychic improvisation" through "free abstract structures which transcend all schematic intent and achieve a new naturalness." Facing page: Klee's "Senecu." Also in Berlin at the time was the Russian Naum Gabo, a member of the Russian abstract movement called Constructivism, which was suppressed by Lenin. Gabo, a trained mathematician, sought to use modern materials to express the meaning of the new technological world. Left: Gabo's "Head of a Woman," a construction in celluloid and metal.

psychology, and anthropology and display awareness of the data these disciplines have made available. Subjecting moral and social doctrines to academic expertise was beneficial. Nazi racist theories never gained credence in the social sciences and were intellectually disreputable from the very beginning; indeed, the Nazis had to subvert the great German universities and expel many of the best scholars and scientists from their academic posts because they denounced Nazi ideology. Both traditional laissez-faire capitalism and doctrinaire Marxism have also been challenged by academic economists, sociologists and historians. Consequently, the Communist party and the state bureaucracy had to control universities in east European countries, and in the United States of the early 1950's, reactionaries like Joseph McCarthy for a short while threatened academic freedom.

The Inner Eye. The abstract movement in art that had originated in Expressionism and Cubism developed in the 1920's and 1930's into a general trend that is often called Surrealism (although strictly speaking the Surrealists were a particular group in Paris in the 1920's). The governing artistic aim of the period was to portray what the inner eye—or psychic as opposed to physical vision—beholds, whether this be a distorted, absurd form, rectangular lines, or private myth. An additional assumption was the autonomy of art—painting does not reflect nature but is itself a distinct nature. These pages show three aspects of the nonrepresentational art of the interwar period. Facing page, top: Piet Mondrian's "Composition in Red, Yellow, and Blue" (1921), a mystical perception of the pure beauty and harmony of line and color. Facing page, bottom: Joan Miró's "Person Throwing a Stone at a Bird" (1926). Miró's work is a symbolic interpretation of nature. Above: Pablo Picasso's "Woman Weeping" (1937). Through what he called "abominable forms," Picasso expressed the ugliness, disorder, and alienation of modern life.

Twentieth-century academic thought has, however, exhibited the defects of its qualities. The compartmentalization of the intellect that began in the late nineteenth century has been greatly intensified. With scholars dissecting and scrutinizing the various parts of the human experience, who could speak for the whole man—for the good life of man and society in their integrated wholes?

One of the grim paradoxes of the twentieth century has been the simultaneous dissemination of fantastic and vicious myths by the extreme Left and Right and the accumulation in the universities of verifiable information on social and individual behavior which thoroughly contradicts these myths. But the extremists provided total views of human nature and social change which the academics, with their enthusiasm for analysis, generally failed to offer. The academics brought into question the old ethics, the old humanism, the old liberalism, but they were tardy and negligent in developing holistic social theories that were both scientifically verifiable and comprehensible and attractive to the common man. Consequently, extremist ideologies proved fatally popular, even to some intellectuals and professors.

In English-speaking countries, the social and behavioral sciences have had a devastat-

COLLECTION HAAGS GEMEENTEMUSEUM, THE HAGUE

COLLECTION OF THE MUSEUM OF MODERN ART, NEW YORK. PURCHASE.

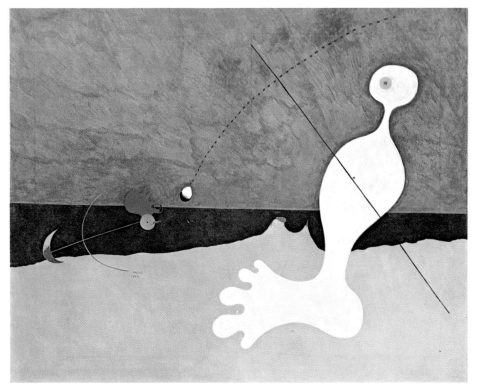

Myth, Psyche, and Terror. Western art at mid-century continued to refine and extend the style and themes of the first quarter of the century. It displayed a growing fascination with primordial myth, an eagerness to communicate psychic experience, and an evocation of the horror of the times. The British abstract school was distinguished by the greatest sculptor of the twentieth century, Henry Moore, who explored mythic themes in a series of earth deities. Left: Moore's "Recumbent Figure" (1938). In the United States, the leading exponent of the so-called Abstract Expressionist school was Jackson Pollock, whose action paintings fulfilled to the highest degree the principle that "the painting has a life of its own." Below: Pollock's "Number 1" (1948). Another American, William de Kooning, effectively combined the themes of primordial myth, psychic experience, and demonic terror that were so central to the modern movement in painting. Facing page: "Woman 1" (1950-1952) by William de Kooning.

COLLECTION OF THE MUSEUM OF MODERN ART, NEW YORK. PURCHASE.

COLLECTION OF THE MUSEUM OF MODERN ART, NEW YORK. PURCHASE.

ing impact on philosophy, which used to provide an integrated view of life. In the face of the vast and often confusing data that these sciences provided, British and American philosophers simply abdicated their social responsibility. They abandoned ethics, metaphysics, and social and political theory as their province and confined themselves to linguistic analysis. Valuable as this scrutiny of terms and the meaning of conceptual phrases has been in

The Humanization of Functionalism. Gropius' and Mies van der Rohe's 1920's functional architecture became the International Style of skyscrapers and factory buildings in the succeeding three decades, and became routinized, vulgarized, and aesthetically exhausted through endless repetition and uninspired imitation. A pioneer functionalist before the First World War, Frank Lloyd Wright inaugurated the movement to humanize functionalism, to incorporate inspiration and personal feeling with the clean lines and bold employment of glass and concrete. Below: the Kaufmann House at Bear Run, Pennsylvania (1936–1937), marks a turning point toward the new "organic" architecture. Wright's evocation of Mayan pyramidal levels, and his efforts to integrate interior living space with outdoor terraces and the waterfall are reminiscent of the Romantics. The same effort to bring human meaning to function inspired the work of Swiss-born Le Corbusier, the most influential architect of the 1940's and 1950's. One of his masterpieces (facing page) was the Church of Notre Dame du Haut, Ronchamp, France (1955) which combines stark concrete walls with dignified monumentality and personal sentiment—the main structure resembles a nun's headdress.

clarifying communication, it leaves men with nothing to communicate about—nothing to believe in, no value system to govern their lives—and therefore vulnerable to emotional commitment to extremist dogmas. The abdication by the "analytic" philosophers of philosophy's traditional role has been a calamity for the twentieth century. If philosophers will not tell us what is justice and virtue, to whom shall we turn? To behaviorist psychologists sending rats through mazes? Or to sociologists studying more effective methods of advertising? Or to anthropologists absorbed in the kinship patterns of New Guinea? Or to the ideologists of the Right and Left, mouthing the dated jargon of Herbert Spencer or Georges Sorel?

A third characteristic of twentieth-century culture has been the perpetuation of modes of thought and feeling that were the product of the new consciousness of the late nineteenth century. The relativism and irrationalism of the age of Nietzsche, Freud, and Weber reached its zenith (or nadir) in the

1920's and 1930's. The motto of these decades might well have been "nothing sacred, nothing true, and nothing good." Moral and social standards were regarded either as the product of class consciousness or as suppressed, unconscious, or semiconscious personal drives. No interpretation of the past was supposed to have a claim to objective validity; it was at best the view of the particular moment, subject to immediate change, or at worst merely a class or national ideology or a private myth. Human nature was regarded as a miscellany of atavistic urges, and human action was viewed as so completely determined by physical and sexual drives as to make a mockery of the Enlightenment view of man as rational and the Romantic faith in the quest for moral and spiritual fulfillment.

The mass murders, unprecedented in human history, perpetrated by the Nazis and the Stalinists demonstrated the pragmatic dangers of extreme relativism and irrationalism. If nothing was good and sacred, how could any ideology, no matter how vicious, be condemned as false? And how could any aggressive act—murder, rape, or pillage—be condemned as inhuman? Freud had tried to show how civilization could absorb and cure its discontents. But the doctrines of relativism and irrationalism in the 1930's perverted Freud's moral intentions—they eroded the dichotomy between reason and unreason; they abandoned the distinction between civilization and savagery. Auschwitz was the consequence, and in the postwar world a quest for the reaffirmation of human values—a search for some principles of good and truth in human life—was launched.

Essentially, the leading thinkers of the contemporary world have tried to regain a kernel of the faith of liberal humanism and rationalism without

The New Monumentalism. Nineteenth-century architects had sought to celebrate the power and enterprise of modern industrial civilization through massive, imposing structures. The result was only a tasteless grandiosity, because they never developed their own style but merely imitated classical and medieval designs in overblown and unwieldy structures. The new functionalism of Gropius and Mies van der Rohe in the 1920's decisively abandoned Victorian Baroque by concentrating on stark and simple lines. Then in the 30's and 40's Wright and Le Corbusier humanized and softened the already redundant puritanism of the International functional style. The next stage in magnificently creative twentieth-century architecture was to apply the concrete and glass materials of functionalism, and the personal expression achieved by Wright and Le Corbusier to monumental structures that celebrated power and technology in a distinctly contemporary way. The new monumentalism in the architecture of the 1960's is exemplified in the IBM Laboratory at La Gaude, France, by Marcel Breuer (below) and in the new City Hall, Toronto, Canada, by Revell and Parkin Associates (facing page).

ignoring the more sophisticated understanding of human nature and society that was the product of the new consciousness or the horror of the two world wars. Many of these thinkers subscribed to a faith called existentialism, which is simply a sadder and wiser, more tragic and less naive version of traditional Western humanism. Albert Camus in 1942 clearly expressed the dilemma of the contemporary era. We are painfully aware of the "absurdity" of human life, the conflict between irrationality and our longing for peace and justice. We cannot deny this awful crisis of the human condition; we have to make the best of it:

At this point of his effort man stands face to face with the irrational. He feels within him his longing for happiness and for reason. The absurd is born of this confrontation between the human need and the unreasonable silence of the world. This must not be forgotten. This must be clung to because the whole consequence of a life can depend on it.[1]

Jean-Paul Sartre's "atheistic existentialism" propounded the same kind of neo-humanism: "There is no human nature, because there is no God to have a conception of it. Man simply is. . . . Man is nothing else but that which he makes of himself."[2]

Even before Camus and Sartre reaffirmed the old faith in man's

1. Albert Camus, *The Myth of Sisyphus.* New York: Knopf, 1955, p. 28.
2. Jean-Paul Sartre, *Existentialism and Humanism,* in M. White, ed., *The Age of Analysis.* New York: Mentor, 1955, p. 124.

The People's Art. Symptomatic of a general cultural bifurcation in mass industrial society, one of the most significant phenomena in twentieth-century art has been the dichotomy between the style of popular art and the style of the major painters and sculptors. The petite bourgeoisie, the working class, and politicians of the extreme Left or the far Right were suspicious of abstract art and often violently hostile to it. They preferred to express didactic or emotional themes in traditional realistic style. Facing page, top: "Woman with Plants" by Grant Wood, typical of the style and theme favored by some American mass-circulation magazines down to the early 1960's. Left: "Hitler in Armor" by Lanziger, an example of Nazi propaganda art. Hitler persecuted and expelled the abstract masters of the Bauhaus school. Below: memorial to Soviet soldiers in Treptow Park, East Berlin, typical of the "socialist realism" that Lenin and Stalin decided was suitable proletarian art. In the 1960's education by schools, museums, and even mass-circulation magazines led to a growing popular recognition of the value of abstract art. And in the radical posters of the period a new, spontaneous popular art was emerging. Facing page, bottom: "Alabama 1965" by Robert Indiana.

nobility, a group of Christian existentialists had revived Augustinian theology. Whether this gave individual man any more external support in his quest for peace and happiness than the secular existentialists allowed him is still being debated. In the first formulation of Christian existentialism by Karl Barth, man's situation was bleak indeed. In his "crisis theology," written in the 1920's, Barth stressed "the eternal qualitative distinction between [human] time and [divine] eternity" as well as "the chasm which separates God and man."[3] But the Christian in the depths of his despair could still hope for "either ascent of man towards God or God's condescendence to man."[3]

3. Quoted in S. P. Schilling, *Contemporary Continental Theologians.* Nashville: Abingdon, 1966, p. 26.

Later, Barth restored the central place of the Incarnation in Christian theology, and the inspiring as well as saving role of Christ in human life has been underlined in both Protestant and Catholic thought in the post-Second World War era. Jesus' life and death is both the means of divine grace and the model for human life. "Man is challenged to participate in the sufferings of God at the hands of a godless world."[4] This statement by Dietrich Bonhoeffer, the Lutheran theologian martyred by the Nazis, enunciates a revived Christian activism that seeks to transform the world through personal commitment to the highest moral act in a particular situation. The new generation of Catholic theologians could not fully accept this existential commitment to a personal quest for fulfillment of God's words — the commands of the institutional Church are authoritative. But the most distinguished of the radical Catholic thinkers, Karl Rahner, insisted that in every situation each Catholic must still ask, "Lord, what do you want me to do?"[5]

The thrust of the postwar existentialism, whether secular or Christian, was toward a vision of liberated individuals joining together in mutual respect and love to build a better society that would take account of the social and behavioral sciences and the horrible lessons of modern history and transcend all of these in a new world community. This vision was expressed around 1950 by the widely venerated dean of German philosophers, Karl Jaspers. The nineteenth-century faith in the rule of law, Jaspers said, was "mere high-sounding words behind which was hidden the sordidness of life that was disclosed by psychoanalysis." In its place he postulated a community based on "our potentiality really to live together, to speak together, through this togetherness to find our way to the truth, and hereby finally to become authentically ourselves."[6]

4. Quoted in D. G. Peerman and M. E. Marty, eds., *A Handbook of Christian Theologians*. Cleveland: World, 1965, p. 483.
5. Quoted in Schilling, *Contemporary Continental Theologians*, p. 222.
6. Karl Jaspers, *The Philosophy of the Future*, in A. Koch, ed., *Philosophy for a Time of Crisis*. New York: Dutton, 1959, pp. 325, 333.

The Contemporary World

ENVIRONMENT ESSAY

By the late 1950's western Europe, with invaluable American aid, had made a spectacular recovery from the devastation of the Second World War. There as in America the demand for material goods seemed insatiable. A generation that had undergone the miseries of the Depression and the hardships of war was now bent on enjoying some of the material benefits modern technology could provide. A stunning array of consumer products became widely available: television sets, transistor radios, Polaroid cameras, wash-and-wear dresses and suits, frozen TV dinners, paperback books. Installment buying made even the most costly of these goods accessible to large sectors of the working class. The poor as well as the rich went in for conspicuous consumption.

Spectacular developments in the chemical industry produced a vast array of new consumer goods, and new "miracle" drugs—antibiotics, antihistamines, tranquilizers—reduced the time lost to illness and increased longevity. The rapid expansion of commercial aviation and the onset of the "jet age" made travel to exotic corners of the earth feasible for many middle-class families. Vacations in distant lands became commonplace as secretaries and schoolteachers took advantage of packaged group tours. The development of prefabricated building units made home ownership possible for a multitude of young married couples. Levittowns or their equivalent sprang up all over America, Japan, and much of Europe.

Atomic energy, the computer, and the jet plane altered both the physical and the mental environment of man. The peaceful use of atomic energy promised unlimited power to electrify and industrialize every corner of the globe. Simultaneously, the development of the atomic and hydrogen bombs forced

men to live under the threat of nuclear holocaust that could annihilate the human species. Previous technological advances had liberated man from physical labor. The computer, an entirely new, self-regulating kind of tool, could eat up the jobs of white-collar as well as blue-collar workers. What sort of culture would men develop with the vastly increased leisure now attainable?

Institutional evidence that the world was shrinking could be seen in the postwar proliferation of international agencies. The World Bank, the International Monetary Fund, the International Development Agency, the International Atomic Energy Agency, NATO, the Organization of American States, the Warsaw Pact, and the United Nations all testified to the fact that defense and economic planning now had to be coordinated and integrated along supranational lines. No nation, not even the most wealthy and prosperous, could any longer go it alone. Technology had made isolationism obsolete.

The Third Industrial Revolution. Momentous developments in science and technology characterized the postwar era. Right: a view of the Renault automobile factory in France, an example of the new vitality of European industry. The destruction caused by the war forced industrialists to start from scratch with new plants, the most modern equipment, and the latest production methods. Above: assembling a missile. Rocket-powered missiles capable of launching communication satellites as well as nuclear warheads across thousands of miles were an important factor in the cold war. Together with other advances in transportation, communication, and propulsion, they contributed to the shrinking of the globe. Facing page: an atom smasher with a generating potential of eight million volts of nuclear energy. The peaceful uses of atomic energy have been continually extended. Agriculture, medicine, mineralogy, and industry have all benefited.

The Crowded Earth. A tide of rising expectations accompanied the postwar population explosion. Facing page, bottom: a university lecture hall in Czechoslovakia. Students must pass grueling examinations to reach this stepping-stone to privilege and prestige. Facing page, top: a housing project in Japan. Although such developments are often ugly, for millions they represent a great improvement in living conditions. Below: airport congestion in the jet age. It is not uncommon for planes to depart and land at the rate of one per minute.

Technological advance promised to make mankind an unbound Prometheus. But with the new promise came new menaces. The population explosion — to which, paradoxically, the new advances in medicine had contributed — continued unchecked precisely in those parts of the world that were least capable of feeding more people. The gains in industrial and agricultural production of every Five-Year Plan in India were wiped out by the increase in population. The teachings of Malthus, the dour eighteenth-century economist, acquired a new and sinister plausibility.

Industrial advance brought with it the very real threat of a fundamental disruption of the earth's ecology. Smog, the product of industrial wastes and automobile fumes, polluted the urban air; alarmed conservationists pointed out that millions of tons of poison were being discharged into the atmosphere each year. Other wastes poured unchecked into rivers and lakes, killing certain species of fish and wildlife and leaving the water unfit for human use. The by-products of postwar progress included larger junk yards and garbage dumps, denuded forests, polluted beaches, litter-strewn parks. Disfunctional ugliness spread across the landscape.

The postwar super-city, the "megalopolis," created unprec-

LIFE PHOTO BY ALFRED EISENSTAEDT

WORLD POPULATION TODAY

Population per square mile

- Over 250
- 125-250
- 25-125
- under 25
- ■ Metropolitan areas over 2,000,000 population

ARCTIC   OCEAN

ATLANTIC

PACIFIC

OCEAN

Montreal
Toronto
Chicago   Detroit   Boston
Cleveland   New York
Philadelphia   Pittsburgh
Washington
San Francisco
Los Angeles

Mexico City

Lima

Sao Paulo   Rio de Janeiro

Sidney

Santiago   Buenos Aires

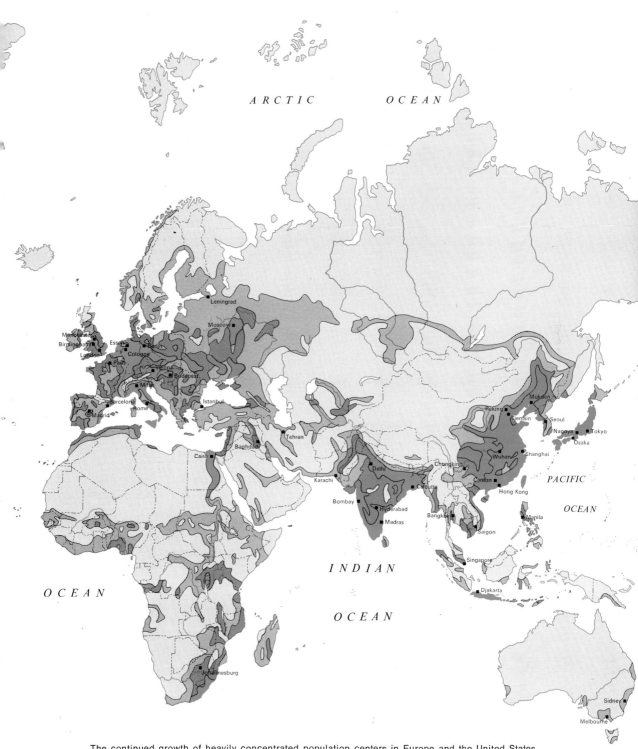

The continued growth of heavily concentrated population centers in Europe and the United States poses critical problems for urban planning. The steady ascent of the demographic curve in many parts of Latin America, Asia, and Africa has placed a perilous pressure on food supply in some areas, has raised grave economic and social issues, and, in the long run, could affect the balance of power in international relations.

The Third World. Certain privileged enclaves in Asia, Africa, and Latin America have become indistinguishable from European centers of industry, urbanization, and art. Above: shipyards in Tokyo. The postwar economic boom in Japan has made that country the industrial and commercial titan of Asia in the second half of the twentieth century. Below: library in Mexico City. The magnificent architecture suggests the great pride the non-European world takes in matching the best that Europe has produced artistically as well as materially. Facing page: building a dam in India. The overriding need of underdeveloped areas such as India to electrify and industrialize has contributed to their determination to maintain a position of ideological neutrality between the Communist bloc and the West. India has received engineers, technicians, and vast sums of money from both the Soviet Union and the United States. Modernization has nevertheless been agonizingly slow, because to accomplish some of its aims, the government has had to overcome prejudices and traditions entrenched for thousands of years.

edented social problems. It seemed impossible to design and allocate living space rationally in the new congestion. Crime rates soared as people were packed together by the tens of thousands in a few city blocks. Ethnic ghettos festered. The drive for success became equated with the "rat race." Middle-class life in the cities and suburbs was glutted with commodities, but to many it seemed to be a life of spiritual desiccation, a new wasteland of loneliness and alienation. The tremendous expansion of the communications media — particularly television in the 1950's — created an entirely new kind of mass culture, marked by standardized, homogenized tastes, life styles, opinions, and values. Conformity was the great byword of the 1950's. It permeated styles of dress, popular songs, voting patterns, and personal behavior.

The American megalopolis — New York city and Los Angeles — was the

vanguard of all these postwar developments. In the early fifties, European intellectuals smugly criticized the vulgarity of American life. By 1960, it could no longer be denied that the same economic, social, and cultural trends were fast emerging in the large European centers and that this way of life was what the European masses, just as much as the American, ardently desired—even those in the socialist heaven of the Soviet Union. The Americanization of the world was under way. Los Angeles appeared to be the destiny of mankind.

The underdeveloped countries of Latin America, Africa, and Asia also craved a mass-consumption economy. But the crucial reforms that would be required to promote industrialization, check population growth, redistribute land, and raise per capita income in these societies often proved elusive. Although the "Third World" had its showcase industries, its dams and its model cities, the culture of misery persisted. Economists spoke grimly of the ever widening gap between the "haves" and the "have-nots" of the world.

I THE BEGINNINGS OF THE COLD WAR

The United Nations

Even before they were sure of victory, Allied statesmen began to make plans to construct a lasting peace. Franklin Roosevelt deserves the major credit for this effort. In 1941 he and Churchill published the Atlantic Charter, a summary of postwar expectations that included a permanent system of international security against aggression. Roosevelt avoided Wilson's political errors: he allowed sentiment for American participation in a postwar organization to build up gradually and in both political parties. In October 1943, at a foreign ministers' meeting in Moscow, the four major Allied belligerents (the United States, Great Britain, Russia, and China) announced their support for such a peace-keeping institution.

The details were settled at inter-Allied conferences during the next year and a half. The meeting at Dumbarton Oaks (August–September 1944) successfully got around Russian reluctance to working with the Chinese at this time, and the basic structure of the United Nations was settled. Its General Assembly was to be open to all members. Because all agreed on the need for unanimity among the permanent members of the Security Council (the United States, Russia, Britain, France, and China), each was given an absolute veto over its decisions. Roosevelt (and to a lesser degree Churchill) saw the need to sidestep the veto in the event of aggression by a permanent member; but Stalin maintained that the veto power was irrevocable. During the San Francisco Conference (April–June 1945) the Russians reversed themselves, however, agreeing that the veto power might be limited by requiring parties to a dispute to abstain from voting. Stalin also abandoned an earlier demand for sixteen seats in the General Assembly, accepting three (for the USSR, the Ukraine, and White Russia). Representatives of fifty countries at San Francisco signed the charter establishing the United Nations.

In 1945 there were vague hopes that the UN would evolve into a world government; but these were soon dashed by hostility between the United States and the Soviet Union and by the insistence of all countries on the prerogatives of their national sovereignty. It quickly became evident that the UN was quite powerless to settle a dispute in which American and Russian interests clashed. Yet the UN did provide the institutional means of resolving conflicts between nations in which neither the United States nor the Soviet Union—nor, preferably, any other major power—felt compelled to take a stand. In the case of serious crises involving the postwar superpowers, the UN did make some contributions to peace. The very necessity of bringing disputes to the Security Council—even if it resulted in long harangues by both sides and eventual deadlock—provided a cooling-off period during which precipitate action was avoided. Also the attendance at the UN of ambassadors from all leading powers provided an easy opportunity for confidential conferences and exchanges of views.

Aside from these peace-keeping functions, the UN made its most important contribution through subsidiary agencies. In the immediate postwar era, the United Nations Relief and Rehabilitation Administration (UNRRA) effectively assisted the homeless and destitute all over the world. The Economic and Social Council (UNESCO) had some remarkable successes in fostering international cooperation in the fields of economic planning, education, and medicine.

Eastern Europe

The first demonstrations of Allied disagreement on the postwar settlement occurred in eastern Europe. As the German army retreated, chaos replaced oppression. The sudden disappearance of Nazi occupation regimes raised the question of who was to form new governments. Several of the prewar governments had been discredited for collaboration with the Nazis; partisan resistance groups tended to be split between Communist and nationalist factions; and governments-in-exile only complicated the picture. Internal dissension left these countries open to outside interference, particularly from the USSR, which had expelled the German forces.

As early as 1944, W. Averill Harriman, the American ambassador in Moscow, had warned Roosevelt of Soviet designs on the territories of neighboring states, particularly Poland. Roosevelt concluded that no one could stop the Russians from taking what they wanted to take in eastern Europe. He was willing to accept preeminent Russian influence there, for he was eager to bring American troops home from the Continent and to secure Russian participation in the Pacific war. Churchill, on the other hand, would have

Gained by the Soviet Union
Gained by Poland
Gained by Yugoslavia
Gained by Rumania

Compared with the redrawing of the map of Europe that followed World War I, the territorial changes after World War II were few. Russian westward expansion was the most significant change. The Soviet Union absorbed Estonia, Latvia, and Lithuania and also regained the territory it had lost in 1918 to Finland, Poland, and Rumania. Poland was compensated at Germany's expense, and Rumania at the expense of Bulgaria. In addition, Yugoslavia gained more territory at the head of the Adriatic. By 1949 Germany had been divided into the Federal Republic (West Germany) and the German Democratic Republic (Communist East Germany). The city of Berlin was also partitioned into western and eastern zones.

preferred to contest the Russian advance into eastern Europe—had the military situation allowed such a course. It did not, and the prime minister was forced to compromise.

During 1944 Churchill approached Stalin with a plan to divide liberated Europe into spheres of influence in which one or another great power would predominate. (At the time, the Russian armies were making an alarming advance into the Balkans.) Stalin accepted and percentages were fixed by which the Soviet Union had the preponderant influence in Rumania and Bulgaria and had 50 per cent influence in Hungary and Yugoslavia. Britain was given control in Greece. It was agreed, too, that the USSR was free to intervene within its sphere against pro-Nazi and pro-Fascist groups and that the governments of neighboring states would be "friendly to Russia." This regional approach, with its tolerance of political interference by one or another of the great powers, had immense consequences for eastern Europe.

Since most of the occupied countries were liberated by the Russians, the

USSR had the major influence on the composition of the provisional governments set up by their citizens. And since it was through these countries that the Germans had attacked Russia, the Soviets understandably considered them of strategic importance to Russian security. Thus the Polish Committee of National Liberation (also known as the Lublin Committee) became the provisional government of Poland, displacing the government in exile that had spent the war years in London. The exile government—after a futile appeal to Roosevelt to intervene on its behalf—had stubbornly refused to accept (or even discuss) the establishment of the Curzon Line as Poland's boundary with the Soviet Union, and the Russian army had stood by while the resistance forces supporting the exile government were destroyed by the Germans.

The decisive elements in the Lublin Committee were the Communists (PPR) and Socialists (PPS), although at the insistence of Churchill and Roosevelt the Polish People's party (or Peasant party, the PSL) of the London exiles was represented. It was not possible for these groups to govern together, and in the elections of 1946 terror and harassment were used to defeat the PSL. The Peasant party then went into opposition, and in the autumn its leader fled to the West. By the end of 1948, purges had eliminated some 75,000 Communists and Socialists who deviated from the Soviet line, and the new Polish United Workers' party was formed. Poland was now a more tractable satellite of the USSR.

In the free elections in Czechoslovakia in May 1946, the Communists won one third of the seats in the Assembly, and their leader, Klement Gottwald, headed the new coalition government. It was not until the next year, however, that their political offensive got under way. Then non-Communist dissidents were rounded up and rival politicians imprisoned and executed. Nonetheless, when the United States announced its Marshall Plan to supply aid to the devastated countries of Europe, Czechoslovakia quickly agreed to participate—too quickly as things turned out. Stalin, fearing that the West would gain influence over participating countries, brought pressure to bear to prevent the eastern European states from accepting American aid. In September 1947, on Stalin's initiative, a meeting of the leaders of various Communist parties was held in Poland. Division of the world into two opposing camps was reported; French and Italian Communists were criticized as parliamentary deviationists; and the Cominform was founded as an "information office" for the various national Communist parties. In response to the threat that participation in the Marshall Plan would bring an end to the Soviet-Czech pact of friendship and mutual aid, the Czech government reversed its decision.

National elections in Czechoslovakia were scheduled for May 1948, but the slow progress of recovery made the Communists fearful of defeat, and in February they called for extraparliamentary mass action. Having gained control of key ministries, including the police, the Communists were in a position to take over the government. The police did nothing to stop harassment of non-Communist political figures. On February 19 an unexpected visit by a leading

Soviet diplomat bespoke the serious possibility of Russian intervention, and the Communists threatened a coup if complete power was not turned over to them. President Benes acceded to this demand, for he believed that Russian support would be necessary in the event of any future German menace. And he knew from his experiences in the late 1930's how hopeless it was to withstand armed aggression alone. That May, elections with a single list of candidates were held, and soon afterward purges began. On May 10, the Czech foreign minister Jan Masaryk — son of the prewar president of Czechoslovakia and, like his father, a liberal — was murdered by Soviet agents who took pains to disguise his death as a suicide.

In the Hungarian elections of November 1945, the Smallholders' party won the majority of seats in the new government. As in Czechoslovakia, however, the Communists were able to control the police and thus to subvert the opposition. In 1947 the Smallholder premier, Ferenc Nagy, was replaced after being implicated in an espionage plot. In January 1948 the Russians arranged a merger of the Social Democrats and the Communists with the latter in control, and single-list elections followed. By 1950 Hungary was completely under Communist domination.

In Rumania, where King Michael had been restored in 1944, the Western powers succeeded in broadening the provisional government to include leaders of the Independent Liberal and National Peasant parties. Elections were delayed until November, and after considerable pressure had been applied to the electorate, an 85 per cent pro-government vote was recorded. The next year a Communist offensive against the opposition parties began, and the National Peasant leader Julius Maniu was condemned to life imprisonment. Elections the following March saw the end of opposition to communism.

The Communist-dominated Fatherland Front in Bulgaria received 80 per cent of the vote in the elections of October 1946. Resolutions passed by its representatives in January 1947 opposed independent political parties, and the leader of the anti-Communist faction was tried and executed on the usual trumped-up treason charges. Potential opposition within the party was then rapidly eliminated by purges, and Bulgaria joined the ranks of the Communist satellites.

Among the countries liberated by the Russians, only Yugoslavia withstood Soviet pressure. There the epic wartime resistance of Tito's Communist party ensured its victory in the elections of November 1945. Initially, the new regime was the most militant in the Communist world. Tito himself was ambitious, envisioning a united Balkan league of Yugoslavia, Bulgaria, and Greece. But his aid to the Greek Communist rebels met with Stalin's disapproval; in early 1948 Stalin wanted Yugoslavia to join in federation only with its poorer neighbors, Bulgaria and Albania. The situation worsened as Tito's ambitious economic plans were criticized in Moscow, and it became clear that Stalin hoped to control Yugoslavia through the more pliable Bulgarian regime. In June, Yugoslavia was expelled from the Cominform. For a time Tito sought to demonstrate to his neighbors his fidelity to Communist ideals, but Russian pressure caused Yugoslav trade with the Communist world to drop to a mere fraction of its previous level. Tito was forced to turn to the West, which willingly supplied him with half a billion dollars in aid during the next few years.

The Truman Doctrine

In Greece, Western intervention prevented a Communist take-over. An agreement at Yalta gave Britain responsibility for supervising Greece's postwar political recovery, but this stopped only temporarily the fighting between the Communist-led leftist resistance and the British-supported Royalists. In the spring of 1946 only half the electorate voted in elections (which Russia refused to help oversee) that were won by the Royalist party. When the monarchy was returned by referendum in September, the working class was deeply alienated, and civil war soon broke out. The Communists (ELAS) were supplied from the Soviet satellites. By the end of 1946 the situation was critical for the Greek government, which had been forced to curtail its efforts at reconstruction to pursue the fighting; and Great Britain, which had been furnishing both military and economic aid, was also in financial difficulties. On February 24, 1947, the British government informed Washington that it would have to pull its forces out of Greece by the end of March. Though surprised by such news, President Truman quickly moved to assume Britain's responsibilities. "This was the time," he wrote later in his memoirs, "to align the United States of America clearly on the side, and at the head, of the free world." In his address to Congress on March 12, 1947, he declared that "it must be the policy of the United States to support free peoples who are resisting attempted subjugation by armed minorities or by outside pressure."

Thus was the Truman Doctrine born. It was also applied to Turkey, which had been under great Soviet pressure. Before Turkey finally entered World War II on the Allied side in February 1945, Russia had begun to advance claims to control of the Bosporus and the Dardanelles and to a base in Thrace. Throughout 1945 and 1946, the Soviet government pressured the Turkish government to accede to these claims; but the United States supported Turkish resistance, and the Republican-controlled Congress authorized $150 million in aid to Turkey, as well as $250 million to Greece. With the United States in the picture, the Greek rebels had little chance of winning, and early in 1948 Stalin ordered Yugoslavia to cease giving aid to the rebels. Harried by his quarrel with Moscow, Tito closed Yugoslavia's border with Greece in the middle of the year, and by the end of 1949 the last of the rebels had retreated to Bulgaria and Rumania. But the Communists had not changed their basic strategy and objectives. They now turned their attention to Germany.

Divided Germany

In Germany the refusal of the West to permit a Communist take-over led to the division of the country. Agreement on the principle of joint and total occupation of the Reich was reached as early as 1943 at a meeting of the Allied foreign ministers in Moscow. At the Yalta Conference four zones were set up, for occupation by the USSR, Great Britain, the United States, and France. Central authorities were to be established for such matters as finance, transport, commerce, and foreign trade.

Neither Russia nor Britain nor the United States wanted Germany to be permanently dismembered. The Soviet Union wanted a unified, Communist-controlled Germany, while Britain hoped for a unified Germany that would be economically viable without posing any threat to Continental security. Roosevelt foresaw a swing back to isolation in the United States after the fighting was concluded; he did not want a settlement that would involve his country in Continental affairs or obligate it to spend large sums on occupation. At the same time, the French government—whose goal was the permanent detachment of the Saar, Rhineland, and Ruhr from Germany—refused to recognize the agreements reached at Yalta and Potsdam, in which it had not participated, and so opposed the political creation of central authorities. In the end a division of Germany was worked out under the pressure of events.

The Allies divided western Germany into three occupied zones; the Soviet army held the eastern half of the country. The western zone commanders were primarily concerned with developing sound local institutions. For three years—from Germany's surrender on May 8, 1945, until the creation of the Federal Republic—the Allies carried out a "de-Nazification" program. It began with the trial for war crimes of top Nazis at Nuremberg from November 1945 until September 1946 and continued with the removal and punishment of other important Nazi leaders. An extensive "reeducation" process effected a significant change in traditional German views of politics and society. Western zone commanders also influenced political reconstruction. In the American zone, provincial elections held during 1946 gave comparable tallies to the moderate and non-Communist Christian Democrats (CDU), Social Democrats (SPD), and Christian Social Union (CSU); in the British sector, elections favored the SPD and CDU. (The French were somewhat slower to revive political activity.)

In the Soviet zone, the Socialist and Communist parties were soon combined into the Socialist Unity party (SED) on orders from Moscow, after the Communists had suffered from identification with the policies of the Soviet occupation. In the October elections in the Soviet zone, the SED was successful in the countryside but was badly defeated in Berlin, where the Socialist (SPD) membership had not followed its leadership into fusion with the Communists. This defeat was a crippling blow to Soviet hopes, for the USSR had expected that strong Communist control in Berlin would evolve into Communist control of the entire country after reunification.

Though within the Soviet zone, Berlin was supposed to be administered by a four-power *Kommandatura* after the war. Moscow had sought to circumvent the *Kommandatura* by establishing an assembly (to control the government) and a police force. But such circumvention of Allied influence in Berlin depended upon political domination there by the Communist-directed SED; the success of the anti-Communist SPD killed the plan. It was too late to return power to the *Kommandatura* (though the Soviets attempted it), and the USSR had to content itself with tightening its hold on the eastern sector of the city.

At the end of 1946, in response to Russian unwillingness to cooperate on German economic problems, the American and British zones were merged economically in the Bizone; and the Western powers made plans to draft a constitution for a federal government for western Germany and to institute long overdue currency reform. The latter the Soviet Union could not accept, as it would cause the value of East German currency to plummet. The Soviets responded to the Western decision by interfering with surface transport to the western sectors of Berlin. This began in April 1948, and in late July the Russians imposed a blockade of all rail, highway, and water traffic. To the surprise of the USSR, the Western powers were able to withstand this pressure, and the West Berlin city government held fast in the face of stepped-up harassment. Throughout the winter an airlift of stupendous magnitude kept the beleaguered sectors of the city supplied with food and fuel. In May 1949 the Berlin blockade was lifted, and the Western powers and the Communists returned to more conventional kinds of confrontation.

Unification was no longer possible. By establishing an armed police force with military equipment in East Germany, the Russians had given the East Germans the means with which to wage a civil war if the country was unified, and the Allies and West Germans knew this. During the blockade the democratically elected city assembly for Berlin had been forced to move into the western sector, and a separate administration had been set up in East Berlin. The division of Berlin became increasingly rigid. In East Germany, the non-Communist parties were purged; a single list of candidates appeared for the elections in the spring of 1949. In West Germany, representatives from the provincial legislatures drafted a federal constitution. The French zone was integrated into the Bizone, and in late summer 1949, general elections were held. The Christian Democrats won a few more seats than the Social Democrats, and Konrad Adenauer (1876–1967)—former mayor of Cologne, with a good record as an anti-Nazi—was made chancellor of the new German Federal Republic.

Coalescence of the West

The Berlin crisis served to spotlight western Europe's vulnerability in the face of Soviet provocations. Other factors also contributed to the coalescence of the United States, Canada, and the western European states in a formal alliance. The rejection by the Soviet Union and its satellites of Marshall Plan aid meant that only the countries of western Europe were receiving this vast assistance, amounting to twelve billion dollars between 1948 and 1953. The governments of these countries, which were liberal and non-Communist (although there were strong Communist opposition parties in France and Italy), naturally looked with favor on a politico-military alliance with their economic benefactor. In the United States the postwar reversion to isolationism that Roosevelt had feared had not occurred. On the contrary, both the Democratic and Republican parties were inspired by a kind of Wilsonian idealism, which involved an active foreign policy and commitments to non-Communist countries so as to contain what seemed to be the dangerous ambitions of Stalin and international communism. Finally, the Communist take-over in Czechoslovakia alarmed western European liberals: Czechoslovakia had been the only eastern European state where a viable system of democracy had existed before the Second World War.

Consequently, in March 1948, after the Czech government had been taken over, a mutual assistance treaty against aggression—not merely renewed German aggression but aggression by any power—was signed at Brussels by Great Britain, France, Belgium, the Netherlands, and Luxembourg. Immediately, the French and British made new suggestions for a program of Atlantic security in which the United States would participate. The North Atlantic Treaty was signed in April 1949. It stipulated that armed attack against any of the signatories (Denmark, Iceland, Italy, Norway, Portugal, Canada, the United States, and the signatories to the Brussels pact) was an attack against them all and that they would all be obliged to aid the victim. Never in peacetime had the United States given such a guarantee. In September the United States Congress approved almost $1.5 billion to supply arms to the North Atlantic Treaty Organization (NATO) countries. But the scene of Soviet-American confrontation was now shifting to the Far East.

Communist Triumph in China and the Korean War

During the war, Japan's occupation of the Chinese mainland had postponed the conflict between the Nationalist government of Chiang Kai-shek (b. 1886) and the Chinese Communists led by Mao Tse-tung (b. 1893), but after the Japanese defeat, the feud burst forth again. Stalin had agreed at Yalta to cooperate with the Nationalist government. Instead, supplies captured by the Russians from the Japanese in Manchuria were allowed to fall into the hands of the Chinese Communist forces. These forces had had considerable success in the northern provinces by December 1945, when General George C. Marshall, army chief of staff in World War II, arrived as President Truman's representative to mediate reluctantly between the two warring factions.

Threatened with the possible loss of American aid, Chiang agreed to a truce. But intermittent heavy fighting occurred the next year while the Communists tried to consolidate their position in northern China. The Nationalists mounted a series of successful campaigns, but the Communists rebounded in January 1947, seizing the offensive against a regime that was drowning in a sea of inflation and corruption. By mid-1947 the tide was turning completely in favor of the Communists, and by December 1949 Chiang and the remaining Nationalist forces withdrew from the mainland to the island of Formosa (Taiwan). China, with its 600 million people, became a Communist state.

The Communist victory created a furor in America, and with congressional elections due in November 1950, the Truman administration was forced by public pressure to resist further Communist expansion in the Far East. At the same time, however, the government was seeking a way to disengage itself from Korean affairs. At the end of World War II it had been agreed that the Soviet Union would disarm all Japanese troops in Korea north of the 38th parallel and American forces would disarm those to the south. The dividing line was by no means intended to be permanent, but, as in Germany, a Communist-controlled administration was rapidly set up in the Russian zone, while the United States supported a rival government in the south. The powers argued for two years, with Russia rejecting any settlement that failed to make the Korean Communist party predominant. In the south elections were held under United Nations supervision, and the United States sought the support of the world organization to bring about unification of the whole country. Nothing came of the UN's efforts. The Western powers recognized the winning party in the south as the legitimate government of Korea, while the Soviet bloc recognized the Communist government of North Korea.

Withdrawal of Russian and American troops followed the elections, and the United States, uncertain of South Korean ambitions, left South Korea weakly armed. Then in January 1950, Secretary of State Dean Acheson described an American defense perimeter in the Pacific that specifically excluded Formosa and Korea. This was interpreted by Korean and Chinese Communists as a reasonable assurance that aggression on their part against South Korea would not meet American military resistance. Accordingly, on June 25, the North Koreans attacked across the 38th parallel—only to find that the United States immediately called on the United Nations to take action. Because the Soviet delegate to the Security Council was at that time boycotting its proceedings, condemnation of North Korea's action was not vetoed, and military assistance by UN members to South Korea was authorized. By September, the North Koreans held nearly all of the peninsula. A UN counteroffensive, manned principally by American troops and directed by General MacArthur, pushed the North Koreans back, intending—with a supporting vote from the General Assembly—to effect unification. As the UN lines approached their borders, the Communist Chinese sent troops into battle alongside the North Koreans. The Chinese were able to force a UN retreat southward, and General MacArthur was unable to win approval for his plan to bomb the enemy's bases inside Chinese territory, because the American government feared that such a move would bring Russia into the conflict. MacArthur was dismissed by President Truman amidst high feeling in the United States, and in July 1951 negotiations for an armistice began. They dragged on until May 1953, when the new Eisenhower administration informed the Chinese Communists that unless they were prepared to sign an armistice, the United States might resort to nuclear weapons. An armistice was signed on July 27.

The Pattern of the Cold War

Thus, less than a decade after World War II, a great part of the world had become divided into opposing camps. In Europe, the demands of the Soviet Union were motivated by a boundless eagerness to secure the triumph of Communist parties in as many countries as possible. But Russian policy, which aroused Western fears, was itself particularly conditioned by fear of possible Western aggression. One must remember that the United States was the only atomic power in the world until 1949 and that the German menace seemed very real to all the states of Europe and probably especially so to Russia. Furthermore, Stalin seems to have interpreted the division of Europe into spheres of influence to mean that he could have a free hand in his, so long as he was similarly generous to the West.

Whatever the sources and aims of Russian policy, the postwar events in eastern Europe and the Korean War were interpreted in the West — and especially in the United States — as evidence of Russia's insatiable appetite for power. By 1947 the American government had decided to resist that aggression. Leading State Department strategists, such as Dean Acheson and George Kennan, formulated a policy of containment: the Soviet Union must be held back by political, economic, and propaganda means (and, if ultimately necessary, by force) until the Soviet leaders abandoned their aggressive aims and attitudes.

The ensuing "cold" (i.e., non-shooting) war, at least down to the early 1960's, was marked by the efforts of both the Soviet Union and the United States to force, persuade, or bribe all other countries of the world to line up within their respective Eastern and Western blocs. The cold war was characterized by feverish propaganda activities on the part of the two superpowers, aimed at domestic as well as foreign audiences. Intellectuals in both countries — but more severely in Russia, with its authoritarian tradition — were called upon to demonstrate their loyalty to the national ideology and condemn the opposition as "decadent bourgeois imperialists" or "Communist aggressors and conspirators." This polarization had a congealing effect on the intellectual life of both countries in the decade after the war. Finally, the cold war was marked by periodic confrontations between the two giants, somewhat similar to the crises that led up to the First and Second World Wars. But the existence of nuclear weapons on both sides (Russia had developed them by 1949) made the prospect of a hot war too frightful to be risked, and conventional warfare seemed all too likely to escalate into nuclear holocaust. Consequently, the menacing gestures, ideological harangues, and momentary crises of the cold war stopped short of World War III. In the 1960's new leadership, a somewhat changed mood in both countries, and a more independent neutralist line taken by other countries began to mitigate the harsh, polarized character of the cold war.

II EUROPEAN RECOVERY

The Shift to State Planning

At the end of the Second World War, governments in eastern and western Europe alike had appalling damage to repair. Moreover, recovery had to be accomplished quickly, for the populations that had withstood so much hardship during the war were expecting—and deserved—immediate relief. Across the face of the Continent, industrial activity was stilled: both resources and equipment had been destroyed, and machinery in working order was generally obsolete. Inflation threatened the struggling national economies. Everywhere, people were hungry and homeless.

Turning away from the principles of traditional capitalism, European governments nationalized critical industries and stepped in to plan the recovery of others. There were many reasons for this radical shift to state control and planning, and they were by no means the same in every country. In France, for example, firms that had collaborated with the Nazi occupation regime (e.g., the Renault firm) were nationalized in a patriotic reaction, and concerns in which Germans had bought up controlling interests during the occupation became the property of the state. There was a widespread conviction in Europe that prewar capitalism had failed either to prepare for war or to provide for prosperity.

In Great Britain, the war had demonstrated that the state could effect tremendous increases in production. It was even more obvious that in many industries, recovery of production levels was not possible without massive modernization and reorganization of existing facilities—change that was beyond the means or initiative of private industry in the immediate postwar years. In addition, serious shortages of capital, plant, and raw materials demanded national control over allocation; existing resources had to be utilized in the most productive manner. Academic economic theory also contributed to the general enthusiasm for state planning. If economists were not socialists, they were often disciples of Keynes, who advocated government investment and control at least until prosperity returned.

Russia and Eastern Europe

In the USSR planning was nothing new, and the inauguration of a fourth Five-Year Plan (to run from 1946 to 1950) was no surprise. But the task of rebuilding the Soviet economy was staggering. The official count put the Russian dead at seven million; much of the countryside of European Russia lay in waste; and 25 million people were homeless, not counting the millions who had been evacuated beyond the Urals. In fact, recovery could not be generated within any reasonable period of time without substantial outside aid.

Almost at once after the end of the war, the United States government announced the end of lend-lease, and the Russians were left to shift for themselves. Stalin promoted Russian recovery by exploiting those countries the Red army had occupied. Seemingly he had no one policy for dealing with them. Sometimes the Russians dismantled the industry and removed it to the Soviet Union; in other instances, the production and economy of the smaller nations were integrated with those of Russia.

Despite the hardships borne by the Russian people, the emphasis remained on heavy industrial products rather than consumer goods. To accomplish industrial expansion, the factories destroyed in western Russia were rebuilt, and in the east more than half the capital investment went into entirely new industrial plants. Collectivization in farming was once again rigorously enforced, and the size of the farms was increased; more and more small farmers were transformed into a rural proletariat. This process met with much the same kind of widespread resistance it had encountered before the war.

By 1950 production of coal, oil, steel, and electrical power exceeded official goals, but the goals for consumer goods had not been achieved. Automobile production, for example, was only 60 per cent of the projected figure, and housing construction was similarly unsatisfactory. Most serious of all, agricultural production fell short of the country's needs.

Economic recovery in the small nations of eastern Europe—the Soviet satellites—was seriously retarded by Russian priorities. The small countries were helpless as the Russian army dismantled and removed to Russia several billion dollars' worth of industrial equipment and complex machine tools. The Soviet Union moved to consolidate its power within these states and to ensure that their economic recovery contributed to that of the USSR. The influence of anti-Communist factions was undermined by economic means: land reform wiped out large landowners and distributed their estates among peasants and farm laborers, while nationalization of large-scale industry eliminated capitalists. Land reform was followed by collectivization (most rapidly in Bulgaria and Yugoslavia), and nationalization was extended to smaller enterprises. At the same time, emphasis was placed on the production of heavy industrial goods.

Importation of consumer goods from the West was not resumed; the bulk of eastern European foreign trade was reoriented eastward. The Russians used their predominant position to obtain the exports of their eastern European neighbors at relatively low prices.

Britain, France, and the Defeated Nations

In Britain the Labour government of Clement Attlee (1883–1967), brought into office by a landslide victory over Churchill and the Conservatives in the election of July 1945, was faced with major postwar problems, including technologically obsolete industries (e.g., coal), a tremendous loss in overseas investments (sold to pay the cost of the war), and a disastrous deficit in international trade. At the end of the war, some 42 per cent of the British labor force was in the armed forces or employed in civilian war production, while only 4 per cent worked in export industries. The Labour government put through a massive program of economic and social reform. First of all, a comprehensive national welfare program—like the one outlined by the economist William Beveridge in his famous report in 1944—was instituted. Second, economic recovery and reconstruction were undertaken on a large scale.

To this end, several important industries were selected for nationalization: notably, coal mining, railroads, electricity, and steel. The Bank of England was also nationalized. Other industries were modernized and reorganized, with the state providing the funds for necessary investments; and industrialists were coaxed to build factories in areas which had high unemployment before the war. The existing schemes of unemployment, sickness, and old age insurance were consolidated and extended, and a free National Health Service was established. British workers, still thinking in terms of prewar days when unemployment was the main danger, were chiefly interested in shortening working hours and preventing mechanization. Their resistance to industrial reorganization was overcome only slowly and with difficulty; wildcat strikes and other labor problems continued to plague the British economy.

Although production started to climb, Britain's balance of payments remained perilous. Its export trade in 1945 was at only 45 per cent of the prewar level, and the decline was aggravated by the abrupt cessation of American lend-lease in September 1945. At the end of the year the United States advanced a loan of $3.75 billion; but that was not enough, and imports had to be cut to the strictest minimum in a program of austerity. The austerity campaign diminished labor's incentive to work harder. Inflationary pressure came from the disproportionate rise in the prices of food and raw material imports in relation to Britain's manufactured exports. In 1949, after a recession in the United States had reduced American imports from Great Britain by one third, it was necessary to devalue the pound from $4.03 to $2.80. This was most unfortunate for the Labour party. It became associated in the voters' minds with the drabness of postwar austerity, and consequently Labour was turned out of office in the election of 1951.

In France the three largest parties in the Assembly of the Fourth Republic after the elections of October 1945 were the Communists, the Socialists, and the MRP (the *Mouvement Républicain Populaire*, a new liberal Catholic party). Within a month the Assembly had unanimously elected Charles de Gaulle head of the provisional government; but the general was soon exasperated with multiparty politics, and in January 1946 he resigned. A Socialist took his place, and France resumed its customary political pattern: a succession of multiparty governments came and went, as coalitions were formed and fell apart. The Communists never headed a government, for no other parties would serve under them; but Communists were given important ministries — including those of armaments, industrial production, and labor — in early postwar governments.

At first all the parties worked together to promote the recovery of production — the Communists expecting to take the credit, since a Communist was head of the ministry of industrial production. There was plenty to do. Transport had to be repaired; agricultural production had fallen, and food shortages hurt the productive capacities of industrial workers; absenteeism and the lingering effects of wartime deportations to Germany produced labor shortages. The excess of currency over available consumer goods created strong inflationary pressure.

War and defeat had convinced a majority of Frenchmen that France could not be a great power unless the traditional economic balance between agriculture and industry gave way to a new emphasis on industry. All the important parties in the Assembly were willing to accept the Monnet Plan, a program of extensive state planning devised by the economist Jean Monnet. This plan projected vast expansion of the steel and machine-tools industries. The United States approved of it, and in May 1946 France was granted a credit of $650 million for the purchase of necessary equipment. Despite delays and setbacks, by 1947 electrical production well exceeded planning goals and coal production was on the way up.

The French government made no attempt to implement a policy of thoroughgoing deflation. Even de Gaulle rejected the idea, for it would have created internal opposition just when France had to assure its allies of French unity and stability. By April 1946 prices had risen so much that real wages were less than 80 per cent of the prewar level. So far the Communists had restrained demands for wage increases (as they were in charge of production recovery), but when they failed to make further gains in the June 1946 elections, they demanded from the government a 25 per cent raise in wage rates and threatened a general strike. A compromise raise of from 18 to 22 per cent was agreed upon, but prices rose still further; by October real wages were only 59 per cent of the prewar level. In early 1947 the Léon Blum government attempted to break this price spiral, but its plans were upset when frost destroyed a large part of the wheat crop. Thus in late 1947 the stage was set for a new series of industrial strikes.

For several weeks in November and December the national unions halted production of coal and severely reduced production in most other industries. Wage increases induced price rises and French exports began to be priced out of the world market. In January 1948 the franc was devalued. Production of food and consumer goods increased, prices began to decline, and foreign trade picked up. A wave of Communist-organized strikes protesting French participation in the Marshall Plan ended in humiliating failure. But political stability did not match French economic success. Although Communists were now excluded from the cabinet, the governments that followed — made up of center factions — were all short-lived. This did not interfere with a successful policy toward the other European states, but it did postpone decisions on crucial domestic and colonial problems.

Like France, Italy had been badly hurt by the war. Homes and public works had been damaged or destroyed; agricultural production had decreased 60 per cent since 1938; livestock had been reduced by 75 per cent. Industry had not suffered so greatly, since most of it was located in northern Italy, which was spared the violent struggle between Allied and German forces that brought ruin to regions in the south. But raw materials had to be imported on a large scale if any increase in industrial production was to be achieved, and the bad relations between workers and management that had surfaced immediately after liberation had to be improved. At the same time, unemployment and underemployment were rising as a result of demobilization and reduced economic activity, while a huge supply of paper currency was causing marked inflation.

The only encouraging sign on the economic horizon was aid from the Allied military government, spent initially for food supplies. UNRRA distributed some $50 million in aid during 1945. In January 1946 it began to furnish food, raw materials, and machinery to revive Italian industry and improve the diet of the people. Between January and June 1946, UNRRA aid to Italy amounted to over $435 million.

Elections in Italy in June 1946 produced a constituent assembly (at the same time a referendum had abolished the monarchy) in which the three largest parties were the Christian Democrats (DC), Socialists (PSIUP), and Communists (PCI). The latter two were allied, and their combined seats slightly outnumbered those of the DC. All three participated in the new government headed by Alcide de Gasperi, an unusually able Christian Democrat. But the government was hamstrung by differences among the parties in the coalition. In May 1947, Gasperi determined to form a minority government of the Christian Democrats, believing that support would be forthcoming from the Right.

The new one-party experiment had the advantage of freeing the Christian Democrats to follow their own policies. Happily, the new minister of the budget, the economist Luigi Einaudi, was able to bring the inflationary spiral under control by restricting bank credit to industry and injecting consumer goods and foodstuffs into the market to lower prices. As confidence was re-gained, the popularity of the Christian Democrats rose, with the result that the Socialist-Communist alliance turned to strikes and other agitation. But the government held firm.

The national elections of April 1948 were contested against the backdrop of the Communist coup in Czechoslovakia and the Anglo-French-American deci-sion to return Trieste to Italy. The United States did all it could to exert its influence in Gasperi's favor, and the Christian Democrats increased their popular vote from 8 million to more than 12.7 million, giving their party an absolute majority. Although recovery was far from complete and the standard of living remained low, political stability, coherent economic policies, and generous foreign aid, especially from the United States, had put Italy solidly on the road to recovery.

The most striking postwar recovery occurred in western Germany, which had sustained a terrific pounding during the war. Allied bombers did extensive damage to housing and agriculture (somewhat less to industry), the railroad network in the Ruhr had been badly hit, and the domestic labor force had been decimated. During Hitler's last stand, in 1945, many cities had been almost leveled.

Profiting from the lesson of the 1920's and 1930's that a Germany revived enough to pay large reparations might easily become a threat to Continental security, the Allies had agreed at the Potsdam Conference to forego maximum reparations. Instead, the industrial (hence, war-making) capacity of the German nation was to be sharply reduced: plant and equipment considered by the Allies to be in excess of Germany's minimum peacetime needs were to be dismantled and transferred to its former victims. Reparations in this form were to be supplied to the USSR and Poland from the Soviet zone. In addi-tion, Russia was to receive 25 per cent of the reparations from the western zones, 15 per cent of which was to be counterbalanced by shipments of food and raw materials from the Soviet zone. Even with reduced industrial ac-tivity, Germany was expected to be self-supporting if trade moved freely between the zones and if the resources of the whole country were pooled to provide the exports to pay for necessary imports.

However, the differences between Russia and the Western powers de-stroyed any chance for national economic unity. Deliveries from East Ger-many to the western zones ceased, and these regions had to import large quantities of foodstuffs and raw materials. The result was that industrial production in West Germany in 1947 was only 40 per cent of the 1936 level, and the occupying powers (particularly Great Britain and the United States) found themselves subsidizing West Germany's balance of payments deficit to the tune of some $500 million.

This state of affairs was considered intolerable by the Western allies. By the end of 1946 they began to remove restrictions on Germany's industrial activity, and in August 1947 substantial increases were authorized. For example, maximum annual steel production was increased from 5.8 million tons for the whole of Germany to 10.7 million tons for the British-American Bizone. Wartime solidarity against the German menace was soon superseded by the Western powers' concern over Russian policy. A strong and prosperous West Germany was now a necessity. By 1950 German economic expansion was under way.

Japan's economic recovery after World War II was initially quite slow, burdened as it was by the terrible devastation of wartime bombardment and by the limitations placed on its industrial system by the occupation forces. But with American aid and encouragement, and with a new middle-class vitality that accompanied the introduction of constitutional monarchy and political democracy, Japan eventually attained a level of economic recovery even more dramatic than that witnessed in the war-torn countries of Europe.

International Economic Planning

The various plans and recovery schemes discussed thus far were almost wholly national in scope and often (from the supranational viewpoint) competing and conflicting. For instance, the Monnet Plan assumed that the Ruhr would supply coal and coke to the French iron industry and that German steel production would be limited. Ruhr coal and coke were not forthcoming (in sufficient quantity) until the end of 1948; and almost immediately thereafter, France's allies authorized an increase in German steel production to which France had to agree, and German steel began to compete with French steel. By the summer of 1947 the United States had extended credits and loans totalling some $7.3 billion to western Europe (in addition to that sent to eastern Europe through UNRRA), and there was a growing conviction that coordinated planning among the European countries was an absolute necessity if American assistance was to be fully effective. Moreover, it was becoming increasingly clear that economic stability and recovery were essential if non-Communist regimes were to be maintained in western Europe.

Some efforts at close economic cooperation dated back to the war years. In July 1944, an International Monetary Conference met at Bretton Woods, New Hampshire, and worked out much-improved international financial arrangements, resolving problems that had exacerbated the Depression. Later that year the European Coal Organization was established in London to allocate coal available for export to western Europe. By the end of 1947 it had been supplanted by the Coal Committee of the Economic Commission for Europe. But the first real step toward economic integration on the European continent was sponsored by the United States. Speaking at Harvard University in June 1947, Secretary of State George C. Marshall proposed a plan whereby the countries that agreed to cooperate economically among themselves would receive monetary assistance from the United States. This plan was open to all countries, regardless of their form of government, but since the Soviet Union demanded that its satellites not participate, it became the basis for recovery of non-Communist states only.

The Marshall Plan was intended to put the economies of the participants on a self-supporting basis while providing a satisfactory standard of living for their citizens. There was to be an overall increase in production, concentrated in such key sectors as coal, steel, food, and transport. Efficiency was to be improved and production costs lowered. Monetary stability would be effected at the same time, so that currencies might be stabilized and made convertible. Finally, economic cooperation was to be extended so that customs unions might eventually be formed. It was estimated that the participating countries would run a dollar deficit of over $22.4 billion during the years 1947–1951. Some $19.3 billion of this would be provided by the United States, and the rest would come as loans from the International Bank for Reconstruction and Development.

The Marshall Plan was perhaps the most remarkable success story of the postwar years. In April 1947, the Organization for European Economic Cooperation (OEEC) was created with sixteen European states and the three western zones of Germany as members. During the next two years the United States Congress authorized some $8 billion in aid to this body. By the end of 1949, annual western European output had expanded by about $30 billion. But despite this good showing, the OEEC made little progress in coordinating the economic policies and plans of its participants. The British Labour government, in particular, pursued a nationalistic line in its planning. France, on the other hand, was willing to adjust the Monnet Plan to contribute as much as possible to the recovery of the Continent as a whole.

Although tentative steps toward economic union had been taken by the Benelux nations (Belgium, the Netherlands, and Luxembourg) and by France and Italy, Great Britain was reluctant to consent to such a plan. The British felt that an economic union with the Continent would weaken Britain's ties with the Commonwealth. In addition, since such a union involved complete free trade within the area (i.e., free movement of goods, capital, and persons), which in turn required similarity of prices and wages, Britain's standard of living and full employment might be endangered. Nonetheless, the European Payments Union was created in September 1950 to facilitate multilateral trade within the participating area. And in May 1950, Robert Schuman, the French foreign minister, announced a plan to coordinate under a single authority the coal and steel production of France, Germany, and any other countries which might agree to participate. This plan heralded a new era in Franco-German relations, based on the willingness of French statesmen to treat Germany as an equal. In exchange for some part of its economic sovereignty, France received a guarantee of an adequate supply of coal for its steel industry. Though once again Great Britain declined to participate, France, Germany, the Benelux nations, and Italy joined in the coal and steel agreement.

The outbreak of war in Korea in the summer of 1950 upset American priorities. Up to that time, economic recovery was the chief goal of American aid to the countries of western Europe. Now the main emphasis was on preparing those states to defend themselves against Communist military aggression. As resources were diverted from economic recovery to arms manufacture, the costs of rearmament necessitated continued American aid to Europe beyond that projected for the Marshall Plan.

III THE DISSOLUTION OF OVERSEAS EMPIRES

The New Nationalism — India and Israel

Around the globe, the postwar years witnessed a veritable explosion of nationalism in the colonial possessions of the Western powers. The transition from colonial to independent status was peaceful in certain instances — if the imperial power was willing to grant independence, and if the colony itself had sufficient unity and sufficient experience in self-government to effect the transition with a minimum of confusion. When these conditions were not met, violence and bloodshed were inevitable.

Britain's willingness to liquidate its empire was mainly induced by the desire to consolidate British commitments by withdrawing British forces from the far-flung corners of the world and thereby save the enormous amounts of capital and materiel that postwar colonial maintenance required. Furthermore, British public opinion, conditioned by the wartime goal of liberating captive peoples, favored decolonization. British colonial rule had depended upon the steady delegation of authority followed by an increasing degree of self-government and finally Commonwealth status with the member state having virtual autonomy. Thus when British colonies, whether in Asia or Africa, were granted their independence, their chances for stable government were far greater than those of former French, Belgian, Portuguese, or Dutch colonies, which had been administered from the mother country and had received little if any preparation for self-rule.

British rule in India had produced a group of Western-educated national leaders, who thought that the subcontinent was ready for self-government. In the 1920's and 1930's the leader of the independence movement was a former lawyer, Mohandas K. Gandhi (1869–1948), who combined saintly nonviolence and love for the Indian masses with intransigent opposition to continued British rule. The catastrophic British defeats at the hands of the Japanese in southeast Asia in 1941 further weakened imperial prestige, and the resumption of nationalist agitation at the end of the war could have been suppressed by no means short of ruthless militarism. This kind of repression the Labour government in London was not willing to undertake; it would have been too costly, and in any case the Labour party had always looked favorably on Indian demands for self-government.

By 1947 the British government had committed itself to independence for India not later than June 1948, but first some provision had to be made for the Muslim minority within the predominantly Hindu population. Proposals ranged from the establishment of an independent Muslim state—Pakistan—to extensive provincial autonomy within a federal system. As negotiations went on, tension between the two groups mounted, and violence increased. In July 1947 the British Parliament rushed through the Independence Act, setting up two independent states which became republics within the Commonwealth. Despite pleas for restraint by Indian leaders, half a million people died in the rioting that followed independence, and some twelve million became refugees. The state of Kashmir remained a problem: some three fourths of its people were Muslims, but its Hindu maharaja had armed the Hindu minority against them, and when Pakistani troops entered Kashmir, Jawaharlal Nehru, the first Indian prime minister, sent in Indian forces. The United Nations negotiated an armistice effective at the beginning of 1949, but no permanent settlement was achieved.

Palestine, which had been controlled by the British since the end of World War I, presented similar problems. In the late nineteenth century, in response to rising anti-Semitism in western Europe and czarist pogroms against the large Jewish population in Russia, a new kind of Jewish nationalism—Zionism—emerged. Initially under the leadership of a Viennese journalist, Theodor Herzl, the Zionist movement sponsored extensive Jewish emigration to Palestine, principally from eastern Europe, before and after World War I. In 1917 a Zionist leader, the distinguished chemist Chaim Weizmann, persuaded the British government to commit itself, in the Balfour Declaration, to a Jewish national home in Palestine, which came under a British mandate at the end of the war. During the 1920's and 1930's the Jews in Palestine—under the leadership of David Ben-Gurion and other socialists of eastern European origin—made tremendous strides in both agriculture and industry. But Palestinian Arab nationalists were aroused by what they regarded as Western intrusion into their land, and chronic strife developed. The rise of Hitler made Palestine all the more important as a Jewish refuge, but to appease the Arabs the British tried to prevent immigration after 1939.

After World War II, demands for virtually unlimited Jewish immigration and the establishment of a Jewish homeland were energetically put forward both by Zionists and by those who felt that such a proposal was only just in view of the Nazi crimes against European Jewry. Still sensitive to Arab opinion, the British authority would not open Palestine to the thousands of homeless Jews who waited in European displaced persons' camps. In the two years immediately following the war, the Jewish community in Palestine set up underground organizations and engaged in guerrilla warfare against the British in a manner reminiscent of the Irish rebellion earlier in the century.

The creation of a Jewish state in Palestine was entirely unacceptable to the Arab nations of the Middle East, who promised military resistance to any efforts in that direction. The British, unwilling to repress the Jewish rebellion by force and unable to effect a compromise between the Jews and Arabs, turned the matter over to the UN. When the General Assembly voted for Palestine's partition into Jewish and Arab states in November 1947 and the British quickly withdrew from the country, war seemed inevitable. Terrorist attacks by both sides became all-out war when the state of Israel was declared on May 14, 1948. UN efforts at reconciliation failed in the face of both sides' determination not to compromise. Only after the Israelis had beaten back the Arab attacks were relatively stable frontiers established. Weizmann became the first president of Israel and Ben-Gurion its first premier. Aided by massive contributions from American Jews, Israel flourished as a Western industrial outpost in the underdeveloped Middle East. But a condition of intermittent warfare characterized the succeeding years of uneasy truce.

Southeast Asia

In southeast Asia, the Japanese occupation — much like Napoleon's conquest of Europe — stimulated existing nationalism and created an intense desire for independence. The Western imperial powers had been publicly humiliated by their defeat, and the puppet native regimes set up under the Japanese convinced many people that they were capable of self-government. The Communists supported the nationalist movements after the war, hoping to eliminate Western power and to direct the local revolutions toward communism. Their goals included frustrating the Marshall Plan by disrupting the flow of raw materials to western Europe.

Of the Western powers, the Americans were opposed to the reestablishment of colonial regimes. The United States readily granted the Philippines complete independence in 1946. The British — as we have seen in the case of India — were willing to cede full independence under conditions of their own choosing. The French were not favorable to independence but were willing to grant considerable autonomy. The Dutch and the Portuguese were resolutely imperialist.

At the end of the war the British offered a constitution and democratic centralized government to Malaya, which was already experiencing guerrilla terror. But the constitution of 1948 left power in the hands of local rulers, all of whom were conservative Malays, and the Malayan Communist party — based predominantly in the large Chinese community — launched a revolt. The conflict between guerrilla terrorists and British forces continued for several years before it was finally brought under control by the British. In 1957, independence was granted Malaya, with a federal constitution that preserved certain traditional Malay advantages over the Chinese population. In August 1963 a Malaysian federation was established that included Singapore, Malaya, and former British territories in Borneo. The new federation immediately faced trouble with Indonesia, which claimed all of Borneo.

The Netherlands tried to maintain control of the East Indies in order to preserve Dutch economic domination of the area's great petroleum and mineral wealth, but Indonesian nationalists in Java and Sumatra declared their independence in 1945, before Allied troops arrived to handle the Japanese surrender. For the next several years there were intermittent hostilities. Under pressure from the United States — which the Dutch deeply resented — a series of plebiscites was held, and in 1949 the independence of Indonesia (consisting chiefly of the former Netherlands East Indies) was officially established.

A commonwealth form of relationship with the Netherlands ended in 1954, and within the next few years some fifty thousand Dutch residents were expelled from the country. This move had disastrous results for the Indonesian economy. President Achmed Sukarno used renewed insurrectionist activity as a pretext to purge his political opponents and strengthen his "directed democracy." In 1960 a new government of anti-Western parties was formed, and subsequently Indonesia entered into agreements to purchase Soviet arms. In 1965, however, a Communist-directed coup was bloodily repressed, and Sukarno was forced to give up his office and powers.

The French attitude toward overseas possessions was predicated on the belief that both France and the colonies would benefit by continued close interrelations. Therefore France offered its colonies a degree of autonomy within a French-dominated federation, but not outright independence. In the French colony of Indochina, a genuine nationalist movement for independence had existed for some years. After World War II the League of the Independence of Vietnam (the Vietminh) — about a tenth of whom, including their leader, Ho Chi Minh, were avowed Communists — clashed with returning French forces. Vietminh numbers in the field doubled by early 1949, despite special French efforts, and the Vietminh's acquisition of Chinese supplies and the arrival of Communist Chinese troops on the northern border of Indochina forced the French to switch a large part of their army to the north. (The army was small to begin with, as the French Left opposed the defense of Indochina.) It also precipitated American aid to the French — for the purpose of defeating the Communists, not restoring the French empire. Yet early in 1953 the Vietminh were able to launch an invasion of Laos.

By early 1954, Communist-inspired guerrilla warfare had succeeded in undermining the French position, and in April 1954 a conference of foreign ministers met in Geneva to bring about an armistice between the French and Communist forces. Soon after the conference convened, the French stronghold at Dien Bien Phu surrendered after a long and costly siege. (The British had refused to endorse an American suggestion to intervene with air and naval forces to save the French.) After a protracted debate, it was finally agreed that Laos and Cambodia should become independent states, that Vietnam should be divided at the 17th parallel, that free elections would be held in all of Vietnam within two years, and that no military buildups would be permitted nor any foreign bases established. The United States and the new republic of South Vietnam, concerned with Communist aggression and subversion, refused to sign the armistice.

In the following years the United States replaced France as the protector of South Vietnam, while Ho Chi Minh sought to extend his authority southward by lending assistance to an underground guerrilla movement. After the Geneva conference, the United States set about consolidating the government of President Ngo Dinh Diem in South Vietnam. Diem's government continued to refuse to hold elections on the ground that they would not be free in North Vietnam. But its own failure to reform land tenure and its perpetuation of arbitrary rule soon gave the Vietminh's successor in the south, the Communist Vietcong, a following, which was extended by systematic terror. A National Front for the Liberation of South Vietnam (NLF) was established in Hanoi in 1960, and late in 1961 the United States began a military build-up in the south. Meanwhile, American relations with the Diem regime deteriorated until in late 1963 the United States approved its overthrow by a military junta. Fighting in South Vietnam settled down to a bloody duel that neither side seemed able to win so long as United States continued assistance to the South Vietnamese and the bounds of conventional warfare were not transgressed.

Africa

Defeat in Indochina persuaded France to try a more moderate tack in Africa. In response to suggestions from the African colonies—which wanted to work toward independence but did not want to be cut off from French aid in the course of modernization—the French Community was created by referendum in 1958. Except for Guinea, which chose immediate independence, all the French colonies in sub-Saharan Africa became autonomous republics in the Community. By 1960 all had moved to full sovereignty, and the Community was significant chiefly as a symbol of continuing French influence in Africa.

In Algeria, however, an important proportion of the population was of European extraction, and these people were determined to retain their hold. Native Muslims, though given the status of French citizens, were denied the equality in administrative affairs that they had been promised, and in October 1954 a group of young militants formed the FLN (*Front de Libération Nationale*) and revolted against the French authorities to obtain independence. The ensuing struggle between the FLN and the French army was accompanied by barbaric behavior on both sides. In 1958 a revolt of the military in Algeria over the indecisiveness of the French government in dealing with the FLN precipitated a national crisis that brought General Charles de Gaulle back to power and replaced the Fourth French Republic with the Fifth. The army fully expected that de Gaulle would insist on the complete integration of Algeria into France. Instead, he immediately moved to increase Muslim participation in the government, to further social and economic development, and to transfer generals whose political convictions regarding Algeria made them unreliable. In September 1959, de Gaulle promised Algeria a choice (after four years of peace) between complete independence, close integration, and a federal arrangement. This proposal stimulated rightist military and civilian extremists in Algeria to renewed acts of insurrection and terror that threatened for a time to extend into France itself. The promised referendum was held in 1962, and it resulted in an overwhelming vote in favor of an independent Algeria. Hundreds of thousands of French Algerians emigrated to France rather than live under the Muslim regime.

The British colonies in Africa gained their independence without revolution, and all the new nations retained membership in the Commonwealth, which was now only a vague alliance of sovereign states that had once been British colonies. The Federation of Rhodesia and Nyasaland, established in 1953, was intended to create a multiracial society; but the reluctance of the European settlers to give up their special position in the government of Southern Rhodesia, coupled with that region's racial policies, roused considerable African hostility, and in 1964 the Federation was officially dissolved. British demands and international economic sanctions under a UN resolution were unable to reverse the course of the white-dominated Rhodesia Front party, which remained in control of Southern Rhodesia and which declared its independence of Britain in 1965 rather than grant equality to the country's black majority.

In 1960 the European electorate of the Union of South Africa—dominated by people of Boer extraction—decided to form a republic, which in 1961 withdrew from the Commonwealth. The African majority was effectively kept in submission by means of the repressive policy of racial separation known as *apartheid* and by tight legal and police controls. White South Africans willingly endured the moral condemnation of much of the rest of the world and weathered economic sanctions, determined to perpetuate their political domination and racial policies.

Belgium pulled hastily out of the Congo in 1960. Unlike Britain, it had failed to give the natives more than a modicum of experience in government, and thus the new country was ripe for civil war. The newly liberated central government, under Premier Patrice Lumumba and President Joseph Kasavubu, was immediately threatened by army mutiny and the separatist efforts of Antoine Gizenga. The Katangan secessionist leader Moise Tshombe obtained European support; chaos and rioting spread; and the Belgian army reoccupied part of the country. Thereupon the central government appealed to the UN. A UN force was sent in, but when it declined to force the submission of the Tshombe regime in Katanga, the Lumumba government turned to the USSR. For a time it seemed probable that the Congo would be the scene of a serious East-West confrontation. Early in 1961 Lumumba, who had been arrested on the orders of Kasavubu, was transferred to Katanga, and shortly thereafter he was murdered. Continued pressure on Tshombe ended the secession in 1963. Only the presence of a UN peace-keeping force inside the country prevented a recurrence of wholesale slaughter.

The dictatorship in Portugal had absolutely no sympathy with the demands of the native population in its colonial possessions. It maintained its position in Angola by force, ignored United Nations and other international appeals for reform, and drove native resistance underground.

IV THE COMMUNIST WORLD IN THE 1950'S

The Soviet Union

With Stalin's death on March 5, 1953, the government of the USSR came under the control of a collective leadership, which ushered in a relatively liberal program. Amnesties were declared, and Stalin's deputy prime minister in charge of internal security was tried and executed. Official control over literature and art relaxed noticeably. Soon, however, rivalry developed between Nikita Khrushchev (b. 1894), the first secretary of the party, and Georgi Malenkov, the chairman of the Soviet council of ministers. The latter represented, in the main, the interests of the managers and technocrats—that elite segment of the population that belonged to the party out of expediency rather than commitment. He believed that the time had come to switch production emphasis from capital to consumer goods. Khrushchev led the faction opposed to such a switch. He was more concerned with expanding agriculture by a "virgin lands" scheme that would extend cultivation to new areas. By February 1955 Malenkov's divergence from Stalinism had sufficiently alienated party sentiment to force his resignation. His place was taken by Marshal Nikolai Bulganin, but Khrushchev soon assumed the commanding role in Russian affairs.

The rise of Khrushchev did not mean an end to de-Stalinization. In February 1956 at a closed meeting of the Twentieth Congress of the Communist party of the Soviet Union, Khrushchev denounced the late leader for his terrible purges of the 1930's, his misjudgment of the Nazi threat, his dictatorial "cult of personality," and his isolation within a vast sycophantic bureaucracy. Khrushchev did not attribute any blame to the Communist party as a whole. In an open session, he put forth the view that capitalism could be overthrown by means short of war. The principle of peaceful coexistence came into being. The relaxation of controls that accompanied de-Stalinization encouraged national liberation movements and liberal tendencies in some satellite countries. These were crushed with the aid of Russian troops.

Khrushchev's attack on Stalinism produced enough opposition in Russia to threaten his own position for a time, but by the summer of 1957 he had stabilized his domination of Soviet bureaucracy, and for a half-dozen years he remained firmly in control. In early 1958, Khrushchev replaced Bulganin as chairman of the Soviet council of ministers. After this triumph, he felt free to reverse his former position and direct more attention to the production of consumer goods. Between the years 1953 and 1958, agricultural output in Russia increased by 50 per cent, thanks to economic incentives for the peasants and to Khrushchev's virgin lands scheme. Still, three to four times more labor was required in the USSR than in the United States for an equal amount of produce. After 1958 stagnation set in, and Khrushchev's attempts to redirect the economy in the interests of satisfying consumer demands fell far short of the country's needs.

Khrushchev's term in office—which ended abruptly in 1964—brought other changes. An attack on the "cult of personality" aimed to widen political participation at the lower levels of Soviet government. An attempt was made to increase the turnover on Soviet elective committees to make sure their personnel did not become rigidified. Propaganda attacks were leveled against corruption, alcoholism, delinquency, and—to show there was continuity in Soviet domestic policy—against religious organizations. Although writers and artists had considerably more freedom than under Stalin, they were still expected to conform to Communist ideology and thereby serve the interests of the state.

Khrushchev's efforts did much to promote Russia's emergence from the harshness and desolation of the Stalinist era. There was a steady rise in popular expectations; economic activity responded to the new incentives and less centralized control, bringing Soviet productivity closer to that of the United States; and Russian technology and science made unprecedented strides, culminating in a space program whose successes were, for a time, a step ahead of American efforts.

Eastern Europe

Relations between the USSR and Yugoslavia improved noticeably after Stalin's death, although the Tito regime preferred to remain neutralist. In 1955, Bulganin and Khrushchev visited Yugoslavia and blamed the rupture on Stalin's policies. After the 1956 Hungarian crisis, however, relations became strained once again. Tito then cultivated commercial and diplomatic ties with other nonaligned nations throughout the world.

Under the Tito regime, Yugoslavia achieved spectacular successes in industrial growth, but in agricultural production it had not attained the prewar levels by the late 1950's, and private peasant holdings remained dominant.

While illiteracy declined from 25 per cent to 5 per cent during the decade, the intellectual ferment and innovation experienced in Russia and the other eastern European nations were not evidenced in Yugoslavia.

The relaxation of strict Stalinism in the USSR promised similar improvements for the other countries of the Eastern bloc. But when forced to choose between the old-line Stalinists of these countries, who were content with Soviet control but reluctant to implement the new policies, and new local leaders, who were eager to adopt the new policies but wanted them accompanied by more freedom, the Russian leaders for the most part chose to work with the former. In East Germany—or the German Democratic Republic as it was called after October 1949—the Ulbricht government was instructed by Moscow to soften the rigorous policy of the Stalinist era. Certain reforms were announced: amnesty for political prisoners, an end to forced collectivization and the antichurch campaign, an easing of traffic restrictions between the zones. This aroused hope among the workers that wages might be raised and production priorities reoriented toward consumer goods. Instead, the Ulbricht government continued to concentrate on heavy industry and even increased the hours of work. On June 16, 1953, a small strike broke out in East Berlin among workers in the building trades. It spread like wildfire. The People's Police (*Vopo*) could not, or would not, control the crowds, and Russian troops had to be used to quell the disturbances. In the afternoon of July 17, Soviet tanks and the *Vopo* opened fire on the demonstrators. Several hundred were killed, and order was restored. Certain reforms were instituted, but the whole world saw that the Communist regime in East Germany depended for its existence not on its popularity with the people but on the power of the Soviet army.

A similar situation arose in Poland in October 1956. This time, publication of Khrushchev's speech to the Twentieth Congress sparked a demonstration for higher wages that rapidly turned into a full-fledged riot. Polish forces were able to put it down, but not without bloodshed. This uneasy situation brought to power Wladyslaw Gomulka—a nationalist who had been imprisoned by Stalin—who for a time followed a semi-independent line. Under Gomulka's regime, the policy of forced collectivization was relaxed. Relations between the Catholic Church and the state reached their warmest in December 1956: religious instruction was made optional in the schools, and clerical appointments were returned to the hands of the Church, which reciprocated by supporting Gomulka. But the situation soon deteriorated. Although there were increased contacts with the West, Poland remained a staunch ally of the Soviets and the government severely limited reform and revisionism.

In Hungary, Imre Nagy, a liberal Communist, became premier in 1953, but two years later the old Stalinist faction was back in power. In 1956 much unrest was produced by discontent with the Stalinist regime and by a harvest failure, and though Moscow attempted a policy of appeasement, the Polish revolt in October sparked a mass demonstration in Budapest. There were calls for solidarity with Poland, free elections, an end to collectivization, and freedom from Russian domination. Soviet troops were called in, but on October 30 they were evacuated from the capital, and Nagy was made premier once again as Soviet appeasement continued.

But when Nagy announced that his country was withdrawing from the Warsaw Pact — an alliance of East European countries — and then asked the UN to take up the Hungarian case, Russia acted swiftly, perhaps encouraged by the international confusion resulting from the Suez crisis then raging in the Middle East. Troops were ordered to return, and a rival pro-Soviet government asked for Russian aid to crush the rebellion. Resistance was fierce and short in the capital, prolonged in some rural areas. In all, some 25,000 Hungarians were killed, and 150,000 fled the country. Nagy was seized and executed in June 1958, and extensive purges were carried out by the Hungarian Communists.

The Rumanian and Bulgarian regimes remained tough and doctrinaire throughout this period. Czechoslovakia experienced much intellectual and student activity in favor of a free press and the right to travel abroad, but there was no outburst at the time of the Hungarian uprising. The Czech Communist party had been thoroughly purged of liberal deviationists, and pro-Russian sentiment was deeply established. Hostility was kept in check by harsh prosecution of dissent accompanied by a sustained attack on the Catholic Church.

V THE WESTERN WORLD IN THE 1950'S

The United States

Harry S. Truman had been elevated to the presidency from the vice-presidential office in April 1945 as a result of Roosevelt's death. His previous career as a senator had gained him some national reputation but had not given him much experience in administration. During his first term as President he exercised strong and effective leadership in foreign policy but encountered trouble with both business and labor on domestic issues.

But the Republican-controlled Eightieth Congress, elected in 1946, played into the President's hands: it rejected extensions of social security and minimum wage legislation, slashed appropriations for western reclamation projects, adopted a discriminatory immigration act, and forced the removal of most price controls so that prices rose sharply. In June 1947, Congress overrode Truman's veto of the conservative Taft-Hartley Labor-Management Relations Act, driving the unions to closer support of the President. Consequently, in the presidential election campaign of 1948, Truman was able to claim that a Republican victory would lead to the reversal of the New Deal.

He defeated his opponent, Governor Thomas E. Dewey of New York, by some two million votes, to the stupefaction of pollsters and political pundits.

From 1948 to 1950 considerable progressive legislation was passed, including the funding of rural reclamation projects, slum clearance, and low-income housing. Truman was authorized to deal with inflation, and a new, somewhat liberalized Displaced Persons Act was passed. Congress refused to pass bills for an adequate farm program, federal aid to education, or fair employment. It did, however, support Truman's "Point Four" program (technical and economic aid to underdeveloped areas), and it did ratify the North Atlantic Treaty.

During Truman's second term, Communist take-overs in eastern Europe and revelations about espionage in the United States dating from the 1930's created an atmosphere of tension and suspicion throughout the country. In February 1950 the junior senator from Wisconsin, Joseph R. McCarthy, announced that 205 known Communists were currently shaping policy in the State Department. The number varied in subsequent speeches, but McCarthy had the ear of a great segment of the nation. He hurled charges left and right without proof, and many of the people he accused lost their jobs without a hearing. McCarthy was a completely irresponsible character assassin, but the Korean War and the failure of the administration's Far East policy made his anti-Communist crusade popular.

The Korean War was the most important issue in the presidential election of 1952. Peace negotiations had been going on for months, while bloody clashes continued. General Eisenhower, the Republican candidate, pledged an early and honorable end to the war, promising to go to Korea himself. He promised, too, to free the Soviet satellites by means short of war and to cut government expenditures. Vice-presidential candidate Richard M. Nixon—who had come to prominence in 1947–1948 during an espionage investigation—capitalized on the cold war spirit and claimed the administration was "soft on Communism." The Democratic candidate, Governor Adlai Stevenson of Illinois, chose to tell various interest groups the hard truth about what they could really expect from the government. Stevenson always came across as an intellectual—not a good thing in those times—and though he won a dedicated following, he had little chance against the enormously popular wartime hero, General Eisenhower, who won by a landslide. The Republicans also gained control of both houses of Congress.

The new President's chief advisers were mostly businessmen, and Eisenhower himself explained that his administration would try to roll back the "creeping socialism" of recent years. Economic controls established during the Korean War were soon lifted, and the development of national resources was largely left to private enterprise. But despite their expressed fiscal conservatism, the Republicans often had recourse to much the same remedies as had their Democratic counterparts. For instance, when their experiment in flexible price supports for farm products failed, compromises were adopted

—with the result that in 1959 the federal government was spending on agriculture considerably more than it had in 1952. The recession of 1953–1954 was remedied by a tax cut, increased social security benefits, and expanded unemployment coverage.

Eisenhower defeated Stevenson again in 1956, though the Democrats regained control of both House and Senate. His second term started off with a historic confrontation between states' rights and the power of the federal government to enforce the law of the land. During his first term, the cause of Negro civil rights had gained ground. In May 1954 the Supreme Court, ruling on *Brown* v. *Board of Education of Topeka*, declared segregation in public schools to be unconstitutional, overturning an 1896 decision. But school integration in the Deep South made no progress. Then, after the Little Rock, Arkansas, school system had been ordered by the Supreme Court to integrate gradually during the 1957–1958 school year, Governor Orville Faubus ordered the National Guard to Central High School on the pretext of threatened violence, and the nine Negro children who had been scheduled to enter were advised to remain at home. Faubus's stand created violence where none had existed, and Eisenhower had to send federal troops to the school to enforce the court-ordered integration.

Brown v. *Board of Education* and the Little Rock crisis were initial steps in an expanding drive for civil rights. Beginning with a successful bus boycott in Montgomery, Alabama, and ultimately leading a huge but dignified march on Washington in 1963, Dr. Martin Luther King, Jr., demonstrated the efficacy of nonviolent protest against the system of white exploitation and suppression of the Negro in America.

The administration's (and indeed the nation's) prestige was shaken when the USSR orbited an artificial satellite, *Sputnik* i, in 1957. Crises over Lebanon and the offshore Chinese islands and a recession in late 1957 combined to produced a huge Democratic success in the 1958 congressional elections. Instead of viewing this as an indication of a rising desire for liberal legislation, Eisenhower used his still substantial influence to block or amend pending reform legislation. The result was a period of political bickering and deadlock.

The presidential campaign of 1960 was highlighted by a series of televised debates between the two candidates, Vice-President Nixon and Senator John F. Kennedy. On television, Kennedy proved himself at least Nixon's equal and dispelled concern over his youth and lack of experience. At a highly publicized meeting with Protestant ministers he allayed fears that his religion —Roman Catholicism—would detract from his performance as President. Many voters, especially younger Americans, were attracted by his vision of a "New Frontier" on which America could regain its momentum for social reform, and his intervention on behalf of Martin Luther King, Jr.—who had just been sentenced to four months at hard labor after taking part in an Atlanta sit-in—solidified the Negro vote in the Democratic camp. In the end, Kennedy defeated Nixon by a margin of less than two tenths of 1 per cent.

Canada

Shortly after 1900, Canada's Liberal prime minister Sir Wilfred Laurier had prophesied that the twentieth century would be Canada's century. There seemed to be good grounds for expecting that Canada would undergo the tremendous industrial expansion that the United States had experienced in the late nineteenth century, with the building of a transcontinental railroad network and the arrival of many eastern and central European immigrants. These optimistic expectations were not borne out until after the Second World War; until that time Canada's economy remained heavily dependent on exports of agricultural produce, for which there was little demand in the 1930's. But by 1950 it was clear that Canada's mineral resources — including oil, copper, uranium, and aluminum — were enormous, and with the exploitation of these resources, Canadians enjoyed unprecedented prosperity, along with renewed immigration, urban growth, and the development of important manufacturing centers. In addition to Montreal, Toronto became one of the fastest growing and most attractive cities on the continent, as well as an important cultural center.

The capital necessary for development of mineral resources and establishment of large industries came mostly from the United States, and by the late 1950's, nationalist feeling in Canada — stimulated by left-wing intellectuals and academics and skillfully exploited by politicians — grew into popular resentment over the seeming probability that the country was becoming an economic and cultural appendage and political satellite of the giant to the south. Economic friction between Canada and its southern neighbor was not new. In the 1950's, specific Canadian grievances and unease centered around the extent of American investment in Canadian industry, American delays in starting work on the St. Lawrence Seaway, and even the comparatively low American duties on Canadian farm and mineral exports.

In the 1950's the Liberal government (which had begun its twenty-three-year tenure in 1935) sought to play a partly independent role in international affairs to offset what was, after all, an unavoidable economic dependence on the United States. Canada's trade with the United States now exceeded its trade with Great Britain, and some 40 per cent of American foreign investment was in Canadian enterprises. But while its foreign policy closely matched that of the United States in fundamentals, Canada carved out its own niche in international affairs. Though an enthusiastic member of NATO, Canada emphasized the alliance's nonmilitary aspects. It sought to serve as an interpreter and mediator between the West and Afro-Asia, and it gave considerable support to UN peace-keeping forces.

The Conservatives, who came to power in 1957, were in essential agreement on both domestic and foreign policy with the Liberals, who were returned to office in 1963 under Lester B. Pearson. In 1968 a vigorous new Liberal prime minister, Pierre Elliott Trudeau, led his party to another victory at the polls.

The New Democratic party, a socialist group, was virulently anti-American but held few seats in Parliament and seemed to have no prospect of supplanting either of the traditional majority parties. The one cloud on the horizon was a vociferous separatist movement among the French-Canadians in the province of Quebec, particularly in Montreal. The French-Canadians had long felt that they had been an underprivileged group in the Canadian Confederation. The federal government's response was to appease French-Canadian dissatisfactions by a variety of concessions, mainly designed to increase economic growth in Quebec, in the expectation that more and better jobs would distract the people there from separatist agitation.

Latin America

Since the end of World War I, Latin America has become steadily more important, both politically and economically. No longer an obscure backwater of the Western world, its phenomenally high yearly population growth and valuable but undeveloped natural resources have combined to make Latin America a source of considerable interest to Western and Communist nations alike. Only a small fraction of its great potential has yet been realized.

A major reason for the persisting underdevelopment of most of Latin America is the political instability that has plagued the area in the twentieth century, as before. Only Mexico achieved a reasonably steady government — one flexible enough to accommodate change without violence. The constitution of 1917 established social and economic reform as a continuing process. For several years after the revolution the Mexican government was hostile to the United States, but from the late 1920's the two nations were generally able to cooperate, especially after World War II, during which Mexico and Brazil were the only Latin American nations to send troops overseas.

Brazil was ruled by the dictator Getulio Vargas for most of the period between 1930 and 1954. A particular victim of the one-crop economy, Brazil suffered great hardship when the world coffee market collapsed after 1929. Since the mid-1950's Brazilian statesmen have attempted to balance their economy through agricultural diversification and industrialization, which has brought the usual social problems in its wake.

Argentina and Chile, with relatively small Indian populations and some excellent agricultural and pastoral land, attracted a steady stream of European immigration and were spared some of the social problems involved in the assimilation of large Indian populations. However, neither Argentina nor Chile enjoyed political stability despite their natural advantages. The government of Argentina cooperated with the Axis during World War II (it was the only Latin American country to maintain diplomatic relations with Germany throughout the war), and in 1946 the country was taken over by Juan Perón. Perón won the workers' support by social and industrial legislation, but he made Argentina a totalitarian military dictatorship. He was ousted in 1955, and succeeding governments achieved neither long tenure nor social and economic reform. Chile, with its rich copper and nitrate mines, was a site of endless labor unrest. Only in the 1960's did a radical government break the power of the old oligarchy, carry out extensive land reform, and attain a measure of political stability.

The discovery of the great petroleum deposits at Lake Maracaibo made Venezuela a rich country, but little of that prosperity trickled down to the Venezuelan poor. Venezuela was a valuable (and well-rewarded) asset to the Allies in World War II, but corruption and coups in the 1950's deprived the common people of the benefits of this great natural resource.

Unlike the United States and Canada, South America had no westward movement into its interior, and there is a striking contrast between the sophisticated, urbanized, and relatively affluent coastal regions and the poor and underdeveloped interior of the continent. Brazil is a partial exception to this phenomenon; in the 1950's the construction of its new capital—Brasilia—on a site far from the coast was a deliberate step in the development of the interior.

A great impediment to progress in Latin America has been the failure of the separate states to cooperate to solve mutual problems. They have looked to the United States for leadership, but beginning with the Pan-American Union of the 1880's, that leadership has been erratic and often self-serving. President Franklin Roosevelt's Good Neighbor Policy, inaugurated in 1933, was intended to replace dollar diplomacy and Yankee imperialism, and it did establish an atmosphere in which the mutual assistance of World War II was feasible. But the Good Neighbor Policy did little or nothing to improve the condition of the Latin American peoples. At Rio de Janeiro in 1947, eighteen Latin American nations joined the United States in a treaty of reciprocal assistance, and in 1948 the Organization of American States was established as a regional agency under the UN to implement the Rio pact. But the OAS was a disappointment to its Latin American members; they bitterly resented the low priority given to their needs.

In Latin America as in Canada, Washington's interest in promoting good relations (particularly out of a concern for hemispheric defense) met with considerable resistance during the 1950's. Once again, the extent to which American investments controlled native industry generated friction. But the situation in Latin America was made radically different by a huge revolutionary potential, generated mainly by the tremendous gulf between a small, wealthy ruling elite and a majority permanently buried in ignorance and brutal poverty. Frequently the national economy in these nations still depended on one or two primary products as exports, and falling world commodity prices could spell disaster. And in contrast to Canada, there was no tradition of peaceful political change by parliamentary means.

The United States was content to work with any government in power, so long as American interests in Latin America were not harmed. In the past, attacks on American holdings had provoked direct intervention, and thus most Latin American regimes were careful not to antagonize their great northern neighbor. The United States did not interfere with the dictatorial Perón regime in Argentina or with military coups in Venezuela and Peru, but it did assist in the overthrow of a regime in Guatemala that appeared to be turning for support to the Communist bloc.

Basic political instability and increasing economic hardship in the second half of the decade contributed to the overthrow of many of the dictatorial regimes that previously held power. The United States did not interfere with the new and more radical regimes, but neither did it offer them the massive economic aid programs (on the order of the Marshall Plan) which they sought.

The chronic economic and political problems of Latin America, combined with a rapidly expanding population and the increasing anger of intellectuals and liberals at reaction and corruption, made for a classic radical revolutionary situation, such as had developed in many other areas in the nineteenth and twentieth centuries. The explosion could have come in any one of a number of countries. It came in Cuba in 1959.

Though in some ways one of the most advanced countries in Latin America, Cuba was ripe for revolution. The Batista regime stagnated in power and oozed corruption. In the late 1950's a young lawyer, Fidel Castro, mounted a guerrilla campaign that won control of the country in January 1959 — after the United States stopped supplying arms to Batista, and Cuban support for his dictatorial regime disappeared. Determined to escape from Cuba's dependence on a single crop — sugar — which provided work for only half the year and thus doomed the laborer to a life of indebtedness, the Castro government was committed to land reform, education, and honest government. Soon, however, it began to use characteristic totalitarian methods to consolidate its power. When in the summer of 1960 the Castro government expropriated property owned by American interests and began receiving economic aid from the Soviet bloc, its relations with the United States deteriorated swiftly. After tolerating all species of militarist, reactionary, and corrupt regimes in Latin America, the American government found itself on bad terms with a new regime that was dedicated to social change of a fundamental nature — but it was a regime that, after assuming power, moved steadily toward the espousal and implementation of Communist principles.

Western Europe

In Britain the strength of the Labour government that had come to power in 1945 was undermined by inflation, by the failure of its nationalization policies to solve the nation's economic ills or to capture the people's imagination, and by the resignation of three of its ministers in protest against what they considered to be too large an expenditure on armaments. The Conservatives came back to power in the elections of October 1951. Winston Churchill was their first prime minister; Anthony Eden replaced him in 1955; and Harold Macmillan took over in 1957.

The Conservatives preserved the Labour government's welfare program virtually intact. But they denationalized the steel industry, expecting that private enterprise would carry Britain toward further economic recovery. All social groups, including the working class, were satisfied with the full employment and general prosperity that prevailed in the 1950's. But in fact these were not years of striking economic growth. Although British living standards were at their highest, those of other countries rose still faster. High external military expenditure (over £ 200 million in 1960) helped to hold down industrial expansion, as did a precarious margin between reserves and liabilities, which forestalled any daring economic ventures that might temporarily upset the economic balance. The ties with the Commonwealth countries were politically cheering but often economically unfortunate. Trade with those countries was not increasing as had been hoped; indeed, the rapid growth of commercial activity in the former colonies sometimes meant that they became Britain's competitors. At the end of the decade, British leaders were giving serious consideration to participation in the Continental economic organization set up in 1957 as the European Economic Community.

In the cold war, Britain ranged itself alongside the United States as a member of NATO and the Southeast Asia Treaty Organization (SEATO). At the same time, Britain maintained an independent atomic deterrent. The Conservative government thought that it would serve the national interest to do so, although it never explained in what circumstances Britain might threaten to use an atomic bomb independently of its allies.

While Britain was suffering from economic problems, the Fourth Republic in France experienced the political instability characteristic of the modern history of that country. The formation of the Pierre Mendès-France government in June 1954 was widely regarded as the beginning of a period of stable government. Composed of a coalition of Radicals and Social Republicans, it also enjoyed the support of the Socialists. Although Mendès-France was able to extricate his country from Indochina, his government foundered during the Algerian conflict, and its divisive effect on the French people continued to contribute to parliamentary and fiscal instability. Guy Mollet, a Socialist, held power from January 1956 to May 1957, but he was unable to resolve the Algerian problem, and his numerous successors likewise failed to achieve any sort of stability.

In Algeria a revolt by the army and the Algerian colonials, outraged at reports that the policy toward the FLN might be softened, brought General de Gaulle back to power in May 1958. The Socialists declined to resist this constitutional but extraparliamentary take-over, as they preferred de Gaulle to the Communists. He accepted the office after receiving decree powers for six months. A new constitution for a Fifth Republic was rapidly drafted and submitted to a popular referendum: it gave the ministers considerable independence of the Assembly and gave the president extensive powers over both the legislature (he had the absolute right of dissolution) and the executive (he appointed his own ministers). Eighty per cent of the voters approved, and in late December 1958 de Gaulle became president of the Fifth Republic for a seven-year term. He then worked for and eventually achieved what had eluded his predecessors: a solution to the Algerian dispute.

Compared to France, the new Federal Republic of Germany was remarkably stable politically. In the 1950's, under a conservative coalition led by Christian Democrat Konrad Adenauer, economic recovery proceeded at a rapid pace. It was based on a government policy of *soziale Marktwirtschaft* (social market economy)—free enterprise tempered by government attention to social welfare. Aided by American subsidies and initially low military expenditures, it succeeded because the remarkably docile laboring population was willing to work long hours, there was an unusually large supply of labor, and both companies and individuals reinvested their profits in business expansion. Between 1950 and 1963 industrial production rose from a base of 100 to 283, and production per working hour more than doubled. Agricultural recovery was also impressive, though by no means up to that of industry. During the early 1960's Germany still found it necessary to import 30 per cent of its food supply.

Despite the Social Democrats' insistence that reunification with East Germany should precede alignment with either bloc, the Adenauer government led West Germany into the Western alliance as a full partner. In May 1955 Allied occupation officially ended, and West Germany obtained full sovereign status. In support of the NATO alliance, and contrary to the sentiments of many Germans, Germany was rearmed, and German contingents were put under the NATO command. Adenauer's policy was vindicated at the polls by decisive election victories in 1953, 1957, and 1961. Extreme right-wing groups mustered only very small support, and Germany's second experiment in democracy seemed to be highly successful. After his retirement, Adenauer was succeeded in 1963 by Ludwig Erhard and in 1966 by Kurt Georg Kiesinger, both Christian Democrats.

Italy's economic success was also impressive, but it did not enjoy the political stability achieved in West Germany. Italian industrial production between 1954 and 1961 increased an average of 9 per cent per year, a triumph for a mixed economy. The state coordinated major investments to promote necessary industries and those with good export prospects. Business was encouraged to invest in the future of the southern part of the country, while the northern industrial areas made substantial gains, particularly in electrical and steel manufacturing. In 1946 and 1947 neutralism had been widely advocated throughout Italy; but to continue its economic recovery, the country badly needed American aid, and its unfortified borders and token military establishment made neutrality seem dangerous. Consequently, Italy participated in both the Marshall Plan and NATO, though its role in the latter was surprisingly small, due to the strength of the Italian Communist party and to the lack of a strong pro-Western leader to replace Gasperi, who retired in 1953 after seven years in office.

European Integration

Whereas after the First World War the western European states adopted ruinously nationalistic policies, after 1945 successful efforts were made to achieve international cooperation. The year 1957 was a landmark in the history of the movement to effect European economic integration. In March representatives of France, West Germany, Italy, and the Benelux countries—the members of the European Coal and Steel Community, which had been set up in 1951 under the Schuman Plan—met at Rome to sign treaties establishing the European Economic Community (a common market) and Euratom (a nuclear energy authority). The EEC treaty bound the signatories to remove all restrictions on their mutual trade by the 1970's (by 1964 all permanent quotas were to be abolished and tariffs reduced by one third). A common external tariff was to be set up to guarantee farmers in the member nations minimum prices for their products, a policy that has been particularly difficult to implement. In order to eliminate differences in labor costs where possible, labor organization was to be made uniform. Financial policies were to be coordinated in the hope that balance-of-payment crises would no longer require unilateral remedies. To minimize the hardships that so much change was bound to cause, an investment bank was set up to aid the development of the more backward national industries, while a social fund was created to finance the retraining of workers whose industries became redundant with the integration. The goals of the EEC were wide-ranging, and they made an important contribution to economic growth. But due at least in part to French obstruction, the political integration that was intended to follow economic cooperation has thus far not taken place.

Because it did not want to compromise its ties with the Commonwealth countries, Great Britain decided against joining the Common Market, as the European Economic Community came to be called. Instead, it attempted to join with other countries outside the Community in a free-trade area that was not bounded by a common external market. The European Free Trade Association was set up in November 1959, with Britain, Austria, Portugal, Switzerland, Norway, Sweden, and Denmark as members. This arrangement did not, however, produce anything like the economic progress achieved by the Common Market.

VI INTERNATIONAL RELATIONS IN THE 1950'S

The Cold War

During the 1950's the cold war of confrontation and crisis continued in all parts of the world. In Europe the unity and military preparedness of the Western bloc in NATO had peaked around 1955 but continued to be sustained by the American presence, and the Soviet Union's hold on its satellites was reaffirmed. In the Far East the Nationalist and Communist Chinese were within striking distance of one another. In the Middle East, America, Britain, France, and the Soviet Union vied for the friendship of the oil-rich Arab states. In Africa, Communist and Western powers competed for influence among the emerging nations. During the Eisenhower administration, American foreign policy involved the strategy of "brinkmanship"; in the words of Secretary of State John Foster Dulles, "The ability to get to the verge without getting into the war is a necessary art." On the Soviet side, de-Stalinization and reiteration of the principle of peaceful coexistence did not imply abandonment of hopes for a growing Communist camp. Nerve-wracking confrontations were unavoidable.

In Europe, continuing tension over Germany and the fear of further Soviet expansion westward prompted the Western bloc to form new mutual defense commitments. Shortly after the outbreak of the Korean conflict, the United States strongly recommended that Germany be rearmed. In response, France produced the Pleven Plan to provide for a European Defense Community with a European army in which the largest national unit would be the battalion; only with thorough integration of any and all German forces was German rearmament at all palatable to the French electorate. The continued instability of the French government, however, forced delay in ratification of the agreement, and when the proposal finally came to a vote in the French Assembly in August 1954, it was defeated. At the last minute Anthony Eden, Britain's foreign secretary, arranged for the Brussels treaties of 1948 to be revived and enlarged under the title of the Western European Union, with Great Britain as a member. This plan had the virtue of quelling fears of German rearmament, and the fears were further reduced when West Germany agreed to forego production or independent use of atomic weapons. Consequently, in May 1955 West Germany became a full partner of NATO.

In the years immediately following Stalin's death, the Russian government evinced a certain caution in international affairs, perhaps because it did not wish to become involved in new commitments until the succession to Stalin was finally settled. Thus the Soviets exerted little influence during the Eisenhower administration's efforts to secure an armistice in the Korean War. Likewise, at the Geneva conference on Far Eastern affairs of April–July

1954, an agreement to end the Indochina conflict was reached in the absence of Russian machinations.

From September to December of 1955, the Chinese Communists bombarded the Nationalist-held islands of Quemoy and Matsu, only a few miles off the Chinese mainland; but when the United States made it clear that the American Seventh Fleet would repulse any outright invasion of the islands, their belligerence was temporarily restrained. In 1958 a new crisis flared up as the Chinese Communists launched another intensive bombardment of Quemoy and Matsu. American warships escorted Nationalist convoys to the islands; and the Seventh Fleet, armed with nuclear weapons, sailed the Formosa Strait. The tension was not relaxed until the American government brought pressure on Chiang Kai-shek to renounce his provocative (yet clearly impractical) plans to use force to regain the mainland.

In April 1954 China and India had agreed to five principles: territorial integrity, nonaggression, noninterference in each other's affairs, equality, and peaceful coexistence. In April of the following year, at an Afro-Asian conference at Bandung, Indonesia, Chou En-lai, the Chinese premier, offered to extend the principles to all Asian and African countries. To the neutralist countries, this looked very favorable as contrasted with the SEATO alliance devised by the United States after the Geneva conference on Indochina in 1954. The signatories of SEATO (Australia, New Zealand, France, Great Britain, the United States, Thailand, Pakistan, and the Philippines) had Communist aggression in mind when they pledged to take collective action in the event of attack on any member state in southeast Asia. Afro-Asian confidence in China's peaceful intentions was shaken in 1959 when China ended Tibetan autonomy, bringing the Communist giant into closer confrontation with India, and when bloody border warfare broke out between India and China in 1962.

In Europe, Germany still remained the principal potential source of East-West conflict; the status of divided Berlin was particularly explosive. In January 1954 a Big Four foreign ministers' conference was held in that city, but no agreement on cold war problems was reached. The USSR continued to demand that the country be unified before elections were held. In May 1955 the entrance of West Germany into NATO as a full partner prompted the Soviet Union to reinforce its ties with the countries of eastern Europe, and on May 14 the Warsaw Pact was signed by East Germany, the Soviet Union, Poland, Czechoslovakia, Hungary, Bulgaria, Rumania, and Albania, establishing a joint military high command.

A summit meeting attended by Eisenhower, Eden, Bulganin, and French premier Edgar Faure was held in Geneva in July. There were discussions of the future of Germany, military security, disarmament, and trade. Despite the lack of any real progress, the amicable atmosphere encouraged an optimistic attitude with regard to relations between the Western and Eastern blocs.

A R C T I C

O C E A N

N O R T H

CANADA

A M E R I C A

UNITED

STATES

PACIFIC

OCEAN

A T L A N T I C

CUBA

DOMINICAN REPUBLIC

⑰

⑱

⑯ GUATEMALA

S O U T H

A M E R I C A

AUSTRALIA

NEW ZEALAND

CRISIS SPOTS

EUROPE

1. Greece: 1944-1949, civil war
2. East Germany; 1948-1949, Berlin Airlift; 1953, uprising and Soviet intervention; 1962, Berlin Wall
3. Poland: 1956, uprising and Soviet intervention
4. Hungary: 1956, revolution and Soviet intervention
5. Cyprus: 1963-1964, Greek-Turkish crisis
6. Czechoslovakia: 1968, Soviet intervention

MIDDLE EAST

7. Egypt: 1956, Suez crisis
8. Lebanon: 1958, U. S. Marine landing
9. Algeria: 1955-1958, insurrection; 1961, independence
10. Yemen: 1962-1967, civil war
11. Israel: 1967, Six days' war with Arab states

AFRICA

12. Kenya: 1952-1959, Mau Mau uprising
13. Congo: 1960-1965, Secession and civil war
14. Rhodesia: 1967, Unilateral Declaration of independence
15. Nigeria: 1967-present, secession and civil war

LATIN AMERICA

16. Guatemala: 1954, pro-Communist government overthrown with U. S. assistance
17. Cuba: 1959, revolution; 1961, Bay of Pigs Invasion; 1962, missile crisis
18. Dominican Republic: 1965, attempted coup forestalled with U.S. assistance

ASIA

19. China: 1945-1949, civil war and Communist victory
20. Formosa: 1949-present, Nationalist Chinese government; 1955/1958, Quemoy and Matsu crisis
21. Philippines; 1949-1955, Huk rebellion
22. Malaya: 1948-1957, Communist rebellion
23. Tibet; 1950, annexed by China
24. Korea: 1950-1953, Korean War
25. Vietnam 1946-1954, French-Indochinese war; 1961-present, Vietnam war
26. India: 1962, Sino-Indian border war;
27. Indian-Pakistani war over Kashmir, 1965
28. Indonesia: 1965, unsuccessful Communist coup
29. Sino-Soviet border dispute, 1969

A R C T I C   O C E A N

ICELAND

NORWAY
SWEDEN

SOVIET UNION

A S I A

GREAT BRITAIN   DENMARK
IRELAND
NETH.
BELG.   GER.
LUX.   ②   POLAND   ③
AUST.   ⑥   CZECH.
FRANCE   ④   HUNG.
SWITZ.   RUM.
ITALY   BULG.
PORTUGAL
GREECE   ①   TURKEY
⑦   SYRIA   LEB.   IRAQ   IRAN
⑧   JORDAN
U.A.R.   ⑪   ISRAEL
(EGYPT)
ALGERIA   ⑨

TIBET   ㉓
㉖   W. PAKISTAN
INDIA   E. PAK.
㉗

CHINA   ⑲

KOREA
㉔

㉙

FORMOSA   ⑳

A F R I C A

⑩   YEMEN

NIGERIA   ⑮
BIAFRA

THE   KENYA
CONGO   ⑫
⑬
KATANGA

RHODESIA
⑭

O C E A N

I N D I A N

O C E A N

THAILAND   VIETNAM
㉕

MALAYA   ㉒

PHILIPPINES   ㉑

I N D O N E S I A   ㉘

AUSTRALIA

THE WORLD IN CRISIS

North Atlantic Treaty Organization (NATO), 1949
Southeast Asia Treaty Organization (SEATO), 1954
Warsaw Treaty Organization (Warsaw Pact), 1955
Central Treaty Organization of the Middle East (CENTO), 1959
Multiple colors indicate membership in more than one organization.
• Countries participating in the Marshall Plan, established in 1947
▪ Countries participating in the Council of Mutual Economic Assistance, established in 1947

Crisis in the Middle East

This optimism was abruptly dissipated by the Hungarian revolt in the autumn of 1956 and also by a critical situation in the Middle East. The Western powers were committed to the existence of the national state of Israel even while they attempted to retain the friendship of the Arab nations. The latter nursed long-standing grievances against the West and would have preferred to remain neutral in the cold war. The leading Arab neutralist was the head of the Egyptian government, Gamal Abdel Nasser. When the United States declined to supply Egypt with the weapons it requested, fearing to upset the balance between Israel and its Arab neighbors, Nasser turned to the Eastern bloc. In September 1955 Egypt arranged to obtain arms from Czechoslovakia. The American government then sought to punish Nasser by withdrawing its offer of a loan to help finance the construction of the huge Aswan dam. When the USSR showed itself in no hurry to supply the necessary capital for this project, Nasser acted to secure it on his own. In late July 1956, he nationalized the Suez Canal Company and closed the canal to Israeli ships.

France and Britain, whose citizens were the chief stockholders in the canal company, led the opposition to the nationalization. On October 29 the Israeli army attacked Egypt, which had allowed terrorists to operate from the Sinai peninsula. The Israelis advanced quickly across the peninsula toward the Suez Canal. The next day the British and French governments demanded that each side pull back ten miles from the canal to create a neutral zone. (It later appeared that the French, and probably also the British, had from the first acted in collusion with the Israeli government.) When the Egyptians refused the Anglo-French demands, British and French troops moved into the canal zone. They had no time to take over the canal, however, for world opinion had mobilized. At the UN the United States and the Soviet Union joined in demanding a cease-fire and the withdrawal of armed forces. Russia also threatened to come to Egypt's assistance. A peace-keeping force was quickly put together by the UN and dispatched to the Sinai peninsula to enforce a truce.

The Eisenhower administration's unequivocal opposition to the Anglo-French Suez venture brought about Anthony Eden's early resignation as British prime minister. The long-run effect of the Suez crises on Anglo-American relations was serious. The British government felt that it had been abandoned by its ally at a critical moment, and British disappointment was reflected in an independent attitude toward American policy in southeast Asia during the 1960's.

After the Suez episode, the United States effectively replaced Britain as the predominant Western power in the Middle East. In 1957, the so-called Eisenhower Doctrine pledged the United States to help any Middle Eastern nation that requested its aid in order to resist armed aggression by a Communist-controlled country. It was applied twice: in April 1957 the United States Sixth Fleet maneuvered in the eastern Mediterranean in support of King Hussein of Jordan, whose regime was threatened from the left, and in July 1958 American troops landed to protect the existing regime in Lebanon. In neither case was there any overt aggression by an outside power.

The Impact of China and the Third World

The end of the decade witnessed a most important development for future international relations: the first overt sign of a Sino-Soviet dispute over foreign policy. At the Moscow conference of Communist parties in 1957, the Russian government was under obligation to the Chinese for the support they had given the USSR during the recent crises in eastern Europe, and out of this meeting came a new assertion of revolutionary vigor. The Russian government renewed demands for an end to the Western military presence in Berlin, but they were firmly rejected by the Eisenhower administration in the summer of 1959, and thereafter Khrushchev seemed to revert to his old belief in coexistence. In September 1959 the Russian leader visited the United States, and the heads of state carried on extremely cordial conversations at Camp David. Before the month was out, Khrushchev made a journey to Peking. He was received without fanfare; there were no declarations of solidarity and unity; indeed, the Russian leader publicly urged China to moderate its foreign policy. Hopes rose in the West that some sort of accommodation between the USSR and the United States would come out of the summit meeting of the Big Four planned for Paris in May 1960.

The cold war was further complicated by the emergence in the 1950's of the so-called Third World. New governments in Asia and Africa were committed to neither side. Rather, they felt free to play the Western powers off against the Soviets, and both the West and the USSR against Communist China, in order to obtain the best military and economic aid, technical assistance, and trade agreements. Poor and underdeveloped in their industrial and commercial capacities, these nations nonetheless represented millions of people in countries with enormous natural potential. Further, even the smallest among them were admitted to the UN soon after achieving statehoood, and the balance of voting power in the General Assembly fell to them. If these nations could work in concert, there was little doubt of their critical impact in international affairs, but there were many problems limiting the effectiveness of their actions, jointly or separately.

The greatest weakness of the Third World nations was the fact that they had been created by imperial powers with little if any regard for ethnic, linguistic, or religious unity. The result was chronic political and social instability such as had racked India and Pakistan since the subcontinent gained its independence in 1947. The new African states established democratic constitutions, but the transfer of power rarely occurred by peaceful political means in these new countries. Military coups and assassinations were frequent. Obviously, the fulfillment of the potential of the Third World awaits the stabilization of the nations that constitute it.

VII THE WORLD IN THE 1960'S

The Superpowers

The cold war confrontations between the United States and the Soviet Union continued in the early 1960's, but as the decade wore on, both of the superpowers were distracted by crises on other frontiers and by internal problems. The harsh polarization of the 1950's began to ease, but the new configuration emerging in international relations was still confused and unclear.

The decade of the 1960's did not open auspiciously in the sphere of international relations. Eleven days before the Paris summit meeting in May of 1960, the Russians announced that an American U-2 plane had been shot down while flying over Russian territory. Moreover, the pilot had been captured and had confessed to being on an espionage mission. Naturally enough, the summit conference opened in an atmosphere of tension. Khrushchev demanded that the flights be halted and that the United States apologize. President Eisenhower would not agree (although the flights had been stopped), and Khrushchev walked out of the conference the next day.

Two years later the United States and the Soviet Union moved as close to war as they had ever come, as a result of the explosive Cuban situation. In 1961 the new Kennedy administration launched an ambitious program of economic aid to Latin America, the Alliance for Progress. It attempted to break away from the traditional policy of working with any existing regime to achieve strategic security and defeat communism; it aimed rather at supplying aid to governments evincing genuine interest in progressive social reform. First, however, Kennedy's government had to deal with a legacy from the Eisenhower administration — a Cuban situation that had steadily deteriorated. In 1960, after Castro nationalized American oil holdings in Cuba, Eisenhower reduced imports of Cuban sugar by 95 per cent; in October all exports to Cuba except medical supplies and certain foodstuffs were halted, and on January 3, 1961, diplomatic relations were severed. At the same time, Cuban exiles in the United States were being trained to mount an invasion. When Kennedy became President, he inherited the plan for exiles to attack Cuba and, after much hesitation, allowed the preparations to continue. The landing of fifteen hundred exiles at the Bay of Pigs in April was a complete fiasco.

In 1962 a crisis developed when the United States learned that Soviet missiles were being installed in Cuba. On October 22 Kennedy announced that all ships bound for Cuba would be stopped and searched to prevent additional offensive weapons from reaching the island and demanded that the missiles already there be removed immediately. He further declared that the United States would tolerate no Russian missiles in the Western Hemisphere and that if a single missile was fired at the United States from Cuba, there would be swift retaliation against the USSR. The United Nations would be asked to oversee the removal of the missiles. The world held its breath as the two nuclear giants faced each other "eyeball to eyeball." Then, at the last moment, a convoy of Soviet ships turned back from the island; the United States gave a pledge not to invade Cuba; the naval blockade was lifted, and Russia removed the missiles.

Another crisis occurred over Berlin. By 1961 the flood of refugees from East Germany to West Berlin was threatening to destroy the East German economy. In August the Communists found a solution: to seal West Berlin off from East Germany by building a wall to divide the city in two. The wall was constructed, and East Germans attempting to escape were shot down. Tension ran high for several months but gradually diminished in 1962. At Christmas 1963 an agreement was made that allowed East Germans to cross into West Berlin to visit their relatives.

Generally, in 1963 there was an easing of tension between the two superpowers, resulting in August in an agreement to a limited ban on nuclear testing. A kind of guarded but mutual admiration seemed to be developing between the American and Russian leaders, even though a meeting between them produced no immediate results. However, on November 22, 1963, Kennedy was assassinated, and in October 1964, Khrushchev fell from power and was replaced by Leonid Brezhnev and Aleksei Kosygin. Khrushchev's moderation and retreat in the Cuban crisis of 1962, as well as his growing unpopularity with the entrenched Communist bureaucracy, played a part in his downfall. At about this time, both the Eastern and Western blocs began to splinter—the Russians had a falling out with Mao and the Chinese Communists, while de Gaulle asserted French intentions to pursue an independent foreign policy.

The Sino-Soviet split that was first apparent to the outside world in 1959 became more pronounced during the sixties. The Chinese were increasingly reluctant to occupy a position subordinate to the USSR in the Communist world, particularly because Russia seemed to be more interested in increasing its own prosperity and physical security by reaching unilateral agreements with the Western powers than in lending material support to other Communist revolutions. Apparent Russian capitulation in the crisis over the placement of Soviet missiles in Cuba gave the Chinese an opportunity to open a personal attack on Khrushchev. When the nuclear test ban treaty was signed in 1963, the Chinese denounced the Russians for entering into an alliance with the imperialists. Nikita Khrushchev's fall from power in 1964 and his replacement by Brezhnev and Kosygin did not heal the Sino-Soviet split.

The Chinese maintained a continuous propaganda campaign against the Soviets, damning them as counterrevolutionaries and revisionists who had sold out to the capitalist West. They held that only in its Maoist form was Marxism-Leninism still perpetuated, and they sought to export this pure ideology to the Communists of other nations. In 1966, China was temporarily distracted by internal turmoil, as the young Red Guard supporters of Mao Tse-tung launched a "cultural" revolution against party officials who dissented from his foreign and domestic policies. Chinese belligerence increased appreciably with their independent development of a hydrogen bomb in 1967 and their work on long-range missiles. Such developments not only worried the Western powers and frightened China's Asian neighbors; they meant that the potential destructiveness of a military confrontation between the two Communist giants could prove far worse for Russia than the Soviets had anticipated. And such conflict seemed more imminent when ideological dispute was accompanied by armed border clashes on the remote Asian frontier between the two countries.

The 1960's also witnessed a feud between the United States and France that was potentially crippling to the Western alliance. De Gaulle's determination to reduce America's influence in Europe was to be expected, for the general had opposed any policies that hampered France's independent action or prevented France from becoming the dominant power in western Europe. In 1964 de Gaulle recognized Communist China, emphasized the cultural links between France and Latin countries throughout the world, and expounded on the need for a third force between Washington and Moscow. Then in March 1966 France decided to withdraw from NATO's military framework. In December of that year the military and political headquarters of NATO moved from Paris to Brussels.

In the second half of the 1960's, additional problems distracted the United States and the Soviet Union from confrontation with each other. The Russian government, now firmly under the control of the party bureaucracy, reverted to a repressive policy against intellectuals who wanted further liberalization of the regime. The same spirit of liberation was at work in the eastern European satellites, and in the spring of 1968 an upheaval within the Czech Communist party threw the Stalinists out of office and brought liberal Marxists to power. The Soviet government—and the Stalinist regime in East Germany —feared the implications of this change as a precedent for upheavals in their own countries. They also were concerned about a possible Czech economic alliance with West Germany. Consequently, in the summer of 1968, echoing (although less violently) the Hungarian crisis of 1956, Russian tanks rolled into Prague, and in the following months the liberal regime was ousted in favor of party conservatives. But this repression angered the Communist parties in France and Italy and further weakened the unity of international Communism.

The United States, meanwhile, had plunged into the divisive imbroglio of the Vietnam War. John Kennedy was succeeded in 1963 by his Vice-President, Lyndon Johnson, who was elected in his own right in 1964 in a sweeping victory over Senator Barry Goldwater of Arizona. Johnson was able to push through the Kennedy domestic program that had stalled in Congress, thus producing the most extensive social legislation since the New Deal. Johnson's administration launched extensive new programs, including aid to education, housing, and urban renewal, medical care for the aged, and several major advances in civil rights. But in August 1964 the war in Vietnam entered a new phase as American aircraft bombed coastal installations in North Vietnam in retaliation for a reported attack on American ships in the Gulf of Tonkin. Though American bombing was widely protested throughout the world, neither the Russians nor the Chinese took any concrete steps to become involved in the fighting. By the end of 1964, the number of American troops in Vietnam exceeded 150,000. During 1966 it rose to 375,000. By 1968 it had reached 575,000.

The increased commitment in Vietnam was justified by the Johnson administration on the basis of the "domino theory" — that if South Vietnam was allowed to fall to the Communists, all the other states in southeast Asia would topple. This view, almost universally accepted by Americans in the 1950's, was now questioned even by prominent senators. By 1968 involvement in Vietnam had become the dominant political issue for most Americans. Its impact on the American economy was enormous, given the tens of billions of dollars devoted to defense expenditures; its cost required the limitation of allocations for sorely needed domestic programs; and it alienated a large proportion of the nation's youth and intellectuals, who saw the war as unjust and ill-conceived. Its most striking political impact was President Johnson's decision in the spring of 1968 to refrain from seeking another term. Free from the stresses of an election campaign, he tried to resolve the Vietnam crisis by ending the bombing of North Vietnam in the fall of 1968. He also initiated peace talks in Paris between the North Vietnamese and American governments, eventually including representatives of the Saigon government and the Vietcong. However, the presidential term of Richard Nixon — who had won the election of 1968 by an even smaller margin than Kennedy in 1960 — began in January 1969 with little concrete progress in the Paris negotiations.

Along with the burden of the Vietnam War, the United States in the late 1960's was disturbed by domestic unrest rising out of racial problems. Growing numbers of black militants called for retaliation against what they saw as systematic violence by the white Establishment. City after city experienced virtual insurrection in the ghettos, and riot police and national guardsmen had to be used to quell the rioting and looting. Black militants also joined forces with opponents of the Vietnam War. Both groups held that continuation of the war deprived the country of funds needed for social reform.

With the Soviet Union distracted by the Chinese menace and threats of revolution in its satellites, and the United States annoyed by de Gaulle and divided internally on foreign policy, the simple polarities of the cold war were fading at the close of the 1960's. Only in the Middle East was some of the old confrontation spirit preserved — but even here the superpowers worked against each other through the Arabs and the Israelis. By 1967, Nasser had drawn closer to Russia, and the Soviets rewarded him with a vast supply of arms. With these, Egypt committed belligerent acts against Israel, and in the Six-Day War of June 1967, the Israelis invaded the Sinai peninsula while the Jordanian, Iraqui, and Syrian forces attacked Israel. Within a week, Israel defeated them all and conquered vast stretches of Arab territory. This victory — won in part with American weapons — was a severe blow for Soviet policy. During the next two years, the United States and the Soviet Union tried to arrange a peace treaty between the Israelis and the Arabs, while at the same time, in cold war tradition, seeking to win the greatest advantage for themselves.

Europe in the 1960's

The astounding recovery of the postwar European economy leveled off somewhat in the 1960's. In West Germany the "economic miracle" faltered momentarily in the economic crisis of 1966 — one outstanding victim being the world-famous firm of Krupp of Essen — and then resumed its dynamic pace. After its auspicious start in 1957, European economic integration made little further progress. In the late 1960's there were several balance-of-payments and currency crises. The European economy was beginning to show signs of wear. Nevertheless, in all western European countries the rate of mass consumption accelerated. European cities — benefiting from slum clearance, new buildings, and the cleaning of historic structures — had never been so beautiful and pleasant. Nor had Europeans ever been so well fed and dressed. Paradoxically, as the European way of life became more Americanized, European governments were more inclined to follow an independent line in foreign policy; their people no longer cared much for ideology but wanted to be left alone to pursue private and family interests.

The contrast in the conditions of everyday life between western and eastern Europe was not as striking as in the 1950's, but it was still quite sharp. In general, the promises made from time to time by Communist leaders in the Soviet Union and its satellites that there would be great improvement in housing and in the quality and quantity of consumer goods were not fulfilled. The Soviet economy was still much stronger in the public than in the private sector, and the dour party functionaries who succeeded Khrushchev in 1964 were actually afraid to move rapidly to a mass-consumption society, for the material enhancement of everyday life might be conducive to political liberalism. That seemed to be the lesson of Czechoslovakia, where prosperity in the late 1950's and the early 1960's culminated in the peaceful political revolution in 1968 that was suppressed by Soviet intervention.

Britain fully participated in the shift to a mass-consumption society. The Conservative government under Harold Macmillan, who had become prime minister in 1957 when Anthony Eden had to resign after the Suez fiasco, favored immediate prosperity and high mass consumption at the cost of postponing efforts to resolve Britain's fundamental problems—a seriously adverse balance of trade, a still retrograde capital plant in industry, a business class that adjusted too slowly to modern technology and commercial methods, and a unionized working class that was selfish and unenterprising. By 1963, although the Conservatives (with some validity) were still telling the British people "you never had it so good," the balance-of-payments problem could no longer be ignored. Britain applied for membership in the Common Market, only to be refused admittance because of de Gaulle's intransigent hostility.

Since the Conservatives seemed to be floundering, the electorate turned to the Labour party, which had been out of office since 1951. In 1964 Labour won a majority of three seats, and in 1965 it gained a decisive majority for only the second time in its history. Harold Wilson, a sometime Oxford economics professor, was the Labour prime minister. His government was pledged to effect long-term structural reform within the country, but it was plagued by a huge balance-of-payments deficit and a serious run on the pound. Wilson was able to get the unions to agree grudgingly to a freeze on wages, and subsequently the pound was devalued from $2.80 to $2.40; but financial troubles persisted. The defection of radical party members combined with the distrust of the unions, on which Labour electoral strength was based, and disastrous showings in the popularity polls contributed to a bleak political outlook for Wilson's government.

In France the de Gaulle regime was shaken in early 1968 by a student revolt in Paris protesting the rigid, centralized system of education at the French universities and the inferiority of staff and equipment. The students were joined by the workers—against the advice of union leaders and the Communist party—in an immense strike that almost realized the old syndicalist dream and was not halted for several weeks. De Gaulle called for new elections, which he won by presenting himself as the only alternative to Communist rule. In November, however, the long-range effects of the strike began to be felt. During the weeks that French industry was idled, the country had continued to import goods at a normal rate, aggravating a balance-of-payments deficit. A run on the franc began, but for the time being de Gaulle refused to devalue the currency. In the spring of 1969, in order to put through relatively minor changes in the French constitution, de Gaulle used his hitherto infallible ploy of forcing the electorate to choose between acceptance of his policy and his resignation. In the absence of a crisis, the French repudiated the de Gaulle-backed plan, and the general resigned. The Gaullist era ended with little expectation of appreciable changes in his long-term policies, but there remained hope of easing French opposition to British membership in the Common Market and the possibility of some revival of French commitment to the Western alliance. In June 1969 Georges Pompidou, a Gaullist, was elected president by a decisive margin.

Prospects and Anxieties

A quarter of a century after the Second World War, both the victorious and the defeated nations had recovered from the terrible depredations and had far outstripped their prewar levels of productivity and consumption. European colonization had been largely liquidated, and the former colonies had taken their places in the United Nations and in the calculations of the great powers. There had been no recurrence of the total war that had twice in the century taxed the capacities and threatened the survival of Western civilization. The existence of two superpowers with the capacity to destroy each other and the rest of the human race as well had precluded all-out war between them.

Nevertheless, war — less than total but still real and terrible — remained endemic in international relations. Conflicts like those in Vietnam and the Middle East not only threatened the involvement of the great powers; they demonstrated the ability of even the smallest nations to resort to war when armed by the superpowers with the most devastating weapons short of atomic bombs.

Within nations, guerrilla warfare developed on the Maoist, Cuban, and Vietcong models meant that political and social stability was to be constantly challenged. And even in relatively stable countries, civil disorders short of armed rebellion required the development of sophisticated crowd-control weapons and techniques and produced the repeated spectacle of police and troops confronting demonstrators — on a Paris street, in a Detroit ghetto, or on the campus of a great university.

When warfare and civil disruptions were not taxing the political and social structure, the threat of famine, overpopulation, and the pollution and destruction of the earth itself raised apprehensions about the prospects for the 1970's. Limited yet constant warfare meant that human and material resources had to be devoted to military needs and were not available to solve the ultimately more critical demands of the demographic and ecological revolutions.

16

HERITAGE
ESSAY

THE CONTEMPORARY ETHOS

Western civilization, which has experienced successive waves of intellectual revolution since the eighteenth century, was faced in the late 1960's with yet another cultural upheaval. The new ethos was passionately proclaimed by radicals in the older generation; it gained fanatical adherents among university students; and, as had occurred in previous intellectual upheavals, it advertised a distinctive life style and was transmuted into demands for political and social change.

Like all previous cultural revolutions, the new ethos of the late 1960's articulated a distinct interpretation of history. Its spokesmen – among them Karl Jaspers and the distinguished British historian Geoffrey Barraclough – claimed that the "post-European age" had dawned. The West, it was said, had lost its hegemony, and a new world culture was forming in which the values of Oriental and African civilizations would challenge Western traditions. From this "conscious counterpoint," as Barraclough wrote in 1964, would come a change in human attitudes – more optimistic, humanitarian, cosmopolitan, life-enhancing, peaceful, and loving. Black intellectual and political leaders in both Africa and the United States made much of this theme, and received an enthusiastic response among the younger generation, both black and white. They asserted that Western civilization is *per se* racist, imperialist, militaristic, technocratic, and materialist. In contrast to the allegedly oppressive philosophy of the West, the philosophy of the non-West, as expressed by an African poet, is pacific and humanitarian:

> Hurrah for those who never invented anything
> hurrah for those who never explored anything
> hurrah for those who never conquered anything
> hurrah for joy
> hurrah for love
> hurrah for the pain of incarnate tears.[1]

1. Quoted in G. Barraclough, *An Introduction to Contemporary History.* London: Watts, 1964, p. 263.

The new ethos proclaimed not only the advent of the post-European age but also the emergence of a "post-industrial" culture and society. Marshall McLuhan declared that the old, rational, "linear" book culture, with which liberalism was associated, had become obsolete in the face of the technological revolution that had altered the means of communication. The electronic age intensified the quality of interpersonal relationships and made the world into a "global village" with a truly cosmopolitan, universally homogeneous culture. Sociologists of more conservative temperament also asserted that the West in the electronic, computer age was experiencing a technological and economic change comparable in significance to that caused by the

The Communist World. The emergence of anti-Stalinist liberal attitudes in the Soviet satellites culminated in the Hungarian Revolution of 1956 (facing page). Although the revolt was put down by Russian arms, the European satellites became increasingly restless; in 1968 the liberal movement in Czechoslovakia had to be suppressed by Russian force. Stalinist communism triumphed in China in 1948 — 1949 under Mao's leadership, but after Stalin's death Mao broke with Stalin's more moderate successors. Right: celebration in Peking, in 1950, of the first anniversary of Mao's triumph. In 1967 a bitter struggle for succession to the ailing Mao developed. Above: public humiliation of Mao's opponents by the Red Guards.

Democratic Leadership. A fortunate characteristic of our era, as compared with the interwar period, has been the generally superior
quality of leadership in democratic countries.
Facing page: Mohandas K. Gandhi, the leader
of nonviolent resistance to colonialism in
India. Below: President John F. Kennedy,
greatly admired by liberals and the young, in
Fort Worth, Texas, in 1963. Both Gandhi and
Kennedy were victims of assassins. Right:
Western statesmen at the funeral of former
West German chancellor Konrad Adenauer in
1967. President Lyndon B. Johnson is second
from the top, President Charles de Gaulle
fourth from the top, and on de Gaulle's right
a later West German chancellor, Kurt Georg
Kiesinger.

Industrial Revolution, whose social and political superstructure would now inevitably be transcended. This view drew quite different conclusions from those propounded by McLuhan: it foresaw not a new humanism but a society in which all achievement and value would lie with the scientist and engineer, who alone had mastered the knowledge that could bring power, wealth, and progress. According to this vision of the new society, student radicals were merely latter-day Luddites whose training in the arts and humanities had been rendered socially useless by technological change. Yet both views heralded a society that superseded the industrial and cultural ambience of the nineteenth century in which Western liberalism had flourished. At the close of the 1960's there was a widespread belief in intellectual and academic circles that a new technological and economic era had begun.

A third historical interpretation delineated in the new ethos—the most easily comprehensible and the most politically relevant one—was that the cold war polarization between the Soviet Union and the United States, and between Stalinism and capitalism, was coming to an end. Furthermore, it was held, this polarization *ought* to terminate immediately because its rigid ideology and brutal power politics inhibited the realization of a global culture and perpetuated the subjection of the Third World (a vague entity that seemed to comprise all the non-white peoples on the earth) to American and Russian domination. It was partly because the American involvement in Vietnam seemed a vestige of the allegedly superseded cold war era that it aroused such fury in the younger generation, not only in the United States but throughout the Western world. Russian intervention in Czechoslovakia in 1968 could be condemned on similar grounds, though it never aroused the volume and intensity of protest that the Vietnam War did; but the devastation of an Asian country by a Western power—whatever the political and moral justification—seemed more inimical to the new ethos than the suppression of liberal Marxists by conservative Communist forces.

The new ethos of the late 1960's propounded not only an interpretation of history but, as with previous Western cultural upheavals, a distinctive ethic, whose motto was "liberation." Norman O. Brown, and many less sophisticated exponents, advocated the liberation of erotic love from the repressive and dehumanizing force of social institutions. Herbert Marcuse—tremendously popular among the younger generation in the late 1960's—condemned industrialism, whether of the capitalist or the socialist variety (though his hostility was vented particularly against the former), and juxtaposed the full realization of the dimensions of human personality and the enslaving drive of industrial-bureaucratic order. Marcuse condemned the traditional liberal protection of free speech for all members of an open society as mere "repressive tolerance"; he thought it morally wrong to protect the political and civil liberties of conservatives. Black nationalists and student radicals who resorted to force and disruption echoed his philosophy.

The late 1960's—not only in America but in almost every country in the Western world—were a time of upheaval, of separation between the old culture and the new, between the reigning and the rising generations, between traditions of the past and hopes for the future. The mood of the late 1960's was a new romanticism, a new humanism, a new anti-institutional anarchism. Everywhere there was a loss of faith in big government, traditional authority, conventional morality and ideology. There was a new spirit of questioning, a new urge to get back to the deepest instincts of the human personality. "Make love, not war"—this vulgarization of the new philosophy was as socially significant and compelling, and as perplexing and terrifying to the old order, as the "rights of man" had been to the *ancien régime* of the eighteenth century. Brown, Marcuse, and also McLuhan spoke to the new generation—the best-educated in human history, uncorrupted by the horrors of depression and war, uncommitted to the ideological clichés of the cold war. It was an existential generation: its members had the luxury of striving for the highest potential of human existence and of judging traditions and social institutions on their merits. They confidently, sometimes arrogantly, regarded themselves as the beautiful and pure in spirit, with the freedom to search for the love that men had always sought for but had previously been driven away from by soul-destroying war, tyranny, and poverty. To the young the Vietnam War represented the return of all the rotten and useless in history, all the tyranny and horror that had diverted men from satisfying their best hopes and deep-

The Emancipation of the Wretched. A main theme of the postwar period was the liberation of Asian, African, and Latin American peoples from colonialism and corrupt dictatorships. The results, however, were not an unmixed blessing. Below: Fidel Castro, liberator of Cuba, exhorting workers in a cement factory. Castro's rule generally improved the condition of the Cuban peasantry and proletariat, but he was not able to put the Cuban economy on a sound footing and his government was heavily dependent on Russian aid. Facing page: Nigerian soldiers in military action against secessionist Biafra, whose people were treated more savagely by the Nigerian government than they had been by British imperial rule.

est faith. The war was viewed as the return of the dragon, the resuscitation of the old order.

The new ethos had at least superficial similarities with the world view of Indian Buddhism, which had always considered the individual as part of a continuous humanity, which had preached "the non-duality of one's self and other selves," which had tended "to alienate the objective natural world and to live in a world of meditation," which had assumed that different philosophies and religions that "seemingly conflict with each other are based on the Absolute One," and which was "indifferent about sexual matters."[2] It is hardly surprising that Indian philosophy and music became fashionable in Western intellectual circles in the late 1960's as never before.

Whatever the parallels between the new ethos and traditional Indian thought, and however encouraging these affinities might be to expectations of the forming of a total world culture, the doctrines that stirred the minds of students and avant-garde intellectuals in the late 1960's were not mainly the consequence of Oriental influence. The new ethos had indigenous roots in some of the central currents of the Western tradition — in Christian mysticism, in the Enlightenment's vision of a happy and peaceful world, in Romanticism's yearning for the

War and Revolution. Above: Israeli troops celebrating their capture of the Moslem holy place, the Dome of the Rock, in Jerusalem during the Arab-Israeli War of 1967. The Israelis justified their attack on the Arabs as self-defense, because Egypt and Syria, with the help of Jordan, intended to destroy Israel. But after their overwhelming victory, the Israelis were unable to make peace with the intransigent Arab governments. Facing page, top: exhibition of the body of Che Guevera, Cuban Communist revolutionary, after his capture and execution by the Bolivian army. Che's execution may have prevented a Communist revolution in Bolivia, but it did nothing to solve the chronic social and economic problems of Latin America. Facing page, bottom: an American soldier guarding a captured enemy in Vietnam during the most unpopular, divisive, and militarily disastrous war in American history.

2. Hajime Nakamura, *Ways of Thinking of Eastern Peoples*. Honolulu: East-West Center Press, 1964, pp. 103, 127, 168, 260.

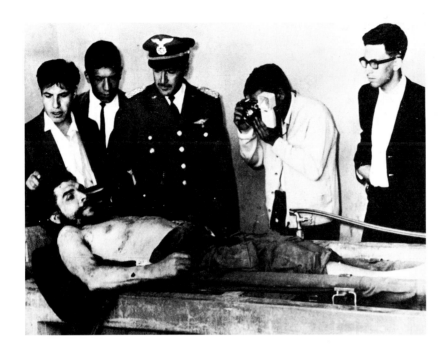

Protest and Confrontation in the United States. Right: anti-Vietnam War demonstration in New York City in 1968. Below: hippies selling an "underground" newspaper in the Haight-Ashbury district of San Francisco, short-lived capital of bohemian hippiedom. Facing page, top: disruption on the campus. Student radicals at the University of Wisconsin block recruitment for the Dow Chemical Company, manufacturer of napalm for the Vietnam War. Facing page, bottom: rioting in Detroit in 1967. In the late 1960's, student radicals, black militants, antiwar demonstrators, and hippies were generally allied against the war and what was called the "military-industrial complex," although each group had particular interests and attitudes that did not coincide with those of the other groups.

union of self and nature and for the union of all individuals in the Absolute Spirit, in anarchism's faith in the spontaneous association of men in a harmonious community when freed from the brutality and oppression of the state, in Nietzsche's life-affirming ethic and Freud's revelation of the primacy of erotic impulses, and in the existential philosophy of Camus, Sartre, and Jaspers.

Essentially, what was happening in the late 1960's was another one of those great upheavals by which Western civilization has periodically renewed itself and redirected its moral and social goals by reasserting those aspects of its heritage

that have been temporarily ignored or subverted. The science, rationalism, and bureaucracy that in the nineteenth century had seemed the salvation of the West were now regarded as impoverishing and brutalizing to the human personality. The new ethos of the late 1960's sought to restore to their central place in Western culture the religious, mystical, compassionate, imaginative, and altruistic ideals that had been tarnished or ignored by industrialism and secularism, by the mechanism and bureaucracy of modern life.

Although in the nineteenth century liberalism had advanced in company with scientism, rationalism, secularism, nationalism, and professionalism, the goal of liberalism from the beginning was nothing else than the liberation of the human spirit and the achievement of international peace and universal brotherhood. It is not to be thought that the new culture of the 1960's, or any subsequent intellectual upheaval, would do other than reinvigorate the liberal faith of the West, give it a new vitality and a fresh inspiration to seek the peace and welfare of the human race.

It is a pernicious misreading of history to identify Western civilization with the racism, imperialism, and capitalism of the late nineteenth and the twentieth century. Even in their heyday, these attitudes and institutions were only one side of the Western world view and way of life. The destiny of Western civilization immeasurably transcends the mistakes of one era. The West has had its confusion, horror, and misery, its moments when antihuman doctrines have seemed on the verge of carrying all before them. But it is the glory of Western civilization that it has never stood still and has never neglected for long the quest for institutions that can contribute to the realization of human freedom. Soon its best minds have recalled the highest ideals of the classical and Christian traditions; they have inspired their contemporaries with the vision of a great age beginning anew, of the establishment of God's Kingdom on earth (or a secular equivalent) in their own time.

Another characteristic of Western civilization has been its blending of extremes, of radicalism with conservatism, of the traditions of the past with the philosophy of the future, of moral absolutism with the institutional exigencies of power and wealth. The great intellectual and moral upheavals have never completely shattered the framework of social and political organization or irrevocably separated one era from all that has gone before. Western civilization has had terrible yet creative upheavals and revolutions that have seemed for a moment to make all of previous history obsolete and irrelevant. And yet when the smoke has cleared and the furious indignation abated, the extremists have given way to the rationalists and moderates, who have restructured the institutions of the past and redirected the ideas of previous eras so as to bring them into harmony with the needs and ideals of the present. The result has never been perfect justice or absolute truth but sufficient justice and enough truth to satisfy the anxieties of the contemporary era while reestablishing the social peace and political order that the progress of civilization requires.

The purpose of the bibliographical essay is to introduce the reader to the important historical literature on the subjects discussed in each chapter and to suggest the main schools of interpretation of major historical problems. Works in foreign languages are listed only when there is no reasonable equivalent in English. Titles marked with an asterisk* are available in paperback.

For the bibliography to the summary *Prologue to Modern History*, dealing with the period 1650–1715, see the bibliographical essays for chapters 14–16 of Volume I.

CHAPTER 1. ABSOLUTISM AND EMPIRE

No single work of synthesis analyzes all facets of eighteenth-century society and government, but valuable introductory surveys are M. S. Anderson, *Europe in the Eighteenth Century* (New York: Holt, 1961), which is strong on political developments, and the more elementary book of the same title by R. J. White* (New York: St. Martin's, 1965). Walter L. Dorn, *Competition for Empire 1740–1763* * (New York: Harper, 1940) is a brilliant example of comparative history that deals with complex issues in a clear and incisive manner. Although on some particular points recent scholarship has offered alternative interpretations, Dorn's work is one of the finest achievements of American scholarship. Another work of synthesis in the same series, Leo Gershoy, *From Despotism to Revolution 1763–1789* * (New York: Harper, 1944) is also learned and immensely valuable for the beginning student. Two volumes in *The New Cambridge Modern History*—Vol. VII: *The Old Regime 1713–1763* and Vol. VIII: *The American and French Revolutions* (Cambridge: Cambridge Univ., 1957, 1965)—are typical of this series: penetrating studies mixed with rather mediocre essays, and generally lacking a synthetic view. A. Goodwin, ed., *The European Nobility in the Eighteenth Century* * (London: Black, 1953) is an important collection of essays in social history, and John Carswell, *The South Sea Bubble* (Stanford: Stanford Univ., 1960) is a thoroughly delightful study that illuminates many facets of early eighteenth-century economy and society. Albert Sorel, *Europe Under the Old Regime* * (New York: Harper, 1964) is a translation of the first chapter of a classic analysis of the mechanism of eighteenth-century international relations. An introduction to eighteenth-century imperialism is provided in the earlier chapters of D. K. Fieldhouse, *The Colonial Empires* (New York: Delacorte, 1967), and important comparative interpretations are offered in A. P. Thornton, *Doctrines of Imperialism* * (New York: Wiley, 1965). The imperial struggle in North America is surveyed in the classic nineteenth-century works of Francis Parkman and in L. H. Gipson, *The British Empire Before the American Revolution* (New York: Knopf, 1938–1969), particularly Volumes VI–XIII. British-French rivalry in India is analyzed in R. C. Majumdar, ed., *The Struggle for Empire* (Bombay: Bharatiya Vidya Bhavan, 1957) and in H. Dodwell, *Dupleix and Clive: The Beginning of Empire* (London: Methuen, 1920). Holden Furber, *John Company at Work* (Cambridge: Harvard Univ., 1951) is an important case study in the character of European imperialism in Asia. Richard Pares, *A West India Fortune* (London: Longmans, 1950) is an absorbing and colorful analysis of colonial society in the Caribbean. For the beginning student, J. H. Plumb, *England in the Eighteenth Century* * (Harmondsworth: Penguin, 1951) is valuable; a more detailed survey is Dorothy Marshall, *Eighteenth Century England* (New York: McKay, 1962). Important for early eighteenth-century British politics is J. H. Plumb, *Sir Robert Walpole*, 2 vols. (London: Cresset, 1956–1960). All advanced study of mid-century British government and politics must begin with the seminal works of Lewis B. Namier, *The Structure of Politics at the Accession of George III*, 2nd ed. (New York: St. Martin's, 1957) and *England in the Age of the American Revolution*, 2nd ed. (New York: Macmillan, 1961). Namier's highly influential and controversial analyses sought to demonstrate that parties and principles were mere facades which covered a power-struggle among aristocratic families and factions. This view has brought Britain within the pattern of the eighteenth-century *ancien régime* and suggested that the differences in the governmental structure of Britain and France were not as great as liberal historians had imagined. On the *ancien régime* in France, a pioneering work of great insight, originally published in 1856, is Alexis de Tocqueville, *The Old Regime and the French Revolution* * (New York: Anchor, 1955), which brilliantly examines the tensions in society and government before the Revolution. A judicious and well-written account, particularly valuable for the beginning student, is Alfred Cobban, *A History of Modern France,* * Vol. I, rev. ed. (London: Cape, 1962). Also useful is J. Lough, *An Introduction to Eighteenth Century France* (London: Longmans, 1960). For the advanced student, important studies of the pressures that existed in French society and the relations between the government and the dominant classes are Franklin L. Ford, *Robe and Sword* (Cambridge: Harvard Univ., 1953); Elinor G. Barber, *The Bourgeoisie in Eighteenth Century France** (Princeton: Princeton Univ., 1955); and Robert Forster, *The Nobility of Toulouse in the Eighteenth Century* (Baltimore: Johns Hopkins Univ., 1960). John C. Gagliardo, *Enlightened Despotism** (New York: Crowell, 1967) is an incisive and careful appraisal, and Geoffrey Bruun, *Enlightened Despots**, 2nd ed. (New York: Holt, 1967) offers good reading. Important for German ideological, cultural, and social trends are W. H. Bruford, *Germany in the Eighteenth Century: The Social Background of the Literary Revival* (Cambridge: Cambridge Univ., 1935) and F. Hertz, *The Development of the German Public Mind,* 2 vols. (New York: Macmillan, 1962). Hajo Holborn, *A History of Modern Germany,* Vol. II (New York: Knopf, 1964) is a reliable survey as are Nicholas Riasanovsky, *A History of Russia* (New York: Oxford Univ., 1963); Michael T. Florinsky, *Russia: A History and an Interpretation* (New York: Macmillan, 1954); and Oscar Halecki, *A History of Poland,* rev. ed. (New York: Roy, 1961). There is no satisfactory survey of the Habsburg empire in the eighteenth century. For the advanced study of eighteenth-century Prussia, Hans Rosenberg, *Bureaucracy, Aristocracy, Autocracy** (Boston: Beacon, 1966) is indispensable; it provides insights into problems of European government and society in general. Richard Herr, *The Eighteenth-Century Revolution in Spain* (Princeton: Princeton Univ., 1958) is valuable for enlightened despotism in that country. Jerome Blum, *Land and Peasant in Russia from the Ninth to the Nineteenth Century* (Princeton: Princeton Univ., 1961) provides a scholarly survey of eighteenth-century Russian economy and society. Biographies of the enlightened despots are legion. On Frederick the Great: Gerhard Ritter (Berkeley: Univ. of Calif., 1969) and G. P. Gooch (New York: Knopf, 1947); on Maria Theresa: G. P. Gooch (New York: Longmans, 1951) and C. L. Morris (New York: Knopf, 1934); on Joseph II: Saul K. Padover, *The Revolutionary Emperor* (New York: Ballou, 1934); on Catherine the Great: G. S. Thomson* (New York, Collier, 1962) and Ian Grey (Philadelphia: Lippincott, 1962). There is a vast library of excellent works on the American Revolution. For the beginning student, E. S. Morgan, *The Birth of the Republic** (Chicago: Univ. of Chicago, 1956) is very helpful, while Richard B. Morris, *The American Revolution Reconsidered* (New York: Harper, 1967) judiciously delineates the problems involved in the advanced study of the subject. On the issues involved in the Revolution, three learned and perceptive works are John C. Miller, *Origins of the American Revolution** (Stanford: Stanford Univ., 1959); Bernard Bailyn, *The Ideological Origins of the American Revolution* (Cambridge, Mass.: Harvard Univ., 1967); and Merrill Jensen, *The Founding of a Nation** (New York: Oxford Univ., 1968). Gordon S. Wood, *The Creation of the American Republic 1776–1787* (Chapel Hill: Univ. of North Carolina, 1969) is an illuminating study. On the impact of the American Revolution in Britain and the reform movement of the 1770's and 1780's, the fol-

lowing are important: Herbert Butterfield, *King George, Lord North, and the People* (London: Bell, 1949); Eugene C. Black, *The Association* (Cambridge: Harvard Univ., 1963); Ian A. Christie, *Wilkes, Wyvill, and Reform* (New York: St. Martin's, 1963); J. S. Watson, *The Reign of George III* (Oxford: Clarendon, 1960); and George Rudé, *Wilkes and Liberty** (Oxford: Oxford Univ., 1962). Robert R. Palmer, *The Age of the Democratic Revolution,* 2 vols. (Princeton: Princeton Univ., 1959–1964) offers in his first volume a richly documented and detailed study of the crisis of the *ancien régime,* arguing that the American Revolution launched the disintegration of aristocratic and absolutist institutions in the Western world. A similar thesis is propounded by Jacques Godechot, *France and the Atlantic Revolution of the Eighteenth Century* (New York: Free Press, 1965).

CHAPTER 2. ENLIGHTENMENT CULTURE

Of all great intellectual movements in modern history, the Enlightenment has been most extensively studied, and the historical literature is of a very high order. An excellent brief introduction is Frank E. Manuel, *The Age of Reason** (Ithaca: Cornell Univ., 1951). More detailed surveys, expert and highly readable, are Paul Hazard, *European Thought in the Eighteenth Century** (New Haven: Yale Univ., 1954) and G. R. Havens, *The Age of Ideas** (New York: Free Press, 1965). A balanced and perceptive analysis, reflecting a profound knowledge of literature, is Lester G. Crocker, *An Age of Crisis* (Baltimore: Johns Hopkins Univ., 1959). Peter Gay, *The Enlightenment: The Rise of Modern Paganism** (New York: Knopf, 1966) is an eloquent and passionate panegyric by a confirmed partisan. Alfred Cobban, *In Search of Humanity* (London: Cape, 1960) is a sympathetic assessment of the political and moral heritage of the Enlightenment. A critical attitude toward the *philosophes* is taken by Carl Becker, *The Heavenly City of the Eighteenth Century Philosophers** (New Haven: Yale Univ., 1932), which claims that Enlightenment thinkers perpetuated the abstract modes of thought characteristic of medieval scholasticism. While the debate on Becker's thesis continues, the trend of scholarship in the 1950's and 1960's has been toward a much more favorable judgment of the *philosophes.* On eighteenth-century theology and popular religious attitudes, important studies are R. R. Palmer, *Catholics and Unbelievers in Eighteenth Century France**, 2nd ed. (New York: Cooper Square, 1961); F. E. Manuel, *The Eighteenth Century Confronts the Gods** (Cambridge: Harvard Univ., 1959); David Bien, *The Calas Affair* (Princeton: Princeton Univ., 1960); and Norman Sykes, *Church and State in Eighteenth-Century England* (Oxford: Clarendon, 1934). For advanced study of eighteenth-century philosophy, Ernst Cassirer, *The Philosophy of the Enlightenment** (Boston: Beacon, 1955) examines the great thinkers in a broad cultural context. For the development of utilitarianism, a work of magisterial scholarship is Elie Halévy, *The Growth of Philosophic Radicalism** (Boston: Beacon, 1955). On eighteenth-century science, a useful compendium is A. Wolf, *A History of*

Science, Technology and Philosophy in the Eighteenth Century, 2nd ed. (London: Allen & Unwin, 1952); Henry Guerlac, Lavoisier, the Crucial Year (Ithaca: Cornell Univ., 1961) is a fascinating study of the Enlightenment scientist at work. There is no entirely satisfactory survey of Enlightenment political, social, and historical thought; important contributions are Kingsley Martin, The Rise of French Liberal Thought*, 2nd ed., ed. J. P. Mayer (New York: New York Univ., 1954); Charles Frankel, The Faith of Reason (New York: King's Crown, 1948); R. V. Sampson, Progress in the Age of Reason (London: Heinemann, 1956); H. Vyverberg, Historical Pessimism in the French Enlightenment (Cambridge: Harvard Univ., 1958); J. B. Black, The Art of History (New York: Crofts, 1926); and Frank E. Manuel, The Prophets of Paris* (Cambridge: Harvard Univ., 1962). Among the many works on individual philosophes, the following are particularly distinguished: Peter Gay, Voltaire's Politics* (Princeton: Princeton Univ., 1959); Lester G. Crocker, ed., Diderot: The Embattled Philosopher (New York: Free Press, 1966); A. M. Wilson, Diderot: The Testing Years, 1713–1759 (New York: Oxford Univ., 1957); Alexander D. Lindsay, Kant (London: Oxford Univ., 1936); Norman K. Smith, The Philosophy of David Hume* (London: Macmillan, 1949); Frederick C. Green, Jean-Jacques Rousseau (Cambridge: Cambridge Univ., 1955); Ernst Cassirer, The Question of Jean-Jacques Rousseau* (New York: Columbia Univ., 1954); Eli Ginzberg, The House of Adam Smith (New York: Octagon, 1964); Mary Mack, Jeremy Bentham (New York: Columbia Univ., 1963). A. R. Humphreys, The Augustan World* (London: Methuen, 1954) is a delightful introduction to the literature and thought of the Enlightenment era. Dorothy Marshall, Dr. Johnson's London* (New York: Wiley, 1967) is a beautiful evocation of the ambience of mid-eighteenth-century London. Valuable for the study of music in the Enlightenment era are M. Bukofzer, Music in the Baroque Era (New York: Norton, 1947); Karl Geiringer, Johann Sebastian Bach (New York: Norton, 1966); and W. J. Turner, Mozart: The Man and His Works,* rev. ed. (New York: Barnes & Noble, 1966). François Fosca, The Eighteenth Century (Geneva: Skira, 1953) is a well-illustrated survey of eighteenth-century painting. I. Schneider, ed., The Enlightenment (New York: Braziller, 1965) is an excellent anthology. Also useful are Crane Brinton, ed., The Portable Age of Reason Reader* (New York: Viking, 1956) and Herbert H. Rowen, From Absolutism to Revolution*, 2nd ed. (New York: Macmillan, 1968).

CHAPTER 3. THE POLITICAL REVOLUTION

The importance and significance of the French Revolution and the Napoleonic era, the vast array of documentary material, and the interest of several great scholars in the period have resulted in an unusually sophisticated body of historical literature. For the beginning student, there are some excellent surveys; but he must be aware at all times that general interpretations of the French Revolution are liable to be influenced by the authors' social and political views.

George Rudé, Revolutionary Europe 1783–1815* (New York: Harper, 1966) is the best brief treatment; the viewpoint is that of the moderate Left. The same attitude prevails in Eric J. Hobsbawm, The Age of Revolution: Europe 1789–1848* (London: Weidenfeld and Nicolson, 1962). A more critical view of the Revolution is taken by Crane Brinton, A Decade of Revolution 1789–99* (New York: Harper, 1944), a subtle, brilliantly written analysis. A balanced survey is Leo Gershoy, The French Revolution and Napoleon (New York: Appleton-Century, 1964). Another excellent survey is Norman Hampson, A Social History of the French Revolution* (Toronto: Univ. of Toronto, 1963), which draws upon much recent research. M. J. Sydenham, The French Revolution* (New York: Putnam, 1965) is also a perceptive synthesis. Advanced study should begin with the work of the two giants of the early twentieth century: Alphonse Aulard, The French Revolution, a Political History, 4 vols. (London: Unwin, 1910) and Albert Mathiez, The French Revolution* (London: Williams & Norgate, 1927) and After Robespierre, the Thermidorian Reaction* (New York: Knopf, 1931). Aulard was the voice of the bourgeois liberal republic, Mathiez the staunch defender of radical Jacobinism. The great historian of the French Revolution in the next generation was Georges Lefebvre. His own commitment was to neo-Marxist doctrine, but his work is distinguished by a balanced treatment of the complex factors that brought on the French Revolution and affected its development. In The Coming of the French Revolution* (Princeton: Princeton Univ., 1947) Lefebvre propounded the now widely accepted thesis that the Revolution was precipitated by an aristocratic reaction. The French Revolution, 2 vols. (New York: Columbia Univ., 1961–1964 and The Thermidorians and the Directory (New York: Random House, 1964) comprise Lefebvre's general history of the Revolution, a work of monumental importance. There is no conservative history of the Revolution of high quality. Louis Madelin, The French Revolution (New York: Putnam, 1916) is occasionally perceptive but substandard as scholarship, and Pierre Gaxotte, The French Revolution (New York: Scribner's, 1932) is blatantly counter-revolutionary and tediously royalist. The best conservative account is still Hippolyte Taine, The French Revolution, 3 vols. (Gloucester: Peter Smith, 1962), which stresses mob action and factional conspiracy. J. L. Talmon, The Origins of Totalitarian Democracy* (London: Secker and Warburg, 1952) presents a provocative and learned argument that the roots of twentieth-century totalitarianism are to be found in Rousseau's philosophy and revolutionary radicalism. The tendency of the younger generation of historians of the French Revolution, disciples of Lefebvre, is to emphasize the central importance of class struggle. Excellent examples of this approach are George Rudé, The Crowd in the French Revolution* (Oxford: Clarendon, 1959) and Albert Soboul, The Parisian Sans-Culottes and the French Revolution (Oxford: Clarendon, 1964). This interpretation is vehemently criticized by Alfred Cobban in The Social Interpretation of the French Revolution* (Cambridge: Cambridge Univ., 1964); Cobban is the only leading recent historian of the Revolution who takes a somewhat critical view of the events in Paris in the 1790's. On the social history of the French Revolution, Richard Cobb's *Les Armées Révolutionnaires* (Paris: Mouton, 1961–1963) is a work of great learning and insight on the composition and attitudes of the revolutionary army, much wider in scope than its title indicates; and Charles Tilly, *The Vendée** (Cambridge: Harvard Univ., 1964) is a careful sociological analysis of the counterrevolutionaries. Important studies of radical groups and leaders are Crane Brinton, *The Jacobins* (New York: Macmillan, 1930), which emphasized the religious type of fervor of the revolutionary Left; M. J. Sydenham, *The Girondins* (London: Athlone, 1961), which argues the revisionist thesis that there was no significant difference between the ideas of the Girondists and those of the Mountain; David Thomson, *The Babeuf Plot* (London: Paul, Trench, Trubner, 1947), a coolly realistic appraisal; Robert R. Palmer, *Twelve Who Ruled** (Princeton: Princeton Univ., 1941), a fascinating portrayal of Robespierre and the Committee of Public Safety; and James M. Thompson, *Robespierre*, 2 vols., (New York: Appleton-Century, 1936) and, in briefer compass, *Robespierre and the French Revolution** (New York: Macmillan, 1953), authoritative biographies. Donald M. Greer, *The Incidence of the Terror During the French Revolution* (Cambridge: Harvard Univ., 1935) is a statistical study of the social background of the victims of the Terror, demonstrating they were not confined to the nobility. The second volume of R. R. Palmer, *The Age of the Democratic Revolution* (*op. cit.*, Chapter 1) depicts the sweep of revolutionary fervor through Europe in the 1790's. A convenient anthology of recent, relevant sociological studies is Jeffrey Kaplow, ed., *New Perspectives on the French Revolution** (New York: Wiley, 1965). Excellent collections of documents from the Revolutionary era are provided by John H. Stewart, ed., *A Documentary Survey of the French Revolution* (New York: Macmillan, 1951) and by J. M. Roberts, ed., *French Revolution Documents, Vol. I: 1787–1792* (New York: Barnes & Noble, 1966). Geoffrey Bruun, *Europe and the French Imperium**, rev. ed. (New York: Harper, 1957) is a well-balanced introduction to the Napoleonic era. The best brief biography of Napoleon is Felix M. Markham, *Napoleon** (New York: New American Library, 1965). Georges Lefebvre, *Napoleon*, 2 vols. (New York: Columbia Univ., 1969) is a magisterial study. J. Holland Rose, *Life of Napoleon I*, 2 vols., 9th ed. (London: Bell, 1924) is still very useful. Pieter Geyl, *Napoleon: For and Against** (New Haven: Yale Univ., 1949) is a fascinating historiographical study, and J. Christopher Herold, ed., *The Mind of Napoleon** (New York: Columbia Univ., 1955) is a skillful and thoroughly delightful anthology of Napoleon's opinions. D. C. Chandler, *The Campaigns of Napoleon* (New York: Macmillan, 1966) offers a detailed study of Napoleon's military career. Important for Napoleonic policy are Harold C. Deutsch, *The Genesis of Napoleonic Imperialism* (Cambridge, Mass.: Harvard Univ., 1938); Owen Connelly, *Napoleon's Satellite Kingdoms* (New York: Free Press, 1965); H. A. L. Fisher, *Studies in Napoleonic Statesmanship: Germany* (Oxford: Clar-

endon, 1903); and Eli Heckscher, *The Continental System* (Gloucester: Peter Smith, 1964). An introduction to the revolutionary and Napoleonic era in Britain is provided by Philip A. Brown, *The French Revolution in English History* (London: Lockwood, 1918) and the relevant chapters in J. S. Watson, *The Reign of George III* (*op. cit.*, Chapter 1). J. Holland Rose, *William Pitt and National Revival* (London: Bell, 1911) and *William Pitt and the Great War* (London: Bell, 1911) discuss many aspects of the period, and Edward P. Thompson, *The Making of the English Working Class** (London: Gollancz, 1963) analyzes the development of contemporary radical movements in Britain. There is no general study of the Napoleonic era in Germany; important aspects are discussed in Guy S. Ford, *Stein and the Era of Reform in Prussia* (Gloucester, Peter Smith, 1922); Walter C. Langsam, *The Napoleonic Wars and German Nationalism in Austria* (New York: AMS, 1930); Robert Ergang, *Herder and the Foundations of German Nationalism* (New York: Columbia Univ., 1931); G. P. Gooch, *Germany and the French Revolution* (New York: Longmans, Green, 1920); and Friedrich Meinecke, *Machiavellism** (New York: Praeger, 1965). Evgenii Tarle, *Napoleon's Invasion of Russia* (New York: Oxford Univ., 1942) is an exciting account, laced with Marxist ideology and Russian nationalist propaganda.

CHAPTER 4. THE ECONOMIC REVOLUTION

Modern scholarship on the Industrial Revolution in Britain begins with Thomas S. Ashton, *The Industrial Revolution**, rev. ed. (New York: Oxford Univ., 1962), still one of the best introductions; Ashton is strongly pro-capitalist and minimizes the alleged deleterious effects of industrialization on the working class. He has written a more detailed account, *An Economic History of England: The Eighteenth Century* (New York: Barnes & Noble, 1955) which also discusses the agricultural revolution. On rural economy and society, valuable studies are Lord Ernle, *English Farming, Past and Present*, 6th ed. (Chicago: Quadrangle, 1961) and G. Mingay, *English Landed Society in the Eighteenth Century* (London: Routledge and Paul, 1963). An excellent introduction to the advanced study of industrialization is Phyllis Deane, *The First Industrial Revolution** (Cambridge: Cambridge Univ., 1965). David Landes, *The Unbound Prometheus* (Cambridge: Cambridge Univ., 1969) – (also partly published in the *Cambridge Economic History of Europe*, Volume VI, Part I, Chapter 5) – is a brilliant and very important comparative study. A pioneering work, Paul Mantoux, *The Industrial Revolution in the Eighteenth Century**, rev. ed. (New York: Macmillan, 1961) is still valuable. Walt W. Rostow, *The Stages of Economic Growth** (Cambridge: Cambridge Univ., 1960) provides an exciting, highly controversial paradigm for the process of industrialization. Phyllis Deane and W. A. Cole, *British Economic Growth 1688–1959*, 2nd ed. (Cambridge: Cambridge Univ., 1968) presents sophisticated statistical analysis. W. H. B. Court, *A Concise Economic History of Britain from 1750 to Recent Times** (Cambridge: Cambridge Univ., 1954) is an authoritative survey, and William O. Henderson, *Britain and Industrial*

Europe 1750–1870, 2nd ed. (Leicester: Leicester Univ., 1965) provides a comparative analysis of the progress of British and Continental industrialization. For French development, Shepherd Clough, *France: A History of National Economics 1789–1939* (New York: Scribner's, 1939) is valuable. Charles Wilson, "The Entrepreneur in the Industrial Revolution in Britain," *Explorations in Entrepreneurial History*, Vol. VII (Cambridge: Harvard Univ., 1954) is an important study of business organization. For critical leftist views of the Industrial Revolution, emphasizing its social ills, see John L. and Barbara Hammond, *The Rise of Modern Industry*, 8th ed. (London: Methuen, 1951) and *The Town Laborer* (London: Longmans, 1920); Eric J. Hobsbawm, *The Age of Revolution* (op. cit., Chapter 1); and — most persuasively — Edward P. Thompson, *The Making of the English Working Class* (op. cit., Chapter 1). For a more favorable view of the effect of the Industrial Revolution on living standards, see R. Max Hartwell, "The Rising Standard of Living in England 1800–1850," *Economic History Review*, Second Series, XIII (1961). This may be supplemented by an ideologically motivated attack on the socialist historians of the Industrial Revolution: Friedrich A. von Hayek, ed., *Capitalism and the Historians** (Chicago: Univ. of Chicago, 1954).

CHAPTER 5. THE AGE OF ROMANTICISM

A general history of the Romantic movement in all its aspects is lacking. A subtle and penetrating inquiry into the nature of Romanticism is Jacques Barzun, *Romanticism and the Modern Ego** (Boston: Little, Brown, 1943). The same author's *Berlioz and the Romantic Century,** 2 vols. (Boston: Little, Brown, 1950) explores many aspects of the cultural world of the early nineteenth century; this very important study is much broader in scope than its title implies. The work of the nineteenth-century scholar, Georg Brandes, *Main Currents in Nineteenth Century Literature*, 6 vols. (London: Heinemann, 1901–1905) is still valuable. Frederick B. Artz, *Reaction and Revolution 1814–1832** (New York: Harper, 1950) and Jacob L. Talmon, *Romanticism and Revolt** (New York: Harcourt, 1967) relate cultural and political change. Useful contributions to the history of British Romanticism are David Daiches, *Critical History of English Literature*, Vol. II (New York: Ronald, 1960); Alfred Cobban, *Edmund Burke and the Revolt Against the Eighteenth Century*, 2nd ed. (New York: Barnes & Noble, 1960); Crane Brinton, *Political Ideas of the English Romanticists** (Ann Arbor: Michigan, 1966); Henry N. Brailsford, *Shelley, Godwin, and Their Circle* (Hamden: Shoe String, 1969); and Geoffrey Faber, *The Oxford Apostles** (Harmondsworth: Penguin, 1954). Raymond Williams, *Culture and Society** (London: Chatto & Windus, 1958) analyzes the intellectual response to the Industrial Revolution. Important studies of German Romanticism are Robert Ergang, *Herder and the Foundations of German Nationalism* (op. cit., Chapter 3); Hans Kohn, *The Mind of Germany** (New York: Scribner, 1960); Leonard Krieger, *The German Idea of Freedom* (Boston: Beacon, 1957); Herbert Marcuse, *Reason and Revolution** 2nd ed. (New York:

Humanities, 1955); Friedrich Meinecke, *Cosmopolitanism and Nationalism* (Princeton: Princeton Univ., 1969); and K. Francke, *A History of German Literature as Determined by Social Forces*, 4th ed. (New York: Holt, 1931). Leading aspects of French Romanticism are studied in Roger Soltau, *French Political Thought of the Nineteenth Century* (New York: Russell, 1959) and G. Boas, *French Philosophies of the Romantic Period* (Baltimore: Johns Hopkins Univ., 1934). Harry Levin, *The Gates of Horn** (New York: Oxford Univ., 1963) is a brilliant study of the major French novelists, and Stanley Mellon, *The Political Uses of History* (Stanford: Stanford Univ., 1958) discusses French historical thought. On German historical thought, Herbert Butterfield, *Man on His Past** (Cambridge: Cambridge Univ., 1955) is an urbane critique, Friedrich Meinecke, *Die Entstehung des Historismus* (Munich: Oldenbourg, 1936) a detailed and partisan account, and T. H. von Laue, *Leopold Ranke, the Formative Years* (Princeton: Princeton Univ., 1950) a perceptive analysis of the ambiguities of Ranke's thought. Morse Peckham, *Beyond the Tragic Vision* (New York: Braziller, 1962) is a sophisticated discussion of Romantic themes in literature, and Jacob L. Talmon, *Political Messianism: The Romantic Phase* (London: Secker & Warburg, 1960) attempts similar projections for political and social thought. American Romanticism is discussed, from three diverse points of view, in Vernon L. Parrington, *Main Currents in American Thought**, Vol. II (New York: Harcourt, 1930); Van Wyck Brooks, *The Flowering of New England** (New York: Dutton, 1940); and Francis O. Mathiesson, *American Renaissance** (New York: Oxford Univ., 1941). There are good general studies of the development of nationalist doctrines and attitudes by two master scholars: Hans Kohn, *The Idea of Nationalism** (New York: Macmillan, 1948) and *Prophets and Peoples: Studies in Nineteenth Century Nationalism** (New York: Macmillan, 1946) and Carlton J. H. Hayes, *The Historical Evolution of Modern Nationalism* (New York: Macmillan, 1950) and *Nationalism: A Religion* (New York: Macmillan, 1960). Maurice Raynal, *The Nineteenth Century: Goya to Gauguin* (New York: Skira, 1951) provides a superb introduction to Romantic painting, and Sir Kenneth Clark, *The Gothic Revival**, 3rd ed. (New York: Holt, 1962) deals with an important movement in Romantic art. On Romantic music, Alfred Einstein, *Music in the Romantic Era* (New York: Norton, 1947) is an authoritative survey, while Barzun's study of Berlioz, cited above, is essential for advanced study. H. E. Hugo, ed., *The Romantic Reader** (New York: Viking, 1957) and M. Peckham, ed., *Romanticism* (New York: Braziller, 1965) are convenient anthologies; the latter identifies Romanticism with leading strands of thought in the later as well as earlier nineteenth century, and the editor's introductory essays are important.

CHAPTER 6. THE IMPACT OF LIBERALISM AND INDUSTRIALISM

Introductory surveys of part or all of the period 1815–1848 are provided in these synthetic works: E. J. Hobs-

bawm, *The Age of Revolution** (*op. cit.*, Chapter 3);
F. B. Artz, *Reaction and Revolution** (*op. cit.*, Chapter 3);
J. L. Talmon, *Romanticism and Revolution** (*op. cit.*,
Chapter 3); and Arthur J. May, *The Age of Metternich
1815–1848**, rev. ed. (New York: Holt, 1963). *The New
Cambridge Modern History*, Vol. X, *The Zenith of European Power* (Cambridge: Cambridge Univ., 1964)
contains several valuable studies. Charles Morazé, *The
Triumph of the Middle Classes** (Cleveland: World,
1966) is an original, often acutely perceptive, neo-
Marxist synthesis of nineteenth-century history. There
is, strangely, no satisfactory history of nineteenth-
century liberalism. Guido de Ruggiero, *The History of
European Liberalism** (Boston: Beacon, 1959) is useful
for the beginning student but superficial and pedestrian. In Harold J. Laski, *The Rise of European Liberalism* (London: Allen & Unwin, 1936), the author's occasional insights are suffocated by Marxist dialectics.
Karl Polanyi, *The Great Transformation** (Boston:
Beacon, 1957) is an unbalanced and idiosyncratic but
often valuable study of the emergence of industrial
society and middle-class liberalism. On the progress of
the Industrial Revolution, the turgid but vastly
learned and authoritative works of J. H. Clapham are
the starting point for advanced study: *Economic History
of Modern Britain*, Vol. I, 4th ed. (Cambridge: Cambridge Univ., 1930) and *The Economic Development of
France and Germany*, 2nd ed. (Cambridge: Cambridge
Univ., 1936). The latter must be supplemented by the
masterful study of Rondo Cameron, *France and the
Economic Development of Europe** (Princeton: Princeton Univ., 1961; abridged ed.*, 1966). Robert Heilbroner, *The Worldly Philosophers**, rev. ed. (New York:
Simon and Schuster, 1961) is a delightfully clear and
comprehensible introduction to the doctrines of economic liberalism; a more detailed treatment is provided by William D. Grampp, *The Manchester School
of Economics* (Stanford: Stanford Univ., 1960), and the
posthumously published lectures of the twentieth-
century economist, W. C. Mitchell, *Types of Economic
Theory*, ed. J. Dorfman (New York: Kelley, 1967) are re-
plete with wide-ranging learning and extraordinary
insights. On the Congress of Vienna and the post-
Napoleonic settlement, Charles K. Webster, *The Congress of Vienna** (New York: Barnes & Noble, 1963)
is valuable. Harold Nicolson, *The Congress of Vienna*
(New York: Harcourt, 1946) is easy reading, and Henry
A. Kissinger, *A World Restored** (London: Weidenfeld and Nicolson, 1957) is an original analysis by
a theorist and part-time practitioner of power politics.
A sympathetic but perceptive treatment of Metternich and post-Napoleonic conservatism is provided
by E. L. Woodward, *Three Studies in European Conservatism* (London: Constable, 1929). Introductory
surveys of British history in the period are Asa Briggs,
*The Age of Improvement** (*op. cit.*, Chapter 3) and
E. L. Woodward, *The Age of Reform*, 2nd ed. (Oxford: Clarendon, 1939). For advanced study, the
starting point is Elie Halévy, *History of the English
People in the Nineteenth Century**, Vols. I–III (London:
Benn, 1949–1952). Volume I, *England in 1815*, is regarded as a classic of twentieth-century historiography; Halévy believed that Benthamism and Wesleyan

religion were the determining modes of thought in
nineteenth-century Britain. S. J. Checkland, *The Rise
of Industrial Society in England* (New York: St.
Martin's, 1964) is extremely valuable for economic and
social development. Important studies of the realities
of British political life are Norman Gash, *Politics in
the Age of Peel* (London: Longmans, 1963); David Cecil,
Melbourne (Indianapolis: Bobbs-Merrill, 1954), a fascinating and beautifully written biography; Norman
McCord, *The Anti-Corn Law League* (London: Allen &
Unwin, 1958); and Herman Ausubel, *John Bright**
(New York: Wiley, 1966), a perceptive and well-balanced study. Asa Briggs, *Chartist Studies* (London:
Macmillan, 1959) examines all aspects of the British
left-wing movement, and Robert L. Schuyler, *The Fall
of the Old Colonial System* (New York: Oxford Univ.,
1945) describes the process of imperial devolution. C.
Woodham Smith, *The Great Hunger** (New York: Harper, 1962) is an engrossing study of the Irish catastrophe that also provides many insights into English
political and social attitudes. Allan Bullock and Maurice Shock, eds., *The Liberal Tradition* (New York: New
York Univ., 1957) is an extremely valuable anthology.
Gordon Wright, *France in Modern Times* (Chicago:
Rand McNally, 1960) is the best survey for the beginning student; Alfred Cobban, *A History of Modern
France**, Vol. II, rev. ed. (London: Cape, 1962–   ) is
also useful; and Denis W. Brogan, *The French Nation
1814–1940** (New York: Harper, 1957) is a clever,
highly personal account. G. Bertier de Sauvigny, *The
Bourbon Restoration* (Philadelphia: Univ. of Pennsyl-
vania, 1967) is a sympathetic interpretation; F. B.
Artz, *France under the Bourbon Restoration*
(Cambridge: Harvard Univ., 1931) is more critical;
Douglas Johnson, *Guizot* (London: Routledge & Paul,
1963) is important for the July Monarchy; and John
Plamenatz, *The Revolutionary Movement in France
1815–1871* (London: Longmans, 1952) surveys liberal
and republican ideas and forces. For an introduction
to German history, standard surveys are Hajo Holborn,
A History of Modern Germany, Vol. II (*op. cit.*, Chapter
1); Koppel S. Pinson, *Modern Germany*, 2nd ed. (New
York: Macmillan, 1966); and A. J. P. Taylor, *The
Course of German History** (New York: Coward-
McCann, 1946), a personal, critical, and often brilliant
essay. Advanced study of German history in the period
should begin with the ardently pro-Prussian account,
Romantic in style, by the nineteenth-century historian
and nationalist thinker, Heinrich von Treitschke,
History of Germany in the Nineteenth Century, 7 vols.
(New York: McBride, Nast, 1915–1919). A careful,
clear, and well-balanced analysis of economic and political change is Theodore S. Hamerow, *Restoration,
Revolution, Reaction** (Princeton: Princeton Univ.,
1958) G. A. Craig, *The Politics of the Prussian Army**
2nd ed. (Oxford: Clarendon, 1964) is a wide-ranging
analysis of the impact of the military on German
political life. Good introductions to Italian history in
the period are A. J. Whyte, *The Evolution of Modern
Italy** (Oxford: Blackwell, 1950) and Gaetano Salve-
mini, *Mazzini** (London: Cape, 1956), an authoritative
biography. Two excellent studies of efforts at reform
and revolution in Russia are Marc Raeff, *Michael Sper-*

ansky (The Hague: M. Nijoff, 1957) and Anatole G. Mazour, *The First Russian Revolution* (Berkeley: Univ. of California, 1937). A highly readable survey of the Habsburg empire is A. J. P. Taylor, *The Hapsburg Monarchy** (London: Hamilton, 1948). An introductory survey of the process of Latin American independence is provided by John B. Trend, *Bolivar and the Independence of Spanish America** (London: Hodder & Stoughton, 1946). Surveys of the development of the United States are the highly readable works of George Dangerfield, *The Era of Good Feelings** (New York: Harcourt, 1952) and *The Awakening of American Nationalism** (New York: Harper & Row, 1965) and, for the Jacksonian period, Glyndon G. Van Deusen, *The Jacksonian Era** (New York: Harper, 1959) and Marvin Meyers, *The Jacksonian Persuasion** (Stanford: Stanford Univ., 1957). On early socialist thought, G. D. H. Cole, *History of Socialist Thought: The Forerunners* (New York: St. Martin's, 1953) is a useful if somewhat uncritical survey; George Lichtheim, *The Origins of Socialism* (New York: Praeger, 1968) is a sophisticated and brilliant analysis, and Frank E. Manuel, *The New World of Henri Saint-Simon** (Cambridge, Mass.: Harvard Univ., 1956), a learned and detailed study of one aspect of the subject. For the 1830's and 1840's, William L. Langer, *Political and Social Upheaval 1832–1852** (New York: Harper, 1969) is a comprehensive survey by a master scholar. On the mid-century revolutions, Priscilla Robertson, *The Revolutions of 1848** (Princeton: Princeton Univ., 1952) is an entertaining comparative account, and Francois Fejto, ed., *The Opening of an Era: 1848* (London: Wingate, 1948) offers a variety of analytical essays, uneven in quality. Lewis B. Namier, *1848: Revolution of the Intellectuals** (London: Cumberlege, 1950) is an acerbic study of the Frankfurt Assembly, while R. J. Rath, *The Viennese Revolution of 1848* (Austin: Univ. of Texas, 1957) is a detailed account of the Austrian upheaval. Donald C. McKay, *The National Workshops* (Cambridge, Mass.: Harvard Univ., 1933) is valuable for the Paris revolution; and George Rudé, *The Crowd in History 1750–1848** (New York: Wiley, 1964), a distinguished essay in comparative history, has an important chapter on Paris in 1848. Arnold Whitridge, *Men in Crisis* (New York: Scribner's, 1949) provides touching and suggestive essays on the mid-century era.

CHAPTER 7. REALISM AND SCIENTISM

R. C. Binkley, *Realism and Nationalism 1852–1871** (New York: Harper, 1935) is a valiant but largely unsuccessful attempt to provide a synthetic view of the 1850's and 1860's. For the beginning student, though it deals only with Britain, the best introduction to the culture of the period is Asa Briggs, *Victorian People** (Chicago: Univ. of Chicago, 1955), a delightful and subtle series of biographical essays. For more detailed study of British culture, with implications for Europe as a whole, major works are Walter E. Houghton, *The Victorian Frame of Mind** (New Haven: Yale Univ., 1957) and W. L. Burn, *The Age of Equipoise** (London: Allen & Unwin, 1964). Georg Brandes, *Main Currents in Nineteenth Century Literature*, 6 vols. (*op. cit.*, Chapter 5) and J. T. Merz, *A History of European Thought in the Nineteenth Century**, 4 vols. (London: Blackwood, 1912–1928), although out-of-date, are still useful sources of information. Morse Peckham, *Beyond the Tragic Vision* (*op. cit.*, Chapter 5) is a brilliant study of modes of thought in European literature, and Walter M. Simon, *European Positivism in the Nineteenth Century* (Ithaca: Cornell Univ., 1963) is a sound analysis of this intellectual trend. R. G. Collingwood, *The Idea of History** (New York: Oxford Univ., 1956) is the best introduction to nineteenth-century historical thought. A brilliant, original, and fascinating account of nineteenth-century science is presented in Charles C. Gillespie, *The Edge of Objectivity** (Princeton: Princeton Univ., 1960); the discussion of Darwin is particularly important. Among the numerous studies of Darwin's life and thought, Gavin de Beers, *Charles Darwin** (New York: Doubleday, 1964) and Gertrude Himmelfarb, *Darwin and the Darwinian Revolution* (London: Chatto & Windus, 1959) are particularly valuable and authoritative, while the intellectual upheaval that centered on Darwinism is trenchantly examined in J. C. Greene, *The Death of Adam* (Ames: Iowa State Univ., 1959) and Loren Eiseley, *Darwin's Century* (Garden City: Doubleday, 1961). The conservative side of social Darwinism is analyzed in perceptive, hostile fashion in Richard Hofstadter, *Social Darwinism in American Thought**, rev. ed. (Boston: Beacon, 1955). Jacques Barzun, *Darwin, Marx, Wagner**, rev. ed. (Garden City: Doubleday, 1958) is a highly readable, critical assessment of the three great system-builders. An extremely detailed account of nineteenth-century Christianity is provided by Kenneth S. Latourette, *Christianity in a Revolutionary Age*, Volumes I–III (New York: Harper, 1958–1962), and the reaction of the Catholic Church to secularism and science is examined in Edward E. Y. Hales, *Pio Nono* (New York: Kenedy, 1954). The best introductions to Marx's life and thought are Isaiah Berlin, *Karl Marx, His Life and Environment**, 2nd ed. (New York: Oxford Univ., 1948); George Lichtheim, *Marxism: An Historical and Critical Study** (New York: Praeger, 1961); and Sidney Hook, *From Hegel to Marx** (New York: Humanities, 1950). There are some excellent studies of the arts in the 1850's and 1860's: J. C. Sloane, *French Painting Between Past and Present* (Princeton: Princeton Univ., 1951); Caesar Grana, *Bohemian versus Bourgeois** (New York: Basic, 1964); Maurice Raynal, *History of Modern Painting*, Vol. I (Geneva: Skira, 1949–1950); H. R. Hitchcock, *Architecture: Nineteenth and Twentieth Centuries* (Harmondsworth: Pelican, 1958); and S. Giedion, *Mechanization Takes Command* (New York: Oxford Univ., 1948). On the middle-class ethos and way of life, in addition to works of Briggs, Houghton, and Burn cited above, the following are important: James A. and Oliver Banks, *Feminism and Family Planning in Victorian England* (Liverpool: Liverpool Univ., 1964); Asa Briggs, *Victorian Cities* (London: Odhams, 1963); Charles Morazé, *Triumph of the Middle Classes* (*op. cit.*, Chapter 6); and Jean Lhomme, *La Grande bourgeoisie au pouvoir* (Paris: Presses Universitaires de France, 1960).

CHAPTER 8. DEMOCRACY AND AUTOCRACY

R. C. Binkley, *Realism and Nationalism 1852–1871* (*op. cit.*, Chapter 7) attempts a synthetic view, arguing that there were federative alternatives to the political and military decisions. A. J. P. Taylor, *The Struggle for Mastery in Europe 1848–1918* (Oxford: Clarendon, 1954) is a well-written survey of international relations. On Britain, Asa Briggs, *The Age of Improvement** (*op. cit.*, Chapter 3) and E. L. Woodward, *The Age of Reform* (*op. cit.*, Chapter 6) are useful introductions. G. M. Trevelyan, *British History in the Nineteenth Century and After*,* new ed. (New York: Longmans, 1946), though somewhat out-of-date, should be read for the insights of a great liberal historian. The most convenient approach to detailed study of British politics in the period is by way of Sir Philip Magnus, *Gladstone** (New York: Dutton, 1954), a superb biography, and Robert Blake, *Disraeli** (New York: St. Martin's, 1966) which is hypercritical of its subject. C. Woodham-Smith, *The Reason Why** (New York: McGraw-Hill, 1954), an absorbing study of a famous incident in the Crimean War, illuminates many aspects of British politics and society in the 1850's. H. J. Hanham, *Elections and Party Management: Politics in the Time of Disraeli and Gladstone* (London: Longmans, 1959) is a dispassionate analysis of political institutions. G. Kitson Clark, *The Making of Victorian England** (Cambridge: Harvard Univ., 1962), offers some interesting general interpretations. A well-balanced introductory survey is J. G. Randall and David Donald, *The Civil War and Reconstruction*, 2nd ed. (Boston: Heath, 1961). The Southern point of view is judiciously presented by Avery O. Craven, *Civil War in the Making** (Baton Rouge: Louisiana State Univ., 1961). Advanced study must begin with the magisterial work of Allan Nevins, *The Ordeal of the Union* (New York: Scribner's, 1947–   ) and *The Emergence of Lincoln*, 2 vols. (New York: Scribner's, 1950). For the South and the Confederacy, Clement Eaton, *Freedom of Thought in the Old South** (New York: P. Smith, 1951) and Douglas S. Freeman, *Robert E. Lee* (New York: Scribner's, 1934–1935) are important. The post-Civil War problems are carefully analyzed in Kenneth M. Stampp, *The Era of Reconstruction** (New York: Knopf, 1965), a synthesis of recent revisionist scholarship. Favorable opinions of Napoleon III are rendered by James M. Thompson, *Louis Napoleon and the Second Empire** (Oxford: Blackwell, 1954) and Roger L. Williams, *Gaslight and Shadow: The World of Napoleon III** (New York: Macmillan, 1957). Mixed but not unsympathetic views are held by Theodore Zeldin, *The Political System of Napoleon III* (New York: St. Martin's, 1958) and Thomas A. B. Corley, *Democratic Despot* (London: Barrie and Rockliff, 1961). A critical view is taken by Lynn M. Case, *French Opinion on War and Diplomacy during the Second Empire* (Philadelphia: Univ. of Pennsylvania, 1954), which shows how Napoleon misunderstood the desires of the French people. Strongly hostile is J. Salwyn Schapiro, *Liberalism and the Challenge of Fascism* (New York: McGraw-Hill, 1949). David Pinkney, *Napoleon III and the Rebuilding of Paris* (Princeton: Princeton Univ.,

1958) is an excellent study of the most positive side of Napoleon's reign. On the Habsburg empire, A. J. P. Taylor, *The Hapsburg Monarchy* (*op. cit.*, Chapter 6) is a smooth introduction; Josef Redlich, *Emperor Francis Joseph of Austria* (New York: Macmillan, 1929) is a sympathetic and valuable biography; and Robert A. Kann, *The Multinational Empire*, 2 vols. (New York: Columbia Univ., 1950) is a detailed study of nationality problems. On czarist Russia, Hugh Seton-Watson, *The Russian Empire: 1801–1917* (Oxford: Clarendon, 1967) is a valuable survey; also important is the same author's *The Decline of Imperial Russia** (London: Methuen, 1952), which provides a detailed study of Alexander II's reign. W. E. Mosse, *Alexander II and the Modernization of Russia** (London: English Univ., 1958) is a sympathetic brief biography. On the peasant problem, authoritative works are Jerome Blum, *Lord and Peasant in Russia* (*op. cit.*, Chapter 1) and Geroid T. Robinson, *Rural Russia under the Old Regime** (New York: Macmillan, 1957). For the beginning student, the most convenient introduction to the Italian unification movement lies in biographies: A. J. Whyte, *The Political Life and Letters of Cavour* (London: Oxford Univ., 1930); Denis Mack Smith, *Garibaldi* (New York: Knopf, 1956); and G. M. Trevelyan, *Garibaldi and the Thousand* (New York: Longmans, 1926) and *Garibaldi and the Making of Italy* (New York: Longmans, 1911). Important analytical studies of Italian unification are Denis Mack Smith, *Cavour and Garibaldi* (Cambridge: Cambridge Univ., 1964) and Raymond Grew, *A Sterner Plan for Italian Unity* (Princeton: Princeton Univ., 1963). The extensive literature on German unification is distinguished by several works of high quality. Theodore S. Hamerow, *Restoration, Revolution, Reaction* (*op. cit.*, Chapter 6) is an expert study of the relations between politics and the economic and social structure, and Gordon A. Craig, *The Politics of the Prussian Army* (*op. cit.*, Chapter 6) synthesizes incisively the political-military relations. William O. Henderson, *The Zollverein* (Chicago: Quadrangle, 1959) is definitive. An important general view by a liberal Austrian scholar is Heinrich Friedjung, *The Struggle for Supremacy in Germany 1859–1866* (New York: Russell, 1966). William N. Medlicott, *Bismarck and Modern Germany** (New York: Harper, 1968) is the best single-volume examination of Bismarck and his era. Erich Eyck, *Bismarck and the German Empire** (London: Allen & Unwin, 1950) is moderately critical of Bismarck, his methods and system. Otto Pflanze, *Bismarck and the Development of Germany* (Princeton: Princeton Univ., 1963) is a convenient survey. For the international aspects of German unification, W. E. Mosse, *The European Powers and the German Question 1848–1871* (Cambridge: Cambridge Univ., 1958) is highly valuable, and George G. Windell, *The Catholics and German Unity 1866–1871* (Minneapolis: Univ. of Minnesota, 1954) illuminates obstacles unification faced. Lawrence D. Steefel, *The Schleswig-Holstein Question* (Cambridge: Harvard Univ., 1932) is an important monograph, and Gordon A. Craig, *The Battle of Königgrätz* (Philadelphia: Lippincott, 1964) a finely tuned work in military history. On the background to the Franco-Prussian War, the work of Robert H. Lord, *The Origins of the War of 1870* (New York: Russell, 1924) is still valuable, and Lawrence D. Steefel, *Bismarck, the Hohenzollern Candidacy, and the Origins of the Franco-German War of 1870* (Cambridge, Mass.: Harvard Univ., 1962) is an important contribution, based on much new material. On the war itself, Michael Howard, *The Franco-Prussian War* (London: Hart-Davis, 1961) provides thorough scholarship and exciting reading.

CHAPTER 9. NATIONALISM AND IMPERIALISM

Until the post-World War II dissolution of the European empires in Asia and Africa, nearly all the works on late nineteenth-century imperialism that were not nationalist or racist propaganda were vehement condemnations, either on moral grounds or from the leftist point of view. Carleton J. H. Hayes, *A Generation of Materialism 1871–1900** (New York: Harper, 1941) is a bitter moral indictment. The leftist theory of imperialism as a critical and decadent stage of capitalism was first articulated by John A. Hobson, *Imperialism: A Study** (London: Allen & Unwin, 1938) and given rigid Marxist form by V. I. Lenin, *Imperialism, the Highest Stage of Capitalism** (New York: International, 1939). Parker T. Moon, *Imperialism and World Politics* (New York: Macmillan, 1926), a thorough condemnation, is typical of older literature. Joseph A. Schumpeter, *Imperialism and the Social Classes** (New York: Meridian, 1955), originally published in 1919, was a pioneering effort at refutation of the Marxist view and is still valuable. More recent literature, while generally not favorable to imperialism, attempts more complex and subtle analysis. William L. Langer, *The Diplomacy of Imperialism* (New York: Knopf, 1935) is a judicious, well-balanced assessment, principally from the standpoint of international relations. William Woodruff, *Impact of Western Man* (New York: St. Martin's, 1967) is an extremely valuable assessment of the consequences of European expansion. James Morris, *Pax Britannica* (London: Faber, 1968) and Barbara W. Tuchman, *The Proud Tower** (New York: Macmillan, 1966) evoke, not without a trace of nostalgia, the ambience of the imperialist era. D. K. Fieldhouse, *The Colonial Empires* (*op. cit.*, Chapter 1) is an authoritative comparative survey, and David S. Landes, *Bankers and Pashas: International Finance and Economic Imperialism* (Cambridge: Harvard Univ., 1958) a fascinating case study. The most important examination of the imperialist ethos is A. P. Thornton, *Doctrines of Imperialism** (*op. cit.*, Chapter 1), a subtle and profound work; also important is J. T. Gallagher and Ronald Robinson, *Africa and the Victorians** (New York: Doubleday, 1968), which attributes the New Imperialism not to economic but to strategic motives. Richard Koebner and Helmut D. Schmidt, *Imperialism: The Story and Significance of a Political Word* (Cambridge: Cambridge Univ., 1964) is an abstract but useful study of ideology. For summary views of European expansion, L. Middleton, *The Rape of Africa* (London: Hale, 1936) and J. T. Pratt, *The*

Expansion of Europe into the Far East (London: Sylvan, 1947) are useful. British imperialism can be studied from the point of view of the home country in A. P. Thornton, *The Imperial Idea and Its Enemies* (New York: St. Martin's, 1959), a brilliant and impartial analysis, and from the colonial viewpoint in the exciting if slightly romanticized account of Charles E. Carrington, *The British Overseas** (Cambridge: Cambridge Univ., 1950). Philip Woodruff, *The Guardians** (New York: Schocken, 1964), a sympathetic treatment of the British ruling group in India, should be compared with the careful and subtly critical view of Michael Edwardes, *British India* (New York: Taplinger, 1968). Important works on French imperialism are Henri Brunschwig, *French Colonialism* (New York: Praeger, 1966); Thomas F. Power, *Jules Ferry and the Renaissance of French Imperialism* (New York: King's Crown, 1944); and John F. Cady, *The Roots of French Imperialism in Eastern Asia* (Ithaca: Cornell, 1954). German imperialism is examined in two studies by Mary E. Townsend, *The Origins of Modern German Colonialism* (New York: Columbia Univ., 1921) and *The Rise and Fall of Germany's Colonial Empire* (New York: Fertig, 1930). Ruth Slade, *King Leopold's Congo* (London: Oxford Univ., 1962) describes imperial exploitation at its worst in Africa, and Victor Purcell, *The Boxer Uprising* (Cambridge: Cambridge Univ., 1963) does the same for China. Excellent studies of American imperialism are Ernest R. May, *Imperial Democracy* (New York: Harcourt, 1961) and Leon Wolff, *Little Brown Brothers* (Garden City: Doubleday, 1961). Russian expansionism is carefully examined in B. H. Sumner, *Russia and the Balkans 1870–1880* (Oxford: Clarendon, 1937) and *Tsardom and Imperialism in the Far East and the Middle East 1880–1914* (Hamden: Shoestring, 1968). On international relations generally, in addition to William L. Langer's work on the period 1890–1902, cited above, the same author's *European Alliances and Alignments 1871–1890*,* 2nd ed. (New York: Knopf, 1950) is essential for advanced study. A. J. P. Taylor, *The Struggle for Mastery in Europe* (*op. cit.*, Chapter 8) is a good introductory survey, with many acute observations. A convenient survey of British domestic history is Robert C. K. Ensor, *England 1870–1914* (Oxford: Clarendon, 1936). Herman Ausubel, *The Late Victorians** (Princeton: Van Nostrand, 1955) is an important reinterpretation, and Helen Lynd, *England in the 1880's* (London: Oxford Univ., 1945) a skillful sociological analysis. Elie Halévy, *Imperialism and the Rise of Labour** (London: Benn, 1949–1951), a detailed and comprehensive older work, is still very valuable. Henry Pelling, *The Origins of the Labour Party** (London: Macmillan, 1954) is the best account of the advance of the Left in Britain. On the Third Republic in France, Denis W. Brogan, *France Under the Republic* (London: Harper, 1940) is discursive, detailed, and perceptive. Important analyses are provided by Roger H. Soltau, *French Parties and Politics 1871–1921* (New York: Russell, 1965) and David Thomson, *Democracy in France Since 1870** (New York: Oxford Univ., 1964). Edward S. Mason, *The Paris Commune* (New York: Macmillan, 1930) and Frank Jellinek, *The Paris Commune of 1871** (London:

Gollancz, 1937) are valuable, and Alistair Horne, *The Fall of Paris** (New York: St. Martin's, 1965) describes dramatically the extinction of the Commune. Robert F. Byrnes, *Prologue to the Dreyfus Affair* (New Brunswick: Rutgers Univ., 1950) illuminates the critical tensions that afflicted the Third Republic. Guy Chapman, *The Dreyfus Case* (London: Hart-Davis, 1955) is a controversial revisionist work; Eugen Weber, *Action française* (Stanford: Stanford Univ., 1962) is a reliable portrait of the extreme Right. P. Spencer, *The Politics of Belief in Nineteenth-Century France* (London: Faber, 1954) is important for the Church's policy. Denis Mack Smith, *Italy, A Modern History* (Ann Arbor: Michigan Univ., 1959) is an excellent political history, and S. William Halperin, *The Separation of Church and State in Italian Thought from Cavour to Mussolini* (Chicago: Univ. of Chicago, 1937) is also valuable. Raymond Carr, *Spain: 1808–1939* (Oxford: Clarendon, 1966) illuminates the Spanish labyrinth. On the German Empire, the best survey is Koppel S. Pinson, *Modern Germany* (op. cit., Chapter 6). Hajo Holborn, *A History of Modern Germany*, Vol. III (New York: Knopf, 1969) contains some valuable chapters. Also useful are J. A. Nichols, *Germany After Bismarck* (Cambridge, Mass.: Harvard Univ., 1958) and Arthur Rosenberg, *Imperial Germany* (Boston: Beacon, 1964). Gordon A. Craig, *From Bismarck to Adenauer** (Baltimore: Johns Hopkins Univ., 1958) provides fine portraits of leading statesmen. Norman Rich, *Friedrich von Holstein*, 2 vols. (Cambridge: Cambridge Univ., 1965) is a vastly detailed political study. On the Habsburg empire, Oscar Jaszi, *The Dissolution of the Habsburg Monarchy** (Chicago: Univ. of Chicago, 1961) is important, especially for Hungary, and Robert A. Kann, *The Multinational Empire* (op. cit., Chapter 8) is diffuse but valuable. On Russia, Hugh Seton-Watson, *The Decline of Imperial Russia* (op. cit., Chapter 8) is a competent synthesis, and Avrahm Yarmolinsky, *The Road to Revolution** (London: Cassell, 1957) and Franco Venturi, *Roots of Revolution** (New York: Knopf, 1960) are fascinating studies of radicalism. Robert F. Byrnes, *Pobedonestsev* (Bloomington: Indiana Univ., 1968) is that historiographical rarity—an intelligent study of reaction. Richard Hough, *The Fleet that Had to Die* (New York: Viking, 1958) is a brilliant account of Russia's naval disaster in the Russo-Japanese War, providing many insights into the problems of czarist government. John A. Garraty, *The New Commonwealth** (New York: Harper, 1968) is a well-informed survey of United States history in the late nineteenth century.

CHAPTER 10. THE DIMENSIONS OF INDUSTRIAL ECONOMY AND SOCIETY

David Landes, *The Unbound Prometheus* (op. cit., Chapter 4) and Rondo E. Cameron, *France and the Economic Development of Europe 1800–1914* (op. cit., Chapter 6) are essential studies. Also important for the expansion of the Industrial Revolution are John H. Clapham, *An Economic History of Modern Britain*, Vols. II and III (Cambridge: Cambridge Univ., 1949); J. D. Chambers, *The Workshop of the World** (New

York: Oxford Univ., 1961); Albert H. Imlah, *Economic Elements in the Pax Britannica* (Cambridge: Harvard Univ., 1958); William O. Henderson, *The Industrial Revolution in Europe** (Chicago: Quadrangle, 1961); Charles J. Singer et al., *A History of Technology*, Vol. V (Oxford: Clarendon, 1954–   ); and Charles P. Kindleberger, *Economic Growth in France and Britain* (Cambridge: Harvard Univ., 1964). Herbert Feis, *Europe, The World's Banker** (New Haven: Yale Univ., 1930) is a comprehensible introduction to finance capitalism, and Herbert Moller, ed., *Population Movements in Modern European History** (New York: Macmillan, 1964) performs the same function for demography. On demographic history in relation to economic change, E. A. Wrigley, *Industrial Growth and Population Change* (Cambridge: Cambridge Univ., 1961) and Carlo M. Cipolla, *The Economic History of World Population** (Baltimore: Penguin, 1962) are major contributions. For urban development, the early twentieth-century work of Adna F. Weber, *The Growth of Cities in the Nineteenth Century** (Ithaca: Cornell Univ., 1963) remains valuable. For detailed portraits of nineteenth-century urban life, Asa Briggs, *Victorian Cities* (op. cit., Chapter 7) and Seymour Mandelbaum, *Boss Tweed's New York** (New York: Wiley, 1965) are illuminating. Provocative interpretive essays on late nineteenth-century industrial society are Thorstein Veblen, *Imperial Germany and the Industrial Revolution**, new ed. (New York: Viking, 1954) and *The Theory of the Leisure Class** (New York: Huebsch, 1945); Lewis Mumford, *Technics and Civilization** (New York: Harcourt, 1934); and, at a more elementary level, Robert Heilbroner, *The Making of Economic Society** (Englewood Cliffs: Prentice-Hall, 1962). H. J. Habakkuk, *American and British Technology in the Nineteenth Century** (Cambridge: Cambridge Univ., 1962) is a fascinating study of the causes for the shift in entrepreneurial leadership. Thomas C. Cochran and William Miller, *The Age of Enterprise** (New York: Macmillan, 1949) is a vivid account of American industrial growth, and Russian economic modernization is described in Theodore H. von Laue, *Sergei Witte and the Industrialization of Russia* (New York: Columbia Univ., 1963). A diffuse and elusive but highly valuable survey of social history is Peter N. Stearns, *European Society in Upheaval** (New York: Macmillan, 1967). The labor movement and socialism has been intensively studied. Edmund Wilson, *To the Finland Station** (New York: Harcourt, 1940) is suggestive and beautifully written, if somewhat out-of-date. A. Fried and R. Saunders, eds., *Socialist Thought** (New York: Doubleday, 1964) is an excellent anthology of theoretical statements by leading socialist spokesmen. Comprehensive surveys are Harry W. Laidler, *Social-Economic Movements* (New York: Crowell, 1949); C. Landauer, *European Socialism*, 2 vols. (Berkeley: Univ. of California, 1959); G. D. H. Cole, *A History of Socialist Thought*, Vol. II (London: Macmillan, 1953–1960); and Edouard Dolléans, *Histoire du mouvement ouvrier*, Vols. II and III (Paris: Colin, 1960). Selig Perlman, *A Theory of the Labor Movement* (New York: Kelley, 1949) is an important analytical work that stresses the division between trade unionism and doctrinaire social-

ism, and David Caute, *The Left in Europe since 1789**
(New York: McGraw-Hill, 1966) is a useful general
survey. The French, British, American, German, and
Spanish labor movements are skillfully examined in,
respectively, Val R. Lorwin, *The French Labor Movement* (Cambridge: Harvard Univ., 1954); Henry Pelling, *A History of British Trade Unionism* (New York:
St. Martin's, 1963); John R. Commons et al., *History of
Labour in the United States*, 4 vols. (New York: Macmillan, 1918–1935); Gerhard Ritter, *Die Arbeiterbewe-
gung in wilhelmischen Reich* (Berlin: Colloquium Verlag, 1959); and Eduardo Comín Colomer, *Historia del
anarquismo español*, 2nd ed. (Barcelona: Editorial
AHR, 1956). The leading revisionist socialists are authoritatively studied in Peter Gay, *The Dilemma of
Democratic Socialism** (New York: Columbia Univ.,
1952), which is concerned with Bernstein, and Harvey
Goldberg, *The Life of Jean Jaurès* (Madison: Univ. of
Wisconsin, 1962). Joseph A. Schumpeter, *Capitalism,
Socialism, and Democracy**, 3rd ed. (New York: Harper, 1950) is a learned and highly theoretical interpretation of the problems of modern industrial society.

CHAPTER 11. THE NEW CONSCIOUSNESS

Gerhard Masur, *Prophets of Yesterday: Studies in European Culture 1890–1914** (New York: Macmillan,
1961) is an excellent introductory survey with many
original insights. Stuart Hughes, *Consciousness and
Society: The Reorientation of European Thought 1890–
1930** (New York: Knopf, 1958) is particularly valuable for social and psychological theories. Carleton J. H.
Hayes, *A Generation of Materialism 1871–1900** (New
York: Harper, 1941) is useful for the beginning student but fundamentally vitiated by the author's arbitrary hostile attitude. George L. Mosse, *The Culture of
Western Europe* (Chicago: Rand McNally, 1961) is valuable for German thought. Important studies of various aspects of irrationalism are Erich Heller, *The Disinherited Mind** (New York: Farrar, Straus and Cudahy,
1957); Karl Löwith, *From Hegel to Nietzsche** (New
York: Holt, 1964); Eric Bentley, *A Century of Hero
Worship*, 2nd ed. (Boston: Beacon, 1957); Mario Praz,
*The Romantic Agony** (London: Oxford Univ., 1951);
and Irving Horowitz, *Radicalism and the Revolt
Against Reason* (London: Routledge & Paul, 1961). A
brilliant if idiosyncratic introduction to philosophy is
Bertrand Russell, *A History of Western Philosophy*
(New York: Simon & Schuster, 1945). Also valuable
are Ralph B. Perry, *The Philosophy of the Recent Past*
(New York: Scribner's, 1926); John Passmore, *A
Hundred Years of Philosophy** (Baltimore: Penguin,
1968); Walter Kaufmann, *Nietzsche** (Princeton:
Princeton Univ., 1950); and Gay W. Allen, *William
James* (New York: Viking, 1967). Authoritative and
comprehensible introductions to the revolution in
physics are C. T. Chase, *The Evolution of Modern
Physics* (Princeton: Von Nostrand, 1947) and Leopold
Infeld, *Albert Einstein: His Work and Its Influence on
our World** (New York: Scribner's, 1950). The shift in
political thought is explored in John Bowle, *Politics
and Opinion in the Nineteenth Century** (London:

Cape, 1954) and Melvin Richter, *The Politics of Conscience* (Cambridge: Harvard Univ., 1964). Anthropological doctrine is expertly analyzed in J. W. Burrow,
Evolution and Society (Cambridge: Cambridge Univ.,
1966) and in Marvin Harris, *The Rise of Anthropological Theory* (New York: Crowell, 1968). Peter J. Pulzer,
*The Rise of Political Anti-Semitism in Germany and
Austria** (New York: Wiley, 1964) is a wide-ranging
study of racist doctrines and movements. A learned,
clear, and highly original account of the development
of sociological theory is Robert A. Nisbet, *The Sociological Tradition* (New York: Basic, 1967). This may be
supplemented by Harry Alpert, *Emile Durkheim and
His Sociology* (New York: Russell, 1961); J. Freund,
The Sociology of Max Weber (New York: Pantheon,
1968); and Rheinhard Bendix, *Max Weber: An Intellectual Portrait** (New York: Doubleday, 1960). For Freud
and the emergence of psychology, the best starting
point is the magisterial work of Ernest Jones, *The Life
and Work of Sigmund Freud*, 3 vols. (New York: Basic,
1953–1961; one vol. abridged ed.*, 1961). Philip Rieff,
*Freud: The Mind of the Moralist** (New York: Viking,
1959) is a sensitive appraisal. Essential for study of
the trends in literature are Edmund Wilson, *Axel's
Castle** (New York: Scribner's, 1931); Ernest J. Sim-
mons, *Dostoevsky** (New York: Vintage, 1962); and
C. M. Bowra, *The Heritage of Symbolism** (London: Macmillan, 1951). The efflorescence in art and architecture
has received excellent analysis in John Rewald, *The
History of Impressionism*, rev. ed. (New York: Museum
of Modern Art, 1962) and *Post-Impressionism*, Vol. I
(New York: Museum of Modern Art, 1956–   );
Stephan T. Madsen, *Art Nouveau* (New York: McGraw-
Hill, 1967); Werner Haftmann, *Painting in the Twentieth Century**, 2 vols. (New York: Praeger, 1965); Niko-
laus Pevsner, *Pioneers of Modern Design**, 2nd ed. (New
York: Museum of Modern Art, 1949); and H. R. Hitch-
cock, *Architecture, Nineteenth and Twentieth Centuries*
(*op. cit.*, Chapter 7). Introductions to the music of the
period are provided by Paul H. Lang, *Music in Western
Civilization* (New York: Norton, 1941); Hugo Leichen-
tritt, *Music, History, and Ideas* (Cambridge: Harvard
Univ., 1954); and Paul Collaer, *A History of Modern
Music** (Cleveland: World, 1961). Two extremely
influential composers are authoritatively studied in
Ernest Newman, *Wagner as Man and Artist** (New
York: Garden City, 1937) and Paul H. Lang, ed., *Stravinsky: A New Appraisal of His Music** (New York:
Norton, 1963). Roger Shattuck, *The Banquet Years**
(New York: Doubleday, 1961) is a beautifully written
evocation of the literary and artistic scene in Paris at
the turn of the century; this is a model of what cul-
tural history should be. Rudolph Binion, *Frau Lou*
(Princeton: Princeton Univ., 1969) is a marvellously
original psychoanalytical study of a key figure in the
Austrian and German intellectual world; this book is a
landmark in historiographical method. Carl Schorske,
"Transformation of the Garden: Ideal and Society in
Austrian Literature," *American Historical Review*, July
1967, is a study of the Viennese ambience, and Samuel
Hynes, *The Edwardian Turn of Mind* (Princeton:
Princeton Univ., 1968) perceptively examines cross-
currents of English culture. Hans Kohn, ed., *The Mod-

ern World,* 2nd ed. (New York: Macmillan, 1968) is an excellent anthology.

CHAPTER 12. THE APOGEE OF WESTERN HEGEMONY

Several of the works cited in the latter part of the bibliographical essay for Chapter 9 are also important for the domestic political history of the immediate pre-World War I period (1905–1914), and many of the books cited for Chapter 11, dealing with intellectual history, illuminate the cultural and social ambience in various countries on the eve of the war. J. M. Roberts, *Europe 1880–1945* (New York: Holt, 1967) is a well-informed, perceptive study. Valuable studies on British government and society in the period are to be found in Simon Nowell-Smith, ed., *Edwardian England 1901–1914* (London: Oxford Univ., 1964); and George Dangerfield, *The Strange Death of Liberal England** (New York: Smith & Hass, 1935) is a superbly colorful portrayal of the turmoil and political conflicts of the period. Roy Jenkins, *Asquith** (New York: Chilmark, 1964) is an interesting but hypercritical biography of the Liberal leader, and Colin Cross, *The Liberals in Power* (London: Barrie, 1963) is a useful survey. A. M. McBrier, *Fabian Socialism and English Politics 1884–1918* (Cambridge: Cambridge Univ., 1962) examines the politics of peaceful change. E. H. Phelps-Brown, *The Growth of British Industrial Relations** (London: Macmillan, 1959) is a sophisticated study of labor relations and welfare programs. The situation in France is illuminated by: Rudolph Binion, *Defeated Leaders* (N. Y.: Columbia Univ., 1960); Michael Curtis, *Three Against the Third Republic* (Princeton: Princeton Univ., 1959); and K. W. Swart, *The Sense of Decadence in Nineteenth-Century France* (The Hague: M. Nijhoff, 1964). Harvey Goldberg, *The Life of Jean Jaurès* (*op. cit.*, Chapter 10) is a careful and detailed biography. The problems in the Habsburg empire are surveyed by Arthur J. May, *The Hapsburg Monarchy* (Cambridge: Harvard Univ., 1951); William A. Jenks, *The Austrian Electoral Reform of 1907* (New York: Columbia Univ., 1950) is an important monograph; and the works of A. J. P. Taylor and R. A. Kann (*op. cit.*, Chapter 8) remain useful for this subject. On Germany, much insight is provided by a leading German editor, Theodore Wolff, *The Eve of 1914* (New York: Knopf, 1936). Carl E. Schorske, *German Social Democracy 1905–1917** (Cambridge: Harvard Univ., 1955) is an outstanding analysis of the radicalization and division of German Marxism, and Lysbeth W. Muncy, *The Junker in the Administration of William II* (Providence: Brown Univ., 1944) is an important contribution to the administrative history of the Wilhelminian era. Lamar Cecil, *Albert Ballin* (Princeton: Princeton Univ., 1967) is an excellent study of a leading German financier that illuminates contemporary economics and politics. On Russia, aside from the general works by Hugh Seton-Watson (*op. cit.*, Chapter 8) and other books cited in Chapter 9, Theodore H. von Laue, *Sergei Witte and the Industrialization of Russia* (*op. cit.*, Chapter 10) is valuable, and Arthur P. Mendel, *Dilemmas of Progress in Tsarist Russia* (Cam-

bridge: Harvard Univ., 1961) is a trenchant account of the difficulties facing advocates of peaceful change. R. K. Massie, *Nicholas and Alexandra** (New York: Atheneum, 1967) is a dramatic narrative of the sorrows and stupidities of the last czar and his consort. On the developing Anglo-German rivalry, Ross J. S. Hoffman, *Great Britain and the German Trade Rivalry* (New York: Russell, 1933) and Sir E. Llewellyn Woodward, *Great Britain and the German Navy* (Hamden: Archon, 1964) are essential studies. Eckhart Kehr, *Schlachtflottenbau und Parteipolitik* (Berlin: Ebering, 1930) is a useful economic interpretation of the naval race. Charles W. Monger, *The End of Isolation* (London: Nelson, 1963) is an authoritative account of British foreign policy from 1900 to 1907, and Arthur J. Marder, *From the Dreadnought to Scapa Flow* (London: Oxford Univ., 1961) is invariably sound and interesting. On the Balkan crisis and Turkish problems, Leften S. Stavrianos, *The Balkans 1815–1914** (New York: Holt, 1963) provides a competent survey; Ernest C. Helmreich, *The Diplomacy of the Balkan Wars* (Cambridge: Harvard Univ., 1938) is a detailed, important analysis; Bernadotte E. Schmitt, *The Annexation of Bosnia 1908–1909* (Cambridge: Cambridge Univ., 1937) is an interesting monograph on a crucial event; Harry N. Howard, *The Partition of Turkey 1913–1923* (New York: Fertig, 1966) is an older work that remains valuable; and Bernard Lewis, *The Emergence of Modern Turkey** (London: Oxford Univ., 1961) is an expert synthesis. Edward M. Earle, *Turkey, the Great Powers, and the Bagdad Railway* (New York: Macmillan, 1923) is a careful account of a contiguous critical problem. The Moroccan issue receives detailed treatment in Eugene N. Anderson, *The First Moroccan Crisis: 1904–1906* (Chicago: Univ. of Chicago, 1930) and I. C. Barlow, *The Agadir Crisis* (Chapel Hill: Univ. of North Carolina, 1940). Important analyses of the relations between public opinion and foreign policy are presented in two works by Eber M. Carroll, *French Public Opinion and Foreign Affairs 1870–1914* (Hamden: Archon, 1964) and *Germany and the Great Powers 1866–1914* (Hamden: Archon, 1966). Perceptive general accounts of international relations are A. J. P. Taylor, *The Struggle for Mastery in Europe* (*op. cit.*, Chapter 8) and L. C. B. Seaman, *From Vienna to Versailles** (New York: Coward-McCann, 1956). On the origins and outbreak of World War I, Dwight E. Lee, ed., *The Outbreak of the First World War**, 2nd ed. (Boston: Heath, 1963) is a valuable collection. Sidney B. Fay, *The Origins of the World War**, 2nd ed. (New York: Macmillan, 1930) remains the outstanding work, more sympathetic to Germany and Austria than the pro-British account of Bernadotte E. Schmitt, *The Coming of the War, 1914*, 2 vols. (New York: Scribner's, 1930), which is careful and detailed but frequently confused and confusing. Pierre Renouvin, *The Immediate Origins of the War* (New Haven: Yale Univ., 1928) is a moderate defense of French policy. The recent, highly controversial work by a German scholar, Fritz Fischer, *Germany's Aims in the First World War** (New York: Norton, 1967), based on new evidence, not only contends that Germany sought Continental hegemony but suggests that it sought war to achieve it. Luigi Albertini, *The Origins of the War of 1914*, 3 vols. (New York: Oxford Univ., 1952–1957) is a vastly detailed, somewhat overrated analysis. On the war itself, A. J. P. Taylor, *The First World War** (New York: Putman, 1964) is a well-written brief account; C. R. M. Crutwell, *A History of the Great War*, 2nd ed. (New York: Oxford Univ., 1936) is dry but useful; and Cyril B. Falls, *The Great War** (New York: Putnam, 1959) is careful and interesting. Winston S. Churchill, *The World Crisis**, 4 vols. (New York: Scribner's, 1923, 1929) remains valuable. On particular aspects of the struggle, Barbara W. Tuchman, *The Guns of August** (New York: Macmillan, 1962) is an exciting account of the early weeks of the war; Leon Wolff, *In Flanders Fields** (New York: Viking, 1958) is a moving portrayal of the carnage on the western front; Alistair Horne, *The Price of Glory: Verdun 1916** (New York: St. Martin's, 1963) is a dramatic narrative; R. M. Watt, *Dare Call It Treason* (New York: Simon & Schuster, 1963) an excellent study of the mutiny in the French army; and Hans Gatzke, *Germany's Drive to the West** (Baltimore: Johns Hopkins Univ., 1950) an important examination of Germany's war aims. Frank P. Chambers, *The War Behind the War* (New York: Harcourt, 1939) is a valuable comparative survey of the home fronts. More recent and detailed studies are J. C. King, *Generals and Politicians* (Berkeley: Univ. of California, 1951), useful for the inner history of French civil-military relations; Arthur Marwick, *The Deluge* (Boston: Little, 1965), an impressionistic and constantly interesting view of wartime Britain; Gerald D. Feldman, *Army, Industry and Labor in Germany, 1914–1918* (Princeton: Princeton Univ., 1966), a study of the extent to which the German army controlled the economy; Z. A. B. Zeman, *The Breakup of the Habsburg Empire 1914–1918* (London: Oxford Univ., 1961), sound and useful; and Arthur J. May, *The Passing of the Hapsburg Monarchy 1914–1918*, 2 vols. (Philadelphia: Univ. of Pennsylvania, 1968), a detailed account. Ernest R. May, *The World War and American Isolation 1914–1917** (Cambridge: Harvard Univ., 1959) is a well-balanced study of how the United States became involved in the war. Arthur S. Link, *Wilson: The Diplomatist**, 2nd ed. (Baltimore: Johns Hopkins Univ., 1957) illuminates key decisions, and Francis L. Loewenheim, ed., *The Historian and the Diplomat* (New York: Harper, 1967) discusses the historical roots of Wilsonian thinking. The literature on the Russian Revolution is extensive. Bertram D. Wolfe, *Three Who Made a Revolution** (New York: Dell, 1964) and Adam B. Ulam, *The Bolsheviks** (New York: Macmillan, 1965) are excellent biographical studies of Lenin and other leading revolutionaries and thereby the best introductions for the beginning student. Isaac Deutscher, *The Prophet Armed** (New York: Oxford Univ., 1954) is a sympathetic account of Trotsky's career to 1921. R. V. Daniels, *Red October* (New York: Scribner's, 1967) is an interesting dramatic narrative. Leon Trotsky, *The History of the Russian Revolution**, 3 vols. (New York: Simon & Schuster, 1937) is, in effect, a detailed memoir by a leading participant, self-serving but important. Two valuable eyewitness accounts are Sir Bernard Pares, *The Fall of*

the Russian Monarchy* (London: Cape, 1939), a sober analysis by a learned British historian of Russia, and John Reed, *Ten Days that Shook the World** (New York: Modern Library, 1960), a feverish but highly perceptive description by a left-wing American journalist. For more advanced study, the detailed analysis provided by Edward H. Carr, *The Bolshevik Revolution 1917–1923,** 3 vols. (New York: Macmillan, 1950–1953) is strong on political matters and sympathetic to the Bolsheviks. George Katkov, *Russia, 1917* (New York: Harper, 1967) is hostile to the Bolsheviks and stresses the importance of German involvement; this remains a moot point. Arno J. Mayer, *Political Origins of the New Diplomacy** (New Haven: Yale Univ., 1959) is a valuable analysis of Allied and Russian Communist thought and policy.

CHAPTER 13. RECONSTRUCTION AND DEPRESSION

Ivo J. Lederer, ed., *The Versailles Settlement** (Boston: Heath, 1960) is a useful anthology of the conflicting assessments of the work of the peace conference. John M. Keynes, *The Economic Consequences of the Peace* (New York: Harcourt, 1920) is a highly influential, controversial, and hostile assessment of the peace settlement by an eminent economist. Étienne Mantoux, *The Carthaginian Peace** (New York: Oxford Univ., 1946) is a detailed response to Keynes's view, and Paul Birdsall, *Versailles Twenty Years After* (New York: Reynal & Hitchcock, 1941) is also a sympathetic appraisal of the peace settlement. Arno J. Mayer, *Politics and Diplomacy of Peacemaking* (New York: Knopf, 1967) is an interesting but tendentious work by a New Left historian, stressing the anti-Bolshevik aims of the peacemakers. Harold Nicolson, *Peacemaking 1919* (New York: Harcourt, 1933) is a memoir and critique by a participant. Herbert Hoover, *The Ordeal of Woodrow Wilson* (New York: McGraw-Hill, 1958) is a sympathetic account of Wilson at Versailles. Ronald B. McCallum, *Public Opinion and the Last Peace* (New York: Oxford Univ., 1944) is an important study of the aftermath of the peace conference. Warren Cohen, *American Revisionists* (Chicago: Univ. of Chicago, 1967) recounts the American battle over the war guilt issue. Elizabeth Wiskemann, *Europe of the Dictators 1919–1945** (New York: Harper, 1966) is a brief survey of interwar politics, particularly in the authoritarian regimes. On Britain in the twenties there are two excellent surveys: C. L. Mowat, *Britain Between the Wars 1918–1940* (Chicago: Univ. of Chicago, 1955), careful and judicious; and A. J. P. Taylor, *England 1914–1945* (New York: Oxford Univ., 1965), perceptive and highly readable. Alfred F. Havighurst, *Twentieth Century Britain** (Evanston, Ill.: Row, Peterson, 1962) is also a useful survey. Robert Graves and Alan Hodge, *The Long Weekend: A Social History of Great Britain 1918–1939** (London: Faber, 1940) and Ronald Blythe, *The Age of Illusion* (London: Hamilton, 1963) are colorful and absorbing accounts of social trends and foibles. Richard W. Lyman, *The First Labor Government* (London: Chapman & Hall, 1957) and Julian Symons, *The General Strike* (London: Cresset, 1957) are valuable studies. Keith Hutchison, *The Decline and Fall of British Capitalism* (London: Cape, 1951) is useful for economic problems. William E. Leuchtenburg, *The Perils of Prosperity** (Chicago: Univ. of Chicago, 1958) is a polished survey of American history in the 1920's. John D. Hicks, *Republican Ascendancy 1921–1933** (New York: Harper, 1960) is a comprehensive account; and Frederick Lewis Allen, *Only Yesterday** (New York: Harper, 1931) is popular, colorful, social history. France in the 1920's is studied in Denis W. Brogan, *France Under the Republic* (*op. cit.*, Chapter 9) and David Thomson, *Democracy in France* (*op. cit.*, Chapter 9). Two ambitious if overly schematic attempts to provide general interpretations of fascism and totalitarianism are Hannah Arendt, *The Origins of Totalitarianism**, 2nd ed. (New York: Meridian, 1965), which finds roots in nineteenth-century racism and imperialism; and Ernest Nolte, *Three Faces of Fascism** (New York: Holt, 1966), a complex sociological and psychological analysis. Koppel S. Pinson, *Modern Germany* (*op. cit.*, Chapter 8) contains some superb chapters on the 1920's. Erich Eyck, *A History of the Weimar Republic*,* 2 vols. (Cambridge: Harvard Univ., 1962–1963) is an important account, sympathetic to the Republic, by a liberal participant. Robert G. L. Waite, *Vanguard of Nazism: The Free Corps Movement in Postwar Germany* (Cambridge: Harvard Univ., 1952) is a valuable study of the extreme Right in Germany in the early 1920's. Harold J. Gordon, Jr., *The Reichswehr and the German Republic* (Princeton: Princeton Univ., 1957) is a careful analysis, rather sympathetic toward the German army leadership. Alexander Gerschenkron, *Bread and Democracy in Germany* (Berkeley: Univ. of California, 1943) is an excellent study of the role of agrarian politics in recent German history. On the politics of the Weimar era, S. William Halperin, *Germany Tried Democracy* (New York: Crowell, 1946) is a valuable introduction; Sir John W. Wheeler-Bennett, *The Wooden Titan* (New York: Morrow, 1936) is an important biography of Hindenburg, based on unpublished sources; Andreas Dorpalen, *Hindenburg and the Weimar Republic* (Princeton: Princeton Univ., 1964) is detailed and important; Henry A. Turner, *Stresemann and the Politics of the Weimar Republic** (Princeton: Princeton Univ., 1963) is useful; and Klaus Epstein, *Matthias Erzberger and the Dilemma of German Democracy* (Princeton: Princeton Univ., 1959) is detailed and frequently apologetic. Alan Bullock, *Hitler: A Study in Tyranny**, 2nd ed. (New York: Harper, 1963) is a well-informed, judicious, and engrossing biography. Karl D. Bracher, *Die Auflösung der Weimarer Republik*, 4th ed. (Stuttgart: Ring-Verlag, 1964) is an important, detailed study of the end of the Republic and Hitler's rise to power. Sir Ivone Kirkpatrick, *Mussolini, A Study in Power* (New York: Hawthorne, 1964) is an interesting, sometimes uncritical biography by a leading British diplomat, and Herman Finer, *Mussolini's Italy** (New York: Holt, 1935) describes the first decade of Fascist rule. On the Soviet Union, Edward H. Carr, *A History of Soviet Russia*, 6 vols. (London: Macmillan, 1950ff) provides a detailed, largely uncritical account. Leonard Schapiro, *The Origin of the Communist Autocracy** (Cambridge: Harvard Univ.,

1955) and *The Communist Party of the Soviet Union** (New York: Random House, 1960) are important, skillful analyses of the development and structure of Bolshevik authoritarianism. Barrington Moore, Jr., *Soviet Politics** (Cambridge: Harvard Univ., 1950) is a valuable study of Stalinist tactics. Isaac Deutscher, *Stalin** 2nd ed. (London: Oxford Univ., 1967) is an apology. David J. Dallin and Boris Nicolaevsky, *Forced Labor in the Soviet Union* (New Haven: Yale Univ., 1947) is a careful, important study. T. H. von Laue, *Why Lenin? Why Stalin?* (Philadelphia: Lippincott, 1964) is a provocative, controversial analysis. Kermit E. McKenzie, *The Comintern and World Revolution* (New York: Columbia Univ., 1964) is a useful study of the international Communist movement. The emergence of the only successful liberal democracy in eastern Europe is described by the first president of Czechoslovakia: Thomas G. Masaryk, *The Making of a State* (London: Allen & Unwin, 1927). On the Depression, John K. Galbraith, *The Great Crash** (Boston: Houghton Mifflin, 1955) is a vivid account by a liberal economist. On international relations, Francis P. Walters, *A History of the League of Nations*, 2 vols. (Oxford: Oxford Univ., 1952) is detailed and valuable but sometimes uncritical; Robert H. Ferrell, *Peace in Their Time: The Origins of the Kellogg-Briand Pact* (New Haven: Yale Univ., 1953) is a careful analysis; Gordon A. Craig and Felix Gilbert, eds., *The Diplomats 1919–1939** (Princeton: Princeton Univ., 1953) provides fine studies of leading diplomats; Kurt Rosenbaum, *Community of Fate: German-Soviet Diplomatic Relations 1922–1928* (Syracuse: Syracuse Univ., 1965) is an important monograph based on unpublished sources; Adam B. Ulam, *Expansion and Coexistence* (New York: Praeger, 1968) is an excellent survey of Soviet foreign policy. George F. Kennan, *American-Soviet Relations 1917–1920*, 2 vols. (Princeton: Princeton Univ., 1956–1958) and *Russia and the West under Lenin and Stalin* (Boston: Little, Brown, 1961) are important, highly personal accounts; and Henry L. Stimson, *The Far Eastern Crisis* (New York: Harper, 1936) is a significant memoir by a former secretary of state.

CHAPTER 14. THE STRUGGLE FOR WORLD POWER

Several of the works cited in Chapter 13, dealing with both domestic politics and international relations, are also important for the 1930's. Of these, on Nazi Germany, Alan Bullock, *Hitler: A Study in Tyranny** is essential. George H. Stein, ed., *Hitler** (Englewood Cliffs: Prentice-Hall, 1968) is a skillful anthology of biographical materials. Sir John W. Wheeler-Bennett, *The Nemesis of Power**, 2nd ed. (New York: St. Martin's, 1964) is a major study of the role of the German army in politics. Franz L. Neumann, *Behemoth** (New York: Octagon, 1963) is a Marxist analysis of the Nazi rise to power, and William S. Allen, *The Nazi Seizure of Power* (Chicago: Quadrangle, 1965) recounts the experience of one middle-sized German town. Guenter Lewy, *The Catholic Church and Nazi Germany** (New York: McGraw-Hill, 1964) is a detailed, judicious study of a highly complex and controversial subject. Arthur

Schweitzer, *Big Business in the Third Reich* (Bloomington: Indiana Univ., 1964) is an important study of the relationship between business executives and Nazi leadership. On Italy, in addition to the works cited for Chapter 13, Richard A. Webster, *The Cross and the Fasces* (Stanford: Stanford Univ., 1960) is a useful account of the relations between Christian democracy and fascism. Frederick W. Deakin, *The Brutal Friendship** (New York: Harper, 1962) is a carefully detailed study of Mussolini's involvement with Hitler. The French Right in the 1930's is analyzed in Charles A. Micaud, *The French Right and Nazi Germany 1933–1939* (New York: Octagon, 1964) and the French Left in Joel Colton, *Léon Blum* (New York: Knopf, 1966) and John T. Marcus, *French Socialism in the Crisis Years* (New York: Praeger, 1958). Martin Wolfe, *The French Franc Between the Wars* (New York: Columbia Univ., 1951) is an important economic analysis. On the Balkans, Robert L. Wolff, *The Balkans in Our Times**, 2nd ed. (Cambridge: Harvard Univ., 1956) is valuable; and Jacob B. Hoptner, *Yugoslavia in Crisis 1934–1941* (New York: Columbia Univ., 1962) is interesting and revealing. For Poland, Josef Korbel, *Poland Between East and West** (Princeton: Princeton Univ., 1963) is essential. In addition to works on the Soviet Union cited for Chapter 13, Robert Conquest, *The Great Terror** (New York: Macmillan, 1968) is a reliable, detailed, and engrossing study of the Stalinist purges. Merle Fainsod, *Smolensk under Soviet Rule* (Cambridge: Harvard Univ., 1958) provides valuable insights into the character of Soviet government. Charles A. Gulick, *Austria from Habsburg to Hitler*, 2 vols. (Berkeley: Univ. of California, 1948) is a highly interesting economic interpretation. On the New Deal era in the United States, William E. Leuchtenburg, *Franklin D. Roosevelt and the New Deal** (New York: Harper, 1964) is the best survey, with excellent chapters on foreign affairs. Arthur M. Schlesinger, Jr., *The Age of Franklin D. Roosevelt*, 3 vols. (Boston: Houghton Mifflin, 1957–1960) is detailed, glossy, and apologetic. Eric F. Goldman, *Rendezvous with Destiny** (New York: Knopf, 1952) is a perceptive, beautifully written history of modern American reform. On the Spanish Civil War, there are two important accounts: Hugh Thomas, *The Spanish Civil War** (New York: Harper, 1961), which strives for impartiality, and Gabriel Jackson, *The Spanish Republic and the Civil War** (Princeton: Princeton Univ., 1965), which views the struggle from the Republican side, though not uncritically. Good surveys of British history in the 1930's are provided in the works of C. L. Mowat and A. J. P. Taylor (*op. cit.*, Chapter 13), although the latter is unreasonably apologetic for the Tories. British history in the period is inevitably bound up with foreign policy. Martin Gilbert and Richard Gott, *The Appeasers* (Boston: Houghton Mifflin, 1962) is the best introductory survey; it is consistently interesting and highly critical. A. L. Rowse, *Appeasement** (New York: Norton, 1961) is a fascinating memoir, also negative in its judgment. The case for Chamberlain, insofar as there might be one, is made by Keith Feiling, *Life of Neville Chamberlain* (London: Macmillan, 1946); Ian MacLeod, *Neville Chamberlain* (New York: Atheneum,

1962); and Sir Samuel Hoare, *Nine Troubled Years* (London: L. Collins, 1954), a memoir by a leading appeaser. A. J. P. Taylor, *Origins of the Second World War** (New York: Atheneum, 1962) is a provocative analysis in which Chamberlain is perversely criticized for not persisting in his appeasement of Hitler. L. B. Namier, *Diplomatic Prelude* (London: Macmillan, 1948) contains excellent critical studies of prewar diplomacy. Sir John W. Wheeler-Bennett, *Munich: Prologue to Tragedy** (New York: Duell, Sloan and Pearce, 1948) remains the best account of the Munich crisis and what led up to it. Francis L. Loewenheim, ed., *Peace or Appeasement? Hitler, Chamberlain and the Munich Crisis** (Boston: Houghton Mifflin, 1965) brings together important documents, excerpts from memoirs, and historical commentaries. Aspects of the crisis are explored in Elizabeth Wiskemann, *Czechs and Germans* (New York: Oxford Univ., 1938) and Radimir Luza, *The Transfer of the Sudeten Germans* (New York: New York Univ., 1964). The French side of appeasement is carefully studied in Arthur H. Furnia, *The Diplomacy of Appeasement* (Washington: University Press, 1960). American foreign policy is described in the authoritative works of William L. Langer and S. Everett Gleason, *The Challenge to Isolation 1937–1940* (New York: Harper, 1952) and *The Undeclared War 1940–41* (New York: Harper, 1953;) Gerhard L. Weinberg, *Germany and the Soviet Union 1939–41* (Leiden: Brill, 1954) is also a judicious and well-researched study. Of the many one-volume histories of World War II, the best perhaps is Basil Collier, *The Second World War* (New York: Morrow, 1967). Winston S. Churchill, *The Second World War**, 6 vols. (Boston: Houghton Mifflin, 1948–1953) is a great work of historical literature. Telford Taylor, *March of Conquest** (New York: Simon and Schuster, 1958) is a valuable account of the German victory in 1940. Alexander Werth, *Russia at War** (New York: Dutton, 1964) is a useful account of the eastern front. Chester Wilmot, *The Struggle for Europe** (New York: Harper, 1952) is an exciting narrative of the Allied march to victory, critical of American generals. On Nazi atrocities, important studies are Raul Hilberg, *The Destruction of the European Jews** (Chicago: Quadrangle, 1961); Hannah Arendt, *Eichmann in Jerusalem** (New York: Viking, 1963); Eugen Kogon, *The Theory and Practice of Hell** (New York: Berkley, 1964); and Alexander Dallin, *German Rule in Russia* (New York: St. Martin's, 1957). George H. Stein, *The Waffen SS* (Ithaca: Cornell Univ., 1966) is a valuable account of a key aspect of the German war machine. H. R. Trevor-Roper, *The Last Days of Hitler** (New York: Macmillan, 1947) describes the final agony of the Third Reich. Robert O. Paxton, *Parades and Politics at Vichy* (Princeton: Princeton Univ., 1966) is a careful, balanced study of wartime France. Gerhard Ritter, *Goerdeler and the German Resistance* (New York: Praeger, 1958) is a sympathetic, somewhat overdrawn account; and Charles F. Delzell, *Mussolini's Enemies* (Princeton: Princeton Univ., 1961) is a valuable study of Italian resistance. Kent R. Greenfield, *American Strategy in World War II* (Baltimore: Johns Hopkins Univ., 1963) provides important essays on United

States military policy. John R. Deane, *The Strange Alliance* (New York: Viking, 1947) and Herbert Feis, *Churchill, Roosevelt, Stalin* (Princeton: Princeton Univ., 1957) describe how East and West got along during the war. Important studies of wartime diplomacy are E. L. Woodward, *British Foreign Policy in the Second World War* (London: H. M. Stationery Off., 1962); John L. Snell, *Illusion and Necessity* (Boston: Houghton Mifflin, 1964); and Philip E. Mosely, *The Kremlin and World Politics* (New York: Vintage, 1960).

CHAPTER 15. TWENTIETH-CENTURY CULTURE

A good survey of twentieth-century physics, containing interesting biographical material and written expressly for the layman, is Barbara Cline, *The Questioners* (New York: Crowell, 1965). Also valuable are Lincoln Barnett, *The Universe and Dr. Einstein* (New York: Mentor, 1952); C. T. Chase, *The Evolution of Modern Physics* (op. cit., Chapter 11); and Bernard Barber, *Science and the Social Order* (New York: Free Press, 1952). The breakthrough in biology is described in the exciting autobiographical account of James Watson, *The Double Helix* (New York: Atheneum, 1968). A clear introduction to twentieth-century philosophy is provided by John Passmore, *A Hundred Years of Philosophy* (op. cit., Chapter 11). Also important are A. J. Ayer et al., *The Revolution in Philosophy* (New York: St. Martin's, 1956); Geoffrey Warnock, *English Philosophy since 1900* (London: Oxford Univ., 1958); Thomas E. Hill, *Contemporary Theories of Knowledge* (New York: Ronald, 1961); Colin Smith, *Contemporary French Philosophy* (New York: Barnes & Noble, 1964); and Albert William Levi, *Philosophy and the Modern World* (Bloomington: Indiana Univ., 1959). Morton White, ed., *The Age of Analysis* (New York: Mentor, 1955) is a convenient, skillfully edited anthology. A. Koch, ed., *Philosophy for a Time of Crisis* (New York: Dutton, 1959) is especially useful for existentialism. Introductions to twentieth-century theology are provided by S. P. Schilling, *Contemporary Continental Theologians* (Nashville: Abingdon, 1966) and D. G. Peerman and M. E. Marty, eds., *A Handbook of Christian Theologians* (Cleveland: World, 1965). Valuable anthologies of the philosophy of history are Hans Meyerhoff, ed., *The Philosophy of History in Our Time* (New York: Anchor, 1959) and Patrick Gardiner, ed., *Theories of History* (Glencoe: Free Press, 1959). On schools of historical interpretation, Fritz Stern, ed., *Varieties of History* (New York: Meridian, 1956) and N. F. Cantor and R. I. Schneider, *How to Study History* (New York: Crowell, 1967) are useful, and Marc Bloch, *The Historian's Craft* (New York: Knopf, 1953) is essential. Edward N. Saveth, ed., *American History and the Social Sciences* (New York: Free Press of Glencoe, 1964) illuminates recent trends. Ved Mehta, *The Fly and the Fly-Bottle* (Boston: Little, Brown, 1962) offers fascinating personal portraits of some British historians, but it is partly misleading in interpretation. On developments in psychology, Franz Alexander and Sheldon T. Selesnick, *The History of Psychiatry* (New York: Harper, 1966) and B. F. Skinner, *Science*

and Human Behavior (New York: Macmillan, 1956) are valuable. Norman MacKenzie, *A Guide to the Social Sciences* (New York: Mentor, 1966) attempts to provide synthetic and critical essays introducing all phases of the social sciences; some are suggestive, others mediocre. On the Keynesian revolution in economics, there are two important works for the layman: Robert Lekachman, *The Age of Keynes* (New York: Random, 1966) and Roy Harrod, *The Life of John Maynard Keynes* (London: Macmillan, 1951), a magisterial, highly sympathetic biography. John K. Galbraith, *The Affluent Society* (Boston: Houghton Mifflin, 1958); Andrew Shonfield, *Modern Capitalism* (New York: Oxford Univ., 1965); and Kenneth E. Boulding, *The Meaning of the Twentieth Century* (New York: Harper, 1964) reflect the recent trend towards an application of economic science to general social and historical questions. Important for the development of sociological theory and social thought in general are Karl Mannheim, *Ideology and Utopia* (New York: Harcourt, 1936); Karl Popper, *The Open Society and Its Enemies*, 4th ed. (Princeton: Princeton Univ., 1963); Raymond Aron, *Main Currents in Sociological Thought,* 2 vols. (New York: Basic, 1965–1967); H. Stuart Hughes, *Consciousness and Society* (op. cit., Chapter 11) and *The Obstructed Path* (New York: Harper, 1968) ; C. Wright Mills, *The Sociological Imagination* (New York: Oxford Univ., 1959); Robert A. Nisbet, *The Quest for Community* (New York: Oxford Univ., 1953); W. Stark, *The Fundamental Forms of Social Thought* (New York: Fordham Univ., 1963); and Erik Erikson, *Childhood and Society*, 2nd ed. (New York: Norton, 1964). Marvin Harris, *The Rise of Anthropological Theory* (op. cit., Chapter 11) is brilliant, vastly learned, up-to-date, and delightfully partisan. Perceptive analyses of key aspects of modern literature are presented in Robert Humphrey, *Stream of Consciousness in the Modern Novel* (Berkeley: Univ. of California, 1954); Richard Hoggart, *The Uses of Literacy* (London: Chatto & Windus, 1957); Raymond Williams, *The Long Revolution* (New York: Columbia Univ., 1961); David Daiches, *The Novel and the Modern World*, rev. ed. (Chicago: Univ. of Chicago, 1960); and Erich Heller, *The Disinherited Mind* (op. cit., Chapter 11). Aspects of the modern ethos are explored in Geoffrey Barraclough, *Introduction to Contemporary History* (London: Watts, 1964); Romano Guardini, *The End of the Modern World* (London: Sheed & Ward, 1957); Alfred Weber, *Farewell to European History* (London: Kegan, Paul, 1948); and C. P. Snow, *The Two Cultures and the Scientific Revolution* (Cambridge: Cambridge Univ., 1959). Werner Haftman, *Painting in the Twentieth Century*, 2 vols. (op. cit., Chapter 11) is a masterly introduction to modern art, throughly satisfactory in every respect. Wylie Sypher, *Rococo to Cubism in Art and Literature* (New York: Random, 1960) is also valuable. Important studies of modern architecture are H. R. Hitchcock, *Architecture, Nineteenth and Twentieth Centuries* (op. cit., Chapter 7) and Vincent Scully, *Modern Architecture* (New York: Braziller, 1961). Many aspects of twentieth-century culture are explored in the essays collected in N. F. Cantor and M. S. Werthman, eds., *A*

History of Popular Culture (New York: Macmillan, 1968; Vol. II of paperback* edition). An important study of twentieth-century music is Aaron Copland's *Music and Imagination* (New York: New American Library, 1957).

CHAPTER 16. THE CONTEMPORARY WORLD

Geoffrey Barraclough, *An Introduction to Contemporary History* (*op. cit.*, Chapter 15) is an important interpretation of the post-World War II era, providing a millennial vision as well as historical insights. Donald C. Watt et al., *A History of the World in the Twentieth Century* (Glenview: Scott, Foresman, 1968) is detailed but heavy reading. Raymond Aron, *The Century of Total War** (New York: Doubleday, 1954) and Hugh Seton-Watson, *Neither War nor Peace** (New York: Praeger, 1960) offer thoughtful perspectives on the international situation. Paul Seabury, *The Rise and Decline of the Cold War* (New York: Basic, 1967) is a valuable and interesting survey. D. F. Fleming, *The Cold War and its Origins, 1917–1960* (New York: Doubleday, 1961) and P. M. S. Blackett, *Atomic Weapons and East-West Relations* (Cambridge: Cambridge Univ., 1956) present leftist, pro-Soviet interpretations. Clark M. Eichelberger, *The U.N.: The First Twenty Years* (New York: Harper, 1965) is a sympathetic appraisal of the UN's record. On the dissolution of the European empires, Rupert Emerson, *From Empire to Nation** (Cambridge: Harvard Univ., 1960) is a careful, important study; Stewart Easton, *The Twilight of European Colonialism* (New York: Holt, 1960) is interesting and valuable; and John Strachey, *The End of Empire** (London: Gollancz, 1959) provides significant insights by a British socialist. International crises are studied in Herman Finer, *Dulles over Suez* (Chicago: Quadrangle, 1964), extremely critical of Dulles; Anthony Eden, *Full Circle* (Boston: Houghton Mifflin, 1960) a persuasive apology, important for Suez and the first Vietnam crisis; Elie Abel, *The Missile Crisis* (Philadelphia: Lippincott, 1966), an interesting account; Joseph Buttinger, *Vietnam: A Dragon Embattled*, 2 vols. (New York: Praeger, 1967), valuable; and Wesley R. Fishel, *Anatomy of a Conflict* (Itasca, Ill.: S. E. Peacock, 1968), the best work on the Vietnam war. On European recovery and economic union, Howard K. Smith, *The State of Europe* (New York: Knopf, 1949) is a valuable study of the postwar situation; F. Roy Willis, *France, Germany, and the New Europe 1945–1963** (Stanford: Stanford Univ., 1965) is a useful survey; William Diebold, Jr., *The Schuman Plan* (New York: Praeger, 1959) is helpful; Hans A. Schmitt, *The Path to European Union* (Baton Rouge: Louisiana State Univ., 1962) is a useful account; and Stephen Grabard, ed., *The New Europe* (Boston: Houghton Mifflin, 1963) contains some perceptive essays. M. M. Postan, *Economic History of Europe, 1945–1965* (Cambridge: Cambridge Univ., 1969) is an authoritative and extremely valuable study. Contemporary Britain's problems are analyzed sympathetically but critically by Anthony Sampson, *Anatomy of Britain**, (New York: Harper, 1962) and in devastating fashion by Max Nic-

olson, *The System* (New York: McGraw-Hill, 1969). Samuel H. Beer, *British Politics in the Collectivist Age* (New York: Knopf, 1965) is a major study of party structure and function. The agonies of the Fourth Republic in France are discussed in Herbert Luethy, *France Against Herself** (New York: Meridian, 1958); Alexander Werth, *France 1940–1955** (London: Hale, 1956), an interesting left-wing view; and Edgar Furniss, *France: Troubled Ally* (New York: Harper, 1960), an important study. Stanley Hoffman et al., *In Search of France** (Cambridge: Harvard Univ., 1963) contains some suggestive essays. Crane Brinton, *Americans and the French* (Cambridge: Harvard Univ., 1968) is a sympathetic analysis. Henry W. Ehrmann, *Politics in France** (Boston: Little, Brown, 1968) is well informed. Alfred J. Rieber, *Stalin and the French Communist Party 1941–1947* (London: Columbia Univ., 1962) provides a careful account of international communism at work in western Europe. On the German Federal Republic, Michael Balfour, *West Germany* (London: Benn, 1968) is a useful introduction; Ralf Dahrendorf, *Society and Democracy in Germany* (New York: Doubleday, 1967) an interesting sociological analysis; and Lewis J. Edinger, *Politics in Germany* (Boston: Little, Brown, 1968) a valuable study of West German politics. H. Stuart Hughes, *The United States and Italy*, rev. ed. (Cambridge: Harvard Univ., 1965) is a suggestive analysis from the left-wing point of view. On postwar eastern Europe, Hugh Seton-Watson, *The East European Revolution** (New York: Praeger, 1950) is a good introduction, and John Lukacs, *The Great Powers and Eastern Europe* (New York: American Book Co., 1953) is independent in judgment. Milovan Djilas, *The New Class** (New York: Praeger, 1957) is a scathing indictment of the Communist system by a Yugoslav Communist. Alex Inkeles and Raymond A. Bauer, *The Soviet Citizen** (Cambridge: Harvard Univ., 1959) is an interesting account of daily life in post-Stalin Russia. Merle Fainsod, *How Russia is Ruled*, 2nd ed. (Cambridge: Harvard Univ., 1963) is a highly informative political analysis. Elliot Goodman, *The Soviet Design for a World State* (New York: Columbia Univ., 1960) is a careful and revealing study. The Communist take-over in Czechoslovakia is described in Josef Korbel, *The Communist Subversion of Czechoslovakia** (Princeton: Princeton Univ., 1964). Contemporary America is surveyed in George E. Mowry, *The Urban Nation** (New York: Hill and Wang, 1965). *The Memoirs of Harry S. Truman*,* 2 vols. (New York: Doubleday, 1955–1956) is highly informative on the United States and world affairs from the close of World War II to the Korean War. Charles E. Bohlen, *The Transformation of American Foreign Policy* (New York: Norton, 1969) is valuable. The new ethos in the United States can be imbibed from three highly influential works: Marshall McLuhan, *Understanding Media** (New York: McGraw-Hill, 1964); Norman O. Brown, *Life Against Death** (Middletown: Wesleyan Univ., 1958); and Herbert Marcuse, *One Dimensional Man** (Boston: Beacon, 1964). The protest movements of the 1960's are surveyed in N. F. Cantor, *The Age of Protest* (New York: Hawthorn, 1969).

INDEX

882